Novell's Encyclopedia
of Networking

Novell's® Encyclopedia of Networking

Kevin Shafer

Novell Press, San Jose

Novell's Encyclopedia of Networking

Published by
Novell Press
2180 Fortune Drive
San Jose, CA 95131

Library of Congress Catalog Card No.: 97-74697

ISBN: 0-7645-4511-6

Printed in the United States of America

Distributed in the United States by IDG Books Worldwide, Inc.

Distributed by Macmillan Canada for Canada; by Contemporanea de Ediciones for Venezuela; by Distribuidora Cuspide for Argentina; by CITEC for Brazil; by Ediciones ZETA S.C.R. Ltda. for Peru; by Editorial Limusa SA for Mexico; by Transworld Publishers Limited in the United Kingdom and Europe; by Academic Bookshop for Egypt; by Levant Distributors S.A.R.L. for Lebanon; by Al Jassim for Saudi Arabia; by Simron Pty. Ltd. for South Africa; by Pustak Mahal for India; by The Computer Bookshop for India; by Toppan Company Ltd. for Japan; by Addison Wesley Publishing Company for Korea; by Longman Singapore Publishers Ltd. for Singapore, Malaysia, Thailand, and Indonesia; by Unalis Corporation for Taiwan; by WS Computer Publishing Company, Inc. for the Philippines; by WoodsLane Pty. Ltd. for Australia; by WoodsLane Enterprises Ltd. for New Zealand. Authorized Sales Agent: Anthony Rudkin Associates for the Middle East and North Africa.

For general information on IDG Books Worldwide's books in the U.S., contact our Consumer Customer Service department at 800-762-2974. For reseller information, including discounts and premium sales, contact our Reseller Customer Service department at 800-434-3422.

For information on where to purchase IDG Books Worldwide's books outside the U.S., contact our International Sales department at 415-655-3078 or fax 415-655-3281.

For information on foreign language translations, contact our Foreign & Subsidiary Rights department at 415-655-3018 or fax 415-655-3281.

For sales inquiries and special prices for bulk quantities, contact our Sales department at 415-655-3200 or write to the address above.

For information on using IDG Books Worldwide's books in the classroom or for ordering examination copies, contact our Educational Sales department at 800-434-2086 or fax 817-251-8174.

For authorization to photocopy items for corporate, personal, or educational use, contact the Copyright Clearance Center, 222 Rosewood Drive, Danvers, MA 01923, or fax 508-750-4470.

For general information on Novell Press books in the U.S., including information on discounts and premiums, contact IDG Books at 800-434-3422 or 415-655-3200. For information on where to purchase Novell Press books outside the U.S., contact IDG Books International at 415-655-3021 or fax 415-655-3295.

John Kilcullen, *President & CEO, IDG Books Worldwide, Inc.*
Brenda McLaughlin, *Senior Vice President & Group Publisher, IDG Books Worldwide, Inc.*
The IDG Books Worldwide logo is a trademark under exclusive license to IDG Books Worldwide, Inc., from International Data Group, Inc.

Rosalie Kearsley, *Publisher, Novell Press, Inc.*
Novell Press and the Novell Press logo are trademarks of Novell, Inc.

Welcome to Novell Press

Novell Press, the world's leading provider of networking books, is the premier source for the most timely and useful information in the networking industry. Novell Press books cover fundamental networking issues as they emerge — from today's Novell and third-party products, to the concepts and strategies that will guide the industry's future. The result is a broad spectrum of titles for the benefit of those involved in networking at any level: end-user, department administrator, developer, systems manager, or network architect.

Novell Press books are written by experts with the full participation of Novell's technical, managerial, and marketing staff. The books are exhaustively reviewed by Novell's own technicians and are published only on the basis of final released software — never on prereleased versions.

Novell Press at IDG is an exciting partnership between two companies at the forefront of the information and communications revolution. The Press is implementing an ambitious publishing program to develop new networking titles centered on the current version of IntranetWare, GroupWise, and on Novell's ManageWise products. Select Novell Press books are translated into 14 languages and are available at bookstores around the world.

K.C. Sue, Publisher, Novell Press, Inc.
Colleen Bluhm, Associate Publisher, Novell Press, Inc.

Novell Press

Publisher
K. C. Sue

Associate Publishers
Rosalie Kearsley
Colleen Bluhm

Acquisitions Editor
Jim Sumser

Managing Editor
Terry Somerson

Development Editor
Ron Hull

Copy Editors
Barry Childs-Helton
Marcia Baker
Nate Holdread
Tim Borek
Donna Scism

Technical Editor
Ken Neff

Project Coordinator
Katy German

Graphics and Production Specialists
Mario F. Amador
Maureen Moore
E. A. Pauw
Mary Penn
Christopher Pimentel
Andreas F. Schueller

Quality Control Specialist
Mick Arellano
Mark Schumann

Proofreader
Jennifer Overmyer

Indexer
Ted Laux

About the Author

Kevin Shafer of Pleasant Hill, California, has been a reporter and columnist for a Midwestern newspaper, a technical editor for the Department of Defense, a managing editor/senior editor for Osborne/McGraw-Hill, and, most recently, a freelance development editor and copy editor for IDG Books Worldwide.

To Dori and Alicia for being my loving and understanding family.

Foreword

Knowledge knows no distinction of social class, gender, age, or experience. Knowledge is a path to understanding for everyone; knowing what something means is the first step toward discovering how it works.

This book is about knowledge and understanding — and is for everyone, whether you are the administrator of a network encompassing the world, or simply the head of a household with computer access to the Internet.

Anyone exposed to the world of networking can attest that here is a universe replete with mind-boggling terminology and concepts. Dialogues between netizens and newbies can escalate into a foreign language seemingly derived from acronyms and abbreviations. In the world of those who speak it, destinations are measured in metrics, a PROM has nothing to do with dancing, and a HAM has nothing to do with food. The wise traveler there knows the value of a reliable translator. *Novell's Encyclopedia of Networking* provides that service, offering a firm underpinning for those who would set up and oversee the operation of a network. Addressing the entire field of networking, this book clarifies concepts, identifies technologies, and untangles the World Wide Web, explaining more than 5,000 terms. Its mission is to help you use the complex — sometimes baffling — professional language of networking to add to your own knowledge.

Preface

A good reference provides answers to questions and problems without providing more information than the reader actually needs. A truly *valuable* reference also provides "one-source shopping" for the reader who has neither the time (nor the desire) to sift through stacks of volumes to find a succinct solution to a complex problem.

Throughout this book, you will find information to expand your knowledge and understanding of the world of network computing. The following topics provide a brief overview of what you will find in this book:

- Acronyms and abbreviations
- Connectivity tools and equipment
- Electrical and electronic terms and concepts
- Electronic mail (e-mail)
- File systems and system architectures
- Hardware cables, cards, connectors, memory, and more
- Industry standards
- Internet addresses, browsers, newsgroups, plug-ins, protocols, and search engines
- Macintosh products
- Measurement systems
- Netscape Navigator
- NetWare and IntranetWare file attributes
- NetWare and IntranetWare file-access and directory-access rights
- NetWare and IntranetWare utilities
- Network administration, including extensive coverage of the NetWare/IntranetWare MONITOR utility
- Novell Directory Services (NDS) objects and properties
- Novell products
- Operating systems such as DOS, OS/2, UNIX, and Windows
- OSI Reference Model
- Protocols and interfaces
- Security
- SNA communication architecture
- Software applications
- Storage media
- Varieties of networks, including ARCnet, ATM, Banyan VINES, DECnet, Token Ring, and others
- World Wide Web (WWW)

This book is a time-saving tool. Information about network computing is readily available in many books and at a vast number of Internet Web sites. This book saves time by compiling a rich collection of information all in one source, with thousands of entries encompassing a complete cross-section of network computing.

How This Book Is Organized

Entries appear in alphabetical order throughout this book. A concise explanation follows each entry, along with pertinent cross-references for those readers who need more information on a topic. When a term or concept has a corresponding abbreviation or acronym, an entry for the abbreviation or acronym also appears, complete with cross-references. All discussions appear with the spelled-out versions of entries.

In addition, appendixes provide quick reference to the following key topics:

- *Appendix A* contains more than 1,200 acronyms and abbreviations.
- *Appendix B* contains the standard American Standard Code for Information Interchange (ASCII) character set.
- *Appendix C* contains a table of Novell Directory Services (NDS) objects and corresponding selectable properties.
- *Appendix D* contains a table of abbreviations used in top-level domains for the Internet.
- *Appendix E* contains a comparative table of NetWare and IntranetWare utilities.
- *Appendix F* contains a comprehensive listing of the Requests for Comments currently available; these online professional discussions helped develop a quarter-century of network technology.
- *Appendix G* contains a graphical review and comparison of the most common network topologies, gathering all their diagrams in one place for easy reference.

A Strategy of Maximum Usability

To supplement its comprehensive coverage, *Novell's Encyclopedia of Networking* is designed to be the most versatile networking reference you and your team have ever used. A new approach makes it an appropriate resource for users of all experience levels:

- Whether you start with the acronym, the abbreviation, or the spelled-out version of term, you get the definition and any cross-references you need. If you see a term spelled out in **boldface type** immediately after an acronym's entry heading, you know an identical entry (with the same cross-references) exists under the spelled-out term. Seasoned professionals can go right to the cross-references; new users have an instant "translation" of the acronym, followed by its explanation. Spelled-out headings for terms include any acronyms in parentheses. If you are instructing new users, you can have them look up either form of the term. You can always find the relevant figure or table under the spelled-out heading, and acronym entries feature cross-references that tell where to find these visual aids.
- When an acronym has two or more meanings, you can untangle them fast. When you see an acronym by itself in a cross-reference, that means it has several meanings and you can find them all in that one entry. In such cases, numbered definitions of the spelled-out terms appear under the heading, in alphabetical order; corresponding numbers identify cross-references. For example, under **NCP** you can find these three definitions: *(1)*

NetWare Core Protocol, (2) *network-control program,* and (3) *Network-Control Protocol.* In such cases, the cross-references are numbered to match the multiple terms; **NCP**, for example, has these cross-references: **(1) network operating system; (1) Novell Directory Services; (2) Systems Network Architecture.** Experienced users know instantly where to go next; novice users can compare and contrast the meanings and immediately tell them apart.

- Nouns-used-as-adjectives pile up rapidly in technical language. To help bring new users up to speed fast, this reference uses punctuation that is more compatible with "Standard English" than is customary in the industry — notably hyphenation to link important pairs of words. Although old hands may find the results a little odd (for example, *File-Allocation Table* and *network-control program* replace *File Allocation Table* and *network control program*), new users may find the meaning more immediately clear and the learning curve a little flatter.

- Network veterans to whom such strings as *Systems Network Architecture message vector data segment* are utterly transparent will be pleased to find that the traditional order of the words remains intact for every term.

Acknowledgments

Putting together a reference source is never easy, and impossible to accomplish without the efforts of many dedicated people. Special thanks to Jim Sumser at IDG Books Worldwide for granting the opportunity to tackle this huge project, and to Dan Blacharski, whose valuable talents, expertise, and input kept the project on schedule. Ron Hull at IDG Books Worldwide deserves a pat on the back for keeping track of this complex process. Barry Childs-Helton and the staff of copy editors at IDG Books Worldwide are to be congratulated for adding the professional polish to what must have seemed a never-ending manuscript. Thanks also go to the folks at Novell, including Ken Neff for his technical review of the material, as well as Lois Dudley, K.C. Sue, and Robin Wheatley for their continuing support.

Table of Contents

& symbols & numbers

& (ampersand)

The *and* sign commonly used in HyperText Markup Language (HTML) documents to indicate special characters.

See also **HyperText Markup Language.**

<> (angle brackets)

Characters in the Structured Query Language (SQL) used to delimit character strings that are names of syntactic elements. Angle brackets are also used in command syntax to denote variable information.

See also **Structure Query Language.**

* (asterisk)

Used as a wildcard character in many operating systems (such as NetWare, DOS, Windows NT, and OS/2) to represent one or more characters in a filename or filename extension. The asterisk may be used in searching or in file operations. For example, the NetWare command NDIR *.DOC lists all files with the .DOC extension. The command NDIR A*.DOC, on the other hand, would list all files with the .DOC extension and starting with the letter *A*.

@ ("at" sign)

A symbol typically used in spreadsheet formulas and e-mail addresses. When used in an e-mail address, it follows the username, as in user@company.com.

\ (backslash)

A character used in some operating systems, such as DOS and NetWare, to separate directory and/or path names in a path statement. In some programming languages, the backslash is used to indicate the character following it is an *escape* code.

// (double slash)

A character used to separate the transport protocol from an Internet address (for example, http://www.idgbooks.com).

μ (mu)

Used to abbreviate the prefix *micro,* meaning 2^{-20}, or one-millionth. For example, microsecond would be abbreviated as μ*sec.*

. and .. (period and double period)

Characters used in some operating systems to refer to the current and parent directories in a hierarchical directory system.

? (question mark)

A character used in some operating systems as a wildcard character that represents a single character in a file or directory name. For example, the DOS command D?G.TXT could apply to DIG.TXT, DOG.TXT, or DUG.TXT. The question mark may also be used in NetWare to access help on a specific topic or command. For example, the NetWare command RENDIR /? displays online help for the RENDIR command.

/ (slash)

A character used in some operating systems (such as UNIX) to separate directory and/or path names in a path statement (for example, UNIX/SUBDCTRY/SUBSUB). In other operating systems, such as DOS or NetWare, the slash is used to separate command line switches (for example, NDIR /DO for the directory only switch of the NetWare NDIR command).

1Base5

An Institute of Electrical and Electronic Engineers (IEEE) 802.3 specification for an Ethernet network operating at 1Mbps. A 1Base5 network uses unshielded twisted-pair (UTP) cabling, uses a physical bus, and attaches nodes to a common cable.

3+

An obsolete operating system from 3Com.

3+Open

An obsolete network operating system from 3Com.

4B/5B encoding

A data-translation scheme that precedes signal encoding in Fiber Distributed Data Interface (FDDI) networks. Under this construct, each group of four bits is represented as a five-bit symbol, which is then associated with a bit pattern. The bit pattern is then encoded using the Non-Return-to-Zero Inverted (NRZI) method, making further electrical encoding more efficient. 4B/5B encoding is significantly more efficient than Manchester signal encoding, which is used in Ethernet networks.

See also **Manchester encoding; Non-Return-to-Zero Inverted.**

5B/6B encoding

A data-translation scheme that precedes signal encoding in 100BaseVG networks. Under this construct, each group of five bits is represented as a six-bit symbol, which is then associated with a bit pattern. The bit pattern is then encoded using the Non-Return-to-Zero (NRZ) method, making further electrical encoding more efficient.

See also **100BaseVG/AnyLAN.**

7-bit/8-bit data

A unit of data typically accepted by serial interfaces. A serial interface can usually be configured to accept *either* 7-bit or 8-bit data.

See also **parity.**

8B/10B encoding

A data translation scheme based on 4B/5B Encoding. 8B/10B Encoding is used to re-code 8-bit patterns into 10-bit symbols. This type of encoding is used in Systems Network Architecture (SNA) networks.

See also **4B/5B Encoding.**

9-track tape

A tape storage format using nine parallel tracks on half-inch magnetic tape. Eight of the tracks are used for data; the ninth is used for parity information. The 9-track tapes are frequently used as mainframe backup systems.

10Base2

An Institute of Electrical and Electronic Engineers (IEEE) 802.3 specification for Ethernet networks using thin coaxial cable.

This specification, also known as *ThinNet*, is often used for small local-area networks (LANs), and offers a throughput of up to 10 megabits per second (Mbps). 10Base2 can support a cable segment as long as 300 meters (about 1,000 feet).

See also **Ethernet; IEEE 802.x; ThinNet.**

10Base5

An Institute of Electrical and Electronic Engineers (IEEE) 802.3 specification for Ethernet networks using thick coaxial cable. This specification, also known as *ThickNet*, can accommodate a larger local-area network (LAN) diameter than 10Base2 and offers a throughput of up to 10 megabits per second (Mbps). 10Base5 can support a cable segment as long as 1,000 meters (about 3,300 feet).

See also **Ethernet; IEEE 802.x; ThickNet.**

10BaseF

An Institute of Electrical and Electronic Engineers (IEEE 802.3) specification for Ethernet networks using fiber-optic cable. This specification offers a throughput of up to 10 megabits per second (Mbps), and is divided into the following three subcategories:

- *10BaseFP (fiber passive)*. Used for desktop connections.
- *10BaseFL (fiber link)*. Used for intermediate hubs and workgroups.
- *10BaseFB (fiber backbone)*. Used for links between buildings.

See also **IEEE 802.x.**

10BaseT

An Institute of Electrical and Electronic Engineers (IEEE) 802.3 specification for Ethernet networks using unshielded twisted-pair (UTP) wiring. This method of wiring provides the network with 10 megabits per second (Mbps) of bandwidth, and typically uses a star topology.

See also **Ethernet; IEEE 802.x; star topology.**

10Basex

A generic designation used to refer to the various types of baseband Ethernet networks.

See also **10Base2; 10Base5; 10BaseF; 10BaseT; Ethernet.**

10Broad36

An Institute of Electrical and Electronic Engineers (IEEE) 802.3 specification for broadband Ethernet networks using 75-ohm coaxial cable, and a bus or tree topology. 10Broad36 networks offer throughput of up to 10 megabits per second (Mbps), and can support cable segments as long as 1,800 meters (about 5,900 feet).

See also **bus network topology; Ethernet; IEEE 802.x; tree topology.**

10-tape rotation method

A method of tape rotation that uses ten tape sets. Each tape set is used for equal time slots over a period of 40 weeks.

16-bit and 32-bit

The number of bits used by an operating system to perform a task. This operating system specification is based on the corresponding hardware platform on which the operating system runs.

56K line

A digital leased line connection that can carry data at 56,000 bits per second (bps).
See also **64K line.**

64K line

Physically the same as a 56K line, except that it offers a higher throughput (about 64,000 bits per second) and usually carries a higher cost.
See also **56K line.**

66-type punch-down block

A device for terminating wires, typically used for telephone systems. The 66-type block has been superseded by the 110-type punch-down block.
See also **110-type punch-down block.**

100Base VG/Any LAN

A proprietary extension of the 100Base VG standard, developed by Hewlett-Packard. 100Base VG is represented by the Institute of Electrical and Electronic Engineers (IEEE) 802.12 specification. Although similar to Ethernet, it cannot be truly called Ethernet because it does not use the Carrier-Sense Multiple-Access/Collision Detection (CSMA/CD) protocol. This architecture supports 100 megabits per second (Mbps) transmission over CAT-3 unshielded twisted-pair (UTP) cabling. 100Base VG supports a demand priority scheme to give priority to data packets over the network. This deterministic access method differs from CSMA/CD's contentious method of handling collisions and attempts to bring greater efficiency to the network. Because it is deterministic, 100Base VG may be more suitable than 100BaseT (Fast Ethernet) for time-sensitive applications, such as videoconferencing.

In an Ethernet network, any node may transmit at any time, and collisions eventually result. On the other hand, 100VG guarantees all stations equal access to the network. In a 100VG network, the hub polls all active ports. When a station requests permission to send data, the hub allows that station to generate one frame, and then go on to the next port, and repeat the process.
See also **100BaseT; Carrier-Sense Multiple-Access/Collision Detection; Ethernet; IEEE 802.**x**.**

100BaseFX

A specification of 100BaseT (Fast Ethernet) that supports two-strand fiber optic cable.
See also **100BaseT; Carrier-Sense Multiple-Access/Collision Detection; Ethernet; IEEE 802.**x**.**

100BaseT

A general classification of the Institute of Electrical and Electronic Engineers (IEEE) 802.3 specification for Ethernet networks that provides the network with 100 megabits per second (Mbps) of bandwidth. 100BaseT retains the Carrier-Sense Multiple-Access/Collision Detection (CSMA/CD) media-access method and can support cable lengths between nodes as long as about 200 meters (about 660 feet). The 100BaseT specification is also known as *Fast Ethernet*.
See also **Fast Ethernet.**

100BaseT4

A specification of 100BaseT (Fast Ethernet) that supports CAT-3, CAT-4, or CAT-5 unshielded twisted-pair (UTP) cabling. 100BaseT4 requires four pairs of wires.

100BaseTX

A specification of 100BaseT (Fast Ethernet) that supports CAT-5 unshielded twisted-pair (UTP) and shielded twisted-pair (STP) cabling. 100BaseTX requires two pairs of wires.

100BaseVG

See **100BaseVG/AnyLAN**.

100BaseX

A generic term used to refer to the various types of Fast Ethernet networks.
See also **100Base VG/Any LAN; 100BaseFX; 100BaseT; 100BaseT4; 100BaseTX; Ethernet; Fast Ethernet; IEEE 802.*x*.*

100Mbps Ethernet

A generic term referring to one of several proposals for running Ethernet at 100Mbps, such as Fast Ethernet and 100Base VG.
See also **Fast Ethernet; 100Base VG/AnyLAN.**

110-type punch-down block

A device used for terminating wires. The block replaces older 66-type blocks, and is often used to connect input and output wires.
See also **66-type punch-down block.**

128-byte file entry

An entry consisting of 128 bytes. For example, a NetWare server that supports both DOS and Macintosh filenames would generate two 128-byte file entries for each file.

193rd bit

A framing bit in a T1 channel. This bit is attached to each group of 192 bits, which represents a single byte from each of the T1 line's 24 channels.
See also **T1.**

802.1

An Institute of Electrical and Electronic Engineers (IEEE) standard for general local-area network (LAN) architecture, internetworking, and network management at the hardware level.
See also **IEEE 802.*x*.*

802.2

An Institute of Electrical and Electronic Engineers (IEEE) standard defining the Logical Link Control (LLC) Layer for a Carrier-Sense Multiple-Access/Collision Detection (CSMA/CD) bus network. LLC establishes an interface between media-access methods and the network layer. LLC functions include framing, addressing, and error control.
See also **IEEE 802.*x*.*

802.3

An Institute of Electrical and Electronic Engineers (IEEE) standard defining the Media Access Control (MAC) Layer for a

Carrier-Sense Multiple-Access/Collision Detection (CSMA/CD) bus network. Although 802.3 is technically not identical to Ethernet, both Ethernet and 802.3 devices can run over the same cable.

See also **IEEE 802.***x***; Media-Access Control.**

802.4

An Institute of Electrical and Electronic Engineers (IEEE) standard defining the Media-Access Control (MAC) Layer for a token-passing bus network.

See also **IEEE 802.***x***; Media-Access Control.**

802.5

An Institute of Electrical and Electronic Engineers (IEEE) standard defining the Media-Access Control (MAC) Layer for a token-passing ring network.

See also **IEEE 802.***x***; Media-Access Control; token passing.**

802.6

An Institute of Electrical and Electronic Engineers (IEEE) standard defining a metro-politan-area network (MAN) on the basis of a 30-mile long fiber-optic ring.

See also **IEEE 802.***x***; metropolitan-area network.**

802.7

An Institute of Electrical and Electronic Engineers (IEEE) Technical Advisory Group (TAG) report on broadband networks.

802.8

An Institute of Electrical and Electronic Engineers (IEEE) Technical Advisory Group (TAG) report on fiber-optic networks.

802.9

An Institute of Electrical and Electronic Engineers (IEEE) standard for integrating voice and data.

802.11

An Institute of Electrical and Electronic Engineers (IEEE) working group concerned with establishing wireless network standards.

802.x

The entire set of Institute of Electrical and Electronic Engineers (IEEE) 802 standards.

See also **IEEE 802.***x***.**

1394 cable

A universal I/O connection for interconnecting multiple digital devices. Often used for connecting video and audio hardware, a 1394 cable is capable of connecting devices at half-duplex rates of up to 400 megabits per second (Mbps). The 1394 cable was originally designed by Apple Computer as a replacement for parallel Small Computer System Interface (SCSI). The medium allows for 16 cable hops of 4.5 meters each, for a 72 meter maximum. The 1394 cable is also known as *firewire*.

See also **Small Computer System Interface.**

3174

A cluster-control unit used with an IBM 3270 display terminal. This is a Systems Network Architecture (SNA) Physical Unit (PU) Type 2.

See also **Systems Network Architecture.**

3270

A family of IBM workstations and printers used with IBM mainframes. These devices rely on either Synchronous Data-Link Control (SDLC) or Binary Synchronous Control (BSC) to communicate with the mainframe host. In Systems Network Architecture (SNA) terms, the 3270 devices are defined as Logical Unit (LU) Types 2 (3270 workstations) and Type 3 (3270 printers).

See also **Binary Synchronous Control; Synchronous Data-Link Control; Systems Network Architecture.**

3270 data stream

A stream in an IBM Systems Network Architecture (SNA) environment where characters are converted and formatted through control characters and attribute settings.

See also **Systems Network Architecture.**

3274

An IBM cluster-control unit for the 3270 workstation family. The 3274 connects one or more 3270 devices with a host computer via a communications control node or Integrated Communications Adapter. In Systems Network Architecture (SNA) terms, the IBM control unit is defined as a Physical Unit (PU) Type 2. These controllers have

been replaced by 3174 controllers in more recent configurations.

See also **Systems Network Architecture.**

3278

An IBM 3270 workstation terminal (LU 2) used to communicate with IBM mainframes.

3279

A color-capable IBM 3270 workstation (LU 2) used to communicate with IBM mainframes.

3705

An IBM communication control node used with IBM 370 series mainframes. The 3705 also includes ports for asynchronous access over dial-up lines and is used to interface the mainframe to 3274 control units. In Systems Network Architecture (SNA) terms, this is a Physical Unit (PU) Type 4.

See also **Systems Network Architecture.**

8086/8088

Intel's 16-bit microprocessor used in early IBM-compatible computers. The 8086 chip was available with clock speeds of 4.77 megahertz (MHz), 8MHz, and 10MHz. The 8088 chip was available with clock speeds of 4.77MHz and 8MHz. These chips contained the equivalent of 29,000 transistors executing 0.33 million instructions per second.

80286

Intel's 16-bit successor to the 8086 chip. The 80286 chip was used in the IBM AT machine, and runs at speeds of 6 megahertz (MHz) to 16MHz. Computers based on the 80286 chip were limited to memory segments of 64K, and could not address more than 1MB of memory.

80386DX

Intel's third-generation 32-bit microprocessor. The chip can run at clock speeds of up to 33MHz. Computers based on the 80386 chip overcame many of the limitations of the 80286, could address as much as 4GB of physical memory and 64TB of virtual memory.

80386SX

Intel's low-end 80386 microprocessor. Its external data bus was only 16 bits instead of 32 bits.

80387

Intel's floating-point coprocessor designed to be used with 80386 computers.

80387SX

Intel's floating-point coprocessor designed to be used with 80386SX computers.

80486DX

Intel's successor to the 80386 microprocessor. With 1,185,000 transistors and clock speeds of up to 50 megahertz (MHz), it could process as many as 41 million instructions per second.

80486DX2

Intel's high-performance overdrive microprocessor for use with systems using 20MHz bus structures. This microprocessor features *speed-doubling technology,* which means it is designed to run twice as fast internally as it does with components external to the chip. The chip offers clock speeds of 50 megahertz (MHz) and 66MHz, with 1.2 million transistors capable or processing 40 million instructions per second.

80486SL

A low-end version of Intel's 80486 microprocessor. The 80486SL included features for power management, and was often used in portable computers.

80486SX

Intel's 80486 microprocessor with no math coprocessor.

80487

Intel's floating-point coprocessor meant to be used with the 80486SX microprocessor. The 80486 microprocessor includes an integrated coprocessor, making the 80487 unnecessary.

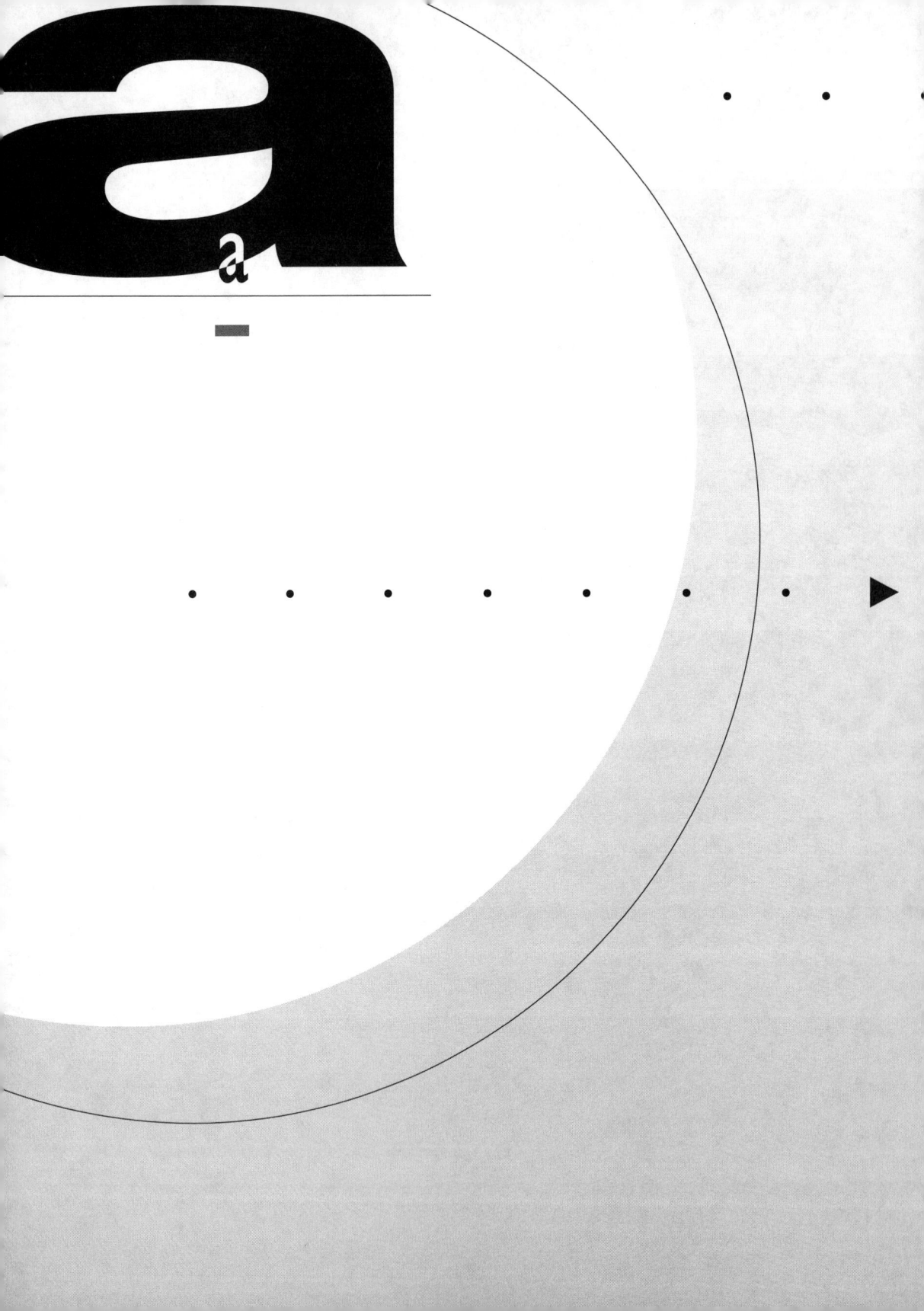

AA

Auto Answer, a modem feature that responds and connects automatically to an incoming call.

AAL

ATM Adaptation Layer, a method of adapting the highest-layer protocols of the OSI Reference Model for transport over an Asynchronous Transfer Mode (ATM) network. An ATM cell itself consists of 53 bytes (48 bytes of payload and a 5-byte header). The AAL determines the format of the cell's payload.

AAL is divided into the following two sublayers:

- *Convergence (CS)*. The CS Sublayer performs message identification and time/clock recovery services. To support data transport over ATM , the CS is subdivided into the Common Part Convergence Sublayer (CPCS) and a Service-Specific Convergence Sublayer (SSCS). AAL service data units are transported between AAL *service access points* (SAPs) throughout the ATM network.
- *Segmentation and Reassembly (SAR)*. The SAR Sublayer divides higher-layer information into 48-byte segments for transport by the ATM cells. When the cell is received, SAR reassembles the segmented ATM cells into larger data units that can then be delivered to the higher layers.

Five AALs have been defined, one for each class of service available in the ATM network, as follows:

- *AAL-1 (ATM Adaptation Layer Type 1)*. This layer is responsible for AAL functions in support of Constant Bit Rate (CBR), time-dependent traffic.
- *AAL-2 (ATM Adaptation Layer Type 2)*. This layer is undefined.
- *AAL-3/4 (ATM Adaptation Layer Type 3/4)*. This layer is responsible for AAL functions in support of Variable Bit Rate (VBR), delay-tolerant data traffic that requires support for sequencing or error detection.
- *AAL-5 (ATM Adaptation Layer Type 5)*. This layer is responsible for AAL functions in support of Variable Bit Rate (VBR), delay-tolerant, connection-oriented traffic that requires little support for sequencing or error detection.

See also **Asynchronous Transfer Mode; Constant Bit Rate; OSI Reference Model; Variable Bit Rate.**

A&B bit signaling

A procedure for T1 transmissions in which one bit from every sixth frame of 24 sub-channels carries supervisory signaling information.
See also **T1.**

AAR

Automatic Alternate Routing, a process by which network traffic is routed automatically to maximize throughput. AAR can also be used to minimize distance and balance channel usage.

AARP

AppleTalk Address-Resolution Protocol, a network-layer protocol in the AppleTalk protocol suite that maps AppleTalk addresses to physical addresses.

See also **AppleTalk; AppleTalk protocols.**

AARP Address-Mapping Table

Used to map AppleTalk node addresses, as well as the addresses of the underlying Data-Link Layer (Layer 2 of the OSI Reference Model) for non-LocalTalk links.

See also **Apple/Talk Address-Resolution Protocol; OSI Reference Model.**

AARP probe packet

A probe packet that asks whether a randomly selected node ID is being used by another node in a nonextended AppleTalk network. If the selected node is being used, the packet chooses a different ID and sends more probe packets. If the selected node is not being used, the sending node uses the node ID.

See also **AppleTalk Address-Resolution Protocol.**

AAUI

Apple Attachment-Unit Interface, an EtherTalk hardware connection included on newer Macintosh computers.

abandon

To cancel or revoke a task. Dialog boxes will often give the user a choice: either accept or abandon input or configuration changes.

A/B box

A hardware switching box used for sharing a peripheral device between two or more computers.

abend

abnormal end, an operating system message issued when a serious problem is detected. Typically an abend stops the computer from proceeding with the program. A hardware or software failure can trigger an abend.

ABI

Application Binary Interface, a specification that outlines the interface between the operating system and a particular hardware platform. In particular, ABI refers to the calls made between applications and the operating system.

ABM

Asynchronous Balanced Mode, an operating mode specified in the High-Level Data-Link Control (HDLC) protocol of the International Standards Organization (ISO). ABM gives equal status to each node in a point-to-point link. Each node therefore functions as both sender and receiver.

See also **High-Level Data-Link Control; International Standards Organization.**

abnormal end (abend)

An operating-system message issued when a serious problem is detected. Typically, an abend stops the computer from proceeding with the program. A hardware or software failure can trigger an abend.

abnormal termination

A system failure, application failure, or other action that causes a program to end unsuccessfully.

abort

To cease a task in progress. For example, if a backup session is aborted, the NetWare SBACKUP utility finishes backing up the files in progress, and then quits without completing the remainder of the backup.

ABORT REMIRROR utility

A NetWare 4.x and IntranetWare server console utility used to stop the remirroring of a logical partition, or to stop the synchronization of data between two mirrored disks. It can also be used to unmirror a mirrored disk.

See also **mirroring; NetWare Loadable Module; NetWare utilities.**

abort timeout

To cease a timeout procedure.

Abort Transaction operation

A command given in conjunction with a Begin Transaction operation. The Begin Transaction operation must come before the Abort Transaction or End Transaction operation.

See also **Begin Transaction operation.**

ABP

Alternate Bipolar, a signal-encoding method in which a positive, negative, or zero voltage is used. A zero voltage usually represents one value and a nonzero voltage represents another.

See also **encoding (signal).**

ABR

area boundary router, a router that attaches an Open Shortest Path First (OSPF) area to the background area. The area boundary router has at least one interface in a routing area and one in the backbone area.

See also **Open Shortest Path First.**

Abstract Syntax

A machine-independent set of language constructs and rules used to describe objects, protocols, and other items.

Abstract Syntax Notation One (ASN.1)

A machine-independent, abstract syntax developed as part of the OSI Reference Model. ASN.1 is used to describe data structures; it functions as a common syntax for sending data between two end systems that use different encoding systems.

See also **Abstract Syntax; OSI Reference Model.**

ABUI

Association of Banyan Users International, a Banyan user group. Members are concerned with hardware and software relating to the Banyan VINES network operating system.

AC

(1) **Alternating Current,** a power supply in which the polarity periodically switches. AC power is typically supplied to most homes and offices in the United States. The amount of power supplied at any time depends on the switching process. A pure AC supply will generate a sine wave over time. In North America, alternating current switches polarity 60 times per second; the rate differs in other countries.

(2) **Access-Control field,** a field used to indicate which users or devices can access a particular file or directory. In Asynchronous Transfer Mode (ATM), the AC field is the first byte in the 5-byte header. In UNIX, the AC field is a 9-bit indicator that shows a file's status.

(3) **Application Context,** a term used in the OSI Reference Model, referring to all the application service elements (ASEs) needed to use an application in a given context.

See also (2) **Asynchronous Transfer Mode;** (3) **OSI Reference Model.**

Accelerated mode

A file-open mode that appeared in NetWare Btrieve before the release of version 6.x and improved response time when updating files. Btrieve version 6.x improved the performance of Normal open mode, making Accelerated mode obsolete.

accelerator board

An add-in board used to replace the main processor with one of higher performance. Use of an accelerator board is often a cost-effective way to upgrade a system.

Acceptable Use Policy (AUP)

A statement or set of rules that limit how a network or computer service is used.

acceptance angle

In fiber optics, a metric that indicates the range over which incoming light is reflected and propagated over the fiber. Factors affecting this angle's size include the refractive indexes of the fiber core, cladding, and surrounding medium.

acceptance cone

The three-dimensional analog of an acceptance angle. The cone is generated by rotating the acceptance angle 360 degrees, using the center of the fiber core as the point of the cone.

See also **acceptance angle.**

access

To retrieve data from a storage device, or to log in to a computer system.

access control

A process that limits access to objects, files, or directories. Typically, access control is achieved through establishing passwords, granting specific privileges, or setting attributes. The operating system uses access control to determine how users, groups of users, or resources can interact with the operating system, files, directories, and network resources. Normally the network administrator assigns each user an appropriate level of access control.

The term denotes a field in a Token Ring token or data frame.

See also **access rights**; **Token Ring**.

Access-Control Decision Function (ACDF)

In an open system, a function used to decide whether to grant access to resources in a given situation.

Access-Control Enforcement Function (ACEF)

In an open system, a function used to enforce decisions of the Access Control Decision Function (ACDF).

Access-Control (AC) field

A field used to indicate which users or devices can access a particular file or directory. In Asynchronous Transfer Mode (ATM), the AC field is the first byte in the 5-byte header. In UNIX, the AC field is a 9-bit indicator that shows a file's status.

See also **Asynchronous Transfer Mode.**

Access-Control Information (ACI)

A specification of the Consultative Committee for International Telegraphy and Telephony (CCITT) X.500 directory services model that ACI refers to the information used to control access to a file or directory.

Access Control list (ACL)

A list of available services that also identifies which users and devices may access those services. In Novell Directory Services (NDS), ACL is an object property; it contains a list of users or devices allowed to access the object, and works with other authentication features to provide network security. An ACL has trustee assignments that include object rights, property rights, and an Inherited Rights Filter (IRF). To modify an ACL for an object, a user must have the appropriate property right. The ACL is a selectable property for the following NDS objects: AFP Server, Alias, Bindery, Bindery Queue, Computer, Country, Directory Map, External Entity, Group, List, Message Routing Group, Messaging Server, NCP Server, Organization, Organizational Role, Organizational Unit, Print Server, Printer, Profile, Queue, Unknown, User, and Volume.

See also **leaf object**; **Novell Directory Services**; **object.**

access-control rights

A system for granting a user access to a file or directory. A user with access control rights can change the trustee assignments and Inherited Rights Filter (IRF) of a directory or file.

access method

A technique for moving data between main storage and an I/O device. In a Systems Network Architecture (SNA) environment, the access method is the software used to control the network's information flow. This term also denotes a method — such as Token Ring or Carrier Sense Multiple Access/Collision Detection (CSMA/CD) — that regulates how, and in what order, a network's nodes may access its transmission media.

See also **Carrier-Sense Multiple-Access/Collision Detection**; **Systems Network Architecture**; **Token Ring.**

access network

A smaller network attached to a backbone network trunk by a gateway or router.

access protocol

A set of rules used by workstations to avoid collisions when transmitting data over the network.

access rate (AR)

A physical rate that indicates the access of the user channel in bits per second. In Frame Relay networks, the offered load is limited by the AR.

See also **Frame Relay network.**

access rights

Properties that specify the use of or access to particular objects, files, or directories — for example, a particular group of rights called a *trustee assignment* can be assigned to a user for a specific file or directory. Access rights may also limit what each user can do with any given resource. A resource may be configured with default access rights that can be overridden by additional rights granted to a specified user. Access rights are system-dependent; each operating environment uses its own nomenclature for them (for example, *access privileges* or *trustee rights*).

Table A.1 lists the access rights available in IntranetWare, the classification of the rights, and where to find more information.

access server

A central computer used for granting access to remote users who connect to the network via modem. The access server gives the remote nodes access to network resources, as if they were directly attached to the network.

access time

The time required to actually request and receive data from a hard drive, figured as the sum of seek time plus drive latency. A lower access time denotes better performance. For example, access time could be reduced by replicating data from a WAN-based access device to a local device.

Access Unit (AU)

Part of the Consultative Committee for International Telegraphy and Telephony (CCITT) X.400 Message Handling System (MHS). An AU is an application process that gives a CCITT-supported service access to a Message Transfer Service (MTS). The MTS then delivers a message to users or services at any site that is accessible through the MHS.

See also **Consultative Committee for International Telegraphy and Telephony; Message Handling System; Message Transfer Service; X.400.**

account

A specification that allows a user to access a workgroup or network. Each user who requires access has an account, which is used to log in to the network and be recognized as a valid participant. User accounts can be configured by the network administrator to grant the holder specific access privileges. A temporary account can be configured to expire at a given date and time. The account can also be used by the administrator to track resource usage.

Table A.1: IntranetWare Access Rights

Right	Directory	File	Object	Property	For More Information
Access control	X	X			See **access-control rights.**
Add Self				X	See **Add Self right.**
Browse			X		See **Browse right.**
Compare				X	See **Compare right.**
Create	X	X	X		See **Create right.**
Delete			X		See **Delete right.**
Delete Self				X	See **Delete Self right.**
Erase	X	X			See **Erase right.**
File Scan	X	X			See **File Scan right.**
Modify	X	X			See **Modify right.**
Read Property				X	See **Read Property right.**
Read	X	X		X	See **Read right.**
Rename Object			X		See **Rename Object right.**
Rename			X		See **Rename right.**
Supervisor	X	X	X	X	See **Supervisor right.**
Write	X	X		X	See **Write right.**

Account Balance

A selectable property for the AFP Server, the Messaging Server object, the NCP Server, the Print Server, and the User objects in Novell Directory Services (NDS).

See also **leaf object; Novell Directory Services; object.**

Account Balance field

A field used by the network administrator to enter a value corresponding to the amount of services granted to a user on a workgroup or network.

Account Locked

A selectable property for the User object in Novell Directory Services (NDS) that locks the user's account to prevent intruders from invading it.

See also **leaf object; Novell Directory Services; object.**

account-management (AM) domain

A subdivision of accounts managed by a single entity.

Account-Metering Function (AMF)

Under the OSI Network-Management Model, the function that tracks each user's resource usage.
    See also **OSI Network-Management Model.**

account policy

A set of rules used to define what rights are granted to which users on the network.

Account Reset Time

A selectable property for the User object in Novell Directory Services (NDS) that tells a user how much time remains before an account is unlocked automatically.
    See also **leaf object; Novell Directory Services; object.**

account restrictions

Limitations on a user's account, which can be configured by the administrator — for example, to set an expiration date, limit access, or require users to enter a password upon login.

account server

A central computer used to control access to a network.

accounting

Tracking and reporting on network resources. The administrator can allocate charges for network services throughout multiple departments, and can assign each user an account balance of available services and resources. NetWare has an accounting option that can be used to charge customers who access a network server. The administrator can charge for five separate services:

- Blocks read from server hard disks
- Blocks written to server hard disks
- Time users are logged in to the server
- Data stored on the server
- Requests accommodated by the server

The administrator can further assign account balances to each user, which would limit the number and amount of services each user can access. Most network operating systems have a built-in accounting utility or can use a third-party add-on package.

Accounting Management

A System-Management Function Area (SMFA) in the OSI Network-Management Model. Accounting Management refers to the administration of network usage, costs, and resource availability.
    See also **OSI Network-Management Model; System-Management Function Area.**

Accumaster Integrator program

AT&T's network-management program. The program collects network information generated by the Network Management Protocol (NMP) and, in turn, generates reports based on this information.

ACDF

Access-Control Decision Function, in an open system, a function used to decide whether to grant access to resources in a given situation.

ACE

Adverse Channel Enhancement, a method of adjusting a modem to compensate for noisy communications lines.

ACEF

Access-Control Enforcement Function, in an open system, a function used to enforce decisions of the Access Control Decision Function (ACDF).

ACF

Advanced Communications Function, a family of IBM software running under Systems Network Architecture (SNA). ACF programs have diverse functions. For example, *ACF/NCP (Network Control Program)* controls communications between network devices and a host machine; *ACF/TCAM (Telecommunications Access Method)* is a VTAM application that handles messages; *ACF/VTAM (Virtual Telecommunications Access Method)* controls communications between terminal and host machines, replacing the earlier *ACF/VTAME (Virtual Telecommunications Access Method-Entry)* program.

See also **Systems Network Architecture; Virtual Telecommunications Access Method.**

ACI

Access-Control Information, a specification of the Consultative Committee for International Telegraphy and Telephony (CCITT) X.500 directory services model that ACI refers to the information used to control access to a file or directory.

ACID

Atomicity, Consistency, Isolation, and Durability, our desirable attributes a transaction should have in a transaction-processing system. *Atomicity* refers to whether a transaction is successful or unsuccessful (that is, either all of the operations take effect or none take effect); a successful transaction *commits* and an unsuccessful transaction *aborts. Consistency* (which is the responsibility of the application program) refers to whether a transaction transforms distributed data from one consistent state to another. *Isolation* refers to whether a transaction appears to execute independently of other transactions that run concurrently. *Durability* (also known as *permanence*) refers to whether the effects of a transaction remain after the transaction is complete. Considered together, these four attributes are often called *ACID properties.*

ACK

A control character (ASCII code 06) that indicates a packet has been received error-free.

Ack Wait timeout

An option used to specify a time value. The SPX Ack Wait timeout is specified in ticks and is set at the server.

ACL

access-control list, a list of available services that also identifies which users and devices may access those services. In Novell Directory Services (NDS), ACL is an object property; it contains a list of users or devices allowed to access the object, and works with other authentication features to provide network security. An ACL has trustee assignments that include object rights, property rights, and an Inherited Rights Filter (IRF). To modify an ACL for an object, a user must have the appropriate property right. The ACL is a selectable property for the following NDS objects: AFP Server, Alias, Bindery, Bindery Queue, Computer, Country, Directory Map, External Entity, Group, List, Message-Routing Group, Messaging Server, NCP Server, Organization, Organizational Role, Organizational Unit, Print Server, Printer, Profile, Queue, Unknown, User, and Volume.

See also **leaf object; Novell Directory Services; object.**

ACL property

Property specifications of the Access Control List. For example, the Write property is needed to change trustees.

See also **access-control list.**

ACONSOLE utility

A NetWare 3.*x* workstation utility that enables the supervisor to access a server through a modem. By doing so, the supervisor can manage the server from that workstation. In NetWare 4.*x*, ACONSOLE was removed and its functions were included in the RCONSOLE utility.

See also **NetWare Loadable Module; NetWare utilities.**

acoustic coupler

A modem with a set of rubber cups that fit over a standard telephone's mouthpiece and earpiece.

across-the-wire migration

A way to upgrade to a higher version of the NetWare operating system using the NetWare Migration Utility. In this type of migration, data files are sent over the network to a destination server.

ACS

Asynchronous Communications Server, a dedicated personal computer or expansion board that provides other nodes on the network with access to serial ports and modems.

ACSE

Association-Control Service Element, an OSI Reference Model service that establishes a relationship between two applications. The ACSE facilitates cooperation and exchange of information between the applications.

See also **OSI Reference Model.**

ACTIVATE SERVER utility

A NetWare 4.*x* and IntranetWare server console utility that loads the Mirrored Server Engine (MSEngine) and synchronizes memory between servers.

See also **MSEngine; NetWare Loadable Module; NetWare utilities.**

active

A term used to indicate when hardware is doing signal processing of any type.

Active Connections

A screen from the NetWare 4.02 MONITOR NetWare Loadable Module (NLM). The screen yields statistical network information, including the number of active connections to each server.

See also **MONITOR; NetWare Loadable Module.**

active hub

A network device used to amplify transmission signals and connect additional nodes to the network.

active hub lights

Physical lights on an active hub. When blinking, the lights indicate that bad packets are being sent over the network.

active link

A device used to connect two network cable segments. Both cable segments must be connected to high-impedance network interface cards.

Active Monitor (AM)

The first station to be started on a Token Ring network. The Active Monitor detects and addresses error conditions in the background, and is responsible for passing and maintaining the token. The performance of the AM is constantly monitored by a Standby Monitor (SM) to guarantee the integrity of the token-passing process.

See also **Standby Monitor; Token Ring.**

Active Monitor Present (AMP)

A Token Ring term. AMP status is determined by a packet issued every three seconds by the ring's active monitor; the packet indicates that the active monitor is still functional.

See also **Token Ring.**

Active Processors

An option from the main menu of the IntranetWare MONITOR NetWare Loadable Module (NLM). Selecting this option shows the number of enabled processors.

See also **MONITOR; NetWare Loadable Module.**

active star topology

A network topology in which a central node cleans and boosts a signal.

See also **star topology.**

active termination

The capability of a Small Computer Systems Interface (SCSI) device to apply or remove terminations.

See also **Small Computer Systems Interface.**

active users

A selectable option found on the Novell Directory Services (NDS) NLIST utility. The parameter shows the users currently logged in to the network.

See also **NLIST utility.**

ActiveX

A group of object-oriented technologies from Microsoft Corporation that adds dynamic features to World Wide Web (WWW) pages and related online presentations.

See also **World Wide Web.**

ActiveX Control

A Microsoft Corporation applet, derived from ActiveX technology, that allows users to build interactive World Wide Web (WWW) pages and networks from components instead of starting from scratch.

See also **applet; ActiveX.**

ACU

(1) **Autocall Unit,** a device used to dial telephone numbers automatically.
(2) **Automatic Client Upgrade,** an IntranetWare feature that allows for automatic upgrading of many existing NetWare workstations to Novell's 32-bit client software.

AD

Administrative Domain, the nodes, routers, and connectors managed by a single administrator.

adapter

A hardware device that connects the computer to a peripheral device. If the personal computer and the peripheral have data buses of different widths, adapters mitigate those differences. For example, you would need a 25-pin-to-9-pin adapter to connect a printer's 25-pin port to a computer's 9-pin port.

adapter cable

A cable used in Token Ring networks to connect the network interface cards to the Multistation Access Unit (MAU).

See also **Multistation Access Unit; Token Ring.**

Adapter Support Interface (ASI)

A standard interface, created by IBM, that allows a Token Ring adapter to communicate with higher-level protocols. ASI contains a Data-Link Layer (Layer 2 of the OSI Reference Model) driver for communicating with the Network Interface Card (NIC), and a Network Layer (Layer 3 of the OSI Reference Model) driver for communicating with network-level protocols.

See also **Network Interface Card; OSI Reference Model; Token Ring.**

Adaptive Differential Pulse Code Modulation (ADPCM)

A process that uses high statistical correlations between consecutive voice samples to create a variable that subdivides the scale of vocal pitch into measurable increments. ADPCM is used to encode analog voice samples into digital signals.

adaptive routing

A method used to reroute messages dynamically through the network by using the best available path.

ADB

Apple Desktop Bus, a serial communications link used to connect low-speed input devices to a Macintosh SE, II, IIx, IIcx, and

SE/30 computer. Up to 16 devices can be daisy-chained to a single Apple Desktop Bus.

ADC

Analog-to-Digital Converter, a device used to convert analog signals to digital signals.

ADCCP

Advanced Data-Communications Control Procedures, an American National Standards Institute (ANSI) standard communications protocol that is bit-oriented, symmetrical, and based on IBM's Synchronous Data-Link Control (SDLC).

See also **American National Standards Institute; Synchronous Data-Link Control.**

add

A term used when including a new device or user in the network.

ADD NAME SPACE utility

A NetWare and IntranetWare server console command used to prepare a NetWare server volume to store OS/2, Macintosh, or UNIX files.

See also **NetWare Loadable Module; NetWare utilities.**

Add Self right

A NetWare property right that gives a trustee the privilege of adding itself as a value of that property. Used only for properties that contain object names as values.

ADDICON utility

An IntranetWare workstation utility that modifies existing Windows 3.1x group (.GRP) files to add icons in the Program Manager group.

See also **NetWare Loadable Module; NetWare utilities.**

ADDMD

Administrative Directory-Management Domain, part of the Consultative Committee for International Telegraphy and Telephony (CCITT) X.500 directory services model. The ADDMD is a set of directory-system agents controlled by a single authority.

See also **Consultative Committee for International Telegraphy and Telephony; X.500.**

add-on board

A circuit board that can be added to a personal computer to give it additional capabilities. For example, memory boards increase the amount of random-access memory (RAM); network boards permit computers to communicate with each other and with a central server.

address

A type of identifier. Addresses can be assigned to network stations and devices, or to locations in memory or disk storage. To receive and reply to messages, each device must have a distinct address.

Address and Control Field compression

A way to minimize unnecessary network overhead. This technique eliminates the All

Stations Address and the Unnumbered Information fields from High-Level Data-Link Control (HDLC) framing on a per-link basis.

address book

A feature of communications programs that stores and arranges electronic mail (e-mail) addresses for future reference.

address bus

The electrical signal lines where memory locations are specified. Each signal line carries one bit. For example, 20 lines on a bus allow access to 1 MB of memory; 32 lines allow access to 4 GB of memory.

Address Field

A frame field that specifies the virtual-circuit numbering or data-link connection identifier, flow control, and frame-discard eligibility. Various local-area network (LAN) topologies may use different sized address fields.

Address Mapping Table

A table generated by the AppleTalk Address-Resolution Protocol to map AppleTalk node addresses.
    See also **AppleTalk Address-Resolution Protocol.**

address mask

Part of the Internet Protocol addressing schema. The address mask, also known as a *subnet mask*, is a group of bits whose values identify a subnetwork. The address mask simplifies the process of referring to members of a given subnet.

address resolution

The process of mapping a hardware-dependent (physical) address to a network (local) address. A Network Interface Card (NIC) contains a table that maps physical addresses to local addresses. To create entries in the table, a network protocol broadcasts a request to a target (local) address and the target responds with its physical address. The NIC then adds the physical address to the table so messages can be sent to the target.
    See also **Address-Resolution Protocol.**

address-resolution cache

An area of memory that contains the entries used to IP addresses to physical addresses. When a node broadcasts an Address Resolution Protocol (ARP) request, a response will be subsequently received and an entry created in the address-resolution cache.

Address-Resolution Protocol (ARP)

A method used to determine the physical address of a target host. A part of the Internet Protocol (IP) and AppleTalk protocol, ARP permits a host that knows only the logical (IP) address of a target host to find the physical (Media-Access Control, or MAC) address of the same target host. The key to this translation is a Network Interface Card (NIC) containing a table that maps IP addresses to MAC addresses for all objects on the network. Entries to table are made automatically when ARP sends a request with the target's IP address. The target issues a response containing its MAC address, and the NIC then adds that MAC address to its ARP table for future reference. (Note: Only networks capable of hardware broadcasts can use ARP.)

Address-Translation Table

A table containing IP addresses and their equivalent physical addresses.

addressed call mode

A mode permitting control signals and commands to establish and terminate calls in the V.25*bis* in-band dialing standard established by the Consultative Committee for International Telegraphy and Telephony (CCIT).

See also **V.25*bis*.**

addressing

A method of assigning numbers for identification purposes. The Media-Access Control (MAC) protocols implemented via hardware define the address of each node on a network segment.

addressing space

The amount of total random-access memory (RAM) available to the operating system in a NetWare 4 server. The space can be further subdivided into domains. The maximum theoretical addressing space is 4GB; practically, however, it is usually much lower.

adjacencies database

A database used in the NetWare Link-Services Protocol (NLSP) to track devices adjacent to a router. The database also tracks the states of each link to the neighboring devices. Each neighboring device responds to the router with a Hello packet, after which the router adds a record of the device to the adjacencies database. If the router fails and the devices stop receiving Hello packets, neighboring devices retain their adjacency for a preconfigured time period.

adjacency

A record kept by a NetWare Link-Services Protocol (NLSP) router concerning its connections to adjacent devices.

adjacency state

In the NetWare Link-Services Protocol (NLSP), the condition of a router's adjacency to neighboring devices. For example, the adjacency state is "down" if the link has been terminated and no Hello packets are being sent.

adjacent channel

The frequency band just before or just after the current channel.

adjacent nodes

Systems Network Architecture (SNA) nodes connected to a given node with no intervening nodes.

See also **Systems Network Architecture.**

ADMD

Administration-Management Domain, a specification of the Consultative Committee for International Telegraphy and Telephony (CCITT) X.400 Message Handling System (MHS) model. An ADMD is a public carrier (such as MCI Mail or AT&T Mail) that can handle any international connection. The ADMD runs in accordance with CCITT guidelines. All the ADMDs in the world combine to form a single, global X.400 network.

See also **Consultative Committee for International Telegraphy and Telephony; Message Handling System; X.400.**

Admin

A Novell Directory Services (NDS) User object, created in the process of installing NetWare 4.*x*, that has special privileges; these include supervisory rights to manage an NDS Directory tree and to create or delete Directory objects. When the Directory tree is first created, ADMIN has a trustee assignment to the [Root] object. Because the trustee assignment includes the Supervisor object right, ADMIN can create and manage any object in the tree. Additional objects can later be given the Supervisor object right if you need to decentralize control of the network. *Caution: Do not delete this object. If the ADMIN object must be deleted, another user must be granted full Directory rights beforehand.*

See **ADMIN object.**

ADMIN object

A Novell Directory Services (NDS) User object, created in the process of installing

NetWare 4.*x*, that has special privileges; these include supervisory rights to manage an NDS Directory tree and to create or delete Directory objects. When the Directory tree is first created, ADMIN has a trustee assignment to the [Root] object. Because the trustee assignment includes the Supervisor object right, ADMIN can create and manage any object in the tree. Additional objects can later be given the Supervisor object right if you need to decentralize control of the network. *Caution: Do not delete this object. If the ADMIN object must be deleted, another user must be granted full Directory rights beforehand.*

administration

Tasks performed by the network supervisor or administrator. The supervisor has access rights to all volumes, directories, and files. These tasks may include configuration management, hardware and software maintenance, and performance monitoring.

Administration-Management Domain (ADMD)

A specification of the Consultative Committee for International Telegraphy and Telephony (CCITT) X.400 Message-Handling System (MHS) model. An ADMD is a public carrier (such as MCI Mail or AT&T Mail) that can handle any international connection. The ADMD runs in accordance with CCITT guidelines. All the ADMDs in the world combine to form a single, global X.400 network.

See also **Consultative Committee for International Telegraphy and Telephony; Message-Handling System; X.400.**

Administrative Directory-Management Domain (ADDMD)

Part of the Consultative Committee for International Telegraphy and Telephony (CCITT) X.500 directory services model. The ADDMD is a set of directory system agents controlled by a single authority.

See also **Consultative Committee for International Telegraphy and Telephony; X.500.**

administrative distance

A rating that measures the trustworthiness of a routing-information source.

Administrative Domain (AD)

The nodes, routers, and connectors managed by a single administrator.

administrative privileges

Special access and modification privileges granted to a user, typically the administrator. Administrative privileges must be granted in the LAN Server domain before accessing LAN Server network information.

administrator

An individual responsible for maintenance and administration of a network. The administrator's tasks usually include setting up the server, creating user accounts, establishing security and maintaining the server. In NetWare 4.*x*, the default account for the administrator is ADMIN. In NetWare 2.*x* and NetWare 3.*x*, the account for the administrator is SUPERVISOR.

See also **ADMIN object.**

administrator object

A Novell Directory Services (NDS) User object, created in the process of installing NetWare 4.*x*, that has special privileges; these include supervisory rights to manage an NDS Directory tree and to create or delete Directory objects. When the Directory tree is first created, ADMIN has a trustee assignment to the [Root] object. Because the trustee assignment includes the Supervisor object right, ADMIN can create and manage any object in the tree. Additional objects can later be given the Supervisor object right if you need to decentralize control of the network. *Caution: Do not delete this object. If the ADMIN object must be deleted, another user must be granted full Directory rights beforehand.*

See **ADMIN object.**

ADN

Advanced Digital Network, a 56-kilobit-per-second leased line.

See also **leased line.**

ADPCM

Adaptive Differential Pulse Code Modulation, a process that uses high statistical correlations between consecutive voice samples to create a variable that subdivides the scale of vocal pitch into measurable increments. ADPCM is used to encode analog voice samples into digital signals.

ADSL

Asymmetric Digital Subscriber Line, a high-speed telecommunications method used to move data over regular telephone lines. ADSL is sometimes used as an alternative to Integrated-Services Digital Network (ISDN) lines.

See also **Integrated-Services Digital Network.**

ADSP

AppleTalk Data-Stream Protocol, part of the AppleTalk protocol suite that establishes full-duplex byte-stream service between sockets. This is a symmetric, connection-oriented protocol. Through ADSP, two processors can open a virtual data pipe for reading and writing information to and from one another.

See also **AppleTalk; AppleTalk protocols.**

ADSP (NLM)

AppleTalk Data-Stream Protocol (NetWare Loadable Module), a NetWare Loadable Module (NLM) that loads the AppleTalk Data Stream Protocol (ADSP) when installing NetWare for Macintosh.

See also **NetWare utilities.**

ADSU

ATM Data-Service Unit, a Data-Service Unit (DSU) used to access an Asynchronous Transfer Mode (ATM) network through a High-Speed Serial Interface (HSSI).

See also **Data Service Unit; Asynchronous Transfer Mode; High-Speed Serial Interface.**

Advanced Communications Function (ACF)

A family of IBM software running under Systems Network Architecture (SNA). ACF programs have diverse functions. For example, *ACF/NCP (Network-Control Program)* controls communications between network devices and a host machine; *ACF/TCAM (Telecommunications Access Method)* is a VTAM application that handles messages; *ACF/VTAM (Virtual Telecommunications Access Method)* controls communications between terminal and host machines, replacing the earlier *ACF/VTAME (Virtual Telecommunications Access Method-Entry)* program.

See also **Systems Network Architecture; Virtual Telecommunications Access Method.**

Advanced Data-Communications Control Procedures (ADCCP)

An American National Standards Institute (ANSI) standard communications protocol that is bit-oriented, symmetrical, and based on IBM's Synchronous Data-Link Control (SDLC).

See also **American National Standards Institute; Synchronous Data-Link Control.**

Advanced Digital Network (ADN)

A 56-kilobit-per-second leased line.
See also **leased line.**

Advanced Function Printing (AFP)

An IBM Systems Application Architecture (SAA) term for the capability to print both text and images.

See also **Systems Application Architecture.**

Advanced Intelligent Network (AIN)

A telecommunications term referring to a sophisticated digital network that does not yet exist.

Advanced Interactive Executive (AIX)

The IBM operating system for UNIX environments. AIX is licensed by IBM and is designed to work on IBM workstations, minicomputers, and mainframes.

Advanced Mobile Phone Service (AMPS)

An analog cellular-telephone service that operates between 825 and 890 megahertz (MHz). Initially developed by AT&T, AMPS uses Frequency-Division Multiplexing (FDM) and is widely used in the United States.

See also **Frequency-Division Multiplexing.**

Advanced Network Services (ANS)

A large, high-speed network on the Internet run by Merit, MCI, and IBM.

See also **Internet.**

Advanced Peer-to-Peer Networking (APPN)

A network architecture defined by IBM's Systems Application Architecture (SAA). APPN facilitates peer communications between microcomputers, without involving a mainframe computer or other Systems Network Architecture (SNA) device. Unlike SNA, APPN supports dynamic packet routing.

See also **Systems Application Architecture; Systems Network Architecture.**

Advanced Peer-to-Peer Internetworking (APPI)

An internetwork architecture defined by IBM's Systems Application Architecture (SAA).

See also **Advanced Peer-to-Peer Networking.**

Advanced Program-to-Program Communications (APPC)

Part of the Systems Network Architecture (SNA) protocol that involves logical unit type 6.2 (LU 6.2) and that allows programs to communicate over the network. APPC facilitates communication between multiple processes in an SNA network, without having to involve a common host system or use terminal emulation. It can be used over an SNA, Ethernet, X.25, or Token Ring network.

See also **Ethernet; logical unit type 6.2; Systems Network Architecture; Token Ring; X.25.**

Advanced Research Projects Agency (ARPA)

The government agency that funded the initial development of the Internet. The agency is now called the Defense Advanced Research Projects Agency (DARPA).

See also **Defense Advanced Research Projects Agency.**

Advanced Research Projects Agency Network (ARPAnet)

The first large, packet-switched wide-area network (WAN). ARPAnet was developed in the 1970s with funding from the Advanced Research Projects Agency (ARPA). ARPAnet was officially decommissioned in 1991.

The ARPAnet project gave birth to Transmission-Control Protocol/Internet Protocol (TCP/IP) and other commonly used network protocols, and eventually became the Internet.

See also **Transmission Control Protocol/Internet Protocol; wide-area network.**

advanced run-length-limited (ARLL) encoding

A method used to store information on a hard disk. ARLL increases the capacity of run-length-limited (RLL) storage and increases the data-transfer rate.

Advanced Services

A set of NetWare Loadable Modules (NLMs) that permit low-level access to the operating system. These services include dynamic array, extended attributes, and hardware management.

Advantage networks

A Digital Equipment Corp. (DEC) networking strategy that adds Transmission-Control Protocol/Internet Protocol (TCP/IP) support to Digital's DECnet Phase V architecture.

For more information about networking products from Digital Equipment Corp., surf the Web to http://www.digital.com/info/internet/networks/index.html.

Adverse Channel Enhancement (ACE)

A method of adjusting a modem to compensate for noisy communications lines.

advertising

A process used by devices on a network to inform other devices of their existence. Under NetWare, devices accomplish advertising via the Service-Advertising Protocol (SAP).

See also **Service-Advertising Protocol.**

AE

Application Entity, under the OSI Reference Model, a process or function that runs all or part of an application. An AE is made up of one or more application service elements (ASEs).

See also **OSI Reference Model.**

AEP

AppleTalk Echo Protocol, part of the AppleTalk protocol suite that exists on the Transport Layer, and is used to determine whether two nodes are connected and available.

See also **AppleTalk; AppleTalk protocols.**

AES Events

A field of the Available Processes & Interrupts screen found on the NetWare 4.02 MONITOR NetWare Loadable Module (NLM). AES stands for Asynchronous Event Scheduler. Through a series of menus and submenus, the MONITOR NLM allows

viewing of various server characteristics and performance of a variety of system maintenance functions.

See also **Available Processes & Interrupts; MONITOR; NetWare Loadable Module.**

AES Process

A field of the Available Processes & Interrupts screen found on the NetWare 4.02 MONITOR NetWare Loadable Module (NLM). AES stands for Asynchronous Event Scheduler. Through a series of menus and submenus, the MONITOR NLM allows viewing of various server characteristics and performance of a variety of system maintenance functions.

See also **Available Processes & Interrupts; MONITOR; NetWare Loadable Module.**

AES Process Call-Backs

A selectable option of the Available Options/Resource Utilization screen of the NetWare 3.12 MONITOR NetWare Loadable Module (NLM). This option, which stands Asynchronous Event Scheduler, permits an NLM to schedule a future event.

See also **MONITOR; NetWare Loadable Module.**

AES Process resource tag

A tag used in the Asynchronous Event Scheduler (AES) process.

AFI

Authority and Format Identifier, under the OSI Reference Model, the part of an

address used for the Network-Layer (Layer 3) Service-Access Point (NSAP). The AFI specifies the administrator responsible for allocating the Initial Domain Identifier (IDI) values.

See also **Initial Domain Identifier; OSI Reference Model.**

AFP

Advanced Function Printing, an IBM Systems Application Architecture (SAA) term for the capability to print both text and images.

See also **Systems Application Architecture.**

AFP (NLM)

A NetWare Loadable Module (NLM) that processes AppleTalk Filing Protocol (AFP) file requests from Macintosh workstations. Once loaded, the AFP NLM establishes the AFP file service environment. The AFP module is loaded from the file server's AUTOEXEC.NCF file.

See also **AppleTalk Filing Protocol; NetWare Loadable Module; NetWare utilities.**

AFP server

A Directory Schema term. The AFP server rebuilds the desktop database in the event of corruption. The AFP server may also function as a NetWare router and AppleTalk server to Apple Macintosh computers on a NetWare network.

See also **AppleTalk Filing Protocol.**

AFP Server object

A leaf object that represents an AFP-based server functioning as a node on the NetWare network. The AFP (AppleTalk Filing Protocol) Server may also function as a NetWare router to Macintosh computers, or as an AppleTalk server to Macintosh computers.

See also **AppleTalk Filing Protocol; leaf object; Novell Directory Services; object.**

AFP shutdown operation

An operation that disconnects all users. After the AFP shutdown operation, the AFP server no longer appears in the Macintosh Chooser.

See also **AppleTalk Filing Protocol.**

AFPCON (NLM)

An AppleTalk File Services utility used to configure the AFP NetWare Loadable Module (NLM) from the server console. The administrator can use APFCON to customize the file services of NetWare for Macintosh to optimize performance.

See also **NetWare Loadable Module; NetWare utilities.**

AFS protocol

A distributed file system, developed at Carnegie-Mellon University, that allows users to easily share and access all files on a network.

See **Andrew File System protocol.**

AFT

Application File Transfer, a prefix used in the International Standardized Profile (ISP)

grouping to identify File Transfer, Access, and Management (FTAM) profiles.

See also **File Transfer, Access, and Management.**

agent

The part of a client/server system that automatically prepares and exchanges information or executes a task on behalf of a client or server application. Examples of agents are NetWare Management Agent, Simple Network-Management Protocol (SNMP) agent, and Target Service Agent (TSA).

See also **NetWare Management Agents; Simple Network-Management Protocol; Target Service Agent.**

aging

The process of systematically removing older items or table entries.

AI

Authentication Information, the information used to determine whether a network user is authorized to access the system.

AIFF

Audio Interchange File Format, a file format used to store and exchange sounds in sound files found on the Internet.

AIM

Analog Intensity Modulation, a modulation method used for communications, that uses light instead of electrical signals. The intensity of the light source varies as a function of the transmitted signal.

AIN

Advanced Intelligent Network, a telecommunications term referring to a sophisticated digital network that does not yet exist.

AIO port driver

An Asynchronous I/O (AIO) port driver used to integrate asynchronous (serial) adapters with such Novell software as NetWare Connect and NetWare (and IntranetWare) MultiProtocol Router.

AIOCOMX (NLM)

A NetWare Loadable Module (NLM) that is a communications port driver to be used with utilities such as Remote Console.

See also **NetWare Loadable Module; NetWare utilities.**

AIS

Alarm-Indication Signal, a signal that indicates the presence of a warning signal on the network. The AIS is used in broadband Integrated-Services Digital Networks (ISDNs) and in the OSI Network-Management Model.

See also **Integrated-Services Digital Network; OSI Network-Management Model.**

AIX

Advanced Interactive Executive, the IBM operating system for UNIX environments. AIX is licensed by IBM and is designed to work on IBM workstations, minicomputers, and mainframes.

AL

Application Layer, the seventh layer in the OSI model. The Application Layer furnishes users with access to the network, and sends a stream of bytes to the Transport Layer (the fourth layer) on the source machine. The Application Layer includes utilities such as file-transfer and terminal-emulation services.

See also **OSI Reference Model.**

alarm

A warning signal used to inform a network administrator of an event. The signal may be audible or visible, and typically calls the administrator's attention to an error or critical situation that has occurred on the network. Alarms can indicate the severity or type of related event, and may trigger an automatic response from network-management software.

Alarm-Indication Signal (AIS)

A signal that indicates the presence of a warning signal on the network. The AIS is used in broadband Integrated-Services Digital Networks (ISDNs) and in the OSI Network-Management Model.

See also **Integrated-Services Digital Network; OSI Network-Management Model.**

Alarm-Reporting Function (ARF)

Under the OSI Network-Management Model, a Systems-Management Function (SMF) service that reports failures, faults, and other problems.

See also **OSI Network-Management Model; Systems-Management Function.**

a-law

A standard from the Consultative Committee for International Telegraphy and Telephony (CCITT) used for converting analog signals to digital (and vice versa) in a Pulse Code Modulation (PCM) system. Used primarily in telephone networks in Europe, a-law is similar to the North American mu-law standard.

See also **Consultative Committee for International Telegraphy and Telephony; mu-law; Pulse Code Modulation.**

alert

An alarm sent by an agent to the administrator, indicating that a problem or other critical event has occurred.

algorithm

A mathematical process used to solve a specific problem. The algorithm consists of a set of well-defined rules or processes. An algorithm can be used to create data compression, or lists of random numbers. For example, a *spanning-tree algorithm* computes open data paths in a network to select a route for a data packet; if one path is inoperable, it finds an alternate path.

alias

An object that points to another object, usually named in an easily recognizable manner. Aliases are meant to simplify access to files and objects by establishing easy-to-recall nicknames for a file or object whose name may be otherwise difficult to recall.

Alias object

A Novell Directory Services (NDS) leaf object that points to the original location of an object in a Directory tree. Using an alias can make a Directory object appear to be in several places within the same Directory. Sometimes an alias names a container object (for example, a container object named *printers* may point to all printers on the network). The Alias object has the following selectable NDS properties: Access-Control List, Aliased-Object Name, Back Link, Bindery, and Object Class.

See also **leaf object; Novell Directory Services; object.**

ALIAS utility

An IntranetWare server console utility that defines a keyword to represent text or a command. When the user types the keyword at the command line, the server replaces the keyword with the text, or executes the command.

See also **NetWare Loadable Module; NetWare utilities.**

Aliased Object Name

A selectable property for the Novell Directory Services (NDS) Alias leaf object, indicating that an object name has been given an alias.

See also **leaf object; Novell Directory Services; object.**

alignment error

A networking error that results from a packet having extra bits. This type of error may be caused by a faulty component or cable.

All-in-1

An office-management software package from Digital Equipment Corporation.

All-in-One Search Page search engine

An Internet metasearch engine that includes 11 search categories and a variety of search tools. Simple text queries are allowed; more complicated searches are possible with the supplied search tools.

See also **metasearch engine.**

All Properties

A property-rights option that grants a trustee specific rights to all properties at once (as opposed to assigning rights individually).

Alloc Short-Term Memory

A selectable option in the Available Options/Resource Utilization screen of the NetWare 3.12 MONITOR NetWare Loadable Module (NLM). This tracked resource is used for short-term memory requests. NLMs with popup windows use Alloc Memory to store menu information previously visible on-screen. When a user returns to a previous menu, the allocated memory immediately returns to the system.

See also **MONITOR; memory; NetWare Loadable Module.**

Allocate Block Count

A field name from the Cache Utilization screen of the MONITOR NetWare Loadable Module (NLM). Through a series of menus and submenus, the MONITOR NLM allows viewing of various server characteristics and performance of a variety of system maintenance functions.

See also **MONITOR; NetWare Loadable Module.**

Allocate Still Waiting

A field name from the Cache Utilization screen of the MONITOR NetWare Loadable Module (NLM). Through a series of menus and submenus, the MONITOR NLM allows viewing of various server characteristics and performance of a variety of system maintenance functions.

See also **MONITOR; NetWare Loadable Module.**

Allocate Wait

A field name from the Cache Utilization screen of the MONITOR NetWare Loadable Module (NLM). Through a series of menus and submenus, the MONITOR NLM allows viewing of various server characteristics and performance of a variety of system maintenance functions.

See also **MONITOR; NetWare Loadable Module.**

Allocated from AVAIL

A field name from the Cache Utilization screen of the MONITOR NetWare Loadable Module (NLM). Through a series of menus and submenus, the MONITOR NLM allows viewing of various server characteristics and performance of a variety of system maintenance functions.

See also **MONITOR; NetWare Loadable Module.**

Allocated from LRU

A field name from the Cache Utilization screen of the MONITOR NetWare Loadable Module (NLM). Through a series of menus and submenus, the MONITOR NLM allows viewing of various server characteristics and performance of a variety of system maintenance functions.

See also **MONITOR; NetWare Loadable Module.**

allocation unit

A NetWare term that denotes an area used to store information from files and tables. An allocation unit may be a block or buffer. A block stores data on disk, and a buffer stores data temporarily in random-access memory (RAM).

ALLOW utility

A NetWare 3.x workstation utility that sets or views rights for a file or directory. This utility has been superseded by the RIGHTS utility in NetWare 4.x.

See also **NetWare Loadable Module; NetWare utilities.**

Allow Unlimited Credit

A Directory Schema term and a selectable property for the AFP Server, Messaging Server, NCP Server, Print Server, and User objects in Novell Directory Services (NDS). As a Directory Services Schema attribute, this parameter allows a user to access and use any network service to which access has been given, without having to have a minimum account balance. The default setting for this parameter is "No." Change to "Yes" to allow unlimited credit.

See also **leaf object; Novell Directory Services; object.**

Allow User to Change Password

A selectable property for the User object in Novell Directory Services (NDS) sometimes abbreviated to "Change Password." The default is set to "Yes." If it is set to "No," the user is not able to change the account's login script with SYSCON.

See also **leaf object; Novell Directory Services; object.**

ALOHA

An access control technique used in transmission-media systems to permit multiple stations to transmit data simultaneously.

alpha testing

The first step in testing a new hardware or software product. The stage precedes *beta testing*, and is usually performed in-house.

alphanumeric

A term that describes the combination of letters, numbers, and sometimes control characters, space characters, or other special characters that make up text.

alt newsgroup

An Internet newsgroup that discusses "alternative" topics, often controversial, that are usually outside the mainstream (such as sexually explicit subjects).

See also **newsgroup.**

Alta Vista search engine

An Internet search engine from Digital Equipment Corporation that tells the user how many matches it found for a search string, provides a hotlinked title and Universal Resource Locator (URL), the first few words of the page's text, a file size, and the date on which Alta Vista inserted the entry into its vast database. Results are ranked and presented with best matches appearing first in the list. Alta Vista provides a capability to search Web sites and Usenet groups.

See also **search engine; Usenet.**

For information about Alta Vista, surf the Web to http://www.altavista.digital.com.

Alternate Bipolar (ABP)

A signal-encoding method in which a positive, negative, or zero voltage is used. A zero voltage usually represents one value and a nonzero voltage represents another.

See also **encoding (signal).**

alternate collating sequence

A sorting sequence that differs from the industry-standard sequence of the American Standard Code for Information Interchange (ASCII). The Btrieve record management system uses an alternate collating sequence to sort keys.

See also **Btrieve.**

Alternate Mark Inversion (AMI)

A signal-encoding mechanism used to detect noise-induced hardware errors: 1 is represented alternately as positive or negative; 0 is represented as zero voltage.

Alternate Route Selection (ARS)

A telephony process used to select a path for transmission.

alternate routing

The use of an alternative communications path if the primary path is unavailable.

Alternating Current (AC)

A power supply in which the polarity periodically switches. AC power is typically supplied to most homes and offices in the United States. The amount of power supplied at any time depends on the switching process. A pure AC supply will generate a sine wave over time. In North America, alternating current switches polarity 60 times per second; the rate differs in other countries.

a.m.

The period between midnight and noon on a 12-hour clock. If a.m. or p.m. is not specified when a user enters a time value, some computer operating systems (such as NetWare) assume military time (a 24-hour clock).

AM

(1) **Account Management,** a subdivision of accounts managed by a single entity.
(2) **Active Monitor,** the first station to be started on a Token Ring network. The Active Monitor detects and addresses error conditions

in the background, and is responsible for passing and maintaining the token. The performance of the AM is constantly monitored by a Standby Monitor (SM) to guarantee the integrity of the token-passing process.

(3) amplitude modulation, a technique that conveys information by varying the amplitude of the carrier signal.

See also **(2) Standby Monitor;** **(2) Token Ring.**

ambiguous filename

A filename in which a wildcard character of ? or * replaces one or more characters. An ambiguous filename may reference more than one file.

AME

Asynchronous Modem Eliminator, also known as a *null modem,* a serial cable and connector with a modified pin configuration that allows two computers to communicate directly without using a physical modem.

America Online (AOL)

An online information service that also provides Internet access, discussion forums, specialized content, and other added value.

 **For information about America Online, surf the Web to** http://www.aol.com.

American National Standards Institute (ANSI)

The standards body responsible for several data communications and terminal stan-

dards. ANSI is the U.S. representative of the Consultative Committee for International Telegraphy and Telephony (CCITT) and the International Standards Organization (ISO).

See also **Consultative Committee for International Telegraphy and Telephony; International Standards Organization.**

American Standard Code for Information Interchange (ASCII)

A 7-bit code employed as a U.S. standard for interchanging data between communications devices. ASCII is commonly used in local-area networks (LANs). The standard ASCII character set has values between 0 and 127, each of which is assigned to a letter, number, or other character; the first 32 characters are control codes. An additional 128 characters, the *extended ASCII character set,* may not have the same functions in all computers or display the same in all programs. Appendix B contains the standard ASCII Character Set.

American Wire Gauge (AWG)

A classification system for copper wire. The values are based on the diameter, or gauge, of the wire; lower gauge numbers correspond to the thicker wires.

AMF

Account-Metering Function, under the OSI Network-Management Model, the function that tracks each user's resource usage.

See also **OSI Network-Management Model.**

AMH

Application Message Handling, under the International Standardized Profile (ISP) model, a prefix identifying Message-Handling System (MHS) actions.
See also **Message-Handling System.**

AMI

Alternate Mark Inversion, a signal-encoding mechanism used to detect noise-induced hardware errors: 1 is represented alternately as positive or negative; 0 is represented as zero voltage.

AMP

Active Monitor Present, a Token Ring term. AMP status is determined by a packet issued every three seconds by the ring's active monitor; the packet indicates that the active monitor is still functional.
See also **Token Ring.**

amplifier

A device used to boost an analog signal.

amplitude

The magnitude of a signal. An electrical signal's amplitude usually is expressed in volts.

amplitude modulation (AM)

A technique that conveys information by varying the amplitude of the carrier signal.

AMPS

Advanced Mobile Phone Service, an analog cellular-telephone service that operates between 825 and 890 megahertz (MHz). Initially developed by AT&T, AMPS uses Frequency-Division Multiplexing (FDM) and is widely used in the United States.
See also **Frequency-Division Multiplexing.**

analog

A term that means proportion or ratio, and also refers to a method of representing values by continuously varying a physical property (such voltage in a circuit). Electronic devices that use this method are called *analog devices;* they can represent an almost-infinite number of values. By contrast, a *digital device* (which maps values onto discrete numbers) can represent a finite range of values based on its capabilities of resolution.

analog communication

A telecommunications system, such as the voice-based telephone system, that uses analog signals to represent information.

Analog Intensity Modulation (AIM)

A modulation method used for communications, that uses light instead of electrical signals. The intensity of the light source varies as a function of the transmitted signal.

analog signal

A continuous, sinusoidal communication (a communication signal that can be represented as a sine wave) often used in the context of transmission methods developed to transmit voice rather than high-speed digital signals.

See also **digital signal.**

Analog Simultaneous Voice Data (ASVD)

A specification standard under consideration by the International Telecommunications Union (ITU) that describes the capability to transmit multimedia data over analog telephone lines. Despite a more restricted bandwidth, ASVD transmission is being considered as an alternative to Integrated-Services Digital Network (ISDN) transmission.

analog-to-digital conversion

The process of converting an analog signal to digital form. This is accomplished with an analog-to-digital converter (ADC) device.

Analog-to-Digital Converter (ADC)

A device used to convert analog signals to digital signals.

anchor

A starting point for a hypertext link that a user clicks to advance to a link location.

See also **hypertext.**

Andrew File System (AFS) protocol

A distributed file system, developed at Carnegie-Mellon University, that allows users to easily share and access all files on a network.

ANF

AppleTalk Networking Forum, a consortium of developers and software vendors whose task is to encapsulate AppleTalk in other protocols such as Transmission-Control Protocol/Internet Protocol (TCP/IP).

See also **Transmission-Control Protocol/Internet Protocol.**

ANI

Automatic Number Identification, a feature that includes the sender's identification number in the transmission. In telephony, this is also known as *caller ID*, and allows the recipient of a phone call to see who is calling before answering the phone. ANI is often tied to a database of caller information, thereby allowing customer-service agents to view a caller's entire record as soon as the call is answered.

Annex D

The American National Standards Institute (ANSI) t1.617 implementation standard that addresses signaling and other network-management functions in a Frame Relay network.

See also **American National Standards Institute; Frame Relay network.**

Anonymous FTP

An Application-Layer (Layer 7 of the OSI Reference Model) protocol of the Transmission Control Protocol/Internet Protocol (TCP/IP) suite that allows a user to retrieve publicly available files from other networks.

See also **OSI Reference Model; Transmission-Control Protocol/Internet Protocol.**

anonymous remailer

A server used to facilitate privacy by maintaining an internal list of anonymous IDs that correspond to valid electronic-mail (e-mail) addresses. An anonymous remailer typically provides this service free of charge, allowing users to send an e-mail to a newsgroup or individual without the recipient becoming aware of the sender's name or e-mail address.

See also **electronic mail; newsgroup.**

ANS

Advanced Network Services, a large, high-speed network on the Internet run by Merit, MCI, and IBM.

See also **Internet.**

ANSI

American National Standards Institute, the standards body responsible for several data communications and terminal standards. ANSI is the U.S. representative of the Consultative Committee for International Telegraphy and Telephony (CCITT) and the International Standards Organization (ISO).

See also **Consultative Committee for International Telegraphy and Telephony; International Standards Organization.**

answer mode

A modem setting that allows the modem to automatically answer an incoming call. The answer mode is determined by the AT command ATS0=n, where n is the number of rings the modem waits before answering the call.

See also **Hayes-compatible modem.**

antivirus program

A type of computer program used to detect and/or remove computer viruses. These programs seek out suspicious activity (such as unnecessary disk access), or look for patterns that indicate the presence of specific viruses. An antivirus program may function as a terminate-and-stay resident (TSR) program that monitors activity constantly; or it may be run on a predetermined schedule. The antivirus program should be updated periodically; new viruses are constantly being released.

See also **terminate-and-stay resident.**

AOL

America Online, an online information service that also provides Internet access, discussion forums, specialized content, and other added value.

For information about America Online, surf the Web to `http://www.aol.com`.

AOM

Application OSI Management, under the International Standardized Profile (ISP) model, a prefix used to denote functions and services for network management.

AOW

Asia and Oceania Workshop, one of three workshops for implementers of the OSI Reference Model. The other workshops are the European Workshop for Open Systems (EWOC) and OSI Implementers Workshop (OIW).

See also **OSI Reference Model.**

AP

Application Process, a program that makes use of Application Layer services under the OSI Reference Model. The AP receives the requested services from the application service elements (ASEs).

See also **OSI Reference Model.**

APD

Avalanche Photodiode, a detector component in a fiber-optic receiver. The APD converts light into electrical energy, emitting an "avalanche" of multiple electrons for each incoming photon.

APDU

Application-Protocol Data Unit, under the OSI Reference Model, a data packet that serves as the exchange unit in the Application Layer (Layer 7).

See also **OSI Reference Model.**

API

Application Program Interface, a set of abstractions that provide easy access to operating-system services and protocols. The application program uses the API to request low-level services from the operating system, usually for data communication, data retrieval, or access to system resources. In GUI-based operating systems, the API will also provide access to the various components of the interface.

APIA

Application Program Interface Association, the organization responsible for writing Application Program Interfaces (APIs) for the Consultative Committee for International Telegraphy and Telephony (CCITT) X.400 Message-Handling System (MHS).

See also **Application Program Interface; Consultative Committee for International Telegraphy and Telephony; Message Handling System; X.400.**

Apollo Domain

A proprietary network-protocol suite from Apollo Computer, used to communicate on proprietary networks.

APPC

Advanced Program-to-Program Communications, part of the Systems Network Architecture (SNA) protocol that involves logical unit type 6.2 (LU 6.2) and that allows programs to communicate over the network. APPC facilitates communication between multiple processes in an SNA network, without having to involve a common host system or use terminal emulation. It can be used over an SNA, Ethernet, X.25, or Token Ring network.

See also **Ethernet; logical unit type 6.2; Systems Network Architecture; Token Ring; X.25.**

Apple

Shortened name for Apple Computer, Inc., a manufacturer of computer hardware (including the Macintosh computer) and software (including the AppleTalk protocol suite).

Apple Attachment-Unit Interface (AAUI)

An EtherTalk hardware connection included on newer Macintosh computers.

Apple Desktop Bus (ADB)

A serial communications link used to connect low-speed input devices to a Macintosh SE, II, IIx, IIcx, and SE/30 computer. Up to 16 devices can be daisy-chained to a single Apple Desktop Bus.

Apple Internet Connection Kit

An Internet browser kit from Apple Computer that contains Netscape Navigator, Claris Emailer Lite, National Center for Supercomputer Applications (NCSA) Telnet, Alladin Stuffit Expander, Newswatcher, Fetch, MacTCP, and Apple Internet Dialer.
See also **browser.**

AppleDouble

An electronic-mail (e-mail) attachment format used with Apple Computers. AppleDouble performs best when sending attachments to recipients who have the capability to read Multipurpose Internet Mail Extensions (MIME).
See also **Multipurpose Internet Mail Extensions.**

AppleShare software

A networking software program from Apple Computer that allows a Macintosh computer to function as a file server in an AppleTalk network. The workstation version of AppleShare allows a Macintosh client to access an AppleShare server. An AppleTalk network file server can be either a Macintosh running AppleShare, or an IBM PC (or compatible) running NetWare for Macintosh.
See also **AppleTalk.**

AppleSingle

An electronic-mail (e-mail) attachment format used with Apple computers.

AppleTalk

A suite of proprietary products and protocols from Apple Computer, based on Carrier-Sense Multiple-Access/Collision Detection (CSMA/CD) protocols. The suite allows hardware and software on an AppleTalk network to communicate, facilitates the routing of data, and supports file and print services. As a layered environment, AppleTalk covers all networking services specified in the OSI Reference Model.
See also **AppleTalk protocols; Carrier-Sense Multiple-Access/Collision Detection; OSI Reference Model.**

For more information, Apple Computer's Web site on networking hardware and software is available at `http://www.abs.apple.com/.`

AppleTalk Address-Resolution Protocol (AARP)

A network-layer protocol in the AppleTalk protocol suite that maps AppleTalk addresses to physical addresses.
See also **AppleTalk; AppleTalk protocols.**

AppleTalk Data-Stream Protocol (ADSP)

Part of the AppleTalk protocol suite that establishes full-duplex, byte-stream service between sockets. This is a symmetric, connection-oriented protocol. Through ADSP, two processors can open a virtual data pipe for reading and writing information to and from one another.

See also **AppleTalk; AppleTalk protocols.**

AppleTalk Echo Protocol (AEP)

Part of the AppleTalk protocol suite that exists on the Transport Layer, and is used to determine whether two nodes are connected and available.

See also **AppleTalk; AppleTalk protocols.**

AppleTalk Extended Remote Printer (ATXRP) module

A NetWare Loadable Module (NLM) called ATXRP.NLM that works with PSERVER to send print jobs from a NetWare client to an AppleTalk printer. This module allows both Macintosh and non-Macintosh users to send print jobs to the same network printer.

See also **NetWare Loadable Module; NetWare utilities.**

AppleTalk File Services module

An NetWare Loadable Module (NLM) called AFP.NLM that allows Macintosh users to share files and applications with non-Macintosh users.

See also **NetWare Loadable Module; NetWare utilities.**

AppleTalk Filing Protocol (ATFP)

Apple Computer's network file system that allows workstations to share files and applications located on an AppleShare file server. Under NetWare, the AFP NetWare Loadable Module (NLM) runs on a NetWare server running NetWare for Macintosh. Under this configuration, ATFP allows the Macintosh users to share files by interacting with the NetWare file system. This term is sometimes also abbreviated "AFP," but has nothing to do with Advanced Function Printing (an IBM term also abbreviated "AFP"). ATFP is loosely based on the OSI Reference Model, and defines the Physical Layer (Layer 1) as LocalTalk, EtherTalk, and TokenTalk; the Network Layer (Layer 3) as Datagram-Delivery Protocol (DDP); the Transport Layer (Layer 4) as AppleTalk Session Protocol; addressing as Name-Binding Protocol; file sharing as AppleShare; and remote access as AppleTalk Remote Access.

Figure A.1 shows the hierarchy of the ATFP file system.

See also **AFP; AFP (NLM); AFP server; AppleTalk; AppleTalk File Services module; AppleTalk protocols; OSI Reference Model.**

AppleTalk module

Novell software that includes an AppleTalk Phase 2 router and required protocols.

AppleTalk network

A computer network based on the AppleTalk protocol. The AppleTalk software is used to link computers, printers, and other devices. A server on an AppleTalk network can be a Macintosh running AppleShare software, or an IBM-compatible PC running NetWare Communication Services software.

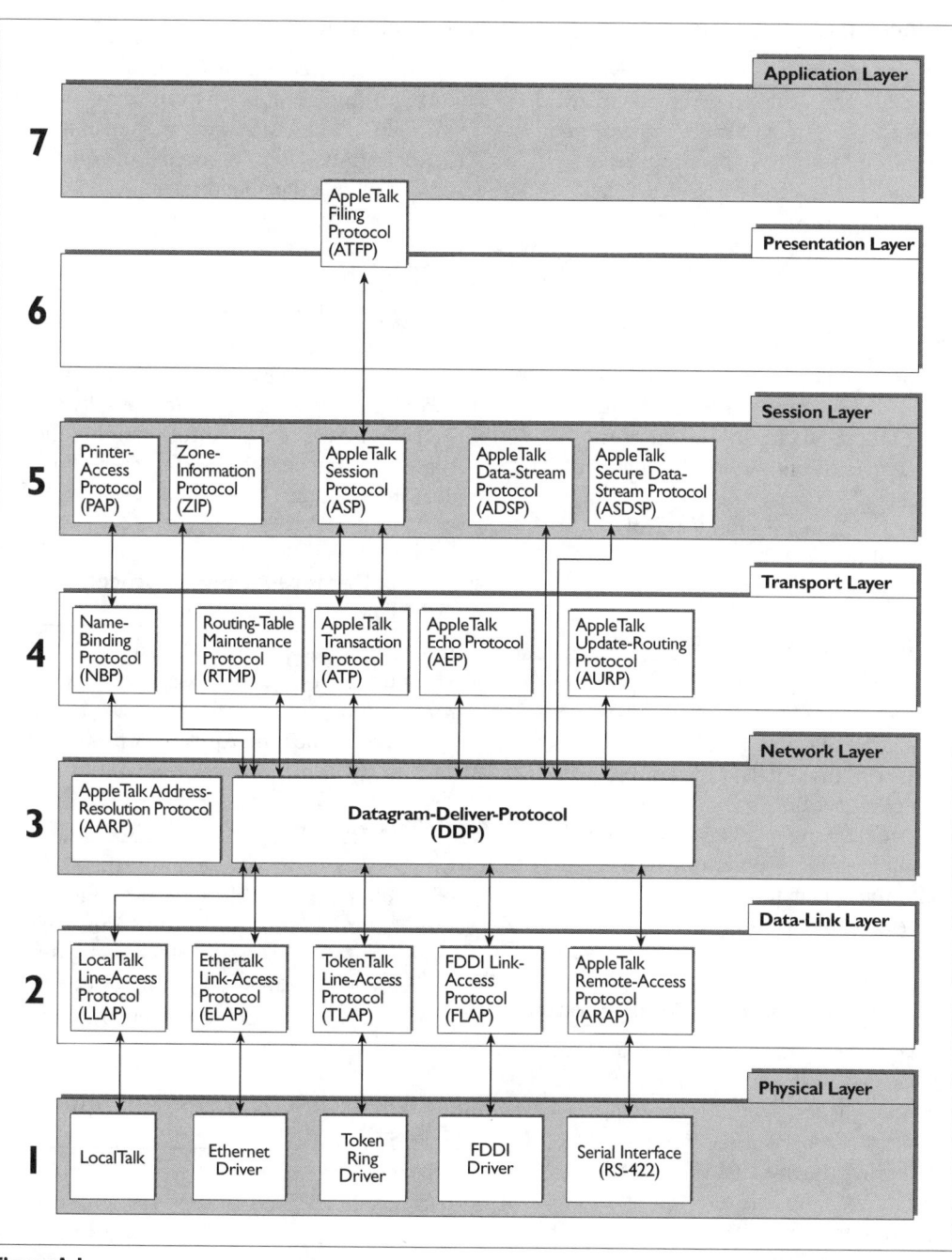

Figure A.1
AppleTalk Hierarchy

AppleTalk Network Zone

A logical grouping of AppleTalk devices. AppleTalk zones are defined by the network administrator. Any given device, such as a Macintosh computer, Apple printer, or NetWare server, can be assigned to an AppleTalk zone.

See **AppleTalk Zone.**

AppleTalk Networking Forum (ANF)

A consortium of developers and software vendors whose task is to encapsulate AppleTalk in other protocols such as Transmission-Control Protocol/Internet Protocol (TCP/IP).

See also **Transmission-Control Protocol/Internet Protocol.**

AppleTalk Phase 2

The most recent version of the AppleTalk protocols. This set of protocols offers more efficient routing algorithms, supports networks with thousands of nodes, provides multiple zones on a network, accommodates Token Ring topologies, and provides cabling for improved performance in a multiprotocol environment.

See also **Token Ring.**

AppleTalk Print Services (ATPS) module

An NetWare Loadable Module (NLM) that allows Macintosh clients to print to NetWare queues. With this module, non-Macintosh clients can also print to AppleTalk printers. The ATPS NLM functions by spooling Macintosh print jobs to the NetWare queue.

See also **NetWare Loadable Module; NetWare utilities.**

AppleTalk printer

A printer connected to an AppleTalk network. An AppleTalk printer can be queried by AppleTalk Print Services, which can then use that printer's font list, even if the queue is serviced by a separate printer.

AppleTalk protocols

A set of rules that specify how the nodes on an AppleTalk network communicate. These protocols control the entire AppleTalk network, including both hardware and software.

Table A.2 lists the protocols found in the AppleTalk Protocol Suite and where to find more information.

AppleTalk Remote-Access Protocol (ARAP)

In the AppleTalk protocol suite, a link-access protocol used to access a network from a remote site over a serial line.

See also **AppleTalk; AppleTalk protocols.**

AppleTalk router

A router that can receive and forward AppleTalk packets on the network. The AppleTalk router can connect the AppleTalk network into an internetwork; all nodes on each network can then access any service or node on any of the connected networks.

AppleTalk Secure Data Stream Protocol (ASDSP)

A Session Layer protocol (Layer 5 of the OSI Reference Model) in the AppleTalk protocol suite. Similar to AppleTalk Data Stream Protocol (ADSP), ASDSP offers more security against unauthorized usage.

See also **AppleTalk; AppleTalk Data-Stream Protocol; AppleTalk protocols; OSI Reference Model.**

AppleTalk Session Protocol (ASP)

Part of the AppleTalk protocol suite, an extension of the AppleTalk Transaction Protocol (ATP) that allows two processes to exchange transactions and commands.

See also **AppleTalk; AppleTalk Transaction Protocol; AppleTalk protocols.**

AppleTalk spooler

An ATPS.NLM component that advertises NetWare print queues on an AppleTalk network. The spooler can accept print jobs from Macintosh clients, and works by creating a logical representation of the queue which becomes visible to Macintosh clients.

See also **AppleTalk Print Services (ATPS) module.**

Table A.2: AppleTalk Protocol Suite

AppleTalk Protocol	For More Information
AppleTalk Address-Resolution Protocol (AARP)	See **AppleTalk Address-Resolution Protocol.**
AppleTalk Data-Stream Protocol (ADSP)	See **AppleTalk Data-Stream Protocol.**
AppleTalk Echo Protocol (AEP)	See **AppleTalk Echo Protocol.**
AppleTalk Filing Protocol (ATFP)	See **AppleTalk Filing Protocol.**
AppleTalk Remote-Access Protocol (ARAP)	See **AppleTalk Remote-Access Protocol.**
AppleTalk Secure Data-Stream Protocol (ASDSP)	See **AppleTalk Secure Data-Stream Protocol.**
AppleTalk Session Protocol (ASP)	See **AppleTalk Session Protocol.**
AppleTalk Transaction Protocol (ATP)	See **AppleTalk Transaction Protocol.**
AppleTalk Update-Based Routing Protocol (AURP)	See **AppleTalk Update-Based Routing Protocol.**
Datagram-Delivery Protocol (DDP)	See **Datagram-Delivery Protocol.**
EtherTalk Link-Access Protocol (ELAP)	See **EtherTalk Link-Access Protocol.**
FDDITalk Link-Access Protocol (FLAP)	See **FDDITalk Link-Access Protocol.**
LocalTalk Link-Access Protocol (LLAP)	See **LocalTalk Link-Access Protocol.**
Name-Binding Protocol (NBP)	See **Name-Binding Protocol.**
Printer-Access Protocol (PAP)	See **Printer-Access Protocol.**
Routing-Table Maintenance Protocol (RTMP)	See **Routing-Table Maintenance Protocol.**
TokenTalk Link-Access Protocol (TLAP)	See **TokenTalk Link-Access Protocol.**
Zone-Information Protocol (ZIP)	See **Zone-Information Protocol.**

AppleTalk stack

The suite of AppleTalk Phase 2 protocols in the AppleTalk module. The AppleTalk stack works with NetWare for Macintosh, and allows Macintosh users to utilize NetWare file and print services.

AppleTalk Transaction Protocol (ATP)

Part of the AppleTalk protocol suite that provides lossless packet delivery from a source socket to a destination socket. ATP enhances the reliability of the Datagram-Delivery Protocol (DDP), which is a best-effort delivery system.

See also **AppleTalk; AppleTalk protocols.**

AppleTalk Update-Based Routing Protocol (AURP)

Part of the AppleTalk protocol suite that functions similarly to the Routing-Table Maintenance Protocol (RTMP), but only sends updates when a change occurs.

See also **AppleTalk; AppleTalk protocols.**

AppleTalk Zone

A logical grouping of AppleTalk devices. AppleTalk zones are defined by the network administrator. Any given device, such as a Macintosh computer, Apple printer, or NetWare server, can be assigned to an AppleTalk zone.

APPLETLK (NLM)

A NetWare Loadable Module (NLM) that includes the AppleTalk protocol stack and router. The APPLETLK module is included in NetWare Multiprotocol Router software, NetWare for Macintosh software, and NetWare Communications Services software.

See also **NetWare Loadable Module; NetWare utilities.**

application

A software program that makes calls to an operating system and manipulates data. An application allows a user to perform a specific task, such as word processing. A stand-alone application runs from a hard disk or floppy disk in a non-networked computer. A network application, on the other hand, can be shared by many users and can access network resources. Applications may also be integrated into complementary suites.

application binary interface (ABI)

A specification that outlines the interface between the operating system and a particular hardware platform. In particular, ABI refers to the calls made between applications and the operating system.

Application Context (AC)

A term used in the OSI Reference Model, referring to all the application service elements (ASEs) needed to use an application in a given context.

See also **OSI Reference Model.**

Application Entity (AE)

Under the OSI Reference Model, a process or function that runs all or part of an application. An AE is made up of one or more application service elements (ASEs).

See also **OSI Reference Model.**

Application File Transfer (AFT)

A prefix used in the International Standardized Profile (ISP) grouping to identify File Transfer, Access, and Management (FTAM) profiles.

See also **File Transfer, Access, and Management.**

application interface

A set of software-based routines or conventions that lets programmers use a given interface as part of an application. Generally, the application interface is used to simplify access to system or networking services.

See also **Application Program Interface.**

Application Layer (OSI model)

The seventh layer in the OSI model. The Application Layer furnishes users with access to the network, and sends a stream of bytes to the Transport Layer (the fourth layer) on the source machine. The Application Layer includes utilities such as file-transfer and terminal-emulation services.

See also **OSI Reference Model.**

Application Message Handling (AMH)

Under the International Standardized Profile (ISP) model, a prefix identifying Message-Handling System (MHS) actions.

See also **Message-Handling System.**

Application object

A leaf object of Novell Directory Services (NDS) that represents a network application in a NetWare Directory tree. Use of Application objects makes network management more efficient, and simplifies common tasks (such as assigning rights or supporting applications).

See also **leaf object; Novell Directory Services; object.**

Application OSI Management (AOM)

Under the International Standardized Profile (ISP) model, a prefix used to denote functions and services for network management.

Application Process (AP)

A program that makes use of Application Layer services under the OSI Reference Model. The AP receives the requested services from the application service elements (ASEs).

See also **OSI Reference Model.**

application program

A program that processes transactions. An application program is sometimes called a *transaction program.*

Application Program Interface (API)

A set of abstractions that provide easy access to operating system services and protocols. The application program uses the API to request low-level services from the operating system, usually for data communication, data retrieval, or access to system resources. In GUI-based operating systems, the API will also provide access to the various components of the interface.

Application Program Interface Association (APIA)

The organization responsible for writing Application Program Interfaces (APIs) for the Consultative Committee for International Telegraphy and Telephony (CCITT) X.400 Message Handling System (MHS).

See also **Application Program Interface; Consultative Committee for International Telegraphy and Telephony; Message Handling System; X.400.**

Application-Protocol Data Unit (APDU)

Under the OSI Reference Model, a data packet that serves as the exchange unit in the Application Layer (Layer 7).

See also **OSI Reference Model.**

application server

A server in a client/server network that runs any applications shared by client workstations. The application server shares the data-processing burden with its clients. A file server, on the other hand, requires the client to run the application and process the data. This computing model often provides for faster data processing, higher reliability, and better data security.

Application Service Element (ASE)

One of several elements in the OSI Reference Model that provide services at the Application Layer (Layer 7). These services are requested by an application process or application entity through a set of predefined Application Programming Interfaces (APIs). The two types of ASEs are *common application service elements* (CASEs) and *specific application service elements* (SASEs). CASEs are more generic, offering services that several different types of applications can use. By contrast, an SASE provides services for a specific application or type of application.

See also **Application Program Interface; OSI Reference Model.**

application subsystem

A set of programs that logs errors, manages incoming communications, loads transaction programs, and provides other services.

Application-Specific Integrated Circuit (ASIC)

A special-purpose chip built from a library of standard circuit cells but containing logic designed for a specific application or device. An ASIC is also known as a *gate array*.

applique

A mounting plate with network connecting hardware that translates communication signals from a network interface into signals expected by the chosen communication standard.

APPN

Advanced Peer-to-Peer Networking, a network architecture defined by IBM's Systems Application Architecture (SAA). APPN facilitates peer communications between microcomputers, without involving a mainframe computer or other Systems Network Architecture (SNA) device. Unlike SNA, APPN supports dynamic packet routing.

See also **Systems Application Architecture; Systems Network Architecture.**

AppNotes

Also known as *NetWare/Novell Application Notes*, a technical journal published by Novell that offers technical information about designing and administering NetWare computing systems.

 **For more information about AppNotes, surf the Web to** `http://www.novell.com/research`.

APPI

Advanced Peer-to-Peer Internetworking, an internetwork architecture defined by IBM's Systems Application Architecture (SAA).

See also **Advanced Peer-to-Peer Networking.**

applet

Generically, any small application embedded as part of a larger application. An applet also refers to a small Java application that can be included in a HyperText Markup Language (HTML) document. When a user accesses an HTML page with a Java-compatible browser, the user can click the applet to transfer the applet code to the user's computer system and have the applet executed by the browser.

See also **HyperText Markup Language; Java.**

AR

access rate, a physical rate that indicates the access of the user channel in bits per second. In Frame Relay networks, the offered load is limited by the AR.

See also **Frame Relay network.**

ARA

Attribute Registration Authority, the organization responsible for allocating unique attribute values in the Consultative Committee for International Telegraphy and Telephony (CCITT) X.400 Message-Handling System (MHS).

See also **Consultative Committee for International Telegraphy and Telephony; Message-Handling System; X.400.**

ARAP

AppleTalk Remote-Access Protocol, in the AppleTalk protocol suite, a link-access protocol used to access a network from a remote site over a serial line.

See also **AppleTalk; AppleTalk protocols.**

arbitration

A set of rules used to resolve conflicting demands for a computer resource.

Archie

An Internet service for gathering, indexing, and displaying information.

architecture

A term with two meanings: (1) the logical structure of a network communications system (made up of protocols, formats, operation sequences, and other specifications), and (2) the physical (hardware) structure of a particular type of computer.

archive

To transfer files to long-term or redundant storage, such as optical disks or magnetic tape. The archive is used to create a backup copy of data that can be used in case the original is damaged. In some archival models, the archive must contain copies of each version of a file.

archive bit

A DOS file attribute that can be set to indicate if a particular file or directory has been modified since the last backup.

Archive Needed (A) attribute

A file attribute set by the NetWare operating system to indicate a file has been changed since the last backup.

archive server

The central computer responsible for the archiving process.

archive site

A node on the Internet that provides access to files.

ARCnet

Attached-Resource Computer Network, a proprietary, token-bus architecture developed in the 1970s by Datapoint Corporation and now widely licensed by third-party vendors. ARCnet is often used in smaller installations, and has a bandwidth of 2.5Mbps. It supports coaxial, twisted-pair, and fiber-optic cable. Although ARCnet typically uses a bus topology, it can also be deployed in a star configuration. ARCnet's advantage over Ethernet is that components are inexpensive and it is simple to configure. It is, however, it is less efficient than Ethernet and not suited to internetworking. A later implementation of ARCnet (ARCnet Plus), offers a throughput of 20Mbps and support for larger data frames.

See also **bus topology**; **star topology.**

ARCnet Trade Association (ATA)

A group of vendors and other organizations that manage the specifications for ARCnet.

 **For general information about the ARCnet Trade Association, surf the Web to** http://www.arcnet.com.

area

Also known as *routing area*, the domain of connected IPX networks that all share a common area address in NetWare Link-Services Protocol (NLSP). All users in one routing area have Network Layer (Layer 3 of the OSI Reference Model) access to the same services.

See also **NetWare Link-Services Protocol**; **OSI Reference Model.**

area address

A 32-bit number and 32-bit mask that define a NetWare Link-Services Protocol (NLSP) routing area.

area-boundary router (ABR)

A router that attaches an Open Shortest Path First (OSPF) area to the background area. The area boundary router has at least one interface in a routing area and one in the backbone area.

See also **Open Shortest Path First.**

area mask

A 32-bit hexadecimal number that indicates how the area network number identifies the routing area and the network within the routing area.

ARF

Alarm-Reporting Function, under the OSI Network-Management Model, a Systems-Management Function (SMF) service that reports failures, faults, and other problems.

See also **OSI Network-Management Model; Systems Management Function.**

ARJ

A DOS file-compression format used to compress multidisk files, designating the compressed file with the .ARJ filename suffix. The program for creating this compression was developed by Robert Jung of ARJ Software.

ARLL

advanced run-length-limited encoding, a method used to store information on a hard disk. ARLL increases the capacity of run-length-limited (RLL) storage and increases the data transfer rate.

ARM

Asynchronous Response Mode, a communications mode specified in the High-Level

Data-Link Control (HDLC) protocol of the International Standards Organization (ISO). An ARM configuration has a secondary (or *slave*) node that can initiate communications with a primary (*master*) node without first having to gain the permission of the master node. ARM differs from *normal response mode* (NRM), which requires the master node to initiate all communications; and *asynchronous balanced mode* (ABM), which grants equal rights to both nodes.

See also **High-Level Data-Link Control; International Standards Organization**

ARP

Address-Resolution Protocol, a method used to determine the physical address of a target host. A part of the Internet Protocol (IP) and AppleTalk protocol, ARP permits a host that knows only the logical (IP) address of a target host to find the physical (Media-Access Control, or MAC) address of the same target host. The key to this translation is a Network Interface Card (NIC) containing a table that maps IP addresses to MAC addresses for all objects on the network. Entries to table are made automatically when ARP sends a request with the target's IP address. The target issues a response containing its MAC address, and the NIC then adds that MAC address to its ARP table for future reference. (*Note: Only networks capable of hardware broadcasts can use ARP.*)

ARPA

Advanced Research Projects Agency, the government agency that funded the initial development of the Internet. The agency is now called the Defense Advanced Research Projects Agency (DARPA).

See also **Defense Advanced Research Projects Agency.**

ARPAnet

Advanced Research Projects Agency Network, the first large, packet-switched wide-area network (WAN). ARPAnet was developed in the 1970s with funding from the Advanced Research Projects Agency (ARPA). ARPAnet was officially decommissioned in 1991. The ARPAnet project gave birth to Transmission-Control Protocol/Internet Protocol (TCP/IP) and other commonly used network protocols, and eventually became the Internet.

See also **Transmission-Control Protocol/Internet Protocol; wide-area network.**

ARQ

Automatic Repeat Request, in communications, a control code that indicates a transmission error has occurred and then requests retransmission.

ARS

(1) Alternate Route Selection, a telephony process used to select a path for transmission.
(2) Automatic Route Selection, in telephony, an automatic process of selecting a path for transmission.

AS

Autonomous System, a set of routers and networks under a single administrative control, but part of a larger network (for exam-

ple, the Internet). The autonomous system is the largest unit in an internetwork topology. The routers communicate using an *interior gateway protocol* (IGP), such as Open Shortest Path First (OSPF). Also referred to as a *routing domain* in the OSI Reference Model.

See also **Interior Gateway Protocol; Open Shortest Path First; OSI Reference Model.**

AS/400

An IBM minicomputer introduced in 1988 to replace the System/36 and System/38 series.

ascending

A logical ordering of database records. Used as an attribute to instruct Btrieve to collate an index in low-to-high order.

See also **Btrieve.**

ASCII

American Standard Code for Information Interchange, a 7-bit code employed as a U.S. standard for interchanging data between communications devices. ASCII is commonly used in local-area networks (LANs). The standard ASCII character set has values between 0 and 127, each of which is assigned to a letter, number, or other character;. the first 32 characters are control codes. An additional 128 characters the *extended ASCII character set*, may not have the same functions in all computers or display the same in all programs. You can find the standard ASCII Character Set in Appendix B.

ASCIIbetical sorting

A sort based on the ASCII strategy of numbers and symbols preceding letters, and uppercase letters preceding lowercase letters.

ASE

Application Service Element, one of several elements in the OSI Reference Model that provide services at the Application Layer (Layer 7). These services are requested by an application process or application entity through a set of predefined Application Program Interfaces (APIs). The two types of ASEs are *common application service elements* (CASEs) and *specific application service elements* (SASEs). CASEs are more generic, offering services that several different types of applications can use. By contrast, an SASE provides services for a specific application or type of application.

See also **Application Program Interface; OSI Reference Model.**

ASI

Adapter Support Interface, a standard interface, created by IBM, that allows a Token Ring adapter to communicate with higher-level protocols. ASI contains a Data Link Layer (Layer 2 of the OSI Reference Model) driver for communicating with the Network Interface Card (NIC), and a Network Layer (Layer 3 of the OSI Reference Model) driver for communicating with network-level protocols.

See also **Network Interface Card; OSI Reference Model; Token Ring.**

Asia and Oceania Workshop (AOW)

One of three workshops for implementers of the OSI Reference Model. The other workshops are the European Workshop for Open Systems (EWOC) and OSI Implementers Workshop (OIW).

See also **OSI Reference Model.**

ASIC

Application-Specific Integrated Circuit. a special-purpose chip built from a library of standard circuit cells but containing logic designed for a specific application or device. An ASIC is also known as a *gate array.*

ASN.1

Abstract Syntax Notation One, a machine-independent, abstract syntax developed as part of the OSI Reference Model. ASN.1 is used to describe data structures; it functions as a common syntax for sending data between two end systems that use different encoding systems.

See also **Abstract Syntax; OSI Reference Model.**

ASP

AppleTalk Session Protocol, part of the AppleTalk protocol suite, an extension of the AppleTalk Transaction Protocol (ATP) that allows two processes to exchange transactions and commands.

See also **AppleTalk; AppleTalk Transaction Protocol; AppleTalk protocols.**

asserted circuit

A circuit that has been closed and has a specific voltage value. Typically an asserted circuit is used to represent a 1.

assigned number

A numerical value used to denote a particular protocol, application, or organization, but not an address. Assigned numbers are assigned by the Internet Assigned-Numbers Authority (IANA).

See also **Internet Assigned-Numbers Authority.**

associated file

A data file connected with a particular job entry.

Association-Control Service Element (ACSE)

An OSI Reference Model service that establishes a relationship between two applications. The ACSE facilitates cooperation and exchange of information between the applications.

See also **OSI Reference Model.**

Association of Banyan Users International (ABUI)

A Banyan user group. Members are concerned with hardware and software relating to the Banyan VINES network operating system.

ASVD

Analog Simultaneous Voice Data, a specification standard under consideration by the International Telecommunications Union (ITU) that describes the capability to transmit multimedia data over analog telephone lines. Despite a more restricted bandwidth, ASVD transmission is being considered as an alternative to Integrated-Services Digital Network (ISDN) transmission.

Asymmetric Digital Subscriber Line (ADSL)

A high-speed telecommunications method used to move data over regular telephone lines. ADSL is sometimes used as an alternative to Integrated-Services Digital Network (ISDN) lines.

See also **Integrated-Services Digital Network.**

asynchronous

A type of data transmission that allows characters or blocks of characters to begin at any time, but each character or block must have an equal time duration. Asynchronous transfer methods place start and stop bits to indicate the beginning and end of each character instead of constantly timing the transmission. This method is more efficient for bursty traffic, and is highly resistant to disruption.

Asynchronous Balanced Mode (ABM)

An operating mode specified in the High-Level Data-Link Control (HDLC) protocol of the International Standards Organization (ISO). ABM gives equal status to each node in a point-to-point link. Each node, therefore, functions as both sender and receiver.

See also **High-Level Data-Link Control; International Standards Organization.**

Asynchronous Communications Server (ACS)

A dedicated personal computer or expansion board that provides other nodes on the network with access to serial ports and modems.

Asynchronous Modem Eliminator (AME)

Also known as a *null modem*, a serial cable and connector with a modified pin configuration that allows two computers to communicate directly without using a physical modem.

Asynchronous Response Mode (ARM)

A communications mode specified in the High-Level Data-Link Control (HDLC) protocol of the International Standards Organization (ISO). An ARM configuration has a secondary (or *slave*) node that can initiate communications with a primary (*master*) node without first having to gain the permission of the master node. ARM differs from *normal response mode* (NRM), which requires the master node to initiate all communications; and *asynchronous balanced mode* (ABM), which grants equal rights to both nodes.

See also **High-Level Data-Link Control; International Standards Organization.**

Asynchronous Time-Division Multiplexing (ATDM)

A variation on the Time-Division Multiplexing (TDM) method of sending information in which time slots are allocated as needed, instead of being preassigned to specific transmitters.

See also **Time-Division Multiplexing.**

Asynchronous Transfer Mode (ATM)

A connection-oriented, packet-switched networking architecture based on broadband ISDN technology. ATM can provide very high bandwidth, dividing data into 53-byte cells (48 bytes of data and a 5-byte header). ATM has three physical-layer specifications: OC-3 (155Mbps), OC-12 (622Mbps), and OC-48 (2.488 Gbps). OC-3 is more common for typical WAN implementations; OC-48 is still largely experimental, though combining sixteen OC-3 switches can effectively create an OC-48 backbone. Although designed to run over large distances and often used as a backbone technology, ATM can also run on desktop units that require extremely high bandwidth to run high-end desktop applications. The 25-Mbps variation of ATM is best suited for desktop connections; its Quality of Service (QoS) guarantees make it usable for many different types of traffic, including voice, data, and video. An existing network running NetWare, Windows, DECnet, TCP/IP, MacTCP, or AppleTalk can connect to an ATM network and run applications without modification, through a technique known as *LAN Emulation* (LANE).

ATM can run on fiber-optic cable or CAT-5 UTP cable, and is deployed using a star topology. ATM offers four QoS levels, each of which can be assigned to particular types of traffic. These four levels are

- *Class A: Constant Bit Rate (CBR)*. This is a "reserved bandwidth" service, and is suited for applications that are intolerant of cell loss.
- *Class B: Variable-Bit-Rate-Real-Time (VBR-RT)*. VBR is also a "reserved bandwidth" service, but instead of generating a constant bit rate, will establish a peak rate, sustainable rate, and maximum burst size.

• *Class C: Variable-Bit-Rate-Non-Real-Time (VBR-NRT).* This level is similar to Class B, but is applied to applications that can tolerate a slight delay, such as video playback or transaction processing.

• *Class D.* This class defines services that use unspecified bit rate (UBR) and available bit rate (ABR). UBR is a non-reserved, "best-effort" service; the network does not allocate resources for a UBR connection. Both UBR and ABR can be applied to traffic that can tolerate more delays or cell loss.

The ATM Forum is the standards body responsible for establishing and promoting ATM standards.

Table A.3 lists related topics and where to find more information. Figure A.2 shows the layers of ATM and Figure A.3 shows a typical ATM implementation.

See also **backbone; star topology.**

For more information, the ATM Forum's Web site is available at `http://www.atmforum.com/.`

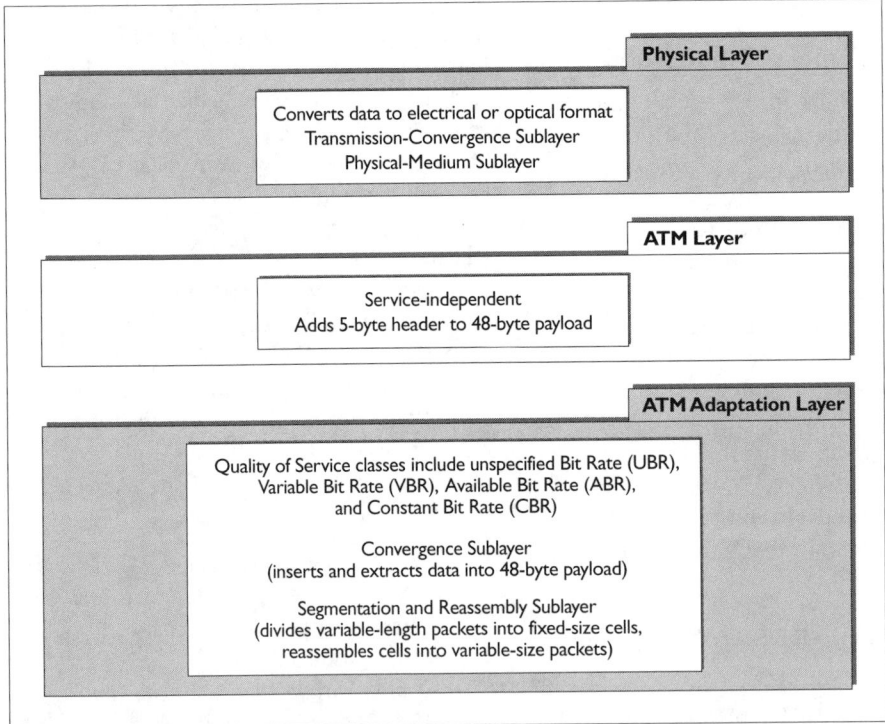

Figure A.2
ATM Layers

asynchronous transmission

A method of transmission under which each character is individually synchronized. The time gap between characters is not a fixed duration. Instead, start bits and stop bits are applied to coordinate data flow.

See also **bisynchronous communication.**

Table A.3: Related ATM Topics	
Topic	**For More Information**
AAL	See **ATM Adaptation Layer.**
AAL-1	See **ATM Adaptation Layer.**
AAL-2	See **ATM Adaptation Layer.**
AAL-3/4	See **ATM Adaptation Layer.**
ABR	See **Available Bit Rate.**
BUS	See **Broadcast and Unknown Server.**
CBR	See **Constant Bit Rate.**
edge device	See **edge device.**
IPNNI	See **Integrated Private Network-to-Network Interface.**
LANE	See **LAN Emulation.**
LECS	See **LAN Emulation Configuration Server.**
LES	See **LAN Server.**
LUNI	See **LAN Emulation User-to-Network Interface.**
leaky bucket	See **leaky bucket.**
MPOA	See **Multiprotocol Over ATM.**
PNNI	See **Private Network-to-Network Interface.**
SVC	See **Switched Virtual Circuit.**
UBR	See **Unspecified Bit Rate.**
UNI	See **User-to-User Network Interface.**
VBR	See **Variable Bit Rate.**
VC	See **Virtual Circuit.**
VLAN	See **Virtual LAN.**

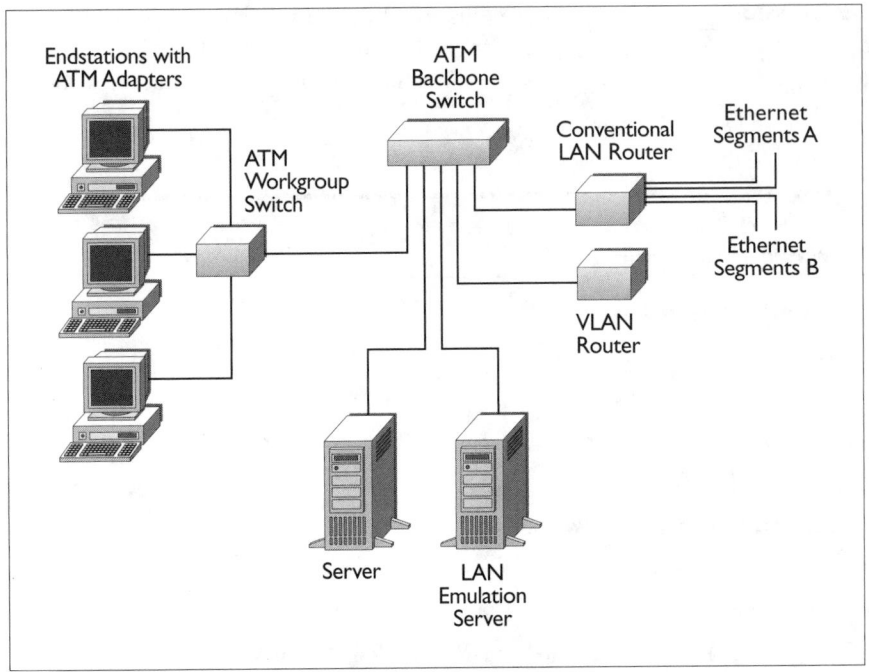

Figure A.3
Typical ATM implementation

AT Command Set

A command set developed by Hayes Microcomputer Products to operate its line of modems. The AT command (short for *attention*) precedes most modem commands. The AT command set is supported by most modem manufacturers, and has become a *de facto* standard. Table A.4 shows the standard AT command set.

See also **Hayes-compatible modem**.

ATA

ARCnet Trade Association, a group of vendors and other organizations that manage the specifications for ARCnet.

For general information about the ARCnet Trade Association, surf the Web to http://www.arcnet.com.

ATCON (NLM)

A NetWare server-based diagnostic utility used to gather information about a server's AppleTalk stack and router, and about other AppleTalk networks on an internetwork.

See also **NetWare Loadable Module; NetWare utilities.**

Table A.4: AT Command Set

Command	Description
+++	Escape code from Online Command state
AT	Attention command that precedes the command line
A/	Repeat the preceding command
A	Answer the call immediately
DT	Dial TouchTone mode
DP	Dial Pulse mode
E	Command echo disabled
E1	Command echo enabled
H	Hang up (on hook)
H1	Off hook
I	Output product code to computer
L	Speaker volume (L0, L1, L2, L3)
M0	Speaker off
M1	Speaker on until Carrier Detect (CD)
M2	Speaker always on
M3	Speaker on from dial to Carrier Detect (CD)
O	Return to online communications
O1	Return to online communications and retrain
Q	Send Result Code messages
Q1	Do not send Result Code messages
Sr?	Read and display contents of register (r)
Sr=n	Set register (r) to value (n) (for example, ATS0=1 equals answer phone on first ring)
V	Result Code messages sent in numeric format
V1	Result Code messages sent in English word format
X	Extended Status mode
Y	Long space disconnect
Z	Reset and reinitialize modem

ATCONFIG (NLM)

A NetWare Loadable Module (NLM) used to configure a newly installed NetWare for Macintosh system.

See also **NetWare Loadable Module; NetWare utilities.**

ATDM

Asynchronous Time-Division Multiplexing, a variation on the Time-Division Multiplexing (TDM) method of sending information in which time slots are allocated as needed, instead of being preassigned to specific transmitters.

See also **Time-Division Multiplexing.**

ATDP

Attention Dial Pulse, a command in the AT command set used to dial a number using a rotary (pulse) telephone.

See also **AT command set.**

ATDT

Attention Dial Tone, a command in the AT command set used to dial a number using a Touch Tone telephone.

See also **AT command set.**

ATFLT (NLM)

A NetWare Loadable Module (NLM) filter that restricts how routers see and communicate with other AppleTalk routers.

See also **NetWare Loadable Module; NetWare utilities.**

ATFP

AppleTalk Filing Protocol, Apple Computer's network file system that allows workstations to share files and applications located on an AppleShare file server. Under NetWare, the AFP NetWare Loadable Module (NLM) runs on a NetWare server running NetWare for Macintosh. Under this configuration, ATFP allows the Macintosh users to share files by interacting with the NetWare file system. This term is sometimes also abbreviated "AFP," but has nothing to do with Advanced Function Printing (an IBM term also abbreviated "AFP"). ATFP is loosely based on the OSI Reference Model, and defines the Physical Layer (Layer 1) as LocalTalk, EtherTalk, and TokenTalk; the Network Layer (Layer 3) as Datagram-Delivery Protocol (DDP); the Transport Layer (Layer 4) as AppleTalk Session Protocol; addressing as Name-Binding Protocol; file sharing as AppleShare; and remote access as AppleTalk Remote Access.

Figure A.1 shows the hierarchy of the ATFP file system.

See also **AppleTalk; AppleTalk File Services module; AppleTalk Filing Protocol (Figure A.1); AppleTalk protocols; OSI Reference Model.**

at-least-once transaction

An AppleTalk Protocol transaction method. An at-least-once transaction guarantees that a request will be executed at least one time.

See also **exactly-once transaction.**

ATM

Asynchronous Transfer Mode, a connection-oriented, packet-switched networking architecture based on broadband ISDN technology. ATM can provide very high bandwidth, dividing data into 53-byte cells (48 bytes of data and a 5-byte header). ATM has three physical-layer specifications: OC-3 (155 Mbps), OC-12 (622 Mbps), and OC-48 (2.488 Gbps). OC-3 is more common for typical WAN implementations; OC-48 is still largely experimental, though combining sixteen OC-3 switches can effectively create, an OC-48 backbone. Although designed to run over large distances and often used as a backbone technology, ATM can also run on desktop units that require extremely high bandwidth to run high-end desktop applications. The 25-Mbps variation of ATM is best suited for desktop connections; its Quality of Service (QoS) guarantees make it usable for many different types of traffic, including voice, data, and video. An existing network running NetWare, Windows, DECnet, TCP/IP, MacTCP, or AppleTalk can connect to an ATM network and run applications without modification, through a technique known as *LAN Emulation* (LANE).

ATM can run on fiber-optic cable or CAT-5 UTP cable, and is deployed using a star topology. ATM offers four QoS levels, each of which can be assigned to particular types of traffic. These four levels are

- *Class A: Constant Bit Rate (CBR).* This is a "reserved bandwidth" service, and is suited for applications that are intolerant of cell loss.
- *Class B: Variable-Bit-Rate-Real-Time (VBR-RT).* VBR is also a "reserved-bandwidth" service, but instead of generating a constant bit rate, will establish a peak rate, sustainable rate, and maximum burst size.

- *Class C: Variable-Bit-Rate-Non-Real-Time (VBR-NRT).* This level is similar to Class B, but is applied to applications that can tolerate a slight delay, such as video playback or transaction processing.
- *Class D.* This class describes services that use unspecified bit rate (UBR) and available bit rate (ABR). UBR is a non-reserved, "best-effort" service; the network does not allocate resources for a UBR connection. Both UBR and ABR can be applied to traffic that can tolerate more delays or cell loss.

The ATM Forum is the standards body responsible for establishing and promoting ATM standards.

Table A.3 lists related topics and where to find more information. Figure A.2 shows the layers of ATM and Figure A.3 shows a typical ATM implementation.

See also **Asynchronous Transfer Mode** (includes **Table A.3, Figure A.2,** and **Figure A.3**); **backbone; star topology.**

For more information, the ATM Forum's Web site is available at `http://www.atmforum.com/`.

ATM Adaptation Layer (AAL)

A method of adapting the highest-layer protocols of the OSI Reference Model for transport over an Asynchronous Transfer Mode (ATM) network. An ATM cell itself consists of 53 bytes (48 bytes of payload and a 5-byte header). The AAL determines the format of the cell's payload.

AAL is divided into the following two sublayers:

- *Convergence (CS).* The CS Sublayer performs message identification and time/clock recovery services. To support data transport over ATM, the CS is subdivided into the Common Part Convergence Sublayer (CPCS) and a Service-Specific Convergence Sublayer (SSCS). AAL service data units are transported between AAL *service access points* (SAPs) throughout the ATM network.
- *Segmentation and Reassembly (SAR).* The SAR Sublayer divides higher-layer information into 48-byte segments for transport by the ATM cells. When the cell is received, SAR reassembles the segmented ATM cells into larger data units that can then be delivered to the higher layers.

Five AALs have been defined, one for each class of service available in the ATM network, as follows:

- *AAL-1 (ATM Adaptation Layer Type 1).* This layer is responsible for AAL functions in support of Constant Bit Rate (CBR), time-dependent traffic.
- *AAL-2 (ATM Adaptation Layer Type 2).* This layer is undefined.
- *AAL-3/4 (ATM Adaptation Layer Type 3/4).* This layer is responsible for AAL functions in support of Variable Bit Rate (VBR), delay-tolerant data traffic that requires support for sequencing or error detection.
- *AAL-5 (ATM Adaptation Layer Type 5).* This layer is responsible for AAL functions in support of Variable Bit Rate (VBR), delay-tolerant, connection-oriented traffic that requires little support for sequencing or error detection.

See also **Asynchronous Transfer Mode; Constant Bit Rate; OSI Reference Model; Variable Bit Rate.**

ATM Data-Service Unit (ADSU)

A Data-Service Unit (DSU) used to access an Asynchronous Transfer Mode (ATM) network through a High-Speed Serial Interface (HSSI).

See also **Asynchronous Transfer Mode; Data-Service Unit; High-Speed Serial Interface.**

Atomicity, Consistency, Isolation, and Durability (ACID)

Four desirable attributes a transaction should have in a transaction-processing system. *Atomicity* refers to whether a transaction is successful or unsuccessful (that is, either all of the operations take effect or none take effect); a successful transaction *commits* and an unsuccessful transaction *aborts*. *Consistency* (which is the responsibility of the application program) refers to whether a transaction transforms distributed data from one consistent state to another. *Isolation* refers to whether a transaction appears to execute independently of other transactions that run concurrently. *Durability* (also known as *permanence*) refers to whether the effects of a transaction remain after the transaction is complete. Considered together, these four attributes are often called *ACID properties.*

ATOTAL utility

In NetWare and IntranetWare, a workstation utility that displays accounting charges for a

given server. In NetWare 3.x, the SYSCON utility is used to set charge rates for the services; in NetWare 4.x, the NETADMIN or NWADMIN utility is used for that function.
See also **NetWare utilities.**

ATP

AppleTalk Transaction Protocol, part of the AppleTalk protocol suite that provides lossless packet delivery from a source socket to a destination socket. ATP enhances the reliability of the Datagram Delivery Protocol (DDP), which is a best-effort delivery system.
See also **AppleTalk; AppleTalk protocols.**

ATPS

AppleTalk Print Services, an NetWare Loadable Module (NLM) that allows Macintosh clients to print to NetWare queues. With this module, non-Macintosh clients can also print to AppleTalk printers. The ATPS NLM functions by spooling Macintosh print jobs to the NetWare queue.
See also **NetWare Loadable Module; NetWare utilities.**

ATPS (NLM)

A NetWare Loadable Module (NLM) that processes print requests from Macintosh and DOS workstations directed to an Apple printer. When this NLM is loaded, it generates a font list for each PostScript spooler. The NLM then responds to each query on the basis of the generated font list.
See also **NetWare Loadable Module; NetWare utilities.**

ATPS print server

A component of the ATPS.NLM that processes print jobs from the NetWare print queue that are directed to an AppleTalk printer. The ATPS print server can direct print jobs from any Macintosh or non-Macintosh client to the AppleTalk printer.

ATPS print spooler

A component of the ATPS.NLM that advertises a NetWare print queue on AppleTalk networks. The spooler, actually a logical representation of a queue, accepts print jobs submitted by Macintosh clients.

ATPSCON (NLM)

The AppleTalk Print Services console utility (ATPSCON.NLM) that configures the ATPS.NLM from the server console. It is used to create and configure spoolers, create and assign print queues, set options, and administer printer servers.
See also **NetWare Loadable Module; NetWare utilities.**

ATTACH utility

A NetWare 3.x server-console utility that connects multiple bindery-based NetWare servers (or NetWare 4 servers using bindery emulation) while the login script is running. Once the workstation has attached to the server, it can access any of the server's services for which it has access privileges. The command is reserved for connecting to subsequent servers after initial connection to the network; it cannot be used to make the initial connection.
See also **login script.**

attach

To create a connection between a workstation and a network server. The server assigns each workstation a connection number, and then attaches each workstation to its LOGIN directory.

Attached-Resource Computer Network (ARCnet)

A proprietary, token-bus architecture developed in the 1970s by Datapoint Corporation and now widely licensed by third-party vendors. ARCnet is often used in smaller installations, and has a bandwidth of 2.5Mbps. It supports coaxial, twisted-pair, and fiber-optic cable. Although ARCnet typically uses a bus topology, it can also be deployed in a star configuration. ARCnet's advantage over Ethernet is that components are inexpensive and it is simple to configure. It is, however, less efficient than Ethernet and not suited to internetworking. A later implementation of ARCnet (ARCnet Plus) offers a throughput of 20Mbps and support for larger data frames.
See also **bus topology; star topology.**

attachment

A separate file included with an electronic-mail (e-mail) message.

Attachment-Unit Interface (AUI)

A universal connector to Ethernet cables.
See also **Ethernet.**

attack scanner

A software package that probes UNIX networks to discover security problems by posing as an intruder trying to steal data or force entry into the network.

Attention Dial Pulse (ATDP)

A command in the AT command set used to dial a number using a rotary (pulse) telephone.
See also **AT command set.**

Attention Dial Tone (ATDT)

A command in the AT command set used to dial a number using a Touch Tone telephone.
See also **AT command set.**

attention message

An AppleTalk Data-Stream Protocol message that allows two transport clients to signal one another outside of the regular data flow. The attention message is made up of a two-byte *attention code* and as much as 570 bytes of data. An attention message is also known in Transport-Layer Interface (TLI) terms as an *expedited transport-service data unit*.
See also **expedited transport-service data unit; Transport-Layer Interface.**

attenuation

A reduction in signal strength caused by electrical losses in the dielectric medium, and by the length of the conductor (the distance the signal must travel). Attenuation is expressed in *decibels per kilometer* (dB/km), and depends on a number of factors, including wire composition, wire size, and the effective range of the signal frequency. Examples of attenuation include (1) the distortion of a digital signal on a network cable, (2) amplitude reduction in an electrical signal without an appreciable change in the information content, or (3) loss of signal strength during the transmission of a signal over a long cable.

attenuation factor

A value used to express the amount of attenuation (signal loss) over a given distance.

ATTOKLLC (NLM)

A NetWare Loadable Module (NLM) that supports Macintosh workstations on a Token Ring network when using NetWare for Macintosh to connect Macintosh workstations to a NetWare network via an AppleTalk router.

See also **NetWare Loadable Module; NetWare utilities.**

attribute

A way to describe access to (and properties of) files and directories. For example, attributes of NetWare files include Read, Write, Create, Delete, and Execute Only. Directory attributes may include Read, Write, Create, Execute, and Hidden. An attribute may also be known as a *flag*. Attributes are applied to files and directories only, not to objects. An attribute cannot be overridden, but may be changed by a user who has the appropriate right.

Table A.5 lists attributes for IntranetWare, their classification, and where to find more information.

Attribute Registration Authority (ARA)

The organization responsible for allocating unique attribute values in the Consultative Committee for International Telegraphy and Telephony (CCITT) X.400 Message-Handling System (MHS).

See also **Consultative Committee for International Telegraphy and Telephony; Message-Handling System; X.400.**

Attribute Security

A component of File System Security that assigns properties to individual files and directories. Also known as a *flag*, such an attribute can override rights granted with trustee assignments, and can be used to prohibit tasks that would otherwise be allowed by effective rights.

attribute type

A set of letters used to distinguish the type of object name in NetWare and IntranetWare.

ATXRP (NLM)

A NetWare Loadable Module (NLM) that enables a NetWare print server to send a print job to an AppleTalk network printer from a NetWare print queue. The AppleTalk Extended Remote Printer (ATXPR) module also allows AppleTalk printers to appear as objects in the Novell Directory Services (NDS) tree.

See also **NetWare Loadable Module; NetWare utilities; Novell Directory Services.**

Table A.5: IntranetWare Attributes

Attribute	Directory	File	For More Information
Archive Needed (A)		X	See **Archive Needed attribute.**
Can't Compress (Cc)		X	See **Can't Compress attribute.**
Compressed (Co)		X	See **Compressed attribute.**
Copy Inhibit (Ci)		X	See **Copy Inhibit attribute.**
Delete Inhibit (Di)	X	X	See **Delete Inhibit attribute.**
Don't Compress (Dc)	X	X	See **Don't Compress attribute.**
Don't Migrate (Dm)	X	X	See **Don't Migrate attribute.**
Don't Suballocate (Ds)		X	See **Don't Suballocate attribute.**
Execute Only (X)		X	See **Execute Only attribute.**
Hidden (H)	X	X	See **Hidden attribute.**
Immediate Compress (Ic)	X	X	See **Immediate Compress attribute.**
Indexed (I)		X	See **Indexed attribute.**
Migrate (M)		X	See **Migrate attribute.**
Normal (N)	X	X	See **Normal attribute.**
Purge (P)	X	X	See **Purge attribute.**
Read Only (Ro)		X	See **Read Only attribute.**
Read Write (Rw)		X	See **Read Write attribute.**
Rename Inhibit (Ri)	X	X	See **Rename Inhibit attribute.**
Shareable (Sh)		X	See **Shareable attribute.**
System (Sy)	X	X	See **System attribute.**
Transactional (T)		X	See **Transactional attribute.**

AU

Access Unit, part of the Consultative Committee for International Telegraphy and Telephony (CCITT) X.400 Message-Handling System (MHS). An AU is an application process that gives a CCITT-supported service access to a Message-Transfer Service (MTS). The MTS then delivers a message to users or services at any site that is accessible through the MHS.

See also **Consultative Committee for International Telegraphy and Telephony; Message-Handling System; Message-Transfer Service; X.400.**

Audio Interchange File Format (AIFF)

A file format used to store and exchange sounds in sound files found on the Internet.

audit

An evaluation of network activity. An audit ensures that network-monitoring and data-gathering processes are functioning properly. This activity is typically independent of the normal network-management function.

Audit Data File

A NetWare system log generated after Auditing is enabled at the volume level or the Novell Directory Services (NDS) container level. The Audit Data File stores a record of audited transactions, as well as all other activities performed by the auditor. The administrator can use the AUDITCON utility to create filters that select specific information from the Audit Data File for reports.

See also **Novell Directory Services.**

audit filter

A feature used by the NetWare AUDITCON utility to view the Audit Data File. The audit filter is used to select or exclude specific events or time periods from a report.

Audit History File

A NetWare system log used to store a record of activities carried out by the auditor. The Audit History File is created when Auditing has been enabled at the volume level or Novell Directory Services (NDS) container level.

See also **Novell Directory Services.**

audit trail

A running record of transactions. This log is generated automatically by several programs and operating systems. The audit trail can be used to track data and determine the origin of any changes made to it.

AUDITCON utility

A NetWare 4.*x* and IntranetWare work-station utility used to filter the Audit Data File to generate reports. It generates a log file that can be used by an independent auditor to verify the accuracy and security of network transactions.

See also **NetWare Loadable Module; NetWare utilities.**

auditing

A process of reviewing network transactions to ensure accuracy and security. An auditor can track network events and activities, but may not open or modify network files unless specifically granted that right by the supervisor.

File or directory events that may be audited include the following:

- Creation, modification, or deletion of a directory or file
- Salvaging, moving, or renaming of a directory or file
- Creation or deletion of a service queue

Server events that may be audited include the following:

- Occurrence of a server failure
- Creation or deletion of Bindery objects
- Mounting or dismounting of volumes
- Modification of security rights

Directory Service events that may be audited include the following:

- Adding or deleting objects
- Moving or renaming objects
- Adding or removing security equivalence
- Tracking User object logins and logouts

Auditing File object

A NetWare leaf object that allows auditing file logs to be managed as objects in the Novell Directory Services (NDS) tree.
See also **leaf object; Novell Directory Services; object.**

auditor

An independent individual with no bias, assigned to verify a network's integrity.

AUI

Attachment-Unit Interface, a universal connector to Ethernet cables.
See also **Ethernet.**

AUI connector

Attachment-Unit Interface connector, a universal connector to Ethernet cables.
See also **Ethernet.**

AUP

Acceptable Use Policy, a statement or set of rules that limit how a network or computer service is used.

AURP

AppleTalk Update-Based Routing Protocol, part of the AppleTalk protocol suite that functions similarly to the Routing-Table Maintenance Protocol (RTMP), but only sends updates when a change occurs.
See also **AppleTalk; AppleTalk protocols.**

AURP (NLM)

A NetWare Loadable Module (NLM) that allows AppleTalk to be tunneled through Internet Protocol (IP), which connects AppleTalk networks through an IP internetwork.
See also **NetWare Loadable Module; NetWare utilities.**

authentication

A way to verify that an object is authorized to send messages or requests to Novell Directory Services (NDS). In NetWare 4.x, authentication guarantees that a given message does indeed originate at the workstation where the data was created; along with login restrictions and access control rights, this feature functions to provide security on the network. From the end-user's perspective, authentication consists of a request for a password and user ID upon login; subsequent operations are authenticated transparently. Although passwords and user IDs are the simplest and most common types of authentication, establishing a login-time restriction can sometimes provide additional security. This technique periodically forces the end-user to log out, log in again, and re-enter the password. Several other authentication mechanisms have been developed, including digital signatures.

See also **Novell Directory Services.**

authentication database

A list of valid remote-system IDs and related Data-Terminal Equipment (DTE) addresses. Each entry in the authentication database indicates a partner that is allowed to communicate with a given interface.

Authentication Information (AI)

The information used to determine whether a network user is authorized to access the system.

authentication system

A server that checks (mostly automatically) the validity of every user and every request on the network. Kerberos, created at MIT, is a distributed authentication system in common use; it uses special keys to encrypt transmissions between itself and a user.

authoring

The process of creating and formatting of a document or World Wide Web (WWW) page, normally by using one of the available programs designed for that purpose.

See also **World Wide Web.**

Authority and Format Identifier (AFI)

Under the OSI Reference Model, the part of an address used for the Network-Layer

(Layer 3) Service-Access Point (NSAP). The AFI specifies the administrator responsible for allocating the Initial Domain Identifier (IDI) values.

See also **Initial Domain Identifier; OSI Reference Model.**

Authority Revocation

A Directory Schema term and a selectable property for the following Novell Directory Services (NDS) objects: External Entity, List, Message-Routing Group, and Messaging Server.

See also **leaf object; Novell Directory Services; object.**

authority zone

A section of the domain-name tree in the Domain-Naming System (DNS) for which one name server is considered the authority.

See also **Domain-Naming System.**

Auto Answer (AA)

A modem feature that responds and connects automatically to an incoming call.

auto endcap

A setting that specifies that captured data should be closed and sent to the printer after exiting an application.

autoanswer

A modem feature for answering incoming calls automatically.

autoauthentication

A client/server utility that lets users access unrestricted resources on the network without a password. If the user attempts to access a restricted resource, however, the utility requests a password.

autobaud

The automatic determination and matching of telecommunications transmission speeds.

Autocall Unit (ACU)

A device used to dial telephone numbers automatically.

autodial

A modem feature for opening a telephone line and placing a call.

AUTOEXEC.BAT

An automatically executing batch file that runs when DOS or OS/2 is booted. AUTOEXEC.BAT may load programs, utilities, or files, issue DOS commands, and trigger a login script.

AUTOEXEC.NCF

A NetWare server's executable batch file used to load modules and set the NetWare operating system configuration. The file holds the server name and internal network number, loads local area network (LAN) drivers and Network Interface Card (NIC) settings, and binds protocols to installed drivers. It may also load NetWare Loadable Modules (NLMs) and make bindery-context settings.

Executable server commands can be included in AUTOEXEC.NCF. If Internetwork Packet Exchange (IPX) is selected as the only protocol during installation, the AUTOEXEC.NCF file contains all LOAD and BIND commands for LAN drivers, NICs, and the IPX protocol.

See also **Internetwork Packet Exchange; NetWare Loadable Module; Network Interface Card.**

Automatic Alternate Routing (AAR)

A process by which network traffic is routed automatically to maximize throughput. AAR can also be used to minimize distance and balance channel usage.

automatic call distributor

A telecommunications device that automatically switches incoming calls to the next available telephone line.

automatic call reconnect

A telecommunications feature that reroutes automatic calls away from a failed trunk line.

Automatic Client Upgrade (ACU)

An IntranetWare feature that allows for automatic upgrading of many existing NetWare workstations to Novell's 32-bit client software.

automatic dial-up

The automatic placement of a telephone call by an individual workstation or network node to a larger network without user intervention.

automatic flow control

A method of controlling data flow over a virtual circuit. Enabled by setting window and packet size, automatic flow control can be negotiated in each direction on a per-call basis.

automatic forwarding

An electronic-mail (e-mail) feature that automatically retransmits incoming messages to another e-mail address.

automatic mailing list

A mailing list maintained by a computer. *See also* **LISTSERV.**

Automatic Number Identification (ANI)

A feature that includes the sender's identification number in the transmission. In telephony, this is also known as *caller ID*, and allows the recipient of a phone call to see who is calling before answering the phone. ANI is often tied to a database of caller information, thereby allowing customer-service agents to view a caller's entire record as soon as the call is answered.

Automatic Repeat Request (ARQ)

In communications, a control code that indicates a transmission error has occurred and then requests retransmission.

automatic rollback

A feature of the Transaction-Tracking System (TTS) that returns a database to its original state. If a network running under

TTS fails when a transaction is in process, the data in the database rolls back to its most recent state.
See also **Transaction-Tracking System.**

Automatic Route Selection (ARS)

In telephony, an automatic process of selecting a path for transmission.

automatic screen destruction

A NetWare Loadable Module (NLM) attribute used to automatically clear the screen displayed on the monitor upon termination of an NLM. Also known as *auto-screen destruction*. If this attribute is disabled, the screen remains open and shows the message `<Press any key to close screen>`.

autonomous confederation

A group of Autonomous Systems (ASs) that trust the reachability or routing information for their network more than they trust reachability or routing information received from other ASs or other confederations.
See also **Autonomous System.**

autonomous switching

A process whereby packets are switched independently without interrupting the system processor. The result of autonomous switching is faster packet processing.
See also **packet switching.**

Autonomous System (AS)

A set of routers and networks under a single administrative control, but part of a larger network (for example, the Internet). The autonomous system is the largest unit in an internetwork topology. The routers communicate using an *interior gateway protocol* (IGP), such as Open Shortest Path First (OSPF). Also referred to as a *routing domain* in the OSI Reference Model.

See also **Interior Gateway Protocol; Open Shortest Path First; OSI Reference Model.**

auto-partition algorithm

An algorithm used by a repeater to automatically disconnect a segment from a network if the segment ceases to function properly.

A/UX

Apple Computer's implementation of UNIX. A/UX contains some Macintosh-specific features, and is based on UNIX System V Release 2 with Berkeley extensions.

AUX

The logical name for an auxiliary device under DOS.

availability

The period of time that a network device or program is ready for use. A device is considered available even if it is currently in use. Availability is determined by the ratio of MTBF to (MTBF + MTTR). MTBR is *mean time before failure*, and MTTR is *mean time to repair*.

See also **mean time between failures; mean time to repair.**

Available Bit Rate (ABR)

A layer-service category for Asynchronous Transfer Mode (ATM). In ABR, ATM layer-transfer characteristics provided by the network may change after a connection is established. When those characteristics change, a flow-control mechanism is specified that supports several types of feedback to control the source rate of transmission.

Available Options

A screen on the NetWare 4.02 MONITOR NetWare Loadable Module (NLM). Through a series of menus and submenus, the MONITOR NLM allows viewing of various server characteristics and performance of a variety of system maintenance functions.

See also **MONITOR; NetWare Loadable Module.**

Available Processes & Interrupts

A screen on the NetWare 4.02 MONITOR NetWare Loadable Module (NLM). Through a series of menus and submenus, the MONITOR NLM allows viewing of various server characteristics and performance of a variety of system maintenance functions.

See also **MONITOR; NetWare Loadable Module.**

Avalanche Photodiode (APD)

A detector component in a fiber-optic receiver. The APD converts light into electrical energy, emitting an "avalanche" of multiple electrons for each incoming photon.

avatar

A visual representation of a user in a shared virtual-reality network.

AWG

American Wire Gauge, a classification system for copper wire. The values are based on the diameter, or gauge, of the wire; lower gauge numbers correspond to the thicker wires.

B channel

The bearer channel in an Integrated Services Digital Network (ISDN) system that can carry voice or data at the rate of 64 kilobits per second (Kbps) in either direction. Multiple B channels can be multiplexed to achieve a higher-rate H channel.

See also **H channel.**

B8ZS

Bipolar with 8-Zero Substitution, a signal-encoding scheme that represents a 1 alternatively as positive and negative voltage, with 0 representing zero voltage. Under the B8ZS encoding scheme, at least one out of every eight bits must be set to 1.

BAC

Basic Access Control, a set of access-control guidelines in the Consultative Committee for International Telegraphy and Telephony (CCITT) X.500 directory services model.

See also **Consultative Committee for International Telegraphy and Telephony; X.500.**

back channel

A channel that sends control information in a direction opposite to that of the primary channel so information can be delivered even when the primary channel may be malfunctioning. A back channel is also known as a *backward channel* or *reverse channel.*

back end

An application running on a server in a client/server network and that does all the processing work for the application. This term is also used to denote a server-based database accessed by front-end, client-side workstations.

See also **front end.**

Back Link attribute

A Novell Directory Services (NDS) property attached to an NDS object when a remote server requires an external reference; the property points back to the actual object. This is a selectable property for the following NDS objects: AFP Server, Alias, Bindery, Bindery Queue, Computer, Country, Directory Map, External Entity, Group, List, Message-Routing Group, Messaging Server, NCP Server, Organization, Organizational Role, Organizational Unit, Print Server, Printer, Profile, Queue, Unknown, User, and Volume.

See also **container object; leaf object; Novell Directory Services; object.**

back pressure

An accumulation of congested information that extends throughout an internetwork.

backbone

The routing structure of an internetwork, made up of the central connection path to which other subnetworks or network segments with lower data-transfer rates can be attached. Using a backbone in an internetwork is an efficient way to reduce network traffic.

backbone bridge topology

A method for using bridges to connect multiple networks. Under this topology, each pair of networks is directly connected with a bridge, thereby allowing any one network to communicate directly with any other network. A *cascaded bridge topology*, on the other hand, does not always allow for a direct connection, and may require one network to go through a middle network to get to a third one.

Figure B.1 shows an example of a backbone bridge topology.

See also **cascaded bridge topology.**

backbone cable

The cable used to form the main trunk of a network. Individual nodes and peripherals can be attached directly to the backbone cable. The four main types of backbone cable are unshielded twisted-pair (UTP), shielded twisted-pair (STP), coaxial, and optical fiber.

See also **coaxial cable; shielded twisted-pair cable; unshielded twisted-pair cable.**

backbone network

A type of central connection path to which other subnetworks (or network segments with lower data rates) can be attached. In this type of network, all systems may be configured to enjoy connectivity to each other as well as the backbone itself. Networks attached to the backbone, known as *access networks*, may require a gateway or router to make the attachment. The backbone network typically uses a higher-speed protocol than the individual segments or subnetworks.

backdoor route

A route used by a border router to send data to a particular nonlocal network specified by the Interior Gateway Protocol (IGP).

See also **Interior Gateway Protocol.**

back-end network

A network used to connect mainframes, minicomputers, and peripherals. A back-end network typically requires high bandwidth, and often employs optical fiber as the transmission medium.

Background Explicit Congestion Notification (BECN)

A notification set by a Frame Relay network indicating that the network is congested in the frame's reverse packet-forwarding direction.

See also **Frame Relay network.**

background noise

An unwanted signal on a line, channel, or circuit.

See also **interference.**

background process

A process, transparent to the end-user, that executes while the end-user is engaged in other activities. The background process uses cycles that the central processing unit (CPU) has available when foreground processes are idle. A background process is allocated lower priority than a foreground process, and cannot accept user input. For example, file compression may be a background process.

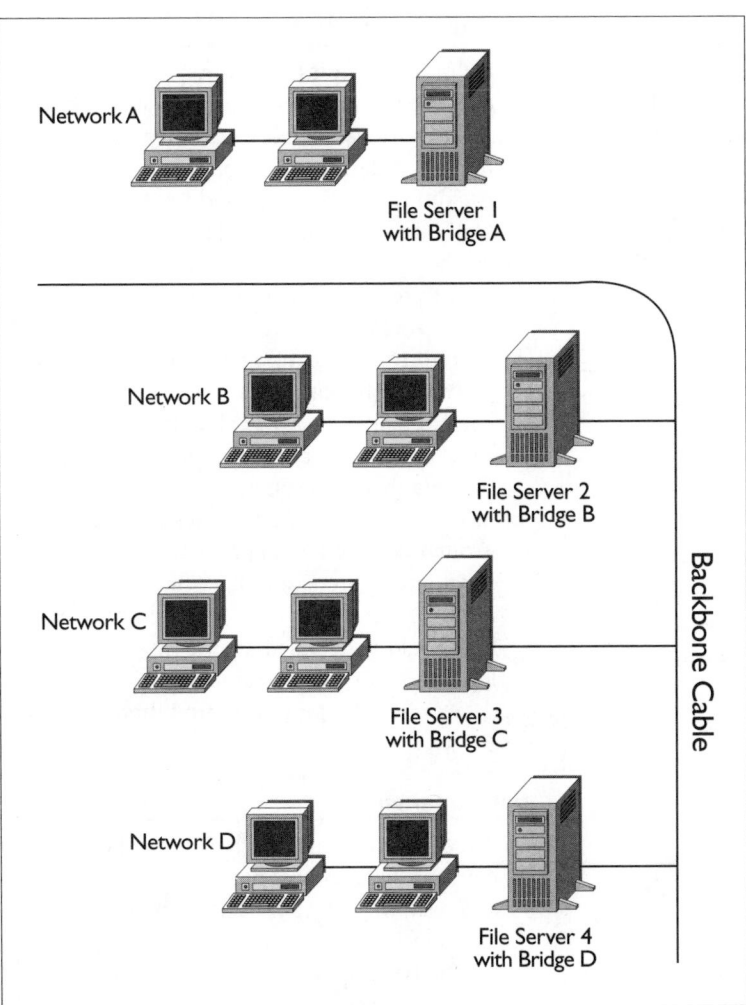

Figure B.1
Backbone bridge topology

backing out

A process in NetWare's Transaction-Tracking
System (TTS) for abandoning an incomplete
database transaction. The backing-out
process prevents related data from being
corrupted by the incomplete transaction.

See also **Transaction-Tracking System.**

backlink

A path returning to a starting point for a
hypertext link that a user has clicked to
advance to a link location.

See also **hypertext.**

backoff

A retransmission delay enforced by the contention of Media-Access Control (MAC) protocols when a node that wants to transmit senses a carrier on the physical medium.
See also **Carrier-Sense Multiple-Access/Carrier Detect; Media-Access Control.**

backplane

A circuit board with slots into which other circuit boards are inserted.

backplate

A metal bracket at one end of a circuit board, normally flush with the casing, that provides cutouts for connectors or switches. Personal computers usually have blank backplates over expansion slots, which are removed when a board is plugged into the slot.

backscattering

Light in a fiber-optic transmission that is reflected back in the direction from which it came.

Backstage

A group of multimedia Web authoring tools from Macromedia, Inc., ranging from a Web-page creator to a package that contains links to mainframe databases.

 **For more information about Backstage, surf the Web to** http://www.macromedia.com.

backup

A duplicate of files, directories, or volumes copied to a storage device (such as a floppy disk, cartridge tape, or hard drive). If the original is destroyed or corrupted, the backup can be retrieved and restored. Method and frequency of backup depend on the age of the data, how many duplicate copies are desired, and the number of backup sessions the administrator is willing to restore. Files that do not change often do not require backing up as often. A *full* backup makes a copy of all data; a *differential* or *incremental* backup only backs up the data that has been added, or data that has changed since the last backup. Backup is often done in a rotation method that distributes current and older files over multiple storage devices. A written backup log should be retained in case the electronic log is destroyed or corrupted.
See also **10-tape rotation method.**

backup engine

A module that runs on a host server and contains the interfaces needed for backing up and restoring data The backup engine reads and translates user requests, determines session type, and activates the appropriate modules to back up and restore files.

backup host

A NetWare server on which a backup program is run. Normally, a backup host has a storage device and storage-device controller.

backup program

An application used to make archives or to back up copies of data files. Operating systems typically have some limited backup functions; more full-featured backup programs are available separately.

backup server

A server system used to carry out shutdowns and backups at regular intervals. Although it need not be a dedicated machine, a backup server runs the backup software. The software notifies all nodes on the network of the impending backup, allows them to end their sessions, and then begins the backup.

backward compatibility

Denotes a software program's capability of working with previous versions. For example, Bindery Emulation gives NetWare 4.x networks backward compatibility with earlier versions of NetWare.

Backward Error Correction (BEC)

An error-correction method in which the error is detected by the recipient, which subsequently requests a retransmission.

backward learning

An information-gathering process often used in algorithms that assume a symmetrical network and infer information about the network on the basis of that assumption.

bad-block revectoring

A data-protection process in which data written to a faulty area of a storage device is retrieved from memory and rewritten to a different area of the device. To prevent sub-

sequent writes to the faulty area, its location is then recorded in a **bad-block table**.

bad-block table

A table kept on the hard disk that lists faulty sectors in a storage device. The operating system refers to this table to ensure that no data is written to faulty sectors.

bad sector

A portion of a hard disk or floppy disk that cannot be used to store data, usually because of physical damage. Operating systems locate and mark bad sectors to prevent them from being used.
See also **bad-block table.**

balanced configuration

A point-to-point configuration in a High-Level Data Link Control (HDLC) network that contains two combined nodes.
See also **High-Level Data-Link Control.**

balun

A hardware device used to adjust impedances for connecting different cable types. The term *balun* is derived from *balanced/un*balanced, because the device is often used to connect twisted-pair cable (balanced) to coaxial (unbalanced) cable. A balun typically has different connectors at each end, allowing the use of twisted-pair wiring with coaxial cable.

bandwidth

The highest signaling rate possible for a given type of connection. Bandwidth is typically expressed in bits per second (bps) for digital circuits. For example, a typical Ethernet network has a maximum bandwidth of 10Mbps. For analog circuits, bandwidth is expressed in hertz (Hz) as the highest possible frequency minus the lowest possible frequency. A higher bandwidth offers greater data-transmission capabilities.

bandwidth-on-demand

The capability of an individual virtual circuit to exceed the Committed Information Rate (CIR) to provide additional bandwidth required by an application. This capability is also known as *dynamic allocation of bandwidth*. *See also* **Committed Information Rate.**

bandwidth reservation

The reservation of call bandwidth for high-bandwidth or high-priority calls in circuit-switched lines.

bang path

An Internet term used to denote a path between two nodes. A bang path is used in a UNIX-to-UNIX Copy Program (UUCP) for electronic mail (e-mail) or Because It's Time Network (BITNET) communications. The path is made up of multiple domain or machine names, separated by exclamation points.

banner page

A page that furnishes information about a print job. Information may include the name of the user initiating the job, and the time and date of printing. The banner page can be printed with each job or suppressed as necessary.

Banyan

Short name for Banyan Systems, Inc., a manufacturer of enterprise networking products, including the VINES operating system.
See also **Virtual Networking System.**

 **For more information about Banyan Systems, surf the Web to** http://www. banyan.com.

barrel connector

A connector used to link two pieces of identical cable in a straight run.

BARRNet

Bay Area Regional Research Network, a San Francisco Bay Area network whose backbone is composed of the University of California at Berkeley, the University of California at Davis, the University of California at San Francisco, the University of California at Santa Cruz, Stanford University, the Lawrence Livermore National Laboratory, and the NASA Ames Research Center.

base address

The starting location for a block of contiguous memory (such as a buffer area, video memory, or the memory area allocated to an I/O port).

base schema

A set of defined object classes in Novell Directory Services (NDS).
See also **Directory Schema; Novell Directory Services; object classes.**

baseband

A network technology using a single carrier frequency that requires all stations attached to a network to participate in every transmission that takes place. A baseband connection sends signals—without modulation—over twisted-pair cable, coaxial cable, or fiber-optic cable. Multiple signals can be sent over the same baseband connection by multiplexing.

See also **broadband.**

baseband network

A type of network (usually run over a short distance) that sends out signals as direct-current pulses, as opposed to modulated signals. A single digital signal occupies the entire bandwidth of the transmission medium. Consequently, nodes in the baseband network can transmit only when the channel is not occupied. Channel sharing can be accomplished, however, through a multiplexing technique. Many PC-based local-area networks (LANs) use baseband techniques.

See also **multiplexing.**

baseline

A reference metric used in performance analysis. In networking, baseline measurements indicate performance levels under what is considered a normal load.

Basic Access Control (BAC)

A set of access-control guidelines in the Consultative Committee for International Telegraphy and Telephony (CCITT) X.500 directory services model.

See also **Consultative Committee for International Telegraphy and Telephony; X.500.**

Basic Encoding Rule (BER)

In Abstract Syntax Notation One (ASN.1), a rule for encoding data elements that specify any ASN.1 element as a byte string. The string includes a Type, Length, and Value field. The Type field indicates an object's class, the Length field indicates the number of bytes used to encode the value, and the Value field indicates the information associated with the ASN.1 object.

See also **Abstract Syntax Notation One.**

Basic Information Unit (BIU)

A Systems Network Architecture (SNA) packet of information, created when the Transmission-Control Layer adds a request/response header to a request/response unit, and then passes the resulting packet to the Path-Control Layer.

See also **Path-Control Layer; Systems Network Architecture.**

Basic Input/Output System (BIOS)

A set of firmware-based programs that allows a computer's central processing unit (CPU) to communicate with printers and other peripherals. These services load automatically each time the computer starts up.

Basic Link Unit (BLU)

A packet of information that exists at the Data-Link layer in a Systems Network Architecture (SNA) network. The BLU is contained in a Synchronous Data-Link Control (SDLC) frame.

See also **Systems Network Architecture; Synchronous Data-Link Control.**

Basic Message-Handling Service (MHS)

In NetWare 3.x, a service in the NetWare MHS group of message-delivery products that provides and delivers messages to users on the same file server. Other products in this group include NetWare Global MHS (which provides message delivery for users at multiple file servers) and NetWare Remote MHS (which provides asynchronous access to an MHS network for laptop computer users).

basic mode

A mode of operation in an Fiber-Distributed Data Interface (FDDI) II network. Under basic mode, only data can be transmitted using packet switching.

See also **Fiber-Distributed Data Interface.**

Basic Rate Access (BRA)

Access to an Integrated-Services Digital Network (ISDN) Basic-Rate Interface. This interface contains two 64 kilobits per second (Kbps) B channels and one 16Kbps D channel. The two B channels handle voice and data; the D channel holds information about the call and the customer.

See also **Basic-Rate Interface; Integrated-Services Digital Network.**

Basic-Rate Interface (BRI)

An interface between a user and an Integrated-Services Digital Network (ISDN) switch. The BRI interface contains two 64 kilobits per second (Kbps) B channels and one 16 Kbps D channel. The two B channels handle voice and data; the D channel holds information about

the call and the customer. BRI is also known as *2B+D* and *Basic-Rate ISDN.*

See also **Integrated-Services Digital Network.**

Basic-Rate ISDN

Basic-Rate Integrated-Services Digital Network, an interface between a user and an Integrated-Services Digital Network (ISDN) switch. The BRI interface contains two 64 kilobit-per-second (Kbps) B channels and one 16Kbps D channel. The two B channels handle voice and data; the D channel holds information about the call and the customer. Basic-Rate ISDN is also known as *2B+D* and BRI.

See also **Integrated-Services Digital Network.**

Basic Telecommunications Access Method (BTAM)

A mostly obsolete method for communicating between IBM mainframes and terminals. BTAM does not support Systems Network Architecture (SNA), and has been replaced by ACF/VTAM as the preferred method of remote communications with IBM mainframes.

See also **Systems Network Architecture.**

Basic Transmission Unit (BTU)

A Systems Network Architecture (SNA) term denoting an aggregate block of one or more path-information units (PIUs) with the same destination. Multiple PIUs can have a single destination, and can be combined into a single packet even when they are not part of the same message.

See also **Systems Network Architecture.**

batch file

An American Standard Code for Information Interchange (ASCII) file containing a sequence of commands. To execute all the commands contained in a batch file, in the order it specifies, a user enters the name of the batch file at the command line. Batch files are often used to initialize the environment, set variables, map drives, and carry out other repetitive system tasks.

See also **American Standard Code for Information Interchange.**

BATCH option

An ITEM option command in a NetWare and IntranetWare NMENU utility file. This option removes the NMENU program from memory before running the called application.

See also **NMENU utility.**

batch-processing server

A server that carries out tasks specified by batch files. The batch-processing server makes it possible to offload time-consuming tasks to an idle workstation. Batch-processing services are typically furnished by third-party software programs. The server does not require a dedicated machine.

baud

A unit referring to the data-transmission speed of a modem or other serial device.

See also **baud rate.**

baud rate

In serial communications, a measurement of signal modulation rate used to indicate the speed at which a signal changes (that is, the number of *state changes per second* on an asynchronous communications channel). A serial port is limited by the baud rate. Baud rate is sometimes incorrectly used to denote *bit rate*, but the two rates are not identical. Both rates are equal *if each signal represents one bit.* If a signal represents several bits, the bit rate is a multiple of the baud rate.

Bay Area Regional Research Network (BARRNet)

A San Francisco Bay Area network whose backbone is composed of the University of California at Berkeley, the University of California at Davis, the University of California at San Francisco, the University of California at Santa Cruz, Stanford University, the Lawrence Livermore National Laboratory, and the NASA Ames Research Center.

 **A comprehensive information source from BARRNet can be found by surfing the Web to the gopher site at** http://gopher.barrnet.net.

BBN

Bolt, Beranek, and Newman, the Massachusetts-based company responsible for development and maintenance of the Advanced Research Projects Agency Network (ARPAnet) and Internet core gateway system.

See also **Advanced Research Projects Agency Network.**

BBS

Bulletin Board System, a computer or group of computers equipped with modems, used to permit access by other computers dialing in from remote locations. BBSs allow users to send messages, get technical support, or access files. Special-interest groups often use BBSs to disseminate information and provide services to members.

 **For a listing of top Bulletin Board Systems on the Internet, surf the Web at** http://dkeep.com/ sbi.htm/.

Bc (committed burst)

The highest number of data bits a network can transfer under normal conditions over a given period of time.

bcc

blind carbon copy; blind courtesy copy, an electronic-mail (e-mail) copy of a message sent to an additional recipient who does not appear on the list of recipients seen by the original addressee.

See also **cc.**

BCC

Block Check Character, a character placed at the end of a block for the purpose of error detection. Each of the BCC's bits is a parity bit for a column of bits in the block.

See also **electronic mail.**

BCD

Binary-Coded Decimal, an encoding mechanism under which each digit is encoded as a four-bit sequence.

BCN

A signaling process used by nodes of a Token Ring network to indicate that a *hard* (serious) *error* has occurred on the network, either at the node itself or at the nodes Nearest Active Upstream Neighbor (NAUN). Beaconing prevents communications from taking place until the error condition has been corrected.

See also **hard error; Nearest Active Upstream Neighbor; Token Ring.**

BCP

Byte-Control Protocols, a protocol that is character-oriented instead of bit-oriented.

BCUG

Bilateral Closed User Group, a facility offering more access control than the standard Closed User Group (CUG). The BCUG limits a CUG relationship to a pair of Data-Terminal Equipment (DTE) units, where access between the DTEs is unlimited, but access to DTEs outside the given pair is not allowed.

See also **Closed User Group.**

Be (excess burst)

Maximum number of uncommitted data bits the network attempts to deliver over a specified period of time.

beaconing

A signaling process used by nodes of a Token Ring network to indicate that a *hard* (serious) *error* has occurred on the network, either at the node itself or at the nodes Nearest Active Upstream Neighbor (NAUN).

Beaconing prevents communications from taking place until the error condition has been corrected.

See also **hard error; Nearest Active Upstream Neighbor; Token Ring.**

BEC

Backward Error Correction, an error-correction method in which the error is detected by the recipient, which subsequently requests a retransmission.

Because It's Time Network (BITNET)

A computer network used to connect more than 1,000 educational institutions in North America and Europe. BITNET provides users at those institutions with easy access to files from remote locations. BITNET uses the Remote Spooling Communications Subsystem (RSCS) and Network Job Entry (NJE) protocols common to IBM mainframes. Consequently, BITNET users must use a gateway to communicate with other networks (such as the Internet).

BECN

Background Explicit Congestion Notification, a notification set by a Frame Relay network indicating that the network is congested in the frame's reverse packet-forwarding direction.

See also **Frame Relay network.**

Begin Transaction operation

A command given in conjunction with an Abort Transaction operation. The Begin Transaction operation must come before the Abort Transaction or End Transaction operation.

See also **Abort Transaction operation.**

bel

A value proportional to the logarithm of the ratio that measures the relative intensity of two levels for an acoustic, electrical, or optical signal. A decibel is one-tenth of a bel.

Bell communications standard

A set of standards for data transmission over telecommunications networks. The standards were developed by AT&T in the 1980s, and have since become a *de facto* standard for modem manufacturers.

Bellcore

An organization responsible for research and development for the following Regional Bell Operating Companies (RBOCs): Ameritech, Bell Atlantic, BellSouth, Nynex, Pacific Telesis, SBC Communications, and US West.

See also **Regional Bell Operating Company.**

Bellman-Ford Algorithm

An algorithm that detects routes through an internetwork by using vectors instead of link states. Also known as the *old ARPAnet algorithm.*

Bell Operating Company (BOC)

One of several local telephone companies that formerly existed in each of seven regions of the United States. A court-ordered deregulation of the telephone industry eliminated BOCs and created seven Regional Bell Holding Companies (RHOCs).

See also **Regional Bell Holding Company.**

benchmark program

An initiative designed to establish a consistent performance metric, against which multiple hardware or software products can be compared.

BER

(1) Basic Encoding Rules, in Abstract Syntax Notation One (ASN.1), a rule for encoding data elements that specify any ASN.1 element as a byte string. The string includes a Type, Length, and Value field. The Type field indicates an object's class, the Length field indicates the number of bytes used to encode the value, and the Value field indicates the information associated with the ASN.1 object.

(2) Bit-Error Rate, the number of erroneous bits per million. The BER depends on the type and length of transmission, and the media involved in the data transfer.

See also **(1) Abstract Syntax Notation One; Bit-Error-Rate Tester.**

Berkeley Internet-Name Domain (BIND)

A domain-name system (DNS) server developed at the University of California, Berkeley. BIND is commonly used on Internet machines.

Berkeley Software Distribution (BSD)

Berkeley Software Distribution UNIX, a UNIX operating system variant developed at the University of California, Berkeley. BSD UNIX offers some enhancements to the original implementation of UNIX designed by AT&T, including virtual memory, networking, and interprocess communications.

Berkeley Software Distribution UNIX (BSD UNIX)

A UNIX operating system variant developed at the University of California, Berkeley. BSD UNIX offers some enhancements to the original implementation of UNIX designed by AT&T, including virtual memory, networking, and interprocess communications.

Bernoulli drive

A high-capacity, removable cartridge drive from Iomega Corporation.

BERT

Bit-Error-Rate Tester, a hardware device used for checking a transmission's Bit Error Rate (BER). The BERT sends a predefined signal, then compares it with the received signal. A BERT may be used for troubleshooting a network's wiring.

best-effort delivery

A type of delivery system common in networks that do not incorporate a sophisticated acknowledgment system to guarantee reliable delivery of information.

beta site

A location where a hardware or software product undergoes pre-release live testing to examine its features and detect flaws before it is released commercially.

beta software

A software product that has been released to a selection of end-users for live testing before the product is released commercially.

beta testing

A process whereby a new hardware or software product is field tested before it is released commercially. Typically, end-users beta-test a product by subjecting it to real-life operating conditions. Flaws that come to light as a result of the beta test are repaired before the program is released commercially.

bfloat

A Btrieve data type used to define a key value. A Btrieve field with a bfloat type contains a single-precision or double-precision real number.
See also **Btrieve.**

BGP

Border Gateway Protocol, a routing protocol designed to replace the External Gateway Protocol (EGP). BGP that interconnects organizational networks and evaluates each possible route for the best available option.
See also **border gateway; External Gateway Protocol; Interior Gateway Protocol.**

BIA

Burned-In Address, a hardware address for a Network Interface Card (NIC), typically assigned by the manufacturer, that is different for each card.

BIB

Bus Interface Board an expansion board that functions as an interface between the computer and the network medium.

big-endian

A term that describes the order in which a word's individual bytes are stored. A big-endian system stores high-order bytes at the lower addresses. Mainframe processors, some Reduced-Instruction-Set-Computing (RISC) machines, and minicomputers use the big-endian system.
See also **little-endian; middle-endian.**

Bilateral Closed User Group (BCUG)

A facility offering more access control than the standard Closed User Group (CUG). The BCUG limits a CUG relationship to a pair of Data-Terminal Equipment (DTE) units, where access between the DTEs is unlimited, but access to DTEs outside the given pair is not allowed.
See also **Closed User Group.**

binary

A numbering system that uses only zeroes and ones.

Binary-Coded Decimal (BCD)

An encoding mechanism under which each digit is encoded as a four-bit sequence.

binary file

A file containing binary information. The data contained in the file is machine-readable, as opposed to human-readable.
See also **binary.**

binary-capable

A term used to describe a channel that allows a printer to receive all 8-bit characters. A binary-capable channel can accommodate both American Standard Code for Information Interchange (ASCII) and binary (that is, PostScript) print jobs.

See also **American Standard Code for Information Interchange; PostScript.**

binary transfer

Transmission of a file using a link configured to expect any type of data or bit pattern.

BIND

Berkeley Internet-Name Domain, a domain-name system (DNS) server developed at the University of California, Berkeley. BIND is commonly used on Internet machines.

bind session

An Advanced Program-to-Program Communications (APPC) process used to establish a session between two logical units (LUs).

See also **Advanced Program-to-Program Communications.**

BIND utility

In NetWare and IntranetWare servers, a console utility that binds a protocol to a Network Interface Card (NIC) or device driver. Without linking the protocol to the interface card or device driver, the interface card or driver cannot process data packets.

See also **NetWare Loadable Module; NetWare utilities.**

bindery

A nonhierarchical network database maintained by the network operating system on each server. Older versions of NetWare use this bindery mechanism to define network entities, including users, print queues, and workgroups. The bindery places these objects in a flat database, as opposed to a hierarchical database such as a Directory tree. The bindery contains three types of components: objects, properties, and property data sets. Objects are users, devices, and other physical or logical entities. Properties are attributes such as full name or login restrictions, and the property data set is the set of values to be stored in the object's property list. NetWare 4.*x* replaces the bindery system with Novell Directory Services (NDS).

Table B.1 compares bindery-based and Directory-based versions of NetWare.

See also **Novell Directory Services.**

bindery context

A NetWare container object that indicates where bindery services are set. *Bindery emulation,* used by Novell Directory Services (NDS) to provide backward compatibility with the older NetWare bindery model, requires a bindery context to be set for each NetWare 4.*x* server.

See also **bindery emulation; container object; Novell Directory Services.**

bindery context level

Denotes a position within the hierarchical framework used in NetWare 4.*x* when bindery emulation is in effect. The *level* of a bindery context represents the default setting that controls object availability and creation.

When the system administrator adds objects to the NetWare network, the bindery context must be appropriately set for each object.

See also **bindery context; bindery emulation; bindery services.**

Bindery Context path

A path statement on a NetWare 4.*x* server that allows the bindery context to be set for up to 16 containers. The Bindery Context SET parameter establishes bindery contexts; a user can enter multiple contexts separated by semicolons. In older versions of NetWare 4, the bindery context can be set for only one container within the Directory tree. Under NetWare 4.1, the bindery context path permits bindery objects located on the NetWare 4.1 server to be located in multiple containers; and furthermore allows NetWare 3.*x* NetWare Loadable Modules (NLMs) that use bindery services to access objects in multiple containers.

See also **NetWare Loadable Module; SET utility.**

bindery emulation

A NetWare 4.*x* feature that permits bindery-based utilities and users to work with Novell Directory Services (NDS) on the same network. Under bindery emulation, NDS emulates the flat structure of the bindery to represent all objects within an Organizational container object. The objects within the container object can then be accessed by NDS objects and by bindery-based clients and servers. As a result, bindery-based programs can access information from NDS. Bindery emulation applies only to leaf objects within the Organizational container object.

See also **bindery services; container object; leaf object; Novell Directory Services; object.**

Table B.I: Bindery-Based Versus Directory-Based Features

Feature	Bindery-Based	Directory-Based
Logical structure	Flat structure	Hierarchical tree
Partitions	None	Distributed database
Replication	None	Partitions replicated
Synchronization	No replicas	Replicas synchronized
Users	Separate accounts on each server	Global account for network
Groups	Server-by-server	Network-wide
Login	Password per server	Network-wide (with authentication)
Printing	No friendly map	User-friendly access
Volumes	Server-specific	Global objects

bindery-emulation user

A NetWare user operating under bindery emulation. A user employing bindery emulation can log in to a server only if that server's bindery context is set to the container where the network's User objects are held.

bindery hopping

A method of viewing objects located in multiple NetWare binderies.

Bindery object

A leaf object that represents an object placed in the Directory tree by an upgrade utility, and that further cannot be identified by Novell Directory Services (NDS). Bindery-based clients need to use older NetWare utilities to gain access to these objects via bindery emulation. The Bindery object is placed for the purpose of backward-compatibility with bindery-based utilities. This object has the Access-Control List, Back Link, Bindery Object Restrictions, Bindery, Bindery Type, Common Name (CN), and Object Class selectable NDS properties.

See also **leaf object; Novell Directory Services; object.**

Bindery Object Restriction

A NetWare Directory Schema term for a single-valued integer attribute used by Bindery objects: an error code that shows why a particular Bindery object cannot be shown as a Directory object. This attribute is also a Novell Directory Services (NDS) selectable property for the Bindery object.

Bindery Property

A NetWare Directory Schema term and a property of the following Novell Directory Services (NDS) objects: AFP Server, Bindery, Bindery Queue, Computer, Country, Directory Map, External Entity, Group, List, Message-Routing Group, Messaging Server, NCP Server, Organization, Organizational Role, Organizational Unit, Print Server, Printer, Profile, Queue, User, and Volume.

See also **leaf object; Novell Directory Services; object.**

Bindery Queue object

A Novell Directory Services (NDS) leaf object that represents a queue placed in a Directory tree by an upgrade utility, which further cannot be identified by Novell Directory Services (NDS). The Bindery Queue object is placed for the purpose of backward-compatibility with bindery-based utilities. This object class has the following selectable properties: Access-Control List (ACL), Back Link, Bindery Property, Bindery Type, Common Name (CN), Description, Device, Host Resource Name, Host Server, Locality, Network Address, Organization, Object Class, Operator, Organizational Unit, Queue Directory, See Also, Server, User, and Volume.

See also **leaf object; Novell Directory Services; object.**

Bindery services

A NetWare 4.x feature that allows bindery-based utilities and clients to coexist with Novell Directory Services (NDS) on the same network. Bindery services emulate a flat database for holding network objects, as opposed to the hierarchical database as is used in NDS.

See also **bindery emulation; Novell Directory Services.**

Bindery Type

A selectable NetWare object property of the Bindery and Bindery Queue objects in Novell Directory Services (NDS).
See also **leaf object; Novell Directory Services; object.**

BINDFIX utility

A NetWare 3.*x* workstation utility for repairing a damaged server bindery. The utility locks the bindery files, then copies them to new files and gives the originals an .OLD extension. After rebuilding the bindery, the utility reopens it so the server can be accessed. The BINDFIX utility has been replaced with the DSREPAIR utility in NetWare 4.*x*.
See also **BINDREST utility; DSREPAIR utility.**

binding

A process that assigns a communications protocol to network boards and local-area network (LAN) drivers (for example, Internet Packet Exchange/Sequenced Packet Exchange to an NE2000 Ethernet adapter). Every board must have a minimum of one communications protocol bound to the LAN driver for that board. It is possible to bind the same protocol stack to multiple LAN drivers on the server.

BINDREST utility

A NetWare 3.*x* workstation utility that deletes the current copy of the bindery and then restores the older copy that existed before running the BINDFIX utility. This function has been replaced with the DSREPAIR utility in NetWare 4.*x*.
See also **BINDFIX utility; DSREPAIR utility.**

binhex

A contraction for "binary hexadecimal" that describes the process of converting nontext files into an American Standard Code for Information Interchange (ASCII) text format. The conversion is often necessary because Internet e-mail cannot be transmitted in a format other than ASCII.
See also **American Standard Code for Information Interchange.**

bionet newsgroup

A type of newsgroup that discusses topics of interest to biologists.

BIOS

Basic Input/Output System, a set of firmware-based programs that allows a computer's central processing unit (CPU) to communicate with printers and other peripherals. These services load automatically each time the computer starts up.

BIOS Extensions

A set of firmware-based services that supplement those furnished by the standard Basic Input/Output System (BIOS).

biphase coding

A bipolar coding scheme in which clocking information is embedded into the synchronous data stream, and then recovered without the need for separate clocking leads.

bipolar

An electrical circuit with both positive and negative polarity.
See also **polarity**; **unipolar.**

Bipolar with 8-Zero Substitution (B8ZS)

A signal-encoding scheme that represents a 1 alternatively as positive and negative voltage, with 0 representing zero voltage. Under the B8ZS encoding scheme, at least one out of every eight bits must be set to 1.

bis

A secondary Consultative Committee for International Telegraphy and Telephony (CCITT) recommendation that serves as an alternative or extension to a primary recommendation. For example, a CCITT classification of a V.42*bis* modem indicates that this modem is a revised version of a V.42 modem.
See also **Consultative Committee for International Telegraphy and Telephony.**

BISDN

A high-speed communications standard for wide-area networks (WANs) that can accommodate high-bandwidth applications (such as video or graphics). Asynchronous Transfer Mode (ATM) is an example of a BISDN-based technology.

See also **Asynchronous Transfer Mode; Integrated-Services Digital Network.**

Bisynchronous Communication (BSC)

A protocol used in mainframe networks under which both sending and receiving devices must be synchronized before transmission begins. Under the bisynchronous model, data is collected into a frame (which contains a header and trailer recognized by the two computers) for synchronization purposes.

bit

The smallest unit of data in a computer. A bit is a type of virtual electronic switch, which is given a value of 0 to indicate an *off* condition, or a value of 1 to indicate an *on* condition. Eight bits equals one byte.
See also **byte.**

bit-array operations

Commands used by NetWare to manipulate bit arrays. NetWare Loadable Modules (NLMs) use bit-array operations to scan bit arrays, and set or clear bits.
See also **NetWare Loadable Module.**

Bit-Error Rate (BER)

The number of erroneous bits per million. The BER depends on the type and length of transmission, and the media involved in the data transfer.

Bit-Error-Rate Tester (BERT)

A hardware device used for checking a transmission's Bit-Error Rate (BER). The

BERT sends a predefined signal, then compares it with the received signal. A BERT may be used for troubleshooting a network's wiring.

bit interval

The amount of time a digital signal is left at one voltage level. The bit interval usually indicates the value of a single bit, though multiple bits can be encoded into one voltage level, making it possible to send multiple bits within a single bit interval.

bit rate

The rate at which bits are transmitted over a communications link. The bit rate is usually represented in bits per second (bps). A higher bit rate indicates a shorter bit interval. Bit rate is sometimes incorrectly used to mean *baud rate*. The two rates are not identical. *Baud rate* indicates the number of signal transitions made in one second. Both rates are equal *if each signal represents one bit*. However, if a signal represents several bits, the bit rate is a multiple of the baud rate.

See also **baud rate.**

bit stuffing

A technique for ensuring that a specific bit pattern does not appear as part of data in a transmission. Bit stuffing involves inserting additional bits, which are removed when the transmission is processed.

bitmap

A binary file in which each bit (or set of bits) corresponds to part of a graphical object such as a font or an image.

bitmap/sequence field

A single-byte field in the AppleTalk Transaction Protocol (ATP) header. The field holds a transaction bitmap, which is used for a Transmission Request (TReq) packet, or a sequence number, which is used for a Transmission Response (TResp) packet.

See also **AppleTalk protocols; AppleTalk Transaction Protocol.**

BITFTP

A popular server to which users can send an electronic mail (e-mail) message to request that a file be mailed by way of e-mail.

See also **FTP-by-mail server.**

BITNET

Because It's Time Network, a computer network used to connect more than 1,000 educational institutions in North America and Europe. BITNET provides users at those institutions with easy access to files from remote locations. BITNET uses the Remote Spooling Communications Subsystem (RSCS) and Network Job Entry (NJE) protocols common to IBM mainframes. Consequently, BITNET users must use a gateway to communicate with other networks (such as the Internet).

bit-oriented protocol

A communications protocol that transmits data as a stream of bits instead of bytes.

Bitronics

A specification developed by Hewlett-Packard Company to allow bidirectional parallel printing on a Centronics-type interface.

See also **Centronics parallel interface.**

bits per second (bps)

A rate that shows the number of bits of information transmitted per second. This metric is similar, but not identical, to *baud rate*.

See also **baud rate; bit rate.**

BitSURFER

A line of Integrated-Services Digital Network (ISDN) terminal adapters from Motorola, Inc.

For more information about networking hardware from Motorola, surf the Web to `http://www.mot.com/ mims/products/isg/ products/isdn.`

BIU

(1) **Basic Information Unit,** a Systems Network Architecture (SNA) packet of information, created when the Transmission-Control Layer adds a request/response header to a request/response unit, and then passes the resulting packet to the Path-Control Layer.

(2) **Bus Interface Unit,** a Network Interface Card (NIC) that functions as an interface between a computer node and the network.

See also (2) **Network Interface Card;** (1) **Path-Control Layer;** (1) **Systems Network Architecture.**

BIX

A commercial online service that provides subscribers access to the Internet, as well as related services such as e-mail, FTP, and Telnet.

biz newsgroup

A type of newsgroup that discusses topics of interest to business and commercial entities.

black hole

In the context of internetwork routing, an area in which packets enter, but do not emerge because of adverse conditions or poor system configuration.

black-tab folder

A folder that appears on screen with a black band on the tab. The band indicates that the particular user accessing the folder has the appropriate access-control rights for modifying that folder's security parameters.

See also **access-control list; access-control rights.**

blackout

A complete loss of electrical power that may be the result of broken power lines or natural disasters.

blank truncation

A Btrieve method of conserving disk space by not storing the trailing blanks in the variable-length portions of records when those records are written to a file.

See also **Btrieve.**

BLAST

Blocked Asynchronous/Synchronous Transmission, a protocol that specifies data transmission in blocks containing a fixed number of bits. The BLAST protocol

simplifies framing and may be used to multiplex transmissions.
See also **multiplexing.**

BLER

Block-Error Rate, a communications error rate based on the proportion of blocks containing errors.

BLERT

Block-Error-Rate Tester, a hardware device that determines a transmission's block-error rate (BLER).

block

A set of continuous bits or bytes that make up a piece of information. The block is the smallest amount of disk space that can be allocated at any one time on a NetWare volume. Block size depends on the volume size, and is set automatically during installation. A NetWare block is usually 4K (although it can be set to 8K, 16K, 32K, or 64K); DOS blocks are usually a multiple of 2K. A disk-allocation block that stores network data; a directory entry block that stores directory information. The term also denotes a capability of preventing a certain right from being exercised. For example, an object's Inherited-Rights Filter can, in some circumstances, block the Supervisor right.

Block-Check Character (BCC)

A character placed at the end of a block for the purpose of error detection. Each of the BCC's bits is a parity bit for a column of bits in the block.

Block-Error Rate (BLER)

A communications error rate based on the proportion of blocks containing errors.

Block-Error-Rate Tester (BLERT)

A hardware device that determines a transmission's block error rate (BLER).

block parity

In serial transmissions, an error-detection method that calculates a place value for each bit in a block of bytes. Block parity (also known as *longitudinal redundancy checking*) is always set to even.

block suballocation

A procedure that allows the last part of several files to share a single disk block. The procedure is meant to make better use of disk space, and divides a partially used disk block into 512-byte suballocation blocks. These suballocation blocks are then used to hold fragments of other files.

Blocked Asynchronous/Synchronous Transmission (BLAST)

A protocol that specifies data transmission in blocks containing a fixed number of bits. The BLAST protocol simplifies framing and may be used to multiplex transmissions.
See also **multiplexing.**

blocking functions

Subroutines that can cause an application to give up control of the central processing unit (CPU). A function in blocking mode waits for a specific event to occur before returning control to the application. Blocking functions are also known as *synchronous functions*.

BLU

Basic Link Unit, a packet of information that exists at the Data-Link layer in a Systems Network Architecture (SNA) network. The BLU is contained in an Synchronous Data Link Control (SDLC) frame.

See also **Systems Network Architecture; Synchronous Data-Link Control.**

Blue Book Ethernet

Ethernet version 2.0 (or Ethernet II), as distinguished from the Ethernet variant defined in the Institute of Electrical and Electronic Engineers (IEEE) 802.3 standard.

See also **Institute of Electrical and Electronic Engineers; IEEE 802.*x*.**

BNC connector

A connecting device with a half-turn locking shell for coaxial cable. The BNC connector is used with thin Ethernet and RG-62 cabling.

BOC

Bell Operating Company, one of several local telephone companies that formerly existed in each of seven regions of the United States. A court-ordered deregulation of the telephone industry eliminated BOCs and created seven Regional Bell Holding Companies (RHOCs).

See also **Regional Bell Holding Company.**

Bolt, Beranek, and Newman

The Massachusetts-based company responsible for development and maintenance of the Advanced Research Projects Agency Network (ARPAnet) and Internet core gateway system.

See also **Advanced Research Projects Agency Network.**

bookmark

An Internet browser device that marks a specific menu or directory and provides the user with easy access to the marked menu or directory. As a feature of some word processing and file-viewing applications, a bookmark allows a user to mark a location in an online document so the user may return to the location quickly.

See also **Internet.**

bookshelf

An icon that represents a set of related books. The texts are available online through Novell DynaText.

Boolean

A logic system that incorporates True or False values combined with AND, OR, and NOT operators. Search engines on the Internet often employ the Boolean logic system by allowing users to specify search strings that include the Boolean operators in order to expand the scope of a search.

boot

The process of starting up a computer. The boot process loads the operating system kernel into the random-access memory (RAM), executes and loads programs, and configures the operating environment.

boot disk

An external disk used to load and start the operating system.

boot files

A set of files that start the operating system and its driver, set environment variables, or execute other system tasks. DOS boot files include AUTOEXEC.BAT and CONFIG.SYS. NetWare server boot files include AUTOEXEC.NCF and STARTUP.NCF.

boot PROM

A nonvolatile type of Programmable Read-Only Memory (PROM) that can be transmitted over a network and contains information for initializing a computer system at startup.

boot ROM

A read-only memory (ROM) chip used to start up a diskless workstation and connect it to the network.

boot sector

In IBM-compatible PCs, a record contained in a storage device (such as a disk) that provides the computer's built-in operating system with basic information about the disk and the version of DOS in use. The boot sector facilitates placing DOS in the computer's memory.

BOOTCONF.SYS

A file used by a workstation employing Remote Reset to determine which remote boot image file to use. BOOTCONF.SYS can be used by a diskless workstation to boot the NetWare operating system.

BOOTP

Bootstrap Protocol, a protocol used by a host computer to obtain its Internet Protocol (IP) address. The host obtains this information by broadcasting a BOOTP request on the local network. The server then receives the request, and replies with a packet that contains the host's address.

See also **Internet Protocol (IP).**

bootstrap program

A program that provides the end-user with a prompt at startup, offering an opportunity to select which disk-image file to boot.

Bootstrap Protocol (BOOTP)

A protocol used by a host computer to obtain its Internet Protocol (IP) address. The host obtains this information by broadcasting a BOOTP request on the local network. The server then receives the request, and replies with a packet that contains the host's address.

See also **Internet Protocol (IP).**

border gateway

An Autonomous System (AS) router that communicates with other AS routers.

See also **Autonomous System.**

Border Gateway Protocol (BGP)

A routing protocol designed to replace the External Gateway Protocol (EGP). BGP interconnects organizational networks and evaluates each possible route for the best available option.

See also **border gateway; External Gateway Protocol; Interior Gateway Protocol.**

bot

A shortened version of the term *robot*, describing a program that responds to network requests by using a specified set of actions or responses.

See also **robot.**

bounce

Occurs when a message moves back and forth between servers indefinitely because of an error condition, or is returned to the sender when undeliverable.

boundary function

A capability of subarea nodes in Systems Network Architecture (SNA) networks that provides protocol support for attached peripheral nodes.

See also **Systems Network Architecture (SNA).**

Boundary-Routing System Architecture

Technology from 3Com that centralizes complex router functions to permit a simpler connection of remote-office local-area networks (LANs) to a central networking site.

For more information about networking products from 3Com, surf the Web to `http://www.3com.com/0file s/products/bguide.`

bozo filter

A feature of a newsreader or electronic-mail (e-mail) program that filters mail by referring to a list of sources from which information is not to be received.

BPDU

Bridge-Protocol Data Unit, a Hello packet in a spanning-tree protocol.

See also **Protocol Data Unit; spanning tree.**

bps

bits per second, a rate that shows the number of bits of information transmitted per second. This metric is similar, but not identical, to *baud rate*.

See also **baud rate; bit rate.**

BRA

Basic-Rate Access, access to an Integrated-Services Digital Network (ISDN) Basic Rate Interface. This interface contains two 64-kilobit-per-second (Kbps) B channels and one 16Kbps D channel. Two B channels handle voice and data; the D channel holds information about the call and the customer.

See also **Basic-Rate Interface; Integrated-Services Digital Network.**

braid shield

A braid or mesh conductor that surrounds the insulation and foil shield in coaxial cable. The braid protects the carrier wire from interference.

branch

A container object and all the objects it contains. In a Novell Directory Services (NDS) Directory tree, the branch can contain other container objects. A branch is also known as a *subtree*.

See also **container object; leaf object; Novell Directory Services; object.**

breakout box

A device connected to a multicore cable for testing signals in a transmission. The breakout box features Light-Emitting Diodes (LEDs) to indicate when a signal is being transmitted.

BRGCON utility

In NetWare 4.*x* and IntranetWare, a server console utility used to view managed objects. Implemented through Simple Network-Management Protocol (SNMP) on a NetWare for OS/2 bridge, the BRGCON utility allows the user to view information on basic bridge configuration, spanning trees for the bridge, transparent bridging, ports, and a table of interfaces.

See also **NetWare Loadable Module; NetWare utilities; Simple Network-Management Protocol.**

BRI

Basic-Rate Interface, an interface between a user and an Integrated-Services Digital Network (ISDN) switch. The BRI interface contains two 64-kilobit-per-second (Kbps) B channels and one 16Kbps D channel. The two B channels handle voice and data; the D channel holds information about the call and the customer. BRI is also known as *2B+D* and *Basic-Rate ISDN*.

See also **Integrated-Services Digital Network.**

bridge

A hardware device that connects two or more physical networks or network segments. A bridge forwards frames between the connecting networks on the basis of information contained in the data-link header. Operating at the Data-Link Layer (Layer 2) of the OSI Reference Model, bridges are transparent to Network-Layer (Layer 3) protocols. (A bridge differs from a *router*, which forwards packets between different network topologies and determines the best path between the two. A router operates at the Network Layer of the OSI Reference Model.) The bridge also functions as a filter, discarding packets intended for the originating network and sending on packets intended for the destination network.

A bridge is protocol-independent, and can, therefore, handle packets from multiple higher-level protocols. It can operate at the Media-Access Control (MAC) sublayer or the Logical-Link Control (LLC) sublayer of the Data-Link Layer. A MAC-Layer bridge can connect only networks using the same architecture; an LLC bridge can connect networks using different architectures.

See also **Media-Access Control; link-level control; OSI Reference Model.**

Bridge-Protocol Data Unit (BPDU)

A Hello packet in a spanning-tree protocol.
See also **Protocol Data Unit; spanning tree.**

broadband

A transmission technology that multiplexes several independent network carriers onto a single cable. Broadband networking permits multiple networks to coexist on a single cable. Because each network conducts its conversations on a different frequency, traffic from one network does not interfere with traffic from the others.

broadband network

A network employing broadband technology to transmit multiple streams of information over long distances over the same cable. The network is divided into multiple channels that can be used concurrently by different networks, using a Frequency-Division Multiplexing (FDM) technique. Each channel is protected from the others by *guard channels*, small bands of unused frequency placed between the data channels.
See also **Frequency-Division Multiplexing.**

broadband transmission

An analog communication technique that uses several communications channels simultaneously. Data in a broadband transmission is modulated into *frequency bands* (*channels*). A *guard band* is a band of unused frequency inserted between these data channels to provide a buffer against interference.
See also **channel.**

broadcast

A transmission method in which all nodes on the network receive a copy of a frame or packet.

Broadcast and Unknown Server (BUS)

An Asynchronous Transfer Mode (ATM) server that handles data sent to a LAN Emulation client, as well as all multicast traffic (and initial unicast frames) sent by a LAN Emulation client.
See also **Asynchronous Transfer Mode; LAN Emulation.**

Broadcast Integrated-Services Digital Network (BISDN)

A high-speed communications standard for wide-area networks (WANs) that can accommodate high-bandwidth applications (such as video or graphics). Asynchronous Transfer Mode (ATM) is an example of a BISDN-based technology.
See also **Asynchronous Transfer Mode; Integrated-Services Digital Network.**

broadcast storm

A condition in which one workstation triggers several other workstations to transmit large numbers of frames at the same time. A broadcast storm can result from loops occurring on a bridged network, and can cause network congestion.

broadcast transmission

A transmission in an AppleTalk network using the LocalTalk architecture and the LocalTalk Link-Access Protocol (LLAP),

where a transmission is sent to every node on the network.

BROADCAST utility

Under NetWare and IntranetWare, a workstation or console utility that allows a user to send messages to other users attached to the server; sets up a workstation to receive all messages, only system messages, or no messages; polls the network for messages; or to send a message to all users logged in or attached to the NetWare server.

broadcast-oriented cable

Cable designed to carry video signals sent from one location in the network. Broadcast-oriented cable is designed for one-way communication.

brouter

A hardware device that combines the functions of a bridge and router, routing some protocols and bridging others. A brouter can operate at either the Data-Link Layer (Layer 2) or Network Layer (Layer 3) of the OSI Reference Model.

See also **bridge; OSI Reference Model; router.**

brownout

A short-term decrease in voltage level that may occur when a piece of heavy machinery is started up. A brownout may cause a computer to crash unless a device such as an uninterruptible power supply (UPS) is in use.

See also **blackout; power conditioning; uninterruptible power supply.**

Browse right

An object right that grants the right to see an object in the Directory tree. Upon installation, if every trustee is granted the Browse right at the Directory tree [Root], all users have unlimited access. The Browse right can be removed from the [Root] object if desired. The Browse right is also known as a *Browse object right*.

See also **access control; access-control list.**

browser

A window in the NetWare Administrator utility that shows objects in the Directory tree; or part of the DOS menu utility that allows users to move around the Directory tree; or an Internet utility (such as Netscape Navigator or Microsoft Internet Explorer) that allows users to view pages on the World Wide Web (WWW).

See also **Internet; NetWare Administrator; World Wide Web; Web browser.**

browser area

The left-hand portion of a Macintosh utility window that contains Browser tools.

Browser tools

Tools for locating NetWare entities in a Macintosh utility window. Browser tools include the Browser, a pop-up menu, and an Open button. These tools can locate volumes, folders, files, users, groups, and print queues.

browser window

A window in the NetWare Administrator utility that shows objects in the Directory tree; or part of the DOS menu utility that allows users to move around the Directory tree; or an Internet utility (such as Netscape Navigator or Microsoft Internet Explorer) that allows users to view pages on the World Wide Web (WWW).

See also **Internet; NetWare Administrator; World Wide Web; Web browser.**

browsing

A way to find objects in a Novell Directory Services (NDS) Directory tree. To find a desired object, a user can browse the Directory tree in either direction to view different parts of the Directory.

BSC

Bisynchronous Communication, a protocol used in mainframe networks under which both sending and receiving devices must be synchronized before transmission begins. Under the bisynchronous model, data is collected into a frame (which contains a header and trailer recognized by the two computers) for synchronization purposes.

BSD

Berkeley Software Distribution, a UNIX operating system variant developed at the University of California, Berkeley. BSD UNIX offers some enhancements to the original implementation of UNIX designed by AT&T, including virtual memory, networking, and interprocess communications.

BSD Socket Layer

A layer in Berkeley Software Distribution UNIX (BSD UNIX) that represents the Application Program Interface (API) between user applications and the networking subsystem of the operating system kernel.

See also **Application Program Interface; Berkeley Software Distribution UNIX.**

BSD UNIX

Berkeley Software Distribution UNIX, a UNIX operating system variant developed at the University of California, Berkeley. BSD UNIX offers some enhancements to the original implementation of UNIX designed by AT&T, including virtual memory, networking, and interprocess communications.

BTAM

Basic Telecommunications Access Method, a mostly obsolete method for communicating between IBM mainframes and terminals. BTAM does not support Systems Network Architecture (SNA), and has been replaced by ACF/VTAM as the preferred method of remote communications with IBM mainframes.

See also **Systems Network Architecture.**

Btrieve

A key-indexed record-management system used for file handling. A function call can be issued from most standard programming languages to invoke Btrieve. The Btrieve program stores data in Btrieve files, which can be recognized by several existing database programs. More than one user or application can access a Btrieve data file at

the same time, and Btrieve maintains file integrity during this concurrent access. The program is available in both client-based and server-based implementations. In addition to record management, Btrieve also includes communications facilities, requesters, utilities, data-protection functions, and support for Novell Directory Services (NDS).

See also **Btrieve Record Manager.**

Btrieve Message Router

A NetWare Loadable Module (NLM) called BROUTER or BDROUTER that allows server-based Btrieve applications to access Btrieve databases on remote servers. In addition, Btrieve Message Routers maintain concurrency controls during transactions that involve Btrieve files on more than one server.

See also **Btrieve; NetWare Loadable Module.**

Btrieve Record Manager

A NetWare software program that returns a status code after every operation an application performs. NetWare accommodates two types of Btrieve Record Manager. A *server-based* version runs on a NetWare server, includes a series of NetWare Loadable Modules (NLMs) for use on the server, and manages data input/output (I/O) with the file system. A *client-based* version runs on a workstation, executes all processing on the workstation, and is included as part of the Btrieve Developer's Kit.

See also **Btrieve; NetWare Loadable Module.**

Btrieve Requester

A program for establishing communications between Btrieve and an application making Btrieve calls. It resides in the workstation in a DOS, OS/2, or Windows environment..

See also **Btrieve.**

BTU

Basic Transmission Unit, a Systems Network Architecture (SNA) term denoting an aggregate block of one or more path information units (PIUs) with the same destination. Multiple PIUs can have a single destination, and can be combined into a single packet even when they are not part of the same message.

See also **Systems Network Architecture.**

BTW

By The Way, an abbreviation indicating an addendum to a message on an online Internet forum.

buffer

An area of a computer's random-access memory (RAM) that temporarily holds data until its disposition. A buffer can be used to mitigate differences in data-flow rates.

See also **memory; random-access memory.**

buffer (fiber-optic cable)

A layer that surrounds the cladding in fiber-optic cabling.

buffered repeater

A device for cleaning and boosting signals before sending them on. A buffered repeater holds a message temporarily if a transmission is already on the network.

bug

A logical or programming error in hardware or software. A software bug can be repaired by altering the program; a hardware bug requires new physical circuits. A bug may cause a wide range of problems, including a crash.

bug fix

A release of hardware or software that corrects known bugs. The bug fix generally does not introduce new features, but is released merely to correct flaws.

built-in command

An operating system command that resides in memory.

built-in groups

Default groups furnished with Windows NT and Windows NT Advanced Server that define a set of rights and permissions for network users.

Bulletin Board System (BBS)

A computer or group of computers equipped with modems, used to permit access by other computers dialing in from remote locations. BBSs allow users to send messages, get technical support, or access files. Special-interest groups often use BBSs to disseminate information and provide services to members.

 **For a listing of top Bulletin Board Systems on the Internet, surf the Web at** `http://dkeep.com/sbi.htm/`.

Bundle bit

A file attribute used during the desktop rebuild process. During this process, NetWare for Macintosh examines files with this attribute to discover associations between icons and file types.

Bundle flag

A file attribute often distributed with Macintosh files. A Bundle flag indicates that the file contains icons that the desktop database rebuilder should collect.

bundled software

Software applications sold with hardware (or with other applications) for a single price.

Burned-In Address (BIA)

A hardware address for a Network Interface Card (NIC), typically assigned by the manufacturer, that is different for each card.

burst

Several units of data that are sent in a single high-speed transmission.

burst mode

A method of transmitting data across a network. In burst mode, data is collected and sent as a unit in a single high-speed transmission. In NetWare, burst mode is synonymous with *packet burst*.

See also **packet burst.**

burst speed

The highest speed at which a device can function without interruption. The burst speed is usually achieved only for short periods of time.

bursty

A term describing data transmitted in short, unequal spurts. Local-area network (LAN) traffic is bursty; short periods of intense activity are interspersed with periods of inactivity.

bus

A path for electrical signals between a central processing unit (CPU) and attached peripherals. Buses are defined by their bit values, speed, and control mechanisms. Also denotes a physical network topology in which all messages are broadcast over a central cable.

BUS

Broadcast and Unknown Server, an Asynchronous Transfer Mode (ATM) server that handles data sent to a LAN Emulation client, as well as all multicast traffic (and initial unicast frames) sent by a LAN Emulation client.

See also **Asynchronous Transfer Mode; LAN Emulation.**

Bus Interface Board (BIB)

An expansion board that functions as an interface between the computer and the network medium.

Bus Interface Unit (BIU)

A Network Interface Card (NIC) that functions as an interface between a computer node and the network.

See also **Network Interface Card.**

bus mastering

A bus-access method that allows a hardware device to take control of the bus and sends data directly to it, without assistance from the central processing unit (CPU). Bus mastering can significantly improve throughput; various architectures support it: MicroChannel Architecture (MCA), Extended Industry-Standard Architecture (EISA), VESA local (V), and Peripheral-Component Interconnect (PCI). Industry-Standard Architecture (ISA) machines, however, do not support bus mastering.

See also **Extended Industry-Standard Architecture; MicroChannel Architecture; Peripheral-Component Interconnect.**

bus network topology

A type of network topology in which all workstations and servers are connected to a central cable. Ethernet networks are often designed with a bus topology.

Figure B.2 shows an example of bus network topology.

By The Way (BTW)

An abbreviation indicating an addendum to a message on an online Internet forum.

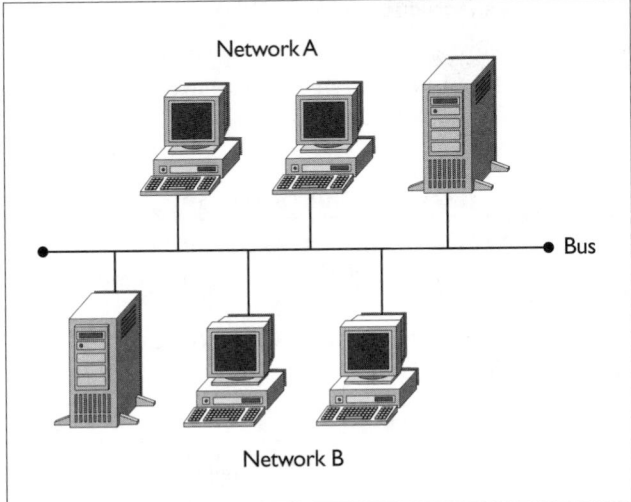

Figure B.2
Bus network topology

bypass

A telephony connection that uses an inter-exchange carrier without going through a local exchange carrier.

bypass printing

A method of printing that runs the print job directly from a client workstation to the printer. Bypass printing circumvents the print queue, and can be prevented by configuring the AppleTalk Print Services (ATPS) NetWare Loadable Module (NLM) and AppleTalk Extended Remote Printer (ATXRP) NLM to hide printers.

See also **AppleTalk Print Services module; ATXRP (NLM); NetWare Loadable Module.**

byte

A unit of data consisting of eight bits, also known as an *octet*. A byte is the amount of storage that represents a single character.

byte reversal

A data-storage format used by IBM personal computers. Byte reversal uses lower-numbered addresses to store the least significant bytes of numeric 16-bit and 32-bit values. (Larger IBM computer systems such as minicomputers and mainframes use the opposite method.)

Byte-Control Protocol (BCP)

A protocol that is character-oriented instead of bit-oriented.

byte-oriented protocol

A communications protocol used to transmit data as a series of bytes, or individual
characters. Many asynchronous protocols
used with modems are byte-oriented.

Byzantine failure

A situation in which a network node fails,
does not disappear from the network, and
continues to operate but functions
improperly.

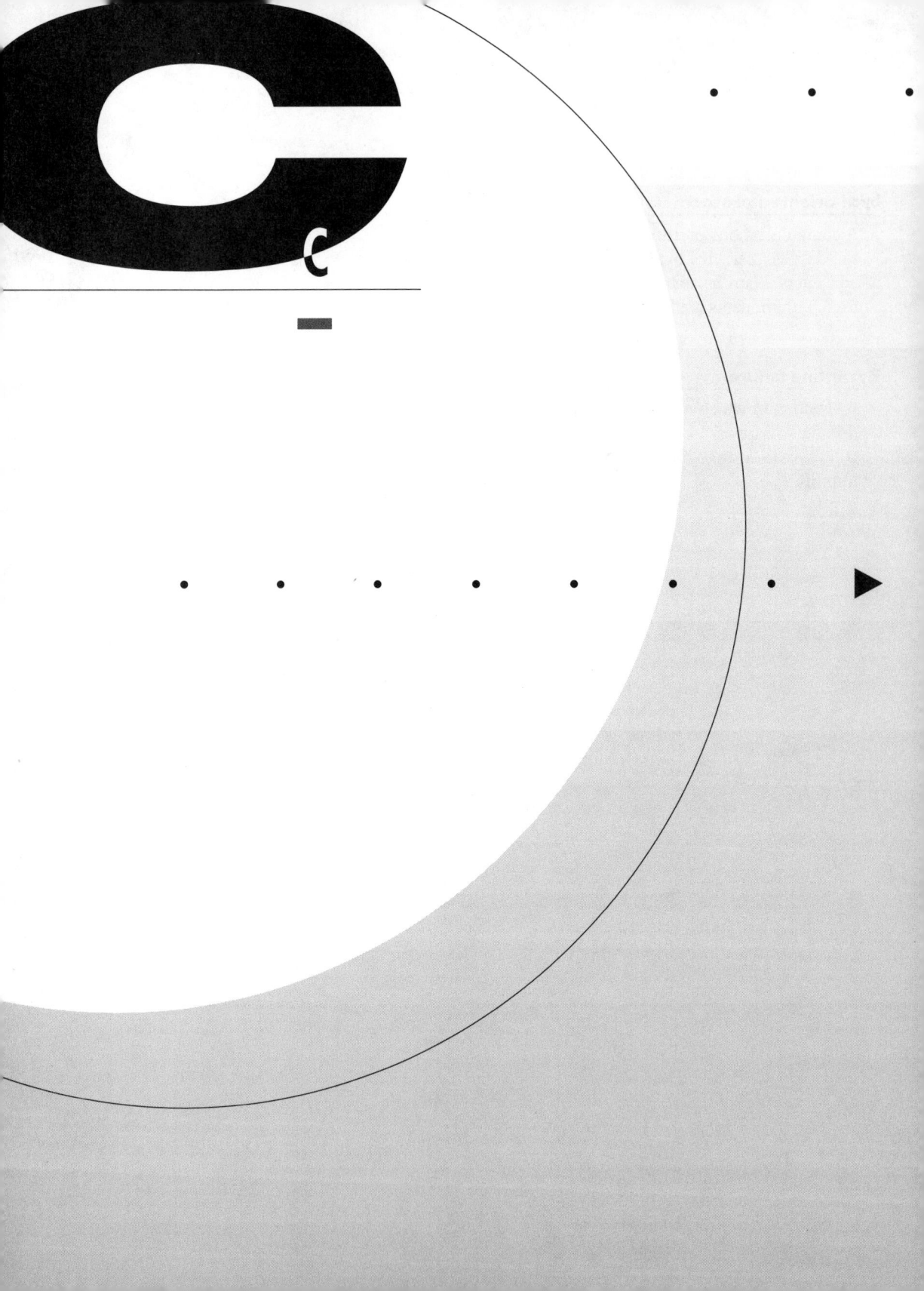

C Library BSD Sockets

In NetWare 3.12, the Available Options/
Resource Utilization screen of the MONI-
TOR NetWare Loadable Module (NLM), a
selectable option that tracks the number of
Berkeley Software Distribution (BSD) UNIX
sockets.

See also **Berkeley Software Distribution
UNIX; MONITOR.**

C2

A level of system security defined by the
National Computer Security Center (NCSC).
To receive a C2 security rating from the
NCSC, a system must meet the following
criteria:

- *Discretionary access control*, the assignment of object-access capabilities on
  the basis of access authorizations
  granted to authenticated users.
- *Object reuse*, a process to ensure
  that the operating system cleanses all
  user-assignable object space and disk
  space *before* reassigning that space to
  another user.
- *Identification and authentication*, a feature that describes how the user is
  identified to the system and how the
  system authenticates the user (as with
  the use of a login password).
- *Auditing*, the process by which the system verifies all or selected security-relat-
  ed events between subjects and objects.
- *System-architecture assurance*, a process
  ensuring that system architecture is
  protected from external interference or
  tampering.
- *Security-testing assurance*, a process
  that ensures the operation of system

security provisions as outlined in
security documentation.
- *Required documentation*, which includes
  the manual of operation that a trusted
  facility must follow.

See also **Orange Book.**

CA

Certificate Authority, the issuer of a chunk
of information used by certain network protocols to secure a network connection. The
information (often embedded in a text file)
enhances network security levels.

CA Private Key

A Directory Schema term for an object
property that can be applied to the following objects in Novell Directory Services
(NDS): External Entity, List, Message-
Routing Group, and Messaging Server.

See also **Novell Directory Services;
object.**

CA Public Key

A Directory Schema term for an object
property that can be applied to the following objects in Novell Directory Services
(NDS): External Entity, List, Message-
Routing Group, and Messaging Server.

See also **Novell Directory Services;
object.**

cable

A linear physical medium used to transmit
information between nodes in a network.
The five main types of cable used in

networking are coaxial, twisted-pair (STP), unshielded twisted-pair (UTP), IBM, and fiber-optic. Cable components include a conductor medium to carry the signal, insulation, and an outer sheath.

Table C.1 lists common cable types and where to find more information.

Table C.1: Cable Types

Cable Type	Use	For More Information
1394	Connects multiple digital devices (such as video and audio hardware)	See **1394 cable**.
adapter	Connects Token Ring Network Interface Card (NIC) to hub or Multistation Access Unit (MAU)	See **adapter cable**.
backbone	Serves as primary cable for connecting networks	See **backbone cable**.
broadcast-oriented	Carries video signals	See **broadcast-oriented cable**.
Category x	Connects telecommunications devices	See **Category x cable**.
CATV	Carries cable television signals	See **CATV cable**.
coaxial	Carries data transmissions	See **coaxial cable**.
data-grade	Carries data transmissions	See **data-grade cable**.
distribution	Serves as intermediate cable for connecting networks	See **distribution cable**.
drop	Connects NIC to a transceiver	See **drop cable**.
feeder	Carries both voice and data signals	See **feeder cable**.
fiber-optic	Connects Fiber Distributed Data Interface networks, long-haul networks, network segments (nodes), mainframe computers to peripherals, and high-speed, high-performance workstations	See **fiber-optic cable**.
horizontal	Connects wiring closet to wall outlet in work area	See **horizontal cable**.
IBM	Connects Token Ring networks, 10BaseT Ethernet networks, ARCnet networks, Integrated-Services Digital Network (ISDN) lines, and some IBM 3270 networks	See **IBM cable**.
patch	Connects two hubs or MAUs	See **patch cable**.

Cable Type	Use	For More Information
plenum	Serves as a fireproof connection through a conduit in a wall, floor, or ceiling	See **plenum cable**.
quad shield	A variation of coaxial cable used where heavy electrical interference can occur	See **quad shield cable**.
quadrax	A variation of coaxial cable (a hybrid of triaxial and twinaxial cable) with same uses as coaxial	See **quadrax cable**.
ribbon	Connects internal disk drives or tape drives	See **ribbon cable**.
riser	Serves as vertical connector (for example, between floors in a building)	See **riser cable**.
shielded twisted-pair	Connects IBM Token Ring networks and ARCnet networks	See **shielded twisted-pair cable**.
thick coax	Connects thick Ethernet networks and cable television	See **thick coax cable**.
thin coaxial	Connects thin Ethernet and ARCnet networks	See **thin coaxial cable**.
transceiver	Connects a NIC to a transceiver in an Ethernet network	See **transceiver cable**.
triaxial	A variation of coaxial cable that adds grounding and improves protection	See **triaxial cable**.
twinaxial	A variation of coaxial cable used to connect IBM and AppleTalk networks	See **twinaxial cable**.
twisted-pair	Connects IBM Token Ring networks, ARCnet networks, 10BaseT networks, and telephone lines	See **twisted-pair cable**.
IBM Type 1	Connects Token Ring networks	See **Type 1-9 cable**.
IBM Type 2	Transmits voice and data	See **Type 1-9 cable**.
IBM Type 3	Connects 16-megabit-per-second (Mbps) networks	See **Type 1-9 cable**.
IBM Type 5	Connects MAUs in a Token Ring network	See **Type 1-9 cable**.
IBM Type 6	Serves as a short-distance patch	See **Type 1-9 cable**.
IBM Type 8	Serves as a flat cable placed beneath a carpet	See **Type 1-9 cable**.
IBM Type 9	Serves as a connector between floors	See **Type 1-9 cable**.
unshielded twisted-pair	Connects 10BaseT networks, ARCnet networks, and telephone lines	See **unshielded twisted-pair cable**.
voice-grade cable	Transmits voice signals	See **voice-grade cable**.

cable modem

An interface box or computer adapter board that enables cable television to serve as a data link.

Cable Retransmission Facility (CRF)

The starting point in a broadband network. End stations can transmit control and error information to the CRF, but not data.

Cable Signal Fault Signature (CSFS)

A unique signal used for testing a line's electrical activity when using time-domain reflectometry. The CSFS may assist a technician in pinpointing the source of a problem.

See also **time-domain reflectometry.**

cable standards

Standards that establish a minimum level of functionality for a cable. Most of these standards have been established by the National Electric Code (NEC) and Underwriters Laboratories (UL). Others have also been specified by the Electronics Industry Association/Telecommunications Industries Association (EIA/TIA), Electrical Testing Laboratory, and Manufacturing Automation Protocol. The NEC specifies safety standards for general-purpose cable used in both residential and commercial environments. Underwriters Laboratories tests cables to determine the conditions under which they function safely.

See also **Electronics Industry Association; Telecommunications Industries Association; Underwriters Laboratories.**

cable tester

An instrument that tests for such cable properties as attenuation, resistance, and characteristic impedance.

cabling system

A specific physical layout of network cable. This portion of a network's physical structure gives the network a characteristic shape (*topology*).

See also **topology.**

cache

A portion of random-access memory (RAM) that can be accessed quickly. The cache is often used to store frequently used blocks of data as a way to minimize the time the central processing unit (CPU) must spend accessing it. Because RAM can be accessed faster than a hard drive, storing frequently used data in RAM improves a system's performance. When a processor references a memory address, the cache first checks to see whether the address holds the desired data. If so, the information is sent directly to the processor.

See also **memory; random-access memory.**

cache buffer

A block of NetWare server memory where files are stored temporarily for quick access. The size of the cache buffer depends on the default block size, which in turn depends on the size of the volume. Because reading data from memory is faster than reading it from disk, the cache buffer facilitates faster access to the data it holds. An operating system uses a cache buffer for several different purposes, including

- Caching a volume's File-Allocation Table (FAT) and suballocation tables in memory
- Caching parts of a Directory-Entry Table (DET)
- Caching parts of files for end-user access
- Creating a hash table for directory names
- Building Turbo FAT indexes for open files that are randomly accessed and have more than 64 regular FAT entries
- Using NetWare Loadable Module (NLM) programs

See also **cache memory; Directory-Entry Table; File-Allocation Table; hashing; NetWare Loadable Module.**

cache buffer pool

The amount of available memory that can be used by the NetWare operating system after the SERVER.EXE file has been loaded into memory. When a NetWare Loadable Module (NLM) is removed from server memory, it returns memory to the cache buffer pool. The memory in the pool can be used for a variety of purposes, including caching the File-Allocation Tables (FATs) for each volume, or creating a hash table of directory information.

See also **cache memory; File-Allocation Table; hashing; memory; NetWare Loadable Module.**

cache controller

A specialized coprocessor that manages cache memory. In some newer processors, cache management is incorporated directly into the main processor.

See also **cache memory; memory.**

cache hit

An event that occurs when a block of disk memory is used for a file.

See also **memory.**

cache memory

Available random-access memory (RAM) that can be used by NetWare to improve server access time. Cache memory allocates RAM for the hash table, File-Allocation Table (FAT), Turbo FAT, suballocation tables, directory cache, temporary storage for files and NLM files, and other functions.

The two types of cache memory are as follows:

- *Directory cache.* This is the area holding the directory entries when the FAT and Directory-Entry Table (DET) are written into the server's memory.
- *File cache.* When a workstation makes a read request to the server, the server executes a hash algorithm to calculate the file's address from a hash table. After the directory entry is located, the server sends the file to the workstation — either directly from server memory, or after retrieval from disk.

See also **Directory-Entry Table; File-Allocation Table; hash table; memory.**

Cache Movable Memory

A selectable option in the Available Options/ Resource Utilization screen of the NetWare 3.12 MONITOR NetWare Loadable Module (NLM). Also, as one of five memory pools available in NetWare 3.1*x*, Cache Movable Memory is used for system tables that grow dynamically, such as the File-Allocation Table (FAT) and Directory-Entry Table (DET).

See also **Directory-Entry Table; File-Allocation Table; MONITOR; NetWare Loadable Module.**

Cache Non-Movable Memory

In NetWare 3.12, a selectable option in the Available Options/Resource Utilization screen of the MONITOR NetWare Loadable Module (NLM). Also, as one of five memory pools in NetWare 3.1x, Cache Non-Movable Memory is used to load modules into memory and to allocate large memory buffers.

See also **MONITOR; NetWare Loadable Module.**

Cache ReCheckBlock Count

A field name in the Cache Utilization screen of the MONITOR NetWare Loadable Module (NLM).

See also **MONITOR; NetWare Loadable Module.**

Cache Utilization

A field name in the Available Options screen of the NetWare 4.02 MONITOR NetWare Loadable Module (NLM). This option provides a view of disk cache block request statistics, including total cache block requests, the number of times a block request had to wait because no cache blocks were available, the number of long-term cache hits, and the number of short-term cache hits.

See also **MONITOR; NetWare Loadable Module.**

caddy

A flat, plastic container used to load a compact disc into some CD-ROM drives.

CAE

Common Application Environment, standards for the operating system, networking protocols, languages, and data management that allow applications to be ported across platforms from different manufacturers.

call

In a networking context, a request issued by a network node to establish communications with another node. In a programming context, the transfer of program execution to some section of code, and then the resumption of program execution from the calling point when instructions in that section of code have been executed.

call authentication

A method of protecting a system against unauthorized access from a remote location. Often the authentication process uses the Password-Authentication Protocol (PAP) or the Challenge-Handshake Authentication Protocol (CHAP).

See also **Challenge-Handshake Authentication Protocol; Password-Authentication Protocol.**

call control

A set of actions that can establish, maintain, or disconnect a wide-area network (WAN)

connection. Call control exists within the Call-Support Layer.
   See also **Call-Support Layer.**

Call-Control Agent

A software module that works with the Call-Support Layer and includes logic for wide-area network (WAN) media-specific connection management.
   See also **Call-Support Layer.**

call packet

A block of data that holds addressing information and other data needed to establish a switched virtual circuit that complies with the X.25 specification of the Consultative Committee for International Telegraphy and Telephony (CCITT).
   See also **Consultative Committee for International Telegraphy and Telephony; X.25.**

call priority

A priority assigned to each origination port in a circuit-switched system. The order of call priorities defines the order in which cells are reconnected.

Call-Request packet

A control packet sent to a Directory-Entry Table (DET) to request initiation of a virtual call.
   See also **Directory-Entry Table.**

call setup time

The time needed to establish a connection between two nodes on a network.

Call-Support Layer

A software module that provides a general interface for controlling wide-area network (WAN) calls.

callback modem

A type of modem that does not answer incoming calls. The caller instead enters a code and hangs up, and the modem returns the call if the code matches an authorized number.

caller ID

A telecommunications feature that includes a sender's identification number in the transmission, so the recipient can see who is calling before the call is answered. Caller ID is also known as *automatic number identification*.
   See also **Automatic Number Identification.**

Calling-Line Identification (CLID)

A feature of the Integrated-Services Digital Network (ISDN) that includes the sender's identification number as part of the transmission, so the recipient knows who is calling before answering the call.
   See also **Automatic Number Identification; caller ID.**

CALLMGR utility

A NetWare utility that monitors the status of wide-area network (WAN) connections. CALLMGR can also be used to start or stop WAN calls manually.

campus-area network (CAN)

A network that connects local-area networks (LANs) from many locations, such as several floors of a building or several buildings. These locations can be physically separated over a great distance. A campus-area network does not require remote communications devices such as modems or telephones, which makes it different from a wide-area network (WAN).

Campus-Wide Information System (CWIS)

An online collection of information concerning a particular school or campus. A CWIS may contain information such as an events calendar, course listing, and job openings. CWISs are often available over the Internet.

CAN

campus area network, a network that connects local-area networks (LANs) from many locations, such as several floors of a building or several buildings. These locations can be physically separated over a great distance. A campus-area network does not require remote communications devices such as modems or telephones, which makes it different from a wide-area network (WAN).

Canadian Standards Association

A Canadian agency responsible for certifying that products comply with Canadian national safety standards.

 **For more information about the Canadian Standards Association, surf the Web to** http://www.csa.com.

cancelbot

A contraction for "cancel robot," a system that automatically sends out messages that request the removal of newsgroup messages.
See also **newsgroup; robot.**

canonicalize

To expand an abbreviated Novell Directory Services (NDS) name to its canonical form, which includes the full naming path and a type specification for each naming component.
See also **Novell Directory Services.**

Can't Compress (Cc) attribute

A NetWare file attribute that produces a status flag to indicate that a file cannot be compressed because doing so would not yield significant space savings.
See also **attribute.**

capacitance

The capability of a nonconductive material to store electricity and to resist voltage changes. Capacitance is measured in microfarads or picofarads. Cable with lower capacitance is considered superior.

capacitor

An electrical component designed to hold a charge. Capacitors are available in several sizes, and typically clean incoming power by absorbing surges and interference.

capacity threshold

A predetermined percentage of a server's hard disk that shows how much of the disk can be used before files must be migrated to a backup storage device.

CAPTURE utility

In NetWare and IntranetWare, a workstation utility that sets printer and printing parameters for use by DOS applications. The utility lets users print to a network printer from a network-unaware application. It can also redirect information to a network file.

card

A printed circuit board or adapter plugged into a computer to add a specialized function or support for a peripheral device.

carriage return

A control character for a hard return as represented by American Standard Code for Information Interchange (ASCII) code 13, which signals the display cursor or print head to return to the first position of the line.

carrier

An analog signal of fixed amplitude and frequency, which with a data-carrying signal forms an output signal used for transmitting data.

carrier band

A communications system that uses the entire bandwidth for one transmission. The signal is modulated before transmission. A baseband system, on the other hand, does not modulate the signal at all; a broadband system divides the bandwidth into channels.
See also **baseband; broadband.**

Carrier Detect (CD)

A signal sent from a modem to a personal computer to indicate that the modem is available for operation.

carrier frequency

The rate at which a carrier signal repeats, measured in hertz (Hz). The carrier frequency is modulated by superimposing a second signal that represents the information being transmitted.

Carrier On

A signal used in Carrier Sense Multiple-Access (CSMA) media-access mechanisms to indicate that the network is in use. If a node detects the Carrier On signal, it waits a random period of time before attempting to transmit.
See also **Carrier-Sense Multiple-Access/ Collision Avoidance; Carrier-Sense Multiple-Access/Collision Detection.**

carrier pulse

A signal that consists of rapid, constant pulses that form the pulse modulation.

Carrier-Sense Multiple-Access/Collision Avoidance (CSMA/CA)

A media-access method that functions at the Media-Access Control (MAC) Sublayer of the OSI Reference Model and is used in Apple LocalTalk networks. Under the CSMA/CA process, before a node transmits on the network, it first listens for activity. If activity is detected, the node waits a random period of time before attempting again. CSMA/CA is *contentious;* the first node that tries to gain access to an unused network is the one allowed to transmit. CSMA/CA has no methods for assigning priority to data. In the event of a collision, LocalTalk passes the problem on to a higher-level protocol. Collision avoidance is less sophisticated than collision detection, and is, therefore, less expensive to build into a chip set.

See also **Carrier-Sense Multiple-Access/Collision Detection; Media-Access Control; OSI Reference Model.**

Carrier-Sense Multiple-Access/Collision Detection (CSMA/CD)

A media-access protocol for dealing with the effects of packet collision. CSMA/CD is used in Ethernet and 802.3 networks, and functions on the Media Access Control (MAC) Sublayer of the OSI Reference Model. In the CSMA/CD model, a node first attempts to detect whether there is traffic on the network. If there is activity, the node waits a random period of time before attempting to transmit. If there is no activity, the node transmits. If two nodes transmit at precisely the same moment, a collision occurs. In the event of a collision, CSMA/CD discards the packets, causes the nodes to cancel their transmissions, and waits a random period of time before attempting to retransmit. CSMA/CD is *contentious;* the first node that tries to gain access to an unused network is allowed to transmit. CSMA/CD has no methods for assigning priority to data.

See also **Media-Access Control; OSI Reference Model.**

carrier signal

An electrical signal that forms the basis of a transmission. The carrier signal does not send any information, although it does have defined properties. The carrier signal is modified (or *modulated*) to transmit information.

carrier wire

A conductive wire that serves as a medium for an electrical signal.

Carrier-Switched Multiplexer (CS-MUX)

A component used in a Fiber Distributed Data Interface (FDDI) network to pass time-dependent data to the architecture's Media-Access Control (MAC) Layer.

See also **Fiber Distributed Data Interface; Media-Access Control; OSI Reference Model.**

Cartridge

A Directory Schema term and a selectable property for the Printer object in Novell Directory Services (NDS).

See also **leaf object; Novell Directory Services; object.**

cartridge

A hardware peripheral device (such as a PostScript cartridge) that attaches to a primary hardware device (such as a printer).

CAS

Communicating Application Specification, a proposed interface standard for fax/modems, developed by Intel and Digital Communications Associates (DCA). CAS competes with the *Class x* hierarchy developed by the Electronic Industries Association (EIA).

See also **Electronic Industries Association.**

cascaded bridge topology

A method of using bridges to connect several networks. In this topology, a middle network serves as an access point between two other networks; the two end networks must go through the middle network to communicate. The advantage of a cascaded bridge topology is that it eliminates the need for one bridge; there is no direct connection between the two end networks.

Figure C.1 shows an example of the cascaded bridge topology.

cascaded star

A network topology that connects multiple hubs in a succession of levels to allow more connections than would be possible in a single level.

cascading

A method of addressing one Interrupt-Request Channel (IRQ) to another IRQ. Cascading is used to avoid losing access to an IRQ in the first bank.

See also **Interrupt-Request Channel.**

case-insensitive

A characteristic applied to information sorting. In a case-insensitive sort, the values of uppercase letters equal the values of lowercase letters.

case-sensitive

A characteristic applied to information sorting. In a case-sensitive sort, the values of uppercase letters are distinct and different from the values of lowercase letters.

Castanet

A group of tools from Marimba, Inc. to create connections that act like broadcast media channels. The product line includes tools for creating, managing, and transmitting content, Java code, and other information over the Internet.

CASTOFF utility

In NetWare 3.*x*, a workstation utility that stops network messages from being displayed on the workstation screen. In NetWare 4.*x*, this utility has been superseded by the SEND utility.

See also **SEND utility.**

CASTON utility

In NetWare 3.*x*, a workstation utility that reverses the CASTOFF command and allows network messages to be displayed on the workstation. In NetWare 4.*x*, the SEND utility supersedes the CASTON utility.

See also **SEND utility.**

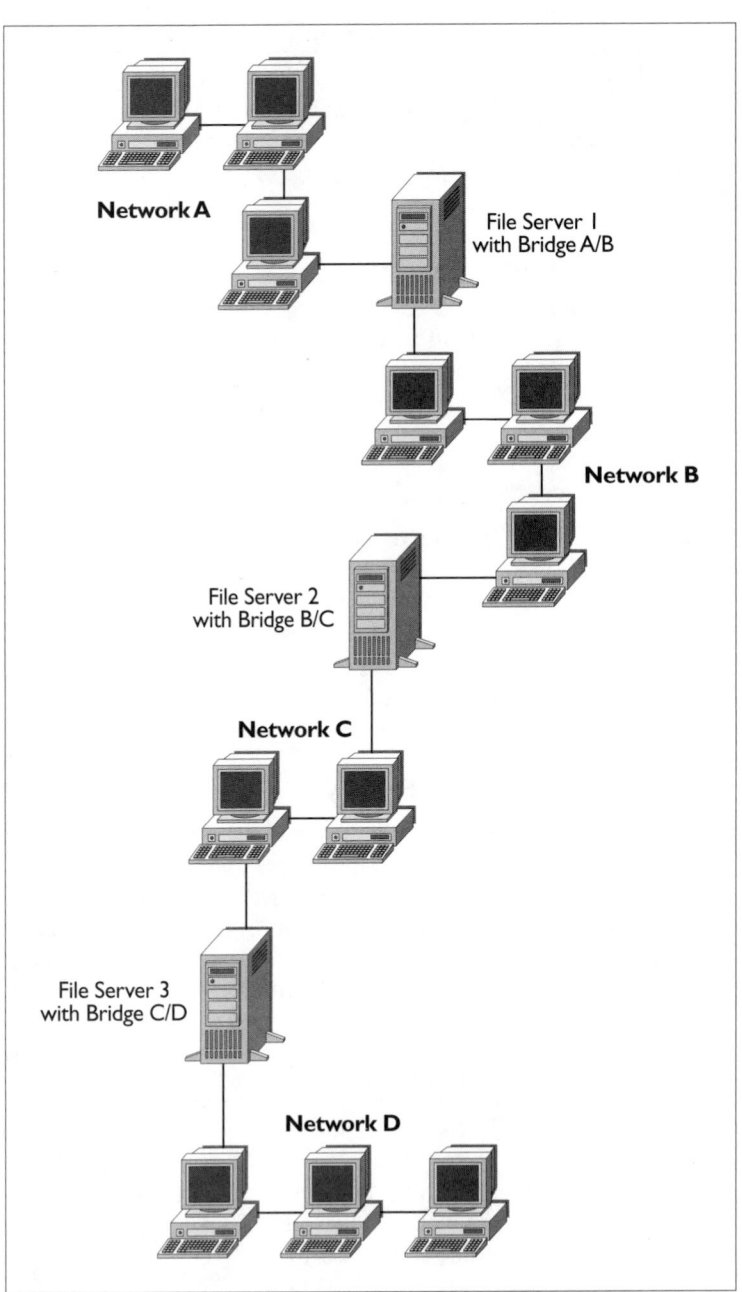

Figure C.1
Cascaded bridge topology

CAT

Common Authentication Technology, a specification for distributed authentication used on the Internet. CAT supports public-key and private-key encryption strategies. Both client and server use a common interface that provides the authentication services. The interface connects to either Distributed Authentication Security Service (DASS) for public-key encryption, or Kerberos for private-key encryption.

See also **Distributed Authentication Security Service; Kerberos.**

Category 1-5

A set of cabling standards (sometimes abbreviated CAT 1-5) established by the Electronics Industry Association/ Telecommunications Industry Association (EIA/TIA).The categories are as follows:

- *Category 1.* Unshielded twisted-pair (UTP) telephone cable.
- *Category 2.* UTP cable for use at speeds of up to 4 megabits per second (Mbps).
- *Category 3.* UTP cable for use at speeds of up to 10Mbps. 10BaseT networks require a minimum of Category 3 cabling.
- *Category 4.* The lowest grade of UTP cabling acceptable for a 16-Mbps Token Ring network.
- *Category 5.* UTP cable for use at speeds of up to 100Mbps.

See also **Electronics Industry Association; Telecommunications Industry Association.**

Category x cable

Refers to the standards established by the Electronics Industry Association/

Telecommunications Industries Association (EIA/TIA) for cabling.

See also **Category 1-5; Electronics Industry Association; Telecommunications Industry Association.**

catenet

A network (such as the Internet) that connects hosts to a diverse set of networks, which are themselves connected with routers.

CATV cable

Community Antenna Television, a broad-band transmission facility using 75-ohm coaxial cable. The cable can carry many television channels, using guard channels to keep them separated.

See also **Cable Television.**

CAU

Controlled-Access Unit, an intelligent access concentrator used in a Token Ring network. The CAU can establish connections for as many as 80 workstations by using pluggable lobe-attachment modules. It can determine whether or not a node is operational, monitor activity, and pass data to the LAN Manager program. The CAU can also connect and disconnect individual nodes.

See also **LAN Manager; Token Ring.**

CAU/LAM

Controlled-Access Unit/Lobe-Attachment Module, an intelligent access concentrator used in a Token Ring network. The CAU can establish connections for as many as 80 workstations by using pluggable lobe-attachment modules. It can determine whether or not a node is operational, monitor activity, and pass data to the LAN Manager program. The CAU can also connect and disconnect individual nodes.

See also **LAN Manager; Token Ring.**

CAV

constant angular velocity, a fixed rotation speed. Hard disks employ a CAV-encoding scheme in which the disk rotates at a constant rate. Under a CAV scheme, sectors toward the center of the disk have a higher density. As the read/write heads move outward, data-transfer rates decrease because the heads must then cover a greater circumference to read the outer sectors.

CBC

Cipher-Block Chaining, an operating mode used by the Data-Encryption Standard (DES).

See also **Data-Encryption Standard.**

CBDS

Connectionless Broadband Data Service, a wide-area network (WAN) technology based on high-speed, packet-switched datagram delivery. CBDS is also known as *Switched Multimegabit Data Service* (*SMDS*).

See also **Switched Multimegabit Data Service.**

CBEMA

Computer Business Manufacturers Association, an organization that furnishes technical committees for work done by other organizations.

CBMS

Computer-Based Messaging System, an older term that denotes a Message-Handling System (MHS) or electronic mail system (e-mail).

See also **Message-Handling System.**

CBR

Constant Bit Rate, a type of Asynchronous Transfer Mode (ATM) connection under the *Class A* Quality of Service (QoS) level. CBR is typically reserved for voice or video, or other data that must be transmitted at a constant rate and is intolerant of loss. CBR is a *reserved-bandwidth* service that generates a steady bit stream.

See also **Asynchronous Transfer Mode.**

CC

Clearing Center, a message-switching element of Electronic Data Interchange (EDI). The Clearing Center transmits documents to their destinations.

See also **Electronic Data Interchange.**

cc:

courtesy copy; carbon copy, in electronic mail (e-mail), a copy of a message that is sent to an additional recipient who appears on the list of recipients seen by the original addressee.

See also **bcc:; electronic mail.**

CCIR

A now-defunct agency in the International Telecommunications Union (ITU) that defined radio communications standards. The CCIR was combined with the

International Frequency-Registration Board (IFRB) to form the International Telecommunications Radiocommunications Standardization Sector (ITU-R).

See also **International Consultative Committee for Radiocommunications; International Telecommunications Union; International Frequency-Registration Board.**

CCIS

Common Channel Interoffice Signaling, a telephone communications transmission method that uses different channels for voice and control signals. A faster, packet-switched mechanism transmits control signals, making it possible to include additional information (such as caller ID or billing information) in the control channel.

See also **caller ID.**

CCITT

Consultative Committee for International Telegraphy and Telephony, a subgroup of the International Telecommunications Union (ITU) that defines data-communications standards. The CCITT is responsible for several communications, telecommunications, and networking standards, including documents that specify X.25, X.400, V.42 and V.42*bis*, and 1.*xxx* Integrated Digital Services Network (ISDN) standards.

There are three main sets of standards:

- *CCITT Groups 1-4*. These are used for facsimile transmissions.
- *CCITT V Series*. These are used for modems, error detection, and correction mechanisms.
- *CCITT X Series*. These are used for local-area networks (LANs).

Many standards appear in documents from both the CCITT and the International Standards Organization (ISO). Although the CCITT is now officially called the *International Telecommunications Union-Telecommunications Standardization Sector* (ITU-TS), it is still commonly referred to as the CCITT. The French name on which the CCITT acronym is based is Comité Consultatif International Téléphonique et Télégraphique.

See also **Integrated-Services Digital Network; International Telecommunications Union; X.25; X.400.**

 **For more information about CCITT, surf the Web to** `http://www.info.itu.ch.`

cc:Mail

Lotus Development Corporation's electronic mail (e-mail) program that works on DOS, Macintosh, Windows, OS/2, and UNIX networks. It includes built-in discussion groups and links to the Internet.

See also **electronic mail.**

 **For more information about networking products from Lotus Development Corporation, surf the Web to** `http://www.lotus.com/` `site.nsf.`

CCRSE

Commitment, Concurrency, and Recovery Service Element, in the OSI Reference Model, an Application Layer (Layer 7) service that implements distributed transactions among many applications.

See also **OSI Reference Model.**

CCS

Common Channel Signaling, a telephone transmission method that uses different channels for voice and control signals. The control signals are sent using a fast, packet-switched technique, making it possible to include additional data (such as caller ID or billing information) in the control channel.

See also **caller ID; Hundreds of Call Seconds.**

CCS 7

Common Channel Signaling 7, an implementation of the Signaling System 7 (SS7) specified by the Consultative Committee for International Telegraphy and Telephony (CCITT). CCS 7 is an Integrated-Services Digital Network (ISDN)-based transmission method that makes special services (such as call-forwarding) available anywhere on a network.

See also **Consultative Committee for International Telegraphy and Telephony; Integrated Services Digital Network.**

CD

(1) **Carrier Detect,** a signal sent from a modem to a personal computer to indicate that the modem is available for operation.
(2) **compact disc,** a nonmagnetic optical disc that stores digital information. A single CD can store 650MB or more of information. Data is stored on the CD as a series of alternating microscopic pits and smooth regions, each with different reflective properties. A laser beam pointed at the disc detects these properties and converts them into digital information.

CD command

A DOS command for changing directories. The CD command changes the current drive directory, and displays the current directory path.

CD utility

In NetWare 4.*x* and IntranetWare, a server console utility that monitors and administers a CD-ROM disc being used as a NetWare volume. With this utility, a CD-ROM volume may be mounted or dismounted, all CD-ROM devices may be listed, all volumes identified on CD-ROM devices may be listed, the root contents of the CD-ROM may be displayed, and hidden index files created by CD-ROM volumes may be purged.

CDA

Communications Decency Act, legislation enacted in 1996 to forbid obscenity and indecency on the Internet. Its constitutionality was challenged in 1997.

CDDI

Copper Distributed Data Interface, a network architecture that implements Fiber Distributed Data Interface (FDDI) specifications on electrical, instead of optical, cable.

See also **Fiber Distributed Data Interface.**

CDEV

A Macintosh program module accessed by clicking an icon in the Control Panel and that allows a user to set or control a hardware or software feature.

CDFS

CD-ROM File System, a specialized file structure used to store information on a compact disc. The File-Allocation Table (FAT) is inadequate for use on a CD-ROM because of the high number of files that may be contained on the CD-ROM.
See also **File-Allocation Table.**

CD-I

Compact Disc-Interactive, a standard compact-disc format for data, text, audio, still video images, and animated graphics.
See also **compact disc.**

CDM

Custom Device Module, the driver component in the NetWare Peripheral Architecture (NPA) that drives the storage devices attached to a host adapter bus.

CDMA

Code-Division Multiple Access, a transmission method that uses codes to fit up to ten times as much data into a channel. Every signal is given a different code; the receiver decodes only signals with appropriate codes. CDMA uses a *soft-handoff* mechanism to avoid lost bits: Both cells transmit transitional bits at the same time on the same frequency, thereby increasing the chance that one of the transmissions will be within range of the receiver. CDMA is not compatible with time-division multiple access (TDMA).
See also **time-division multiple access.**

CDPD

Cellular Digital Packet Data, a cellular communications method for sending data that transmits over any cellular channel currently not in use in an attempt to achieve a greater level of efficiency.

CD-ROM

Compact Disc Read-Only Memory, an optical storage device that can store up to 650MB of data. Often CD-ROMs store large multimedia applications, encyclopedias, or large reference works, and libraries of fonts or clip art. Many large software applications are distributed on CD-ROM. A CD-ROM uses a constant-linear-velocity encoding scheme to store data in one spiral track divided into segments of equal length.

CDROM (NLM)

In NetWare 3.*x* and later versions, a NetWare Loadable Module (NLM) server console utility that accesses a CD-ROM as a read-only volume on a file server. This NLM allows users to mount a volume represented by a CD-ROM and access the data stored on it.
See also **NetWare Loadable Module.**

CD-ROM drive

A hardware peripheral for reading compact discs. A CD-ROM drive may be connected to an individual workstation or to a network. If the drive is connected to the network, a compact disc can be shared among many users.
See also **compact disc; Compact Disc Read-Only Memory.**

CD-ROM Extended Architecture (CD-ROM/XA)

An extension to the CD-ROM format developed by Microsoft, Philips, and Sony. CD-ROM/XA facilitates storage of audio and visual information on a compact disc, thereby enabling users to play audio while viewing visual data.

See also **compact disc; Compact Disc Read-Only Memory.**

CD-ROM File System (CDFS)

A specialized file structure used to store information on a compact disc. The File-Allocation Table (FAT) is inadequate for use on a CD-ROM because of the high number of files that may be contained on the CD-ROM.

See also **File-Allocation Table.**

CD-ROM/XA

CD-ROM Extended Architecture, an extension to the CD-ROM format developed by Microsoft, Philips, and Sony. CD-ROM/XA facilitates storage of audio and visual information on a compact disc, thereby enabling users to play audio while viewing visual data.

CDM

Custom Device Module, the driver component in the NetWare Peripheral Architecture (NPA) that drives the storage devices attached to a host adapter bus.

See also **host adapter bus; NetWare Peripheral Architecture.**

cell

A fixed-length data packet.

cell (ATM)

The individual unit of data used in transmitting information in an Asynchronous Transfer Mode (ATM) network. An ATM cell contains a uniform 53 bytes, 48 of which are used for data and five for header information. Use of a fixed-length cell offers a number of advantages, and facilitates the Quality of Service (QoS) guarantees inherent in the ATM network. In a network with variable-length packets, on the other hand, a high-priority smaller packet may be behind a larger, low-priority packet on the network medium, which would cause delay and the possible late arrival of the high-priority packet.

See also **Asynchronous Transfer Mode.**

Cell-Loss Priority (CLP)

In an Asynchronous Transfer Mode (ATM) network, a bit value that specifies whether a particular cell can be discarded if necessary. ATM's traffic policing function uses a buffering technique, known as a *leaky bucket*, where traffic flows (or leaks) out of a buffer (or bucket) at a constant rate, regardless of how fast it flows into the bucket. If the buffer starts to overflow, the ATM switch polices the buffer by examining the Cell-Loss Priority bit that exists in the header of every ATM cell. This bit identifies cells that can be discarded if necessary.

See also **Asynchronous Transfer Mode.**

cell relay

A type of packet transmission used in a Broadcast Integrated-Service Digital Network (BISDN).

See also **Broadcast Integrated-Service Digital Network; Asynchronous Transfer Mode.**

cell-switched network

A type of network that offers the advantages of both circuit-switching and packet-switching. A cell-switched network offers guaranteed bandwidth, as well as the efficiency inherent in a packet-switched network. Asynchronous Transfer Mode (ATM) is a type of cell-switched network.

See also **Asynchronous Transfer Mode.**

cellular communications

A wireless communications technology. In the cellular model, the communications area is divided into smaller geographical areas (called *cells*), and transmissions are passed between cells until they reach their final destinations. Every cell has an antenna to pick up signals from the adjacent cells or callers.

Cellular Digital Packet Data (CDPD)

A cellular communications method for sending data that transmits over any cellular channel currently not in use in an attempt to achieve a greater level of efficiency.

cellular network

A type of wireless network that operates in the 825 to 890 megahertz (MHz) range. A cellular network uses individual stations, or cells, to pass signals from the sender, between stations, and eventually to the recipient. A cellular data network competes with cellular voice channels for bandwidth. To utilize the channel as fully as possible, some mechanisms send data in the same channels used for voice. A cellular network may be advantageous for companies with a limited number of nodes in separate buildings.

cellular radio

A telecommunications technology that uses radio transmissions to access a telephone network through a series of cells (transmission areas).

See also **cellular communications.**

Cello

A program from Cornell Law School that provides access to the Internet by using Windows on a personal computer. The program is similar to Mosaic.

See also **Mosaic.**

CELP

Code-Excited Linear Predictive Coding, a variant of the Linear Predictive Coding (LPC) voice-encoding algorithm, capable of generating digital voice output at 4,800 bits per second (bps).

See also **Linear Predictive Coding.**

Central Exchange

Services offered to a company by the local telephone company. All switching takes place in the telephone company's central office, as opposed to the customer's site.

See also **Centrex.**

Central Office (CO)

The nearest telephone switching station that provides switching services, dial tone services, private lines, and Centrex. Telephone customers are directly connected to a CO, which in turn connects them to the rest of the telecommunications system.

See also **Centrex.**

central processing

A network configuration where a single server processes tasks for several workstations. All the workstations in this configuration can communicate with the server, and all share the computing power of the central processor. Because the workstations share the server's processing power, central processing networks with more workstations operate slower than networks with fewer workstations.

central processing unit (CPU)

The part of a computer that processes data. This term typically refers to the computer's chassis and all its attached components.

centralized network

A type of network where a single machine controls network activity. A mainframe-based network is usually centralized.

Centrex (Central Exchange)

Services offered to a company by the local telephone company. All switching takes place in the telephone company's central office, as opposed to the customer's site.

Centronics parallel interface

A 36-pin interface used for connecting a personal computer to a peripheral device. The Centronics parallel interface uses eight parallel data lines, and additional lines for status and control information.

See also **parallel printer interface.**

CEPT

Conférence Européene des Postes et Télécommunications, an association of 26 European organizations that recommends communications standards to the Consultative Committee for International Telegraphy and Telephony (CCIT).

See also **Consultative Committee for International Telegraphy and Telephony; Postal Telephone and Telegraph.**

CERN

Conseil Européen pour la Récherche Nucléaire, the original name for an organization now known as the European Laboratory for Particle Physics in Switzerland, where Tim Berners-Lee developed a system (part of what is now known as the World Wide Web) to enhance the availability of research to remote users.

 **For more information about CERN, surf the Web to** `http://www.cern.ch/cern.`

CERT

Computer Emergency Response Team, an Internet group formed by the Defense Advanced Research Projects Agency (DARPA) to respond to security problems on the Internet. Administrators can get information and assistance on security issues from CERT, and the organization offers a number of tools and documents about network security at its FTP site.

See also **Defense Advanced Research Projects Agency.**

 **For more information about the Computer Emergency Response Team, surf the Web to** http://www.cert.org.

certificate

Information used by the Secure-Sockets Layer (SSL) protocol to establish a secure connection. To create a valid SSL, both sides must have a valid Security Certificate. The information contained in a Security Certificate includes to whom the certificate belongs, who issued the certificate, some sort of unique identification (such as a serial number), dates the certificate is valid, and an encrypted "fingerprint" that can be used to verify the contents of the certificate.

See also **Security Certificate; Secure-Sockets Layer.**

Certificate Authority (CA)

The issuer of a chunk of information used by certain network protocols to secure a network connection. The information (often embedded in a text file) enhances network security levels.

Certificate Revocation

A Directory Schema term and a selectable property for the External Entity, List, Message-Routing Group, and Messaging Server objects in Novell Directory Services (NDS).

See also **leaf object; Novell Directory Services; object.**

Certificate Validity Interval

A Directory Schema term and a selectable property for the following objects in Novell Directory Services (NDS): External Entity, List, Message-Routing Group, and Messaging Server.

See also **leaf object; Novell Directory Services; object.**

Certified Novell Administrator (CNA)

Formerly known as *Certified NetWare Administrator*, a certificate program in which users responsible for daily network operations take classes and pass tests to achieve the CNA designation. Students can also earn the designation of CNE, Enterprise Certified Novell Engineer, Certified Novell Administrator, or Certified Novell Instructor.

See also **Certified Novell Engineer; Enterprise Certified Novell Engineer; Certified Novell Administrator; Certified Novell Instructor; Master CNE.**

 **For more information about Novell's certification curriculum, surf the Web to** http://education.novell.com.

Certified Novell Engineer (CNE)

Formerly known as *Certified NetWare Engineer*, a certificate program in which users take classes and pass tests to achieve the CNE designation. CNEs are certified to provide support for NetWare and IntranetWare networks, including system design, installation, and maintenance.

Certified Novell Instructor (CNI)

Formerly known as *Certified NetWare Instructor*, a certificate program in which users take classes and pass tests to achieve the CNI designation. CNIs are certified to teach Novell courses.

Certified Novell Technician (CNT)

Formerly known as *Certified NetWare Technician*, a certificate program in which users take classes and pass tests to achieve the CNT designation.

CFB

Cipher Feedback, an operating mode used by the Data-Encryption Standard (DES).
See also **Data-Encryption Standard.**

CGI

Common Gateway Interface, a platform-independent interface used by a HyperText Transfer Protocol (HTTP)-based information server to run external programs. A CGI program receives client requests and responds with the requested information. In NetWare, the CGI is the feature that allows the NetWare Web Server to modify Web pages before they are sent to a browser.
See also **HyperText Transfer Protocol; Local Common Gateway Interface; NetWare Web Server.**

chaining

The act of grouping together Systems Network Architecture (SNA) Request/Response Units (RUs) to aid in error recovery.
See also **Request/Response Units; Systems Network Architecture.**

Challenge-Handshake Authentication Protocol (CHAP)

An inbound call-protection method that allows a receiving node to initiate a challenge sequence, which is then modified by the caller before the call can take place.

Chameleon

A Windows software program that allows users to connect directly to the Internet through a Serial-Line Internet Protocol (SLIP) Internet provider.
See also **Serial-Line Internet Protocol (SLIP).**

change-direction protocol

A data flow control protocol in a Systems Network Architecture (SNA) network used when the logical unit (LU) stops sending requests, and sends a signal indicating that it has done so to the receiving LU. The LU then prepares to receive requests.
See also **Systems Network Architecture.**

channel

A logical or physical path for transmitting electromagnetic signals. The path may include a host bus adapter, cables, and storage devices. A *communications channel* is used to transmit data or voice. A *disk channel* includes the components that connect a hard drive to an operating environment. A channel is also known as *line* or *link*.

channel attachment

The direct connection of data channels (or Input/Output channels) to a computer.

channel bank

A device that multiplexes several low-speed signals into one high-speed signal.
See also **multiplexing.**

channel operator (chan-op)

A person who starts an Internet Relay Chat (IRC) session and controls such parameters as public accessibility and who can participate.
See also **Internet Relay Chat.**

channel service unit (CSU)

A Digital Signal Processor (DSP) that performs transmit-and-receive filtering, signal shaping, longitudinal balance, voltage isolation, equalization, and remote loopback testing for digital transmission. The CSU functions as a buffer between customer premises equipment (CPE) and the public carrier wide-area network (WAN), preventing a faulty CPE from affecting the public carrier's system. The CSU takes data from a Digital Data Service (DDS) line and hands it off to a Data Service Unit (DSU), which then interfaces with computer equipment. A CSU may be combined with a DSU to form a single Integrated Service Unit (ISU).
See also **Digital Data Service; Digital Service Unit; Digital Signal Processor; Integrated Service Unit; loopback testing.**

CHAOSnet protocol

A network protocol used primarily in the artificial intelligence community. CHAOSnet was developed at the Massachusetts Institute of Technology (MIT).

CHAP

Challenge-Handshake Authentication Protocol, an inbound call-protection method that allows a receiving node to initiate a challenge sequence, which is then modified by the caller before the call can take place.

character

In the context of computer science, a group of eight binary digits that function together as a single unit. This group represents a single letter or symbol in an encoding scheme, such as American Standard Code for Information Interchange (ASCII) or Extended Binary-Coded Decimal Interchange Code (EBCDIC). A character is also known as a *byte* or *octet.*
See also **American Standard Code for Information Interchange; Extended Binary-Coded Decimal Interchange Code.**

character code

A code that represents an alphanumeric character in a character set, such as American Standard Code for Information Interchange (ASCII) or Extended Binary-Coded Decimal Interchange Code (EBCDIC).
See also **American Standard Code for Information Interchange; Extended Binary-Coded Decimal Interchange Code.**

character length

The number of bits that form a character. The standard American Standard Code for Information Interchange (ASCII) character set requires a character length of seven bits for transmissions.
See also **American Standard Code for Information Interchange.**

Character-Manipulation Services

A set of American National Standards Institute (ANSI) functions for testing alphanumeric characters. These services can convert alphanumeric characters between uppercase and lowercase, or to convert multibyte characters into wide-character codes.

See also **American National Standards Institute.**

character mode

A video adapter mode used in personal computers. A personal computer in character mode display characters on the screen from the built-in character set, but not show graphics or a mouse pointer. Character mode is also referred to as *text mode.*

character set

A group of letters, numbers, or symbols, such as American Standard Code for Information Interchange (ASCII) or Extended Binary-Coded Decimal Interchange Code (EBCDIC), used by a computer.

See also **American Standard Code for Information Interchange; Extended Binary-Coded Decimal Interchange Code.**

character string

An array of any number of adjacent characters followed by a NULL character. The NULL character marks the end of the string.

character-based interface

An operating system or application that uses only text characters for the user interface.

Character-Oriented Windows Interface (COW)

A Systems Application Architecture (SAA) compatible interface used in the OS/2 operating system.

See also **Systems Application Architecture.**

characters per second (cps)

The number of characters that are transmitted every second during a data transfer.

chat

A real-time online conversation with other network users.

chat room

An Internet site where real-time online conversations with other network users take place.

chatter

An error condition in which a flawed network board may cause the Packet Receive Buffer count to climb quickly.

CHDIR command

A DOS command for changing directories. The CHDIR command changes the current drive directory, and displays the current directory path. The CHDIR command is sometimes abbreviated as the CD command.

CheaperNet

A 10Base-2 thin coaxial cable network. This term is derived from the fact that thin coaxial cable is less expensive than thick coaxial cable.

See also **10Base-2; Thin-Net.**

checkbox

In a graphical user interface (GUI), a box used to select options. When a checkbox option has been selected, an *x* appears in the box.

See also **graphical user interface.**

checksum

A calculation that keeps a running total of the bits of a transmitted message as a means of detecting errors in transmission. This value is transmitted with the message, and the recipient then recalculates the checksum and compares it to the received value. A checksum can detect most errors in a packet, although it is not as accurate as a *cyclical redundancy check (CRC)* calculation.

See also **cyclical redundancy check.**

child

A data set with no subordinates, or the lowest level of a directory structure.

See also **parent.**

child document

A file or document called up by a World Wide Web (WWW) browser to fill a frame under the direction of a layout document (called the *parent document*).

See also **browser; Web browser.**

child VLM

A NetWare Virtual Loadable Module (VLM) that handles a specific implementation of a logical group of functions.

See also **Virtual Loadable Module.**

chip creep

The loss of a solid electrical connection between an integrated circuit and its socket. Chip creep can result from frequent temperature changes.

CHKDIR utility

In NetWare 3.*x*, a workstation utility that displays a volume or directory's space limit, maximum storage capacity, space currently in use, and amount of free space. In NetWare 4.*x*, CHKDIR has been superseded by the NDIR utility.

See also **NDIR utility.**

CHKVOL utility

In NetWare 3.*x*, a console utility for workstations and servers that displays volume information, total disk space allowed for a volume, space in use, space occupied by deleted files that have not yet been purged, free space, remaining free space, and space available to the user. In NetWare 4.*x*, NDIR has superseded CHKVOL.

See also **NDIR utility.**

chmod

A UNIX command that sets who can read, write, or execute a file, as well as other technical parameters.

choke packet

A packet that tells a transmitter that congestion exists on the network and that the transmitter should reduce its sending rate.

Chooser

A Desk Accessory (DA) utility that permits Macintosh users to access network devices, including file servers and printers.

chromatic dispersion

The dispersion of a light signal in a fiber-optic transmission. Chromatic dispersion is the result of the different propagation speeds of the light at different wavelengths.

CHRP

Common Hardware-Reference Platform, an open hardware architecture (originally designed by IBM) that ensures compatibility among compliant systems built by different manufacturers.

chunk

An arbitrary portion of a record or piece of programming code, usually specified by offset and length.

CICS

Customer Information Control System, a transaction-processing subsystem used on IBM mainframes. CICS supports IBM's Systems Network Architecture (SNA).

See also **Systems Network Architecture.**

CICS/VS

Customer Information Control System for Virtual Storage, a host program that runs on the IBM System/370. This program can be used in a communications network.

CIDR

Classless Interdomain Routing, a routing strategy that allows organizations or corporations that have more than 256 nodes on a network, but fewer than 65,536 nodes, to be able to use a special Class C Internet address. This strategy allows the assignment of consecutive Class C addresses to these organizations and corporations in such a way that routers view the cluster as a "supernetwork" rather than viewing the entire organizational or corporate network as a separate network (which would require a Class B address). The strategy was developed to address the inadequate number of Class B Internet addresses.

See also **Class B network address; Class C network address; IP address.**

CineWeb

A plug-in from Digigami for World Wide Web (WWW), Netscape Navigator-compatible browsers that allows quicker viewing of QuickTime, Video for Windows, Motion Pictures Experts Group (MPEG), and Autodesk Animator downloadable files.

See also **Netscape Navigator; plug-in.**

Cipher-Block Chaining (CBC)

An operating mode used by the Data-Encryption Standard (DES).

See also **Data-Encryption Standard.**

Cipher Feedback (CFB)

An operating mode used by the Data-Encryption Standard (DES).
See also **Data-Encryption Standard.**

ciphertext

Text that has been encrypted to make it impossible to read without the key to the encryption scheme.

CIPX

Compressed Internet Packet Exchange, a variant of the Novell Internet Packet Exchange (IPX) protocol that uses a compressed header of between 1 and 7 octets (provided that only the IPX header is compressed); a 30-octet header is normally characteristic of IPX packets. CIPX compression can speed up transmissions over slow wide-area network (WAN) lines.
See also **Compressed Internet Packet Exchange (CIPX) protocol; header compression; Internet Packet Exchange.**

CIR

Committed Information Rate, a Frame Relay network term indicating the rate of information, measured in bits per second (bps), at which the network transfers data on a virtual circuit under normal conditions. If network activity exceeds the CIR, the Frame Relay controller marks packets to indicate whether they can be discarded.
See also **Frame Relay network.**

circuit

A closed path that carries an electrical current.

circuit board

A flat board on which electrical components are mounted and interconnected to form a circuit. The board is constructed of an insulating material such as epoxy or phenolic resin. Interconnection between the components usually is made with patterns of copper foil that may appear on one or both sides of the board.

circuit switching

A technique for establishing a nonsharable, temporary connection between two end devices.

circuit-switched network

A type of connection-oriented network in which a temporary dedicated circuit is established between two nodes. The circuit provides a guaranteed level of bandwidth for the connection, and is disabled when the transmission is completed. The public telephone system is an example of a circuit-switched network.

CIS

CompuServe Information Service, a commercial information service providing access to the Internet and other value-added features including discussion forums, online communities, and information resources.

 **To find out more about CompuServe, surf the Web to** http://world.compuserve.com.

CISC

Complex-Instruction-Set Computing, a processor-design strategy that gives the processor a large number of powerful assembly-language instructions. These instructions may be complex and may slow down overall processing.

See also **Reduced-Instruction-Set Computing.**

Cisco

Short name for Cisco Systems, Inc., a manufacturer of routers, local-area network (LAN) switches, Asynchronous Transfer Mode (ATM) switches, dial-up access servers, and network-management software.

For more information about Cisco Systems, surf the Web to `http://www.cisco.com/texthome.htm.`

City

A Directory Schema term and a selectable property for the User object in Novell Directory Services (NDS).

See also **leaf object; Novell Directory Services; object.**

CIX

Commercial Internet Exchange, a nonprofit trade association of Public Data Internetwork service providers.

For more information on the Commercial Internet Exchange, surf the Web to `http://www.cix.org.`

cladding

The material that surrounds the fiber core in a fiber-optic cable. Cladding has a lower refraction index than that of the core; light that hits the cladding reflects back to the core and can continue on its path.

clamping time

The amount of time a surge protector requires to deal with a voltage spike or surge, and then return the voltage to an acceptable level.

See also **spike; surge.**

ClariNews

A Clarinet Communications service that provides news releases and press releases in a private Usenet hierarchy.

See also **Usenet.**

Class A Certification

A Federal Communications Commission (FCC) certification for industrial, commercial, or office equipment. The Class A commercial certification is not as restrictive as the Class B certification.

See also **Class B Certification; Federal Communications Commission.**

Class A network address

An Internet address class used for networks with as many as 16.8 million nodes. This class has 128 addresses available.

See also **Classless Interdomain Routing; IP address.**

Class B Certification

A Federal Communications Commission (FCC) certification for computer equipment intended for home use. The Class B certification is more restrictive than the commercial Class A certification.

See also **Class A Certification; Federal Communications Commission.**

Class B network address

An Internet address class used for networks with up to 65,536 nodes. This class has 16,384 addresses available.

See also **Classless Interdomain Routing; IP address.**

Class C network address

An Internet address class used for networks with up to 255 nodes. This class has 2 million addresses available.

See also **Classless Interdomain Routing; IP address.**

Class D network address

An Internet address class used for multicast networks. This class has 268.4 million addresses available.

See also **IP address.**

Classless Interdomain Routing (CIDR)

A routing strategy that allows organizations or corporations that have more than 256 nodes on a network, but fewer than 65,536 nodes, to be able to use a special Class C Internet address. This strategy allows the assignment of consecutive Class C addresses to these organizations and corporations in such a way that routers view the cluster as a "supernetwork" rather than viewing the entire organizational or corporate network as a separate network (which would require a Class B address). The strategy was developed to address the inadequate number of Class B Internet addresses.

See also **Class B network address; Class C network address; IP address.**

Clear Request packet

A control packet sent to Data-Terminal Equipment (DTE) to request that a virtual call be terminated.

See also **Data-Terminal Equipment.**

CLEAR STATION utility

In NetWare and IntranetWare, a server console utility that clears the connection if a workstation crashes while still logged on to the server. The CLEAR STATION utility closes all open files on the workstation, and erases any workstation information stored in tables on the server.

Clear To Send (CTS)

A control signal generated by data-communications hardware to indicate readiness to transmit data. The CTS signal is usually sent in response to a Request To Send (RTS) signal issued by a node requesting to transmit data over the network.

See also **Request To Send.**

Clearing Center (CC)

A message-switching element of Electronic Data Interchange (EDI). The Clearing Center transmits documents to their destinations.

See also **Electronic Data Interchange.**

Clearinghouse Protocol

A protocol in the Xerox Network Systems (XNS) protocol suite used in the Presentation Layer (Layer 6) of the OSI Reference Model.

See also **OSI Reference Model; Xerox Network Systems.**

clear-text User-Authentication Module (clear-text UAM)

A type of authentication that does not use password encryption. The network interprets each user's password as entered, and is, therefore, more vulnerable to detection.

CLI

command-line interface, an interface between a user who is typing commands and a computer program or operating system receiving instructions from the user.

CLIB.IMP

A file that contains all public symbols made available by the NetWare Loadable Module (NLM) C Interface. The CLIB.IMP is similar to a standard C object library. The CLIB.IMP does not actually include the C object code, however. It only lists the function names in the NLM C Interface.

See also **NetWare Loadable Module.**

CLIB utility

In NetWare and IntranetWare, a server console utility that allows the network administrator to load CLIB routines and functions.

See also **CLIB.IMP.**

CLID

Calling-Line Identification, a feature of the Integrated-Services Digital Network (ISDN) that includes the sender's identification number as part of the transmission, so the recipient knows who is calling before answering the call.

See also **Automatic Number Identification; caller ID.**

client

A workstation capable of gaining access to network services. In other contexts, the term can refer to a software application (such as network-connectivity software or the Btrieve engine) that runs on a given workstation.

client application

In Object Linking and Embedding (OLE), the application that starts the server application for the purpose of manipulating linked or embedded information.

See also **Object Linking and Embedding.**

Client 16

Workstation-connectivity software that provides 16-bit DOS or Windows 3.*x* access to NetWare 2.2, NetWare 3.12, and NetWare 4.11 servers that have Open Data-Link Interface (ODI) drivers, Virtual Loadable Modules (VLMs), and the NET.CFG file.

See also **NET.CFG; Open Data-Link Interface; Virtual Loadable Module.**

Client 32

Workstation-connectivity software that provides 32-bit access to NetWare 2.2, NetWare

3.12, and NetWare 4.11 servers from Windows 95, Windows 3.1, or DOS. Client 32 provides a graphical utility to log in from Windows, or the capability to access network files and printers through Windows 95 dialog boxes such as Network Neighborhood or Windows Explorer.

See also **Windows 95.**

client type

Refers to the operating system that the client machine runs. For example, under NetWare, client types can include DOS, Macintosh, OS/2, UNIX, and Windows.

client-based application

An application executed from the client machine (or workstation) in a network.

client-server model

A type of network configuration that distributes intelligence from the server to the individual workstations on the network. In this model, the client requests services from the servers, which receive the requests and return data or results. The server is typically a more powerful computer, with the client being a desktop machine. Processing can occur on the client, the server, on both client and server (as *distributed processing*) on many machines. A client-server application can be divided into a *front end* (which runs on the client) and a *back end* (which runs on the server). The front-end includes an interface that lets end-users make requests and issue commands to be carried out at the back end.

See also **back end; front end; local-area network.**

client-server network

A network that dedicates at least one personal computer to function as a server. The server runs the network operating system, controls communication, and manages shared resources. The clients, on the other hand, are individual user workstations that share those resources while connected to the network.

Figure C.2 shows an example of a client-server network.

See also **client-server model; local-area network.**

client-server operating system

An operating system that runs on a server in a client-server network. This operating system is responsible for coordinating how clients access the resources of the server. NetWare 3.*x* and NetWare 4.*x* are client-server operating systems.

CLNP

Connectionless Network Protocol, an Open Systems Interconnection (OSI) protocol that provides the OSI Connectionless Network Service. In the OSI model, CLNP is the functional equivalent of the NetWare Internet Packet Exchange (IPX) protocol and the Internet Protocol (IP). CLNP datagrams include destination information along with each unit of data; a direct connection is unnecessary.

See also **Internet Packet Exchange; Internet Protocol; OSI Reference Model.**

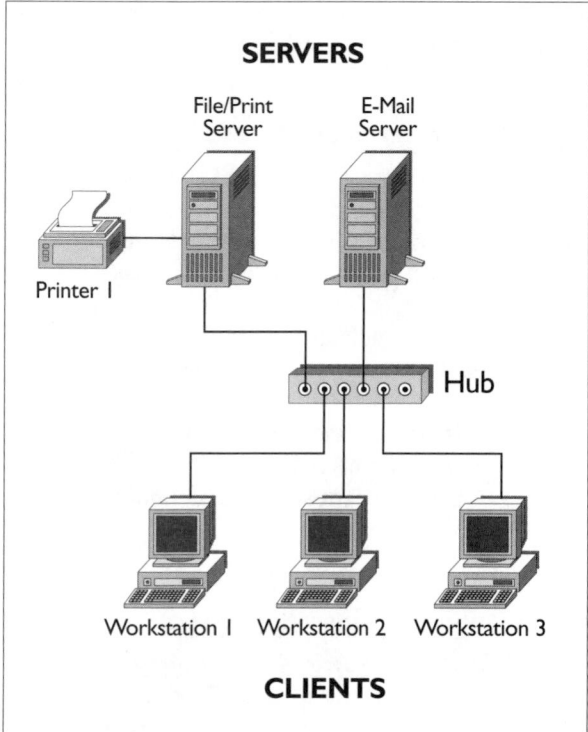

SERVERS

File/Print Server　　E-Mail Server

Printer 1

Hub

Workstation 1　Workstation 2　Workstation 3

CLIENTS

Figure C.2
Client-server network

CLNS

Connectionless-Mode Network Service, in the OSI Reference Model, a service on the Network Layer (Layer 3) where data transmission can occur without a fixed connection between source and destination. In this model, packets are independent, may reach their destinations through multiple paths, and may arrive out of order. Consequently, each packet carries the destination address. Most local-area networks (LANs) operate in connectionless mode.

See also **local-area network; OSI Reference Model.**

clock

An electronic circuit that generates periodic pulses used to synchronize information flow through a computer's internal communications channels.

clock doubling

A technique used by some processors to process data internally at double the speed used when communicating with other system components.

clock rate

A measurement of processing efficiency, expressed in megahertz (MHz).
See also **clock speed.**

clock speed

A measurement of processing efficiency, expressed in megahertz (MHz).

clocking

A method of time-synchronizing a system's communications data.

clone

A hardware device that uses the same physical architecture (structure) as another.

CLONE command

A command that creates a new, empty Btrieve file with the same file specifications as an existing file.
See also **Btrieve.**

closed architecture

A hardware design that does not allow user-supplied or third-party additions.

Closed User Group (CUG)

A facility for configuring virtual private networks within a larger public network. A CUG allows an administrator to collect many Data-Terminal Equipment (DTE) devices into one logical group. That group's ability to receive or make outgoing calls can then be restricted.
See also **Data-Terminal Equipment.**

CLP

Cell-Loss Priority, in an Asynchronous Transfer Mode (ATM) network, a bit value that specifies whether a particular cell can be discarded if necessary. ATM's traffic policing function uses a buffering technique, known as a *leaky bucket*, where traffic flows (or leaks) out of a buffer (or bucket) at a constant rate, regardless of how fast it flows into the bucket. If the buffer starts to overflow, the ATM switch polices the buffer by examining the Cell Loss Priority bit that exists in the header of every ATM cell. This bit identifies cells that can be discarded if necessary.
See also **Asynchronous Transfer Mode.**

CLS command

In NetWare and IntranetWare, a server console command that clears the console screen of messages. A similar command is available in DOS.

CLTP

Connectionless Transport Protocol, in an Asynchronous Transfer Mode (ATM) network, a bit value that specifies whether a particular cell can be discarded if necessary. ATM's traffic policing function uses a buffering technique, known as a *leaky bucket*, where traffic flows (or leaks) out of a buffer (or bucket) at a constant rate, regardless of how fast it flows into the bucket. If the buffer starts to overflow, the ATM switch polices the buffer by examining the Cell-Loss Priority bit that exists in the header of every ATM cell. This bit identifies cells that can be discarded if necessary.
See also **Asynchronous Transfer Mode.**

CLTS

Connectionless Transport Service, in the OSI Reference Model, a best-effort transport service on the Transport Layer (Layer 4) CLTS uses end-to-end addressing and error checking; it does not guarantee delivery.

See also **OSI Reference Model.**

CLU

Command Line Utility, a utility accessed through a single-word command.

cluster

A group of I/O devices in a Systems Network Architecture (SNA) network that shares a communications path to the host machine. A *cluster controller* manages the communications between the cluster and the host.

See also **Systems Network Architecture.**

cluster controller

An IBM-compatible device for attaching 3270-class terminals. The cluster controller can be channel-attached to a host system, or may communicate with the host via Synchronous Data-Link Control (SDLC).

See also **Synchronous Data-Link Control.**

CLV

constant linear velocity, a changing rotation speed. To ensure a constant data density, CD-ROM drives use a CLV-encoding scheme in which the disc rotates at a varying rate. Data on a CD is stored in a single, spiral track divided into equal segments. To read the data

at a constant rate, the CD-ROM drive changes its speed of rotation according to where the read head is on the disc.

See also **Compact Disc Read-Only Memory.**

CMC

Common Mail Calls, an Application Program Interface (API) that enables message-handling agents to communicate with post offices in a manner independent of hardware platforms, operating systems, e-mail systems, and messaging protocols. Common Mail Calls are also known as *common messaging calls.*

See also **Application Program Interface.**

CMIP

Common Management-Information Protocol, the OSI Network-Management Model information protocol for network monitoring and control information. CMIP includes specifications for accounting management, configuration management, fault management, performance management, and security management. CMIP is not widely used because of the widespread commercial availability of products on the basis of Simple Network-Management Protocol (SNMP).

See also **OSI Network-Management Model; Simple Network-Management Protocol.**

CMIPDU

Common Management-Information-Protocol Data Unit, a packet conforming to the Common Management Information Protocol (CMIP). The packet's contents

depend on the Common Management-Information Service Element (CMISE) request.

See also **Common Management-Information Protocol; Common Management-Information Service Element; OSI Network-Management Model.**

CMIPM

In the OSI Network-Management Model, an application that can accept operations from a Common Management-Information Service Element (CMISE) user, and initiate the appropriate actions for responding with valid Common Management-Information Protocol (CMIP) packets.

See also **Common Management-Information Machine; Common Management-Information Protocol; Common Management-Information Service Element; OSI Network-Management Model.**

CMIS

Common Management-Information Service, the specification used in the OSI Network Management Model for network monitoring and control.

See also **Common Management-Information Protocol; OSI Network Management Model.**

CMISE

Common Management-Information Service Element, an entity that furnishes network management and control services under the OSI Network Management Model. The seven types of CMISEs are

Action, Cancel Get, Create, Delete, Event Report, Get, and Set. The system-management functions use these services to carry out specific tasks.

See also **OSI Network-Management Model.**

CMNS

Connection-Mode Network Service, a service that extends local X.25 switching to such networks as Ethernet, Fiber Distributed Data Interface (FDDI), and Token Ring.

See also **Ethernet; Fiber Distributed Data Interface; Token Ring; X.25.**

CMOS

Complementary Metal-Oxide Semiconductor, a battery-powered memory chip that holds system configuration parameters when the computer is shut down. The CMOS chip is usually located on the system board.

CMOS RAM

Memory that stores system-configuration data. CMOS random-access memory (RAM) uses a battery-powered chip to retain the date, time, and other system information when the computer system is shut down.

See also **memory; random-access memory.**

CMOT

Common Management-Information Services and Protocol Over TCP/IP, an initiative that attempted to implement two services of the Open Systems Interconnection (OSI) framework — Common Management-Information Service (CMIS) and Common

Management-Information Protocol (CMIP) — over the TCP/IP suite. CMOT was never implemented due to widespread usage of Simple Network-Management Protocol (SNMP) and the complexities of porting the OSI model to TCP/IP.

See also **Common Management-Information Protocol; Common Management-Information Service; OSI Network-Management Model; Simple Network-Management Protocol.**

CMS

Conversational Monitor System, a Systems Network Architecture (SNA) subsystem used for managing interactive sessions.

See also **Systems Network Architecture.**

CMT

Connection Management, a process in the Fiber Distributed Data Interface (FDDI) that handles the transition of a ring through its various states.

See also **Common Name; Fiber Distributed Data Interface.**

CNA

Certified Novell Administrator, formerly known as *Certified NetWare Administrator*, a certificate program in which users responsible for daily network operations take classes and pass tests to achieve the CNA designation. Students can also earn the designation of CNE, Enterprise Certified Novell Engineer, Certified Novell Administrator, or Certified Novell Instructor.

See also **Certified Novell Engineer; Enterprise Certified Novell Engineer;** **Certified Novell Administrator; Certified Novell Instructor; Master CNE.**

 **For more information about Novell's certification curriculum, surf the Web to** `http://education.novell.com.`

CNE

Formerly known as *Certified NetWare Engineer*, a certificate program in which users take classes and pass tests to achieve the CNE designation. CNEs are certified to provide support for NetWare and IntranetWare networks, including system design, installation, and maintenance.

CNE Professional Association (CNEPA)

An association of CNEs that offers its members such benefits as technical workshops, subscriptions, and admission to network-related events.

CNI

Certified Novell Instructor, formerly known as *Certified NetWare Instructor*, a certificate program in which users take classes and pass tests to achieve the CNI designation. CNIs are certified to teach Novell courses.

CNT

Certified Novell Technician, formerly known as *Certified NetWare Technician*, a certificate program in which users take classes and pass tests to achieve the CNT designation.

CO

Central Office, the nearest telephone switching station that provides switching services, dial tone services, private lines, and Centrex. Telephone customers are directly connected to a CO, which in turn connects them to the rest of the telecommunications system.

See also **Centrex.**

coax booster

A hardware device that strengthens the signal carried over a coaxial cable. A coax booster makes it possible to run cable over greater distances with a minimum of signal loss.

coaxial cable

A type of cable that uses a central solid wire surrounded by insulation. A braided-wire conductor sheath surrounds the insulation, and a plastic jacket surrounds the sheath. Coaxial cable can accommodate high bandwidth and is resistant to interference. Thus, it is well-suited to computer networking. Variations of coaxial cable include quad-shield, quadrax, thick coaxial, thin coaxial, triaxial, and twinaxial.

See also **cable; quad-shield cable; quadrax cable; thick coaxial cable; thin coaxial cable; triaxial cable; twinaxial cable.**

COCF

Connection-Oriented Convergence Function, a function of the Distributed-Queue Dual-Bus (DQDB) network architecture that prepares data going into or out of a connection-oriented service. The service establishes a fixed connection, sends the data, and then breaks the connection.

See also **Distributed-Queue Dual-Bus.**

code-division multiple access (CDMA)

A transmission method that uses codes to fit up to ten times as much data into a channel. Every signal is given a different code; the receiver decodes only signals with appropriate codes. CDMA uses a *soft-handoff* mechanism to avoid lost bits: Both cells transmit transitional bits at the same time on the same frequency, thereby increasing the chance that one of the transmissions will be within range of the receiver. CDMA is not compatible with time-division multiple access (TDMA).

See also **time-division multiple access.**

Code-Excited Linear Predictive Coding (CELP)

A variant of the Linear Predictive Coding (LPC) voice-encoding algorithm, capable of generating digital voice output at 4,800 bits per second (bps).

See also **Linear Predictive Coding.**

code page

A table that stores a character set in support of a language script. Some operating systems support many code pages, and allow users to switch from one to another. A single-byte code page stores up to 256 codes to represent lowercase and uppercase letters, numbers, and symbols. Differences between code pages may result in unreadable text. The 850 common code page has been established to remedy this incompatibility between character sets; it can handle most character sets of the Roman script. The Unicode code page goes even further, supporting 64,000 characters in the Roman, Chinese, and other character sets.

See also **Unicode.**

code-page switching

An operating system mechanism that allows users to switch between character sets employed by different languages.

code/decode (codec)

A device or method that converts analog signals to digital signals. Codecs are used in digital telephone systems to transmit voice over digital lines.

cold boot

The process of starting up a computer that begins after the power is switched on.

See also **warm boot.**

Cold Boot Loader

A program on a NetWare file server that automatically loads NetWare after a cold boot.

collapsed backbone

A local-area network (LAN) architecture in which the backplane of a device acts as a network backbone by routing traffic between nodes and other hubs in a multiple-LAN environment.

See also **backplane; local-area network (LAN).**

collapsed directory

A directory in which the subdirectories are not displayed.

collision

A conflict between two network packets that results when two devices transmit data at the same time. Depending on the type of network, the originating stations may attempt to retransmit after a collision.

collision detection and avoidance

The act of detecting and/or avoiding a collision of two data packets. In an Ethernet network, a collision occurs when signals from two nodes are transmitted on to the network at the same time. In such a case, the packets are discarded and must be retransmitted.

Collisions are detected by checking the direct current (DC) voltage level on the line. If the level is higher than expected, a collision is occurring. Under the Carrier-Sense Multiple-Access/Collision Detection (CSMA/CD) method, collisions are detected by monitoring the transmission line for a special signal that indicates the collision has occurred.

Collision avoidance results when nodes send a special signal to indicate that the line is being used, so no other nodes transmit. Under CSMA/CD, nodes use the Ready To Send (RTS) and Clear To Send (CTS) signals to indicate the network's state of readiness.

See also **Carrier-Sense Multiple-Access/Collision Detection; Clear To Send; Ready To Send.**

COLORPAL utility

In NetWare and IntranetWare, a workstation utility that sets screen colors for character-based menus. The COLORPAL utility provides options for changing colors on the active window border, the active window text, the alert-window text and border, background and inactive windows, the error-window text and border, the help-window text and border, a key name and description, a quick-help area, a screen header, and the selection bar.

COM

Common Object Model, an object-oriented, open architecture that permits client-server applications that run on different platforms to communicate transparently with one another. COM was developed jointly by Microsoft and Digital Equipment Corporation (DEC) as a way of allowing networks using Microsoft's Object Linking and Embedding (OLE) technology to communicate with networks using DEC's ObjectBroker technology. COM's goal is to allow machines that run Windows operating systems or the Macintosh operating system to communicate with machines that run UNIX.

See also **Object Linking and Embedding.**

com (commercial)

A suffix attached to an Internet address of a site maintained by a commercial organization or individual.

See also **IP address.**

COM port

An asynchronous serial port on an IBM PC-compatible computer.

combiner

A fiber-optic coupler device that combines many incoming signals into one outgoing signal.

command

A short program used for a specific task.

command button

An icon in a graphical utility for carrying out a specific action.

command file

A user-defined file containing a sequence of commands. A command file can execute a frequently used command or a sequence of commands.

command format

Instructions showing how to type a command at the keyboard. Command format is also known as *syntax.*

command-history buffer

A portion of memory that saves command strings entered from the keyboard. This buffer allows previously entered commands to be retrieved by using the up arrow and down arrow keys, edited, and then re-executed.

command interpreter

Part of an operating system that displays a command prompt on the screen. Also known as a *command interpreter,* the command processor interprets and executes any valid command issued by the user, retrieves requested files, and displays error messages.

See **command processor.**

command line

A command, followed by additional information, given to the computer one at a time. The command line ends when the Enter key is pressed.

command-line argument

A parameter that changes the default mode of a command. A command-line switch is commonly made up of one or more letters that follow the slash character / in a command. In UNIX, the command-line switch is a character that follows a hyphen in a command. A command-line switch is also known as a *command-line argument.*

See **command-line switch.**

command-line interface (CLI)

An interface between a user who is typing commands and a computer program or operating system receiving instructions from the user.

command-line switch

A parameter that changes the default mode of a command. A command-line switch is commonly made up of one or more letters that follow the slash character / in a command. In UNIX, the command-line switch is a character that follows a hyphen in a command. A command-line switch is also known as a *command-line argument.*

command-line utility (CLU)

A utility accessed through a single-word command.

command processor

Part of an operating system that displays a command prompt on the screen. Also known as a *command interpreter,* the command processor interprets and executes any valid command issued by the user, retrieves requested files, and displays error messages.

command prompt

A screen symbol that indicates the operating system is ready to receive input.

Commercial Internet Exchange (CIX)

A nonprofit trade association of Public Data Internetwork service providers.

 **For more information about the Commercial Internet Exchange, surf the Web to** `http://www.cix.org.`

CommExec object

An object in NetWare for Systems Application Architecture (SAA) that provides management capabilities and rights (network privileges) for the [Root] level of the Novell Directory Services (NDS) Directory tree.

See also **Novell Directory Services; Systems Application Architecture.**

committed burst (Bc)

The highest number of data bits that a network can transfer under typical conditions, over a given period of time.

Commitment, Concurrency, and Recovery Service Element (CCRSE)

In the OSI Reference Model, an Application Layer (Layer 7) service that implements distributed transactions among many applications.

See also **OSI Reference Model.**

committed burst size

The highest number of data bits a network can transfer under normal conditions, over a given period of time.

committed information rate (CIR)

A Frame Relay network term indicating the rate of information, measured in bits per second (bps), at which the network transfers data on a virtual circuit under normal conditions. If network activity exceeds the CIR, the Frame Relay controller marks packets to indicate whether they can be discarded.

See also **Frame Relay network.**

Common Applications Environment (CAE)

Standards for the operating system, networking protocols, languages, and data management that allow applications to be ported across platforms from different manufacturers.

Common Authentication Technology (CAT)

A specification for distributed authentication used on the Internet. CAT supports public-key and private-key encryption strategies. Both client and server use a common interface that provides the authentication services. The interface connects to either Distributed-Authentication Security Service (DASS) for public-key encryption, or Kerberos for private-key encryption.

See also **Distributed-Authentication Security Service; Kerberos.**

common carrier

A private company that provides communications services to the public. A telephone company is an example of a common carrier.

Common Channel Interoffice Signaling (CCIS)

A telephone communications transmission method that uses different channels for voice and control signals. A faster, packet-switched mechanism transmits control signals, making it possible to include additional information (such as caller ID or billing information) in the control channel.

See also **caller ID.**

Common Channel Signaling (CCS)

A telephone transmission method that uses different channels for voice and control signals. The control signals are sent using a fast, packet-switched technique, making it possible to include additional data (such as caller ID or billing information) in the control channel.

See also **caller ID.**

Common Channel Signaling 7 (CCS 7)

An implementation of the Signaling System 7 (SS7) specified by the Consultative Committee for International Telegraphy and Telephony (CCITT). CCS 7 is an Integrated Services Digital Network (ISDN)-based transmission method that makes special services (such as call-forwarding) available anywhere on a network.

See also **Consultative Committee for International Telegraphy and Telephony; Integrated Services Digital Network.**

Common Gateway Interface (CGI)

A platform-independent interface used by a HyperText Transfer Protocol (HTTP)-based information server to run external programs. A CGI program receives client requests and responds with the requested information. In NetWare, the CGI is the feature that allows the NetWare Web Server to modify Web pages before they are sent to a browser.

See also **HyperText Transfer Protocol; Local Common Gateway Interface; NetWare Web Server.**

Common Hardware-Reference Platform (CHRP)

An open hardware architecture (originally designed by IBM) that ensures compatibility among compliant systems built by different manufacturers.

Common Mail Calls (CMC)

An Application Program Interface (API) that enables message-handling agents to communicate with post offices in a manner independent of hardware platforms, operating systems, e-mail systems, and messaging protocols. Common Mail Calls are also known as *common messaging calls.*

See also **Application Program Interface.**

Common Management-Information Machine (CMIPM)

In the OSI Network-Management Model, an application that can accept operations from a Common Management-Information Service Element (CMISE) user, and initiate the appropriate actions for responding with valid Common Management-Information Protocol (CMIP) packets.

See also **Common Management-Information Protocol; Common Management-Information Service Element; OSI Network-Management Model.**

Common Management-Information Protocol (CMIP)

The OSI Network-Management Model information protocol for network monitoring and control information. CMIP includes specifications for accounting management, configuration management, fault management, performance management, and security management. CMIP is not widely used because of the widespread commercial availability of products on the basis of Simple Network-Management Protocol (SNMP).

See also **OSI Network-Management Model; Simple Network-Management Protocol.**

Common Management-Information-Protocol Data Unit (CMIPDU)

A packet conforming to the Common Management-Information Protocol (CMIP). The packet's contents depends on the Common Management-Information Service Element (CMISE) request.

See also **Common Management-Information Protocol; Common Management-Information Service Element; OSI Network-Management Model.**

Common Management-Information Service (CMIS)

The specification used in the OSI Network-Management Model for network monitoring and control.

See also **Common Management-Information Protocol; OSI Network-Management Model.**

Common Management-Information Service Element (CMISE)

An entity that furnishes network management and control services under the OSI Network-Management Model. The seven types of CMISEs are Action, Cancel Get, Create, Delete, Event Report, Get, and Set. The system-management functions use these services to carry out specific tasks.

See also **OSI Network-Management Model.**

Common Management-Information Services and Protocol Over TCP/IP (CMOT)

An initiative that attempted to implement two services of the Open Systems Interconnection (OSI) framework — Common Management-Information Service (CMIS) and Common Management-Information Protocol (CMIP) — over the TCP/IP suite. CMOT was never implemented due to widespread usage of Simple Network-Management Protocol (SNMP) and the complexities of porting the OSI model to TCP/IP.

See also **Common Management-Information Protocol; Common Management-Information Service; OSI Network-Management Model; Simple Network-Management Protocol.**

Common Name (CN)

The naming attribute that denotes leaf objects in Novell Directory Services (NDS). For a user object, the Common Name is the user's login name.

See also **leaf object; Novell Directory Services.**

Common Object Model (COM)

An object-oriented, open architecture that permits client-server applications that run on different platforms to communicate transparently with one another. COM was developed jointly by Microsoft and Digital Equipment Corporation (DEC) as a way of allowing networks using Microsoft's Object Linking and Embedding (OLE) technology to communicate with networks using DEC's ObjectBroker technology. COM's goal is to allow machines that run Windows operating systems or the Macintosh operating system to communicate with machines that run UNIX.

See also **Object Linking and Embedding.**

Common Object-Request Broker Architecture (CORBA)

A multiplatform architecture, developed by the Object-Management Group, that permits object-oriented applications to communicate and exchange data regardless of their hardware platforms. CORBA employs Object-Request Brokers (ORBs) to establish communications between objects, and to invoke methods on behalf of objects. A standard Interface-Definition Language (the CORBA IDL) defines an object's interface. The CORBA 2.0 specification includes an interoperability standard, which allows different vendors' objects to interoperate.

See also **Object-Request Broker.**

For more information about CORBA, surf the Web to `http://www.acl.lanl.gov/corba.`

Common Program Interface for Communications (CPIC)

A set of Application Program Interfaces (APIs) for program-to-program communications used in IBM's Systems Application Architecture (SAA).

See also **Application Program Interface; Systems Application Architecture.**

Common User Access (CUA)

In IBM Systems Application Architecture (SAA), a common set of specifications for user interfaces, providing a consistent look and feel for all applications and platforms.

See also **Systems Application Architecture.**

Communicating Application Specification (CAS)

A proposed interface standard for fax/modems, developed by Intel and Digital Communications Associates (DCA). CAS competes with the *Class x* hierarchy developed by the Electronic Industries Association (EIA).

See also **Electronic Industries Association.**

communication

The process of transferring data from one device to another in a computer system.

communication protocol

A set of rules used by a program or operating system to communicate between endpoints. A communication protocol facilitates the packaging, transmission, and delivery of information. Communication protocols may be workstation-based or server-based.

See also **protocol.**

communication-protocol stack

A protocol that defines the rules for sending and receiving information by a network device. The stack furnishes routing and connection services by adding information to any packet that passes through it.

See also **protocol.**

communication server

A type of server that provides access to modems and telephone lines. The communication server can be a dedicated machine

or can reside on a workstation. It runs applications necessary to establish connections, prepare files, and send or receive data. A communication server can also provide terminal-emulation services for mainframe access.

communication services

A basic network service that facilitates connections between two or more nodes.

communications buffers

The area in a file server's memory that temporarily holds data packets arriving from workstations. Communications buffers are also known as *packet-receive buffers*.
See also **memory.**

communications channel

A pathway that employs a specific set of signals and methods for transferring data between workstation and printer.

communications controller

A machine attached to the host computer in a Systems Network Architecture (SNA) network that processes communications destined for the host. Also known as a *front-end processor*.
See also **Systems Network Architecture.**

Communications Decency Act (CDA)

Legislation enacted in 1996 to forbid obscenity and indecency on the Internet. Its constitutionality was challenged in 1997.

communications line

A physical connection (such as cable or circuit) that links one or more devices to another device.

communications NLM

A NetWare Loadable Module (NLM) that establishes communications with other systems and remote networks.
See also **NetWare Loadable Module.**

communications parameters

A group of settings that must be set before computers can communicate over an asynchronous connection. Communications parameters include baud rate, number of data bits, number of stop bits, and parity.
See also **parity.**

communications port

An asynchronous serial port on an IBM PC-compatible computer.
See also **COM port.**

communications program

A personal computer program that enables a user to call up and communicate with other computers.

communications/modem server

A network server with one or more modems that can be shared by users on the network.
See also **modem.**

community

A logical group of Simple Network-Management Protocol (SNMP) and Network-Management System (NMS) devices located in the same administrative domain.

See also **Network-Management System; Simple Network-Management Protocol.**

Community Antenna Television, or Cable Television (CATV)

A broadband transmission facility using 75-ohm coaxial cable. The cable can carry many television channels, using guard channels to keep them separated.

comp newsgroup

A type of newsgroup that discusses topics of interest to computer users.

To access a computer newsgroup that discusses topics about the World Wide Web, surf over to `http://comp.infosystems.www.`

compact disc (CD)

A nonmagnetic optical disc that stores digital information. A single CD can store 650MB or more of information. Data is stored on the CD as a series of alternating microscopic pits and smooth regions, each with different reflective properties. A laser beam pointed at the disc detects these properties and converts them into digital information.

Compact Disc Read-Only Memory (CD-ROM)

An optical storage device that can store up to 650MB of data. Often CD-ROMs store large multimedia applications, encyclopedias, or large reference works, and libraries of fonts or clip art. Many large software applications are distributed on CD-ROM. A CD-ROM uses a constant-linear-velocity encoding scheme to store data in one spiral track divided into segments of equal length.

Compact Disc-Interactive (CDI)

A standard compact-disc format for data, text, audio, still video images, and animated graphics.

See also **compact disc.**

companding

A contraction of "*com*pressing" and "ex*panding*," referring to a Pulse Code Modulation (PCM) process of logically rounding an analog signal sample value to scale-step decimal values on a nonlinear scale. The decimal values are then coded into binary equivalents. The process is reversed at the receiving terminal.

See also **Pulse Code Modulation.**

Compare right

A NetWare property right that indicates the holder has the right to compare another value to a value of the given property to see whether they are equal. The Compare right can be applied to an operation to yield a value of *True* or *False*, but not the actual value of the property.

compatibility

The shared capability of two or more devices or programs to work together. Compatibility may be built into some products; with others, it must be achieved through additional drivers or filters.

compatible

A term that describes a computer (also known as a *clone*) whose architecture is compatible with that of the IBM PC. This term also describes a peripheral device, data file, or application program that can either work with or understand the same commands, formats, or languages as another.

Complementary Metal-Oxide Semiconductor (CMOS)

A battery-powered memory chip that holds system configuration parameters when the computer is shut down. The CMOS chip is usually located on the system board.

complete name

In Novell Directory Services (NDS), a NetWare object's common name, followed by a period, the name of the container object, another period, and so on through all succeeding container objects down to the root of the Directory tree.

Complete-Sequence-Number PDU (CSNP)

A Protocol Data Unit (PDU) sent by a designated router to an Open Shortest Path First (OSPF) network to maintain database synchronization.

See also **Open Shortest Path First; Protocol Data Unit.**

Complex-Instruction-Set Computing (CISC)

A processor-design strategy that gives the processor a large number of powerful assembly-language instructions. These instructions may be complex and may slow down overall processing.

See also **Reduced-Instruction-Set Computing.**

complex network

A network with different platforms. A complex network can contain Macintosh, DOS, OS/2, UNIX, Windows, and other platforms, typically in a wide-area network (WAN) configuration.

See also **wide-area network.**

component

An element of hardware or software combined with other elements to form complete systems, functions, or programs.

compress

To enable a storage medium to hold more online data by removing redundant information.

Compressed (Co) attribute

A NetWare file attribute that indicates a file has been compressed by generating a status-flag attribute.

See also **attribute.**

Compressed Internet Packet Exchange (CIPX) protocol

A variant of the Novell Internet Packet Exchange (IPX) protocol that uses a compressed header of between 1 and 7 octets (provided that only the IPX header is compressed); a 30-octet header is normally characteristic of IPX packets. CIPX compression can speed up transmissions over slow wide-area network (WAN) lines.

See also **header compression; Internet Packet Exchange.**

Compressed Serial-Line Interface Protocol (CSLIP)

A variant of the Serial-Line Interface Protocol (SLIP) that uses the Van Jacobsen compression strategy to compress packet headers. CSLIP is used to transmit Internet Protocol (IP) packets over serial-line connections.

See also **Serial-Line Interface Protocol.**

compression

The process of compacting information. Because compressed files take up less space, more files can be placed on a storage medium. Files must be decompressed before use.

CompuServe Information Service (CIS)

A commercial information service providing access to the Internet and other value-added features including discussion forums, online communities, and information resources.

 **To find out more about CompuServe, surf the Web to** http://world.compuserve.com.

CompuServe NetLauncher

An Internet starter kit from CompuServe that includes an Internet access provider, connection software, and Web browser. The NetLauncher program is started after the user exits the CompuServe Information Manager program.

computation bound

A state under which the processor's speed limits the speed of a program's execution.

computer

In a general context, any machine that accepts structured input, uses prescribed rules to process the input, and produces results as output. In the context of NetWare, a Directory Schema term. Individual computers on a network are known as *nodes* or *stations*. A node can be a PC, minicomputer, or mainframe.

Computer Business Manufacturers Association (CBEMA)

An organization that furnishes technical committees for work done by other organizations.

Computer Emergency Response Team (CERT)

An Internet group formed by the Defense Advanced Research Projects Agency (DARPA) to respond to security problems on the Internet. Administrators can get information and assistance on security issues from CERT, and the organization offers a number of tools and documents about network security at its FTP site.

See also **Defense Advanced Research Projects Agency.**

For more information about the Computer Emergency Response Team, surf the Web to `http://www.cert.org.`

Computer object

A NetWare leaf object representing a computer on the network. The Computer object's properties can hold information such as the physical computer's serial number, or the name of the person to whom the computer is assigned. The Computer object has the following selectable properties in Novell Directory Services (NDS): Access Control List, Back Link, Bindery, Common Name (CN), Description, Locality (L), Network Address, Object Class, Operator, Organization (O), Organizational Unit (OU), Owner, See Also, Serial Number, Server, and Status.

See also **leaf object; Novell Directory Services; object.**

Computer Science Network (CSNET)

An internetwork consisting of universities, research institutions, and commercial concerns. CSNET merged with Because It's Time Network (BITNET) to form the Corporation for Research and Educational Networking (CREN).

See also **Because It's Time Network; Corporation for Research and Educational Networking.**

Computer-Based Messaging System (CBMS)

An older term that denotes a Message-Handling System (MHS) or electronic mail system (e-mail).

See also **Message-Handling System.**

Computer-Telephone Integration (CTI)

A technology that integrates telephone services into a computer to achieve greater productivity. CTI technology is often employed in customer service areas, and includes features such as caller ID and automatic dialing.

See also **automatic dialing; caller ID.**

Computer-to-PBX Interface (CPI)

An interface used by a computer to communicate with a Private Branch Exchange (PBX).

See also **Private Branch Exchange.**

concentrator

A hardware device with a single bus and many connections. A concentrator (sometimes called a *hub* or *wiring center*) can send many input channels out to fewer output channels, and can store the input data until an output channel becomes available. When employed as a hub, a concentrator is a termination point for the cables connected to nodes in the network, and forms the basic topology of the network. Concentrators may also connect different network elements with different cabling schemes or architectures. A concentrator may also include a processor, network monitoring features, and many boards (each functioning as one hub).

concurrency controls

A set of Btrieve methods for resolving conflicts when two applications try to access the same data. Concurrency controls may include record locking or transaction control, and guarantee data-file integrity.

See also **Btrieve.**

concurrent

A condition under which two or more programs are accessing the processor at the same time. Processes that run concurrently must share system resources.

conditioned analog line

Analog line formed by adding devices to improve the electrical signal.

conditional search

A search that locates information in a database or file on the basis of a given set of criteria.

conductor

A material that can carry an electrical current.

conference

A logical meeting place where computer users interact over the network.

Conférence Européene des Postes et Télécommunications (CEPT)

An association of 26 European organizations that recommends communications standards to the Consultative Committee for International Telegraphy and Telephony (CCIT).

See also **Consultative Committee for International Telegraphy and Telephony; Postal Telephone and Telegraph.**

CONFIG utility

In NetWare and IntranetWare, a server console utility that displays configuration information: the server's name and network identification number, information on which local-area network (LAN) drivers are loaded, Network Interface Card (NIC) information, and the server's Directory tree and bindery context.

CONFIG.SYS

A configuration file executed by the DOS operating system upon start-up. Located in the root directory of the default boot disk, the CONFIG.SYS file contains the basic commands that set up the system for operation. Some applications or hardware peripherals require an explicit statement they must add to the CONFIG.SYS file to function.

configuration (hardware)

The way network hardware is used and connected. *Hardware* may include servers, workstations, printers, cables, network boards, routers, and other devices. Hardware configuration may include a specification for the hardware installed in (or attached to) the computer, and parameters for an add-in board.

configuration (router)

Settings and parameters established to configure a NetWare server as a router. Accomplished with the INETCFG utility, these settings can configure AppleTalk or TCP/IP packet routing across network segments. Router-configuration settings can also configure Internetwork Packet Exchange/Sequenced Packet Exchange (IPX/SPX) parameters, load and bind protocols to network boards, enable Network Link-Services Protocol (NLSP), and display recent console messages.

See also **AppleTalk; INETCFG; Internetwork Packet Exchange/Sequenced Packet Exchange; Network Link Services Protocol.**

configuration (server)

Settings and parameters that specify how the network server is used. In NetWare, the server configuration parameters are selected through the INSTALL NetWare Loadable Module (NLM). Configuration includes loading and binding the drivers for disks, CD-ROMs, and local-area networks (LANs). In addition, the server configuration can assign an IPX internal or external network number; partitions the hard disk; creates and mounts NetWare volumes; modifies volume segments, enables file compression, or installs Novell Directory Services (NDS).

See also **INSTALL; NetWare Loadable Module; Novell Directory Services.**

configuration (software)

Settings and parameters that specify how network software is used. Software configuration may include a specification on how the software is installed, as well as preference options, default settings, and a set of configuration files.

configuration command

In NetWare and IntranetWare, a server console utility that displays configuration information: the server's name and network identification number, information on which local-area network (LAN) drivers are loaded, Network Interface Card (NIC) information, and the server's Directory tree and bindery context.

See also **CONFIG utility.**

configuration file

A file containing commands that set up the computing environment. The configuration file executes automatically upon startup.

See also **CONFIG.SYS.**

Configuration Management

Of the five OSI Network-Management Model domains, the one that manages networked applications and user access. Configuration Management encompasses several tasks, including identifying objects on the network, and determining information about those objects. The process of configuration management may also include the storage and reporting of this information, modifying the parameters of the objects' settings, and managing relationships between objects. According to the OSI Network-Management Model, any object has four operational states: Active, Busy, Disabled, and Enabled.

See also **OSI Network-Management Model.**

configuration options

Btrieve specifications that are defined when Btrieve is loaded. These options control how Btrieve operates, and can be changed from the Setup utility.
See also **Btrieve.**

configuration services

A network service in a control point and in the physical unit. Configuration services activate, deactivate, and maintain the status of physical units, links, and link stations.

configured router

A router configured on the network, instead of from a seed router.
See also **seed router.**

confirmation

An application's acknowledgment that data has been received.

confirmation box

A box that appears when a user exits a menu utility or creates, modifies, or deletes an item. The confirmation box gives the user the options of proceeding with the previously specified task or canceling it.

conformance options

A set of options that provide access to an expert set of parameters used to control Packet- and Frame-level operations. Conformance options include parameters for changing the frame-reject operation and setting the length of a clear confirmation packet.

Conformance-Testing Service (CTS)

A series of programs that test how well a product implements a particular protocol as per specifications set by the International Standards Organization (ISO).
See also **International Standards Organization.**

congestion

A state in which excessive traffic is occurring on the network. In a congested network, individual packets may arrive late at their destinations, and performance may be adversely affected.

congestion control

The use of mechanisms designed to limit excessive traffic, usually by providing network switches with a way to signal the router to slow a transmission.
See also **Background Explicit Congestion Notification; Forward Explicit Congestion Notification.**

CONLOG (NLM)

In NetWare 4.*x* and IntranetWare, a server console utility that captures all console messages generated at the server and writes those messages to a log file. Console messages can identify errors that may occur during system initialization.
See also **NetWare Loadable Module.**

connect

To establish an authenticated connection to a server.

connect time

The amount of time a node has been connected to a server.

Connected Items pane

The top pane of the Macintosh Workspace. This area contains a snapshot of each item or device currently employed by the user, as well as the utilities that administer them.

connection

The state that exists when two devices on a network are communicating.

Connection Information

In NetWare and IntranetWare, a field name from the Available Options screen of the MONITOR NetWare Loadable Module (NLM). This field contains options for listing active connections, listing licensed and unlicensed connections, listing physical record locks for users, clearing a connection, listing open files, listing the record-lock status of open files, and sending a message to a workstation connection.

See also **locking; MONITOR; NetWare Loadable Module.**

Connection Management (CMT)

A process in the Fiber Distributed Data Interface (FDDI) that handles the transition of a ring through its various states.

See also **Fiber Distributed Data Interface.**

Connection-Mode Network Service (CMNS)

A service that extends local X.25 switching to such networks as Ethernet, Fiber Distributed Data Interface (FDDI), and Token Ring.

See also **Ethernet; Fiber Distributed Data Interface; Token Ring; X.25.**

connection number

A number assigned to the workstations, printers, or applications attached to a NetWare server. The connection numbers may be different each time the device is attached. A connection number may also assign a process.

connection services

A set of services that obtain information about a workstation or other device currently using the services of the file server.

connectionless

In the Internet Protocol (IP), a type of datagram delivery that transmits all packets independently of other packets. Communication takes place without having first established a direct connection. In a connectionless networking scheme, each packet contains addressing information.

See also **Connectionless Network Protocol; Datagram-Delivery Protocol; Internet Protocol.**

Connectionless Broadband Data Service (CBDS)

A wide-area network (WAN) technology based on high-speed, packet-switched datagram delivery. CBDS is also known as *Switched Multimegabit Data Service (SMDS)*.

See also **Switched Multimegabit Data Service.**

Connectionless-Mode Network Service (CLNS)

In the OSI Reference Model, a service on the Network Layer (Layer 3) where data transmission can occur without a fixed connection between source and destination. In this model, packets are independent, may reach their destinations through multiple paths, and may arrive out of order. Consequently, each packet carries the destination address. Most local-area networks (LANs) operate in connectionless mode.

See also **local-area network; OSI Reference Model.**

Connectionless Network Protocol (CLNP)

An Open Systems Interconnection (OSI) protocol that provides the OSI Connectionless Network Service. In the OSI model, CLNP is the functional equivalent of the NetWare Internet Packet Exchange (IPX) protocol and the Internet Protocol (IP). CLNP datagrams include destination information along with each unit of data; a direct connection is unnecessary.

See also **Internet Packet Exchange; Internet Protocol; OSI Reference Model.**

connectionless service

A network service that transmits data packets without first arranging a predetermined path between the source and destination. Each packet of a transmission may take a different route to reach its destination; no guaranteed delivery or priority services are available. A connectionless service is defined in the Network Layer (Layer 3) and Transport Layer (Layer 4) of the OSI Reference Model.

See also **OSI Reference Model.**

Connectionless Transport Protocol (CLTP)

In an Asynchronous Transfer Mode (ATM) network, a bit value that specifies whether a particular cell can be discarded if necessary. ATM's traffic policing function uses a buffering technique, known as a leaky bucket, where traffic flows (or leaks) out of a buffer (or bucket) at a constant rate, regardless of how fast it flows into the bucket. If the buffer starts to overflow, the ATM switch polices the buffer by examining the Cell-Loss Priority bit that exists in the header of every ATM cell. This bit identifies cells that can be discarded if necessary.

See also **Asynchronous Transfer Mode.**

Connectionless Transport Service (CLTS)

In the OSI Reference Model, a best-effort transport service on the Transport Layer (Layer 4). CLTS uses end-to-end addressing and error checking; it does not guarantee delivery.

See also **OSI Reference Model.**

connection-oriented

A term that describes data transfer without the existence of a virtual circuit.

Connection-Oriented Convergence Function (COCF)

A function of the Distributed-Queue Dual-Bus (DQDB) network architecture that prepares data going into or out of a connection-oriented service. The service establishes a fixed connection, sends the data, and then breaks the connection.
See also **Distributed-Queue Dual-Bus.**

Connection-Oriented Network Protocol (CONP)

A protocol in the OSI Reference Model that provides connection-oriented operations to upper-level protocols.
See also **OSI Reference Model.**

Connection-Oriented Network Service (CONS)

A network service where transmissions of data occur after a predetermined path has been determined between source and destination. In a connection-oriented service, packets reach their destination in the order in which they were sent. Asynchronous Transfer Mode (ATM) is a connection-oriented service.
See also **Asynchronous Transfer Mode.**

connectivity

The ability to connect computers, sometimes with many architectures, on a single network for the purpose of sharing resources.

connector

A device that provides a physical link between two components.

Table C.2 lists common connector types, their uses, and where to find more information.

CONP

Connection-Oriented Network Protocol, a protocol in the OSI Reference Model that provides connection-oriented operations to upper-level protocols.
See also **OSI Reference Model.**

CONS

Connection-Mode Network Service, a service that extends local X.25 switching to such networks as Ethernet, Fiber Distributed Data Interface (FDDI), and Token Ring.
See also **Ethernet; Fiber Distributed Data Interface; Token Ring; X.25.**

Conseil Européen pour la Récherche Nucléaire (CERN)

The original name for an organization now known as the European Laboratory for Particle Physics in Switzerland, where Tim Berners-Lee developed a system (part of what is now known as the World Wide Web) to enhance the availability of research to remote users.

For more information about CERN, surf the Web to http://www.cern.ch/cern.

Table C.2: Common Connector Types

Connector Type	Use	For More Information
AUI (attachment unit interface)	Links a drop cable to a network interface card (NIC)	See **AUI (Attachment-Unit Interface) connector**.
barrel	Links two segments of cable in a straight run	See **barrel connector**.
BNC (bayonet nut connector)	Links Ethernet thin coaxial cables, or link twinaxial cable segments	See **BNC connector**.
D-4	Links fiber-optic cable	See **D-4 connector**.
DIN	Links a keyboard to a personal computer, or links components on a LocalTalk network	See **DIN connector**.
D-type	Links serial, parallel, and video components	See **D-type connector**.
elbow	Links two sections of cable in a corner, or to change the direction of a cable linkage	See **elbow connector**.
ESCON (Enterprise System Connection Architecture)	Links fiber-optic cable	See **ESCON connector**.
F	Links cables in a broadband Ethernet network or a broadband token bus network	See **F connector**.
FC	Links fiber-optic cable	See **FC connector**.
fiber-optic	Links two segments of the optical core of fiber-optic cable	See **fiber-optic connector**.
IBM Data	Links components of a Token Ring network	See **IBM Data connector**.
ISO 8877	Links telephones to the wall or to modems	See **ISO 8877 connector**.
L-to-T	Links two Frequency-Division Multiplexing (FDM) groups into a single Time-Division Multiplexing (TDM) group	See **L-to-T Connector**.
MIC	Links fiber-optic cable in a Fiber Distributed Data Interface (FDDI) network	See **Medium Interface Connector**.
N-Series	Links coaxial thick cable	See **N-Series connector**.
RJ-xx	Links telephones to the wall or to modems	See **RJ-xx connector**.
SC (subscriber connector)	Links fiber-optic cable connectors	See **subscriber connector**.

Connector Type	Use	For More Information
SMA	Links fiber-optic cable	See **SMA connector**.
straight-tip	Links fiber-optic cable	See **straight-tip connector**.
T	Attaches a device to a section of cable	See **T connector**.
TNC (threaded-nut connector)	Links Ethernet thin coaxial cables, or links twinaxial cable segments	See **threaded-nut connector**.

console

The monitor and keyboard used to view and control server or host activity.

console operator

A user who has been given rights to manage the NetWare server.

constant angular velocity (CAV)

A fixed rotation speed. Hard disks employ a CAV-encoding scheme in which the disk rotates at a constant rate. Under a CAV scheme, sectors toward the center of the disk have a higher density. As the read/write heads move outward, data-transfer rates decrease because the heads must then cover a greater circumference to read the outer sectors.

Constant Bit Rate (CBR)

A type of Asynchronous Transfer Mode (ATM) connection under the *Class A* Quality of Service (QoS) level. CBR is typically reserved for voice or video, or other data that must be transmitted at a constant rate

and is intolerant of loss. CBR is a *reserved-bandwidth* service that generates a steady bit stream.

See also **Asynchronous Transfer Mode.**

constant linear velocity (CLV)

A changing rotation speed. To ensure a constant data density, CD-ROM drives use a CLV-encoding scheme in which the disc rotates at a varying rate. Data on a CD is stored in a single, spiral track divided into equal segments. To read the data at a constant rate, the CD-ROM drive changes its speed of rotation according to where the read head is on the disc.

See also **Compact Disc Read-Only Memory.**

Consultative Committee for International Telegraphy and Telephony (CCITT)

A subgroup of the International Telecommunications Union (ITU) that defines data-communications standards. The CCITT is responsible for several communications, telecommunications, and networking standards, including documents that specify

X.25, X.400, V.42 and V.42*bis*, and 1.*xxx*
Integrated-Services Digital Network (ISDN)
standards.

There are three main sets of standards:

- *CCITT Groups 1-4.* These are used for
  facsimile transmissions.
- *CCITT V Series.* These are used for
  modems, error detection, and
  correction mechanisms.
- *CCITT X Series.* These are used for
  local-area networks (LANs).

Many standards appear in documents
from both the CCITT and the International
Standards Organization (ISO). Although
the CCITT is now officially called the
*International Telecommunications Union-
Telecommunications Standardization Sector*
(ITU-TS), it is still commonly referred to as
the CCITT. The French name on which the
CCITT acronym is based is Comité Con-
sultatif International Téléphonique et
Télégraphique.

See also **Integrated-Services Digital Network; International Telecommunications
Union; X.25; X.400.**

**For more information
about CCITT, surf the Web
to** http://www.info.itu.ch.

container

A high-level object (also known as a *parent*)
used to organize other objects in the Novell
Directory Services (NDS) Directory tree. The
three types of container objects are Country
(C), Organization (O), and Organizational
Unit (OU).

See also **container object; Novell
Directory Services.**

Container login script

A script that sets the environment for all
users within a given container.

container object

In NetWare 4.*x* and IntranetWare, a high-
level object capable of holding other
objects. A container object is used to logically organize other objects in the Novell
Directory Services (NDS) Directory tree.
Table C.3 lists the four types of container
objects, their uses, and where to find more
information.

The Country and Locality container
objects are optional, and are used mainly by
companies that extend across geographical
boundaries. The Organization container
object is used to organize other objects in
the Directory tree, and the Organizational
Unit container object is used to organize
leaf objects in the Directory tree.

See also **leaf object; Novell Directory
Services.**

contention

The state that occurs in some media-access
methods where nodes compete to gain
access to the network. In a contention-based
access method, the first node to seek access
is the one that gets the privilege of transmitting. Carrier-Sense Multiple-Access/Collision
Detect (CSMA/CD) is a contention-based
access method. Token Ring, on the other
hand, gives all nodes an equal opportunity
to transmit by passing a token among them.

See also **Carrier-Sense Multiple-
Access/Collision Detect; Token Ring.**

Table C.3: Container Objects

Object	Use	For More Information
[Root]	A special object that appears at the top of the Novell Directory Services (NDS) Directory tree	See **[Root] object**.
Country (C)	Uses a two-letter designation to define where a company is located	See **Country (C) object**.
Locality (L)	Not currently supported by NetWare utilities, can define a locality (L) or a state (S)	See **Locality (L) object**.
Organization (O)	Defines the name of a company	See **Organization (O) object**.
Organizational Unit (OU)	Defines the locations, departments, divisions, or workgroups of a company	See **Organizational Unit (OU) object**.

contention-loser polarity

A designation indicating that a logical unit (LU) is the *contention loser* for a session.
See also **logical unit**.

contention-winner polarity

A designation indicating that a logical unit (LU) is the *contention winner* for a session. When a requesting LU indicates that it should be the loser in the event of a contention, the responding LU automatically accepts the status of contention winner.
See also **logical unit**.

context

In NetWare 4.*x* or IntranetWare, the location of an object within its container in the Novell Directory Services (NDS) Directory tree. If an object is moved from one container object to another, it has changed contexts.

See also **container object; leaf object; Novell Directory Services**.

context switching

Switching between applications without ending the first application. Context switching allows users to work with many applications simultaneously. It differs from *multitasking* because only one program is active at a time.
See also **multitasking**.

context-sensitive help

Help information concerning a current item or task that can be accessed by an end-user.

continuous operation

A Btrieve feature that permits users to back up data files while they are still open. During this process, Btrieve opens the active file in read-only mode, and then permits the backup utility to access the file's static image.

See also **Btrieve.**

control character

A special formatting character often used in word processing programs. The character is generated by pressing the Control (Ctrl) key along with an additional key.

control code

A sequence of characters used for hardware control. Control codes are also known as *setup strings* or *escape sequences.*

control-information byte

The first byte in an AppleTalk Transaction Protocol (ATP) header. This byte holds the packet's function code, XO bit, EOM bit, and STS bit.

See also **AppleTalk Transaction Protocol.**

control packet

A link-control or network-control packet that establishes encapsulation format options, packet-size limitations, link setup, peer authentication, or protocol management in the OSI Reference Model Network Layer (Layer 3).

See also **OSI Reference Model.**

Control Panel

A Macintosh desk accessory used to change the speaker volume, mouse tracking, color display, or other parameters. System controls are kept in the Control Panel grouping in Windows 95.

control point

A control point in a host node that provides network services for dependent nodes.

See also **System-Services Control Point.**

Control Unit Terminal (CUT)

An operating mode for terminals that allows one session per terminal.

Controlled-Access Unit (CAU)

An intelligent access concentrator used in a Token Ring network. The CAU can establish connections for as many as 80 workstations by using pluggable lobe-attachment modules. It can determine whether or not a node is operational, monitor activity, and pass data to the LAN Manager program. The CAU can also connect and disconnect individual nodes.

See also **LAN Manager; Token Ring.**

Controlled-Access Unit/Lobe-Attachment Module (CAU/LAM)

A box, providing ports to which new nodes can be attached, that is plugged into the Controlled-Access Unit (CAU) in a Token Ring network.

See also **Controlled-Access Unit; Token Ring.**

controller

In mainframe computers, a device that regulates communications between a host computer and the terminals accessing it. In

personal computers, a device responsible for accessing other devices (for example, a hard disk controller lets the computer access and manage the hard disk).

controller address

A number used by the operating system to locate the controller on a disk channel. The address is usually set physically by moving jumpers on the disk controller board.

controller board

A hardware device that allows a computer to communicate with a peripheral device. The controller board manages input/output (I/O), and regulates the operation of the peripheral device. In some newer devices, controller circuitry is built in and a separate board is not needed.

conventional memory

Computer memory below 640K. The operating system and applications are typically loaded into conventional memory. Conventional memory is also known as *base memory* or *random-access memory (RAM)*.

See also **memory; memory management.**

convergence

A Novell Directory Schema term and selectable property, indicating the synchronization process undertaken by a network after a route change.

convergence rate

The rate at which NetWare Link-Services Protocol (NLSP) routing information

converges on all NLSP routers on the Internet Packet Exchange (IPX) internetwork. This rate is set at the *NLSP Rate of Convergence* parameter.

See also **NetWare Link-Services Protocol; Internet Packet Exchange.**

convergence time

The time necessary to propagate routing information throughout a NetWare Link-Services Protocol (NLSP) network.

See also **NetWare Link-Services Protocol.**

conversation

As a logical process, communication between two transaction programs in a Type 6.2 LU-LU session.

See also **logical unit Type 6.2.**

Conversational Monitor System (CMS)

A Systems Network Architecture (SNA) subsystem used for managing interactive sessions.

See also **Systems Network Architecture.**

conversational transaction

Occurs when two or more applications communicate using the services of logical units (LUs).

convert

To change the format of a document or piece of data without changing the underlying content. A common example is converting a document created with one software program (say, a word processor) into a format recognizable by another software program (such as a spreadsheet).

cookie

A piece of information sent by a World Wide Web (WWW) server to a Web browser, saved by the browser, and returned to the server whenever the browser makes additional requests from the server. Cookies are used by Web servers to store information about services and users who access the server through a particular browser.

See also **Web browser.**

cooperative multitasking

A type of multitasking in which all applications share system resources. A cooperative multitasking operating system maintains a list of active applications and an execution order. When one application is operating, others cannot run until the first application returns control to the operating system.

cooperative processing

A method that allows an application to execute its various tasks on different machines. Cooperative processing is sometimes used in client-server computing, for example, when the front end of an application executes on the client and the back end on the server.

Copper Distributed Data Interface (CDDI)

A network architecture that implements Fiber Distributed Data Interface (FDDI) specifications on electrical, instead of optical, cable.

See also **Fiber Distributed Data Interface.**

coprocessor

A microprocessor chip that carries out a specific group of tasks for another processor. Coprocessors are often used for floating-point arithmetic, graphics, disk management, or input/output (I/O).

Copy Inhibit (Ci) attribute

A NetWare file attribute that prohibits users from copying the file.

See also **attribute.**

CORBA

Common Object-Request Broker Architecture, a multiplatform architecture, developed by the Object Management Group, that permits object-oriented applications to communicate and exchange data regardless of their hardware platforms. CORBA employs Object-Request Brokers (ORBs) to establish communications between objects, and to invoke methods on behalf of objects. A standard Interface-Definition Language (the CORBA IDL) defines an object's interface. The CORBA 2.0 specification includes an interoperability standard, which allows different vendors' objects to interoperate.

See also **Object-Request Broker.**

For more information about CORBA, surf the Web to `http://www.acl.lanl.gov/ corba.`

core

The transparent central fiber in a fiber-optic cable, through which the light signal travels. The core is surrounded by cladding, which reflects light back into the core.

core gateway

A primary router on the Internet, historically one of a set of gateways or routers operated by the Internet Network Operations Center (INOC). As a central part of routing on the Internet, the core-gateway system requires that all groups advertise paths to their networks from a core gateway.

corona wire

A thin wire in a laser printer that emits an electrical charge to attract toner to the paper.

Corporation for Open Systems (COS)

A group involved in testing and promoting products that support the OSI Reference Model.

See also **OSI Reference Model.**

Corporation for Open Systems Interconnection Networking in Europe (COSINE)

A European project to build a communication network consisting of scientific and industrial organizations.

Corporation for Research and Educational Networking (CREN)

A research organization concerned with the ongoing operation of the Internet.

 **For more information on CREN, log on to its Web site at** `http://www.cren.net`.

COS

Corporation for Open Systems, a group involved in testing and promoting products that support the OSI Reference Model.

See also **OSI Reference Model.**

COSINE

Corporation for Open Systems Interconnection Networking in Europe, a European project to build a communication network consisting of scientific and industrial organizations.

Cosmo

A line of products from Silicon Graphics enabling World Wide Web (WWW), Netscape Navigator-compatible browsers to show three-dimensional simulations constructed with the Virtual-Reality Modeling Language (VRML).

See also **Netscape Navigator; Virtual-Reality Modeling Language.**

cost

A metric applied to a circuit, which indicates the likelihood that traffic will be routed over that circuit. Cost is defined in terms of *hop count*.

See also **hop count.**

count to infinity

An artifact that can occur in distance-vector routing. A count-to-infinity condition occurs if a network becomes unreachable because routers are relying on incorrect information.

country code

A two-letter abbreviation used in the last part of an Internet address to signify country (for locations outside the United States).

See also **IP address.**

Country Name

A NetWare Directory Schema term that defines the name of the country in which a company resides.

Country (C) object

A Novell Directory Services (NDS) optional container object that designates the country in which a given network resides. The Country object is necessary only for global networks that exist across several countries. This object has the following selectable NDS properties: Access-Control List (ACL), Back Link, Bindery Property, Description, and Object Class.

See also **container object; Novell Directory Services; object.**

coupler

A device for transferring energy among many channels. In a fiber-optic network, a coupler routes an incoming signal to many outgoing paths, or routes many incoming paths into a single outbound path. A coupler may have one of several designs, including

- *Tee coupler.* Divides the incoming signal into two outgoing signals.
- *Star coupler.* Divides the signal into more than two signals.

COW

Character-Oriented Windows Interface, a Systems Application Architecture (SAA) compatible interface used in the OS/2 operating system.

See also **Systems Application Architecture.**

CPE

Customer Premises Equipment, hardware leased or owned by the customer, and used at the customer's location.

CPI

Computer-to-PBX Interface, an interface used by a computer to communicate with a Private Branch Exchange (PBX).

See also **Private Branch Exchange.**

CPIC

Common Programming Interface for Communications, a set of Application Program Interfaces (APIs) for program-to-program communications used in IBM's Systems Application Architecture (SAA).

See also **Application Program Interface; Systems Application Architecture.**

cps

characters per second, the number of characters that are transmitted every second during a data transfer.

CPU

Central Processing Unit, the part of a computer that processes data. This term typically refers to the computer's chassis and all its attached components.

cracker

An individual who attempts to gain unauthorized access into a network or computer system.

crash

A condition that occurs when a program unexpectedly stops because of a hardware failure or a software error. The computer must usually be restarted to recover from a crash, and unsaved work is usually lost.

CRC

cyclical redundancy check, an error-checking value. Every Ethernet frame includes a CRC to guarantee data integrity.
See also **Ethernet.**

Create right

A NetWare directory right or file right. An object Create right grants the user the right to create new objects in the Novell Directory Services (NDS) Directory tree. A File system Create right grants a user the right to create new files or subdirectories.

See also **Directory tree; Novell Directory Services.**

Creator code

A four-character code held by every Macintosh file. The Creator code identifies the application that created the file.

CREN

Corporation for Research and Educational Networking, a research organization concerned with the ongoing operation of the Internet.

 **For more information on CREN, log on to its Web site at** http://www.cren.net.

Crescendo

A line of plug-in products from LiveUpdate that allows files on a Netscape Navigator or Microsoft Internet Explorer Web browser to play Musical Instrument Digital Interface (MIDI) files.
See also **Internet Explorer; Netscape Navigator; Web browser.**

CRF

Cable Retransmission Facility, the starting point in a broadband network. End stations can transmit control and error information to the CRF, but not data.

crimper

A small tool for crimping the end of a cable to attach the cable to a connector.

critical error

A program error that causes an application to stop until the error condition is corrected.

critical path

A chain of links needed to accomplish a given task. Outlining a critical path may be useful in spotting where bottlenecks may occur.

Cross-Certificate Pair

A NetWare Directory Schema term and selectable property for the External Entity, List, Message-Routing Group, and Messaging Server objects in Novell Directory Services (NDS). Cross-Certificate Pair is a set of public keys that allows public-key verification to supersede the normal certification hierarchy.

See also **leaf object; Novell Directory Services; object.**

crosspost

Directing a single news article to more than one Usenet newsgroup by using a newsreader program.

See also **newsreader; Usenet.**

cross wye

A cable that switches from one wiring sequence to another, thereby changing the pin assignments of the incoming cable.

cross-connect device

A connection between a horizontal cable running from a machine, to the cable running to the network hub. A cross-connect is the connection that exists between two punch-down blocks.

See also **punch-down block.**

cross-referenced

A condition where items or topics may have related details in another text, and are so referenced.

crosstalk

Interference that exists when two wires are in physical proximity. *Far-end crosstalk (FEXT)* is interference in a wire at the receiving end of a signal sent on a different wire. *Near-end crosstalk (NEXT)* is interference in a wire at the transmitting end of a signal sent over a different wire.

CSA

Canadian Standards Association, a Canadian agency responsible for certifying that products comply with Canadian national safety standards.

For more information about the Canadian Standards Association, surf the Web to http://www.csa.com.

CSFS

Cable Signal Fault Signature, a unique signal used for testing a line's electrical activity when using time-domain reflectometry. The CSFS may assist a technician in pinpointing the source of a problem.

See also **time-domain reflectometry.**

CSLIP

Compressed Serial-Line Interface Protocol, a variant of the Serial-Line Interface Protocol (SLIP) that uses the Van Jacobsen compression strategy to compress packet headers. CSLIP is used to transmit Internet Protocol (IP) packets over serial line connections.

See also **Serial-Line Interface Protocol.**

CSMA/CA

Carrier-Sense Multiple-Access/Collision Avoidance, a media-access method that functions at the Media-Access Control (MAC) Sublayer of the OSI Reference Model and is used in Apple LocalTalk networks. Under the CSMA/CA process, before a node transmits on the network, it first listens for activity. If activity is detected, the node waits a random period of time before attempting again. CSMA/CA is *contentious;* the first node that tries to gain access to an unused network is the one allowed to transmit. CSMA/CA has no methods for assigning priority to data. In the event of a collision, LocalTalk passes the problem on to a higher-level protocol. Collision avoidance is less sophisticated than collision detection, and is, therefore, less expensive to build into a chip set.

See also **Carrier-Sense Multiple-Access/Collision Detection; Media-Access Control; OSI Reference Model.**

CSMA/CD

Carrier-Sense Multiple-Access/Collision Detect, a media-access protocol for dealing with the effects of packet collision. CSMA/CD is used in Ethernet and 802.3 networks, and functions on the Media Access Control (MAC) Sublayer of the OSI Reference Model. In the CSMA/CD model, a node first attempts to detect whether there is traffic on the network. If there is activity, the node waits a random period of time before attempting to transmit. If there is no activity, the node transmits. If two nodes transmit at precisely the same moment, a collision occurs. In the event of a collision, CSMA/CD discards the packets, causes the nodes to cancel their transmissions, and waits a random period of time before attempting to retransmit. CSMA/CD is *contentious;* the first node that tries to gain access to an unused network is allowed to transmit. CSMA/CD has no methods for assigning priority to data.

See also **Media-Access Control; OSI Reference Model.**

CS-MUX

Carrier-Switched Multiplexer, a component used in a Fiber Distributed Data Interface (FDDI) network to pass time-dependent data to the architecture's Media-Access Control (MAC) Layer.

See also **Fiber Distributed Data Interface; Media-Access Control; OSI Reference Model.**

CSNET

Computer Science Network, an internetwork consisting of universities, research institutions, and commercial concerns. CSNET merged with Because It's Time Network (BITNET) to form the Corporation for Research and Educational Networking (CREN).

See also **Because It's Time Network; Corporation for Research and Educational Networking.**

CSNP

Complete-Sequence-Number PDU, a Protocol Data Unit (PDU) sent by a designated router to an Open Shortest Path First (OSPF) network to maintain database synchronization.

See also **Open Shortest Path First; Protocol Data Unit.**

CSU

channel service unit, a Digital Signal Processor (DSP) that performs transmit-and-receive filtering, signal shaping, longitudinal balance, voltage isolation, equalization, and remote loopback testing for digital transmission. The CSU functions as a buffer between customer premises equipment (CPE) and the public carrier wide-area network (WAN), preventing a faulty CPE from affecting the public carrier's system. The CSU takes data from a Digital Data Service (DDS) line and hands it off to a Data Service Unit (DSU), which then interfaces with computer equipment. A CSU may be combined with a DSU to form a single Integrated-Service Unit (ISU).

See also **Digital Data Service; Digital Service Unit; Digital Signal Processor; Integrated-Service Unit; loopback testing.**

CTI

Computer-Telephone Integration, a technology that integrates telephone services into a computer to achieve greater productivity. CTI technology is often employed in customer service areas, and includes features such as caller ID and automatic dialing.

See also **automatic dialing; caller ID.**

Ctrl-Alt-Del

A combination of three keys (Ctrl, Alt, and Delete) that triggers a warm boot of IBM-compatible computers.

See also **warm boot.**

Ctrl-Break

A key combination (Ctrl and C) used to interrupt a process
See **Ctrl-C.**

Ctrl-C

A key combination (Ctrl and C) used to interrupt a process.

CTS

(1) Clear To Send, a control signal generated by data-communications hardware to indicate readiness transmit data. The CTS signal is usually sent in response to a Request To Send (RTS) signal issued by a node requesting to transmit data over the network. **(2) Conformance-Testing Service,** a series of programs that test how well a product implements a particular protocol as per specifications set by the International Standards Organization (ISO).

See also **(1) Request To Send; (2) International Standards Organization.**

CUA

Common User Access, in IBM Systems Application Architecture (SAA), a common set of specifications for user interfaces, providing a consistent look and feel for all applications and platforms.

See also **Systems Application Architecture.**

CUG

Closed User Group, a facility for configuring virtual private networks within a larger public network. A CUG allows an administrator to collect many Data-Terminal Equipment (DTE) devices into one logical group. That group's ability to receive or make outgoing calls can then be restricted.
See also **Data-Terminal Equipment.**

current context

The current position of an object in a Novell Directory Services (NDS) Directory tree.
See also **Directory tree; Novell Directory Services.**

current directory

The current position on the disk, used by the operating system to locate files. If the PROMPT PG command is added to the AUTOEXEC.BAT file, the command line displays the current directory.

current disk drive

The drive presently used by the operating system to locate files. The current disk drive letter is displayed in the system prompt.

Current Disk Requests

A field name in the Cache Utilization screen of the MONITOR NetWare Loadable Module (NLM), indicating the number of disk requests the server is waiting to service.
See also **MONITOR; NetWare Loadable Module.**

Current Licensed Connections

In NetWare 4.x and IntranetWare, an option from the MONITOR NetWare Loadable Module (NLM) screen that can be used by a network administrator to determine how many licensed connections are active. These connections count toward the limit on the NetWare license.
See also **MONITOR; NetWare Loadable Module.**

cursor coupling

In NetWare 3.x and NetWare 4.x, a feature of the Screen Handling Services that manages the server's logical screens, by specifying that the input and output cursors should occupy the same position.

cursor-movement keys

The arrow keys on a keyboard that control the cursor.

CU-SeeMe

A videoconferencing program enabling users to carry on real-time, video-enhanced conversations with other users. Originally released as freeware by Cornell University, commercial distribution is now handled by White Pine Software.

 **To find out more about CU-SeeMe, surf the Web to** http://www.wpine.com.

custom backup

A way of storing files in which only selected portions of files are archived. In a custom

backup, the *exclude* and *include* options
indicate what subsets to backup or restore.

Custom Device Module (CDM)

The driver component in the NetWare
Peripheral Architecture (NPA) that drives
the storage devices attached to a host
adapter bus.
    See also **host adapter bus; NetWare
Peripheral Architecture.**

Customer Information Control System (CICS)

A transaction-processing subsystem used on
IBM mainframes. CICS supports IBM's
Systems Network Architecture (SNA).
    See also **Systems Network Architecture.**

Customer Information Control System for Virtual Storage (CICS/VS)

A host program that runs on the IBM
System/370. This program can be used in a
communications network.

Customer Premises Equipment (CPE)

Hardware leased or owned by the customer,
and used at the customer's location.

CUT

Control Unit Terminal, an operating
mode for terminals that allows one session
per terminal.

cut-off wavelength

In single-mode fiber optics, the shortest
wavelength at which a signal takes a single
path through the core.

cut-through switching

A type of Token Ring switching in which
data is forwarded as soon as the first 20 to
30 bytes of a frame have been received.
These first few bytes contain the Media-
Access Control (MAC) Layer destination
address information, and must be received
before data is transmitted. After the header
has been read, a connection is established
between the input and output ports, and
transmission begins immediately. This technique significantly decreases latency, and
differs from *store-and-forward switching*
(which uses a buffering technique to receive
an entire frame into memory before forwarding). Cut-through switching is also
known as *on-the-fly switching*.
    See also **Media-Access Control;
Token Ring.**

CWIS

Campus-Wide Information System, an
online collection of information concerning
a particular school or campus. A CWIS may
contain information such as an events calendar, course listing, and job openings. CWISs
are often available over the Internet.

CX utility

In NetWare 4.*x* and IntranetWare, a workstation utility that changes context in the
Novell Directory Services (NDS) Directory

tree, or to view containers and leaf objects in a Directory tree structure. The CX command is similar to the DOS CD and DIR commands in that the CX utility changes contexts (in a manner similar to the changing of DOS directories) and allows a view of all objects below a given container (similar to viewing a DOS directory).

Cyberhub

A line of servers and Windows plug-ins from Black Sun Interactive that enables Web browsers to create and participate in simulated online worlds on the basis of the Virtual-Reality Modeling Language (VRML).
See also **Virtual-Reality Modeling Language; Web browser.**

Cyberjack

A suite of Internet tools from Delrina that includes a Web browser, links to Gopher and File-Transfer Protocol (FTP) sites, and general-purpose utilities (such as a file compression-decompression program).

cyberspace

A term describing information resources available through computer networks. The term was coined by William Gibson in his novel *Neuromancer*.

cycle (FDDI II)

In a Fiber Distributed Data Interface (FDDI) II network in hybrid mode, a 12,500-bit protocol data unit (packet). Such a cycle provides the framework for the FDDI

transmission. The cycle is repeated 8,000 times per second, generating a bandwidth of 100 megabits per second (Mbps) for the network. The cycle contains a *preamble* (which establishes synchronization), *cycle header* (which specifies how the cycle is used), *dedicated packet group* (used for packet control), and the *wideband channel* (used for the actual data transmission).
See also **Fiber Distributed Data Interface.**

cycle (periodic analog signal)

A complete repetition of a periodic analog signal. A cycle is the movement of a signal from its peak to its low point and back to the peak.

cyclical redundancy check (CRC)

An error-checking value. Every Ethernet frame includes a CRC to guarantee data integrity.
See also **Ethernet.**

cylinder

A group of concentric tracks on a hard disk that organizes data. The cylinders are numbered according to the tracks they reference.

D channel

A signaling channel in an Integrated-Services Digital Network (ISDN) connection. The D channel controls signals, and to send information about the call being placed. The D channel has a data rate of 16 kilobits per second (Kbps) in Basic-Rate Interface (BRI) ISDN, and 64Kbps for Primary Rate Interface (PRI).

See also **Basic-Rate Interface; Integrated-Services Digital Network; Primary Rate Interface.**

D-4 connector

A fiber-optic connector with a threaded coupling nut. The D-4 connector is used for single-mode or multimode fiber cable.

D4 framing

A method of identifying individual channels in a DS-1 channel. D4 framing combines twelve 193-bit frames into a single D4 superframe, such that each DS-1 channel comprises two D4 superframes. Every 193rd bit identifies the individual (DS-0) channels.

See also **DS-x.**

DA

Destination Address, the address in a packet header that identifies the recipient of that packet.

DAA

Data-Access Arrangement, a telephony device used to protect the public telephone network against user equipment that does not meet Federal Communications Commission (FCC) standards.

See also **Federal Communications Commission.**

DAC

(1) Digital-to-Analog Converter, a hardware device used to convert a digital signal to an analog signal.
(2) Dual-Attachment Concentrator, a concentrator used in an Fiber Distributed Data Interface (FDDI) to attach single-attachment stations or station clusters to the FDDI rings.

See also **(2) Fiber Distributed Data Interface.**

DACS

Digital Access and Cross-Connect System, In digital communications, a mechanism used to switch a 64 kilobit-per-second (Kbps) DS-0 channel from one T1 line to another.

See also **DS-x; T1.**

daemon

A background process capable of initializing other processes with little or no input from the user. Daemons typically provide services (such as printing or server advertising) in the UNIX environment. Other daemon processes may perform some administrative functions or access the host file system. On an IBM-compatible personal computer, a daemon typically runs from the CONFIG.SYS file at system startup, and need not be executed again.

daily full backup

A backup strategy that backs up all data on the network at the end of every day; each day's data occupies a separate tape.

daisy chain

A serial linkage among a series of components, as in bus-based networks. Devices may be daisy-chained if they are connected to a Small Computer System Interface (SCSI) adapter. Daisy-chaining is also known as *cascading*.

See also **bus network topology; cascading.**

DAL

Data-Access Language, an extension of the Structured Query Language (SQL) database language used in Macintosh-based client-server environments. DAL establishes a uniform level of access to any SQL-compliant database.

See also **Structured Query Language.**

DAL server

A server that uses Data-Access Language.

DAM

Data-Access Manager, a feature of the Macintosh System 7 operating system that accesses network databases by mediating between an application and the database it needs to access. DAM relies on database extensions to communicate with the database.

DAMA

Demand-Assigned Multiple Access, a way to allocate access to communications channels. Under a DAMA configuration, idle channels are combined in a pool. When a channel is requested, an idle channel is selected, given the requested bandwidth, and assigned to the requesting party.

DAN

departmental-area network, a network that services a single department. This terminology usually applies only to government agencies.

DAP

Directory-Access Protocol, an X.500 Directory Services protocol. The DAP establishes communications between a Directory User Agent (DUA) and a Directory System Agent (DSA).

See also **Directory System Agent: Directory User Agent; X.500.**

dark fiber

A fiber-optic cable that is not carrying a signal, or fiber-optic cable through which no light is transmitted.

DARPA

Defense Advanced Research Projects Agency, the United States government agency that funded the Advanced Research Projects Agency Network (ARPAnet). ARPAnet was a network of government agencies and universities that later became the Internet. DARPA was originally termed Advanced Research Projects Agency (ARPA), and is part of the United States Department of Defense (DoD).

See also **Advanced Research Projects Agency Network.**

DAS

(1) Disk Array Subsystem, the combination of cabling, circuitry, and the carriage required for using multiple hard disks.
(2) Dual-Attachment Station, in Fiber Distributed Data Interface (FDDI) networks, a station or node connected to both the primary and secondary rings. A station can be directly connected to the FDDI ring through a port on the DAS, with no concentrator required. A single-attachment station, on the other hand, must be attached to a concentrator.
(3) Dynamically Assigned Socket, an AppleTalk socket in the numeric range of 128 through 254. Values between 1 and 127 are retained for use by statically assigned sockets. The socket value is assigned to a particular client upon request. The socket is the entity used to facilitate communication between programs or processes. Any process running on a node can request a DAS value; while that process is executing, its assigned value cannot be employed by any other socket.

See also **(3) AppleTalk; (2) Fiber Distributed Data Interface.**

DASS

Distributed-Authentication Security Service, A system for authenticating users logging into a network from unattended

workstations. DASS relies on public-key encryption to provide security.

See also **public-key encryption system.**

DAT

Digital Audio Tape, a storage medium often used for network backups. Using the Data/DAT logical recording format (which supports random data reads and writes) DAT permits data to be updated in place. Modified data need not be rewritten to a new location. DAT is often deployed on a small audiotape cassette, most commonly a 4-millimeter tape in a helical-scan drive.

data

Any entity that conveys meaning. For example, computer data is stored as a series of electrical charges arranged in patterns that convey information.

Data-Access Arrangement (DAA)

A telephony device used to protect the public telephone network against user equipment that does not meet Federal Communications Commission (FCC) standards.

See also **Federal Communications Commission.**

Data-Access Language (DAL)

An extension of the Structured Query Language (SQL) database language used in Macintosh-based client-server environments. DAL establishes a uniform level of access to any SQL-compliant database.

See also **Structured Query Language.**

Data-Access Manager (DAM)

A feature of the Macintosh System 7 operating system that accesses network databases by mediating between an application and the database it needs to access. DAM relies on database extensions to communicate with the database.

data bit

The number of bits that defines a character on a serial data transmission. Usually this number is seven or eight. When connecting two computers by way of a COM port, the data-bit parameter must be set the same at both ends. In serial communications, information is sent in a stream of bits, or a *frame*. Each frame is made up of start bits, data bits, a parity bit, and stop bits. Whether the data-bit parameter is set to seven or eight depends on the parity bit, which can be set to zero or one.

See also **parity.**

data bus

The internal bus used by devices and system components to communicate with the central processing unit (CPU). The first personal computers used an Industry Standard Architecture (ISA) bus, which ran at 4.77 megahertz (MHz). The ISA bus was later extended to form the Extended Industry Standard Architecture (EISA). Other bus architectures include the proprietary IBM MicroChannel bus, Video Electronics Standards Association (VESA) bus, and Peripheral Component Interconnect (PCI) bus.

See also **Extended Industry-Standard Architecture; Industry-Standard**

Architecture; Peripheral-Component Interconnect; Video Electronics Standards Association.

Data-Carrier Detect (DCD)

A telecommunications signal in an RS-232 connection, asserted (or marked as True) if the modem detects a signal with a frequency that is appropriate for the modem being used.

data channel

A Systems Network Architecture (SNA) device that connects a processor and main storage with peripherals.

See also **Systems Network Architecture.**

Data-Circuit-Terminating Equipment (DCE)

A device associated with a single network port responsible for establishing, maintaining, and terminating a connection with Data-Terminal Equipment (DTE).

See also **Data-Terminal Equipment.**

data communications

The transmission of information electronically over a physical medium. The sender of the information encodes and transmits the data, and the recipient receives and decodes it. The data may be transmitted in any one of several different methods, including point-to-point, switched, broadcast, multicast, store-and-forward, time-division multiplexed, or frequency-division multiplexed.

See also **broadcast; multicast; multiplexing; point-to-point connection; store-and-forward.**

data-communications equipment (DCE)

Network equipment that establishes, maintains, and terminates a data-communications session. The DCE is connected to the Data-Terminal Equipment (DTE) located on the customer premises.

See also **Data-Terminal Equipment.**

data compression

A way to compress information for transfer over a communications link to facilitate a faster transfer. Data compression requires both peers to support a common compression methodology. Compression typically involves the elimination of redundant information. Compression may be based on patterns in bit sequences, patterns of occurrences of byte values, or commonly occurring words or phrases. *Lossless compression* allows all information to be recovered by the recipient. A *lossy compression* scheme discards less relevant data. A lossy scheme can achieve a much higher compression ratio.

See also **lossless compression; lossy compression.**

data connector (Type 1)

A connector used with Type 1 cable and used in Token Ring network wiring centers.
See also **Token Ring.**

Data-Definition Language (DDL)

A language that describes data and its relationships.

Data-Encryption Algorithm (DEA)

An algorithm that encrypts data for the Data-Encryption Standard (DES). This process divides a message into 64-bit blocks, each one of which is encrypted separately and one character at a time. Each character is scrambled 16 times during the encryption process, and the encryption method constantly changes. The key lays out the details of the scrambling process.
See also **Data-Encryption Standard.**

Data-Encryption Key (DEK)

A value that encrypts data. The Data-Encryption Algorithm uses the DEK to encode a message. The DEK can also decrypt the message once it has been received. Some encryption methods use a different key for encrypting and decrypting.
See also **decryption; encryption.**

Data-Encryption Standard (DES)

A standard encryption methodology that scrambles data into unintelligible code for safe transmission over a public network. DES relies on a 64-bit key and a private-key encryption methodology to convert text into encrypted form. The messages are divided into 64-bit blocks, which are encrypted separately using the Data-Encryption Algorithm (DEA). In this private key strategy, only the sender and receiver know the key used to encrypt the data. The encryption algorithm is publicly known. Although it is difficult to break the code, if an unauthorized individual learns the key, there is no way to prevent that individual from using it.

The DES can operate in one of the following four progressively complex modes: Electronic Cookbook (ECB), Cipher-Block

Chaining (CBC), Cipher Feedback (CFB), and Output Feedback (OFB). Under ECB, the encryption process is the same for each data block, and repeated patterns are always encoded in the same manner. CBC encrypts each block on the basis of the encryption of the previous block. CFB is still more complex, and dependent on pseudo-random values. The most complex, OFB, is similar to CFB, and is often used to encrypt satellite communications.

See also **Cipher-Block Chaining; Cipher Feedback; Electronic Cookbook; Output Feedback.**

Data-Exchange Interface (DXI)

An interface between a router and a Data Service Unit (DSU) that performs segmentation and reassembly.

data file

A file that contains information as opposed to executable code.

Data-Flow Control Layer (SNA model)

The fifth layer (Layer 5) of IBM's Systems Network Architecture (SNA) that defines the more general aspects of the connection. Methods used for recovering lost data execute in this layer, and the rules for packet acknowledgment are also specified here.

See also **Systems Network Architecture.**

data fork

Part of a Macintosh file that contains user-specified information. The data fork is one

of two parts of a Macintosh file, with the other one being the resource fork.

See also **resource fork.**

data link

The components and medium required to establish communications between two network workstations. The medium is generally comprised of fiber or wire, and the components are the transmission devices and receiving devices at both ends of the link.

Data-Link Connection Identifier (DLCI)

A 10-bit routing address used by the virtual circuit in a Frame Relay network. The DLCI is used at either the User-to-Network Interface (UNI) or the Network-Network Interface (NNI). With this identified, both user and network management platforms can identify a frame as originating from a particular Permanent Virtual Circuit (PVC). The DLCI multiplexes multiple PVCs over a single physical circuit.

See also **Frame Relay network; Network-Network Interface; User-to-Network Interface; Permanent Virtual Circuit.**

Data-Link Control (DLC)

A protocol in IBM's Systems Network Architecture (SNA) used to manage the physical connection and ensure that messages reach their destinations.

See also **Systems Network Architecture.**

Data-Link Control Layer

The second layer (Layer 2) of the seven-layer Systems Network Architecture (SNA) communications model that contains the link stations that schedule data transfer over a link between two nodes, and executes an error-control mechanism for that link. Furthermore, the Data-Link Control Layer defines the protocols that send data over the Physical Layer (Layer 1). Synchronous Data-Link Control (SDLC) is an example of a Data-Link Control Layer function.

See also **Synchronous Data-Link Control; Systems Network Architecture.**

Data-Link Layer (OSI model)

The second layer (Layer 2) in the seven-layer OSI Reference Model. The Data Link Layer packages and addresses data, and controls transmission flow over communication lines.

See also **OSI Reference Model.**

Data-Link Services (DLS)

The services provided at the second (Data-Link) Layer of the OSI Reference Model.

data migration

The transfer of inactive or infrequently used data to less-expensive storage media. Under NetWare, data migration moves data from the NetWare volume to tape, optical disc, or another near-line or off-line media. Although the data is physically located on this alternative media, the operating system still sees it as residing on the volume. The process of data migration frees up hard disk space for files that are more frequently accessed, while still giving users a way to access those files that are less frequently used.

Data-Network-Identification Code (DNIC)

A unique four-digit value assigned to public networks and public network services.

Data Over Voice (DOV)

A communications strategy for sending data over a voice channel at the same time a voice transmission is taking place.

data packet

A defined block that contains data and that also typically includes administrative information (such as addresses) in the packet header or footer. The structure of data packets may be more specifically defined for different protocols.

Data-Personal-Communications Services (Data-PCS)

A wireless communications service that was proposed by Apple Computer, and that involved requesting the Federal Communications Commission (FCC) to set aside a 40 megahertz (MHz) bandwidth in the 140MHz range between 1.85 and 1.99 gigahertz (GHz). The bandwidth would be used for wireless communications sent via radio waves.

See also **Federal Communications Commission.**

data processing (DP)

Processing typically done by minicomputers or mainframes in a data center.

data protection

A way to guarantee the safety of data on the network. NetWare offers data protection by keeping duplicate file directories, and by redirecting data from bad blocks to more reliable blocks on the hard disk. Although duplexing or mirroring may be one part of a data-protection scheme, by itself, either of these techniques are still inadequate and should be used along with a regular backup scheme. Mirroring stores duplicate copies of data on separate disks, but on the same controller channel. Duplexing, which is more reliable, stores duplicate data on separate disks on separate controller channels.

NetWare facilitates data protection by protecting information about where data is located. The operating system maintains duplicate copies of the hard disk's Directory-Entry Table (DET) and File-Allocation Table (FAT), which contain address information about where data can be stored or retrieved. In addition, data must be protected against physical surface defects. A NetWare hard disk stores data in blocks of 4K, 8K, 16K, 32K, or 64K. Storage blocks may occasionally fail. NetWare and other operating systems offer ways to prevent data from being written to bad blocks.

See also **Directory-Entry Table; File-Allocation Table.**

data rate

The speed at which data bits are sent and received. Data rate is usually measured in bits per second (bps). Usually, the data rate in bps is approximately equivalent to the baud rate divided by ten.

data reliability

Part of the NetWare System Fault Tolerance (SFT) features, which helps to protect the network data by guaranteeing that the data is read correctly, and is written to and stored on good media.

See also **System Fault Tolerance.**

data requester

A NetWare Loadable Module (NLM) that sends data between the backup engine and the Target Service Agent (TSA). The data requester is also known as *Storage-Management Data Requester* (SMDR).

See also **NetWare Loadable Module; Storage-Management Data Requester; TSA Resources.**

Data-Service Unit/Channel-Service Unit (DSU/CSU)

In a digital telecommunications network, two components of a Data-Communications Equipment (DCE) device that provide access to digital services over a variety of lines. The DSU connects to the Data-Terminal Equipment (DTE) through a synchronous serial interface, formats data for transmission, and controls data flow between the network and the CSU. The CSU terminates the long-distance connection at the user's end, processes digital signals, tests remote loopback, and functions as a buffer to prevent nonstandard customer-premises equipment from bringing down the public carrier's network.

See also **Data-Communications Equipment; Data-Terminal Equipment.**

data set

A term used by the telephone company to refer to a modem.

Data Set Ready (DSR)

A signal sent from a modem to indicate that the modem is ready to function.

data sink

The recipient of a data transmission.

data source

The sender of a data transmission.

Data-Stream Compatibility (DSC)

A minimal printing mode used in IBM's Systems Network Architecture (SNA).
See also **Systems Network Architecture.**

data switch

A location or physical device that routes data to a destination. In a switching network, a data switch groups data together and routes it on the basis of network traffic or other predetermined criteria.

Data-Switching Equipment (DSE)

Physical equipment used in a switching network.

Data-Terminal Equipment (DTE)

A network-attached, customer premises, or end-user hardware device that operates in packet mode and connects with the Data-Communications Equipment (DCE) to establish data communications.
See also **Data-Communications Equipment.**

Data Terminal Ready (DTR)

A signal from a modem indicating that a device is ready to send and receive data.

data transfer

Sending data between devices, such as from a storage device to a processor.

data transparency

A data-transmission strategy meant to guarantee that data is not misinterpreted as control signals. Any bit or byte sequence that could potentially be interpreted as a flag or command is modified before transmission, and then restored to its original sequence upon receipt.
See also **flag.**

Data Under Voice (DUV)

A telecommunications strategy for sending voice and data over the same line.

data warehousing

A method of storing large amounts of historical transaction processing data in a central location for subsequent analysis and reporting. The data warehouse is usually accessed with a multidimensional database product capable of examining raw data, spotting business and marketing trends, and generating comparative reports. The data warehouse can be quite large, sometimes in the multiple gigabytes, or in some cases, terabytes. The warehouse uses *metadata* (or information about data) to allow this large amount of information to be turned into something more meaningful. A variation of the data warehouse is the *data mart*, which separates the information into several different categories.

database

A set of one or more records or files compiled into a single type of structure or format. A database usually contains indexed files or records that pertain to a related subject or given application, and allows single or multiple users to accept, store, and provide data. The records of a database can be accessed, edited, or retrieved by way of a query language, such as Structured Query Language (SQL).

A *flat-file database* holds all information in a single file that contains individual records. The records are not organized in any meaningful way; instead, a lookup table is used to find and manipulate the flat-file records. A *relational database*, on the other hand, organizes data as a set of tables, with rows representing records and columns representing individual fields. A newer type of database, an *object-oriented database*, organizes information into objects, each of which contains properties and specifies allowable operations. Other types of databases include an *inverted-list database*, *hierarchical database*, *network database*, and *distributed database*.

See also **Structured Query Language.**

database-management system (DBMS)

A software application that controls data in a database. The DBMS organizes, stores, and retrieves data; as well as to apply security and data integrity to the database. A DBMS typically includes features for reporting, importing and exporting data from external applications, and a data-manipulation language used to query the database.

database model

A method used by a database-management system. The database model organizes the structure of the database.

database server

A database application that follows the client-server model. The application is divided into a *front end* that runs on the user workstation, and a *back end* that runs on a server or host. The front end interacts with the user, collects data, and displays data to the end-user. The back end performs compute-intensive tasks (such as data analysis and manipulation).

database TSA

A NetWare database Target Service Agent (TSA) that sends commands and data between the host server (where the NetWare SBACKUP utility resides) and the database (where the data to be backed up resides).

See also **Storage-Management Services; Target Service Agent.**

Data-Compression Protocol

A set of rules and methodologies that compress data before transmission.

data-encoding scheme

A method used by a hard-disk controller to store information on a hard or floppy disk.

data-grade cable

Twisted-pair cable that can be used for data transmission. Data-grade cable encompasses Categories 2, 3, 4, and 5.
See also **cable.**

datagram

A packet containing information and address information. The datagram is a type of packet routed through a packet-switching network. The information, or data, held by the datagram is referred to as the *payload*, and the addressing information is usually contained in a header. Because datagrams hold address information, they do not need to arrive in consecutive order. Datagrams are common to connectionless transmission mechanisms.

Datagram-Delivery Protocol (DDP)

An AppleTalk protocol that establishes a best-effort, socket-to-socket delivery service for sending datagrams across an AppleTalk internetwork. DDP operates at the Network Layer (Layer 3) of the OSI Reference Model, and prepares data packets for sending on through the network medium.
See also **AppleTalk protocols; OSI Reference Model.**

Datakit VCS

AT&T's data-switch device that can be linked to X.25 networks, and that offers communications channels ranging from 9.6

kilobits per second (Kbps) to 8 megabits per second (Mbps).
See also **X.25.**

DATANET I

A packet-switched network located in the Netherlands.

DATAPAC

A packet-switched network located in Canada.

Data-PCS

Data-Personal-Communications Services, a wireless communications service that was proposed by Apple Computer, and that involved requesting the Federal Communications Commission (FCC) to set aside a 40 megahertz (MHz) bandwidth in the 140 MHz range between 1.85 and 1.99 gigahertz (GHz). The bandwidth would be used for wireless communications sent via radio waves.
See also **Federal Communications Commission.**

Dataphone Digital Service (DDS)

A four-wire digital communications service from AT&T that operates at speeds ranging from 2,400 bits per second (bps) to 56 kilobits per second (Kbps) over a point-to-point connection. No modem is required, but a Data-Service Unit/Channel-Service Unit (DSU/CSU) is needed at the interface between the digital lines and the customer equipment. DDS is often used to establish a point-to-point link in a wide-area network (WAN).

See also **Data-Service Unit/Channel-Service Unit.**

dataset

A collection of data collected by a software agent, generally relative to a particular network function or device. NetWare further defines a dataset as manipulable by the SBACKUP utility. A dataset can contain different items or records, depending on the Target Service Agent (TSA) to which it is related.

See also **SBACKUP utility; Target Service Agent.**

Date Password Expires

A Directory Schema term in Novell Directory Services (NDS).

See also **Novell Directory Services.**

Datex-l

A public circuit-switched network located in Germany.

Datex-p

A public packet-switched network located in Germany.

daylight-saving time (DST)

The practice of setting clocks an hour ahead to provide an extra hour of daylight at the end of workdays during spring, summer, and fall.

Days Between Forced Changes

A Directory Schema term and selectable property for the User object in Novell Directory Services (NDS). In NetWare networks that require periodic password changes for security purposes, the Days Between Forced Changes parameter can be changed by entering a new value.

See also **leaf object; Novell Directory Services; object.**

DBMS

database-management system, a software application that controls data in a database. The DBMS organizes, stores, and retrieves data; as well as to apply security and data integrity to the database. A DBMS typically includes features for reporting, importing and exporting data from external applications, and a data-manipulation language used to query the database.

DBS

direct-broadcast satellite, a satellite that broadcasts signals directly to subscribers without having to go through a central station first.

DC

Direct Current, electrical power that travels only in one direction, often used in batteries and electronic components.

See also **Alternating Current.**

DC-2000

A quarter-inch tape cartridge used in tape backup systems. The DC-2000 can store up to 250MB of compressed data.

DCA

(1) Defense Communications Agency, a United States government organization responsible for Defense Data Networks (DDNs) such as MILnet.

(2) Document-Content Architecture, a data-stream architecture defined by IBM, used in text documents, and consisting of three standard formats. The *Revisable-Form Text* (RFT) format is used for text that can still be edited; the *Final-Form Text* (FFT) standard is used for text that has already been formatted for a given output device and can no longer be edited; and the *Mixed-Form Text* (MFT) format applies to documents that may contain graphics or other types of data in addition to text.

See also **(1) MILnet.**

DCB

disk coprocessor board, an intelligent board that functions as an interface between the host microprocessor and the disk controller. This board can increase performance by relieving the host microprocessor of data storage and retrieval tasks. The DCB has been replaced by a Host Bus Adapter (HBA) in newer versions of NetWare.

See also **Host Bus Adapter.**

DCD

Data-Carrier Detect, a telecommunications signal in an RS-232 connection, asserted (or marked as True) if the modem detects a signal with a frequency that is appropriate for the modem being used.

DCDB file

Domain-Control Database, an IBM file associated with the LAN Manager and LAN Server applications.

See also **LAN Manager; LAN Server.**

DCE

(1) Data-Communications Equipment, network equipment that establishes, maintains, and terminates a data-communications session. The DCE is connected to the Data-Terminal Equipment (DTE) located on the customer premises.

(2) Data-Circuit-Terminating Equipment, a device associated with a single network port responsible for establishing, maintaining, and terminating a connection with Data-Terminal Equipment (DTE).

(3) Distributed Computing Environment, an open networking architecture designed by the Open Software Foundation (OSF). The OSF is a consortium of vendors that includes Digital Equipment Corporation, Hewlett-Packard, and IBM. DCE provides all of the elements needed to distribute applications and their functions across a network transparently. Under the DCE model, the network would appear to the end-user as a single entity. This makes all of the network's resources transparently available to every user.

See also **(1) and (2) Data-Terminal Equipment.**

DCS

(1) Defined Context Set, a Consultative Committee for International Telegraphy and Telephony (CCITT) X.216 recommendation that establishes a context for the delivery and usage of services on the Presentation Layer (Layer 6) of the OSI Reference Model (2) **Digital Cross-Connect System**, in digital telephony, a switch that to switches a digital channel from one device to another by cross-connecting the digital channels. The cross-connection takes place at the slowest rate common to the two lines involved.

See also (1) **Consultative Committee for International Telegraphy and Telephony**; (1) **OSI Reference Model.**

DDB

Distributed Database, a database that provides services to all network applications and users over different platforms. The distributed database may be stored on different hard disks in different locations.

DDBMS

Distributed Database-Management System, the software used to reference a distributed database.

DDCMP

Digital Data-Communications Message Protocol, a byte-oriented, link-layer synchronous protocol designed by Digital Equipment Corporation as the primary data-link component in DECnet.

See also **DECnet.**

DDD

direct distance dialing, dialing a long-distance number without going through an operator.

DDE

Dynamic Data Exchange, a technique used for application-to-application communications, available on the Microsoft Windows, Macintosh System 7, and OS/2 operating systems. Two DDE-compliant applications can exchange data and commands by DDE conversations, or two-way connections that take place between the applications. A DDE conversation does not require any user intervention. DDE has been superseded by Object Linking and Embedding (OLE).

See also **Object Linking and Embedding.**

DDL

Data-Definition Language, a language that describes data and its relationships.

DDM

Distributed Data Management, a service of IBM's Systems Network Architecture (SNA) used to allow file sharing and remote file access in the network.

See also **Systems Network Architecture.**

DDN

Defense Data Network, the network that connects military installations. The DDN encompasses MILnet and Advanced Research Projects Agency Network (ARPAnet), and the Transmission-Control Protocol/Internet Protocol (TCP/IP) protocols they employ.

See also **Advanced Research Projects Agency Network; MILnet.**

DDN NIC

Defense-Data-Network Network Information Center, the control center of the Defense Data Network (DDN). The DDN is a global network used by the United States Department of Defense, part of which is accessible through the Internet and part of which is classified. The DDN NIC provides information and services through the Internet. Its functions include assigning numbers to domains, assigning IP network addresses, and functioning as a repository for Requests for Comments concerning the Internet community.

See also **IP address; Request for Comments.**

 **For more information about the Defense-Data-Network Network Information Center, surf the Web to** `http://rs.internic.net/nsf/nis/sectionL.html.`

DDP

(1) Datagram-Delivery Protocol, an AppleTalk protocol that establishes a best-effort, socket-to-socket delivery service for sending datagrams across an AppleTalk internetwork. DDP operates at the Network Layer (Layer 3) of the OSI Reference Model, and prepares data packets for sending on through the network medium.

(2) Distributed Data Processing, a way of processing data where the work is distributed across multiple computers.

See also **(1) AppleTalk protocols; (1) OSI Reference Model.**

DDS

(1) Dataphone Digital Service, a four-wire digital communications service from AT&T that operates at speeds ranging from 2,400 bits per second (bps) to 56 kilobits per second (Kbps) over a point-to-point connection. No modem is required, but a Data-Service Unit/Channel-Service Unit (DSU/CSU) is needed at the interface between the digital lines and the customer equipment. DDS is often used to establish a point-to-point link in a wide-area network (WAN).

(2) Digital Data Service, leased lines that can accommodate a transmission rate of between 2.4 kilobits per second (Kbps) and 56 Kbps.

See also **(1) Data Service Unit/Channel Service Unit.**

DE

Discard Eligibility, a Frame Relay network term. The DE bit is set by an end node to indicate that certain frames can be discarded in the event of network congestion.

See also **Frame Relay network.**

de facto standard

A standard that has come about through widespread usage, instead of through an official standards organization.

de jure standard

A standard that has come about through the formal processes of an official standards organization.

DEA

Data-Encryption Algorithm, an algorithm that encrypts data for the Data-Encryption Standard (DES). This process divides a message into 64-bit blocks, each one of which is encrypted separately and one character at a time. Each character is scrambled 16 times during the encryption process, and the encryption method constantly changes. The key lays out the details of the scrambling process.

See also **Data-Encryption Standard.**

deadlock

A condition that occurs when multiple network nodes are waiting for messages from each other and cannot continue processing. Deadlock can also occur when multiple applications are attempting to lock the same files at the same time. Deadlock can be alleviated either by ending the transaction or by releasing the record locks.

debug screen

A troubleshooting screen, accessible from an assembly or C program with a special key sequence. The screen is usually hidden unless the file server is at a breakpoint.

debugger

A program utility used by application developers to identify problems in program code.

DEC Alpha

A 64-bit, Reduced-Instruction-Set-Computing (RISC)-based computer system from Digital Equipment Corporation. The DEC Alpha was introduced in 1992, and uses a superscalar design that allows the processor to execute more than one instruction for each clock cycle. The Alpha can be used in symmetrical multiprocessing environments. The Alpha chip is deployed in both workstations and servers. The most recent iteration of the Alpha chip, the 21164, can run at speeds of up to 500 megahertz (MHz), and supports the Digital UNIX, Windows NT, and OpenVMS operating systems.

DEC Management-Control Center (DECmcc)

The network-management software used in Digital Equipment Corporation's DECnet networks.

See also **DECnet.**

decentralized network

A distributed network.

decibel (dB)

One-tenth of a bel. A decibel is a logarithmic unit of measurement that indicates a signal's intensity.

See also **bel.**

decimal

A base-10 numbering system that uses the numbers zero through nine.

DECmcc

DEC Management-Control Center, the network-management software used in

Digital Equipment Corporation's DECnet networks.

See also **DECnet.**

DECnet

Digital Equipment Corporation's set of proprietary networking protocols. DECnet is used in Digital's VAX line of computers to exchange messages and data. The newest DECnet implementation, DECnet Phase V, merges itself with the standard OSI protocols in an attempt to establish interoperability with any other OSI-compliant network code. Phase IV, which was introduced in 1982, roughly corresponded to the OSI Reference Model. The eight layers of DECnet Phase IV were: Physical, Data-Link, Routing, End-to-End Communications,

Session Control, Network Application, Network-Management, and User. DECnet Phase V was introduced to comply more rigorously to the seven-layer OSI Reference Model.

Figure D.1 compares DECnet Phase IV and Phase V to the OSI Reference Model. *See also* **OSI Reference Model.**

decryption

The act of unscrambling or decoding encrypted data.

dedicated circuit

A circuit that connects a user's location directly to a telephone company's point of presence.

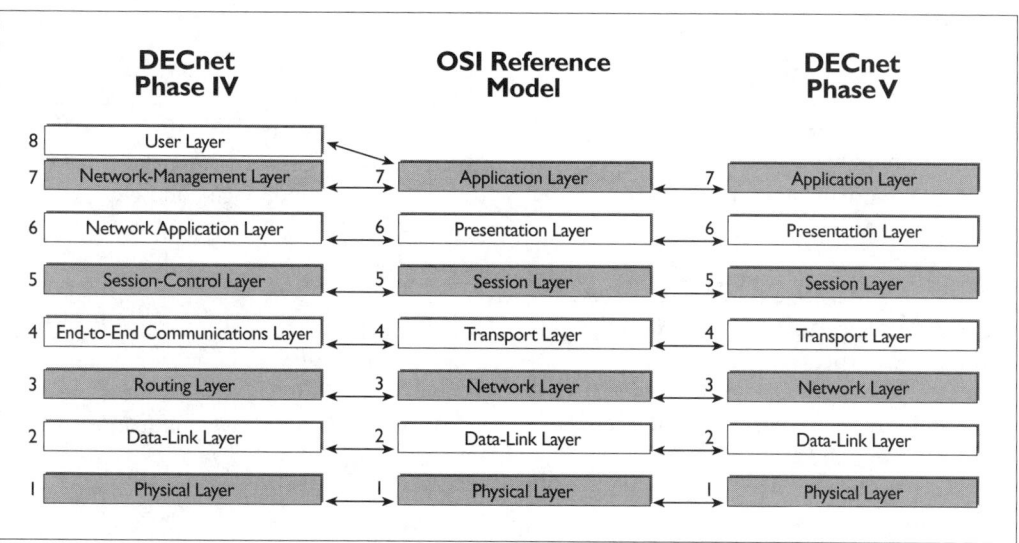

Figure D.1
DECnet Phase IV, Phase V, and the OSI Reference Model

dedicated line

A leased or private communications line. A dedicated line, as a permanent connection between two points, is always available. Types of dedicated line services include Dataphone Digital Services, 56/64 Kbps lines, fractional T1 lines, and T1/E1 lines.
See also **T1.**

dedicated router

A device whose sole function is to operate as a router. A dedicated router cannot function as a workstation or a server at the same time, and is considered more reliable. For example, if a workstation is also functioning as a router, an application on the workstation could hang — causing the router function to stop operating.
See also **nondedicated router.**

dedicated server

A network computer that functions solely as a server. The dedicated server performs tasks such as storing files, printing, and managing communications.
See also **nondedicated server.**

Dedicated Token Ring (DTR)

A Token Ring specification outlined in the Institute of Electrical and Electronic Engineers (IEEE) 802.5r specification that allows full-duplex connections, and establishes a connection speed of up to 32 megabits per second (Mbps). By enabling full-duplex communications, the token-passing mechanism is bypassed and communication can take place between a device and a switch port at any time.

See also **full duplex; IEEE 802.***x***;**
Token Ring.

DeepV

A World Wide Web (WWW) Windows browser plug-in from Hands Off that displays three-dimensional images in a compact format.

default

A preset option or value usually meant to accommodate the most common configuration used by the most users. Defaults can usually be changed by users to reflect a new value.

default directory

A standard directory created and used by an operating system or by an application.

default drive

The drive a workstation uses after initial startup or login. On a network, the default drive is assigned upon login, and is identified by the drive prompt.

default login script

A script containing very basic commands such as drive mappings. This script is pre-coded into the LOGIN.EXE command, and cannot be edited. Users may, however, choose to write an alternative login script that supersedes the default login script.
See also **login script.**

default path

A path used by a router to send a packet when the packet does not contain any routing instructions, and the router does not have a predefined path. The default path usually sends the packet to another router that has more detailed routing information.

See also **packet; router.**

Default Profile

A selectable property of the User object in Novell Directory Services (NDS).

See also **leaf object; Novell Directory Services; object.**

Default Queue

A Directory Schema term and selectable property for the Printer object in Novell Directory Services (NDS). The Default Queue is the queue specified in the current print job's configuration. All print jobs are automatically sent to the default queue unless the user specifies otherwise.

See also **leaf object; Novell Directory Services; object.**

default route

An entry in a routing table that can redirect frames for which a next hop has not been explicitly listed in the table.

Default Server

A Directory Schema term and a selectable property for the User object in Novell Directory Services (NDS). The default server is the server to which a user attaches upon

login, and is specified in the NET.CFG file in NetWare. For IntranetWare Windows 95 and Windows NT clients, the default server can be specified in the network properties.

See also **leaf object; NET.CFG; Novell Directory Services; object.**

default value

A preset value used for a parameter or other type of setting. The default value is usually meant to accommodate the most common configuration used by the most users. Default values can usually be changed by users to reflect a new value.

default zone

The zone to which a device belongs in an AppleTalk Phase 2 network until it has been assigned to a specific zone. If no default zone has been defined, the first zone name on the zone list becomes the default zone. Every zone list has a default zone.

See also **AppleTalk Phase 2.**

Defense Advanced Research Projects Agency (DARPA)

The United States government agency that funded the Advanced Research Projects Agency Network (ARPAnet). ARPAnet was a network of government agencies and universities that later became the Internet. DARPA was originally termed Advanced Research Projects Agency (ARPA), and is part of the United States Department of Defense (DoD).

See also **Advanced Research Projects Agency Network.**

Defense Communications Agency (DCA)

A United States government organization responsible for Defense Data Networks (DDNs) such as MILnet.

See also **MILnet.**

Defense Data Network (DDN)

The network that connects military installations. The DDN encompasses MILnet and Advanced Research Projects Agency Network (ARPAnet), and the Transmission Control Protocol/Internet Protocol (TCP/IP) protocols they employ.

See also **Advanced Research Projects Agency Network; MILnet.**

Defense-Data-Network Network Information Center (DDN NIC)

The control center of the Defense Data Network (DDN). The DDN is a global network used by the United States Department of Defense, part of which is accessible through the Internet and part of which is classified. The DDN NIC provides information and services through the Internet. Its functions include assigning numbers to domains, assigning IP network addresses, and functioning as a repository for Requests for Comments concerning the Internet community.

See also **Appendix F; IP address; Request for Comments.**

For more information about the Defense-Data-Network Network Information Center, surf the Web to http://rs.internic.net/ nsf/nis/sectionL.html.

deferral time

A specification of the Carrier-Sense Multiple-Access (CSMA) media-access method the period of time a node waits before attempting to access the network after a packet collision. The deferral time depends on a random number and on the network's level of activity.

See also **Carrier-Sense Multiple-Access/Collision Detect.**

Deferred Procedure Call (DPC)

A condition in effect when Windows NT or Windows NT Advanced Server calls a task that is less important than the function currently executing. Consequently, execution of the called function is delayed until the higher-priority functions are completed.

Defined Context Set (DCS)

A Consultative Committee for International Telegraphy and Telephony (CCITT) X.216 recommendation that establishes a context for the delivery and usage of services on the Presentation Layer (Layer 6) of the OSI Reference Model.

See also **Consultative Committee for International Telegraphy and Telephony; OSI Reference Model.**

definition file

A file that contains linking information about a NetWare Loadable Module (NLM). The definition file may contain the names of the object files to link, and the name of the executable to create. This file includes a set of keywords for directing the NetWare linker as it creates the executable.

See also **NetWare Loadable Module.**

defragmentation

Reorganizing and rewriting files so that they occupy a large, contiguous area on a disk instead of multiple smaller areas. When a file is continuously updated over a period of time, the file may be written into different areas of the disk. This fragmentation of files can lead to delays in loading the file. Defragmentation consolidates the file fragments into a contiguous area, and allows for faster access.

See also **fragmentation.**

defragmenter

A software utility that rewrites files so that they occupy a large, contiguous area on a disk instead of multiple smaller areas. A defragmenter can improve performance that has been lost because of fragmentation.

See also **fragmentation.**

DEK

Data-Encryption Key, a value that encrypts data. The Data-Encryption Algorithm uses the DEK to encode a message. The DEK can also decrypt the message once it has been received. Some encryption methods use a different key for encrypting and decrypting.

See also **decryption; encryption.**

delay

The time required to send a byte of data from one system to another. Delay is usually measured in microseconds.

delay distortion

Signal distortion caused by the relative difference in speed of the various components of that signal.

delete

Removing a file from a disk, or an item from a file. File deletion can be done through operating system commands or directly from some applications. When a file is deleted, it is not immediately removed from the disk, which allows for the possibility of recovering a deleted file if it was deleted accidentally.

Delete Inhibit (Di) attribute

A selectable NetWare file system attribute. This attribute prohibits users from erasing a particular directory or file, even if that user has the Erase right. A file that has been assigned the Delete Inhibit attribute cannot be deleted by any user, including the owner of the file or the system supervisor.

See also **attribute.**

Delete right

An object right in Novell Directory Services (NDS) that provides a user with the privilege of deleting a particular object from the Directory tree. A container object cannot be deleted unless the objects within the container are deleted first. Furthermore, the Write right for existing object properties must also be granted before objects can be deleted.

See also **container object; Novell Directory Services; Write right.**

Delete Self right

A property right in Novell Directory Services (NDS) that provides a trustee with the privilege of removing itself as a value of the property. The Delete Self right is used only for properties for which the User object can be listed as a value.

See also **leaf object; Novell Directory Services; object; trustee rights.**

DELETED.SAV directory

A hidden Novell NetWare directory located on the SYS volume used as a temporary place to store deleted (but not purged) directories. Deleted files and directories can be recovered through this directory, using the NetWare 3.*x* SALVAGE utility or the NetWare 4.*x* FILER utility.

See also **FILER utility; SALVAGE utility.**

delimiter

A symbol or other character that indicates that a command, command parameter, or data field has begun or ended. A delimiter is commonly represented as a comma (,), period (.), slash (/), backslash (\), hyphen (-), or colon (:).

delivery-confirmation bit

A component of a user packet that acknowledges receipt of a complete packet sequence. The deliver confirmation bit can be set to one to indicate that an acknowledgment is sent from the recipient to the sender. The delivery confirmation bit is also known as the *D-bit*.

Delphi Internet

A commercial online service that offers access to the Internet, electronic mail (e-mail), File Transfer Protocol (FTP), and Telnet services.

See also **electronic mail; File Transfer Protocol; Telnet.**

 **For more information about Delphi Internet, surf the Web to** `http://www.delphi.com`.

Demand-Assigned Multiple Access (DAMA)

A way to allocate access to communications channels. Under a DAMA configuration, idle channels are combined in a pool. When a channel is requested, an idle channel is selected, given the requested bandwidth, and assigned to the requesting party.

demand paging

A type of virtual memory management that reads pages of information into memory from disk as they are needed by a program.

demand priority

The media-access method used in 100BaseVG, a 100 Mbps networking implementation similar to Ethernet but originally designed by Hewlett-Packard. The demand priority scheme differs from the Carrier-Sense Multiple-Access/Collision Detection (CSMA/CD) method used in Institute of Electrical and Electronic Engineers (IEEE) 802.3 Ethernet, in that packet collisions are avoided by using the hub for controlling network access. Because network access centers around the hub, a 100BaseVG network must be deployed in a star topology.

Whereas CSMA/CD is a contentious methodology in which packets collide and are re-sent, demand priority guarantees each node access to the network at regular intervals. The network hub polls all active ports. When a node requests permission from the hub to send data, the hub allows it to send one frame and then moves on to the next port to repeat the process. A node can mark its data as high priority, and the hub immediately gives that node access to the network.

Demand priority avoids the possibility of standard priority packets getting constantly left behind, however, by keeping track of access requests. If standard priority packets are waiting too long for network access, the hub automatically upgrades those packets to high priority. Under this mechanism, nodes that do not need to transmit are left alone, and do not have to generate overhead by passing tokens or being polled. Furthermore, packet collisions are avoided because only one node can access the network segment at a time.

See also **100BaseVG; Carrier-Sense Multiple-Access/Collision Detection; hub; IEEE 802.*x*.**

Demand-Protocol Architecture (DPA)

A feature of Microsoft's LAN Manager network operating system that makes it possible to load or unload protocol stacks dynamically. DPA makes it possible to support multiple network environments in the same machine.

See also **LAN Manager.**

demarcation point

The point at which the customer-premises equipment (CPE) ends and the telephone company's equipment begins.

demodulation

The process of recovering data from a previously modulated carrier frequency. Demodulation is accomplished by converting analog signals into digital signals.

See also **modem.**

demultiplexer

A hardware device that separates multiplexed material sent from a single input into discrete elements. The demultiplexer then sends these elements to multiple output paths.

See also **multiplexing.**

de-ossification

The process of converting definitions that conform to the OSI Network-Management Model into definitions that conform to the Internet Protocol (IP) network-management model.

See also **OSI Network-Management Model.**

Department

A Directory Schema term in Novell Directory Services (NDS).

See also **Novell Directory Services.**

Department of Defense (DoD)

The United States governmental agency that has been responsible for funding and development of communications protocols.

departmental LAN

A small or medium-sized local-area network (LAN) of as many as about 30 users. The nodes on the departmental LAN all share local resources.

departmental-area network (DAN)

A network that services a single department. This terminology usually applies only to government agencies.

dependent LU

A Logical Unit (LU) that has an active session to an LU within the Systems Network Architecture (SNA) host system. The dependent LU is unable to send BINDS.

See also **Systems Network Architecture.**

DES

Data-Encryption Standard, a standard encryption methodology that scrambles data into unintelligible code for safe transmission over a public network. DES relies on a 64-bit key and a private-key encryption methodology to convert text into encrypted form. The messages are divided into 64-bit blocks, which are encrypted separately using the Data Encryption Algorithm (DEA). In this private key strategy, only the sender and receiver know the key used to encrypt the data. The encryption algorithm is publicly known. Although it is difficult to break the code, if an unauthorized individual learns the key, there is no way to prevent that individual from using it.

The DES can operate in one of the following four progressively complex modes: Electronic Cookbook (ECB), Cipher-Block Chaining (CBC), Cipher Feedback (CFB), and Output Feedback (OFB). Under ECB, the encryption process is the same for each data block, and repeated patterns are always encoded in the same manner. CBC encrypts each block on the basis of the encryption of the previous block. CFB is still more complex, and dependent on pseudo-random values. The most complex, OFB, is similar to CFB, and is often used to encrypt satellite communications.

See also **Cipher-Block Chaining; Cipher Feedback; Electronic Cookbook; Output Feedback.**

Description

A Directory Schema term and selectable property for the AFP Server, Bindery Queue, Computer, Country, Directory Map, External Entity, Group, List, Message-Routing Group, Messaging Server, Organization, Organizational Role, Organizational Unit, Print Server, Printer, Profile, Queue, User, and Volume objects in Novell Directory Services (NDS). Description is an optional attribute of the NDS Schema that may be used; for example, to contain the full name of the country, the Country Name attribute can contain only a two-letter code.

See also **container object; leaf object; Novell Directory Services; object.**

description file

An American Standard Code for Information Interchange (ASCII) file used by the CREATE, INDEX, and SINDEX Maintenance utility commands in NetWare.

designated router

A NetWare Link-Services Protocol (NLSP) router responsible for exchanges of link state information between all other NLSP routers on the local-area network (LAN). The designated router is the router with the highest priority.

In Open Shortest Path First (OSPF) protocol networks, a router that generates a link state advertisement for a multiaccess network, and reduces the number of adjacencies required on a multiaccess network.

See also **NetWare Link-Services Protocol; Open Shortest Path First.**

desk accessory

A small application that can be selected from the Apple operating system menu while within another application. Examples of desk accessories are the Macintosh Calculator, Scrapbook, and Chooser.

desktop

Generically, a workstation that resides on a user's desk. In the Apple Macintosh and Microsoft Windows environments, the term refers to the interface that shows a graphical representation of files and programs that are located on the workstation.

desktop computer

A small, microprocessor-based computer system that usually sits on a desktop. A desktop computer is also called a *microcomputer* or *personal computer*.

desktop database

A database maintained by the server in an AppleTalk network. This database holds information that associates files with icons, and documents with applications. Under the AppleTalk Filing Protocol (ATFP), every server must maintain a desktop database.

See also **AppleTalk; AppleTalk Filing Protocol.**

Desktop-Management Interface (DMI)

A standard, supported by several vendors, used to automate the process of identifying a personal computer (both hardware and software) to the network. No user intervention is required. The DMI identifies information about any personal computer component, including manufacturer, component name, version, serial number, and installation date and time.

Destination Address (DA)

The address in a packet header that identifies the recipient of that packet.

Destination ID (DID)

The address of a destination node in an Attached-Resource Computer Network (ARCnet) packet.

See also **Attached-Resource Computer Network.**

destination node

Under the OSI Reference Model, a node that represents the host computers at each end of a connection. In a packet-switching network, the destination node is the node attached to the Data-Terminal Equipment (DTE).

See also **Data-Terminal Equipment; OSI Reference Model.**

destination server

The NetWare 4.*x* server to which data files, bindery files, and other data are migrated during an upgrade from a server running an earlier version of the operating system.

destructive test

A surface test that functions as a disk format, destroying data and making multiple passes over the disk surface for the purpose of reading and writing test patterns.

DET

Directory-Entry Table, a table located on a network volume that contains information about files, directories, directory trustees, or other directory entries for the particular volume on which it is located. The directory table may occupy one or more blocks on the volume; each block contains 4K of data and can hold 128 directory entries (each 32 bytes long).

detail

A FLAG option that offers a view of file or directory details.

Details dialog box

A dialog box from the NetWare Administrator utility that appears when the user double-clicks on an object. It can also be found by selecting Details from the File menu after selecting an object. The dialog box shows the Novell Directory Services (NDS) properties of an object.

See also **NetWare Administrator; Novell Directory Services; object.**

Detect Intruder

A selectable property for the Organization and Organizational Unit objects of Novell Directory Services (NDS). Detect Intruder is an optional password restriction used to detect an intruder who is attempting to use someone else's account without using the proper password. If this property has been selected, the user account makes a record of all attempts to log in with an incorrect password.

See also **container object; Novell Directory Services; object.**

developer environment

A complete set of tools that allows a programmer to create a computer program. The developer environment includes a programming language, and other components such as a compiler, debugger, text editor, and code libraries.

device

Any hardware attached to a computer, such as a printer, mouse, or Network Interface Card (NIC).

See also **Network Interface Card.**

Device

A Directory Schema term and selectable property for the Bindery Queue and Queue objects of Novell Directory Services (NDS).

See also **leaf object; Novell Directory Services; object.**

device dependence

A requirement that a specific device be present before a program can function.

device driver

A software program (or firmware) that establishes an interface between the operating system and a peripheral device, and controls the software routines that make the peripherals work. NetWare uses two types of device drivers: disk drivers, and NetWare Peripheral Architecture (NPA) drivers. *Disk drivers* establish an interface with the adapter that connects to a disk drive by an internal cable. NetWare's Media Manager uses the *NPA drivers* — also known as Host Adapter Modules (HAMs) or Custom Device Modules (CDMs) — to track storage devices and media. HAMs establish an interface with the host adapter; the CDM drives the storage devices attached to the host adapter.

See also **Media Manager; NetWare Peripheral Architecture; NMAGENT utility.**

device independence

The ability to produce similar results across multiple environments, without having to have specific hardware. For example, UNIX is *device-independent* because it can run on a wide range of computer platforms.

Device-Independent Backup Interface (DIBI)

An interface meant to simplify the process of moving backed-up data from one environment to another on the same network.

device name

A name used by the operating system to identify a peripheral or other component.

device numbering

A way to identify devices that may entail three different numbering schemes: the physical address, device code, or the logical device number. The drive establishes the *physical address* when it reads the address set by jumpers (or by software-based configuration). The *device code* is determined by the driver ID, driver load instance, disk number, and controller number. The *logical device number* is determined by the order in which disk drivers are loaded.

Device object

A Novell Directory Services (NDS) subclass that represents a computer, peripheral, or other component on a Directory tree.

See also **Novell Directory Services.**

device sharing

A method of sharing a centrally located device such as a printer or storage peripheral. Device sharing presents a more efficient way to use network resources.

DFS

Distributed File System, a file system in which files located on multiple machines appear to an end-user as if they were all in a single location.

DFT

Distributed-Function Terminal, a terminal mode in IBM's System Network Architecture (SNA) capable of supporting as many as five sessions, thereby allowing the user to access five applications through the same terminal.

DFWMAC

Distributed-Foundation Wireless Media-Access Control, a data-link-layer protocol for wireless local-area networks (LANs).

DHCP

Dynamic Host-Configuration Protocol, a protocol that dynamically assigns Internet Protocol (IP) addresses to Windows-based personal computers in a local-area network (LAN). DHCP allows the administrator to assign a set of IP addresses. Then each client requests an IP address from the DHCP server, uses it only as long as necessary, and returns it to the address pool.

DHCPCFG (NLM)

Dynamic Host-Configuration Protocol NLM, in IntranetWare, a server console NetWare Loadable Module (NLM) that manages server configuration under the NetWare Dynamic Host-Configuration Protocol (DHCP).

See also **NetWare Loadable Module.**

DIA

Document-Interchange Architecture, a set of services defined by IBM designed to make it easier to use documents throughout multiple IBM computing environments. The four services of DIA include Application-Processing Services (APS), Document-Distribution Services (DDS), Document-Library Services (DLS), and File-Transfer Service (FTS).

diagnostic program

An application that tests computer hardware and peripherals to detect *hard faults* and *soft faults*. Most computers run a simple diagnostic program at startup.

dial backup

A configured backup serial line through a circuit-switched connection, used to protect wide-area networks (WANs) from down-time. If the WAN link goes down, the serial line can still transmit data until the link is restored.

dial-back

A security mechanism meant to prevent unauthorized dial-up access to the network. Network-based software retains a list of authorized users and the numbers from which they may call. If a user needs access to the network, the server receives the user's call, receives the login information, and then terminates the connection. Then the software refers to the dial-up table and calls the number back to re-establish connection.

Dialed-Number Identification Service (DNIS)

A character string that indicates the number dialed by the caller, and specifies how the call should be handled by the Private Branch Exchange (PBX).

See also **Private Branch Exchange.**

dial-in/dial-out server

A dedicated personal computer or expansion board that provides other nodes on the network with access to serial ports and modems.

See also **asynchronous communications server.**

dialog box

A window in a graphical application that usually appears when the application requires some sort of additional input from the user before carrying out a task.

dial-on-demand routing

A routing process that provides on-demand network connections through the Public Switched Telephone Network (PSTN).

See also **Public Switched Telephone Network.**

dial-up

Accessing a telephone circuit through manual or automatic dialing sequences.

dial-up access

A way to temporarily connect a remote workstation to a server over a standard telephone connection.

dial-up connection

A connection to the public data network (PDN) often used by personal computer users to access data from remote hosts. A dial-up connection usually carries a slower rate than a leased line.

See also **public data network.**

dial-up line

A nondedicated communications line that can be accessed through dial-up facilities. The public telephone network is composed of dial-up lines. A dial-up connection is temporary — established at the time of dial-up, destroyed when the call is terminated.

dial-up service

A type of account with an Internet service provider (ISP) that allows a personal computer to connect to the Internet using a modem and the public telephone network. Normally, the user makes this connection by placing a phone call to a *system port connection point* (a pool of modems); the call may not be long distance and the line may be busy if all modems are in use.

See also **Internet service provider.**

DIB

Directory Information Base, a database used to hold Directory Services information in the X.500 Directory Services model. The DIB can be partitioned and stored in separate locations. In this model, the DIB is accessed by Directory System Agents (DSAs) on behalf of Directory User Agents (DUAs).

See also **Directory System Agent: Directory User Agent; X.500.**

DIBI

Device-Independent Backup Interface, an interface meant to simplify the process of moving backed-up data from one environment to another on the same network.

dibit

A bit pair treated as a single unit.

DID

(1) Destination ID, the address of a destination node in an Attached-Resource Computer Network (ARCnet) packet.
(2) direct inward dialing, a system in which an external caller dials a number in a Private Branch Exchange (PBX) directly, without first going through the switchboard.

See also also **(1) Attached-Resource Computer Network; (2) Private Branch Exchange.**

dielectric

A nonconducting material used to form an insulating layer around conductive wire in either coaxial or twisted-pair cable. The dielectric material can be rubber or certain types of plastic.

differential backup

A backup that archives only new files or those modified since the last full backup. Files that require differential backup are marked with a *modify bit* to point them out to the backup utility.

differential encoding

A digital coding technique that denotes a binary value by a signal change rather than by a particular signal level.

differential Manchester encoding

A digital coding scheme that uses a transition in the middle of a bit time for clocking; the transition at the beginning of the bit time denotes a zero. Differential Manchester encoding is popular in Token Ring networks.

See also **Token Ring.**

digerati

A term (probably derived from "literati") that refers to people considered knowledgeable about the "digital revolution."

digest

A compilation of messages posted to a mailing list over a period of time. A digest provides the receiver with one big message instead of numerous smaller messages.

digital

The representation of information by zeroes and ones. Data characters in a digital stream are discrete electrical pulses or signal levels.

See also **analog.**

Digital Access and Cross-Connect System (DACS)

In digital communications, a mechanism used to switch a 64 kilobit-per-second (Kbps) DS-0 channel from one T1 line to another.

See also **DS-*x*; T1.**

Digital Audio Tape (DAT)

A storage medium often used for network backups. Using the Data/DAT logical recording format (which supports random data reads and writes), DAT permits data to be updated in place. Modified data need not be rewritten to a new location. DAT is often deployed on a small audiotape cassette, most commonly a 4-millimeter tape in a helical-scan drive.

digital cash

An electronic payment system found on the Internet that allows payments to be made without traditional cash transactions.

digital circuit

A line that transmits data in unmodulated square waves that represent values of zero or one.

digital communication

A method of telecommunications that uses digital signals in the form of binary values to represent information. A digital signal is encoded as a discrete value, represented as a zero or a one. The binary values are encoded as different voltage or current levels. Analog signals, by contrast, represent information as variations in a continuous waveform.

Digital Cross-Connect System (DCS)

In digital telephony, a switch that switches a digital channel from one device to another by cross-connecting the digital channels. The cross-connection takes place at the slowest rate common to the two lines involved.

Digital Data-Communications Message Protocol (DDCMP)

A byte-oriented, link-layer synchronous protocol designed by Digital Equipment Corporation as the primary data-link component in DECnet.

See also **DECnet.**

Digital Data Service (DDS)

Leased lines that can accommodate a transmission rate of between 2.4 kilobits per second (Kbps) and 56 Kbps.

digital ID

An element assigned by a certification authority and attached to an electronic message. A digital ID authenticates the message and sender through such information as sender's name, address, organization, and public key; as well as by digital signature, serial number, and limits on the validity period.

Digital-Intel-Xerox (DIX)

Refers to the three companies (Digital Equipment Corporation, Intel, and Xerox) whose early research led to the development of the Blue Book Ethernet standard. The term was often used to identify a type of connector on a Network Interface Card (NIC).

See also **Blue Book Ethernet; Network Interface Card.**

Digital Multiplexed Interface (DMI)

A T1 interface between a Private Branch Exchange (PBX) and a computer.
See also **Private Branch Exchange; T1.**

Digital Network Architecture (DNA)

Digital Equipment Corporation's layered architecture used in DECnet.
See also **DECnet.**

Digital Service (DS)

A telecommunications service that uses digital signaling and is defined as a North American service using a five-level transmission hierarchy. A DS relies on Pulse Code Modulation (PCM) to encode analog signals in digital form. The five levels of digital services are DS-0 (64Kbps), DS-1 (1.544Mbps), DS-2 (6.312Mbps), DS-3 (44.736Mbps), and DS-4 (274.176Mbps).
See also **DS-x; Pulse Code Modulation.**

Digital Service Unit (DSU)

A device that sits between a user's Data-Terminal Equipment (DTE) and a common carrier's digital circuits. The DSU formats data for transmission on the public carrier's wide-area network (WAN). The DSU is required to connect to carrier services such as Frame Relay or Switched Multimegabit Data Service (SMDS)
See also **Data-Terminal Equipment; Frame Relay network; Switched Multimegabit Data Service.**

Digital Signal Cross-Connect Between Levels 1 and 3 (DSX1/3)

An interface that connects DS-1 and DS-3 signals.
See also **DS-x.**

Digital Signal Processor (DSP)

A device used to extract and process elements from a digital stream.
See also **DSP.**

digital signature

A unique value assigned to a particular transaction. Designed to be impossible to forge, this security method verifies the identity of the sender and origin of the message.

Digital Simultaneous Voice and Data (DSVD)

A standard used in terminal adapters that allows a user to talk over a telephone line being used simultaneously to transmit data.

Digital Speech Interpolation (DSI)

A method of improving the efficiency of a communications channel. By sending transmissions during the quiet periods that normally occur in a voice conversation, DIS can double the number of voice signals a line can carry.

Digital Termination Service (DTS)

A service that allows the private network to access the carrier networks with digital microwave equipment.

d

digital-to-analog converter (DAC)

A hardware device used to convert a digital signal to an analog signal.

Dijkstra's algorithm

An Open Shortest Path First (OSPF) routing algorithm that uses path length to determine a shortest-path spanning tree. Dijkstra's algorithm is commonly used in link-state routing algorithms.
See also **link-state routing algorithm; Open Shortest Path First.**

dimmed command

A command displayed in light gray in the graphical user interface (GUI). A command is dimmed when it is not currently available.
See also **graphical user interface.**

DIN connector

A connector that complies with the German Deutsche Industrie Norm (DIN) standards body. Some Macintosh computers use a DIN connector as the serial port connector; some IBM computers use a DIN connector to connect the keyboard to the system unit.
See also **connector.**

DIP

dual in-line package, a type of switch that can have one of two settings. DIP switches provide an alternative to jumper settings that are used to configure components. DIP switches are common in dot matrix printers, modems, and other peripherals.

direct-broadcast satellite (DBS)

A satellite that broadcasts signals directly to subscribers without having to go through a central station first.

direct connection

An immediate connection to the network. In wide-area networking, a direct connection does not go through a local carrier.

Direct Current (DC)

Electrical power that travels only in one direction, often used in batteries and electronic components.
See also **Alternating Current.**

direct distance dialing (DDD)

Dialing a long-distance number without going through an operator.

direct inward dialing (DID)

A system in which an external caller dials a number in a Private Branch Exchange (PBX) directly, without first going through the switchboard.
See also **Private Branch Exchange.**

direct link

A circuit that connects two stations directly, with no intervening nodes or stations.

Direct Memory Access (DMA)

A circuit used to facilitate data transfer between a device and system memory. A special processor called the *DMA controller chip* is required to manage DMA because the computer's central processing unit (CPU) is not involved in the transaction.

direct outward dialing (DOD)

A system in which an internal caller dials an outside number in a Private Branch Exchange (PBX) directly, without first going through the switchboard.

See also **Private Branch Exchange.**

direct wave

In wireless communications, a wave that requires a direct line of sight between sender and recipient.

direct-control switching

A network-switching system that establishes the packet path directly through network signals, instead of through a central controller or hub.

directed search

A search request sent to a node known to contain a resource, to determine the continued existence of the resource while determining routing information about the node.

directed transmission

In AppleTalk networks using LocalTalk, a transmission intended for one specific node. In infrared communications, a way of aiming a signal at a central reflective target.

See also **AppleTalk; infrared transmission; LocalTalk.**

directional coupler

A type of coupler that can send a split signal in only one direction.

directory

A disk structure that contains files. Generically, a directory is a way to organize and group files for easier access by placing them in a logical order and related subsections. A directory can contain many levels of subdirectories in a tree-like structure. The term can also refer to the Directory database in NetWare. The Novell directory organizes the Novell Directory Services (NDS) objects in a hierarchical tree structure called the *Directory tree.*

See also **Directory tree; NetWare Directory; Novell Directory Services.**

Directory access-control request

A NetWare Directory Services request that sets access rights to Novell Directory Services (NDS) objects.

See also **NetWare Directory; Novell Directory Services.**

Directory-Access Protocol (DAP)

An X.500 Directory Services protocol. The DAP establishes communications between a Directory User Agent (DUA) and a Directory System Agent (DSA).

See also **Directory System Agent; Directory User Agent; X.500.**

directory attributes

A set of eight properties that can be assigned to NetWare Directories to establish File

System security. The Directory attributes detail how users may manage a Directory. Table D.1 shows the directory attributes and provides a description of each.

See also **attribute; NetWare Directory.**

directory cache

Part of the server memory that holds frequently requested directory entries copied from the disk directory tables. The purpose of the cache is to facilitate faster access to a file's location.

directory caching

A feature of NetWare that improves performance by writing copies of the File-Allocation Table (FAT) and Directory-Entry Table (DET) into the network server's memory. This allows a file's location to be read directly from memory, instead of accessing it from a physical disk.

See also **Directory-Entry Table; File-Allocation Table.**

directory entry

A record containing the basic information about directories and files on a NetWare server. Directory entries may include names, owners, date and time of last update, and location on the hard disk. The directory entries are located in a directory table on the network hard disk.

Directory-Entry Table (DET)

A table located on a network volume that contains information about files, directories, directory trustees, or other directory entries for the particular volume on which it is located. The directory table may occupy one or more blocks on the volume; each block contains 4K of data and can hold 128 directory entries (each 32 bytes long).

Table D.1: Directory Attributes

Attribute	Description
Delete Inhibit (Di)	Prevents the directory from being deleted.
Don't Compress (Dc)	Prevents the directory from being compressed.
Don't Migrate (Dm)	Prevents a directory from being moved from the server's hard disk to another storage medium.
Hidden (H)	Hides a directory so the DIR command does not list it.
Immediate Compress (Ic)	Compresses every file in a directory as each file is closed.
Purge (P)	Flags a directory to be erased from the system as soon as it is deleted.
Rename Inhibit (Ri)	Prevents a directory name from being modified.
System (Sy)	Hides the directory so the DIR command does not make it visible.

directory hashing

A NetWare feature used to improve performance by indexing file locations on a disk to reduce the time needed to locate a file. Instead of conducting a sequential search, a directory-hashing feature makes a calculation to predict a file's address.

directory ID

An AppleTalk feature that assigns a unique value to a directory when that directory is created.

See also **AppleTalk.**

Directory Information Base (DIB)

A database used to hold Directory Services information in the X.500 Directory Services model. The DIB can be partitioned and stored in separate locations. In this model, the DIB is accessed by Directory System Agents (DSAs) on behalf of Directory User Agents (DUAs).

See also **Directory System Agent; Directory User Agent; X.500.**

Directory Information Tree (DIT)

The structure that holds the information for a Directory Information Base (DIB) in the X.500 Directory Services model. If a DIT is large, the information contained in it may be distributed to provide faster access. A DIT's objects can be used to represent intermediate categories or specific objects. The DIT does not contain the objects themselves; it holds information about the objects. The DIT supports both retrieval and modification; and any DIT operation may be configured to apply to one entry or a group of entries. End-users can access the DIT's

information through a Directory User Agent (DUA) or Directory System Agent (DSA).

See also **Directory System Agent; Directory User Agent; X.500.**

Directory-Management Domain (DMD)

In the X.500 Directory-Management Services scheme, a set of Directory System Agents (DSAs) managed by a single organization.

See also **Directory System Agent; X.500.**

directory-management request

A request that controls the physical distribution of the Novell Directory Services (NDS) database. Administrators use these requests to install new Directory partitions and manage their replicas. Directory management requests include Add Partition, Add Replica, List Replicas, Remove Partition, Synchronize Replicas, Create a New Partition, and Merge Partition.

See also **Novell Directory Services.**

Directory Map object

A Directory Schema term and a leaf object in Novell Directory Services (NDS), referring to a directory on a volume. The Directory Map object specifies a path on a volume. It permits the drive to be mapped to a given application without requiring the actual path and volume where the application is physically located. A Directory Map is often used in login scripts to avoid having to map a drive to a specific directory path. The Directory Map object has the following selectable properties in NDS: Access-Control List, Back Link, Bindery, Common Name (CN), Description, Host Resource, Host

Server, Locality (L), Name, Object Class, Organization (O), Organizational Unit (OU), Path, and See Also.

See also **leaf object; Novell Directory Services; object.**

directory node

An addressable entity on a NetWare network, containing information about a directory. The directory node is a 128-byte entry contained in the server's Directory-Entry Table (DET). The directory node includes the directory name, attributes, Inherited-Rights Mask, creation date and time, creator's object ID, link to parent directory, and link to the trustee node.

See also **directory attributes; Directory-Entry Table; Inherited-Rights Mask; trustee node.**

Directory object

A set of properties stored in the Novell Directory Services (NDS) Directory database. The three types of directory objects are the *root object*, *container objects*, and *leaf objects*. A directory object can represent a physical or a logical network resource. Although it represents the resource, the Directory object does not contain the actual resource—only information about how to use it.

See also **container object; leaf object; Novell Directory Services; object.**

Directory partition

A logical division of the NetWare Directory database that forms a unit of data in the Directory tree. This unit is then used to store and replicate Directory information.

Each partition contains a container object, all objects contained therein, and data about those objects (such as properties and rights). The Directory partition does not contain any information about the file system, nor about the directories contained in the file system. To optimize the capability (through distributed operations) of accessing different areas of the Directory, each Directory partition can be replicated and stored at many locations. Figure N.2 shows an example of default Directory partitions.

See also **NetWare Directory partition.**

directory path

A character string indicating the position of a file within the file system. The directory path lists the server name, volume name, and name of each directory that leads to the file system directory to which access is desired.

Directory replica

A copy of a NetWare Directory partition that provides a means for storing the NetWare Directory Database (NDD) on several servers across the network without having to duplicate the entire database for each server. An unlimited number of replicas can be created for each Directory partition and can be stored on any server. Directory replicas eliminate a single point of failure on the network and provide faster access to information across a wide-area network (WAN) link.

Table D.1 shows the four types of Directory replicas.

See also **Master replica; NetWare Directory Database; NetWare Directory replica, Read-Only replica; Read/Write replica; Subordinate replica.**

Table D.1: Directory Replica Types

Type	Description
Master replica	Used to create a new Directory partition in the Directory database, or to read and update Directory information. Only one master replica may be created for each partition.
Read/write replica	Used to read or update Directory information.
Read-only replica	Used to view (but not modify) Directory information.
Subordinate replica	Automatically added on the server by Novell Directory Services (NDS) if a parent Directory partition has either a Master, Read/Write, or Read-Only replica on the server and the child partition does not.

directory rights

Rights used to control the actions a NetWare trustee can take with a given directory. Directory rights are not assigned to Novell Directory Services (NDS) objects; they are part of the file system. A User object can be granted directory rights to a directory on a volume.

See also **Novell Directory Services; trustee rights.**

Directory root

An object in the NetWare Directory tree. The directory root establishes the highest point of access for different Country and Organization objects. It also permits trustee assignments to grant rights to the entire Directory tree.

See also **Novell Directory Services; trustee rights.**

Directory Schema

The set of rules defining how to create the Novell Directory Services (NDS) Directory tree and store information in the Directory database. The schema defines attribute information, inheritance, naming, and subordination. *Attribute information* concerns the different types of information that can be associated with an object. *Inheritance* specifies which objects can inherit the properties and rights of other objects, and naming determines the structure of the Directory tree. *Subordination* determines the location of objects in the Directory tree.

See also **Novell Directory Services.**

directory server

A software application that can access directory information and directory services for other nodes on the network.

Directory Service Area (DSA)

The calling area covered by a directory service.

Directory Services (DS)

A feature of NetWare 4.*x*; a global, distributed, replicated database that retains information about all resources in the network. The Directory Services feature centrally manages any size network through a hierarchical, tree-like representation. Other directory services include the X.500 standard and the Domain-Naming System (DNS).

See also **Domain-Naming System; Novell Directory Services; X.500.**

Directory Services request

A request made to NetWare's Directory database by users or network supervisors. The three types of Directory Services requests are as follows: End-users or administrators make *directory-access requests* to create, modify, or retrieve objects. *Directory access-control requests* set the access rights to Directory objects. Administrators make *directory-management requests* to enact management functions (such as partitioning) that pertain to the physical distribution of the Directory's database.

directory structure

A hierarchical structure that represents how NetWare directories are related to each other on a volume. The term can also be used to refer to the relationship of Novell Directory Services (NDS) partitions in the Directory database.

See also **Novell Directory Services.**

directory-structure duplication

A feature of NetWare used to protect data from the effects of hardware failure. The feature copies the Directory-Entry Table (DET) and File-Allocation Table (FAT) to separate areas of the hard disk. If the primary copy is destroyed, the operating system accesses the secondary copy.

See also **Directory-Entry Table; File-Allocation Table.**

Directory synchronization

Maintaining multiple instances of a NetWare Directory and ensuring that all are properly updated.

Directory System Agent (DSA)

Software used in the X.500 Directory Services model for accessing, using, and updating the Directory Information Base (DIB) or Directory Information Tree (DIT).

See also **Directory Information Base; Directory Information Tree; X.500.**

Directory System Protocol (DSP)

A protocol used by Directory System Agents (DSAs) to communicate with each other.

See also **Directory System Agent.**

directory table

A table located on a network volume that contains information about files, directories, directory trustees, or other directory entries for the particular volume on which it is located. The directory table may occupy one or more blocks on the volume; each block contains 4K of data and can hold 128 directory entries (each 32 bytes long).

See also **Directory-Entry Table.**

Directory tree

A hierarchical structure representing objects in a directory services database. The Directory tree shows container objects, which are used to organize the network, and leaf objects that represent individual resources. The X.500 specification developed by the Institute of Electronic and Electrical Engineers (IEEE) provides a standard method for organizing information in a directory tree pattern so that it is globally available. Novell Directory Services (NDS) is a directory service that complies with the X.500 specification.

See also **Institute of Electronic and Electrical Engineers; Novell Directory Services; X.500.**

Directory tree name

A name assigned during installation to each NetWare Directory tree. The Directory tree name can be up to 32 characters. Characters can be uppercase or lowercase letters, numbers, and hyphens, but may not contain a space or a trailing underscore.

Directory User Agent (DUA)

A program used in the X.500 Directory Services model for accessing directory services and that establishes an interface between an end-user and a Directory System Agent (DSA), which retrieves the requested services.

See also **Directory System Agent; X.500.**

directory verification

A feature of NetWare used to protect data from the effects of hardware failure. Directory verification occurs whenever the server is started up. During this verification, the operating system performs a consistency check to ensure that duplicate sets of Directory-Entry Table (DET) and File-Allocation Table (FAT) are identical.

See also **Directory-Entry Table; File-Allocation Table.**

dirty cache block

A temporary memory storage space that contains updated information not yet written to disk. These blocks are sent to the disk when a client write operation completely fills a cache block, or after an Aged Write default value has been reached.

dirty cache buffers

File blocks that exist in memory and are waiting to be written to disk.

DIS

Draft International Standard, an early version of a proposed standard from a formal standards organization. The DIS is submitted to committee members for comment before the standard is formally ratified.

disable

To turn off a function. A graphical user interface (GUI) typically shows disabled menu commands in gray to indicate that they are unavailable.

See also **dimmed command; graphical user interface.**

DISABLE LOGIN utility

In NetWare 3.*x* and NetWare 4.*x*, a server console utility that prevents users from logging in to the file server, and is usually executed prior to server maintenance. Once maintenance is complete, the ENABLE LOGIN utility once again allow users to log in.

See also **ENABLE LOGIN utility.**

DISABLE TTS utility

In NetWare 3.*x* and NetWare 4.*x*, a server console utility that turns off the NetWare Transaction-Tracking System (TTS) after an ENABLE TTS command has been issued. The DISABLE TTS utility is used primarily by application developers who must test transactional applications with TTS disabled.

See also **ENABLE TTS utility; Transaction-Tracking System.**

Discard Eligibility (DE)

A Frame Relay network term. The DE bit is set by an end node to indicate that certain frames can be discarded in the event of network congestion.

See also **Frame Relay network.**

disk

A plate-like storage medium magnetically encoded. A disk may take the form of a *hard disk* (usually installed within a computer system), a *floppy disk* (removable and has less storage capacity), a *CD-ROM* (which cannot be written to or erased), or an *optical disc* (which can be erasable and writable).

disk accelerator

Another term for disk cache, an area of random-access memory (RAM) used to store frequently accessed data. A disk cache increases performance by relieving an application from having to constantly reaccess data from a physical disk. When an application requests information from the hard drive, the disk cache program first checks to see whether the information exists in the cache memory. If so, the information is loaded from the cache memory instead of from the hard disk.

Disk Adapter Locks

In the Available Options/Resource Utilization screen of the NetWare 3.12 MONITOR NetWare Loadable Module (NLM), a tracked resource used to track loadable modules needing information about disk adapters, controllers, or host bus adapters.

See also **MONITOR; NetWare Loadable Module.**

disk-allocation block

A data-storage unit used by network volumes. Disk-allocation blocks may be 4K, 8K, 16K, 32K, or 64K in size, and may vary in size between volumes. One volume, however, can have only one block size. The disk-allocation block represents the smallest file size for that volume, unless suballocation is used.

Disk Array Subsystem (DAS)

The combination of cabling, circuitry, and the carriage required for using multiple hard disks.

disk cache

An area of random-access memory (RAM) used to store frequently accessed data. A disk cache increases performance by relieving an application from having to constantly reaccess data from a physical disk. When an application requests information from the hard drive, the disk-cache program first checks to see whether the information exists in the cache memory. If so, the information is loaded from the cache memory instead of from the hard disk.

disk controller

A hardware device used to control how data is written to and retrieved from an attached hard disk. The disk controller regulates the movement of the physical disk head as it reads data from the disk or writes data to it.

disk coprocessor board (DCB)

An intelligent board that functions as an interface between the host microprocessor and the disk controller. This board can increase performance by relieving the host microprocessor of data storage and retrieval tasks. The DCB has been replaced by a Host Bus Adapter (HBA) in newer versions of NetWare.

See also **Host Bus Adapter.**

disk drive

A peripheral storage device that reads from and writes to magnetic or optical discs. The operating system assigns a unique name to each installed drive.

Disk Drive Locks

In NetWare 3.12, a tracked resource in the Available Options/Resource Utilization screen of the MONITOR NetWare Loadable Module (NLM); the feature tracks loadable modules that require information about the hard disks.

See also **MONITOR; NetWare Loadable Module.**

disk driver

A program that facilitates communication between the disk controller and the server's central processing unit (CPU), or between the operating system and hard disks.

disk duplexing

A data-protection scheme that duplicates data onto two hard disks, each one on a separate disk channel. If the first hard disk fails, the second one takes over automatically. Besides protection, disk duplexing also writes data to both the original hard disk and to the duplicate hard disk simultaneously. This can facilitate faster access by allowing split seeks, whereby a read request is sent to whichever disk is capable of responding first.

Figure D.2 shows disk duplexing in NetWare.

See also **disk mirroring.**

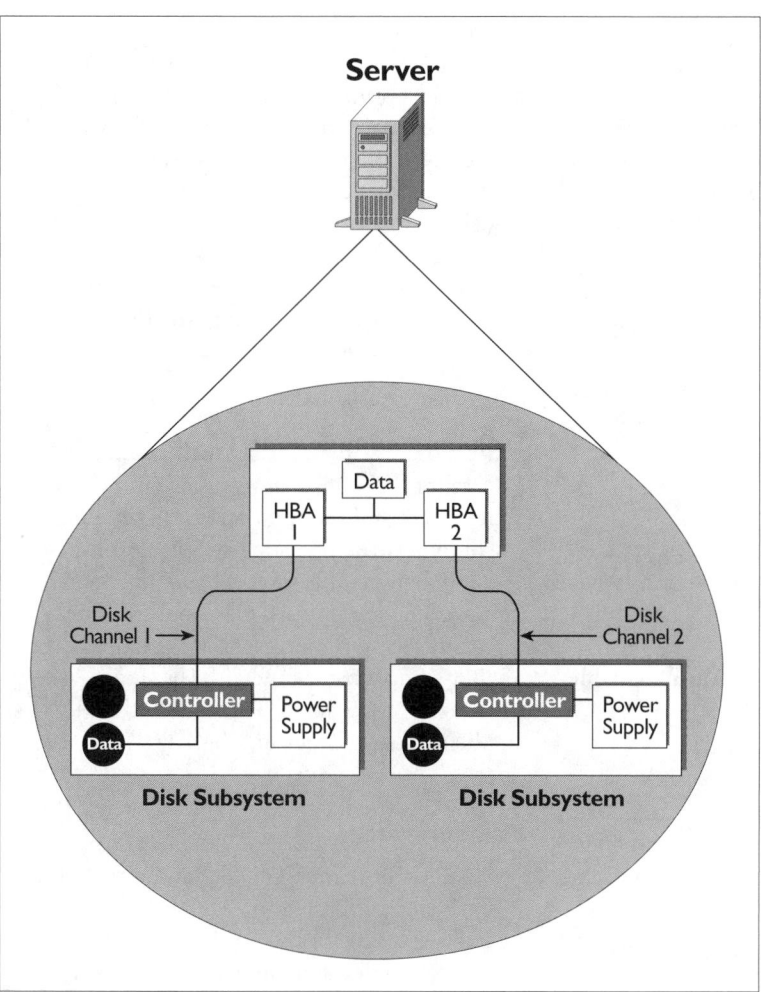

Figure D.2
Disk duplexing in NetWare

Disk File-System Partition Locks

In NetWare 3.12, a tracked resource in the Available Options/Resource Utilization screen of the MONITOR NetWare Loadable Module (NLM); the feature tracks loadable modules that require access to information about logical partitions.

See also MONITOR; NetWare Loadable Module.

disk format

A way of preparing and structuring a disk so it can receive data from a particular operating system. Disk formatting is a function of the operating system. Usually, a disk formatted by one operating system cannot be read by a different operating system without a special translation utility. Hard-disk formats include File-Allocation Table (FAT), which applies to the DOS and NetWare operating systems; High-Performance File System (HPFS) for the OS/2 operating system; Hierarchical File System (HFS) for the Macintosh operating system; and many others.

See also **File-Allocation Table; Hierarchical File System; High-Performance File System.**

Disk Information

A field name in the Available Options screen of the NetWare 4.02 MONITOR NetWare Loadable Module (NLM).

See also **MONITOR; NetWare Loadable Module.**

disk interface board

An add-on board that functions as an interface between a host microprocessor and the disk controller. A disk interface board is also known as a *disk coprocessor board* (DCB) or a *Host Bus Adapter* (HBA).

See also **disk coprocessor board; Host Bus Adapter.**

disk mirroring

A procedure that involves duplicating data from a NetWare partition on one hard disk to the NetWare partition on another disk. Disk mirroring pairs multiple hard disks on the same channel, and like disk duplexing, writes data to both the original and sec-

ondary disk. If the original disk fails, the secondary disk automatically takes over. Disk mirroring cannot protect against failures that occur along the channel between the disks and the NetWare server, because the duplicate disks exist on the same channel.

Figure D.3 shows disk mirroring in NetWare.

See also **disk duplexing; MIRROR STATUS utility; mirroring.**

Disk Operating System (DOS)

A set of programs that manage computer resources and the applications that run on a computer. The operating system establishes a link between the physical computer and associated peripherals, files, and the applications being run on them. DOS is used on IBM-compatible computers. The more common DOS implementations include Microsoft's MS-DOS and IBM's PC-DOS.

disk optimizer

A utility for rearranging files and directories for better performance. A defragmenter utility is a type of disk optimizer.

See also **defragmenter.**

disk partition

A logical subdivision of a hard disk. One disk can have multiple partitions, with each partition having a unique name. In the NetWare operating system, a NetWare disk partition is created on each hard disk, and volumes are then created from the NetWare partitions.

See also **NetWare Directory partition.**

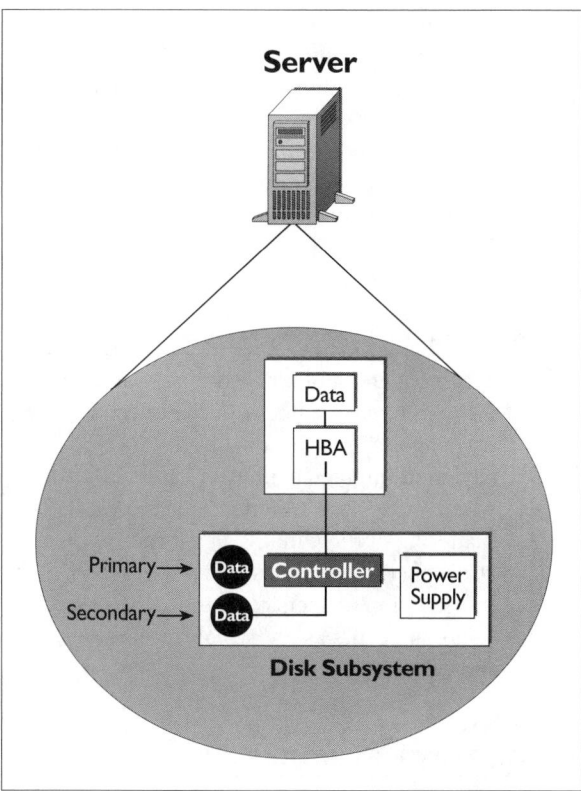

Figure D.3
Disk mirroring in NetWare

Disk Raw-Partition Locks

A tracked resource in the Available Options/Resource Utilization screen of the NetWare 3.12 MONITOR NetWare Loadable Module (NLM); the feature tracks access to disk partitions.

See also **MONITOR; NetWare Loadable Module.**

disk striping

A data-storage strategy that combines partitions on multiple hard disks into a single volume. Because each partition is on a separate disk, multiple partitions can be read from or written to simultaneously.

disk striping with parity

A disk-striping strategy that distributes parity information across multiple hard disk partitions. In the event of a failed partition, the information on the other partitions can reconstruct the missing data.

disk subsystem

An external unit that can be attached to a server and that contains any combination of hard drives, tape drives, or optical drives. A disk subsystem gives the server additional storage capacity.

diskette

A disk that can be removed from a drive. A diskette is also known as a *floppy disk*.

diskless workstation

A networked computer with no local disk storage capacity. A diskless workstation boots from a network file server, and also loads all of its programs from the file server.

DISKSET utility

In NetWare 3.x, a server console utility that adds a hard disk's identification and configuration information to the host bus adapter's Electrical-Erasable Programmable Read-Only Memory (EEPROM) chip. This utility is used when installing a new disk subsystem or when replacing a hard disk on the server.

DISMOUNT utility

In NetWare 3.x and NetWare 4.x, a server console utility that unloads a volume from the server to allow the disk to be repaired or replaced. The volume can then be reloaded using the MOUNT command.
See also **MOUNT utility.**

DISOSS

Distributed Office-Supported System, an IBM mainframe-based software package that offers users a variety of document preparation and electronic-mail (e-mail) features. The DISOSS system allows documents created by different products to be shared among different IBM systems. The DISOSS system is often used as a way to transmit documents between IBM systems and non-IBM systems.

dispersion

The broadening of a light signal as it travels through fiber in a fiber-optic connection. Dispersion is proportional to distance traveled, and imposes a limit on bandwidth. In wireless communications, dispersion is the scattering of the wireless signal caused by atmospheric conditions. In an electrical transmission, dispersion is the signal distortion that occurs as the signal travels along the wire.

DISPLAY NETWORKS utility

In NetWare 3.x and NetWare 4.x, a server console utility that lists all networks and assigned network numbers that the NetWare server's internal router recognizes.

DISPLAY SERVERS utility

In NetWare 3.x and NetWare 4.x, a server console utility that lists all servers and services being advertised by Service-Advertising Protocol (SAP) packets.
See also **Service-Advertising Protocol.**

disruptive test

A network diagnostic test that requires ordinary network activity to cease before it can be run.

distance vector

An algorithm used to disseminate routing information to routers on the network. Routers employing this algorithm only retain the information necessary to reach the next router destination on the network.

distance-vector algorithm

The class of routing algorithms that broadcast routing information periodically, instead of sending information only when a change occurs in a route. Routers use this algorithm to exchange information about accessible networks with neighboring routers.

distance-vector protocol

The protocol used to derive best path information from the information contained in adjacent nodes. Some examples of distance vector protocols include Internet Protocol (IP), Routing-Information Protocol (RIP), Internet Packet Exchange Routing-Information Protocol (IPX RIP), and Routing-Table Maintenance Protocol (RTMP).
See also **Internet Protocol; Internet Packet Exchange; Routing-Information Protocol; Routing-Table Maintenance Protocol.**

distinguished name

The complete path from an object to the [Root] of the Novell Directory Services (NDS) Directory tree. A distinguished name, which uniquely identifies each object in the NDS Directory tree, is a combination of an object's common name and context.
See also **common name; Novell Directory Services.**

distortion

An undesirable change in a signal that may be caused by attenuation, crosstalk, interference, or delay.

distortion delay

Fluctuating and nonuniform transmission speeds of the components of a communications signal through a transmission medium.

distributed applications

Applications that operate in a distributed computing environment and that may contain modules running on different computer systems.

distributed architecture

A processor configuration in which the processors are contained in multiple devices. Each processor can function independently, or in cooperation with other elements.

Distributed-Authentication Security Service (DASS)

A system for authenticating users logging in to a network from unattended workstations. DASS relies on public-key encryption to provide security.
See also **public-key encryption system.**

distributed computing

A method of computing that distributes processing between multiple devices.

Distributed Computing Environment (DCE)

An open networking architecture designed by the Open Software Foundation (OSF). The OSF is a consortium of vendors that includes Digital Equipment Corporation, Hewlett-Packard, and IBM. DCE provides all of the elements needed to distribute applications and their functions across a network transparently. Under the DCE model, the network would appear to the end-user as a single entity. This makes all of the network's resources transparently available to every user.

Distributed Data Management (DDM)

A service of IBM's Systems Network Architecture (SNA) used to allow file sharing and remote file access in the network.

See also **Systems Network Architecture.**

Distributed Data Processing (DDP)

A way of processing data where the work is distributed across multiple computers.

distributed database (DDB)

A database that provides services to all network applications and users over different platforms. The distributed database may be stored on different hard disks in different locations.

Distributed Database-Management System (DDBMS)

The software used to reference a distributed database.

Distributed File System (DFS)

A file system in which files located on multiple machines appear to an end-user as if they were all in a single location.

Distributed-Foundation Wireless Media-Access Control (DFWMAC)

A data-link-layer protocol for wireless local-area networks (LANs).

Distributed-Function Terminal (DFT)

A terminal mode in IBM's System Network Architecture (SNA) capable of supporting as many as five sessions, thereby allowing the user to access five applications through the same terminal.

distributed network

A type of network where processing is distributed to multiple computers instead of being carried out by a single computer. Processing may be shared between clients, file servers, print servers, or application servers. The distributed model promotes efficiency by dynamically assigning processing, depending on the existing workload and specific task.

Distributed Network Architecture (DNA)

A network architecture developed by Digital Equipment Corporation (DEC), whereby processing and services are distributed across the network, instead of being located in a single host. DNA is the framework for all of DEC's communications products.

Distributed Office-Applications Model (DOAM)

An Open Systems Interface (OSI) model used for several application-layer processes. The functions of DOAM include document filing and retrieval (DFR), document printing application (DPA), Message-Oriented Text Interchange System (MOTIS), and referenced data transfer (RDT).

See also **Message-Oriented Text Interchange System.**

Distributed Office-Supported System (DISOSS)

An IBM mainframe-based software package that offers users a variety of document preparation and electronic-mail (e-mail) features. The DISOSS system allows documents created by different products to be shared among different IBM systems. The DISOSS system is often used as a way to transmit documents between IBM systems and non-IBM systems.

distributed processing

A technique used to allow multiple networked computers to jointly complete a task. In a distributed processing model, different nodes are assigned responsibility for specialized tasks.

Distributed-Queue Dual-Bus (DQDB)

A network architecture defined in the Institute of Electronic and Electrical Engineers (IEEE) 802.6 Metropolitan-Area Network (MAN) standard. DQDB is the main platform used for Synchronous Multimegabit Data Service (SMDS) access. DQDB, like Asynchronous Transfer Mode (ATM), uses a fixed-size, 53-byte cell to hold data and addressing information. DQDB establishes a Media-Access Control (MAC)-layer protocol that allows multiple systems to interconnect through two unidirectional logical buses. A network node may transmit and receive on one or both buses, depending on the location of the node in relation to the bus. It can also be used to establish a private, fiber-based MAN that can support data, voice, and video. The DQDB consists of the protocol syntax, and the distributed queuing algorithm used for shared medium access control. Generally, DQDB requires fiber-optic cable, and can support a transmission speed of up to 50 megabits per second (Mbps).

See also **Asynchronous Transfer Mode; Institute of Electronic and Electrical Engineers; IEEE 802.x; Media-Access Control; Metropolitan-Area Network.**

Distributed Relational Data Architecture (DRDA)

A distributed database architecture designed by IBM that forms the basis of the database management features offered by IBM's SystemView network management software.

See also **SystemView.**

distributed star topology

A physical topology with two or more hubs having workstations connected in a star arrangement around each one. Figure D.4 shows an example of distributed star topology.

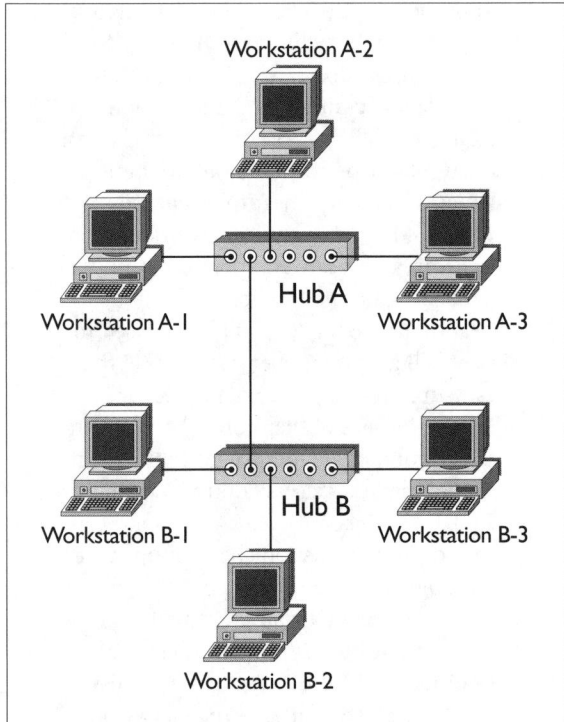

Figure D.4
Distributed star topology

Distributed System-Object Model (DSOM)

A system designed by IBM for sharing objects across a network. DSOM is compliant with the Common Object-Request Broker Architecture (CORBA) model.

See also **Common Object-Request Broker Architecture.**

Distributed Systems Architecture (DSA)

A network architecture designed by Honeywell that complies with Open System Interconnection (OSI) standards.

distributed system

Multiple, autonomous, linked computers that can (through proper software) give the appearance of being a single, integrated computer system. Unlike a centralized system (in which multiple personal computers are connected to a single host machine), a distributed system entails computers that may be parts of local-area networks (LANs), wide-area networks (WANs), or global-area networks (GANs). The Internet and automated teller machines (ATM) networks are examples of distributed systems.

See also **centralized network.**

distributed transaction-processing services

A set of services used to allow transaction programs to communicate with each other and to access remote resources. These services also facilitate synchronization and error recovery.

distribution cable

A cable used in a broadband network over intermediate distances, or for establishing branches off of a network backbone.

distribution frame

The location where wiring from multiple network components is concentrated.

Distribution List (DL)

A Directory Schema term. In the X.400 Message-Handling System (MHS), the DL is used for sending a message to multiple recipients with a single transmission.
See also **Message-Handling System; X.400.**

Distribution List object

In NetWare, a Novell Directory Services (NDS) leaf object that represents a list of mail recipients. The Distribution List object allows an individual to avoid having to enter in names of multiple recipients; simply entering in the name of the Distribution List object disseminates the message to all members of the list.
See also **Novell Directory Services.**

DIT

Directory Information Tree, the structure that holds the information for a Directory Information Base (DIB) in the X.500 Directory Services model. If a DIT is large, the information contained in it may be distributed to provide faster access. A DIT's objects can be used to represent intermediate categories or specific objects. The DIT does not contain the objects themselves; it holds information about the objects. The DIT supports both retrieval and modification; and any DIT operation may be configured to apply to one entry or a group of entries. End-users can access the DIT's information through a Directory User Agent (DUA) or Directory System Agent (DSA).
See also **Directory System Agent: Directory User Agent; X.500.**

diversity

A strategy used in microwave communications to protect against equipment failure. *Frequency diversity* allocates a separate frequency band that can be used if the primary band is unavailable because of noise or interference. *Space diversity*, on the other hand, sets up two receiving antennas in close proximity to each other, so that if the primary antenna fails, the secondary one can be used.

DIX

Digital-Intel-Xerox, refers to the three companies (Digital Equipment Corporation, Intel, and Xerox) whose early research led to the development of the Blue Book Ethernet standard. The term was often used to identify a type of connector on a Network Interface Card (NIC).

See also **Blue Book Ethernet; Network Interface Card.**

D-type connector

A type of connector that uses pins and sockets to establish contact. D-type connectors are commonly used for both serial and parallel ports on personal computers.
See also **connector.**

dB

decibel, one-tenth of a bel. A decibel is a logarithmic unit of measurement that indicates a signal's intensity.
See also **bel.**

DL

Distribution List, a Directory Schema term. In the X.400 Message-Handling System (MHS), the DL is used for sending a message to multiple recipients with a single transmission.
See also **Message-Handling System; X.400.**

DLC

Data-Link Control, a protocol in IBM's Systems Network Architecture (SNA) used to manage the physical connection and ensure that messages reach their destinations.
See also **Systems Network Architecture.**

DLCI

Data-Link Connection Identifier, a 10-bit routing address used by the virtual circuit in a Frame Relay network. The DLCI is used at either the User-to-Network Interface (UNI) or the Network-Network Interface (NNI). With this identified, both user and network management platforms can identify a frame as originating from a particular Permanent Virtual Circuit (PVC). The DLCI multiplexes multiple PVCs over a single physical circuit.
See also **Frame Relay network; Network-Network Interface; User-to-Network Interface; Permanent Virtual Circuit.**

DLL

Dynamic Link Library, a program library that holds related modules of compiled executable functions that can be called by other programs. The DLL model allows the developer to insert a pointer to the DLL, as opposed to inserting the full program code into an application. An application reads the functions in the DLL at runtime, and several applications can use the same DLL. DLLs are used in Microsoft Windows and IBM's OS/2 operating systems.

DLS

Data-Link Services, the services provided at the second (Data-Link) Layer of the OSI Reference Model.

DMA

Direct Memory Access, a circuit used to facilitate data transfer between a device and system memory. A special processor called the *DMA controller chip* is required to manage DMA because the computer's central processing unit (CPU) is not involved in the transaction.

DMD

Directory-Management Domain, in the X.500 Directory-Management Services scheme, a set of Directory System Agents (DSAs) managed by a single organization.

See also **Directory System Agent; X.500.**

DMI

(1) Desktop-Management Interface, a standard, supported by several vendors, used to automate the process of identifying a personal computer (both hardware and software) to the network. No user intervention is required. The DMI identifies information about any personal computer component, including manufacturer, component name, version, serial number, and installation date and time.
(2) Digital Multiplexed Interface, a T1 interface between a Private Branch Exchange (PBX) and a computer.

See also **(2) Private Branch Exchange; (2) T1.**

DNA

(1) Digital Network Architecture, Digital Equipment Corporation's layered architecture used in DECnet.
(2) Distributed Network Architecture, a network architecture developed by Digital Equipment Corporation (DEC) whereby processing and services are distributed across the network, instead of being located in a single host. DNA is the framework for all of DEC's communications products.

See also **(1) DECnet.**

DNIC

Data-Network Identification Code, a unique four-digit value assigned to public networks and public network services.

DNIS

Dialed-Number Identification Service, a character string that indicates the number dialed by the caller, and specifies how the call should be handled by the Private Branch Exchange (PBX).

See also **Private Branch Exchange.**

DNS

Domain-Naming System, a distributed naming service that provides information about the Internet Protocol (IP) addresses and domain names of all computers on a network. The DNS server translates symbolic, easy-to-remember names into numeric IP addresses. Commonly used on the Internet, DNS domains may be based on geography or organization. The topmost domain is standardized, and includes the domain names *com* (commercial organization), *edu* (educational institution), *gov* (government agency), *int* (international organization), *mil* (United States military), *net* (networking organization), and *org* (nonprofit organization).

See also **Internet Protocol; IP address.**

Do_BTRV

A NetWare Loadable Module (NLM) Behavior Testing utility that simulates the Btrieve record management of multiple network database users for testing purposes. It generates a database with two indices, fill the database with records, and performs various functions on the database. Do_BTRV is included in the Novell NLM Certification Kit.

See also **NetWare Loadable Module.**

Do_File

A NetWare Loadable Module (NLM) Behavior Testing utility that simulates the file-accessing activity of multiple network users for testing purposes. It creates a new network file, copies data into it, closes and copies it, and executes other file functions. Do_File is included in the Novell NLM Certification Kit.

See also **NetWare Loadable Module.**

Do_Play

A NetWare Loadable Module (NLM) Behavior Testing utility; a keystroke-automation utility used to automatically execute DOS applications. It was designed for use with batch files, and is often used to automate the exercising procedure of a NetWare application that needs to use a DOS workstation application.

See also **NetWare Loadable Module.**

Do_Print

A NetWare Loadable Module (NLM) Behavior Testing utility that simulates file printing activity of multiple network users to re-create a typical end-user environment for testing purposes. The Do_Print utility is included in the Novell NLM Certification Kit.

See also **NetWare Loadable Module.**

Do_Rec

A NetWare Loadable Module (NLM) Behavior Testing utility; a DOS-based key-

capture program, used to record the keystrokes used to execute a DOS application. It is often used to automate a behavior testing procedure. The Do_Rec utility is included in the NLM Certification Kit.

See also **NetWare Loadable Module.**

DOAM

Distributed Office-Applications Model, an Open Systems Interface (OSI) model used for several application-layer processes. The functions of DOAM include document filing and retrieval (DFR), document printing application (DPA), Message-Oriented Text Interchange System (MOTIS), and referenced data transfer (RDT).

See also **Message-Oriented Text Interchange System.**

Document Content Architecture (DCA)

A data-stream architecture defined by IBM, used in text documents, and consisting of three standard formats. The *Revisable Form Text* (RFT) format is used for text that can still be edited; the *Final Form Text* (FFT) standard is used for text that has already been formatted for a given output device and can no longer be edited; and the *Mixed Form Text* (MFT) format applies to documents that may contain graphics or other types of data in addition to text.

Document-Interchange Architecture (DIA)

A set of services defined by IBM designed to make it easier to use documents throughout multiple IBM computing environments. The four services of DIA include Application-Processing Services (APS), Document-

Distribution Services (DDS), Document-Library Services (DLS), and File-Transfer Service (FTS).

document management

Management of a large collection of electronic documents through a specific software program. Document management software may provide services for version control, check-in and check-out, text-string or phrase searching, and other features.

Document Transfer and Manipulation (DTAM)

Specifications for nontelephone and non-telegraph communications services (such as telex, fax transmissions, and telewriting) that define three service classes (bulk transfer, document manipulation, and bulk transfer and manipulation), primitive functional units for each service class, and related communications support functions.

documentation

A piece of reference material that accompanies computer software or hardware. Documentation may be printed or online, and may include tutorials, specifications, troubleshooting details, or other references.

DOD

Direct Outward Dialing, a system in which an internal caller dials an outside number in a Private Branch Exchange (PBX) directly, without first going through the switchboard. *See also* **Private Branch Exchange.**

DoD

Department of Defense, the United States governmental agency that has been responsible for funding and development of communications protocols.

domain

A logical group of network servers that appear to end-users as a single network server. When used in the context of the Internet, domain refers to an element of the Domain Naming System (DNS) naming hierarchy. In NetWare, domain refers to the memory segment within NetWare used to separate NetWare Loadable Modules (NLMs) from the operating system. NetWare 4.1 has two domains: OS, and OS_PROTECTED. The OS_PROTECTED domain prevents a malfunctioning NLM from writing to memory it should not have access to, thereby preventing it from potentially bringing down the system. The OS domains were removed in NetWare 4.11 because of improvements in the operating system.
See also **Domain-Naming System; NetWare Loadable Module.**

DOMAIN (NLM)

In NetWare 4.1, a server console utility that establishes a protected operating-system domain, allows viewing of the current domain — as well as the NetWare Loadable Modules (NLMs) in the domain — and also changes the current domain, or permits some misbehaved NLMs to be loaded. NLMs are typically developed and tested in this area, so any errors that exist do not corrupt the system. The OS domains were

removed in NetWare 4.11 because of improvements in the operating system.
See also **NetWare Loadable Module.**

Domain-Control Database (DCDB) file

An IBM file associated with the LAN Manager and LAN Server applications.
See also **LAN Manager; LAN Server.**

Domain-Naming System (DNS)

A distributed naming service that provides information about the Internet Protocol (IP) addresses and domain names of all computers on a network. The DNS server translates symbolic, easy-to-remember names into numeric IP addresses. Commonly used on the Internet, DNS domains may be based on geography or organization. The top-most domain is standardized, and includes the domain names *com* (commercial organization), *edu* (educational institution), *gov* (government agency), *int* (international organization), *mil* (United States military), *net* (networking organization), and *org* (nonprofit organization).
See also **Internet Protocol; IP address.**

domain server

An Internet computer that translates between Internet domain names (such as *xyz.abc.com*) and Internet numerical addresses (such as *123.456.78.0*).
See also **Internet address.**

Domain-Specific Part (DSP)

Part of the address for the Network Service-Access Point (NSAP) in the OSI Reference

Model. The DSP is the address within the domain.
See also **Network Service-Access Point; OSI Reference Model.**

DOMPAC

A packet-switched network located in French Guyana.

Don't Compress (Dc) attribute

A NetWare file system directory attribute used to prevent files from being compressed.
See also **attribute; directory attribute; file compression.**

Don't Migrate (Dm) attribute

A NetWare file system directory attribute and file attribute used to prevent files from being migrated to secondary storage devices such as a tape drive or optical disc.
See also **attribute; directory attribute; file compression.**

Don't Suballocate (Ds) attribute

A NetWare file system attribute that prevents a file from being suballocated, even if suballocation has been enabled.
See also **attribute; directory attribute; Novell Directory Services; suballocation.**

DOS

Disk Operating System, a set of programs that manage computer resources and the applications that run on a computer. The operating system establishes a link between the physical computer and associated

peripherals, files, and the applications being run on them. DOS is used on IBM-compatible computers. The more common DOS implementations include Microsoft's MS-DOS and IBM's PC-DOS.

DOS boot record

A record used by the read-only memory (ROM)-Basic Input/Output System (BIOS) to determine from which device to boot. The boot record can reside on a floppy disk, local hard disk, or remote boot chip. ROM-BIOS runs a program from the boot record to determine the disk format, and the location of system files and directories. ROM-BIOS is then able to load system files and the command processor.

See also **Basic Input/Output System; read-only memory.**

DOS client

A workstation that boots with DOS, and accesses the network through the NetWare DOS Requester software or a NetWare shell.

See also **NetWare DOS Requester; NetWare shell.**

DOS device

A storage unit (such as a disk drive or tape-backup unit) compatible with the DOS disk format.

DOS DIR command

A DOS command used to view the contents of a directory.

DOS extenders

A software program that allows DOS programs to be executed in protected mode and therefore use extended memory.

See also **memory.**

DOS menu utility

A utility where options are presented in a character-based menu.

DOS partition functions

A set of features used to allow access to files in the DOS partition of a NetWare server's disk. They are used primarily to install new software from the DOS partition to the NetWare partition. These functions adversely affect server performance, and should be used only when necessary. Therefore, if a file in the DOS partition is accessed frequently, it should be moved into the NetWare partition.

DOS prompt

A screen prompt that indicates that DOS is operational. The DOS prompt shows the current drive letter, a colon, and a greater-than symbol (>), but can be customized using the PROMPT command.

DOS Protected-Mode Interface (DPMI)

A Microsoft interface specification that establishes a DOS extension, which allows DOS programs to run in protected mode and therefore use extended memory. Protected mode allows programs to run as DOS tasks on their own, or under Windows

3.*x*. It provides these enhancements on 80286 and higher processors.

See also **memory.**

DOS Requester

The DOS client software written for the NetWare 2.*x*, NetWare 3.*x*, and NetWare 4.*x* operating systems, used to connect the workstation to network services. The DOS Requester replaces the NETX.COM shell from previous releases of NetWare. It mediates between applications, DOS, and NetWare, and consists of a Terminate-and-Stay-Resident (TSR) manager and multiple Virtual Loadable Modules (VLMs). DOS can call the DOS Requester to execute a network-based task that DOS would be incapable of executing by itself.

See also **NetWare DOS Requester; NETX.COM; Virtual Loadable Module.**

DOS setup routine

A routine used to set up the system configuration of a DOS client or NetWare server. This routine records the system's built-in hardware features and available system memory, and allows the user to set parameters such as the date and time, password, and keyboard speed.

DOS text utility

A DOS utility that provides instructions to the network. The command line and DOS menu utilities are both types of DOS text utilities.

DOS version

The version number and type of DOS being used. Different implementations of DOS (such as Novell DOS and MS DOS) are not compatible.

DOSGEN utility

In NetWare and IntraNetWare, a workstation utility that creates a DOS boot file in the SYS:LOGIN directory on the server. The workstation's boot files are then copied into the server's SYS:LOGIN directory so that the workstation can boot from the server.

dot address

Four groups of numbers in an Internet Protocol (IP) address that are separated by periods (or dots) where each group represents the decimal equivalent of the corresponding 8 bits of the 32-bit IP address. A dot address (for example, 117.127.137.147) is also known as *dotted quad* or *dotted quad address*.

See also **IP address.**

dot-matrix printer

A type of printer that forms characters and images from patterns of dots.

dotted decimal

The notation system used to represent four-byte Internet Protocol (IP) addresses.

See also **dot address; IP address.**

double buffering

Using two buffers for input and output. Double buffering improves performance and increases throughput. In this type of system, one buffer is being processed while the other is still being filled.

DOV

Data Over Voice, a communications strategy for sending data over a voice channel at the same time a voice transmission is taking place.

down

To shut down a server or other network device.

DOWN utility

In NetWare and IntranetWare, a server console utility that shuts down a NetWare server. The DOWN utility protects data integrity by closing open files and writing all cache buffers to disk before shutting down the system.

downgrading

The process of converting a message from the 1988 X.400 Message-Handling System (MHS) to one that can be used by a system using the 1984 version of X.400.
See also **Message-Handling System; X.400.**

downlink

A telecommunications link between a satellite and Earth station or stations.

downlink station

A group of communications equipment designed to receive and transmit signals to and from satellites.

download

The act of copying a file to a computer or peripheral device. For example, fonts can be downloaded directly to a printer, or a file downloaded from a host computer to a client computer. Both host and recipient must use the same communications protocol in order for a download to take place.

downsizing

In networking, a technique that offloads applications from proprietary mainframe platforms to a network of smaller, less expensive microcomputers. A common downsizing strategy replaces or supplements mainframes with a client-server architecture.
See also **client-server model.**

Downstream Physical Unit (DSPU)

A device in a ring topology that lies in the direction in which packets are traveling.
See also **ring topology.**

downtime

The amount of time a server, network, or other device is inoperable. A machine unavailable is not necessarily down; it may simply be unavailable because of heavy activity.

downward compatibility

Another term for backward compatibility.

DP

(1) **data processing,** processing typically done by minicomputers or mainframes in a data center.

(2) draft proposal, a preliminary version of a standard circulated by a formal standards organization or committee, comments and criticisms are received and considered, and the proposal may be subsequently edited.

DPA

Demand-Protocol Architecture, a feature of Microsoft's LAN Manager network operating system that makes it possible to load or unload protocol stacks dynamically. DPA makes it possible to support multiple network environments in the same machine.

See also **LAN Manager.**

DPC

Deferred Procedure Call, a condition in effect when Windows NT or Windows NT Advanced Server calls a task that is less important than the function currently executing. Consequently, execution of the called function is delayed until the higher-priority functions are completed.

DPMI

DOS Protected-Mode Interface, a Microsoft interface specification that establishes a DOS extension, which allows DOS programs to run in protected mode and therefore use extended memory. Protected mode allows programs to run as DOS tasks on their own, or under Windows 3.*x*. It provides these enhancements on 80286 and higher processors.

See also **memory.**

DQDB

Distributed-Queue Dual-Bus, a network architecture defined in the Institute of Electronic and Electrical Engineers (IEEE) 802.6 Metropolitan-Area Network (MAN) standard. DQDB is the main platform used for Synchronous Multimegabit Data Service (SMDS) access. DQDB, like Asynchronous Transfer Mode (ATM), uses a fixed-size, 53-byte cell to hold data and addressing information. DQDB establishes a Media-Access Control (MAC)-layer protocol that allows multiple systems to interconnect through two unidirectional logical buses. A network node may transmit and receive on one or both buses, depending on the location of the node in relation to the bus. It can also be used to establish a private, fiber-based MAN that can support data, voice, and video. The DQDB consists of the protocol syntax, and the distributed queuing algorithm used for shared medium access control. Generally, DQDB requires fiber-optic cable, and can support a transmission speed of up to 50 megabits per second (Mbps).

See also **Asynchronous Transfer Mode; Institute of Electronic and Electrical Engineers; IEEE 802.***x***; Media-Access Control; Metropolitan-Area Network.**

Draft International Standard (DIS)

An early version of a proposed standard from a formal standards organization. The DIS is submitted to committee members for comment before the standard is formally ratified.

Draft Proposal (DP)

A preliminary version of a standard circulated by a formal standards organization or committee, comments and criticisms are

received and considered, and the proposal may be subsequently edited.

drag-and-drop function

A mouse pointer operation that allows a user to select an object and move it to a new location. Drag-and-drop is often used to simplify file operations. For example, dragging a file to a printer icon causes the document to print.

DRAM

Dynamic Random-Access Memory, a type of chip memory that stores information in capacitors. The chip's charge must be renewed periodically. DRAM is slower, but less expensive than static RAM (SRAM), and more widely used by personal computer manufacturers.

DRDA

Distributed Relational Data Architecture, a distributed database architecture designed by IBM that forms the basis of the database management features offered by IBM's SystemView network management software.
See also **SystemView.**

drive

Refers to either a physical, logical, or virtual drive. A *physical drive* is a physical storage device (such as a disk drive or tape drive) to which data can be written, or from which it can be read. A *logical drive* identifies a specific directory located on the physical drive. A *virtual drive* may take the form of a random-access memory (RAM) disk, and mimics a physical drive.

drive array

A group of hard drives used in a single Redundant Array of Inexpensive Disks (RAID) configuration.
See also **Redundant Array of Inexpensive Disks.**

drive letter

A letter used to show that a specific disk drive is active.

drive mapping

A function whereby a pointer is established to point to a specific location in the file system. The pointer is represented as a letter assigned to a directory path on a volume. The path identifies the location of a directory, and includes the volume, directory, and any subdirectories that lead to the desired directory. Drive mappings are created for the purpose of following these paths. NetWare can recognize four types of drive mappings: local drive mappings, network drive mappings, network search drive mappings, and Directory Map objects. *Local drive mappings* are paths to local media, such as a hard disk. *Network drive mappings* point to volumes or directories on the network. *Network search drive mappings* point to network directories that are to be searched when a file is not found in the current directory. *Directory Map objects* permit a drive to be mapped to an application without having to know the actual path to where the application is physically located. Furthermore, drive mappings can be either temporary or permanent. To make the mappings permanent, MAP commands must be placed in the login script, or marked as permanent in the graphical login utility.
See also **MAP utility.**

driver

An application that establishes an interface between the operating system and a peripheral device. Drivers can be created for almost any type of device, including printers, Small Computer System Interface (SCSI) devices, or Network Interface Cards (NICs). Specialized drivers support a single model of one device for one program; but more generic drivers are also created for use with multiple device models.

See also **Network Interface Card; Small Computer System Interface.**

droid

A contraction for "software android" that refers to a program performing tasks on behalf of a user usually within preset parameters and without user intervention.

drop

An attachment to a horizontal cabling system, usually the point at which a computer is connected to the network transmission medium.

drop box

A folder in an AppleShare server used to grant write privileges.

drop-box folder

In NetWare, a folder for which a user has Create and File Scan rights. Users can copy files into the folder, but cannot see the folder's contents, delete files contained in the folder, or search the folder. A Macintosh folder marked with a belt around it is a drop-box folder.

drop cable

A four-pair Attachment-Unit Interface (AUI) cable used to connect network interface cards. The drop cable is connected to the network cable by a clamp.

See also **Attachment-Unit Interface.**

drop set

All the components required to connect a computer or peripheral to horizontal cabling. The drop set includes at least the cable and an adapter.

drop side

All the components required to connect a computer or peripheral to the patch panel or punch-down block that connects to the distribution frame.

See also **punch-down block.**

dropout

The temporary loss of a transmission signal.

DS

(1) Digital Service, a telecommunications service that uses digital signaling and is defined as a North American service using a five-level transmission hierarchy. A DS relies on Pulse Code Modulation (PCM) to encode analog signals in digital form. The five levels of digital services are DS-0 (64Kbps), DS-1 (1.544Mbps), DS-2 (6.312Mbps), DS-3 (44.736Mbps), and DS-4 (274.176Mbps). **(2) Directory Services,** a feature of NetWare 4.x a global, distributed, replicated database that retains information about all resources in the network. The Directory Services feature centrally manages any size network through a hierarchical, tree-like representation. Other directory services include the X.500 standard and the Domain-Naming System (DNS).

See also (2) **Domain-Naming System;** (1) **DS-*x*;** (2) **Novell Directory Services;** (1) **Pulse Code Modulation; X.500.**

DS (NLM)

A NetWare Loadable Module (NLM) that loads Novell Directory Services (NDS) on the network server. This NLM is loaded automatically when the server is started up.

See also **NetWare Loadable Module; Novell Directory Services.**

DS Login menu

A menu that can be accessed by clicking the tree icon in the Novell Directory Services (NDS) menu bar. The DS Login menu lets users check their NDS status, log in to the Directory, change the NDS password, and log out of the directory. When a user logs in to Directory Services via the DS Login menu, the user is not connecting to any given server, but is instead logging directly in to the Directory Services tree.

See also **Novell Directory Services.**

DS MIGRATE utility

In IntranetWare, a Windows workstation utility that upgrades a NetWare 2.*x* or NetWare 3.*x* server bindery by migrating information to an existing Directory tree. DS MIGRATE uses a three-step process: discover, model, and configure. Migrated bindery information can be modeled and configured as appropriate for the Directory tree.

DS Revision

A selectable property for the NCP Server object in Novell Directory Services (NDS).

See also **leaf object; Novell Directory Services; object.**

DS-*x*

Digital Service, a North American service specifying a five-level transmission hierarchy for telecommunications service using digital signaling. The five levels of digital services are as follows:

- *DS-0* – 64 kilobits per second (Kbps)
- *DS-1* – 1.544 megabits per second (Mbps) for United States; 2.108Mbps for Europe
- *DS-2* – 6.312Mbps
- *DS-3* – 44.736Mbps
- *DS-4* – 274.176Mbps

DSA

(1) **Directory Service Area,** the calling area covered by a directory service.
(2) **Directory System Agent,** software used in the X.500 Directory Services model for accessing, using, and updating the Directory Information Base (DIB) or Directory Information Tree (DIT).
(3) **Distributed Systems Architecture,** a network architecture designed by Honeywell that complies with Open System Interconnection (OSI) standards.

See also (2) **Directory Information Base;** (2) **Directory Information Tree;** (2) **X.500.**

DSC

Data-Stream Compatibility, a minimal printing mode used in IBM's Systems Network Architecture (SNA).

See also **Systems Network Architecture.**

DSE

Data-Switching Equipment, physical equipment used in a switching network.

DSI

Digital Speech Interpolation, a method of improving the efficiency of a communications channel. By sending transmissions during the quiet periods that normally occur in a voice conversation, DIS can double the number of voice signals a line can carry.

DSMERGE utility

In NetWare 4.*x* and IntranetWare, a utility that creates a single Directory tree from two separate trees, renames the tree to verify that all servers in the tree are responding properly and have the same tree name, and allows the viewing of time synchronization information. The DSMERGE utility merges the two directories at the root. The DSMERGE utility function must be executed before objects can be moved from one tree to another.

DSOM

Distributed System-Object Model, a system designed by IBM for sharing objects across a network. DSOM is compliant with the Common Object-Request Broker Architecture (CORBA) model.

See also **Common Object-Request Broker Architecture.**

DSP

(1) Digital Signal Processor, a device used to extract and process elements from a digital stream.
(2) Directory System Protocol, a protocol used by Directory System Agents (DSAs) to communicate with each other.
(3) Domain-Specific Part, part of the address for the Network Service-Access Point (NSAP) in the OSI Reference Model. The DSP is the address within the domain.

See also **(2) Directory System Agent;
(3) Network Service-Access Point;
(3) OSI Reference Model.**

DSPACE utility

In NetWare 3.*x*, a workstation utility that lists and changes a current file server's attachments, limits a user's disk space on a volume, and limits disk space in a directory.

DSPU

Downstream Physical Unit, a device in a ring topology that lies in the direction in which packets are traveling.

See also **ring topology.**

DSR

Data Set Ready, a signal sent from a modem to indicate that the modem is ready to function.

DSREPAIR utility

In NetWare 4.x and IntranetWare, a server console utility that repairs and corrects problems in the Directory Information Database (DIB). The utility only works on that portion of the database stored on the server where the utility has been executed. To repair the entire database, the utility must be run on each server that holds part of the database.

DST

daylight-saving time, the practice of setting clocks an hour ahead to provide an extra hour of daylight at the end of workdays during spring, summer, and fall.

DSU

Digital Service Unit, a device that sits between a user's Data-Terminal Equipment (DTE) and a common carrier's digital circuits. The DSU formats data for transmission on the public carrier's wide-area network (WAN). The DSU is required to connect to carrier services such as Frame Relay or Switched Multimegabit Data Service (SMDS)

See also **Data-Terminal Equipment; Frame Relay network; Switched Multimegabit Data Service.**

DSU/CSU

Data-Service Unit/Channel-Service Unit, in a digital telecommunications network, two components of a Data-Communications Equipment (DCE) device that provide access to digital services over a variety of lines. The DSU connects to the Data-Terminal Equipment (DTE) through a synchronous serial

interface, formats data for transmission, and controls data flow between the network and the CSU. The CSU terminates the long-distance connection at the user's end, processes digital signals, tests remote loopback, and functions as a buffer to prevent nonstandard customer-premises equipment from bringing down the public carrier's network.

See also **Data-Communications Equipment; Data-Terminal Equipment.**

DSVD

Digital Simultaneous Voice and Data, a standard used in terminal adapters that allows a user to talk over a telephone line being used simultaneously to transmit data.

DSX1/3

Digital Signal Cross-Connect Between Levels 1 and 3, an interface that connects DS-1 and DS-3 signals.

See also **DS-x.**

DTAM

Document Transfer and Manipulation, specifications for nontelephone and nontelegraph communications services (such as telex, fax transmissions, and telewriting) that define three service classes (bulk transfer, document manipulation, and bulk transfer and manipulation), primitive functional units for each service class, and related communications support functions.

DTE

Data-Terminal Equipment, a network-attached, customer premises, or end-user hardware device that operates in packet mode and connects with the Data-Communications Equipment (DCE) to establish data communications.

See also **Data-Communications Equipment.**

DTMF

Dual-Tone Multifrequency, a telephone technology used to create 16 separate tones from 8 frequencies. The 16 tones are used to provide a unique tone for each of the 12 base buttons on a Touch Tone telephone, plus four additional keys.

DTR

(1) Data Terminal Ready, a signal from a modem indicating that a device is ready to send and receive data.

(2) Dedicated Token Ring, a Token Ring specification outlined in the Institute of Electrical and Electronic Engineers (IEEE) 802.5r specification that allows full-duplex connections, and establishes a connection speed of up to 32 megabits per second (Mbps). By enabling full-duplex communications, the token-passing mechanism is bypassed and communication can take place between a device and a switch port at any time.

See also **(2) full duplex; (2) IEEE 802.x; (2) Token Ring.**

DTS

Digital-Termination Service, a service that allows the private network to access the carrier networks with digital microwave equipment.

DUA

Directory User Agent, A program used in the X.500 Directory Services model for accessing directory services and that establishes an interface between an end-user and a Directory System Agent (DSA), which retrieves the requested services.

See also **Directory System Agent; X.500.**

dual cable system

A networking configuration that connects a node to the network through more than one physical link. The value of this configuration is that if one link fails, the station is still able to communicate through the additional link.

dual homing

An Fiber Distributed Data Interface (FDDI) technique that uses redundant concentrators to improve reliability. Under this configuration, the server is attached to both concentrators, which are both connected to a dual-attached FDDI ring. Dual homing provides an alternative route to the FDDI network, in case the primary route is unavailable.

See also **Fiber Distributed Data Interface.**

dual in-line package (DIP)

A type of switch that can have one of two settings. DIP switches provide an alternative to jumper settings that are used to configure components. DIP switches are common in dot matrix printers, modems, and other peripherals.

dual processing

A System Fault Tolerance (SFT) III configuration that assigns different parts of an
operating system to separate processors. A
server with dual processing capability has
two central processing units (CPUs)
installed.

See also **System Fault Tolerance.**

Dual-Tone Multifrequency (DTMF)

A telephone technology used to create 16
separate tones from 8 frequencies. The 16
tones are used to provide a unique tone for
each of the 12 base buttons on a Touch
Tone telephone, plus four additional keys.

Dual-Attachment Concentrator (DAC)

A concentrator used in a Fiber Distributed
Data Interface (FDDI) to attach single-attachment stations or station clusters to the FDDI
rings.

See also **Fiber Distributed Data
Interface.**

dual-attachment station (DAS)

In Fiber Distributed Data Interface (FDDI)
networks, a station or node connected to
both the primary and secondary rings. A
station can be directly connected to the
FDDI ring through a port on the DAS, with
no concentrator required. A single-attachment station, on the other hand, must be
attached to a concentrator.

See also **Fiber Distributed Data
Interface.**

dumb terminal

A monitor and keyboard with limited capabilities, used mainly for displaying and
editing data.

duplexing

A method of duplicating data to protect it.
Disk duplexing involves copying one set of
data onto two hard disks on two separate
disk channels. Duplexing is preferable to
mirroring, which copies data onto two hard
disks on the same disk channel.

Duplicate FATs and DETs

A feature of the Data Reliability function that
duplicates the File-Allocation Table (FAT)
and Directory-Entry Table (DET), both of
which contain data-address information.
The duplication is meant to help prevent
data loss.

See also **Directory-Entry Table; File-
Allocation Table.**

duty cycle

The proportion of a time period in an
electrical signal, when the signal is on and
represented by a bit value of one.

DUV

Data Under Voice, a telecommunications
strategy for sending voice and data over the
same line.

DXI

Data-Exchange Interface, An interface
between a router and a Data Service Unit

(DSU) that performs segmentation and reassembly.

dynamic

A term describing processes that change over time.

dynamic address resolution

The process of using an address resolution protocol to determine and store address information on demand.

dynamic addressing

An AppleTalk networking strategy under which network nodes automatically select unique addresses. Under this scheme, a node continues to try new addresses until it finds one that is not in use.

See also **AppleTalk.**

dynamic configuration

A way to allocate resources according to current needs and resource availability. NetWare servers dynamically configure the following parameters: directory cache buffers, file locks, kernel processes, kernel semaphores, maximum number of open files, memory for NetWare Loadable Module (NLM) programs, router/server advertising, routing buffers, service processes, Transaction-Tracking Service (TTS) transactions, and turbo FAT index tables.

See also **NetWare Loadable Module; Transaction-Tracking Service.**

Dynamic Data Exchange (DDE)

A technique used for application-to-application communications, available on the Microsoft Windows, Macintosh System 7, and OS/2 operating systems. Two DDE-compliant applications can exchange data and commands by DDE conversations, or two-way connections that take place between the applications. A DDE conversation does not require any user intervention. DDE has been superseded by Object Linking and Embedding (OLE).

See also **Object Linking and Embedding.**

Dynamic Host-Configuration Protocol (DHCP)

A protocol that dynamically assigns Internet Protocol (IP) addresses to Windows-based personal computers in a local-area network (LAN). DHCP allows the administrator to assign a set of IP addresses. Then each client requests an IP address from the DHCP server, uses it only as long as necessary, and returns it to the address pool.

Dynamic Link Library (DLL)

A program library that holds related modules of compiled executable functions that can be called by other programs. The DLL model allows the developer to insert a pointer to the DLL, as opposed to inserting the full program code into an application. An application reads the functions in the DLL at runtime, and several applications can use the same DLL. DLLs are used in Microsoft Windows and IBM's OS/2 operating systems.

dynamic link routine

A program that can be loaded on demand and terminated automatically. The dynamic link routine is a function of the OS/2 and Microsoft Windows 3.*x* operating systems.

dynamic memory

Memory used for random-access memory (RAM) that continuously rewrites all stored information. All data is lost from dynamic memory when the system shuts down.
See also **memory.**

Dynamic Random-Access Memory (DRAM)

A type of chip memory that stores information in capacitors. The chip's charge must be renewed periodically. DRAM is slower, but less expensive than static RAM (SRAM), and more widely used by personal computer manufacturers.

dynamic routing

The automatic rerouting of data transmissions to maximize throughput or to balance traffic. The automatic routing decisions are based on available data about current network traffic.

Dynamically Assigned Socket (DAS)

An AppleTalk socket in the numeric range of 128 through 254. Values between 1 and 127 are retained for use by statically assigned sockets. The socket value is assigned to a particular client upon request. The socket is the entity used to facilitate communication between programs or processes. Any process running on a node can request a DAS value; while that process is executing, its assigned value cannot be employed by any other socket.
See also **AppleTalk.**

DynaText

An electronic document viewer provided in NetWare and IntranetWare that provides a graphical user interface (GUI) for reading online manuals on workstations throughout the network.

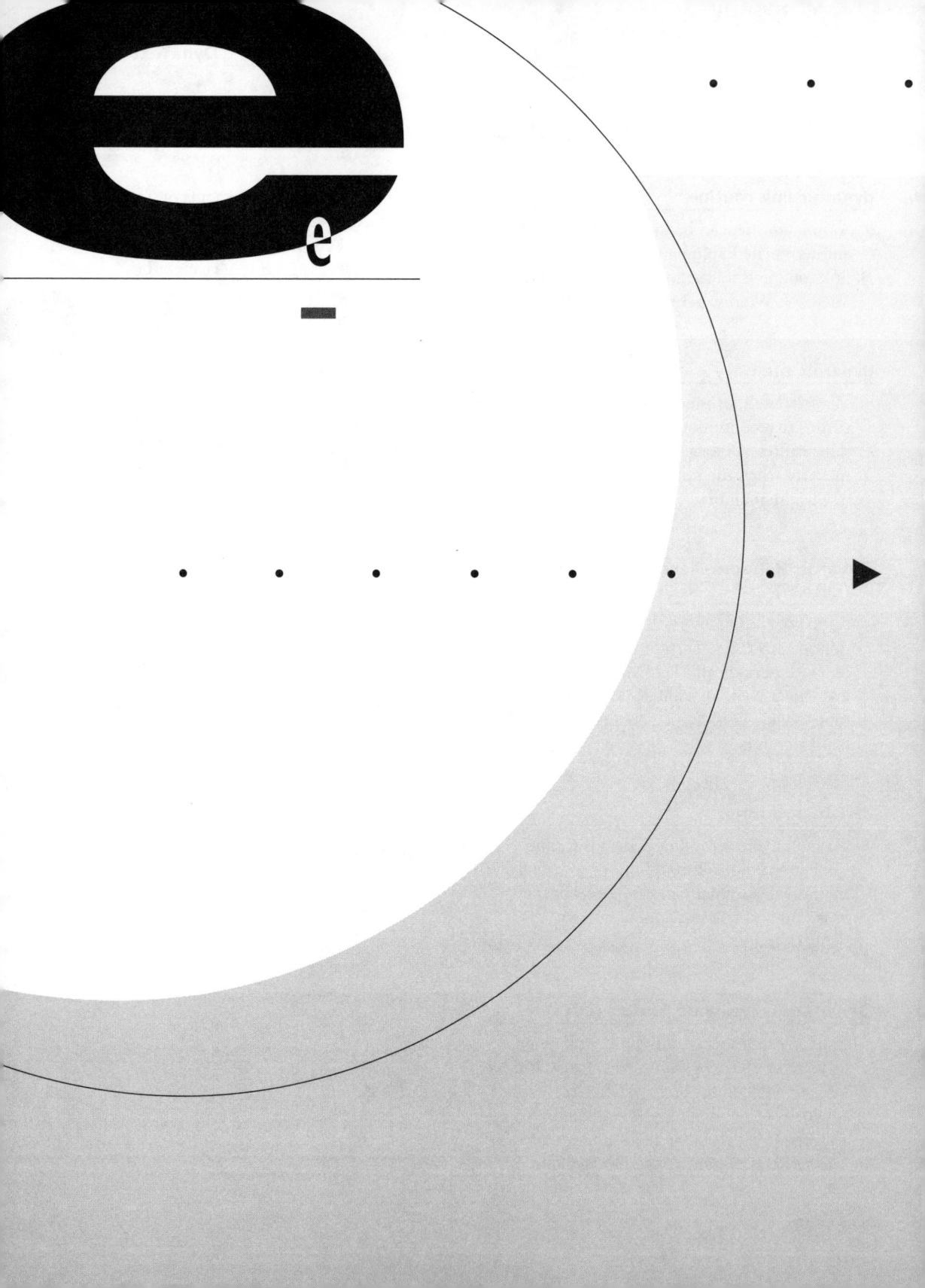

E

exa-, a prefix used to indicate one quintillion, or 10^{18}. When applied to computing, it refers to the power of two closest to one quintillion.

E channel

A 64-kilobit-per-second (Kbps) circuit-switching control channel in an Integrated-Services Digital Network (ISDN).

See also **Integrated-Services Digital Network.**

E&M signaling

A standard signaling method often used in interoffice and toll trunk lines.

E.164

A Consultative Committee for International Telegraphy and Telephony (CCITT) recommendation for an evolution of telephone numbers in international telecommunications numbering. This specification especially affects Integrated-Services Digital Network (ISDN), Broadcast Integrated-Services Digital Network (BISDN), and Switched Multimegabit Data Service (SMDS) networks.

See also **Broadcast Integrated-Services Digital Network; Integrated-Services Digital Network; Switched Multimegabit Data Service.**

E1 carrier

A transport channel used to carry 30 voice channels, each one running at 64 kilobits per second (Kbps), for a total of 2,048 megabits per second (Mbps). It also holds two additional 64Kbps channels for signaling. E1 links can be multiplexed into single larger links. The E1 configuration is commonly used in Europe, Mexico, and South America, and is similar to the T carrier channels used in North America.

See also **T1.**

Early Token Release (ETR)

A control process used in Token Ring networks that allows multiple packets to travel in the ring at the same time. A standard Token Ring network only allows the single node that holds the token to transmit, so that only one packet is traveling in the ring at any given time; and the token can be passed only after the packet has been received. Under ETR, the token is released immediately after the sending node releases the packet into the ring.

See also **Token Ring.**

EARN

European Academic and Research Network, a European network used to provide file transfer and electronic mail (e-mail) services to universities and research institutions.

Earth station

The ground-based end of a satellite communications system. The Earth station includes an antenna and receiver, and is used to communicate with an orbiting satellite. The Earth station can send signals to the satellite, which in turn relays them to another Earth station.

e-cash (electronic cash)

An electronic payment system that offers many of the same benefits of traditional cash transactions.

E3

A transmission rate (34 megabits per second) that is the highest rate generally available in the European digital infrastructure.

EB

exabyte, a unit of measure equaling one quintillion bytes.

EBCDIC

Extended Binary-Coded Decimal Interchange Code, a character set that has 256 characters, with each character represented by an 8-bit pattern. The character set, defined by IBM, includes values for control functions and graphics. It is commonly used on IBM mainframes and minicomputers, and differs from American Standard Code for Information Interchange (ASCII) in that placement of the letters of the alphabet is discontinuous. There is no direct match that can be achieved when converting between ASCII and EBCDIC, because each character set contains some unique characters.

See also **American Standard Code for Information Interchange.**

ECB

(1) Electronic Cookbook, an operating mode used in the Data-Encryption Standard (DES).

(2) Event-Control Block, an entity used to control events relating to the transmission and reception of Internetwork Packet Exchange/Sequenced Packet Exchange (IPX/SPX) packets and sessions.

See also **(1) Data-Encryption Standard; (2) Internetwork Packet Exchange; (2) Sequenced Packet Exchange.**

ECC

error-correction code, an entity used to control events relating to the transmission sand reception of Internetwork Packet Exchange/Sequenced Packet Exchange (IPX/SPX) packets and sessions.

See also **Internetwork Packet Exchange; Sequenced Packet Exchange.**

echo

A type of distortion that occurs when a transmitted packet is reflected back to the sender. An echo may occur if there is an electrical mismatch between the sender and recipient. Echo can also refer to a mechanism used to test network nodes, where each receiving station on the network sends a message back to the host.

echo cancellation

A mechanism used to control echoes on communications links. With echo cancellation, a modem checks for a delayed duplication of the original signal, and then adds a reversed version of the transmission to the channel on which the information was received. This removes the echo without adversely affecting the original transmission.

Echo/Echo Reply

A network-management mechanism that determines whether network nodes are capable of receiving transmissions, or whether the network connection is functioning properly. An echo signal is issued, and the sender waits for an echo reply, which indicates that the receiving node is operational.

Echoplex

A verification mode in which keyboard codes are echoed back to a terminal screen when the appropriate signal is returned from the other end of the line to indicate that the characters were received correctly.

Echospeech

A plug-in from Echo Speech for Windows and Macintosh World Wide Web (WWW) browsers that adds speech-optimized streaming audio to Internet Web sites.
See also **Web browser.**

ECL

Emitter-Coupled Logic, an entity used to control events relating to the transmission and reception of Internetwork Packet Exchange/Sequenced Packet Exchange (IPX/SPX) packets and sessions.
See also **Internetwork Packet Exchange; Sequenced Packet Exchange.**

ECMA

European Computer Manufacturers Association, an entity used to control events relating to the transmission and reception of Internetwork Packet Exchange/Sequenced Packet Exchange (IPX/SPX) packets and sessions.
See also **Internetwork Packet Exchange; Sequenced Packet Exchange.**

ECN

Explicit Congestion Notification, a Frame Relay mechanism used to indicate when the network is congested. This mechanism uses two bit values to indicate the congested condition. The Backward Explicit Congestion Notification (BECN) bit value is included in Frame Relay headers that are traveling in the direction opposite the congestion, in an attempt to inform source nodes that a congested condition is occurring downline. The Forward Explicit Congestion Notification (FECN) bit value is included in Frame Relay headers that are traveling toward the congestion, in an attempt to inform destination nodes that a congested condition is occurring ahead.

ECNE

Enterprise CNE, an individual with the CNE designation who has also been certified by Novell to support enterprise-wide networks. This certification has been superseded by the Master CNE.

ECTP

Ethernet Configuration-Test Protocol, a protocol used to determine whether a network conforms to the Blue Book Ethernet standard.

ED

End Delimiter, a field in a Token Ring token or data frame, used to indicate the end of the token or frame.

See also **Token Ring.**

EDI

Electronic Data Interchange, a way to electronically exchange standardized business documents such as bills of material, purchase orders, or invoices. An EDI network can be established using Open Systems Interconnection (OSI) standards, or through one of several proprietary products that are commercially available. EDI may also take place over the Internet, although more security-conscious users often prefer to use a private, value-added network.

EDIFACT

Electronic Data Interchange for Administration, Commerce, and Transport, a United Nations data exchange standard designed to be a multi-industry standard for electronic data interchange (EDI).

See also **electronic data interchange.**

EDIT (NLM)

In NetWare and IntranetWare, a server console utility used to create and edit text files (of up to 8K in size) on either a DOS or NetWare partition. This NetWare Loadable Module (NLM) is useful for creating .NCF batch files that automatically execute server commands.

See also **NetWare Loadable Module.**

EDITOR

A program used to create and edit ASCII text files.

EDO

Extended Data Out, dynamic random-access memory (DRAM) that improves memory speed and performance by altering the timing and sequence of signals that activate the circuitry for accessing memory locations.

EDP

electronic data processing, processing typically done by minicomputers or mainframes in a data center.

See **data processing.**

edu (educational)

A suffix for an Internet address that indicates the host computer is run by an educational institution (probably a college or university) and that the host computer probably is in the United States.

See also **IP address.**

EEMA

European Electronic-Mail Association, a European trade group made up of developers and vendors of electronic mail (e-mail) products.

EEMS

Enhanced Expanded-Memory Specification, a revised version of the Expanded-Memory Specification (EMS). EEMS allows

DOS applications to use more than 640K of memory.

See also **memory.**

EEPROM

Enhanced Erasable/Programmable Read-Only Memory, a type of read-only memory that allows old data to be erased by writing over it.

EFF

Electronic Frontier Foundation, a public policy organization whose goals include preserving the public availability of electronic networks (such as the Internet).

effective bandwidth

The strongest portion of a communications channel's signal.

Effective Isotropic Radiated Power (EIRP)

The relative strength of a signal received at the Earth station portion of a satellite communications system. This value is measured in decibels.

See also **Earth station.**

effective rights

The rights a Novell Directory Services (NDS) or bindery object can exercise to view or modify a given directory, file, or object. Every time an object attempts a task relating to a directory, file, or other object, the NetWare operating system calculates the seeking object's effective rights. If an object has no explicitly stated effective rights, at least it has the rights granted to [Public] or to the group EVERYONE. The following four factors determine the effective rights to a file or directory:

- An object's trustee assignments to the file or directory
- Inherited rights from an object's trustee assignments to parent directories
- Trustee assignments of Group objects to which a User object belongs
- Trustee assignments of objects in the User object's *Security Equal To* list.

See also **NetWare Directory; Novell Directory Services; trustee rights.**

effective throughput

The practical number of data bits that can be sent over a given period of time.

EFS

(1) End Frame Sequence, the last field in a Token Ring packet.
(2) Error-Free Second, a second of transmission that contains no errors. The number of EFSs that occur over a given period of time may be used as an indicator of transmission quality.

See also **(1) Token Ring.**

EGA

Enhanced Graphics Adapter, an IBM video-display standard that requires a digital RGB Enhanced Color Display, and provides medium-level resolution for both text and graphics. The EGA standard has been superseded by Video Graphics Array (VGA).

See also **Video Graphics Array.**

EGP

External Gateway Protocol, a protocol used by gateways in an internetwork to exchange network reachability information between autonomous systems. EGP is used in the Internet core system, and is part of the Transmission-Control Protocol/Internet Protocol (TCP/IP) suite.

See also **Transmission-Control Protocol/Internet Protocol.**

EGP peer

An Exterior Gateway Protocol (EGP) peer. When an EGP peer uses an Interior Gateway Protocol (IGP) distance vector algorithm to disseminate information about routing, continuous changes may make the algorithm unstable.

See also **Exterior Gateway Protocol; Interior Gateway Protocol.**

EIA

Electronic Industries Association, a standards organization that establishes standards for cabling.

See also **cable.**

EIB

Enterprise Information Base, a database used in an enterprise network to hold management and performance information about the network. Data held in the EIB is often accessed by network management software.

EIRP

Effective Isotropic Radiated Power, the relative strength of a signal received at the Earth station portion of a satellite communications system. This value is measured in decibels.

See also **Earth station.**

EISA

Extended Industry-Standard Architecture, a 32-bit bus standard that is compatible with Industry-Standard Architecture (ISA). Developed to allow input/output (I/O) to keep pace with faster processors, EISA also allows multiple processors to share the same bus.

See also **Industry-Standard Architecture.**

EKTS

Electronic Key Telephone System, a key telephone system using electrical switches.

ELAP

EtherTalk Link Access Protocol, an AppleTalk link-access protocol used for EtherTalk, and exists at the Data Link Layer (Layer 2) of the OSI Reference Model.

elbow connector

A connector with a right angle used to connect wires in a corner.

See also **connector.**

electrical signal

An electrical current sent as a waveform. Communications can take place over an electrical signal by superimposing a modulating signal over a fixed carrier signal. Information can be represented by

changing, or modulating, the superimposed signal in different ways relative to the fixed signal.

Electrifier

A plug-in from Lari Software for Windows and Macintosh World Wide Web (WWW) browsers that displays graphics created with the company's Lightning Draw graphics tools (based on Apple Computer's QuickDraw GX technology). The graphics are vector images, which means they are composed of lines and shapes instead of dots.

See also **Web browser.**

electromagnetic interference (EMI)

A type of interference that may emanate from motors or other power supplies in close proximity to a computer. Electromagnetic interference may cause computer errors.

Electronic Cookbook (ECB)

An operating mode used in the Data-Encryption Standard (DES).

See also **Data-Encryption Standard.**

Electronic Data Interchange (EDI)

A way to electronically exchange standardized business documents such as bills of material, purchase orders, or invoices. An EDI network can be established using Open Systems Interconnection (OSI) standards, or through one of several proprietary products that are commercially available. EDI may also take place over the Internet, although more security-conscious users often prefer to use a private, value-added network.

Electronic Data Interchange for Administration, Commerce, and Transport (EDIFACT)

A United Nations data exchange standard designed to be a multi-industry standard for electronic data interchange (EDI).

See also **electronic data interchange.**

electronic data processing (EDP)

Processing typically done by minicomputers or mainframes in a data center.

See **data processing.**

Electronic Frontier Foundation (EFF)

A public policy organization whose goals include preserving the public availability of electronic networks (such as the Internet).

Electronic Industries Association (EIA)

A standards organization that establishes standards for cabling.

See also **cable.**

Electronic Key Telephone System (EKTS)

A key telephone system using electrical switches.

electronic mail (e-mail)

A method used to send files and messages between workstations. One user can send a message to another user or group of users on the same system. E-mail systems can be implemented on a peer-to-peer network, client-server architecture, mainframe computer, dial-up service, or through the Internet.

See also **dial-up service; mailbox; mail-enabled application.**

Electronic Mail Association (EMA)

A trade group consisting of developers and vendors of electronic-mail (e-mail) products.

electronic mailbox

A directory in an electronic-mail (e-mail) software system used to store a user's messages.
See also **electronic mail; dial-up service; mailbox; mail-enabled application.**

Electronic Switched Network (ESN)

A telecommunications service used by private networks that establishes an automatic switching mechanism between Private Branch Exchanges (PBXs), so that one PBX can call any other PBX in the network without a dedicated connection.
See also **Private Branch Exchange.**

electronic switching

Making circuit connections electronically, as opposed to electromechanically.

electrostatic discharge (ESD)

Charges generated by static electricity. An electrostatic discharge as low as 30 volts may harm a computer component.

elevator seeking

A way to organize how data is read from a hard disk storage device by logically organizing disk operations as they arrive at the server for processing. This mechanism can improve disk channel performance, by minimizing back-and-forth movements of the physical disk head. Elevator seeking accomplishes this efficiency by queuing disk-read and disk-write requests for a given drive. The operating system then prioritizes the requests on the basis of the drive's head position, and fulfills them according to the current position of the drive head.

ELF

extremely low-frequency emission, radiation emitted by a computer monitor or other electronic appliance. An ELF emission ranges from between 5 Hertz (Hz) and 2,000Hz, and decline as a function of the square of the distance from its source.

Elm

An electronic-mail (e-mail) reader for systems operating in the UNIX environment.
See also **electronic mail.**

ELS NetWare

Entry-Level System NetWare, an early version of NetWare meant for smaller networks. ELS NetWare was discontinued in 1991, and has been superseded by Personal NetWare.
See also **Personal NetWare.**

e-mail

electronic mail, a method used to send files and messages between workstations. One user can send a message to another user or

group of users on the same system. E-mail systems can be implemented on a peer-to-peer network, client-server architecture, mainframe computer, dial-up service, or through the Internet.

See also **dial-up service; mailbox; mail-enabled application.**

E-Mail Address

A Directory Schema term; also, in Novell Directory Services (NDS), a selectable property for the following objects: External Entity, Group, Message-Routing Group, Organization, Organizational Role, Organizational Unit, and User. An e-mail address implements a standardized addressing scheme for the purpose of sending a message from one station to another over a network.

See also **container object; leaf object; Novell Directory Services; object.**

EMA

(1) **Electronic Mail Association,** a trade group consisting of developers and vendors of electronic mail (e-mail) products.
(2) **Enterprise Management Architecture,** Digital Equipment Corporation's network-management model designed to manage multivendor enterprise networks, and to comply with the International Standards Organization (ISO) Common Management-Information Protocol (CMIP) standard. EMA is implemented in Digital's DEC Management Control Center (DECmcc) product.

See also (2) **Common Management-Information Protocol;** (2) **DEC Management Control Center.**

embedded SCSI

A hard disk with a Small Computer System Interface (SCSI) and hard disk controller both built into the unit.

See also **Small Computer System Interface.**

EMI

electromagnetic interference, a type of interference that may emanate from motors or other power supplies in close proximity to a computer. Electromagnetic interference may cause computer errors.

Emissary

A suite of Internet tools from Wollongong that includes a World Wide Web (WWW) browser, an electronic-mail (e-mail) client, a newsreader, and ftp access. The package features a customizable toolbar, dialer setup, changing menus (when moving from one function to the next), hot lists containing popular Web Universal Resource Locator (URL) addresses, and an automatic e-mail filing system.

See also **electronic mail; newsreader; Web browser.**

 **For more information about Emissary, surf the Web to** `http://www.attachmate.com/products&services/internet/edsk2ws.htm`.

Emitter-Coupled Logic (ECL)

A logical scheme for high-speed digital circuitry.

EMM

Expanded-Memory Manager, a device driver used to support the software portion of the Expanded-Memory Specification (EMS). This driver creates a block of addresses, used to swap data into and out of as needed.

See also **Expanded-Memory Specification; memory.**

emoticon

A group of symbols often used within electronic-mail (e-mail) messages. Emoticons often convey an emotion, such as irony, joy, displeasure, or anger. Many emoticons must be viewed sideways to understand their meaning. One of the most common emoticons, which indicates happiness, is written as : -)

EMS

Expanded-Memory Specification, the standard method of accessing expanded memory. This specification allows programs running on Intel 8086 processors to access up to 32MB of expanded memory.

See also **memory.**

emulation

Making one device or software program appear as though it were another device or software program. For example, terminal emulation programs allow a personal computer to pose as a mainframe computer terminal.

emulation mode

A network control program function that enables the program to perform activities equivalent to those performed by a transmission control unit.

enable

To prepare a software program or hardware device for a task. A menu command enabled is typically shown in black type.

ENABLE LOGIN utility

In NetWare and IntranetWare, a server console utility that re-enables logins after they have been disabled using the DISABLE LOGIN command, or that enables the administrator's account when the account has been locked by the intruder detection function.

See also **DISABLE LOGIN utility.**

ENABLE TTS utility

A NetWare and IntranetWare server console utility that reestablishes the Transaction-Tracking System (TTS) after it has been disabled with the DISABLE TTS utility.

See also **DISABLE TTS utility; Transaction-Tracking System.**

Encapsulated PostScript (EPS)

The file format used by the PostScript page-description language, service-independent so images can be transferred between different applications. Images can also be sized and then output to different printers. An EPS file contains PostScript commands, and an optional preview image stored in PICT or TIFF format. An EPS file can be printed only to a PostScript-compatible printer.

encapsulation

A technique whereby one protocol is enveloped within a second protocol for transmission.

encapsulation bridging

A bridge that carries Ethernet frames from one router to another across different media, such as serial lines and Fiber Distributed Data Interface (FDDI) lines.

See also **bridge; Fiber Distributed Data Interface; translation bridging.**

encode

To represent characters or values in an alternative format.

encoding (signal)

A set of rules used to represent characters or values in an alternative format. A common type of signal encoding represents different voltage levels as either a zero or one. This simple mechanism forms the basis of binary transmissions. There are numerous types of encoding schemes, including Alternate Mark Inversion (AMI), Bipolar with 8-Zero Substitution (B8ZS), Differential Manchester, Manchester, Non-Return-to-Zero (NRZ), and Return to Zero (RZ).

See also **Alternate Mark Inversion; Bipolar with 8-Zero Substitution; differential Manchester encoding; Manchester encoding; Non-Return-to-Zero; Return to Zero.**

encryption

A process used to transform text into an unreadable form (known as *ciphertext*) that can then be decoded using a conversion algorithm and predefined bit value (known as a *key*). The simplest type of encryption simply uses a single key, and the recipient must know both the encryption algorithm and key to decrypt the message. *Private-key encryption* uses a private key, which only the sender and recipient know, and a public encryption algorithm. *Public-key encryption*, on the other hand, uses two halves of a bit sequence, each one constituting a key. One key is placed in an accessible public-key library. The other key is only known to an individual.

end bracket

Part of a circuit board with slots used to plug in other boards.

End Delimiter (ED)

A field in a Token Ring token or data frame, used to indicate the end of the token or frame.

See also **Token Ring.**

End Frame Sequence (EFS)

The last field in a Token Ring packet.

See also **Token Ring.**

end node

The computer or other hardware unit that exists at the origin and destination of network traffic. The end node does not relay traffic to other nodes.

end-of-content (EOC)

A character used to indicate the end of a message or a page.

End Office (EO)

A Central Office in a telecommunications network where subscribers' lines terminate and are connected with other exchanges.

end system (ES)

Under the OSI Reference Model, the computer that contains application processes that can communicate through all seven layers of the OSI model. An end system is sometimes referred to as an *end node*.
See also **OSI Reference Model.**

End-System-to-Intermediate-System (ES-IS)

The connection between an end system (or user station) and an intermediate system (or the routing element in an internetwork).

ENDCAP utility

A NetWare 3.*x* workstation utility that frees a workstation's printer port after information was sent to the printer with the CAPTURE command. The ENDCAP function has been included in the CAPTURE command in NetWare 4.*x*.
See also **CAPTURE utility.**

end-of-file (EOF)

A code placed after the last byte in a file. The EOF code indicates that no more data follows after that point.

end-of-text (ETX)

A character used to indicate the end of a text file.

end-of-transmission (EOT)

A character used to indicate the end of a transmission.

End-to-End Routing

A routing strategy that predetermines a message's full route before the message is sent.

end-user

An individual who uses an application on his or her own workstation.

Energy Services Network (ESnet)

An internetwork that spans across multiple nations of the world.

engine

The core of a database or other application.

Enhanced Erasable/Programmable Read-Only Memory (EEPROM)

A type of read-only memory that allows old data to be erased by writing over it.

Enhanced Expanded-Memory Specification (EEMS)

A revised version of the Expanded-Memory Specification (EMS). EEMS allows DOS applications to use more than 640K of memory.
See also **memory.**

Enhanced Graphics Adapter (EGA)

An IBM video display standard that requires a digital RGB Enhanced Color Display, and provides medium-level resolution for both text and graphics. The EGA standard has been superseded by Video Graphics Array (VGA).

See also **Video Graphics Array.**

Enhanced Parallel Port (EPP)

A parallel port with a signal rate of up to 16 megabits per second (Mbps).

Enhanced Small-Device Interface (ESDI)

A standard used to interface a bus controller with a hard drive. ESDI has, in most cases, been replaced by Small Computer System Interface (SCSI).

See also **Small Computer System Interface.**

ENS

Enterprise Network Services, Banyan Systems' software product (based on its StreetTalk Directory Service) that supports Internetwork Packet Exchange/Sequenced Packet Exchange (IPX/SPX), and includes the StreetTalk Directory Assistance, Banyan Security Service, and Banyan Network-Management applications. ENS can be used by StreetTalk users to track servers running operating systems other than VINES.

enterprise

An entire business group or organization, including remote offices.

Enterprise CNE (ECNE)

An individual with the CNE designation who has also been certified by Novell to support enterprise-wide networks. This certification has been superseded by the Master CNE.

enterprise computing

A method of connecting all a company's computing resources, including those in remote locations. The enterprise network may encompass several different computing platforms and operating systems.

Enterprise Information Base (EIB)

A database used in an enterprise network to hold management and performance information about the network. Data held in the EIB is often accessed by network management software.

Enterprise Management Architecture (EMA)

Digital Equipment Corporation's network-management model designed to manage multivendor enterprise networks, and to comply with the International Standards Organization (ISO) Common Management-Information Protocol (CMIP) standard. EMA is implemented in Digital's DEC Management Control Center (DECmcc) product.

See also **Common Management-Information Protocol; DEC Management Control Center.**

enterprise network

An internetwork that connects multiple sites and runs mission-critical applications.

Enterprise Network Services (ENS)

Banyan Systems' software product (based on its StreetTalk Directory Service) that supports Internetwork Packet Exchange/Sequenced Packet Exchange (IPX/SPX), and includes the StreetTalk Directory Assistance, Banyan Security Service, and Banyan Network-Management applications. ENS can be used by StreetTalk users to track servers running operating systems other than VINES.

See also **Internetwork Packet Exchange; Sequenced Packet Exchange; StreetTalk Directory Service; Virtual Networking System.**

Enterprise System Connection Architecture (ESCON)

A fiber-optic communications channel, developed by IBM, that connects mainframes and peripheral devices and uses multimode fiber with a light-emitting diode (LED) as a light source.

entity

An abstract device (such as a program or a function) that implements services or functions used by other entities at higher layers; and requests services or functions from other entities at lower layers.

entrance facilities

The spot where a building's wiring meets the external wiring.

entry box

A box in a DOS menu utility or Windows application into which text is entered.

Entry-Level System (ELS) NetWare

An early version of NetWare meant for smaller networks. ELS NetWare was discontinued in 1991, and has been superseded by Personal NetWare.

See also **Personal NetWare.**

entry point

The point where a network node is connected to a network. When applied to software, entry point refers to the point where a program starts to execute.

entry state

A value in a routing table in an AppleTalk network. The entry state shows the status of a path.

See also **AppleTalk.**

envelope

Information added to a data packet to ensure that it reaches its destination, and arrives without error. The envelope is usually added in the form of a data-packet header.

envelope delay distortion

The amount of delay between different frequencies in an electrical signal.

environment

Generically, all the hardware and software resources available to a user. This term can also refer to the specific operating system needed to execute a program.

environment variable

A variable used to define the current operating system environment. The name of the environment variable is case-sensitive.

environmental security

A method of protecting the entire data processing environment. Environmental security involves protecting against both accidental or deliberate harm that may threaten data in any way.

EO

End Office, a Central Office in a telecommunications network where subscribers' lines terminate and are connected with other exchanges.

EOC

end-of-content, a character used to indicate the end of a message or a page.

EOF

end-of-file, a code placed after the last byte in a file. The EOF code indicates that no more data follows after that point.

EOM (end-of-message) bit

A bit in an AppleTalk Data-Stream Protocol (ADSP) header that indicates that the previous packet was the last one in a single message.
See also **AppleTalk Data-Stream Protocol.**

EOT

end-of-transmission, a character used to indicate the end of a transmission.

EPP

Enhanced Parallel Port, a parallel port with a signal rate of up to 16 megabits per second (Mbps).

EPS

Encapsulated PostScript, the file format used by the PostScript page-description language, service-independent so images can be transferred between different applications. Images can also be sized and then output to different printers. An EPS file contains PostScript commands, and an optional preview image stored in PICT or TIFF format. An EPS file can be printed only to a PostScript-compatible printer.

equalization

Balancing a circuit by reducing frequency and phase distortion.

Erase right

A NetWare and IntranetWare directory and file right that grants a user the right to delete a directory, subdirectory, or file. However, a user with the Erase right cannot erase a file if the Delete Inhibit attribute is enabled.
See also **Delete Inhibit attribute.**

Erlang

A metric that shows the current usage of a communications channel relative to its total capacity. One Erlang is equal to 36 CCS (hundreds of call-seconds).

ERP

Exterior Routing Protocol, a protocol used by gateways in an internetwork to exchange network reachability information between autonomous systems. ERP is used in the Internet core system, and is part of the Transmission-Control Protocol/Internet Protocol (TCP/IP) suite.

See also **Transmission-Control Protocol/Internet Protocol.**

error

The difference between what is expected and what actually occurs. Computer operating systems report unexpected or illegal events by issuing error codes. In telecommunications, an error may be caused by noise or distortion.

error control

A method of ensuring that data transmissions from a source are received at the destination without any errors.

error-correction code (ECC)

A type of code used to detect or correct communications transmission errors.

error detection and correction

The process of determining whether a bit (or bits) has changed during a transmission, and of correcting those errors. There are numerous methods for both detection and correction. The cyclical redundancy check (CRC)

is a common error-detection method, based on a factor of the original bit pattern. The sender computes a CRC value and adds it to the data packet; the recipient then computes a CRC value on the basis of the received data packet. If the two CRC values are equal, there was no error in transmission.

See also **cyclical redundancy check.**

error-free second (EFS)

A second of transmission that contains no errors. The number of EFSs that occur over a given period of time may be used as an indicator of transmission quality.

error handling

The method used by a program to handle errors that occur when the program runs. Error handling accommodates unexpected events or incorrectly entered data, often by issuing a dialog box to request that the user take appropriate action.

error log exit

A routine in the NetWare Advanced Program-to-Program Communications (APPC) DOS extension, used to log errors during a conversation.

See also **Advanced Program-to-Program Communications (APPC).**

error message

A message issued by the operating system to indicate the existence of an error.

See also **error.**

error rate

The ratio between the number of incorrectly-received bits and the total number of bits in a transmission.

error-correcting protocol

One of many communications protocols used to detect and correct transmission errors.

ES

end system, under the OSI Reference Model, the computer that contains application processes that can communicate through all seven layers of the OSI model. An end system is sometimes referred to as an *end node*.
See also **OSI Reference Model.**

Escape sequence

A sequence of characters that begins with the Escape character, and followed by one or more additional characters. This sequence is meant to perform a specific task, and is often used to control monitors or printers.

ESCON

Enterprise System Connection Architecture, a fiber-optic communications channel, developed by IBM, that connects mainframes and peripheral devices and uses multimode fiber with a light-emitting diode (LED) as a light source.

ESCON (Enterprise System Connection Architecture) connector

A fiber-optic connector used with multimode fiber in a channel that complies with

IBM Enterprise System Connection Architecture (ESCON).
See also **connector; Enterprise System Connection Architecture.**

ESDI

Enhanced Small-Device Interface, a standard used to interface a bus controller with a hard drive. ESDI has, in most cases, been replaced by Small Computer System Interface (SCSI).
See also **Small Computer System Interface.**

ES-IS

End-System-to-Intermediate-System, the connection between an end system (or user station) and an intermediate system (or the routing element in an internetwork).

ESD

Electrostatic discharge, charges generated by static electricity. An electrostatic discharge as low as 30 volts may harm a computer component.

ESF

Extended Superframe-Format Framing, a method used to frame a DS-1 channel that groups 24 frames into a single superframe, such that one DS-1 channel holds one superframe.
See also **DS-x.**

ESN

Electronic Switched Network, a telecommunications service used by private networks that establishes an automatic switching mechanism between Private Branch Exchanges (PBXs), so that one PBX can call any other PBX in the network without a dedicated connection.

See also **Private Branch Exchange.**

ESNet

Energy Services Network, an internetwork that spans across multiple nations of the world.

Establishment Controller

An IBM device used to support multiple devices for the purpose of communicating with a mainframe host computer.

Ethernet

A type of shared-media, local-area network (LAN), originally developed in 1974 by Bob Metcalfe, founder of 3Com. Ethernet uses a bus or star topology, and is a packet-switching, contention-oriented network. Ethernet is based on the Carrier-Sense Multiple-Access/Collision Detection (CSMA/CD) media-access method. (CSMA/CD detects packet collisions and causes the transmitting nodes to automatically retransmit after a random period of time.)

The Institute of Electronic and Electrical Engineers (IEEE) Ethernet standard, 802.3, has since been significantly extended to include Fast Ethernet, Gigabit Ethernet, and IsoEthernet. The still-common 10Base-T Ethernet standard was introduced in 1990, and allows Ethernet to operate over a standard twisted-pair telephone wire. This standard operates with a throughput of 10 megabits per second (Mbps). Xerox intro-

duced the first Ethernet LAN in 1981; 3Com introduced the first Ethernet adapter card the year after.

Table E.1 compares features of major types of Ethernet.

See also **Carrier-Sense Multiple-Access/Collision Detection; connector; Fast Ethernet; Gigabit Ethernet; IsoEthernet; IEEE 802.*x*.**

 **For more information about Ethernet, surf the Web to** http://wwwhost.ots.utexas.edu/ethernet.

Ethernet configuration

The network setup that facilitates communications over an Ethernet environment.

Ethernet Configuration-Test Protocol (ECTP)

A protocol used to determine whether a network conforms to the Blue Book Ethernet standard.

See also **Blue Book Ethernet.**

Ethernet meltdown

When traffic on an Ethernet network reaches its maximum capacity.

Ethernet packet

A variable-length packet transmitted over an Ethernet network. The packet includes a synchronization preamble, destination address, source address, type-code indicator, data field, and cyclical redundancy check (CRC).

See also **cyclical redundancy check; network address; network number; preamble; type code.**

EtherTalk

An AppleTalk-based Ethernet network that may be nonextended (EtherTalk 1.0, also known as Blue Book Ethernet) or extended (EtherTalk 2.0). EtherTalk works with the AppleShare network operating system, and runs over coaxial cable at 10 megabits per second (Mbps).

See also **Blue Book Ethernet; Ethernet.**

EtherTalk Link-Access Protocol (ELAP)

An AppleTalk link-access protocol used for EtherTalk, ELAP exists at the Data-Link Layer (Layer 2) of the OSI Reference Model.

See also **AppleTalk protocols; OSI Reference Model.**

ETR

Early Token Release, a control process used in Token Ring networks that allows multiple packets to travel in the ring at the same time. A standard Token Ring network only allows the single node that holds the token to transmit, so that only one packet is traveling in the ring at any given time; and the token can be passed only after the packet has been received. Under ETR, the token is released immediately after the sending node releases the packet into the ring.

See also **Token Ring.**

ETSI

European Telecommunications Standards Institute, a European standards organization that recommends telecommunications standards.

Table E.I: Ethernet Features Comparison

Ethernet Type	Connectors	Topology	Cable Type
Twisted-Pair Ethernet (1Base5, 10BaseT)	RJ-45	Star	Unshielded twisted-pair (UTP)
Thick Ethernet (10Base5)	N-Series barrel, elbow	Bus	Thick (3/8-inch) 50-ohm coaxial
Thin Ethernet (10Base2)	BNC (T-connector, barrel, elbow)	Bus	Thin (3/16-inch) 50-ohm coaxial
Fiber-Optic Ethernet (10BaseF, 10BaseFB, 10BaseFP, 10BaseFL)	F, FC	Star	Fiber-optic
Broadband Ethernet (10Broad36)	F	Star	75-ohm (CATV) coaxial
Fast Ethernet (100BaseVG, 100BaseT, 100BaseT4, 100BaseTX, 100BaseFX)	RJ-45	Star	UTP

ETX

end-of-text, a character used to indicate the end of a text file.

Eudora

An electronic-mail (e-mail) client program from Qualcomm that runs on Windows and Macintosh platforms. Eudora runs on systems that have full-time Internet connections and those without full-time Internet connections, and features automatic notification upon receipt of electronic mail. A shareware version of this program, Eudora Light, is available for downloading from the Internet.

See also **electronic mail.**

 **For more information about Eudora, surf the Web to** `http://www.eudora.com.`

EUnet

A UNIX-based network located in Europe designed to provide interconnection and electronic-mail (e-mail) services. This network began as an extension of Usenet.

See also **electronic mail; Usenet.**

Euronet

A networking scheme originally proposed by countries belonging to the European Common Market.

European Academic and Research Network (EARN)

A European network used to provide file transfer and electronic-mail (e-mail) services to universities and research institutions.

European Computer Manufacturers Association (ECMA)

A trade organization that provides standards organizations with technical committees.

European Electronic Mail Association (EEMA)

A European trade group made up of developers and vendors of electronic mail (e-mail) products.

European Telecommunications Standards Institute (ETSI)

A European standards organization that recommends telecommunications standards.

European Workshop for Open Systems (EWOS)

A regional workshop for implementers of the OSI Reference Model.

See also **OSI Reference Model.**

even parity

A parity setting where if the sum of all the bits set to 1 is even, the parity bit is set to 0; and if the sum of all the bits set to 1 is odd, the parity bit is set to 1.

See also **parity; parity bit.**

event

Either a response to the occurrence of a significant task on the network (such as the completion of a request for information), or a message that indicates operational irregularities in physical elements of a network.

Event Control Block (ECB)

An entity used to control events relating to the transmission and reception of Inter-network Packet Exchange/Sequenced Packet Exchange (IPX/SPX) packets and sessions.

See also **Internetwork Packet Exchange; Sequenced Packet Exchange.**

Event Notification Call-Backs

In NetWare 3.12, a tracked resource and selectable option in the Available Options/Resource Utilization screen of the MONITOR NetWare Loadable Module (NLM). This option gives modules the capability to detect when a system event occurs.

See also **MONITOR; NetWare Loadable Module.**

event reporting

A network-management function. Event reporting uses software agents to gather information on all objects being managed by that agent. The agent then generates a report and issues it to the network-management package.

eWorld search engine

An online Internet service from Apple Computer that uses a World Wide Web (WWW) browser from InterCon, offers electronic-mail (e-mail) capabilities, and may be connected to the Internet either by configuring a modem or by using a direct network link.

See also **Web browser.**

For more information about eWorld, surf the Web to http://www.eworld.com.

EWOS

European Workshop for Open Systems, a regional workshop for implementers of the OSI Reference Model.

See also **OSI Reference Model.**

exa-

A prefix (abbreviated E) used to indicate one quintillion, or 10^{18}. When applied to computing, it refers to the power of two closest to one quintillion.

exabyte (EB)

A unit of measure equaling one quintillion bytes.

exactly-once transaction

An AppleTalk Transaction Protocol (ATP) transaction method that guarantees a request is only implemented one time.

See also **AppleTalk protocols; AppleTalk Transaction Protocol.**

excess burst size (Be)

The highest number of uncommitted data bits that a network can attempt to send over a given period of time.

exchange

An area serviced by a central telecommunications office. An exchange services a sequential block of telephone numbers.

Exchange

A shortened name for the Microsoft Exchange program, a line of mail servers and clients offering groupware applications and supporting connection to standard Internet electronic mail. This product is part of the Microsoft BackOffice Suite of products. Microsoft Exchange runs on a Windows NT Server.

 **For more information about Microsoft Exchange, surf the Web to** `http://www. microsoft.com/products/ default.asp.`

exchange carrier

A company that provides telecommunications services within a given exchange.

Excite search engine

A World Wide Web (WWW) search engine that allows users to enter traditional keyword searches or concept searches to surf the Web, Usenet, Usenet classifieds, and a database of Web site reviews. The results of a search are a hotlinked title and a summary, but no Universal Resource Locator (URL) address is included.

See also **Usenet; World Wide Web.**

 **For more information about Excite, surf the Web to** `http://www.excite.com.`

executable

A program that can be operated by the computer. An executable program in DOS usually has the filename extension .EXE or .COM.

executable code

A series of instructions contained in a program that can be operated by the computer.

Execute Only (X) attribute

A NetWare file attribute that prevents a file from being copied. This attribute cannot be removed; instead, the file must be copied over with an identical file that does not have the Execute Only attribute set.

EXIT utility

In NetWare and IntranetWare, a server console utility used to return to the DOS partition after shutting down the server.

expandability

A system's capability to encompass additional hardware or software (such as more memory, larger disk drives, or new adapters).

expanded memory

A way of allowing a program to access up to 32MB of memory outside of conventional memory. Early personal computers were restricted to 1MB (640K for applications and 384K for system use). Expanded memory allows these personal computers to go beyond that level by swapping address blocks in which data can be swapped in and out as needed.

See also **memory.**

Expanded-Memory Manager (EMM)

A device driver used to support the software portion of the Expanded-Memory Specification (EMS). This driver creates a block of addresses, swapping data into and out of it as needed.

See also **Expanded-Memory Specification; memory.**

Expanded-Memory Specification (EMS)

The standard method of accessing expanded memory. This specification allows programs running on Intel 8086 processors to access up to 32MB of expanded memory.

See also **memory.**

expansion

Increasing a microcomputer's capabilities by adding hardware that can perform a certain task that could not otherwise be done with the basic system.

expansion board

See **adapter.**

expansion bus

A common pathway between hardware devices. A bus is used to connect a central processing unit (CPU) to its main memory, and to the memory residing in its peripheral devices' control units; and can, therefore, transfer data from the motherboard to plug-in peripherals. The expansion bus can be used to expand the basic personal computer system by use of adapter cards. There are several different types of expansion buses, including Industry-Standard Architecture

(ISA), Extended Industry-Standard Architecture (EISA), Micro-Channel Architecture (MCA), Peripheral-Component Interconnect (PCI), Video Electronics Standards Association (VESA), and Personal Computer Memory Card International Association (PCMCIA).

See also **Extended Industry-Standard Architecture; Industry-Standard Architecture; Micro-Channel Architecture; Peripheral-Component Interconnect; Personal Computer Memory Card International Association; Video Electronics Standards Association.**

expansion chassis

A hardware structure that includes a power supply and a backplane.

expansion slot

A connector on the expansion bus that allows an adapter to gain access to the system bus.

expansion unit

An external housing unit that adds additional expansion slots to a portable computer.

expedited delivery

An option set by a given protocol layer to tell another protocol layer to handle specific data more rapidly.

Expedited Transport-Service Data Unit (ETSDU)

An Attention message in an AppleTalk Data-Stream Protocol (ADSP) network. The message allows two transport clients to send a signal to each other outside of the regular flow of data.

See also **AppleTalk Data-Stream Protocol.**

expert parameter

The parameters used to provide precise control over Packet Layer and Frame Layer operations. Expert parameters can be used to configure the advanced settings of a specific wide-area network (WAN) call destination, or to configure Permanent Virtual Circuits (PVCs).

See also **Permanent Virtual Circuit; WAN call destination.**

Explicit Congestion Notification (ECN)

A Frame Relay mechanism used to indicate when the network is congested. This mechanism uses two bit values to indicate the congested condition. The Backward Explicit Congestion Notification (BECN) bit value is included in Frame Relay headers that are traveling in the direction opposite the congestion, in an attempt to inform source nodes that a congested condition is occurring downline. The Forward Explicit Congestion Notification (FECN) bit value is included in Frame Relay headers that are traveling toward the congestion, in an attempt to inform destination nodes that a congested condition is occurring ahead.

See also **Backward Explicit Congestion Notification; Forward Explicit Congestion Notification.**

explicit route

A route from a Systems Network Architecture (SNA) source subarea to a destination subarea, as specified by a list of subarea nodes and transmission groups that connect the two.

See also **Systems Network Architecture.**

explicit trustee assignments

The Novell Directory Service (NDS) object rights that are granted exclusively to an object in the Directory tree. An explicit trustee assignment overrides any trustee assignments made higher up in the Directory tree.

See also **NetWare Directory; Novell Directory Services; trustee assignment.**

Explore

A suite of Internet tools and utilities from FTP Software that includes a World Wide Web (WWW) browser, electronic-mail (e-mail) client, ftp client, Gopher client, Telnet client, and a Network News-Transfer Protocol (NNTP) newsreader.

See also **electronic mail; Gopher; Network News-Transfer Protocol; Telnet; Web browser.**

explorer frame

A method used in Token Ring networks to determine the best route between a source and destination.

See also **Token Ring.**

extant number

A sequential set of numbers referring to one page of the extended directory space.

extended addressing

An AppleTalk Phase 2 mechanism that assigns 8-bit node numbers and 16-bit network numbers to each workstation.

Extended AppleTalk network

An AppleTalk network that supports the AppleTalk Phase 2 extensions, including zone lists and network ranges.
See also **AppleTalk; AppleTalk Phase 2.**

Extended Binary-Coded Decimal Interchange Code (EBCDIC)

A character set that has 256 characters, with each character represented by an 8-bit pattern. The character set, defined by IBM, includes values for control functions and graphics. It is commonly used on IBM mainframes and minicomputers, and differs from American Standard Code for Information Interchange (ASCII) in that placement of the letters of the alphabet is discontinuous. There is no direct match that can be achieved when converting between ASCII and EBCDIC, because each character set contains some unique characters.
See also **American Standard Code for Information Interchange.**

Extended Data Out (EDO)

Dynamic random-access memory (DRAM) that improves memory speed and performance by altering the timing and sequence of signals that activate the circuitry for accessing memory locations.

Extended Industry-Standard Architecture (EISA)

A 32-bit bus standard that is compatible with Industry Standard Architecture (ISA). Developed to allow input/output (I/O) to keep pace with faster processors, EISA also allows multiple processors to share the same bus.
See also **Industry-Standard Architecture.**

extended memory

The memory above 1MB on 80286, 80386, and 80486 personal computers. Some applications require extended memory to operate on those platforms.
See also **memory.**

extended memory manager

A software utility required for a personal computer to make use of extended memory.
See also **memory.**

Extended-Memory Specification (XMS)

The standard used to allow personal computers to access extended memory. DOS and Windows include an extended memory device driver called HIMEM.SYS, used to gain access to extended memory.
See also **memory.**

extended network

An AppleTalk Phase 2 network on high-speed media that can support the Phase 2 addressing extensions of the network range and zones list.
See also **AppleTalk; AppleTalk Phase 2.**

Extended Superframe-Format Framing (ESF)

A method used to frame a DS-1 channel that groups 24 frames into a single superframe, such that one DS-1 channel holds one superframe.

See also **DS-x.**

extensible MIB

A Management Information Base (MIB) in a Simple Network Management Protocol (SNMP) environment that can be defined by individual vendors to allow new variables.

See also **Management Information Base; Simple Network Management Protocol.**

extension mapping

A type of mapping used to attach Macintosh application information to a non-Macintosh file. Extension mapping allows a Macintosh user to access a non-Macintosh file and automatically open the specified application.

Exterior Gateway Protocol (EGP)

A protocol used by gateways in an internetwork to exchange network reachability information between autonomous systems. EGP is used in the Internet core system, and is part of the Transmission-Control Protocol/Internet Protocol (TCP/IP) suite.

See also **Transmission-Control Protocol/Internet Protocol.**

exterior router

An AppleTalk network router that routes packets to a non-AppleTalk protocol, from which packets may be transmitted by tunneling.

See also **AppleTalk; interior router.**

Exterior Routing Protocol (ERP)

A protocol used by gateways in an internetwork to exchange network reachability information between autonomous systems. ERP is used in the Internet core system, and is part of the Transmission-Control Protocol/Internet Protocol (TCP/IP) suite.

See also **Transmission-Control Protocol/Internet Protocol.**

external command

A command not automatically loaded into memory because it is used less frequently than other commands.

External Data Representation (XDR)

A machine-independent syntax developed by Sun Microsystems as part of their Network File System (NFS), and used to describe data structures.

External Entity object

A leaf object representing a nonnative Novell Directory Services (NDS) object imported into NDS, or registered into NDS. NetWare Message-Handling Service (MHS) uses External Entity objects to represent users from non-NDS environments, and thereby creating a fully integrated address book. This object has the Access-Control List, Authority Revocation, Back Link,

Bindery, CA Private Key, CA Public Key, Certificate Revocation, Certificate Validity Interval, Common Name (CN), Cross-Certificate Pair, Description, E-Mail Address, External Name, Facsimile Telephone Number, Group Membership, Last Referenced Time, Locality (L), Obituary, Object Class, Organizational Unit (OU), Physical Delivery Office Name, Postal Address, Postal Code, Reference, Revision, S, SA, See Also, and Title selectable properties in NDS.

See also **leaf object; NetWare MHS Services; Novell Directory Services; object.**

External Name

A Directory Schema term and a selectable property for the External Entity object in Novell Directory Services (NDS).

See also **leaf object; Novell Directory Services; object.**

External Synchronizer

A Directory Schema term in Novell Directory Services (NDS).

See also **Directory Schema; Novell Directory Services.**

extremely low-frequency emission (ELF)

Radiation emitted by a computer monitor or other electronic appliance. An ELF emission ranges from between 5 Hertz (Hz) and 2,000Hz, and decline as a function of the square of the distance from its source.

EZ-Find at The River

A World Wide Web (WWW) metasearch engine that allows users to submit several queries to a variety of 11 available search engines in rapid succession, which it processes sequentially.

See also **World Wide Web.**

 **For more information about EZ-Find at the River, surf the Web to** `http://www.theriver.com/TheRiver/Explore/ezfind.html`.

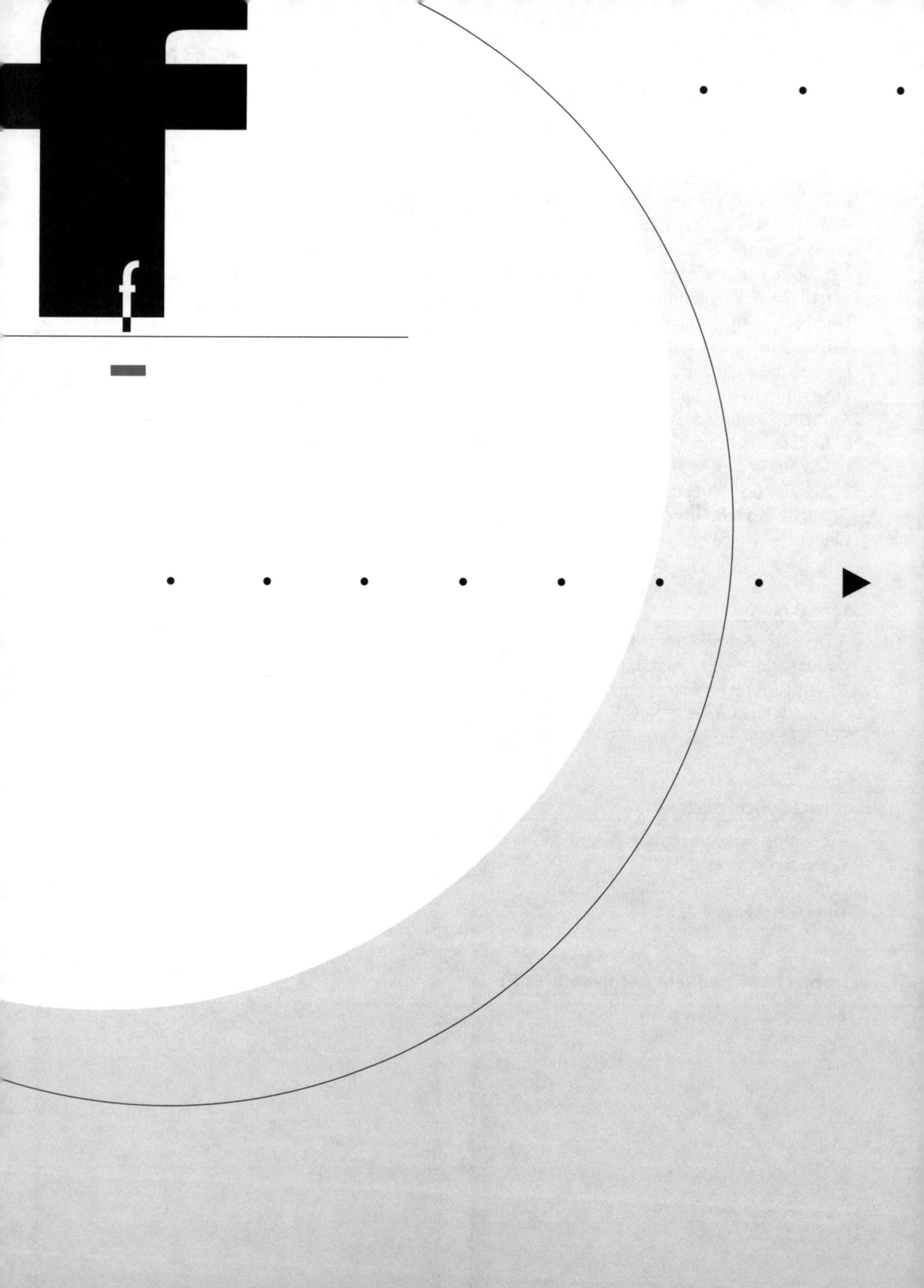

F connector

A connector used in broadband Ethernet networks and broadband token-bus networks.

See also **Ethernet.**

facility

A transmission link between two stations in a telephone communications system. In an X.25 network, a facility is a packet field through which users request network services.

See also **X.25.**

facility bypass

A telecommunications method of bypassing the telephone company's central office.

Facility Data Link (FDL)

Part of an Extended Superframe-Format (ESF) that is a 4-kilobit-per-second (Kbps) communications link between a sender's station and the telephone company's monitors. The 4Kbps band is made by taking half of the ESF's framing bits and using them to establish the link.

See also **Extended Superframe-Format Framing.**

facsimile (fax)

An electronic reproduction of a document sent over a telephone line through a specialized hardware device or computer add-in board.

Facsimile Telephone Number

A selectable property for the External Entity, Organization, Organizational Role, Organizational Unit, and User objects in Novell Directory Services (NDS).

See also **leaf object; Novell Directory Services; object.**

fading

The decrease of a wireless or electrical signal that may occur because of an obstruction blocking the transmitter or receiver's antenna, interference from other signals, or increased distance from the source of transmission.

FADU

File-Access Data Unit, part of the Open Systems Interconnection (OSI) File Transfer, Access, and Management (FTAM) service. FADU is a packet that holds information about accessing a directory tree in a particular file system.

See also **File Transfer, Access, and Management.**

fail-soft system

A system designed to cause the least amount of damage possible in the event of failure. A fail-soft system shuts down all nonessential functions and operates at a reduced capacity until the problem has been resolved.

failure handling

A NetWare System Fault Tolerance III (SFT III) process used to prevent system downtime caused by a single hardware failure.

SFT III allows a mirrored server (a *secondary server*) to automatically take over if the first server (the *primary server*) fails. The process is transparent to end-users, although a slight pause may be noticeable as SFT III switches from the primary to the secondary server.

See also **System Fault Tolerance.**

fake root

A subdirectory that functions as a root directory. Under NetWare, the network administrator can map a drive to a fake root. This capability allows the administrator to install an application in a subdirectory *even if it requires installation at the root,* which is sometimes desirable for security reasons. The fake-root function is useful for applications that cannot be executed from a subdirectory. Assigning user rights at the root level poses a security risk, however; using a fake root overcomes the security problem.

FAL

File-Access Listener, a program in Digital Equipment Company's DECnet environment that implements the Data-Access Protocol (DAP) and can accept remote requests for local files (issued from any process that can use the DAP).

See also **DECnet.**

fall time

The amount of time required for an electrical signal to move from 90 percent to 10 percent. This value is used to establish a maximum transmission speed.

fan switching

A process of using a route cache to expedite packet switching through a router.

fanout

A communications configuration in which there are more output lines than input lines.

FAQ

Frequently Asked Questions, a collection of commonly asked questions with answers on any given topic, typically found on the Internet. A FAQ is posted to give newcomers or novices information about a particular topic, to minimize the number of questions that have to be asked individually.

Far-End Block Error (FEBE)

An error reported to the sender by the receiver in a Broadcast Integrated-Service Digital Network (BISDN) network. The error is determined by computing a checksum at the receiving end and comparing it with a checksum generated by the sender. If the two numbers do not match, an error is assumed, and an FEBE message is sent.

See also **Broadcast Integrated-Service Digital Network; checksum.**

Far-End Crosstalk (FEXT)

Interference in which a transmitted signal leaks from one wire into the transmitted signal of another.

Far-End Receive Failure (FERF)

A signal sent upstream in a Broadcast Integrated-Service Digital Network (BISDN) network that indicates an error has occurred downstream.

Fast Ethernet

An extension of the Institute of Electronic and Electrical Engineers (IEEE) Ethernet standard that operates at 100 megabits per second (Mbps). Fast Ethernet is structurally very similar to 10Mbps Ethernet, but achieves its tenfold increase by dividing the bit-timing (or the amount of time a bit requires for transmission) by 10. It uses the same packet format, supports twisted-pair copper wire, and uses the same error-detection methods. However, maximum cable lengths are shorter than a 10BaseT implementation. Cable length is limited to 100 meters between the repeater and workstation, and only two repeater hops are allowed between any two workstations. Fast Ethernet is typically deployed in a star topology with a central hub. A Fast Ethernet network can include both 10Mbps and 100Mbps connections.

See also **10BaseT; Ethernet.**

Fast Link Pulse (FLP)

One of a series of identical startup signals sent by an Ethernet device capable of supporting a transmission rate of 100 megabits per second (Mbps). These signals are used in a Fast Ethernet network.

See also **Fast Ethernet.**

Fast Local Internet Protocol (FLIP)

An Internet Protocol (IP) developed as an alternative to Transmission-Control Protocol

(TCP) to offer better security and network-management capabilities for internetworks made up of large-scale distributed systems.

See also **Internet Protocol; Transmission-Control Protocol.**

Fast Packet-Switching (FPS)

A switching strategy that realizes higher throughput by simplifying the switching process. FPS uses fixed-size packets and simplified addresses. In addition, error checking and acknowledgment is left to higher-level protocols. FPS is used in certain frame and cell-relay implementations such as Asynchronous Transfer Mode (ATM).

See also **Asynchronous Transfer Mode.**

fast select

A facility used to expand the Call and Clear User fields beyond a 16-octet limit to 128 octets. Fast select is often used in point-of-sale (POS) and other transaction-oriented applications.

See also **point of sale.**

Fast-Connect Circuit Switching

The use of fast electronic switching devices to establish a circuit between two stations.

FastPath

A high-speed gateway between AppleTalk and Ethernet networks.

See also **AppleTalk; Ethernet; gateway.**

FAT

File-Allocation Table, an index that includes a list of pointers to show the physical disk areas at which the pieces of a file are located. The FAT groups together files that may be held in multiple, noncontiguous blocks.

See also **Turbo File-Allocation Table.**

fatal error

An unrecoverable error that prevents a given system or application task from being accomplished.

fault

A physical or logical abnormal condition in a communications link.

fault management

One of five of the basic System-Management Function Areas (SMFAs) found in the OSI Network-Management Model. Fault management detects, diagnoses, and corrects network faults. Network-management software applications can detect faults, by either requiring nodes to report faults or by polling all nodes on the network periodically. Sometimes the system corrects the fault automatically, although some faults may require manual intervention.

See also **OSI Network-Management Model.**

fault point

A location at which a fault can occur.

fault tolerance

A data-protection scheme that ensures the continued operation of the network. Fault tolerance may encompass several preventative measures, including duplicating data on multiple storage devices to protect it against hazardous events. Fault tolerance may also involve distributing the NetWare Directory database (NDD) between multiple servers to ensure that access to object information continues if the primary server fails. Other types of fault tolerance may include running dual cabling systems, or writing data to separate channels.

See also **NetWare Directory database; primary server.**

fax

facsimile, an electronic reproduction of a document sent over a telephone line through a specialized hardware device or computer add-in board.

fax board

An add-in adapter used to convert electronic documents into fax format and transmit them over a telephone line.

fax device

A hardware device used to send and receive faxes on the network or over telephone lines. A fax device can be a separate device, or it may take the form of an add-in Network Interface Card (NIC). A fax board converts an existing electronic document into an appropriate format for transmission.

See also **Network Interface Card.**

fax modem

An internal computer modem that includes internal fax capabilities. A fax modem accepts electronic text or graphics files, and converts them into fax format for transmission. A fax modem fits into a personal computer expansion slot and provides most of the same features as a freestanding fax machine.

See also **modem.**

Fax Number

A selectable property for the User object in Novell Directory Services (NDS).

See also **leaf object; Novell Directory Services; object.**

fax server

A server that provides the network with fax transmission and reception services.

FBE

Free Buffer Enquiry, a server that provides the network with fax transmission and reception services.

FC

Frame Control, a field in a Token Ring data packet that presents a value used to indicate whether the frame is a Media-Access Control (MAC) Layer (a sublayer of the Data-Link Layer of the OSI Reference Model) management packet, or whether it carries logical link control data.

See also **Media-Access Control; OSI Reference Model; packet.**

FC connector

A connector used for fiber-optic cable. An FC connector has a threaded coupling nut and a ceramic ferrule for holding the fiber.

FCC

Federal Communications Commission, a federal agency that develops guidelines for the operation of communications and other electronic equipment. The FCC also allocates bandwidth for FM radio broadcasting and television, long-distance telecommunications, and short-haul transmissions.

FCC certification

Approval granted by the Federal Communications Commission (FCC) that indicates a particular computer meets FCC standards for radio frequency interference (RFI) emissions. *Class A certification* applies to mainframes and minicomputers and other computers used in commercial settings; *Class B certification,* which is stricter, applies to personal computers and laptops used in the home and office.

See also **Class A certification; Class B certification.**

FCONSOLE utility

In NetWare 3.*x,* a server console utility that supervisors use to broadcast messages, view user connection information, access information from the network server to fine-tune its performance, or shut down the file server. With FCONSOLE, an operator can control the server from any station on the network.

FCS

(1) **Fiber Channel Standard,** the optical-fiber specification in a Fiber Distributed Data Interface (FDDI) network architecture. (2) **Frame-Check Sequence,** a value used to check for errors in a message transmitted over a network. The FCS calculates a value on the basis of the packet's contents,

and stores the value within the packet in a separate FCS field. The recipient recalculates the value and compares it against the value contained in the FCS field. If the two numbers match, the transmission is assumed to be error-free.

See also (1) **Fibre Channel**; (2) **packet.**

FDDI

Fiber Distributed Data Interface, a high-speed local-area network (LAN) standard specified by the American National Standards Institute (ANSI) X3T9.5 committee. FDDI uses fiber-optic cable, which transmits light generated from a laser or Light-Emitting Diode (LED) to realize a data speed of 100 megabits per second (Mbps). An FDDI network uses either multimode or single-mode fiber-optic cable and is built on a dual-ring topology. It uses a token-passing mechanism for media access and can be used in a backbone network, back-end network that connects mainframes and mini-computers, or a front-end network that connects high-speed workstations

FDDI II

A proposed standard from the American National Standards Institute (ANSI) to enhance the Fiber Distributed Data Interface (FDDI) by providing isochronous transmission for connectionless data circuits and for connection-oriented voice and video circuits.

See also **American National Standards Institute; Fiber Distributed Data Interface.**

FDDITalk

Apple Computer's implementation of the Fiber Distributed Data Interface (FDDI)

protocol that includes the protocols and drivers for use in an AppleTalk network.

See also **AppleTalk; Fiber Distributed Data Interface.**

FDDITalk Link-Access Protocol (FLAP)

The AppleTalk Data-Link Layer (Layer 2 of the OSI Reference Model) protocol portion of FDDITalk.

See also **AppleTalk; FDDITalk; OSI Reference Model.**

FDL

Facility Data Link, part of an Extended Superframe Format (ESF) that is a 4-kilobit-per-second (Kbps) communications link between a sender's station and the telephone company's monitors. The 4Kbps band is made by taking half of the ESF's framing bits and using them to establish the link.

See also **Extended Superframe-Format Framing.**

FDM

Frequency-Division Multiplexing, a type of multiplexing that divides a medium's bandwidth into separate frequency ranges. Each separate frequency is divided by a guard channel that protects it from interference from the other frequencies.

See also **multiplexing.**

FDMA

Frequency-Division Multiple Access, a method of dividing a large bandwidth into multiple channels.

FDX

full duplex, a process whereby two data streams flow in opposite directions simultaneously. In a full-duplex system, the recipient node can send control data back to the sender; the sender continues to transmit data.
See also **half duplex.**

FEBE

Far-End Block Error, an error reported to the sender by the receiver in a Broadcast Integrated-Service Digital Network (BISDN) network. The error is determined by computing a checksum at the receiving end and comparing it with a checksum generated by the sender. If the two numbers do not match, an error is assumed, and a FEBE message is sent.
See also **Broadcast Integrated-Service Digital Network; checksum.**

FEC

Forward Error Correction, an error-correction mechanism that provides the transmission enough information to allow the recipient to locate and correct any bit-level errors that occur during transmission.

FECN

Forward Explicit Congestion Notification, a bit set by a Frame Relay network to indicate that congestion is occurring in the packet-forwarding direction.
See also **Frame Relay network.**

Federal Communications Commission (FCC)

A federal agency that develops guidelines for the operation of communications and other electronic equipment. The FCC also allocates bandwidth for FM radio broadcasting and television, long-distance telecommunications, and short-haul transmissions.

 **For more information about the FCC, surf the Web to** http://www.fcc.gov.

Federal Information Exchange (FIX)

A connection between the public Internet and one of the federal government's internetworks.

Federal Networking Council (FNC)

A committee made up of representatives from multiple government agencies that have networks connected to the Internet.

 **For more information about the Federal Networking Council, surf the Web to** http://www.fnc.gov.

feed

A circuit over which data is sent to a central station or along a network backbone.

feeder cable

A 25-pair cable used to carry voice and data signals.

FEP

Front-End Processor, in a Systems Network Architecture (SNA) network, a component that controls access to the host computer (usually a mainframe), and is typically attached to the host by a direct channel. The FEP is used to offload certain tasks from the host, such as monitoring links or establishing connections.

See also **Systems Network Architecture.**

FERF

Far-End Receive Failure, a signal sent upstream in a Broadcast Integrated-Service Digital Network (BISDN) network that indicates an error has occurred downstream.

ferrule

A component that keeps the optical core and cladding of a fiber-optic connection immobile. The ferrule is made of ceramic, plastic, or stainless steel, and is glued to the cladding with epoxy.

See also **cladding.**

Fetch

A Macintosh client program used for the File-Transfer Protocol (FTP) that features a graphical user interface (GUI), drag-and-drop transfers, multiple simultaneous downloads, and compatibility with a variety of system resources, file types, and configurations.

FEXT

Far-End Crosstalk, interference in which a transmitted signal leaks from one wire into the transmitted signal of another.

fiber bandwidth

A metric measurement that reflects a fiber-optic cable's capacity to carry data. Fiber bandwidth is expressed in megahertz

(MHz) or megabits per second (Mbps) per kilometer.

fiber bundle

A collection of fibers that are routed together in fiber-optic transmissions. The two types of fiber bundles are a *flexible bundle* (which are bundled at either end of a fiber-optic cable, but are free to move between the endpoints) and a *rigid bundle* (which are melted together to form a single rod bent into a specific shape during manufacturing).

Fiber Channel

Also **Fibre Channel,** a fiber-optic channel standard that can also be used for networking. Its three primary uses are clustering, linking processors to storage arrays, and creating a local-area network (LAN) backbone. The American National Standards Institute (ANSI) Fibre Channel standard supports several different grades of fiber-optic cable, and uses a 4B/8B signal encoding scheme. Bandwidth can range from 100 megabits per second (Mbps) to 1 gigabit per second (Gbps). Originally, the ANSI standard was termed "Fiber Channel" (with the American spelling), and was later changed to the French spelling ("Fibre") to reflect the fact that the standard was expanded to include copper cabling.

See also **4B/5B Encoding; 8B/10B Encoding; American National Standards Institute; bandwidth.**

Fiber Channel Standard (FCS)

The optical fiber specification in a Fiber Distributed Data Interface (FDDI) network architecture.

See also **FCS; Fibre Channel.**

Fiber Distributed Data Interface (FDDI)

A high-speed local-area network (LAN) standard specified by the American National Standards Institute (ANSI) X3T9.5 committee. FDDI uses fiber-optic cable, which transmits light generated from a laser or light-emitting diode (LED) to realize a data speed of 100 megabits per second (Mbps). A FDDI network uses either multimode or single-mode fiber-optic cable and is built on a dual-ring topology. It uses a token-passing mechanism for media access and can be used in a backbone network, back-end network that connects mainframes and minicomputers, or a front-end network that connects high-speed workstations.

Fiber-Optic Inter-Repeater Link (FOIRL)

A device used to connect fiber-optic cable to an Attachment Unit Interface (AUI) in an Ethernet installation.

See also **Attachment Unit Interface; Ethernet.**

fiber optics

A communications technology that transmits data along a focused beam of light over a glass or plastic fiber. Fiber optics offers an advantage over copper media, in that it allows for greater distances and a higher bandwidth, and it is immune to electromagnetic interference (EMI).

See also **electromagnetic interference.**

fiber-optic cable

A transmission medium made of glass- or plastic-fiber strands, surrounded by a protected jacket. Fiber-optic cable facili-

tates a high-bandwidth transmission by modulating a focused light source through the fiber.

fiber-optic connector

A connector used to create a physical link between two segments of optical core. Each fiber is held in place by a ferrule, and the end of the cut fiber is polished before the connection is made.

See also **ferrule.**

Fibre Channel

A fiber-optic channel standard that can also be used for networking. Its three primary uses are clustering, linking processors to storage arrays, and creating a local-area network (LAN) backbone. The American National Standards Institute (ANSI) Fibre Channel standard supports several different grades of fiber-optic cable, and uses a 4B/8B signal encoding scheme. Bandwidth can range from 100 megabits per second (Mbps) to 1 gigabit per second (Gbps). Originally, the ANSI standard was termed "Fiber Channel" (with the American spelling), and was later changed to the French spelling ("Fibre") to reflect the fact that the standard was expanded to include copper cabling.

See also **4B/5B Encoding; 8B/10B Encoding; American National Standards Institute; bandwidth.**

FID4

Format Identifier 4, a format used by a transmission header in Systems Network Architecture (SNA) to encapsulate a message between SNA subarea nodes that are capable of supporting virtual and explicit routes, as well as transmission groups.

See also **Systems Network Architecture.**

FIDONET

A worldwide network of Bulletin Board Systems (BBSs) in which each individual BBS represents a node on the network.

field

The smallest unit of data in a database file or networking packet.

FIFO

First In, First Out, a processing strategy under which the first element to be added to a queue ("first in") is the first one to be processed ("first out").

See also **Last In, First Out.**

file

A set of records stored on a disk.

File-Access Data Unit (FADU)

Part of the Open Systems Interconnection (OSI) File Transfer, Access, and Management (FTAM) service. FADU is a packet that holds information about accessing a directory tree in a particular file system.

See also **File Transfer, Access, and Management.**

File-Access Listener (FAL)

A program in Digital Equipment Company's DECnet environment that implements the

Data-Access Protocol (DAP) and can accept remote requests for local files (issued from any process that can use the DAP).

See also **DECnet.**

File-Allocation Table (FAT)

An index that includes a list of pointers to show the physical disk areas at which the pieces of a file are located. The FAT groups together files that may be held in multiple, noncontiguous blocks.

See also **Turbo File-Allocation Table.**

file attribute

A particular value associated with a file. The file attribute may indicate what types of actions are allowed to be performed on the file, or who may access the file. Table F.1 shows the file attributes for NetWare and provides a description of each.

See also **attribute.**

file-cache buffer pool

A memory buffer in a NetWare server used to store frequently used files.

file caching

Using system random-access memory (RAM) to improve file access time. File caching reserves a portion of RAM to hold frequently accessed files so they do not have to be continually accessed from the physical storage media. Whenever an application requests a file, the operating system first looks in the cache to see whether the file is there. If it is, the file is retrieved from cache instead of from the physical storage device.

See also **cache; cache memory.**

Table F.1: File Attributes

Attribute	Description
Archive Needed (A)	Identifies files modified since the most recent backup (assigned automatically).
Copy Inhibit (Ci)	Prevents Macintosh users from copying a file.
Delete Inhibit (Di)	Prevents the file from being deleted.
Don't Compress (Dc)	Prevents the file from being compressed.
Don't Migrate (Dm)	Prevents a file from being migrated from the server's hard disk to another storage medium.
Don't Suballocate (Ds)	Prevents data from being suballocated.
Hidden (H)	Hides a file so it cannot be listed by using the DIR command.
Index (I)	Allows large files to be accessed quickly by indexing files with more than 64 File-Allocation Table (FAT) entries (set automatically).
Immediate Compress (Ic)	Compresses every file in a file as each file is closed.
Purge (P)	Flags a file to be erased from the system as soon as it is deleted.
Read Only (Ro)	Prevents a file from being modified.
Read/Write (Rw)	Allows writing to a file.
Rename Inhibit (Ri)	Prevents a filename from being modified.
Shareable (Sh)	Allows more than one user to simultaneously access a file.
System (Sy)	Hides the file so it cannot be seen by using the DIR command.
Transactional (T)	Allows a file to be tracked and protected by the Transaction-Tracking System (TTS).
Execute Only (X)	Prevents a file from being copied, modified, or backed up.

file compression

A method used to store more data on the storage medium than would otherwise be possible. This method compresses files that are not used, or files that are infrequently used. File compression can be done by some operating systems (including NetWare 4.x), although standalone compression applications are also available.

See also **compression; lossless compression; lossy compression.**

File Engine Services

A set of functions that provide NetWare Loadable Modules (NLMs) with access to non-DOS name spaces.

See also **NetWare Loadable Module.**

file format

The structure of a file. Different programs and operating systems employ different file formats.

file fragmentation

A process used by the operating system to make use of all available disk space. Files become fragmented when they are stored in several noncontiguous places on a physical disk. However, highly fragmented files take longer to read because the disk head must move over several different locations on the disk.

See also **defragmentation.**

file handle

A number that refers to or identifies a file.

file indexing

The process of indexing File-Allocation Table (FAT) entries to access large files faster. File indexing allows an application to go directly to a specific block of a file, instead of scanning through all consecutive blocks.

See also **File-Allocation Table.**

file locking

A process used to ensure that a file is updated correctly before another application or process can access the file. Once a file has been locked, it cannot be accessed by any other connection.

filename

The name used by a file on a disk for reference purposes. Every file in a directory has a unique filename, although files in different directories can use the same name because they are specified along with the directory path.

See also **filename extension.**

file node

A 128-byte addressable network entry that includes information about a file. The entry is located in the server's Directory-Entry Table (DET), and includes the filename, attributes, file size, creation date and time, and other management data.

See also **Directory-Entry Table.**

File Open/Lock Activity

In NetWare and IntranetWare, a field in the Available Options screen of the MONITOR NetWare Loadable Module (NLM). This field allows checking the status of a file, checking the file's lock activity and status, viewing which workstations have open files, viewing mounted volumes, viewing the directories on each mounted volume, and viewing the files in a directory.

See also **NetWare Loadable Module; MONITOR.**

file recovery

The process of recovering deleted or damaged files.

file rights

Assigned rights that control a trustee's access to a file and the operations that can be performed on it.

See also **access control; access rights.**

File Scan right

In NetWare and IntranetWare, a directory right and file right that grants a user the right to see the directory and file by using the DIR or NDIR command.

See also **access rights.**

file server

A central computer that runs the network's operating-system software and stores files that can be accessed by client computers on the same network.

File-Server Environment Services

A set of function calls used to let applications set server parameters and view information about the servers. Applications can use these calls to enable or disable transaction tracking, set server time and date, or prohibit or allow users to log in.

File Service Process (FSP)

A process that executes file-handling requests on a NetWare file server.

file sharing

A networking feature that permits multiple users to access the same file simultaneously.

file specification (filespec)

A denotation that includes the drive letter, path name, directory name, and filename.

file system

A method used by the network operating system to organize data on the hard disk. The file system gives each file a filename and stores it in a specific location within a file hierarchy for easy access. The file system uses a path or directory structure to organize files hierarchically. Table F.2 shows some common file systems. Table F.3 shows a breakdown of the major components found in the Novell file system, and Figure F.1 shows how those components fit together by using a metaphor of an office filing system.

See also **Distributed File System; Hierarchical File System; High-Performance File System; Installable File System; Macintosh File System; Network File System; NT File System.**

File System Security rights

A set of assigned NetWare rights used to control access to a given file or directory. File System Security rights can be inherited from another directory. These rights include Supervisor, Read, Write, Create, Erase, Modify, File Scan, and Access Control rights.

See also **access rights.**

file transfer

The process of copying a file from one location to another. To transfer a file over the network, the file is divided into *packets*. Depending on whether the file is being sent between two incompatible operating systems, the file may need to be reformatted or translated upon receipt.

See also **packet.**

Table F.2: Common File Systems

File system	Description
Andrew File System (AFS)	Distributed file system for large networks.
CD-ROM File System	Stores information about files on compact disc (CD).
File-Allocation Table (FAT)	A file system used by versions of the DOS and Windows 3.x operating systems.
FAT32	An enhanced file system used by recent versions of Windows 95.
Hierarchical File System (HFS)	A file system used by the Macintosh System 7 operating system.
High-Performance File System (HPFS)	A file system used by the OS/2 operating system.
Network File System (NFS)	Distributed file system found in UNIX operating systems.
NT File System (NTFS)	A file system used by Windows NT and the NT Advanced File Server.

Table F.3: Components of the Novell File System

Component	Description
Volume	The highest level that refers to a partition and that may encompass any amount of space from a hard disk or multiple hard disks.
Directory	An intermediate level, containing other directories or files.
File	The level at which a user or a process works.

File-Transfer Protocol (FTP)

Part of the Transmission-Control Protocol/ Internet Protocol (TCP/IP) suite of protocols. FTP is used to transmit information between stations, and to prevent errors in the transmission. FTP transmits data between stations in packets.

See also **Transmission-Control Protocol/Internet Protocol.**

File-Transfer Service (FTS)

A service in the Application Layer (Layer 7) of the OSI Reference Model that is responsible for handling files and transferring them between locations. File-transfer services may include Electronic Data Interchange (EDI), the Message-Handling System (MHS), transaction processing, or virtual-terminal applications.

See also **Application Layer; Electronic Data Interchange; Message-Handling System; OSI Reference Model.**

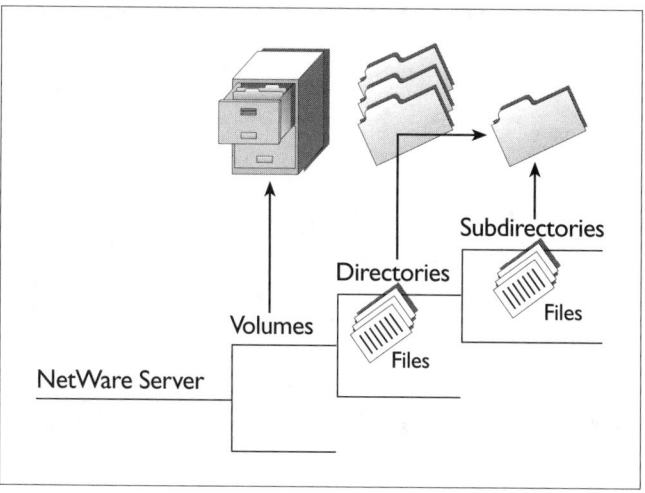

Figure F.1
NetWare File System

File Transfer, Access, and Management (FTAM)

The Open Systems Interconnection (OSI) remote file service protocol used for transferring and accessing files on different types of computers that are also FTAM compliant.
See also **Open Systems Interconnection.**

file-compression program

An application that compresses files so that they take up a smaller amount of storage space. Some operating systems have file compression utilities built in, although several standalone file-compression programs are also available.
See also **compression; lossless compression; lossy compression.**

file-conversion program

An application used to convert files from one format into another. A file-conversion program may convert files between the formats of two different applications, or between the formats of two different operating systems.

FILELINK utility

A Novell DOS utility used to transfer files between two serially connected computers, where one computer runs in master mode and the other in slave mode.

filename extension

The extension that appears after the period in a filename. The extension typically indicates the type of file. Table F.4 lists common filename extensions for DOS and Table F.5 lists common filename extensions for IntranetWare.
See also **filename.**

Table F.4: DOS Filename Extensions Used by IntranetWare

Extension	File Type
.BAT	Executable batch file
.COM	Executable command file
.DAT	ASCII data file
.ERR	Error log file
.EXE	Executable file
.HLP	Help screens in a menu or graphical utility
.MSG	Message file
.OVL	Overlay file (used with IntranetWare menu utilities)
.SYS	Operating system or driver file
.TXT	ASCII text file

Table F.5: IntranetWare-Specific Filename Extensions

Extension	File Type
.001	Unicode table
.DSK	Server disk driver
.LAN	Server LAN driver
.MSG	Text messages (for international versions)
.NAM	Name-space file
.NCF	Server-executable batch file used to load modules and set the NetWare OS configuration
.NDS	Novell Directory Services file
.NLM	NetWare Loadable Module program
.PDF	Printer-definition file
.Q	Print-job file
.QDR	Print-queue-definition directory

FILER utility

In NetWare and IntranetWare, a workstation utility that manages the NetWare file system. The FILER utility can be used to execute most file-related tasks, such as viewing file and directory information, modifying attributes, and searching for files. Table F.6 shows some of the available options in the FILER utility and a description of those options.

FILTCFG (NLM)

In NetWare 4.x and IntranetWare, a server utility that sets up and configures filters for Internetwork Packet Exchange (IPX), Transmission-Control Protocol/Internet Protocol (TCP/IP), and AppleTalk protocols. Filters help to control what type of information is sent and received by a router, to limit specific kinds of traffic to a certain portion of the network, and to provide security. NetWare 4.x uses the following filter types:

- *Packet forwarding.* Used for IPX and TCP/IP, this filter restricts access to services by filtering out any data packets the restricted location sends to the service location.
- *Service information.* Used for IPX and AppleTalk, this filter restricts service advertisement on a router's internetwork. The two types of service information filters are *service-advertisement filters* (which limit service advertisements sent by a router for a specified set of services to a specified set of networks) and *service-acceptance filters* (which limit the acceptance of service advertisements received by the router for a specified set of services at a specified set of networks).
- *Routing information.* Used for IPX, TCP/IP, and AppleTalk, this filter restricts the exchange of routing information between routers by limiting the routes added to the routing tables of specified routers.

See also **AppleTalk; Internetwork Packet Exchange; Transmission-Control Protocol/Internet Protocol.**

filtering

A task accomplished by a network router. With filtering active, the router discards certain types of packets, or packets that originate from (or are destined for) specific locations.

filtering rate

The speed at which packets are checked and discarded by a router.

Finder

An Apple Macintosh application used to start up other programs, manage documents and applications, and manipulate files.
See also **Macintosh.**

Find-It search engine

A World Wide Web (WWW) search engine from iTools that provides access to multiple search engines, but forces a user to reenter a search query for each engine.
See also **search engine.**

Finger

An Internet service used to gather information about a person associated with given user identification information.

Table F.6: FILER Available Options

Option	Description
Manage files and directories	Modifies or views files; changes the current directory or server; modifies, adds, or views directories; modifies, adds, or views subdirectories; modifies or views rights for files and directories; views trustees for files and directories.
Manage according to search pattern	Views files or directories according to a search pattern.
Select current directory	Sets current context, volume object, and new path.
View volume information	Views owner, creation date, creation time, volume type, total kilobytes available, maximum directory entries, and entries available.
Salvage deleted files	Sets confirmation defaults when files are modified, file attributes, and notification if extended attributes are lost.
Purge deleted files	Permanently removes deleted files from the system.
Set default filer options	Retrieves deleted files that have not been purged.

Fire Phasers

A NetWare login script command. The Fire Phasers command makes a noise using the workstation's speaker. It is most often used to alert the user to read a message or to take an action.

See also **login script.**

firewall

A routing mechanism that prevents certain broadcast messages from passing into a particular network or subnetwork.

firewire

The Institute of Electronic and Electrical Engineers (IEEE) 1394 standard, originally created by Apple Computer, that offers a high-speed method of connecting peripheral devices to a host computer. It is often used for video equipment.

See also **Institute of Electronic and Electrical Engineers.**

firmware

Software instructions that are set permanently into an integrated circuit.

First In, First Out (FIFO)

A processing strategy under which the first element to be added to a queue ("first in") is the first one to be processed ("first out").

See also **Last In, First Out.**

first-level file

A file opened at the operating-system level by using the **open**, **sopen**, or **create** function.

First-Level Interrupt Handler (FLIH)

A network device that determines which device or channel is the source of an interrupt. After making that determination, the FLIH then invokes a second-level interrupt handler to process the request behind the interrupt.

See also **interrupt; interrupt handler.**

FIX

Federal Information Exchange, a connection between the public Internet and one of the federal government's internetworks.

fix

A piece of add-on code that resolves a bug or defect in a previous release of the software. Fixes are typically incorporated into future releases.

fixed disk

See **hard disk.**

Fixed Priority-Oriented Demand Assignment (FPODA)

A network access protocol that requires stations to reserve slots on the network.

fixed routing

A routing mechanism under which packets are transmitted between source and destination over a fixed, permanent path.

flag

Assigned to a folder or file, a property or value that represents a given condition. A flag consists of a single bit, usually set to "on" or "off," or to "yes" or "no." Flags can be used to filter out packets or to determine the rules for access and use of a particular file or directory. A flag is also known as an *attribute*.

See also **attribute.**

flag byte

A bit sequence used to mark the start or end of a frame.

flag character

In an X.25 packet-switching network, a character added to the beginning and end of each Link-Access Procedure, Balanced (LAPB) protocol frame to indicate its boundaries.

See also **Link-Access Procedure, Balanced; X.25.**

FLAG utility

In NetWare and IntranetWare, a file and workstation utility that sets attributes for a directory or file. This utility allows a user to view or modify file and directory attributes to determine which operations can be performed with the file or directory; modify the owner of a file or directory; and view or modify the search mode of executable files to determine how a program uses search drives when looking for a file.

See also **attribute; search mode.**

FLAGDIR utility

In NetWare 3.x, a command-line utility used to view or modify the attributes of subdirectories in a given directory. A user must be logged in to a file server before using FLAGDIR and must be on a network drive to set attributes. To change the attributes of a directory or volume, a user must have the Modify right for that directory or volume. The attributes that can be changed include Normal (N), Hidden (H), System (Sy), Purge (P), Delete Inhibit (Di), Rename Inhibit (Ri), and Help. FLAGDIR has been superseded by the FLAG utility in NetWare 4.x.

See also **attribute; directory attributes; FLAG utility; volume.**

flame

Slang for a rude, insulting, and emotionally charged electronic-mail (e-mail) message.

See also **electronic mail.**

flame war

An online discussion that has degenerated into a heated series of personal attacks against the participants.

flamebait

A comment or statement posted to a mailing list, newsgroup, or other online forum, and intended to elicit highly emotional postings from other participants.

FLAP

FDDITalk Link-Access Protocol, the AppleTalk Data-Link Layer (Layer 2 of the OSI Reference Model) protocol portion of FDDITalk.

See also **AppleTalk; FDDITalk; OSI Reference Model.**

flapping

A problem in routing that occurs when an advertised route between two nodes alternates (or *flaps*) back and forth between two paths. Flapping usually is caused by a network problem that causes intermittent interface failures.

Flash EPROM

Intel's Erasable/Programmable Read-Only Memory (EPROM) technology incorporating a nonvolatile memory storage that can be electrically erased in the circuit and then reprogrammed.

See also **EEPROM.**

flash memory

A type of nonvolatile random-access memory (RAM) that retains its contents after the power for the computer has been shut off. Flash memory can be erased or reprogrammed, and is often used to store configuration information.

See also **memory; random-access memory.**

flash update

An asynchronous routing update sent in response to a change in network topology.

FlashWare

A line of Precepts Software products used to produce real-time video over internal corporate intranetworks or over the Internet.

 **For more information about FlashWare, surf the Web to** `http://www.precept.com/forms/flshwr.htm`.

flat name structure

A naming structure that gives each file a unique name. In a flat structure, there is no logical relationship between names; the names are accessible through a table lookup procedure.

flc

A sophisticated version of a *fli* animation file.
See also **fli**.

fli

An animation file in Autodesk Animator format that can be viewed on many Web browsers by adding the proper plug-in software. This name is an abbreviation for the slang word for a movie, "flick."
See also **Web browser**.

FLIH

First-Level Interrupt Handler, a network device that determines which device or channel is the source of an interrupt. After making that determination, the FLIH then invokes a second-level interrupt handler to process the request behind the interrupt.

FLIP

Fast Local Internet Protocol, an Internet Protocol (IP) developed as an alternative to Transmission-Control Protocol (TCP) to offer better security and network-management capabilities for internetworks made up of large-scale distributed systems.
See also **Internet Protocol; Transmission-Control Protocol.**

floating-point unit (FPU)

A math coprocessor chip used for floating-point arithmetic.

floating-point coprocessor

A secondary processor that performs floating-point arithmetic faster than the main processor. Some processors integrate the floating-point unit directly into the main processor instead of using a separate chip.
See also **80387; 80487.**

flooding

A process used by a link-state router to build and maintain a logical map of the entire network by sending a packet with information about its links to all other link state routers on the network. Each link-state router then combines its own information with the information gained from other routers.
See also **link-state router.**

floppy disk

An inexpensive, polyester-based, low-capacity removable memory disk. Floppy disks are often distinguished as $5^{1}/_{4}$ or $3^{1}/_{2}$ disks, which refers to their size (in inches).

flow control

The process used to manage the rate at which data travels between network components. Flow control imposes an optimal transmission rate to minimize network congestion. It is used most often when the transmitting device is significantly faster than the receiving device.

flow-control negotiation

The process of negotiating the window size and maximum packet size of individual calls in each direction.

FLP

Fast-Link Pulse, one of a series of identical startup signals sent by an Ethernet device capable of supporting a transmission rate of 100 megabits per second (Mbps). These signals are used in a Fast Ethernet network.
See also **Fast Ethernet.**

flux budget

The amount of light that can be lost between adjacent nodes in a Fiber Distributed Data Interface (FDDI) network without causing the transmission to degrade.
See also **Fiber Distributed Data Interface.**

FNC

Federal Networking Council, a committee made up of representatives from multiple government agencies that have networks connected to the Internet.

focal point

In IBM's Network-Management Architecture (NMA), the node (usually a mainframe host) that runs the network-management software.
See also **Network-Management Architecture.**

foil shield

A thin aluminum shield that surrounds the dielectric in coaxial cable. The foil shield is surrounded by a braided shield that is, in turn, surrounded by a plastic or rubber jacket.
See also **coaxial cable; dielectric.**

FOIRL

Fiber-Optic Inter-Repeater Link, a device used to connect fiber-optic cable to an Attachment Unit Interface (AUI) in an Ethernet installation.
See also **Attachment Unit Interface; Ethernet.**

folder

An operating system container that holds documents, applications, and other subfolders. A folder is the equivalent of a subdirectory and is used to organize information on the desktop.

followup

A public reply to a Usenet newsgroup posting that includes a link back to the original posting.
See also **newsgroup; Usenet.**

font

A set of characters of the same typeface, style, stroke weight, and size. A font should not be confused with a typeface, which refers to the actual design of the characters.

font list

A list of a printer's resident fonts.

footprint

In satellite communications, the area of Earth covered by a radio signal transmitted from the satellite. In networking, footprint is the amount of random-access memory (RAM) that an application uses during execution.

See also **random-access memory.**

For Your Information (FYI)

A short document containing information about topics of importance to Internet users.

foreground process

A process currently operating and being controlled interactively by the user. A foreground process gets the highest priority from the computer's central processing unit (CPU).

See also **background process; central processing unit.**

foreign E-mail address

A NetWare Directory Schema term that specifies an object's mailbox when it resides in a foreign electronic-mail (e-mail) system. An object is limited to only one foreign e-mail address.

See also **electronic mail.**

foreign E-mail alias

A NetWare Directory Schema term that specifies an object's aliases as they are known by a foreign electronic-mail (e-mail) system. An object can have one foreign e-mail alias for each foreign e-mail address.

See also **electronic mail.**

Foreign Exchange (FX)

A line that connects a subscriber's telephone to a central office other than the one that would normally provide service to the subscriber's region.

forge

The act of intentionally misrepresenting an electronic-mail (e-mail) message so that it appears to have come from someone else.

fork

A file component in the Apple Macintosh File System (MFS). The two types of forks are a *data fork* (which holds data) and a *resource fork* (which contains application-specific information).

See also **data fork; Macintosh File System; resource fork.**

form (printer)

In NetWare, the name and size of the paper used for a print job.

form (screen)

A specification for the layout of data or menu options on a video screen.

form feed

A print-job option that requests the printer to add an extra sheet of blank paper at the end of a print job.
See also **LPT1.**

format

An operating-system process that prepares a data disk for use.

Format Identifier 4 (FID4)

A format used by a transmission header in Systems Network Architecture (SNA) to encapsulate a message between SNA subarea nodes that are capable of supporting virtual and explicit routes, as well as transmission groups.
See also **Systems Network Architecture.**

formatter

A printer function that converts print data to dot patterns.

forms

World Wide Web (WWW) pages or sections of pages that collect text from a user and send data back to a host or server for processing.

forms-based

World Wide Web (WWW) screens or programs that use forms in a HyperText Transfer Protocol (HTTP) language to solicit input from a user.

forward channel

A communications path that carries a transmission from a call initiator to a called party.

Forward Error Correction (FEC)

An error-correction mechanism that provides the transmission enough information to allow the recipient to locate and correct any bit-level errors that occur during transmission.

Forward Explicit Congestion Notification (FECN)

A bit set by a Frame Relay network to indicate that congestion is occurring in the packet-forwarding direction.
See also **Frame Relay network.**

forward file

A file created to tell an electronic-mail (e-mail) program to send any incoming messages to another e-mail address.

forwarding

The process of sending a data packet or message to another destination. Forwarding can take place in a network bridge, router, or gateway. The network device first reads the packet and checks the address and protocol in the packet header, and then forwards it to the destination on the basis of the information it finds.

Fourier transform

A technique that uses a time-series pattern to evaluate the importance of various frequency cycles.

four-wire circuit

A circuit comprised of two pairs of conducting wires, used for telephone communications. One pair is used for transmitting, the other for receiving.

FPODA

Fixed Priority-Oriented Demand Assignment, a network access protocol that requires stations to reserve slots on the network.

FPS

Fast Packet-Switching, a switching strategy that realizes higher throughput by simplifying the switching process. FPS uses fixed-size packets and simplified addresses. In addition, error checking and acknowledgment is left to higher-level protocols. FPS is used in certain frame and cell-relay implementations such as Asynchronous Transfer Mode (ATM).
See also **Asynchronous Transfer Mode.**

FPSM utility

A NetWare Loadable Module (NLM) in IntranetWare that contains a library of C programming language functions to provide floating-point support for NLM programs. The FPSM utility is automatically loaded by any NLM that needs it.
See also **NetWare Loadable Module.**

FPU

floating-point unit, a math coprocessor chip used for floating-point arithmetic.

FQDN

Fully Qualified Domain Name, the full name for a machine on the Internet. The FQDN includes the machine's name and the domain name.
See also **IP address.**

fractional T1 (FT1)

A digital-communications line derived from a larger 1.544-megabit-per-second (Mbps) T1 line. A fractional T1 can have a bandwidth of 384, 512, or 768 kilobits per second (Kbps). Up to twenty-four 64 Kbps fractional T1 lines can be derived from a full T1 line.
See also **T1.**

fragment

A piece of a packet that has been broken down to smaller components for transmission.

fragmentation

The process of breaking a packet into smaller pieces to accommodate the transport requirements of the physical network medium. Fragmentation involves breaking up the data into individual parts, each of which is combined with a header for additional processing. This term also describes a condition in which parts of a disk file are scattered over different areas of a disk, particularly a hard disk. This condition usually occurs when files are deleted and new files are added.
See also **header; packet.**

frame

A packet data format consisting of streams of bits. A frame includes start bits, data bits, an optional parity bit, and stop bits in addition to the payload. Figure F.2 shows a comparison of different frame formats and the components of each.

See also **packet; parity.**

Frame-Check Sequence (FCS)

A value used to check for errors in a message transmitted over a network. The FCS calculates a value on the basis of the packet's contents, and stores the value within the packet in a separate FCS field. The recipient recalculates the value and compares it against the value contained in the FCS field. If the two numbers match, the transmission is assumed to be error-free.

See also **FCS; packet.**

Frame Control (FC)

A field in a Token Ring data packet that presents a value used to indicate whether the frame is a Media-Access Control (MAC) Layer (a sublayer of the Data-Link Layer of the OSI Reference Model) management packet, or whether it carries logical link control data.

See also **Media-Access Control; OSI Reference Model; packet.**

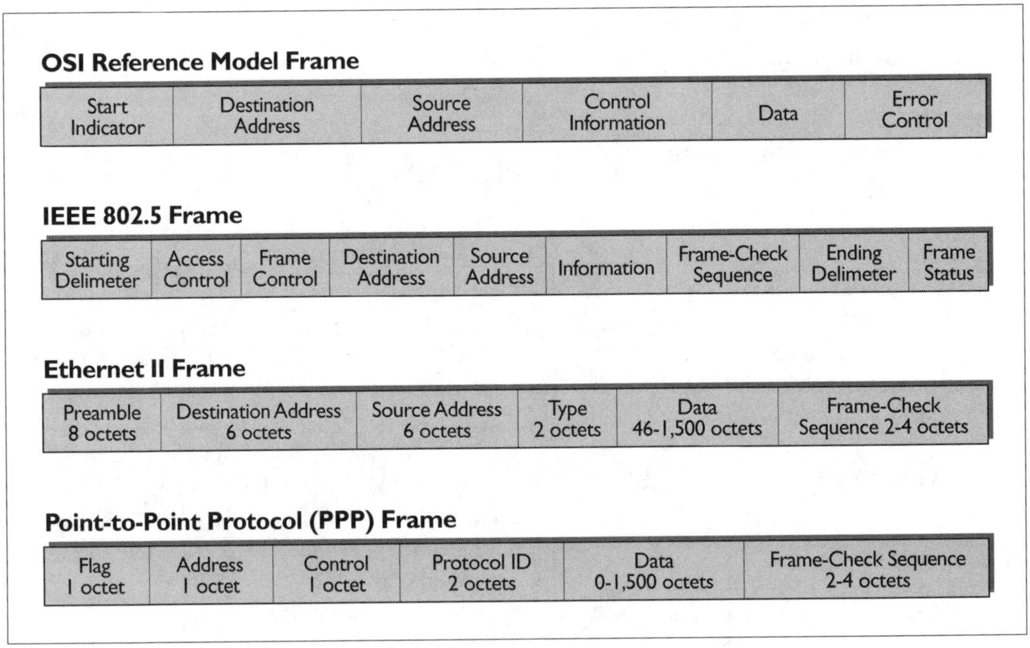

OSI Reference Model Frame

Start Indicator	Destination Address	Source Address	Control Information	Data	Error Control

IEEE 802.5 Frame

Starting Delimeter	Access Control	Frame Control	Destination Address	Source Address	Information	Frame-Check Sequence	Ending Delimeter	Frame Status

Ethernet II Frame

Preamble 8 octets	Destination Address 6 octets	Source Address 6 octets	Type 2 octets	Data 46-1,500 octets	Frame-Check Sequence 2-4 octets

Point-to-Point Protocol (PPP) Frame

Flag 1 octet	Address 1 octet	Control 1 octet	Protocol ID 2 octets	Data 0-1,500 octets	Frame-Check Sequence 2-4 octets

Figure F.2
Frame Comparison

Frame Layer

An X.25 layer that transports data over a physical link and corrects link errors. The Frame Layer is also called the *Link Layer*.
See also **X.25**.

Frame-Reject Response (FRMR)

A frame used to indicate that an unacceptable frame has been received.

Frame Relay network

A type of wide-area network (WAN) system that uses permanent circuits between end points. Through statistical multiplexing, transmission resources are allocated only when active communications are taking place over the circuit. This scheme contrasts with systems that use only Time-Division Multiplexing (TDM) techniques to support multiple data streams. Frame Relay implements fast packet-switching and offers a high throughput, because Data-Link Layer protocols can save time by foregoing the use of error-checking algorithms, leaving these to higher protocol layers. Frame Relay includes a cyclical redundancy check (CRC) algorithm to detect corrupted bits, but does not incorporate any mechanisms to correct bad data. Frame Relay is usually used for sending data only and is well-suited to bursty transmissions. There are, however, some innovations that allow the transmission of voice traffic over a Frame Relay network. The technology uses variable-length packets with small headers. Frame Relay was originally conceived as a protocol for Integrated-Services Digital Networks (ISDNs) in 1984. In 1990, a consortium of Cisco Systems, StrataCom, Northern Telecom, and Digital Equipment Corporation (DEC) developed a specification that extended the basic Frame Relay specification to provide additional capabilities for complex internetworking environments. The extensions were referred to collectively as the *Local Management Interface (LMI)*.
See also **bursty; cyclical redundancy check; Data-Link Layer; Local Management Interface; OSI Network-Management Model; OSI Reference Model; Time-Division Multiplexing; wide-area network**.

Frame Status (FS)

A field appearing in a Token Ring data packet.
See also **Token Ring**.

frame switching

The process of transporting High-Level Data-Link Control (HDLC) frames over a network.
See also **High-Level Data-Link Control**.

framing

The process that inserts start and stop bits before and after data has been transmitted. Framing is used in asynchronous communications to delimit data.
See also **parity**.

Free Agent

A Windows-based newsreader from Forte, Inc. that includes online and offline operation, threaded and unthreaded display, and a multiple-window display.
See also **newsreader**.

For more information about Free Agent, surf the Web to `http://www.forteinc.com/agent/freagent.htm.`

Free Buffer Enquiry (FBE)

A field appearing in an Attached-Resource Computer Network (ARCnet) frame.

See also **Attached-Resource Computer Network.**

free memory

The portion of computer memory not currently in use. Free memory is what remains after the operating system and device drivers have been loaded.

See also **memory.**

Free Software Foundation (FSF)

An organization that creates freely available software. The organization is well-known in the UNIX world for its GNU operating environment.

free space attenuation

The amount of signal loss that occurs between sender and recipient in a wireless connection.

freenet

Any of several free online systems, the first one of which was created at the University of Cleveland that offers local community information and limited Internet access.

freeware

A software program that (although the author still retains rights or ownership) may be used without payment. Freeware differs from *shareware* (which usually includes a trial period but requires some sort of payment to the author) and from *public-domain software* (for which the author relinquishes all rights).

frequency

A metric that indicates the number of times a cycle repeats within a given period. Frequency is usually expressed in *hertz (Hz)*.

See also **hertz.**

frequency band

A range of frequencies in which a transmission takes place.

frequency converter

A device used to convert between frequency ranges in a broadband system.

See also **broadband transmission.**

frequency delay

A signaling delay that may occur when signals operating at different frequencies travel at different speeds through a medium. Frequency delay may cause signal distortion but may be corrected with an equalizer.

See also **equalization.**

Frequency-Division Multiple Access (FDMA)

A method of dividing a large bandwidth into multiple channels.

Frequency-Division Multiplexing (FDM)

A type of multiplexing that divides a medium's bandwidth into separate frequency ranges. Each separate frequency is divided by a guard channel that protects it from interference from the other frequencies.

See also **multiplexing.**

frequency translator

An analog device used in a broadband cable system. The frequency translator is used to convert one block of frequencies to another.

frequency-agile modem

A type of modem used in broadband systems capable of switching frequencies to allow communications to take place over multiple channels at different times.

Frequently Asked Questions (FAQ)

A collection of commonly asked questions with answers on any given topic, typically found on the Internet. A FAQ (pronounced "fack") is posted to give newcomers or novices information about a particular topic, to minimize the number of questions that have to be asked individually.

FRMR

Frame-Reject Response, a frame used to indicate that an unacceptable frame has been received.

frogging

The process of inverting signal frequencies in a broadband transmission. Frogging is used to equalize distortion.

See also **equalization.**

front-end application

A network application, typically deployed on a client workstation, that works with a back-end application running on a server.

See also **back end.**

front-end network

A type of network consisting of specialized, high-performance workstations. A front-end network is usually connected with optical fiber.

See also **back-end network.**

Front-End Processor (FEP)

In a Systems Network Architecture (SNA) network, a component that controls access to the host computer (usually a mainframe), and is typically attached to the host by a direct channel. The FEP is used to offload certain tasks from the host, such as monitoring links or establishing connections.

See also **Systems Network Architecture.**

FrontPage

Microsoft's Windows-based World Wide Web (WWW) page design program that, under the right conditions, does not require a knowledge of Perl or other program based on the Common Gateway Interface.

See also **Common Gateway Interface; Perl; World Wide Web.**

FS

Frame Status, a field appearing in a Token Ring data packet.

See also **Token Ring.**

FSF

Free Software Foundation, an organization that creates freely available software. The organization is well-known in the UNIX world for its GNU operating environment.

FSP

File-Service Process, a process that executes file-handling requests on a NetWare file server.

FT1

Fractional T1, a digital-communications line derived from a larger 1.544-megabit-per-second (Mbps) T1 line. A fractional T1 can have a bandwidth of 384, 512, or 768 kilobits per second (Kbps). Up to twenty-four 64 Kbps fractional T1 lines can be derived from a full T1 line.
See also **T1.**

FTAM

File Transfer, Access, and Management, the Open Systems Interconnection (OSI) remote file service protocol used for transferring and accessing files on different types of computers that are also FTAM compliant.
See also **Open Systems Interconnection.**

FTP

File-Transfer Protocol, part of the Transmission-Control Protocol/ Internet Protocol (TCP/IP) suite of protocols. FTP is used to transmit information between stations, and to prevent errors in the transmis-

sion. FTP transmits data between stations in packets.
See also **Transmission-Control Protocol/Internet Protocol.**

FTP-by-mail

A process in which a user sends a message to a server to request that a file be mailed to the user by way of electronic mail (e-mail). This process is used when only e-mail access to the Internet is available.

FTS

File-Transfer Service, a service in the Application Layer (Layer 7 of the OSI Reference Model) that is responsible for handling files and transferring them between locations. File-transfer services may include Electronic Data Interchange (EDI), the Message-Handling System (MHS), transaction processing, or virtual-terminal applications.

full backup

A copy of all files contained in a server. A full backup copies all files, directories, and management information to a separate backup media.

full duplex (FDX)

A process whereby two data streams flow in opposite directions simultaneously. In a full-duplex system, the recipient node can send control data back to the sender; the sender continues to transmit data.
See also **half duplex.**

Full Name

A selectable property for the following objects in Novell Directory Services (NDS): AFP Server, Group, Message Routing Group, Messaging Server, NCP Server, Print Server, and User.

See also **leaf object; Novell Directory Services; object.**

full-page display

A monitor capable of displaying a full page of text at one time without requiring the user to scroll up or down.

Fully Qualified Domain Name (FQDN)

The full name for a machine on the Internet. The FQDN includes the machine's name and the domain name.

See also **IP address.**

function keys

Programmable keys on a keyboard that can be assigned to perform specialized tasks.

function-management header

An optional field at the beginning of a request unit. The function management header carries logical unit (LU) control information.

Function-Management Layer

In IBM's Systems Network Architecture (SNA) model, the communications layer that formats presentations and communicates with the Data-Flow Control Layer. End-users deal directly with the Function-Management Layer.

See also **Systems Network Architecture.**

fusing

A laser printer process that bonds toner to the paper by using a heated fusing roller and a pressure roller to melt the toner, and then press it onto the paper.

Fuzzball

An LSI-11 computer system from Digital Equipment Corporation (DEC) that runs Internet Protocol (IP) gateway software and is used on the National Science Foundation Network (NSFnet) as backbone packet switches.

See also **Internet Protocol; National Science Foundation Network.**

FX (Foreign Exchange)

Foreign Exchange, a line that connects a subscriber's telephone to a central office other than the one that would normally provide service to the subscriber's region.

FYI

For Your Information, a short document containing information about topics of importance to Internet users.

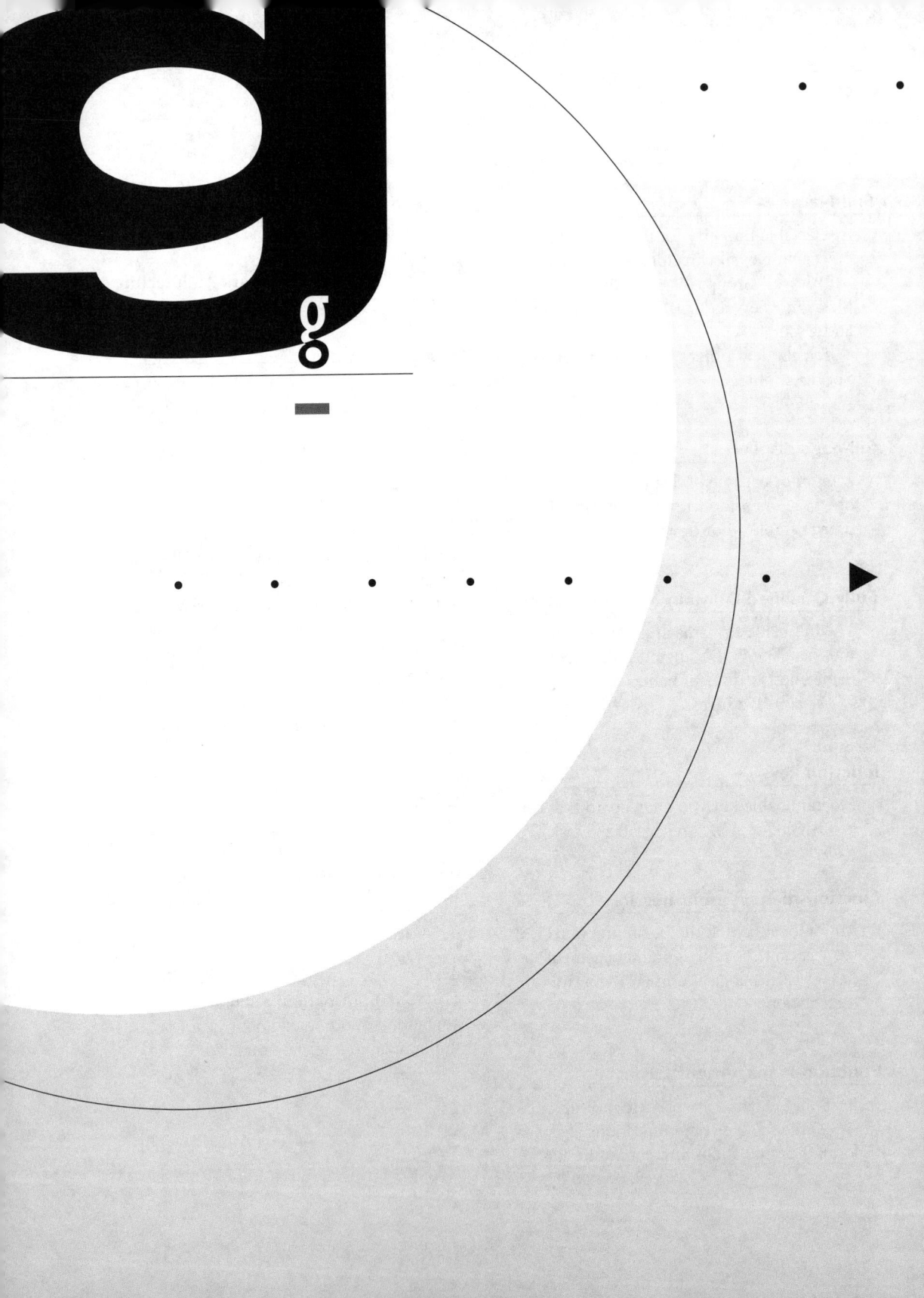

G

Abbreviation for *giga*, or one billion.

G.703

An electrical and mechanical specification from the Consultative Committee for International Telegraphy and Telephony (CCITT) that defines a connection between a telephone company and Data-Terminal Equipment (DTE).

See also **Consultative Committee for International Telegraphy and Telephony; Data-Terminal Equipment.**

gain

An increase in an electrical signal's voltage as a result of amplification.

GAN

global-area network, a type of network that spans multiple countries and supports international data formats.

See also **local-area network; wide-area network.**

garbage collection

Deallocating memory blocks that are no longer in use.

Gatedaemon

A program that routes packets on the Internet and supports several routing protocols.

gateway

A link between two dissimilar networks that maps information between the two networks or subnetworks through a routing table. A gateway is usually a combination of hardware and software, and runs on the following layers of the OSI Reference Model: Application (Layer 7), Presentation (Layer 6), and Session (Layer 5). An *address gateway* connects networks with different directory spaces, a *protocol gateway* connects networks that use different protocols. A third type, the *format gateway,* connects networks that use different representation schemes — for example, American Standard Code for Information Interchange (ASCII) and Extended Binary-Coded Decimal Interchange Code (EBCDIC).

See also **American Standard Code for Information Interchange; Extended Binary-Coded Decimal Interchange Code; OSI Reference Model; router.**

gateway host

In Systems Network Architecture (SNA), a host node that contains a *system-services control point (SSCP)* for a gateway.

See also **Systems Network Architecture; system-services control point.**

gateway NCP

A network-control program (NCP) connecting two or more Systems Network Architecture (SNA) networks. A gateway NCP translates addresses for cross-network data transmissions.

See also **network-control program; Systems Network Architecture.**

gateway server

A type of server that provides users with network access to resources in remote environments.

Gateway-to-Gateway Protocol (GGP)

A protocol used in MILnet that uses a distributed shortest-path algorithm to specify how core routers exchange reachability and routing information.

See also **MILnet.**

gauge

A metric that indicates the diameter of electrical wire. Higher gauge numbers indicate thinner wire. Table G.1 shows common wire gauges and their approximate diameters (measured in millimeters).

See also **American Wire Gauge.**

Table G.1: Gauges and Measurements

Gauge	Diameter (mm)
30	0.26
24	0.51
22	0.64
20	0.81
18	1.02
16	1.29
14	1.63
12	2.05

Gaussian noises

Noise in an electrical signal that results from the vibration of atoms and molecules. Gaussian noise increases with temperature, and occurs on all frequencies.

GB

gigabyte, a unit that measures memory or physical storage. A gigabyte equals about one billion bytes, or more precisely, 2^{30} bytes.

Gb

gigabit, a unit of measurement that usually measures transmission speeds in optical links. A gigabit equals about one billion bits, or more precisely, 2^{10} bits.

GDMO

Guidelines for the Definition of Managed Objects, an International Standards Organization (ISO) specification that establishes a type of notation that describes managed objects and the actions taken to manage them.

GDS

General Data Stream, a format used for mapped data in IBM's Advanced Program-to-Program Communications (APPC) architecture. High-level application data is converted to GDS format before transmission.

gender changer

A connector used to connect two cables of the same gender (two male connectors or two female connectors).

See also **female connector; jack; male connector.**

General Data Stream (GDS)

A format used for mapped data in IBM's Advanced Program-to-Program Communications (APPC) architecture. High-level application data is converted to GDS format before transmission.

See also **Advanced Program-to-Program Communications.**

General Format Identifier (GFI)

A field in an X.25 packet that indicates the packet's format.

See also **X.25.**

general help screen

An online help screen that provides general information about a specific task or function.

general service query

A query that requires a response from every qualified server. The query can specify all servers, or servers of a given type. All qualified servers respond to the query with an identification packet.

General Switch Telephone Network (GSTN)

A public telephone network.

General-Purpose Interface Bus (GPIB)

A parallel interface often used to connect scientific equipment to computers.

Generational Qualifier

A NetWare Directory Schema term and a selectable property for User object in Novell Directory Services (NDS).

See also **leaf object; Novell Directory Services; object.**

Generic Flow Control (GFC)

A protocol used in Asynchronous Transfer Mode (ATM) networking. GFC ensures that all nodes are given access to the transmission medium.

See also **Asynchronous Transfer Mode.**

GEnie

An online Internet service from General Electric.

geosynchronous orbit

The orbit of a satellite whose velocity that matches the speed of Earth's rotation, causing the satellite's position to remain stationary relative to a specific point on Earth's surface.

GETO

In IntranetWare, an IntranetWare GETx control command in a menu file. The GETO command prompts the user for optional input.

See also **GETx command.**

GETP

In IntranetWare, a GETx control command in a menu file. The GETP command prompts the user for programmed input.
See also **GETx command.**

GETR

In IntranetWare, an IntranetWare GETx control command in a menu file. The GETR command prompts the user for required input.
See also **GETx command.**

GETx command

A set of IntranetWare control commands in a menu file that prompt the user for input by displaying an entry box that contains specific instructions.
See also **GetO; GETP; GETR.**

GFC

Generic Flow Control, a protocol used in Asynchronous Transfer Mode (ATM) networking. GFC ensures that all nodes are given access to the transmission medium.
See also **Asynchronous Transfer Mode.**

GFI

General Format Identifier, a field in an X.25 packet that indicates the packet's format.
See also **X.25.**

GGP

Gateway-to-Gateway Protocol, a protocol used in MILnet that uses a distributed shortest-path algorithm to specify how core

routers exchange reachability and routing information.
See also **MILnet.**

GID

A selectable property for the Group and Message-Routing Group objects in Novell Directory Services (NDS).
See also **leaf object; Novell Directory Services; object.**

GIF

Graphics Interchange Format, a graphics format, originally designed for CompuServe Information Services, widely used on the Internet for standalone graphic documents and for graphic elements in Web pages. The GIF (pronounced "jiff") format specifies a raster view of compressed images
See also **CompuServe Information Service; Web browser.**

gigabit (Gb)

A unit of measurement that usually measures transmission speeds in optical links. A gigabit equals about one billion bits, or more precisely, 2^{10} bits.

gigabyte (GB)

A unit that measures memory or physical storage. A gigabyte equals about one billion bytes, or more precisely, 2^{30} bytes.

Given Name

A NetWare Directory Schema term and a selectable property for User object in Novell Directory Services (NDS).

See also **leaf object; Novell Directory Services; object.**

glare

An error condition that occurs in a bidirectional telephone circuit when an incoming and an outgoing call connect because of a crossed connection.

Global Chat

A Windows and UNIX program from Quarterdeck Corporation used to access Internet Relay Chat (IRC) services.
See also **Internet Relay Chat.**

global group

A function of Windows NT Advanced Server; a group of users who have access to the servers and workstations in their own domain, as well as in other domains.
See also **domain; Windows NT Advanced Server.**

global kill file

A file that tells a newsreader which articles to skip, applying the same criteria to all newsgroups to which a user subscribes.

global login

A type of login that permits a user to log in to the network itself instead of individual servers. A global login provides access to all network resources.

global name

A name in a network known to all the network's nodes and servers.

global naming service

A network service that provides a way to name the resources attached to a file server. Banyan's StreetTalk service and Novell Directory Services (NDS) use global naming.
See also **Novell Directory Services.**

global network

An international network that encompasses all offices of a multinational company. Global networks must address unique problems, including working in multiple languages, standards, and currencies.

global pseudo-preemption

A NetWare system parameter that blocks all threads and processes after a certain number of read or write system calls have been executed.

global tree

A network directory tree using Abstract Syntax Notation One (ASN.1) to represent network-management objects. The tree's main subtrees are administered by The Consultative Committee for International Telegraphy and Telephony (CCITT), International Standards Organization (ISO), and by a joint ISO-CCITT committee.
See also **Abstract Syntax Notation One; Consultative Committee for International Telegraphy and Telephony; International Standards Organization.**

global-area network (GAN)

A type of network that spans multiple countries and supports international data formats.

See also **local-area network; wide-area network.**

GMT

Greenwich Mean Time, the time at the Greenwich observatory, used as a global standard reference time. GMT is also known as *Universal Coordinated Time*.

GNNWorks

A World Wide Web (WWW) browser from America Online that integrates news and mail services, as well as dial-up access. GNNWorks uses a card-catalog metaphor, the conceptual equivalent of a bookmark list or a hotlink list. As the user visits a Web site, a new card is created. Tabs at the bottom of the screen show the different sites entered in the card catalog. Multiple catalogues facilitate easy organization; a master catalogue tracks all individual Web sites visited.

See also **Web browser.**

 **For more information about GNNWorks, surf the Web to** http://www.gnn.com.

GNU

A collection of freeware programs from the Free Software Foundation, and particularly programs that offer a functional equivalent to the programs and utilities found in UNIX operating systems.

 **For more information about the Free Software Foundation, surf the Web to** http://www.gnu.ai.mit. edu.

Gopher

A distributed Internet service that provides access to hierarchically organized information in a database, catalog, newsgroup, or other system. Gopher servers are accessible through TELNET or through a Gopher client. A Gopher client can access information on any Gopher server through a single menu system.

Gopherspace

A term that encompasses all Gopher menus on the Internet.

GoS

Grade of Service, a telephony metric that indicates performance levels, referring to the probability of delay before a call can be connected.

GOSIP

Government OSI Profile, the United States government's representation of the OSI Reference Model. Government contractors usually have to comply with GOSIP, which includes specifications for interoperation among systems, and mutual access among users in different government agencies.

See also **OSI Reference Model.**

gov (government)

A suffix attached to the Internet addresses sites maintained by parts of the government (most likely the federal government), as opposed to a company or educational institution.

See also **IP address.**

Government OSI Profile (GOSIP)

The United States government's representation of the OSI Reference Model. Government contractors usually have to comply with GOSIP, which includes specifications for interoperation among systems, and mutual access among users in different government agencies.

See also **OSI Reference Model.**

 **For more information about GOSIP, surf the Web to** `http://jitcemh.army.mil/ppd/gosip.htm.`

GPIB

General-Purpose Interface Bus, a parallel interface often used to connect scientific equipment to computers.

grace login

A login that can be performed during the period between notifying a user to change passwords and disabling the user's account if the password has not been changed.

grade of service (GoS)

A telephony metric that indicates performance levels, referring to the probability of delay before a call can be connected.

graded-index fiber

A fiber-optic cable that has several layers of cladding, each with a different refractive index. Graded-index fiber provides a cleaner signal than does single-step fiber.

See also **refractive index.**

GRANT

A NetWare 3.*x* workstation utility that gives users or groups trustee rights to use files and directories.

See also **trustee rights.**

graphical user interface (GUI)

An operating environment that uses graphics to identify its features and controls. GUIs such as Microsoft Windows, Motif, and Macintosh present commands and information through a series of icons that the user clicks on or manipulates. GUI-based applications utilize a consistent set of menus, dialog boxes, and other graphical components to execute within portions of the screen delineated as windows.

graphical utility

A utility used by network administrators to manage the network through a graphical operating environment such as Windows or OS/2.

graphics accelerator board

An expansion board with a graphics coprocessor and other video circuitry. To improve system performance, the graphics accelerator board offloads most graphics-processing tasks from the main processor to the graphics coprocessor.

graphics coprocessor

A graphics chip designed to speed up the processing of graphics and the display of high-resolution images.

Graphics Interchange Format (GIF)

A graphics format, originally designed for CompuServe Information Services, widely used on the Internet for standalone graphic documents and for graphic elements in Web pages. The GIF (pronounced "jiff") format specifies a raster view of compressed images.
　See also **CompuServe Information Service; Web browser.**

graphics mode

A video adapter mode that creates screen displays a pixel at a time instead of a character at a time.

green box

A version of NetWare specific to a locale or created in a foreign language.

Greenwich Mean Time (GMT)

The time at the Greenwich observatory, used as a global standard reference time. GMT is also known as *Universal Coordinated Time.*

ground

A reference voltage used for other voltages in an electrical system. A ground establishes a common return path for an electrical current. All networks and network segments must be grounded.

ground start

A signaling mechanism used in telecommunications to establish a dial tone and prevent collisions between incoming and outgoing calls, normally by grounding the circuit in a Private Branch Exchange (PBX).
　See also **Private Branch Exchange.**

ground station

Communications equipment that sends and receives signals to and from satellites. A ground station is also known as a *downlink station.*

ground wave

A low-frequency radio signal used in wireless communications. The ground wave travels over the surface of the Earth.

group

A set of network users who share applications, have similar needs, and can be managed collectively.

group (telecommunications)

A type of broadband communications channel that consists of twelve 4-kilohertz (KHz) voice channels, for a total of 48KHz. Each channel uses a different carrier frequency. All channels are transmitted simultaneously, using Frequency-Division Multiplexing (FDM).
　See also **Frequency-Division Multiplexing.**

group address

A single address that refers to multiple network devices. A group address is also known as a *multiple address*.

group delay

A communication signal problem caused by nonuniform transmission speeds of a signal's components through a transmission medium.

Group Membership

A NetWare Directory Schema term, and a selectable property for External Entity and User objects in Novell Directory Services (NDS).

See also **leaf object; Novell Directory Services; object.**

Group object

A leaf object in the Novell Directory Services (NDS) structure, used to administer network users as a group rather than as individuals. The Group object lists multiple User objects; an action taken on a Group object applies to every member of the group. In NDS, the Group object has the following selectable properties: Access-Control List, Back Link, Bindery, Common Name (CN), Description, E-Mail Address, Full Name, GID, Locality, Login Script, Mailbox ID, Mailbox Location, Member, Object Class, Organization (O), Organizational Unit (OU), Owner, Profile, Profile Membership, and See Also.

See also **leaf object; Novell Directory Services; object.**

group reply

A response to an electronic-mail (e-mail) message, sent to the person who sent the original message and to all others who appear on its distribution list.

groupware

A type of software that allows several network users (or small groups of users) to access and manipulate objects concurrently and work collaboratively on a project. Typically groupware includes functions for scheduling, messaging, and document management.

GroupWise

Novell's groupware software offering that includes features such as electronic-mail (e-mail), directory services, and support for threaded group discussions. Other features include group scheduling, document management, and replication. Users of GroupWise can also manage and track documents; a check-in-and-check-out facility allows several members of the workgroup to access documents from a central repository. An add-on program adds capabilities of workflow management.

GSTN

General Switch Telephone Network, a public telephone network.

guaranteed bandwidth

The capacity of a network to transmit continuously at a given speed. Guaranteed bandwidth is essential for delay-insensitive applications such as voice or video.

guard band

A small band of frequency that separates multiple bands in a broadband transmission. The guard band prevents interference between the multiple communications channels.

guard time

A period of silence that occurs between transmissions in a Time-Division Multiplexing (TDM) signaling system. The guard time compensates for signal distortion and helps maintain synchronization.

See also **Time-Division Multiplexing.**

Guest

A special type of network account that allows unregistered users to access the network. A guest account enjoys only limited access rights.

GUEST

A username with no password and limited rights. The GUEST username is created automatically when NetWare 3.x is installed, and allows a user without a registered user name to log in to the network. GUEST is a member of the EVERYONE group. Any trustee assignments made to the EVERYONE group apply to the GUEST user.

GUI

graphical user interface, an operating environment that uses graphics to identify its features and controls. GUIs such as Microsoft Windows, Motif, and Macintosh present commands and information through a series of icons that the user clicks on or

manipulates. GUI-based applications utilize a consistent set of menus, dialog boxes, and other graphical components to execute within portions of the screen delineated as windows.

guided media

Transmission media that constrain, or focus, the communications signal.

Guidelines for the Definition of Managed Objects (GDMO)

An International Standards Organization (ISO) specification that establishes a type of notation that describes managed objects and the actions taken to manage them.

Gzip

A lossless compression utility for UNIX files, developed by the Free Software Foundation as part of the GNU project. Files compressed with this utility usually have the .GZ suffix.

See also **lossless compression.**

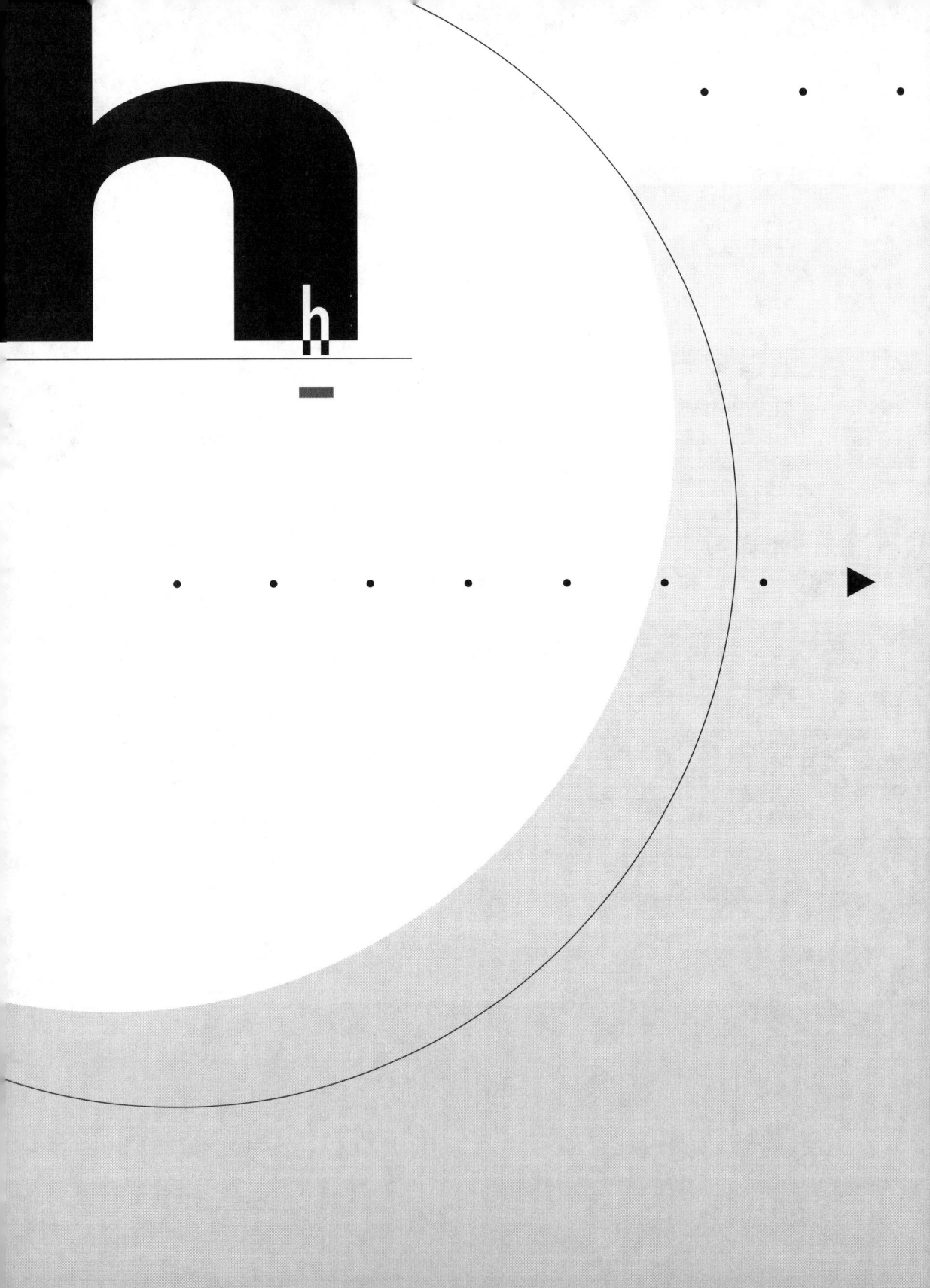

h

H Channel

A higher-rate ISDN channel that can be leased as single units and then subdivided into multiple, lower-bandwidth channels. H channels are appropriate for high-bandwidth transmissions such as video or graphics. The types of H channels include the following:

- H0. This channel equals six B channels of 64 kilobits per second (Kbps) each, for a total of 384 Kbps.
- H10. This channel equals 23 B channels, and comprises a single Primary Rate Interface (PRI) line of 1.472Mbps.
- H11. This channel consists of 23 B channels and one D channel, which is used for signaling, for a total of 1.536Mbps.
- H12. This channel equals 30 B channels, and comprises a European PRI of 1.92Mbps.

See also **B channel.**

hacker

Originally, a self-taught computer user who "hacks" through the steps involved in creating a program, running a network, or other technology-related task. Later, the term came to refer to an individual who breaks into other people's computers for the purpose of theft or vandalism.

HAL

Hardware Abstraction Layer, a function of Microsoft Windows NT and NT Advanced Server that acts as an interface between the operating-system kernel and specific hardware, to make NT transportable to other machines. Under HAL, every piece of hardware looks the same to higher layers.

See also **Windows NT; Windows NT Advanced Server.**

half bridge

One of a pair of bridges that are separated by a telecommunications link in a wide area network (WAN). A half bridge is not connected directly to another network, but instead, is connected to another half bridge via telephone or long-distance cable.

half duplex (HDX)

A type of communications in which transmission can go in either direction, but only one direction at a time. The entire bandwidth is used for the one-way transmission. (By contrast, *full duplex* divides the bandwidth between the two directions.)

See also **full duplex.**

half gateway

A device designed to perform half the functions of a full gateway (which is often divided into halves to simplify design and maintenance).

See also **gateway.**

half router

One of a pair of routers separated by a telecommunications link. To nonrouter stations, the pair of routers appears as a single router.

See also **router.**

half-open connection

An incomplete connection in which only half of the link is established.

half-session

A component providing data-flow control and transmission control for one session of a network-addressable unit (NAU).

See also **network-addressable unit.**

HALT utility

In NetWare 4.*x* and IntranetWare, a server console utility used on System Fault Tolerance (SFT) III servers. This utility shuts down an IOEngine on one SFT III server, leaving the other IOEngine running. The HALT utility only works when SFT III servers are mirrored.

See also **mirroring; IOEngine; System Fault Tolerance.**

HAM

Host Adapter Module, a driver component used to drive specific host adapter hardware in the NetWare Peripheral Architecture (NPA).

See also **Custom Device Module; NetWare Peripheral Architecture.**

Hamming code

A forward error-correcting technique that inserts additional bits at predefined locations in a transmission. The calculated value of these additional bits makes it possible to determine whether an error has occurred during transmission.

hand-held computer

A portable computer, small enough to fit into a hand or pocket. Hand-held computers are often used for specialized applications for which the user must be highly mobile (such as patient care or inventory control). Hand-held computers also often have multiple input methods (such as bar-code scanning devices or pen-based mechanisms).

See also **portable computer.**

handle

A pointer used to identify a computer resource or feature. The number of handles allowed is limited by the operating system.

hand-off

The transfer of a connection between cells in cellular communications. The hand-off time (which can be from 200 to 1,200 milliseconds) accounts for the short delay sometimes experienced when talking on a cellular telephone.

See also **cellular communications.**

handset

The part of a telephone that contains the transmitter and receiver, held during use of the telephone.

handshaking

The exchange between two data-communications systems that takes place before data transmission. The handshaking procedure guarantees that the devices on both ends of the connection are synchronized, and coordinates each phase of the data-exchange transaction. The process of hardware handshaking uses the Request To Send (RTS) and Clear To Send (CTS) pins to control transmissions; software handshaking uses XON/XOFF characters to signal start and stop times.

See also **Clear To Send; Request To Send; XON/XOFF.**

hang

Another term for **deadlock**.

hard-coded

Software that does not allow future expansion.

hard disk

A magnetic data-storage device. Data can be read from, and written to, a hard disk; the disk can be attached to a stand-alone, local workstation, or to a networked workstation. The capacity of the hard disk depends on the *cylinders*, concentric storage areas similar to a floppy disk's tracks. A greater number of cylinders yields greater storage capacity. A hard disk has higher storage capacity and faster access time than a floppy disk.

See also **cylinder; sector; track.**

Hard Disk and Channel Reliability

A feature of System Fault Tolerance (SFT) that guarantees the integrity of data through disk-mirroring and disk-duplexing facilities.

See also **disk duplexing; disk mirroring; System Fault Tolerance.**

hard-disk controller

An expansion board used to control a hard drive. A hard-disk controller may manage multiple hard disks, floppy disks, and tape drives within the same system.

See also **controller.**

hard-disk interface

A way of accessing data stored on a hard disk. Hard-disk interfaces include the ST-506 Interface, Enhanced Small-Device Interface (ESDI), Integrated-Drive Electronics (IDE), and Small Computer Systems Interface (SCSI).

See also **Enhanced Small-Device Interface; Integrated-Drive Electronics; Small Computer Systems Interface; ST-506.**

hard-disk type

A number used to define hard-disk characteristics. The hard-disk type is stored in a computer's Complementary Metal-Oxide Semiconductor (CMOS) random-access memory (RAM); it defines the hard disk's number of read/write heads, number of cylinders on the disk, and other information.

See also **Complementary Metal-Oxide Semiconductor; cylinder; random-access memory; memory.**

hard drive

The storage device that holds the hard disk. The drive rotates the disk at speeds of up to 3,600 revolutions per minute (rpm), and places a read/write head on a thin cushion of air immediately above the disk. The entire unit is sealed to protect it from contaminants.

See also **hard disk.**

hard error

A serious error that occurs in a Token Ring and could bring down the network.
See also **soft error; Token Ring.**

hard reset

A system reset done mechanically by shutting off the power and turning it on again, or by pressing a reset button. A hard reset may be necessary if the Ctrl-Alt-Del key combination does not work.

hardware

Physical computer devices; network hardware may include nodes, cabling, and other peripherals such as printers or storage devices.
See also **software.**

Hardware Abstraction Layer (HAL)

A function of Microsoft Windows NT and NT Advanced Server that acts as an interface between the operating-system kernel and specific hardware, to make NT transportable to other machines. Under HAL, every piece of hardware looks the same to higher layers.
See also **Windows NT; Windows NT Advanced Server.**

hardware address

A number assigned to a Network Interface Card (NIC) by a manufacturer or network administrator. The hardware address identifies the local device address to the rest of the network.
See also **logical address; network address; Network Interface Card; physical address.**

hardware handshaking

A handshaking procedure that takes place between two hardware devices. Hardware handshaking uses an additional pair of serial port wires to accommodate flow control.
See also **serial port; XON/XOFF.**

hardware interrupt

A request for service, generated by a hardware device.

Hardware Interrupt Handlers

In NetWare 3.12, a resource that appears in the Available Options/Resource Utilization screen of MONITOR NetWare Loadable Module (NLM), which tracks loadable modules and hardware use that may cause an interrupt. Local-area network (LAN) drivers and disk drivers that require interrupts also use this resource.
See also **MONITOR; NetWare Loadable Module.**

hardware dependence

A requirement that a particular piece of hardware be present before an application can function.

hardware independence

The capability of a software application to run in multiple environments without requiring specific hardware.

hard-wired

A system designed in such a way that future expansion has been made impossible.
See also **hard-coded.**

Harmonica

A cabling device used to convert a 25-pair cable into multiple 2-pair, 3-pair, or 4-pair cables.

Harmonica Block

A wiring block used to connect a limited number of RJ-11 plugs into a single wiring center.

See also **RJ-*xx***.

hashing

A way of quickly predicting a file's address by calculating the address in cache memory and on the hard disk. If a workstation must read a file on the server, the server performs a hash algorithm to predict an address on a hash table. This method is often much more efficient than searching for a file sequentially.

HAT

Huge Variable-Length Record Allocation Table, an array of pointers to the variable-length portion of a Btrieve record. The HAT is a linked list.

See also **Btrieve.**

Hayes-compatible modem

Any modem that recognizes the standard AT Command Set.

See also **AT Command Set; modem.**

HBA

Host Bus Adapter, a device that functions as an interface between a host microprocessor and the disk controller. During data storage and retrieval, the HBA is used to offload tasks from the host microprocessor, thereby improving performance. The HBA, along with its disk subsystems, make up a *disk channel.* NetWare can accommodate five host-adapter channels, with four controllers on each channel and eight drives attached to each controller.

HCSS

High-Capacity Storage System, a storage system used to extend the NetWare server's storage capacity. HCSS integrates an optical disc library or *jukebox* into the NetWare file system, and transfers files between the server's hard disk (which is faster) and the slower, high-capacity devices contained in the library. The process is completely transparent to the end-user, to whom files still appear to be stored on the file server, even if they are stored in the external jukebox. This method migrates data files off of the hard disk when data stored on it reaches a specified capacity; least-accessed files migrate to the jukebox. HCSS utilizes a cache on the server's hard disk to temporarily store files from the jukebox that are frequently accessed.

See also **jukebox.**

HCSS utility

In NetWare 4.*x* and IntranetWare, a server console utility that provides a view of current High-Capacity Storage System (HCSS) commands and current settings, and allows the changing of the current HCSS settings.

See also **High-Capacity Storage System.**

HDH

HDLC Distance Host, a means of running the High-Level Data-Link Control (HDLC) protocol over synchronous serial links instead of over special HDLC hardware.

See also **High-Level Data-Link Control.**

HDLC

High-Level Data-Link Control, a bit-oriented, synchronous protocol. HDLC is used in the Data-Link Layer (Layer 2) of the OSI Reference Model. HDLC is very similar to Synchronous Data-Link Control (SDLC), and is used for high-level, synchronous connections to X.25 packet-based networks. In HDLC, messages are sent in frames of variable sizes.

See also **OSI Reference Model; Synchronous Data-Link Control; X.25.**

HDLC Distance Host

A means of running the High-Level Data-Link Control (HDLC) protocol over synchronous serial links instead of over special HDLC hardware.

See also **High-Level Data-Link Control.**

HDX

half duplex, a type of communications in which transmission can go in either direction, but only one direction at a time. The entire bandwidth is used for the one-way transmission. (By contrast, *full duplex* divides the bandwidth between the two directions.)

See also **full duplex.**

head

In a hard drive, a physical device that reads data from, and writes data to, the platter. Two heads may exist in the drive, one on each side of the platter. The movement of the head is governed by the disk controller.

See also **platter.**

head end

The starting point for a broadband transmission to end-users. Recipients of the transmission can usually transmit control and error information back to the head end, but no data.

header

Information at the beginning of a data packet. The header typically includes addressing and control information.

See also **packet.**

header compression

A set of compression options designed to cut nonessential data from the frame format. Header compression helps maximize bandwidth on Public Switched Telephone Network (PSTN) connections.

See also **Public Switched Telephone Network.**

Header-Error Control (HEC)

In an Asynchronous Transfer Mode (ATM) cell header, an 8-bit field used to detect errors in the header. The value of the HEC field is calculated using the other 32 bits of the header.

See also **Asynchronous Transfer Mode.**

heartbeat

A test function used in Ethernet networks to determine signal quality.

See also **Ethernet; Signal-Quality Error.**

HEC

Header-Error Control, in an Asynchronous Transfer Mode (ATM) cell header, an 8-bit field used to detect errors in the header. The value of the HEC field is calculated using the other 32 bits of the header.

See also **Asynchronous Transfer Mode.**

HELLO

A routing protocol that allows trusting packet switches to discover routes with minimal delays, particularly in the National Science Foundation Network (NSFnet).

See also **National Science Foundation Network.**

Hello interval

In Open Shortest Path First (OSPF) networks, the number of seconds between transmissions of Hello packets.

See also **Open Shortest Path First.**

Hello packet

In Open Shortest Path First (OSPF) networks, a protocol that establishes and maintains neighbor relationships.

See also **Open Shortest Path First.**

help button

In a graphical user interface (GUI), a feature typically offered on a dialog box to give the user access to context-sensitive, online help about a particular feature.

See also **Graphical User Interface.**

Help Desk

A central site where queries are answered, sometimes fully or partially automated. A Help Desk is often staffed by support personnel who have the knowledge and resources to answer questions about software or hardware products and troubleshoot problems. Specialized Help Desk software may offer a prepared body of knowledge, or may allow an administrator to put knowledge into the system so the Help Desk staff can readily locate and disseminate needed information.

help key

A special key used to gain access to online help. The <F1> key is usually designated as the help key.

help menu

The part of a graphical utility's menu bar used to access online help.

HELP utility

In NetWare 4.*x* and IntranetWare, a server console utility that provides information about NetWare Loadable Modules (NLMs) and other server utilities. The HELP utility also shows syntax, a brief description, and an example for each console command.

See also **NetWare Loadable Module.**

helper address

An address configured on an interface to which broadcasts received in that interface are sent.

helper application

A program that a World Wide Web (WWW) browser calls on to perform a specific task. Most Web browsers now use *plug-in applications* loaded from within the browser.

 **For more information about helper applications from Netscape Communications, surf the Web to** http://home.netscape.com/assist/helper_apps.

HEMS

High-Level Entity-Management System, a network-management protocol that was once a prospective standard for the Internet. The Simple Gateway-Monitoring Protocol (SGMP) and Common Management-Information Services Protocol Over TCP/IP (CMOT) were selected instead as Internet standards.

See also **Common Management-Information Services Protocol Over TCP/IP; Simple Gateway -Monitoring Protocol.**

HEPnet

High-Energy Physics Network, a worldwide research network for laboratories specializing in high-energy physics work.

hermaphroditic

A standard Token Ring connection that has both plug (male) and socket (female) connecting components.
See also **Token Ring.**

hertz (Hz)

A unit of electrical frequency equal to one cycle per second.

heterogeneous network

A network using multiple protocols at the Network Layer (Layer 3 of the OSI Reference Model). A heterogeneous network may contain components from different vendors.
See also **OSI Reference Model.**

Heterogeneous LAN Management (HLM)

A capability allowing the management of local-area networks (LANs) that contain dissimilar devices and run different protocols on different machines.

hexadecimal

A system of numeric notation used to denote addresses in computer memory. Hexadecimal is a base-16 system in which the numbers 0 through 9 are represented by the numerals themselves, and the base-10 numbers 10 through 15 are represented by letters A through F. A leading *0x* (zero and *x*) or a trailing uppercase *H* indicates that a number is hexadecimal. For example, the decimal number 10 would be represented in hexadecimal as either 0xa or aH.

HFS

Hierarchical File System, the standard Macintosh file structure, used to manage files and directories.

HFS CD-ROM module

In NetWare for Macintosh, a module that controls an individual computer's use of CD-ROM discs. The HFS CD-ROM module stores CD-ROM information, otherwise inaccessible to Macintosh users except through the disc volume itself, in a separate area of the hard disk.

HFSCD (NLM)

In IntranetWare, a server console NetWare Loadable Module (NLM) that controls the interaction between NetWare for Macintosh and a CD-ROM drive. With this NLM, all workstations on the network can share data stored on a CD-ROM. A CD-ROM can be mounted as a NetWare for Macintosh volume. After files have been copied from the CD-ROM to the hard disk, file access is performed at the speed of the hard disk, rather than at the slower access speed of the CD-ROM.

See also **NetWare for Macintosh.**

HFSCDCON (NLM)

In IntranetWare, a server console NetWare Loadable Module (NLM) that configures the HFS CD-ROM module. This NLM allows a user to view a list of scanned compact discs, monitors the status of each one, and mounts one or more discs. While using this utility to set up the CD-ROM drive, a user can specify whether the CD-ROM should be automatically mounted, whether NetWare for

Macintosh should automatically scan the CD-ROM's Directory tree, the number of days a CD-ROM file can remain inactive before it is removed from the hard-disk volume, and the maximum amount of disk space on the network that NetWare for Macintosh can use for storing CD-ROM data.

HFSLFS (NLM)

A NetWare Loadable Module (NLM) that allows the CD-ROM NLM to support CD-ROMs that have been formatted with the High-Performance File System (HPFS).

See also **High-Performance File System.**

HGopher

A Windows client that allows the retrieval and viewing of Gopher files on the Internet. This program allows a user to copy multiple windows into a viewer simultaneously while browsing other windows.

hiccup

An error in transmission that occurs when data has been dropped and must be retransmitted. A hiccup is commonly caused by momentary line or port interference, buffer overflow, power loss, or power surge.

Hidden (H) attribute

A DOS or OS/2 attribute that, when switched on, hides files from view in a standard directory listing. This attribute also prevents the specified file from being deleted or copied. In NetWare and IntranetWare, the Hidden (H) attribute may be used on files and directories.

See also **attribute.**

hidden file

A file for which the Hidden (H) attribute has been set. A hidden file does not appear in a standard directory listing.

hierarchical addressing

An addressing scheme that partitions a network into sections. The section identifier makes up one part of each destination address, and the destination identifier makes up another. Hierarchical addressing permits destination identifiers to be reused in different sections.

Hierarchical File System (HFS)

The standard Macintosh file structure, used to manage files and directories.

hierarchical name structure

A naming strategy that depends on a hierarchical relationship, as among files or network entities.

hierarchical routing

A type of routing that distinguishes several network levels. The Internet, for example, may contain three routing levels in its hierarchical routing system: backbone, midlevel, and stub.

See also **backbone; Internet; stub network.**

Hierarchical Storage Management (HSM)

A data-management system that transparently migrates files to progressively less expensive media, depending on frequency of access. Files accessed most frequently are stored on high-speed media; those accessed less frequently may be stored on tape or optical media. End-users need not know the physical location of a file to access it.

hierarchy

A logical structuring of elements in a series of branches emanating downward, starting from a root or top-level node; each successive node can have none, one, or multiple branches leading to subsidiary nodes. Only one path leads from a lower-level node back to the root or top-level node. Figure H.1 shows an example of the hierarchy used in Novell Directory Services (NDS).

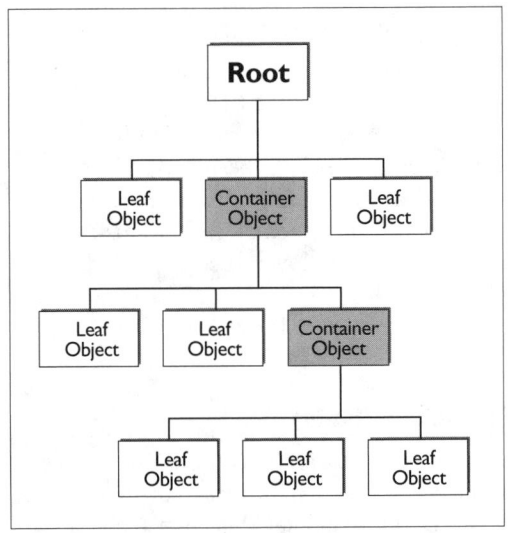

Figure H.1
Hierarchy in Novell Directory Services (NDS)

High-Convergence Sync Interval

A Directory Schema term in Novell Directory Services (NDS).

See also **Novell Directory Services.**

high memory

A generic term for memory above conventional memory. High memory can indicate system memory, extended memory, or expanded memory.

See also **memory.**

high memory area (HMA)

The first 64K of extended memory between 1,024K and 1,088K. The HMA can be directly addressed by DOS in Real mode if a separate device driver is used. HMA provides additional memory addressed directly by DOS and functions in a fashion similar to conventional memory. HMA is available on computers that have 80286, 80386, and 80486 microprocessors with more than 1,024K of random-access memory (RAM) installed.

See also **memory.**

High-Performance File System (HPFS)

A file system that supports long filenames and high-level caching mechanisms. HPFS is used by the OS/2 operating system, and supports filenames of up to 255 characters. It can accommodate high-capacity hard disks, and uses advanced caching methods for faster access.

High-Performance Parallel Interface (HiPPI)

A type of channel connection originally designed to connect supercomputers with mainframes. It has also become useful in high-performance applications such as cinematic special effects and scientific visualization. The connection-oriented mechanism offers transmission rates of up to 1.6 gigabits per second (Gbps). HiPPI can work with several other local-area network (LAN) mechanisms to create a very high-speed wide-area network (WAN).

See also **local-area network; wide-area network.**

High Sierra standard

A subset of the International Standards Organization (ISO) 9660 standard often used by CD-ROM manufacturers.

See also **International Standards Organization.**

High-Capacity Storage System (HCSS)

A storage system used to extend the NetWare server's storage capacity. HCSS integrates an optical-disc library (or *jukebox*) into the NetWare file system, and transfers files between the server's hard disk (which is faster) and the slower, high-capacity devices contained in the library. The process is completely transparent to the end-user, to whom files still appear to be stored on the file server, even if they are stored in the external jukebox. This method migrates data files off of the hard disk when data stored on it reaches a specified capacity; least-accessed files migrate to the jukebox. HCSS utilizes a cache on the server's hard disk to temporarily store files from the jukebox that are frequently accessed.

See also **jukebox.**

high-end

Any full-featured product, typically the most expensive and feature-rich product in a company's product family.

High-Energy Physics Network (HEPnet)

A worldwide research network for laboratories specializing in high-energy physics work.

High-Level Data-Link Control (HLDC)

A bit-oriented, synchronous protocol. HDLC is used in the Data-Link Layer (Layer 2) of the OSI Reference Model. HDLC is very similar to Synchronous Data-Link Control (SDLC), and is used for high-level, synchronous connections to X.25 packet-based networks. In HDLC, messages are sent in frames of variable sizes.

See also **OSI Reference Model; Synchronous Data-Link Control; X.25.**

High-Level Entity-Management System (HEMS)

A network-management protocol that was once a prospective standard for the Internet. The Simple Gateway-Monitoring Protocol (SGMP) and Common Management-Information Services Protocol Over TCP/IP (CMOT) were selected instead as Internet standards.

See also **Common Management-Information Services Protocol Over**

TCP/IP; Simple Gateway-Monitoring Protocol.

high-level language

A machine-independent programming language that uses English-like syntax. A high-level statement corresponds to multiple assembly-language instructions.

High-Level-Language Application Program Interface (HLLAPI)

An Application Program Interface (API) designed to be used with high-level languages such as C, Pascal, and BASIC. The computer-based API can establish an interface between a mainframe computer and an application on a personal computer.

See also **Application Program Interface.**

high-speed circuit

A telecommunications circuit with a fast transmission rate of 20 kilobits per second (Kbps) or more, a rate faster than what is typically needed for voice communication.

High-Speed Command Interface (HSCI)

A single-ported interface controller from Cisco Systems that provides full-duplex, synchronous serial communications at 52 megabits per second (Mbps).

High-Speed Local-Area Network (HSLAN)

Any of several high-speed transmission architectures that function at 100 megabits per second (Mbps) or faster. Fast Ethernet,

Gigabit Ethernet, Fiber Distributed Data Interface (FDDI), and Asynchronous Transfer Mode (ATM) are all examples of HSLANs.

See also **Asynchronous Transfer Mode; fast Ethernet; Fiber Distributed Data Interface.**

High-Speed Serial Interface (HSSI)

Serial connections transmitting at more than 20 kilobits per second (Kbps).

high-usage trunk group

A cable group used as the primary path between two switching stations in a telecommunications network.

Higher Privileges

In Novell Directory Services (NDS), a Directory Schema term and selectable property for the User object.

See also **leaf object; Novell Directory Services; object.**

HiPPI

High-Performance Parallel Interface, a type of channel connection originally designed to connect supercomputers with mainframes. It has also become useful in high-performance applications such as cinematic special effects and scientific visualization. The connection-oriented mechanism offers transmission rates of up to 1.6 gigabits per second (Gbps). HiPPI can work with several other local-area network (LAN) mechanisms to create a very high-speed wide-area network (WAN).

See also **local-area network; wide-area network.**

history list

A list of Uniform Resource Locator (URL) addresses visited during a session on the Internet, with the most recent World Wide Web (WWW) site listed first. Most Web browsers allow entries in the history list to be moved to a *bookmark list.*

See also **bookmark; Uniform Resource Locator; Web browser; World Wide Web.**

history menu

A feature of Novell ElectroText and DynaText that allows users to retrace their steps through a document or documents.

See also **DynaText; Novell ElectroText.**

hit

Either a temporary change in the phase or amplitude of a signal that can create distortion and cause errors, or the successful return of an item that meets a specified search criteria.

See also **search engine.**

HLLAPI

High-Level-Language Application Program Interface, an Application Program Interface (API) designed to be used with high-level languages such as C, Pascal, and BASIC. The computer-based API can establish an interface between a mainframe computer and an application on a personal computer.

See also **Application Program Interface.**

HLM

Heterogeneous LAN Management, a capability allowing the management of local-area networks (LANs) that contain dissimilar devices and run different protocols on different machines.

HMA

high memory area, the first 64K of extended memory between 1,024K and 1,088K. The HMA can be directly addressed by DOS in Real mode if a separate device driver is used. HMA provides additional memory addressed directly by DOS and functions in a fashion similar to conventional memory. HMA is available on computers that have 80286, 80386, and 80486 microprocessors with more than 1,024K of random-access memory (RAM) installed.

See also **memory.**

HMUX

Hybrid Multiplexer, in Fiber Distributed Data Interface (FDDI) II networks, a component of the Media-Access Control (MAC) Layer that multiplexes network data from the MAC Layer, as well as time-dependent data such as voice or video.

See also **Media-Access Control; Fiber Distributed Data Interface.**

hogging

A state that occurs when a transmitting node consumes a large percentage of the network's available bandwidth.

holding time

The amount of time a call is in control of a communications channel.

hold-down

A state of a route in which the router neither advertises the route nor believes any advertisement about the route for a specified length of time. A hold-down is used to flush out bad information about a route from all routers in the network. When a link to a route fails, the route can be placed in a hold-down mode.

See also **router.**

hole in the tree

In NetWare or IntranetWare, a security feature used in trustee assignments that prevents users with rights in one branch of the Novell Directory Services (NDS) Directory tree from browsing the entire Directory tree.

See also **Novell Directory Services; trustee assignment.**

Home Directory

A selectable property for the User object in Novell Directory Services (NDS).

See also **leaf object; Novell Directory Services; object.**

home directory

A private network directory in a NetWare network. The network supervisor can create a home directory for a user, if the user's login directory maps a drive to the home directory.

home page

The first page (or opening page) of a World Wide Web (WWW) site that typically introduces a visitor to what is available on that site.
See also **Web site; World Wide Web.**

home run

A cable running from a wallplate to a distribution frame.
See also **distribution frame.**

homogeneous network

A network using a single protocol at the Network Layer (Layer 3 of the OSI Reference Model). A homogeneous network runs a single operating system, and consists of devices purchased from a single manufacturer.
See also **OSI Reference Model.**

homologation

The compliance and conformity of a product or a specification to standards established by recognized international organizations, which enables portability of products and services across international boundaries.

hooked vector

An intercepted interrupt vector that points to a replacement interrupt service routine (ISR) instead of the original service routine.
See also **interrupt service routine.**

hop

The distance traveled by a packet between routers or other network devices as it travels to its final destination.

hop count

The number of routers or other network devices a data packet must pass through to reach its final destination. One hop equals the transmission of a packet across one router.

horizontal cable

A cable defined by the Electronics Industry Association/Telecommunications Industry Association (EIA/TIA) 568 specification that runs from a wiring closet or distribution frame, to a wall outlet in a work area. Horizontal cable is usually installed inside the walls, floors, or ceiling.
See also **distribution frame; Electronics Industry Association; Telecommunications Industry Association; wiring closet.**

host

A network server or central computer to which other nodes, storage devices, or controllers are attached. The host provides services to other computers. In a mainframe environment, a *front-end processor* or controller may sit between the host and the terminals it controls.
See also **front end.**

host adapter

A Network Interface Card (NIC) in a host server, used to control a storage device.
See also **Network Interface Card.**

Host Adapter Module (HAM)

A driver component used to drive specific host adapter hardware in the NetWare Peripheral Architecture (NPA).
See also **Custom Device Module; NetWare Peripheral Architecture.**

Host Bus Adapter (HBA)

A device that functions as an interface between a host microprocessor and the disk controller. During data storage and retrieval, the HBA is used to offload tasks from the host microprocessor, thereby improving performance. The HBA, along with its disk subsystems, make up a *disk channel*. NetWare can accommodate five host-adapter channels, with four controllers on each channel and eight drives attached to each controller.

Host Device

In Novell Directory Services (NDS), a Directory Schema term and a selectable property for the following NDS objects: AFP Server, Messaging Server, NCP Server, Print Server, and Printer.
See also **leaf object; Novell Directory Services; object.**

Host Name Database

A database that contains all names, aliases, and network addresses of the computers on the network.

host node

A subarea node that includes a systems services control point (SSCP).
See also **systems services control point.**

host order

The order in which integers and shorts are stored on a given host processor.
See also **integer.**

Host Resource

A selectable property for the Directory Map object in Novell Directory Services (NDS).
See also **leaf object; Novell Directory Services; object.**

Host Resource Name

A NetWare Directory Schema term and a selectable property for the following Novell Directory Services (NDS) objects: Bindery Queue, Queue, and Volume.
See also **leaf object; Novell Directory Services; object.**

Host Server

A NetWare Directory Schema term and a selectable property for the following Novell Directory Services (NDS) objects: Bindery Queue, Directory Map, Queue, and Volume.
See also **leaf object; Novell Directory Services; object.**

host server

A NetWare or other network server with a host adapter and storage device.

host table

A list that contains Transmission-Control Protocol/Internet Protocol (TCP/IP) hosts on a network, along with their network addresses.

host-based network

Any type of network in which control is centralized in a mainframe computer.

hostname

An Internet term for a machine's name. The hostname is part of the Fully Qualified Domain Name (FQDN).
See also **Fully Qualified Domain Name.**

host-to-host

A layer in the Transmission-Control Protocol/Internet Protocol (TCP/IP) suite.
See also **Transmission-Control Protocol/Internet Protocol.**

host-to-terminal

A type of connection in which multiple terminals are connected to a single host machine.

Hot Fix feature

A NetWare feature used to protect data in the event of hardware failure. Hot Fix allocates a portion of the hard disk's storage capacity as a redirection area. If the read-after-write verification finds a bad data block on the disk, Hot Fix redirects the data away from the bad block to the redirection area. Hot Fix then marks the block as bad; the server makes no further attempts to store data in the bad block in the future.
See also **System Fault Tolerance.**

hot key

A keystroke or key combination that triggers a particular task.

hot-line service

A private, point-to-point telecommunications link. A hot-line service does not require dialing.

Hot-Potato Algorithm

A network routing algorithm used to route a packet to the output line with the shortest queue.

hot standby

A microwave communications strategy that connects two transmitters and two receivers to an antenna. If one unit malfunctions, the hot standby immediately takes over the duties of the primary unit.

HotJava

An interactive, Java-based World Wide Web (WWW) browser created by Sun Microsystems' SunSoft Division. The browsing environment is highly customizable, and can create dedicated information applications such as kiosks or self-service information sites.
See also **Java; Web browser; World Wide Web.**

HotDog

An editor for HyperText Markup Language (HTML) from Sausage Software, used to create World Wide Web (WWW) pages. HotDog includes a full list of menus and button bars for HTML commands.

See also **HyperText Markup Language; World Wide Web.**

For more information about HotDog, surf the Web to `http://www.sausage.com/store/sstop/htmls/top1t2.htm`.

hotlist

A list of World Wide Web (WWW) locations about a particular topic, arranged to allow the user to jump to the Web site (or add to a bookmark list) by clicking an item.

See also **bookmark; World Wide Web.**

hot-swapping

A Redundant Array of Inexpensive Disks (RAID) technique that deals with the failure of an array by activating a spare drive and rebuilding the data from another drive in the array that has failed.

See also **Redundant Array of Inexpensive Disks.**

HPFS

High-Performance File System, a file system that supports long filenames and high-level caching mechanisms. HPFS is used by the OS/2 operating system, and supports filenames of up to 255 characters. It can accommodate high-capacity hard disks, and uses advanced caching methods for faster access.

HiPPI

High-Performance Parallel Interface, a type of channel connection originally designed to connect supercomputers with mainframes. It has also become useful in high-performance applications such as cinematic special effects and scientific visualization. The connection-oriented mechanism offers transmission rates of up to 1.6 gigabits per second (Gbps). HiPPI can work with several other local-area network (LAN) mechanisms to create a very high-speed wide-area network (WAN).

HSCI

High-Speed Communications Interface, a single-ported interface controller from Cisco Systems that provides full-duplex, synchronous serial communications at 52 megabits per second (Mbps).

HSLAN

High-Speed Local-Area Network, any of several high-speed transmission architectures that function at 100 megabits per second (Mbps) or faster. Fast Ethernet, Gigabit Ethernet, Fiber Distributed Data Interface (FDDI), and Asynchronous Transfer Mode (ATM) are all examples of HSLANs.

See also **Asynchronous Transfer Mode; fast Ethernet; Fiber Distributed Data Interface.**

HSM

Hierarchical Storage Management, a data-management system that transparently migrates files to progressively less expensive media, depending on frequency of access. Files accessed most frequently are stored on high-speed media; those accessed less frequently may be stored on tape or optical media. End-users need not know the physical location of a file to access it.

HSSI

High-Speed Serial Interface, serial connections transmitting at more than 20 kilobits per second (Kbps).

HTML

HyperText Markup Language, a set of markup codes (or *tags*) inserted in a text file to make the file viewable through a World Wide Web (WWW) browser. The individual tags tell the browser how to display the text. HTML is an official standard; Microsoft, Netscape Communications, and other companies have added proprietary extensions to HTML to enhance its functionality.

See also **Web browser; World Wide Web.**

HTTP

HyperText Transfer Protocol, a collection of rules for exchanging information on the World Wide Web (WWW), under which any file can contain a hyperlink to another file, or another location within the same file.

See also **hyperlink; hypertext; World Wide Web.**

HTTPD

HyperText Transfer Protocol Daemon, a program that exists on a World Wide Web (WWW) server and accommodates client requests for files.

See also **World Wide Web.**

hub

A network device that modifies transmission signals and permits the network to be expanded. A hub is often located in a wiring closet and is a point of concentration for wiring. An *active hub* amplifies transmission signals; a *passive hub* does not, instead splitting the signals. Either type allows workstations to be added to the network, but a passive hub (because it does not amplify) must be connected directly to a station or to an active hub. Typically a hub connects nodes with a common architecture such as Ethernet or Token Ring. A *concentrator*, which is sometimes mistakenly referred to as a hub, can accommodate multiple architectures.

See also **concentrator; Ethernet; Token Ring; wiring closet.**

hub and spoke

A network topology that connects multiple peripheral components directly to a common central component.

hub card

A multiport card used in a 10BaseT network. A hub card can be used in place of a hub.

See also **10BaseT.**

Huffman coding

A lossless method of encoding data according to the relative frequency of the data's individual elements. Huffman coding is frequently used for text files and fax transmissions.

See also **lossless compression.**

Huge Variable-Length Record (HVLR)

A record larger than 64K. Btrieve can perform record operations on portions of a HVLR without having to use the full record.
See also **Btrieve.**

Huge Variable-Length Record Allocation Table (HAT)

An array of pointers to the variable-length portion of a Btrieve record. The HAT is a linked list.
See also **Btrieve.**

Hundred Call Seconds (CCS)

A measure of line activity in telephone communications. One CCS is equal to 100 seconds of conversation on a single line. One hour of conversation on a single line equals 36 CCS (one *Erlang*).

hunt group

A group of telecommunications lines accessed in succession to find the first available line.

HVLR

Huge Variable-Length Record, a record larger than 64K. Btrieve can perform record operations on portions of a HVLR without having to use the full record.
See also **Btrieve.**

hybrid circuit

A telephone wiring circuit in a 4-wire cable. The hybrid circuit divides the 4-wire cable into two 2-wire paths.

hybrid mode

In a network using Fiber Distributed Data Interface (FDDI) II network, a mode of operation that allows data and voice to be transmitted over the same network. In hybrid mode, packet-based and circuit-switched services are both available.
See also **Fiber Distributed Data Interface.**

Hybrid Multiplexer (HMUX)

In Fiber Distributed Data Interface (FDDI) II networks, a component of the Media-Access Control (MAC) Layer that multiplexes network data from the MAC Layer, as well as time-dependent data such as voice or video.
See also **Media-Access Control; Fiber Distributed Data Interface.**

hybrid network

A network that mixes two or more topologies.

hybrid topology

A network based on two or more physical topologies such as a star-wired ring topology.

hyperlink

A link in a hypertext system used to move to another file, or another location within the same file.
See also **hypertext.**

hypermedia

A combination of data, text, and other elements in a hypertext system. Hypermedia links together different elements, allowing users to move easily from one to another. Multiple connections make additional material, resources, and related topics easy to access.

See also **hypertext.**

HyperStudio

A World Wide Web (WWW) browser plug-in from Roger Wagner Publishing for Macintosh-based and Windows-based systems. HyperStudio allows users to interact with and create multimedia projects.

See also **Web browser.**

 **For more information about HyperStudio, surf the Web to** `http://www.hyperstudio.com`.

hypertext

A way of retrieving and presenting information on the basis of a dynamic index. Hypertext linkage and retrieval is generally nonlinear and nonsequential, providing a convenient way for users to jump to sections of related text.

HyperText Markup Language (HTML)

A set of markup codes (or *tags*) inserted in a text file to make the file viewable through a World Wide Web (WWW) browser. The individual tags tell the browser how to display the text. HTML is an official standard; Microsoft, Netscape Communications, and other companies have added proprietary extensions to HTML to enhance its functionality.

See also **Web browser; World Wide Web.**

HyperText Transfer Protocol (HTTP)

A collection of rules for exchanging information on the World Wide Web (WWW), under which any file can contain a hyperlink to another file, or another location within the same file.

See also **hyperlink; hypertext; World Wide Web.**

HyperText-Transfer-Protocol Daemon (HTTPD)

A program that exists on a World Wide Web (WWW) server and accommodates client requests for files.

See also **World Wide Web.**

HYTELNET

An Internet program used to find out what resources are available.

Hz

hertz, a unit of electrical frequency equal to one cycle per second.

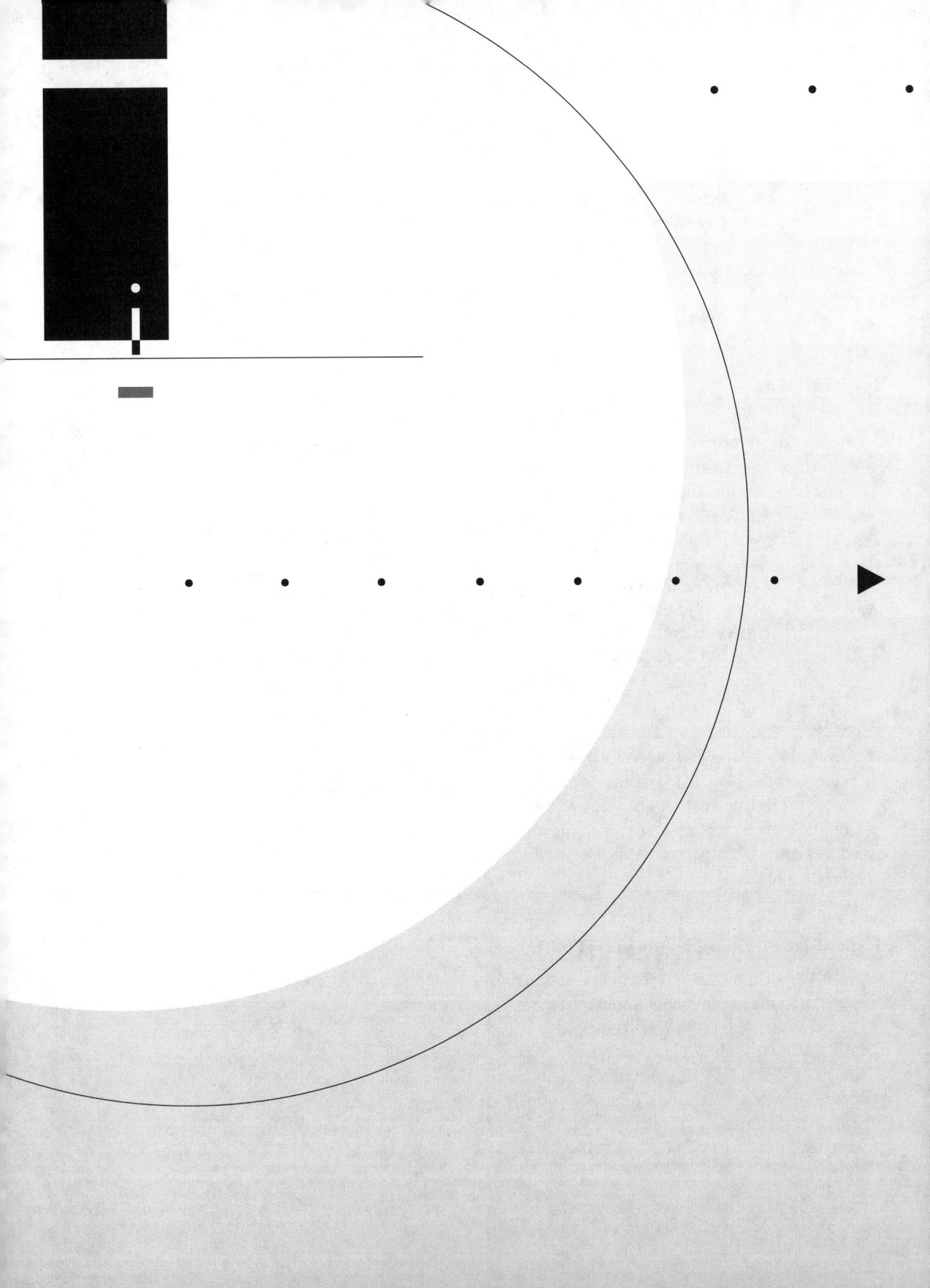

I frame

Information frame, a frame used to transfer packet information and flow-control data.
See also packet.

I/O

input/output, the transfer of data between a computer and its attached peripheral devices.

I/O bound

The state that exists when the speed of the input/output (I/O) port limits the speed of a program's execution.

I/O Request Packet (IRP)

A packet used in Windows NT and Windows NT Advanced Server to provide communication between drivers.
See also **Windows NT; Windows NT Advanced Server.**

IA5

International Alphabet 5, a 7-bit code defining the character set used for message transfers in the Consultative Committee for International Telegraphy and Telephony (CCITT) X.400 Message-Handling System (MHS). IA5 is similar to American Standard Code for Information Interchange (ASCII), but allows for international characters.
See also **American Standard Code for Information Interchange; Consultative Committee for International Telegraphy and Telephony; Message-Handling System; X.400.**

IAB

Internet Architecture Board, the coordinating committee that oversees management of the Internet. IAB consists of two subcommittees; the Internet Engineering Task Force (IETF), and the Internet Research Task Force (IRTF). The IETF recommends standards and protocols for use on the Internet; and the IRTF researches new Internet-related technologies. The Internet Engineering Steering Group (IESG) is the executive committee for the IETF. The Internet Research Steering Group (IRSG) is the executive committee for the IRTF. The name of this group formerly was the *Internet Activities Board.*

IAC

Inter-Application Communication, a feature of the Macintosh System 7 operating system that permits independent software applications to share information. IAC consists of the Publish-and-Subscribe feature (which enables users to create documents made up of components created by multiple applications) and Apple events (which permits one application to take control over another one).

IANA

Internet Assigned-Numbers Authority, A group, operated by the University of Southern California Information Sciences Institute, responsible for assigning values for networks and attributes, and ensuring that every identifier is unique.
See also **Internet Network-Information Center.**

IAP

Internet access provider, a company that provides access to the Internet. The IAP has a point of presence on the Internet, and sometimes has its own high-speed leased lines. An IAP is also commonly known as an *Internet service provider* (ISP).

See also **Internet; Internet service provider.**

IBM cable

The cabling system designed by IBM. Cable types are referred to as Type 1 through Type 9, and are used for Token Ring and general-purpose wiring. IBM cable types are as follows:

- *Type 1.* Shielded twisted-pair (STP), used in Token Ring networks.
- *Type 2.* Four pairs of unshielded solid wire and two pairs of shielded solid wire.
- *Type 3.* Unshielded twisted-pair (UTP), with two, three, or four pairs of solid wire.
- *Type 4.* Undefined.
- *Type 5.* Fiber-optic cable.
- *Type 6.* Shielded twisted-pair (STP), with two pairs of stranded wire.
- *Type 7.* Undefined.
- *Type 8.* Shielded twisted-pair, with two pairs of flat solid wire.
- *Type 9.* Shielded twisted-pair (STP), with two pairs of solid or stranded wire, covered with a plenum jacket.

IBM data connector

A type of data connector used in IBM Token Ring networks. An IBM data connector attaches a node to a Multistation Access Unit (MAU), wallplate, or patch panel.

See also **Mau; Multistation Access Unit; Token Ring.**

IBM Network Management (IBMNM)

A network-management protocol used in an IBM Token Ring network.

See also **Token Ring.**

IBMNM

IBM Network Management, a network management protocol used in an IBM Token Ring network.

See also **Token Ring.**

IC

integrated circuit, a small semiconductor with multiple electrical components. An integrated circuit is also known as a *computer chip.*

ICMP

Internet Control-Message Protocol, part of the Internet Protocol (IP) used to handle link-level error and control messages. Gateways and hosts use the ICMP to send problem reports concerning datagrams back to the source.

ICMP error message

An Internet Control-Message Protocol
(ICMP) packet that contains information
about network failures.
See also **Internet Control-Message
Protocol.**

ICMP Router-Discovery Protocol (IRDP)

A protocol similar to the End System-to-
Intermediate-System (ES-IS) protocol that
enables a host to determine a default gateway by using a router address. The difference between ES-IS and IRDP is that the
latter uses the Internet Protocol (IP).
See also **End System-to-Intermediate
System.**

icon

A graphical representation of an object,
application, or device. A group icon represents several objects, applications, or
devices. End-users can manipulate the
icons, typically by moving a mouse or
pointing device, to trigger an action or to
access data.
See also **graphical user interface.**

IconAuthor

A World Wide Web (WWW) browser
plug-in from Aimtech for Windows-based
browsers that plays multimedia files created
with Aimtech's multimedia authoring tool.
See also **Netscape Navigator; Web
browser.**

**For more information about
IconAuthor, surf the Web to**
`http://www.aimtech.com/
iconauthor.`

IDA

Integrated Digital Access, a method of
providing access to multiple digital channels
(such as voice, video, and data channels).

IDAPI

**Integrated-Database Application
Programming Interface,** a standard for
interfaces between front-end and back-end
database applications. IDAPI was proposed
as an alternative to Microsoft's Open
Database Connectivity (ODBC) standard by
Borland, IBM, and Novell.
See also **Open Database Connectivity.**

IDC

insulation-displacement contact, a cabling
contact in which the connector cuts into the
cable's insulation to make contact with the
wire.
See also **vampire tap.**

IDE

Integrated-Drive Electronics, an interface
standard for hard disk drives that replaces
the ST-506, and places controller hardware
on the drive for better performance. An IDE
bus has a 40-pin connector.

identifier variable

A variable used in a login script. The identifier variable is used to enter in a variable, as
opposed to a specific name, in a login script
command. As a result, multiple users can
use the same script.
See also **login script.**

IDF

intermediate distribution frame, an intermediate wiring location. The IDF is connected to a main distribution frame at one end, and to end-users on the other end.
See also **distribution frame.**

IDG

Inter-Dialog Gap, the minimum gap between dialogs in a LocalTalk network.
See also **LocalTalk.**

IDI

Initial Domain Identifier, the portion of a network address, as specified in the OSI Reference Model, that represents the domain.
See also **OSI Reference Model.**

idle cell

A cell in an Asynchronous Transfer Mode (ATM) network transmitted for the purpose of keeping network traffic at a specific level.
See also **Asynchronous Transfer Mode.**

IDN

Integrated Digital Network, A network using digital signaling and digital circuits.

IDP

Internet Datagram Packet, a protocol for the Network Layer (Layer 3) of the OSI Reference Model. IDP is part of the Xerox Network Systems (XNS) protocol suite

that routes data or packets from a variety of transport protocols, such as Routing-Information Protocol (RIP), Packet-Exchange Protocol (PEP), and Sequenced Packet Protocol (SPP).
See also **OSI Reference Model; Packet-Exchange Protocol; Routing-Information Protocol; Sequenced-Packet Protocol; Xerox Network Systems.**

IDPR

Interdomain Policy Routing, an experimental interdomain routing protocol under consideration by the Internet Engineering Task Force (IETF) that encapsulates traffic between autonomous systems (ASs) and routes the traffic according to the policies established by each AS along the path.
See also **autonomous system; Internet Engineering Task Force.**

IDRP

IS-IS Interdomain Routing Protocol, an Open Systems Interconnection (OSI) protocol that determines how routers communicate with other routers in different domains.
See also **Open Systems Interconnection.**

IDT

Interrupt Dispatch Table, a table used by the Windows NT and Windows NT Advanced Server operating systems to locate the appropriate routine for handling a given interrupt.
See also **Windows NT; Windows NT Advanced Server.**

IDU

Interface Data Unit, a data structure specified in the OSI Reference Model. The IDU is
a structure passed between layers, when one
layer is providing a service to an entity in a
higher layer.

See also **OSI Reference Model.**

IEC

**International Electrotechnical
Commission,** an international standards
organization that sets electrical standards.

IEEE

**Institute of Electrical and Electronic
Engineers,** a standards organization that
establishes networking standards for
cabling, electrical topology, physical topology, and access schemes. The IEEE established the 802.5 and 802.3 protocols.

See also **IEEE 802.x.**

IEEE 802.x

A family of protocols included in specifications from the Institute of Electrical and
Electronic Engineers (IEEE). Table I.1
shows some of the common IEEE 802.x
specifications.

Table I.1: IEEE 802.x Specifications	
Specification	**Description**
IEEE 802.1	An access-control standard for bridges linking 802.3, 802.4, and 802.5 networks.
IEEE 802.2	The standard specifying the Logical-Link Control (LLC) sublayer of the Data-Link Layer (Layer 2 of the OSI Reference Model), for use with 802.3, 802.4, and 802.5 networks.
IEEE 802.3	A standard defining the Media-Access Control (MAC) Layer for a Carrier-Sense Multiple Access/Collision Detection (CSMA/CD) bus network, such as Ethernet.
IEEE 802.4	A standard defining the Media-Access Control (MAC) Layer for a token-passing bus network.
IEEE 802.5	A standard defining the Media-Access Control (MAC) Layer for a token-passing ring network model such as IBM Token Ring.
IEEE 802.6	A standard for metropolitan-area networks (MANs) based on fiber-optic rings.

See also **Carrier-Sense Multiple-Access/Collision Detection; Institute of Electrical and
Electronic Engineers; Logical-Link Control; Media-Access Control; metropolitan-area network; OSI Reference Model.**

IESG

Internet Engineering Steering Group, the executive committee of the Internet Engineering Task Force (IETF).

See also **Internet Engineering Task Force.**

IETF

Internet Engineering Task Force, the Internet Activities Board task force that addresses the short-term engineering concerns of the Internet. The IETF is responsible for the Remote Network-Monitoring Management-Information Base (RMON MIB), a standard for monitoring network activity.

IFG

Interframe Gap, the maximum time period that can exist between consecutive frames or packets.

IFIP

International Federation for Information Processing, an organization that researches preliminary Open Systems Interconnection (OSI) standardization procedures and is responsible for formalizing the Message-Handling System (MHS) specifications found in the X.400 specification.

See also **Message-Handling System; Open Systems Interconnection; X.400.**

IFRB

International Frequency-Registration Board, an agency of the International Telecommunications Union (ITU) that allocates frequency bands in the electromagnetic spectrum. This agency was combined with the International Consultative Committee for Radiocommunications (CCIR) to form the International Telecommunications Radiocommunications Standardization Sector (ITU-R).

See also **International Telecommunications Union; International Frequency-Registration Board.**

IFS

Installable File System, a file system that can be dynamically loaded into an existing operating system. An IFS is used to make newer releases of operating systems backward-compatible with older versions.

See also **backward compatibility.**

IGP

Interior Gateway Protocol, a protocol used to exchange routing table information between routers in the Internet. Two IGPs are the Routing-Information Protocol (RIP) and Open Shortest Path First (OSPF).

See also **Routing-Information Protocol; Open Shortest Path First.**

IGRP

Interior Gateway Routing Protocol, a protocol used to exchange routing table information between routers in the Internet. Two IGPs are the Routing-Information Protocol (RIP) and Open Shortest Path First (OSPF).

See also **Routing-Information Protocol; Open Shortest Path First.**

IHL

Internet Header Length, a four-bit field in the Internet Protocol (IP) datagram. The value in the IHL specifies the length of the datagram header.

IIH

IS-IS Hello, message packets that are sent to all Intermediate System (IS) network nodes to maintain adjacencies.
See also **Intermediate System; Intermediate-System-to-Intermediate-System.**

ILMI

Interim Local Management Interface, an interface specification from the Asynchronous Transfer Mode (ATM) Forum group that outlines the incorporation of net-work-management capabilities into the ATM User-to-Network Interface (UNI).
See also **Asynchronous Transfer Mode; User-to-Network Interface.**

"I'm Alive" Packet

A diagnostic packet sent by a NetWare System Fault Tolerance (SFT) III server. The "I'm Alive" packet is sent over the internet-work connection to allow servers to check each other's status. Every SFT III server sends the packet to other servers over the IPX cable at the rate of 18 times per second.
See also **System Fault Tolerance.**

IMAC

Isochronous Media-Access Control, a Media-Access Control (MAC) element in the Fiber Distributed Data Interface (FDDI) II architecture. IMAC can accommodate delay-insensitive data, such as voice or video, which is received through a circuit-switched multiplexer.
See also **Fiber Distributed Data Interface; Media-Access Control.**

image file

A file that contains a single image sent to a user's computer by a host computer on the World Wide Web (WWW) as part of a Web page.
See also **World Wide Web.**

imagemap

A World Wide Web (WWW) picture report-ing by subregion any clicks of a mouse.
See also **World Wide Web.**

IMAP

Internet Message-Access Protocol, A client/server protocol for receiving electronic mail (e-mail) from a local server. Under IMAP, mail is received and held by an Internet server, and subsequently retrieved, searched, read, or deleted by the client.

Immediate Compress (Ic) attribute

In NetWare 4.*x*, a directory and file-system attribute that causes a file or directory to be compressed as soon as the operating system can do so, without having to wait for a specific event to trigger the compression.
See also **attribute.**

immediate delivery

An electronic-mail (e-mail) feature in which a program sends a message immediately when a user indicates composition is complete.

See also **electronic mail.**

immediate purge

A NetWare restoration option, formally known as *Immediate purge of deleted files.*

IMP

Interface Message Processor, internet packet-switched nodes. This term is no longer used. The current terms include *packet-switched nodes, packet switches,* or *switches.*

impairment

The degradation of an electrical signal.

impedance

Resistance to an Alternating Current (AC) in a wire. Impedance is measured in ohms, and is a function of signal frequency.

See also **Alternating Current; ohm.**

implicit congestion notification

A method of detecting network congestion. Transmission-Control Protocol (TCP), for example, uses an implicit congestion notification method to infer when the network is in a congested state.

See also **Transmission-Control Protocol.**

implicit transaction tracking

A function that works transparently with existing multiuser software, uses record locking, and requires no coding on the part of the developer.

See also **record locking.**

Improved Mobile Telephone Service (IMTS)

A mobile telephony services that allows a mobile telephone user to dial directly to a standard wired telephone.

IMR

Internet Monthly Report, a report containing news and recent technology developments posted monthly on the Internet.

IMS

Information-Management Systems, IBM's mainframe-based database-management and communications software used in Systems Network Architecture (SNA) networks.

See also **Systems Network Architecture.**

IMTS

Improved Mobile Telephone Service, a mobile telephony service that allows the user of a mobile telephone to dial directly to a standard wired telephone.

inband signaling

A transmission containing signal and control information, sent within the regular data channel instead of in a separate frequency.

inbound service-advertisement filter

A service-information filter used to limit acceptance of service advertisements received by a router.

See also **router; Service-Advertising Protocol.**

inbox

A component of an electronic-mail (e-mail) application program where incoming messages are stored for later viewing.

See also **electronic mail; mailbox.**

Incorrect Login Attempt

A Directory Schema term and a selectable property for the User object in Novell Directory Services (NDS).

See also **leaf object; Novell Directory Services; object.**

Incorrect Login Count

A Directory Schema term in Novell Directory Services (NDS).

See also **Novell Directory Services.**

incremental backup

A data backup methodology that backs up only those files that have been modified or created since the most recent backup.

independent LU

An logical unit (LU) that does not require an active session to another LU within a Systems Network Architecture (SNA) host system.

See also **logical unit; Systems Network Architecture.**

Independent Telephone Company (ITC)

A local exchange carrier that is not one of the Regional Bell Operating Companies (RBOCs).

See also **Regional Bell Holding Company; Regional Bell Operating Company.**

index

A key or group of keys used by a database program to sort files.

See also **key.**

index balancing

The process of searching for available space in a sibling index page, when one index page becomes full.

index of refraction

A metric that indicates the degree to which light travels at a different speed through a particular medium.

Indexed (I) attribute

A NetWare file attribute set when a file exceeds a fixed size, and indicates that the file has been indexed for fast access.

See also **attribute.**

inductor

An electrical component used to minimize noise caused by interference. Inductors are typically found in line conditioners or surge protectors.

See also **power conditioning; surge protector.**

Industrial, Scientific, and Medical (ISM)

The three ranges of frequency the Federal Communications Commission (FCC) made available for unlicensed spread-spectrum communications. Prior to the FCC's action, which took place in 1985, these frequencies were allocated for industrial, scientific, and medical use. The frequencies are, specifically, 902 – 928 megahertz (MHz), 2.4 – 2.5 gigahertz (GHz), and 5.8 – 5.9GHz.

See also **Federal Communications Commission; spread-spectrum transmission.**

Industry-Standard Architecture (ISA)

An industry-standard bus design, commonly used on the IBM PC/XT. The ISA design uses plug-in cards and expansion slots, and can accommodate both 8-bit and 16-bit cards.

INETCFG (NLM)

In NetWare 4.*x* and IntranetWare, a server console NetWare Loadable Module (NLM) used for installing Novell internetworking products. This utility permits a network administrator to configure interface boards and network protocols.

See also **NetWare Loadable Module.**

information frame (I frame)

A frame used to transfer packet information and flow-control data.

See also **packet.**

Information-Management Systems (IMS)

IBM's mainframe-based database-management and communications software used in Systems Network Architecture (SNA) networks.

See also **Systems Network Architecture.**

Information Systems Network (ISN)

AT&T's high-speed switching network that can accommodate both voice and data, and can be connected to most standard network architectures.

InfoSeek Guide search engine

A World Wide Web (WWW) search engine that returns up to 100 results ranked in the order of relevance to a search query entered by the user. In addition to the relevance rating, InfoSeek Guide provides a linkable title, an outline, an abstract, and a universal resource listing (URL) for every page that it returns.

See also **search engine; World Wide Web.**

For more information about InfoSeek Guide, surf the Web to http://www.infoseek.com.

infrared network

A wireless network that uses infrared transmission methods to transfer information.
See also **wireless network.**

infrared transmission

A type of wireless communications that can be used only in small areas, such as a single office. Light waves below the visual spectrum are used to connect devices in a network, instead of traditional cabling. The devices must have a line-of-sight connection (no obstacles can impede the path between sender and receiver).
See also **line-of-sight communications; wireless network.**

Inherited ACL

A Directory Schema term in Novell Directory Services (NDS).
See also **Novell Directory Services.**

Inherited-Rights Filter (IRF)

A list of rights that can apply to a NetWare file, directory, or object. The IRF controls the rights that a trustee can inherit from parent directories or container objects. In its default state, the IRF allows all rights to be inherited. However, the IRF does not grant rights, but rather only allows or revokes them. The IRF may be ignored if a trustee has an explicit trustee assignment to a given file, directory, or object. The IRF is part of the access control list (ACL), and to change an object's IRF, a user must have the Write property right to the ACL property of that object. The IRF is used to prevent rights from automatically moving between objects.

See also **access-control list; container object; Novell Directory Services; rights; trustee assignment.**

Inherited-Rights Mask (IRM)

A NetWare 3.*x* feature, used to filter out specific rights. The IRM is used as a security measure to determine which trustee rights can be carried over into a new subdirectory.
See also **trustee assignment; trustee rights.**

Initial Domain Identifier (IDI)

The portion of a network address, as specified in the OSI Reference Model, that represents the domain.
See also **OSI Reference Model.**

initialize

The process of preparing a new floppy or hard disk for use. The process erases any previously stored information. In DOS systems, initializing is referred to as *formatting*.

INITIALIZE SYSTEM utility

In NetWare 4.*x* and IntranetWare, a server console utility that enables the multiprotocol router (MPR) configuration by executing all commands in the NETINFO.CFG file.
See also **multiprotocol router; NETINFO.CFG file.**

Initials

A Directory Schema term and a selectable property for the User object in Novell Directory Services (NDS).

See also **leaf object; Novell Directory Services; object.**

Inktomi search engine

A World Wide Web (WWW) search engine that returns up to 20 results ranked in the order of relevance to a search query entered by the user. In addition, Inktomi assigns a relevance rating on how significant terms included in the search string are in the found document, with scores ranging from 0 to 1,000.

See also **search engine; World Wide Web.**

For more information about Inktomi, surf the Web to http://www.inktomi.com/products.html.

inline

A portion of a World Wide Web (WWW) page containing images or sounds that are automatically downloaded as part of the page rather than shown only when a link to the image or sound is selected.

See also **World Wide Web (WWW).**

InnerWeb Publisher

A discontinued product from Novell used for publishing information on an intranetwork.

INOC

Internet Network-Operations Center, a group responsible in the early days of the Internet for monitoring and controlling core gateways.

In-Place Upgrade NLM

A server-based NetWare Loadable Module (NLM) that enables users to change a NetWare 2.1x or higher server to a NetWare 4.1 server, without having to purchase additional hardware.

See also **NetWare Loadable Module.**

input

Any type of information that moves into a computer, usually from a keyboard or other input device.

input cursor

A cursor on a NetWare Loadable Module (NLM) screen that indicates the starting column or row position where input is taken. The input cursor and output cursor can be placed in two different locations on the screen, for situations in which input is accepted in one field and output is shown in a different field.

See also **NetWare Loadable Module.**

input/output (I/O)

The transfer of data between a computer and its attached peripheral devices.

Input/Output Engine (IOEngine)

Part of the NetWare System Fault Tolerance (SFT) III operating system that handles physical processes (such as network input and output), hardware interrupts, and device drivers. SFT III consists of two parts: the IOEngine and the MSEngine (Mirrored Server Engine). The IOEngine routes packets between the network and the MSEngine. The IOEngine appears as a standard NetWare router to the network workstations.

See also **MSEngine; System Fault Tolerance.**

insertion loss

A signal loss, measured in decibels, that occurs at a point of connection.

inset box

A box in a DOS menu utility used to display information. The information in the inset box cannot be changed.

inside wire

Wiring that runs between workstations and other devices on the customer premises, and the point at which the public wiring starts.

install

To configure hardware or software for use. Software applications usually come with an installation program, which automatically copies all the necessary files into the appropriate directories. The install program may then assist the user in configuring the program to match the target system.

INSTALL (NLM)

In NetWare and IntranetWare, a server console NetWare Loadable Module (NLM) used to initiate the installation of NetWare or IntranetWare, and enable or disable data migration. INSTALL can be used to create, delete, and manage hard disk partitions, install NetWare and NLMs, load drivers, and change server startup and configuration files.

See also **NetWare Loadable Module.**

Installable File System (IFS)

A file system that can be dynamically loaded into an existing operating system. An IFS is used to make newer releases of operating systems backward-compatible with older versions.

See also **backward compatibility.**

installation program

An application used to install and configure another application. The installation program may guide the user through a series of configuration options, and usually copies all of the correct files into the appropriate directories.

Institute of Electrical and Electronic Engineers (IEEE)

A standards organization that establishes networking standards for cabling, electrical topology, physical topology, and access schemes. The IEEE established the 802.5 and 802.3 protocols.

See also **IEEE 802.x.**

instruction set

A set of machine-language instructions that a processor executes.

See also **machine language.**

Insulation-Displacement Contact (IDC)

A cabling contact in which the connector cuts into the cable's insulation to make contact with the wire.

See also **vampire tap.**

int (international)

A suffix on an Internet address that indicates the address belongs to an international organization.

See also **Internet address.**

INT 14H

A personal computer hardware interrupt used to reroute messages from the serial port to the Network Interface Card (NIC). This interrupt is used by some terminal-emulation applications.

See also **hardware interrupt; Network Interface Card; serial port; terminal emulation.**

INT 21H

A DOS interrupt that performs a variety of functions, including getting a segment for use by a control program, reading the computer keyboard, writing to the monitor display, and writing to printer.

See also **hardware interrupt.**

INTAP

Interoperability Technology Association for Information Processing, a Japanese organization formed to develop Open Systems Interconnection (OSI) profiles and conformance tests.

See also **Open Systems Interconnection.**

integer

A whole number. Integers are often used in programming languages as data types for numbering or counting. For example, an integer may be described as long or short, depending on the number of bytes of memory it is stored in. A short integer would cover a shorter range of numbers than a long integer. Integers require fewer bits for representation, so a computer can perform calculations involving integers faster than calculations for floating-point numbers.

integral controller

A controller built into a mainframe computer.

integrated circuit (IC)

A small semiconductor with multiple electrical components. An integrated circuit is also known as a *computer chip.*

Integrated-Database Application Programing Interface (IDAPI)

A standard for interfaces between front-end and back-end database applications. IDAPI was proposed as an alternative to Microsoft's Open Database Connectivity (ODBC) standard by Borland, IBM, and Novell.

See also **Open Database Connectivity.**

Integrated Digital Access (IDA)

A method of providing access to multiple digital channels (such as voice, video, and data channels).

Integrated Digital Network (IDN)

A network using digital signaling and digital circuits.

Integrated Drive Electronics (IDE)

An interface standard for hard disk drives that replaces the ST-506, and places controller hardware on the drive for better performance. An IDE bus has a 40-pin connector.

Integrated IS-IS Protocol

A protocol used to establish communications between routers in an autonomous system or routing domain. Integrated IS-IS is a version of the Intermediate-System-to-Intermediate-System (IS-IS) protocol that uses a single routing algorithm to support more protocols on the Network Layer (Layer 3 of the OSI Reference Model) than Connectionless Network Protocol (CLNP). The Integrated IS-IS protocol can be used in either a Transmission-Control Protocol/Internet Protocol (TCP/IP) or Open Systems Interconnection (OSI) environment.

See also **Open Systems Interconnection; OSI Reference Model; Transmissio- Control Protocol/Internet Protocol.**

integrated service unit (ISU)

A device that combines a channel service unit (CSU) and a data service unit (DSU). The ISU interfaces computers and terminals with Digital Data Service (DDS) lines.

See also **channel service unit; data service unit; Digital Data Service.**

Integrated-Services Digital Network (ISDN)

A set of Consultative Committee for International Telegraphy and Telephony (CCITT) standards for digital networking. ISDN involves the digitizing of a telephone network so that voice, data, text, graphics, music, video, and other source files can be provided to users from a single terminal over existing telephone wiring. ISDN requires special adapters to translate between analog and digital signals. Transmission rates are based on the amount of multiplexed Bearer channels ("B" channels), which are 64 kilobits per second (Kbps) each. The Basic-Rate Interface (BRI) consists of two B channels and a single 16 Kbps D channel. The D channel is used to carry signaling information. The Primary-Rate Interface (PRI) consists of 23 B channels and one D channel, for a total of 1.536 megabits per second (Mbps).

See also **B channel; Basic-Rate Interface; Consultative Committee for International Telegraphy and Telephony; D channel; Primary-Rate Interface.**

integrated software

An application program that combines the functionality of different applications (such as a word processor, spreadsheet, and database) into a single offering. An integrated software package usually has a consistent user interface across all modules, and permits users to transfer data between the different modules easily.

integrated terminal

A terminal that can accommodate multiple transmission streams.

Integrated Voice and Data (IVD)

The integration of voice and data traffic in a single network. Primarily, this consists of the integration of Integrated-Services Digital Network (ISDN) and local-area network (LAN) architectures, and is overseen by the Institute of Electrical and Electronic Engineers (IEEE) 802.9 working group.

See also 802.9; Institute of Electrical and Electronic Engineers; Integrated-Services Digital Network.

integrity control

A way to guarantee that data is accurate. Methods of integrity control may include concurrency controls and shadow paging.

Intel byte order

The byte order used by the Intel 186 processor family. In the Intel byte order, integers are stored in a most-significant byte last pattern.

intellectual property

Any special knowledge or information that can be bought or sold, or can be considered to be an economic asset to the holder.

intelligent hub

A physical hub device that combines the functions of a hub with processing capabilities.

See also hub.

Intelligent Peripheral Interface (IPI)

A hard disk interface that can accommodate a transfer rate of up to 25 megabits per second (Mbps), and offers a high storage capacity.

Intelligent-Printer Data Stream (IPDS)

A printing mode in a Systems Network Architecture (SNA) network that provides access to multiple Advanced-Function Printing (AFP) features simultaneously.

See also Advanced-Function Printing; Systems Network Architecture.

intelligent terminal

A terminal connected to a mainframe or other central host computer. An intelligent terminal possesses some local computing capabilities, and can execute certain tasks independently of the host. However, the intelligent terminal usually lacks local disk storage.

Interactive Voice Response (IVR)

A type of Computer-Telephone Integration (CTI) that allows end-users to input information using a TouchTone telephone. The IVR system uses a synthesized computer voice to interact with the caller.

See also Computer-Telephone Integration.

Inter-Application Communication (IAC)

A feature of the Macintosh System 7 operating system that permits independent software applications to share information. IAC consists of the Publish-and-Subscribe feature (which enables users to create documents made up of components created by multiple applications) and Apple events (which permit one application to take control over another one).

InterAp

An Internet tools package from Stac that includes a Web Navigator World Wide Web (WWW) browser with scripting capabilities to automate tasks and to exchange data with other applications.

See also **Web browser.**

interconnect company

A company that sells telecommunications equipment for connecting to telephone lines. Equipment sold by the interconnect company must be registered with the telephone company before installation.

Inter-Dialog Gap (IDG)

The minimum gap between dialogs in a LocalTalk network.

See also **LocalTalk.**

Interdomain Policy Routing (IDPR)

An experimental interdomain routing protocol under consideration by the Internet Engineering Task Force (IETF) that encapsulates traffic between autonomous systems

(ASs) and routes the traffic according to the policies established by each AS along the path.

See also **autonomous system; Internet Engineering Task Force.**

Interdomain Routing Protocol (IRP)

An Internet protocol defined by the International Standards Organization (ISO) that routes packets between different domains in an internetwork. Based on the Border Gateway Protocol (BGP), IRP is designed to operate seamlessly with End-System-to-End-System (ES-ES) and Intermediate-System-to-Intermediate-System (IS-IS) protocols.

See also **Border Gateway Protocol; Intermediate-System-to-Intermediate-System.**

Interexchange Carrier (IXC)

A long-distance telephone carrier.

interface

The point at which a physical or logical connection is made between two elements. In hardware, an interface refers to the physical connection between circuits or devices. In software, an interface is a software connection between two applications or two application functions.

Interface Data Unit (IDU)

A data structure specified in the OSI Reference Model. The IDU is a structure passed between layers, when one layer is

providing a service to an entity in a higher layer.
See also **OSI Reference Model.**

interface group

A group of interfaces that permits protocols to request an X.25 virtual circuit (VC) through any interface in the group, without having to specify one specific interface.
See also **virtual circuit; X.25.**

Interface Message Processor (IMP)

Internet packet-switched nodes. This term is no longer used. The current terms include *packet-switched nodes*, *packet switches*, or *switches*.

interface standard

Any standard method of connecting two or more elements with different functions. Personal computers employ several interface standards, including Small Computer System Interface (SCSI), Integrated Drive Electronics (IDE), and Enhanced Small-Device Interface (ESDI).
See also **Enhanced Small-Device Interface; Integrated Drive Electronics; Small Computer System Interface.**

interference

An external factor that may adversely influence data being transmitted along a circuit. Interference may come from a variety of sources, including magnetic fields.
See also **electromagnetic interference; radio-frequency interference.**

Interframe Gap (IFG)

The maximum time period that can exist between consecutive frames or packets.

Interim Local-Management Interface (ILMI)

An interface specification from the Asynchronous Transfer Mode (ATM) Forum group that outlines the incorporation of network-management capabilities into the ATM User-to-Network Interface (UNI).
See also **Asynchronous Transfer Mode; User-to-Network Interface.**

Interior Gateway Protocol (IGP)

A protocol used to exchange routing table information between routers in the Internet. Two IGPs are the Routing-Information Protocol (RIP) and Open Shortest Path First (OSPF).
See also **Routing-Information Protocol; Open Shortest Path First.**

Interior Gateway Routing Protocol (IGRP)

A protocol used by routers to communicate with each other in an autonomous system having arbitrarily complex topology and consisting of media with diverse bandwidth and delay characteristics. Originally designed by Cisco Systems to work in Internet Protocol (IP) networks, IGRP was later ported to run in the Open System Interconnection (OSI) Connectionless-Network Protocol (CLNP) networks. Because it is a distance vector routing protocol, each router IGRP sends all or a portion of its routing table in a routing update message at regular intervals to each of its neighboring routers. Routers then use this information to calculate distances to all nodes located in the network. Features incorporated in IGRP that are designed to enhance stability include hold-downs, split horizons, and poison-reverse updates.

See also **distance-vector protocol; hold-down; Internet Protocol; Open Systems Interconnection; poison-reverse updates; split-horizon routing.**

interior router

An AppleTalk network router that routes packets between networks.

See also **AppleTalk; exterior router.**

InterLATA

A set of telephony services, provided by Interexchange Carriers (IXCs), that move between two or more exchanges. Each exchange is known as a Local Access and Transport Area (LATA).

See also **Interexchange Carrier; Local Access and Transport Area.**

interleave

Transmitting pulses from two or more digital sources in a time-division sequence over a single circuit. When applied to random-access memory (RAM), the interleaving process divides dynamic RAM into two separate memory banks, so the processor can read one while the other is being refreshed. In hard disks, the sector interleave refers to the ordering of sectors within a track.

See also **Dynamic Random-Access Memory; sector; track.**

INTERLNK

A DOS command that connects two computers using their parallel or serial ports, thereby allowing them to share disk or printer ports. The INTERLNK command is available on DOS 6 and later versions. DOS 6 must be present on at least one of the two computers, and a three-wire serial cable, seven-wire null-modem cable, or bidirectional parallel cable is required. Furthermore, the CONFIG.SYS file must be edited to include the INTERLNK.EXE device driver.

See also **CONFIG.SYS.**

intermediate cross-connect

A cross-connect between wiring closets.

See also **wiring closet.**

intermediate distribution frame (IDF)

An intermediate wiring location. The IDF is connected to a main distribution frame at one end, and to end-users on the other end.

See also **distribution frame.**

intermediate node

A node that can provide intermediate routing services in a Systems Network Architecture (SNA) network.

See also **Systems Network Architecture.**

Intermediate Routing Node (IRN)

A Systems Network Architecture (SNA) sub-area node that has the capability of intermediate routing.

See also **Systems Network Architecture.**

Intermediate System (IS)

A network entity specified in the OSI Reference Model. The IS functions as an intermediary between multiple subnetworks. Repeaters and bridges are examples of intermediate systems.

See also **OSI Reference Model.**

Intermediate-System-to-Intermediate-System (IS-IS)

An Open Systems Interconnection (OSI) link-state routing protocol. IS-IS allows intermediate systems to exchange routing information. The IS-IS protocol floods the network with link-state information to build a complete, consistent picture of the network topology. This protocol uses IS-IS Hello packets, Link-State Packets (LSPs), and Sequence Numbers Packets (SNPs) for data transmission.

See also **Hello packet; Link-State Packet; link state routing algorithm; Open Systems Interconnection.**

internal command

An operating system command that resides in memory. An internal command does not have to be loaded from disk, and, therefore, can respond quickly.

internal modem

A modem that plugs into a computer's expansion bus.

See also **modem.**

internal network

A virtual, logical network made up of the AppleTalk protocol stack and the AppleTalk router.

See also **AppleTalk.**

Internal Organization of the Network Layer (IONL)

A Network-Layer (Layer 3) specification of the OSI Reference Model. IONL divides the Network Layer into three sublayers: Subnetwork Access, Subnetwork-Dependent, and Subnetwork-Independent. The Subnetwork Access sublayer establishes an interface over which data is sent across the subnetwork or network. The Subnetwork-Dependent sublayer assumes a specific subnetwork architecture, and the Subnetwork-Independent sublayer provides for internetworking of the layers above itself.

See also **OSI Reference Model.**

internal PAD

A packet assembler/disassembler (PAD) in a packet-switching network that exists inside of a packet-switching node.

See also **packet assembler/disassembler.**

internal routing

A routing mechanism used by NetWare to provide access to two or more networks from a single file server. The server has one Network Interface Card (NIC) for each network. This mechanism allows two networks using different protocols to become part of the same internetwork.

See also **Network Interface Card.**

International Alphabet 5 (IA5)

A 7-bit code defining the character set used for message transfers in the Consultative Committee for International Telegraphy and Telephony (CCITT) X.400 Message-Handling System (MHS). IA5 is similar to American Standard Code for Information Interchange (ASCII), but allows for international characters.

See also **American Standard Code for Information Interchange; Consultative Committee for International Telegraphy and Telephony; Message-Handling System; X.400.**

International Consultative Committee for Radiocommunications (CCIR)

A now-defunct agency in the International Telecommunications Union (ITU) that defined radio communications standards. The CCIR was combined with the International Frequency-Registration Board (IFRB) to form the International Telecommunications Radiocommunications Standardization Sector (ITU-R).

See also **International Telecommunications Union; International Frequency-Registration Board.**

International Electrotechnical Commission (IEC)

An international standards organization that sets electrical standards.

International Federation for Information Processing (IFIP)

An organization that researches preliminary Open Systems Interconnection (OSI) standardization procedures and is responsible

for formalizing the Message-Handling System (MHS) specifications found in the X.400 specification.

See also **Message-Handling System; Open Systems Interconnection; X.400.**

International Frequency-Registration Board (IFRB)

An agency of the International Telecommunications Union (ITU) that allocates frequency bands in the electromagnetic spectrum. This agency was combined with the International Consultative Committee for Radiocommunications (CCIR) to form the International Telecommunications Radiocommunications Standardization Sector (ITU-R).

See also **International Telecommunications Union; International Consultative Committee for Radio communications (CCIR).**

international numbering plan

A Consultative Committee for International Telegraphy and Telephony (CCITT) telecommunications standard for allocating telephone numbers around the world.

See also **Consultative Committee for International Telegraphy and Telephony.**

International Reference Version (IRV)

A variation of the International Alphabet 5 (IA5) character-encoding mechanism.

See also **International Alphabet 5.**

International Standardization Organization (ISO)

A Geneva-based organization that develops standards for international data communications, information exchange, and other types of commercial activity. The United States member of ISO is the American National Standards Institute (ANSI). ISO is well known for the seven-layer Open Systems Interconnection (OSI) model for computer-to-computer communications. Figure I.1 shows the organization of the ISO.

International Standardization Profile (ISP)

A subset of a specification still under review during the formalization process. The ISP is also known as a *functional standard*.

International Standards Organization Development Environment (ISODE)

A device used in digital telephone services. The ISODE is made up of the channel service unit (CSU) and the digital service unit (DSU), and is used in place of a modem on a Digital Data Service (DDS) connection.

See also **channel service unit; data service unit; Digital Data Service.**

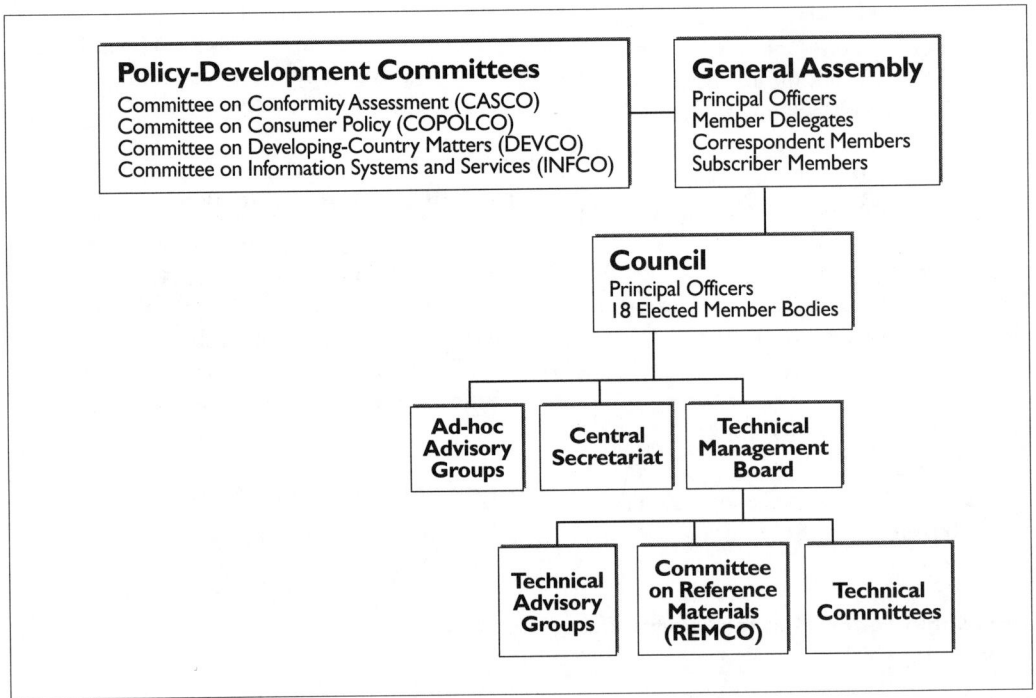

Figure I.1
ISO Organization
See also **American National Standards Institute; OSI Reference Model.**

International Telecommunications Union (ITU)

A United Nations agency that develops international telecommunications standards. The ITU has three subagencies: the Consultative Committee for International Telegraphy and Telephony (CCITT), International Frequency-Registration Board (IFRB), and International Consultative Committee for Radiocommunications (CCIR).

See also **Consultative Committee for International Telegraphy and Telephony; International Frequency-Registration Board; International Consultative Committee for Radiocommunications.**

For more information about the International Telecommunications Union, surf the Web to http://www.itu.ch.

internationalization

A process that permits software to be adapted for use with multiple languages.

Internet

The worldwide internetwork formed by the Defense Advanced Research Projects Agency (DARPA), and the Transmission-Control Protocol/Internet Protocol (TCP/IP) protocols it uses. Originally created to link research and military defense networks such as the National Science Foundation Network (NSFnet) and MILnet, the Internet has evolved into a collection of networks and routers that use TCP/IP, and function as a single, virtual network. The Internet uses a three-tiered structure shown in Table I.2.

Overseeing activities of the Internet are the Internet Society (ISOC), the Internet Architecture Board (IAB), the Internet Engineering Study Group (IESG), and the Internet Research Study Group (IRSG).

See also **Internet Architecture Board; World Wide Web.**

Table I.2: Three Tiers of the Internet

Tier	Description
Backbone	The highest level of the Internet hierarchy. The backbone uses a very high bandwidth to carry traffic and perform routing for the intermediate (transit) networks.
Transit networks	The next level in the Internet hierarchy. The transit networks (also known as regional networks) carry data and perform routing for the stub networks.
Stub networks	The local level in the Internet hierarchy. The stub networks include local-area networks (LANs) and metropolitan-area networks (MANs) carry packets between hosts, but not between networks.

internet

In general usage, any interconnected set of networks. Network users on an internet (or *internetwork*) can share information and peripherals. Types of internetworks include local-area-network-to-local-area-network (LAN-to-LAN), LAN-to-mainframe, and LAN-to-wide-area-network (WAN).

See also **local-area network; wide-area network.**

Internet Access Provider (IAP)

A company that provides access to the Internet. The IAP has a point of presence on the Internet, and sometimes has its own high-speed leased lines. An IAP is also commonly known as an *Internet service provider* (ISP).

See also **Internet; Internet service provider.**

Internet Activities Board (IAB)

Internet Architecture Board, the coordinating committee that oversees management of the Internet. IAB consists of two subcommittees; the Internet Engineering Task Force (IETF), and the Internet Research Task Force (IRTF). The IETF recommends standards and protocols for use on the Internet; and the IRTF researches new Internet-related technologies. The Internet Engineering Steering Group (IESG) is the executive committee for the IETF. The Internet Research Steering Group (IRSG) is the executive committee for the IRTF. The name of this group formerly was the *Internet Activities Board.*

Internet address

A 32-bit address assigned to Transmission-Control Protocol/Internet Protocol (TCP/IP) Internet hosts that consists of information about the document type and about the protocol used to transport it, the domain name of the machine on which the document is found, and the document's name represented as an absolute path to the file. Electronic-mail (e-mail) addresses often contain the domain name information following an "at symbol" (@).

See also **IP address.**

Internet Architecture Board (IAB)

The coordinating committee that oversees management of the Internet. IAB consists of two subcommittees: the Internet Engineering Task Force (IETF), and the Internet Research Task Force (IRTF). The IETF recommends standards and protocols for use on the Internet; and the IRTF researches new Internet-related technologies. The Internet Engineering Steering Group (IESG) is the executive committee for the IETF. The Internet Research Steering Group (IRSG) is the executive committee for the IRTF. The name of this group formerly was the *Internet Activities Board.*

Internet Assigned-Numbers Authority (IANA)

A group, operated by the University of Southern California Information Sciences Institute, responsible for assigning values for networks and attributes, and ensuring that every identifier is unique.

See also **Internet Network-Information Center.**

Internet Chameleon

An package that includes 18 Internet tools, including a World Wide Web (WWW) browser, connection software, electronic mail (e-mail) client software, a newsgroup enabler, lookup tools, diagnostic tools, a real-time chat utility, and an Internet address book.

See also **Web browser.**

Internet Control-Message Protocol (ICMP)

Part of the Internet Protocol (IP) used to handle link-level error and control messages. Gateways and hosts use the ICMP to send problem reports concerning datagrams back to the source.

Internet Datagram Packet (IDP)

A protocol for the Network Layer (Layer 3) of the OSI Reference Model. IDP is part of the Xerox Network Systems (XNS) protocol suite that routes data or packets from a variety of transport protocols, such as Routing Information Protocol (RIP), Packet-Exchange Protocol (PEP), and Sequenced-Packet Protocol (SPP).

See also **OSI Reference Model; Packet-Exchange Protocol; Routing-Information Protocol; Sequenced Packet Protocol; Xerox Network Systems.**

Internet Engineering Steering Group (IESG)

The executive committee of the Internet Engineering Task Force (IETF).

See also **Internet Engineering Task Force.**

Internet Engineering Task Force (IETF)

The Internet Activities Board task force that addresses the short-term engineering concerns of the Internet. The IETF is responsible for the Remote Network-Monitoring Management-Information Base (RMON MIB), a standard for monitoring network activity.

Internet Explorer

A World Wide Web (WWW) browser from Microsoft that includes a feature allowing Web page designers to position Graphics Interchange Format (GIF) images in the background of a page and that includes enhancements for multimedia elements. Internet Explorer runs on a Windows 95 and Windows NT platform.

See also **Web browser.**

Internet Header Length (IHL)

A four-bit field in the Internet Protocol (IP) datagram. The value in the IHL specifies the length of the datagram header.

Internet In A Box

A 16-bit World Wide Web (WWW) browser package from CompuServe that includes the Web browser, newsreader, electronic mail (e-mail), dialer, network manager, and configuration tools. A Windows 95 version of this program is called Mosaic In A Box.

See also **Mosaic In A Box; Web browser.**

Internet Message-Access Protocol (IMAP)

A client/server protocol for receiving electronic mail (e-mail) from a local server. Under IMAP, mail is received and held by an Internet server, and subsequently retrieved, searched, read, or deleted by the client.

Internet message server

Software that provides access to the Internet over network bridges. A dedicated machine is not required to establish this type of connection.

Internet Monthly Report (IMR)

A report containing news and recent technology developments posted monthly on the Internet.

Internet Network Information Center (InterNIC)

A central organization responsible for allocating and maintaining World Wide Web (WWW) domain names. This organization works as a cooperative effort between AT&T, the National Science Foundation (NSF), and Network Solutions, Inc. AT&T supports the Directory and Database Services, which entails overseeing a Directory of Directories, white pages services, and publicly accessible databases. The NSF is responsible for maintaining Net Scout services, which entails the publication of Scout Report and Net happenings.

Network Solutions sponsors Registration Services, Support Services, and Net Scout Services. The InterNIC Registration Services registers second-level domain names to be used on the Internet. The second-level domain name consists of a unique name (not to exceed 22-characters) followed by a three-letter, top-level-domain abbreviation. Figure I.2 shows the process involved for getting an Internet address.

internet network library

A library that contains functions used in Transmission Control Protocol/Internet Protocol (TCP/IP) programming.

Internet Network-Operations Center (INOC)

A group responsible in the early days of the Internet for monitoring and controlling core gateways.

Internetwork Packet-Exchange Open Data Interface (IPXODI)

A module that takes workstation requests that the DOS Requester determines are for the network, packages them with addressing information, and transfers them to the Link Support Layer (LSL). Each packet must have an initialized header, which specifies the target network, origin, and what happens after delivery. IPXODI transmits data packets as datagrams (therefore it can send them only on a best-effort basis).

See also **Link-Support Layer.**

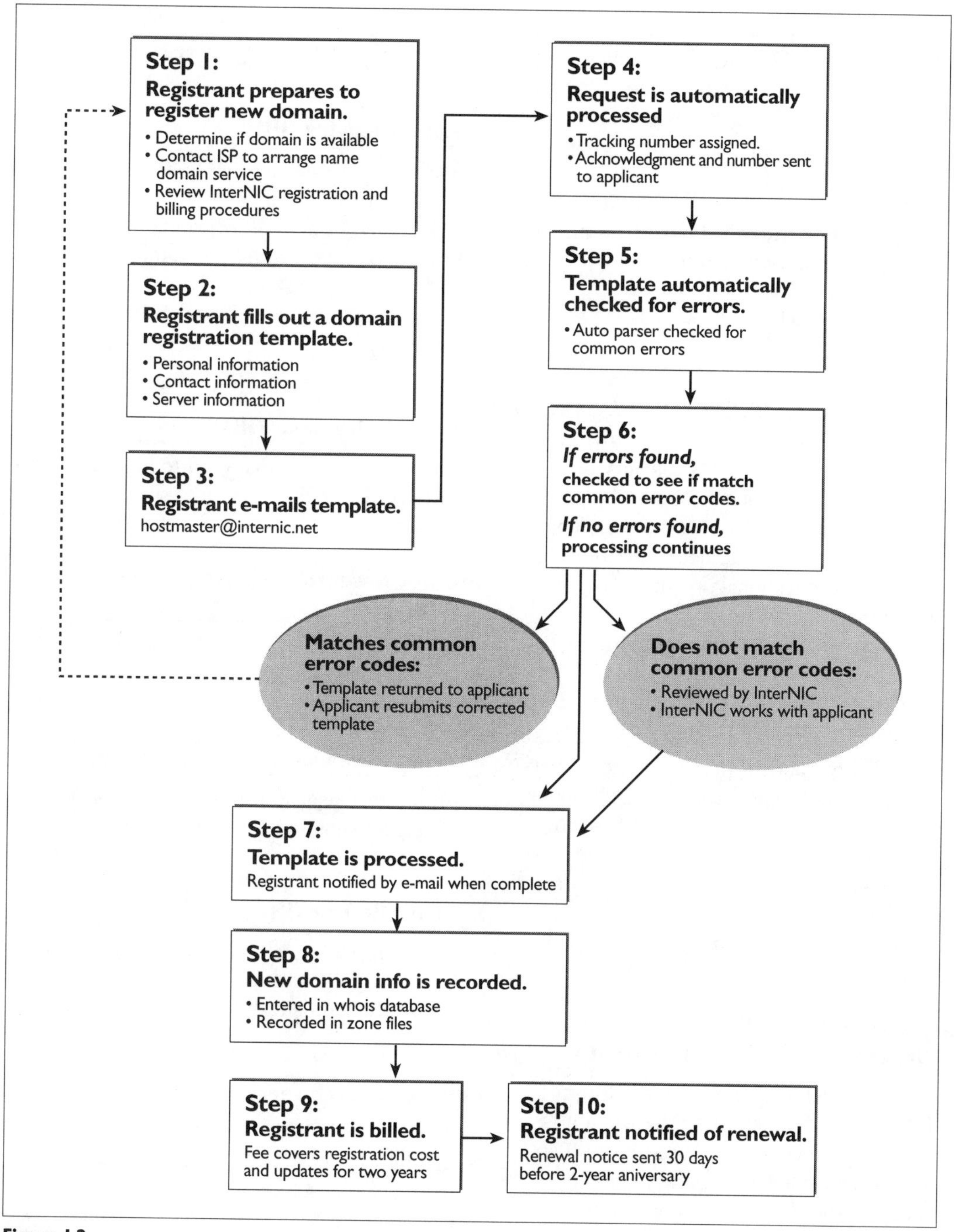

Step 1:

Registrant prepares to register new domain.

- Determine if domain is available
- Contact ISP to arrange name domain service
- Review InterNIC registration and billing procedures

Step 2:

Registrant fills out a domain registration template.

- Personal information
- Contact information
- Server information

Step 3:

Registrant e-mails template.
hostmaster@internic.net

Step 4:

Request is automatically processed

- Tracking number assigned.
- Acknowledgment and number sent to applicant

Step 5:

Template automatically checked for errors.

- Auto parser checked for common errors

Step 6:

If errors found,
checked to see if match common error codes.

If no errors found,
processing continues

Matches common error codes:

- Template returned to applicant
- Applicant resubmits corrected template

Does not match common error codes:

- Reviewed by InterNIC
- InterNIC works with applicant

Step 7:

Template is processed.
Registrant notified by e-mail when complete

Step 8:

New domain info is recorded.

- Entered in whois database
- Recorded in zone files

Step 9:

Registrant is billed.
Fee covers registration cost and updates for two years

Step 10:

Registrant notified of renewal.
Renewal notice sent 30 days before 2-year aniversary

Figure 1.2
InterNIC Approval Process

Internet Phone

A program from VocalTec that enables a personal computer equipped with a multimedia audio card to communicate with other computers on the Internet as if it were a telephone.

For more information about Internet Phone, surf the Web to `http://www.vocaltec.com`.

Internet presence provider (IPP)

A company or organization that provides access to the Internet. This category of Internet providers includes both Internet service providers (ISPs) and internal departments that manage Internet connections for companies, educational organizations, or government agencies.

See also **Internet service provider.**

Internet Protocol (IP)

An industry standard protocol suite. IP permits multivendor nodes in a heterogeneous network to communicate. IP is a Session Layer (Layer 5 of the OSI Reference Model) protocol that defines how packets are organized and handled.

See also **OSI Reference Model.**

Internet Protocol Next Generation/version 6 (IPng/IPv6)

The proposed next version of the Internet Protocol. IPv6 supersedes IPv4 when it is approved. The major new features in IPv6 include expanded addressing capability, simplified header format, more support for extensions and options, flow labeling, authentication and privacy features.

Internet Registry (IR)

A centralized database that holds the network addresses of all autonomous systems on the Internet. The IR is maintained by the Internet Assigned-Numbers Authority (IANA).

See also **Internet Assigned-Numbers Authority.**

Internet Relay Chat (IRC)

An Internet service that used to hold multiparty conferences.

Internet Research Steering Group (IRSG)

An Internet-related group that oversees the Internet Research Task Force (IRTF).

Internet Research Task Force (IRTF)

An Internet-related group, the function of which is to conduct long-term research.

Internet Router (IR)

A device in an AppleTalk internetwork that is used to filter and route packets.

See also **AppleTalk.**

Internet Search search engine

A World Wide Web (WWW) search engine that returns results ranked in the order of relevance to a search query entered by the user. Internet Search provides a linkable title, an abstract, and a universal resource listing (URL) for every page that it returns.

See also **search engine; World Wide Web.**

Internet service provider (ISP)

A commercial organization that provides access to the Internet, sometimes in a package that includes software, consulting, and technical support.

See also **Internet presence provider.**

Internet Sleuth search engine

A World Wide Web (WWW) metasearch engine that provides a multithreaded search site that feeds search terms simultaneously to other search engines (such as Lycos, Infoseek Guide, and AltaVista).

See also **search engine.**

Internet Society

An international organization dedicated to promoting the Internet as a means for communication and collaboration, and that provides a platform for the discussion of administration issues regarding the Internet.

 **For more information about the Internet Society, surf the Web to** http://www.isoc.org.

Internet Society News (ISN)

The Internet Society's official newsletter.

Internet Standard (IS)

An Internet specification that has been formally evaluated and tested. The specification must first go through the Proposed Standard and Draft Standard stages, where significant testing is implemented, before it becomes an official Internet Standard.

Internet Talk Radio (ITR)

An audio multicast broadcast over the Internet.

Internet(1)

A subtree administered by the Internet Architecture Board, designated with the numeral 1.

See also **Internet Architecture Board.**

internetwork

Two or more networks connected by routers, bridges, or gateways. All users on an internetwork can use all of the resources of any connected network, so long as the appropriate privileges have been granted. Internetworking may involve connecting two local-area networks (LANs), connecting a LAN to a mainframe, or connecting a LAN to a wide-area network (WAN).

See also **local-area network; wide-area network.**

internetwork link

A connection between two or more networks. The different types of internetwork links include bridges, routers, brouters (bridge/routers), gateways, and switches, which may be used to connect similar or dissimilar networks. Whereas bridges and routers are used to connect identical or similar networks, a gateway can be employed to connect dissimilar networks. A switch, on the other hand, is a type of multiport bridge or gateway used to connect more than two networks.

Internetwork Packet Exchange (IPX)

A Novell communications protocol used to send data packets to a requested internetwork destination. IPX routes outgoing data packets across a network, reads assigned addresses of returning data, and sends it to the proper area within the operating system. IPX is capable of routing data packets through physically different networks and workstations, and is a best-effort delivery service.

Internetworking Configuration utility

INETCFG, in NetWare 4.*x* and IntranetWare, a server console NetWare Loadable Module (NLM) used for installing Novell internetworking products. This utility permits a network administrator to configure interface boards and network protocols.

See also **NetWare Loadable Module.**

Internetworking Unit (IWU)

An intermediate system that functions as an intermediary between two subnetworks.

InterNIC

Internet Network Information Center, a central organization responsible for allocating and maintaining World Wide Web (WWW) domain names. This organization works as a cooperative effort between AT&T, the National Science Foundation (NSF), and Network Solutions, Inc. AT&T supports the Directory and Database Services, which entails overseeing a Directory of Directories, white pages services, and publicly accessible databases. The NSF is responsible for maintaining Net Scout services, which entails the publication of Scout Report and Net-happenings. Network Solutions sponsors Registration Services, Support Services, and Net Scout Services. The InterNIC Registration Services registers second-level domain names to be used on the Internet. The second-level domain name consists of a unique name (not to exceed 22-characters) followed by a three-letter, top-level-domain abbreviation. Figure I.2 shows the process involved for getting an Internet address.

Interoffice Channel (IOC)

A communications link that exists between two telephone carrier central offices.

interoperability

The ability of multivendor devices in a heterogeneous network to communicate and share data. In an interoperable system, one user does not need to know the particulars of the operating system running on a device from which data is being accessed. Adherence to open standards, as opposed to proprietary protocols, promotes interoperability.

Interoperability Technology Association for Information Processing (INTAP)

A Japanese organization formed to develop Open Systems Interconnection (OSI) profiles and conformance tests.

See also **Open Systems Interconnection.**

Interpersonal Messaging (IPM)

One of two major components of the X.400 Message-Handling System (MHS) that covers ordinary business or personal correspondence. The IPM elements consist of a heading (such as name and address) and a body (which is the content of the message). IPM messages are sent and received over the Interpersonal Messaging Service. The other major component of MHS is the Message-Transfer System (MTS).

See also **Message-Handling System; Message-Transfer System; X.400.**

Interpersonal Messaging Service (IPMS)

A user-to-user service in the 1984 version of the X.400 Message-Handling System (MHS) specification. IPMS provides for electronic mail (e-mail).

See also **Message-Handling System; X.400.**

Interprocess Communication (IPC)

Methods used to pass information between two programs running on the same computer under a multitasking operating system. IPC may also refer to information being passed between two programs running on a network.

Inter-Repeater Link (IRL)

A cable segment between two repeaters in an Ethernet network. No nodes are attached to the IRL.

See also **Ethernet.**

Interrupt Dispatch Table (IDT)

A table used by the Windows NT and Windows NT Advanced Server operating systems to locate the appropriate routine for handling a given interrupt.

See also **Windows NT; Windows NT Advanced Server.**

interrupt

A halt in a computer process triggered by an external event. The interrupt stops normal processing, and can take the form of an internal hardware interrupt, external hardware interrupt, or software interrupt. An interrupt is also known as a *trap*.

interrupt character

A character or combination of characters entered from the keyboard to interrupt processing on the computer. Common interrupt character combinations include Ctrl+C, Ctrl+D, and Ctrl+].

interrupt controller

An integrated circuit (IC) that processes and prioritizes hardware interrupts.

See also **integrated circuit; interrupt.**

interrupt handler

A software routine executed automatically when an interrupt occurs.

See also **interrupt.**

interrupt mode

A printer configuration option that sends a signal through the data port when it is ready to accept another character for transmission to the printer.

Interrupt-Request Channel (IRQ)

A signal protocol used by hardware devices. The IRQ allows the hardware device to communicate to the system that attention is required.

Interrupt-Request Level (IRQL)

A service of Microsoft Windows NT and Windows NT Advanced Server that reflects a level of priority for interrupt request lines. Interrupts below the specified level are masked; interrupts above the level are handled.

See also **Windows NT; Windows NT Advanced Server.**

interrupt service routine (ISR)

A routine that processes an interrupt, and then returns control to the process that was suspended when the interrupt occurred.

Interrupt Time Call-Backs

In NetWare 3.12, a tracked resource that appears as an option in the Available Options/Resource Utilization screen of the MONITOR NetWare Loadable Module (NLM). This resource tracks the NLMs containing processes that take place at regular intervals.

See also **NetWare Loadable Module; MONITOR.**

interrupt vector table

A list of addresses for interrupt handlers.

INTERSVR

A DOS command contained in MS-DOS 6 and higher. INTERSVR starts the server program used to transfer files between computers using the INTERLNK command.

See also **INTERLNK.**

InterVu

A World Wide Web (WWW) browser plug-in for Windows-based versions of Netscape Navigator and compatible browsers that plays digital movie files in Motion Pictures Experts Group (MPEG) format.

See also **Motion Pictures Experts Group; Netscape Navigator; Web browser.**

intra-area routing

A term used to describe routing within an area on a DECnet network.

See also **DECnet routing.**

intraexchange carrier

A local telephone company that handles calls within an exchange, or intraLATA calls.

See also **intraLATA; Local Access and Transport Area.**

intraframe encoding

A compression scheme used in video signal transmission. Intraframe encoding encodes only those parts of the video frame that have changed.

IntraLATA

The telephony circuits within a single Local Access and Transport Area (LATA).
See also **Local Access and Transport Area.**

IntranetWare

A software bundle from Novell that includes the NetWare 4.*x* network operating system, and is designed to create an intranet from an existing network infrastructure. IntranetWare is designed to allow both Internet Protocol (IP) and Internetwork Packet Exchange (IPX) access to intranet resources such as Web servers, FTP servers, and wide-area network (WAN) connections to the Internet. All services of the intranetwork platform are included (such as file, print, directory, messaging, Web publishing, security, connectivity, and management). Like its predecessors, IntranetWare incorporates Novell Directory Services (NDS) for management and security.
See also **NetWare.**

intranetwork link

The connection between two elements in the same network.

intruder

An unauthorized user who has accessed, or is attempting to access, a computer system.

Intruder Address

A selectable property for the User object in Novell Directory Services (NDS).
See also **leaf object; Novell Directory Services; object.**

Intruder Attempt Reset Interval

A Directory Schema term and a selectable property for the Organization and Organizational Unit objects in Novell Directory Services (NDS).
See also **container object; Novell Directory Services; object.**

Intruder Limit

A NetWare login security option used to prevent intruders from guessing passwords by setting a limit on the number of incorrect passwords that can be entered in a given time period.
See also **intruder.**

intruder lockout

The act of locking a user account after the NetWare Intruder Limit has been reached or other restrictions have been violated.

Intruder Lockout (OU)

A selectable property for the Organizational Unit (OU) object in Novell Directory Services (NDS).
See also **container object; Novell Directory Services; object.**

Intruder-Lockout Reset Interval

A Directory Schema term and a selectable property for the Organization object in Novell Directory Services (NDS).

See also **container object; Novell Directory Services; object.**

Inverse ARP (Address-Resolution Protocol)

A protocol that can learn the IP address of a remote node's Data-Link Connection Identifier (DLCI).

See also **Data-Link Connection Identifier; IP address.**

inverted backbone

A type of network architecture in which the hub and routers sit at the center of the network, and network segments are attached to the hub.

See also **hub; router.**

Invitation to Transmit (ITT)

A token frame in an Attached-Resource Computer Network (ARCnet) network.

See also **Attached-Resource Computer Network.**

Inward Wide-Area Telephone Service (INWATS)

An "800" telephone service, where the party being called is billed for the call.

INWATS

Inward Wide Area Telephone Service, an "800" telephone service, where the party being called is billed for the call.

IOEngine

Input/Output Engine, part of the NetWare System Fault Tolerance (SFT) III operating system that handles physical processes (such as network input and output), hardware interrupts, and device drivers. SFT III consists of two parts; the IOEngine and the MSEngine (Mirrored Server Engine). The IOEngine routes packets between the network and the MSEngine. The IOEngine appears as a standard NetWare router to the network workstations.

See also **MSEngine; System Fault Tolerance.**

IOC

Interoffice channel, a communications link that exists between two telephone carrier central offices.

IONL

Internal Organization of the Network Layer, a Network Layer (Layer 3) specification of the OSI Reference Model. IONL divides the Network Layer into three sublayers: Subnetwork Access, Subnetwork-Dependent, and Subnetwork-Independent. The Subnetwork Access sublayer establishes an interface over which data is sent across the subnetwork or network. The Subnetwork-Dependent sublayer assumes a specific subnetwork architecture, and the Subnetwork-Independent sublayer provides for internetworking of the layers above itself.

See also **OSI Reference Model.**

IP

Internet Protocol, an industry-standard protocol suite. IP permits multivendor nodes in a heterogeneous network to communicate. IP is a Session Layer (Layer 5 of the OSI Reference Model) protocol that defines how packets are organized and handled.

See also **OSI Reference Model.**

IP address

An Internet Protocol (IP) address is assigned to every system in a TCP/IP network. The IP address is a network-level address, and is 4 bytes (32 bits) long. The IP address can be divided into two parts: an IP network address and a local host address. IP addresses are assigned by the Internet Assigned-Numbers Authority (IANA), and are hierarchical in nature. The five classes of IP addresses are shown in Table I.3. These are referred to as Class A through E. Class A is used for large networks, B for medium-sized networks, and C for smaller networks. Class D addresses are reserved for multicast addresses, and class E is a reserved class used for experimental purposes.

Table I.3: IP Address Classes

Level	Available Addresses (Decimal Notation)	Examples (h=host address; n=network address)	Description
Class A	1 to 126	1.h.h.h to 126.h.h.h	Uses 7 bits assigned for the network address and 24 bits for the local host address. A maximum of 16,777,214 hosts are possible on this class of network, and 127 addresses are available. All Class A addresses have been assigned.
Class B	128 to 191 (address 127 is reserved for a loopback test)	128.n.h.h to 191.n.h.h	Uses 14 bits assigned for the network address and 16 bits for the local host address. A maximum of 65,534 hosts are possible on this class of network, and 16,383 addresses are available. Most Class A addresses have been assigned.
Class C	192 to 223	192.n.n.h to 223.n.n.h	Uses 21 bits assigned for the network address and 16 bits for the local host address. A maximum of 254 hosts are possible on this class of network, and 2 million addresses are available.
Class D			Reserved for multicasting.
Class E			Reserved for future use.

See also **Internet Network Information Center; IP address formats.**

IP address formats

The 4 bytes (32 bits) in an IP address that identify the type of network connection. As shown in Figure I.3, the division of the bytes determines the class of the address. IP addresses are often converted from binary format to dotted decimal notation, with each of the 4 bytes converted to the equivalent decimal value from 0 to 255. For example, the address 10001111 01010111 11000111 00100001 converts to the equivalent address of 143.87.199.33. No host address and no network address can consist entirely of bytes with values of 0. The network address of 127 is reserved as a *loopback address* (the message is sent back to the sending process). The final byte in an IP address cannot be 0 or 255.

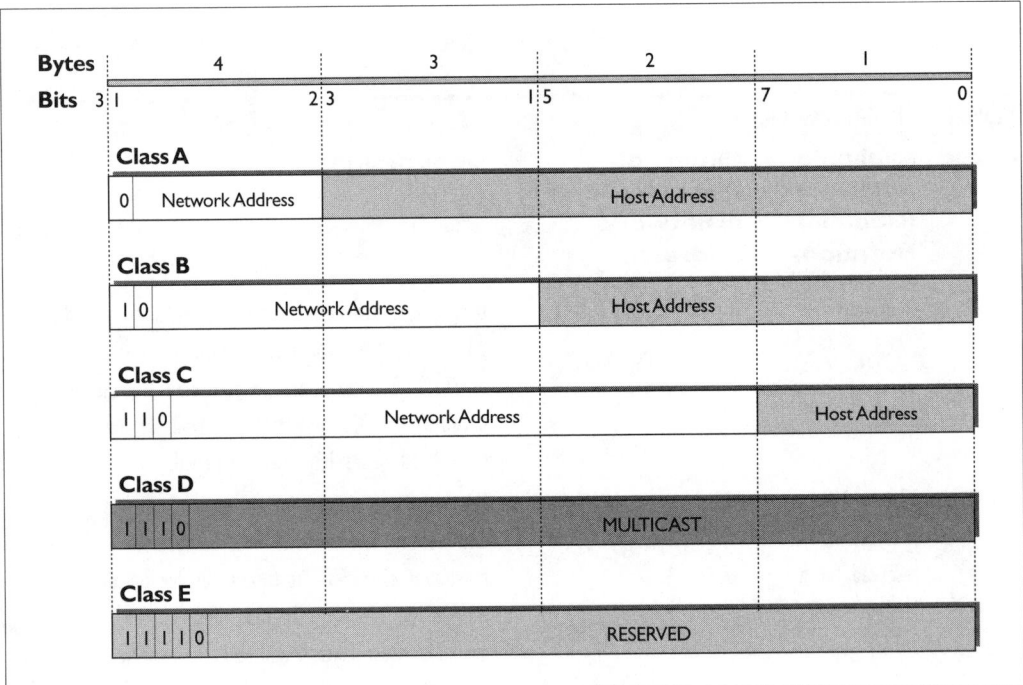

Figure I.3
IP address formats

See also **IP address**.

IP host address

Part of the 4-byte IP address. The IP host address is unique for every node on a network.

IP network address

Part of the 4-byte IP address. The IP network address is the same for all nodes on one network.

IP number

IP address formats, the 4 bytes (32 bits) in an IP address that identify the type of network connection. The division of the bytes determines the class of the address. IP addresses are often converted from binary format to dotted decimal notation, with each of the 4 bytes converted to the equivalent decimal value from 0 to 255. For example, the address 10001111 01010111 11000111 00100001 converts to the equivalent address of 143.87.199.33. No host address and no network address can consist entirely of bytes with values of 0. The network address of 127 is reserved as a *loopback address* (the message is sent back to the sending process). The final byte in an IP address cannot be 0 or 255.

See also **IP address formats** (includes **Figure I.3**).

IP Security Option (IPSO)

A part of the Internet Protocol (IP) that specifies how security levels are defined on a per-interface basis.

See also **Internet Protocol.**

IP tunneling

A method used to allow two or more Internetwork Packet Exchange (IPX) networks to exchange IPX packets through an Internet Protocol (IP) internetwork. IP tunneling encapsulates IPX packets in a User-Datagram Protocol (UDP) datagram for transmission across the IP internetwork.

See also **Internetwork Packet Exchange; User Datagram Protocol.**

IPC

Interprocess Communication, methods used to pass information between two programs running on the same computer under a multitasking operating system. IPC may also refer to information being passed between two programs running on a network.

IPCONFIG (NLM)

A NetWare Loadable Module (NLM) used to configure Internet Protocol (IP) static routes when using NetWare/IP.

See also **NetWare Loadable Module; NetWare/IP.**

IPDS

Intelligent Printer Data Stream, methods used to pass information between two programs running on the same computer under a multitasking operating system. IPC may also refer to information being passed between two programs running on a network.

IPFLT (NLM)

A NetWare Loadable Module (NLM) used to restrict how routers see and communicate with other Internet Protocol (IP) routers.
See also **NetWare Loadable Module.**

IPI

Intelligent Peripheral Interface, a hard disk interface that can accommodate a transfer rate of up to 25 megabits per second (Mbps), and offers a high storage capacity.

IPM

Interpersonal Messaging, one of two major components of the X.400 Message-Handling System (MHS) that covers ordinary business or personal correspondence. The IPM elements consist of a heading (such as name and address) and a body (which is the content of the message). IPM messages are sent and received over the Interpersonal Messaging Service. The other major component of MHS is the Message-Transfer System (MTS).
See also **Message-Handling System; Message-Transfer System; X.400.**

IPMS

Interpersonal Messaging Service, or System, a user-to-user service in the 1984 version of the X.400 Message-Handling System (MHS) specification. IPMS provides for electronic mail (e-mail).
See also **Message-Handling System; X.400.**

IPng/IPv6

Internet Protocol Next Generation/version 6, the proposed next version of the Internet Protocol. IPv6 supersede IPv4 when it is approved. The major new features in IPv6 include expanded addressing capability, simplified header format, more support for extensions and options, flow labeling, authentication and privacy features.

IPP

Internet presence provider, a company or organization that provides access to the Internet. This category of Internet providers includes both Internet service providers (ISPs) and internal departments that manage Internet connections for companies, educational organizations, or government agencies.
See also **Internet service provider.**

IPSO

IP Security Option, a part of the Internet Protocol (IP) that specifies how security levels are defined on a per-interface basis.
See also **Internet Protocol.**

IPX

Internetwork Packet Exchange, a module that takes workstation requests that the DOS Requester determines are for the network, packages them with addressing information, and transfers them to the Link-Support Layer (LSL). Each packet must have an initialized header, which specifies the target network, origin, and what happens after delivery. IPXODI transmits data packets as datagrams, and can therefore send them only on a best-effort basis.
See also **Link-Support Layer.**

IPX address

A network address used in Novell NetWare networks that includes a 4-byte network number, a 6-byte node number, and a 2-byte socket number. The network number is assigned to every segment on the LAN. The node number identifies a specific system, and is usually assigned by the manufacturer. The socket number distinguishes processes within one computer.

IPX external network number

A network number used to identify a network cable segment on a NetWare network. The IPX external network is expressed in hexadecimal format, and is between one and eight digits. It is assigned when the Internetwork Packet Exchange (IPX) protocol is bound to a Network Interface Card (NIC) in the server.

See also **Internetwork Packet Exchange; Network Interface Card.**

IPX internal network number

A network number used to identify a NetWare server. Every server on the network has a unique IPX internal network number. The IPX internal network number is expressed in hexadecimal format, and is between one and eight digits.

IPX internetwork address

A 12-byte number used in NetWare networks expressed in hexadecimal format, and consists of three parts. The first part is 4 bytes, and consists of the IPX external network number; and the second part is 6

bytes and is a node number. The third part is a 2-byte socket number.

See also **IPX address.**

IPX Sockets

In NetWare 3.12, a tracked resource that appears as an option in the Available Options/Resource Utilization screen of the MONITOR NetWare Loadable Module (NLM). This resource display tracks NLMs that have established a socket connection between two devices, with a different socket handling each type of communication.

See also **NetWare Loadable Module; MONITOR.**

IPXCON (NLM)

In NetWare 4.*x* and IntranetWare, a server console NetWare Loadable Module (NLM) that monitors and troubleshoots Internetwork Packet Exchange (IPX) routers and network segments throughout an IPX network. With this NLM, a user can view the status of an IPX router or network segment, view all paths through which IPX packets can flow, locate all active IPX routers on the network, and monitor remote IPX routers running NetWare IPX Router software.

See also **Internetwork Packet Exchange; NetWare Loadable Module; router.**

IPXFLT (NLM)

A NetWare Loadable Module (NLM) used to restrict how routers see and communicate with other Internetwork Packet Exchange (IPX) routers.

See also **NetWare Loadable Module.**

IPXODI

Internet Packet-Exchange Open Data Interface, a module that takes workstation requests that the DOS Requester determines are for the network, packages them with addressing information, and transfers them to the Link-Support Layer (LSL). Each packet must have an initialized header, which specifies the target network, origin, and what happens after delivery. IPXODI transmits data packets as datagrams, and can therefore send them only on a best-effort basis.

See also **Link-Support Layer.**

IPXPING (NLM)

In NetWare 4.*x* and IntranetWare, a server console NetWare Loadable Module (NLM) that checks connectivity to an Internetwork Packet Exchange (IPX) server on an internetwork. This NLM sends an IPX ping request packet to an IPX target node (either a server or a workstation). When the target node receives the request packet, it returns a reply packet.

See also **Internetwork Packet Exchange; NetWare Loadable Module.**

IPXS (NLM)

In NetWare and IntranetWare, a server console NetWare Loadable Module (NLM) that provides the Internetwork Packet Exchange (IPX) protocol to NLM programs requiring a STREAMS-based version of IPX. When using the IPXS utility, the STREAMS utility is automatically loaded.

See also **Internetwork Packet Exchange; NetWare Loadable Module; STREAMS utility.**

IR

Internet Registry, Internet Router, a centralized database that holds the network addresses of all autonomous systems on the Internet. The IR is maintained by the Internet Assigned-Numbers Authority (IANA).

See also **Internet-Assigned Numbers Authority.**

IRC

Internet Relay Chat, an Internet service that used to hold multiparty conferences.

IRDP

ICMP Router-Discovery Protocol, a protocol similar to the End System-to-Intermediate-System (ES-IS) protocol that enables a host to determine a default gateway by using a router address. The difference between ES-IS and IRDP is that the latter uses the Internet Protocol (IP).

See also **End System-to-Intermediate-System.**

IRF

Inherited-Rights Filter, a list of rights that can apply to a NetWare file, directory, or object. The IRF controls the rights that a trustee can inherit from parent directories or container objects. In its default state, the IRF allows all rights to be inherited. However, the IRF does not grant rights, but rather only allows or revokes them. The IRF may be ignored if a trustee has an explicit trustee assignment to a given file, directory or object. The IRF is part of the access control list (ACL), and to change an object's IRF, a user must have the Write property right to the ACL property of that object. The IRF is used to prevent rights from automatically moving between objects.

See also **access-control list; container object; Novell Directory Services; rights; trustee assignment.**

Iridium Project

A project being led by Motorola to establish worldwide mobile communications. The Iridium Project will place 77 satellites in orbit to facilitate point-to-point communications between any two locations on Earth.

IRL

Inter-Repeater Link, a cable segment between two repeaters in an Ethernet network. No nodes are attached to the IRL.

See also Ethernet.

IRM

Inherited-Rights Mask, a NetWare 3.*x* feature, used to filter out specific rights. The IRM is used as a security measure to determine which trustee rights can be carried over into a new subdirectory.

See also **trustee assignment; trustee rights.**

IRN

Intermediate Routing Node, a Systems Network Architecture (SNA) subarea node that has the capability of intermediate routing.

See also **Systems Network Architecture.**

IRP

(1) I/O Request Packet, a packet used in Windows NT and Windows NT Advanced Server to provide communication between drivers.

(2) Interdomain Routing Protocol, an Internet protocol defined by the International Standards Organization (ISO) that routes packets between different domains in an internetwork. Based on the Border Gateway Protocol (BGP), IRP is designed to operate seamlessly with End System to End System (ES-ES) and Intermediate System to Intermediate System (IS-IS) protocols.

See also **(1) Windows NT; (1) Windows NT Advanced Server; (2) Border Gateway Protocol; (2) Intermediate-System-to-Intermediate-System.**

IRQ

Interrupt-Request Channel, a signal protocol used by hardware devices. The IRQ allows the hardware device to communicate to the system that attention is required.

IRQL

Interrupt-Request Level, a service of Microsoft Windows NT and Windows NT Advanced Server that reflects a level of priority for interrupt-request lines. Interrupts below the specified level are masked; interrupts above the level are handled.

See also **Windows NT; Windows NT Advanced Server.**

IRSG

Internet Research Steering Group, a group that oversees the Internet Research Task Force (IRTF).

IRTF

Internet Research Task Force, a group whose function is to conduct long-term, Internet-related research.

IRV

International Reference Version, a variation of the International Alphabet 5 (IA5) character-encoding mechanism.
See also **International Alphabet 5.**

IS

(1) Intermediate System, a network entity specified in the OSI Reference Model. The IS functions as an intermediary between multiple subnetworks. Repeaters and bridges are examples of intermediate systems.
(2) Internet Standard, an Internet specification that has been formally evaluated and tested. The specification must first go through the Proposed Standard and Draft Standard stages, where significant testing is implemented, before it becomes an official Internet Standard.
See also **OSI Reference Model.**

ISA

Industry-Standard Architecture, an industry-standard bus design, commonly used on the IBM PC/XT. The ISA design uses plug-in cards and expansion slots, and can accommodate both 8-bit and 16-bit cards.

isarithmic flow control

A flow-control process that sends permits through a network, the possession of which grants a node the right to transmit information.

ISDN

Integrated-Services Digital Network, a set of Consultative Committee for International Telegraphy and Telephony (CCITT) standards for digital networking. ISDN involves the digitizing of a telephone network so that voice, data, text, graphics, music, video, and other source files can be provided to users from a single terminal over existing telephone wiring. ISDN requires special adapters to translate between analog and digital signals. Transmission rates are based on the amount of multiplexed Bearer channels ("B" channels), which are 64 kilobits per second (Kbps) each. The Basic-Rate Interface (BRI) consists of two B channels and a single 16Kbps D channel. The D channel is used to carry signaling information. The Primary-Rate Interface (PRI) consists of 23 B channels and one D channel, for a total of 1.536 megabits per second (Mbps).
See also **B channel; Basic-Rate Interface; Consultative Committee for International Telegraphy and Telephony; D channel; Primary-Rate Interface.**

IS-IS Hello (IIH)

Message packets that are sent to all Intermediate System (IS) network nodes to maintain adjacencies.
See also **Intermediate System; Intermediate-System-to-Intermediate-System.**

IS-IS

Intermediate System to Intermediate System, an Open Systems Interconnection (OSI) link-state routing protocol. IS-IS allows intermediate systems to exchange routing information. The IS-IS protocol floods the network with link-state information to build a complete, consistent picture of the network topology. This protocol uses IS-IS Hello packets, Link-State Packets (LSPs), and Sequence-Numbers Packets (SNPs) for data transmission.

See also **Hello packet; Link-State Packet; link-state routing algorithm; Open Systems Interconnection.**

IS-IS Interdomain Routing Protocol (IDRP)

An Open Systems Interconnection (OSI) protocol that determines how routers communicate with other routers in different domains.

See also **Open Systems Interconnection.**

ISA

Industry-Standard Architecture, an industry-standard bus design, commonly used on the IBM PC/XT. The ISA design uses plug-in cards and expansion slots, and can accommodate both 8-bit and 16-bit cards.

ISM

Industrial, Scientific, and Medical, the three ranges of frequency the Federal Communications Commission (FCC) made available for unlicensed spread-spectrum communications. Prior to the FCC's action, which took place in 1985, these frequencies were allocated for industrial, scientific, and

medical use. The frequencies are, specifically: 902 – 928 megahertz (MHz), 2.4 – 2.5 gigahertz (GHz), and 5.8 – 5.9GHz.

See also **Federal Communications Commission; spread-spectrum transmission.**

ISN

(1) Information Systems Network, AT&T's high-speed switching network that can accommodate both voice and data, and can be connected to most standard network architectures.

(2) Internet Society News, the Internet Society's official newsletter.

ISO

International Standards Organization, a device used in digital telephone services. The ISODE is made up of the channel service unit (CSU) and the digital service unit (DSU), and is used in place of a modem on a Digital Data Service (DDS) connection.

See also **channel service unit; data service unit; Digital Data Service.**

ISO 8877 connector

A variation of the RJ-45 connector that is compatible with international standards.

See also **RJ-*xx* connector.**

Iso(1)

Part of the global tree of networking information. Iso(1) is a top-level subtree administered by the International Standards Organization (ISO).

See also **International Standards Organization.**

isochronous

A time-sensitive transmission. Isochronous transmission places a constant time interval between transmissions, regardless of whether they are synchronous or asynchronous. In this manner, asynchronous data can be transmitted over a synchronous link.

Isochronous Media-Access Control (IMAC)

A Media-Access Control (MAC) element in the Fiber Distributed Data Interface (FDDI) II architecture. IMAC can accommodate delay-insensitive data, such as voice or video, which is received through a circuit-switched multiplexer.

See also **Fiber Distributed Data Interface; Media-Access Control.**

ISOCON

A NetWare utility for managing the OSI protocol stack in a multiprotocol network.

ISODE

International Standards Organization Development Environment, a device used in digital telephone services. The ISODE is made up of the channel service unit (CSU) and the digital service unit (DSU), and is used in place of a modem on a Digital Data Service (DDS) connection.

See also **channel service unit; data service unit; Digital Data Service.**

isoEthernet

The Institute of Electrical and Electronic Engineers (IEEE) 802.9a standard used to transmit delay-insensitive, multimedia traffic over the same wiring used on 10BaseT Ethernet. IsoEthernet uses an encoding scheme common to Fiber Distributed Data Interface (FDDI) to squeeze an extra 6.144 megabits per second (Mbps) of bandwidth out of the 10Mbps 10BaseT connection. This additional bandwidth is used to isolate delay-insensitive traffic from the contention-oriented Ethernet data traffic. IsoEthernet can be deployed using existing cabling, and requires a separate isoEthernet hub and isoEthernet network adapter cards.

See also **10BaseT; Ethernet; Fiber Distributed Data Interface; IEEE 802.x; Institute of Electrical and Electronic Engineers.**

isolation

A type of power conditioning that protects against noise by using ferro-resonant isolation transformers to mitigate voltage irregularities.

See also **power conditioning.**

ISP

(1) International Standardization Profile, a subset of a specification still under review during the formalization process. The ISP is also known as a *functional standard.*

(2) Internet service provider, a commercial organization that provides access to the Internet, sometimes in a package that includes software, consulting, and technical support.

See also **Internet presence provider.**

ISR

Interrupt service routine, a routine that processes an interrupt, and then returns control to the process that was suspended when the interrupt occurred.

ISU

integrated service unit, a device that combines a channel service unit (CSU) and a data service unit (DSU). The ISU interfaces computers and terminals with Digital Data Service (DDS) lines.

See also **channel service unit; data service unit; Digital Data Service.**

ITC

Independent Telephone Company, a local exchange carrier that is not one of the Regional Bell Operating Companies (RBOCs).

See also **Regional Bell Holding Company; Regional Bell Operating Company.**

ITEM

An Organizational command in an NMENU menu source file. The ITEM command tells the program that a choice follows.

See also **NMENU utility.**

ITR

Internet Talk Radio, an audio multicast broadcast over the Internet.

ITT

Invitation to Transmit, a token frame in an Attached-Resource Computer Network (ARCnet) network.

See also **Attached-Resource Computer Network.**

ITU

International Telecommunications Union, a United Nations agency that develops international telecommunications standards. The ITU has three subagencies; the Consultative Committee for International Telegraphy and Telephony (CCITT), International Frequency-Registration Board (IFRB), and International Consultative Committee for Radiocommunications (CCIR).

See also **Consultative Committee for International Telegraphy and Telephony; International Frequency-Registration Board; International Consultative Committee for Radiocommunications.**

IVD

Integrated Voice and Data, the integration of voice and data traffic in a single network. Primarily, this consists of the integration of Integrated-Services Digital Network (ISDN) and local-area network (LAN) architectures. ICVD is overseen by the Institute of Electrical and Electronic Engineers (IEEE) 802.9 working group.

See also **802.9; Institute of Electrical and Electronic Engineers; Integrated Services Digital Network.**

IVR

Interactive Voice Response, a type of
Computer-Telephone Integration (CTI) that
allows end-users to input information using
a TouchTone telephone. The IVR system
uses a synthesized computer voice to interact with the caller.

See also **Computer-Telephone
Integration.**

IWU

Internetworking Unit, an intermediate system that functions as an intermediary
between two subnetworks.

IXC

Interexchange Carrier, a long-distance
telephone carrier.

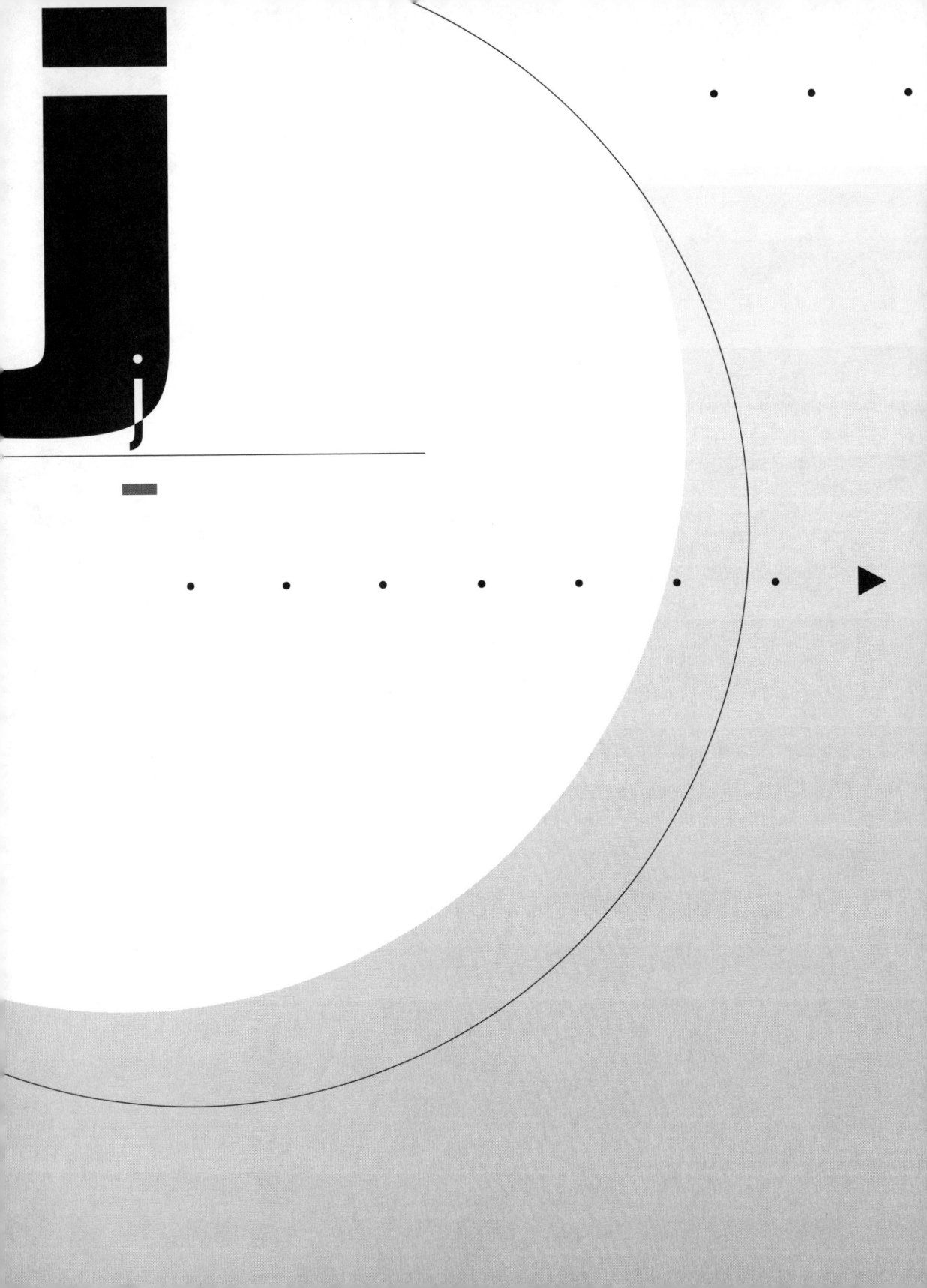

jabber

A meaningless transmission continuously generated by a network device. Jabber is usually the result of a hardware malfunction or user error.

jabber detector

A device that helps to prevent a node from sending continuous and meaningless transmissions in a Carrier-Sense Multiple-Access/ Collision Detection (CSMA/CD) media-access network.

See also **Carrier-Sense Multiple-Access/Collision Detection.**

jabber packet

An oversized packet (larger than 1,518 bytes) in an Ethernet network that contains a bad CRC (cyclical redundancy check) value. The transmission is meaningless and is usually caused by a hardware malfunction.

See also **Ethernet.**

jack

A female connector with sockets or slots. A male connector is called a *plug*.

jack in

A term popularized by William Gibson in the novel *Neuromancer* that means to connect to a particular facet of the Internet, to a virtual-reality space, or to an active social information line.

jacket

An outer covering on a cable. The material used to construct this outer covering is a major factor in determining the relative safety of the cable.

See also **cable.**

jam signal

A signal on an Ethernet network telling other nodes that a packet collision has occurred.

See also **Ethernet.**

jamming

A radiation in a specific range of frequencies that inhibits or prevents signals in that frequency range from being used. Deliberate jamming is also called *active jamming*; unintentional jamming is also called *passive jamming*.

JANET

Joint Academic Network, an X.25 network maintained by academic institutions in Great Britain to provide worldwide electronic mail (e-mail) access through other networks.

See also **X.25.**

Japan Standards Association (JSA)

A Japanese equivalent to the American National Standards Institute (ANSI).

See also **American National Standards Institute.**

Japanese UNIX Network (JUNET)

A Japanese research network used by commercial institutions and organizations.

jargon file

A file containing technical terminology and various idioms inherent to computing.

For more information about the jargon file, surf the Web to http://www.ccil.org/jargon/jargon.html.

Java

A programming language released by Sun Microsystems in 1995, used to write general-purpose programs and programs designed to run specifically on the Internet or on intranets. The general-purpose programs (called *Java applications*) can be run standalone. The Internet or intranet programs (called *applets*) must be run from within a Web browser.

See also **applet; Java Development Kit; Web browser.**

Java Development Kit (JDK)

A software development kit (SDK) available from Sun Microsystems that contains development tools to write, test, and debug Java applications and applets.

See also **applet.**

Download the IntranetWare SDK for Java at http://developer.novell.com/net2000/java/sdk/sdk.htm.

JavaScript

A Java scripting language from Sun Microsystems and Netscape Communications that facilitates adding interactive features to a Web page.

See also **Java.**

JCL

Job-Control Language, a command language providing the required instructions for a specific operating system to run a specific application program.

JDA

Joint Development Agreement, a now-defunct agreement between International Business Machines (IBM) and Microsoft Corporation to jointly develop operating system technologies.

JDK

Java Development Kit, a software development kit (SDK) available from Sun Microsystems that contains development tools to write, test, and debug Java applications and applets.

See also **applet.**

JEDI

Joint Electronic Data Interchange, a task force representing the United Nations in Electronic Data Interchange (EDI) meetings and events.

See also **Electronic Data Interchange.**

jitter

A signal variation in timing caused by the constancy of a source clock rate or differences between a source's clock and a receiver's clock. Two types of jitter are *phase jitter* (in which the signal is out of phase) and *amplitude jitter* (in which the amplitude of the signal varies).

Job-Control Language (JCL)

A command language providing the required instructions for a specific operating system to run a specific application program.

job server

A server that uses software to manage a network or special-purpose queue of jobs and that does not require a dedicated machine. A job server itself can be a dedicated machine.
See also **server.**

Job Transfer and Manipulation (JTM)

A file-transfer service defined in the Application Layer (Layer 7 of the OSI Reference Model), which enables an application to perform data processing on a remote machine.
See also **OSI Reference Model.**

John Von Neumann Center Network (JVNCnet)

A network in the Northeastern United States that provides T1 and slower serial links for midlevel networking services.
See also **T1.**

Joint Academic Network (JANET)

An X.25 network maintained by academic institutions in Great Britain to provide worldwide electronic mail (e-mail) access through other networks.
See also **X.25.**

Joint Development Agreement (JDA)

A now-defunct agreement between International Business Machines (IBM) and Microsoft Corporation to jointly develop operating system technologies.

Joint Electronic Data Interchange (JEDI)

A task force representing the United Nations in Electronic Data Interchange (EDI) meetings and events.
See also **Electronic Data Interchange.**

Joint Photographic Experts Group (JPEG)

An International Standards Organization (ISO)/International Telecommunications Union (ITU) standard that compresses files containing still images. To achieve compression ratio as high as 100:1, JPEG (pronounced *JAY-peg*) first performs a discrete cosine transformation by using frequencies to break down image data. JPEG then quantifies these frequencies to adjust the number of bits used to represent various frequencies (also known as *adjusting the granularity*). JPEG then uses a lossy algorithm (which means the granularity of rarely used frequencies can be dropped out during the compression) to compress the files.
See also **International Standards Organization; International Telecommunications Union.**

Joint Technical Committee (JTC)

A committee formed by the International Standards Organization (ISO) and the International Electrotechnical Commission (IEC) to address such issues as the Open Systems Interconnection (OSI) model.

See also **International Standards Organization; International Electrotechnical Commission.**

Jonzy's Universal Gopher Hierarchy Excavation and Display (Jughead)

A program capable of limiting an Internet search to a selection of Gopher services by searching only higher-level menus in servers. This search must point to a Gopher client on a Jughead server.

See also **Gopher; Internet.**

journaling

A process that enables fast restarts as needed by logging network system activity.

JPEG

Joint Photographic Experts Group, an International Standards Organization (ISO)/International Telecommunications Union (ITU) standard that compresses files containing still images. To achieve compression ratio as high as 100:1, JPEG (pronounced *JAY-peg*) first performs a discrete cosine transformation by using frequencies to break down image data. JPEG then quantifies these frequencies to adjust the number of bits used to represent various frequencies (also known as *adjusting the granularity*). JPEG then uses a lossy algorithm (which means the granularity of rarely used fre-

quencies can be dropped out during the compression) to compress the files.

See also **International Standards Organization, International Telecommunications Union.**

JSA

Japan Standards Association, a Japanese equivalent to the American National Standards Institute (ANSI).

See also **American National Standards Institute.**

JTC

Joint Technical Committee, a committee formed by the International Standards Organization (ISO) and the International Electrotechnical Commission (IEC) to address such issues as the Open Systems Interconnection (OSI) model.

See also **International Standards Organization, International Electrotechnical Commission.**

JTM

Job Transfer and Manipulation, a file-transfer service defined in the Application Layer (Layer 7) of the OSI Reference Model, which enables an application to perform data processing on a remote machine.

See also **OSI Reference Model.**

Jughead

Jonzy's Universal Gopher Hierarchy Excavation and Display, a program capable of limiting an Internet search to a selection of Gopher services by searching only higher-

level menus in servers. This search must point to a Gopher client on a Jughead server.
See also **Gopher; Internet.**

gate through three-dimensional panoramic graphics images.
See also **authoring; Web browser.**

jukebox

A high-capacity storage device that uses an autochanger to mount and dismount optical disks.
See also **high-capacity storage system.**

jumbo group

A multichannel telecommunications group that consists of six master groups (collections of a large number of channels). Using 3,600 voice channels, the jumbo group simultaneously transmits over a broadband connection.

jumper

A wire or metal bridge used to close a circuit and establish an electrical connection.

jumper block

A group (also called a *block*) of jumpers.

JUNET

Japanese UNIX Network, a Japanese research network used by commercial institutions and organizations.

Jutvision

A line of 32-bit Windows authoring tools, Web browser plug-ins, and player programs from Visdyn Software that create and navi-

JVNCnet

John Von Neumann Center Network, a network in the Northeastern United States that provides T1 and slower serial links for midlevel networking services.
See also **T1.**

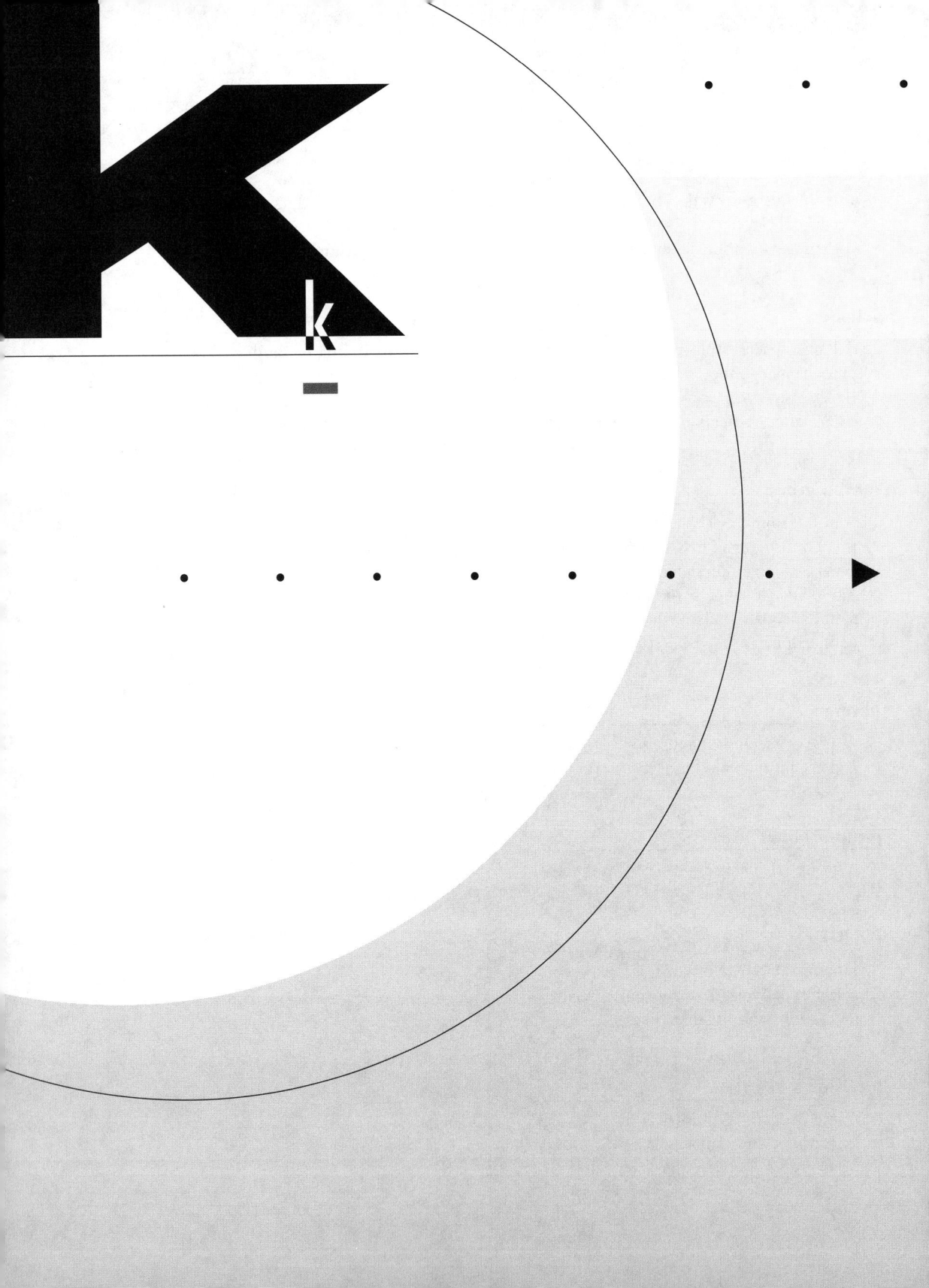

K

An abbreviation for *kilo*, which has a metric equivalent of 1,000. This abbreviation is often combined with other abbreviations in computing, such as *KB* or *Kb*.

See also **kilobyte; kilobit.**

k12 newsgroup

A type of newsgroup that discusses topics of interest to elementary through high school students and teachers.

KA9Q

An RFC 1208 specification that implements the Transmission-Control Protocol/Internet Protocol (TCP/IP) suite for packet radio systems.

See also **Transmission-Control Protocol/Internet Protocol.**

Karn's algorithm

An algorithm improving round-trip time estimations by helping protocols in the OSI Reference Model's Transport Layer (Layer 4) distinguish between good and bad round-trip time samples.

See also **OSI Reference Model.**

KB

kilobyte, a unit of measure equaling 2^{10} (or 1,024) bytes, most commonly used in the context of computer memory or disk storage capacity.

Kb

kilobit, a unit of measure equaling 2^{10} (or 1,024) bits.

kbit/s

kilobits per second, a unit of measure equaling 2^{10} (or 1,024) bits of data being transferred to and from peripheral devices every second.

kbyte/s

kilobytes per second, a unit of measure equaling 2^{10} (or 1,024) bytes of data being transferred to and from peripheral devices every second.

KDC

Key-Distribution Center, a center responsible for storing, managing, and distributing encryption keys.

keep-alive packet

An Echo Request packet sent to a remote peer, often generating an Echo Response packet being sent back from the remote peer. This is a continuous test at the access interface, sent at a specified interval.

Kerberos

A network-security system that verifies a user is legitimate when logging in to a network and when requesting a service from the network. Using private-key encryption methods, Kerberos encrypts transmissions between Kerberos and a user by using special keys called *tickets*. The Massachusetts Institute of Technology (MIT) designed this system to provide authentication for users accessing a network from an unattended workstation.

See also **private-key encryption.**

Kermit

A file-transfer protocol commonly used on Bulletin Board Systems (BBSs).

See also **Bulletin Board System.**

kernel

The portion of an operating system responsible for managing system resources.

key

A group (or multiple groups) of bytes characterized by physical location in a database record. A key provides the access to a data value and provides a means of sorting database records.

In encryption, a key is a conversion algorithm and predefined bit value used to decipher text encrypted in an unreadable form (known as *ciphertext*). The simplest type of encryption uses a single key, and the recipient must know both the encryption algorithm and key to decrypt the message. *Private-key encryption* uses a private key, which only the sender and recipient know, and a public encryption algorithm. *Public-key encryption*, on the other hand, uses two halves of a bit sequence, each one constituting a key: One key is placed in an accessible public-key library; the other key is only known to an individual.

key combination

A combination of keystrokes that provides keyboard access to menu commands. A key combination enables the user to bypass using a mouse to select from menus, which may accelerate user interface with an application program.

Key-Distribution Center (KDC)

A center responsible for storing, managing, and distributing encryption keys.

Key-Management Protocol (KMP)

A protocol used to check security keys in a secure network.

key redefinition

The assignment of different functions to specific keys by an application program.

Key Telephone System (KTS)

An arrangement of multiline telephones that enables users to access a central office or Private Branch Exchange (PBX) by pressing keys. Users can put a caller on hold, call or answer a selected line, talk over an intercom, or transfer calls to another line.

See also **Private Branch Exchange.**

KEYB (NLM)

A NetWare 4.*x* and IntranetWare console utility that provides selection of nationality or language for the keyboard on the network server.

keyboard buffer

Computer system memory used to store the most recently typed keys on a keyboard. This is also known as a *type-ahead buffer*.

Keyboard Send and Receive (KSR)

A communication device consisting of a printer and a keyboard. The KSR prints messages as they are received and transmits messages as they are typed at the keyboard.

keyboard template

A plastic overlay fitting over the keys of a keyboard to help a novice user learn the functions of certain keys that are specific to an application program.

keying

The asymmetrical shaping of a component to ensure it is connected properly to another component. A common example of keying is modular telephone jacks.

keystroke information

Information appearing at the bottom of a screen in a DOS menu utility that provides information about the keys available to the user when accessing information on the screen.

keywords

Designated words or terms in a programming language or operating system reserved for particular functions or operations. Also known as *reserved words*.

kill file

A data file designed to filter out Internet news postings or electronic mail (e-mail) from certain persons or about certain topics.

killer channel

A digital telecommunications channel that overlaps and interferes with other channels because its timing is off.

kilobaud

A unit of measure equaling 1,000 baud. See also **baud; baud rate.**

kilobit (Kbit)

A unit of measure equaling 2^{10} (or 1,024) bits.

kilobits per second (kbit/s)

A unit of measure equaling 2^{10} (or 1,024) bits of data being transferred to and from peripheral devices every second.

kilobyte (KB or K)

A unit of measure equaling 2^{10} (or 1,024) bytes, most commonly used in the context of computer memory or disk storage capacity.

kilobytes per second (kbyte/s)

A unit of measure equaling 2^{10} (or 1,024) bytes of data being transferred to and from peripheral devices every second.

KIS

Knowbot Information Services, an Internet service designed to query directory services to retrieve requested information.

KMP

Key-Management Protocol, a protocol used to check security keys in a secure network.

Knowbot

A program that tracks down information. This is a combination of the term *knowledge robot*.

Knowbot Information Services (KIS)

An Internet service designed to query directory services to retrieve requested information.

Koan

A line of Windows and ActiveX music-creation tools and Web browser plug-ins from Sseyo Ltd.

KSR

Keyboard Send and Receive, a communication device consisting of a printer and a keyboard. The KSR prints messages as they are received and transmits messages as they are typed at the keyboard.

KTS

Key Telephone System, an arrangement of multiline telephones that enables users to access a central office or Private Branch Exchange (PBX) by pressing keys. Users can put a caller on hold, call or answer a selected line, talk over an intercom, or transfer calls to another line.

See also **Private Branch Exchange.**

k

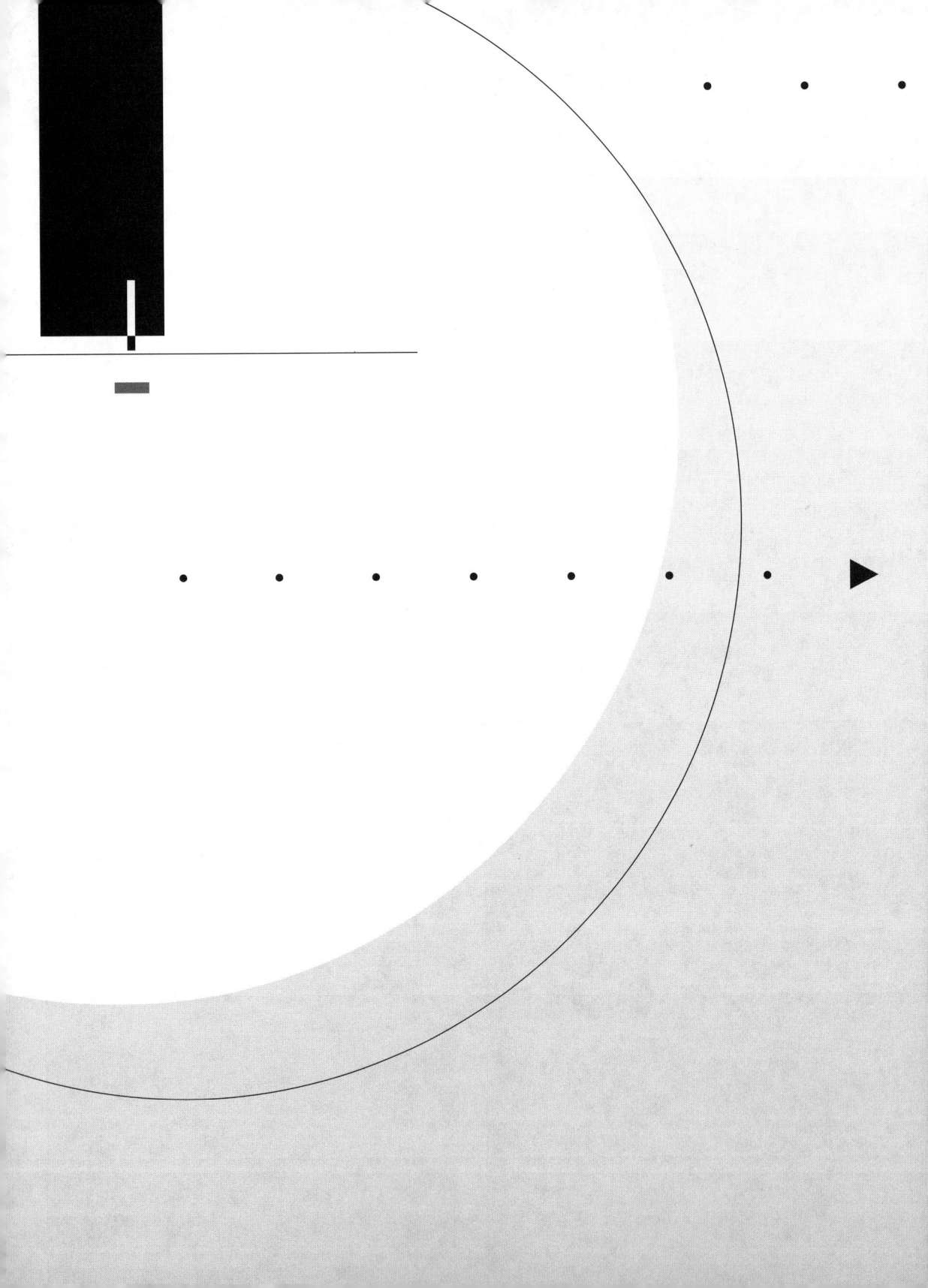

L Multiplex (LMX)

A hierarchy of telecommunications channel groupings representing a group, super group, master group, and jumbo group.

LAA

Locally Administered Address, a parameter used by a 3174 controller to determine whether a node can access a mainframe computer connected to a Token Ring network.

See also **3174; Token Ring.**

LAM

Lobe-Attachment Module, a Token Ring network box that has multiple interfaces to which as many as 20 *lobes* (nodes) can be attached. A LAM is functionally similar to a Multistation-Attachment Unit (MAU), although the MAU can have only eight lobes attached. When a LAM is daisy-chained and connected to a Controlled-Access Unit (CAU), each CAU can handle as many as 4 LAMs, which yields a potential for 80 lobes.

See also **Controlled-Access Unit; Multistation-Attachment Unit.**

LAMA

Local Automatic Message Accounting, an accounting method used by a local telephone company to generate automatic billing for local and toll calls. The method requires the Automatic Number Identification (ANI) capability.

See also **Automatic Number Identification.**

LAN

local-area network, a system in which personal computers and electronic office equipment are linked together (usually with a wiring-based cabling scheme) within a small area to form a network. Users can then communicate with each other, share resources (such as data storage and printers), and access remote computers or other networks. Local-area networks are usually either server-based and peer-based.

In the *server-based LAN,* a dedicated server is connected to various workstations, which request services from the server. The *network operating system* (which determines higher-level protocols and available services) augments the operating system on the workstations, so the server then controls access to some of the network resources. Common network operating systems for server-based LANs include NetWare and IntranetWare from Novell; LAN Manager and Windows NT Advanced Server from Microsoft; LAN Server from IBM; and VINES from Banyan Systems.

The *peer-to-peer-based* (or simply *peer-based*) *LAN,* each node in the network can initiate actions, access other nodes, and provide services for other nodes without first acquiring permission from the server. The network operating system often runs under the native operating system of the individual workstations. Common network operating systems for peer-to-peer LANs include Personal NetWare from Novell, Windows for Workgroups from Microsoft, LANstep from Hayes Microcomputer Products, and LANtastic from Artisoft.

The physical *topology* of the LAN determines the cabling scheme used to physically connect the nodes of the networks.

Common physical topologies include bus, ring, star, tree, and star-wired. The logical topology of the LAN determines how information is passed from one node to the others on the network. The two most common logical topologies are *bus* (in which information is broadcast to all nodes at the same time) and *ring* (in which information is passed from node to node until it reaches its destination).

Setting up a LAN requires specific hardware and software. Hardware requirements include personal computers, Network Interface Cards (NICs), cables, connectors, wiring centers, and safety devices (such as an uninterruptible power supply). Software requirements include hardware-specific drivers, the network operating system, workstation software (such as shells, redirectors, requestors, or client software), applications, management programs, diagnostic programs, and backup software.

See also **Client 16; Client 32; LAN Manager; LANstep; LANtastic; local-area network** (includes **Figure L.1**); **NetWare DOS Requester; NetWare Requester for OS/2; NetWare Shell; Network Interface card; network operating system; Personal NetWare; Windows for Workgroups; Windows NT Advanced Server.**

LAN adapter

A circuit board installed on each local-area network (LAN) workstation that allows the workstations to communicate with each other and with NetWare servers.

See also **adapter; LAN interface board; network adapter.**

LAN Automation Option (LANAO)

An optional add-on to NetView that simplifies the management of one or more Token Ring networks in the IBM Network-Management Architecture (NMA).

See also **NetView; Network-Management Architecture.**

LAN Bridge Server (LBS)

A Token Ring network server that tracks (and provides access to) any bridges connected to the network.

See also **Token Ring.**

LAN driver

A software component that serves as a link between a server's or a workstation's operating system and the physical parts of a local area network (LAN). Written to the Open Data-Link Interface (ODI) specification, LAN drivers in NetWare 4.*x* connect directly to the ODI model's Link-Support Layer (LSL), which serves as an intermediary between the drivers and communication protocols.

See also **Open Data-Link Interface.**

Lan Driver Information

In NetWare 4.02, the name of a screen appearing in the MONITOR NetWare Loadable Module (NLM).

See also **NetWare Loadable Module; MONITOR.**

LAN interface board

An interface board installed on each local area network (LAN) workstation that allows the workstations to communicate with each other and with NetWare servers.

See also **adapter; LAN adapter; network adapter.**

LAN inventory package

A software program that automatically creates an inventory of the components and configurations on a local area network (LAN), and then updates the inventory when changes are made to the network.

LAN Manager

A Microsoft server-based network operating system that supports various low-level network architectures (such as ARCnet, Ethernet, and Token Ring). LAN Manager has not been updated since the introduction of Windows NT and Windows NT Advanced Server.

LAN Manager for UNIX (LMU)

A Microsoft server-based network operating system that supports the UNIX operating system.

LAN Network Manager (LNM)

A Systems Application Architecture (SAA)-compliant, IBM product that manages Token Ring networks by using both the Common Management-Information Protocol (CMIP) and the Simple Network-Management Protocol (SNMP). While running under OS/2, LNM can act as an entry point for NetView.

See also **Common Management-Information Protocol; NetView; Simple Network-Management Protocol; System Application Architecture.**

LAN Server

IBM's server-based network operating system, based on Microsoft's LAN Manager, that supports servers running in the OS/2 environment.

LAN Traffic Monitor (LTM)

A device that monitors the traffic activity in a local-area network (LAN) system.

LAN Workgroup

A server-based connectivity package from Novell that provides NetWare users with transparent access to networked Transmission-Control Protocol/Internet Protocol (TCP/IP) resources from their workstations. Features include transparent file sharing, terminal emulation, remote command execution, remote printing, network information utilities, and support for all standard application programming interfaces (APIs).

See also **Transmission-Control Protocol/Internet Protocol.**

 **For more information about networking products from Novell, surf the Web to** `http://voyager.provo.novell.com/catalog/bl_cat.htm`.

LAN WorkPlace

A desktop-connectivity package from Novell that provides concurrent access to Transmission Control Protocol/Internet Protocol (TCP/IP), NetWare, and Internet resources. Features include terminal emulation, graphical file transfer, transparent Network File

System (NFS) file sharing, and Netscape Navigator.

See also **Transmission Control Protocol/Internet Protocol.**

LAN/MAN Management Protocol

A local-area network (LAN) protocol that provides Common Management-Information Service/Common Management-Information Protocol (CMIS/CMIP) network management services by implementing them directly into the Logical-Link Control (LLC) sublayer of the Data-Link Layer (Layer 2) of the OSI Reference Model. Because it provides Application Level (Level 7) services and bypasses the intervening four layers to use LLC services, LLMP cannot use routers. The original name of this protocol was *CMIS/CMIP Over LLC*, also known as *CMOL*.

See also **Common Management-Information Service; Common Management-Information Protocol; Logical-Link Control; OSI Reference Model.**

LAN/RM

Local-Area Network Reference Model, a description of a local-area network (LAN) as defined by 802.*x* specification set of the Institute of Electrical and Electronic Engineers (IEEE).

See also **IEEE 802.x.**

LAN/WAN Information

In NetWare 4.02, a field name appearing in the Available Options screen of the MONITOR NetWare Loadable Module (NLM).

See also **NetWare Loadable Module; MONITOR.**

LANalyzer

A software-only network analysis product from Novell that monitors traffic on an Ethernet or Token Ring segment, and then stores information about the segment and each station attached to it. The analysis is often used for planning network growth, monitoring and optimizing network performance, and troubleshooting network problems.

See also **Ethernet; Token Ring.**

LANAO

LAN Automation Option, an optional add-on to NetView that simplifies the management of one or more Token Ring networks in the IBM Network Management Architecture (NMA).

See also **NetView; Network Management Architecture.**

land line

A telephone line that relies on transmissions across wires and cables, as opposed to transmissions via satellite.

language

A series of instructions that can be processed and executed by a computer.

Language

In Novell Directory Services (NDS), a Directory Schema term and a selectable property for the User object.

See also **leaf object; Novell Directory Services; object.**

language enabling

A process during the internationalization of NetWare that involves isolating message strings (such as error messages and menu items) from the source code and placing them in Language Modules. One of the most valuable uses of language enabling is the capability of retrieving program messages in one of any number of languages at run time.

Language Identification Number (LIN)

A number assigned to non-English versions of NetWare Loadable Modules (NLMs) as a means of identification.

LANGUAGE utility

A NetWare 4.*x* and IntranetWare server console utility that sets the language to be used by the network server or NetWare Loadable Modules (NLMs).

See also **NetWare Loadable Module.**

LANstep

A peer-to-peer networking environment from Hayes Microcomputer Products that distributes network services over one or more nondedicated servers. Through a centralized database of available services called LANstep Smart Directory Services, users may access a service by name without having to specify the location of the server that provides the services. Although it provides its own operating system, LANstep does allow DOS and Windows applications to execute.

LANtastic

A peer-to-peer operating system from Artisoft that supports networks ranging in size from two nodes to a few hundred nodes. All stations on the network can share files with all other stations, or the configuration can be set so that one personal computer acts as a dedicated file server. The system runs as a DOS process and uses the DOS file system, but can provide limited multitasking in some configurations.

LAP

Link-Access Procedure, a bit-oriented, data-link-level protocol from the Consultative Committee for International Telegraphy and Telephony (CCITT), used for communications between devices designated as Data Communications Equipment (DCE) and Data Terminal Equipment (DTE).

See also **Consultative Committee for International Telegraphy and Telephony; Data-Communications Equipment; Data-Terminal Equipment.**

LAP-B Protocol

Link-Access Procedure, Balanced Protocol, a bit-oriented, data-link protocol from the Consultative Committee for International Telegraphy and Telephony (CCITT) used to link terminals and computers to packet-switched networks. This protocol is similar to the Synchronous Data-Link Control (SDLC) protocol and is equivalent to the High-Level Data-Link Control (HDLC) asynchronous balanced mode.

See also **Consultative Committee for International Telegraphy and Telephony; High-Level Data-Link Control; Synchronous Data-Link Control.**

LAPD

Link-Access Protocol, D channel, a bit-oriented, data-link protocol from the Consultative Committee for International Telegraphy and Telephony (CCITT) used on the Integrated-Services Digital Network (ISDN) D channel.

See also **Integrated-Services Digital Network; Link-Access Procedure.**

laptop computer

A battery-operated, portable computer with a flat screen and keyboard that fold together. Some models are equipped with hardware that allows the user to plug the laptop into a desktop computer system.

See also **portable computer.**

Large Internet Packet (LIP)

A functionality that increases the size of internetwork packets beyond 576 bytes. Prior to NetWare 4.0, when the workstation initiated a negotiation with the NetWare server, and the server detected a router between it and the workstation, the server limited the packet size to 576 bytes. With the introduction of NetWare 4.0 and subsequent versions, LIP allowed the workstation to determine the packet size on the basis of maximum size supported by the router. The larger packet size is supported by Ethernet and Token Ring networks.

See also **Ethernet; Token Ring.**

Large Internet Packet Exchange (LIPX)

A process that allows larger packet sizes to increase throughput on networks.

See also **Large Internet Packet.**

Laser Prep file

A file containing a dictionary of PostScript shorthand commands used by the LaserWriter driver on the Macintosh, which downloads the file to initialize the printer before sending a print job. Usually the Macintosh operating system handles this task transparently.

laser transmission

A wireless communications technique in which laser beams of light are transmitted in pulses over a narrow path to a receiver, which translates the pulses into bits. This type of transmission offers high bandwidths and is not subjected to interference or jamming.

Last In, First Out (LIFO)

A programming queuing strategy in which the element added most recently ("last in") is the element removed first ("first out").

Last Login Time

A Directory Schema term and a selectable property for the User object in Novell Directory Services (NDS).

See also **leaf object; Novell Directory Services; User object.**

last mile

A telephony term used to describe the link between a customer's site and the local telephone company's central office, often the most expensive and least efficient stretch in a telephone company's cabling system.

Last Name

A selectable property for the User object in Novell Directory Services (NDS).

See also **leaf object; Novell Directory Services; User object.**

Last Referenced Time

In Novell Directory Services (NDS), a selectable property for the following objects: External Entity, List, Message-Routing Group, and Messaging Server.

See also **leaf object; Novell Directory Services; User object.**

LASTDRIVE

A DOS command used in the CONFIG.SYS file to specify the maximum number of drives that can be accessed on a computer system, a number often set by networking software.

LAT

Local-Area Transport, a protocol from Digital Equipment Corporation (DEC) that provides for high-speed, asynchronous communication among hosts and terminal servers on an Ethernet network.

See also **Ethernet.**

LATA

Local Access and Transport Area, a geographical and administrative area for which a local telephone company is responsible.

latency

The amount of time before a requested network or communications channel is available for transmission, or the amount of time required for a transmission to reach its destination.

layer

A group of related capabilities or services that build upon each other in an operating, communications, or networking environment. Through a communications process of well-defined interfaces, each layer provides services to the layer above it and uses services of the layers below it. Layers communicate across machines by using a predefined protocol, such as Transmission-Control Protocol/Internet Protocol (TCP/IP). However, the communication takes place only at the lowest-level layer on each machine, and then is spread upward to the appropriate layers. For example, each layer within the TCP/IP suite has various functions that are independent of the other layers. Each layer expects to receive certain services from the layer beneath it, and provides certain services to the layer above it.

See also **Transmission-Control Protocol/Internet Protocol.**

Layer-Management Entity (LME)

A mechanism by which the seven layers in the OSI Reference Model can communicate with each other to exchange information and to access management elements at different layers. An LME is also known as a *hook.*

See also **OSI Reference Model.**

LBRV

Low-Bit-Rate Voice, a digitized voice signal sent at a transmission speed below a channel capacity of 64,000 bits per second (bps).

LBS

LAN Bridge Server, a Token Ring network server that tracks and provides access to any bridges connected to the network.

See also **Token Ring.**

LBT/LWT

Listen Before Talk, a fundamental rule for the Carrier-Sense Multiple-Access/Collision Detect (CSMA/CD) media-access method. LBT requires that when a node has a packet to send on to the network, it must first listen for a special signal indicating the network is in use. Should no such signal be detected, the node can begin transmitting.

See also **Carrier-Sense Multiple-Access/Collision Detect; Listen While Talk.**

LC

Local Channel, a digital telecommunications link between a customer's site and the central office of the telephone company.

LCC/LCD

Lost Calls Cleared, a call-handling method in which blocked calls are lost or discarded.

See also **Lost Calls Delayed.**

LCD

(1) **liquid crystal display**, a type of screen display in which electric current is applied to align electrodes surrounding rod-shaped crystals in a special liquid. As current is applied, the orientation of the electrodes changes to produce dark areas on the screen display. This technology is common for portable computers.

(2) **Lost Calls Delayed**, a call-handling method in which blocked calls are queued for later processing or are delayed.

See also (1) **portable computer**; (2) **Lost Calls Cleared.**

LCGI

Local Common Gateway Interface, a feature that allows the NetWare Web Server to modify Web pages before sending them to a browser.

See also **Common Gateway Interface; NetWare Web Server.**

LCN

Logical Channel Number, a unique number assigned to each virtual circuit (VC) and attached to each packet in a call. The LCN differentiates the packet from other packets generated by users issuing other calls.

See also **virtual circuit**.

LCP

Link-Control Protocol, procedures for establishing, configuring, testing, and terminating the operation of data-link connections. LCP also automates the configuration of serial links for bridges and routers over wide-area networks (WANs).

LCR

(1) **Least-Cost Routing**, a feature of a Private Branch Exchange (PBX) telephone system that selects the most economical path to a destination.

(2) **Line-Control Register**, a register in a universal asynchronous receiver/transmitter

(UART) that specifies a parity type.

See also (1) **Private Branch Exchange**; (2) **universal asynchronous receiver/transmitter.**

LDDS

Limited-Distance Data Service, a class of telecommunications service that provides digital transmission capabilities over short distances through the use of line drivers instead of modems.

See also **line driver.**

LDM

Limited-Distance Modem, a short-haul modem designed for high-speed transmissions of more than 1 megabit per second (Mbps) over distances of less than 20 miles.

See also **short-haul modem.**

leaf object

A NetWare object that resides at the bottom of the Novell Directory Services (NDS) tree and does not contain any other objects. Certain properties are associated with each type of leaf object and differentiate the various leaf object classes. Table L.1 shows the seven categories of leaf objects supported by IntranetWare and the objects included in those categories.

leaf site

A computer that receives newsfeeds from Usenet groups on the Internet, but that does not pass these feeds on to other computers.

See also **Internet; Usenet.**

learning router

A router's interface that is configured to learn its configuration from a configured router on the same network. A learning router is also known as a *non-seed router*.

leased line

A communications line leased on a monthly basis from a public data network (PDN) vendor.

See also **public data network.**

Least-Cost Routing (LCR)

A feature of a Private Branch Exchange (PBX) telephone system that selects the most economical path to a destination.

See also **Private Branch Exchange.**

Least Recently Used (LRU)

A file-migration algorithm allowing files that have not been accessed during the longest period of time to be transferred first.

least-significant bit (LSB)

A bit corresponding to the lowest order of two (2^0) in a bit sequence, whose location depends on the context and on the ordering within a word.

See also **most-significant bit.**

LEC

Local Exchange Carrier, a company that provides local communications connections or long-distance connections through an Interexchange Carrier (IXC).

See also **Interexchange Carrier.**

Table L.1: Leaf Objects

Leaf Object Category	Objects Included	For More Information
User	User	See **User object.**
	User Template	See **User Template object.**
	Group	See **Group object.**
	Organizational Role	See **Organizational Role object.**
	Profile	See **Profile object.**
Server	NetWare Server	See **NetWare Server object.**
	Volume	See **Volume object.**
	Directory Map	See **Directory Map object.**
Printer	Printer	See **Printer object.**
	Print Queue	See **Print Queue object.**
Messaging	Messaging Server	See **Messaging Server object.**
	Message-Routing Group	See **Message-Routing Group object.**
	Distribution List	See **Distribution List object.**
	External Entity	See **External Entity object.**
Network Services	Application	See **Network Services object.**
	Auditing File	See **Auditing File object.**
	License Service Provider	See **License Service Provider object.**
Informational	AFP Server	See **AFP Server object.**
	Computer	See **Computer object.**
Miscellaneous	Alias	See **Alias object.**
	Unknown	See **Unknown object.**
	Bindery	See **Bindery object.**
	Bindery Queue	See **Bindery Queue object.**

LED

light-emitting diode, a semiconductor device that converts electrical energy into light. This device is commonly used in calculator displays and as "activity lights" on computers and modems.

legacy wiring

Wiring installed in a business or residence before the installation of a network system.

LEN

Low-Entry Networking, a term describing IBM's peer-to-peer configuration for Systems Network Architecture (SNA) networks.
See also **peer-to-peer; Systems Network Architecture.**

LEOS

Acronym for *Low-Earth-Orbit Satellite.*

level 1 routing

An interaction of routers within the same routing area.
See also **routing area.**

level 2 routing

An interaction of routers between established routing areas within an organization that forms a *routing domain* controlled by a single administrative unit.
See also **routing domain.**

level 3 routing

An interaction of routers between routing domains controlled by different administrative units.
See also **routing domain.**

LFN

Long Fat Network, a long-distance network that has bandwidths of several hundred megabits per second, which can cause performance and packet-loss problems with protocols in the Transmission-Control Protocol/ Internet Protocol (TCP/IP) protocol suite.
See also **Transmission-Control Protocol/Internet Protocol.**

library NLM applications

A collection of NetWare Loadable Module (NLM) applications that export functions that can be called by other NLM applications.
See also **NetWare Loadable Module.**

License Service Provider (LSP) object

In IntranetWare, a leaf object created when a License Service Provider (LSP) is registered with Novell Directory Services (NDS) to represent a server that has loaded the NetWare Licensing Services (NLS) NetWare Loadable Module (NLM). The NLS NLM enables administrators to track and control the use of licensed applications on the network.
See also **leaf object; object.**

Licensed Connections

A field name from the Cache Utilization screen appearing in the MONITOR NetWare Loadable Module (NLM).

See also **NetWare Loadable Module; MONITOR.**

LID

Local Injection/Detection, in fiber optics, a device used to align fibers when splicing them together.

lifetime

A representation of the length of time a particular value, feature, or link should be considered valid.

LIFO

Last In, First Out, a programming queuing strategy in which the element added most recently ("last in") is the element removed first ("first out").

light-emitting diode (LED)

A semiconductor device that converts electrical energy into light. This device is commonly used in calculator displays and as "activity lights" on computers and modems.

light-wave communication

A term describing fiber-optic cables and light generated by light-emitting diodes (LEDs) or lasers.

Lightweight Presentation Protocol (LPP)

A Presentation Layer (Layer 6 of the OSI Reference Model) protocol for use in the Common Management-Information Services (CMIS) Over TCP/IP (or *CMOT*) network management scheme. The CMOT scheme was never completed.

See also **Common Management-Information Services Over TCP/IP; OSI Reference Model.**

Lightweight Protocol

A high-speed internetwork protocol that combines routing and transport services in a more streamlined fashion than traditional Network Layer (Layer 3 of the OSI Reference Model) or Transport Layer (Layer 4) protocols. This protocol uses fixed header and trailer sizes; a more efficient checksum and error-correction method; error checking at endpoints (rather than after each transmission); and connection-oriented transmissions. The overall effect of these features is a faster transmission of data.

See also **OSI Reference Model.**

Limit Grace Logins

A selectable property for the Novell Directory Services (NDS) User object that limits the number of times a user can log in to the network without using a password.

See also **leaf object; Novell Directory Services; object.**

Limited-Distance Data Service (LDDS)

A class of telecommunications service that provides digital transmission capabilities over short distances through the use of line drivers instead of modems.

See also **line driver.**

Limited-Distance Modem (LDM)

A short-haul modem designed for high-speed transmissions of more than 1 megabit per second (Mbps) over distances of less than 20 miles.

See also **short-haul modem.**

limited resource link

A resource defined by a device operator to remain active only when the resource is being used.

LIMS

Lotus-Intel-Microsoft Specifications, a specification that calls for the allocation of expanded memory on special chips, and then maps the expanded memory into 16K pages allocated in the area of system memory between 640K and 1MB. This specification was originally developed by a joint consortium of Lotus, Intel, and Microsoft to work around a restriction on 8086 computers that could not operate in protected mode because more memory was needed to access addresses above 1MB.

See also **memory.**

LIN

Language Identification Number, a number assigned to non-English versions of NetWare Loadable Modules (NLMs) as a means of identification.

line

A circuit, channel, or link that carries signals for data or voice communications.

See also **channel; link.**

line adapter

A communications device designed to convert a digital signal into a form suitable for transmission over a communications channel.

line analyzer

A device used to troubleshoot and monitor load by displaying information about a transmission on a communications channel.

line card

A card that serves as an interface between a communications line and a device.

line circuit

A circuit that determines whether a telephone line is on-hook or off-hook and that handles the origination and termination of calls.

See also **Off Hook.**

line conditioner

A device that minimizes voltage-supply fluctuations, detects reversed polarity, detects a missing ground, and detects an overloaded neutral wire. A line conditioner is also known as a *voltage regulator*, *power conditioner*, and *line stabilizer/line conditioner (LS/LC)*.

Line-Control Register (LCR)

A register in a universal asynchronous receiver/transmitter (UART) that specifies a parity type.

See also **universal asynchronous receiver/transmitter.**

line driver

A communications hardware device that extends the transmission range between computers connected on a leased line. The line driver, which includes a transmitter and a receiver, is used for digital communications. One line driver is required at each end of the communications line.

line group

A term describing multiple telephone lines that can be activated or deactivated as a group.

line hit

A brief burst of interference on an electrical transmission line.

Line Insulation Test (LIT)

A test to check telephone lines automatically for short circuits, grounds, and interference.

line level

The power (measured in decibels) of an electrical signal at a particular point in the transmission path.

line load

A percentage of capacity usage a telephone line is getting at a particular time.

line monitor

A telecommunications device that can record and display all transmissions on the line to which it is attached.

Line Printer Daemon (LPD)

A UNIX daemon program that controls printing from a machine or network by knowing to which printer or print queue it is sending a job and making necessary adjustments.
    See also **daemon.**

line-sharing device

A multiplexing device that provides the capability for two or more devices to share the same communications line.
    See also **multiplexing.**

line speed

The transmission speed a telephone line supports at a given Grade of Service (GoS).
    See also **Grade of Service.**

line status

A setting that indicates whether a telephone is on-hook or off-hook.
    See also **Off Hook.**

line-termination equipment

Line cards, modems, multiplexers, hubs, and concentrators that can be used to send telecommunications signals.

line turnaround (LTA)

The amount of time in half-duplex (HDX) communications that it takes to set the line to reverse the transmission direction.
    See also **half duplex.**

Linear Predictive Coding (LPC)

A voice-encoding algorithm used in narrow-band transmissions of secure telephone units (STU-III) and that can produce a digitized voice signal at 2,400 bits per second (bps). Code-Excited Linear Predictive Coding (CELP) is a variation of LPC and can produce digitized voice signals at 4,800 bps.

See also **Code-Excited Linear Predictive Coding.**

line-of-sight communications

A communications process in which a signal from one location is transmitted to another location through the open air without reflection off a satellite or off the Earth.

LNI

Local Network Interconnect, a concentrator that supports multiple devices or communications controllers, whether standalone or attached to Ethernet cable.

link

A channel or line (usually a point-to-point line) on a network. In the context of NetWare Link-Services Protocol (NLSP), a link is a pointer to Designated Router pseudonode.

See also **NetWare Link-Services Protocol.**

Link-Access Procedure (LAP)

A bit-oriented, data-link-level protocol from the Consultative Committee for Interna-

tional Telegraphy and Telephony (CCITT), used for communications between devices designated as Data Communications Equipment (DCE) and Data Terminal Equipment (DTE).

See also **Consultative Committee for International Telegraphy and Telephony; Data-Communications Equipment; Data-Terminal Equipment.**

Link-Access Procedure, Balanced (LAPB) Protocol

A bit-oriented, data-link protocol from the Consultative Committee for International Telegraphy and Telephony (CCITT) used to link terminals and computers to packet-switched networks. This protocol is similar to the Synchronous Data-Link Control (SDLC) protocol and is equivalent to the High-Level Data-Link Control (HDLC) asynchronous balanced mode.

See also **Consultative Committee for International Telegraphy and Telephony; High-Level Data-Link Control; Synchronous Data-Link Control.**

Link-Access Procedure, D Channel (LAPD)

A bit-oriented, data-link protocol from the Consultative Committee for International Telegraphy and Telephony (CCITT) used on the Integrated-Services Digital Network (ISDN) D channel.

See also **Integrated-Services Digital Network; Link-Access Procedure.**

link connection

Equipment used to provide two-way communication from one link station to other link stations.

See also **line; link; link station.**

Link-Control Protocol (LCP)

Procedures for establishing, configuring, testing, and terminating the operation of data-link connections. LCP also automates the configuration of serial links for bridges and routers over wide-area networks (WANs).

link driver

Software that provides an interface between a Network Interface Card (NIC) and the operating system of a computer. The link driver is specific to the type of NIC installed on the computer.

See also **Network Interface Card.**

Link Layer

A shortened name sometimes used to refer to the Data-Link Layer (Layer 2) of the OSI Reference Model.

See also **Data-Link Layer; OSI Reference Model.**

link level

A part of the Consultative Committee for International Telegraphy and Telephony (CCITT) X.25 standard that defines the link protocol. The CCITT recommends the Link-Access Procedure (LAP) and Link-Access Procedure, Balanced (LAPB) protocols.

See also **Consultative Committee for International Telegraphy and Telephony;**

Link-Access Procedure; Link-Access Procedure, Balanced; X.25.

Link-Service Access Point (LSAP)

A Service Access Point (SAP) in the Logical-Link-Control (LLC) sublayer of the Data-Link Layer (Layer 2) in the OSI Reference Model.

See also **Logical-Link Control; OSI Reference Model; Service-Access Point.**

Link-Services Layer (LSL)

A component of the Open Data-Link Interface (ODI) model responsible for routing packets between local-area network (LAN) boards that use varied multiple-link interface drivers (MLIDs) and protocol stacks.

See also **Open Data-Link Interface.**

Link-State Packet (LSP)

In a NetWare Link-Services Protocol (NLSP) network, a link-state protocol packet that contains information about all the connections for a router (including information about all neighbors for that packet), broadcast to all other routers in the internetwork.

See also **link-state protocol; link-state router; neighbor; neighboring router; NetWare Link-Services Protocol.**

link-state protocol

A routing protocol under which a router sends information on the state of all its packets to all nodes of the internetwork, thereby reducing routing loops and network traffic. However, this approach does require more memory than the distance-vector algorithm. Examples of a link-state protocol include NetWare Link-Services Protocol (NLSP) and AppleTalk.

See also **AppleTalk; distance-vector protocol; link-state router; NetWare Link-Services Protocol.**

link-state router

A router that sends a packet containing information about all its links to all link-state routers on the network, which uses this information to build the network map. The network is said to have "converged" when all link-state routers have the same map of the network.

See also **link-state protocol.**

link-state routing algorithm

An algorithm that builds and maintains a logical map of a network system.

See also **link-state protocol; link-state router.**

link station

A combination of hardware and software that enables a node to attach to and provide control for a link. The two types of link stations are a *primary link station* and *secondary link station*.

See also **link; primary link station; secondary link station.**

link-station address

The sending and receiving addresses for network nodes. Although each sending address must be unique, multiple receiving addresses may be associated with each node.

Link-Support Layer (LSL)

An intermediary between drivers for the server or router on a local-area network (LAN) and the communications protocols (such as Internet Packet Exchange, AppleTalk Filing Protocol, and Transmission Control Protocol/Internet Protocol). A component of Novell's Open Data-Link Interface (ODI) specification, the LSL is an intermediate layer between the Network Interface Card's LAN driver and the protocol stacks. The LSL is responsible for directing packets from the LAN driver to the appropriate protocol stack, or from any of the available protocol stacks to the LAN driver.

See also **Network Interface Card; Open Data-Link Interface.**

link-level protocol

A set of rules and procedures defining communications methods over a channel, circuit, or link.

See also **channel; circuit; link.**

Linux

A clone of the UNIX operating system that is a multiuser, multitasking environment designed to work on Intel 386, 486, and Pentium computer systems. Unlike other versions of UNIX, Linux is capable of coexisting with DOS.

LIP

Large Internet Packet, a functionality that increases the size of internetwork packets beyond 576 bytes. Prior to NetWare 4.0, when the workstation initiated a negotiation with the NetWare server, and the server detected a router between it and the workstation, the server limited the packet size to 576 bytes. With the introduction of NetWare 4.0 and subsequent versions, LIP allowed the workstation to determine the packet size on the basis of maximum size supported by the router. The larger packet size is supported by Ethernet and Token Ring networks.

See also **Ethernet; Token Ring.**

liquid crystal display (LCD)

A type of screen display in which electric current is applied to align electrodes surrounding rod-shaped crystals in a special liquid. As current is applied, the orientation of the electrodes changes to produce dark areas on the screen display. This technology is common for portable computers.

See also **portable computer.**

list box

A section of a screen display in a graphical utility window that contains a list of items from which to choose.

LIST DEVICES utility

A server console utility in NetWare 4.*x* and IntranetWare that displays a list of devices on the server and allows the registration of new devices with the server.

See also **NetWare Loadable Module; NetWare utility.**

List object

In IntranetWare, an object that represents an unordered set of object names in the Novell Directory Services (NDS) Directory tree and that allows the user to logically group other objects. This object has the Access Control List, Authority Revocation, Back Link, Bindery, CA Private Key, CA Public Key, Certificate Revocation, Certificate Validity Interval, Common Name (CN), Cross Certificate Pair, Description, Last Referenced Time, Locality (L), Mailbox ID, Member, Obituary, Object Class, Organization (O), Organizational Unit (OU), Owner, Reference, Revision, and See Also selectable NDS properties.

See also **leaf object; Novell Directory Services; object.**

LISTDIR utility

A NetWare 3.*x* file utility that provides a view of a directory's subdirectories, of each subdirectory's Inherited Rights Mask (IRM), of each subdirectory's effective rights, of each subdirectory's creation date, and of subsequent subdirectories. A file server must be attached before this utility can be used to view the subdirectories of any directory on that file server.

Listen Before Talk (LBT)

A fundamental rule for the Carrier-Sense Multiple-Access/Collision Detect (CSMA/CD) media-access method. LBT requires that when a node has a packet to send on to the network, it must first listen for a special signal indicating the network is in use. Should no such signal be detected, the node can begin transmitting.

See also **Carrier-Sense Multiple-Access/Collision Detect; Listen While Talk.**

Listen While Talk (LWT)

A fundamental rule for the Carrier-Sense Multiple-Access/Collision Detect (CSMA/CD) media-access method. LWT requires that when a node has a packet to send on to the network, it must first listen for a special signal indicating the network is in use, and continue to listen, even while transmitting.

See also **Carrier-Sense Multiple-Access/Collision Detect; Listen Before Talk.**

LISTSERV

A group of computer programs that automatically manages mailing lists, distributes messages posted to the list, and adds or deletes members.

LIT

Line Insulation Test, a test to check telephone lines automatically for short circuits, grounds, and interference.

little-endian

A term that describes the order in which a word's individual bytes are stored. A little-endian system stores low-order bytes at the lower addresses. Computers with Intel processors (such as the 80286, 80386, and 80486), as well as VAX and PDP-11 computers, use the little-endian system.

See also **big-endian; middle-endian.**

Live3D

A Web browser plug-in from Netscape Communications that enables Netscape Navigator-compatible browsers to show three-dimensional simulations and environments based on Virtual-Reality Modeling Language (VRML).

See also **Netscape Navigator; Virtual-Reality Modeling Language; Web browser.**

 **For more information about networking products from Netscape Communications, surf the Web to** http://www.netscape.com.

LLAP

LocalTalk Link-Access Protocol, a link-access protocol found in the AppleTalk suite of protocols and used in LocalTalk networks.
See also **AppleTalk; LocalTalk network.**

LLC

Logical-Link Control, a protocol and packet format commonly used in Systems Network Architecture (SNA) networks and more widely supported than the Synchronous Data-Link Control (SDLC) protocol.
See also **Synchronous Data-Link Control; Systems Network Architecture.**

LLC2

Logical-Link Control Type 2, a protocol and packet format commonly used in Systems Network Architecture (SNA) networks and more widely supported than the Synchronous Data-Link Control (SDLC) protocol.
See also **Synchronous Data-Link Control; Systems Network Architecture.**

LME

Layer-Management Entity, a mechanism by which the seven layers in the OSI Reference Model can communicate with each other to exchange information and to access management elements at different layers. An LME is also known as a *hook*.

See also **OSI Reference Model.**

LMI

Local Management Interface, an interface specification that provides for the exchange of management-related information between a network and a hardware device.

LMMP

LAN/MAN Management Protocol, a local-area network (LAN) protocol that provides Common Management-Information Service/Common Management-Information Protocol (CMIS/CMIP) network management services by implementing them directly into the Logical-Link Control (LLC) sublayer of the Data-Link Layer (Layer 2) of the OSI Reference Model. Because it provides Application level (level 7) services and bypasses the intervening four layers to use LLC services, LLMP cannot use routers. The original name of this protocol was CMIS/CMIP over LLC, and so it is also known as *CMOL*.

See also **Common Management-Information Service; Common Management Information Protocol; Logical-Link Control; OSI Reference Model.**

LMU

LAN Manager for UNIX, a Microsoft server-based network operating system that supports the UNIX operating system.

LMX

L Multiplex, a hierarchy of telecommunications channel groupings representing a group, super group, master group, and jumbo group.

LNM

LAN Network Manager, a Systems Application Architecture (SAA)-compliant, IBM product that manages Token Ring networks by using both the Common Management-Information Protocol (CMIP) and the Simple Network-Management Protocol (SNMP). While running under OS/2, LNM can act as an entry point for NetView.

See also **Common Management-Information Protocol; NetView; Simple Network-Management Protocol; System Application Architecture.**

load balancing

A scheme that distributes network traffic among parallel paths, providing redundancy while efficiently using available bandwidth.

load sharing

A process in which two or more remote bridges share their traffic load in a parallel configuration; if one bridge fails, traffic can be routed to the next parallel bridge.

See also **bridge.**

LOAD utility

In NetWare and IntranetWare, a console utility that links loadable modules to the operating system. These loadable modules include disk drivers, local-area network (LAN) drivers, NetWare Loadable Modules

(NLMs), and name-space NLMs. When the module is loaded, it links itself to the system and allocates a portion of the system's resources for its own use. When the module is unloaded, the system resources are returned to the system.

See also **LAN driver; NetWare Loadable Module; name-space NLM.**

loadable module

A program loaded and unloaded from a server or workstation while the operating system is running. Two common types of loadable modules are NetWare Loadable Modules (NLMs) and Virtual Loadable Modules (VLMs).

See also **NetWare Loadable Module; Virtual Loadable Module.**

loading

A process during which NetWare Loadable Modules (NLMs) are linked to the NetWare operating system and system resources are allocated to the NLMs.

See also **LOAD utility; NetWare Loadable Module.**

loading coil

A device attached to copper cabling that reduces distortion of analog signals. It is not possible to transmit digital signals across copper cables when loading coils are attached.

lobe

A synonym for "node" in the context of Token Ring networks.

Lobe-Attachment Module (LAM)

A Token Ring network box that has multiple interfaces to which as many as 20 *lobes* (nodes) can be attached. A LAM is functionally similar to a Multistation-Attachment Unit (MAU), although the MAU can have only eight lobes attached. When a LAM is daisy-chained and connected to a Controlled-Access Unit (CAU), each CAU can handle as many as 4 LAMs, which yields a potential for 80 lobes.

See also **Controlled-Access Unit; Multistation-Attachment Unit.**

local

A term used to describe a communications device that can be accessed directly (as opposed to through a communications line), an information processing operation performed by a computer not installed in a remote location, or a programming variable used in only one part of a program (such as in a subroutine).

See also **remote computing.**

Local Access and Transport Area (LATA)

A geographical and administrative area for which a local telephone company is responsible.

local acknowledgment

The process of an intermediate network node terminating a Data-Link Layer (Layer 2 of the OSI Reference Model) session for an end host. Local acknowledgments reduce network overhead.

See also **OSI Reference Model.**

local-area network (LAN)

A system in which personal computers and electronic office equipment are linked together (usually with a wiring-based cabling scheme) within a small area to form a network. Users can then communicate with each other, share resources (such as data storage and printers), and access remote computers or other networks. Figure L.1 shows an example of the *server-based LAN* and the *peer-to-peer LAN*.

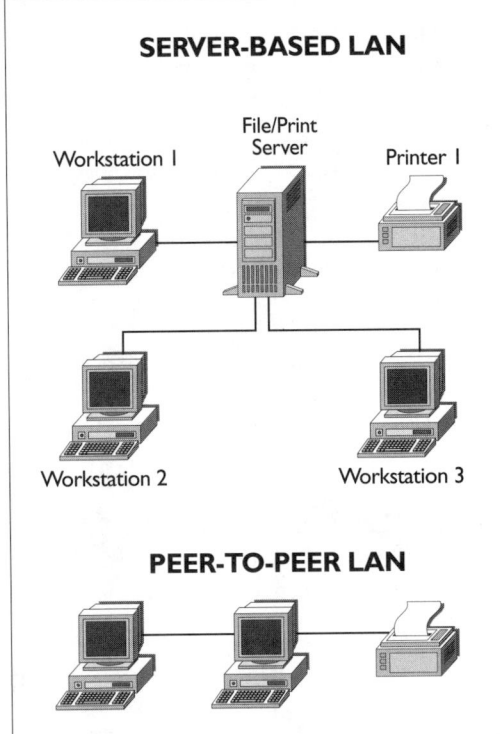

SERVER-BASED LAN

File/Print Server

Workstation 1   Printer 1

Workstation 2   Workstation 3

PEER-TO-PEER LAN

Figure L.I
LAN configurations

In a *server-based LAN,* a dedicated server is connected to various workstations, which request services from the server. The *network operating system* (which determines higher-level protocols and available services)

augments the operating system on the workstations, so the server then controls access to some of the network resources. Common network operating systems for server-based LANs include NetWare and IntranetWare from Novell; LAN Manager and Windows NT Advanced Server from Microsoft; LAN Server from IBM; and VINES from Banyan Systems.

In a *peer-to-peer-based* (or simply *peer-based*) LAN, each node in the network can initiate actions, access other nodes, and provide services for other nodes without first acquiring permission from the server. The network operating system often runs under the native operating system of the individual workstations. Common network operating systems for peer-to-peer LANs include Personal NetWare from Novell, Windows for Workgroups from Microsoft, LANstep from Hayes Microcomputer Products, and LANtastic from Artisoft.

The physical *topology* of the LAN determines the cabling scheme used to physically connect the nodes of the networks. Common physical topologies include bus, ring, star, tree, and star-wired. The logical topology of the LAN determines how information is passed from one node to the others on the network. The two most common logical topologies are *bus* (in which information is broadcast to all nodes at the same time) and *ring* (in which information is passed from node to node until it reaches its destination). Setting up a LAN requires specific hardware and software. Hardware requirements include personal computers, Network Interface Cards (NICs), cables, connectors, wiring centers, and safety devices (such as an uninterruptible power supply). Software requirements include hardware-specific drivers, the network operating system, workstation software (such as shells, redirectors, requestors, or client software), applications, management programs, diagnostic programs, and backup software.

See also **Client 16; Client 32; LAN Manager; LANstep; LANtastic; NetWare DOS Requester; NetWare Requester for OS/2; NetWare shell; network interface card; network operating system; Personal NetWare; Windows for Workgroups; Windows NT Advanced Server.**

Local Automatic-Message Accounting (LAMA)

An accounting method used by a local telephone company to generate automatic billing for local and toll calls. The method requires the Automatic Number Identification (ANI) capability.

See also **Automatic Number Identification.**

local bridge

A bridge directly interconnecting networks in the same geographical area.

local bus

A 32-bit path directly connecting the central processing unit (CPU) to memory, video, and disk controllers in an IBM (or compatible) personal computer. Local bus architecture allows the transfer of data from the CPU to memory, video, and disk controllers (and vice versa) at the speed of the CPU. This represents an improvement over older bus architectures in which microprocessor speeds outpaced internal bus speeds, slowing the computer and creating a narrow data stream in and out of the CPU. Local-bus architecture is found in Peripheral-

Component Interconnect (PCI) and Video Electronics Standards Association (VESA) buses.

See also **Peripheral-Component Interconnect; Video Electronics Standards Association.**

local carrier

A company that provides local communications connections or long-distance connections through an Interexchange Carrier (IXC). A local carrier is also known as a *Local Exchange Carrier* (*LEC*).

See also **Interexchange Carrier.**

Local Channel (LC)

A digital telecommunications link between a customer's site and the central office of the telephone company.

Local Common Gateway Interface (LCGI)

A feature that allows the NetWare Web Server to modify Web pages before sending them to a browser.

See also **Common Gateway Interface; NetWare Web Server.**

local disk

A disk attached to a network workstation rather than to a file server.

local drive

A storage device physically contained in, or attached to, a workstation. A local drive is also known as a *physical drive*.

local drive mapping

A path to local media (such as a hard disk drive and floppy disk drives). Some versions of DOS, for example, reserve drives A: through E: for local drive mappings.

Local Exchange Carrier (LEC)

A company that provides local communications connections or long-distance connections through an Interexchange Carrier (IXC).
See also **Interexchange Carrier.**

local group

A Windows NT Advanced Server group that has rights and permissions granted to only the resources of a server in the group's domain.
See also **Windows NT Advanced Server.**

Local Injection/Detection (LID)

In fiber optics, a device used to align fibers when splicing them together.

local loop

The portion of a communications circuit connecting subscriber equipment to equipment in a local telephone exchange or local telephone company's central office.

Local Management Interface (LMI)

An interface specification that provides for the exchange of management-related information between a network and a hardware device.

local name

A name known only to a single server or domain in an internetwork or in a network.

Local Network Interconnect (LNI)

A concentrator that supports multiple devices or communications controllers, whether standalone or attached to Ethernet cable.

local printer

A printer attached directly to a port on a network's print server.
See also **remote printer.**

local semaphore

An interprocess communication signal between NetWare Loadable Module (NLM) applications running on a single server. Such signals control resources, synchronize thread execution, and queue threads. A local semaphore differs from a *network semaphore*, which applies resources available to servers and workstations on the network.
See also **NetWare Loadable Module; semaphore; thread.**

local-transaction program

An application program in a Systems Network Architecture (SNA) network that performs transactions with one or more programs at the logical unit.
See also **logical unit; Systems Network Architecture.**

Local-Area Network Reference Model (LAN/RM)

A description of a local-area network (LAN) as defined by 802.*x* specification set of the Institute of Electrical and Electronic Engineers (IEEE).

See also **IEEE 802.*x*.**

Local-Area Transport (LAT)

A protocol from Digital Equipment Corporation (DEC) that provides for high-speed, asynchronous communication among hosts and terminal servers on an Ethernet network.

See also **Ethernet.**

Locality (L) object

A NetWare container object that defines geographic locations in the Novell Directory Services (NDS) Directory tree. Because this object is not currently enabled by Novell's NWADMIN or NETADMIN utilities, it is not visible through the current utilities. However, third-party programs are available to define and view this class.

See also **container object; Novell Directory Services; object.**

localization

The preparation of hard-copy and online documentation to be used in locations that use non-English languages.

localization toolkit

A package containing the tools third-party vendors need for translating NetWare into non-English versions.

Locally Administered Address (LAA)

A parameter used by a 3174 controller to determine whether a node can access a mainframe computer connected to a Token Ring network.

See also **3174; Token Ring.**

LocalTalk Link-Access Protocol (LLAP)

A link-access protocol found in the AppleTalk suite of protocols and used in LocalTalk networks.

See also **AppleTalk; LocalTalk network.**

LocalTalk network

A proprietary network architecture from Apple Computer, Inc., that consists of a system of twisted-pair cables, cable extenders, and connectors (DB-9, DIN-8, or DIN-3) that connects computers and network devices to create an AppleTalk network. Using Carrier-Sense Multiple-Access/Collision Avoidance (CSMA/CA) and the LocalTalk Link-Access Protocol (LLAP), up to 255 nodes can be separated by up to 1,000 feet. LocalTalk operates at the Data-Link Layer (Layer 2) and Physical Layer (Layer 1) of the OSI Reference Model.

See also **AppleTalk; Carrier-Sense Multiple-Access/Collision; OSI Reference Model.**

Location

A NetWare Directory Schema term and a selectable property for the User object in Novell Directory Services (NDS).

Lock File Server Console

In NetWare 4.02, a field name from the Available Options screen of the MONITOR NetWare Loadable Module (NLM).

See also **NetWare Loadable Module; MONITOR.**

Locked By Intruder

A NetWare Directory Schema term and a selectable property for the User object in Novell Directory Services (NDS).

See also **Novell Directory Services.**

locked file

A file whose attributes have been set so the file may be opened and read, but not written to, deleted, or changed in any way.

locking

A process to ensure that two network users or programs cannot try to access the same data simultaneously. An *advisory lock* issues a warning, and can be overridden. A *physical lock*, on the other hand, is a control mechanism that cannot be overwritten. Four types of locks can be used. With a *file lock*, a file server prevents users from accessing any part of a file while another user is accessing the same file. With a *record lock*, a file server prevents users from accessing a record in a file while another user is accessing the same record. With a *logical lock*, logical units (LUs) in a file are inaccessible. With a *physical lock*, sectors or groups of sectors on a hard disk are inaccessible.

Lockout After Detection

A NetWare Directory Schema term and a selectable property for the Organization and Organizational Unit objects in Novell Directory Services (NDS).

See also **Novell Directory Services.**

log in

The act of entering a username and password to gain access to a network system such as the Novell Directory Services (NDS) Directory tree or a NetWare server.

See also **log out; password; username.**

log off

log out, the act of terminating a session on a network system by sending a terminating message or command. The system may respond with informational messages such as the total resources consumed during the session, or the total time between logging in and logging out.

See also **log in.**

log on

log in, the act of entering a username and password to gain access to a network system such as the Novell Directory Services (NDS) Directory tree or a NetWare server.

See also **log out; password; username.**

log out

The act of terminating a session on a network system by sending a terminating message or command. The system may respond with informational messages such as the total resources consumed during the session, or the total time between logging in and logging out.

See also **log in.**

logical address

A network or node address assigned during installation of a network or addition of a workstation. The installation software assigns a logical address; the hardware manufacturer assigns a hardware address.

logical channel

A mechanism that allows multiple, simultaneous virtual circuits (VCs) across one physical link on a network.

See also **virtual circuit.**

Logical Channel Number (LCN)

A unique number assigned to each virtual circuit (VC) and attached to each packet in a call. The LCN differentiates the packet from other packets generated by users issuing other calls.

See also **virtual circuit.**

logical device name

A name used by the operating system to identify a DOS device.

logical drive

An internal representation used by an operating system to refer to an actual disk device or to a group of directories specified by the DOS SUBST command.

Logical-Link Control Type 2 (LLC2)

A protocol and packet format commonly used in Systems Network Architecture (SNA) networks and more widely supported than the Synchronous Data-Link Control (SDLC) protocol.

See also **Synchronous Data-Link Control; Systems Network Architecture.**

logical memory

Memory that appears contiguous to NetWare 4.*x* processes, but that may not have contiguous addresses.

See also **memory.**

logical number

A number assigned by a software installation program to a hardware device. This logical number assignment is made according to such conditions as which other devices are attached to the network and the order in which those devices were attached.

logical partition

A part of a NetWare or IntranetWare physical partition, measured from the beginning of a data area to the end of that same data area.

See also **physical partition.**

logical ring

A network that may be cabled physically as a star topology, but is treated logically as a ring topology.

See also **ring topology; star topology.**

logical topology

A network's logical layout that specifies which path information takes through a network, how the information is transmitted, and how the elements in the network communicate with each other. The two most common types of logical topology are *bus* and *ring*.

See also **bus topology; ring topology.**

logical unit (LU)

A terminal-emulation program or application in a Systems Network Architecture (SNA) network that can communicate with host systems and applications (Type 0, 1, 2, 3, 4, or 7) or with other logical units of the same type (Type 6.0, 6.1, or 6.2).

See also **Systems Network Architecture.**

Logical Unit Type 6.2

An architectural base for Advanced Program-to-Program Communications (APPC) that supports sessions between two applications in a Distributed Data Processing (DDP) environment.

See also **Advanced Program-to-Program Communications; Distributed Data Processing.**

Logical-Link Control (LLC)

A sublayer in the Local Area Network Reference Model (LAN/RM) that provides an interface and services for the network-layer protocols, and mediates between the higher-level protocols and lower media-access protocols. The LLC resides above the Media Access Control (MAC) sublayer, and, when combined, the LLC and MAC sublayers are equivalent to the Data-Link Layer (Layer 2 of the OSI Reference Model). The LLC is similar to the Synchronous Data-Link Control (SDLC) link-layer protocol.

See also **Media-Access Control; OSI Reference Model; Synchronous Data-Link Control.**

login

A procedure of entering a username and password to gain access to a network system such as the Novell Directory Services (NDS) Directory tree or a NetWare server.

See also **logout; password; username.**

Login Allowed Time Map

A NetWare Directory Schema term and a selectable property for the User object in Novell Directory Services (NDS).

See also **Novell Directory Services.**

LOGIN directory

A directory (SYS:LOGIN) that contains LOGIN, NLIST, and other utilities. Created during the installation of NetWare or IntranetWare, the LOGIN directory can be used to log in and to view a list of available servers.

See also **LOGIN utility; NLIST utility.**

Login Disabled

A NetWare selectable property for the User object in Novell Directory Services (NDS).

See also **leaf object; Novell Directory Services; object.**

Login Expiration Date and Time

A NetWare selectable property for the User object in Novell Directory Services (NDS).
See also **leaf object; Novell Directory Services; object.**

Login Expiration Time

A NetWare selectable property for the User object in Novell Directory Services (NDS).
See also **leaf object; Novell Directory Services; object.**

Login Grace Limit

A NetWare selectable property for the User object in Novell Directory Services (NDS).
See also **leaf object; Novell Directory Services; object.**

Login Grace Remaining

A NetWare selectable property for the User object in Novell Directory Services (NDS).
See also **leaf object; Novell Directory Services; object.**

Login Intruder Address

A NetWare selectable property for the User object in Novell Directory Services (NDS).
See also **leaf object; Novell Directory Services; object.**

Login Intruder Attempts

A NetWare selectable property for the User object in Novell Directory Services (NDS).
See also **leaf object; Novell Directory Services; object.**

Login Intruder Limit

A NetWare selectable property for the Organization and Organizational Unit objects in Novell Directory Services (NDS).
See also **leaf object; Novell Directory Services; object.**

Login Intruder Reset Time

A NetWare selectable property for the User object in Novell Directory Services (NDS).
See also **leaf object; Novell Directory Services; object.**

Login Maximum Simultaneous

A NetWare selectable property for the User object in Novell Directory Services (NDS).
See also **leaf object; Novell Directory Services; object.**

login name

A unique name that each user is required to use at login to identify the user.
See also **username; password.**

login restrictions

A set of restrictions on user accounts that control access to the network. In NetWare, login restrictions include a password requirement, account limits, disk space limits, a limited number of connections allowed, and time limits.

login script

A NetWare file containing a list of commands that organize a user's network environment when issued by the user upon logging in to the network. Login scripts can map drives, display messages, set environment variables, and execute programs or menus.

Container login scripts, which are assigned to Container objects, execute first and set general environments for all users in a container. *Profile login scripts,* assigned to Profile objects, execute after container login scripts and set environments for multiple users. *User login scripts,* assigned to User objects, set environments that are specific to a single user (such as menu options) and execute after Container and Profile login scripts.

A default login script created by the LOGIN utility executes the first time a user logs in and contains only essential commands (such as a drive mapping to NetWare utilities). The default login script also executes when a user does not have an individual User login script.

Table L.2 shows some of the common commands found in login scripts. Figure L.2 shows the correlation between types of login scripts.

See also **leaf object; mapping; object.**

Login Script

A NetWare Directory Schema term and a selectable property for the following objects in Novell Directory Services (NDS): Group, Message Routing Group, Organization, Organizational Unit, Profile, and User.

See also **Novell Directory Services.**

login security

A system that controls initial access to the network and provides continued verification of the identity of the user.

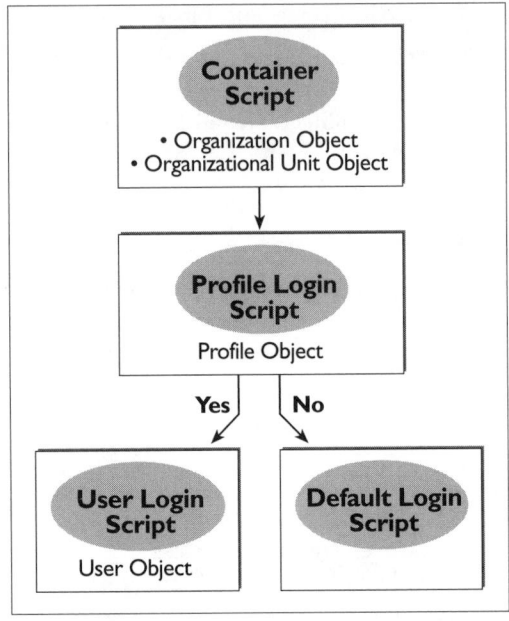

Figure L.2
Login Scripts

Login Time

A NetWare Directory Schema term and a selectable property for the User object in Novell Directory Services (NDS).

See also **leaf object; Novell Directory Services; object.**

Login Time Restrictions

A NetWare Directory Schema term and a selectable property for the User object in Novell Directory Services (NDS).

See also **leaf object; Novell Directory Services; object.**

Table L.2: Common Login Script Commands

Command	Description
ATTACH	Uses bindery services to attach workstations to bindery-based NetWare servers (NetWare 2.x or NetWare 3.x).
COMSPEC	Specifies the directory where the DOS command processor (COMMAND.COM file) is loaded. Used only when users run DOS from the network.
EXIT	Terminates execution of the LOGIN utility and then executes an external program.
FIRE PHASERS	Emits a "phaser" sound.
IF..THEN	Under certain conditions, performs a specified action.
MAP	Maps drives and search drives to network directories and to Novell Directory Services (NDS) objects.
PAUSE	Invokes a pause in the execution of the login script.
SET	Sets environment variables.
WRITE	Displays messages on the screen of the workstation when the user logs in.

LOGIN utility

A NetWare and IntranetWare workstation utility that provides access to the network by logging in to a server and running a login script. Users are allowed to log in to only one server at a time. When the LOGIN utility is invoked, the user is logged out from all other servers.

logout

A procedure that terminates access to a network system by breaking the network connection and deleting drives mapped to the network.

See also **login**.

LOGOUT utility

A NetWare and IntranetWare workstation utility that terminates access to and exits the network system or logs out of a server.

Long Fat Network (LFN)

A long-distance network that has bandwidths of several hundred megabits per second, which can cause performance and packet-loss problems with protocols in the Transmission Control Protocol/Internet Protocol (TCP/IP) protocol suite.

See also **Transmission Control Protocol/Internet Protocol.**

long machine type

A six-letter name that represents a DOS machine brand in NetWare (for example,

IBM_PC for an IBM computer). The same long machine type name is used as a subdirectory name when more than one brand of workstation is used (for example, IBM_PC subdirectory for IBM workstations and COMPAQ subdirectory for COMPAQ workstations). If more than one version of DOS is used at various workstations, separate subdirectories must be created for each machine type.

Long Term Cache Dirty Hits

A field name in the "Cache Utilization" screen of the MONITOR NetWare Loadable Module (NLM).

See also **NetWare Loadable Module; MONITOR.**

LONG.NAM (NLM)

In NetWare 4.11 and later versions, a NetWare Loadable Module (NLM) that enables support for OS/2, Windows NT, and Windows 95 long filenames on the file server.

long-haul carrier

A description of the cabling and signaling specifications for a carrier system responsible for long-distance telecommunications signals. Coaxial cabling and analog signaling are characteristics of this carrier, and they provide tremendous capacity, but are expensive to use.

long-haul microwave communications

Microwave transmissions over distances of 25 to 30 miles.

long-haul modem

A communications device capable of transmitting information over long distances.

longitudinal redundancy checking

In serial transmissions, an error-detection method that calculates a place value for each bit in a block of bytes. Longitudinal redundancy checking (also known as *block parity*) is always set to even.

See also **block parity.**

Look-Ahead Queuing

In telephony, an automatic call-distribution feature that involves a secondary queue checking for congestion before traffic is switched to it.

Look-Back Queuing

In telephony, an automatic call-distribution feature that involves a secondary queue checking to see whether congestion on a primary queue has cleared so calls can be returned to the primary queue.

loop

A circuit between a customer's location and a telephone company's central office.

loop timing

In digital communications, a synchronization method that extracts timing information from incoming pulses.

loopback

A diagnostic test that transmits a signal across a medium while the sending device waits for the return of the signal.

loopback mode

An operating mode that allows testing of a line by sending a signal back to its origin instead of sending it on to a destination.

loopback plug

A special connector used to perform echo testing.

See also **echo**.

Loose Source and Record Route (LSRR)

An Internet Protocol (IP) option that enables a datagram's source to specify routing information and to record the datagram route. This option is used as a security measure because it ensures that datagrams travel over only those routes that have a level of security commensurate with that of the datagram.

See also **Internet Protocol**.

loss

A disappearance of a packet or call during transmission. Loss sometimes occurs during periods of heavy network traffic or because of an addressing error.

loss budget

A combination of all the factors contributing to the loss of a signal between the source and destination.

lossless compression

A data-compression method that rearranges or recodes data in a more compact fashion, in such a way that no data is lost when the file is decompressed. The *Lempel-Ziv* (or LZ) *Algorithm*, which searches for redundant strings of data and converts them to smaller tokens, is a common algorithm used by lossless compression programs.

lossy compression

A data-compression method that discards any data the compression mechanism decides is not needed, which results in the loss of some original data when the file is decompressed.

Lost Calls Cleared (LCC)

A call-handling method in which blocked calls are lost or discarded.

Lost Calls Delayed (LCD)

A call-handling method in which blocked calls are queued for later processing or are delayed.

Lotus-Intel-Microsoft Specifications (LIMS)

A specification that calls for the allocation of expanded memory on special chips, and then maps the expanded memory into 16K pages allocated in the area of system memory between 640K and 1MB. This specification was originally developed by a joint consortium of Lotus, Intel, and Microsoft to work around a restriction on 8086 computers that could not operate in protected mode because more memory was needed to access addresses above 1MB.

See also **memory.**

Lotus Notes

A distributed client-server database application from Lotus Development Corporation that allows users to view information in individualized ways, and to expand the database according to individual preferences. A Notes server runs the Notes configuration at a particular installation and enforces access privileges as it handles client requests. Lotus Notes also includes electronic mail and allows the development of custom applications.

 **For more information about networking products from Lotus Development Corporation, surf the Web to** `http://www.lotus.com/ site.nsf`.

Lotus SmartSuite

An application suite from Lotus Development Corporation that includes Lotus 1-2-3 (a spreadsheet program), Approach (a relational database program), Freelance Graphics (a presentation program), Word Pro (a word processing program), ScreenCam (a video recording program for playback through Freelance Graphics), and SmartCenter (a suite-integration utility). All applications are now available in 32-bit versions for Windows 95 and Windows NT platforms.

Low-Bit-Rate Voice (LBRV)

A digitized voice signal sent at a transmission speed below a channel capacity of 64,000 bits per second (bps).

low-end

An inexpensive product from the lower end of a company's product list. Such products usually have limited capabilities and features.

See also **high-end.**

Low-Entry Networking (LEN)

A term describing IBM's peer-to-peer configuration for Systems Network Architecture (SNA) networks.

See also **peer-to-peer; Systems Network Architecture.**

lower memory

The lowest portion of conventional memory, in which the operating system and installable device drivers are commonly loaded.

See also **memory.**

low-level language

A programming language (such as assembly language) that is close to machine language.

low-level protocol

A protocol at the Physical Layer (Layer 1) or Data-Link Layer (Layer 2) of the OSI Reference Model.

See also **OSI Reference Model.**

low-speed modem

A modem that operates at speeds of 600 bits per second (bps) or less.

LPC

Linear Predictive Coding, a voice-encoding algorithm used in narrowband transmissions of secure telephone units (STU-III) and that can produce a digitized voice signal at 2,400 bits per second (bps). Code-Excited Linear Predictive Coding (CELP) is a variation of LPC and can produce digitized voice signals at 4,800 bps.

See also **Code-Excited Linear Predictive Coding.**

LPD

Line Printer Daemon, a UNIX daemon program that controls printing from a machine or network by knowing to which printer or print queue it is sending a job and making necessary adjustments.

See also **daemon.**

LPP

Lightweight Presentation Protocol, a Presentation Layer (Layer 6 of the OSI Reference Model) protocol for use in the Common Management-Information Services (CMIS) Over TCP/IP (or *CMOT*) network management scheme. The CMOT scheme was never completed.

See also **Common Management-Information Services Over TCP/IP; OSI Reference Model.**

LPT

The logical name that DOS assigns to a line printer connected to a personal computer through parallel printer ports.

LRU

Least Recently Used, a file-migration algorithm allowing files that have not been accessed during the longest period of time to be transferred first.

LRU Sitting Time

In NetWare, a field name in the Cache Utilization screen of the MONITOR NetWare Loadable Module (NLM).

See also **NetWare Loadable Module; MONITOR.**

LSAP

Link-Service-Access Point, a Service-Access Point (SAP) in the Logical-Link-Control (LLC) sublayer of the Data-Link Layer (Layer 2) in the OSI Reference Model.

See also **Logical-Link Control; OSI Reference Model; Service-Access Point.**

LSB

Least-significant bit, a bit corresponding to the lowest order of two (2^0) in a bit sequence, whose location depends on the context and on the ordering within a word.

See also **most-significant bit.**

LSL

(1) **Link-Services Layer,** a component of the Open Data-Link Interface (ODI) model

responsible for routing packets between local-area network (LAN) boards that use varied multiple-link interface drivers (MLIDs) and protocol stacks.

(2) Link-Support Layer, an intermediary between drivers for the server or router on a local-area network (LAN) and the communications protocols (such as Internet Packet Exchange, AppleTalk Filing Protocol, and Transmission-Control Protocol/Internet Protocol). A component of Novell's Open Data-Link Interface (ODI) specification, the LSL is an intermediate layer between the Network Interface Card's LAN driver and the protocol stacks. The LSL is responsible for directing packets from the LAN driver to the appropriate protocol stack, or from any of the available protocol stacks to the LAN driver.

See also **(2) Network Interface Card; (1) and (2) Open Data-Link Interface.**

LSL AES Event Call-Backs

In NetWare 3.12, a tracked resource that appears as an option in the Available Options/Resource Utilization screen of the MONITOR NetWare Loadable Module (NLM). This Asynchronous Event Service (AES) resource allows LAN drivers to schedule a future event.

See also **NetWare Loadable Module; MONITOR.**

LSL Default Protocol Stacks

In NetWare 3.12, a tracked resource that appears as an option in the Available Options/Resource Utilization screen of the MONITOR NetWare Loadable Module (NLM). This resource tracks protocol NLMs that register to receive all packets that no

other protocol claims.

See also **NetWare Loadable Module; MONITOR.**

LSL Packet-Receive Buffers

In NetWare 3.12, a tracked resource that appears as an option in the Available Options/Resource Utilization screen of the MONITOR NetWare Loadable Module (NLM). This resource tracks which LAN driver is using a particular packet receive buffer so that the buffers can be freed when the LAN driver is unloaded.

See also **NetWare Loadable Module; MONITOR.**

LSL Pre-Scan Protocol Stacks

In NetWare 3.12, a tracked resource that appears as an option in the Available Options/Resource Utilization screen of the MONITOR NetWare Loadable Module (NLM). This resource tracks protocol NLMs that register to pre-scan all incoming packets to determine if the packets belong to the NLMs.

See also **NetWare Loadable Module; MONITOR.**

LSL Protocol Stacks

In NetWare 3.12, a tracked resource that appears as an option in the "Available Options/Resource Utilization" screen of the MONITOR NetWare Loadable Module (NLM). This resource tracks protocol NLMs that register as protocol stacks.

See also **NetWare Loadable Module; MONITOR.**

LSLC32 (NLM)

A Link-Support Layer (LSL) NetWare Loadable Module (NLM) file that enables a 32-bit workstation to communicate with different protocols. The module for 16-bit workstations is called LSL.COM.

See also **Link-Support Layer.**

LSP

(1) **License Service Provider,** in IntranetWare, a leaf object created when a License Service Provider (LSP) is registered with Novell Directory Services (NDS) to represent a server that has loaded the NetWare Licensing Services (NLS) NetWare Loadable Module (NLM). The NLS NLM enables administrators to track and control the use of licensed applications on the network. (2) **Link-State Packet,** in a NetWare Link-Services Protocol (NLSP) network, a link-state protocol packet that contains information about all the connections for a router (including information about all neighbors for that packet), broadcast to all other routers in the internetwork.

See also **(1) leaf object; (2) link-state protocol; (2) link-state router; (2) neighbor; (2) neighboring router; (2) NetWare Link-Services Protocol; (1) object.**

LSRR

Loose Source and Record Route, an Internet Protocol (IP) option that enables a datagram's source to specify routing information and to record the datagram route. This option is used as a security measure because it ensures that datagrams travel over only those routes that have a level of security commensurate with that of the datagram.

See also **Internet Protocol.**

L-to-T Connector

A telecommunications component used to connect two (analog) Frequency-Division Multiplexing (FDM) groups into a single (digital) Time-Division Multiplexing (TDM) group.

See also **Frequency-Division Multiplexing; Time-Division Multiplexing.**

LTA

line turnaround, the amount of time in half-duplex (HDX) communications that it takes to set the line to reverse the transmission direction.

See also **half duplex.**

LTM

LAN Traffic Monitor, a device that monitors the traffic activity in a local-area network (LAN) system.

LU

Logical Unit, a terminal-emulation program or application in a Systems Network Architecture (SNA) network that can communicate with host systems and applications (Type 0, 1, 2, 3, 4, or 7) or with other logical units of the same type (Type 6.0, 6.1, or 6.2).

See also **Systems Network Architecture.**

LU 6.2

Logical Unit Type 6.2, an architectural base for Advanced Program-to-Program Communications (APPC) that supports sessions between two applications in a Distributed Data Processing (DDP) environment.

See also **Advanced Program-to-Program Communications; Distributed Data**

lurking

Listening in on a network or internetwork discussion by a user forum, special-interest group, or newsgroup, without participating.

LWT

Listen While Talk, a fundamental rule for the Carrier-Sense Multiple-Access/Collision Detect (CSMA/CD) media-access method. LWT requires that when a node has a packet to send on to the network, it must first listen for a special signal indicating the network is in use, and continue to listen, even while transmitting.

See also **Carrier-Sense Multiple-Access/Collision Detect; Listen Before Talk.**

Lycos search engine

A World Wide Web (WWW) search engine that returns results ranked in their order of relevance to a search query entered by the user. In addition to the relevance rating, Lycos indicates how many terms in the original search string were matched, which is helpful because Lycos searches for any specified term, and not all specified terms. By default, Lycos provides a linkable title, an outline, an abstract, and a universal resource listing (URL) for every page that it returns.

 **For more information about Lycos, surf the Web to** `http://www.lycos.com.`

Lynx

A World Wide Web (WWW) character-based (hypertext file reader) browser for users on both UNIX and Virtual Memory System (VMS) platforms who are connected to those systems through cursor-addressable, character-cell terminals or emulators.

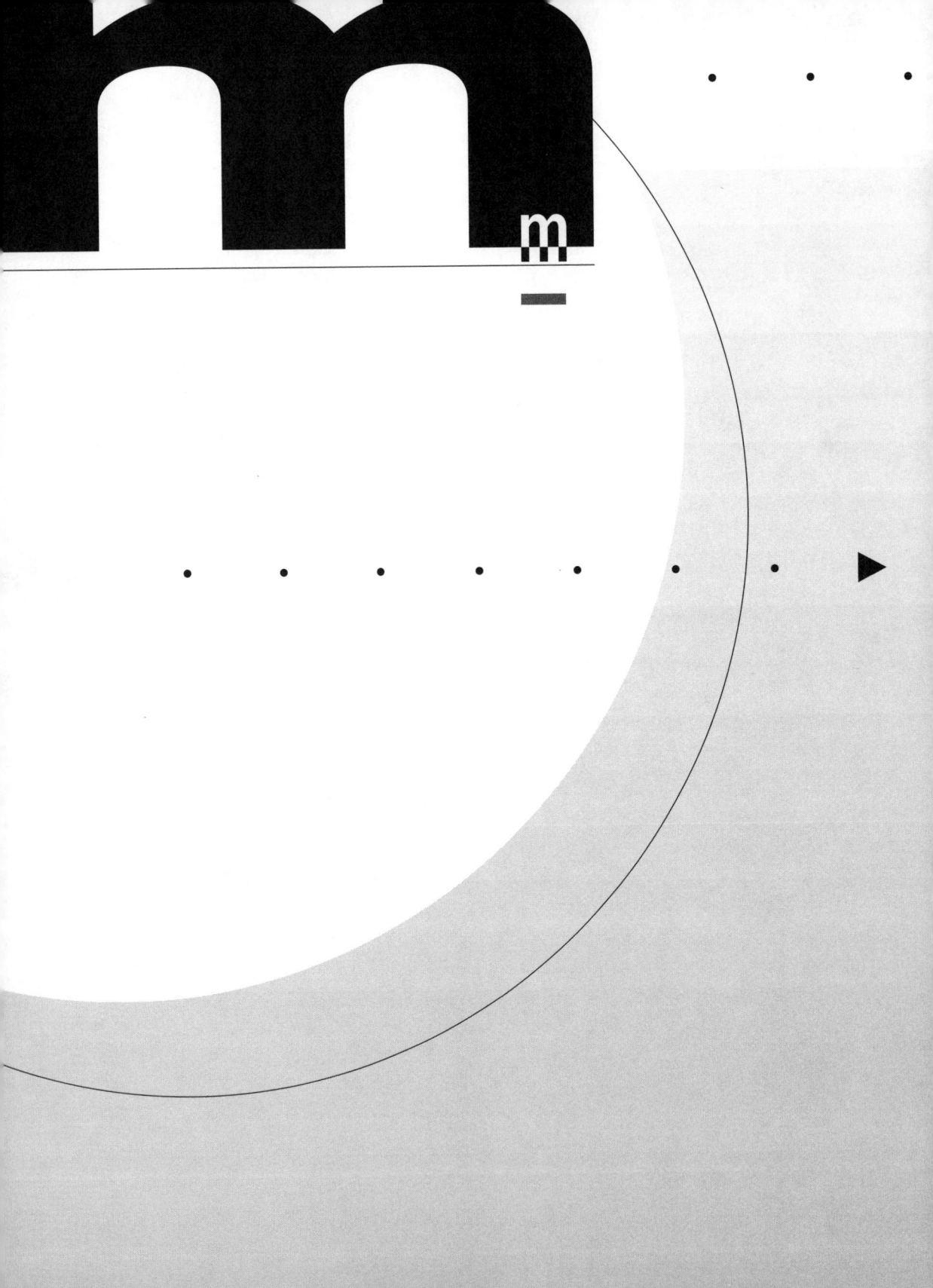

M13

A telecommunications method used to multiplex 28 T1 channels into 1 T3 channel.
See also **T1 multiplexer; T3 channel.**

MAC

Media-Access Control, one of two sublayers of the Data-Link Layer (Layer 2 of the OSI Reference Model) that controls the use of network hardware and governs access to transmission media. This sublayer is defined in the Institute of Electronic and Electrical Engineers (IEEE) 802.*x* set of local-area network (LAN) standards. The other sublayer in the Data-Link Layer is the Logical-Link Control (LLC) Sublayer.
See also **Data-Link Layer; Institute of Electronic and Electrical Engineers; Logical-Link Control; OSI Reference Model.**

MAC Convergence Function (MCF)

A Distributed-Queue Dual-Bus (DQDB) network function that prepares data from a connectionless service.
See also **connectionless service.**

MAC Sublayer

Media-Access Control, one of two sublayers of the Data-Link Layer (Layer 2 of the OSI Reference Model) that controls the use of network hardware and governs access to transmission media. This sublayer is defined in the Institute of Electronic and Electrical Engineers (IEEE) 802.*x* set of local-area network (LAN) standards. The other sublayer in the Data-Link Layer is the Logical-Link Control (LLC) Sublayer.

See also **Data-Link Layer; Institute of Electronic and Electrical Engineers; Logical-Link Control; OSI Reference Model.**

MAC.NAM (NLM)

A NetWare Loadable Module (NLM) that loads support for the long filenames and file formats of the Macintosh operating system onto the NetWare server. This NLM is used in conjunction with the ADD NAME SPACE console command, which assigns the name space to a particular volume.

MacBinary

A Macintosh file-transfer protocol that ensures the proper transmission of Macintosh files over a modem.
See also **modem.**

MACFILE (NLM)

In IntranetWare, a file utility that provides support for the Macintosh operating system on a NetWare server. This NetWare Loadable Module (NLM) provides maintenance for the Macintosh operating system desktop database.
See also **NetWare Loadable Module.**

Mach

A variation of the UNIX operating system that supports multitasking and multiprocessing. Mach was the first operating system to use a microkernel as an alternative to the traditional operating system kernel.
See also **kernel; multiprocessing; multitasking; UNIX.**

machine language

A native binary language used internally by a computer. Machine language is the result of high-level programming code being assembled, compiled, or interpreted into a format the computer uses to process instructions.

MacHTTP

A Macintosh program for supplying World Wide Web (WWW) pages over the Internet to browser clients. Initially released as shareware, the program now is available from the StarNine division of Quarterdeck. The *HTTP* in this product name stands for *HyperText Transfer Protocol*.

See also **HyperText Transfer Protocol; Web browser.**

Macintosh

A personal computer from Apple Computer, Inc., that features a user-friendly *graphical user interface* (GUI) and uses a proprietary operating system to simulate the user's desktop on-screen display. Because all but the earliest models of the Macintosh have built-in networking capabilities, no Network Interface Card (NIC) or adapters are required. A Macintosh is also known as a *Mac*.

Macintosh client

A Macintosh computer that has been attached to a NetWare for Macintosh network. Using AppleTalk, a Macintosh client can store data on and retrieve data from a NetWare for Macintosh server. A Macintosh client also is capable of running executable network files, sharing files with other clients, and monitoring queues.

Macintosh File System (MFS)

A system for storing Macintosh files in a flat structure common on early models of the Macintosh computer. Newer models use a hierarchical file structure but can still read disks created with the flat-file structure.

See also **Hierarchical File System.**

Macintosh files

Macintosh computer files that contain a data fork (information specified by the user) and a resource fork (file information, including Macintosh-specific information such as the windows and icons used with the file). Macintosh clients on a NetWare or IntranetWare network system access both the data and resource forks of requested Macintosh files, because both forks are required for the Macintosh to read the file. Non-Macintosh clients, on the other hand, access only the data fork of a Macintosh file. When Macintosh clients copy Macintosh files from one location to another on a NetWare server (either by using the NCOPY command or by dragging and dropping), both the data fork and the resource fork are copied. In order for Macintosh files to be stored on a NetWare server, the MAC.NAM NetWare Loadable Module (NLM) must be linked with the NetWare operating computer.

See also **MAC.NAM; MACFILE.**

Macintosh user

A general term describing a user at a Macintosh workstation.

MacIPX

An implementation of the Internet Packet Exchange (IPX) designed for NetWare for Macintosh networks. Configuration for MacIPX is performed through the MacIPX control panel.

MacNCP

An implementation of the NetWare Core Protocol (NCP) designed for NetWare for Macintosh networks. Configuration for MacNCP is performed through the MacIPX control panel, which enables a user to specify and verify a username, a Novell Directory Services (NDS) context, and a preferred Directory tree.

See also **NCP; NetWare Core Protocol; Novell Directory Services.**

MacNDS

A suite of client software packages for NetWare for Macintosh that includes MacIPX, MacNCP, the NetWare User-Authentication Method (UAM), and NetWare aliases.

See also **MacIPX; MacNCP; User-Authentication Method.**

macro

A collection of keystroke commands and instructions stored in a file and executed by typing a single command at the command line. A macro automates a complex or repet-

itive sequence of application commands and is similar to login scripts that are executed through NetWare.

See also **login script.**

MacTCP

A Macintosh version of the Transmission-Control Protocol/Internet Protocol (TCP/IP) suite used to connect a Macintosh to the Internet and to intranetworks.

See also **Transmission-Control Protocol/Internet Protocol.**

MacWeb

A Macintosh World Wide Web (WWW) browser from TradeWave Corporation that integrates with the company's TradeWave Galaxy package, which is a combination of business-oriented Web pages and Internet tools (including publishing software). The package offers built-in newsreaders and electronic mail (e-mail) support.

See also **newsreader; Web browser.**

MacZilla

A Macintosh Netscape Navigator plug-in from Knowledge Engineering that plays back digital movies and audio.

MAGAZINE utility

In NetWare 4.*x* and IntranetWare, a server console utility that issues the prompts *Insert Magazine* and *Remove Magazine*, which refer to hardware devices holding several pieces of media. The user may respond that the media is inserted, not inserted, removed, or not removed.

mail

In the context of electronic communications, messages sent to one or more recipients by electronic mail (e-mail), voicemail, or videomail. Mail can be read by the recipient at a later time.

mail bridge

A connecting device that filters mail transmissions between networks. Criteria is specified to determine what mail is passed between the networks.

mail-delivery system

An electronic-mail system that may include a *mail server* (a program for managing mail delivery), a *mail directory* (the directory on the network system designated for electronic mail), a *mailbox* (a user's repository to store messages), and a *mail exploder* (a program, also known as a *mailbot*, that delivers messages to all recipients on a mailing list).

See also **electronic mail; mailbox, mail bridge; mailbot.**

MAIL directory

NetWare's SYS:MAIL directory, created during network installation and used by electronic-mail programs compatible with NetWare. For versions prior to NetWare 4.*x*, the MAIL directory was a repository for user login scripts. Upgrading from older versions to NetWare 4.*x* still retains the old user subdirectories in the MAIL directory, but the login scripts become a property of the new User object. New users created under NetWare 4.*x* do not have subdirectories in the MAIL directory.

See also **login script.**

Mail Exchange record (MX)

A data structure in the Internet Domain-Naming System (DNS) that indicates which machines can handle electronic mail (e-mail) for a particular region of the Internet.

See also **Domain-Naming System; Internet.**

mail filter

An electronic-mail (e-mail) option that provides for the selection of some combination of messages to be placed at the beginning of a list, to be forwarded, to be ignored, and to be deleted.

mail reflector

An electronic-mail (e-mail) feature that sends messages and documents in response to e-mail requests. A mail reflector is also known as a *mailbot*.

See also **LISTSRV; mailbot.**

mail server

A program that manages the delivery of electronic mail (e-mail) or other information upon request. A mail server often is considered part of a mail-delivery system.

See also **electronic mail; mail-delivery system.**

mail-stop information

A term describing a facet of addressing in Novell Directory Services (NDS). A mail stop can be recorded for each User object.

Mail-Transfer Agent (MTA)

A component of the electronic-mail (e-mail) system found in the Transmission-Control Protocol/Internet Protocol (TCP/IP) suite. An MTA provides an interface between users (and applications) and the e-mail system, sends and receives messages, and forwards messages between mail servers. Different MTAs communicate with each other using the Simple Mail-Transfer Protocol (SMTP). Users interact with MTAs through user agents, which communicate with the MTA using a protocol such as Post Office Protocol Version 3 (POP3).

See also **electronic mail; Post Office Protocol 3; Transmission-Control Protocol/Internet Protocol; Simple Mail-Transfer Protocol.**

mailbomb

Either a large number of files or one large file sent to an electronic-mail (e-mail) address in an effort to crash the recipient's e-mail system.

mailbot

A program that automatically sends electronic-mail (e-mail) messages or automatically replies to e-mail messages. The term is a contraction for *mail robot.*

mailbox

A repository for the storage of electronic-mail (e-mail) messages. A mailbox does not automatically appear as part of an e-mail package, but rather must be configured through a service provider or by the administrator of an interoffice network.

Mailbox ID

A Directory Schema term and a selectable property for the following objects in Novell Directory Services (NDS): Group, List, Message-Routing Group, Organization, Organizational Role, Organizational Unit, and User. The NetWare utility used to administer mailbox information (either NetWare Administrator or NETADMIN) assigns a unique name (up to eight characters of the object's name) to an object's mailbox in the NetWare Messaging Database.

See also **container object; leaf object; Novell Directory Services; object.**

Mailbox Location

A Directory Schema term and a selectable property for the following objects in Novell Directory Services (NDS): Group, Message-Routing Group, Organization, Organizational Role, Organizational Unit, and User. Mailbox Location is the name of the Messaging Server where an object's mailbox resides.

See also **container object; leaf object; Novell Directory Services; object.**

mail-enabled application

An application that includes an electronic-mail (e-mail) function and other functions (such as contact-management software, intelligent mail handling, and workflow automation).

Mailing Label Information

A selectable property for the User object in Novell Directory Services (NDS).

See also **leaf object; Novell Directory Services; object.**

mailing list

A type of electronic-mail (e-mail) address that remails any incoming mail to a list of recipients, known as *subscribers*. Because mailing lists are topic-specific, subscribers can pick mailing lists of interest.

mailto

A World Wide Web (WWW) page feature that creates a pre-addressed electronic-mail (e-mail) form (including a link to the Web page) that visitors may use to return feedback, report errors, or participate in surveys.

See also **World Wide Web.**

Main Distribution Frame (MDF)

A central distribution point (usually a wiring closet) for the wiring of a building. An MDF may be connected directly to a user's workstation or to an intermediate distribution point.

See also **wiring closet.**

main function

A developer-written function that executes as the initial thread of a NetWare Loadable Module (NLM). Program execution begins with the main function.

main menu

The first menu that appears when running a utility, especially a DOS-based utility in NetWare or IntranetWare.

mainframe system

A large-scale, multiuser computer system managing large amounts of data and computing tasks. A mainframe system normally is supplied complete with peripherals and software by companies such as Burroughs, Control Data, IBM, Univac, and others.

Maintenance-Operation Protocol (MOP)

A protocol from Digital Equipment Corporation that provides a way to perform primitive maintenance operations on a DECnet network system.

See also **DECnet.**

maintenance release

A low-level update to software that includes minor bug fixes or the addition of minor features. A higher-level update that fixes major bugs or introduces major features is called a major release. Version numbers on the software indicate the level of the update. For example, software with a release version number of 4.0 indicates a major release; a version number of 4.1 indicates a maintenance release.

major resource

A resource defined by NetWare's Target Service Agent (TSA) that contains data to be backed up as a group (such as data on a server or volume). A major resource is recognized by the SBACKUP NetWare Loadable Module (NLM).

See also **minor resource; NetWare Loadable Module; SBACKUP; Target Service Agent.**

MAKEUSER utility

In NetWare 3.12, a server console utility that allows a supervisor or workgroup manager to create and delete users on a regular basis or when many users must be created. The supervisor or workgroup manager creates a USR file containing keywords necessary to create and assign rights and restrictions to new users or to delete existing users.

Malachi

A product from En Technology that enables the downloading of software through a television set. Malachi components include an adapter for a personal computer, a cable to connect the computer with the television, and software.

male connector

A cable connector with pins that are designed to engage with the sockets on a female connector.

See also **female connector; jack.**

MAN

metropolitan-area network, a network that spans a larger geographical area than a local-area network (LAN) but a smaller geographic area than a wide-area network (WAN).

See also **local-area network; wide-area network.**

managed object

A network device managed by either network-management software or a protocol suite such as Simple Network-Management Protocol (SNMP).

See also **Simple Network-Management Protocol.**

Management Domain (MD)

An area defined by the X.400 Message-Handling System (MHS) from the Consultative Committee for International Telegraphy and Telephony (CCITT), whose message-handling capabilities operate under the control of a single management domain. The two types of MDs are the Administrative Management Domain (ADMD) and the Private Management Domain (PRMD).

See also **Administrative Management Domain; Consultative Committee for International Telegraphy and Telephony; Message-Handling System; Private Management Domain; X.400.**

Management Information Base (MIB)

A database of network-management information and objects used by the Common Management-Information Protocol (CMIP) and the Simple Network-Management Protocol (SNMP). Each network-management service has its own set of objects for different types of devices or for different network-management protocols.

See also **Common Management-Information Protocol; Simple Network-Management Protocol.**

Management Information System (MIS)

A computer-based information system within a company that integrates data from all the departments it serves and provides company management with necessary decision-making data, tracks progress, and solves problems.

management services

Functions for the System Network Architecture (SNA) that are distributed among network components to manage and control an SNA network.

See also **System Network Architecture.**

ManageWise

Novell's network-management software package that includes NetWare and Windows NT server management, desktop management, network analysis, automated network inventory, remote control, software management, and virus prevention. The product is designed to detect and repair such network problems as printing problems, limited access to applications, slow network response time, disk failures, limited storage space on the server, and critical node monitoring. ManageWise also monitors more than 2,000 server conditions, including the network directory, disk drives, volumes, memory, logged-in users, and installed-and-running software.

managing process

Software that initiates network requests for data from managing agents (programs monitoring the activity of workstations) and per-

forms any analysis on the data. The managing process software operates on a dedicated machine known as the managing station.

Manchester encoding

A digital scheme used in Ethernet networks to encode data and timing signals in the same transmitted data stream. Manchester encoding uses a mid-bit-time transition for clocking; a 1 denotes a high level during the first half of the bit time.

manual key

A modified form of the null key used to exclude particular records from a database index. In Btrieve, for example, if every byte of one segment in a manual key contains a null value, then Btrieve excludes the key from the index.

See also **Btrieve; null key.**

Manufacturing Automation Protocol (MAP)

A specification outlining the automation of tasks in a computer-integrated manufacturing or factory environment. MAP was originally formulated by General Motors to assist in procurement.

Manufacturing Message Service (MMS)

A service, used in automated production lines, that enables a computer application on a control machine to communicate with an application on a slave machine.

map

In the context of NetWare, the assignment of a drive letter or directory path by a DOS or OS/2 client on a NetWare volume. For example, if a client maps drive F to the SYS:MARKETNG/PRODUCT subdirectory, then that subdirectory is accessed each time the client changes to drive F.

In the context of the Internet, a map is a list of actual addresses used for message delivery in lieu of certain nominal or symbolic addresses. A map also refers to a specific region on a Web page that reports coordinates of any mouse clicks within its border, enabling server programs to respond accordingly.

See also **Web page.**

MAP

Manufacturing Automation Protocol, a specification outlining the automation of tasks in a computer-integrated manufacturing or factory environment. MAP was originally formulated by General Motors to assist in procurement.

MAP utility

In NetWare and IntranetWare, a workstation utility that enables users to view drive mappings, create (or change) network or search drive mappings, or map a drive to a fake root directory for applications that require a root directory. If drive mappings are not included in the login script, they must be manually re-created each time the user logs in. As many as 26 mappings (including local drives) are allowed. Search drive mappings begin at the end of the alphabet with the letter Z and work backward.

See also **map; mapping.**

MAPI

(1) Messaging Application Program Interface, a messaging-service and mail-service interface from Microsoft that provides functions for Microsoft Mail within a Windows application.

(2) Microsoft API, an Application Program Interface (API) from Microsoft that adds messaging capabilities to any Windows application by handling the details of directory service and message storage and forwarding.

See also **(1) Microsoft Mail; (2) Application Program Interface.**

mapped conversation

A conversation occurring between two transaction programs that are using the Advanced Program-to-Program Communication (APPC) Application Program Interface (API).

mapping

The assignment of a drive letter to a particular logical disk drive.

margin

An allowance for signal loss through attenuation or simply over time during a signal transmission.

Mariner

A World Wide Web (WWW) browser from NCD Software. Mariner includes an access-control feature that enables users to lock out certain Uniform Resource Locators (URLs) that may be deemed inappropriate for children.

See also **Web browser.**

mark parity

A parity setting in which the parity bit is always set to 1 and as the eighth bit.

See also **parity bit.**

markup tag

A formatting or inclusion tag in an editing program that serves as an instruction to a processing or reading program. A markup tag is not visible until the file is passed through an appropriate program. A familiar use of markup tags occurs in the HyperText Markup Language (HTML) used to create Web pages, where tags represent document layout instructions and links to other places in a file. Markup tags are placed within angle brackets (< >).

See also **HyperText Markup Language; Web home page; Web browser.**

masquerade

A threat to network security imposed by either a program that purports to perform a function other than one it is intended to perform or a user pretending to be someone else.

master-key password

A security password that controls access to the entire operating system. When a computer system is started, the operating system prompts for the master key password.

See also **password.**

master replica

A Novell Directory Services (NDS) Directory replica that contains the first instance of partition information and is used to change the structure of the Directory tree in relation to that partition. Other Directory replica types include Read/Write replicas, Read-Only replicas, and subordinate replicas. Although many Directory replicas can exist, only one master replica is allowed, and it always is considered the most accurate Directory replica.

See also **Read-Only replica; Read/Write replica; subordinate replica; Novell Directory Services.**

MATHLIB utility

In NetWare and IntranetWare, a server console utility that provides mathematical functions to CLIB (the NetWare Loadable Module C interface utility). This utility is used on servers that have a math coprocessor installed. Both the STREAMS and CLIB utilities must be loaded before MATHLIB can be loaded.

MATHLIBC utility

In NetWare 4.*x* and IntranetWare, a server console utility that provides mathematical functions to CLIB (the NetWare Loadable Module C interface utility). This utility automatically uses a floating-point emulator and works on servers that do not have a math coprocessor installed. Both the STREAMS and CLIB utilities must be loaded before MATHLIBC can be loaded.

mating

The joining of two connectors to complete a circuit or establish a network link. Mating usually occurs between male and female connectors.

See also **connector; connectivity; jack.**

MAU

(1) **Medium-Attachment Unit,** a device that detects collisions and injects bits onto the network. The MAU works on the Physical Layer (Layer 1) of the OSI Reference Model and complies with the Institute of Electronic and Electrical Engineers (IEEE) 802.3 standard.

(2) **Multistation Access Unit,** a multiport wiring hub used on Token Ring networks that can connect as many as eight nodes (or lobes) to a ring network. An MAU is also known as a Controlled-Access Unit (CAU).

See also (1) **Collision Detection and Avoidance;** (1) **IEEE 802.x;** (1) **OSI Reference Model;** (2) **Controlled-Access Unit;** (2) **Token Ring.**

maxdata

A term describing the maximum data size for a frame on a network link.

Maximum Connections

A Directory Schema term and a selectable property for the User object in Novell Directory Services (NDS).

See also **leaf object; Novell Directory Services; object.**

Maximum-Receive Unit (MRU)

An option in the Link-Control Protocol (LCP). The MRU enables a sender to inform a peer that the sender can receive larger frames than specified in the default, or to request that the peer send smaller frames.

See also **Link-Control Protocol.**

Maximum-Rights Mask (MRM)

A NetWare 2.2 list of trustee directory rights granted to users. The MRM has been replaced by the Inherited-Rights Mask (IRM) in NetWare 3.x and the Inherited-Rights Filter in NetWare 4.x.

Table M.1 lists the access rights available in NetWare 2.2.

Table M.1: NetWare 2.2 Access Rights

Right	Description
Access Control (A)	Change trustee assignments and the MRM.
Create (C)	Create a new file or directory.
Erase (E)	Delete a file or directory.
File Scan (F)	See files in directory listings.
Modify (M)	Change a file or directory name or attributes, but not content.
Read (R)	Open and read a file.
Write (W)	Open and write to a file.

See also **access rights; Inherited-Rights Mask; Inherited-Rights Filter.**

Maximum-Transmission Unit (MTU)

Specified in bytes, the largest packet size that can be sent on a physical network medium. As an example, the MTU for Ethernet is 1,500 bytes.

MB

(Also **M**) **megabyte,** a unit of measure equaling 2^{20} (or 1,048,576) bytes most commonly used in the context of computer memory or disk storage capacity. A megabyte equals 1,024 kilobytes.
See also **kilobyte.**

Mb

(Also *Mbit*) **megabit,** a unit of measure equaling 2^{20} (or 1,048,576) binary digits (or bits) often used as an equivalent to 1 million bits.
See also **kilobit.**

mBED

mBED Software's line of multimedia Web-page-authoring tools and Web browser plug-ins that enables the user to create multimedia Web sites.
See also **Web page.**

M-bit

The **more-data mark,** a bit that is a component of a user packet and, when set, identifies the next packet sent as a logical continuation of the data contained in the current packet.

Mbit/s

Megabits per second, a unit of measure equaling 2^{20} (or 1,048,576) bits of data being transferred to and from peripheral devices every second.

MBONE

Multicast Backbone, a multicast, virtual network that adds live audio and video capabilities to the Internet. An MBONE network is organized as clusters of networks connected by *tunnels* (paths between end-points that support multicast transmissions); these networks support multicast Internet Protocol (IP) transmissions.
See also **Internet Protocol; virtual network.**

Mbps

Megabits per second, a unit of measure equaling 2^{20} (or 1,048,576) bits of data being transferred to and from peripheral devices every second.

MCA

MicroChannel Architecture, an IBM bus developed for higher models of the PS/2 line of computers that includes 32-bit transfer and software configuration of expansion boards.

MCF

MAC Convergence Function, a Distributed-Queue Dual-Bus (DQDB) network function that prepares data from a connectionless service.
See also **connectionless service.**

MCI

Media-Control Interface, an interface used to control multimedia files and devices.

MCI Mail

An electronic-mail (e-mail) system from MCI that provides links to the Internet. More than one user may have the same username within the MCI e-mail system.

MD

Management Domain, an area defined by the X.400 Message-Handling System (MHS) from the Consultative Committee for International Telegraphy and Telephony (CCITT), whose message-handling capabilities operate under the control of a single management domain. The two types of MDs are the Administrative Management Domain (ADMD) and the Private Management Domain (PRMD).

See also **Administrative Management Domain; Consultative Committee for International Telegraphy and Telephony; Message-Handling System; Private Management Domain; X.400.**

MD5

Message Digest 5 Algorithm, a proposed encryption method for the Simple Network-Management Protocol (SNMP) that uses a message, an authentication key, and time information to formulate a checksum value known as a *digest*.

See also **Simple Network-Management Protocol.**

MDF

Main Distribution Frame, a central distribution point (usually a wiring closet) for the wiring of a building. An MDF may be connected directly to a user's workstation or to an intermediate distribution point.

See also **wiring closet.**

mean time between failures (MTBF)

A statistically derived average length of time (expressed in thousands or tens of thousands of hours) that a computer system or component operates before failing.

mean time to repair (MTTR)

A statistically derived average length of time it takes to repair a failing computer system or component.

media

The plural of *medium*, a term describing the physical paths over which communications flow (for example, copper wires, coaxial cables, or fiber-optic cables).

See also **medium.**

Media-Access Control (MAC)

One of two sublayers of the Data-Link Layer (Layer 2 of the OSI Reference Model) that controls the use of network hardware and governs access to transmission media. This sublayer is defined in the Institute of Electronic and Electrical Engineers (IEEE) 802.*x* set of local-area network (LAN) standards. The other sublayer in the Data-Link Layer is the Logical-Link Control (LLC) Sublayer.

See also **Data-Link Layer; Institute of Electronic and Electrical Engineers; Logical-Link Control; OSI Reference Model.**

Media-Control Interface (MCI)

An interface used to control multimedia files and devices.

media filter

A device that converts a Token Ring adapter board output signal to work with a specific type of wiring.
See also **cable; Token Ring.**

media label

A label describing the information contained on electronic media.

media-management NLM

A type of NetWare Loadable Module (NLM) that supports NetWare's High-Capacity Storage System (HCCS) by providing access to alternative types of media.
See also **High-Capacity Storage System; NetWare Loadable Module.**

Media Manager (MM)

A NetWare database that tracks all peripheral storage devices and media attached to NetWare servers and enables applications to access or gain information from the devices and media. This database receives input/output requests from applications and converts them to messages compatible with the NetWare Peripheral Architecture (NPA).

See also **NetWare Peripheral Architecture.**

media-set ID

Identification information attached to electronic media to help identify their contents. The media-set ID is commonly used for backup tape cartridges.

MEDIA utility

In NetWare 4.*x* and IntranetWare, a server console utility that responds to the *Insert Media* and *Remove Media* prompts. The user may respond that the medium is inserted, not inserted, removed, or not removed.

media-access method

A strategy on the Data-Link Layer (Layer 2) of the OSI Reference Model that network nodes use to access a network transmission medium. A common media-access method is Carrier-Sense Multiple-Access/Collision Detection (CSMA/CD).
See also **Carrier-Sense Multiple-Access/Collision Detection; OSI Reference Model.**

medium

Physical components of a network system (usually cables or wires) that carry information from one point to another.

Medium-Attachment Unit (MAU)

A device that detects collisions and injects bits onto the network. The MAU works on the Physical Layer (Layer 1) of the OSI

Reference Model and complies with the Institute of Electronic and Electrical Engineers (IEEE) 802.3 standard.

See also **Collision Detection and Avoidance; IEEE 802.x; MAU; OSI Reference Model.**

Medium-Interface Connector (MIC)

A connector conforming to the Fiber Distributed Data Interface (FDDI) *de facto* standard.

See also **de facto standard; Fiber Distributed Data Interface.**

megabit (Mbit)

A unit of measure equaling 2^{20} (or 1,048,576) binary digits (or bits) often used as an equivalent to 1 million bits. Another abbreviation is **Mb**.

See also **kilobit.**

megabits per second (Mbit/s, Mbps)

A unit of measure equaling 2^{20} (or 1,048,576) bits of data being transferred to and from peripheral devices every second.

See also **kilobits per second.**

megabyte (MB)

A unit of measure equaling 2^{20} (or 1,048,576) bytes most commonly used in the context of computer memory or disk storage capacity. A megabyte equals 1,024 kilobytes; it can also be abbreviated as *M*.

See also **kilobyte.**

megahertz (MHz)

A unit of measure equaling one million cycles per second. The speed at which a computer's processor operates (the *clock speed*) is often expressed in megahertz.

Member

In Novell Directory Services (NDS), a Directory Schema term and a selectable property for the Group, List, and Message-Routing Group objects.

See also **leaf object; Novell Directory Services; object.**

MEMMAP utility

A NetWare Loadable Module (NLM) that displays the addresses of the code and data area of each NLM currently loaded on the file server. This utility is useful in translating reported memory access information.

See also **NetWare Loadable Module.**

Memory

In Novell Directory Services (NDS), a Directory Schema term and a selectable property for the Printer object.

See also **leaf object; Novell Directory Services; object.**

memory

A capacity of internal dynamic data storage that can be accessed by a computer's operating system. Two types of memory are read-only memory (ROM) and random-access memory (RAM).

ROM is installed on the computer's motherboard by the manufacturer and contains firmware such as the computer Basic Input/Output System (BIOS).

RAM accepts and holds binary data, including the data being operated on and the program that directs the operations performed. RAM stores the information and accesses any part of the information upon request.

Table M.2 shows the types of RAM found in DOS. Figure M.1 shows how memory is addressed in personal computers running DOS.

memory address

An exact memory location that stores a particular data item or program instruction.

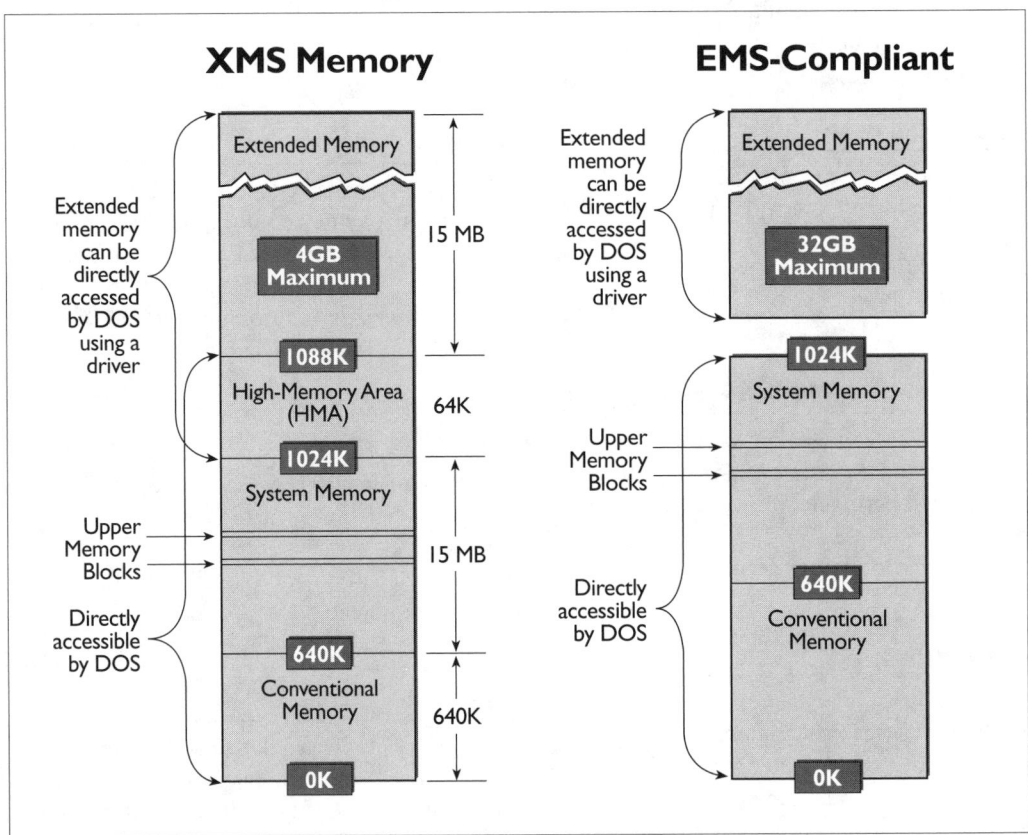

Figure M.1
Memory addressing in DOS

Table M.2: DOS Memory Types

Type	Description
Conventional Memory (also known as *low DOS memory* or *base memory*)	Located below 640K. Devoted to running programs and applications.
Expanded Memory	Located outside normal address space of DOS. Can be addressed in 16K units (also known as pages) in areas known as page frames. Designed to store data and numbers. Available for computers that have 8086, 8088, and 80286 microprocessors through memory boards compliant with the expanded memory specification (EMS). Available for computers that have 80386 and 80486 microprocessors through EMS emulators.
Extended Memory	Located above the 1MB address limit of DOS. Used for RAM disks and disk caching routines. Computers that have 80286 microprocessors can address up to 16MB of extended memory. Computers that have 80386 and 80486 microprocessors can address up to 4GB of extended memory. With DOS drivers, extended memory from 1,024K to 1,088K (defined as the high-memory area, or HMA) can be addressed. DOS extenders that comply with the extended memory specification (XMS) can address memory above 1,088K.
Upper Memory	Can mean system memory (between 640K and 1,024K), HMA (1,024K to 1,088K), extended memory (above 1,024K), or expanded memory (also above 1,024K).
High-Memory Area (HMA)	Located in the first 64K of extended memory (1,024K to 1,088K). Can be addressed directly by DOS in real mode by using such device drivers as HIMEM.SYS. Provides additional memory addressed directly by DOS and functions in a fashion similar to conventional memory. Available on computers that have 80286, 80386, and 80486 microprocessors with more than 1,024K of RAM installed.
System Memory (also known as *high DOS memory*, *high memory*, *HMA*, or *upper memory*)	Located between 640K and 1,024K. Not usually addressed by DOS or applications. Can be addressed by computers with 80386 or 80486 microprocessors that use special control programs to make upper memory blocks (UMBs) in system memory.
Upper Memory Block (UMB)	Located between 640K and 1,024K. Directly addressed by DOS and applications. Defined by the XMS specification and created by a driver (such as EMM386.EXE by converting unused address spaces in system memory to UMBs.

memory allocation

The reservation of specific memory locations in random-access memory (RAM) for processes, instructions, and data. During the installation of a computer system, the installer allocates memory for such items as disk caches, RAM disks, extended memory, and expanded memory. Operating systems and applications allocate memory to meet certain requirements but can use only memory that is actually available. Memory is reallocated between resources to optimize performance.

An example of memory allocation is NetWare's use of memory allocation pools. NetWare 3.*x* uses five or more memory allocation pools. During continuous operation of a NetWare 3.*x* server, applications may run out of memory because memory is not always released back to the operating system. NetWare 4.*x* alleviates this problem by using only one allocation memory pool so that memory-management operations are reduced.

memory board

An add-on card or board that increases the amount of random-access memory (RAM) within a personal computer.

memory buffer

An area of memory that serves as a temporary storage site for data. Buffers often are used to compensate for differences between transmission and processing speeds or to hold data until a peripheral device becomes available.

See also **memory.**

memory cache

A high-speed memory area on a microprocessor storing commonly used code or data that comes from slower memory. A memory cache eliminates the need to access a computer system's main memory to fetch instructions.

See also **memory.**

memory chip

A computer chip holding data or program instructions. A random-access memory (RAM) chip stores the information temporarily, and a read-only memory (ROM) chip stores the information permanently.

See also **memory; random-access memory; read-only memory.**

memory disk

A designated portion of random-access memory (RAM) made to act like a fast disk drive. A memory disk is also known as a *RAM disk* or a *virtual disk*.

memory dump

A printed, displayed, or saved copy of the status of a specific internal memory area in a computer that shows the values of the variables stored in that memory area.

See also **memory address.**

memory management

A process of managing the manner in which a computer handles memory and memory allocation.

See also **memory; memory allocation.**

memory-management unit (MMU)

The part of a computer microprocessor responsible for managing the mapping of virtual memory addresses to actual physical addresses. The MMU can be a separate chip (as was the case in early Intel or Motorola microprocessors) or part of the central processing unit (CPU) chip.

See also **central processing unit; physical memory; virtual memory.**

memory map

The organization and allocation of computer memory. A memory map provides an indication of how much memory is being used by the operating system and underlying application programs.

MEMORY MAP utility

In NetWare 4.*x* and IntranetWare, a server console utility that displays the amount of memory allocated to DOS and to the server.

memory pool

A finite supply of memory (not necessarily contiguous) reserved for specific NetWare function requests and for file caching.

See also **memory allocation.**

memory protection

A NetWare 4.*x* process that protects NetWare server memory from corruption by NetWare Loadable Modules (NLMs). This process uses the DOMAIN NLM to create the OS_PROTECTED domain, which provides limited entry points into the

default OS domain (thereby protecting the operating-system memory from unauthorized access). The need for the DOMAIN NLM was eliminated in NetWare 4.11.

See also **DOMAIN.**

MEMORY utility

In NetWare and IntranetWare, a server console utility that displays the total amount of installed memory that the operating system can address. NetWare 3.1 and later versions address memory above 16MB on Extended Industry-Standard Architecture (EISA) bus computers. All versions of NetWare can address memory only up to 16MB on Industry-Standard Architecture (ISA) bus computers. NetWare 4.1 can address up to 64MB on a Peripheral-Connect Interconnect (PCI) computer.

Memory Utilization

In NetWare 4.02, a field name in the Available Options screen of the NetWare Loadable Module (NLM).

See also **MONITOR; NetWare Loadable Module.**

MENU utility

A text utility through which a NetWare network administrator can create customized menus for other users. In NetWare 3.12 and NetWare 4.*x*, the MENU utility was replaced by the enhanced NMENU utility.

See also **NMENU utility.**

menu command

A command in a menu source code file indicating the beginning of a menu.

menu utility

A utility enabling NetWare users to access workstation utilities from the DOS or OS/2 operating system. Options are presented as items in a menu rather than by icons or other graphical elements.

MENUCNVT utility

In IntranetWare, a workstation utility that converts menu programs created with the MENU utility in NetWare 3.12 into menu programs supported by IntranetWare's NMENU utility.

MENUMAKE utility

In IntranetWare, a workstation utility that creates a menu program for users to use when they work on the network. This utility actually compiles text utility files into a menu program.

MERIT

A regional network located in Michigan and affiliated with Advanced Network Services (ANS).

See also **Advanced Network Services.**

mesh network topology

A physical network topology in which at least two paths lead to and from each network node. This type of topology provides backup connections in the event of connection failures between nodes.

Figure M.2 shows an example of mesh network topology.

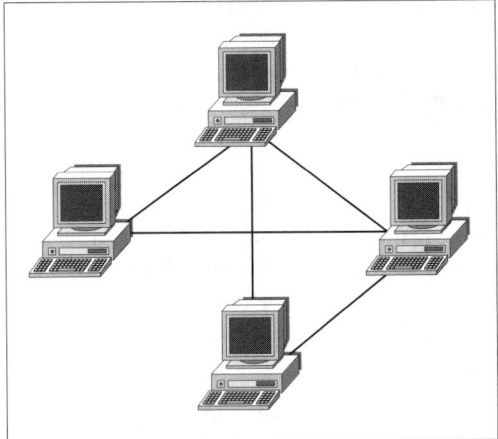

Figure M.2
Mesh network topology

message

A logical grouping of information at the Application Layer (Layer 7) of the OSI Reference Model.

See also **OSI Reference Model.**

message channel

A form of multitasking, interprocess communication that allows two programs running on the same computer to share information.

Message Digest 5 Algorithm (MD5)

A proposed encryption method for the Simple Network-Management Protocol (SNMP) that uses a message, an authentication key, and time information to formulate a checksum value known as a *digest*.

See also **Simple Network-Management Protocol.**

Message-Handling System (MHS)

A store-and-forward technology from Novell that handles the sending of electronic mail (e-mail) messages, fax services, calendar and scheduling services, and workflow automation. NetWare Global MHS also offers optional modules for accessing such messaging environments as UNIX, Transmission-Control Protocol/Internet Protocol (TCP/IP), Open Systems Interconnect (OSI), IBM mainframes, Macintosh, and OS/2. MHS has largely been superseded by Novell's GroupWise system.

See also **GroupWise; Open Systems Interconnect; Transmission-Control Protocol/Internet Protocol; UNIX.**

message packet

A network communications unit of information.

Message-Routing Group

In Novell Directory Services (NDS), a selectable property for the Messaging Server object.

See also **leaf object; Novell Directory Services; object.**

Message-Routing Group object

In NetWare and IntranetWare, a leaf object in Novell Directory Services (NDS) that represents a group of messaging servers that can send and receive messages among themselves. A Message-Routing Group object can have the following properties: Access-Control List, Authority Revocation, Back Link, Bindery, CA Private Key, CA Public Key, Certificate Revocation, Certificate-Validity Interval, Common Name (CN), Cross-Certificate Pair, Description, E-Mail Address, Full Name, GID, Last Referenced Time, Locality (L), Login Script, Mailbox ID, Mailbox Location, Member, Obituary, Object Class, Organization (O), Organizational Unit (OU), Owner, Profile, Profile Membership, Reference, Revision, and See Also.

See also **leaf object; Novell Directory Services; object.**

Message Server

In Novell Directory Services (NDS), a Directory Schema term and a selectable property for the User object.

See also **leaf object; Novell Directory Services; object.**

Message Store (MS)

A component specified in the Consultative Committee for International Telegraphy and Telephony (CCITT) X.400 Message-Handling System (MHS) in which electronic mail (e-mail) is stored either until it is retrieved by a User Agent (UA) or until an allowable storage time expires.

See also **Consultative Committee for International Telegraphy and Telephony; Message-Handling System; User Agent; X.400.**

message switching

A switching technique that involves sending network messages from node to node, with each message being stored at a node until a forwarding path becomes available.

message system

A communications protocol that resides on top of the Internetwork Packet Exchange (IPX) and provides an engine that enables a network node to send messages to other nodes. Access to the message system is provided in a set of Application Program Interfaces (APIs).

See also **Application Program Interface; Internetwork Packet Exchange.**

Message Tools

A contraction of Message-Enabling Tools, a set of programs that manage the enabling and translation of software string resources. These tools extract text strings from such resources as error messages and menu items, displaying them from the source code so that they can be translated and reinserted.

Message-Transfer Agent (MTA)

A component specified in the Consultative Committee for International Telegraphy and Telephony (CCITT) X.400 Message-Handling System (MHS) that stores (or forwards) electronic-mail (e-mail) messages to a User Agent (UA), another MTA, or to some other authorized recipient.

See also **Consultative Committee for International Telegraphy and Telephony; Message-Handling System; MTA; User Agent; X.400.**

Message-Transfer Layer (MTL)

A component specified by the Consultative Committee for International Telegraphy and Telephony (CCITT) in its X.400 Message-Handling System (MHS) specification. The MTL represents one of two sublayers of the Application Layer (Layer 7) in the OSI Reference Model and provides access to transfer services across a network. The other sublayer (which resides above the MTL) is the User-Agent Layer (UAL).

See also **Consultative Committee for International Telegraphy and Telephony; Message-Handling System; OSI Reference Model; User Agent; User-Agent Layer; X.400.**

Message-Transfer Service (MTS)

A component specified in the Consultative Committee for International Telegraphy and Telephony (CCITT) X.400 Message-Handling System (MHS) that processes requests from Access Units (AUs), Message Stores (MSs), Message-Transfer Agents (MTAs), and User Agents (UAs).

See also **Access Units; Consultative Committee for International Telegraphy and Telephony; Message-Handling System; Message Stores; Message-Transfer Agents; User Agent; X.400.**

message unit

A unit of data processed by any layer on a network.

Message-Oriented Text-Interchange System (MOTIS)

A Message-Handling System (MHS) developed by the International Standards Organization (ISO). The basic MOTIS elements are compatible with the Consultative Committee for International Telegraphy and Telephony (CCITT) X.400 MHS specifications.

See also **Consultative Committee for International Telegraphy and Telephony; International Standards Organization; Message-Handling System; X.400.**

message-switched network

A network configured so that messages from multiple users can travel along the network at the same time. Also known as a *store-and-forward network*, this system stores messages temporarily and then forwards the messages through routing (or switching) to a destination. In contrast to *packet-switched networks* (in which individual packets are passed to a destination and reassembled there), a message-switched network collects an entire message before forwarding it to a destination.

See also **packet switching; store-and-forward.**

Messaging Application Program Interface (MAPI)

A messaging-service and mail-service interface from Microsoft that provides functions for Microsoft Mail within a Windows application.

See also **MAPI; Microsoft Mail.**

Messaging-Database Location

A Directory Schema term and a selectable property for the Messaging Server object in Novell Directory Services (NDS).

See also **leaf object; Novell Directory Services; object.**

Messaging Server

A Directory Schema term and a selectable property for the NCP Server object in Novell Directory Services (NDS).

See also **leaf object; Novell Directory Services; object.**

Message Server object

In NetWare and IntranetWare, a leaf object in Novell Directory Services (NDS) that represents a messaging server that resides on a NetWare server. When NetWare or IntranetWare is first installed, this object is automatically created and placed in the same Directory tree context as the NetWare Server leaf object. Different types of messaging servers provide different types of connectivity or operate in different environments. NetWare 4, for example, includes a NetWare Basic MHS server, which services messages between NetWare 4 network users. A Global MHS server supports communication across asynchronous links with non-MHS environments (such as Simple Mail-Transfer Protocol, Systems Network Architecture Distribution Services, and X.400).

A Message Server object can have the following properties: Access-Control List, Account Balance, Allow Unlimited Credit, Authority Revocation, Back Link, Bindery,

CA Private Key, CA Public Key, Certificate Revocation, Certificate-Validity Interval, Common Name (CN), Cross Certificate Pair, Description, Full Name, Host Device, Last Referenced Time, Locality (L), Message-Routing Group, Messaging-Database Location, Messaging Server Type, Minimum Account Balance, Network Address, Obituary, Object Class, Organization (O), Organizational Unit (OU), Postmaster, Private Key, Public Key, Reference, Resource, Revision, Security Equals To, Security Flags, See Also, Status, Supported Services, and User Version.

See also **leaf object; Novell Directory Services; object.**

Messaging Server Type

In Novell Directory Services (NDS), a Directory Schema term and a selectable property for the Messaging Server object.

See also **leaf object; Novell Directory Services; object.**

MetaCrawler search engine

A World Wide Web (WWW) search engine from go2net that provides a multithreaded search site that feeds search terms simultaneously to other search engines (such as Lycos, Infoseek Guide, and Inktomi). MetaCrawler compiles all search results from all sources and eliminates any redundancies.

See also **search engine.**

 **For more information, visit Metacrawler's Web site at** `http:// www.metacrawler.com/.`

Metal-Oxide Varistor (MOV)

In an electrical line conditioner or surge protector, a component that intercepts high-voltage spikes from an incoming power supply.

See also **line conditioner; spike.**

metaverse

A term coined by author Neal Stephenson that originally meant a virtual electronic reality but has grown to mean an abstract universe composed of all ideas, messages, and actions circulating through electronic networks.

metering

A process of tracking software availability and use across a network to ensure that software licenses are not being violated or to predict when new copies (or licenses) of a software product must be purchased.

method

A procedure in an object-oriented language that an object executes when it receives a message.

metropolitan-area network (MAN)

A network that spans a larger geographical area than a local-area network (LAN) but a smaller geographic area than a wide-area network (WAN).

See also **local-area network; wide-area network.**

MFM

Modified Frequency Modulation, an encoding scheme used on 40MB or smaller hard-disk drives.

MFS

Macintosh File System, a system for storing Macintosh files in a flat structure common on early models of the Macintosh computer. Newer models use a hierarchical file structure but can still read disks created with the flat-file structure.

See also **Hierarchical File System.**

MHS

Message-Handling System, a store-and-forward technology from Novell that handles the sending of electronic mail (e-mail) messages, fax services, calendar and scheduling services, and workflow automation. NetWare Global MHS also offers optional modules for accessing such messaging environments as UNIX, Transmission-Control Protocol/Internet Protocol (TCP/IP), Open Systems Interconnect (OSI), IBM mainframes, Macintosh, and OS/2. MHS has largely been superseded by Novell's GroupWise system.

See also **GroupWise; Open Systems Interconnect; Transmission-Control Protocol/Internet Protocol; UNIX.**

MHSV

Multimedia Home-Space Viewer, a Windows or Macintosh plug-in for Netscape Navigator (and compatible browsers) that navigates through three-dimensional environments. MHSV is from Paragraph.

See also **Netscape Navigator.**

MHz

megahertz, a unit of measure equaling one million cycles per second. The speed at which a computer's processor operates (the *clock speed*) is often expressed in megahertz.

MIB

Management Information Base, a database of network-management information and objects used by the Common Management-Information Protocol (CMIP) and the Simple Network-Management Protocol (SNMP). Each network-management service has its own set of objects for different types of devices or for different network-management protocols.

See also **Common Management-Information Protocol; Simple Network-Management Protocol.**

MIC

Medium-Interface Connector, a connector conforming to the Fiber Distributed Data Interface (FDDI) *de facto* standard.

See also ***de facto*** **standard; Fiber Distributed Data Interface.**

MicroChannel Architecture (MCA)

An IBM bus developed for higher models of the PS/2 line of computers that includes 32-bit transfer and software configuration of expansion boards.

microbend

A flaw in fiber-optic cable in which tiny bends have occurred in the fiber, which can affect transmissions.

MicroChannel

A proprietary bus architecture from IBM that allows the use of software to set addresses and interrupts for hardware devices. Expansion boards for Micro-Channel Architecture (MCA) are not compatible with machines that have Industry-Standard Architecture (ISA) or Extended Industry-Standard Architecture (EISA) configurations.

See also **Extended Industry-Standard Architecture; Industry-Standard Architecture.**

microcode

A set of low-level instructions that specify what a computer microprocessor does when it executes machine-language code.

See also **machine-language instruction.**

Microcom Networking Protocol (MNP)

A ten-level set of communications protocols from Microcom used as a standard of data compression as well as error detection and correction. The ten levels follow:

- *Levels 1 to 4* define hardware error control.
- *Level 5* describes a 2:1 data-compression method.
- *Level 6* describes a communication protocol beginning with V.22*bis* modulation and switching to V.29 when possible.
- *Level 7* describes a 3:1 data-compression method.
- *Level 8* is undefined.

- *Level 9* contains a proprietary technique for providing good performance over a variety of types of links.
- *Level 10* describes an error-control protocol often used on noisy links.

microcomputer

A computer based on a single-chip microprocessor.

microcrack

A flaw in fiber-optic cable in which tiny cracks have developed in the fiber, which can affect transmissions.

microkernel

A streamlined operating-system kernel that processes only scheduling, loading, and running of tasks; modules running on top of the microkernel run all other operating-system tasks. The microkernel was developed at Carnegie-Mellon University as part of the Mach operating system.

See also **kernel.**

micron

A unit of measure equaling one-millionth of a meter, or 1/25,000 of an inch.

microprocessor

A central processing unit (CPU) that appears on one computer chip. A microprocessor is also known as a *processor*.

Microsoft

A shortened name for Microsoft Corporation, a manufacturer of software applications, operating systems, and some hardware.

Microsoft API (MAPI)

An Application Program Interface (API) from Microsoft that adds messaging capabilities to any Windows application by handling the details of directory service and message storage and forwarding.
See also **MAPI.**

Microsoft Disk Operating System (MS-DOS)

A single-user, single-tasking operating system for personal computers that allocates system resources through either a command line or shell interface. Although similar to IBM's PC-DOS, file sizes and names of device drivers do differ between the two systems.
See also **Disk Operating System.**

Microsoft Mail

An electronic-mail (e-mail) package from Microsoft that is part of Microsoft Office, Windows for Workgroups, and Windows 95. Microsoft Mail is compatible with the Messaging Application Program Interface (MAPI) from Microsoft.
See also **Messaging Application Program Interface; Microsoft Office; Windows 95; Windows for Workgroups.**

Microsoft Network (MSN)

An online service from Microsoft that enables users to exchange messages, read news, seek answers to technical questions, download software, and connect to the Internet.
See also **Windows 95.**

Microsoft Office

An integrated suite of office applications that includes Microsoft's Word (word processing), Excel (spreadsheet), PowerPoint (presentations), Mail (electronic mail), and Access (database) applications.

 **For more information about Microsoft Office, surf the Web to** http://www.microsoft.com/products/default.htm.

Microsoft Windows

(1) **Windows 3.x,** an operating system from Microsoft Corporation that features a multitasking graphical user interface (GUI) environment running on DOS-based computers and a standard interface based on drop-down menus, windowed regions on the screen, and a pointing device (such as a mouse). The three main components of Windows 3.x are the Program Manager (the primary shell program that manages the execution of applications and task switching), the Print Manager (which coordinates printing), and the File Manager (which manages files, directories, and disks). The standard Windows package includes a Write program (word processing), Paint program (graphics), Terminal program (communications), and other utilities.

(2) Windows 95, an operating system from Microsoft that supports preemptive multitasking (multitasking under the control of the operating system) and multithreading (the capability to run multiple parts of a program). Included with the Windows 95 package is the Microsoft Network (MSN), which is an online service package providing electronic mail support, chat forums, Internet access, and information services. In addition to MSN, Windows 95 provides built-in support for peer-to-peer networking, as well as support for Transmission-Control Protocol/Internet Protocol (TCP/IP), Internetwork Packet Exchange/Sequenced Packet Exchange (IPX/SPX), Network Basic Input/Output Service Extended User Interface (NetBEUI), Network-Driver Interface Specification (NDIS), Open Data-Link Interface (ODI), File-Transfer Protocol (FTP), Telnet, Serial-Line Internet Protocol (SLIP), and Point-to-Point Protocol (PPP). Windows 95 is the successor to Windows 3.*x*.

(3) Windows NT, a 32-bit, multitasking, portable operating system introduced by Microsoft in 1993. Based on the Windows graphical user interface (GUI), Windows NT runs Windows and DOS applications, runs OS/2 16-bit applications, and includes 32-bit programs specifically designed to run under Windows NT. This operating system supports the DOS File-Allocation Table (FAT) system, the OS/2 High-Performance File System (HPFS), and its own NT File System (NTFS), as well as multiprocessing, Object Linking and Embedding (OLE), and peer-to-peer networking. Windows NT uses preemptive multitasking with applications capable of executing multiple threads.

(4) Windows NT Advanced Server, a version of the Windows NT operating system that features centralized network management, security functions, disk mirroring, and support for Redundant Array of Inexpensive Disks (RAID) and uninterruptible power supply (UPS).

(5) Windows for Workgroups, a Microsoft application based on the Windows 3.*x* graphical user interface (GUI) that includes added functions for limited networking of computers to allow users to share files, exchange electronic mail (e-mail), maintain a collective calendar of events, and so on.

See also **(1) graphical user interface; (2) File-Transfer Protocol; (2) Internetwork Packet Exchange/Sequenced Packet Exchange; (2) Microsoft Network; (2) Network Basic Input/Output Service Extended User Interface; (2) Open Data-Link Interface; (2) Point-to-Point Protocol; (2) Serial-Line Internet Protocol; (2) Telnet; (2) Transmission-Control Protocol/Internet Protocol; (3) File-Allocation Table; (3) Graphical User Interface; (3) High-Performance File System; (3) NT File System; (3) Object Linking and Embedding; (3) Windows NT** (includes **Figure W.1**).

micro-to-mainframe

A connection between a personal computer (or microcomputer) and a mainframe-based network. This connection includes terminal-emulation software that enables the microcomputer to access data and applications on the mainframe system.

microwave network

A wireless network that uses microwave transmissions to transmit signals between nodes on the network.

See also **microwave transmission.**

microwave transmission

A transmission that occurs in a high bandwidth above 1 gigahertz (GHz) in the electromagnetic spectrum and used in a wireless network. A microwave transmission requires a line of sight between the sender and receiver but can use Earth-based or satellite receivers.

See also **line of sight.**

MID

Information at the beginning of a data packet, (also known as a *Message ID* or a *header*), that typically includes addressing and control information.

See also **header; packet.**

middle-endian

A term that describes the order in which a word's individual bytes are stored. A big-endian system stores high-order bytes at the lower addresses; a little-endian system stores low-order bytes at the lower addresses. Middle-endian systems store somewhere in between.

See also **big-endian; little-endian.**

middleware

Hardware or software that resides between an application program and the computer operating system or the network operating system. Common examples of middleware are a network shell or Common Object-Request Broker Architecture (CORBA).

See also **Common Object-Request Broker Architecture.**

MIDI

Musical Instrument Digital Interface, a music-file format including strings of messages that can be sent to a sound card, built-in sound system, or external device for translation back into musical notes and rhythms.

Midplug

Yamaha's Windows-based plug-in for Netscape Navigator and compatible browsers that enables a browser to play music provided in the Musical Instrument Digital Interface (MIDI) format.

See also **Musical Instrument Digital Interface; Netscape Navigator.**

midsplit

A broadband cable system in which the available frequencies are split into two groups: one for transmission and one for reception.

MIGPRINT utility

In IntranetWare, a workstation utility (from the DOS prompt) that migrates printers, print queues, print-job configurations, and print servers from a NetWare 2.*x* or NetWare 3.*x* source server into an IntranetWare Directory tree. The MIGPRINT utility is to be used only after an across-the-

wire migration of bindery information has been performed with the MIGRATE utility.
See also **MIGRATE utility.**

MIGRATE utility

In IntranetWare, a workstation utility (from the DOS prompt) that migrates NetWare 2.*x* or NetWare 3.*x* information and data files into an IntranetWare Directory tree. The two types of migration are across-the-wire and same-server.
See also **migration.**

Migrated (M) attribute

A NetWare status flag, set automatically, indicating that a file has migrated.

migration

In the context of the NetWare operating system, the conversion of servers from NetWare 2.*x* or NetWare 3.*x* (or from another operating system) to NetWare 4.*x*. (This is not the same as *data migration*, which entails moving files to near-line or offline storage devices.)

In the context of a NetWare protocol, migration is the conversion of a server, router, or network from the Internetwork Packet Exchange (IPX) protocol to NetWare Link-Services Protocol (NLSP), or from Transmission-Control Protocol/Internet Protocol (TCP/IP) to the Open Shortest Path First (OSPF) protocol.
See also **data migration; Internetwork Packet Exchange; NetWare Link-Services Protocol; Open Shortest Path First; Transmission-Control Protocol/Internet Protocol.**

mil (military)

A suffix on an Internet address that indicates the host computer is run under the jurisdiction of the U.S. Department of Defense (DoD).
See also **Department of Defense; Internet address.**

million instructions per second (MIPS)

A measurement used to gauge the speed of a computer's central processing unit (CPU).

millisecond (ms, msec)

A unit of measure equal to one-thousandth of a second.

millivolt (mv)

A unit of measure equal to one-thousandth of a volt.

MILnet

A network appearing on the Internet, originally used for unclassified military information.
See also **Defense Data Network.**

MIME

Multipurpose Internet Mail Extensions, a specification that enables Internet users to send multipart and multimedia messages. Electronic-mail (e-mail) applications that have MIME can send PostScript images, binary files, audio messages, and digital video over the Internet.

minicomputer

A medium-sized computer capable of running multitasking operations and managing more than 100 users simultaneously.

See also **mainframe system; microcomputer.**

mini-hard disk

A hard disk mounted on a Type III PC Card (also known as a *PCMCIA card*).

Minimum Account Balance

In Novell Directory Services (NDS), a selectable property for the following objects: AFP Server, Messaging Server, NCP Server, Print Server, and User.

See also **leaf object; Novell Directory Services; object.**

Minimum Password Length

A Directory Schema term for Novell Directory Services (NDS).

Minimum Spanning Tree (MST)

The shortest set of network or internetwork connections that includes all possible connections but does not contain any loops.

minor resource

A resource defined by NetWare's Target Service Agent (TSA) and located in the Novell Directory Services (NDS) Directory tree below a selected major resource. A major resource is recognized by the SBACKUP NetWare Loadable Module (NLM).

See also **major resource; NetWare Loadable Module; SBACKUP; Target Service Agent.**

MIPS

Million instructions per second, a measurement used to gauge the speed of a computer's central processing unit (CPU).

MIRROR STATUS utility

In NetWare 4.*x* and IntranetWare, a server console utility used to view the status of mirrored disk partitions and the percentage of mirrored data on each partition.

See also **mirroring.**

Mirrored Server Engine (MSEngine)

One of two parts of NetWare's System Fault Tolerance III (SFT III) operating system responsible for handling such nonphysical processes as the NetWare file system, queue management, and the Directory. The other part of SFT III is the Input/Output Engine (IOEngine). Both the primary server and the secondary server share the same MSEngine. By keeping track of active network processes, the MSEngine provides uninterrupted service if the primary server fails and the secondary server takes over.

See also **Input/Output Engine; System Fault Tolerance.**

Mirrored Server Link (MSL)

A connection in NetWare's System Fault Tolerance III (SFT III) primary and secondary servers that manages server synchronization. The MSL requires a bus extension from the primary Input/Output Engine (IOEngine) to the secondary IOEngine, with a direct connection made through fiber-optic cable.

See also **Input/Output Engine; Mirrored Server Engine; System Fault Tolerance.**

mirroring

A process of duplicating data from the NetWare partition on one hard disk drive to the NetWare partition on another hard disk drive. This duplication provides fault tolerance for a file system.

See also **fault tolerance; partition.**

MIS

Management Information System, a computer-based information system within a company that integrates data from all the departments it serves and provides company management with necessary decision-making data, tracks progress, and solves problems.

misc newsgroup

An Internet newsgroup that discusses topics that do not fit any of the other newsgroup types.

See also **newsgroup.**

mission-critical application

A computer application vital to the operation of a company.

MJ

Modular Jack, a female connector (with sockets or slots) used to connect voice cables to a faceplate. An example of an MJ is a telephone jack.

MKS Internet Anywhere

An integrated package that includes a World Wide Web (WWW) browser, mail software, newsreader, and ftp client software. The Web browser is a licensed version of Spyglass Enhanced Mosaic, with larger icons that more accurately represent their functions.

See also **newsreader; Web browser.**

MLI

Multiple-Link Interface, a part of a generic network driver that sits under the Link-Support Layer (LSL) in Open Data-Link Interface (ODI) and that deals with Network Interface Cards (NICs) supporting ODI.

See also **Multiple-Link Interface Driver; Network Interface Card; Open Data-Link Interface.**

MLID

Multiple-Link Interface Driver, a device driver that handles the sending and receiving of packets to and from a physical or logical local-area network medium. The MLID complies with the Open Data-Link Interface (ODI) specification.

See also **Open Data-Link Interface.**

MLP

Multilink Procedures protocol, a protocol used in networks that have multiple connections running in parallel. This protocol oversees the use of a point-to-point protocol such as Link-Access Procedure Balanced (LAPB) or High-Level Data-Link Control (HDLC) to help balance the loads on connections.

See also **High-Level Data-Link Control; Link-Access Procedure Balanced.**

MLT

Multiple Logical Terminals, a feature of the IBM 3174 establishment controller in the Systems Network Architecture (SNA) environment that enables components to support simultaneous multiple network sessions.

See also **Systems Network Architecture.**

MM

Media Manager, a NetWare database that tracks all peripheral storage devices and media attached to NetWare servers and enables applications to access or gain information from the devices and media. This database receives input/output requests from applications and converts them to messages compatible with the NetWare Peripheral Architecture (NPA).

See also **NetWare Peripheral Architecture.**

MMF

Multimode Fiber, an optical fiber that supports the propagation of multiple frequencies of light.

MMJ

Modified Modular Jack, a cable developed by Digital Equipment Corporation. The MMJ is a variant of the RJ-*xx* jacks and is designed for use in premises cabling.

MMS

Manufacturing Message Service, a service used in automated production lines, enabling a computer application on a control machine to communicate with an application on a slave machine.

MMT

Multimedia Multiparty Teleconferencing, a process that allows for the transfer of data, voice, and video transmissions in a teleconferencing environment.

MMU

memory-management unit, the part of a computer microprocessor responsible for managing the mapping of virtual memory addresses to actual physical addresses. The MMU can be a separate chip (as was the case in early Intel or Motorola microprocessors) or part of the central processing unit (CPU) chip.

See also **central processing unit; physical memory; virtual memory.**

mnemonic

An easy-to-remember name or abbreviation that represents a long or complex programming instruction.

MNP

Microcom Networking Protocol, a ten-level set of communications protocols from Microcom used as a standard of data compression as well as error detection and correction. The ten levels follow:

- *Levels 1 to 4* define hardware error control.
- *Level 5* describes a 2:1 data-compression method.
- *Level 6* describes a communication protocol beginning with V.22*bis* modulation and switching to V.29 when possible.
- *Level 7* describes a 3:1 data-compression method.
- *Level 8* is undefined.
- *Level 9* contains a proprietary technique for providing good performance over a variety of types of links.
- *Level 10* describes an error-control protocol often used on noisy links.

mobile computing

The establishment of links to a network by remote users.

Mobile-Telephone Switching Office (MTSO)

A central computer that monitors all cellular communication transmissions and adjusts channel assignment to accommodate the fluctuating quality of signals.

Mobitex

A collection of wireless networks maintained by RAM Mobile Data that connects more than 6,000 cities.

modal dispersion

The gradual spreading of a fiber-optic signal with increasing distance.

mode

A set of parameters that defines properties of a network session.

mode name

A name used by a program to request a specific set of network properties that the program wants to use for a network-session conversation.

modem

A contraction for *modulator/demodulator* that describes a device used to convert digital data into analog (or waveform) signals for transmission along analog signal carriers. The device also converts received analog signals into digital data to be used by a computer. A *digital modem* merely transmits digital signals; it does not translate back and forth between analog and digital formats.

Figure M.3 shows the evolution of modem speeds defined by International Telecommunications Union (ITU) specifications.

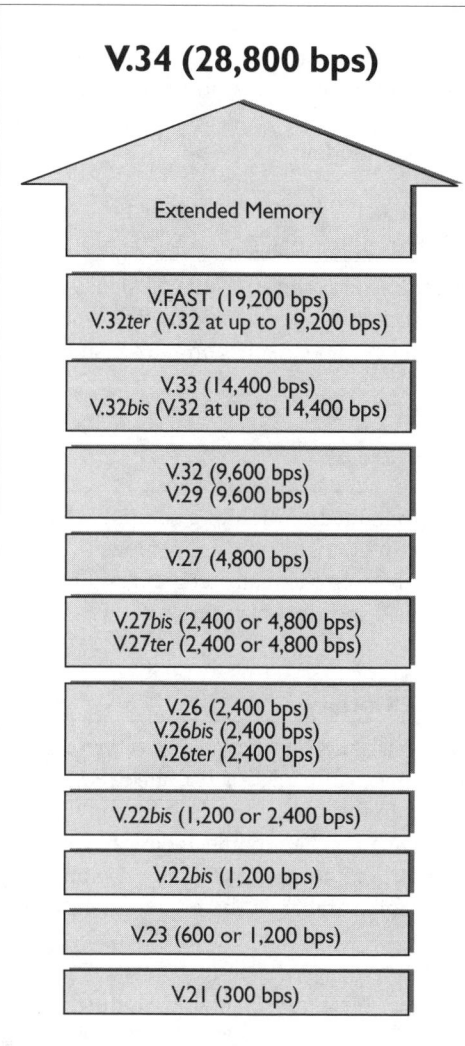

Figure M.3
Evolution of modem speeds

simply may be a null-modem cable connecting the serial ports on two computers. In a synchronous system, a modem eliminator must also provide functions to synchronize communications.

See also **null modem.**

modem server

A synonym for an **Asynchronous Communications Server** (ACS).

moderated mailing list

A mailing list for which incoming messages have been approved by a designated person.
See also **mailing list.**

moderated newsgroup

A newsgroup for which postings have been approved by a designated person.
See also **newsgroup.**

moderator

A person responsible for reviewing mailing list messages and newsgroup postings and deciding which ones to release to the public.

modem eliminator

A device enabling two computers to be linked without the use of modems. In an asynchronous system, a modem eliminator

modifiable

A key attribute that enables a user to modify a key field during an update to a file.
See also **attribute.**

Modified Frequency Modulation (MFM)

An encoding scheme used on 40MB or smaller hard-disk drives.

Modified Modular Jack (MMJ)

A cable developed by Digital Equipment Corporation. The MMJ is a variant of the RJ-*xx* jacks and is designed for use in premises cabling.

See also **Modular Jack; premises cabling.**

Modify bit

A file attribute set by the operating system when a file is changed, indicating that file data has been modified. In NetWare, the Modify bit is called the Archive Needed Attribute and appears as an *A* whenever file attributes are listed. Modify bits are checked by backup programs to back up only those files for which the Modify bit has been set.

Modify right

In IntranetWare, a file-access and directory-access right that grants the privilege of changing the attributes or name of a file or directory.

See also **access rights.**

Modular Jack (MJ)

A female connector (with sockets or slots) used to connect voice cables to a faceplate. An example of an MJ is a telephone jack.

modularity

Characterized by the quality of being composed of self-supporting pieces that can be used independently.

modulation

The process of converting digital signals to analog signals by modulating a carrier frequency.

See also **modem.**

Modulation protocol

A protocol that modulates digital signals for transmission over telephone lines and depends on the transmission rates it supports.

module

A self-contained portion of a computer program written, tested, and compiled separately from the main program and that performs a specific operation.

MODULES utility

In NetWare and IntranetWare, a server console utility that displays a list of currently loaded modules, with the list showing the short name for the module, a descriptive string (or long name) for the module, and the version number (if the module is a disk driver, LAN driver, or NetWare Loadable Module).

See also **NetWare Loadable Module.**

Modulo 8 or 128

A numbering method for packet sequences that controls the numbering of sequential data packets in a window.

MONITOR (NLM)

In NetWare and IntranetWare, a server console utility that enables the viewing of server activity, locking of the server console, assessment of random-access memory (RAM) and central processing unit (CPU) utilization, and optimization of memory through garbage collection.

The MONITOR NetWare Loadable Module (NLM) main screen displays two menus of information. Table M.3 shows the options from the *General Information* menu, the versions of NetWare in which the options appear, and comments on the general use of the option. Table M.4 shows the entries listed in the *Available Options* window, the versions of NetWare in which the options appear, and the tasks performed by the option.

MOO

MUD, Object-Oriented, a multiuser, text-based role-playing environment.

See also **Multi-User Dimension; Multiuser Shared Hallucination; Multiuser Simulated Environment.**

MOP

Maintenance-Operation Protocol, a protocol from Digital Equipment Corporation that provides a way to perform primitive maintenance operations on a DECnet network system.

See also **DECnet.**

more-data mark (M-bit)

A bit that is a component of a user packet and, when set, identifies the next packet sent as a logical continuation of the data contained in the current packet.

Mosaic

A World Wide Web (WWW) browser originally developed as shareware at the National Center for Supercomputing Applications (NCSA) and now licensed to third-party commercial vendors.

See also **Mosaic In A Box; NCSA Mosaic; Quarterdeck Mosaic; Spyglass Enhanced Mosaic; Web browser.**

For more information about Mosaic, surf the Web to `http://www.ncsa.uiuc.edu/sdg/software/mosaic.`

Mosaic In A Box

An inexpensive World Wide Web (WWW) browser from CompuServe that provides a unique CompuServe Wallet (a tool for making online shopping more secure) and is designed specifically for Windows 95.

See also **Web browser.**

Most Significant Bit (MSB)

A bit corresponding to the highest power of 2 in a bit sequence. The MSB's location depends on the context and the ordering of bits within a word.

Table M.3: MONITOR Available Options Window

Option	Ver. 3.12	Ver. 4.10	Ver. 4.11	Description
File Server Up Time	x			Length of time the file server has been running since it was last booted.
Server Up Time		x	x	Length of time the server has been running since it was last booted.
Active Processors			x	Number of enabled processors.
Utilization	x	x	x	For uniprocessor servers, reflects CPU utilization. For multiprocessor servers, the average utilization of all active processors.
Original Cache Buffers	x	x	x	Number of cache buffers available when server is booted (represented as the number of blocks installed as cache memory on the server). Default: 4K.
Total Cache Buffers	x	x	x	Number of blocks available for file caching (decreases as modules are loaded).
Dirty Cache Buffers	x	x	x	Number of file blocks in memory waiting to be written to disk.
Current Disk Requests	x	x	x	Number of disk requests waiting in a queue to be written to disk.
Packet-Receive Buffers	x	x	x	Number of buffers available to handle station requests. Default: 10.
Directory-Cache Buffers	x	x	x	Number of buffers allocated to handle directory caching.
Service Processes	x	x		Number of task handlers allocated for station requests. When memory is allocated for service processes, it remains allocated until the file server is shut down.
Maximum Service Processes		x	x	Number of task handlers allocated to service client requests. When memory is allocated for service processes, it remains allocated until the file server is shut down. Each service process requires 4K of RAM.
Current Service Processes	x	x	x	Number of service processes currently allocated. Performance is adversely affected when this number matches Maximum Service Processes.
Connections in Use		x		Number of stations currently attached to file server.
Maximum Licensed Connections		x	x	Maximum possible number of licensed service connections, which matches the number-of-users version of NetWare.
Current Licensed Connections		x	x	Number of current licensed connections, which counts toward the limit on NetWare license.
Open Files	x	x	x	Number of files accessed by the file server and by workstations.

Table M.4: MONITOR Available Options Menu

Option	Ver. 3.12	Ver. 4.10	Ver. 4.11	Tasks
Connection Information	x	x	x	List active connections.
		x	x	List licensed and unlicensed connections.
	x	x	x	List physical record locks for user.
	x	x	x	Clear a connection.
	x	x	x	List open files.
		x	x	List record lock status of open files.
			x	Send a message to a workstation connection.
Disk Information	x	x	x	List system hard disks.
	x	x	x	List volume segments per hard disk.
	x	x	x	Change the *Read After Write Verify* status of the hard disk.
	x	x	x	Flash the hard-disk light.
			x	Change the drive-light status.
	x	x	x	Activate/deactivate a hard disk.
	x	x	x	Mount/dismount a removable media device.
	x	x	x	Lock/unlock a removable media device.
LAN (WAN) Information	x	x	x	List LAN drivers and statistics.
		x	x	View the LAN driver version and the protocols bound to it.
		x	x	View node and network address.

(continued)

MONITOR Available Options Menu (continued)

Option	Ver. 3.12	Ver. 4.10	Ver. 4.11	Tasks
System Module Information	x	x	x	List system modules.
		x	x	List size of module code and data image.
	x	x	x	List resources used by system modules.
		x	x	View resource tag memory usage.
Lock File Server Console	x	x	x	Lock the file server console.
	x	x	x	Unlock the file server console.
File Open/Lock Activity	x			Check the status of a file.
		x	x	Check a file's lock activity and status.
		x	x	View which stations have open files.
	x			View mounted volumes.
		x	x	View mounted volumes and directories on each volume.
		x	x	View files in a directory.
Cache Utilization		x	x	View disk cache block-request statistics.
Processor Utilization	x	x	x	Check the server's processor utilization.
		x	x	View a histogram of selected processes.

(continued)

Option	Ver. 3.12	Ver. 4.10	Ver. 4.11	Tasks
Resource Utilization	x	x	x	View memory statistics.
	x	x	x	View tracked resources.
Memory Utilization		x	x	View allocated memory information for entire system or one selected system module.
		x	x	View memory statistics.
		x	x	Perform garbage collection.
Scheduling Information		x	x	View and change the priority of a process.
		x	x	View number of times a process ran.
Multiprocessor Information			x	Access information about processors, threads, and mutexes.
Server Parameters			x	Set values for server parameters.
Exit	x	x		Exit MONITOR.

motherboard

The main circuit board in a computer that contains the central processing unit (CPU), a coprocessor (and support chips), device controllers, memory, and expansion slots.

Motif

A graphical user interface (GUI) for UNIX computers.
See also **graphical user interface.**

Motion Pictures Experts Group (MPEG)

A standard set by International Standards Organization/International Telecommunications Union (ISO/ITU) for compressing video files. MPEG requires a fast computer or a plug-in MPEG board for an existing computer.
See also **International Standardization Organization (ISO); International Telecommunications Union (ITU).**

For more information about MPEG, surf the Web to `http://www.eit.com/creations/techinfo/mpeg.`

MOTIS

Message-Oriented Text-Interchange System, a Message-Handling System (MHS) developed by the International Standards Organization (ISO). The basic MOTIS elements are compatible with the Consultative Committee for International Telegraphy and Telephony (CCITT) X.400 MHS specifications.

See also **Consultative Committee for International Telegraphy and Telephony; International Standards Organization; Message-Handling System; X.400.**

mount

The process of inserting a CD-ROM disc into a CD-ROM drive so that the Hierarchical File System (HFS) CD-ROM module knows that the CD-ROM drive exists.

MOUNT utility

In NetWare and IntranetWare, a server console utility that makes volumes available to users. Volumes can be mounted and dismounted while the server runs. This utility is also used to mount all volumes residing on a removable drive when such a drive has been replaced.
See also **volume.**

mouse

A computer input device with one or more buttons, used with programs designed for a graphical user interface (GUI) to move the cursor around the screen display. A mouse can be one of four types: a bus mouse (requires a separate expansion board in the computer), a serial mouse (plugs into a serial port), a regular mouse (plugs into a mouse port), and a wireless mouse.
See also **graphical user interface.**

mouse pointer

In programs that use a graphical user interface (GUI), a small symbol that appears on the monitor screen and whose movement is controlled by a mouse. The mouse pointer indicates a position on the display screen.

See also **graphical user interface.**

MOV

Metal-Oxide Varistor, in an electrical line conditioner or surge protector, a component that intercepts high-voltage spikes from an incoming power supply.

See also **line conditioner; spike.**

MovieStar

A plug-in for Windows and Macintosh Netscape Navigator (and compatible) browsers that plays digital movies and simulated virtual reality environments. MovieStar is from Intelligence At Large.

See also **Netscape Navigator.**

 **For more information about MovieStar, Intelligence At Large's Web site can be found at** http://www.ialsoft.com/.

Mozilla

The original code name used for the development team at Netscape Communications for what became the Netscape Navigator Web browser. The name is sometimes used to refer to the fire-breathing dragon mascot at Netscape.

See also **Netscape Navigator.**

MP protocol

Multilink Point-to-Point protocol, an extension of the Point-to-Point Protocol (PPP) used to split a signal, send it along multiple channels, and then reassemble and sequence it at the common destination for the channels.

See also **Point-to-Point Protocol.**

MPDRIVER (NLM)

In IntranetWare, a server console utility that enables processors in a multiprocessor server running NetWare Symmetric Multiprocessing (SMP) software. This NetWare Loadable Module (NLM) is used to enable and disable individual processors dynamically after NetWare SMP has been installed.

See also **NetWare Loadable Module.**

MPEG

Motion Pictures Experts Group, a standard set by International Standards Organization/International Telecommunications Union (ISO/ITU) for compressing video files. MPEG requires a fast computer or a plug-in MPEG board for an existing computer.

See also **International Standardization Organization (ISO); International Telecommunications Union (ITU).**

MPI

Multiple-Protocol Interface, the top part of the Link-Support Layer (LSL) of the Open Data-Link Interface (ODI) specification that provides support for local-area network (LAN) drivers.

See also **Link-Support Layer; Open Data-Link Interface.**

MPOA

Multiprotocol Over ATM, an effort of the ATM Forum to standardize protocols to run multiple network layers over Asynchronous Transfer Mode (ATM) networks.

See also **Asynchronous Transfer Mode.**

MPR

NetWare Multiprotocol Router, a software-based bridge and router combination (*brouter*) that can concurrently route Internetwork Packet Exchange (IPX), Transmission-Control Protocol/Internet Protocol (TCP/IP), and AppleTalk across both local-area networks (LANs) and wide-area networks (WANs). The NetWare Multiprotocol Router operates on personal computers with 80386, 80486, or Pentium microprocessors, and supports Ethernet, Token Ring, Fiber Distributed Data Interface (FDDI), fast Ethernet, and ARCnet network topologies.

See also **AppleTalk; ARCnet; Ethernet; Fiber Distributed Data Interface; Internetwork Packet Exchange; Transmission-Control Protocol/Internet Protocol.**

MRM

Maximum-Rights Mask, a NetWare 2.2 list of trustee directory rights granted to users. The MRM has been replaced by the Inherited-Rights Mask (IRM) in NetWare 3.*x* and the Inherited-Rights Filter in NetWare 4.*x*.

See also **access rights; Inherited-Rights Mask; Inherited-Rights Filter; Maximum-Rights Mask** (includes **Table M.1**).

MRU

Maximum-Receive Unit, an option in the Link-Control Protocol (LCP). The MRU enables a sender to inform a peer that the sender can receive larger frames than specified in the default, or to request that the peer send smaller frames.

See also **Link-Control Protocol.**

MS

Message Store, a component specified in the Consultative Committee for International Telegraphy and Telephony (CCITT) X.400 Message-Handling System (MHS) in which electronic mail (e-mail) is stored either until it is retrieved by a User Agent (UA) or until an allowable storage time expires.

See also **Consultative Committee for International Telegraphy and Telephony; Message-Handling System; User Agent; X.400.**

ms

Millisecond, a unit of measure equal to one-thousandth of a second.

MS-DOS

Microsoft Disk Operating System, a single-user, single-tasking operating system for personal computers that allocates system resources through either a command line or shell interface. Although similar to IBM's PC-DOS, file sizes and names of device drivers do differ between the two systems.

See also **Disk Operating System.**

MSEngine

Mirrored Server Engine, one of two parts of NetWare's System Fault Tolerance III (SFT III) operating system responsible for handling such nonphysical processes as the NetWare file system, queue management, and the Directory. The other part of SFT III is the Input/Output Engine (IOEngine). Both the primary server and the secondary server share the same MSEngine. By keeping track of active network processes, the MSEngine provides uninterrupted service if the primary server fails and the secondary server takes over.

See also **Input/Output Engine; System Fault Tolerance.**

MS Windows client

A NetWare workstation that boots with the DOS operating system and gains access to the network through either the NetWare DOS Requester (in NetWare 4.*x*) or a NetWare shell (in NetWare versions previous to NetWare 4.*x*). While running Windows, the workstation computer (with client software) can perform networking tasks in the Windows environment, including mapping drives, capturing printer ports, sending messages, and changing contexts.

See also **DOS Requester; NetWare DOS Requester.**

MSAU

Multi-Station-Access Unit (alternate spelling of **Multistation-Access Unit**), a multiport wiring hub used on Token Ring networks that can connect as many as eight nodes (or lobes) to a ring network. A Multistation-Access Unit is also known as a *Controlled-Access Unit (CAU)*.

See also **Controlled-Access Unit; MAU; Token Ring.**

MSB

Most Significant Bit, a bit corresponding to the highest power of 2 in a bit sequence. The MSB's location depends on the context and the ordering of bits within a word.

msec

Millisecond, a unit of measure equal to one-thousandth of a second.

MSERVER utility

In NetWare 4.*x* and IntranetWare, a server console utility that loads the IOEngine on each NetWare SFT III server. This utility is executed at the DOS prompt of each SFT III server. MSERVER executes the IOSTART.NCF and IOAUTO.NCF files.

See also **IOEngine.**

MSL

Mirrored Server Link, a connection in NetWare's System Fault Tolerance III (SFT III) primary and secondary servers that manages server synchronization. The MSL requires a bus extension from the primary Input/Output Engine (IOEngine) to the secondary IOEngine, with a direct connection made through fiber-optic cable.

See also **Input/Output Engine; Mirrored Server Engine; System Fault Tolerance.**

MSM

Media-Support Module (another name for the **Novell Generic Media-Support Module**). In NetWare 4.02, a field name that appears in the System Modules menu in the MONITOR NetWare Loadable Module (NLM).

See also **MONITOR; NetWare Loadable Module.**

MSN

Microsoft Network, an online service from Microsoft that enables users to exchange messages, read news, seek answers to technical questions, download software, and connect to the Internet.

See also **Windows 95.**

MST

Minimum Spanning Tree, the shortest set of network or internetwork connections that includes all possible connections but does not contain any loops.

MTA

(1) Mail-Transfer Agent, a component of the electronic-mail (e-mail) system found in the Transmission-Control Protocol/Internet Protocol (TCP/IP) suite. An MTA provides an interface between users (and applications) and the e-mail system, sends and receives messages, and forwards messages between mail servers. Different MTAs communicate with each other using the Simple Mail-Transfer Protocol (SMTP). Users interact with MTAs through user agents, which communicate with the MTA using a protocol such as Post Office Protocol Version 3 (POP3).

(2) Message-Transfer Agent, a component specified in the Consultative Committee for International Telegraphy and Telephony (CCITT) X.400 Message-Handling System (MHS) that stores (or forwards) electronic-mail (e-mail) messages to a User Agent (UA), another MTA, or to some other authorized recipient.

See also **(1) electronic mail; (1) Post Office Protocol 3; (1) Transmission-Control Protocol/Internet Protocol; (1) Simple Mail-Transfer Protocol; (2) Consultative Committee for International Telegraphy and Telephony; (2) Message-Handling System; (2) User Agent; (2) X.400.**

MTBF

Mean time between failures, a statistically derived average length of time (expressed in thousands or tens of thousands of hours) that a computer system or component operates before failing.

MTL

Message-Transfer Layer, a component specified in the Consultative Committee for International Telegraphy and Telephony (CCITT) X.400 Message-Handling System (MHS) that represents one of two sublayers of the Application Layer (Layer 7) in the OSI Reference Model and provides access to transfer services across a network. The other sublayer (which resides above the MTL) is the User Agent Layer (UAL).

See also **Consultative Committee for International Telegraphy and Telephony; Message-Handling System; OSI Reference Model; User Agent; User-Agent Layer; X.400.**

MTS

Message-Transfer Service, a component specified in the Consultative Committee for International Telegraphy and Telephony (CCITT) X.400 Message-Handling System (MHS) that processes requests from Access Units (AUs), Message Stores (MSs), Message-Transfer Agents (MTAs), and User Agents (UAs).

See also **Access Units; Consultative Committee for International Telegraphy and Telephony; Message-Handling System; Message Stores; Message-Transfer Agents; User Agent; X.400.**

MTSO

Mobile-Telephone Switching Office, a central computer that monitors all cellular communication transmissions and adjusts channel assignment to accommodate the fluctuating quality of signals.

MTTR

Mean time to repair, a statistically derived average length of time it takes to repair a failing computer system or component.

MTU

Maximum-Transmission Unit, specified in bytes, the largest packet size that can be sent on a physical network medium. As an example, the MTU for Ethernet is 1,500 bytes.

MUD

Multi-User Dimension, a multiuser simulation environment in which a user can create things that stay after the user leaves. Other users can interact with these things in the original user's absence, thus building a simulated environment gradually and collectively.

MUD, Object-Oriented (MOO)

A multiuser, text-based role-playing environment.
See also **Multi-User Dimension.**

mu-law

A companding standard used in North America for conversion between analog and digital signals in Pulse Code Modulation (PCM) systems.
See also **companding; Pulse Code Modulation.**

multicast

A transmission method in which multiple (but not all) nodes on the network receive a copy of a frame or packet.
See also **broadcast.**

multicast address

An address referring to multiple network devices. A multicast address is also known as a *group address*.
See also **IP address.**

Multicast Backbone (MBONE)

A multicast, virtual network that adds live audio and video capabilities to the Internet. An MBONE network is organized as clusters of networks connected by *tunnels* (paths between endpoints that support multicast transmissions) and that support multicast Internet Protocol (IP) transmissions.

See also **Internet Protocol; virtual network.**

multi-CPU architecture

A computer architecture in which multiple microprocessors work together on the same task or separately on different tasks.

multidrop connection

A network connection that utilizes a single line to connect multiple nodes. The Ethernet bus topology uses a multidrop connection.

See also **bus topology.**

multidrop line

A line or circuit often found in a Systems Network Architecture (SNA) network that connects several nodes on a single logical link. A multidrop line is also known as a *multipoint line.*

See also **Systems Network Architecture.**

MultiFinder

A multitasking operating system for the Macintosh computer under which several applications (including background applications) can be open at the same time.

multi-homed host

An Internet connection scheme in which a single machine is connected to multiple data links, possibly over multiple networks.

multihoming

An Intermediate-System-to-Intermediate-System (IS-IS) addressing scheme that supports the assignment of multiple data links or area addresses.

See also **Intermediate-System-to-Intermediate-System.**

multilayer

A printed circuit board that has several layers of circuitry laminated together to form a single board.

Multilink Point-to-Point protocol (MP protocol)

An extension of the Point-to-Point Protocol (PPP) used to split a signal, send it along multiple channels, and then reassemble and sequence it at the common destination for the channels.

See also **Point-to-Point Protocol.**

Multilink Procedures (MLP) protocol

A protocol used in networks that have multiple connections running in parallel. This protocol oversees the use of a point-to-point protocol such as Link-Access Procedure Balanced (LAPB) or High-Level Data-Link Control (HDLC) to help balance the loads on connections.

See also **High-Level Data-Link Control; Link-Access Procedure Balanced.**

multimedia

A computer technology that incorporates video, animation, sound, graphics, and text with user interaction.

multimedia extension

Operating system software that extends an application interface to include video, animation, sound, graphics, and text. A multimedia extension also includes commands for synchronization and device control.

Multimedia Home-Space Viewer (MHSV)

A Windows or Macintosh plug-in for Netscape Navigator (and compatible browsers) that navigates through three-dimensional environments. MHSV is from Paragraph.
See also **Netscape Navigator.**

Multimedia Multiparty Teleconferencing (MMT)

A process that allows for the transfer of data, voice, and video transmissions in a teleconferencing environment.

Multimode Fiber (MMF)

An optical fiber that supports the propagation of multiple frequencies of light.

multipart

An electronic-mail (e-mail) format description indicating that the contents of the message represent several different objects.

multipath

A term describing radio communications signals that are reflected back and are out of phase with each other.

multiple access

A term describing simultaneous access to the same file by multiple users on a network. Multiple access usually entails only the reading of files with some sort of locking mechanism employed to prevent users from interfering with each other while trying to modify the file.

multiple-domain network

A Systems Network Architecture (SNA) network that controls multiple system service access points (SSCPs).
See also **system service access points; Systems Network Architecture.**

Multiple-Link Interface (MLI)

A part of a generic network driver that sits under the Link-Support Layer (LSL) in Open Data-Link Interface (ODI) and that deals with Network Interface Cards (NICs) supporting ODI.
See also **Multiple-Link Interface Driver; Network Interface Card; Open Data-Link Interface.**

Multiple-Link Interface Driver (MLID)

A device driver that handles the sending and receiving of packets to and from a physical or logical local-area network medium. The MLID complies with the Open Data-Link Interface (ODI) specification.
See also **Open Data-Link Interface.**

Multiple Logical Terminals (MLT)

A feature of the IBM 3174 establishment controller in the Systems Network Architecture (SNA) environment that enables components to support simultaneous multiple network sessions.

See also **Systems Network Architecture.**

multiple name-space support

A method allowing various workstations running different operating systems to create their own familiar naming conventions. Operating systems such as DOS, Macintosh, OS/2, UNIX, and Windows each have unique naming conventions for files, including name length, allowable characters, case-sensitivity, data and resource forks, length of filename extensions, and so on. This method allows each file stored on a given volume to have a name that any workstation (regardless of the workstation's operating system) can recognize.

Multiple-Protocol Interface (MPI)

The top part of the Link-Support Layer (LSL) of the Open Data-Link Interface (ODI) specification that provides support for local-area network (LAN) drivers.

See also **Link-Support Layer; Open Data-Link Interface.**

multiple protocols

A scenario under which more than one standard is used by a program or operating system for communication between two or more entities on a network.

Multiple Uniform-Naming Convention Provider (MUP)

A Windows NT driver that determines which network to access when an application requests permission to open a remote file.

See also **Windows NT.**

Multiple Virtual Storage (MVS)

An operating system used by IBM computers for large host systems.

multiple-byte character

A character made up of two or more bytes in situations in which a language includes more than the 256 characters that one byte can allow. The American Standard Code for Information Interchange (ASCII) character set includes 256 characters. If a language (such as some Asian languages) includes more than 256 characters, then more than one byte is necessary to accommodate all the characters in the language.

multiplexer

A device that accepts multiple electronic transmission signals and combines them into one high-speed transmission. A multiplexer, also known as a mux, is often used to allow remote terminals to communicate with front-end processor ports over a single circuit.

multiplexing

A method allowing a single communications circuit to take the place of several parallel communications circuits.

multiplexor VLM

A Virtual Loadable Module (VLM) that routes calls to a child VLM. The two types of VLMs are *multiplexor VLMs* and *child VLMs*.

See also **Virtual Loadable Module.**

multipoint connection

A network connection involving multiple nodes connected by a single line.

See also **bus topology; multidrop line.**

multipoint line

A communications line or circuit that interconnects several nodes of a network system.

See also **point-to-point line.**

multiport repeater

An Ethernet network repeater that connects multiple network nodes in parallel.

multiprocessing

A computer operating system that has the capability to use more than one central processing unit (CPU) in a single computer. The two types of multiprocessing are

- *Asymmetrical multiprocessing.* The program designer must specify the processor to be used when running the program.
- *Symmetrical multiprocessing.* The operating system dynamically assigns tasks to the next available processor.

multiprotocol encapsulation

A method used by protocols on the Network Layer (Layer 3) of the OSI Reference Model in which a layer adds control information to the protocol data unit (PDU) from the preceding layer. Multiprotocol encapsulation is also sometimes used to envelop one protocol inside another to facilitate transmission.

See also **OSI Reference Model; protocol data unit.**

Multiprotocol Over ATM

An effort of the ATM Forum to standardize protocols to run multiple network layers over Asynchronous Transfer Mode (ATM) networks.

See also **Asynchronous Transfer Mode.**

 **For more information about Multiprotocol over ATM, the ATM Forum's Web site is available at** `http://www.atmforum.com/`.

Multiprotocol Router (MPR)

NetWare Multiprotocol Router, a software-based bridge and router combination (*brouter*) that can concurrently route Internetwork Packet Exchange (IPX), Transmission-Control Protocol/Internet Protocol (TCP/IP), and AppleTalk across both local-area networks (LANs) and wide-area networks (WANs). The NetWare Multiprotocol Router operates on personal computers with 80386, 80486, or Pentium microprocessors, and supports Ethernet,

Token Ring, Fiber Distributed Data Interface (FDDI), fast Ethernet, and ARCnet network topologies.

See also **AppleTalk; ARCnet; Ethernet; Fiber Distributed Data Interface; Internetwork Packet Exchange; Transmission-Control Protocol/Internet Protocol.**

Multipurpose Internet Mail Extensions (MIME)

A specification that enables Internet users to send multipart and multimedia messages. Electronic-mail (e-mail) applications that have MIME can send PostScript images, binary files, audio messages, and digital video over the Internet.

multiserver network

A single network with two or more NetWare servers in which users can access any NetWare server to which they have rights. A multiserver network should not be confused with an *internetwork*, in which two or more networks are linked through a router.

See also **internetwork.**

Multistation Access Unit (MAU)

A multiport wiring hub used on Token Ring networks that can connect as many as eight nodes (or lobes) to a ring network. A Multistation Access Unit is also known as a *Controlled-Access Unit (CAU)*.

See also **Controlled-Access Unit; MAU; Token Ring.**

multitasking

The capability of a computer to run more than one application simultaneously and to switch between the applications while they continue to run.

multithreading

A concurrent processing of several threads inside the same program, thus freeing one thread from waiting for another thread to finish processing before it can start.

See also **thread.**

multiuser

A term describing an operating system that supports more than one simultaneous user. Network systems are an example of multiuser environments.

Multi-User Dimension (MUD)

A multiuser simulation environment in which a user can create things that stay after the user leaves. Other users can interact with these things in the original user's absence, thus building a simulated environment gradually and collectively.

See also **MOO.**

Multiuser Shared Hallucination (MUSH)

An interactive simulation that enables multiple users to add features or objects using a scripting or programming language.

See also **MOO; Multi-User Dimension.**

Multiuser Simulated Environment (MUSE)

A multiuser, computer-moderated, interactive simulation that enables multiple users to add features or objects using a scripting or programming language. A MUSE usually has more features for users to add with fewer built-in dialogues, implying that the interaction is a game.

See also **MOO; Multi-User Dimension.**

multivendor network

A network made up of different components manufactured by different vendors.

MUP

Multiple Uniform-Naming Convention Provider, a Windows NT driver that determines which network to access when an application requests permission to open a remote file.

See also **Windows NT.**

MUSE

Multiuser Simulated Environment, a multiuser, computer-moderated, interactive simulation that enables multiple users to add features or objects using a scripting or programming language. A MUSE usually has more features for users to add with fewer built-in dialogues, implying that the interaction is a game.

MUSH

Multiuser Shared Hallucination, an interactive simulation that enables multiple users to add features or objects using a scripting or programming language.

Musical Instrument Digital Interface (MIDI)

A music-file format including strings of messages that can be sent to a sound card, built-in sound system, or external device for translation back into musical notes and rhythms.

mutex

A locking mechanism (mutual exclusion lock) associated with a Symmetric Multiprocessing (SMP) data structure that prevents a thread from accessing the data structure if it is already in use.

mux

A variation of the term **multiplexer**.

MUX Multiplier

A telecommunications device used to funnel multiple signals onto a single channel.

mv

millivolt, a unit of measure equal to one-thousandth of a volt.

MVS

Multiple Virtual Storage, an operating system used by IBM computers for large host systems.

MX

Mail Exchange record, a data structure in the Internet Domain-Naming System (DNS) that indicates which machines can handle electronic mail (e-mail) for a particular region of the Internet.

See also **Domain-Naming System; Internet.**

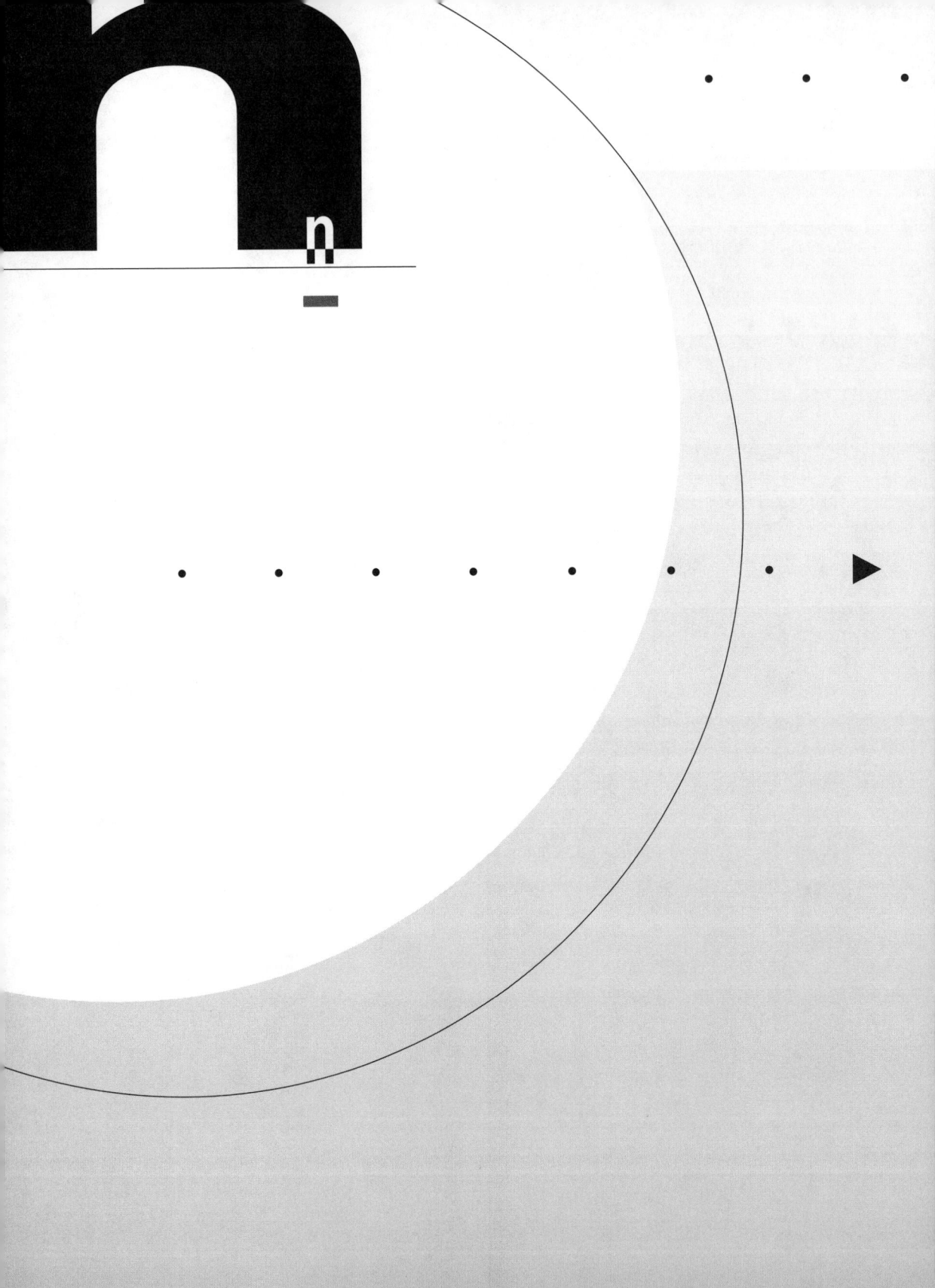

n

An abbreviation for the prefix **nano-** that represents an order of magnitude equivalent to 2^{-30}, or about one-billionth.

N-1

An intrauniversity network, located in Japan, that connects X.25 mainframe computer networks.

See also **X.25.**

NA

Numerical aperture, a range of angles over which a fiber-optic core can receive incoming light.

NAC

Network-Access Controller, a device that provides access to a network, either for another network or for remote callers.

NACSIS

National Center for Science Information Systems, a Japanese network considered a successor to the N-1 network, which is an intrauniversity network linking X.25 mainframe computers.

See also **N-1; X.25.**

NAEC

Novell Authorized Education Centers, an independent training organization that meets Novell education standards and is authorized to teach Novell-developed courses with Certified Novell Instructors (CNIs).

See also **Certified Novell Instructor.**

Nagle's algorithm

A combination of two congestion-control algorithms used in Transmission-Control Protocol (TCP) networks. One algorithm reduces a sending window and another limits small datagrams.

See also **datagram; Transmission-Control Protocol.**

NAK

negative acknowledgment, a Return signal reporting an error in a message that has been received.

See also **error detection and correction.**

NAL

Novell Application Launcher, in IntranetWare, a Windows workstation utility that runs applications associated with Novell Directory Services (NDS) Application leaf objects. The NAL utility allows a user to view Application objects and run the associated application. Those Application objects created and managed by the network supervisor (through the NetWare Application Manager utility) appear as NetWare-delivered applications in the main window of NAL.

See also **Application object; leaf object; NetWare Application Manager utility; Novell Directory Services.**

NAM

NetWare Application Manager, in IntranetWare, a Windows workstation utility included with the Novell Application Launcher (NAL) that creates and manages Novell Directory Services (NDS) Application leaf objects through the NetWare

Administrator utility. The Application object is first created with the NetWare Administrator utility, which allows a network supervisor to choose from assigned object classes and properties. After the Application object properties are set, an executable file is associated with the object; this file allocates resources such as drive mappings or printer ports.

See also **Application object; leaf object; NetWare Administrator utility; Novell Directory Services.**

Name

In Novell Directory Services (NDS), a NetWare Directory Schema term and a selectable property for the Directory Map object.

See also **leaf object; Novell Directory Services; object.**

name binding

The association of a name for each Network Visible Entity (NVE) with its Internet address.

See also **IP address; Network Visible Entity.**

Name-Binding Protocol (NBP)

An AppleTalk protocol that converts entity names into their corresponding Internet addresses. For example, the Macintosh Chooser Desk Accessory and the ATCON NetWare Loadable Module (NLM) use NBP to locate AppleTalk entities.

See also **AppleTalk; Internet address.**

name caching

A method of using a router to store remotely discovered host names for future use in packet-forwarding decisions.

name context

The position of an object within the Novell Directory Services (NDS) Directory tree.

See also **container object; leaf object; Novell Directory Services; object.**

name resolution

The process of associating a network location with a name assigned by a NetWare network administrator.

name server

A network server that resolves network names into network addresses.

See also **network address; network name.**

name-space NLMs

A set of NetWare Loadable Modules (NLMs) that allow storage of non-DOS files on a NetWare server under a folder name or filename that a user expects to see them, even if the files were created on a platform different from that of the viewing workstation. NetWare uses a different name space for different platforms.

The names of the NLMs have a .NAM extension (for example, LONG.NAM, OS2.NAM, MAC.NAM, FTAM.NAM, and NFS.NAM). To store non-DOS file types on a NetWare volume, the name space NLM must be loaded (and the name space added to the volume) through use of the ADD NAME SPACE console command. The NetWare installation program automatically places the MAC.NAM and OS2.NAM files in the SYS:SYSTEM directory.

name-space format

A filename format that is unique to a specific operating system. For example, DOS, Macintosh, Network Filing System (NFS), and OS/2 each have different name-space formats.

name type

A distinction made between different objects in Novell Directory Services (NDS). For example, the name type of an Organization object is O; an Organizational Unit object is OU.

See also **container object; leaf object; Novell Directory Services; object.**

NAME utility

In NetWare and IntranetWare, a server console utility that displays the name of the NetWare server.

named pipe

The means by which a client communicates with advanced client-server applications such as Microsoft SQL Server and Microsoft Comm Server software. NetWare Client workstations most frequently communicate with client-server applications by using the Interprocess Communications (IPC) protocol for named pipes.

See also **Interprocess Communications.**

Named Pipes Extender for DOS

A terminate-and-stay-resident (TSR) program for DOS that extends the capability of DOS in NetWare to include the use of remote named pipes. The Named Pipes Extender for DOS is also known as the *Named Pipes DOS Extender (DOSNP)* or *Named Pipes extender.*

See also **named pipe; terminate-and-stay-resident.**

Namer

A Macintosh application used to name and rename printers. This program appears on the LaserWriter or ImageWriter installation disks.

names directory (ND)

A database that contains the mappings of all Network-Visible Entities (NVEs) with their Internet addresses.

See also **Internet address; Network-Visible Entity.**

names table

A table in each network node that contains the mappings of all Network-Visible Entities (NVEs) in that node, complete with their Internet addresses.

See also **Internet address; Network-Visible Entity.**

naming service

A network service that names resources on the network to access the resources by that name, which allows correspondence between a network entity and a name, rather than having to remember network addresses. A *local naming service* associates resources to a single server; a *global naming service* associates resources with an entire network or internetwork.

NAMPS

Narrowband Analog Mobile-Phone Service, a communications standard from Motorola that combines the Advanced Mobile Home-Service (AMPS) cellular standard with digital signaling information.

See also **Advanced Mobile-Phone Service.**

nano-

An order of magnitude equivalent to 2^{-30}, or about one-billionth.

nanosecond (ns)

A unit of measure equal to one-billionth of a second.

Narrowband Analog Mobile-Phone Service (NAMPS)

A communications standard from Motorola that combines the Advanced Mobile Home-Service (AMPS) cellular standard with digital signaling information.

See also **Advanced Mobile Home-Service.**

narrowband

A voice-grade communications transmission channel of 2,400 bits per second (bps) or less.

Narrowband ISDN (NISDN)

A term describing ordinary Integrated-Services Digital Network (ISDN) architecture in which narrowband transmissions are used.

See also **Integrated-Services Digital Network; narrowband.**

NAS

Network Application Support, specifications from Digital Equipment Corporation designed to use international standards to support a uniform environment for software running on different platforms. The NAS specifications contrast with IBM's Systems Application Architecture (SAA) in that SAA provides proprietary protocols to support multiple platforms.

See also **Systems Application Architecture.**

NASI

NetWare Asynchronous Services Interface, specifications for accessing NetWare communications servers. The NASI Software Developer's Kit (SDK) can be used to build applications running on this interface.

National Center for Science Information Systems (NACSIS)

A Japanese network considered a successor to the N-1 network, which is an intra-university network linking X.25 mainframe computers.

See also **N-1; X.25.**

National Center for Supercomputer Applications (NCSA)

A University of Illinois at Urbana-Champaign computing center that provides information and resources for the World Wide Web (WWW).

National Computer Security Center (NCSC)

A branch of the United States National Security Agency (NSA) responsible for defining security standards for computer products. The Orange Book produced by the Department of Defense (DoD) lists seven levels of security.

See also **Department of Defense; Orange Book.**

National Information Infrastructure (NII)

A term describing an anticipated combination of the Internet with public networks to form a seamless communications web, including all the necessary protocols, access software, applications software, the information itself, and service providers.

National Institute of Standards and Technology (NIST)

A United States government agency responsible for supporting and cataloging a variety of standards. The NIST was formerly known as the National Bureau of Standards (NBS).

National Research and Education Network (NREN)

A network being developed as a state-of-the-art network for research organizations and educational institutions.

National Science Foundation (NSF)

A United States government agency that provides funding for scientific research and controls the National Science Foundation Network (NSFnet) to provide support for educational and scientific research.

National Voluntary Laboratory Accreditation Program (NVLAP)

The United States' part of a group of centers that develop automated software to test compliance with X.400 and X.500 standards. Other parts of the group are located in the United Kingdom (the National Computer Center), France (Alcatel), and Germany (Danet GmbH).

See also **X.400; X.500.**

NAU

network-addressable unit, a logical unit (LU), physical unit (PU), or system-services control point (SSCP) that is the origin or destination of information transmitted through the path-control network in a Systems Network Architecture (SNA) environment.

See also **logical unit; physical unit; Systems Network Architecture; system-services control point.**

NAUN

Nearest Active Upstream Neighbor, a Token Ring node from which another node receives packets and the token. Token Ring nodes receive transmissions only from a NAUN.

See also **Token Ring.**

NBP

Name-Binding Protocol, an AppleTalk protocol that converts entity names into their corresponding Internet addresses. For example, the Macintosh Chooser Desk Accessory and the ATCON NetWare Loadable Module (NLM) use NBP to locate AppleTalk entities.

See also **AppleTalk; Internet address.**

NCB

Network-Control Block, a packet structure used in the NetBIOS transport protocol.

See also **Network Basic Input/Output System.**

NCC

Network-Control Center, a designated network workstation in charge of network management, which receives reports from agent processes running on workstations.

See also **managing process.**

NCCF

Network Communications Control Facility, a component of IBM's NetView network-management software that monitors and controls the operation of a network.

See also **NetView.**

NCCP

Novell College Credit Program, in which Novell issues an official transcript upon completion of NetWare certification courses reviewed by the American Council on Education (ACE) and that may result in college course credit being awarded for taking the courses and passing the certification examinations.

NCF file

A NetWare configuration file (NCF) that can be used by the network administrator to automate network server commands. These files are similar to DOS batch files.

NCompass

A group of World Wide Web (WWW) browser plug-ins from NCompass Labs that facilitate building and using elements based on Microsoft's ActiveX Controls technology.

NControl

An automation tool set, included in Novell's NLM Certification Kit, used to automate the execution of DOS, Windows, OS/2, and NetWare Loadable Module (NLM) applications that contain their own user interfaces. NControl is sometimes used to test software products.

NCOPY utility

A NetWare and IntranetWare file utility that allows a user to copy files or directories from one location to another. The NCOPY utility allows the use of drive letters instead of directory paths to specify source and target paths, and allows the use of wildcard characters.

NCP

(1) **NetWare Core Protocol,** procedures that are followed by a server's NetWare operating system to accept and respond to workstation requests. NCPs exist for every service that a station might request from a server. Requests are formed using the exact guidelines of a specific service protocol and the server handles the request according to the protocol rules. Requests that are commonly serviced include creating or destroying a service connection, manipulating directories and files, opening semaphores, altering the Novell Directory Services (NDS) Directory tree, and printing.

(2) **network-control program,** a program that provides routing, error control, testing, and addressing of Systems Network Architecture (SNA) devices.

(3) **Network-Control Protocol,** a program that manages basic networking functions for a network; NetWare Core Protocol (see Definition 1 in this entry) is an example.

See also **(1) network operating system; (1) Novell Directory Services; (2) Systems Network Architecture.**

NCP Extensions

A resource appearing in the Available Options/Resource Utilization screen of the NetWare 3.12 MONITOR NetWare Loadable Module (NLM) that tracks loadable modules that define their own NetWare Control Protocols (NCPs).

See also **MONITOR; NetWare Control Protocol; NetWare Loadable Module.**

NCP Packet Signature

A NetWare security feature that prevents forgery of NetWare Core Protocol (NCP) by requiring the server and the user's workstation to attach a "signature" to each NCP packet, which changes with every packet. If an NCP packet contains in incorrect signature, the packet is discarded without breaking the workstation's connection to the server. This feature protects both servers and workstations from unauthorized access or the attempted use of unauthorized network privileges.

See also **NetWare Core Protocol.**

NCP Server object

In Novell Directory Services (NDS), an object automatically created for any IntranetWare server being upgraded or installed in IntranetWare that represents any server providing NetWare Core Protocol (NCP) transport and session servers. This object is in a subclass of the Server object. An NCP Server object can have the Access-Control List, Account Balance, Allow Unlimited Credit, Back Link, Bindery, Common Name (CN), DS Revision, Full Name, Host Device, Locality (L), Messaging Server, Minimum Account Balance, Network Address, Object Class, Operator, Organization (O), Organizational Unit (OU), Private Key, Public Key, Resource, Security Equals To, Security Flags, See Also, Status, Supported Services, User, and Version selectable NDS properties.

See also **Novell Directory Services; Server object.**

NCS

(1) **Network-Control System,** a software tool that monitors and modifies network activity. NCS software is generally found on older network systems that incorporate a low-speed, secondary data channel created with Time-Division Multiplexing (TDM).

(2) **Novell Consulting Services,** a department at Novell providing custom software development, network auditing, network-systems design, and distributed application-design services.

See also (1) **Time-Division Multiplexing.**

NCSA

National Center for Supercomputer Applications, a University of Illinois at Urbana-Champaign computing center that provides information and resources for the World Wide Web (WWW).

NCSA Mosaic

A World Wide Web (WWW) browser from the National Center for Supercomputer Applications (NCSA) that offers customizable disk caching and random-access memory (RAM) caching. Two unique features of NCSA Mosaic are Collaborate (which allows the linking of other Web browsers) and Mosaic Astroturf (which allows the setting of the browser to follow a series of links). NCSA Mosaic was one of the first Web browsers.

See also **Web browser.**

For more information about NCSA Mosaic, surf the Web to `http://www.ncsa.uiuc.edu/sdg/software/mosaic.`

NCSC

National Computer Security Center, a branch of the United States National Security Agency (NSA) responsible for defining security standards for computer products. The Orange Book produced by the Department of Defense (DoD) lists seven levels of security.

See also **Department of Defense; Orange Book.**

NCUPDATE utility

In NetWare 4.*x* and IntranetWare, a workstation utility that automatically updates a user's NET.CFG file with a new name context after a container has been moved or renamed. Although NCUPDATE can be run from the command line, it is designed to be run from a Container login script. The network supervisor places a command to run NCUPDATE in the login script of a container by using either NetWare Administrator or NETADMIN.

See also **Container login script; NetWare Administrator.**

ND

Names directory, a database that contains the mappings of all Network-Visible Entities (NVEs) with their Internet addresses.

See also **Internet address; Network-Visible Entity.**

NDD

NetWare Directory Database, a NetWare system database that includes information about all the objects in Novell Directory Services. The information appears in a hierarchically organized tree structure. The NetWare Directory is also known as the *NetWare Directory*, the *Directory*, or the *Directory tree.*

See also **Novell Directory Services.**

NDIR utility

In NetWare and IntranetWare, a file and workstation utility that allows viewing of information about files (such as date, size, owner, attributes, and archive information), about directories (such as creation date, owner, subdirectories, Inherited-Rights Filter, and effective rights), and about volumes. In addition, this utility provides the capability to sort information according to creation date, owner, file or directory attributes, and so on. To view several files in the default directory, separate each filename from the others with a comma. Wildcard characters are acceptable with this utility.

See also **attribute; Inherited-Rights Filter.**

NDIS

Network Driver-Interface Specification, a specification developed jointly by 3Com and Microsoft to standardize the interface used between a Network Interface Cards (NIC) and the underlying operating system, as well as to provide protocol multiplexing so that multiple protocol stacks may be used at one time.

See also **Network Interface Card.**

NDPS

Novell Distributed Print Services, in IntranetWare, a distributed service designed for complex print-management and production requirements, and that consists of client, server, and connectivity components seamlessly linking and sharing network printers with applications. With NDPS, the NetWare Administrator provides management and control of printers, eliminating the need to create and configure Print Queue, Printer, and Print Server leaf objects.

See also **leaf object.**

NDS

Novell Directory Services, in NetWare and IntranetWare, a relational database distributed across the entire network, providing global access to all network resources regardless their locations. NDS uses a distributed database (called the NetWare Directory database, or simply the Directory) to store all network resources as objects. Users log in to a multiserver network and view the entire network as a single information system, which improves user productivity and diminishes administrative costs.

NDS organizes users, groups, printers, servers, volumes, and other physical network devices into a hierarchical tree structure. The NDS tree (also known as the Directory tree) is what allows resources to be managed and displayed in a single view. The Directory tree is managed through objects and their associated properties.

See **Novell Directory Services** (includes **Figure N.3** and **Table N.11**).

NDS MANAGER utility

In IntranetWare, a Windows workstation utility that manages Novell Directory Services (NDS) partitions and replicas on a NetWare server. The utility provides partitioning and replication services for the NDS database, server and workstation services from a single client location, and version update capabilities. The NDS MANAGER utility can be run as a standalone utility (from the SYS:PUBLIC directory) or can be configured to run as a tool under the Tools menu in NetWare Administrator.

See also **NetWare Administrator; Novell Directory Services; partition; replica.**

NE2000

A proprietary Novell Network Interface Card (NIC) used on Ethernet networks.
See also **Ethernet; Network Interface Card.**

NEAP

Novell Educational Academic Partner, a college or university that provides Novell-authorized courses in a semester- or quarter-length curriculum and authorized to teach Novell-developed courses with Certified Novell Instructors (CNIs).
See also **Certified Novell Instructor.**

near-end crosstalk (NEXT)

Interference that occurs close to a connector at either end of a cable. NEXT is usually measured near the source of a test signal.

Nearest Active Upstream Neighbor (NAUN)

A Token Ring node from which another node receives packets and the token. Token Ring nodes receive transmissions only from a NAUN.
See also **Token Ring.**

NEARnet

A New-England-area regional network that connects the National Science Foundation Network (NSFnet), many universities, and several major corporations.
See also **National Science Foundation.**

negative acknowledgment (NAK)

A Return signal reporting an error in a message that has been received.
See also **error detection and correction.**

negotiable BIND

A Request/Response Unit (RU) that enables two logical-unit-to-logical unit (LU-LU) half sessions to negotiate the parameters of a network session when the LUs are activating a session.

neighbor

Under NetWare Link-Services Protocol (NLSP), a router capable of forming an adjacency with another NLSP router. Two NLSP routers are considered neighbors when they can communicate without the aid of an intermediary router.
See also **adjacency; NetWare Link-Services Protocol.**

neighboring router

Two routers in the Open Shortest Path First (OPSF) protocol that share a route to the same network.

See also **Open Shortest Path First.**

NEP

Noise-Equivalent Power, the amount of optical power needed by a fiber-optic receiver to produce an electric current as strong as the receiver's base noise level.

See also **fiber optics.**

NET

Network Entity Title, a network address defined in the OSI Reference Model and used in Connectionless-Mode Network Service (CLNS) networks.

See also **Connectionless-Mode Network Service; OSI Reference Model.**

net (network)

A suffix on an Internet address that indicates the address belongs to a network provider or a consortium of research laboratories. Internet service providers (ISPs) often have names with the *net* suffix.

See also **IP address; Internet service provider.**

NET.CFG

NetWare's workstation boot file containing configuration values that adjust the operating parameters of the NetWare DOS Requester, Internet Packet Exchange (IPX), and other workstation software. Created with a text editor that uses the American Standard Code for Information Interchange (ASCII), NET.CFG must be included on the workstation's boot disk with other boot files. NET.CFG (which is similar to the CONFIG.SYS file in DOS) replaces the SHELL.CFG file used in earlier versions of NetWare.

See also **Internet Packet Exchange; NetWare DOS Requester.**

NETADMIN utility

In Intranetware, a workstation utility that manages Novell Directory Services (NDS) objects and their properties by allowing users to view, create, move, delete, and assign rights to any NDS object under their jurisdiction. Table N.1 shows the options available under the main NETADMIN menu and describes their uses.

Information provided by NETADMIN is displayed in windows that represent layers of the Directory tree. Users select the level of the tree either by browsing the tree or by choosing the Search option from the main menu.

See also **Alias object; container object; Directory tree; leaf object; Novell Directory Services.**

NetBEUI

Network Basic Input/Output System, Extended User Interface, an implementation of IBM's Network Basic Input/Output System (NetBIOS) transport protocol that communicates with a network through Microsoft's Network Driver-Interface Specification (NDIS) for the Network Interface Card (NIC). Microsoft's LAN Server and LAN Manager use NetBEUI.

See also **LAN Manager; LAN Server; Network Driver-Interface Specification.**

Table N.1: NETADMIN Options

Option	Description
Manage objects	Provides for management of objects, properties, object rights, file system rights.
Manage according to search pattern	Provides for selection of individual or groups of objects to view or manage. Provides for selection of a view of Alias objects.
Change context	Provides the capability to change where a user is in the Directory tree structure.
Search	Provides search capabilities for any NDS object or object class, with wildcard characters being accepted.

NetBIOS

Network Basic Input Output System, generically, the standard protocol used as an interface for applications developed to run peer-to-peer communications on an IBM personal computer network and a Token Ring network. The NetWare Client for DOS and MS Windows program includes a NetBIOS driver that is an emulator, allowing NetWare Internetwork Packet Exchange (IPX) to interface with two NetBIOS interrupts. This driver is an emulator because it does not transmit NetBIOS packets, but rather the packets are encapsulated as IPX packets, which are themselves transmitted.

See also **NetWare Client for DOS and MS Windows; Internetwork Packet Exchange; Token Ring.**

NetBIOS Extended User Interface (NetBEUI)

An implementation of IBM's Network Basic Input/Output System (NetBIOS) transport protocol that communicates with a network through Microsoft's Network Driver-Interface Specification (NDIS) for the Network Interface Card (NIC). Microsoft's LAN Server and LAN Manager use NetBEUI.

See also **LAN Manager; LAN Server; Network Driver-Interface Specification.**

NETBIOS command

A NetWare workstation command that allows users to view the NetWare version information, view which interrupts are currently in use, determine if NETBIOS has been loaded, and unload NETBIOS.

NETBIOS.EXE

A NetBIOS driver in the NetWare Client for DOS and MS Windows program. NETBIOS.EXE is an emulator that allows NetWare Internetwork Packet Exchange (IPX) to interface with two NetBIOS interrupts. This driver is an emulator because it does not transmit NetBIOS packets, but rather the packets are encapsulated as IPX packets, which are themselves transmitted.

See also **NetWare Client for DOS and MS Windows; Internetwork Packet Exchange; Token Ring.**

NetCruiser

A suite of Internet applications from NetCom that includes a World Wide Web (WWW) browser; a Network News-Transfer Protocol (NNTP) newsreader; gopher, ftp, Telnet, and finger applications; and an Internet Relay Chat (IRC) client.

See also **Internet Relay Chat; Network News-Transfer Protocol; Telnet; Web browser.**

Netfind

A telephone-directory-style search engine used to find people with Internet addresses.

NETINFO.CFG

In NetWare, an executable batch file that resides on the server and stores LOAD and BIND commands associated with protocol configuration when the INETCFG NetWare Loadable Module (NLM) is used to configure the protocols. If INETCFG is not used, the LOAD and BIND commands are placed in the AUTOEXEC.NCF file. The NET-INFO.CFG file is located on the NetWare partition of the server's hard disk.

See also **AUTOEXEC.NCF; INETCFG; NetWare Loadable Module.**

netiquette

A set of unwritten rules that govern the use of electronic mail (e-mail) and other network services. The term is a contraction of "network etiquette."

netizen

A term that describes a citizen of the Internet, or someone who uses network resources.

NetMC

A World Wide Web (WWW) browser plug-in from NEC for Windows-based versions of Netscape Navigator and compatible browsers that plays multimedia presentations created with the NetMC multimedia authoring tool.

See also **Netscape Navigator; Web browser.**

Netnews

A term used to describe Usenet newsgroups.
See also **newsgroup; Usenet.**

Netopia

Integrated-Service Data Network (ISDN) modems from Farallon Communications that combine terminal-adapter and network interfaces.

See also **Integrated-Service Data Network.**

NetPartner

An AT&T network-management system that monitors voice and data links for wide-area networks (WANs).

Netscape

Shortened name for Netscape Communications, the developer and manufacturer of such World Wide Web (WWW) products as Netscape Navigator, a popular Web browser.

See also **Netscape Navigator; Web browser.**

Netscape Extensions

Rules and standards established by Netscape Communications for content and appearance of HyperText Markup Language (HTML) pages on the World Wide Web (WWW), including tables, style sheets, and frames.

See also **HyperText Markup Language; markup tab; Web home page.**

Netscape Media Player

A World Wide Web (WWW) browser plug-in from Netscape Communications for Netscape Navigator that plays multimedia created with Netscape MediaServer. Versions are available for Windows, Macintosh, and UNIX platforms.

See also **Netscape Navigator; Web browser.**

Netscape Navigator

A World Wide Web (WWW) browser from Netscape Communications that features a variety of plug-ins for increased functionality, as well as multiplatform support.

The plug-ins provide three-dimensional, multimedia, and collaboration tools. Live3D, a Virtual-Reality Modeling Language (VRML) plug-in, provides the capability to view and navigate three-dimensional worlds from within Navigator windows. Other plug-ins provide the capability to listen to Audio-Interchange File Format (AIFF), Musical Instrument Digital Interface (MIDI), waveform audio, and multimedia audio files. The Navigator Mail and News software provides extended support for HyperText Markup Language (HTML) files.

Netscape Navigator comes in versions for the Windows, Macintosh, and UNIX environments.

See also **Audio-Interchange File Format; HyperText Markup Language; Musical Instrument Digital Interface; Virtual-Reality Modeling Language; Web browser.**

 **For more information about Netscape Navigator and related products, surf the Web to** `http:// www.netscape.com/comprod/ products/navigator/ index.html.`

NetShark

A World Wide Web (WWW) browser from InterCon Systems used in both the eWorld and America Online commercial services. The Web browser provides a selection of prechosen Web sites and an electronic mail (e-mail) client.

See also **Web browser.**

NetSync cluster

A group that includes 1 NetWare 4.*x* server running the NETSYNC4 NetWare Loadable Module (NLM) and up to 12 NetWare 3.*x* servers attached to it.

See also **NETSYNC4; NetWare Loadable Module.**

NETSYNC3 (NLM)

In NetWare 4.*x* and IntranetWare, a NetWare Loadable Module (NLM) loaded on a NetWare 3 file server console to enable the NetWare Bindery Synchronizer. NETSYNC3 copies the NetWare 3 server's bindery information to a NetWare 4.*x* server's bindery context, and communicates with the NetWare 4.*x* server to receive updates to Directory information. NETSYNC3 moves printing objects and converts the NetWare 3 PRINTDEF database into a database compatible with NetWare 4.*x*. The NLM then creates the NETSYNC working directory under SYS:SYSTEM for NetSync log files. The NETSYNC3 utility should be added to the AUTOEXEC.NCF file on the NetWare 3 server so that it can run continuously.

See also **AUTOEXEC.NCF; NetWare Loadable Module; PRINTDEF utility.**

NETSYNC4 (NLM)

In NetWare 4.*x* and IntranetWare, a NetWare Loadable Module (NLM) that is loaded on a NetWare 4.1 "host" server console to enable the NetWare Bindery Synchronizer. NETSYNC4 authorizes NetWare 3 servers to be part of the NetSync cluster. It also receives information from the NetWare 3 binderies and continually downloads updated Directory information to all attached NetWare 3 servers.

See also **NetSync cluster; NetWare Loadable Module.**

NETUSER utility

In NetWare 4.*x* and IntranetWare, a workstation utility that manages network tasks. Table N.2 shows the available options on the NETUSER main menu and provides a description of each.

Table N.2: NETUSER Options

Option	Description
Printing	Provides for capturing ports to printers or print queues. Sends, modifies, pauses, and deletes print jobs after a port has been captured.
Messages	Provides for the sending of messages to users or groups, as well as enabling or disabling incoming messages.
Drives	Provides for the management of drive and search mappings. Provides a view of effective rights on selected drives.
Attachments	Provides the capability to manage network attachments, change a password, view server information, or change a login script.
Change Context	Provides the capability to set a current context when logged in to a Directory tree.

NetView

An IBM software product that monitors Systems Network Architecture (SNA) networks. NetView includes access services, a performance monitor, a session monitor, a hardware monitor, a status monitor, a distribution manager, a host command facility, a Help Desk facility, and customization facilities. This product runs as a Virtual Telecommunications Access Method (VTAM) application on the mainframe computer serving as the network manager.

See also **Network Communications Control Facility; Network-Management Architecture; Systems Network Architecture; Virtual Telecommunications Access Method.**

NetWare

A local-area network (LAN)/wide-area network (WAN) operating system from Novell that uses the NetWare Core Protocol (NCP), Internetwork Packet Exchange (IPX), and Sequenced Packet Exchange (SPX) protocols to transparently share services across dissimilar platforms. NetWare servers can support DOS, Windows, UNIX, and OS/2 clients, or Macintosh workstations. The Novell Directory Services (NDS) feature provides a scheme for arranging the entire network into a unified structure, as well as organizing network resources for easy access and centralized administration of the network.

Since its introduction in the early 1980s, NetWare has been released in a number of versions, including the following:

- *NetWare 86*. The first shipped version of NetWare designed for Intel 8086 processors used a modified implementation of the Xerox networking

software called the Internetwork Packet Exchange (IPX).
- *NetWare 2*. This release included a modification to the Xerox networking software called Sequence Packet Exchange (SPX) and provided support for the Macintosh.
- *NetWare 3*. This release is a client-server implementation written to support the Intel 80386 processor. NetWare 3 is a 32-bit implementation of NetWare and includes support for additional Network Interface Cards (NICs), encapsulation of IPX/SPX packets within a Transmission-Control Protocol/Internet Protocol (TCP/IP) network, and a number of bug fixes. NetWare 3.12 is the latest release of this version.
- *NetWare 4*. This release features an Enterprise LAN/WAN support, a global naming scheme (NDS), improved remote access capabilities, enhanced security features, and central network administration. NetWare 4.1 is the latest release of this version.
- *IntranetWare*. This latest release features the NetWare 4.11 operating system along with added Internet capabilities, including a Web server, NetBasic tool, Netscape Navigator Web browser, and Novell Java platform. In addition, the NetWare Distributed Printing Services (NDPS) has been introduced.

Table N.3 compares features of various releases of NetWare. Figure N.1 shows how NetWare fits into the OSI Reference Model. *See also* **OSI Reference Model.**

For more information about NetWare and IntranetWare products, surf the Web to http://www.novell.com/ intranetware.

Table N.3: NetWare and IntranetWare Feature Comparison

Feature	NetWare 3.12	NetWare 4.1	IntranetWare
INTRANET/INTERNET			
NetBasic tool	No	No	Yes
Netscape browser	No	No	Yes
Novell Java platform	No	No	Yes
Web server	No	No	Yes
ARCHITECTURE			
Maximum number of user connections per server	250	1,000	1,000
Nondedicated server	No	Yes (NetWare for OS/2)	Yes (IntranetWare for OS/2)
INSTALLATION			
Automated choice and configuration of protocols	No	No	Yes
Hardware autodetection	No	No	Yes
Install from CD-ROM	No	Yes	Yes
MIGRATION			
Graphical Administration	No	Yes	Yes
NDS modeling with DS MIGRATE utility	No	No	Yes
NetWare file-migration utility	No	No	Yes
LICENSING SERVICES			
Licensing Services	No	No	Yes
NetWare for Macintosh user licenses included	5	Limited to total number of new user licenses	Matches the number of IntranetWare user licenses

(continued)

Table N.3: NetWare and IntranetWare Feature Comparison (continued)

Feature	NetWare 3.12	NetWare 4.1	IntranetWare
SERVER OPERATING SYSTEM			
Abend Recovery	No	No	Yes
Memory protection	No	Yes	Yes
Symmetric Multiprocessing	No	OEM-supplied	Yes
NOVELL DIRECTORY SERVICES (NDS)			
Directory Services	No	Yes	Yes
NetWare Administrator	No	Limited	Yes
Partition Management	No	PARTMGR and Partition Manager	NDS Manager
SECURITY SERVICES			
AUDITCON utility	No	Limited	Additional events
Network C2	No	No	Yes
Restrict login to specific Macintosh addresses	No	Yes	Yes
RSA Public Key/Private Key	No	Yes	Yes
Security auditing	No	Yes	Yes
Single login to network	No	Yes	Yes
PRINT SERVICES			
Maximum shared printers	16 per print server	256 per print server	256 per print server
NetWare Administrator "Quick Setup"	No	No	Yes
NetWare Distributed Print Services (NDPS)	No	No	Yes
Print management	Bindery-based	Directory-base	Directory-based
RAM used with remote printer	4K to 20K	4.6K to 5.4K	4.6K to 5.4K

Feature	NetWare 3.12	NetWare 4.1	IntranetWare
FILE SERVICES			
Additive licensing	No	Yes	Yes
Automatic file compression	No	Yes	Yes
Block suballocation	No	Yes	Yes
High-Capacity Storage System (HCSS)	No	Yes	Yes
NetWare Peripheral Architecture (NPA)	No	Yes	Yes
Support for long filenames	Yes	OS/2	Windows 95, Windows NT, OS/2
Volume capacity		2 million directory entries	16 million directory entries
CONNECTIVITY SERVICES			
Dynamic Host-Control Protocol (DHCP) support	Add-on	Add-on	Yes
Internet service provider (ISP) connectivity	No	No	Leased line, Frame Relay, ISDN
IP/IPX gateway	No	No	Yes
Large Internet Packet (LIP)	Add-on	Yes	Yes
Load and bind multiple protocols at installation	No	TCP/IP, AppleTalk, IPX	TCP/IP, AppleTalk, IPX
Multiprotocol routing	Add-on	Add-on	Integrated support for PPP, ISDN, Frame Relay, ATM, X.25
Packet-burst protocol	Add-on	Yes	Yes
Protocol management	Limited	Yes	Yes
TCP/IP	Add-on	Add-on	Yes
APPLICATION SERVICES			
Developer Net 2000	No	No	Yes
Novell Application Launcher (NAL)	No	No	Yes

(continued)

Table N.3: NetWare and IntranetWare Feature Comparison (continued)

Feature	NetWare 3.12	NetWare 4.1	IntranetWare
NETWORK MANAGEMENT			Yes
GUI utility with view of entire network	No	Yes	Yes
Integrated messaging	No	Yes	Yes
NetWare Link-Services Protocol (NLSP)	Add-on	Yes	Yes
Remote-console modem callback	No	Yes	Yes
Remote-console session security	No	Yes	Yes
STORAGE MANAGEMENT SERVICES			
End-user graphical-user-interface (GUI) tools	No	Yes	Yes
SBACKUP utility	Limited	Limited	Yes
Target Service Agents (TSAs)	Limited	DOS, Windows 3.1x, OS/2	DOS, Windows 3.1x, Windows 95, OS/2, Mac
CLIENT SUPPORT			
Embedded international language support	No	Yes	Yes
LPT ports on client	LPT-1 to LPT-3	LPT-1 to LPT-9	LPT-1 to LPT-9
NetWare DOS Requester support	Yes	Yes	Yes

NetWare Access Server

Novell's application-server software that network managers use to provide users on remote networks and local-area networks (LANs) with access to all NetWare LAN resources, including Systems Network Architecture (SNA) and Transmission-Control Protocol/Internet Protocol (TCP/IP) applications.

See also **Systems Network Architecture; Transmission-Control Protocol/Internet Protocol.**

NetWare Administrator (NWADMIN) utility

In NetWare 4.x and IntranetWare, a Windows and OS/2 workstation utility that performs supervisory tasks available in the FILER, NETADMIN, PARTMGR, and PCONSOLE utilities. The NetWare Administrator utility allows a network supervisor to create users and groups; create, delete, move, and rename Novell Directory Services (NDS) objects; assign rights in the Directory tree and in the file

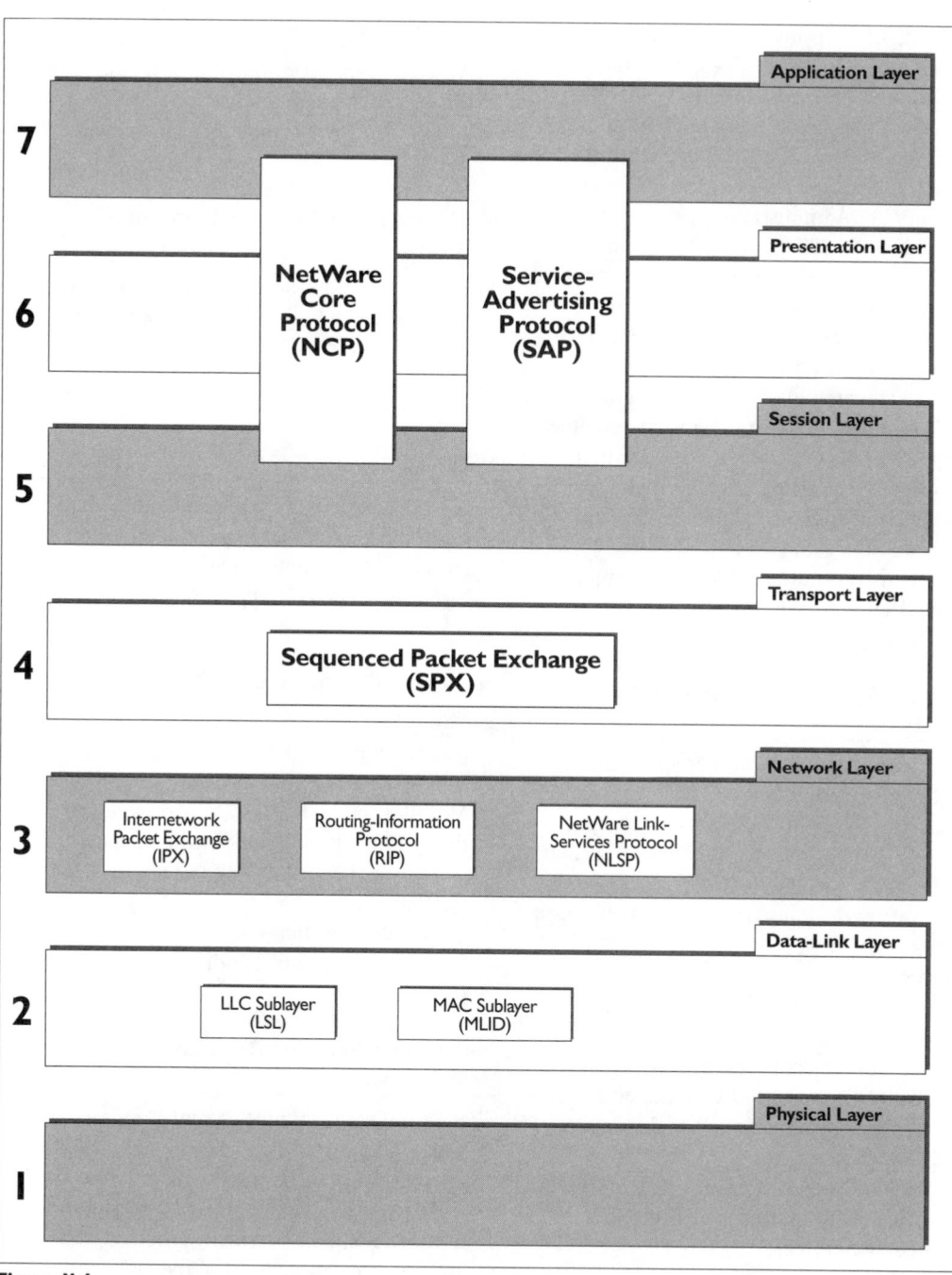

Figure N.1
NetWare and the OSI Reference Model

system; set up print services; and set up and manage NDS partitions and replicas.

When NetWare or IntranetWare is first installed, files for the Windows version of NetWare Administrator are copied to the SYS:PUBLIC directory. For the OS/2 version of NetWare Administrator, the files are copied to the SYS:PUBLIC/OS2 directory.

This utility uses a graphical user interface (GUI) and runs as a multiple-document-interface (MDI) application. By using a menu bar and a browser, supervisors are able to view the file system of a server in the current Directory tree; open a container object and view the objects that are in it; view an object dialog (which provides object details) of a container object; and view an object dialog of a leaf object.

See also **container object; leaf object; Novell Directory Services; object.**

NetWare Application Manager (NAM) utility

In IntranetWare, a Windows workstation utility included with the Novell Application Launcher (NAL) that creates and manages Novell Directory Services (NDS) Application leaf objects through the NetWare Administrator utility. The Application object is first created with the NetWare Administrator utility, which allows a network supervisor to choose from assigned object classes and properties. After the Application object properties are set, an executable file is associated with the object; this file allocates resources such as drive mappings or printer ports.

See also **Application object; leaf object; NetWare Administrator utility; Novell Directory Services.**

NetWare Application Notes

A Novell support resource now included in the *Novell Support Connection* CD-ROM. *See also* **Novell Support Connection.**

NetWare Asynchronous Services Interface (NASI)

Specifications for accessing NetWare communications servers. The NASI Software Developer's Kit (SDK) can be used to build applications running on this interface.

NetWare Buyer's Guide

A Novell support resource, now known as the *Novell Buyer's Guide*, included in the *Novell Support Connection* CD-ROM. *See also* **Novell Support Connection.**

NetWare C Interface for NLM applications

A core set of Application Program Interfaces (APIs) for NetWare Loadable Modules (NLMs). These APIs provide a direct programming link to the operating system services for NetWare 3.*x* and NetWare 4.*x*.

See also **Application Program Interface; NetWare Loadable Module.**

NetWare Client for DOS and MS Windows

Software connecting DOS and Windows workstations with the NetWare network to allow users at those workstations to use network resources. Table N.4 shows the four terminate-and-stay-resident programs that are the core components of the DOS and Windows environment.

Table N.4: Key Components of NetWare Client for DOS and Windows

Component	Program	Description
Link-Support Layer (LSL)	LSL.COM	Puts packaged requests from the IPXODI driver into the proper transmission format for the physical network on which the workstations run. Takes replies for the workstation clients from the network, removes network-specific information, and passes the reply to IPXODI.
NetWare DOS Requester	VLM.EXE	DOS-based software that provides the interface between DOS and the network.
ODI LAN driver	NE2000.COM (for NE2000 Network Interface Cards)	Sends requests received from the LSL and forwards them to the network, as well as receiving replies from the network and passing them to the LSL software.
Transport protocol	IPXODI.COM	Delivers requests and replies between the workstations and the network. Handles packet sequencing and acknowledgment for a client-server connection.

See also **Link-Support Layer; NE2000; NetWare DOS Requester.**

NetWare Client for OS/2

Software that connects OS/2 workstations with the NetWare network to allow users at those workstations to use network resources. NetWare Client for OS/2 directs network requests from the workstations to the network, and allows applications servers to communicate with their workstations without using a NetWare server.

NetWare Connect

A NetWare add-on product that enables remote users of Windows, DOS, and Macintosh computers to dial in and access all resources available on a NetWare network, as well as enabling network users to dial out to connect to remote computers, bulletin boards, X.25 and Integrated-Services Digital Network (ISDN) services, and other asynchronous hosts.

NetWare Connection

A monthly user publication produced by NetWare Users International (NUI) that provides a forum for the exchange of information among CNEs and other users of NetWare and related products.

NetWare Console Monitor

In NetWare 4.02, a field name that appears in the System Modules menu in the MONITOR NetWare Loadable Module (NLM).

See also **MONITOR; NetWare Loadable Module.**

NetWare Control Center

A NetWare for Macintosh administrative utility that helps to manage users, groups, and security on a NetWare file server from a Macintosh client.

NetWare Core Protocol (NCP)

Procedures that are followed by a server's NetWare operating system to accept and respond to workstation requests. NCPs exist for every service that a station might request from a server. Requests are formed using the exact guidelines of a specific service protocol and the server handles the request according to the protocol rules. Requests that are commonly serviced include creating or destroying a service connection, manipulating directories and files, opening semaphores, altering the Novell Directory Services (NDS) Directory tree, and printing.

See also **NCP; network operating system; Novell Directory Services.**

NetWare desk accessory

A Macintosh desk accessory that enables a NetWare for Macintosh user to send messages to other users, as well as to view or administer print jobs from a Macintosh workstation.

NetWare Directory

A NetWare system database that includes information about all the objects in Novell Directory Services. The information appears in a hierarchically organized tree structure. The NetWare Directory is also known as the *NetWare Directory Database*, the *Directory*, or the *Directory tree*. Note that the *D* is usually capitalized to distinguish the NetWare Directory from a file-system directory.

See also **Novell Directory Services.**

NetWare Directory Browser utility

In IntranetWare, a Macintosh workstation utility that allows the selection of objects from the Directory tree. Using the NetWare Directory Browser utility, users can see all objects in a Directory tree, provided the objects have not been hidden. By using the NetWare Directory Browser to save Server, Volume, Printer, and Print Queue objects, and then hiding the Browser, a network supervisor can create custom NetWare Client configurations for individual users.

NetWare Directory Database (NDD)

A NetWare system database that includes information about all the objects in Novell Directory Services. The information appears in a hierarchically organized tree structure. The NetWare Directory is also known as the *NetWare Directory*, the *Directory*, or the *Directory tree*.

See also **Novell Directory Services.**

NetWare Directory partition

A logical division of the NetWare Directory database that forms a unit of data in the Directory tree. This unit is then used to store and replicate Directory information. Each partition contains a container object, all objects contained therein, and data about those objects (such as properties and rights). The Directory partition does not contain any information about the file system, nor about the directories contained in the file system. To optimize the capability (through distributed operations) of accessing different areas of the Directory, each Directory partition can be replicated and stored at many locations. Figure N.2 shows an example of default Directory partitions.

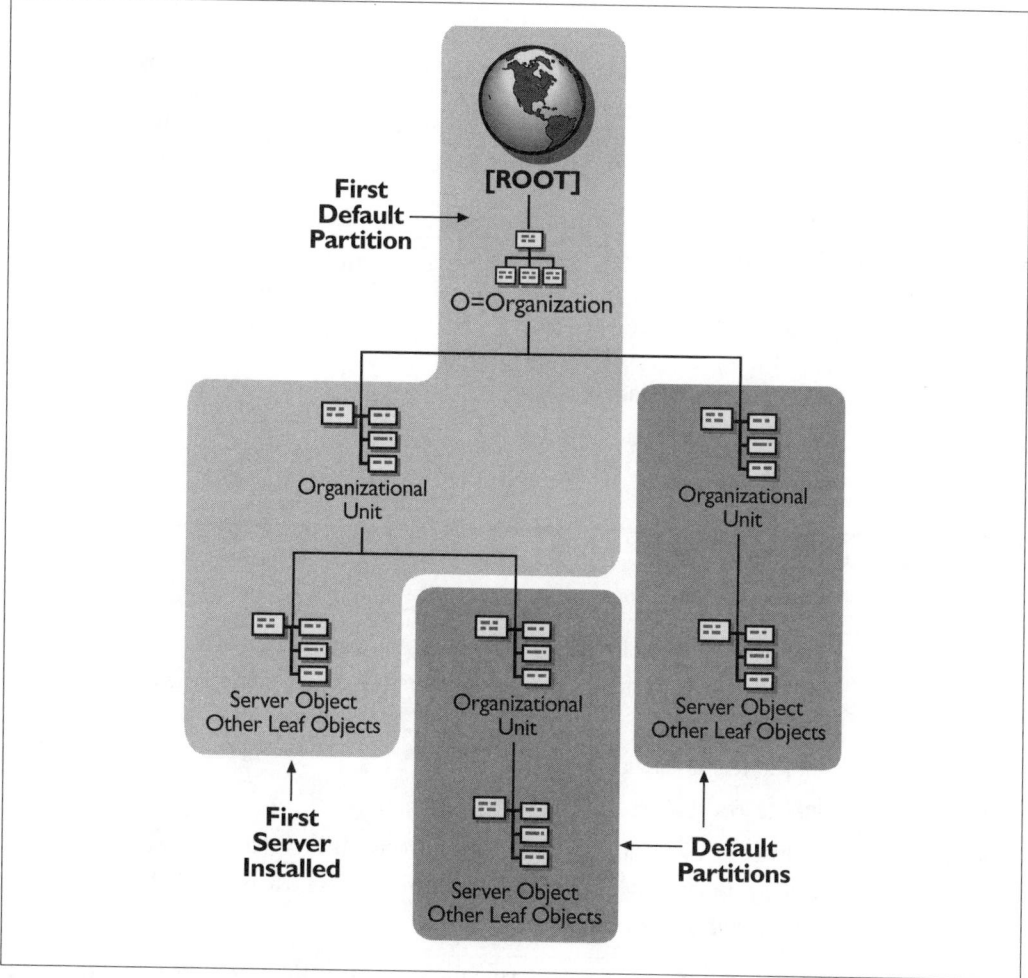

Figure N.2
Default Directory partitions

See also **container object; Novell Directory Services; object.**

NetWare Directory replica

A copy of a NetWare Directory partition that provides a means for storing the NetWare Directory Database (NDD) on several servers across the network without having to duplicate the entire database for each server. An unlimited number of replicas can be created for each Directory partition and can be stored on any server. Directory replicas eliminate a single point of failure on the network and provide faster access to information across a wide-area network (WAN) link.

Table N.5 shows the four types of Directory replicas.

NetWare Domain Protection

A field name in the System Modules menu of the NetWare 4.02 MONITOR NetWare Loadable Module (NLM).

See also **MONITOR; NetWare Loadable Module.**

NetWare DOS Requester

A group of Virtual Loadable Module (VLM) files and a single executable file (VLM.EXE) that together provide NetWare support for DOS and Windows client workstations. The VLM files are grouped into the DOS Redirection Layer, the Service-Protocol Layer, and the Transport-Protocol Layer, all of which are described in Table N.6. The VLM Manager (VLM.EXE) controls communication and memory issues between the individual layers, and is responsible for loading the required VLMs and for disbursing requests to individual modules.

NetWare Express

A private electronic information service no longer provided by Novell.

Table N.5: Directory Replica Types

Type	Description
Master replica	Used to create a new Directory partition in the Directory database, or to read and update Directory information. Only one master replica may be created for each partition.
Read/write replica	Used to read or update Directory information.
Read-only replica	Used to view (but not modify) Directory information.
Subordinate replica	Automatically added on the server by Novell Directory Services (NDS) if a parent Directory partition has either a Master, Read/Write, or Read-only replica on the server and the child partition does not.

See also **Master replica; NetWare Directory Database; Read-Only replica; Read/Write replica; Subordinate replica**.

Table N.6: DOS Requester Layers

Layer	Module	Description
DOS-Redirection Layer	REDIR.VLM	Provides DOS services through the DOS redirector.
Service-Protocol Layer	NWP.VLM	Handles network implementation through the BIND.VLM (for NetWare 2 and NetWare 3 bindery servers), NDS.VLM (for NetWare 4 NDS servers), or PNW.NLM (for Personal NetWare servers) child VLMs.
	RSA.VLM	Provides system-level background security authentication for the workstation.
	FIO.VLM	Provides file-transfer protocol.
	PRINT.VLM	Provides print services using the FIO module for file writes and provides print redirection.
Transport-Protocol Layer	IPXNCP.VLM	Provides the Internetwork Packet Exchange (IPX) protocol as a transfer medium.
	AUTO.VLM	Reconnects a client workstation to a server, and rebuilds the workstation environment to its original state.

See also **NetWare Client for DOS and Windows; Virtual Loadable Module.**

NetWare File-Migration utility

In IntranetWare, a Windows workstation utility that migrates files from NetWare 3.1*x* servers to NetWare 4.11 servers. This utility can still be used after the NetWare 3.1*x* bindery has been migrated by using the DS MIGRATE utility. NetWare File-Migration utility runs under the NetWare Administrator utility.

See also **DS MIGRATE utility; NetWare Administrator utility.**

NetWare for Macintosh

A collection of NetWare Loadable Modules (NLMs) used to provide file handling, printing, network administration, and AppleTalk routing for Macintosh clients on a NetWare network. These NLMs allow Macintosh users to access such network resources as Novell Directory Services (NDS), applications, and network printers to use NetWare features while working in the Macintosh environment.

See also **AppleTalk; MAC.NAM; MAC-FILE; NetWare Loadable Module.**

NetWare for SAA

A group of NetWare Loadable Modules (NLMs) making up a gateway package that provides connectivity to Systems Network Architecture (SNA) networks. With proper access privileges, users can gain access to applications and data on mainframe or midrange computers while working under the DOS, Windows, OS/2, or UNIX operating systems, or while working on a Macintosh computer. NetWare for SAA supports up to several hundred sessions for each gateway.

NetWare for UNIX

A software program that enables users working under the UNIX operating system to utilize the features of a NetWare network (such as file handling, printing, and backup services). Formerly known as Portable NetWare, NetWare for UNIX is sold by third-party vendors.

NetWare Hub Services

A software package from Novell that manages any hub card that complies with the NetWare Hub-Management Interface (HMI) standard.
See also hub.

NetWare Internet-Access Server (NIAS)

An enhanced version of the NetWare Multiprotocol Router that offers a single wide-area network (WAN) connection and Internetwork Packet Exchange/Internet Protocol (IPX/IP) gateway functions. NIAS is included in the IntranetWare product.

See also Internet Protocol; Internetwork Packet Exchange; IntranetWare; NetWare Multiprotocol Router.

NetWare ISA Device Driver

In NetWare 4.02, a field name from the System Modules menu in the MONITOR NetWare Loadable Module (NLM).
See also **MONITOR; NetWare Loadable Module.**

NetWare Licensing Services (NLS)

A distributed network service enabling NetWare administrators to monitor and control the use of licensed applications on a NetWare network. The enterprise service architecture of this service consists of client components that support different platforms and system components that reside on network servers. NLS also includes a license-metering tool and libraries that export licensing-service functionality to developers of other licensing services.

NetWare Link-Services Protocol (NLSP)

Novell's derivation of the Intermediate-System-to-Intermediate-System (IS-IS) link-state routing protocol. NLSP transfers information between routers and makes routing decisions on the basis of that information. NLSP routers exchange link information (such as network connectivity, path costs, Internetwork Packet Exchange network numbers, and media types) with peer routers to build and maintain a logical map of the network. NLSP multicasts routing information only when a route is changed or service on the network is changed. NLSP routers use the Routing-Information Protocol (RIP).

See also **Intermediate-System-to-Intermediate-System; link-state router; Routing-Information Protocol.**

NetWare Link/X.25

Novell's implementation of X.25 for the NetWare Multiprotocol Router.

See also **NetWare Multiprotocol Router; X.25.**

NetWare Lite

A DOS-based, peer-to-peer version of the NetWare network operating system that makes drives, files, and printers available to all DOS and Windows users in the network. Although it supports up to 255 nodes on the network, NetWare Lite is limited to a maximum of 25 simultaneous users. NetWare Lite has been replaced by the Personal NetWare product.

See also **peer-to-peer network.**

NetWare Loadable Module (NLM)

One of a set of NetWare programs loaded (some automatically) and unloaded from server memory while the server is running. When an NLM is loaded, the program is dynamically linked to the operating system, and the NetWare server allocates a portion of memory to it. The amount of memory allocated depends on the task the NLM is designed to perform. Control of the memo-

ry and all other allocated resources are returned to the operating system when the NLM is unloaded. While some NLMs (such as utilities) can be loaded, used, and then unloaded, others (such as local-area network drivers and disk-driver NLMs) must be loaded each time the server is started. Commands to load the latter NLMs are stored in the STARTUP.NCF and AUTOEXEC.NCF files.

Table N.7 shows four common types of NLM programs.

During NetWare installation, most NLM programs are copied to SYS:SYSTEM. As the needs arise, users may copy additional NLMs into the SYS:SYSTEM directory, any network directory on the NetWare server, or a DOS drive of the NetWare server.

NetWare Loadable Module utilities

NetWare Loadable Modules (NLMs) that are used to monitor the server and to change configuration options.

NetWare Login utility

In IntranetWare, a Windows workstation utility that accesses a NetWare Directory tree or NetWare server, and runs a login script. The NetWare Login utility, by default, runs whenever Windows is started. However, the utility can be started at any time by choosing the NetWare Login icon in Windows.

See also **login script.**

Table N.7: NLM Program Types

Type	Filename Extension	Description
Disk driver	.DSK	Controls communication between the operating system and hard drives. May be loaded and unloaded while the server is running.
Local-area network (LAN) driver	.LAN	Controls communication between the operating system and Network Interface Cards (NICs). May be loaded and unloaded while the server is running, and while users are logged in to the network.
Management utilities and server-application module	.NLM	Allows administrators and users to change and monitor configuration options. May be loaded and unloaded while the server is running.
Name-space support	.NAM	Allows non-DOS naming conventions to be stored in the Directory and in the file naming system.

NetWare managed node

A NetWare 4.x server that has the NetWare Management software enabled, thus making more information available to management-console software than is available with Internetwork Packet Exchange/Sequenced Packet Exchange (IPX/SPX) function calls.

See also **Internetwork Packet Exchange; NetWare Management Agents; Sequenced Packet Exchange.**

NetWare Management Agent (NMA)

A group of NetWare Loadable Module (NLM) programs that provides information about the configuration of a server (including the NLM programs installed, printers, print queues, hard disks, disk controllers, and drivers), statistics on server traffic, statistics on server memory, and specifications on alarm settings for server errors and events. By loading the NetWare Management Agent, network administrators can monitor, manage, and maintain all network servers from a single console.

See also **NMA.**

NetWare Management System (NMS)

A system that manages a NetWare network by using a network-management protocol and building a map of network resources. NMS has been replaced by the ManageWise product.

See also **ManageWise; NMAGENT utility.**

NetWare MHS Services

Services that allow users to exchange electronic mail, share calendars, schedule events, and so on, electronically across a NetWare network. To provide these services, NetWare uses a messaging server, a Distribution List object, a Message-Routing Group object, an External Entity object, and a Postmaster.

See also **Distribution List object; External Entity object, Message-Routing Group object; Postmaster.**

NetWare Migration utility

A NetWare 4.*x* workstation utility the allows the transfer of network information from a NetWare 2.*x* or NetWare 3.*x* server to an existing NetWare 4.*x* server on the same network. This can be either an across-the-wire migration or a same-server migration.

See also **across-the-wire migration; same-server migration.**

NetWare Mobile

An integrated client environment for mobile computing and remote access that provides access to available services on a NetWare network. NetWare Mobile includes an enhanced dialer (to simplify NetWare network connections), a Mobile File assistant (to help manage files), location profiling, and graphical administration tools.

NetWare Monitor

In NetWare for OS/2, a graphical utility that runs under OS/2 Presentation Manager and that monitors resources on a NetWare for OS/2 server. The NetWare Monitor is also known as *PMMON* because the PMMON.EXE file is used to run the utility.

NetWare Multiprotocol Router

A software-based bridge and router combination (*brouter*) that can concurrently route Internetwork Packet Exchange (IPX), Transmission-Control Protocol/Internet Protocol (TCP/IP), and AppleTalk across both local-area networks (LANs) and wide-area networks (WANs). The NetWare Multiprotocol Router operates on personal computers with 80386, 80486, or Pentium microprocessors, and supports Ethernet, Token Ring, Fiber Distributed Data Interface (FDDI), fast Ethernet, and ARCnet network topologies.

See also **AppleTalk; ARCnet; Ethernet; Fiber Distributed Data Interface; Internetwork Packet Exchange; Transmission-Control Protocol/Internet Protocol.**

NetWare Multiprotocol Router Plus

Software that provides wide-area network (WAN) connectivity for dispersed heterogeneous networks over T1, fractional T1, X.25, and low-speed synchronous leased lines. This product replaces NetWare Link/64, NetWare Link/T1, and NetWare Link/X.25.

See also **heterogeneous network; T1; X.25.**

NetWare Name Service (NNS)

A predecessor to Novell Directory Services (NDS) that consisted of a set of specialized utilities designed to work with NetWare 2 and NetWare 3 networks to provide a more transparent access to resources in NetWare installations. NNS is no longer available and no longer supported.

See also **Novell Directory Services.**

NetWare NFS

A collection of NetWare Loadable Modules (NLMs) used to integrate UNIX systems transparently with NetWare 4.*x* file systems and resources. NetWare NFS provides UNIX users with access to the NetWare environment from their native UNIX operating system. NetWare NFS uses the Network File System (NFS) Application-Layer protocol from Sun Microsystems.

See also **Network File System; NFS.**

NetWare NFS Gateway

Software installed on a NetWare server that allows NetWare clients to access files on a Network File System (NFS) server and that makes the files appear as though they are on the NetWare server.

NetWare NLM Utility User Interface

In NetWare 4.02, a field name from the System Modules menu in the MONITOR NetWare Loadable Module (NLM).

See also **MONITOR; NetWare Loadable Module.**

NetWare Notify

A startup document on a Macintosh workstation running the NetWare client software that enables users to receive brief messages.

NetWare operating system

Novell's network operating system that runs on the server and provides to the NetWare network file and record locking, security, print spooling, and interprocess communications, while determining performance, multivendor support, and reliability of the network.

NetWare OS Loader

In NetWare 4.02, a field name from the System Modules menu in the MONITOR NetWare Loadable Module (NLM).

See also **MONITOR; NetWare Loadable Module.**

NetWare partition (disk)

A partition created on each NetWare network hard disk, from which NetWare volumes are created. A NetWare disk partition is a subdivision of a hard disk and should not be confused with a NetWare Directory partition.

See also **NetWare Directory partition; partition.**

NetWare Peripheral Architecture (NPA)

An extension of the Media Manager (MM) that provides broader and more flexible driver support for host adapters and storage devices. NPA distinguishes between two types of driver support: Host Adapter

Module (HAM) and Custom Device Module (CDM). The HAM drives the host adapter hardware and provides functionality to route requests to the bus where a specified device is attached. The Host Adapter Interface (HAI) provides an interface for HAMs to communicate with the MM. The CDM drives storage devices or autochanges attached to a host adapter bus. The Custom Device Interface (CDI) provides an interface for CDMs to communicate with the MM.

See also **Media Manager.**

NetWare Print Chooser utility

In IntranetWare, a Macintosh workstation utility that chooses and configures a Novell Directory Services (NDS) Printer or Print Queue object.

See also **leaf object; Novell Directory Services; Printer object; Print Queue object.**

NetWare protocols and transports

Components of NetWare software that enable client workstations and servers to communicate and be understood on the network. A protocol manages data and a transport manages application messages. Table N.8 shows the protocols provided with NetWare Client software and where to find more information.

Table N.8: NetWare Client Protocols

Protocol	For More Information
Address-Resolution Protocol (ARP)	See **Address-Resolution Protocol.**
Bootstrap Protocol (BOOTP)	See **Bootstrap Protocol.**
Internet Control-Message Protocol (ICMP)	See **Internet Control-Message Protocol.**
Internetwork Packet Exchange (IPX)	See **Internetwork Packet Exchange.**
Management Information Base (MIB)	See **Management Information Base.**
Network Basic Input/Output System (NetBIOS)	See **Network Basic Input/Output System.**
Remote Program Load (RPL)	See **Remote Program Load.**
Reverse Address-Resolution Protocol (RARP)	See **Reverse Address-Resolution Protocol.**
Sequenced Packet Exchange (SPX)	See **Sequenced Packet Exchange.**
System Network Architecture (SNA)	See **System Network Architecture.**
Transmission-Control Protocol (TCP)	See **Transmission-Control Protocol.**
User-Datagram Protocol (UDP)	See **User-Datagram Protocol.**
Xerox Network System (XNS)	See **Xerox Network System.**

NetWare Remote Console

(1) **RCONSOLE utility,** in NetWare and IntranetWare, a workstation utility that allows a user to load and unload NetWare Loadable Modules (NLMs), execute console commands, and copy files to NetWare directories or to non-NetWare partitions during a remote console session. This utility does not, however, allow the user to transfer files from a server. Remote servers can be accessed on the same network (which is a direct connection) or through a modem or null modem cable (which is an asynchronous connection). The RCONSOLE utility can be executed from a local hard drive or from a network drive, and the user does not need Supervisor object rights to the remote server.

(2) **Remote Console,** Novell software that enables a network supervisor to manage servers from a workstation. The software is invoked using the RCONSOLE utility.

See also (1) **NetWare Loadable Module;** (2) **remote console management.**

NetWare Remote Console SPS Driver

In NetWare 4.02, a field name from the System Modules menu in the MONITOR NetWare Loadable Module (NLM).

See also **MONITOR; NetWare Loadable Module.**

NetWare Requester for OS/2

Software running on an OS/2 workstation that enables the workstation to connect to a NetWare network and that allows application servers to communicate with the workstations without involving NetWare.

NetWare rights package

A feature of the Rights utility that provides a particular set of NetWare rights. Among the available rights packages are User, Owner, Private, Drop, View Only, and Custom.

NetWare Runtime

A single-user version of the NetWare $4.x$ operating system that can be used as a dedicated applications server with NetWare Loadable Modules (NLMs) installed on it, thus freeing the remaining NetWare servers for other network tasks. Network clients attach to an NLM running on top of NetWare Runtime. That NLM provides to the client required services through Application Program Interfaces (APIs).

See also **Application Program Interface; NetWare Loadable Module.**

NetWare server

A computer that runs the NetWare operating system software, regulates communications among personal computers attached to it, and manages such shared network resources as printers and volumes.

NetWare server console operator

A NetWare $3.x$ user (or member of a group) to whom the network supervisor has delegated certain rights in managing the NetWare server through the use of the FCONSOLE.EXE utility.

NetWare Server for OS/2

Device drivers allowing the NetWare 4.*x* operating system to operate as a nondedicated server on a computer running under the OS/2 operating system. NetWare Server for OS/2 runs as an independent operating system on an OS/2 computer. Although it is not a process controlled by OS/2, it does share the hard disk, memory, and CD-ROM drive with OS/2. NetWare Server for OS/2 works with NetWare Client for OS/2.

See also **NetWare Client for OS/2.**

NetWare Server object

A leaf object in Novell Directory Services (NDS) that represents a server running NetWare on the network and that can be referenced by other objects (such as a Volume object) to help identify their locations.

See also **leaf object; Novell Directory Services; object.**

NetWare Server TSA

A Target Service Agent (TSA) that passes requests for data generated within SBACKUP to the NetWare server where the data resides, and then returns to SBACKUP the requested data through the Storage-Management Data Requester (SMDR).

See also **SBACKUP; Storage-Management Data Requester; Target Service Agent.**

NetWare shell

A NetWare program, loaded into the memory of each workstation, that builds itself around DOS to intercept the workstation's network requests and reroute them to a NetWare server. The NetWare shell works only on versions prior to NetWare 4.0.

See also **shell.**

NetWare SQL

An access system for relational databases, based on Structured Query Language (SQL), and residing at the NetWare server as a NetWare Loadable Module (NLM). This NLM allows users to run applications that are designed to manage shared data files.

See also **NetWare Loadable Module; Structured Query Language.**

NetWare STREAMS

A set of NetWare services that enable user processes to create STREAMS messages, to send the messages to neighboring kernel modules and drivers, and to receive the contents of such messages from kernel modules and drivers.

See also **STREAMS utility.**

NetWare TCP/IP

A group of NetWare Loadable Modules (NLMs) that implement the Transmission-Control Protocol/Internet Protocol (TCP/IP) suite to provide routing services for workstations by using the TCP/IP format.

See also **NetWare Loadable Module; Transmission-Control Protocol/Internet Protocol.**

NetWare Telephony Services

A software/hardware package designed to integrate a NetWare network with a telephone private branch exchange (PBX). A hardware link is administered through the NetWare server and is used for all communication between the network and the PBX. Workstations must be configured with the proper software and must communicate with the PBX only through the server.

See also **private branch exchange.**

NetWare Tools (OS/2) utility

In IntranetWare, an OS/2 workstation utility that provides access to network resources. This utility enables users to map drives, manage printer connections, manage the Directory tree, manage server connections, display network users, and send messages.

NetWare TSA (OS/2)

In IntranetWare, an OS/2 workstation module that allows the hard drive on the workstation to be accessed by the SBACKUP utility or another backup program for backup to the network. This utility allows users to specify which users can access a particular workstation's hard drive, the password for access to the hard drive, and which specific partitions on the hard drive are available for backup.

NetWare UAM

A User-Authentication Method (UAM) that provides password encryption, allows Novell Directory Services (NDS) authentication, and enables NetWare users to enter passwords that are longer than six characters while working on a Macintosh workstation.

See also **User-Authentication Method.**

NetWare UNIX Client (NUC)

Software that enables the NetWare operating system to provide services to UnixWare users and applications, and that allows UnixWare users to access remote directories, files, and printers on NetWare servers as if they were in the UNIX environment.

NetWare User Tools utility

In IntranetWare, a Windows workstation utility that provides services for capturing a printer, printing, sending a network message, mapping a drive, changing a password, attaching to a NetWare server, authenticating to a Novell Directory Services (NDS) tree, and changing NetWare Client settings. When the NetWare Administrator utility is installed, the NetWare User Tools utility is copied to the SYS:PUBLIC directory. When NetWare Client 32 is installed on client workstation, a Windows Program Manager group called NetWare Tools is created and a NetWare User Tools icon is added to the group. The NetWare User Tools utility is started either by double-clicking this icon, or by selecting the File option from Program Manager or File Manager, choosing the Run option, and then specifying the full path to NWUser on the network server.

See also **NetWare Administrator utility; Novell Directory Services.**

NetWare Users International (NUI)

A nonprofit organization that facilitates communication between Novell and NetWare users by organizing user groups, discussion gatherings, and trade shows. Although sponsored by Novell, NUI is independent and not a part of the Novell corporate structure.

NetWare utilities

In NetWare, the server console, workstation, or file-management programs used to perform specific tasks on the network. *Server console utilities* execute on the server console, *workstation utilities* execute on the workstation (although they are installed on the server), and *file-management utilities* execute programs to manipulate files. NetWare utilities are often NetWare Loadable Modules (NLMs) or Virtual Loadable Modules (VLMs).

See also **NetWare Loadable Modules; Virtual Loadable Modules.**

NetWare volume

A physical amount of NetWare server hard-disk storage space that has a fixed size. A NetWare volume sits at the same level as a DOS root directory, the highest level of the NetWare directory structure.

NetWare Volume Mounter utility

In IntranetWare, a Macintosh workstation utility that mounts a NetWare volume.

NetWare Web Server

A component of IntranetWare integrated with Novell Directory Services (NDS) to provide the capability of building a World Wide Web (WWW) site on a corporate intranetwork and the Internet. Through NDS authentication and multiple-access control, the NetWare Web Server provides security to prevent unauthorized break-ins from inside or outside an organization. A Secure Sockets Layer (SSL) uses public key/private key encryption to encode the entire dialogue between the Web browser and the NetWare server. The NetWare Web Server also includes Internet Protocol (IP) address, username, host name, directory, document, NDS user, and NDS group filters.

See also **IP address; Novell Directory Services; Web browser; World Wide Web.**

For more information about the NetWare Web Server, surf the Web to `http://www.novell.com/icd/nip/nwsflyer.html`.

NetWare/IP

A group of NetWare Loadable Modules (NLMs) providing Internet Protocol (IP) support for NetWare 3.*x* and NetWare 4.*x* servers. NetWare/IP allows a NetWare server to function as a gateway between NetWare and Transmission-Control Protocol/Internet Protocol (TCP/IP) networks.

See also **Internet Protocol; Transmission-Control Protocol/Internet Protocol.**

NetWare-encrypted password

A password encoded by the NetWare User-Authentication Method (UAM) software on a Macintosh workstation before it can be sent to the NetWare server.

NetWire

An electronic information service from Novell that provides access to product information, services information, and time-sensitive technical information for NetWare users. NetWire began as Novell's forum on CompuServe and has since been integrated with the Novell Support Connection on the World Wide Web (WWW).

network

A group of computers communicating with each other, sharing peripherals, and accessing remote hosts or other networks. For example, a NetWare network (which consists of workstations, peripherals, and one or more NetWare servers) provides users with the capability to send messages between workstations, share files, and protect files through a security system. Workstations are often called *nodes* (or *lobes*) and connect to one or more *servers*. The physical layout of a network is called a *topology,* the means of connection is often by *cables,* and the means of communication between nodes is often through *protocols.* Table N.9 shows different types of network classifications.

Table N.9: Network Classifications

Classification	Abbreviation	Description
Campus-area network	CAN	Connects network nodes that are geographically located at multiple locations and that does not require remote communications devices.
Global-area network	GAN	Connects network nodes that are geographically located in multiple countries.
Local-area network	LAN	Connects network nodes that are geographically located within a relatively small distance from each other and that allows users to share files, printers, and other network resources.
Metropolitan-area network	MAN	Connects network nodes that are geographically located within 50 to 75 miles of each other.
Wide-area network	WAN	Connects network nodes that are geographically located over large areas and that usually include remote bridges or routers to connect groups of nodes by telephone or other dedicated lines.

See also **cable; internetwork; intranetwork; node; server; protocol; topology.**

Network-Access Controller (NAC)

A device that provides access to a network, either for another network or for remote callers.

network activity indicators

Two arrows appearing in the upper-left corner of a Macintosh computer display screen that blink to indicate network activity (such as sending a message or copying a file to a server).

network adapter

Hardware installed in workstation and server computers that enables them to communicate on a network. A network adapter is commonly referred to as a *Network Interface Card (NIC)*.

See also **adapter; network; Network Interface Card.**

Network Address

A NetWare Directory Schema term and a selectable property for the following objects in Novell Directory Services (NDS): AFP Server, Bindery Queue, Computer, Messaging Server, NCP Server, Print Server, Printer, Queue, and User.

See also **leaf object; Novell Directory Services; object.**

network address

An eight-digit, hexadecimal number that uniquely identifies a network cable segment, or a unique number that represents a network device.

Network Address Restrictions

A NetWare Directory Schema term and a selectable property for the Printer and User objects in Novell Directory Services (NDS).

See also **leaf object; Novell Directory Services; object.**

network-addressable unit (NAU)

A logical unit (LU), physical unit (PU), or system-services control point (SSCP) that is the origin or destination of information transmitted through the path-control network in a Systems Network Architecture (SNA) environment.

See also **logical unit; physical unit; Systems Network Architecture; system-services control point.**

network administration

Management tasks (including assigning addresses to devices, maintaining network data files across a network, and setting up of internetwork routing) related to the software and hardware connecting a network. Network administration can also include system tasks related to server management (including starting up and shutting down the network system, adding or removing user accounts, and backing up and restoring network server data).

network analyzer

A software product, or a combination of software and hardware, that monitors the activity of a network and the workstations attached to the network and that provides summaries or long-term trends of network activity and performance. The software-hardware combination may include a Network Interface Card (NIC) used to directly test the network.

See also **LANalyzer.**

Network Application Support (NAS)

Specifications from Digital Equipment Corporation designed to use international standards to support a uniform environment for software running on different platforms. The NAS specifications contrast with IBM's Systems Application Architecture (SAA) in that SAA provides proprietary protocols to support multiple platforms.

See also **Systems Application Architecture.**

network architecture

A framework of principles that facilitates the operation, maintenance, and growth of a communications network by isolating user programs and applications from network details. Network architecture includes protocols and software that help to organize functions, data formats, and procedures for a network system.

Table N.10 shows common network architectures and where to find more information.

network backbone

A central cabling system that attaches servers and routers on a network and that handles all network traffic. Because of its configuration (all servers connected to a central cable), the network backbone often decreases the time needed for transmission of packets and decreases the amount of traffic on a network.

See also **backbone topology.**

Table N.10: Common Network Architectures	
Architecture	**For More Information**
ARCnet	See **Attached-Resource Computer Network.**
ATM	See **Asynchronous Transfer Mode.**
Ethernet	See **Ethernet.**
FDDI	See **Fiber Distributed Data Interface.**
Token Ring	See **Token Ring.**

See also **network; protocol.**

Network Basic Input/Output System (NetBIOS)

Generically, the standard protocol used as an interface for applications developed to run peer-to-peer communications on an IBM personal computer network and a Token Ring network. The NetWare Client for DOS and MS Windows program includes a NetBIOS driver that is an emulator, allowing NetWare Internetwork Packet Exchange (IPX) to interface with two NetBIOS interrupts. This driver is an emulator because it does not transmit NetBIOS packets, but rather the packets are encapsulated as IPX packets, which are themselves transmitted.

See also **NetWare Client for DOS and MS Windows; Internetwork Packet Exchange; Token Ring.**

Network Basic Input/Output System, Extended User Interface (NetBEUI)

An implementation of IBM's Network Basic Input/Output System (NetBIOS) transport protocol that communicates with a network through Microsoft's Network Driver-Interface Specification (NDIS) for the Network Interface Card (NIC). Microsoft's LAN Server and LAN Manager use NetBEUI.

See also **LAN Manager; LAN Server; Network Driver-Interface Specification.**

network board

A circuit board installed in a NetWare network workstation computer to allow it to communicate with other workstations and with a NetWare server. This term is also known as a *Network Interface Card (NIC)*

or *network card* when used in documentation from companies other than Novell.

See also **Network Interface Card.**

network communication

The process of workstations on a network requesting data and services from another workstation through a communications medium such as a cable.

Network Communications Control Facility (NCCF)

A component of IBM's NetView network-management software that monitors and controls the operation of a network.

See also **NetView.**

network computing

A multivendor networking environment incorporating local-area network (LAN) and wide-area network (WAN) technologies to provide enterprise network connectivity.

See also **enterprise network; local-area network; wide-area network.**

network-connection software

Software files that must be loaded on a network workstation computer in order for the workstation to be connected to the network.

Network-Control Block (NCB)

A packet structure used in the NetBIOS transport protocol.

See also **Network Basic Input/Output System.**

Network-Control Center (NCC)

A designated network workstation in charge of network management, which receives reports from agent processes running on workstations.

See also **managing process.**

network-control program (NCP)

A program that provides routing, error control, testing, and addressing of Systems Network Architecture (SNA) devices.

See also **NCP; Systems Network Architecture.**

Network-Control Protocol (NCP)

A program such as NetWare Core Protocol (NCP) that manages basic networking functions for a network.

See also **NCP; NetWare Core Protocol.**

Network-Control System (NCS)

A software tool that monitors and modifies network activity. NCS software is generally found on older network systems that incorporate a low-speed, secondary data channel created with Time-Division Multiplexing (TDM).

See also **Time-Division Multiplexing.**

network device driver

Software that controls the coordination between the physical functions of a Network Interface Card (NIC) and other workstation hardware or software on a network.

network direct printer

A printer or print queue server from a third-party vendor that connects directly to a network such as NetWare. Installation utilities usually supplied by the vendor configure the device to recognize network print components and communicate with the network.

network directory

A directory located not on the computer being used, but rather on another computer in a network. A network directory is also known as a *shared folder* in a Macintosh environment.

network drive

An internal representation used by an operating system to refer to an actual disk device or to a group of directories specified by the DOS SUBST command. A network drive is also known as a *logical drive.*

Network Driver-Interface Specification (NDIS)

A specification developed jointly by 3Com and Microsoft to standardize the interface used between a Network Interface Cards (NIC) and the underlying operating system, as well as to provide protocol multiplexing so multiple protocol stacks may be used at one time.

See also **Network Interface Card.**

Network Entity Title (NET)

A network address defined in the OSI Reference Model and used in Connectionless-Mode Network Service (CLNS) networks.

See also **Connectionless-Mode Network Service; OSI Reference Model.**

Network File System (NFS)

An Application-Layer protocol form Sun Microsystems. Implemented by Novell as an optional NetWare product, *NetWare NFS* is a distributed file-system protocol used to access NetWare file systems and NetWare print queues on UNIX systems.

See also **NetWare NFS; NFS.**

network hardware

Hardware used to create a network that includes computers (for both workstations and servers) and related equipment (including circuit boards, keyboards, and monitors), connection equipment (including cables, wiring centers, connectors, repeaters, transceivers, bridges, routers, and gateways), and auxiliary components (including peripheral devices, safety devices, and tools).

Network Information Center (NIC)

A central authority responsible for assigning all Internet addresses. The NIC is also known as the *Internet Network Information Center* (InterNIC).

See also **Internet Network Information Center; NIC.**

 **For more information about InterNIC, surf the Web to** `http://rs.internic.net.`

Network Information Services (NIS)

A UNIX security and file-access database usually found in the UNIX host files /etc/hosts, /etc/passwd, and /etc/group. The NIS is also known as the *Yellow Pages.*

network interface

A boundary that exists between a network carrier and a local installation.

network interface board

Hardware (usually an internal circuit board, often termed a *Network Interface Card* or *NIC* in NetWare applications) that provides the interface between a device (such as a printer or computer) and the network's transmission media.

See also **Network Interface Card; NIC.**

Network Interface Card (NIC)

A hardware interface between a device (such as a printer or computer) and the network's transmission media. A NIC communicates through drivers with network node software (such as a network shell or operating system) on one end and with network cabling to separate nodes on the other end. Chips on the board provide support for different varieties of network architectures (such as Ethernet or Token Ring), which, in turn, determines features and restrictions for the NIC. On the outgoing end of the connection, a NIC (in a workstation) translates user requests into a form suitable for transmission across the network. On the incoming end of the connection, the NIC monitors the network and checks to see whether the packet's destination address matches the NIC node address, if the packet's destination address indicates it is being broadcast to all nodes on the network, or if the packet's destination address indicates it is being multicast to a group of nodes on the network. A NIC is also known as a *LAN adapter, LAN card, network board, Network Interface Module (NIM), Network Interface Unit (NUI)*, or *network adapter.*

See also **network architecture; NIC.**

Network Interface Module (NIM)

Another name for Network Interface Card. *See also* **Network Interface Card.**

Network Interface Unit (NIU)

Another name for Network Interface Card. *See also* **Network Interface Card.**

Network Layer (OSI model)

The third layer (Layer 3) in the OSI Reference Model. The Network Layer ensures that information arrives at its intended destination and smoothes out differences between network media so that higher layers in the model (the Transport, Session, Presentation, and Application Layers) do not need to account for the distinctions.

See also **OSI Reference Model.**

network management

A process that ensures consistent reliability and availability of a network, and ensures the timely transmission of data across a network. Network management can be assigned to dedicated devices or to general-purpose devices.

Network-Management Architecture (NMA)

In IBM's NetView package, a centralized, mainframe-oriented model for network management. NMA provides configuration management, problem management, performance and accounting management, and change management.

See also **NetView; NMA.**

Network-Management Entity (NME)

Software or hardware in the OSI network-management model that provides a network node with the capability to collect, store, and report data about the node's activity.

Network-Management Managers

In NetWare 3.12, a resource that appears in the Available Options/Resource Utilization screen of the MONITOR NetWare Loadable Module (NLM), tracking the number of network-management managers the NMAGENT NLM has allocated.

See also **MONITOR; NetWare Loadable Module; NMAGENT.**

Network-Management NLM

A NetWare Loadable Module (NLM) that tracks information about network equipment, warns of impending problems, and allows remote management of the network.

See also **NetWare Loadable Module.**

Network-Management Objects

In NetWare 3.12, a resource appearing in the Available Options/Resource Utilization screen of the MONITOR NetWare Loadable Module (NLM). The resource tracks the number of network-management objects the NMAGENT NLM has allocated.
See also **MONITOR; NetWare Loadable Module; NMAGENT.**

Network-Management Protocol (NMP)

A protocol from AT&T that controls certain network devices (such as modems or T1 multiplexers).
See also **T1 multiplexer.**

network-management services function

A set of programs in a Systems Network Architecture (SNA) network that receives network-management data, alerts, and problem-determination statistics from Network-Management Vector Transport (NMVT) Request/Response Units (RUs).
See also **Network-Management Vector Transport; Request/Response Unit; Systems Network Architecture.**

Network-Management Triggers

In NetWare 3.12, a resource that appears in the Available Options/Resource Utilization screen of the MONITOR NetWare Loadable Module (NLM). This resource tracks the number of network-management triggers the NMAGENT NLM has allocated.
See also **MONITOR; NetWare Loadable Module; NMAGENT.**

Network-Management Vector Transport (NMVT)

A protocol in Systems Network Architecture (SNA) networks used to exchange network-management data.
See also **Systems Network Architecture.**

network modem

A modem equipped with a Network Interface Card (NIC), directly connected to a network as a *node*. Remote callers access the network through this node.

network monitoring

A network-management function that constantly checks the network and reports any problems.

network name

A symbolic identifier that the network uses to identify a network-addressable unit (NAU), a link station, or both.

Network News-Transfer Protocol (NNTP)

A protocol used by news servers, interactive enough to allow the servers to select which newsgroups and articles they want. This protocol saves on network traffic and on file deletions.

network node (NN)

A personal computer (either a server or workstation), router, printer, or fax machine connected to a network by a Network Interface Card (NIC) and a local-area network (LAN) driver.

See also **Network Interface Card; LAN driver.**

network number

A number that uniquely identifies a network cable segment. In an AppleTalk network, the network number is a decimal integer between 1 and 65,279. In a NetWare network, the network number is a hexadecimal number that starts with the character pair 0x or 0X and is specified with or without trailing zeros. In a Transmission-Control Protocol/Internet Protocol (TCP/IP) network, this is simply the number of the network. A network number is also known as the *IPX external network number.*

See also **AppleTalk; network numbering; Transmission-Control Protocol/Internet Protocol.**

network numbering

A system of numbers that identifies servers, Network Interface Cards (NICs), and cable segments on a network. In NetWare, this system includes an IPX external number (which identifies a network cable segment), an IPX internal network number (which identifies an individual NetWare 4.*x* server), and a node number (which identifies a NIC).

Network Operating Center (NOC)

An organization or a site responsible for the maintenance of a network.

network operating system (NOS)

Software installed on a network server that coordinates network activities, regulates who can access which files on the network, who can make changes to data, and who can use network resources (such as a shared printer).

Network Packet-Switch Interface (NPSI)

An interface used in Systems Network Architecture (SNA) networks.

See also **Systems Network Architecture.**

network printer

A printer shared by workstations (or nodes) across a network.

Network Printing-Alliance Protocol (NPAP)

A proposed bidirectional protocol standard that allows the exchange of configuration information and other data independent of the Printer-Control Language (PCL) or the Page-Description Language (PDL) in use on the network.

See also **Page-Description Language; Printer-Control Language.**

network queue

A group of network jobs waiting to be processed. *Jobs* contain data interpreted only by the job creator or the job server.

network range

A continuous range of decimal integers between 1 and 65,279 (such as 1-10) assigned to each extended network supporting AppleTalk.

See also **AppleTalk; network number.**

network search-drive mapping

A pointer to a directory that contains applications, operating system files, and so forth that allow execution of a program even if it is not physically located in that directory. The mapping enables the operating system to locate the file.

See also **MAP utility.**

network server

A dedicated computer on a local-area network (LAN) that provides access to (and storage for) files and data, while also managing shared resources for the network.

Network-Services Access Point (NSAP)

The location in the OSI Reference Model through which a Transport Layer (Layer 4) entity can get access to Network Layer (Layer 3) services. Each NSAP is assigned a unique network address.

See also **OSI Reference Model.**

Network Services objects

A group of Novell Directory Services (NDS) leaf objects that allow a network administrator to manage a network. This group includes the User Template object (which is used to create User objects), the Application object (which allows the management of applications as objects), the Auditing File object (which allows the management of an auditing log file as an object), and the License Service Provider object (which represents a network server with the NetWare Licensing Services NetWare Loadable Module loaded).

See also **leaf object; Novell Directory Services; object.**

Network-Services Protocol (NSP)

A proprietary protocol from Digital Equipment Corporation (used in DECnet networks) that works on the Transport Layer (Layer 4) of the OSI Reference Model.

See also **DECnet; OSI Reference Model.**

network station

A machine linked to a network that may be either a workstation or a server. A network station is also known as a *node*.

network supervisor

A generic term describing the person responsible for configuring the NetWare server, workstations, user access, printing, and so forth.

network topology

The physical arrangement of nodes on a network and including such topologies as bus topology, cascaded bridge, distributed star, hybrid, logical, mesh, physical, ring, star, star-wired ring, and tree.

See also **bus topology; cascaded bridge topology; distributed star topology; hybrid topology; logical topology; mesh topology; physical topology; ring topology; star topology; star-wired ring topology; tree topology.**

network traffic

The load of transmitted data carried by network connections, or channels.

See also **channel.**

Network-Visible Entity (NVE)

An AppleTalk network resource or process accessible through the Datagram-Delivery Protocol (DDP).

See also **AppleTalk; Datagram-Delivery Protocol.**

network-aware application

An application created on a network and that can access such network services as printing.

network byte order

A byte order commonly used in AppleTalk networks that specifies integers must be stored most-significant-byte-first.

See also **AppleTalk.**

Network-Network Interface (NNI)

The interconnection used in a Frame Relay network that enables users who are subscribing to different frame relay providers to communicate with one another.

See also **Frame Relay network.**

NETX.VLM

A Virtual Loadable Module (VLM) in the NetWare DOS Requester that provides backward compatibility with NETx.COM (and other older versions of the network shell), directing user and application requests to DOS or to the network.

See also **NetWare DOS Requester; NETx.COM.**

NETx.COM

A network shell program for versions prior to NetWare 4.*x* used to establish a connection with the operating system running on the NetWare server. Earlier versions of the program were named NET3.COM, NET4.COM, and NET5.COM, which correspond to the major versions of DOS 3, DOS 4, and DOS 5. NETx.COM was replaced in later versions of NetWare with the NetWare DOS Requester.

See also **NetWare DOS Requester.**

newbie

A term used to describe a person who is new to the Internet or to a particular area of the Internet, particularly someone who is new to a Usenet newsgroup.

See also **Internet; newsgroup; Usenet.**

News

An Internet information-sharing service that allows users to exchange messages about topics of mutual interest and to view messages posted by other users. News is also known as *Netnews, Network News,* or *Usenet News.*

See also **Usenet.**

news newsgroup

An Internet newsgroup that discusses topics about Internet newsgroups.

See also **newsgroup.**

news server

An Internet computer that accesses Usenet newsgroups and allows the user to read the information contained in the newsgroup.

See also **newsgroup.**

Newsadmin (news administrator)

A person responsible for managing system Usenet newsgroups (including deciding which newsgroups to carry, how long to keep bulletins, and the exchange of news-feeds with other systems) for an Internet service provider (ISP) or for an internal intranetwork site.

See also **Internet service provider; Usenet.**

newsgroup

A distributed bulletin board system (BBS) on the Internet that provides discussion groups and information about particular topics. Usenet news, for example, is a sys-

tem that distributes thousands of newsgroups across the Internet.

See also **Usenet.**

newsgroup kill file

A file telling a newsreader which articles a user wants to read and which to discard.

See also **newsreader.**

newsreader

A program that retrieves, organizes, and displays messages or articles from newsgroups. A newsreader can select newsgroups, select newsgroup articles, provide viewing of newsgroup articles, and post articles (or responses to an article). Types of newsreaders include character-based, windowed, threaded (which arrange articles so that the evolution of original article and responses can be viewed), and online (which provides viewing while connected to the Internet).

See also **newsgroup.**

NEXT

Interference that occurs close to a connector at either end of a cable. NEXT is usually measured near the source of a test signal.

See **near-end crosstalk.**

Next ID

In an Attached-Resource Computer Network (ARCnet) frame, the address of the next node to receive a token.

See also **Attached-Resource Computer Network.**

Next-Station Addressing (NSA)

In a Fiber Distributed Data Interface (FDDI) network, an addressing mode by which a workstation can send a packet to the next workstation in the ring without having to know that workstation's network address.

See also **Fiber Distributed Data Interface.**

NeXTSTEP

An object-oriented variant of the UNIX operating system in which only a micro-kernel operating system stays loaded; other services are provided in modules that can be loaded as needed. NeXTSTEP supports Transmission-Control Protocol/Internet Protocol (TCP/IP) networks, and includes software that allows a NeXTSTEP machine to access file and print services on a NetWare or AppleTalk network.

NFS

(1) **Network File System,** an Application-Layer file-system protocol from Sun Microsystems.
(2) **NetWare NFS,** an optional NetWare product that implements Network File System. As a distributed file-system protocol used to access NetWare file systems and NetWare print queues on UNIX systems, NetWare NFS is a collection of NetWare Loadable Modules (NLMs) that provide UNIX users with access to the NetWare environment from their native UNIX operating system. For example, NetWare NFS integrates UNIX systems transparently with NetWare 4.*x* file systems and resources.

NFS.NAM

A NetWare Loadable Module (NLM) that loads support for UNIX long filenames onto the server.

NIAS

NetWare Internet-Access Server, an enhanced version of the NetWare Multiprotocol Router that offers a single wide-area network (WAN) connection and Internetwork Packet Exchange/Internet Protocol (IPX/IP) gateway functions. NIAS is included in the IntranetWare product.

See also **Internet Protocol; Internetwork Packet Exchange; IntranetWare; NetWare Multiprotocol Router.**

NIC

(1) **Network Information Center,** a central authority responsible for assigning all Internet addresses. The Network Information Center is also known as the *Internet Network Information Center (InterNIC).*
(2) **Network Interface Card,** a hardware interface between a device (such as a printer or computer) and the network's transmission media. A NIC communicates through drivers with network node software (such as a network shell or operating system) on one end and with network cabling to separate nodes on the other end. Chips on the board provide support for different varieties of network architectures (such as Ethernet or Token Ring), which, in turn, determines features and restrictions for the NIC. On the outgoing end of the connection, a NIC (in a workstation) translates user requests into a form suitable for transmission across the

network. On the incoming end of the connection, the NIC monitors the network and checks to see whether the packet's destination address matches the NIC node address, if the packet's destination address indicates it is being broadcast to all nodes on the network, or if the packet's destination address indicates it is being multicast to a group of nodes on the network. A NIC is also known as a *LAN adapter, LAN card, network board, Network Interface Module (NIM), Network Interface Unit (NUI),* or *network adapter.*

See also **(1) Internet Network Information Center; (2) network architecture.**

NID

Next ID, in an Attached-Resource Computer Network (ARCnet) frame, the address of the next node to receive a token.

See also **Attached-Resource Computer Network.**

NII

National Information Infrastructure, a term describing an anticipated combination of the Internet with public networks to form a seamless communications web, including all the necessary protocols, access software, applications software, the information itself, and service providers.

NIM

Network Interface Module, another name for **Network Interface Card**.

NIS

Network Information Services, a UNIX security and file-access database usually found in the UNIX host files /etc/hosts, /etc/passwd, and /etc/group. The NIS is also known as the *Yellow Pages*.

NISDN

Narrowband ISDN, a term describing ordinary Integrated-Services Digital Network (ISDN) architecture in which narrowband transmissions are used.

See also **Integrated-Services Digital Network; narrowband.**

NIST

National Institute of Standards and Technology, a United States government agency responsible for supporting and cataloging a variety of standards. The NIST was formerly known as the National Bureau of Standards (NBS).

NIT (NLM)

In IntranetWare, a NetWare Loadable Module (NLM) that provides a set of interface tools required by other NLM programs. This NLM is automatically loaded by any other NLM that requires it.

See also **NetWare Loadable Module.**

nitwork

A colloquial term that describes the collection of details that must be considered to keep a network functioning properly.

NIU

Network Interface Unit, another name for **Network Interface Card**.

NLICLEAR.NLM

In NetWare 3.x, a NetWare Loadable Module (NLM) that clears incomplete and unauthenticated logins so that they can be reused.

NLIST utility

In NetWare 4.x and IntranetWare, a workstation utility that views information about objects (such as users, groups, volumes, servers, and so on) and searches on objects and object properties. By searching on objects and properties, this utility can provide a view of a specific group of objects (such as a group of all users whose passwords expire on a certain date).

See also **object**.

NLM

NetWare Loadable Module, one of a set of NetWare programs loaded (some automatically) and unloaded from server memory while the server is running. When an NLM is loaded, the program is dynamically linked to the operating system, and the NetWare server allocates a portion of memory to it. The amount of memory allocated depends on the task the NLM is designed to perform. Control of the memory and all other allocated resources are returned to the operating system when the NLM is unloaded. While some NLMs (such as utilities) can be loaded, used, and then unloaded, others (such as local-area network drivers and disk driver NLMs) must be loaded each time the server is started. Commands to load the latter NLMs are stored in the STARTUP.NCF and AUTOEXEC.NCF files.

See **NetWare Loadable Module** (includes **Table N.7**).

NLM global data items

NetWare Loadable Module (NLM) data items for which only one value has been assigned and that are global to all thread groups and threads of the NLM. If a change is made to the values of NLM global data items, all thread groups and threads in the NLM are affected.

See also **NetWare Loadable Module; thread; thread group.**

NLM screens

Regular or popup screens that appear during the execution of a NetWare Loadable Module (NLM) and that contain instructional or error information about the NLM or about the function the NLM is performing.

See also **NetWare Loadable Module.**

NLMLIB utility

In IntranetWare, a NetWare Loadable Module (NLM) that contains a library of functions providing run-time support for other NLM programs. The NLMLIB utility is loaded automatically by any NLM that requires it.

See also **NetWare Loadable Module.**

NLS

NetWare Licensing Services, a distributed network service enabling NetWare administrators to monitor and control the use of licensed applications on a NetWare network. The enterprise service architecture of this service consists of client components that support different platforms and system components that reside on network servers. NLS also includes a license-metering tool and libraries that export licensing-service functionality to developers of other licensing services.

NLS MANAGER utility

In IntranetWare, a Windows workstation utility that manages NetWare Licensing Services (NLS). This utility provides for installing a license certificate, creating a metering certificate, viewing licensing information, viewing license certificate details, assigning users to license certificates, viewing or changing a license certificate's owner, and viewing License Service Provider (LSP) Server information.

See also **NetWare Licensing Services.**

NLSP

NetWare Link-Services Protocol, Novell's derivation of the Intermediate System-to-Intermediate System (IS-IS) link-state routing protocol. NLSP transfers information between routers and makes routing decisions on the basis of that information. NLSP routers exchange link information (such as network connectivity, path costs, Internetwork Packet Exchange network numbers, and media types) with peer routers to build and maintain a logical map

of the network. NLSP multicasts routing information only when a route is changed or service on the network is changed. NLSP routers use the Routing-Information Protocol (RIP).

See also **Intermediate-System-to-Intermediate-System; link-state router; Routing-Information Protocol.**

NMA

(1) NetWare Management Agent, a group of NetWare Loadable Module (NLM) programs that provides information about the configuration of a server (including the NLM programs installed, printers, print queues, hard disks, disk controllers, and drivers), statistics on server traffic, statistics on server memory, and specifications on alarm settings for server errors and events. By loading the NetWare Management Agent, network administrators can monitor, manage, and maintain all network servers from a single console.

(2) Network-Management Architecture, in IBM's NetView package, a centralized, mainframe-oriented model for network management. NMA provides configuration management, problem management, performance and accounting management, and change management.

See also **(2) NetView; (1) NetWare Loadable Module.**

NMAGENT utility

In NetWare 3.12, a server console utility that allows local-area network (LAN) drivers to register and pass configuration parameters before the LAN drivers can be loaded.

NME

Network-Management Entity, software or hardware in the OSI network-management model that provides a network node with the capability to collect, store, and report data about the node's activity.

NMENU utility

In NetWare and IntranetWare, a workstation utility that enables the customization of menus. NMENU can only be used with menu files that already exist. To use NMENU on these menu files, Read and File Scan rights are required.

NMP

Network-Management Protocol, a protocol from AT&T that controls certain network devices (such as modems or T1 multiplexers).

See also **T1 multiplexer.**

NMS

NetWare Management System, a system that manages a NetWare network by using a network-management protocol and building a map of network resources. NMS has been replaced by the ManageWise product.

See also **ManageWise; NMAGENT utility.**

NMVT

Network-Management Vector Transport, a protocol in Systems Network Architecture (SNA) networks used to exchange network-management data.

See also **Systems Network Architecture.**

NN

Network node, a personal computer (either a server or workstation), router, printer, or fax machine connected to a network by a Network Interface Card (NIC) and a local-area network (LAN) driver.

See also **Network Interface Card; LAN driver.**

nn

A UNIX newsreader that features a fast summary presentation of pending articles and is popular at some academic sites with direct UNIX connections.

NNI

Network-Network Interface, the interconnection used in a Frame Relay network that enables users who are subscribing to different frame relay providers to communicate with one another.

See also **Frame Relay network.**

NNS

NetWare Name Service, a predecessor to Novell Directory Services (NDS) that consisted of a set of specialized utilities designed to work with NetWare 2 and NetWare 3 networks to provide a more transparent access to resources in NetWare installations. NNS is no longer available and no longer supported.

See also **Novell Directory Services.**

NNS Domain

A NetWare Directory Schema term and a selectable property for the Organization and Organizational Unit objects in Novell Directory Services (NDS).

See also **container object; Novell Directory Services; object.**

NNTP

Network News-Transfer Protocol, a protocol used by news servers, interactive enough to allow the servers to select which newsgroups and articles they want. This protocol saves on network traffic and on file deletions.

NoAutoendcap

A specification that captured data should not be closed and sent to a printer after exiting an application, which allows more information to be added to a print job.

NoBanner

A specification indicating that no banner page should be printed.

NOC

Network Operating Center, an organization or a site responsible for the maintenance of a network.

NOCLEAR

An ITEM command option in an NMENU utility menu source file that keeps the current DOS screen display on the screen while other tasks are being performed in the background.

See also **NMENU utility.**

node

Any addressable entity on a network (including any device that has been assigned a network address and is capable of sending and receiving information), or an endpoint of a link or junction common to two or more links on a network. The term sometimes refers to an actual device such as a server, router, workstation, or network printer. Nodes can also be host processors, communications controllers, or terminals. If a node is not a computer, it must have a Network Interface Card (NIC) preinstalled.

See also **Network Interface Card; node address; node number.**

node address

A combination of a node number with the network number to form a unique node address.

See also **node number.**

node number

A unique 8-bit node number acquired dynamically by a node when it connects to the network (which the node tries to use when it reconnects to the network). The node number is assigned to a Network Interface Card (NIC). Each node must have at least one NIC, by which the node is connected to the network. Depending on the type of NIC, node numbers are assigned in different ways. For example, node numbers for Ethernet and Token Ring NICs are preset

by the manufacturer. Node numbers for ARCnet NICs are set with jumpers and switches.
See also **Network Interface Card.**

node schematic

A graphical representation of a node (or NetWare server) that displays network boards, server disks, volumes, queues, users, NetWare Loadable Modules (NLMs), and event and alert messages. This representation is the main graphical display in the NetWare Management System (NMS) software.
See also **node; NetWare Loadable Module; NetWare Management System.**

Node-to-Node Routing

A method that routes a packet from its source node to its destination, instead of routing a packet to the router nearest to the destination node.

NOECHO

An ITEM command option in an NMENU utility source file that prevents a user from seeing the menu item command when typed on the screen at the DOS prompt.

NoFormFeed

A specification indicating that a printer should not add blank paper to the end of a print job.

noise

An unwanted low-voltage, low-current, high-frequency signal that occurs between two points in a transmission circuit.

Noise-Equivalent Power (NEP)

Amount of optical power needed by a fiber-optic receiver to produce an electric current as strong as the receiver's base noise level.
See also **fiber optics.**

Nominal Velocity of Propagation (NVP)

A speed expressed as a percentage or fraction of the speed of light in a vacuum, used to measure signal movement through a cable.

nonblocking functions

Functions that do not cause a caller to relinquish control.

nonblocking mode

A mode of execution that allows a function to return immediately if a specific event is not pending or has not occurred. Nonblocking mode is also known as *asynchronous execution*.

nondedicated router

An external router that can function simultaneously as a router and as a workstation.

nondedicated server

A network server that runs the network functions and performs as a workstation.

nondisruptive test

A network-management diagnostic or performance test that can be run in the background, and that has little or no effect on normal network activity.

nonextended AppleTalk network

An AppleTalk network not supporting Phase 2 extensions (such as zone lists and network ranges).
See also **AppleTalk Phase 2.**

non-Macintosh client

A NetWare term describing a DOS, Windows, or OS/2 client communicating with the network through an Internetwork Packet-Exchange (IPX) connection.
See also **Internetwork Packet Exchange.**

non-Macintosh user

A NetWare term describing a user working at a DOS, Windows, OS/2, or UNIX workstation.

NoNOTIfy

A specification indicating that a user does not receive a message when a print job has completed.

nonpreemptive environment

A fast, real-time, multitasking network environment in which threads are scheduled according to priority levels and are executed on a run-to-completion basis.
See also **thread.**

nonrepudiation

A network-security measure in which a sender cannot deny having sent a message and a recipient cannot deny having received the message.

Non-Return-to-Zero (NRZ)

A binary encoding scheme that represents ones and zeros as opposite and alternating high and low voltages, with no return to reference (or zero) voltage between encoded bits.
See also **Return to Zero.**

Non-Return-to-Zero Inverted (NRZI)

A binary encoding scheme that inverts a signal on a one and leaves the signal unchanged for a zero. A change in voltage indicates a one bit and the absence of a change in voltage indicates a zero bit.
See also **Return to Zero; Return-to-Zero Inverted.**

non-seed router

A router's interface configured to learn its configuration from a configured router on the same network. A non-seed router is also known as a *learning router*.

nonshareable

A term describing a file, device, or process available to only one user at a time.

nonswitched line

A connection between systems or devices that can be made without dialing.

nonvolatile memory

A type of computer memory that retains its contents when a computer is shut down. For example, *read-only memory* (ROM), *erasable programmable-read-only memory* (EPROM), and *electrically erasable-*

programmable-read-only memory (EEP-ROM) are all nonvolatile memory types.
See also **memory.**

nonvolatile RAM (NVRAM)

Random-access memory (RAM) that retains its contents when a computer is shut down, sometimes used to store configuration information.
See also **memory.**

Normal (N) attribute

A file attribute that is set by the NetWare operating system to indicate that no other NetWare attributes have been set.

Normal Response Mode (NRM)

A High-Level Data-Link Control (HDLC) mode used on links with one primary station and one or more secondary stations and that allows secondary stations to transmit only if they first receive poll information from the primary station.
See also **High-Level Data-Link Control; polling.**

normal termination

A termination resulting in the successful execution of a program.

Northwest Net

A regional network in the Northwest United States, Alaska, Montana, and North Dakota that connects all major universities in the region, as well as such major corporations as Boeing International and Sequent Computer.

NOS

network operating system, software installed on a network server that coordinates network activities, regulates who can access which files on the network, who can make changes to data, and who can use network resources (such as a shared printer).

NoTabs

A specification indicating that no spaces be allocated to tabs in a text print job.

notarization

The use of a notary (a trusted third party) to verify that a communication between two entities is legitimate.

notebook computer

A portable computer with a flat-screen display and keyboard that fold together for easier transportation. Notebook computers can run from battery power or can be plugged into an alternating current (AC) power source. Notebook computers often use Personal Computer Memory Card International Association (PCMIA) expansion connections for additional peripheral devices such as modems, fax modems, and network connections.
See also **portable computer.**

Notify

A selectable property for the Printer object in Novell Directory Services (NDS).
See also **leaf object; Novell Directory Services; object.**

Notify List Users

A list of users that appears in the properties of the Printer object and represents those users who are to be notified when the printer experiences an error.

notwork

A term describing a network that is not functioning properly or not functioning at all.

Novell Alliance Program

A partnership formed between Novell and professional service companies that provides customers with comprehensive network design and support services.

Novell Application Launcher (NAL) utility

In IntranetWare, a Windows workstation utility that runs applications associated with Novell Directory Services (NDS) Application leaf objects. The NAL utility allows a user to view Application objects and run the associated application. Those Application objects created and managed by the network supervisor (through the NetWare Application Manager utility) appear as NetWare-delivered applications in the main window of NAL.

See also **Application object; leaf object; NetWare Application Manager utility; Novell Directory Services.**

Novell *ApplNotes*

Novell's monthly technical journal that includes information about designing, implementing, and managing NetWare-

based computer systems. This publication was formerly known as NetWare *Application Notes.*

See also **Novell Support Connection.**

Novell AppWare

A software layer developed by Novell that makes network services more easily available to all developers, regardless of the operating system or user interface for which the developers are writing. AppWare is no longer sold by Novell.

Novell Authorized Education Centers (NAEC)

An independent training organization that meets Novell education standards and is authorized to teach Novell-developed courses with Certified Novell Instructors (CNIs).

See also **Certified Novell Instructor.**

To locate the NAEC nearest you, surf the Web to `http://db.netpub.com/ nov_edu/x/naecloc.`

Novell Authorized Reseller

A person or company that has received authorization to sell NetWare network products.

Novell *Buyer's Guide*

A Novell reference guide containing information about Novell products and services, as well as information about Novell's role in the network computing industry. This guide

was formerly known as the *NetWare Buyer's Guide*.

See also **Novell Support Connection.**

Novell College Credit Program (NCCP)

A program in which Novell issues an official transcript upon completion of NetWare certification courses reviewed by the American Council on Education (ACE) and that may result in college course credit being awarded for taking the courses and passing the certification examinations.

Novell Consulting Services (NCS)

A department at Novell providing custom software development, network auditing, network systems design, and distributed application-design services.

Novell Directory Services (NDS)

In NetWare and IntranetWare, a relational database distributed across the entire network, providing global access to all network resources regardless their locations. NDS uses a distributed database (called the NetWare Directory database, or simply the Directory) to store all network resources as objects. Users log in to a multiserver network and view the entire network as a single information system, which improves user productivity and diminishes administrative costs.

NDS organizes users, groups, printers, servers, volumes, and other physical network devices into a hierarchical tree structure. The NDS tree (also known as the Directory tree) is what allows resources to be managed and displayed in a single view. Figure N.3 shows an example of an NDS Directory tree. The

Directory tree is managed through objects and their associated properties.

NDS replaces the bindery found in NetWare 3.*x* networks. NDS is distributed and can be replicated on multiple servers, whereas the bindery in NetWare 3.*x* is a flat structure in which resources belong to a single server.

Table N.11 shows some of the key features found in NDS.

 **For more information about NDS, surf the Web to** http://www.novell.com/ nds/flyer.html.

Novell Distributed Print Services (NDPS)

In IntranetWare, a distributed service designed for complex print-management and production requirements, and that consists of client, server, and connectivity components seamlessly linking and sharing network printers with applications. With NDPS, the NetWare Administrator provides management and control of printers, eliminating the need to create and configure Print Queue, Printer, and Print Server leaf objects.

See also **leaf object.**

Novell DOS 7

A version of DOS developed by Digital Research (which was, at the time, a subsidiary of Novell) that provides improvements in the memory-management, multitasking, and networking capabilities of other versions of DOS, and includes utilities to improve system performance through disk compression.

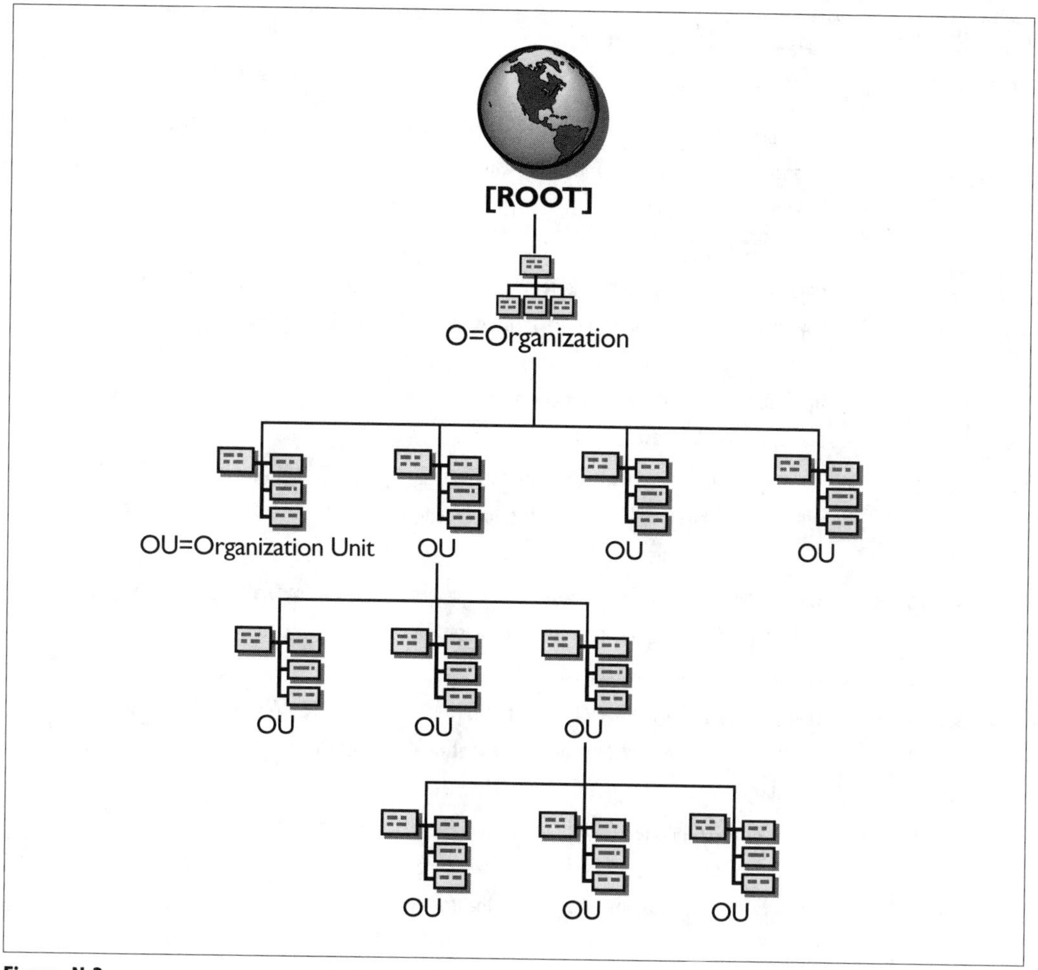

[ROOT]

O=Organization

OU=Organization Unit   OU   OU   OU

OU   OU   OU

OU   OU   OU

Figure N.3
NDS Directory tree

Table N.11: Key Features of NDS

Feature	Description	For More Information
Authentication	Users may log in to the network and gain access to any server, volume, or printer to which they have rights. User trustee rights restrict access within the network.	See **authentication.**
Objects	Objects that represent network resources (either physical entities or logical entities) consist of categories of information (properties) and data in those properties. All this information is stored in the Directory database.	See **container object; leaf object; object.**
Directory tree	This logical, hierarchical tree organization starts with a root object and branches out to container objects and leaf objects.	See **Directory tree.**
Directory partitions	These subdivisions of the Directory database are created by default upon installation of a server in a new context of the Directory tree.	See **NetWare Directory partition.**
Directory replicas	These copies of each Directory partition are stored on many servers throughout the network to improve access and provide fault tolerance.	See **NetWare Directory replica.**
Time synchronization	This feature establishes the order of events in NDS and ensures that when an event takes place, the Directory replicas are updated in the correct order.	See **time synchronization.**
Bindery compatibility	This feature provides compatibility with earlier, bindery-based versions of NetWare that may co-exist with NDS on the network.	See **bindery.**

Novell Educational Academic Partner (NEAP)

A college or university that provides Novell-authorized courses in a semester- or quarter-length curriculum and authorized to teach Novell-developed courses with Certified Novell Instructors (CNIs).

See also **Certified Novell Instructor.**

Novell ElectroText

Online NetWare documentation that provides access to documents from a NetWare workstation. This documentation includes all manuals in the NetWare 4.*x* documentation set (except the *Quick Access Guide*).

Novell ElectroText viewer

A Windows-based online help system that includes NetWare 4.*x* documentation.

Novell Ethernet Topology-Support Module

In NetWare 4.02, a field name that appears in the System Modules menu in the MONI-TOR NetWare Loadable Module (NLM).

See also **MONITOR; NetWare Loadable Module.**

Novell Generic Media-Support Module

In NetWare 4.02, a field name that appears in the System Modules menu in the MONI-TOR NetWare Loadable Module (NLM).

See also **MONITOR; NetWare Loadable Module.**

Novell Labs

An agency at Novell working with manufacturers to test and certify hardware and software components designed to interface with NetWare networks.

Novell NE2000

In NetWare 4.02, a field name that appears in the System Modules menu in the MONI-TOR NetWare Loadable Module (NLM).

See also **MONITOR; NetWare Loadable Module.**

Novell OEM Partners

Original Equipment Manufacturers (OEMs) in partnerships with Novell that provide sales and support services for NetWare networks.

Novell research reports

Reports based on technical research conducted by Novell, exploring such topics as network backup and security.

Novell reseller

Novell Authorized Reseller, a person or company that has received authorization to sell NetWare network products.

Novell Support Connection

Formerly known as the *Novell Support Encyclopedia* (NSE) and *Novell Support Encyclopedia, Professional Edition* (NSEPro), a CD-ROM that contains Novell technical information documents, Novell Labs hardware and software test bulletins, online product manuals, *Novell AppNotes* (also known as *NetWare Application Notes*), the *Novell Buyer's Guide* (also known as *NetWare Buyer's Guide*), and Novell corporate information, as well as patches, fixes, and drivers for NetWare.

Novell Support Encyclopedia (NSE)

A CD-ROM from Novell, now known as *Novell Support Connection,* that contains Novell technical information documents. *See also Novell Support Connection.*

Novell Support Encyclopedia, Professional Edition (NSEPro)

A CD-ROM from Novell, now known as *Novell Support Connection,* that contains Novell technical information documents. *See also Novell Support Connection.*

Novell Technical Support (NTS)

A Novell department consisting of customer support representatives and support engineers that provides service to end users and to independent service providers.

Novell Virtual Terminals (NVT)

A two-part application program allowing DOS clients to access applications running on a NetWare Application server. One part of the program is for the DOS system and the other is for the UnixWare Application server.

NPA

NetWare Peripheral Architecture, an extension of the Media Manager (MM) that provides broader and more flexible driver support for host adapters and storage devices. NPA distinguishes between two types of driver support: Host Adapter Module (HAM) and Custom-Device Module (CDM). The HAM drives the host adapter hardware and provides functionality to route requests to the bus where a specified device is attached. The Host Adapter Interface (HAI) provides an interface for HAMs to communicate with the MM. The CDM drives storage devices or autochanges attached to a host adapter bus. The Custom-Device Interface (CDI) provides an interface for CDMs to communicate with the MM. *See also* **Media Manager.**

NPAMS (NLM)

In NetWare 4.*x* and IntranetWare, a server console utility that enables the mounting of a CD-ROM drive as a NetWare volume. The name of this NetWare Loadable Module (NLM) is an abbreviation for NetWare Peripheral Architecture Mirrored Server (NPAMS). This is a custom device module required to mount a CD-ROM drive as a System Fault Tolerance III (SFT III) volume. *See also* **NetWare Loadable Module; NetWare Peripheral Architecture; System Fault Tolerance.**

NPAP

Network Printing-Alliance Protocol, a proposed bidirectional protocol standard that allows the exchange of configuration information and other data independent of the Printer-Control Language (PCL) or the Page-Description Language (PDL) in use on the network.

See also **Page-Description Language; Printer-Control Language.**

NPATH utility

In NetWare 4.*x* and IntranetWare, a workstation utility that views the NetWare search sequence for a file, which helps troubleshoot why a search is turning up an incorrect version of a file, why the file can not be located, or why the file is displaying in a foreign language.

NPDN

A low-speed, circuit-switched, public network located in Nordic countries.

NPRINT utility

In NetWare and IntranetWare, a workstation utility that prints plain text files or files that were created outside of a particular application.

NPRINTER (NLM)

In NetWare 4.*x* and IntranetWare, a NetWare Loadable Module (NLM) that allows the attachment of a printer to a NetWare server. Multiple NPRINTER NLMs are allowed to be loaded on a NetWare server.

See also **NetWare Loadable Module.**

NPRINTER.EXE utility

In NetWare 4.*x* and IntranetWare, a workstation utility used to attach a printer to a workstation.

NPSI

Network Packet-Switch Interface, an interface used in Systems Network Architecture (SNA) networks.

See also **Systems Network Architecture.**

NPTWIN95.EXE utility

In IntranetWare, a Windows 95 workstation utility that loads software to route jobs out of a print queue through the proper port on the workstation to the printer.

NREN

National Research and Education Network, a network being developed as a state-of-the-art network for research organizations and educational institutions.

NRM

Normal Response Mode, a High-Level Data-Link Control (HDLC) mode used on links with one primary station and one or more secondary stations and that allows secondary stations to transmit only if they first receive poll information from the primary station.

See also **High-Level Data-Link Control; polling.**

NRZ

Non-Return-to-Zero, a binary encoding scheme that represents ones and zeros as opposite and alternating high and low voltages, with no return to reference (or zero) voltage between encoded bits.

See also **Non-Return-to-Zero Inverted; Return to Zero.**

NRZI

Non-Return-to-Zero Inverted, a binary encoding scheme that inverts a signal on a one and leaves the signal unchanged for a zero. A change in voltage indicates a one bit and the absence of a change in voltage indicates a zero bit.

See also **Non-Return-to-Zero; Return to Zero; Return-to-Zero Inverted.**

ns

nanosecond, a unit of measure equal to one-billionth of a second.

NS header

A part of the network services (NS) Request/Response Unit (RU) that identifies the type of RU.

N-Series connector

A connector similar to a threaded-nut connector (TNC), but with a fatter barrel and a thinner plug, used to connect thick coaxial cables in a thick Ethernet network.

See also **connector; Ethernet.**

NSA

Next-Station Addressing, in a Fiber Distributed Data Interface (FDDI) network, an addressing mode by which a workstation can send a packet to the next workstation in the ring without having to know that workstation's network address.

See also **Fiber Distributed Data Interface.**

NSAP

Network-Service Access Point, the location in the OSI Reference Model through which a Transport Layer (Layer 4) entity can get access to Network Layer (Layer 3) services. Each NSAP is assigned a unique network address.

See also **OSI Reference Model.**

NSE

Novell Support Encyclopedia, now part of the *Novell Support Connection* CD-ROM.
See Novell Support Connection.

NSEPro

Novell Support Encyclopedia Professional Edition, now part of the *Novell Support Connection* CD-ROM.
See Novell Support Connection.

NSF

National Science Foundation, a United States, government agency that provides funding for scientific research.

NSFnet

The National Science Foundation Network, a network administered and controlled by the National Science Foundation to provide support for educational and scientific research.

See also **NEARnet.**

NSP

Network-Services Protocol, a proprietary protocol from Digital Equipment Corporation (used in DECnet networks) that works on the Transport Layer (Layer 4) of the OSI Reference Model.

See also **DECnet; OSI Reference Model.**

NT Application object

A Novell Directory Services (NDS) leaf object used to represent any object using Windows NT as the workstation operating system.

See also **leaf object; Novell Directory Services; object.**

NT File System (NTFS)

The native file system for the Windows NT operating system that features up to 256 characters for filenames, a system of permissions for file sharing, a transaction log, the OS/2 File-Allocation Table (FAT), and the OS/2 High-Performance File System (HPFS).

See also **File-Allocation Table; High-Performance File System; Windows NT.**

NTFS

NT File System, the native file system for the Windows NT operating system that features up to 256 characters for filenames, a system of permissions for file sharing, a transaction log, the OS/2 File-Allocation Table (FAT), and the OS/2 High-Performance File System (HPFS).

See also **File-Allocation Table; High-Performance File System; Windows NT.**

NTS

Novell Technical Support, a Novell department consisting of customer support representatives and support engineers that provides service to end users and to independent service providers.

NuBus

A bus specification providing expansion capabilities for a Macintosh computer that supports 32-bit data and address transfer. Slots on the Macintosh for NuBus are used to provide video capabilities, extra memory, and networking capabilities.

NUC

NetWare UNIX Client, software that enables the NetWare operating system to provide services to UnixWare users and applications, and that allows UnixWare users to access remote directories, files, and printers on NetWare servers as if they were in the UNIX environment.

NUI

NetWare Users International, a nonprofit organization that facilitates communication between Novell and NetWare users by organizing user groups, discussion gatherings, and trade shows. Although sponsored by Novell, NUI is independent and not a part of the Novell corporate structure.

null key

A key field in Btrieve that can be a user-defined character. Btrieve distinguishes between any-segment null keys (called a manual key) and all-segment null keys (which were simply called null keys in earlier versions of Btrieve). The any-segment null key does not include a particular record in the index if the value of any key segment of that record matches a null value. The all-segment null key excludes a particular record from the index only if the value of all key segments of that record matches a null value.

See also **Btrieve.**

null modem

A serial cable and connector with a modified RS-232 configuration that enables two computers to communicate directly without a modem as an intermediary device. The pin configuration of the connecting cable is crossed over so that the wires used for sending by one computer are used for receiving data by the other computer.

numerical aperture (NA)

A range of angles over which a fiber-optic core can receive incoming light.

Numeris

A public Integrated-Services Digital Network (ISDN) located in France.

See also **Integrated-Services Digital Network.**

NUT

An interface for NetWare Loadable Modules (NLMs) in NetWare 3.x that must be loaded on NetWare 3.x servers in order for some NLMs to operate.

See also **NetWare Loadable Module.**

NVE

Network-Visible Entity, an AppleTalk network resource or process accessible through the Datagram-Delivery Protocol (DDP).

See also **AppleTalk; Datagram-Delivery Protocol.**

NVER utility

In NetWare and IntranetWare, a workstation utility that allows users to view version information (for both a workstation and attached servers) and to view NetWare Requester for OS/2 version information for OS/2 and attached servers.

See also **NetWare Requester for OS/2.**

NVLAP

National Voluntary Laboratory Accreditation Program, the United States part of a group of centers that develop automated software to test compliance with X.400 and X.500 standards. Other parts of the group are located in the United Kingdom (the National Computer Center), France (Alcatel), and Germany (Danet GmbH).

See also **X.400; X.500.**

NVP

Nominal Velocity of Propagation, a speed expressed as a percentage or fraction of the speed of light in a vacuum, used to measure signal movement through a cable.

NVRAM

nonvolatile RAM, random-access memory (RAM) that retains its contents when a computer is shut down, sometimes used to store configuration information.
See also **memory.**

NVT

Novell Virtual Terminals, a two-part application program allowing DOS clients to access applications running on a NetWare Application server. One part of the program is for the DOS system and the other is for the UnixWare Application server.

NWADMIN

NetWare Administrator, in NetWare 4.*x* and IntranetWare, a Windows and OS/2 workstation utility that performs supervisory tasks available in the FILER, NETADMIN, PARTMGR, and PCONSOLE utilities. The NetWare Administrator utility allows a network supervisor to create users and groups; create, delete, move, and rename Novell Directory Services (NDS) objects; assign rights in the Directory tree and in the file system; set up print services; and set up and manage NDS partitions and replicas.

When NetWare or IntranetWare is first installed, files for the Windows version of NetWare Administrator are copied to the SYS:PUBLIC directory. For the OS/2 version of NetWare Administrator, the files are copied to the SYS:PUBLIC/OS2 directory.

This utility uses a Graphical User Interface (GUI) and runs as a multiple-document interface (MDI) application. By using a menu bar and a browser, supervisors are able to view the file system of a server in the current Directory tree; open a container object and view the objects that are in it; view an object dialog (which provides object details) of a container object; and view an object dialog of a leaf object.
See also **container object; leaf object; Novell Directory Services; object.**

NWIP (NLM)

A NetWare Loadable Module (NLM) in IntranetWare that supports NetWare/IP on the server.
See also **NetWare/IP.**

NWIPCFG (NLM)

In IntranetWare, a NetWare Loadable Module (NLM) that configures and manages the NetWare/IP server software. This NLM allows users to configure a NetWare server as a NetWare Domain-Naming System (DNS) client, configure the NetWare/IP server software, and start the NetWare/IP service.
See also **Domain-Naming System; NetWare/IP.**

NWPA (NLM)

A NetWare Loadable Module (NLM) that allows the NetWare server to support NetWare Peripheral Architecture (NPA), which allows disk drivers and CD-ROM drivers to work with NetWare.

See also **NetWare Peripheral Architecture.**

NWSNUT

An interface for NetWare Loadable Modules (NLMs) in NetWare 4.*x* that must be loaded on NetWare 4.*x* servers in order for some NLMs to operate.

See also **NetWare Loadable Module.**

NWSTART utility

In IntranetWare, an OS/2 workstation utility that starts NetWare Client for OS/2 on an OS/2 workstation when the DISCONNECT ON parameter (which prevents NetWare Client for OS/2 from making a network connection when the workstation is started) is included in the NET.CFG file.

See also **NetWare Client for OS/2; NET.CFG.**

NWSTOP utility

In IntranetWare, an OS/2 workstation utility that disconnects NetWare Client for OS/2 without having to turn off the workstation computer.

See also **NetWare Client for OS/2.**

NWXTRACT utility

A NetWare and IntranetWare workstation utility that extracts and copies files from a CD-ROM drive, or from installation diskettes, to the network or to local drives.

Nyquist Sampling Theorem

A theorem that postulates it is possible to reconstruct analog signals from samples if enough samples are taken.

NYSERNet

A New York state network using a T1 backbone to connect the National Science Foundation Network (NSFnet), many universities, and several major corporations.

See also **National Science Foundation; T1.**

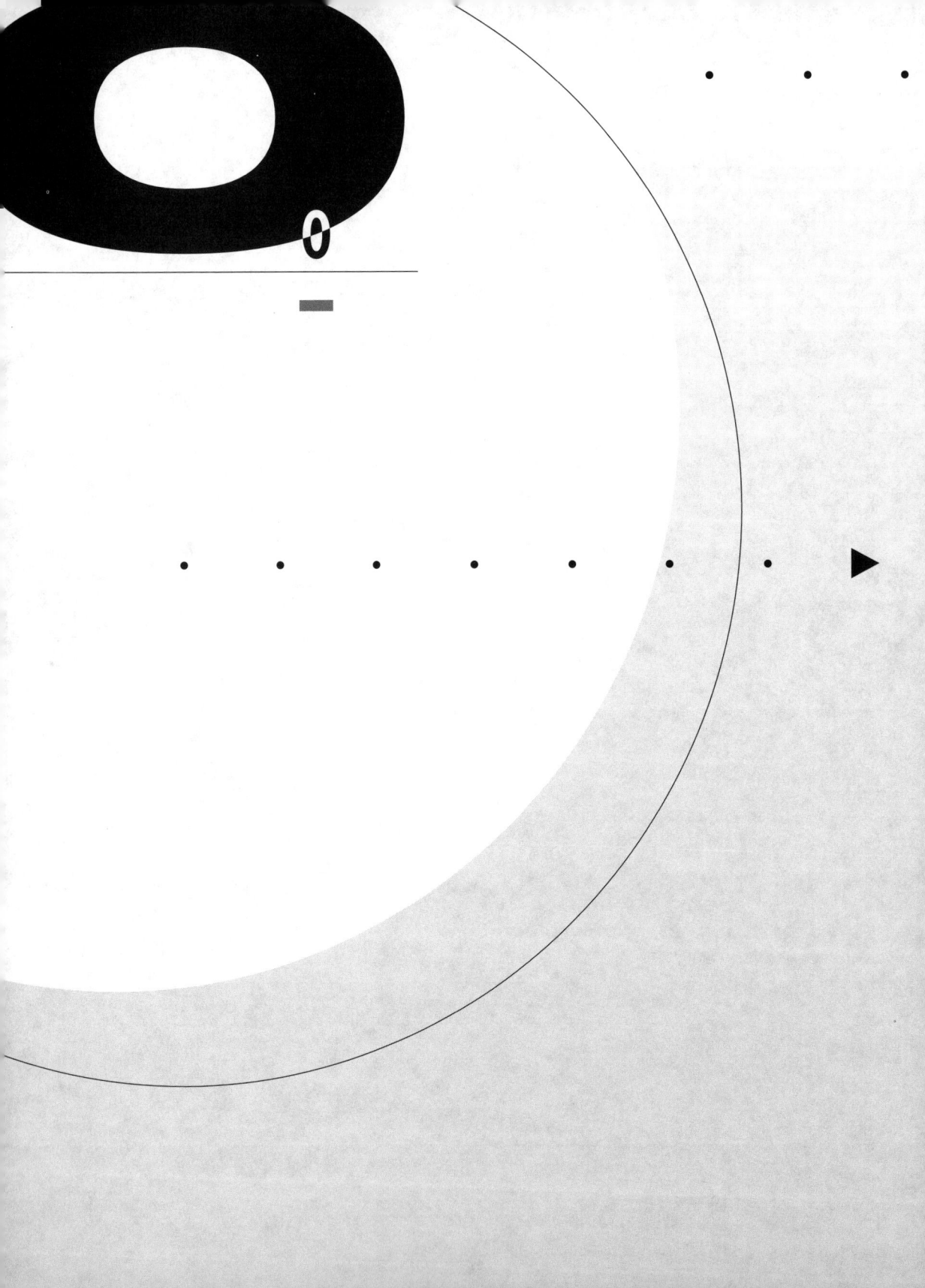

O

NetWare's common name abbreviation for the Organization leaf object in Novell Directory Services (NDS).

See also **Organization; Organization object.**

OAI

Open Application Interface, a telephonic interface that can be programmed and changed to affect the operation of a Private Branch Exchange (PBX).

See also **Private Branch Exchange.**

OAM

Operation, Administration, and Management package, a menu-based interface in UnixWare used to access a suite of system administration and maintenance utilities. These utilities can monitor network performance, detect network defects, protect the network operating system, report on network failures, and localize network faults.

See also **UnixWare operating system.**

OARnet

Ohio Academic Resources Network, a network connecting sites that include the Ohio supercomputer center in Columbus.

Obituary

In NetWare, a Directory Schema term used to avoid name collisions during certain operations. Obituary is a selectable property for the External Entity, List, Message Routing Group, and Messaging Server objects in Novell Directory Services (NDS).

See also **leaf object; Novell Directory Services; object.**

object

A structure in Novell Directory Services (NDS) that stores information about a network resource. An object consists of categories of information (or *properties*), as well as the data in those properties. Objects can represent *physical entities* (such as a user or a printer) or *logical entities* (such as groups or print queues). The object stores information about the entity, but is not the actual entity itself. The two types of objects are *container objects* (which hold other objects) and *leaf objects* (located at the ends of branches and not containing other objects.) Table O.1 shows the types of NDS objects, as well as the actual NDS objects that fall within each object type. Appendix C contains a list of objects and corresponding properties that may be selected for each.

Table O.1: Object Types

Container Objects	Leaf Objects
Country (C)	AFP Server
Organization (O)	Alias
Organizational Unit (OU)	Bindery
	Bindery Queue
	Computer
	Directory Map
	(continued)

Table 0.1: Object Types (continued)	
Container Objects	**Leaf Objects**
	Distribution List
	External Entity
	Group
	Message-Routing Group
	Messaging Server
	NCP Server
	Organizational Role
	Print Queue
	Print Server
	Printer
	Profile
	Unknown
	User
	Volume

Leaf objects have a common name, but container objects are referred to by their Organizational Unit name, Organization name, or Country name. The *complete name* of an object consists of its common name (if it has one), followed by a period, followed by the name of the container object, followed by a period, and so on, up through all container objects to the [Root] object of the Directory tree. The *context* of an object is the position of the object within its container object. Moving objects from one container to another is called *changing contexts*.

See also **container object; leaf object; common name; Novell Directory Services.**

object class

A defined list of objects (such as servers, users, and print queues) found in Novell Directory Services (NDS).

See also **container object; leaf object; Novell Directory Services; object; object property.**

Object Class

A NetWare Directory Schema term and a selectable property for the following objects in Novell Directory Services (NDS): AFP Server, Alias, Bindery, Bindery Queue, Computer, Country, Directory Map, External Entity, Group, List, Message-Routing Group, Messaging Server, NCP Server, Organization, Organizational Role, Organizational Unit, Print Server, Printer, Profile, Queue, Unknown, User, and Volume.

See also **container object; leaf object; Novell Directory Services; object.**

object instance

An instance of an object type bound to a value. This term is used in the context of network management.

Object Linking and Embedding (OLE)

A specification defining how Microsoft Windows applications can link to a document file a reference to an actual object, or embed an object into a document file by making a copy of the object at the desired location. This specification requires OLE support to be written into the Windows applications, with the lowest version of OLE involved by any of the applications determining the capabilities of the application interface. The OLE specification enables objects from different programs to be linked and embedded in a separate application, and it enables the user to edit the object using the application that created the object.

object property

The identification of categories of information about a NetWare or IntranetWare object. Table O.2 shows selectable properties for Novell Directory Services (NDS) objects. Appendix C contains a list of objects and corresponding properties that may be selected for each.

See also **container object; leaf object; Novell Directory Services; object.**

Object-Request Broker (ORB)

A service developed by the Object-Management Group (OMG) as part of the Common Object-Request Broker Architecture (CORBA) specification that enables existing applications to communicate with object-oriented applications. An ORB enables applications to request network services without first knowing the directory structure of the environment from which the service is being requested.

See also **Common Object-Request Broker Architecture; object-oriented program.**

object rights

An object's assigned qualities that define what control the object has over directories, files, or other Novell Directory Services (NDS) objects.

See also **container object; leaf object; Novell Directory Services; object.**

Object Trustees (ACL)

A NetWare Directory Schema term and a selectable property for User object in Novell Directory Services (NDS).

See also **leaf object; Novell Directory Services; object.**

object type

Classification of a Novell Directory Services (NDS) object as a user, user group, file server, and so on.

See also **container object; leaf object; Novell Directory Services; object.**

ObjectBroker

A package from Digital Equipment Corporation that enables transparent communication between object-oriented applications running on different hardware and enables developers to create object-oriented applications and services to be distributed across a network.

See also **Object Linking and Embedding; object-oriented program.**

Table 0.2: NDS Object Properties

Property, A-H	Property, H-M	Property, M-P	Property, P-V
Access-Control List	Home Directory	Memory	Private Key
Account Balance	Host Device	Message-Routing Group	Profile
Account Locked	Host Resource	Message Server	Profile Membership
Account Reset Time	Host Resource Name	Messaging-Database Location	Public Key
Aliased Object Name	Host Server	Messaging Server	Queue
Allow Unlimited Credit	Incorrect Login Attempts	Messaging-Server Type	Queue Directory
Allow User to Change Password	Initials	Minimum Account Balance	Reference
Authority Revocation	Intruder Address	Name	Remaining Grace Logins
Back Link	Intruder-Attempt Reset Interval	Network Address	Require a Password
Bindery-Object Restrictions	Intruder Lockout OU	Network Address Restrictions	Require a Unique Password
Bindery Property	Intruder-Lockout Reset Interval	NNS Domain	Reset Interval
Bindery Type	Language	Notify	Resource
CA Private Key	Last Login Time	Obituary	Revision
CA Public Key	Last Name	Object Class	Role Occupant
Cartridge	Last Referenced Time	Object Trustees (ACL)	SA
Certificate Revocation	Limit Grace Logins	Operator	SAP Name
Certificate-Validity Interval	Locality (L)	Organization (O)	Security Equals To
City	Location	Organizational Unit (OU)	Security Equivalences
Common Name (CN)	Locked By Intruder	Owner	Security Flags

Property, A-H	Property, H-M	Property, M-P	Property, P-V
Country (C)	Lockout After Detection	Page-Description Language	See Also
Cross-Certificate Pair	Login Allowed Time Map	Password Allow Change	Serial Number
Days Between Forced Changes	Login Disabled	Password-Expiration Date and Time	Server
Default Profile	Login-Expiration Date and Time	Password-Expiration Interval	Server Holds
Default Queue	Login-Expiration Time	Password-Expiration Time	State or Province
Default Server	Login Grace Limit	Password Minimum Length	Status
Description	Login Grace Remaining	Password Required	Street
Detect Intruder	Login Intruder Address	Password Unique Required	Supervisor
Device	Login Intruder Attempts	Passwords Used	Supported Connections
DS Revision	Login Intruder Limit	Path	Supported Services
E-Mail Address	Login Intruder Reset Time	Physical-Delivery Office Name	Supported Typefaces
External Name	Login Maximum Simultaneous	Postal Address	Surname
Facsimile Telephone Number	Login Script	Postal Code	Telephone
Fax Number	Login Time	Postal Office Box	Telephone Number
Full Name	Login-Time Restrictions	Postmaster	Title
Generational Qualifier	Mailbox ID	Print	Type Creator Map
GID	Mailbox Location	Print-Job Configuration	User
Given Name	Mailing-Label Information	Print Server	User ID (UID)
Group Membership	Maximum Connections	Printer Configuration	User Version
Higher Privileges	Member	Printer Control	Version
			Volume

object-oriented

Any computer system, operating system, programming language, application, or graphical user interface (GUI) that supports the use of objects.

See also **object.**

object-oriented graphics

Images constructed from individual components (such as lines, arcs, circles, and squares) that are defined mathematically rather than as a set of dots. Users may manipulate a part of the image without redrawing, and may resize or rotate the image without any distortion. Object-oriented graphics are also known as *vector graphics* or *structured graphics*.

See also **vector graphics (images).**

object-oriented programming (OOP)

A programming model in which the program is viewed as a set of self-contained objects (objects containing both data and code) interacting with other objects by passing messages from one to another. This model also enables the programmer to create procedures that work with objects whose exact type may not be known until the program is run. Objects are incorporated in the program by making them part of a layered hierarchy.

Occupant

A NetWare Directory Schema term in Novell Directory Services (NDS).

See also **Novell Directory Services.**

OCR

optical character recognition, a capability provided by a standard optical scanner and special software that enables a computer to recognize printed or typed characters.

octet

A group of eight binary digits that are operated on as a unit. An octet, also known as a *byte* or a *character,* generally is used when describing frame or packet formats.

ODA

Open Document Architecture, an Open Systems Interconnection (OSI) specification (ISO 8613) from the International Standards Organization (ISO) defining how documents (especially documents containing fonts, graphics, and text) are electronically transmitted. This specification outlines three levels of document representation: Level 1 (for text-only data), Level 2 (for text and graphics generated in a word processing program), and Level 3 (for text and graphics generated in a desktop-publishing program). The specification primarily addresses the logical representation of the document.

ODBC

Open Database Connectivity, a Microsoft Application Programming Interface (API) that defines how databases are accessed in the Windows environment.

odd parity

A communications error-checking method in which the sum of all the 1 bits in the byte plus the parity bit must be odd. When the total is already odd, the parity bit is set to 0. When the total is even, the parity bit is set to 1.

See also **parity bit.**

ODI

Open Data-Link Interface, a driver specification developed by Novell to enable a single workstation to communicate transparently with several different protocol stacks while using a single local-area network (LAN) board and a single LAN driver. ODI enables a workstation to access several protocol-specific applications and services at the same time and also allows communication between devices with different frame formats. The ODI architecture consists of three major components: Multiple-Link Interface Driver (MLID), Link-Support Layer (LSL), and communication protocol stacks. In addition, the Media-Support Module (MSM), Topology-Specific Module (TSM), and Hardware-Specific Module (HSM) are subcomponents of the MLID.

See also **Open Database Connectivity** (includes **Table O.3** and **Figure O.2**).

ODI/NDIS Support (ODINSUP)

An interface that enables the Open Data-Link Interface (ODI) to coexist with network driver-interfaces that comply with the Network Driver-Interface Specification (NDIS). ODINSUP permits the connection of a workstation to dissimilar networks; the networks can appear as one. NDIS protocol stacks can communicate through the ODI Link-Support Layer (LSL) and Multiple-Link Interface Driver (MLID), which permits both NDIS and ODI protocol stacks to

coexist on the same system and to use a single MLID. ODINSUP enables a user to utilize a wider variety of programs without being concerned with compatibility and without having to reconfigure or reboot a workstation to switch from one network to another. Figure O.1 shows ODINSUP.

ODINSUP

Another name for **ODI/NDIS Support.**

OEM

original equipment manufacturer, the original manufacturer of hardware subsystems or hardware components. The OEM often contracts to supply subsystems or components to a value-added reseller (VAR).

See also **value-added reseller.**

OFB

Output Feedback, a Data-Encryption Standard (DES) operating mode.

See also **Data-Encryption Standard.**

Off Hook (OH)

An indication that a telephone line is in use.

OFF utility

In NetWare and IntranetWare, a server console utility that clears the console screen.

office drop

A network cable connected to a workstation node.

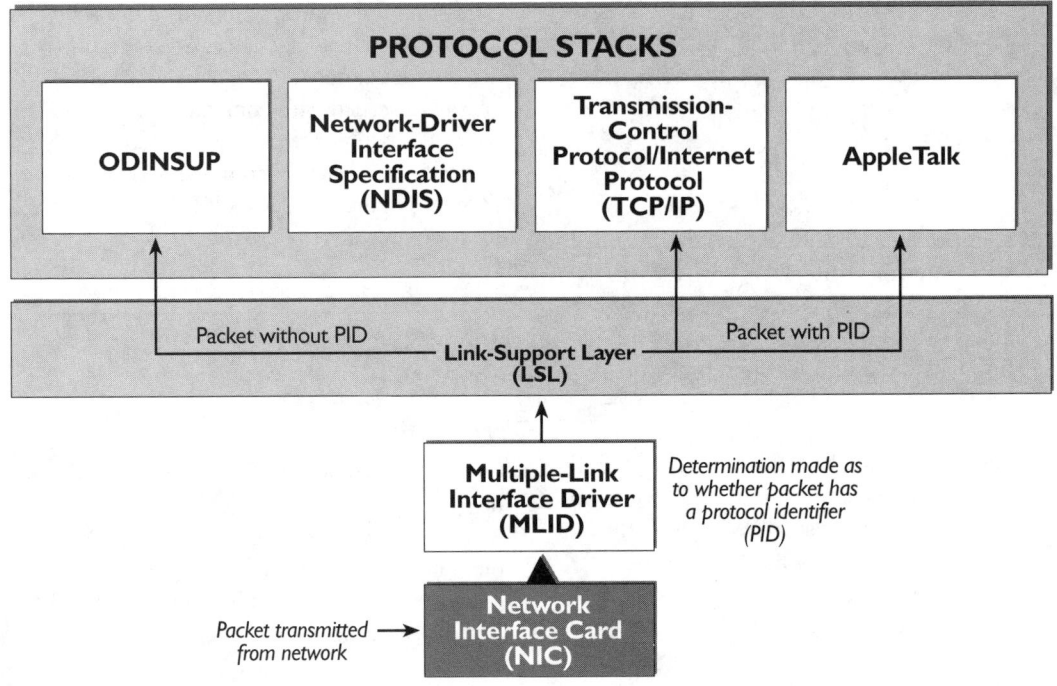

PROTOCOL STACKS

| ODINSUP | Network-Driver Interface Specification (NDIS) | Transmission-Control Protocol/Internet Protocol (TCP/IP) | AppleTalk |

Packet without PID   Packet with PID

Link-Support Layer (LSL)

Multiple-Link Interface Driver (MLID)

Determination made as to whether packet has a protocol identifier (PID)

Packet transmitted from network →

Network Interface Card (NIC)

Figure 0.1
ODINSUP

> *See also* **Link-Support Layer; Multiple-Link Interface Driver; Open Data-Link Interface.**

offline

The condition of a computer system or peripheral device that is unavailable for use.

offline mail reader

A program that enables a user to read and reply to electronic mail (e-mail) messages from a local copy of the message in the user's mailbox by retrieving messages from the mailbox on the host machine and storing the message on a local disk or in memory until the user is ready to read it.

offline newsreader

A newsreader that can download files from a newsgroup and enables a user to review the postings at a later time, which results in lower connect charges but may result in usage of a significant amount of system storage space.

> *See also* **newsgroup.**

offline UPS

A backup *uninterruptible power supply* (UPS) unit not configured to activate automatically should a power outage occur.

offspring count

The number of subdirectories and files located in a directory.

OFNP

Optical Fiber, Nonconductive Plenum, a specification from the Underwriters Laboratory (UL) that defines certain safety criteria for optical fiber.

See also **Underwriters Laboratory.**

OFNR

Optical Fiber, Nonconductive Riser, a specification from the Underwriters Laboratory (UL) that defines certain safety criteria for optical fiber.

See also **Underwriters Laboratory.**

OH

Off Hook, an indication that a telephone line is in use.

Ohio Academic Resources Network (OARnet)

A network connecting sites that include the Ohio supercomputer center in Columbus.

ohm

An electrical unit of resistance that is the counterpart to friction, represented by the uppercase Greek letter omega Ω. For example, a resistance of 1 ohm passes 1 ampere of current when 1 volt is applied.

OIM

OSI Internet Management, an organization responsible for specifying ways in which the protocols of the OSI Network-Management Model can be used to manage Transmission-Control Protocol/Internet Protocol (TCP/IP) networks.

See also **Transmission-Control Protocol/Internet Protocol.**

OIW

OSI Implementers Workshop, a regional workshop representing North America for implementers of the OSI Reference Model. Other workshops include the European Workshop for Open Systems (EWOS), which represents Europe, and the Asia and Oceania Workshop (AOW), which represents the Asiatic region.

See also **OSI Reference Model.**

OLE

Object Linking and Embedding, a specification defining how Microsoft Windows applications can link to a document file a reference to an actual object, or embed an object into a document file by making a copy of the object at the desired location. This specification requires OLE support to be written into the Windows applications, with the lowest version of OLE involved by any of the applications determining the capabilities of the application interface. The OLE specification enables objects from different programs to be linked and embedded in a separate application, enabling the user to edit the object using the application that created the object.

OLiVR

A World Wide Web (WWW) browser plug-in for Netscape Navigator from OLiVR Corporation that plays movies created with the company's authoring tools. OLiVR employs a fractal compression technology that extracts and transmits as much detail from the movie source as can be accommodated over each Internet connection.

See also **Netscape Navigator; Web browser.**

on the fly

An idiom that connotes being on the run, in a hurry, on the spur of the moment, while at the same time being very busy or continuously active. Tasks performed on the fly are often done while other processes are active.

on-demand call

A call activated by the presence of data traffic directed to or through a remote peer system.

on-demand connection

A type of connection that uses static routing information to advertise the presence of an exterior network and provides occasional access to a remote system (as opposed to permanent access). This type of connection minimizes a connection expense and maximizes network resources.

on-demand SVC

A virtual circuit, shut down after data has been transmitted over a Switched Virtual Circuit (SVC), that remains down until more data is queued up for sending (at which time a connection is re-established).

on-the-fly switching

A switching process performed on the spur of the moment, while the switch is very busy or continuously active.

ONC

Open-Network Computing, a distributed computing model that uses the Sun Microsystems Network File System (NFS) for handling files distributed over remote locations by using Remote Procedure Calls (RPCs). This model is supported in most UNIX environments, including Novell's UnixWare.

See also **Network File System; Remote Procedure Call.**

ones density

A measurement that compares the number of ones in a transmission with the total number of digital time slots transmitted. Certain specifications restrict the number of consecutive zeros that may appear in a transmission.

one-time login

A configuration of the network operating system that enables a user to enter a username and password when the computer starts up and that entry allows login to the network.

online

A term describing the capability to perform operations on a computer, the availability of a peripheral device to be used, or a communications computer connected to a remote computer over a network or modem link.

See also **offline.**

online help

The availability of information about network functions and concepts from any workstation on the network.

online UPS

A backup uninterruptible power supply (UPS) unit configured to automatically activate should a power outage occur.

OnLive!

A line of World Wide Web (WWW) browser plug-ins from OnLive Technologies for Netscape Navigator and compatible browsers that presents computer-based conference calls when viewing Web pages with the company's matching software.
See also **Netscape Navigator; Web browser.**

ONN

Open Network Node, a part of the Advanced Peer-to-Peer Internetworking (APPI) standard that provides directory and routing services for Advanced Peer-to-Peer Networking (APPN) end nodes and low-entry nodes.
See also **Advanced Peer-to-Peer Internetworking; Advanced Peer-to-Peer Networking.**

OOP

Object-oriented programming, a programming model in which the program is viewed as a set of self-contained objects (objects containing both data and code) interacting with other objects by passing messages from one to another. This model also enables the programmer to create procedures that work with objects whose exact type may not be known until the program is run. Objects are incorporated in the program by making them part of a layered hierarchy.

open

A networking environment in which the specifications for elements or interfaces have been made publicly available in order for third-party vendors to create compatible or competing products. This term may also describe a gap or separation in the conductive material of a cable.

Open Application Interface (OAI)

A telephonic interface that can be programmed and changed to affect the operation of a Private Branch Exchange (PBX).
See also **Private Branch Exchange.**

open architecture

An architectural design that makes network hardware and software compatible with components from a variety of vendors.

Open Book Repository

A collection of online text maintained by the Online Books Initiative and that contains the text of books, journals, and other reference works.

For more information about the Online Book Repository, surf the Web to `http://www.obi.std.com.`

open circuit

A medium's transmission path that has been broken and that usually prevents network communication.

Open Database Connectivity (ODBC)

A Microsoft Application Program Interface (API) defining how databases are accessed in the Windows environment.

Open Data-Link Interface (ODI)

A driver specification developed by Novell to enable a single workstation to communicate transparently with several different protocol stacks while using a single local-area network (LAN) board and a single LAN driver. ODI enables a workstation to access several protocol-specific applications and services at the same time and also allows communication between devices with different frame formats. The ODI architecture consists of three major components: Multiple-Link Interface Driver (MLID), Link-Support Layer (LSL), and communication protocol stacks. In addition, the Media-Support Module (MSM), Topology-Specific Module (TSM), and Hardware-Specific Module (HSM) are subcomponents of the MLID. Table O.3 describes each of these components. Figure O.2 shows the ODI model.

Table O.3: ODI Architectural Components

Component	Description
Multiple-Link Interface Driver (MLID)	A LAN board driver designed to remove Media-Access Control (MAC) header information from a packet and pass the packet to the Link-Support Layer (LSL).
Media-Support Module (MSM)	Standardizes and manages primary details concerning the interface between the MLID, LSL, and operating system.
Topology-Specific Module	Manages operations unique to a specific media type. Multiple frame support implemented here.
Hardware-Specific Module	Handles all hardware interactions, including adapter initialization, reset, shutdown, and removal, as well as packet reception and transmission.
Link-Support Layer (LSL)	Responsible for determining to which protocol stack a packet should be delivered, for transmitting a packet sent from the protocol stack, and for tracking the various protocols and MLID software on the system.
Protocol Stack	Because the LSL has a Multiple-Protocol Interface (MPI), it can communicate with a variety of protocol stacks without making the stack that receives a packet aware of the media or LAN board type.

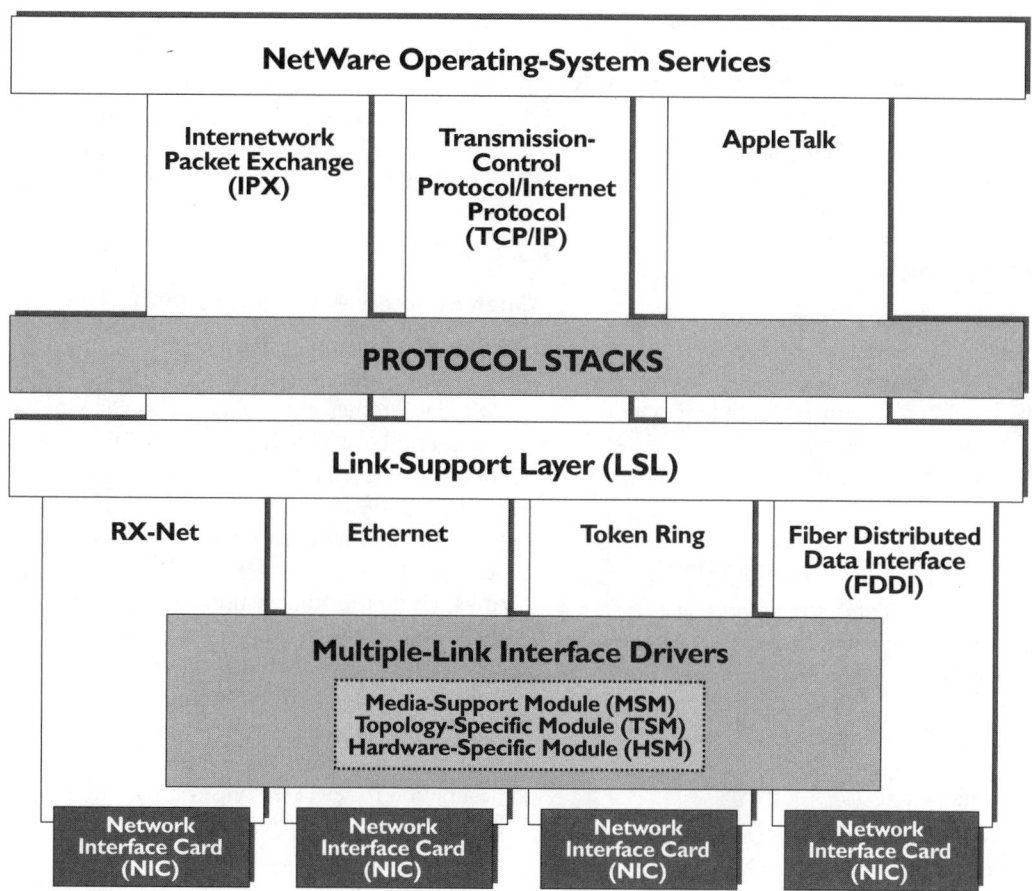

NetWare Operating-System Services

| Internetwork Packet Exchange (IPX) | Transmission-Control Protocol/Internet Protocol (TCP/IP) | AppleTalk |

PROTOCOL STACKS

Link-Support Layer (LSL)

| RX-Net | Ethernet | Token Ring | Fiber Distributed Data Interface (FDDI) |

Multiple-Link Interface Drivers

Media-Support Module (MSM)
Topology-Specific Module (TSM)
Hardware-Specific Module (HSM)

| Network Interface Card (NIC) | Network Interface Card (NIC) | Network Interface Card (NIC) | Network Interface Card (NIC) |

Figure 0.2
ODI model

See also **ODI/NDIS Support.**

Open Document Architecture (ODA)

An Open Systems Interconnection (OSI) specification (ISO 8613) from the International Standards Organization (ISO) defining how documents (especially documents containing fonts, graphics, and text) are electronically transmitted. This specification outlines three levels of document repre-

sentation: Level 1 (for text-only data), Level 2 (for text and graphics generated in a word-processing program), and Level 3 (for text and graphics generated in a desktop-publishing program). The specification primarily addresses the logical representation of the document.

Open Files

A field name that appears in the Cache Utilization menu in the MONITOR NetWare Loadable Module (NLM).

See also **MONITOR; NetWare Loadable Module.**

OPEN LOOK

A nonproprietary *graphical user interface (GUI)* from AT&T for two-dimensional and three-dimensional graphics; as implemented by Sun Microsystems, it includes a window manager and a toolkit.

See also **graphical user interface.**

Open-Network Computing (ONC)

A distributed computing model that uses the Sun Microsystems Network File System (NFS) for handling files distributed over remote locations by using Remote Procedure Calls (RPCs). This model is supported in most UNIX environments, including Novell's UnixWare.

See also **Network File System; Remote Procedure Call.**

Open Network Node (ONN)

A part of the Advanced Peer-to-Peer Internetworking (APPI) standard that provides directory and routing services for Advanced Peer-to-Peer Networking (APPN) end nodes and low-entry nodes.

See also **Advanced Peer-to-Peer Internetworking; Advanced Peer-to-Peer Networking.**

open pipe

A path between a sender and receiver in a circuit-switched and leased-line communications network that indicates data can flow directly between two locations, rather than being broken into packets and routed by various paths.

Open Shortest Path First (OSPF)

A link-state internal gateway protocol that is part of the Transmission-Control Protocol/Internet Protocol (TCP/IP) suite. Using link-state advertisements, OSPF routers exchange information (such as information about the attached interfaces, metrics used, and other variables) about the state of their network connections and links. Using this information to construct the topology of the internetwork, the OSPF routers are able to then determine routing information for delivery of packets. All this information is stored in a link-state database, which the router examines for each destination to select the shortest path to serve as the route to that destination. The OSPF method is considered superior to distance vector routing protocols, which have little knowledge about the topology of the network.

open system

A networking system in which the specifications for elements or interfaces have been made publicly available in order for third-party vendors to create compatible or competing products.

Open System Testing Consortium (OSTC)

A European organization responsible for developing a suite of tests for testing conformance to the International Telecommunications Union (ITU) X.400 Message-Handling System (MHS) recommendations.

See also **International Telecommunications Union; Message-Handling System; X.400.**

Open Systems Interconnection (OSI)

An international program created by the International Standards Organization (ISO) and the Consultative Committee for International Telegraphy and Telephony (CCITT) to standardize data networking and to facilitate the interoperability of multivendor equipment. Under this standardization, an *open system* is one that supports the OSI Reference Model for connecting systems on a network and for transmitting information on these systems. The theory behind this program is to outline all aspects of computer-to-computer communication from the lowest level of signaling techniques to high-level interactions in support of specific applications.

See also **OSI Reference Model.**

Open-Systems Message Exchange (OSME)

An IBM application that provides the capability to exchange messages complying to the International Telecommunications Union (ITU) Message-Handling System (MHS) X.400 specification.

See also **International Telecommunications Union; Message-Handling System; X.400.**

Open Text search engine

An Internet search engine that provides World Wide Web (WWW) search options for Simple Search (which searches for documents containing an exact phrase), Power Search (which allows the use of Boolean and proximity operators in the search string), and Weighted Search (which enables the user to specify how to weigh the search results). Search results provide a hotlinked title, an abstract, a numerical score, a file size, and a Uniform Resource Locator (URL).

See also **search engine; Uniform Resource Locator.**

operating system (OS)

Software that manages a computer system by such tasks as controlling data storage, controlling input and output to and from the keyboard (or other peripheral devices), and controlling the execution of compatible applications.

See also **network operating system.**

operating-system I/O services

Services in NetWare responsible for performing input/output (I/O) functions at the operating system level. These services reference files by using a *file handle* that is returned when a file is opened. The file handle is then passed to other functions.

operating-system-protected (OSP) domain

A reserved portion of system memory used to run untested third-party NetWare Loadable Modules (NLMs) on NetWare 4.1 servers.

See also **memory; NetWare Loadable Module.**

Operation, Administration and Management (OAM) package

A menu-based interface in UnixWare used to access a suite of system administration and maintenance utilities. These utilities can monitor network performance, detect network defects, protect the network operating system, report on network failures, and localize network faults.

See also **UnixWare operating system.**

Operator

In NetWare, a Directory Schema term and a selectable property for the Bindery Queue, Computer, NCP Server, Print Server, Printer, and Queue objects in Novell Directory Services (NDS).

See also **leaf object; Novell Directory Services; object.**

operator hold

A hold placed by a print-queue operator on a print job.

optical character recognition (OCR)

A capability provided by a standard optical scanner and special software that enables a computer to recognize printed or typed characters.

optical disc

A type of removable media that can be one- or two-sided, read-only or read-write, and is used as the media type for the High-Capacity Storage System (HCCS).

See also **High-Capacity Storage System.**

Table 0.4: Optical Drives

Drive	Description
Compact Disc Read-Only Memory (CD-ROM)	A medium with a storage capacity of approximately 600MB. Optional jukebox versions can hold from 5 to 100 compact discs.
Write Once, Read Many (WORM)	A high-capacity storage medium with recording capabilities. Data can be written only once to a location but can be read from the location many times.
Erasable Optical (EO)	A read-write medium that stores data in an optical format. NetWare 4.x supports the High-Capacity Storage System (HCSS), which allows network files to be stored on EO disks rather than on a hard drive.
Optical Read-Only Memory (OROM)	A storage medium that can be read by a magneto-optical drive.
Magneto-Optical (MO)	A general classification of storage media that use optical means to store data.

See also **compact disc; Compact Disc Read-Only Memory; Write Once, Read Many.**

optical-disc library

A high-capacity storage device that uses an autochanger mechanism to mount and dismount optical discs. An optical-disc library is also known as a *jukebox*.

optical drive

A device that provides mass storage through optical or magneto-optical encoding of data. Table O.4 shows several types of optical drives.

Optical Fiber, Nonconductive Plenum (OFNP)

A specification from the Underwriters Laboratory (UL) that defines certain safety criteria for optical fiber.
See also **Underwriters Laboratory.**

Optical Fiber, Nonconductive Riser (OFNR)

A specification from the Underwriters Laboratory (UL) that defines certain safety criteria for optical fiber.
See also **Underwriters Laboratory.**

optical switch

A high-speed communications switch that uses light to carry out a switching function.

Optical Time-Domain Reflectometer (OTDR)

A fiber-optic communications tool that tests a light signal and analyzes the cable that carries it by sending out a light signal and checking the amount and type of light that reflects back.

Orange Book

A document originally entitled "The Department of Defense Trusted Computer System Evaluation Criteria" (TCSEC), originally designed to provide network-security guidelines for developers and administrators. By listing basic requirements for very low and very high levels of security, the Orange Book provides evaluation criteria for different divisions of security. Criteria are hierarchically divided into Divisions D, C, B, and A. Division A represents systems with the most comprehensive security. Divisions C and B also have subdivisions known as *classes*, hierarchically arranged within divisions. Table O.5 shows the four divisions of security outlined by the Orange Book, as well as certain classes.

 **For more information about the Orange Book, surf the Web to** http://www.v-one.com/pubs/obook/obook.htm.

ORB

Object-Request Broker, a service developed by the Object-Management Group (OMG) as part of the Common Object-Request Broker Architecture (CORBA) specification that enables existing applications to communicate with object-oriented applications. An ORB enables applications to request network services without first knowing the directory structure of the environment from which the service is being requested.
See also **Common Object-Request Broker Architecture; object-oriented program.**

Table 0.5: Orange Book Security Levels

Division	Class	Description
A	AI	Systems must satisfy all the requirements for class B3, with no additional architectural features being required. However, these systems must meet a formal design specification, include specified verification techniques, be subjected to stringent configuration management, and follow strict guidelines for distributing the system to remote sites.
B	B3	Systems must satisfy all the requirements for class B2, and must also be able to mediate all accesses of subjects to objects, be tamperproof, and be small enough to be subjected to testing and analysis. A security administrator is suggested, audit mechanisms are expanded to signal security-relevant events, and system-recovery procedures are required.
	B2	Systems contain all the security features required for class BI, except that the discretionary and mandatory control enforcement must be extended to all components in the system. The system must have carefully structured *protection-critical* and *non-protection-critical* elements. Class B2 systems are relatively impervious to penetration by intruders.
	BI	Systems contain all the security features required for class C2; most also have an informal statement of the security policy model, data labeling, and mandatory access control over named subjects and objects. In addition, the system must provide the capability of labeling exported information.
C	C2	Systems are more discretionary about the separation of users and data. This class denotes an environment in which users are individually accountable for their actions through login procedures, auditing of security-relevant issues, and resource isolation.
	CI	Systems nominally satisfy discretionary security requirements for the separation of users and data. This class denotes an environment in which cooperating users process data at the same level of sensitivity.
D		Systems have been evaluated but fail to meet requirements for a higher evaluation class.

order of magnitude

A change in the numerical value of a number, reflected as a multiple of a reference value. The two most common reference values are expressed as decimal (base 10) or binary (base 2) values. Prefixes indicating orders of magnitude are often combined with computer measurements (for example, a *kilobyte* represents 1,000 bytes) as a means of expressing a large number of the unit of measurement. Table O.6 lists some common orders of magnitude used in computing environments.

org (organization)

A suffix on an Internet address (.ORG), indicating the address belongs to a noncommercial organization. The collection of all

addresses of this type is sometimes called an *org domain* or an *org hierarchy*.

See also **Internet address; Internet service provider.**

Organization

In NetWare, a Directory Schema term and a selectable property for the following objects in Novell Directory Services (NDS): AFP Server, Bindery Queue, Computer, Directory Map, Group, List, Message-Routing Group, Messaging Server, NCP Server, Organization, Print Server, Printer, Profile, Queue, and Volume.

See also **leaf object; Novell Directory Services; object.**

Table O.6: Orders of Magnitude

Measurement	Abbreviation	Binary	Decimal	Example
exa-	E	2^{60}	10^{18}	1,000,000,000,000,000,000
peta-	P	2^{50}	10^{15}	1,000,000,000,000,000
tera-	T	2^{40}	10^{12}	1,000,000,000,000
giga-	G	2^{30}	10^{9}	1,000,000,000
mega-	M	2^{20}	10^{6}	1,000,000
kilo-	K	2^{10}	10^{3}	1,000
milli-	m	2^{-10}	10^{-3}	0.001
micro-	μ	2^{-20}	10^{-6}	0.000001
nano-	n	2^{-30}	10^{-9}	0.000000001
pico-	p	2^{-40}	10^{-12}	0.000000000001
femto-	f	2^{-50}	10^{-15}	0.000000000000001
atta-	a	2^{-60}	10^{-18}	0.000000000000000001

Organization Name

In NetWare, a Directory Schema term in Novell Directory Services (NDS).

See also **Novell Directory Services.**

Organization (O) object

In Novell Directory Services (NDS), a container object required in every Directory tree. An Organization object designates a company, a division of a company, a university or college with several departments, and so on. An Organization object must be placed directly below the [Root] object in the NDS hierarchy, unless a Country or Locality object is used. An Organization object has the following selectable NDS properties: Access-Control List, Back Link, Bindery, Description, Detect Intruder, E-Mail Address, Facsimile Telephone Number, Intruder-Attempt Reset Interval, Intruder-Lockout Reset Interval, Locality, Lockout After Detection, Login-Intruder Limit, Login Script, Mailbox ID, Mailbox Location, NNS Domain, Object Class, Organization, Physical-Delivery Office Name, Postal Address, Postal Code, Postal Office Box, Print-Job Configuration, Printer Control, Supervisor, SA, See Also, Supervisor (S), and Telephone Number.

See also **container object; Novell Directory Services; object; [Root].**

organizational command

An NMENU utility file source command that establishes the content and organization of menu programs.

See also **NMENU utility.**

Organizational Person

A NetWare Directory Schema term in Novell Directory Services (NDS).

See also **Novell Directory Services.**

Organizational Person object

A Novell Directory Services (NDS) leaf object that is one of two subclasses defined in the X.500 standard (the other is the Residential Person object). The Organizational Person object defines anyone who either represents or is in some way associated with a particular organization.

See also **leaf object; Novell Directory Services; object.**

Organizational Role

A NetWare Directory Schema term in Novell Directory Services (NDS).

See also **Novell Directory Services.**

Organizational Role object

A Novell Directory Services (NDS) leaf object that defines a position or role with an organization object or container object. Object or file rights are granted to the role itself and not to the occupants who may belong to the role. An Organizational Role object has the following selectable NDS properties: Access-Control List, Back Link, Bindery, Common Name (CN), Description, E-Mail Address, Facsimile Telephone Number, Locality, Mailbox ID, Mailbox Location, Object Class, Organizational Unit (OU), Physical Delivery Office Name, Postal Address, Postal Code, Postal Office Box, Role Occupant, Supervisor, SA, See Also, and Telephone Number.

See also **leaf object; Novell Directory Services; object.**

Organizational Unit

In NetWare, a Directory Schema term and a selectable property for the following objects in Novell Directory Services (NDS): AFP Server, Bindery Queue, Computer, Directory Map, External Entity, Group, List, Message Routing Group, Messaging Server, NCP Server, Organizational Role, Print Server, Printer, Profile, Queue, User, and Volume.

See also **leaf object; Novell Directory Services; object.**

Organizational Unit (OU) object

A Novell Directory Services (NDS) container object that allows the organization of leaf objects and represents a division, a business unit, or a project team. Organizational Unit objects contain other Organizational Unit (OU) objects, leaf objects, or any NDS object type except the [Root], Country, or Organization objects. An Organizational Unit object has the following selectable NDS properties: Access-Control List, Back Link, Bindery, Description, Detect Intruder, E-Mail Address, Facsimile Telephone Number, Intruder Attempt Reset Interval, Intruder Lockout OU, Locality, Lockout After Detection, Login Intruder Limit, Login Script, Mailbox ID, Mailbox Location, NNS Domain, Object Class, Physical Delivery Office Name, Postal Address, Postal Code, Postal Office Box, Print Job Configuration, Printer Control, Reset Interval, Supervisor, SA, See Also, and Telephone Number.

See also **container object; Novell Directory Services; object.**

Origin server

A World Wide Web (WWW) server on which a particular resource resides or can be created.

See also **World Wide Web.**

Original Cache Buffers

A field name appearing in the Cache Utilization menu in the MONITOR NetWare Loadable Module (NLM).

See also **MONITOR; NetWare Loadable Module.**

original equipment manufacturer (OEM)

The original manufacturer of hardware subsystems or hardware components. The OEM often contracts to supply subsystems or components to a value-added reseller (VAR).

See also **value-added reseller.**

originate mode

A mode on a device initiating a call and waiting for a remote device to respond.

OS

operating system, software that manages a computer system by such tasks as controlling data storage, controlling input and output to and from the keyboard (or other peripheral devices), and controlling the execution of compatible applications.

See also **network operating system.**

OS kernel

The core of an operating system that provides the most essential and basic system services (such as memory management).

OS/2

A 32-bit operating system from IBM that uses a graphical user interface (GUI), supports true preemptive multitasking, multiple threads, and nonsegmented memory addressing. OS/2 provides support for the DOS File-Allocation Table (FAT) and its own High-Performance File System (HPFS), as well as such add-on file systems as the CD-ROM File System (CDFS). Two useful features of OS/2 are long filename support and extended attribute support. Microsoft's LAN Manager and LAN Server network operating systems are built on OS/2.

See also **File-Allocation Table; graphical user interface; High-Performance File System; LAN Manager; LAN Server.**

 **For more information about operating systems from IBM, surf the Web to** http://www.software.ibm.com/os.

OS/2 client

A computer that runs on the OS/2 operating system platform and that connects to the network by using the NetWare Client for OS/2 software. This computer has the capability to store and retrieve data from the network, as well as run executable network files.

See also **NetWare Client for OS/2.**

OS/2 Requester

Part of the software that connects a computer running the OS/2 operating system to a NetWare network. The OS/2 Requester enables OS/2 users to share network resources.

OSF/Motif

A nonproprietary graphical user interface (GUI) standard from the Open Software Foundation (OSF) that includes a window manager and a toolkit.

OSI

Open Systems Interconnection, an international program created by the International Standards Organization (ISO) and the Consultative Committee for International Telegraphy and Telephony (CCITT) to standardize data networking and to facilitate the interoperability of multivendor equipment. Under this standardization, an *open system* is one that supports the OSI Reference Model for connecting systems on a network and for transmitting information on these systems. The theory behind this program is to outline all aspects of computer-to-computer communication, from the lowest level of signaling techniques to high-level interactions in support of specific applications.

See also **OSI Reference Model.**

OSI Government Systems Interconnection Protocol (OSI GOSIP)

A specification based on the OSI Reference Model that must be followed for purchases made for government installations, particularly purchases that involve networking products or services.

See also **OSI Reference Model.**

OSI Implementers Workshop (OIW)

A regional workshop representing North America for implementers of the OSI

Reference Model. Other workshops include the European Workshop for Open Systems (EWOS), which represents Europe, and the Asia and Oceania Workshop (AOW), which represents the Asiatic region.

See also **OSI Reference Model.**

OSI Internet Management (OIM)

An organization responsible for specifying ways in which the protocols of the OSI Network-Management Model can be used to manage Transmission-Control Protocol/Internet Protocol (TCP/IP) networks.

See also **Transmission-Control Protocol/Internet Protocol.**

OSI network address

A network address in the OSI Reference Model associated with an entity in the Transport Layer (Layer 4). The address, which may be up to 20 bytes long, contains a standardized initial domain part and a domain-specific part (which falls under the control of the network administrator).

See also **OSI Reference Model.**

OSI Network-Management Model

Concepts and guidelines developed by the International Standards Organization (ISO) to be used as a basis for various aspects of network management. The basic configuration outlines a manager system communicating with a managed system to manage a resource contained in or controlled by the managed system. The three real-world building blocks for this model include a manager, agent, and managed object. This model defines how the Common Management-Information Protocol (CMIP)

can be used effectively to manage all kinds of resources. Two types of standards are outlined in this model:

- *Communications standards* define how manager and agent systems communicate through the Application Layer (Layer 7) of the OSI Reference Model to the Presentation Layer (Layer 6) by using CMIP.
- *Management information standards* define how particular resources can be managed over a communications interface.

The four major components of the OSI Network-Management Model are as follows (see Figure O.3):

- *Systems-Management Application Process (SMAP)* carries out the network-management functions on a single machine.
- *Systems-Management Application Entity (SMAE)* communicates with other network nodes (including the network manager) through Common Management-Information Protocol (CMIP) packets.
- *Layer-Management Entity (LME)* provides network-management functions.
- *Management Information Base (MIB)* contains the network-management information received from each node.

A task passes from SMAP through the Systems-Management Interface (SMI) to the SMAE. Within the SMAE, the Systems-Management-Application Service Element (SMASE) contains the Systems-Management Function Areas (SMFAs) and the Systems-Management Functions (SMFs). Table O.7 shows the SMFAs and Table O.8 shows the SMFs.

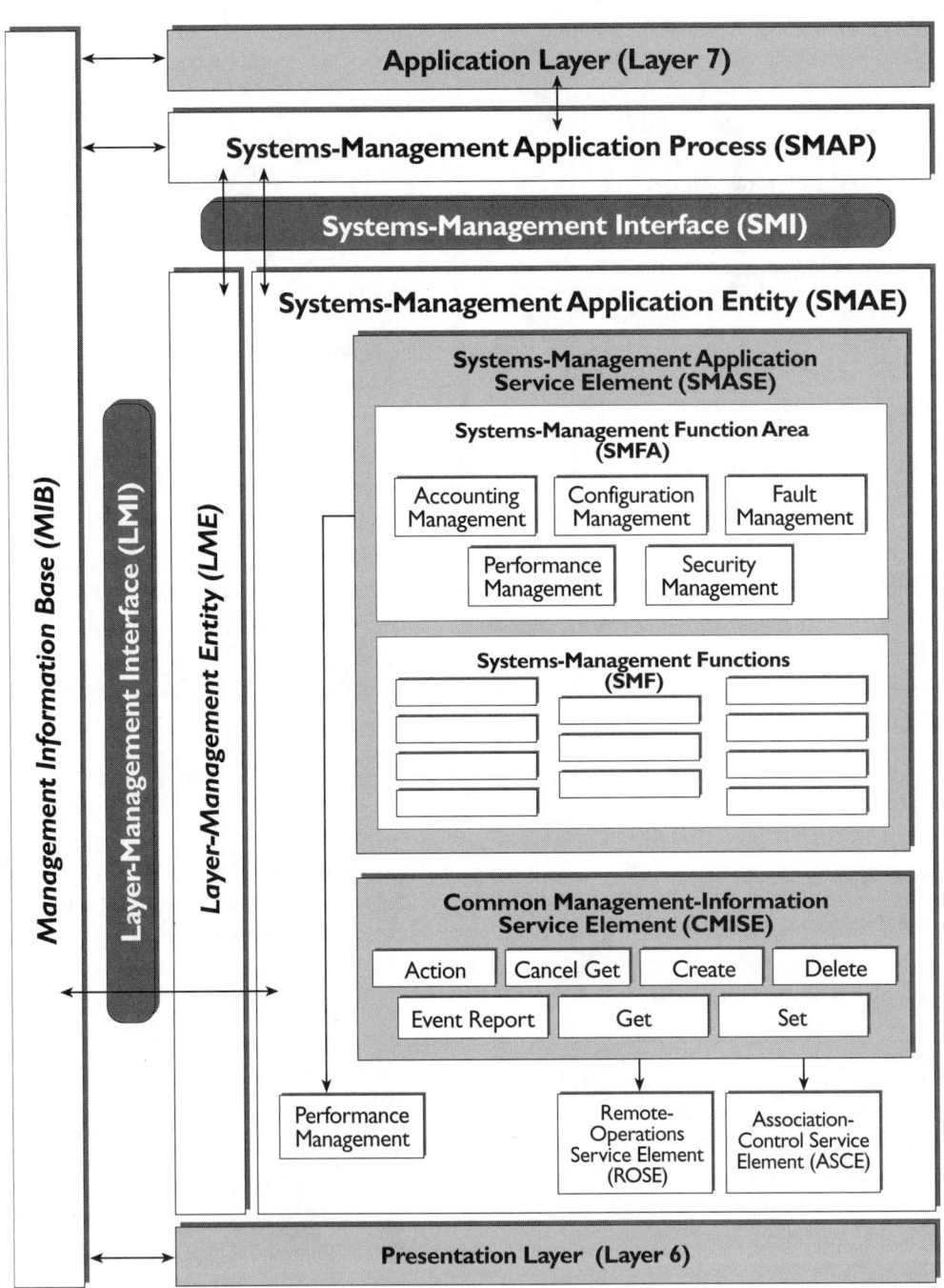

Figure 0.3
OSI Network-Management Model

Table O.7: System-Management Functions (SMFs)

Domain	Description
Accounting Management	Measures network utilization parameters to aid in the regulation of users or groups of users.
Configuration Management	Monitors network and system configuration information to track and manage the effects of various hardware and software versions.
Fault Management	Detects, logs, notifies users of, and fixes network problems.
Performance Management	Measures and makes available various aspects of network performance.
Security Management	Controls access to network resources according to local guidelines to protect against intruders.

Table O.8: System-Management Functions (SMFs)

Function	Description
Access Control	Controls access to management information and operations.
Account Metering	Tracks resource usage, generates accounting and billing for such usage, and enforces accounting limitations.
Alarm Reporting	Provides information about faults, errors, or other network-operation abnormalities.
Event Reporting	Selects events to be reported.
Log Control	Specifies what to do with report logs.
Object Management	Creates, deletes, examines, and updates objects.
Relationship Management	Establishes, monitors, and views the relationships of objects.
Security Alarm Reporting	Provides information about faults, errors, or other network-security abnormalities.
Security Audit Trail	Specifies events and formats to be used in security log.
State Management	Monitors the management states of objects.
Summarization	Analyzes and summarizes network-management information.
Test Management	Tests network components and services.
Workload Monitoring	Monitors objects and attributes.

The SMASE functions rely on the Common-Management Service Element (CMISE) to perform certain services, including Action, Cancel Get, Create, Delete, Event Report, Get, and Set. The CMISE relies on the Association-Control Service Element (ACSE) and the Remote-Operations Service Element (ROSE) to accomplish some of its tasks. SMASE can also bypass CMISE completely and use the Application-Service Element (ASE) to perform services. The OSI Network-Management Model is also known as the *ISO Network-Management Model*.

See also **Common Management-Information Protocol; International Standards Organization; OSI Reference Model.**

OSI presentation address

A network address in the OSI Reference Model associated with an entity in the Application Layer (Layer 7). The OSI presentation address consists of an OSI network address and of selectors identifying Service Access Points (SAPs) for the Presentation Layer (Layer 6), Session Layer (Layer 5), and Transport Layer (Layer 4) of the OSI Reference Model.

See also **OSI network address; OSI Reference Model; Service-Access Points.**

OSI Reference Model

A computer network system model developed by the International Standards Organization (ISO) to standardize the interconnection of open computer systems (computer systems that are open for communication with other systems). The model defines seven specific layers, specifies how each layer can be addressed, and outlines the specific services and protocols each

layer can use. The following principles were applied to define the seven layers:

- Whenever a different level of abstraction was needed, a layer was created.
- Each layer was designed to perform a well-defined function, which included internationally standardized protocols.
- Layer boundaries were designed to minimize information flow across the boundaries.
- The total number of layers was determined to be large enough that distinct functions could be defined clearly, but small enough that the overall architectural model did not become unwieldy.

Each layer of the model uses certain protocols, and certain exchange units. Table O.9 shows the seven layers of the OSI Reference Model, a description of each, examples of the protocols used, and the exchange units used.

In addition to the seven major layers, the OSI Reference Model also includes *sublayers* within the Data-Link Layer (Layer 2) and Network Layer (Layer 3). The sublayers within the Data-Link Layer are as follows:

- *Media-Access Control (MAC),* the lower sublayer, controls media-access issues such as whether to use token passing and contention.
- *Logical-Link Control (LLC),* the higher sublayer, controls issues such as error control, flow control, and framing.

The sublayers of the Network Layer include the following:

- Access Sublayer (Layer 4)
- Intranetwork Sublayer (Layer 3)
- Harmonizing Sublayer (Layer 2)
- Internetwork Sublayer (Layer 1)

Figure O.4 shows the OSI Reference Model.

Table 0.9: OSI Reference Model

Layer	Description	Protocol Example	Exchange Unit
Application (Layer 7)	Provides services to application processes outside the scope of the OSI Reference Model (such as word processing programs or spreadsheet programs). This layer identifies and establishes the availability of communications partners, synchronizes the applications, establishes agreement on procedures for error control and data integrity, and determines the existence of sufficient resources for the intended communication.	Simple Mail-Transfer Protocol (SMTP); File-Transfer Protocol (FTP)	Application-Protocol Data Unit (APDU)
Presentation (Layer 6)	Used to negotiate and establish the encoding of values for transferring structured data types (an operation called *transfer syntax*). This layer is responsible for communicating with the Session Layer and for managing the transfer syntax.	External-Data Representation (XDR)	Presentation-Protocol Data Unit (PPDU)
Session (Layer 5)	Establishes a network connection between users by managing ordinary data transport and providing enhanced services to certain applications. Some of the services provided are dialog control (which means managing whose turn it is to communicate across the network), token management (which means managing the exchange of tokens to determine which side can perform critical operations), and synchronization (which means inserting checkpoints into the data stream to monitor the transmission of data).	Transmission-Control Protocol (TCP); AppleTalk Data-Stream Protocol (ADSP)	Session-Protocol Data Unit (SPDU)
Transport (Layer 4)	Accepts data from the Session Layer, splits it up into smaller units (if necessary), and ensures accurate arrival at the destination. Through this layer, a source computer communicates with a destination computer, using message headers and control	Transmission-Control Protocol (TCP); User Datagram Protocol (UDP); Sequenced Packet Exchange (SPX);	Transport-Protocol Data Unit (TPDU)

(continued)

(Table 0.9: continued)

Layer	Description	Protocol Example	Exchange Unit
	messages. This layer provides connection-management services (which allow a Transport Layer user to create and maintain a data path to a correspondent Transport Layer user) and data-transfer services (which provide a way to exchange data between a pair of Transport Layer users).	AppleTalk File-Transfer Protocol (ATFP)	
Network (Layer 3)	Routes information from one networked computer to another. These computers may be located on the same network or on different networks. Of primary concern is how packets are routed from source to destination; this layer ensures that congestion does not occur on the network and that heterogeneous networks can communicate with each other.	Internet Protocol (IP); Datagram-Delivery Protocol (DDP); Internetwork Packet Exchange (IPX)	Packet
Data-Link (Layer 2)	Provides a reliable means of data transmission across the Physical Layer by breaking the data into frames, transmitting the frames sequentially, and processing the acknowledged frames sent back by the receiver. This layer provides error control by creating and recognizing frame boundaries and errors associated with this information. Special bit patterns are attached to the beginning and end of the frames, and are constantly checked for accuracy.	Point-to-Point Protocol (PPP); EtherTalk Link-Access Protocol (ELAP); Serial-Line Interface Protocol (SLIP); LocalTalk Link-Access Protocol (LLAP)	Frame
Physical (Layer 1)	Provides a physical connection (as well as a means to activate and deactivate the connection) for the transmission of data among network entities. Design issues considered here are mechanical, electrical, and procedural interfaces, as well as the physical transmission medium. The services provided include the establishment of a connection and the transmission of bits over a physical medium to the Data-Link Layer.		Bit

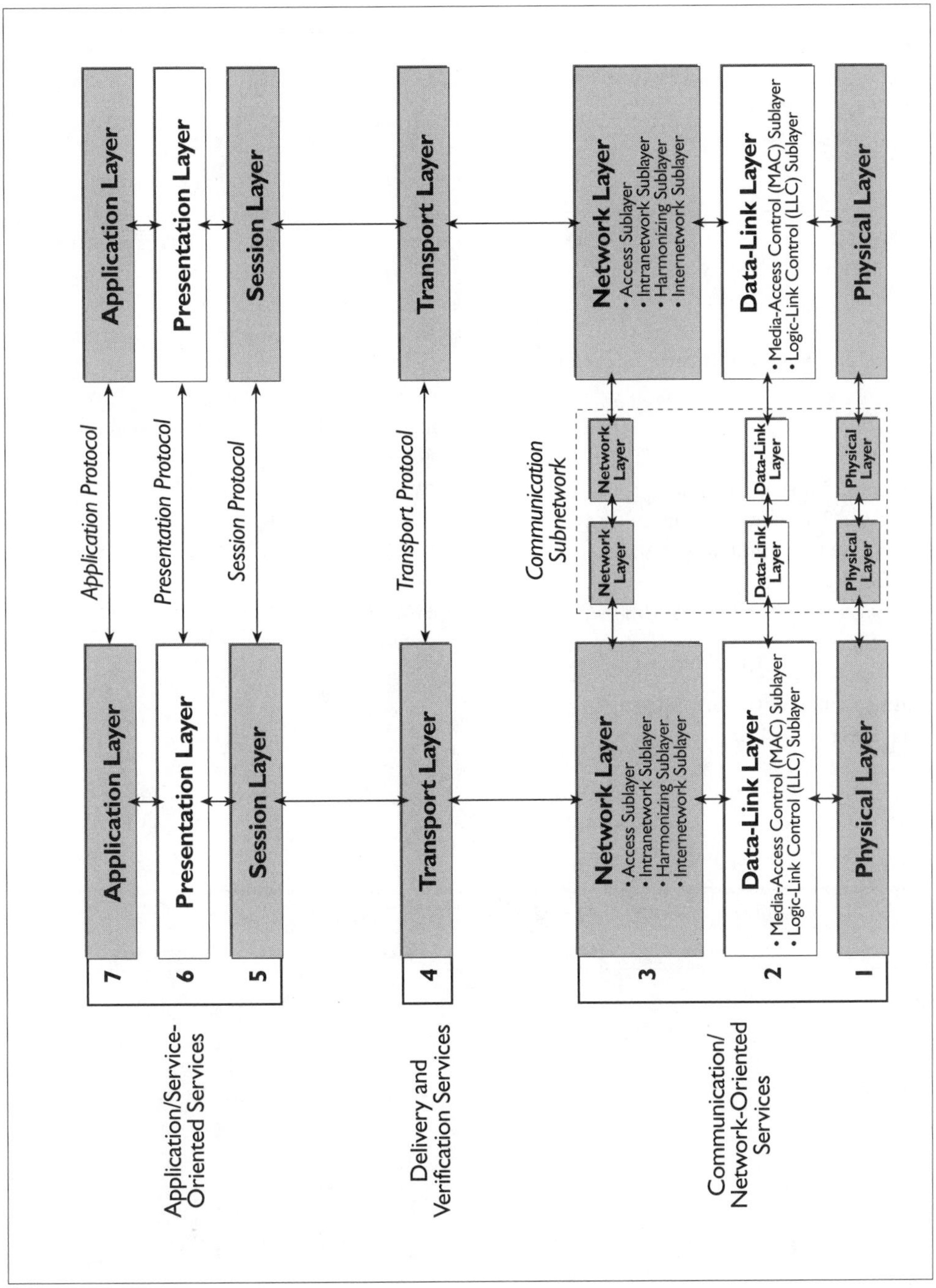

Application Layer 7

Presentation Layer 6

Session Layer 5

Application/Service-Oriented Services

Transport Layer 4

Delivery and Verification Services

Network Layer 3
- Access Sublayer
- Intranetwork Sublayer
- Harmonizing Sublayer
- Internetwork Sublayer

Data-Link Layer 2
- Media-Access Control (MAC) Sublayer
- Logic-Link Control (LLC) Sublayer

Physical Layer 1

Communication/Network-Oriented Services

Application Layer

Presentation Layer

Session Layer

Transport Layer

Network Layer
- Access Sublayer
- Intranetwork Sublayer
- Harmonizing Sublayer
- Internetwork Sublayer

Data-Link Layer
- Media-Access Control (MAC) Sublayer
- Logic-Link Control (LLC) Sublayer

Physical Layer

Application Protocol

Presentation Protocol

Session Protocol

Transport Protocol

Communication Subnetwork

Network Layer   Network Layer

Data-Link Layer   Data-Link Layer

Physical Layer   Physical Layer

Figure 0.4
OSI Reference Model

Specific internetworking devices are used for each level of the OSI Reference Model. Table O.10 shows how certain devices match up with the model.

OSINET

An association responsible for the international promotion of Open Systems Interconnection (OSI) in vendor architectures.

See also **Open Systems Interconnection.**

OSME

Open Systems Message Exchange, an IBM application that provides the capability to exchange messages complying to the International Telecommunications Union (ITU) Message-Handling System (MHS) X.400 specification.

See also **International Telecommunications Union; Message-Handling System; X.400.**

OSPF

Open Shortest Path First, a link-state internal gateway protocol that is part of the Transmission-Control Protocol/Internet Protocol (TCP/IP) suite. Using link-state advertisements, OSPF routers exchange information (such as information about the attached interfaces, metrics used, and other variables) about the state of their network connections and links. Using this information to construct the topology of the internetwork, the OSPF routers are able to then determine routing information for delivery of packets. All this information is stored in a link-state database, which the router examines for each destination to select the shortest path to serve as the route to that destination. The OSPF method is considered superior to distance vector routing protocols, which have little knowledge about the topology of the network.

Table O.10: Internetworking Devices and the OSI Reference Model

Layer	Repeater	Bridge	Router	Gateway
Application				X
Presentation				X
Session				X
Transport				X
Network			X	X
Data-Link		X (at MAC sublayer)	X	X
Physical	X	X	X	X

OSTC

Open System Testing Consortium, a European organization responsible for developing a suite of tests for testing conformance to the International Telecommunications Union (ITU) X.400 Message-Handling System (MHS) recommendations.

See also **International Telecommunications Union; Message-Handling System; X.400.**

OTDR

Optical Time-Domain Reflectometer, a fiber-optic communications tool that tests a light signal and analyzes the cable that carries it by sending out a light signal and checking the amount and type of light that reflects back.

Other Names

In NetWare, a Directory Schema term in Novell Directory Services (NDS).

See also **Novell Directory Services.**

outbound service-advertisement filter

A filter that limits the service advertisements propagated by the router to a selected set of services at a selected set of networks.

See also **service advertising.**

outframe

The maximum number of outstanding frames allowed in a Systems Network Architecture (SNA) server at any time.

See also **Systems Network Architecture.**

outline

A window in an online document (in ElectroText or DynaText format) that displays the table of contents, list of figures, or list of tables.

out-of-band communication

A diagnostic or management process that uses frequencies outside the range being used for data or message communications.

output

Data sent by a computer to a peripheral device (such as a console, hard disk, or printer).

output cursor

A cursor indicating the starting row and column position on the computer display screen where the output goes when a function that writes to the display screen is called.

Output Feedback (OFB)

A Data-Encryption Standard (DES) operating mode.

See also **Data-Encryption Standard.**

outsourcing

A policy of subcontracting a company's data-processing operations to outside vendors rather than maintaining internal departments to perform the operations.

Owner

In Novell Directory Services (NDS), a selectable property for the Computer, Group, List, Message-Routing Group, and Printer objects.

See also **leaf object; Novell Directory Services; object.**

owner name

An assigned password that protects data files from unauthorized access by Btrieve applications. The owner name can be set through the Btrieve Maintenance utility.

See also **Btrieve.**

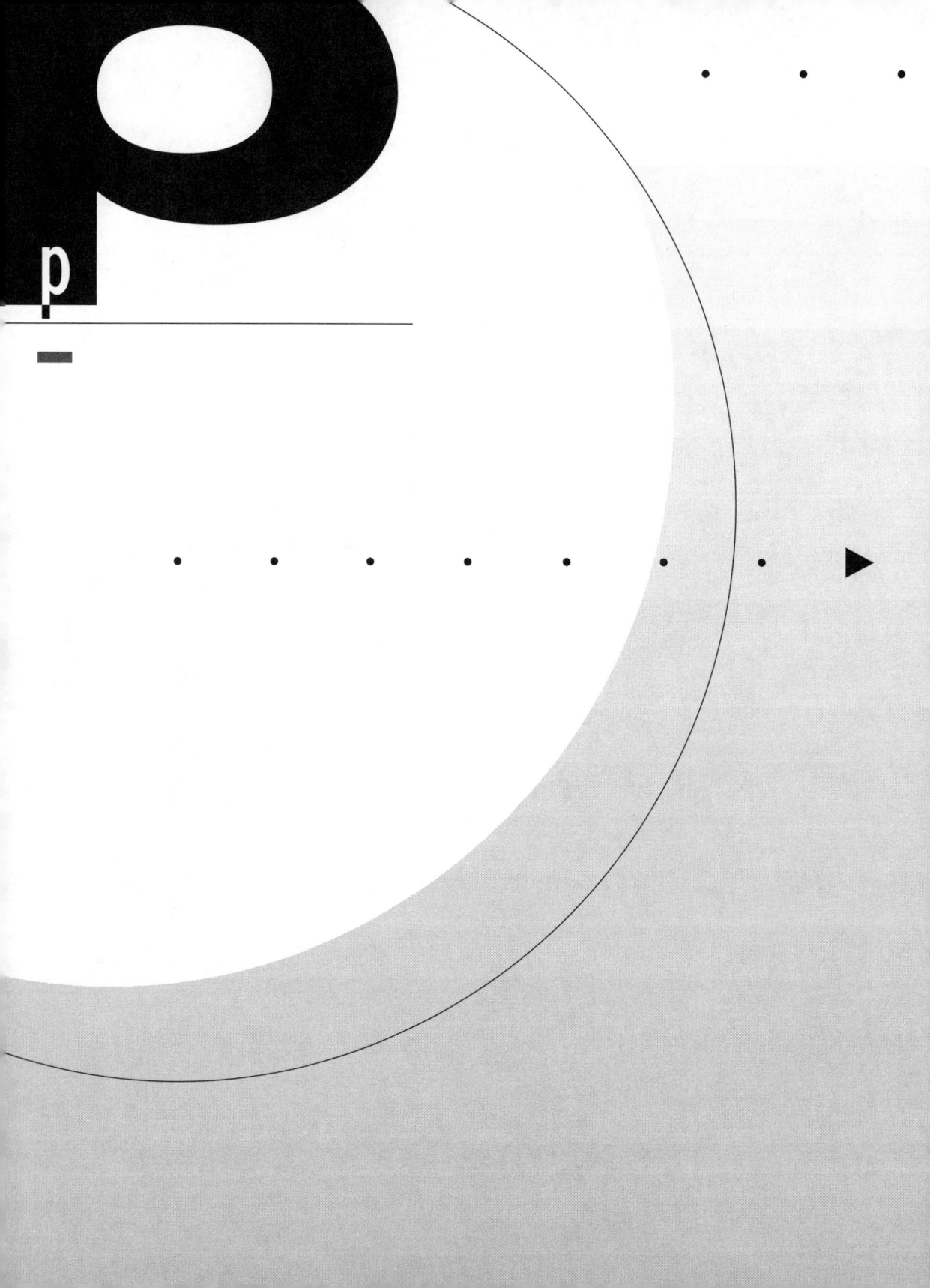

p.m.

A Latin abbreviation for *post meridiem*, which means afternoon. Unless "a.m." or "p.m." is used when specifying times, NetWare assumes the value to be military time (24-hour time format).

PABX

Private Automatic Branch Exchange, a telephone system offering automatic switching and other communications capabilities. Because almost all telephone systems are now automatic, this term is often replaced with a synonym, **Private Branch Exchange (PBX)**.

PAC

Privilege-Attribute Certificate, a certificate that specifies the privileges granted to a user and is checked to determine whether the user should be granted access to a requested service (or to the network).

PACE

Priority Access-Control Enabled, a proprietary variant of the Ethernet architecture designed to set priorities for the transmission of time-sensitive materials; the highest priority is granted to data that must be sent at a constant rate to be readable. PACE was developed by 3Com and other collaborators.
See also **Ethernet.**

pacing

A method of controlling network traffic in a Systems Network Architecture (SNA) net-work by limiting the amount of data a program can send or receive at one time to prevent overrunning of logical unit (LU) buffers.
See also **Systems Network Architecture.**

pacing window size

The number of Request/Response Units (RUs) a program is allowed to send before permission is required to send more in a Systems Network Architecture (SNA) network.
See also **Systems Network Architecture.**

packet

A unit of information used in network communication. Messages sent between network devices are formed into a header and data portion that together make up a packet. Headers are appended to the data portion as the packet travels through the communication layers. The packet might contain a request for service, information on how to handle the request, and the data to be serviced. If a message exceeds a maximum packet size, it is partitioned and carried as several packets. When the packets arrive at the prescribed destination, the packets are reassembled into a complete message, the headers are stripped off in reverse order, and the request is serviced.
See also **Large Internet Packet.**

packet assembler/disassembler (PAD)

A device or program that creates packets of data for transmission and removes data from received packets. The PAD is most common in data networks using packets that meet the X.25 specification of the

Consultative Committee for International Telegraphy and Telephony (CCITT).

See also **Consultative Committee for International Telegraphy and Telephony; X.25.**

packet buffer

An area where incoming packets are held until a receiving device can process the data.

See also **buffer; packet-receive buffer.**

packet burst

A method of transmitting data across a NetWare network in which data is collected and sent as a unit in a single high-speed transmission. Packet burst is also known as *burst mode*.

Packet-Burst Protocol (PBP)

A protocol (which is built on top of the Internetwork Packet Exchange) that speeds the transfer of multiple-packet NetWare Core Protocol (NCP) file reads and writes between a workstation and a NetWare server by eliminating the need to sequence and acknowledge each packet. Because it enables a server or workstation to send a whole set (or burst) of packets before it requires acknowledgment, PBP is more efficient than the one request-one response protocol used in early versions of NetWare and reduces network traffic. Dropped packets are monitored by PBP; retransmissions are only performed for missing packets.

See also **Internetwork Packet Exchange; NetWare Core Protocol.**

packet driver

A program for computers operating in the DOS and Windows environments that connects network software to Network Interface Cards (NICs). An Open Data-Link Interface (ODI) driver is an example of a packet driver.

See also **Network Interface Card; Open Data-Link Interface.**

Packet-Exchange Protocol (PEP)

A Xerox Network Systems (XNS) protocol used at the Transport Level (Level 4 of the OSI Reference Model).

See also **OSI Reference Model; Xerox Network Systems.**

packet filter

A process in which bridges perform such traffic-control functions as limiting protocol-specific traffic to one segment of the network and isolating electronic-mail (e-mail) domains. After a network administrator sets packet-filter specifications for each bridge, the bridge can either accept or reject any packet matching the specifications.

packet forwarding

The copying of a packet from one interface to another through the use of an intermediate system.

packet frame

Information added to a packet to ensure the packet is properly and accurately transmitted across a network. The format of the information contained in the packet frame depends on the physical medium on which the data travels.

Packet InterNet Groper (PING)

A program that tests the accessibility of destinations by sending the destinations an Internet Control-Message Protocol (ICMP) echo request and waiting for a reply.

See also **Internet Control-Message Protocol.**

Packet Layer

Under the X.25 specification of Consultative Committee for International Telegraphy and Telephony (CCITT), the layer of a packet-switched network that controls call setup and clearing, packet transfer, and network facility selection.

See also **Consultative Committee for International Telegraphy and Telephony; X.25.**

Packet-Level Procedure (PAP)

A full-duplex protocol for the transfer of packets between a computer and a modem on an X.25 network.

See also **PAP; X.25.**

Packet-Level Protocol (PLP)

A full-duplex protocol specifying the details of data transfer between a sender and receiver on an X.25 network that supports error detection and correction, packet sequencing, and transfer-rate adjustment.

See also **full duplex; X.25.**

packet radio network

A network using radio waves to transmit packets of information.

packet-receive buffer

A special area set aside in the NetWare server's memory that temporarily holds data packets arriving from various workstations until the server is ready to process them and send them to their destinations. Although the default range of packet-receive buffers (set during server installation) should be satisfactory, the following parameters may be set during installation to increase the range:

- *Maximum packet buffers* resets the maximum number of packet receive buffers allocated by the operating system.
- *Minimum packet-receive buffers* resets the minimum number of packet-receive buffers allocated by the operating system.
- *New packet-receive buffer time* establishes the amount of time the operating system must wait before allocating packet-receive buffers on an as-needed basis.

packet size

The size of an incoming or outgoing data packet.

Packet-Switch Node (PSN)

A dedicated machine that accepts and routes packets in a packet-switching network.

packet-switched network

A configuration of independent, interconnected computers that use packets to transmit information to each other.

See also **packet; packet switching.**

packet switching

The division of data communications messages into finite-sized packets, which are forwarded over different circuit paths and reassembled into the message before the message is passed on to the receiving terminal or device.

See also **packet; packet-switched network.**

packet-switching service

A commercial company offering packet-switching network services to paid subscribers. CompuServe is an example of a packet-switching service.

See also **CompuServe Information Service.**

PACNET

A packet-switched network located in New Zealand.

PAD

packet assembler/disassembler, a device or program that creates packets of data for transmission and removes data from received packets. The PAD is most common in data networks using packets that meet the X.25 specification of the Consultative Committee for International Telegraphy and Telephony (CCITT).

See also **Consultative Committee for International Telegraphy and Telephony; X.25.**

page

A collection of information (such as text, graphics, and sounds) organized for presentation on the World Wide Web (WWW). Also, a contiguous chunk of memory of a predefined size that may be allocated on an as-needed basis, usually in some area of random-access memory (RAM).

See also **memory; page-mode RAM; paging; random-access memory; World Wide Web.**

Page-Description Language

In Novell Directory Services (NDS), a NetWare Directory Schema term and a selectable property for the Printer object.

See also **leaf object; Novell Directory Services; object.**

Page-Description Language (PDL)

Commands that control the reproduction of text and graphic images on a printed page. Adobe PostScript is an example of a PDL.

See also **PostScript.**

paged memory-management unit (PMMU)

A specialized microprocessor chip that manages virtual memory.

See also **virtual memory.**

page-mode RAM

A system in which specialized Dynamic Random-Access Memory (DRAM) microprocessor chips divide memory so that consecutive accesses to memory addresses in the same chunk of memory result in a page-mode cycle that takes about half the processing time of a regular DRAM cycle.

See also **Dynamic Random-Access Memory; page.**

pager

A feature that breaks up information solicited from the World Wide Web (WWW) into chunks that can be viewed one screen at a time.

See also **paging**; **World Wide Web (WWW)**.

paging

A NetWare feature that allows memory to be assigned noncontiguously (rather than in large blocks of contiguously addressed pages) by using memory segmentation. *Page tables* map physical addresses to logical memory; each table entry corresponds to a *memory page* (equivalent to 4K of random-access memory). A group of page tables is known as a *domain*. Paging in NetWare is used for memory protection.

See also **memory**; **NetWare Domain Protection**; **random-access memory**.

palmtop computer

A "miniature," battery-operated, portable computer that can be held in the palm of one hand. Palmtops usually experience less power duration from their batteries, and do not include floppy disk drives or hard-disk drives.

See also **portable computer**.

PAM

Pulse Amplitude Modulation, a digital-to-analog conversion scheme in which a modulating wave modulates the amplitude of a pulse stream.

See also **pulse**; **Pulse Code Modulation**.

PAP

(1) Packet-Level Procedure, a full-duplex protocol for the transfer of packets between a computer and a modem on an X.25 network.

(2) Password-Authentication Protocol, a method of validating a network node's inbound call by comparing an exchange of peer ID/password pairs against a list of authorized pairs.

(3) Printer-Access Protocol, a part of the AppleTalk protocol suite that enables Macintosh clients and NetWare for Macintosh servers to communicate with printers on an AppleTalk network.

See also **(1) X.25**; **(2) password**; **(3) AppleTalk**; **(3) AppleTalk protocols**; **(3) NetWare for Macintosh**.

parallel channel

A channel with a channel-to-control unit input/output (I/O) interface, using bus-and-tag cables as a transmission medium.

parallel port

A printer interface that transmits data in parallel, 7 or 8 bits at a time. The parallel port is often used to connect a parallel printer to a computer workstation.

See also **port**; **portable**.

parallel printer

A printer that accepts data routed on a bus in *parallel format* (7 or 8 bits at a time), rather than in *serial format* (1 bit at a time).

See also **serial printer**.

parallel printer interface

An interface that accepts data routed on a bus in parallel format, 7 or 8 bits at a time. The parallel printer interface is faster and easier to configure than a serial printer interface. However, if the printer cable extends beyond 10 feet, the data transfer can be unreliable.

See also **serial; serial printer.**

parallel processing

A computing method in which two or more microprocessors operate simultaneously while working on different aspects of the same program and sharing the computational load for high-speed processing.

parallel sessions

Two or more network sessions concurrently active between the same two *logical units* (LUs) in a Systems Network Architecture (SNA) network, with each session capable of having a different set of session parameters.

See also **Systems Network Architecture.**

parallel tasking

A technology from 3Com that allows network adapters to transmit data to the network before an entire frame has been loaded into the adapter buffer from the computer. Parallel tasking also allows the transmission of data to a computer's main memory before an entire frame has been received from the network. This boosts throughput because a frame can reside on the network, the adapter, and in computer memory all at the same time.

parallel transmission

A simultaneous transmission of all bits that make up a character or byte.

parameter

A critical item of information required by a program, utility, or Application Program Interface (API) to perform a prescribed operation.

See also **Application Program Interface.**

Parameter RAM (PRAM)

An area of random-access memory (RAM) in an AppleTalk network that stores configuration information (such as a node's network address).

PARC Universal Protocol (PUP)

A protocol developed at the Xerox Palo Alto Research Center (PARC), similar to Internet Protocol (IP).

See also **Internet Protocol.**

parent

A data set that can have subordinate data sets.

parent container

In NetWare or IntranetWare, a high-level container object holding other objects in the Novell Directory Services (NDS) Directory tree. The three types of parent containers are Country, Organization, and Organizational Unit.

See also **container object; Novell Directory Services; object.**

parent directory

A directory structure in a hierarchical directory system that appears immediately above a subdirectory or current directory. The double period (. .) symbol is shorthand for the name of the parent directory.

parent objects

In Novell Directory Services (NDS), container objects that contain other objects.
See also **container object; Novell Directory Services; object; parent container.**

parity

A method that uses an extra or redundant bit, inserted after the data bits but before the stop bit (or bits), to check for errors in transmitted data. Parity settings on both communicating computers must match. Table P.1 shows the types of parity and provides a brief description of each. Figure P.1 shows an example of parity.

parity bit

An extra (or redundant) bit in a byte (8 bits), used for error checking in data transmission.
See also **parity.**

parity checking

A checking method applied to a character or a series of characters and that adds a parity bit to check for data-transmission errors.
See also **parity; parity bit.**

parity error

A mismatch that occurs in parity bits and indicates an error in data transmission.
See also **parity; parity bit.**

Partial Sequence Number PDU (PSNP)

A Protocol Data Unit (PDU) that requests Link-State Packets (LSPs) from one Intermediate System (IS) to another.
See also **Protocol Data Unit; Intermediate System; Link-State Packet.**

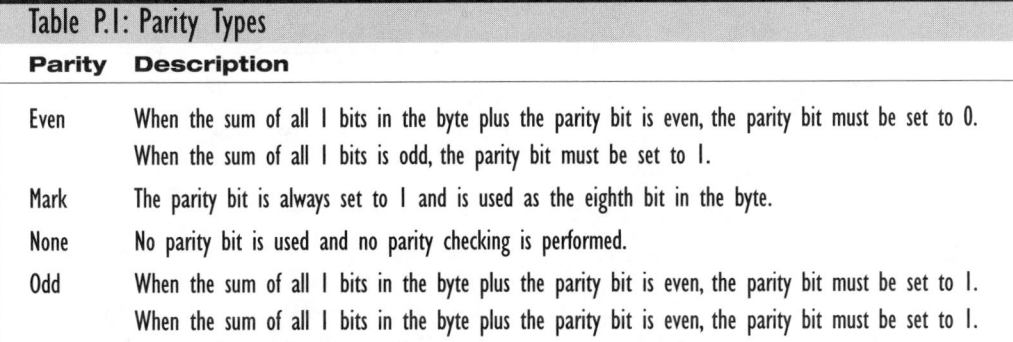

Table P.1: Parity Types

Parity	Description
Even	When the sum of all 1 bits in the byte plus the parity bit is even, the parity bit must be set to 0. When the sum of all 1 bits is odd, the parity bit must be set to 1.
Mark	The parity bit is always set to 1 and is used as the eighth bit in the byte.
None	No parity bit is used and no parity checking is performed.
Odd	When the sum of all 1 bits in the byte plus the parity bit is even, the parity bit must be set to 1. When the sum of all 1 bits in the byte plus the parity bit is even, the parity bit must be set to 1.
Space	The parity bit is set to 0 and used as the eighth bit in the byte.

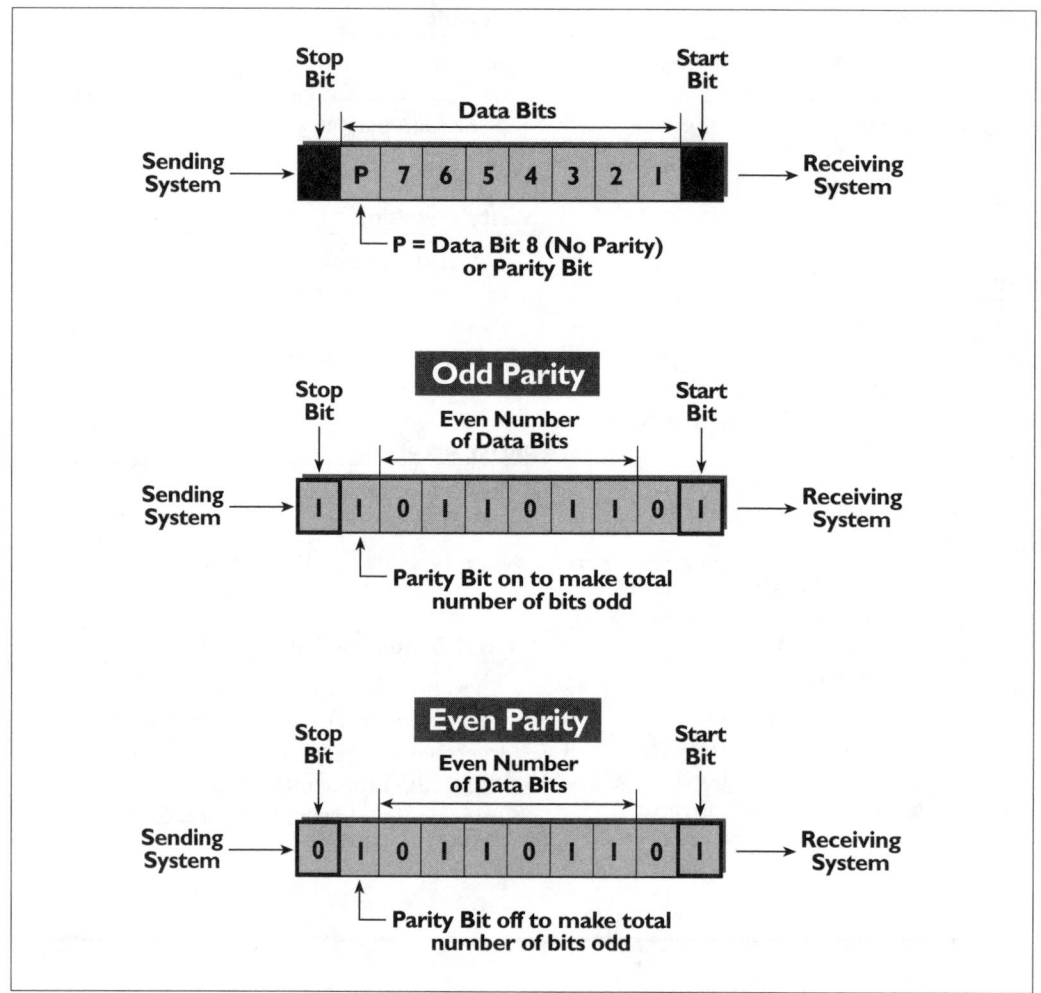

Figure P.1
Parity, Even and Odd

See also **parity bit**.

partition

Either a logical division of the NetWare Directory database (NDD) or a logical unit into which the hard disk on a personal computer or NetWare server can be divided. In NetWare, a partition forms a distinct unit of data in the Directory tree that is used to store and replicate Directory information. Although each NetWare Directory partition consists of a container object, all objects contained in it, and information about those objects, these partitions do not contain any information about the file system or about the directories and files contained there.

See also **NetWare Directory database; NetWare Directory partition.**

Partition Control

In Novell Directory Services (NDS), a Directory Schema attribute that tracks the states of split-and-join operations on partitions.

Partition-Creation Time

In Novell Directory Services (NDS), a Directory Schema term that identifies the particular incarnation of a partition's list of replicas.

partition management

A method used to manage NetWare Directory partitions and replicas, allowing division of the Directory into partitions and management of various Directory replicas of the partitions. With partition management, a user can create, merge, and move Directory partitions; display partitions and partition details; as well as add, delete, synchronize, and display Directory replicas.

See also **NetWare Directory partition; NetWare Directory replica.**

PARTMGR utility

In NetWare and IntranetWare, a workstation utility used to manage partitions and their directories.

See also **NetWare Directory partition.**

passive concurrency

A type of concurrency control in which a task does not perform any type of explicit locking.

passive coupler

In fiber-optic communications, an optical-signal redirector that splits a signal as requested and passes the weakened signal on to all fibers, which results in signal loss.

passive hub

A device that splits a transmission signal and allows more workstations to be added to a network topology.

passive star coupler

An optical-signal redirector in fiber-optic communications, created by fusing multiple optical fibers together; their meeting point is used as the center of a passive-star network topology.

passive star topology

A network configuration in which multiple nodes are connected to a central hub that passes signals on but does not process the signal in any way. This is the opposite of an *active star topology*, which processes signals before passing them on.

See also **active star topology.**

password

Characters typed in by a user when logging in to a network. NetWare enables the network supervisor to specify whether passwords are required, to assign passwords to users, to specify whether passwords must be unique, and to specify whether passwords must be changed periodically. In NetWare 4.x, login passwords are encrypted at the workstation in a format that only the NetWare server can decode, which helps to prevent intruders from accessing network files.

Password Allow Change

In Novell Directory Services (NDS), a selectable property for the User object that determines whether the user logged in under an account can change the password for that account.

See also **leaf object; Novell Directory Services; object.**

Password-Authentication Protocol (PAP)

A method of validating a network node's inbound call by comparing an exchange of peer ID/password pairs against a list of authorized pairs.

See also **PAP; password.**

Password-Expiration Date and Time

In Novell Directory Services (NDS), a selectable property for the User object.

See also **leaf object; Novell Directory Services; object; password.**

Password-Expiration Interval

In Novell Directory Services (NDS), a selectable property for the User object that specifies the time interval after which a password expires.

See also **leaf object; Novell Directory Services; object; password.**

Password-Expiration Time

In Novell Directory Services (NDS), a selectable property for the User object that specifies the next time a password expires.

See also **leaf object; Novell Directory Services; object; password.**

password file

A file containing all passwords used to log in to a network system. This file is usually encoded to restrict access to sensitive network data.

Password Minimum Length

A selectable property for the User object in Novell Directory Services (NDS) that specifies the minimum length for a clear-text password.

See also **leaf object; Novell Directory Services; object; password.**

password protection

A protection scheme that guards network access by requiring one or more passwords before a user is allowed to log in.

Password Required

In Novell Directory Services (NDS), a selectable property for the User object specifying that a password is required to log in to the network.

See also **leaf object; Novell Directory Services; object; password.**

Password Unique Required

In Novell Directory Services (NDS), a selectable property for the User object that specifies when a password is changed it must be different from those defined in the Passwords Used selectable property.

See also **leaf object; Novell Directory Services; object; password.**

Passwords Used

In Novell Directory Services (NDS), a NetWare Directory Schema term and a selectable property for the User object that specifies previously used passwords.

See also **leaf object; Novell Directory Services; object; password.**

patch

An additional segment of programming code that improves how a product works for a specific situation and that may or may not be included in a future release of the product.

patch cable

A cable used in Token Ring networks that connects Multistation Access Units (MAUs) to each other.

See also **Multistation Access Unit; Token Ring.**

patch panel

A wiring center that provides for the interconnection of twisted-pair or coaxial cables without connecting the cable to a punch-down block.

See also **punch-down block.**

path

The complete location (including drive,

directory, and subdirectory) of a file or directory in the file system.

Path

In Novell Directory Services (NDS), a NetWare Directory Schema term and a selectable property for the Directory Map object.

See also **leaf object; Novell Directory Services; object.**

Path-Control Layer (SNA model)

The third layer (Layer 3) in the Systems Network Architecture (SNA) communications model. The Path-Control Layer creates a logical channel between two network nodes.

See also **Systems Network Architecture.**

path-control network

The routing portion of a Systems Network Architecture (SNA) network.

See also **Systems Network Architecture.**

path cost

An arbitrary value used by a routing algorithm to determine the best path to a destination.

Path Information Unit (PIU)

A packet created in a Systems Network Architecture (SNA) network when the Path-Control Layer (Layer 3) adds a transmission header to a basic information unit (BIU) from the Transmission-Control Layer (Layer 4).

See also **Basic Information Unit; Systems Network Architecture.**

pathname

Identification of a file that includes the server name, volume, directory path, and filename.
See also **directory path.**

PathWorks

A network operating system from Digital Equipment Corporation (DEC), based on Microsoft LAN Manager.
See also **LAN Manager.**

PAUDIT utility

A NetWare 3.*x* workstation utility for viewing system accounting records. This utility also records each time an intruder is detected trying to log in to the file server.

PAUSE

A DOS command that temporarily suspends batch processing, displays an optional message, and prompts the user to press any key to continue.

payload

The data portion of an Asynchronous Transfer Mode (ATM) packet (or cell).
See also **Asynchronous Transfer Mode.**

Table P.2: PC Card Features

Feature	Description
Card Information Structure (CIS)	Describes characteristics and capabilities for automatic configuration by the host system.
CardBus	Enables 32-bit bus mastering and operational speeds of up to 33 megahertz (MHz).
Direct Memory Access (DMA)	Enables DMA technology directly in the hardware when matched with a corresponding host system.
Execute In Place (XIP)	Enables operating system and applications to run directly from PC card.
Low-voltage operation	Enables a 3.3-volt and a 5-volt operation.
Plug and Play	Allows a PC Card to be inserted or removed while the system is on because of the extended length of the contact pins for power and ground.
Power management	Enables an interface to Advanced Power Management (APM).
Zoomed Video (ZV)	Allows the PC Card to write video data directly to a Video Graphics Array (VGA) controller.

See also **Personal Computer Memory Card International Association.**

PBP

Packet-Burst Protocol, a protocol (built on top of the Internetwork Packet Exchange) that speeds the transfer of multiple-packet NetWare Core Protocol (NCP) file reads and writes between a workstation and a NetWare server by eliminating the need to sequence and acknowledge each packet. Because it enables a server or workstation to send a whole set (or burst) of packets before it requires acknowledgment, PBP is more efficient than the one request-one response protocol used in early versions of NetWare and reduces network traffic. Dropped packets are monitored by PBP; retransmissions are only performed for missing packets.

See also **Internetwork Packet Exchange; NetWare Core Protocol.**

PBX

Private Branch Exchange, a telephone system that provides interoffice connections from one extension to another, as well as connections to an external telephone network. PBX switching can be automatic or manual (done by an operator).

See also **PABX.**

PC

(1) *personal computer,* often IBM-compatible.
(2) **physical contact,** a term describing a condition where cable and fiber elements in optical fiber are actually touching and making a connection.

PC card

A card conforming the Personal Computer Memory Card International Association (PCMCIA) standard that uses a 68-pin connector with longer power and ground pins (which always engage before the signal pins). Table P.2 shows some of the features of the PC Card.

PC card slot

An opening in the case of a portable computer that is designed to accept a PC card. A PC card slot is also known as a *PCMCIA slot.*

See also **portable computer.**

PCI

(1) **Peripheral-Component Interconnect,** an Intel specification defining a local bus that allows as many as ten PCI-compliant expansion cards to be plugged into the motherboard of a computer. One of the expansion cards must be a PCI controller card, which exchanges information with the computer's processor and enables certain intelligent PCI adapters to perform tasks concurrently with the main processor by using bus-mastering techniques.
(2) **Protocol-Control Information,** protocol-dependent information added to a data packet in the OSI Reference Model before the packet can be passed to a lower level for processing.

See also **(1) bus mastering; controller board; (1) motherboard; (2) OSI Reference Model.**

PCL

(1) **Printer-Control Language,** a Page-Description Language (PDL) used by the Hewlett-Packard LaserJet and other compatible printers.

(2) Procedure Coverage Logger, a utility in the NetWare Loadable Module (NLM) Certification Kit used to verify that a product's actual exercising procedure provides adequate coverage of the functions declared in the source code.

See also **(1) Page-Description Language.**

PCM

Pulse Code Modulation, the transmission of analog information that has been sampled into digital form and encoded with a fixed number of bits.

See also **Pulse Amplitude Modulation.**

PCMCIA

Personal Computer Memory Card International Association, a nonprofit organization formed in 1989 that developed a standard for credit-card sized, plug-in adapters designed for use in portable computers. In addition to hardware standards, the organization also established Socket Services software to provide a standard interface to the hardware, as well as Card Services software to coordinate access to PC cards.

See also **PC card.**

PCMCIA modem

A modem that works on a PC card.

See also **PC card.**

PCONSOLE utility

A NetWare and IntranetWare workstation utility that is the administrative utility for NetWare print services. Through the graphi-

cal interface of NetWare Administrator, the PCONSOLE utility performs the following tasks:

- Creates, assigns, modifies, deletes, and monitors print queues, print servers, and printers
- Sends, monitors, modifies, pauses, resumes, and deletes print jobs
- Installs basic print services through Quick Setup
- Enables and provides a view of the print server auditing log
- Changes the Novell Directory Services context

See also **NetWare Administrator.**

PCS

(1) Personal Communications Services, a class of applications that includes wireless communications for users of portable computers.

(2) plastic-clad silica, optical fiber that features a glass core and plastic cladding.

See also **(2) cladding.**

PD stats

problem-determination statistics, under Systems Network Architecture (SNA), statistics used by the network-management function to determine and diagnose problems associated with the communication links used for network sessions.

See also **Systems Network Architecture.**

PDA

personal digital assistant, a battery-operated palmtop computer (which means it fits in the palm of one hand) that features a pen-based interface for personal organization software with fax and electronic-mail (e-mail) facilities.

See also **portable computer.**

PDAU

Physical-Delivery Access Unit, in an X.400 Message-Handling System (MHS) as specified by the Consultative Committee for International Telegraphy and Telephony (CCITT), an application process that enables a Message-Transfer System (MTS) to deliver an image of a letter to any location accessible through the MHS.

See also **Consultative Committee for International Telegraphy and Telephony; Message-Handling System; Message-Transfer System; X.400.**

PDL

Page-Description Language, in Novell Directory Services (NDS), a NetWare Directory Schema term and a selectable property for the Printer object.

See also **leaf object; Novell Directory Services; object.**

PDN

Public Data Network, a data network available for use by the general public.

PDP

Professional Developers Program, a joint program between Novell and independent developers of computer applications to provide direct access to various NetWare services and centralized network resources.

PDP has been replaced by the Developer Net program.

PDS

(1) Premises Distribution System, either a cabling system encompassing an entire building, or the name of AT&T's premises wiring system.

(2) Processor Direct Slot, a general-purpose expansion slot in Macintosh computers that is connected directly to the microprocessor instead of indirectly by a bus (as with a NuBus system).

See also **(1) premises network; (2) NuBus.**

PDU

Protocol Data Unit, a packet exchanged between devices within a specified layer of the OSI Reference Model. A PDU communicates with the same layer of the OSI Reference Model on another machine.

See also **OSI Reference Model.**

PDU lifetime

A value indicating the number of routers a Protocol Data Unit (PDU) can use before it reaches it destination. If the PDU exceeds this value, it is discarded. PDU Lifetime is invoked to keep PDUs from continuously traveling around a network without ever reaching a destination.

See also **Protocol Data Unit.**

peak load

A value expressed in one of several performance measures (such as number of packets or bits per second) that defines a maximum amount of traffic a network can handle.

peer

A device that has equal communications capabilities with another device.

peer hub

A hub installed on a Network Interface Card (NIC) that plugs into an expansion slot on a computer.

See also **Network Interface Card.**

peer layers

In a layered network architecture, corresponding layers on two connected nodes that communicate with each other at a particular layer, using a protocol supported by that layer.

See also **OSI Reference Model; Systems Network Architecture.**

peer-to-peer

A type of direct communication between two devices on the same communications level of a network without intervention by any intermediary devices (such as a host or server).

peer-to-peer network

A network in which each node can initiate actions, access other nodes, and provide services for other nodes without first acquiring permission from the server. The network operating system often runs under the native operating system of the individual workstations. Common network operating systems for peer-to-peer local-area networks

(LANs) include Personal NetWare from Novell, Windows for Workgroups from Microsoft, LANstep from Hayes Microcomputer Products, and LANtastic from Artisoft.

See also **local-area network; network.**

PEM

Privacy-Enhanced Mail, one of two enhancements to Internet mail-message formatting introduced in RFC 822 that provides mechanisms for encrypting, signing, and authenticating messages to ensure that electronic mail (e-mail) is reasonably secure from intruders. The other enhancement was Multipurpose Internet Mail Extensions (MIME).

See also **Multipurpose Internet-Mail Extensions.**

pen computer

A computer that accepts handwriting as input, incorporating pattern-recognition software that translates marks made on the computer screen with a special pen-like stylus. The stylus can also be used to make menu selections.

Pentium

Intel's 64-bit microprocessor chip, the next-generation follow-up to the 80486 microprocessor chip. Features include an 8K instruction code, data caches, a built-in floating-point coprocessor, a memory-management unit (MMU), and dual pipelining (which allows the processing of more than one instruction per clock cycle).

See also **80486; floating-point coprocessor; memory-management unit.**

PEP

Packet-Exchange Protocol, a Xerox Network Systems (XNS) protocol used at the Transport Level (Level 4 of the OSI Reference Model).

See also **OSI Reference Model; Xerox Network Systems.**

performance management

As defined by the International Standards Organization (ISO) and the Consultative Committee for International Telegraphy and Telephony (CCITT), a part of the OSI Network-Management Model that performs the following functions:

- Monitors day-to-day activity on the network
- Gathers and logs data on the basis of day-to-day activity of the network
- Stores the performance data in a database to be used for network optimization and expansion
- Analyzes the performance data to identify bottlenecks
- Changes configuration settings of the network to optimize performance

See also **OSI Network-Management Model.**

performance tuning

The capability to monitor and analyze the performance of a computer system, and to adjust the configuration of the system to obtain optimum performance.

peripheral

A CD-ROM drive, fax machine, hard-disk drive, modem, optical drive, printer, tape

drive, or other device that can be attached to a file server, workstation, standalone server, or the network itself to provide additional services to network users.

Peripheral-Component Interconnect (PCI)

An Intel specification defining a local bus that allows as many as ten PCI-compliant expansion cards to be plugged into the motherboard of a computer. One of the expansion cards must be a PCI controller card, which exchanges information with the computer's processor and enables certain intelligent PCI adapters to perform tasks concurrently with the main processor by using bus-mastering techniques.

See also **bus mastering; controller board; motherboard; PCI.**

peripheral node

A network node in a Systems Network Architecture (SNA) network that depends upon an intermediate or host node to provide network services for its dependent *logical units* (LUs), but has no intermediate routing function assigned to it.

See also **Systems Network Architecture.**

peripheral router

A router that connects a network to a larger internetwork.

PERL

A script programming language designed to process system-oriented tasks in the UNIX environment. This language is widely used to create Common Gateway Interface (CGI) programs that can be ported between the NetWare Web Server and UNIX servers.

See also **Common Gateway Interface.**

Permanent Memory

One of five NetWare memory pools used by the operating system for permanent tables. The Permanent Memory pool is a source of memory for the Semi-Permanent Memory pool and the Alloc Short-Term Memory pool.

See also **MONITOR; NetWare Loadable Module; NMAGENT.**

permanent SVC

A switched virtual circuit (SVC) that remains in a connected state until a user or application disconnects it.

permanent swap file

A file used to store parts of running programs that have been swapped out of memory to make room for other running programs. Once created, a permanent swap file can be used repeatedly in virtual-memory operations that use hard-disk space in place of random-access memory (RAM).

See also **random-access memory; virtual memory.**

permanent virtual circuit (PVC)

A communications path between two fixed end points continuously available and similar to a leased line.

See also **leased line; PVC.**

permission

A privilege to access certain system resources, granted to a user on the basis of rights given to the user's account by the network administrator.

See also **access rights.**

Person

A NetWare Directory Schema term in Novell Directory Services (NDS).

See also **Novell Directory Services.**

Person object

A Novell Directory Services (NDS) leaf object that contains the more common attributes of the Organizational Person and Residential Person objects.

See also **leaf object; Novell Directory Services; object.**

Personal Communications Services (PCS)

A class of applications that includes wireless communications for users of portable computers.

See also **PCS.**

Personal Computer Memory Card International Association (PCMCIA)

A nonprofit organization formed in 1989 that developed a standard for credit-card sized, plug-in adapters designed for use in portable computers. In addition to hardware standards, the organization also established Socket Services software to provide a standard interface to the hardware, as well as

Card Services software to coordinate access to PC cards.

See also **PC card.**

For more information about PCMCIA, surf the Web to `http://www.pc-card.com`.

personal digital assistant (PDA)

A battery-operated palmtop computer (which means it fits in palm of one hand) that features a pen-based interface for personal organization software with fax and electronic-mail (e-mail) facilities.

See also **portable computer.**

Personal Identification Number (PIN)

A unique number or code assigned to identify individuals as they perform network transactions (such as banking from an automated teller machine).

Personal Information Manager (PIM)

A software package that integrates word processing, database, and other modules to enable users to store notes, memos, names and addresses, appointments, to-do lists, and other organizational activities.

Personal NetWare

Peer-to-peer network software released by Novell in 1994 that provides DOS and Windows users with the capability to share printers, files, and other resources, and to run standard applications. Personal NetWare replaced NetWare Lite.

For more information about Personal NetWare, surf the Web to `http://voyager.provo.novell.com/catalog/qr/sne14210.html`.

pervasive computing

A still-futuristic concept that anticipates computers will be readily available in most environments, that all computers will have the capability to interconnect with other computers, and that users will have access to information (and to other users) from anywhere at any time. The basis for this interconnection will be networking and internetworking, and the tools necessary for this interconnection will be easy to use.

peta-

An order of magnitude that represents 10^{15} in the base-10 system or 2^{50} in the base-2 system.

PGP

Pretty Good Privacy, a software program — available as shareware — that encrypts files using a private-key encryption algorithm, sends and receives encrypted electronic mail (e-mail), creates and verifies digital signatures, and manages (creates, certifies, and revokes) keys. Despite patent, licensing, import, and export restrictions, PGP is available over the Internet; most versions carry licensing restrictions on usage and distribution.

phase

A reference (expressed in degrees or radians) to a portion of an entire signal period that is used to offset the start of a signal.

phase jitter

A distortion of signal phase caused by random fluctuations in signal frequency and that makes it difficult to synchronize the signal.

Phase-Lock Loop (PLL)

In a Token Ring network, a function that automatically ensures accurate signal timing.
See also **Token Ring.**

PhoneNet

A telephone-wire version of AppleTalk whose adapters and wiring are less expensive than those found in LocalTalk.
See also **AppleTalk; LocalTalk.**

photodetector

A fiber-optic communications component that registers incoming light; its sensitivity has an influence on the transmission properties of a connection.

photodiode

In a fiber-optic communications receiver, the component that converts light signals into electrical signals.

PHY

(1) The physical sublayer in a Fiber Distributed Data Interface (FDDI) network.
(2) A fiber-optic cable used in FDDI.
See also **Fiber Distributed Data Interface.**

physical address

The address of a network device as defined in the Data-Link Layer (Layer 2) of the OSI Reference Model.
See also **Data-Link Layer; OSI Reference Model.**

physical connection

A hardware connection between two computer devices.

physical contact (PC)

A term describing a condition where cable and fiber elements in optical fiber are actually touching and making a connection.
See also **PC.**

Physical-Control Layer (SNA model)

The first layer (Layer 1) in the Systems Network Architecture (SNA) communications model. The Physical Control Layer provides a serial or parallel interface to the network.
See also **Systems Network Architecture.**

Physical-Delivery Office Name

In Novell Directory Services (NDS), a selectable property for the following objects:

External Entity, Organization, Organizational Role, Organizational Unit, and User.

See also **container object; leaf object; Novell Directory Services; object.**

Physical-Delivery Access Unit (PDAU)

In an X.400 Message-Handling System (MHS) as specified by the Consultative Committee for International Telegraphy and Telephony (CCITT), an application process that enables a Message-Transfer System (MTS) to deliver an image of a letter to any location accessible through the MHS.

See also **Consultative Committee for International Telegraphy and Telephony; Message-Handling System; Message-Transfer System; X.400.**

physical drive

A physical (as opposed to conceptual or logical) device in a computer that performs actual magnetic or optical operations on the storage medium. The physical drive may be divided into several *logical drives* (logical processes that function as though they were separate disk drives).

See also **logical drive.**

Physical Layer (OSI model)

The first layer (Layer 1) in the OSI Reference Model. The Physical Layer details the protocols that govern transmission media and signals.

See also **OSI Reference Model.**

Physical-Layer Convergence Procedure (PLCP)

In the Distributed-Queue Dual-Bus (DQDB) network architecture, a function that maps high-level packets into a uniform format for transmission through a particular configuration.

See also **Distributed-Queue Dual-Bus.**

Physical-Layer Signaling (PLS)

The highest component of the Physical Layer (Layer 1) in the OSI Reference Model that provides an interface between the Physical Layer and the Media-Access Control (MAC) sublayer of the Data-Link Layer (Layer 2).

See also **OSI Reference Model; PLS.**

physical medium

In the OSI Reference Model, a medium that provides a physical means of transmitting data. An interface for the physical medium is supplied at the bottom of the Physical Layer (Layer 1) of the OSI Reference Model; the model itself does not provide specifications for physical media.

See also **OSI Reference Model.**

physical-media-dependent (PMD)

A physical layer in most networking architectures that is responsible for the actual connection between two locations.

physical memory

Random-access memory (RAM) chips installed in a computer system. NetWare addresses physical memory in 4K blocks called *pages.*

See also **memory; page.**

physical network management (PNM)

The maintenance and management of the physical components of a network, such as computers, cabling, connectors, power supply, telephones, fax machines, and other devices.

physical node address

The address of a file server's Network Interface Card (NIC) on a local-area network (LAN).

See also **Network Interface Card.**

physical partition

A hard-disk partition created for the use of the operating system. The hard disk can contain several physical partitions for numerous operating systems.

See also **partition.**

physical topology

A wiring layout for a network that specifies how network elements are electrically interconnected and what happens when a network node fails. The three main types of physical topology are a *logical bus topology* (including bus, star, and tree topologies), a *logical ring topology* (including Token Ring), and a *hybrid topology* (which is a combination of different topologies). Physical topologies are also classified by the manner in which nodes are connected to each other, including a *point-to-point connection* (in which two nodes are directly linked together) and a *multipoint connection* (in which multiple nodes are connected to a single node).

See also **bus topology; star topology; tree topology; Token Ring.**

physical unit (PU)

In Systems Network Architecture (SNA), a node that supports one or more logical units (LUs).

See also **logical unit; Systems Network Architecture.**

physical-unit services

Components of the physical unit (PU) that provide configuration services and maintenance services for sessions that involve the control points of system services.

Physics Network (PHYSNET)

A group of physics-research networks connected through the DECnet topology.

See also **DECnet.**

PIC

Primary Interexchange Carrier, a long-distance telephone-service carrier to which a user may subscribe.

Pico

A text-editor program originally designed as an editing tool for the Pine electronic-mail (e-mail) program. Pico is now available as a separate package for UNIX systems. Program features include cut-and-paste, full text justification, searching, spell checking, and a file browser.

See also **Pine.**

PID

Protocol ID, a field in a Sub-Network Access Protocol (SNAP) header that helps to identify

a distinct routed or bridged protocol.
See also **Sub-Network Access Protocol.**

piggybacking

A transmission process that includes acknowledgment packets within ordinary data packets.

PIM

Personal Information Manager, a software package that integrates word processing, database, and other modules to enable users to store notes, memos, names and addresses, appointments, to-do lists, and other organizational activities.

pin

In some types of cable connectors, the male lead (usually one of many leads running through the cable).

PIN

Personal Identification Number, a unique number or code assigned to identify individuals as they perform network transactions (such as banking from an automated teller machine).

pin-compatible

When an electronic component has the exact number and configuration of connecting pins used by a different device.

Pine

A mail program used on an electronic-mail (e-mail) reader called elm for systems operating in the UNIX environment.

PING

(1) **Packet InterNet Groper,** a program that tests the accessibility of destinations by sending the destinations an Internet Control-Message Protocol (ICMP) echo request and waiting for a reply.
(2) **PING (NLM).** In NetWare 4.*x* and IntranetWare, a server console utility that sends an Internet Control-Message Protocol (ICMP) echo-request packet to an Internet Protocol (IP) node on an internetwork. If the target node receives the echo-request packet, it sends back a reply packet. This NetWare Loadable Module (NLM) determines whether an IP node is reachable on the internetwork
See also **(1) Internet Control-Message Protocol; (2) Internet Control-Message Protocol; (2) NetWare Loadable Module.**

ping packet

A packet containing an Echo message or Echo Reply message sent by using the Internet Control-Message Protocol (ICMP) to monitor the performance of network nodes.
See also **Internet Control-Message Protocol.**

ping-ponging

A term describing the actions of a packet in a two-node routing loop.

pinout

The function associated with a specific pin; each pin in a multipin connector has a pinout. Figure P.2 shows a pinout configuration for 25-pin and 9-pin serial cables.

PIP

Abbreviation for *program-initialization parameter.*

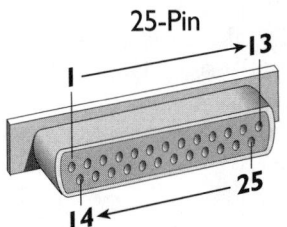
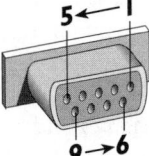

Pin	Function
1	Protective Ground
2	Transmit Data
3	Receive Data
4	Request to Send
5	Clear to Send
6	Data Set Ready
7	Signal Ground / Common Return
8	Received Line Signal Detect
9	+ Voltage
10	- Voltage
11	Unused
12	Secondary Received Line Signal Indicator
13	Secondary Clear to Send
14	Secondary Transmit Data
15	DCE Transmitter Signal Element Timing
16	Secondary Receive Data
17	Receiver Signal Element Timing
18	Unused
19	Secondary Request to Send
20	Data Terminal Ready
21	Signal Quality Detect
22	Ring Indicator
23	Data Signal Rate Selector
24	DTE Transmitter Signal Element Timing
25	Unused

Pin	Function
1	Carrier Detect
2	Receive Data
3	Transmit Data
4	Data Terminal Ready
5	System Ground
6	Data Set Ready
7	Request to Send
8	Clear to Send
9	Ring Indicator

Figure P.2
Pinout Configurations

pipe

A section of computer memory used by one command to pass processing information to a second command.

Pipeline USA

An Internet service provider (ISP) located in New York City that uses a special, Windows-based browser (also called Pipeline) with its own interface protocol.
See also **Internet service provider; Web browser.**

pipelining

The fetching and encoding of instructions to ensure that a processor need not wait to carry out the instructions; as soon as one instruction is executed, another instruction is ready.

piping

A process in which the output of one program immediately becomes the input for another program.

PIR

Protocol-Independent Routing, the routing of packets without regard to packet format or the protocol being used.

PIU

Path Information Unit, a packet created in a Systems Network Architecture (SNA) network when the Path-Control Layer (Layer 3) adds a transmission header to a basic information unit (BIU) from the Transmission-Control Layer (Layer 4).
See also **Basic Information Unit; Systems Network Architecture.**

pkgadd

A UnixWare command to simplify the process of installing third-party software and extensions for the operating system.
See also **UnixWare.**

PKZIP

A shareware file-compression program for computers that run in the DOS environment. PKZIP enables users to compress several files into one ZIP file. Files are decompressed by using the PKUNZIP shareware program. (A Windows version of this program is called WinZip.)
See also **WinZip.**

plain folder

An icon depicting a white folder with no markings. If an icon appears as a plain folder, NetWare users may open the folder to view its contents.

Plain Old Telephone Service (POTS)

The standard analog telephone service provided by many telephone companies.

plaintext

Unencoded text, as opposed to encrypted text.

plastic-clad silica (PCS)

Optical fiber that features a glass core and plastic cladding.

See also **cladding; PCS.**

platform

A generic reference to all possible choices for some specific part of a computing environment (such as the NetWare network operating-system platform or the DOS operating-system platform).

platform-specific routers

Routers used on a specific type of network architecture, usually proprietary.

platter

A round metal surface on a hard disk. Multiple platters may be stacked on a hard disk with a read/write head for each side of the platter with the group of read/write heads moving in unison to the same track number on each platter side. Figure P.3 shows the location of platters on a hard-disk drive.

PLCP

Physical-Layer Convergence Procedure, in the Distributed-Queue Dual-Bus (DQDB) network architecture, a function that maps high-level packets into a uniform format for transmission through a particular configuration.

See also **Distributed-Queue Dual-Bus.**

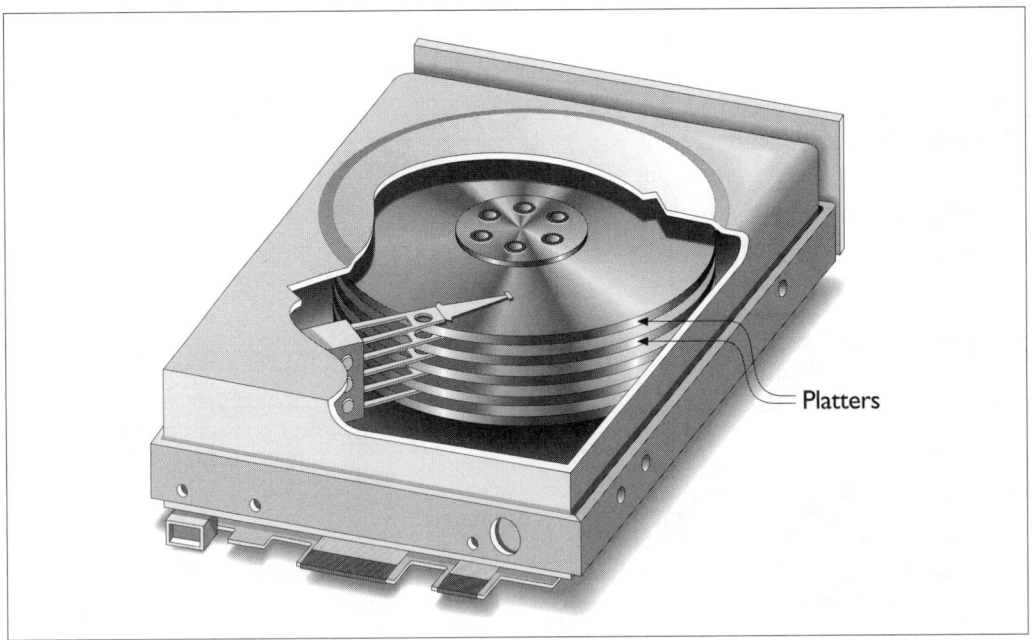

Platters

Figure P.3
Platters on a hard-disk drive

plenum

A type of air shaft or duct used for ventilation in a building.

plenum cable

A cable that runs through a plenum. Subjected to stringent standards, plenum cable must have a jacket made of fire-resistant material that does not exude toxic chemicals when exposed to heat.

plesiochronous

Corresponding events in digital signaling that happen at the same *rate* in two timing-synchronization systems, but not necessarily at the same *time*. Although the clocks on the two systems run at the same speed, they are not synchronized to the same time reference.

PLL

Phase-Lock Loop, in a Token Ring network, a function that automatically ensures accurate signal timing.

See also **Token Ring.**

plotter

A graphics-rendering device used to draw charts, diagrams, and so on.

PLP

Packet-Level Protocol, a full-duplex protocol specifying the details of data transfer between a sender and receiver on an X.25 network that supports error detection and correction, packet sequencing, and transfer-rate adjustment.

See also **full duplex; X.25.**

PLS

(1) Physical-Layer Signaling, the highest component of the Physical Layer (Layer 1) in the OSI Reference Model that provides an interface between the Physical Layer and the Media-Access Control (MAC) sublayer of the Data-Link Layer (Layer 2).

(2) Primary link station, in a network that complies with the Synchronous Data-Link Control (SDLC) protocol, the link station that controls the link. The PLS initiates communications with another PLS or with a secondary link station (SLS). Each link has only one PLS.

See also **(1) OSI Reference Model; (2) secondary link station; (2) Synchronous Data-Link Control.**

PLU

Primary logical unit, a logical unit (LU) containing the primary half-session for a particular LU-to-LU session.

See also **half-session; secondary logical unit.**

plug

A male connector with pins that fit into the sockets of a female connector.

Plug and Play

A standard defining automatic techniques that simplify the process of configuring a personal computer, often found in Industry-Standard Architecture (ISA) expansion boards. The standard was developed jointly by Compaq Computer Corporation, Microsoft, Intel, and Phoenix Technologies.

See also **Industry-Standard Architecture.**

plug-compatible

A hardware device that works in exactly the same manner as a device manufactured by a different company.

plug-in

A software program installed with (or inside) another program, designed to add optional functionality.

PMD

Physical-media-dependent, a physical layer in most networking architectures that is responsible for the actual connection between two locations.

PMMON (NetWare Monitor)

In NetWare 4.x and IntranetWare, a server console utility used on a NetWare Server for OS/2 to monitor the OS/2 operating system. In NetWare Server for OS/2, PMMON allocates memory and sets performance-tuning levels for the central processing unit (CPU), tracking many of the same server statistics that the MONITOR utility does in NetWare 4. Although MONITOR should be used in most cases for monitoring NetWare Server for OS/2, PMMON should be used to monitor CPU utilization between NetWare Server for OS/2 and the OS/2 operating system. PMMON displays the following statistics:

- NetWare Server for OS/2 use
- Original, total, dirty, and directory cache buffers
- Packet-receive buffers
- Service processes
- Percent of OS/2 CPU and NetWare CPU use

- Disk requests
- Connections in use
- Number of open files

See also **MONITOR; NetWare Server for OS/2.**

PMMU

paged memory-management unit, a specialized microprocessor chip that manages virtual memory.

See also **virtual memory.**

PNM

physical network management, the maintenance and management of the physical components of a network, such as computers, cabling, connectors, power supply, telephones, fax machines, and other devices.

PNNI

Private Network-to-Network Interface, a routing information protocol that enables multivendor Asynchronous Transfer Mode (ATM) switches to be integrated in the same network.

See also **Asynchronous Transfer Mode.**

point of presence (POP)

A connection serviced by a local or long-distance telephone company.

See also **POP.**

point-to-point connection

A direct connection between two network nodes without any intervening nodes or switches, or a direct connection between two networks.

point-to-point line

A switched or nonswitched communication line or circuit that connects a single node in a remote network with another node.

Point-to-Point Protocol (PPP)

An industry-standard protocol enabling point-to-point transmissions of routed data from router to router, or from host to network, on local-area networks (LANs) by using a synchronous or asynchronous serial interface. PPP is a successor to Serial Line-Interface Protocol (SLIP).

See also **Serial Line-Interface Protocol.**

Point-to-Point Protocol Remote-Node Services (PPPRNS)

A protocol that supports Point-to-Point Protocol (PPP) connections to remote network nodes.

poison-reverse updates

Routing loops sent to defeat large routing loops and to specifically indicate that a network or subnetwork is unreachable, rather than implying that a network is unreachable by excluding it in routing updates.

polarity

A designation indicating that a logical unit (LU) is the *contention winner* or *loser* for a session in a network that complies with Systems Network Architecture (SNA). When a requesting LU indicates that it should be the loser in the event of a contention, the responding LU automatically accepts the status of contention winner.

See also **logical unit; Systems Network Architecture.**

poll interval

A time interval (expressed in seconds) between the nonbroadcast, multiaccess transmission of a Hello packet to a network neighbor that has become inactive.

Poll Procedure Call-Backs

In NetWare 3.12, a resource appearing in the Available Options/Resource Utilization screen of the MONITOR NetWare Loadable Module (NLM). The resource identifies the loadable modules that have processes executing at defined intervals.

See also **MONITOR; NetWare Loadable Module; NMAGENT.**

Poll/Final bit (P/F)

A bit used in such protocols as High-Level Data-Link Control (HDLC) and Synchronous Data-Link Control (SDLC) to indicate the function of a frame. When a frame is a command, a 1 in this bit indicates a poll. When a frame is a response, a 1 in this bit indicates that the current frame is the last frame in the response.

See also **High-Level Data-Link Control; Synchronous Data-Link Control.**

polled mode

A printer configuration option that allows a port driver to periodically check (or poll) the data port to determine whether the data port is ready to accept data for transmission to a printer. Status of the port is indicated with a flag and queries are made at each timer tick (18 times per second) on the central processing unit (CPU). Although it may significantly slow other tasks at a workstation, polled mode does eliminate any possibility of interrupt conflicts among different network hardware configurations by allowing users to set up a printer without having to determine to which interrupt the port is set or even if the port supports interrupts.

See also **port driver.**

polling

Contacting the nodes on a network, periodically and sequentially, by sending an inquiry to ask whether a given node wants to transmit; if it does, the node returns an acknowledgment to enable the transmission to start. The three common types of polling are *roll-call polling* (a master station locates the next node to call by consulting a polling list), *hub polling* (one node in *poll mode* polls the next node in a sequence), and *token-passing polling* (a sequenced node receives a token and can transmit or pass the token to the next device in the sequence).

See also **Token Ring.**

POP

(1) Point of presence, a connection serviced by a local or long-distance telephone company.

(2) Post Office Protocol, conventions and rules according to which electronic-mail (e-mail) programs running on a computer workstation (called an *e-mail client*) communicate with e-mail server programs on the network (called a *mailbox*). Messages sent to the client are stored in the mailbox for later retrieval by the client.

See also **(2) electronic mail; mailbox; (2) POP server.**

POP server

A program that uses the Post Office Protocol (POP) to transfer electronic mail (e-mail) to and from an e-mail client program on a network. The address of the POP server is often required when securing and configuring an Internet account with an Internet service provider (ISP).

See also **Internet service provider; Post Office Protocol.**

popup screen

A menu or other graphical display laid over the screen currently displayed on a computer monitor.

port

In hardware, a connecting component allowing a microprocessor to communicate with a compatible peripheral. In software, a memory address identifying a physical circuit that is used to transfer information between a microprocessor and a peripheral.

See also **parallel port; portable.**

port driver

A software driver responsible for routing jobs from the print queue and through the proper port to a printer. NetWare 4.*x* and IntranetWare use the NPRINTER NetWare Loadable Module (NLM) as a port driver.

See also **NetWare Loadable Module; NPRINTER.**

port multiplier

A *concentrator* that connects multiple devices to a network.

port number

The number assigned to network computers to identify them while they communicate on the Internet.

port selector

A hardware device (or software) responsible for selecting — either randomly or according to predefined criteria — a particular port for use in a communications session.

port switching

Transparently switching from one port to another in response to port malfunction or overload.

portable

(1) Said of hardware small enough to be carried, as is a **portable computer**.
(2) Said of a program that can be moved easily from one computing environment to another with minimal changes (for example, a program *is portable to Windows* or *can be ported to Windows*).

portable computer

A battery-powered computer designed to be carried easily from location to location. Types of portable computers include *laptop computers* (which have an extended battery life), *notebook computers* (which are smaller than a laptop and can fit into a briefcase), and *palmtop computers* (often specifically designed for a particular function, small enough to fit in the palm of a hand).

Table P.3 shows a comparison of portable computers.

Table P.3: Comparison of Portable Computers

Type	Power Source	Approximate Weight	Features
Transportable	House current	15 to 35 pounds	Floppy disk drive, hard-disk drive, standard monitor
Laptop	House current or batteries	8 to 15 pounds	Floppy disk drive, flat liquid-crystal display (LCD) or plasma monitor
Notebook	Batteries or transformer pack	2 to 8 pounds	RAM drive or EPROM
Palmtop	Batteries or transformer pack	Less than 2 pounds	Small size

See also **laptop computer; notebook computer; palmtop computer.**

portable modem

An external modem with a compact design that allows easy transportation and can be plugged into any computer.

Portable Operating System Interface (POSIX)

A standard originally developed by the Institute of Electrical and Electronics Engineers (IEEE) to provide a common interface to UNIX systems. POSIX now encompasses the interface between applications and operating systems in a variety of environments.

See also **Institute of Electrical and Electronic Engineers.**

POST

power-on self test, a set of computer diagnostic programs designed to ensure that major system components are present and operating correctly. These programs are stored in read-only memory (ROM) and loaded before the operating system when the computer is started up. When the POST detects a problem, system startup is halted and a message is displayed on the screen.

post office

An intermediate storage location for messages in a Message-Handling System (MHS) where messages are held until they are retrieved by a user or sent to a designated destination.

See also **Message-Handling System.**

Post Office Protocol (POP)

Conventions and rules according to which electronic-mail (e-mail) programs running on a computer workstation (called an *e-mail client*) communicate with e-mail server programs on the network (called a *mailbox*). Messages sent to the client are stored in the mailbox for later retrieval by the client.

See also **electronic mail; mailbox; POP; POP server.**

Post, Telephone, and Telegraph (PTT)

A government agency found in many European countries that provides postal, telephonic, telegraphic, and other communications services.

Postal (Zip) Code

In Novell Directory Services (NDS), a NetWare Directory Schema term and a selectable property for the External Entity, Organization, Organizational Role, Organizational Unit, and User objects.

See also **container object; leaf object; Novell Directory Services; object.**

Postal Address

In Novell Directory Services (NDS), a selectable property for the External Entity, Organization, Organizational Role, Organizational Unit, and User objects.

See also **container object; leaf object; Novell Directory Services; object.**

Postal Office Box

In Novell Directory Services (NDS), a
NetWare Directory Schema term and a
selectable property for the Organization,
Organizational Role, Organizational Unit,
and User objects.

See also **container object; leaf object;
Novell Directory Services; object.**

postamble

A sequence of bits or fields — which may
include an error-checking field, specific
flags, or a predefined bit sequence — to
indicate the end of a message or packet. A
postamble is also known as a *trailer*.

See also **trailer.**

posting

In the context of NetWare, a method in
which an Advanced Program-to-Program
Communications (APPC) process enables a
transaction program to check whether a
specific amount of data is available in the
receive buffer of a logical unit (LU). In the
context of Internet communications, a posting is an article in a newsgroup.

See also **Advanced Program-to-Program
Communications.**

Postmaster

In Novell Directory Services (NDS), a
NetWare Directory Schema term and a
selectable property for the Messaging Server
object.

See also **leaf object; Novell Directory
Services; object; Postmaster.**

Postmaster

A NetWare user who has the Supervisor
access right to the NetWare Message-
Handling Service (MHS) Messaging Server
object, the Read access right to the Message
Routing Group in which the NetWare MHS
Messaging Server object is located. In
Novell Directory Services (NDS), the
Postmaster also has the Supervisor access
right to the Mailbox Location, Mailbox ID,
and E-Mail Address properties for users of
the NetWare MHS Messaging Server object.
When certain types of errors occur, Basic
NetWare MHS sends a message to the
Postmaster's electronic-mail (e-mail) box.

Postmaster General

A NetWare user who has the Supervisor
access right to the NetWare Message
Routing Group in which the user resides,
and who can add a messaging server to
(or remove it from) the Message Routing
Group. More than one Postmaster General
can be assigned to a Message-Routing
Group.

PostScript

A Page-Description Language (PDL) from
Adobe Systems that codes text to control
fonts, text formatting, graphic images, page
layout, and other aspects of printed images.
PostScript is implemented on several different types of printers and applications.

See also **Encapsulated PostScript.**

PostScript Printer-Definition File (PPD)

A file that contains model information about a PostScript printer, which a print spooler can use to answer PostScript queries from a network.

See also **Encapsulated PostScript; PostScript.**

POTS

Plain Old Telephone Service, the standard analog telephone service provided by many telephone companies.

power budget

A measurable difference between the power of a transmitter and the sensitivity of a receiver. A power budget determines the amount of signal loss that can be allowed in a transmission and the maximum distance a signal can reliably travel.

power conditioning

Methods used to protect sensitive network hardware components from the ill effects of a disruption in electrical power supply (known as a *power disturbance*). Table P.4 shows common power disturbances and the available types of protection.

power supply

A computer component that converts the electrical power supplied at a wall outlet to a lower voltage for use by the computer.

power surge

A sudden increase in line voltage, usually caused by a nearby electrical appliance or by the restoration of power after an outage.

power-on self test (POST)

Computer diagnostic programs designed to ensure that major system components are present and operating correctly. These programs are stored in read-only memory (ROM) and loaded before the operating system when the computer is started up. When the POST detects a problem, system startup is halted and a message is displayed on the screen.

Table P.4: Power Conditioning

Disturbance	Description	Protection	Protection Device
Transient, spike, or surge	Short, but extreme, burst of voltage	Suppression	Surge protector
Noise, static	Small change in voltage	Isolation	Ferro-resonant isolation transformers
Blackout, brownout	Temporary drop or loss of power	Regulation	uninterruptible power supply (UPS)

See also **surge protector; uninterruptible power supply.**

PowerPC

A microprocessor chip with Reduced Instruction-Set Computing (RISC) architecture, jointly developed by Apple Computer, IBM, and Motorola. The PowerPC features 32-bit processing, which enables it to handle more than one set of instructions at a time. Since the introduction of the PowerPC 601 chip in 1993, the following five generations of this chip have been released:

- *601* featured clock speeds of 60MHz (for the Power Macintosh 6100 computer), 66MHz (for the Power Macintosh 7100), and 80MHz (for the Power Macintosh 8100).
- *603* was less expensive, smaller, and more energy-efficient — but slower — than the 601.
- *603e,* an upgrade of the 603 chip, includes a larger chunk of level 1 cache memory. This chip is smaller and runs cooler than any other PowerPC chips.
- *604* is faster than the 601 and 603 chips, with clock speeds of up to 166MHz.
- *604e,* a revision of the 604 chip, has twice as much internal cache memory and can initiate four instructions per clock cycle.

PPD

PostScript Printer-Definition File, a file that contains model information about a PostScript printer, which a print spooler can use to answer PostScript queries from a network.

See also **Encapsulated PostScript; PostScript.**

PPP

Point-to-Point Protocol, an industry-standard protocol enabling point-to-point transmissions of routed data from router to router, or from host to network, on local-area networks (LANs) by using a synchronous or asynchronous serial interface. PPP is a successor to Serial Line-Interface Protocol (SLIP).

See also **Serial Line-Interface Protocol.**

PPPRNS

Point-to-Point Protocol Remote-Node Services, a protocol that supports Point-to-Point Protocol (PPP) connections to remote network nodes.

PRAM

Parameter RAM, an area of random-access memory (RAM) in an AppleTalk network that stores configuration information (such as a node's network address).

preamble

A sequence of bits or fields in a message or packet, containing source and destination addresses, information about packet type or size, special signals, or a predefined bit sequence to indicate the start of the message or packet. A preamble is also known as a *header.*

See also **header.**

preemptive multitasking

A method whereby an operating system executes a task for a specific period of time (determined by a preset priority), preempts the task, and provides another task with access to the central processing unit (CPU) for a prescribed amount of time. In this type of processing, no task is allowed to exceed its allotted time interval.

pre-help portal

A portal with a display message appearing on the monitor screen for an extended period of time. A message such as Press <F1> for help is an example of a pre-help portal.

pre-imaging

Storing the image of a file page before updating a record on the page. In Btrieve, pre-imaging provides recovery capabilities in the event that a file is damaged or a system failure occurs before a file can be updated.

See also **Btrieve.**

PRELUDE.OBJ

An object file in the NetWare Loadable Module (NLM) Software Development Kit (SDK) that contains routines to initialize and terminate NLM applications.

See also **NetWare Loadable Module.**

Premises Distribution System (PDS)

Either a cabling system encompassing an entire building, or the name of AT&T's premises-wiring system.

See also **PDS.**

premises network

A network confined to a single building but that encompasses the entire building.

Presentation Layer (OSI model)

The sixth layer (Layer 6) in the OSI Reference Model. The Presentation Layer is responsible for communicating with the Session Layer (Layer 5) and for managing the negotiation and establishment of the encoded values for the transfer of structured data types.

See also **OSI Reference Model.**

Presentation-Services Layer (SNA model)

The sixth layer (Layer 6) in the Systems Network Architecture (SNA) communications model. The Presentation-Services Layer provides data information and formatting services to the network.

See also **Systems Network Architecture.**

Pretty Good Privacy (PGP)

A software program, available as shareware, that encrypts files using a private-key encryption algorithm, sends and receives encrypted electronic mail (e-mail), creates and verifies digital signatures, and manages (creates, certifies, and revokes) keys. Despite patent, licensing, import, and export restrictions, PGP is available over the Internet; most versions carry licensing restrictions on usage and distribution.

PRI

(1) Primary-Rate Interface, another name for Primary-Rate ISDN.

(2) Primary-Rate ISDN, one of two service categories provided by an Integrated-Services Digital Network (ISDN) that provides *bearer channels* (also known a *B channels*) and *data channels* (also known as *D channels*), both of which are capable of speeds of 64 kilobits per second (Kbps). When combined, the 1.544 megabit-per-second (Mbps) speed is equivalent to that of a T1 channel. The other service category provided by ISDN is known as Bit-Rate Interface (BRI).

See also **(2) Bit-Rate Interface; (2) Integrated-Services; (2) Digital Network; (2) T1.**

primary half-session

The half-session on the network node that sends a session activation request.

See also **half-session; secondary half-session.**

Primary Interexchange Carrier (PIC)

A long-distance telephone service carrier to which a user may subscribe.

primary link station (PLS)

In a network that complies with the Synchronous Data-Link Control (SDLC) protocol, the link station that controls the link. The PLS initiates communications with another PLS or with a secondary link station (SLS). Each link has only one PLS.

See also **PLS; secondary link station; Synchronous Data-Link Control.**

primary logical unit (PLU)

A logical unit (LU) containing the primary half-session for a particular LU-to-LU session.

See also **half-session; secondary logical unit.**

Primary-Rate Interface (PRI)

Another term for **Primary-Rate ISDN.**

Primary-Rate ISDN (PRI)

One of two service categories provided by an Integrated-Services Digital Network (ISDN) that provides *bearer channels* (also known a *B channels*) and *data channels* (also known as *D channels*), both of which are capable of speeds of 64 kilobits per second (Kbps). When combined, the 1.544 megabit-per-second (Mbps) speed is equivalent to that of a T1 channel. The other service category provided by ISDN is known as Bit-Rate Interface (BRI).

See also **Bit-Rate Interface; Integrated-Services Digital Network; PRI; T1.**

primary server

Under NetWare System Fault Tolerance III (SFT III), a server that network stations see, and to which they send requests for network services. (Routers send packets to the primary server because it is the only server they see.) The IOEngine in the primary server determines the order and type of events sent to the MSEngine, and only the primary server can send reply packets to network workstations. By contrast, the SFT III secondary server is the server activated after the primary server. Either server may function as a primary server; system failure determines the role of each. When the primary server fails, the secondary server becomes the new primary server. When the failed server is then restored, it becomes the secondary server.

See also **IOEngine; MSEngine; secondary server; System Fault Tolerance.**

primary station

In such protocols as High-Level Data-Link Control (HDLC) and Synchronous Data-Link Control (SDLC), a station that performs management functions, controls the transmission activity of secondary stations, and receives responses from secondary stations. A primary station is also known as a *primary link station.*

See also **High-Level Data-Link Control; primary link station; secondary link station; Synchronous Data-Link Control.**

primary time server

A server responsible for synchronizing the time with at least one other Primary time server (or Reference time server) and for providing the time to Secondary time servers and workstations.

See also **reference time server; secondary time server.**

Print

In Novell Directory Services (NDS), a NetWare Directory Schema term and a selectable property for the Print Server object.

See also **leaf object; Novell Directory Services; object.**

print device

Any printer, plotter, or other peripheral device that prints from the network.

print-device definition

A function or mode, defined in a Printer-Definition File (PDF), that corresponds to a printer, plotter, or other peripheral. A print-device definition supplies the necessary control sequences for setting or resetting the printer, as well as for controlling such features as boldface, emphasis, italics, print size, font selection, and colors.. It enables the user to specify modes for use in print-job configurations, which prepare the printer for a print job, combine functions, reset the printer to default settings, and so forth. Print definitions are required for proper performance by a printer and must be imported into NetWare print services by using the NetWare Administrator or PRINTDEF utilities.

See also **NetWare Administrator; PRINTDEF utility.**

print driver

A software driver that converts print jobs into a format recognizable by the type of printer being used.

print header

Transport-control codes that precede data to a print queue and match the modes defined by the NetWare PRINTDEF utility. The default size for a print header is 64 bytes.

See also **print tail; PRINTDEF utility.**

print job

A file sent by Novell Directory Services (NDS) — or through bindery services — and stored in a print-queue directory to await printing. Each print job is assigned a unique filename: a variation of the first four characters of the print-queue directory identification, four more numerals, and a .Q filename extension. Print jobs are handled on a first-in, first out (FIFO) basis by the print queue.

See also **print queue.**

print-job configuration

A set of options used to determine how a job is printed. These options can include the printer to be used, print queue to be used, number of copies to print, whether to use a banner page, specific printer form, and print-device mode. In NetWare, print-job configurations can be created through the NetWare Administrator and PRINTCON utilities.

See also **banner page; NetWare Administrator utility; PRINTCON utility.**

Print-Job Configuration

In Novell Directory Services (NDS), a NetWare Directory Schema term and a selectable property for the Organization, Organizational Unit, and User objects.

See also **container object; leaf object; Novell Directory Services; object.**

print-job list

A list accessible from NetWare's PCONSOLE, NETUSER, or NetWare Administrator utilities that shows all print jobs currently in the print queue.

See also **NETUSER; NetWare Administrator; PCONSOLE; print queue.**

Print Manager

A print-job-management utility in Windows 3.*x* that queues any documents to be printed on a network printer. This utility enables users to change the order of the print queue or to remove print jobs from the queue. Print Manager only works with Windows applications.

print queue

A network directory that stores print jobs and that has a printer assigned to it, which receives the print jobs from the print server. When the printer is ready, the print server removes the print job from the directory (print queue) and sends it to the printer. The only limitation on the number of print jobs a print queue can hold is disk space. In NetWare, all print queues are assigned names, each is a random number (representing the print-queue identification seen through the NetWare Administrator utility) followed by the .QDR extension. All print-queue directories in NetWare contain files (with .SYS and .SRV filename extensions) that are flagged as system files and hidden files.

See also **print job; print server.**

print-queue operator

A user (usually designated by the NetWare network administrator) who can edit other users' print jobs, delete print jobs from the print queue, modify the print-queue status, and change the order in which print jobs are serviced.

print-queue polling time

A time interval that a print server waits between checking the print queue for jobs that are ready for printing.

See also **print server.**

print-queue sampling interval

In NetWare, a period specified in the PCONSOLE utility as the amount of time a print server waits between checking the print queues for print jobs ready to be printed. The default is 15 seconds.

See also **PCONSOLE utility.**

print server

A program that takes print jobs from a print queue and sends them to a network printer. In NetWare 4.*x* and IntranetWare, print servers run through the PSERVER NetWare Loadable Module (NLM) on a NetWare server; they can service up to 255 printers that have any number of print queues assigned. In NetWare 3.*x*, print servers are loaded through either PSERVER (on a file server) or PSERVER.EXE (on a dedicated workstation).

See also **print job; print queue; PSERVER.**

Print Server

In Novell Directory Services (NDS), a NetWare Directory Schema term and a selectable property for the Printer object.

See also **leaf object; Novell Directory Services; object.**

Print Server object

In Novell Directory Services (NDS), a leaf object that represents a network print server. This object should be placed in the same container as printers and print queues with which it is associated. This object has the following selectable NDS properties: Access-Control List, Account Balance, Allow Unlimited Credit, Back Link, Bindery, Common Name (CN), Description, Full Name, Host Device, Locality, Minimum Account Balance, Network Address, Object Class, Operator, Organization, Organizational Unit, Print, Private Key, Public Key, Resource, SAP Name, Security Equals To, Security Flags, See Also, Status, User, and Version.

See also **leaf object; Novell Directory Services; object.**

Print Server operator

A user (or member of a group) delegated rights by the NetWare network administrator to manage the print server by controlling notify lists, printers, and print-queue assignments.

See also **print queue; print server.**

print spooler

Operating-system software that coordinates the print jobs sent to a shared printer when the printer is busy.

print tail

Transport-control codes that follow a print header to a print queue and that match modes defined by the NetWare PRINTDEF utility. The default size for a print tail is 16 bytes.

See also **print header; PRINTDEF utility.**

PRINTCON utility

In NetWare and IntranetWare, a workstation utility that creates or modifies print-job configurations to specify a default printer and other options for users of CAPTURE, NPRINT, NETUSER, or PCONSOLE. The PRINTCON utility can also change the current User or container object in Novell Directory Services, or change the NetWare server in bindery mode.

PRINTDEF utility

In NetWare and IntranetWare, a workstation utility that views, modifies, imports, or exports print-device definitions, as well as monitoring, modifying, or creating printer forms.

printer

A peripheral or piece of hardware used to produce printed material. A printer may be attached directly to the network, to the printer port of a NetWare server, or the printer port of a computer workstation. A network printer-port driver is required to pass a print job from the network to the printer; the type of driver depends on the method of attachment to the network. Printers attached directly to the network store their own printer-port drivers. Printers attached to a NetWare server must have the NPRINTER NetWare Loadable Module (NLM) loaded on the NetWare server. Printers attached to the computer workstation must have the NPRINTER.EXE file loaded at the workstation.

See also **NetWare Loadable Module; NPRINTER (NLM); NPRINTER.EXE utility; printer-port driver.**

Printer-Access Protocol (PAP)

A part of the AppleTalk protocol suite that enables Macintosh clients and NetWare for Macintosh servers to communicate with printers on an AppleTalk network.

See also **AppleTalk; AppleTalk protocols; NetWare for Macintosh; PAP.**

Printer Configuration

In Novell Directory Services (NDS), a NetWare Directory Schema term and a selectable property for the Printer object.

See also **leaf object; Novell Directory Services; object.**

Printer Control

In Novell Directory Services (NDS), a NetWare Directory Schema term and a selectable property for the Organization, Organizational Unit, and User objects.

See also **container object; leaf object; Novell Directory Services; object.**

Printer-Control Language (PCL)

A Page-Description Language (PDL) used by the Hewlett-Packard LaserJet and other compatible printers.

See also **Page-Description Language; PCL.**

printer definition

A set of printer-control characters specific to a particular brand or model of printer, used to format printer output to produce bold, italic, and centered text.

printer emulation

A printer characteristic that enables the printer to behave like a printer from another manufacturer by changing modes.

printer form

An option in NetWare print services that allows the designation of a *form* to indicate the type of paper on which a job is to be printed. If the paper loaded in the printer does not match the printer-form designation, the job is not printed.

printer mode

A sequence of print functions that defines the style, size, boldness, and orientation of typefaces used in a printed file. A printer mode is also known as a *printer command, control sequence,* or *escape sequence.*

Printer object

In Novell Directory Services (NDS), a leaf object that represents a physical printing device on the network. Every printer should have a corresponding NDS object, which should be placed in the same container as those of the users who print to it. This object has the following selectable NDS properties: Access-Control List, Back Link, Bindery, Cartridge, Common Name (CN), Default Queue, Description, Host Device, Locality, Memory, Network Address, Network Address Restrictions, Notify, Object Class, Operator, Organization, Organizational Unit, Owner, Page-Description Language, Print Server, Printer Configuration, Queue, See Also, Serial Number, Status, and Supported Typefaces.

See also **leaf object; Novell Directory Services; object.**

printer server

An AppleTalk Print Services (ATPS) entity that services a single print queue and sends jobs to a single printer on an AppleTalk network.

See also **AppleTalk; AppleTalk protocols.**

printing

The process of transferring data from computer files (in the form of print jobs) to a print queue, through a print server, and finally to a printer for output on paper. Several printers can be shared across a network to facilitate printing from all nodes.

printing object

Novell Directory Services (NDS) objects (including the Print Server object and the Printer object) that have certain properties that contain information about the physical resources they represent.

See also **Novell Directory Services; object; property.**

Priority Access-Control Enabled (PACE)

A proprietary variant of the Ethernet architecture designed to set priorities for the transmission of time-sensitive materials; the highest priority is granted to data that must be sent at a constant rate to be readable. PACE was developed by 3Com and other collaborators.

See also **Ethernet.**

priority queuing

The setting of priorities for frames in an output queue on the basis of various routing features such as packet size and interface type.

Privacy-Enhanced Mail (PEM)

One of two enhancements to Internet mail-message formatting introduced in RFC 822 that provides mechanisms for encrypting, signing, and authenticating messages to ensure that electronic mail (e-mail) is reasonable secure from intruders. The other enhancement was Multipurpose Internet Mail Extensions (MIME).

See also **Multipurpose Internet Mail Extensions.**

Private Automatic Branch Exchange (PABX)

A telephone system offering automatic switching and other communications capabilities. Because almost all telephone systems are now automatic, this term is often replaced with a synonym, **Private Branch Exchange (PBX).**

Private Branch Exchange (PBX)

A telephone system that provides interoffice connections from one extension to another, as well as connections to an external telephone network. PBX switching can be automatic or manual (done by an operator).

Private Key

In Novell Directory Services (NDS), a NetWare Directory Schema term and a selectable property for the AFP Server, Messaging Server, NCP Server, Print Server, and User objects.

See also **leaf object; Novell Directory Services; object.**

private leased circuit

A leased communications circuit that is always available and that connects a company communications network with a remote site.

Private Management Domain (PRMD)

An electronic-mail (e-mail) system or a Message-Handling System (MHS), operated by a private organization, that complies with the X.400 communications model.

See also **Message-Handling System; X.400.**

Private Network-to-Network Interface (PNNI)

A routing information protocol that enables multivendor Asynchronous Transfer Mode (ATM) switches to be integrated in the same network.

See also **Asynchronous Transfer Mode.**

private-key encryption system

An encryption method that uses a conversion algorithm and predefined bit value (called a *key*) known only to sender and receiver. Private-key encryption is also called *one-key encryption* or *single-key encryption*.

See also **encryption; public-key encryption system.**

Privilege-Attribute Certificate (PAC)

A certificate that specifies the privileges granted to a user and is checked to determine whether the user should be granted access to a requested service (or to the network).

privilege level (microprocessor)

A scheme for protecting Intel microprocessors that assigns addresses to specific tasks and, from within the tasks, protects the operating system (and special processor registers) from access by applications. Four privilege levels are defined within a task. Ring 0, the innermost ring, is assigned as the most-trusted level. Ring 3, the outermost ring, is least trusted, and is available to applications. Rings 1 and 2 are reserved for the operating system and its extensions. Privilege levels are maintained by circuitry found in the memory-management unit (MMU).

In NetWare 4.1, Novell recommends running the NetWare operating system in the OS domain (level 0) and any untested NetWare Loadable Modules (NLMs) in the OS_PROTECTED domain (level 3). After an NLM has been tested and proven reliable, it can be run in level 0. Because of enhancements to the memory handling, this is no longer necessary in NetWare 4.11.

A privilege level is also known as a *protection ring*. Figure P.4 shows the privilege-level protection scheme.

See also **memory-management unit.**

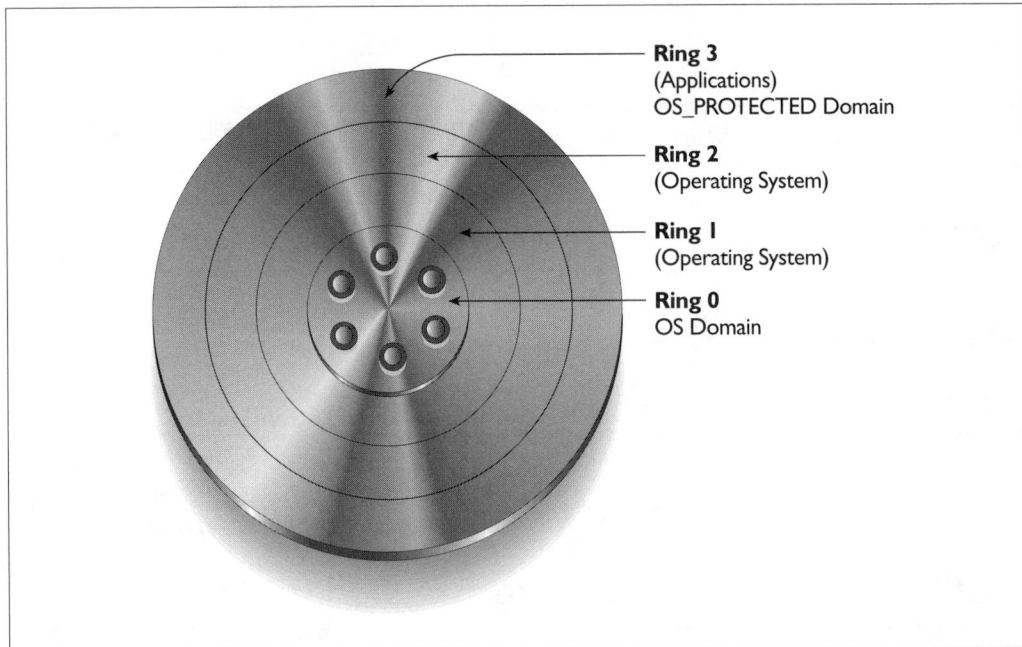

Ring 3
(Applications)
OS_PROTECTED Domain

Ring 2
(Operating System)

Ring 1
(Operating System)

Ring 0
OS Domain

Figure P.4
Privilege levels

privilege level (network)

Rights granted to a user by the network administrator so the user can execute various functions on the network.

See also **access rights.**

privileged mode

A mode of the operating system that allows certain device drivers and the operating system to manipulate parts of the system (such as memory or input/output ports).

PRMD

Private Management Domain, an electronic-mail (e-mail) system or a Message-Handling System (MHS), operated by a private organization, that complies with the X.400 communications model.

See also **Message-Handling System;** **X.400.**

PRN

A logical device name assigned to a printer in the DOS and OS/2 environments. This assignment usually is made to the parallel port, known on most systems as LPT1.

See also **parallel port; LPT1.**

probe

An AppleTalk network packet sent to the remote end of the network to request an acknowledgment from the end node. This packet is used to determine the end of the network and to verify that the node is functioning properly.

See also **AppleTalk.**

problem-determination statistics (PD Stats)

Under Systems Network Architecture (SNA), statistics used by the network-management function to determine and diagnose problems associated with the communication links used for network sessions.

See also **Systems Network Architecture.**

Procedure Coverage Logger (PCL)

A utility in the NetWare Loadable Module (NLM) Certification Kit used to verify that a product's actual exercising procedure provides adequate coverage of the functions declared in the source code.

See also **PCL.**

process

A program (or portion of a program) that executes on a host computer in a multitasking network environment.

Processes

In NetWare 3.12, a resource in the Available Options/Resource Utilization screen of the MONITOR NetWare Loadable Module (NLM) that tracks loadable modules that start processes. This resource ensures that the process is deleted once the module is unloaded.

See also **MONITOR; NetWare Loadable Module; NMAGENT.**

Processor Exception Handlers

In NetWare 3.12, a resource appearing in the Available Options/Resource Utilization

screen of the MONITOR NetWare Loadable Module (NLM) that tracks exceptions to the rules the hardware detects.

See also **MONITOR; NetWare Loadable Module; NMAGENT.**

Processor Utilization

In NetWare 4.02, a field name that appears in the Available Options menu in the MONITOR NetWare Loadable Module (NLM).

See also **MONITOR; NetWare Loadable Module.**

Processor Direct Slot (PDS)

A general-purpose expansion slot in Macintosh computers that is connected directly to the microprocessor instead of indirectly by a bus (as with a NuBus system).

See also **NuBus; PDS.**

Prodigy

An Internet service provider (ISP), operated by IBM and Sears, that uses a special Web browser and that enables users to create their own Web home pages.

See also **Web browser; Web home page.**

 **For more information about Prodigy, surf the Web to** http://www.prodigy.com.

Professional Developers Program (PDP)

A joint program between Novell and independent developers of computer applications to provide direct access to various NetWare services and centralized network resources. PDP has been replaced by the Developer Net program.

Profile

In Novell Directory Services (NDS), a NetWare Directory Schema term and a selectable property for the Group, Message Routing Group, and User objects.

See also **leaf object; Novell Directory Services; object.**

Profile login script

A script that sets the NetWare environment for a group of users who have identical login script needs. If Profile login script is used (it is optional), it executes after a Container login script and before a User login script.

See also **Container login script; login script; User login script.**

Profile Membership

In Novell Directory Services (NDS), a selectable property for the following objects: Group, Message-Routing Group, and User.

See also **leaf object; Novell Directory Services; object.**

Profile object

In Novell Directory Services (NDS), a leaf object that contains a login script that can be utilized by users who must share common login-script commands but are not located in the same portion of the Directory tree. The Profile login script executes after the Container login script and before the User login script. This object has the following selectable NDS properties: Access-Control List, Back Link, Bindery, Common Name (CN), Description, Locality, Login Script, Object Class, Organization, Organizational Unit, and See Also.

See also **leaf object; login script; Novell Directory Services; object.**

program

Specially coded instructions that perform a specific task when carried out by a computer.

program link

An icon or symbol that appears on a monitor screen and, when double-clicked, runs preset executable files. Program links often are used to display graphics or to download files.
See also **hyperlink; hypertext.**

Program Manager

A Windows 3.*x* shell that enables a user to organize programs and applications, create groups, and serves as the basis for running the Windows 3.*x* program.
See also **shell; Windows.**

programming language

A language used specifically to create a program of instructions that a computer can execute to perform a prescribed task. More than 200 programming languages currently are used, including BASIC, C, C++, FORTRAN, and Pascal.

Project 21

A project created by the International Maritime Satellite Organization that calls for 30 to 40 satellites to provide point-to-point communications between any two locations on Earth.

promiscuous mode

An operating mode on a Network Interface Card (NIC) that allows any packet to be passed to a higher layer regardless of whether the packet has been addressed to a node.
See also **Network Interface Card.**

prompt

A character or message that appears on the computer monitor display screen and that requires a response from the user. Examples of prompts include the *DOS prompt* (which displays the current drive letter followed by the > symbol), the *OS/2 prompt* (which displays the current drive mapping in brackets), and the NetWare *server console prompt* (which displays a colon). The DOS and OS/2 prompts can be customized; the NetWare prompt cannot be changed.

propagation delay

A value indicating the amount of time required for a signal to pass through a component (or from one component to another).

property

Characteristics of objects in Novell Directory Services (NDS) that hold information about the object. NDS requires only those properties entered when a new object is created (such as properties that name the object, or properties required to create the object). A property can contain multiple values (such as the Telephone Number property, which contains numerous telephone numbers).

Appendix C contains a complete list of NDS properties and the objects for which

the properties can be selected.
See also **Novell Directory Services;
object.**

property groups

A group of Novell Directory Services (NDS)
properties organized by function.

property rights

Rights that apply to an object property in
Novell Directory Services (NDS).
See also **Novell Directory Services;
object.**

proprietary server

A server designed to be used with hardware
and software from a particular vendor and
running a proprietary operating system.

proprietary software

Software designed specifically to run on a
particular computer system and not readily
available to the public.

Prospero

A collection of protocols and embedded
software (from the Information Sciences
Institute at the University of Southern
California) that provides tools for accessing,
organizing, and using files that may be
located in diverse remote locations.

 **For more information about
Prospero, surf the Web to**
`http://gost.isi.edu/info/
prospero.`

Protect

A NetWare Loadable Module (NLM) used to
detect suspicious memory access by one or
more NLMs, used to test client-server applications and to debug products.

protected mode

A mode that provides multitasking capabilities by allocating memory to various processes that run concurrently; memory used by
one process is not allowed to overlap memory used by another process. Computers
equipped with Intel's 80286, 80386, 80486,
and Pentium microprocessors run in protected mode by default. However, computers
equipped with these microprocessors can
also be set to run in *real mode*, which means
they are subjected to the same memory
constraints of an 8086 machine (only
1MB of memory and only one process
or application running at one time).

protection ring

Another term for **privilege level.**

protocol

Conventions or rules that determine how a
program or operating system communicates
between two endpoints. A protocol defines
the procedures to follow as data is transmitted or received across a network, including
the format, timing, sequence, and error
checking used on the network. Table P.5
shows some common protocols and where
to find more information.

Table P.5: Common Network Protocols

Protocol	For More Information
Address-Resolution Protocol (ARP)	See **Address-Resolution Protocol**.
Andrew File-System protocol (AFS protocol)	See **Andrew File-System protocol**.
AppleTalk Address-Resolution Protocol (AARP)	See **AppleTalk Address-Resolution Protocol**.
AppleTalk Data-Stream Protocol (ADSP)	See **AppleTalk Data-Stream Protocol**.
AppleTalk Echo Protocol (AEP)	See **AppleTalk Echo Protocol**.
AppleTalk Filing Protocol (ATFP)	See **AppleTalk Filing Protocol**.
AppleTalk protocols	See **AppleTalk protocols**.
AppleTalk Remote-Access Protocol (ARAP)	See **AppleTalk Remote-Access Protocol**.
AppleTalk Secure Data-Stream Protocol (ASDSP)	See **AppleTalk Secure Data-Stream Protocol**.
AppleTalk Session Protocol (ASP)	See **AppleTalk Session Protocol**.
AppleTalk Transaction Protocol (ATP)	See **AppleTalk Transaction Protocol**.
AppleTalk Update-Based Routing Protocol (AURP)	See **AppleTalk Update-Based Routing Protocol**.
Bootstrap Protocol (BOOTP)	See **Bootstrap Protocol**.
Border Gateway Protocol (BGP)	See **Border Gateway Protocol**.
Byte-Control Protocol (BCP)	See **Byte-Control Protocol**.
Challenge Handshake-Authentication Protocol (CHAP)	See **Challenge Handshake-Authentication Protocol**.
Common Management-Information Protocol (CMIP)	See **Common Management-Information Protocol**.
Common Management-Information Protocol Data Unit (CMIPDU)	See **Common Management-Information Protocol Data Unit**.
Common Management-Information Services and Protocol Over TCP/IP (CMOT)	See **Common Management-Information Services and Protocol Over TCP/IP**.

(continued)

Table P.5: Common Network Protocols (continued)

Protocol	For More Information
Compressed Internet Packet-Exchange (IPX) Protocol (CIPX Protocol)	See **Compressed Internet Packet-Exchange Protocol.**
Compressed Serial-Line Interface Protocol (CSLIP)	See **Compressed Serial-Line Interface Protocol.**
Connection-Oriented Network Protocol (CONP)	See **Connection-Oriented Network Protocol.**
Connectionless Network Protocol (CLNP)	See **Connectionless Network Protocol.**
Connectionless Transport Protocol (CLTP)	See **Connectionless Transport Protocol.**
Datagram Delivery Protocol (DDP)	See **Datagram Delivery Protocol.**
Digital Data-Communications Message Protocol (DDCMP)	See **Digital Data-Communications Message Protocol.**
Directory-Access Protocol (DAP)	See **Directory-Access Protocol.**
Directory System Protocol (DSP)	See **Directory System Protocol.**
Dynamic Host Configuration Protocol (DHCP)	See **Dynamic Host Configuration Protocol.**
Ethernet Configuration-Test Protocol (ECTP)	See **Ethernet Configuration-Test Protocol.**
EtherTalk Link-Access Protocol (ELAP)	See **EtherTalk Link-Access Protocol.**
Exterior Gateway Protocol (EGP)	See **Exterior Gateway Protocol.**
Exterior Routing Protocol (ERP)	See **Exterior Routing Protocol.**
Fast Local-Internet Protocol (FLIP)	See **Fast Local-Internet Protocol.**
FDDITalk Link-Access Protocol (FLAP)	See **FDDITalk Link-Access Protocol.**
File-Transfer Protocol (FTP)	See **File-Transfer Protocol.**
Gateway-to-Gateway Protocol (GGP)	See **Gateway-to-Gateway Protocol.**
HyperText Transfer Protocol (HTTP)	See **HyperText Transfer Protocol.**
ICMP Router-Discovery Protocol (IRDP)	See **ICMP Router-Discovery Protocol.**

Protocol	For More Information
Interdomain Routing Protocol (IRP)	See Interdomain Routing Protocol.
Interior Gateway Protocol (IGP)	See Interior Gateway Protocol.
Interior Gateway-Routing Protocol (IGRP)	See Interior Gateway-Routing Protocol.
Internet Control-Message Protocol (ICMP)	See Internet Control-Message Protocol.
Internet Message-Access Protocol (IMAP)	See Internet Message-Access Protocol.
Internet Protocol (IP)	See Internet Protocol.
LAN/MAN-Management Protocol (LMMP)	See LAN/MAN-Management Protocol.
Link-Access Procedure, Balanced (LAPB Protocol)	See Link-Access Procedure, Balanced.
Link-Access Protocol (LAP)	See Link-Access Protocol.
Link-Control Protocol (LCP)	See Link-Control Protocol.
LocalTalk Link-Access Protocol (LLAP)	See LocalTalk Link-Access Protocol.
Multilink Point-to-Point Protocol (MP protocol)	See Multilink Point-to-Point Protocol.
Multiprotocol Over ATM (MPOA)	See Multiprotocol Over ATM.
Name-Binding Protocol (NBP)	See Name-Binding Protocol.
NetWare Core Protocol (NCP)	See NetWare Core Protocol.
NetWare Link-Services Protocol (NLSP)	See NetWare Link-Services Protocol.
Network-Control Protocol (NCP)	See Network-Control Protocol.
Network-Management Protocol (NMP)	See Network-Management Protocol.
Network News-Transfer Protocol (NNTP)	See Network News-Transfer Protocol.
Network Printing-Alliance Protocol (NPAP)	See Network Printing-Alliance Protocol.
Network Services Protocol (NSP)	See Network Services Protocol.

(continued)

Table P.5: Common Network Protocols (continued)

Protocol	For More Information
OSI Government Systems Interconnection Protocol (OSI GOSIP)	See **OSI Government Systems Interconnection Protocol.**
Packet-Burst Protocol (PBP)	See **Packet-Burst Protocol.**
Packet-Exchange Protocol (PEP)	See **Packet-Exchange Protocol.**
Packet-Level Protocol (PLP)	See **Packet-Level Protocol.**
Password-Authentication Protocol (PAP)	See **Password-Authentication Protocol.**
Point-to-Point Protocol (PPP)	See **Point-to-Point Protocol.**
Point-to-Point Protocol Remote-Node Services (PPPRNS)	See **Point-to-Point Protocol Remote-Node Services.**
Post Office Protocol 3 (POP3)	See **Post Office Protocol 3.**
Printer-Access Protocol (PAP)	See **Printer-Access Protocol.**
Reverse Address-Resolution Protocol (RARP)	See **Reverse Address-Resolution Protocol.**
Router-Discovery Protocol	See **Router-Discovery Protocol.**
Router Information Protocol (RIP)	See **Router Information Protocol.**
Routing Information Protocol (RIP)	See **Routing Information Protocol.**
Routing-Table Maintenance Protocol (RTMP)	See **Routing-Table Maintenance Protocol.**
Routing Table Protocol (RTP)	See **Routing Table Protocol.**
Secure-Sockets Layer Protocol (SSL Protocol)	See **Secure-Sockets Layer Protocol.**
Sequenced Packet Protocol (SPP)	See **Sequenced Packet Protocol.**
Serial-Line Internet Protocol (SLIP)	See **Serial-Line Internet Protocol.**
Service-Advertising Protocol (SAP)	See **Service-Advertising Protocol.**
Simple Gateway-Monitoring Protocol (SGMP)	See **Simple Gateway-Monitoring Protocol.**

Protocol	For More Information
Simple Mail-Transfer Protocol (SMTP)	See **Simple Mail-Transfer Protocol.**
Simple Network-Management Protocol (SNMP)	See **Simple Network-Management Protocol.**
Simple Network-Time Protocol (SNTP)	See **Simple Network-Time Protocol.**
Sub-Network Access Protocol (SNAP)	See **Sub-Network Access Protocol.**
Technical Office Protocol (TOP)	See **Technical Office Protocol.**
TokenTalk Link-Access Protocol (TLAP)	See **TokenTalk Link-Access Protocol.**
Transmission-Control Protocol (TCP)	See **Transmission-Control Protocol.**
Transmission-Control Protocol/Internetwork Protocol (TCP/IP)	See **Transmission-Control Protocol/Internetwork Protocol.**
Trivial File-Transfer Protocol (TFTP)	See **Trivial File-Transfer Protocol.**
Upper-Layer Protocol (ULP)	See **Upper-Layer Protocol.**
User Datagram Protocol (UDP)	See **User Datagram Protocol.**
Virtual-Terminal Protocol (VTP)	See **Virtual-Terminal Protocol.**
X display Manager Control Protocol (XDMCP)	See **X display Manager Control Protocol.**
Xpress Transfer Protocol (XTP)	See **Xpress Transfer Protocol.**
Zone-Information Protocol (ZIP)	See **Zone-Information Protocol.**

protocol address

An address in the Network Layer (Layer 3) of the OSI Reference Model. The protocol address refers to a logical (rather than physical) network device.

See also **OSI Reference Model.**

protocol analyzer

A hardware-software combination (or simply software) used to capture and examine network traffic. Novell's LANalyzer is an example of a software-based protocol analyzer.

See also **LANalyzer.**

protocol client

An application or a protocol that solicits and receives the services of another protocol.

Protocol-Control Information (PCI)

Protocol-dependent information added to a data packet in the OSI Reference Model before the packet can be passed to a lower level for processing.

See also **OSI Reference Model; PCI.**

protocol converter

A hardware-software combination used to connect two dissimilar networks by converting from one protocol to another.

Protocol Data Unit (PDU)

A packet exchanged between devices within a specified layer of the OSI Reference Model. A PDU communicates with the same layer of the OSI Reference Model on another machine.

See also **OSI Reference Model.**

protocol-dependent

A process or component based on a software address, or available in the Network Layer (Layer 3) of the OSI Reference Model, that is specific to the protocol used in the Network Layer.

See also **Network Layer; OSI Reference Model.**

Protocol element

A command for performing File-Transfer Protocol (FTP) operations at the protocol level.

See also **File-Transfer Protocol.**

protocol field compression

A process that reduces Protocol ID field from the two-byte framing standard set by the High-Level Data-Link Control (HDLC) Protocol to a single byte. Protocol field compression is one way to reduce unnecessary overhead when using low-bandwidth links.

See also **High-Level Data-Link Control.**

Protocol ID (PID)

A field in a Sub-Network Access Protocol (SNAP) header that helps to identify a distinct routed or bridged protocol.

See also **Sub-Network Access Protocol.**

protocol-independent

A process or component that is not based on a software address, not available in the Network Layer (Layer 3) of the OSI Reference Model, and not specific to any protocol used in the Network Layer.

See also **Network Layer; OSI Reference Model.**

protocol stack

A suite of protocols that includes all layers required to perform transmission and receipt of data packets.

See also **protocol suite.**

protocol suite

A collection of networking protocols providing all communications and services required to enable computers to exchange messages and other information. A protocol suite usually accomplishes this by managing physical connections, communications services, and application support.

protocol translator

A means, whether software or a network device, of converting one protocol into another similar protocol.

PROTOCOL utility

In NetWare and IntranetWare, a server console utility that views the protocols registered on the NetWare server and registers additional protocols or frame types. Local-area network (LAN) drivers automatically load the Internetwork Packet Exchange (IPX) protocol; other protocol stacks register themselves. Similarly, each LAN driver automatically registers a frame type when it is loaded.

See also **Internetwork Packet Exchange.**

Protocol-Independent Routing (PIR)

The routing of packets without regard to packet format or the protocol being used.

provider options

Options made available through a particular transport provider (such as Datagram Delivery Protocol or AppleTalk Data-Stream Protocol), accessible only through the Transport-Layer Interface (TLI).

See also **AppleTalk Data-Stream Protocol; Datagram-Delivery Protocol; Transport-Layer Interface.**

proxy

An element responding on behalf of another element and requesting the use of a particular protocol. A proxy is also known as a *proxy agent.*

proxy ARP

The process of a router replying to an Address-Resolution Protocol (ARP) request from a host on behalf of the ARP target host. This process was effective in subnetted Internet Protocol (IP) networks with hosts that did not recognize the subnetting; knowledge of subnets was limited to subnet routers, and the hosts could see only the IP network. When the subnet routers reply to ARP requests from hosts on behalf of other hosts (on other subnets reachable through the router), the hosts that originate the requests need not know about the subnets attached to the network. This use of proxy ARP is called *ARP subnet routers.* Because most IP hosts now understand subnetting, the use of ARP subnet routers has been minimized. The most common use of proxy ARP today is in *stub networks.*

See also **Address-Resolution Protocol; stub network.**

proxy protocol

A protocol used on the World Wide Web (WWW) whenever a proxy server initiates communication with another proxy server through a firewall.

See also **World Wide Web.**

proxy server

A server that acts on behalf of another server.

PSC utility

In NetWare and IntranetWare, a workstation utility used to view network-printer information, control network printers, and control the print server.

PSERVER (NLM)

In NetWare 4.*x* and IntranetWare, a server console utility used to monitor and manage printers and print queues.

pseudo hop count

Under NetWare System Fault Tolerance III (SFT III), the number of hops a primary server adds to the true hop count when advertising the route to the Mirrored Server Engine (MSEngine). A pseudo hop count becomes necessary when the SFT III servers reside on different network segments and the hop count for one server is higher than for another server. The primary server advertises an artificially high hop count (the true hop count plus a pseudo hop count) to ensure that packets are rerouted properly in the event that one server fails. If the primary server does fail, the surviving server advertises the true hop count, which is immedi-

ately recognized by routers as the best route to the MSEngine. The *total hop count* (true hop count plus pseudo hop count) cannot exceed 16.

See also **Mirrored Server Engine; primary server; System Fault Tolerance.**

pseudo preemption count

A NetWare system parameter determining the number of times that threads are allowed to make file-read or file-write system calls before they are forced to relinquish control.

pseudo preemption time

A NetWare system parameter indicating the amount of time (in 0.84-microsecond increments) that a NetWare Loadable Module (NLM) process may run before it is forced to relinquish control.

pseudo volume

In NetWare for Macintosh, the process of a CD-ROM copying files from a compact disc to the server's hard disk, and then creating a partition (the pseudo volume). Although the pseudo volume looks like a separate volume on the Macintosh desktop, it now contains the CD-ROM files and directory structure.

pseudonode

Under NetWare Link-Services Protocol (NLSP), a fictitious router that represents an entire local-area network (LAN) in the link-state database.

See also **NetWare Link-Services Protocol.**

pseudo-switched link

In a Public Switched Telephone Network (PSTN), a dial-up communications link established by using a pair of synchronous modems.

See also **dial-up connection; Public Switched Telephone Network.**

pseudoterminal

A computer terminal that does not really exist. Some programs such as Telnet may use a pseudoterminal to log in a user and run commands.

PSI

A large commercial Internet network. PSI stands for *Performance Systems International.*

PSN

Packet Switch Node, a dedicated machine that accepts and routes packets in a packet-switching network.

PSNP

Partial Sequence Number PDU, a Protocol Data Unit (PDU) that requests Link-State Packets (LSPs) from one Intermediate System (IS) to another.

See also **Protocol Data Unit; Intermediate System; Link-State Packet.**

PSTN

Public Switched Telephone Network, a telephone-communications service provider with switched-circuit lines that offers unre-

stricted access, an attribute that emphasizes the importance of inbound authentication for a network.

PTM

Pulse Time Modulation, encoding an analog signal for conversion to digital format by varying a time-dependent feature of a pulse.

See also **pulse; Pulse Amplitude Modulation; Pulse Code Modulation.**

PTT

Post, Telephone, and Telegraph, a government agency found in many European countries that provides postal, telephonic, telegraphic, and other communications services.

PU

Physical unit, in Systems Network Architecture (SNA), a node that supports one or more logical units (LUs).

See also **logical unit; Systems Network Architecture.**

PU 2.1

In a peer-oriented network, a type of physical unit (PU) that connects Systems Network Architecture (SNA) nodes.

See also **physical unit; Systems Network Architecture.**

public data network (PDN)

A data network available for use by the general public.

PUBLIC directory

A directory created on the SYS: volume during NetWare installation that allows general access to the network, as well as containing NetWare utilities and programs for network users. The location of this directory for DOS users is SYS:PUBLIC; for OS/2 users, the location is SYS:PUBLIC/OS2.

public files

NetWare utilities, help files, some message and data files, and any other files that must be accessed by all NetWare users. The files usually are located in the SYS:PUBLIC directory for DOS users and the SYS:PUBLIC/OS2 directory for OS/2 users.

Public Key

In Novell Directory Services (NDS), a NetWare Directory Schema term and a selectable property for the AFP Server, Messaging Server, NCP Server, Print Server, and User objects.

See also **leaf object; Novell Directory Services; object; public-key encryption system.**

public-key encryption system

An encryption method that uses a conversion algorithm, a predefined bit value (called a *key*) known only to a single user, and a key known by the public. Public-key encryption is also known as *double-key encryption*.

See also **encryption; private-key encryption system.**

public service provider

An Internet service provider (ISP) that offers connection time that can be paid for by the hour or by the month.

See also **Internet service provider.**

Public Switched Telephone Network (PSTN)

A telephone communications service provider with switched-circuit lines that offers unrestricted access, an attribute that emphasizes the importance of inbound authentication for a network.

[Public] trustee

A special trustee in NetWare that can be added to any Novell Directory Services (NDS) object, directory, or file, and that, by default, includes the Read right and the File Scan right. When [Public] becomes a trustee of an object, directory, or file, all NDS objects effectively are granted rights to that object, directory, or file. [Public] must always be entered enclosed in brackets; its use is restricted to trustee assignments. Like any other trustee, [Public] may be added or deleted, and an Inherited-Rights Filter (IRF) blocks inherited rights for [Public].

See also **Inherited-Rights Filter; trustee; trustee rights.**

pulse

A brief variation in voltage or current level, characterized by the amplitude of change and the duration of the change. A pulse *rise time* is measured as the amount of time needed to change the level from 10 percent to 90 percent of maximum; a *fall time* is measured as the amount of time needed to change the level from 90 percent back down to 10 percent.

See also **Pulse Amplitude Modulation.**

Pulse Amplitude Modulation (PAM)

A digital-to-analog conversion scheme in which a modulating wave modulates the amplitude of a pulse stream.

See also **pulse; Pulse Code Modulation.**

pulse carrier

A signal used as the basis for pulse modulation; it consists of a series of rapid, constant pulses.

See also **pulse.**

Pulse Code Modulation (PCM)

The transmission of analog information that has been sampled into digital form and encoded with a fixed number of bits.

See also **pulse; Pulse Amplitude Modulation; Pulse Time Modulation.**

pulse density

A measurement that compares the number of ones in a transmission with the total number of digital time slots transmitted. Certain specifications restrict the number of consecutive zeros that may appear in a transmission.

Pulse Time Modulation (PTM)

Encoding an analog signal for conversion to digital format by varying a time-dependent feature of a pulse.

See also **pulse; Pulse Amplitude Modulation; Pulse Code Modulation.**

punch-down block

Also known as a **patch panel**, a device with metal tabs used to puncture the casing on twisted-pair cable and to make electrical contact for wires on the cable, thereby establishing a *cross-connection* between the block and other blocks or connections with specific devices.

PUP

PARC Universal Protocol, a protocol developed at the Xerox Palo Alto Research Center (PARC), similar to Internet Protocol (IP).

See also **Internet Protocol.**

PUPGRADE (NLM)

In NetWare 3.*x*, a server console and workstation utility that upgrades NetWare 3 print servers and printers to Novell Directory Services (NDS) objects. This NetWare Loadable Module (NLM) also upgrades NetWare 3 PRINTCON and PRINTDEF databases to NetWare 4 format.

See also **PRINTCON utility; PRINTDEF utility.**

purge

The removal of previously deleted files from a disk or directory.

Purge (P) attribute

A NetWare file-system attribute that causes NetWare to purge a directory or file when it is deleted.

PURGE utility

In NetWare and IntranetWare, a workstation utility that permanently removes previously deleted files from the file system. To operate the PURGE utility successfully, the user must have the proper Delete rights in a specified directory. If the user has the Delete right at the root, the user can use PURGE to remove all deleted files from the entire volume.

PVC

(1) **Permanent Virtual Circuit,** a communications path between two fixed end points continuously available and similar to a leased line.

(2) *polyvinylchloride*, a plastic used in the manufacture of some magnetic recording media.

See also (1) **leased line.**

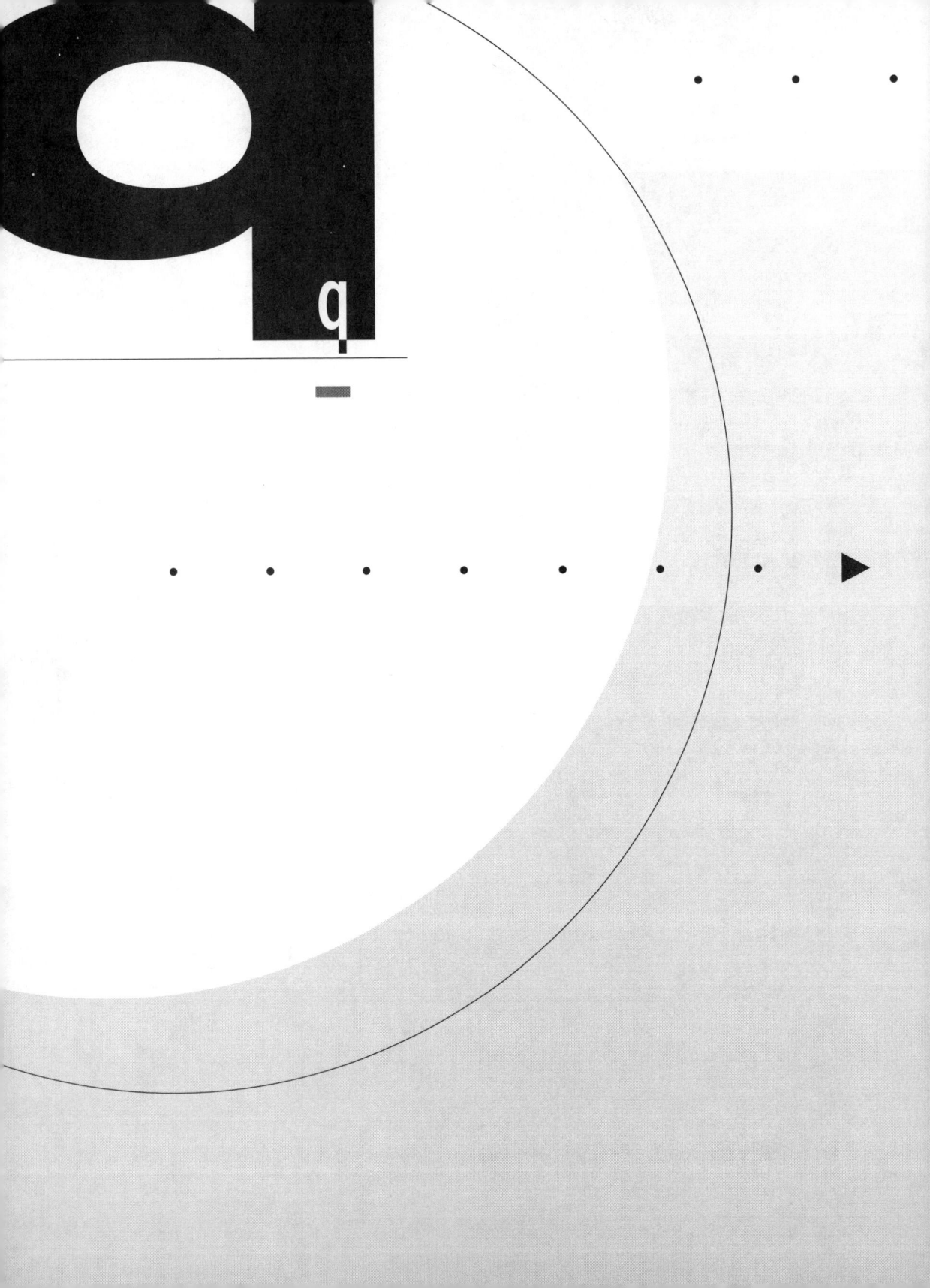

Q.920/Q.921

Specifications for Integrated-Services Digital Networks (ISDNs) that define the User-to-Network Interface (UNI) in the Data-Link Layer (Layer 2) of the OSI Reference Model.

See also **Integrated-Services Digital Network; OSI Reference Model; User-to-Network Interface.**

Q.931

A recommended standard from the Consultative Committee for International Telegraphy and Telephony (CCITT) that defines signaling to set up an Integrated-Services Digital Network (ISDN) connection.

See also **Consultative Committee for International Telegraphy and Telephony; Integrated-Services Digital Network.**

Q.93B

A recommended standard from the Consultative Committee for International Telegraphy and Telephony (CCITT) that defines signaling to set up an Asynchronous Transfer Mode (ATM) connection.

See also **Asynchronous Transfer Mode; Consultative Committee for International Telegraphy and Telephony.**

Q-bit

qualifier bit, a component of a user packet that determines whether the user data field contains data for the user or high-level control information.

See also **packet.**

QIC

quarter-inch cartridge, standards developed by the Quarter-Inch Cartridge Drive Standards trade association that specify tapes commonly used in backup operations. Two of the most common are a QIC 40 (a tape that writes 10,000 bits per inch on 20 tracks) or QIC 80 (a tape that writes 14,700 bits per inch on 28 tracks) to back up as much as 250MB of compressed information from a small-to-medium hard-disk system. The QIC 1350 tape format can back up as much as 1.35GB of compressed information and the QIC 2100 tapes can back up as much as 2.1GB of compressed information.

QLCC

Qualified Link-Level Control, a protocol enabling Systems Network Architecture (SNA) packets to be transmitted over X.25 links.

See also **Systems Network Architecture; X.25.**

QMS

Queue-Management Services, a built-in component of the NetWare operating system that provides developers with a set of Application Program Interface (API) calls to handle queue operations from any type of application. QMS is commonly used for print servers, batch job servers, archive servers, file-copying servers, and compiling servers.

See also **Application Program Interface.**

QMS events

A NetWare auditing option that tracks activities (such as requests to create or destroy) that affect print queues.

See also **print queue.**

QoS

Quality of Service, a set of parameters in Asynchronous Transfer Mode (ATM) networks that describe a transmission with such values as allowable delay variation in cell transmission and allowable cell loss versus total cells transmitted.

See also **Asynchronous Transfer Mode.**

quad

A cable that has two twisted pairs of wires (four in all) with each wire separately insulated.

quad-shield cable

Coaxial cable that has four layers of shielding (alternating layers of foil and braid shields), used in industrial settings where heavy electrical interference can occur.

quadbit

A group of 4 bits transmitted, processed, and interpreted as a single bit.

quadrature amplitude modulation

A data-encoding technique for modems operating at 2,400 bits per second (bps) that uses a combination of phase and amplitude change to encode multiple bits on a single carrier signal.

quadrax cable

A hybrid of triaxial and twinaxial cable that has extra wire with dielectric and has extra shielding.

Qualified Link-Level Control (QLCC) protocol

A protocol enabling Systems Network Architecture (SNA) packets to be transmitted over X.25 links.

See also **Systems Network Architecture; X.25.**

qualifier bit (Q-bit)

A component of a user packet that determines whether the user data field contains data for the user or high-level control information.

See also **packet.**

Quality of Service (QoS)

A set of parameters in Asynchronous Transfer Mode (ATM) networks that describe a transmission with such values as allowable delay variation in cell transmission and allowable cell loss versus total cells transmitted.

See also **Asynchronous Transfer Mode.**

quantizing

The digital-signal process of converting a Pulse Amplitude Modulation (PAM) signal to a Pulse Code Modulation (PCM) signal.

See also **Pulse Amplitude Modulation; Pulse Code Modulation.**

Quarterdeck Mosaic

A World Wide Web (WWW) browser from Quarterdeck Corporation that stores a history list by session and by total usage (across sessions) and features hot lists with an entry's creation date, Multipurpose Internet Mail Extensions (MIME) type, and header information. Quarterdeck Mosaic is part of the InternetSuite package of Internet tools.

See also **Multipurpose Internet Mail Extensions; Web browser.**

 **For more information about Quarterdeck Mosaic, surf the Web to** `http:// arachnid.qdeck.com/ qdeck/products/QMosaic.`

quarter-inch cartridge (QIC)

Standards developed by the Quarter-Inch Cartridge Drive Standards trade association that specify tapes commonly used in backup operations. Two of the most common are a QIC 40 (a tape that writes 10,000 bits per inch on 20 tracks) or QIC 80 (a tape that writes 14,700 bits per inch on 28 tracks) to back up as much as 250MB of compressed information from a small-to-medium hard-disk system. The QIC 1350 tape format can back up as much as 1.35GB of compressed information and the QIC 2100 tapes can back up as much as 2.1GB of compressed information.

quartet signaling

A 100BaseVG Ethernet strategy developed by Hewlett-Packard and AT&T that simultaneously uses four wire pairs and relies on the fact that the pairs need not be used for sending and receiving at the same time. Demand priority in the 100BaseVG implementation enables hubs to handle the network access for network nodes, so wire availability is guaranteed. Quartet signaling offers four times as many channels as ordinary Ethernet and uses 5B/6B encoding.

See also **5B/6B encoding; 100BaseVG.**

query

A message that inquires about the value of some variable or set of variables.

query language

A programming language found in database-management systems (DBMSs) that enables a user to extract and display specific information from the database. The Structured Query Language is an international query language.

See also **database-management system; Structured Query Language.**

queue

An area of the network operating system that contains a list or line formed by items waiting for service (such as tasks waiting to be performed, stations waiting for connections, messages waiting for transmission, or jobs waiting to be printed).

Queue

A selectable property for the Printer object in Novell Directory Services (NDS).

See also **leaf object; Novell Directory Services; object.**

Queue Directory

A NetWare Directory Schema term and a selectable property for the Bindery Queue and Queue objects in Novell Directory Services (NDS).

See also **leaf object; Novell Directory Services; object.**

Queue-Management Services (QMS)

A built-in component of the NetWare operating system that provides developers with a set of Application Program Interface (API) calls to handle queue operations from any type of application. QMS is commonly used for print servers, batch job servers, archive servers, file copying servers, and compiling servers.

See also **Application Program Interface**.

Queue object

A NetWare leaf object representing a print queue on the network or, more specifically, the directories where print jobs are sent to be serviced by a printer. The Queue object has the Access-Control List, Back Link, Bindery, Common Name (CN), Description, Device, Host Resource Name, Host Server, Locality, Network Address, Object Class, Operator, Organization (O), Organizational Unit (OU), Queue Directory, See Also, Server, User, and Volume selectable properties in Novell Directory Services (NDS).

See also **leaf object; Novell Directory Services; object.**

queue operator

A NetWare user who has rights to manage all jobs in a queue. The queue operator can view information about the queue and jobs in the queue, place a print job on hold, release the print job from a hold, determine the date and time a job prints, and delete a print job.

queue polling time

Another term for **queue sampling interval**.

queue sampling interval

A time period the print server waits between checking the print queues for jobs that are ready and waiting to be printed.

See also **print queue; print server.**

queue server mode

An operating mode found on network-direct printers and hardware queue servers that allows the device to directly access the print queue.

queue services

Services that allow applications to create and manipulate queues for controlling jobs and services on the network.

queue user

A NetWare user who can place his or her own print jobs on hold, release the print jobs from a hold, determine the date and time jobs are to be printed, and delete print jobs.

queuing delay

A time period that data must wait before transmission onto a statistically multiplexed physical circuit.

queuing theory

Scientific principles applied to the formation or lack of formation of network congestion or congestion at an interface.

QuickDraw printer

A type of printer used with a Macintosh printer that does not have PostScript capabilities.

QuickTime

An architecture developed by Apple Computer that works with time-based data types (such as sound and video) to synchronize multiple tracks of sound and pictures. QuickTime is a common data format that can be created on one type of computer and played back on another. Versions are available for both Macintosh and Windows.

QuickTime plug-in

A plug-in from Apple Computer, Inc. for Netscape Navigator-compatible World Wide Web (WWW) browsers, that displays movies in Apple's cross-platform QuickTime format. This plug-in is available for both Windows and Macintosh environments.

See also **Netscape Navigator; QuickTime.**

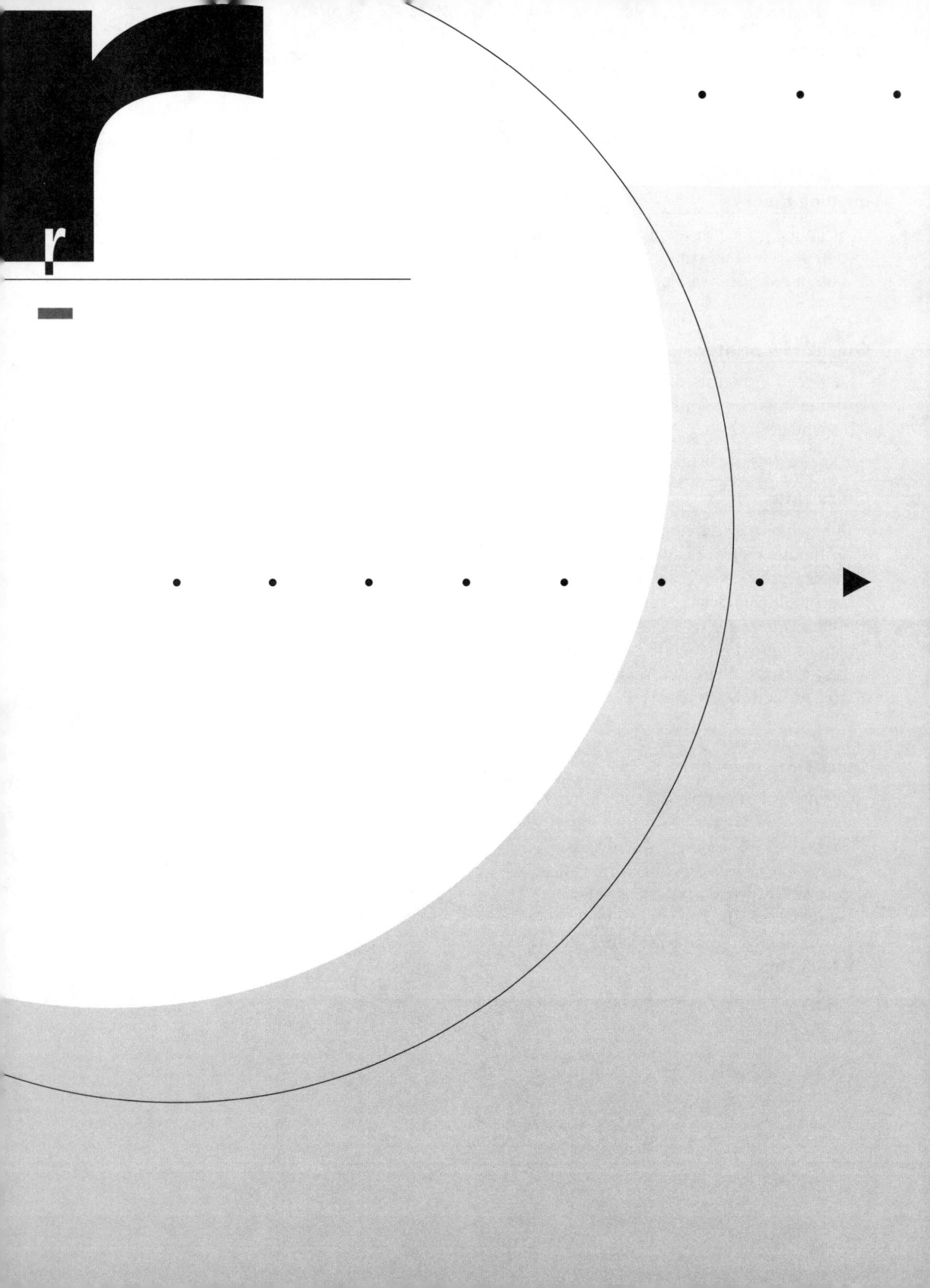

RACE

Research and Development Program in Advanced Communications in Europe, a project that explores the development of broadband networking capabilities in Europe.

rack-mount server

A motherboard installed in a large rack to provide power to several computers and that supports symmetric multiprocessing. A rack-mount server is often used in large network installations where many servers would clutter limited space.

radio button

A round button in a graphical utility that represents a selection option and, when selected, appears on the monitor display screen as a darkened circle.

radio frequency (RF)

A generic reference to frequencies that respond to radio transmissions (such as Cable Television and broadband networks).

radio-frequency interference (RFI)

A noise source often caused by cordless telephones, intercoms, or electrical motors.

radio network

A wireless network in which communications are accomplished with single-frequency or spread-spectrum radio wave transmissions that are broadcast in all directions.

radio paging

The use of radio waves in a remote signaling process that involves contacting and activating a paging device that beeps when contacted.

RAID

Redundant Array of Inexpensive Drives, a disk-subsystem architecture combining two or more standard physical drives into a single logical drive to achieve data redundancy. This architecture is used to provide fault tolerance in the event that one or more drives fail.

See also **disk mirroring; disk striping; mirroring; RAID** (includes **Table R.3**).

RAM

Random-access memory, an internal dynamic storage area of a computer's memory that can be addressed by the operating system. This area of memory is used by programs and drivers to execute instructions and to hold data temporarily.

See also **memory; random-access memory** (includes **Table R.1**).

RAM chip

A semiconductor storage medium that can be either dynamic RAM (whose capacitors must have their electrical charge refreshed every millisecond) or static RAM (whose capacitors retain their charge as long as power is applied).

See also **random-access memory.**

RAM disk

An area of computer memory managed by a special device driver and used as a simulated disk with higher operating speed than a regular hard disk. Because random-access memory (RAM) is volatile, a RAM disk loses all its contents when power is turned off for the computer.

See also **random-access memory.**

random access

A process in which a storage device can go directly to a required memory address without having to read from the beginning each time data is requested. A random-access device reads information directly by accessing the appropriate memory address.

See also **sequential access.**

random-access memory (RAM)

An internal dynamic storage area of a computer's memory that can be addressed by the operating system. This area of memory is used by programs and drivers to execute instructions and to hold data temporarily. Table R.1 shows the three common types of RAM.

See also **memory.**

RARE

Réseaux Associés pour la Récherche Européenne, a consortium of European universities and research centers that promotes an advanced scientific telecommunications infrastructure.

RARP

Reverse Address-Resolution Protocol, a process that determines an Internet address from a Data-Link address in a Transmission-Control Protocol/Internet Protocol (TCP/IP) network. This process provides the reverse functionality of an Ethernet function in which a router determines an 8-bit Media-Access Control (MAC) or local Data-Link Layer (Layer 2 of the OSI Reference Model) address for a device with which it is attempting to communicate. The process of determining the local Data-Link address from an Internet address is known as *address resolution*.

See also **data link; IP address; OSI Reference Model; Transmission-Control Protocol/Internet Protocol.**

RAS

Remote-Access Services, a Windows NT service that provides limited wide-area networking (WAN) capabilities, such as remote access and packet routing. Types of WAN connections supported by RAS include Integrated-Services Digital Networks (ISDNs), modems, and X.25 links.

See also **Integrated-Services Digital Network; Windows NT; X.25.**

RBHC

Regional Bell Holding Company, one of seven telephone companies created after the divestiture of AT&T in 1984 and that crosses state lines.

See also **Regional Bell Holding Company** (includes **Figure R.1**).

Table R.1: Types of RAM

Type	Abbreviation	Description
Dynamic RAM	DRAM	Must be periodically refreshed.
Static RAM	SRAM	Retains contents as long as power is supplied.
Video RAM	VRAM	Provides memory for graphics processing or temporary image storage.

RBOC

Regional Bell Operating Company, one of seven telephone companies created after the divestiture of AT&T in 1984. Each RBOC exists within the boundaries of only one state.

RC5 encryption algorithm

A secret-key encryption algorithm using a variable-length key and relying heavily on data-dependent rotations of bit values for its encoding method. This algorithm uses separate algorithms for expanding the secret key, performing encryption, and performing decryption.

RCGI

Remote Common-Gateway Interface, a feature that allows the NetWare Web Server to modify Web pages before sending them to a browser.

RCONSOLE utility

In NetWare and IntranetWare, a workstation utility that allows a user to load and unload NetWare Loadable Modules (NLMs), execute console commands, and copy files to NetWare directories or to non-NetWare par-

titions during a remote console session. This utility does not, however, allow the user to transfer files from a server. Remote servers can be accessed on the same network (which is a direct connection) or through a modem or null modem cable (which is an asynchronous connection). The RCONSOLE utility can be executed from a local hard drive or from a network drive, and the user does not need Supervisor object rights to the remote server.

See also **NetWare Loadable Module.**

rcp

A command (**Remote Copy**) used on UNIX systems to copy files from one computer to another.

RDA

Remote Database Access, an Open Systems Interconnection (OSI) specification outlining remote access to databases located across a network.

See also **Open Systems Interconnection; remote access.**

RDN

Relative Distinguished Name, in NetWare or IntranetWare, a context from an object to another object in the Novell Directory Services (NDS) Directory tree.

See also **distinguished name; Novell Directory Services.**

read-after-write verification

A method used to ensure that data written to the hard disk matches the original data still residing in computer memory. If a match is made, the data is released from computer memory. If a match is not made, the hard disk block location is recognized as bad. In NetWare, Hot Fix then redirects the data to a good block location within the Hot Fix Redirection Area.

See also **Hot Fix feature.**

Read-Only (Ro) attribute

A NetWare file attribute producing a status flag indicating that no one can write to a file.

See also **attribute.**

Read-Only replica

A NetWare Directory replica used to view, but not modify, information about the Directory.

See also **NetWare Directory replica.**

Read right

A NetWare directory, file, and property right that grants a user the right to open and read directories and files, as well as the right to read the values of a property.

See also **access rights.**

Read Write (Rw) attribute

A NetWare file attribute producing a status flag indicating that a file can be read or modified.

See also **attribute.**

Read/Write replica

A NetWare Directory replica used to read or update information about the Directory (such as adding or deleting objects).

See also **NetWare Directory replica.**

ReadBind

A NetWare Loadable Module (NLM) Behavior Testing utility used to view the contents of a file server's bindery and that verifies the bindery objects are properly implemented.

README file

A text file included on disks from a software manufacturer that contains important information about the software (such as last-minute information not included in the software documentation).

read-only

A file mode that allows viewing the contents of the file but does not allow a user to insert, update, or delete any information.

read-only memory (ROM)

Computer memory chips whose contents can be executed and read but cannot be changed. Table R.2 shows four types of ROM.

Table R.2: Types of ROM

Type	Abbreviation	Description
Electronically Erasable Programmable ROM	EEPROM	Old data is erased by writing over it.
Erasable Programmable ROM	EPROM	Old data is erased by shining ultraviolet light on the chip.
Programmable ROM	PROM	Can be programmed once, but cannot be changed after programming.
Mask ROM	MROM	Programmed during manufacturing and cannot be changed.

See also **memory.**

real mode

A mode on computers with an Intel 80286, 80386, or 80486 microprocessor that allows the computer to emulate a computer with an 8086 microprocessor. While an 8086 microprocessor uses a 20-bit address bus and can address up to 1MB of memory, the 80286, 80386, and 80486 microprocessors are capable of multitasking and addressing more than 1MB of memory. While running in real mode, the 80286, 80386, and 80486 microprocessors become subject to the same 8086 memory constraints and are able to process only one task at a time.

See also **80286; 80386; 80486; memory.**

real-time

Describes a computer system that generates output almost simultaneously with corresponding inputs.

RealAudio

A technology and set of World Wide Web (WWW) browser plug-in products from Progressive Networks that delivers audio clips, broadcasts audio events, and produces audio-enhanced Web pages over the Internet.

See also **Web browser; World Wide Web.**

For more information about RealAudio, surf the Web to `http://www.realaudio.com.`

reassembly

The putting back together of a datagram message at the destination after it has been fragmented either at the source or at an intermediate node.

reboot

The process of restarting a computer and reloading the operating system.

rec (recreation)

A suffix on an Internet address that indicates the address belongs to a subject group including mainstream sports, culture, and entertainment. However, this Internet hierarchy can contain more exotic topic areas that may be unsuitable for younger users.

See also **Internet address.**

rec newsgroup

A type of newsgroup that discusses recreational topics.

See also **newsgroup.**

Receive Data (RXD)

As defined by the RS-232-C standard, a hardware signal that carries data from one device to another.

See also **RS-232-C.**

Receive Only (RO)

A setting that indicates a device can receive transmission data but cannot transmit any data.

receive pacing

Pacing the rate at which a component is receiving information.

Received Up To

A NetWare Directory Schema term in Novell Directory Services (NDS).

receiver

The one of three major communications system components designed to capture or store transmission data and then convert it to visual or acoustic form. The other two major components in a communications system are a transmitter and a communications channel.

Receiver Ready packet

A control packet sent to Data-Terminal Equipment (DTE) that indicates a receiving DTE is ready for a call.

See also **control packet; Data-Terminal Equipment.**

reconfiguration burst

A special bit pattern transmitted repeatedly over an Attached-Resource Computer Network (ARCnet) whenever a node wants to force the creation of a new token or when a new node is added to the network.

See also **Attached-Resource Computer Network (ARCnet).**

record

A set of logically associated data items in a database, usually the unit transferred between an application and a database-management system (DBMS). A record is often a collection of database fields.

See also **database; database-management system; field.**

record locking

A NetWare operating system feature that prevents different users from gaining simultaneous access to the same record in a shared file. This feature prevents overlapping disk writes in a multiuser environment.

Record Manager

A Btrieve feature that maintains records in a data file. A server-based Record Manager in Btrieve resides at the server and handles data input/output with the file system. A client-based Record Manager in Btrieve resides at the workstation and handles data input/output with the file system through operating system calls.

See also **Btrieve.**

rectifier

A device designed to convert alternating current (AC) into direct current (DC).

recursion

The capability of a programming language subroutine to call itself.

recursive

A term used to describe commands or routines that call themselves.

recursive copying

A process that copies a specified source directory to a destination directory in a manner that keeps all directories and files exactly as they were on the source logical drive. Utilities that incorporate recursive copying include XCOPY and BACKUP in DOS and OS/2, as well as NCOPY in NetWare.

See also **NCOPY utility.**

Red Book

A term used to describe the telecommunications standards published by the Consultative Committee for International Telegraphy and Telephony (CCITT) in 1985. Also, a term used to describe the National Security Agency's "Trusted Network Interpretation" companion to the Orange Book.

See also **Consultative Committee for International Telegraphy and Telephony; Orange Book.**

red box

A package containing the standard U.S. format English version of Novell products.

redirect

A process in the Internet Control-Message Protocol (ICMP) or the End-System-to-Intermediate-System (ES-IS) protocol that enables a router to tell a host to use another router for better effectiveness.

See also **End-System-to-Intermediate-System; Internet Control-Message Protocol.**

redirection

A diversion of data or other signals from a default or intended destination to a new destination.

redirection area

A space on a hard disk set aside for the Hot Fix feature to send data redirected from faulty disk blocks. The redirection area is also known as the *Hot Fix Redirection Area.*

See also **Hot Fix feature.**

redirection reference

A mapping of a logical device name (such as LPT1) to a network printer that makes it possible for an application that is not network-aware to send print jobs to a network printer.

See also **LPT1.**

redirector

A networking program that intercepts requests from another program or from a user and directs them to the appropriate environment. NetWare DOS Requester is an example of a redirector.

See also **NetWare DOS Requester.**

redistribution

The process of allowing routing information from one routing protocol to be distributed in update messages from another routing protocol.

Reduced-Instruction-Set Computing (RISC)

A type of microprocessor chip that recognizes usually fewer than 128 assembly-language instructions and is commonly used in workstations because it can be designed to run faster than a Complex-Instruction-Set-Computing (CISC) chip.

See also **Complex-Instruction-Set Computing.**

redundancy

Either a duplicate capacity used when a failure occurs, or having more than one path to a signal point.

Redundant Array of Inexpensive Drives (RAID)

A disk-subsystem architecture combining two or more standard physical drives into a single logical drive to achieve data redundancy. This architecture is used to provide fault tolerance in the event that one or more drives fail. Table R.3 shows the different levels of RAID architecture.

See also **disk mirroring; disk striping; mirroring.**

Redwood

A proposed networking environment from Banyan Systems for extended enterprise networks, based in part on StreetTalk and Intelligent Messaging (Banyan's existing networking tools).

reentrant

A program technique allowing one copy of a program to be loaded into memory and shared with another program. Reentrant code often used in operating system service routines (so that only one copy of the code is needed) and in multithreaded applications (where different events take place concurrently in the computer).

See also **multithreading.**

Reference

In Novell Directory Services (NDS), a selectable property for the External Entity, List, Message-Routing Group, and Messaging Server objects.

See also **leaf object; Novell Directory Services; object.**

Reference time server

A NetWare server responsible for providing a time to which all other time servers and workstations synchronize.

See also **time server.**

referential integrity (RI)

An assurance that when a Structured Query Language (SQL) field in one table references a field in another table, changes to these fields will be synchronized.

TABLE R.3: RAID Architecture Levels

Level	Description
RAID 0	This level (which incorporates data striping, disk spanning, or bit interleaving) includes data written block by block across each drive, or data blocks written to the next available disk.
RAID 1	This level (which incorporates disk mirroring or disk duplexing) includes two hard disks of equal capacity that duplicate the contents of one another.
RAID 2	This level (which incorporates data striping or bit interleaving) includes bits written to different drives with checksum information written to special checksum drives.
RAID 3	This level (which incorporates data striping, bit interleaving, and parity checking) includes bits written to different drives and a single parity bit written to a parity drive.
RAID 4	This level (at which data striping, bit interleaving, and parity checking take place) includes data written to different drives, a single parity bit written to a parity drive, and an entire block (sector) of data written to each hard disk each time.
RAID 5	This level (which incorporates data striping, bit interleaving, and distributed parity) includes data written to different drives, an entire block (or sector) of data written to each hard disk each time, and parity data added to another sector.

See also **RI**; **Structured Query Language**.

refractive index

A measurement indicating the degree to which light travels at a different speed in a given medium. Refractive index is also known as *index of refraction*.

Regional Bell Holding Company (RBHC)

One of seven telephone companies created after the divestiture of AT&T in 1984 and that crosses state lines. Figure R.1 shows the geographic location of RBHCs across the United States.

Regional Bell Operating Company (RBOC)

One of seven telephone companies created after the divestiture of AT&T in 1984, each

of which exists within the boundaries of only one state.

register insertion

A media-access method in which a node that wants to transmit inserts a register (or a buffer) containing a packet into the data stream of a ring at an appropriate point in the stream. This method is used in older ring topologies, but has been replaced in newer ring networks with token passing.
See also **ring**; **ring topology**; **string**.

REGISTER MEMORY utility

In NetWare and IntranetWare, a server console utility that configures the operating system to recognize installed memory above

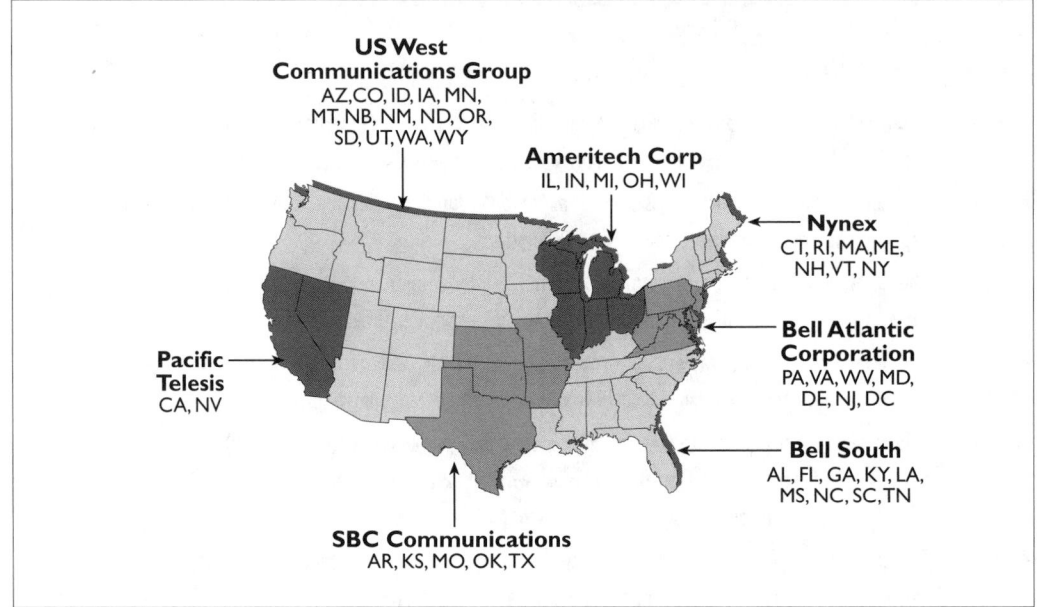

Figure R.1
RBHC locations

the amount of memory automatically registered. All memory is registered by NetWare and IntranetWare according to the bus type recognized by the system. For an Industry-Standard Architecture (ISA) bus, up to 16MB of memory is recognized. For an Extended Industry-Standard Architecture (EISA) or a Microchannel Architecture (MCA) bus, all the memory present is recognized. For a Peripheral-Component Interconnect (PCI) bus, up to 64MB of memory is recognized.

See also **Extended Industry-Standard Architecture; Industry-Standard Architecture; Microchannel Architecture; Peripheral-Component Interconnect.**

Registered Disk Adapters

In NetWare 3.12, a resource appearing in the Available Options/Resource Utilization screen of the MONITOR NetWare Loadable Module (NLM) that tracks configuration options of disk drivers (such as interrupts, memory addresses, input/output ports, slots, and Direct Memory Addresses).

See also **MONITOR; NetWare Loadable Module.**

Registered Hardware Options

In NetWare 3.12, a resource appearing in the Available Options/Resource Utilization screen of the MONITOR NetWare Loadable Module (NLM) that tracks local-area network (LAN) drivers that request interrupts, memory addresses, input/output port, slots, and Direct Memory Addresses (DMAs).

See also **LAN driver; MONITOR; NetWare Loadable Module.**

Registered MLID Boards

In NetWare 3.12, a resource appearing in the Available Options/Resource Utilization screen of the MONITOR NetWare Loadable Module (NLM) that tracks the number of local-area network (LAN) drivers that have been loaded and ensures that a LAN driver's resources are returned to the operating system when the driver is unloaded.

See also **LAN driver; MONITOR; NetWare Loadable Module.**

registered resources

Network resources that can be monitored and managed by a management software program designed to work with NetWare Management Agent. The registration process involves key software, hardware, and data components identifying themselves to the NetWare Management Agent.

See also **NetWare Management Agents.**

regulation

A power-conditioning process (such as that used by an Uninterruptible Power Supply) that protects against blackouts and brownouts.

See also **power conditioning.**

REINITIALIZE SYSTEM utility

In NetWare 4.*x* and IntranetWare, a server console utility that enables configuration

changes made since the commands in the NETINFO.CFG file were executed. This utility compares the current NETINFO.CFG file with a previous version and, if it finds any new commands in the current file, executes those commands. This utility also informs any NetWare Loadable Module (NLM) registered with the Simple Network Management Protocol (SNMP) that it is executing these commands, which enables any NLM storing configuration information outside of NETINFO.CFG to know that configuration changes have taken place.

See also **NETINFO.CFG; NetWare Loadable Module; Simple Network-Management Protocol.**

relational database

A database model with data organized as a set of two-dimensional tables represented by rows (which represent records, or collections of information about a specific topic) and columns (which represent fields, or items that make up a record). Data in a relational database always appears from the point of view of the user.

Relative Distinguished Name (RDN)

In NetWare or IntranetWare, a context from an object to another object in the Novell Directory Services (NDS) Directory tree.

See also **distinguished name; Novell Directory Services.**

relay

An electrical switch designed to allow a small current to control a larger current.

relay point

A point in a packet-switching network at which packets or messages are switched to other circuits or channels.

relaying

One of two major functions of the Network Layer (Layer 3) of the OSI Reference Model that moves data between a source and destination along a path determined by a routing process. The other major function of the Network Layer is routing.

See also **OSI Reference Model.**

release timer

A device used by an exactly-once transaction under AppleTalk Transaction Protocol (ATP) to determine when to eliminate entries from its transactions list.

See also **AppleTalk Transaction Protocol; exactly-once transaction.**

reliability

A ratio of expected keep-alive packets to received keep-alive packets used as a routing metric. A high ratio indicates a reliable line.

See also **keep-alive packet.**

Reliable Transfer

A transfer mode in the OSI Reference Model that guarantees either that a message will be transmitted without error or that a user will be notified if the message could not be transferred without error.

See also **OSI Reference Model.**

Reliable-Transfer Service Element (RTSE)

An Application Service Element (ASE) in the Application Layer (Layer 7) of the OSI Reference Model that ensures that Protocol Data Units (PDUs) are transferred reliably between applications.

See also **Application Service Element; OSI Reference Model; Protocol Data Unit.**

Remaining Grace Login

In Novell Directory Services (NDS), a NetWare Directory Schema term and a selectable property for the User object.

See also **leaf object; Novell Directory Services; object.**

REMAPID (NLM)

In NetWare 4.*x* and IntranetWare, a NetWare Loadable Module (NLM) that assists the NETSYNC3 utility in handling password changes. This NLM is automatically loaded by NETSYNC3 on every NetWare 3.*x* server in the NetSync cluster and must remain loaded even after NETSYNC3 is unloaded so that users can continue to log in to the NetWare 3.*x* server.

See also **NetWare Loadable Module; NETSYNC3.**

REMIRROR PARTITION utility

A NetWare and IntranetWare server console utility that starts the remirroring of a logical partition. This utility is used only when automatic remirroring has ceased.

See also **mirroring; disk partition.**

REMOTE (NLM)

A server console NetWare Loadable Module (NLM) that allows remote access to the NetWare server from a workstation. REMOTE must be loaded on the server before the RCONSOLE utility can be used to access a server from a workstation. The execution of REMOTE establishes a password that must be entered when RCONSOLE is executed at the workstation.

See also **NetWare Loadable Module; RCONSOLE utility.**

remote access

Access to network resources that are not physically located on the same site network topology.

Remote-Access Services (RAS)

A Windows NT service that provides limited wide-area networking (WAN) capabilities, such as remote access and packet routing. Types of WAN connections supported by RAS include Integrated-Services Digital Networks (ISDNs), modems, and X.25 links.

See also **Integrated-Services Digital Network; Windows NT; X.25.**

remote boot

A method in which NetWare uses a remote image file to boot a diskless workstation (a client workstation that does not need a floppy or hard drive to function on the network). The diskless workstation relies on a Programmable Read-Only Memory (PROM) chip installed in its Network Interface Card (NIC) to communicate with the boot server.

See also **Network Interface Card; Remote Program Load.**

remote bridge

A bridge connecting physically disparate network nodes on a wide-area network (WAN).

See also **bridge.**

Remote Common-Gateway Interface (RCGI)

A feature that allows the NetWare Web Server to modify Web pages before sending them to a browser.

remote computing

Computing performed from a remote location by way of either a remote node (where a user dials in through an access server and becomes another node on the network) or remote control (where a user dials in from a remote location to access his or her own computer).

remote connection

A connection (often utilizing a telephone line and modems) between a local-area network (LAN) on one end and a workstation (or other network) on the other end. Because no network cabling is involved, a remote connection can often cover great distances.

Remote Console

Novell software that enables a network supervisor to manage servers from a workstation. The software is invoked using the RCONSOLE utility.

See also **RCONSOLE utility; remote console management.**

remote-console management

The ability of a NetWare network supervisor to manage servers from a workstation by using console commands as if the supervisor were at the server console; scanning directories and editing text files in both NetWare and non-NetWare partitions on a server; transferring files to (but not from) a server; shutting down a server; or installing or upgrading NetWare on a remote server. Remote-console management is accomplished by using the RCONSOLE utility.

See also **RCONSOLE.**

Remote Database Access (RDA)

An Open Systems Interconnection (OSI) specification outlining remote access to databases located across a network.

See also **Open Systems Interconnection; remote access.**

remote dialback

A security feature available on networks that have dial-in access.

remote digital-loopback test

A modem capability allowing an entire circuit to be tested.

See also **loopback.**

Remote File Service (RFS)

A Distributed File System (DFS) network protocol allowing computer programs to use network resources as though they were local services.

See also **Distributed File System.**

Remote Job Entry (RJE)

The transmission of data and commands from a remote location to a centralized host computer to facilitate processing.

Remote Network Monitoring (RMON)

A proposed standard for the use of remote monitors, designed to supplement network-management information obtained and used in the Simple Network-Management Protocol (SNMP), particularly by providing functions for getting information about operation and performance of entire networks (or subnetworks) on an internetwork.

See also **Simple Network-Management Protocol.**

remote node

A form of remote access on Internet Protocol (IP) and Internetwork Packet Exchange (IPX) networks in which a device dials in to the network and acts like a peer on the target network.

See also **Internet Protocol; Internetwork Packet Exchange.**

Remote-Operations Service Element (ROSE)

In the Application Layer (Layer 7) of the OSI Reference Model, an Application Service Element (ASE) that supports interactive cooperation between two applications. An application that requests the association is known as an *initiator* (or an *invoker*) and that responding to the request is known as the *responder* (or *performer*). Once an association is established, the applications must agree on one of the following five operation classes: Class 1 (for synchronous interactions) reports both success and failure; Class 2 (for asynchronous interactions) reports both success and failure; Class 3 (for asynchronous interactions) reports only failures; Class 4 (for asynchronous interactions) reports only successes; and Class 5 (for asynchronous interactions) reports neither successes nor failures. In addition, the applications must agree on one of the following three association classes: Class 1 indicates only the initiator can invoke operations; Class 2 indicates only the responder can invoke operations; Class 3 indicates either the initiator or the responder can invoke operations. Although ROSE provides a mechanism to enable applications to cooperate, it does not provide a means for carrying out the actual operations.

See also **Application Service Element; OSI Network-Management Model; OSI Reference Model.**

Remote Password Generator (RPG)

A device that generates a unique password each time a user logs in to a network by using a special number created by the network and the user's Personal Identification Number (PIN).

See also **password; Personal Identification Number.**

remote printer

A NetWare network printer not directly attached to a network server, but attached instead to a workstation or directly to the network.

remote-printer mode

An operating mode for network-direct printers or hardware queue servers that are connected to a printer and then to the network

(or are installed in a port at the printer) to function in a manner similar to a workstation running the NetWare 4.*x* NPRINTER or NetWare 3.*x* RPRINTER utilities. Devices configured for remote printer mode are then controlled by a NetWare print server.

See also **NPRINTER; RPRINTER utility.**

Remote Procedure Call (RPC)

A mechanism allowing a procedure on one computer to be used in a transparent manner by a program running on another computer.

Remote Program Load (RPL)

A process in which an image of a bootable floppy disk is stored on a NetWare volume so that remote boot workstations can use the image to start up at the system prompt. A Programmable Read-Only Memory (PROM) chip in the Network Interface Card (NIC) of the workstation allows the workstation to communicate with the boot server. When the workstation is started, it uses the boot image to load the DOS system and the NetWare Client files required to connect to the network.

See also **Network Interface Card; remote boot.**

Remote Reset

A Novell software program that allows a user to boot a DOS workstation from a remote boot image file on a NetWare server. To use Remote Reset, a user must install a Remote Reset Programmable Read-Only Memory (PROM) chip on the workstation's Network Interface Card (NIC) and then run the DOSGEN utility, which then uploads the workstation boot files into a remote image file in the server's LOGIN directory.

See also **DOSGEN utility; Network Interface Card; remote boot.**

remote resource

Any device available through the network even though it is not attached to a local node.

Remote Server Sessions

In NetWare 3.12, a resource appearing in the Available Options/Resource Utilization screen of the MONITOR NetWare Loadable Module (NLM); the resource tracks the number of remote servers that have at least one remote connection.
See also **MONITOR; NetWare Loadable Module.**

remote server support

A function on a NetWare server that provides a NetWare Loadable Module (NLM) with the ability to access other servers on the network.
See also **NetWare Loadable Module.**

Remote Source-Route Bridging (RSRB)

A process of sending a packet over a wide-area network (WAN) route that has been predetermined entirely in real time prior to the sending of the packet.

remote terminal

A terminal geographically located away from a network, usually connected to the network by way of a modem and telephone line.

remote transaction program

A partner transaction program that uses a remote logical unit (LU) in a Systems Network Architecture (SNA) network.
See also **logical unit; Systems Network Architecture; transaction program.**

remote user

A user who is geographically located away from a network and who accesses the network by way of a modem and telephone line.

remote workstation

A stand-alone computer or a workstation that connects to a local-area network (LAN) by a router or through a remote asynchronous connection.

remote-control program

A program that provides an interface between two computers so that when they are linked together (by way of a serial cable, modem-to-modem communication link, or network connection), one computer can control the operation of the other computer. Each computer runs a copy of the remote-control program.

REMOVE DOS utility

A NetWare and IntranetWare server console utility that removes DOS from server memory and causes the server to be cold booted with the EXIT command. This utility frees additional memory for file caching when available memory on the server is low because the memory for DOS is returned to the operating system. The REMOVE

DOS utility allows those who are using RCONSOLE to reboot the server remotely.
See also **memory; RCONSOLE.**

REMOVE utility

A NetWare 3.*x* workstation utility that deletes a user or group from the trustee list of a file or directory. To remove a user or group from the trustee list of a file or directory on a server, a user must be attached to the file server and must have the Access-Control right in that directory.
See also **rights; trustee rights.**

Rename Inhibit (Ri) attribute

A NetWare directory and file attribute producing a status flag that prevents any user from renaming the directory or the file.
See also **attribute.**

Rename right

A NetWare object right that grants a user the right to change the name of an object (which, in effect, changes the naming of the property).
See also **access rights.**

RENDIR utility

A NetWare and IntranetWare workstation utility that allows users to rename a directory.

repeater

A device functioning at the Physical Layer (Layer 1) of the OSI Reference Model that indiscriminately passes all signals from one network segment to another and recondi-

tions the signal to extend the distance between two hosts.
See also **OSI Reference Model.**

replacement variable

Variables entered in batch files that are replaced by defined parameter values entered in the command line when the batch file is executed.
See also **batch file.**

replica

A copy of a NetWare Directory partition that provides a means for storing the NetWare Directory database (NDD) on several servers across the network without having to duplicate the entire database for each server. An unlimited number of replicas can be created for each Directory partition and can be stored on any server. Directory replicas eliminate a single point of failure on the network and provide faster access to information across a wide-area network (WAN) link.
See also **NetWare Directory database.**

replica synchronization

A process that ensures replicas of the NetWare Directory partition contain the same information as other replicas of that partition.
See also **NetWare Directory partition; NetWare Directory replica.**

repudiation

A denial by either a sending node that a network transmission message was sent or by a receiving node that a network transmission message was received.

Request for Comments (RFC)

A procedure in the Internet community that involves the submission of a series of documents containing protocol descriptions, model descriptions, and experimental results for review by experts.

See also **Appendix F; Internet.**

For more information about RFCs, surf the Web to http://www.uwaterloo.ca/ uw_infoserv/rfc.html.

Request To Send (RTS)

A hardware signal sent from a potential transmission sender to a destination and that indicates the transmitter is ready to send a transmission. The receiver sends a Clear To Send (CTS) signal when it is ready to receive the transmission. These signals are used in the Carrier-Sense Multiple-Access/Collision Avoidance (CSMA/CA) method commonly used in LocalTalk networks.

See also **Carrier-Sense Multiple-Access/Collision Avoidance; Clear To Send; LocalTalk.**

Request/Response Header (RH)

Control information that precedes a Request/Response Unit (RU), that specifies the type of RU, and that contains control information associated with that RU.

See also **Request/Response Unit.**

Request/Response Unit (RU)

A message unit containing such control information as a request code, function-management headers, end-user data, or a combination of these types of information.

requester

A workstation program that passes requests from an application to a server-based application.

Require a Password

A NetWare Directory Schema term and a selectable property for the User object in Novell Directory Services (NDS).

See also **leaf object; Novell Directory Services; object.**

Require a Unique Password

A selectable property for the User object in Novell Directory Services (NDS).

See also **leaf object; Novell Directory Services; object.**

Require Unique Passwords

A NetWare Directory Schema term.

Research and Development Program in Advanced Communications in Europe (RACE)

A project that explores the development of broadband networking capabilities in Europe.

Réseaux Associés pour la Réchérche Européenne (RARE)

A consortium of European universities and research centers that promotes an advanced scientific telecommunications infrastructure.

reservation protocol

A communications protocol that enables a network node to assume exclusive control of a channel for a limited period of time.

reserved memory

The area of DOS memory between 640K and 1MB used to store system and video information. Reserved memory is also known as *upper memory*.

See also **memory.**

reserved word

A designated word or term in a programming language or operating system reserved for particular functions or operations. A reserved word is also known as a *keyword*.

Reset Interval

A selectable property for the Organizational Unit (OU) object in Novell Directory Services (NDS).

See also **container object; Novell Directory Services; object.**

Reset request packet

A control packet sent to Data-Terminal Equipment (DTE) to request the resetting of a virtual call.

See also **Data-Terminal Equipment.**

RESET ROUTER utility

In NetWare and IntranetWare, a server console utility that resets the router table in the server if the table has become inaccurate or corrupted in some way. A router updates the routing table on a preset periodic basis; by contrast, this utility resets the router table immediately.

See also **router; routing table.**

residual error

A communication error that occurs or survives despite the presence of a system error-correction mechanism.

resistance

A conducting medium's degree of opposition to the flow of electricity in a circuit.

resource

Any of a variety of manageable components of a network. Table R.4 shows some examples of NetWare network resources.

Resource

A NetWare Directory Schema term and a selectable property for the following objects in Novell Directory Services (NDS): AFP Server, Messaging Server, NCP Server, and Print Server.

See also **leaf object; Novell Directory Services; object.**

resource fork

Part of a Macintosh file that contains file resources, including Macintosh-specific information (such as the windows and icons used with the file). The resource fork is one of two parts of a Macintosh file, with the other one being the *data fork*.

See also **data fork.**

Table R.4: NetWare Network Resources

Resource Type	Examples
Networking components	Cabling, hubs, concentrators, adapters, Network Interface Cards (NICs)
Hardware components	Servers, workstations, hard disks, printers
Major software components	NetWare operating system, file services, mail services, queue services, communications services
Minor software components	Protocols, gateways, disk drivers, local-area network (LAN) drivers (controlled by the operating system)
Data structures	Volumes, queues, users, processes, security

Resource object

An object class in Novell Directory Services (NDS) that identifies the logical resources available on the network.

See also **logical unit.**

resource tag

Operating-system tags used to ensure that allocated NetWare server resources (such as screens and allocated memory) are properly returned to the operating system upon termination of a NetWare Loadable Module (NLM). The NLM requests a resource from the NetWare server for each kind of resource it uses and then assigns it a resource tag name.

See also **NetWare Loadable Module.**

Resource Utilization

In NetWare 4.02, a field name appearing in the Available Options screen of the MONITOR NetWare Loadable Module (NLM).

See also **MONITOR; NetWare Loadable Module.**

responder

A socket client in AppleTalk Transaction Protocol (ATP) that performs a service for a requester and sends a TResp packet as notification that the service was performed.

See also **AppleTalk Transaction Protocol; requester.**

response mode

A communications mode in which a device receives a call and must respond to the call.

response time

The amount of time elapsing between sending a network transmission request and actually receiving the data.

response unit

A response by a logical unit (LU) to one or more request units that indicates the successful receipt of data or indicates an error condition.

See also **logical unit.**

responsible LU

A logical unit (LU) that deactivates a session when it is no longer being used by two LUs for a conversation.

See also **logical unit.**

Restart Request packet

A control packet sent to Data-Terminal Equipment (DTE) to request the restarting of a virtual call.

See also **Data-Terminal Equipment.**

RESTART SERVER utility

In NetWare 4.*x* and IntranetWare, a server console utility that restarts a server, which is useful when troubleshooting procedures require the server to be frequently shut down.

RESTART utility

In NetWare 4.*x* and IntranetWare, a server console utility that reloads the IOEngine on one NetWare System Fault Tolerance III (SFT III) server (while leaving the other server running), or forces a server to switch over from primary to secondary status. This utility only works when the SFT III servers have been properly *mirrored*, and can only be run from the appropriate IOEngine.

See also **IOEngine; mirroring; System Fault Tolerance.**

restore

To retrieve data previously copied or backed up to a storage medium.

resynchronization

A NetWare process in which servers that comply with System Fault Tolerance III (SFT III) are returned to a mirrored (identical) state. *Mirroring* is the process of duplicating data from the NetWare partition on one hard-disk drive (a *primary server*) to the NetWare partition on another hard disk drive (a *secondary server*). When a primary server fails, the secondary server takes over. When both servers are restored to operation, they resynchronize memory images and mirror disks automatically. Both servers are continually polling each other so that each server is aware of the state of the other server. If a server runs in an unmirrored state, it searches for a partner. When it detects a partner on the other end of a mirrored server link, it automatically attempts to synchronize with the other server and return to a mirrored state.

See also **fault tolerance; mirroring; partition.**

retry count

A number that represents how many requests the Network Basic Input/Output System (NetBIOS) transmits for connections, or how many failed communications it retransmits.

See also **Network Basic Input/Output System.**

return (reflection) loss

A value expressed as a ratio in decibels (dB) that indicates the amount of a signal lost because it is reflected back toward the sender.

return band

A one-directional, Frequency-Division Multiplexing (FDM) channel over which a remote device responds to a central controller.

See also **Frequency-Division Multiplexing.**

return code

A code returned by Advanced Program-to-Program Communications (APPC) to the issuer of a verb to indicate the results of the execution of that verb.

See also **Advanced Program-to-Program Communications.**

Return to Zero (RZ)

A self-clocking method of signal-encoding; RZ involves voltage returning to a neutral (or zero) state halfway through each bit interval.

Return-to-Zero Inverted (RZI)

An inverted version of Return-to-Zero (RZ) in which 1 and 0 are exchanged in the signal descriptions.

Reverse Address-Resolution Protocol (RARP)

A process that determines an Internet address from a Data-Link address in a Transmission-Control Protocol/Internet Protocol (TCP/IP) network. This process provides the reverse functionality of an Ethernet function in which a router determines an 8-bit Media-Access Control (MAC) or local Data-Link Layer (Layer 2 of the OSI Reference Model) address for a device with which it is attempting to communicate. The process of determining the local Data-Link address from an Internet address is known as *address resolution.*

See also **data link; IP address; OSI Reference Model; Transmission-Control Protocol/Internet Protocol.**

reverse charging

A facility specified in a Call-Request packet by the calling Data-Terminal Equipment (DTE). Reverse charging is the equivalent of a collect telephone call.

See also **Call-Request packet; Data-Terminal Equipment.**

Revision

A NetWare Directory Schema term and a selectable property for the External Entity, List, Message-Routing Group, and Messaging Server objects in Novell Directory Services (NDS).

See also **leaf object; Novell Directory Services; object.**

REVOKE utility

In NetWare 3.*x*, a workstation utility that revokes trustee rights from a user or group in a file or a directory. A user must be attached to a file server before revoking trustee rights in a file or directory on that server, and must have Access Control rights in that file or directory. Only one user or one group can have trustee rights revoked with each invocation of the REVOKE utility.

See also **rights; trustee rights.**

RF

radio frequency, a generic reference to frequencies that respond to radio transmissions (such as Cable Television and broadband networks).

RFC

Request for Comments, a procedure in the Internet community that involves the submission of a series of documents containing protocol descriptions, model descriptions, and experimental results for review by experts.

See also **Appendix F; Internet; Request for Comments** (includes **Smart Link**).

RFI

Radio-frequency interference, a noise source often caused by cordless telephones, intercoms, or electrical motors.

RFS

Remote File Service, a Distributed File System (DFS) network protocol allowing computer programs to use network resources as though they were local services.

See also **Distributed File System.**

RH

Request/Response Header, control information that precedes a Request/Response Unit (RU), that specifies the type of RU, and that contains control information associated with that RU.

See also **Request/Response Unit.**

RI

(1) referential integrity, an assurance that when a Structured Query Language (SQL) field in one table references a field in

another table, changes to these fields will be synchronized.
(2) Ring Indicator, a signal that indicates an incoming call.

See also **(1) Structured Query Language; (2) Ring In/Ring Out.**

RI/RO

Ring In/Ring Out, a port through which a Token Ring Multistation Access Unit (MAU) can be connected (Ring In) and a port through which the MAU can be connected to another MAU (Ring Out).

See also **Multistation Access Unit; Token Ring.**

ribbon cable

A type of cable, typically used for connecting internal disks or tape drives, that has wires placed side-by-side in the insulation material rather than twisted together inside a circular insulation.

See also **cable.**

RIF

Routing-Information Field, a field that appears in the header of a packet that complies with the 802.5 standard set by the Institute of Electronic and Electrical Engineers (IEEE). The RIF is used by a source-route bridge to determine through which Token Ring network segments a packet must transmit.

See also **802.5; IEEE 802.x; Institute of Electronic and Electrical Engineers; Token Ring.**

rights

Qualities that determine what a Novell Directory Services (NDS) object can do with directories, files, other objects, or properties of objects. An object can only perform operations if it has the rights to perform those operations, which are granted to a specific directory, file, or object by *trustee assignments*. Each object has a list of who has rights to the object and what rights the object has to other objects. *Directory rights* apply to the NetWare file system directory (as well as subdirectories within the directory) and are considered part of the file system. *File rights* only apply to the file to which they are assigned. A trustee must have the Access-Control right to a directory or file to grant directory or file rights to other objects. *Object rights* apply to NDS objects, but do not affect the properties of an object. *Property rights* apply to the properties of an NDS object. A trustee must have the Write, Add Self, Delete Self, or Supervisor right to the Access Control List property of the object to grant object or property rights to other objects.

Table R.5 provides a list of IntranetWare rights, what type of rights are available, and a brief description of the right.

See also **access rights.**

RIGHTS utility

A NetWare and IntranetWare workstation utility that allows a user to view or modify user or group rights for files, directories, and volumes.

rightsizing

Matching the goals of a corporation with the available computing and networking solu-

tions to maximize business effectiveness in reaching that goal.

ring

The attachment of network nodes in a closed loop with data being transmitted from node to node around the loop, always in the same direction.

ring group

A collection of Token Ring interfaces on one or more routers in a bridged Token Ring network.

See also **Token Ring.**

Ring In/Ring Out (RI/RO)

A port through which a Token Ring Multistation Access Unit (MAU) can be connected (Ring In) and a port through which the MAU can be connected to another MAU (Ring Out).

See also **Multistation-Access Unit; Token Ring.**

Ring Indicator (RI)

A signal that indicates an incoming call.

ring latency

In a network that complies with Token Ring topology or with the 802.5 standard set by Institute of Electronic and Electrical Engineers (IEEE), the amount of time required for a signal to propagate once around a ring.

See also **802.5; IEEE 802.x; Institute of Electronic and Electrical Engineers; ring; Token Ring.**

ring monitor

A centralized management tool used on Token Ring or Institute of Electronic and Electrical Engineers (IEEE) 802.5 networks.

See also 802.5; IEEE 802.x; Institute of Electronic and Electrical Engineers; Token Ring.

Table R.5: IntranetWare Rights

Right	Type	Description
Access Control	Directory, File	Grants the right to change the trustee assignments and Inherited Rights Filter (IRF) of a directory or file.
Add Self	Property	Grants a trustee the right to add itself as a value of the property.
Browse	Object	Grants the right to see an object in the Directory tree.
Compare	Property	Grants the right to compare any value to a value of the property.
Create	Directory, File, Object	Grants the right to create a directory, file, or object, or to salvage them after they have been deleted.
Delete	Object	Grants the right to delete the object from the Directory Tree.
Delete Self	Property	Grants a trustee the right to remove itself as a value of the property.
Erase	Directory, File	Grants the right to erase (or delete) a file or directory.
File Scan	Directory, File	Grants the right to see a directory (including its files and subdirectories) or a file.
Modify	Directory, File	Grants the right to change the attributes or name of a directory (including its files and subdirectories) or file.
Read Property	Property	Grants the right to read the values of the property.
Read	Directory, File, Property	Grants the right to open and read a directory, file, or property.
Rename	Object	Grants the right to change the name of an object.
Supervisor	Directory, File, Object, Property	Grants all rights to directories, files, objects, and properties.
Write	Directory, File, Property	Grants the right to add, change, or remove any values of the directory, file, or property.

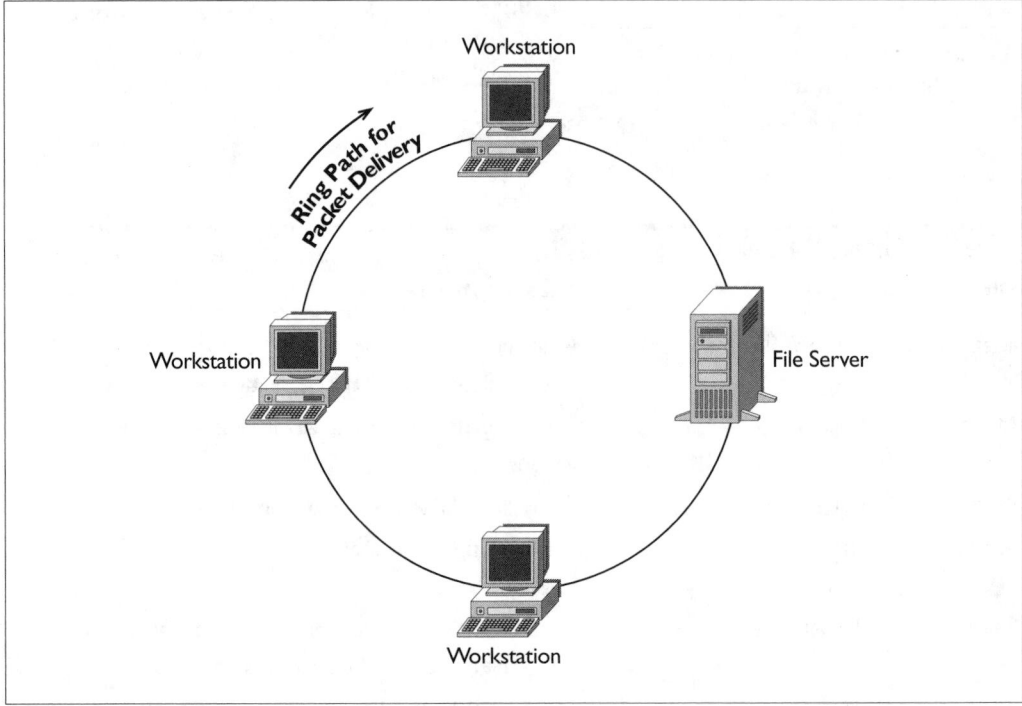

Figure R.2
Ring topology

See also **star-wired ring topology; Token Ring.**

ring topology

A network topology that has the characteristics of a logical topology (packets are transmitted sequentially from node to node in a predefined order) and a physical topology (each node is connected to two other nodes). In a ring topology, nodes are positioned in a closed loop. Information is transmitted on a one-way path around the loop so that a node receives packets from exactly one other node, a node transmits packets to exactly one other node, and the initiating node is the last to receive a packet. Each node in the ring can act as a repeater, thus capable of boosting a transmission signal before passing it along. Cable requirements are minimal for a ring topology. However, if one node fails, the entire ring fails and, because communication is one-way, diagnosing or troubleshooting problems becomes difficult.

Figure R.2 shows an example of ring topology.

RIP

Routing-Information Protocol, a routing protocol in which routers use routing tables to determine the most cost-efficient route (the route involving the fewest hops) to a destination. RIP routers periodically broadcast messages that contain routing update information about each network it can reach, and the cost (or the number of hop counts) to reach that network. The routing update information is kept in the routing table that includes the ultimate destination, the next hop on the way to that destination, and a metric (which indicates the distance in number of hops to the destination). The router that sent the routing update message is considered the next router (or hop) on the route to the network. A router determines the destination route on the basis of the fewest hop counts needed to reach the destination. As changes occur to the network (such as topology changes), a new route to a destination may prove to be more cost-efficient. Thus, the routing tables are constantly updated and routers always choose the most efficient route to a destination. TCP/IP allows a maximum of 15 hop counts to reach a destination.

See also **RIP (IPX); RIP (TCP/IP); RIP II (TCP/IP).**

RIP (IPX)

NetWare's implementation of the Routing-Information Protocol (RIP) with Internet Packet Exchange (IPX) protocol.

See also **Routing-Information Protocol.**

RIP (TCP/IP)

A distance-vector gateway protocol for Transmission-Control Protocol/Internet Protocol (TCP/IP) networks in which routers determine and use the most efficient routes to nodes on the network. The TCP/IP Routing-Information Protocol (RIP) router

periodically broadcasts messages that contain routing update information about each network it can reach, and the cost (or the number of hop counts) to reach that network. The routing update information is kept in the routing table, with the router that sent the routing update message being remembered as the next router (or hop) on the route to the network. A router determines the destination route on the basis of the fewest hop counts needed to reach the destination. TCP/IP allows a maximum of 15 hop counts to reach a destination.

See also **RIP II.**

RIP II (TCP/IP)

A Routing-Information Protocol (RIP) enhancement that includes the subnetwork mask in its routing information. RIP is not able to advertise information about subnetworks, so routers are limited to advertising only networking (and not subnetworking) routes. RIP II can support subnets, and can be used in those network topologies requiring variable-length subnet masks.

See also **RIP (TCP/IP).**

RISC

Reduced-Instruction-Set Computing, a type of microprocessor chip that recognizes usually fewer than 128 assembly-language instructions. Commonly used in workstations, it can be designed to run faster than a Complex-Instruction-Set-Computing (CISC) chip.

See also **Complex-Instruction-Set Computing.**

rise time

A time increment that an electrical signal takes to go from 10 percent of its level to 90 percent, which is used when setting the upper limit on the maximum transmission speed supported by the signal.

See also **fall time.**

riser cable

Cable strung vertically, such as in an elevator shaft of a building. Because such areas can be a source of electrical interference, optical fiber is usually the cable of choice for riser cables.

Rivesi, Shamir, Adleman (RSA) Algorithm

A patented public-key encryption algorithm that bears the name of its inventors.

RJ-*xx*

A modular connection mechanism that allows for up to eight wires dedicated to carry different signals. Table R.6 shows the three most common types of RJ-*xx* mechanisms.

RJ-*xx* connector

A connector for RJ-*xx* mechanisms that catches and locks a plug (the male component) in place with an overhanging element in the jack (the female component) connector.

Table R.6: RJ-*xx* Types

Type	Description
RJ-11	A four-wire (two-pair) connection with the two central wires being tip (green wire) and ring (red wire) lines.
RJ-12	A six-wire (three-pair) connection that uses the same-sized plug (male component) and jack (female component).
RJ-45	An eight-wire (four-pair) connection commonly used for data transmission over unshielded twisted-pair (UTP) cable and leased-line telephone connections.

RJE

Remote Job Entry, the transmission of data and commands from a remote location to a centralized host computer to facilitate processing.

RLL

run-length-limited, an encoding scheme used to store information on a hard disk that effectively doubles the hard disk's storage capacity in contrast with older schemes such as Modified Frequency Modulation (MFM).

See also **Modified Frequency Modulation.**

rlogin

A remote login service found on Berkeley Software Distribution (BSD) UNIX operating systems comparable to the Internet's Telnet service.

See also **Berkeley Software Distribution UNIX.**

RMON

Remote Network Monitoring, a proposed standard for the use of remote monitors, designed to supplement network-management information obtained and used in the Simple Network-Management Protocol (SNMP), particularly by providing functions for getting information about operation and performance of entire networks (or subnetworks) on an internetwork.

See also **Simple Network-Management Protocol.**

RMS

(1) Root Mean Square, a value associated with Alternating Current (AC) voltage as it is actually measured. This value can be calculated by multiplying the peak voltage in the circuit by 0.070707.
(2) *RMS*, a portion of the Digital Electronics Corporation (DEC) operating system that handles files.

RO

Receive Only, a setting that indicates a device can receive transmission data but cannot transmit any data.

roamer

A cellular telephone user who uses services in multiple calling areas during the course of one call.

robot

A program that automatically performs a task ordinarily performed by a person. A mailbot is an example of a type of robot.
See also **mailbot.**

Role Occupant

A selectable property for the Organizational Unit (OU) object in Novell Directory Services (NDS).
See also **container object; Novell Directory Services; object.**

roll-back

The database process of aborting a transaction and undoing all changes made to a file during the transaction. Roll-back restores a file to the state it was in prior to the transaction.

roll-forward

The database process of re-creating data in the database by rerunning all the transactions listed in a transaction log.

roll-in

The process of transferring data from an auxiliary memory to the computer's central memory.
See also **memory.**

ROM

read-only memory, computer memory chips whose contents can be executed and read but cannot be changed.
See also **read-only memory** (includes **Table R.2**).

ROM BIOS

Software that provides routines to perform basic input/output (I/O) operations on an IBM or IBM-compatible computer.

root bridge

A device appointed by a spanning tree to determine which managed bridges to block in the spanning tree topology.
See also **spanning tree.**

root directory

In a hierarchical directory structure, the highest directory level. In NetWare, the root directory is the volume.

Root Mean Square (RMS)

A value associated with Alternating Current (AC) voltage as it is actually measured. This value can be calculated by multiplying the peak voltage in the circuit by 0.070707.
See also **RMS.**

[Root] object

A Novell Directory Services (NDS) container object that provides the highest point of access to different Country and Organization objects, and allows trustee assignments granting rights to the entire NetWare Directory tree. The Country, Organization, and Alias objects can be created at the [Root] object. The [Root] object is merely a placeholder that contains no information.
See also **container object; Novell Directory Services; object.**

ROSE

Remote-Operations Service Element, in the Application Layer (Layer 7) of the OSI Reference Model, an Application Service Element (ASE) that supports interactive cooperation between two applications. An application that requests the association is known as an *initiator* (or an *invoker*) and that responding to the request is known as the *responder* (or *performer*). Once an association is established, the applications must agree on one of the following five operation classes: Class 1 (for synchronous interactions) reports both success and failure; Class 2 (for asynchronous interactions) reports both success and failure; Class 3 (for asynchronous interactions) reports only failures; Class 4 (for asynchronous interactions) reports only successes; and Class 5 (for asynchronous interactions) reports neither successes nor failures. In addition, the applications must agree on one of the following three association classes: Class 1 indicates only the initiator can invoke operations; Class 2 indicates only the responder can invoke operations; Class 3 indicates either the initiator or the responder can invoke operations. Although ROSE provides a mechanism to enable applications to cooperate, it does not provide a means for carrying out the actual operations.
See also **Application Service Element; OSI Network-Management Model; OSI Reference Model.**

Round-Trip Time (RTT)

The total amount of time required for a network communication to travel from the source to the destination and back, including the amount of time required to process the message at the destination and generate a reply. Routing algorithms sometimes use RTT in calculating the most efficient route.

route

A path through an internetwork that determines which computers are accessible from other computers across the network.

route discovery

A process that determines the possible routes on a source-routing network from the source to a destination node.

route extension

A Systems Network Architecture (SNA) path from the destination subarea node through peripheral equipment to a network addressable unit (NAU).

See also **network-addressable unit; Systems Network Architecture.**

ROUTE utility

In NetWare and IntranetWare, a server console utility that passes frames from NetWare through IBM-compatible source route bridges on a Token Ring network. This utility enables the operating system to track and configure source routing information.

See also **source routing; Token Ring.**

routed protocol

A protocol for which a router understands the logical internetwork as perceived by the protocol in order for the router to route that protocol.

router

A workstation or NetWare server that runs software to manage the exchange of information between network cabling systems. A NetWare router, which runs on a NetWare server, connects separate network cabling topologies or separate networks by way of the server's NetWare operating system. By default, NetWare automatically routes Internet Packet-Exchange/Sequenced Packet-Exchange (IPX/SPX) packets, although it can be enabled for nonrouting Transmission-Control Protocol/Internet Protocol (TCP/IP) and AppleTalk protocols. The two types of routers are a *local router*, which is used within the cable limitations of a local-area network (LAN) driver, and a *remote router*, which is connected beyond its driver limitations or through a modem.

Figure R.3 shows an example of a router.

See also **routing; Routing-Information Protocol; routing metric; routing table.**

Router-Discovery Protocol

A feature of the Transmission-Control Protocol/Internet Protocol (TCP/IP) suite that allows hosts to find routers on locally attached networks and that alleviates the need to configure hosts with a routing table or a default router.

See also **routing table; Transmission-Control Protocol/Internet Protocol.**

router screen

A screen display activated when the NetWare TRACK ON server console utility is invoked.

See also **TRACK ON utility.**

routing

The process of moving information (in the form of data packets) across an internetwork from source to destination. This process occurs at the Network Layer (Layer 3) of the OSI Reference Model and can be contrasted to *bridging*, which occurs at the Data-Link Layer (Layer 2). Routing involves the determination of the most efficient routing path and the transport of packet information through the network. Routing algorithms use *metrics* (such as hop counts, or path lengths) to determine the optimal path to a destination and store routing

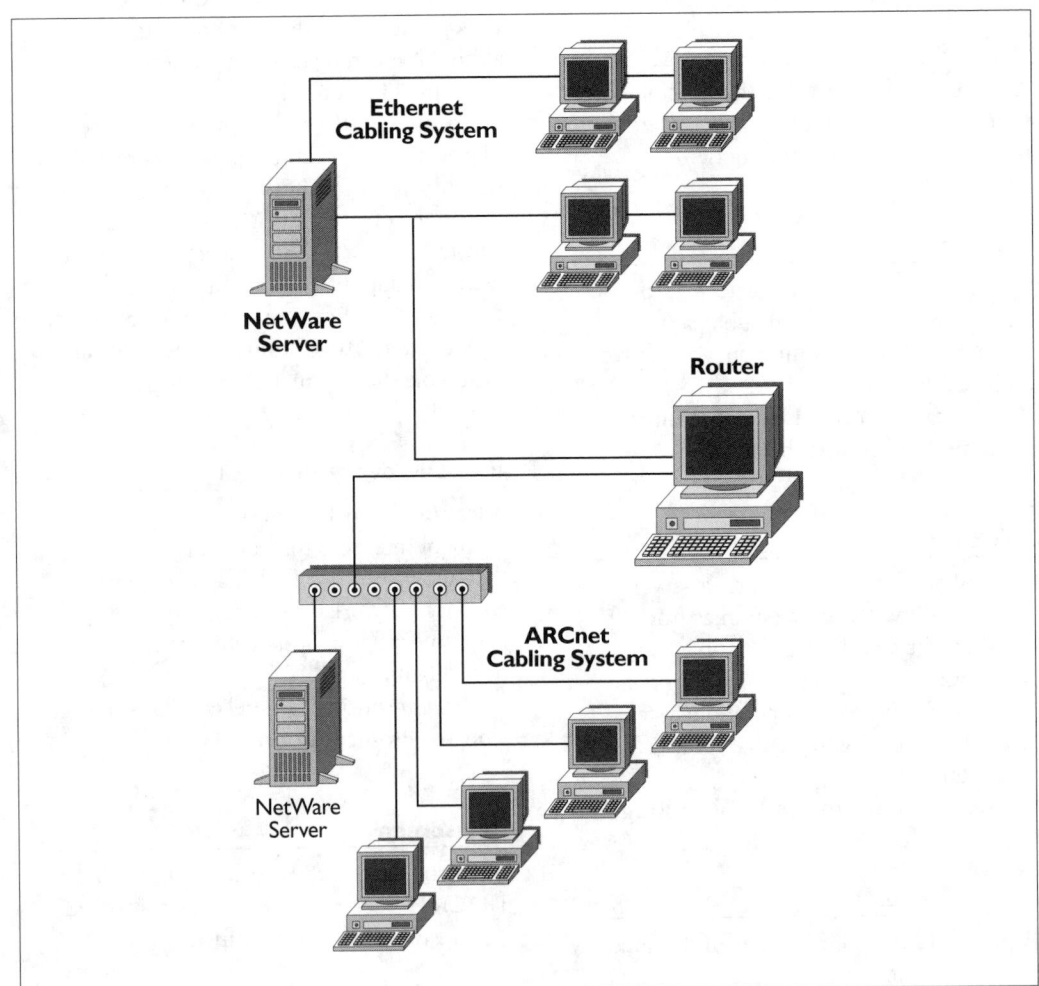

Figure R.3
Router

information in *routing tables*. These tables help to determine the optimal path to a destination. Transportation of the packet is accomplished by determining the address of the destination and sending the packet to that destination address.

See also **router; Routing-Information Protocol; routing metric; routing table.**

routing area

An administrative domain of Internetwork Packet Exchange (IPX) networks that all have the same area address. The routing area provides users with access to services in the Network Layer (Layer 3) of the OSI Reference Model.

See also **Internet Packet Exchange; OSI Reference Model.**

routing bridge

A bridge used on the Media-Access Control (MAC) sublayer of the Data-Link Layer (Layer 2) of the OSI Reference Model that uses methods from the Network Layer (Layer 3) to determine the topology of a network.

See also **OSI Reference Model.**

routing buffer

A portion of NetWare file server random-access memory (RAM) used as a temporary storage area of packets until they can be processed by the server or sent on to the network. The routing buffer is also known as a *communication buffer*.

See also **random-access memory.**

routing domain

A collection of routing areas that are connected by level 2 routers. Routers within the same domain communicate by way of a common intradomain routing protocol known as an *Interior Gateway Protocol* (IGP), such as Intermediate System-to-Intermediate System (IS-IS) protocol. Routers in different domains communicate by way of a common interdomain routing protocol known as an *Exterior Gateway Protocol* (EGP), such as the IS-IS Interdomain Routing Protocol (IDRP).

See also **Exterior-Gateway Protocol; Interior-Gateway Protocol; Intermediate-System-to-Intermediate-System; IS-IS Interdomain Routing Protocol; level-2 routing; routing area.**

Routing-Information Field (RIF)

A field that appears in the header of a packet that complies with the 802.5 standard set by the Institute of Electronic and Electrical Engineers (IEEE). The RIF is used by a source-route bridge to determine through which Token Ring network segments a packet must transmit.

See also **802.5; IEEE 802.x; Institute of Electronic and Electrical Engineers; Token Ring.**

routing-information filter

A filter designed to restrict the exchange of routing information between routers to provide more network security and to reduce network bandwidth consumed by the periodic exchange of routing information between routers.

Routing-Information Protocol (RIP)

A routing protocol in which routers use routing tables to determine the most cost-efficient route (the route involving the fewest hops) to a destination. RIP routers periodically broadcast messages that contain routing update information about each network it can reach, and the cost (or the number of hop counts) to reach that network. The routing update information is kept in the routing table that includes the ultimate destination, the next hop on the way to that destination, and a metric (which indicates the distance in number of hops to the destination). The router that sent the routing update message is considered the next router (or hop) on the route to the network. A router determines the destination route on the basis of the fewest hop counts needed to reach the destination. As changes occur to the network (such as topology changes), a new route to a destination may prove to be more cost-efficient. Thus, the routing tables are constantly updated and routers always choose the most efficient route to a destination. TCP/IP allows a maximum of 15 hop counts to reach a destination.

See also **RIP (IPX); RIP (TCP/IP); RIP II (TCP/IP).**

Routing-Information Table

A table that contains information (such as network numbers, routes to a particular destination, and metrics that are associated with those routes) that a router uses to determine the best possible route to use to forward packets to destinations.

See also **router; routing metric; Routing-Information Protocol.**

routing metric

A measurement that determines the preference between two routes generated by the same protocol to the same destination. Metric information includes reliability, delay, bandwidth, load, Maximum-Transmission Units (MTUs), communications costs, and hop count.

See also **hop count; Maximum-Transmission Unit.**

routing protocol

A protocol that uses a special routing algorithm and Routing-Information Tables to enable the routing of packets from source to destination.

routing table

Another term for **Routing-Information Table.**

Routing-Table Maintenance Protocol (RTMP)

An AppleTalk routing protocol in the Transport Layer (Layer 4) of the OSI Reference Model that provides for the moving packets between networks. RTMP was derived from the Routing-Information Protocol (RIP).

See also **AppleTalk; OSI Reference Model; Routing-Information Protocol.**

Routing-Table Protocol (RTP)

A routing protocol used in Banyan Virtual Network System (VINES) networks that includes delay as a part of the Routing-Information Table.

See also **Virtual Networking System.**

routing update

A message sent by a router at prescribed intervals of time to indicate network reachability and associated cost information.
See also **Routing-Information Protocol.**

RPC

Remote Procedure Call, a mechanism allowing a procedure on one computer to be used in a transparent manner by a program running on another computer.

RPG

Remote Password Generator, a device that generates a unique password each time a user logs into a network by using a special number created by the network and the user's Personal Identification Number (PIN).
See also **password; Personal Identification Number.**

RPL

(1) **Remote Program Load,** a process in which an image of a bootable floppy disk is stored on a NetWare volume so that remote-boot workstations can use the image to start up at the system prompt. A Programmable Read-Only Memory (PROM) chip in the Network Interface Card (NIC) of the workstation allows the workstation to communicate with the boot server. When the workstation is started, it uses the boot image to load the DOS system and the NetWare Client files required to connect to the network.
(2) **RPL (NLM),** in NetWare 4.*x* and IntranetWare, a server console NetWare Loadable Module (NLM) that enables remote booting of diskless workstations that have Network Interface Cards (NICs) installed. This NLM provides the Remote Program Load protocol (RPL) stack to the server.
See also (1) **Network Interface Card;** (1) **remote boot;** (2) **NetWare Loadable Module;** (2) **Network Interface Card;** (2) **Remote Program Load.**

RPL (NLM)

In NetWare 4.*x* and IntranetWare, a server console NetWare Loadable Module (NLM) that enables remote booting of diskless workstations that have Network Interface Cards (NICs) installed. This NLM provides the Remote Program Load protocol (RPL) stack to the server.
See also **NetWare Loadable Module; Network Interface Card; Remote Program Load.**

RPRINTER utility

In NetWare 3.*x*, a server console utility that connects a remote printer to or disconnects a remote printer from a print server.
See also **print server; remote printer.**

RS/6000

A set of 32-bit chips used in IBM Reduced-Instruction-Set Computing (RISC) workstations that features a superscalar design with four separate 16K data-cache units and an 8K instruction cache. Together with Apple and Motorola, IBM developed a single-chip version of the RS/6000 called the *PowerPC.*
See also **Reduced-Instruction-Set Computing; PowerPC.**

RS232 (NLM)

In NetWare and IntranetWare, a server console NetWare Loadable Module (NLM) that sets up a communication port for remote management over a modem or null-modem cable. This NLM is an asynchronous communications driver.

See also **NetWare Loadable Module.**

RS-232-C

A recommended standard interface from the Electronic Industries Association (EIA) that defines electrical, functional, and mechanical characteristics of asynchronous transmissions between Data-Terminal Equipment (DTE) and a peripheral device. The RS-232-C is a 25-pin or 9-pin DB connector.

See also **Data-Terminal Equipment; Electronic Industries Association; pinout.**

RS-422

A recommended standard interface from the Electronic Industries Association (EIA) that defines electrical and functional characteristics of balanced serial interface, but does not specify a connector. The RS-422 is used on the serial port of a Macintosh computer.

See also **Electronic Industries Association.**

RS-423

A recommended standard interface from the Electronic Industries Association (EIA) that defines electrical and functional characteristics of unbalanced serial interface, but does not specify a connector.

See also **Electronic Industries Association.**

RS-449

A recommended standard interface from the Electronic Industries Association (EIA) that defines electrical, functional, and mechanical characteristics of synchronous transmissions in a serial binary data interchange. The RS-449 is a 37-pin or 9-pin DB connector.

See also **Electronic Industries Association.**

RS-485

A recommended standard interface from the Electronic Industries Association (EIA) that defines electrical and functional characteristics of balanced serial interface, but does not specify a connector. The RS-485 uses tri-state drivers rather than the dual-state drivers found in the RS-422, and is used in multipoint applications.

See also **Electronic Industries Association.**

RS-530

A recommended standard interface from the Electronic Industries Association (EIA) that defines electrical and functional characteristics of serial binary data transmission, either synchronously or asynchronously. The RS-530 uses a 25-pin DB connector.

See also **Electronic Industries Association.**

RSA

The **Rivesi, Shamir, Adleman Algorithm,** a patented public-key encryption algorithm that bears the name of its inventors.

RSPX (NLM)

In NetWare and IntranetWare, a server console NetWare Loadable Module (NLM) that allows the RCONSOLE utility to access a server over a direct connection by loading the Sequenced Packet Exchange (SPX) driver and advertising the server to the workstation.

See also **NetWare Loadable Module; RCONSOLE utility; Sequenced Packet Exchange.**

RSRB

Remote Source-Route Bridging, a process of sending a packet over a wide-area network (WAN) route that has been predetermined entirely in real time prior to the sending of the packet.

RTDM (NLM)

In NetWare for Macintosh Real-Time Data Migration (RTDM), a NetWare Loadable Module (NLM) that copies a Macintosh CD-ROM file to a NetWare volume.

See also **NetWare for Macintosh.**

RTEL

A "reverse Telnet" software package from Lantronix that allows a host using Transmission-Control Protocol/Internet Protocol (TCP/IP) to establish a session with a device attached to a terminal server port.

See also **Transmission-Control Protocol/Internet Protocol.**

 **For more information about Lantronix products, surf the Web to** http://www.lantronix.com/htmfiles/prodinfo/prodhome.htm.

RTMP

Routing-Table Maintenance Protocol, an AppleTalk routing protocol in the Transport Layer (Layer 4) of the OSI Reference Model that provides for the moving packets between networks. RTMP was derived from the Routing-Information Protocol (RIP).

See also **AppleTalk; OSI Reference Model; Routing-Information Protocol.**

RTP

Routing-Table Protocol, a routing protocol used in Banyan Virtual Network System (VINES) networks that includes delay as a part of the Routing-Information Table.

See also **Virtual Networking System.**

RTS

Request To Send, a hardware signal sent from a potential transmission sender to a destination and that indicates the transmitter is ready to send a transmission. The receiver sends a Clear To Send (CTS) signal when it is ready to receive the transmission. These signals are used in the Carrier-Sense Multiple-Access/Collision Avoidance (CSMA/CA) method commonly used in LocalTalk networks.

See also **Carrier-Sense Multiple-Access/Collision Avoidance; Clear To Send; LocalTalk.**

RTSE

Reliable-Transfer Service Element, an Application Service Element (ASE) in the Application Layer (Layer 7) of the OSI Reference Model that ensures that

Protocol Data Units (PDUs) are transferred reliably between applications.

See also **Application Service Element; OSI Reference Model; Protocol Data Unit.**

RTT

Round-Trip Time, the total amount of time required for a network communication to travel from the source to the destination and back, including the amount of time required to process the message at the destination and generate a reply. Routing algorithms sometimes use RTT in calculating the most efficient route.

RU

Request/Response Unit, a message unit containing such control information as a request code, function-management headers, end-user data, or a combination of these types of information.

RUB

A device jointly developed by Cisco Systems and SynOptics Communications that combines the capabilities of a **router** and a **hub.**

run-length-limited (RLL)

An encoding scheme used to store information on a hard disk that effectively doubles the hard disk's storage capacity in contrast with older schemes such as Modified Frequency Modulation (MFM).

See also **Modified Frequency Modulation.**

runt packet

A packet that has too few bits.

RXD

Receive Data, as defined by the RS-232-C standard, a hardware signal that carries data from one device to another.

See also **RS-232-C.**

RZ

Return to Zero, a self-clocking method of signal-encoding; RZ involves voltage returning to a neutral (or zero) state halfway through each bit interval.

RZI

Return-to-Zero Inverted, an inverted version of Return-to-Zero (RZ) in which 1 and 0 are exchanged in the signal descriptions.

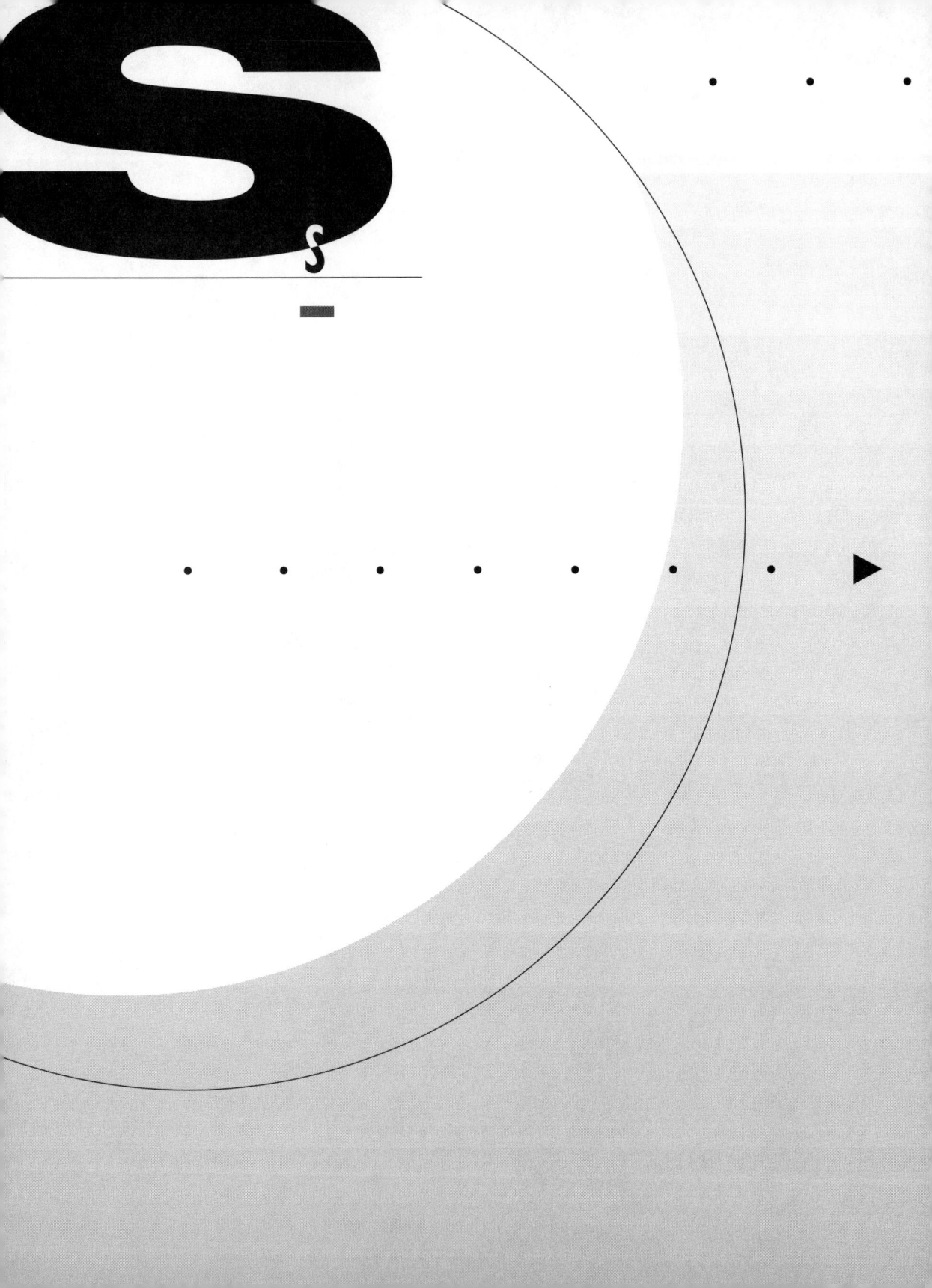

S

A selectable property for the following objects in Novell Directory Services (NDS): External Entity, Organization (O), Organizational Role, Organizational Unit (OU), and User.

See also **container object; leaf object; Novell Directory Services; object.**

SA

A selectable property for the following objects in Novell Directory Services (NDS): External Entity, Organization (O), Organizational Role, Organizational Unit (OU), and User.

See also **container object; leaf object; Novell Directory Services; object.**

SA

Source Address, a packet-header field whose value represents the address of the node sending the packet.

See also **Destination Address.**

SAA

Systems Application Architecture, a set of IBM standards introduced in 1987 that defines a set of interfaces (and protocols) for future IBM software. The three main components of SAA are *Common User Access* (CUA), which defines a graphical user interface (GUI) for products designed for object-oriented environments; *Common Programming Interface* (CPI), which includes application program interfaces (APIs) and Structured Query Language (SQL); and *Common Communications Support* (CCS), which provides a common set of communications protocols.

See also **Application Program Interface; graphical user interface; Structured Query Language; Application Architecture.**

SAC

(1) Simplified Access Control, access-control guidelines presented in the Consultative Committee for International Telegraphy and Telephony (CCITT) X.500 Directory Services model. **(2) Single-Attachment Concentrator,** a Fiber Distributed Data Interface (FDDI) network concentrator that serves as a termination point for a Single-Attachment Station (SAS) and that attaches to the FDDI network through a Dual-Attachment Concentrator (DAC).

See also **(1) Consultative Committee for International Telegraphy and Telephony; (2) Dual-Attachment Concentrator; (2) Fiber Distributed Data Interface; (2) Single-Attachment Station. (1) X.500;**

safety device

A device designed to protect network system hardware from drastic deviations or fluctuations in the electrical power supply.

sag

A drop in line voltage between 70 percent and 90 percent of the nominal voltage over a short period of time.

SALVAGE utility

In NetWare 3.x, a file utility that provides a view of all deleted files, recovers (or purges) files that have been erased from the workstation, and restores files to their original directories or to the DELETED.SAV directory. Every deleted file is stored in the directory from which it was deleted until the server needs disk space. Any salvaged file is restored (along with original trustee rights) to the directory from which it was deleted, unless that directory was deleted, in which case the file is restored to the DELETED.SAV directory.

salvageable files

NetWare files that have been deleted by users but are recoverable.

same-server migration

A method of using a single network server to upgrade a network to NetWare 4.x; a workstation hard disk temporarily holds bindery information.

Sampled Servo (SS)

A recording technique for compact discs in which the contents are stored on a single, spiral track.

SAP

(1) **Service-Access Point,** an interface between layers in the OSI Reference Model through which an entity at a particular layer can provide services to the processes at the layer above. SAPs, which are assigned by the Institute for Electrical and Electronic Engineers (IEEE), each have their own unique address that can also be used as the access point to the service's user (the entity at the next highest level). SAPs are often labeled according to the layer being discussed (for example, PSAP for the Presentation Layer, SSAP for the Session Layer, TSAP for the Transport Layer, NSAP for the Network Layer, DSAP for the Data-Link Layer, and PhSAP for the Physical Layer).

(2) **Service-Advertising Protocol,** a Novell protocol used by servers to advertise their services to the network, which allows routers to create and maintain a database of current internetwork server information. Routers broadcast SAP updates to all other routers on the network to keep all routers synchronized. Workstations broadcast SAP request packets to query the network to find a server.

See also **(1) OSI Reference Model; (2) router; (2) routing.**

SAP filtering

Under Service-Advertising Protocol (SAP), a scheme in which a user can filter multiple Novell Directory Service (NDS) objects by first finding a server and opening its bindery to reveal the names of more objects. This scheme helps to prevent the lists of servers and Directory trees from becoming too large, and also improves network security by not revealing all Directory trees and network servers.

See also **Novell Directory Services; Service-Advertising Protocol.**

SAP Name

In Novell Directory Services (NDS), a NetWare Directory Schema term and a selectable property for the Print Server object.

See also **leaf object; Novell Directory Services; object.**

SAPONET-P

A public packet-switching data network located in South Africa.

SAR

Segmentation and Reassembly, a process that involves segmenting data frames into Asynchronous Transfer Mode (ATM) cells at the transmitter and reassembling them into their original format at the receiver.

See also **Asynchronous Transfer Mode.**

SAS

Single-Attachment Station, a Fiber Distributed Data Interface (FDDI) network node that lacks the physical ports necessary to attach directly to both the primary and secondary rings on the network and that, instead, attaches to a concentrator.

See also **Fiber Distributed Data Interface.**

SATAN

Security-Analysis Tool for Auditing Networks, a set of networking-security tools that consists of Hypertext Markup Language (HTML) files, shell scripts, and programs written in the C programming language, Perl, and Expect. These programs are used to write additional HTML files that probe networks to determine a network's configuration (and weak points), probe network weaknesses to determine vulnerability, and generate a report. Because SATAN is readily available to both system administrators and to potential network intruders, its use has become controversial.

See also **SATAN** (includes **Smart Link**).

satellite communications

A communications process that relays signals from geostationary orbiting satellites to multiple Earth-based stations, offering a high-bandwidth, cost-efficient communications system with relatively long propagation and broadcast capabilities.

Saved Items pane

The lower pane in a Macintosh workstation monitor display, containing the entities and utilities represented in a session file.

SavvySearch search engine

A World Wide Web (WWW) metasearch engine that allows users to specify search terms and to have 10 to 50 results submitted from 23 different Web search engines.

See also **search engine; World Wide Web.**

SBACKUP (NLM)

In NetWare and IntranetWare, a server console NetWare Loadable Module (NLM) that backsup and restores specified data on a server or a workstation, or to a specified service.

See also **NetWare Loadable Module; Storage Management Services.**

SC

Subscriber Connector, a device that connects two components by plugging one connector into the other and that establishes a connection that must be broken (for example, by pressing a button or releasing a hatch). An SC works with either single-mode or multimode fiber.

Scalar Processor Architecture (SPARC)

A 32-bit Reduced-Instruction-Set-Computing (RISC) processor from Sun Microsystems, used in SPARCstation workstations.

See also **Reduced-Instruction-Set-Computing; SPARCstation.**

scaling

The process of adding more nodes to expand a network.

scan

In a NetWare context, the process by which NetWare for Macintosh copies a Directory tree from a compact disc to a NetWare volume on the server so that Macintosh workstations can display folders and files on the compact disc.

SCAN FOR NEW DEVICES utility

In NetWare 4.*x* and IntranetWare, a server console utility that registers new devices with the Media Manager (MM) so that they are available to the operating system. This utility is used after the server has been booted and when the devices that have been added do not appear with the LIST DEVICES command.

See also **Media Manager.**

scattering

A method of communication or of gathering information in which an intelligent fixed disk device controller issues multiple simultaneous requests to different drives connected to the same controller.

SCHDELAY (NLM)

In NetWare 4.*x* and IntranetWare, a server console NetWare Loadable Module (NLM) that sets priorities for server processes, schedules processes to use less of the server's central processing unit (CPU), and slows processes when the server is busy.

See also **NetWare Loadable Module.**

Scheduling Information

A field name that appears in the MONITOR NetWare Loadable Module (NLM) for NetWare 4.02.

See also **MONITOR; NetWare Loadable Module.**

schema

The rules that define how the Novell Directory Services (NDS) Directory tree is created, and how information is stored in the Directory database. The schema defines attribute information, inheritance, naming, and subordination. Attribute information concerns the different types of information that can be associated with an object. Inheritance specifies which objects can inherit the properties and rights of other objects, and naming determines the structure of the directory tree. Subordination determines the location of objects in the directory tree.

See also **Novell Directory Services.**

sci newsgroup

An Internet newsgroup that discusses scientific topics.

See also **newsgroup.**

SCR

Signal-to-crosstalk ratio, a ratio value representing the decibel level of a signal to the noise in a twisted-pair cable. The SCR is calculated specifically as the ratio between near-end crosstalk (NEXT) and the attenuation on a cable.

See also **near-end crosstalk.**

screen attributes

A set of attributes that determines the behavior of a screen.

screen-handling services

Services that make it possible to manage special features of the logical screen of a server, including the ability to create new screens with a variety of different attributes and the ability to manipulate the screen.

Screen Input Call-Backs

In NetWare 3.12, a resource appearing in the Available Options/Resource Utilization screen of the MONITOR NetWare Loadable Module (NLM) that tracks NLMs that use an alternate method for key input from a console screen. The TRACK ON utility uses this resource.

See also **MONITOR; NetWare Loadable Module; TRACK ON utility.**

screen names

Names for screens that can be specified by a NetWare linker directive file.

Screens

In NetWare 3.12, a resource appearing in the Available Options/Resource Utilization screen of the MONITOR NetWare Loadable Module (NLM) that tracks how many screens an NLM has created or opened on the file server console.

See also **MONITOR; NetWare Loadable Module.**

script

A small program invoked at a particular time, such as a login script or a macro program that contains commonly used or frequently used commands.

See also **Container login script; login script; Profile login script; System login script.**

scroll

To move text up or down on a screen display while reading it.

scroll bar

In a graphical utility, an on-screen bar beside a list box that enables the user to move up and down the list by clicking.

SCS

SNA Character Stream, a printing mode in the Systems Network Architecture (SNA)

model that provides various printing and formatting capabilities.

See also **Systems Network Architecture.**

SCSI

Small Computer System Interface, an industry standard outlining the interconnection of peripheral devices (such as hard disk drives and tape backup systems) and their controllers to a microprocessor. The standard defines both hardware and software specifications for communication between a host computer and a peripheral device. A large degree of compatibility between SCSI (pronounced "scuzzy") devices is common.

See also **SCSI bus; SCSI disconnect; SCSI terminator.**

SCSI bus

A Small Computer System Interface (SCSI) with a 50-pin connector (as opposed to an Integrated-Drive Electronics, or IDE, 40-pin connector) that connects Host Bus Adapters (HBAs) to controllers and hard disks. A SCSI bus requires the use of proper termination equipment and requires that proper addresses be used for all connected peripheral devices.

See also **Small Computer System Interface; SCSI terminator.**

SCSI disconnect

In NetWare, a feature of a Small Computer-System Interconnect (SCSI) driver that tells a disk to prepare for input/output (I/O) operations. The SCSI driver can send messages to other hard disks or perform I/O operations to other hard disks while the

disk is preparing for I/O. When the disk is ready, it sends a message back to the SCSI driver that it is ready to send or receive data. This signals the driver that the disk is ready for I/O and the driver then performs the I/O.

See also **Small Computer-System Interface.**

SCSI terminator

A device used in Small Computer System Interface (SCSI) connections that prevents signals from echoing on the SCSI bus.

See also **SCSI bus; Small Computer System Interface.**

SD

Start Delimiter, a field that appears in a Token Ring data or token packet.

See also **Token Ring.**

SDDI

Shielded Distributed Data Interface, a network configuration that uses *shielded twisted-pair (STP)* cabling for the Fiber Distributed Data Interface (FDDI) architecture and protocols.

See also **Fiber Distributed Data Interface; shielded twisted-pair cable.**

SDF

Sub-Distribution Frame, an intermediate wiring center connected by backbone cable to a Main Distribution Frame (MDF).

See also **Main Distribution Frame.**

SDI or SMSDI

storage-device interface, a set of routines that enables the NetWare SBACKUP utility to access various storage devices and media. In the event that more than one storage device is attached to the host, the SDI provides SBACKUP with a list of storage devices and media.

See also **SBACKUP.**

SDLC

Synchronous Data-Link Control, a protocol developed by IBM in the mid-1970s to support a variety of link types and topologies. SDLC can be used with point-to-point and multipoint links, bounded and unbounded media, half-duplex and full-duplex transmissions, and circuit-switched and packet-switched networks. SDLC identifies *primary* network nodes as those controlling the operation of other stations and *secondary* network nodes as those being controlled by a primary network node. These nodes can be placed in a *point-to-point configuration* (which involves only a primary and secondary node), a *multipoint configuration* (which involves one primary and multiple secondary nodes), a *loop configuration* (which involves a primary node connected to the first and last secondary nodes in a loop topology), and a *hub go-ahead configuration* (which involves the primary node using an outbound channel and the secondary nodes using an inbound channel).

SDSU

SMS Data-Service Unit, a data-service unit that provides access to Switched Multimegabit Data Service (SMDS) through a High-Speed Serial Interface (HSSI) or through some other serial interface.

See also **High-Speed Serial Interface; Switched Multimegabit Data Service.**

SDU

Service Data Unit, a packet passed as a service-request parameter from one layer in the OSI Reference Model to a layer below it.

See also **OSI Reference Model.**

search

A query of information on a network or in a database.

search algorithm

A search sequence used by NetWare workstation utilities to find and then load message files in DOS and Unicode messages in OS/2.

See also **search drive; SEARCH utility.**

search criteria

Values specified when making a search query that tell the network system or database to match the requested values.

search drive

A drive supported only from DOS workstations that the NetWare operating system searches when a requested file is not found in the current directory. This feature allows a user to access an application file or data located in a directory other than the current directory.

See also **drive mapping.**

search engine

A World Wide Web (WWW) location that uses search criteria specified by a user to compile a list of Web sites that mention words or phrases specified in the search criteria. Some search engines use Web robots to search through and index hypertext documents available on the WWW; others simply gather information available from indexes.

See also **robot; World Wide Web.**

search mode

A mode specifying how a program uses search drives when looking for a data file.

See also **search drive.**

search path

A list indicating to the operating system which directories to search if a requested program is not found in the current directory.

SEARCH utility

In NetWare and IntranetWare, a server console utility that provides a view of the current search paths for the operating system, adds or deletes search paths, and tells the server where to look for NetWare Loadable Module (NLM) files and NetWare configuration files (NCF).

See also **NCF file; NetWare Loadable Module.**

seat

Configuration of a telephone line, port, and telephone on a computer system.

second source

An alternative supplier for an identical piece of computer hardware.

secondary half-session

A half-session on a node that receives the session-activation request.

See also **half-session; primary half-session.**

secondary link station (SLS)

A link station (other than the primary link station) that can exchange data with a primary link station, but not with other secondary link stations.

See also **primary link station.**

secondary logical unit (SLU)

A logical unit (LU) containing the secondary half-session for a particular logical-unit-to-logical-unit (LU-LU) session.

See also **half-session; logical unit; secondary half-session.**

secondary server

Under NetWare System Fault Tolerance III (SFT III), a server that receives a mirrored copy of the memory and disk from the primary server (the first server activated on the system) and is activated after the primary server, and that splits multiple read requests with the primary server. Unless it is on the same network segment as the primary server, the secondary server acts as a router for the local network segments to which it is directly attached. If it is on the same network segment as the primary server, the secondary server does not perform any routing. The designation of primary server versus secondary server is handled by the system. When the primary server fails, the secondary server becomes the new primary server. When the failed server is restored, it becomes the new secondary server.

See also **mirroring; primary server.**

Secondary time server

A NetWare server that provides the time to workstations after it has received the time from a Single-Reference, Primary, or Reference time server.

See also **Primary time server; Reference time server; Single-Reference time server.**

second-level files

Files that are opened at the stream level with the *fopen, fdopen,* and *freopen* commands.

See also **first-level files.**

secret-key encryption

A data-encryption scheme used to encrypt and decrypt messages in which a single key is known only to the sender or receiver.

sector

A subdivision of a track on a hard-disk drive. Figure S.1 shows hard-disk sectors.

SECURE CONSOLE utility

In NetWare and IntranetWare, a server console utility that increases network security by preventing NetWare Loadable Modules (NLMs) from being loaded from any directory other than SYS:SYSTEM, preventing keyboard entry into the operating system debugger, and preventing the server date and time from being changed. Unless the SECURE CONSOLE utility is used, an NLM can be loaded from a DOS partition, a diskette drive, or any directory on a

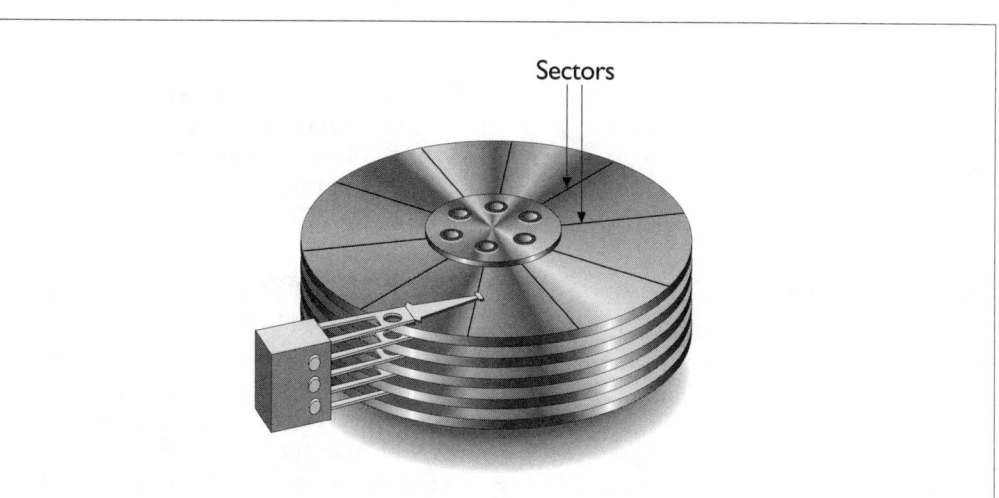

Sectors

Figure S.1
Hard-disk sectors

NetWare volume, which means that anyone having access to the server console could load an NLM.

See also **NetWare Loadable Module.**

Secure Electronic Transactions (SET) protocol

A protocol developed by VISA and MasterCard that allows for credit card transactions to be conducted across the Internet.

Secure-Sockets Layer (SSL) protocol

A protocol designed by Netscape Communications that provides for encrypted authenticated communications across the Internet between World Wide Web (WWW) browsers and servers. A Uniform Resource Locator (URL) that begins with *http* indicates an SSL connection. With an SSL connection, each side is required to have a Security Certificate, the information from which is used to encrypt a message. This ensures that only the intended recipient can decode the message, that the message has not been tampered with, and that the message did indeed originate from the source that it claims to have come from.

See also **Security Certificate; Uniform Resource Locator; World Wide Web; Web browser.**

secure transmission

An exchange of messages that has the assurance that the message was sent by the person or system it claims to be and that has the assurance that only the intended recipient can read the message. A secure transmission mode is common on many Web browsers.

See also **Secure-Sockets Layer protocol; Web browser.**

security

Elements in NetWare and IntranetWare that control access to the network or to specific information on the network. Security can be classified into the six categories shown in Table S.1

Security-Analysis Tool for Auditing Networks (SATAN)

A set of networking-security tools that consists of HyperText Markup Language (HTML) files, shell scripts, and programs written in the C programming language, Perl, and Expect. These programs are used to write additional HTML files that probe networks to determine a network's configuration (and weak points), probe network weaknesses to determine vulnerability, and generate a report. Because SATAN is readily available to both system administrators and to potential network intruders, its use has become controversial.

 **For more information about SATAN, surf the Web to** `http://www.fish.com/ satan.`

Security Certificate

Information used by the Secure-Sockets Layer (SSL) protocol to establish a secure connection. To create a valid SSL, both sides must have a valid Security Certificate. The information contained in a Security Certificate includes to whom the certificate belongs, who issued the certificate, some sort of unique identification (such as a serial

Table S.1: Security Categories

Category	Description
Login security	Controls which users can access the network. This security feature requires the knowledge of the name of a User object and the correct password (if required) to log in to the network.
Trustees security	Designates the users who can access directories, files, or objects. A trustee is a User or Group object who has been granted access to a directory. Access to the system is granted through trustee assignments.
Rights security	Determines the level of access for each trustee. Rights determine the type of access a trustee has to a directory, file, or object.
Inheritance security	Passes rights from higher to lower levels. With inheritance, rights granted in a trustee assignment apply to objects, directories, and files below the assignment. Inheritance applies to both directories (and files) on a volume and objects in the Directory tree.
Attributes security	Describes the characteristics of directories and files. Attributes describe characteristics of a file or a directory and tell the operating system what actions are allowed.
Effective-rights security	Lists a user's actual rights to a directory, file, or object. Effective rights are calculated to a directory, file, or object whenever an action is taken.

See also **attribute; effective rights; Orange Book; rights; trustee.**

number), dates the certificate is valid, and an encrypted "fingerprint" that can be used to verify the contents of the certificate.

See also **Secure-Sockets Layer.**

Security Equals To

In Novell Directory Services (NDS), a NetWare Directory Schema term and a selectable property for the AFP Server, Messaging Server, NCP Server, Print Server, and User objects. This property provides a user with temporary access to the same information or rights that another user has access to.

See also **leaf object; Novell Directory Services; object.**

security equivalence

A Novell Directory Services (NDS) property of every User object that lists other objects. A user is granted all rights that any object in that list is granted, including object rights, file rights, and directory rights.

See also **access rights.**

Security Equivalences

A selectable property for the User object in Novell Directory Services (NDS).

See also **leaf object; Novell Directory Services; object.**

Security Flags

In Novell Directory Services (NDS), a selectable property for the AFP Server, Messaging Server, NCP Server, Print Server, and User objects.

See also **leaf object; Novell Directory Services; object.**

Security Management

One of five network-management domains described in the OSI Network Management Model that controls access to network resources according to local guidelines to protect against intruders. To accomplish this control, all access points to the network are defined and efforts are made to ensure that these points cannot be breached or compromised. Access points include the network nodes, cables, air waves, and programs. An authentication process (which is not specified in the OSI Network Management Model) restricts access by unauthorized users and alarm signals are used to alert of any breach or compromise to network security.

See also **OSI Network Management Model.**

SECURITY utility

In NetWare 3.*x*, a workstation utility that checks for possible file server security violations by examining the bindery and reporting potential security violations. Supervisor rights are required to run this utility because it is run from the SYS:SYSTEM directory. This utility identifies potential security problems on the network, but does not correct them.

See also **Media Manager.**

See Also

A NetWare Directory Schema term and a selectable property for the following objects in Novell Directory Services (NDS): AFP Server, Bindery Queue, Computer, Directory Map, External Entity, Group, List, Message Routing Group, Messaging Server, NCP Server, Organization (O), Organizational Role, Organizational Unit (OU), Print Server, Printer, Profile, Queue, User, and Volume.

See also **container object; leaf object; Novell Directory Services; object.**

seed router

An AppleTalk router that defines the range of network numbers for all routers in a network segment. Each AppleTalk network segment is required to have at least one seed router. A seed router is also known as a *configured router*.

See also **AppleTalk; router.**

seek time

The amount of time that elapses while a hard disk drive's read/write head searches for a given track.

See also **sector; track.**

segment

A discrete portion of a network or a local-area network (LAN) that has no routers or bridges.

See also **local-area network.**

segmentation

Setting a maximum limit for the amount of memory to be used by a process. Segmentation assigns memory from a large block of physically contiguous memory.
See also **memory.**

Segmentation and Reassembly (SAR)

A process that involves segmenting data frames into Asynchronous Transfer Mode (ATM) cells at the transmitter and reassembling them into their original format at the receiver.
See also **Asynchronous Transfer Mode.**

Selected Properties

A property right found in Novell Directory Services (NDS).
See also **Novell Directory Services.**

Selected Property rights

An option allowing the assignment of property rights to individual Novell Directory Services (NDS) objects in a NetWare Directory tree.
See also **Directory tree; Novell Directory Services.**

selector

A value used at a specific layer of the OSI Reference Model to distinguish each of the Service-Access Points (SAPs) through which an entity at that level provides services to the layer above it.
See also **OSI Reference Model; Service-Access Point.**

semaphore

In multiprocessor environments, an integer value used to prevent data corruption by coordinating the activities of programs and processes. Semaphores help to synchronize interprocess communications by ensuring that certain event sequences do or do not occur. Semaphores can also be used to restrict the number of users who have access to a resource by setting an upper limit. When the upper limit is reached, the semaphore denies access by additional users. An *event semaphore* allows a thread to tell other threads that an event has occurred and that it is safe for the threads to resume execution. A *mutual-exclusion semaphore* protects system resources from simultaneous access by several processes. A *multiple-wait semaphore* allows threads to wait for multiple events to take place, or for multiple resources to become free.

Semaphores

In NetWare 3.12 , a resource appearing in the Available Options/Resource Utilization screen of the MONITOR NetWare Loadable Module (NLM); it tracks the number of NLMs that use semaphores.
See also **MONITOR; NetWare Loadable Module; semaphore.**

Semi-Permanent Memory

In NetWare 3.12, a resource appearing in the Available Options/Resource Utilization screen of the MONITOR NetWare Loadable Module (NLM) that allocates small amounts of memory that an NLM expects to use for a long time.
See also **MONITOR; NetWare Loadable Module.**

SEND utility

In NetWare 4.x and IntranetWare, a server console and workstation utility that sends messages to users attached to a server, sets a workstation to receive messages, provides a view of the current broadcast mode at the client, polls for messages, and sends messages to users. This utility can set a workstation to receive all messages, only system messages, or no messages at all. It can send messages to all users who are logged in or attached to a NetWare server, or to a list of users or connection numbers.

sense code

Code indicating what type of error has occurred in the running of a program and sent to a partner node in function-management headers or negative responses.

Sentry

A NetWare Loadable Module (NLM) Behavior Testing utility that monitors time slices and central processing unit (CPU) utilization time for NLMs. The major purpose of this utility is to ensure that an NLM meets the maximum allowed time slice requirement of NLM behavior testing.
See also **NetWare Loadable Module.**

sequence number

A number appearing in the bitmap/sequence header of an AppleTalk Transaction Protocol (ATP) header of a Transaction Response (TResp) packet that indicates the position of the TResp packet in a TResp message.

Sequenced Packet Exchange (SPX)

A NetWare protocol that enhances the Novell Internetwork Packet Exchange (IPX) protocol. To ensure successful packet delivery, SPX requests verification from a destination that data has been received, compares a verification value to a value calculated before transmission, and, by matching those two numbers, acknowledges the packet arrived and that it arrived intact. SPX also has the capability of tracking data transmissions consisting of more than one packet (a transmission that has been split into several packets). If no acknowledgment is received within a specified amount of time, SPX retransmits the packets. If retransmissions fail to produce an acknowledgment, SPX notifies the operator that the connection has failed. SPX is derived from the Xerox Packet Protocol.
See also **Internetwork Packet Exchange.**

Sequenced-Packet Protocol (SPP)

In the Xerox Network System (XNS), a protocol for the Transport Layer (Layer 4) of the OSI Reference Model.
See also **OSI Reference Model; Xerox Network System.**

sequential access

An access method used by some storage devices in which the device starts at the beginning of the medium to find a specific storage location.

serial

Performing tasks one after the other.

serial communication

Transmission of data from one device to another, one bit at a time, over a single line. The NetWare standard for serial communication is the RS-232 standard, which includes the parameters listed in Table S.2.

Serial-Line Internet Protocol (SLIP)

An Internet protocol designed to run Internet Protocol (IP) over serial lines that connect two network systems. SLIP is being replaced by Point-to-Point Protocol (PPP).
See also **Point-to-Point Protocol.**

Serial Number

A NetWare Directory Schema term and a selectable property for the AFP Server, Country (C), and Printer objects in Novell Directory Services (NDS).
See also **leaf object; Novell Directory Services; object.**

serial port

A port (typically COM1 or COM2 on IBM-compatible systems) that allows the asynchronous transmission of data, one bit at a time.
See also **COM port; parallel port.**

serial printer

A printer that uses a serial interface to a network. Because a serial printer accepts data transferred a bit at a time and assembled into bytes using handshaking techniques, it may perform slower than a parallel printer.

serial transmission

The transmission of data one bit at a time, one after the other, on the same wire.

serialization

A process of assigning serial numbers to software to prevent unlawful duplication of the product.

Table S.2: RS-232 Communication Parameters

Parameter	Description
Baud rate	Indicates the signal modulation rate, or the speed at which the signal changes.
Character length	Indicates the number of data bits used to form a character.
Parity	Indicates an error-checking method to be used in data transmission.
Stop bit	Indicates a signal denoting the end of a particular character.
XON/XOFF	Indicates a method that prevents the sending system from transmitting data faster than the receiving system can accept it.

See also **baud rate; character length; parity; RS-232-C; stop bit; XON/XOFF.**

server

A network computer used by multiple users to share access to files, printing, communications, and other services. In a large network, a server may run the network operating system (such as a *NetWare server* running the NetWare operating system); in smaller networks, the server may run a personal computer operating system in tandem with peer-to-peer networking software.

See also **NetWare server; print server.**

Server

In Novell Directory Services (NDS), a NetWare Directory Schema term and a selectable property for the Bindery Queue, Computer, and Queue objects.

See also **leaf object; Novell Directory Services; object.**

server application

An application that creates Object Linking and Embedding (OLE) objects.

See also **Object Linking and Embedding.**

server console

A monitor-keyboard combination that enables a user to view network traffic, send messages, set configuration parameters, shut down a network server, and (in the case of NetWare) load and unload NetWare Loadable Module (NLM) programs.

See also **NetWare Loadable Module.**

Server Holds

A NetWare Directory Schema term and a selectable property for the User object in Novell Directory Services (NDS). This property contains the number of accounting charges pending while a server performs a chargeable action.

See also **leaf object; Novell Directory Services; object.**

server manager

A user with rights to manage a Personal NetWare server and to change its configuration.

See also **Personal NetWare.**

Server Message Block (SMB)

Microsoft's network protocol for distributed file systems, which lets one computer use the files and resources of another computer as if the two machines were locally connected.

server mirroring

A NetWare System Fault Tolerance III (SFT III) configuration in which a secondary (identical) server immediately takes over network operations when a primary server fails. The two servers must be connected by a mirrored server link and, as long as this link is in place, can reside on different network segments.

See also **mirroring; primary server; secondary server; System Fault Tolerance.**

Server object

A Novell Directory Services (NDS) leaf object that represents a server.

See also **leaf object; Novell Directory Services; object.**

server owner

A person responsible for the computer on which a Personal NetWare server is loaded.

See also **Personal NetWare.**

server protocol

Procedures and processes that a network server follows to accept and respond to service requests from workstations.

Server-Session Socket (SSS)

In AppleTalk networks, a protocol in the Session Layer (Layer 5) of the OSI Reference Model that contains the number of the socket to which Session Layer packets are sent.

See also **AppleTalk; OSI Reference Model; socket.**

Server Side Includes (SSI)

Commands that enable authors of World Wide Web (WWW) pages to insert variables in their Web pages (such as text from another file or the current date and time).

See also **World Wide Web; Web home page.**

Server Up Time

A field name appearing in the Cache Utilization screen of the MONITOR NetWare Loadable Module (NLM).

See also **MONITOR; NetWare Loadable Module.**

SERVER utility

In NetWare and IntranetWare, a utility that boots NetWare on a server, executes the STARTUP.NCF file, mounts the SYS: volume, executes the AUTOEXEC.NCF file, and executes the INITSYS.NCF file (a DOS-executable file that boots the NetWare operating system).

See also **AUTOEXEC.NCF; STARTUP.NCF.**

server-based network

The use of one or more network nodes as dedicated servers through which other nodes must go to access resources on other workstations.

See also **peer-to-peer network.**

service

A task or operation made available through an application or systems program and that includes network services (or those that include file services to control file access and storage), print services, communications services, fax services, archive services, and backup services.

Service-Access Point (SAP)

An interface between layers in the OSI Reference Model through which an entity at a particular layer can provide services to the processes at the layer above. SAPs, which are assigned by the Institute for Electrical and Electronic Engineers (IEEE), each have their own unique address that can also be used as the access point to the service's user (the entity at the next highest level). SAPs are often labeled according to the layer being discussed (for example, PSAP for the Presentation Layer, SSAP for the Session Layer, TSAP for the Transport Layer, NSAP for the Network Layer, DSAP for the Data-Link Layer, and PhSAP for the Physical Layer).

See also **OSI Reference Model; SAP.**

Service Advertising

In NetWare 3.12, a resource appearing in the Available Options/Resource Utilization screen of the MONITOR NetWare Loadable Module (NLM) that tracks the number of times an NLM advertises itself over the network (usually 1 or 0).

See also **MONITOR; NetWare Loadable Module.**

Service-Advertising Protocol (SAP)

A Novell protocol used by servers to advertise their services to the network, which allows routers to create and maintain a database of current internetwork server information. Routers broadcast SAP updates to all other routers on the network to keep all routers synchronized. Workstations broadcast SAP request packets to query the network to find a server.

See also **router; routing; SAP.**

service bureau

A company that provides support services (such as data processing or software development) as an outside vendor to its customers, thus providing a means for companies to avoid high equipment and personnel costs associated with running similar in-house services.

Service-Connection Task Numbers

In NetWare 3.12, a resource appearing in the Available Options/Resource Utilization screen of the MONITOR NetWare Loadable Module (NLM) that tracks the task numbers assigned to an NLM for use on a connection.

See also **MONITOR; NetWare Loadable Module.**

Service Connections

In NetWare 3.12, a resource appearing in the Available Options/Resource Utilization screen of the MONITOR NetWare Loadable Module (NLM) that tracks the number of all attached and logged-in users on the network.

See also **MONITOR; NetWare Loadable Module.**

Service Data Unit (SDU)

A packet passed as a service-request parameter from one layer in the OSI Reference Model to a layer below it.

See also **OSI Reference Model.**

Service HyperText Transfer Protocol (SHTTP)

A secure version of the HyperText Transfer Protocol (HTTP) that provides encryption services, a digital signature, and authentication. SHTTP provides end-to-end secure communications.

See also **authentication; digital signature; encryption; HyperText Transfer Protocol.**

service information filter

A filter that restricts service access by filtering out any packets that advertise the services. A service information filter keeps applications from discovering the locations of services, but does not restrict access to the services if the application already knows their locations.

service point

Software through which a non-IBM device or a network can communicate with a network manager in IBM's Network-Management Architecture (NMA) model.

See also **Network-Management Architecture.**

Service Processes

A field name appearing in the Cache Utilization screen of the MONITOR NetWare Loadable Module (NLM).

See also **MONITOR; NetWare Loadable Module.**

service provider

A company or individual who provides access to a network or to another service. Service providers are distinguished by the modem speeds they can handle, whether the access telephone number is local or long-distance, the types of access protocols they support, and, in the case of an Internet service provider (ISP), the range of Internet usage capabilities they support.

See also **Internet service provider.**

servlet

A small, specialized server program, particularly a program acting as a component or helper application for larger software applications.

SERVMAN (NLM)

In NetWare 4.x and IntranetWare, a server console NetWare Loadable Module (NLM) that provides a view of and configures system parameters, changes system parameter values, and provides a view of volume, storage, network, adapter, device, and disk partition information. The main screen for SERVMAN (or Server Manager) displays statistics about the server, such as processor use, processor speed, and number of NLMs loaded. An Available Options screen provides access to more information, as shown in Table S.3.

session

Either a connection between two network-addressable units (NAUs), or the time between turning on a computer and turning it off.

See also **network-addressable unit.**

session activation

The exchange of an activation request and a positive response between network-addressable units (NAUs).

See also **network-addressable unit.**

Table S.3: SERVMAN Available Options

Option	Description
Server parameters	Provides a view of operating system parameters and provides a means to change system parameter values in the AUTOEXEC.NCF and STARTUP.NCF files.
Storage information	Provides a view of adapter, device, and partition information.
Volume information	Provides information about volumes mounted on the server.
Network information	Provides network information such as number of packets received and transmitted.

See also **AUTOEXEC.NCF; NetWare Loadable Module; STARTUP.NCF.**

session deactivation

The exchange of a deactivation request and a response between a network-addressable units (NAUs).
See also **network-addressable unit.**

session file

A file that contains the names and locations of NetWare for Macintosh entities most frequently used, and the utility used to work with each one.

Session Layer (OSI model)

The fifth layer (Layer 5) in the seven-layer OSI Reference Model. The Session Layer allows dialog control between end systems and handles problems that are not communication issues.
See also **OSI Reference Model.**

session parameters

Parameters specifying or constraining protocols between two network-addressable units (NAUs).
See also **network-addressable units; session.**

session partner

Either of two network-addressable units (NAUs) participating in a network session.
See also **network-addressable units; session.**

SESSION utility

In NetWare 3.x, a workstation utility that changes to another file server, provides information on (and allows modification of) drive mappings, provides a view of groups on the network, sends messages to groups, provides a means to modify search drives, allows selection of a default drive, and lists user information.

SET protocol

Secure Electronic Transactions, a protocol developed by VISA and MasterCard that allows for credit card transactions to be conducted across the Internet.

SET TIME utility

In NetWare and IntranetWare, a server console utility that sets the date and time kept by the server. This utility is used most appropriately on a Reference or Single Reference time server. Changing the time on a Primary, Reference, or Single Reference time server affects the time on all other servers that refer to that time server.

See also **Primary time server; Reference time server; Single Reference time server.**

SET TIME ZONE utility

In NetWare 4.*x* and IntranetWare, a server console utility that configures time zone information, which is critical to time synchronization in Novell Directory Services (NDS). If the time zone is not set, no standard abbreviations are used and the time zone offset is set to zero.

See also **Novell Directory Services.**

SET utility

In NetWare 4.*x* and IntranetWare, a server console utility that provides a view of and allows the configuration of operating system parameters. Table S.4 shows the 14 major categories of parameters used and provides a brief description of each.

See also **NetWare Core Protocol; Novell Directory Services; System Fault Tolerance; TIMESYNC; Transaction-Tracking System.**

Settable Parameters

In NetWare 3.12, a resource appearing in the Available Options/Resource Utilization screen of the MONITOR NetWare Loadable Module (NLM). The resource tracks NLMs that add SET parameters and ensures that when the NLM is unloaded, the SET parameters are also unloaded.

See also **MONITOR; NetWare Loadable Module; SET utility.**

SETPASS utility

In NetWare and IntranetWare, a workstation utility that sets a user's password.

Sets

A NetWare Loadable Module (NLM) Behavior Testing utility that provides a menu-driven interface for changing system parameters of the NetWare 3.*x* operating system.

See also **NetWare Loadable Module.**

settle time

The time it takes to stabilize the head on a hard disk drive above the track.

See also **hard drive.**

SETTTS utility

In NetWare and IntranetWare, a workstation utility that sets the logical and physical record locks for the Transaction-Tracking System (TTS), as well as providing a view of the logical and physical record locks.

See also **Transaction-Tracking System.**

SETUP

A menu-driven program that usually allows the changing of a computer's standard system configuration.

SETUPDOC utility

In IntranetWare, a Windows 3.*x* workstation utility that installs and deletes document collections (and DynaText viewers), configures viewers to access document collections, and creates viewer icons at individual workstations.

Table S.4: SET Parameters

Category	Description	Parameters
Communications Parameters	Control settings for communication buffers.	Maximum Packet-Receive Buffers; Minimum Packet-Receive Buffers; Maximum Physical-Receive Packet Size; IPX NetBIOS Replication Option; Maximum Interrupt Events; Reply to Get Nearest Server; Number of Watchdog Packets; Delay Between Watchdog Packets; Delay Before First Watchdog Packet; New Packet-Receive-Buffer Wait Time; Console-Display Watchdog Logouts
Directory-Caching Parameters	Provide faster directory access by holding entries from the Directory table in memory.	Dirty-Directory-Cache Delay Time; Maximum Concurrent Directory-Cache Writes; Directory-Cache-Allocation Wait Time; Directory-Cache Buffer Nonreferenced Delay; Maximum Directory-Cache Buffers; Minimum Directory-Cache Buffers; Maximum Number of Internal Directory Handles; Maximum Number of Directory Handles
Disk Parameters	Control part of the Hot Fix redirection area.	Enable Disk-Read-After-Write Verify; Remirror Block Size; Concurrent Remirror Requests; Mirrored-Devices-Are-Out-of-Sync Message Frequency; Ignore Disk Geometry; Enable IO-Handicap Attribute
Error-Handling Parameters	Control the size of error logs and what happens when the logs exceed the specified size.	Server Log-File State; Volume Log-File State; Volume TTS Log-File State; Server Log-File Overflow Size; Volume Log-File Overflow Size; Volume TTS Log-File Overflow Size; Enable Deadlock Detection; Auto-Restart-After-Abend Delay Time; Auto Restart After Abend
File-Caching Parameters	Provide faster file access by holding files (or portions of files) in memory.	Read-Ahead Enabled; Read-Ahead LRU Sitting-Time Threshold; Minimum File-Cache Buffers; Maximum Concurrent Disk-Cache Writes; Dirty-Disk-Cache Delay Time; Minimum File-Cache-Report Threshold

(continued)

Parameter	Description	Parameters
File-System Parameters	Provide warnings when volumes are almost full, control file purging, control the reuse of Turbo File-Allocation Tables (Turbo FATs), and control file compression.	Minimum File-Delete Wait Time; File-Delete Wait Time; Allow Deletion of Active Directories; Maximum Percent of Volume Space Allowed for Extended Attributes; Maximum Extended Attributes per File or Path; Fast Volume Mounts; Maximum Percent of Volume Used by Directory; Immediate Purge of Deleted Files; Maximum Subdirectory Tree-Depth; Volume-Low-Warn All Users; Volume-Low-Warning Reset Threshold; Volume-Low-Warning Threshold; Turbo FAT Re-Use Wait Time; Compression Daily-Check Stop Hour; Compression Daily-Check Starting Hour; Minimum Compression-Percentage Gain; Enable File Compression; Maximum Concurrent Compressions; Convert-Compressed-to-Uncompressed Option; Decompress Percent-Disk-Space-Free to Allow Commit; Decompress Free-Space-Warning Interval; Deleted-Files Compression Option; Days Untouched Before Compression; Allow Unowned Files to Be Extended
Lock Parameters	Control how many open files are allowed for each workstation, how many open files are allowed for the system, how many record locks are allowed for each connection, and how many record locks are allowed on the system.	Maximum Record Locks Per Connection; Maximum File Locks Per Connection; Maximum Record Locks; Maximum File Locks
Memory Parameters	Control the size of the dynamic memory pool and the automatic registering of memory on computers using the Extended Industry-Standard Architecture (EISA) bus.	Allow Invalid Pointers; Read-Fault Notification; Read-Fault Emulation; Write-Fault Notification; Write-Fault Emulation; Garbage-Collection Interval; Number of Frees for Garbage Collection; Minimum Free Memory for Garbage Collection; Alloc-Memory Check Flag; Auto-Register Memory Above 16 Megabytes; Reserved Buffers Below 16 Megabytes

(continued)

Table S.4: SET Parameters (continued)

Category	Description	Parameters
NetWare Core Protocol (NCP) Parameters	Control NCP packets, control boundary checking, and assign NCP Server Packet-Signature levels.	NCP File Commit; Display NCP Bad-Component Warnings; Reject NCP Packets with Bad Components; Display NCP Bad-Length Warnings; Reject NCP Packets with Bad Lengths; Maximum Outstanding NCP Searches; NCP Packet-Signature Option; Enable IPX Checksums; Allow Change to Client Rights; Allow LIP
Novell Directory Services (NDS) Parameters	Control the NDS trace file, set time intervals for maintenance processes, set NDS synchronization, specify the number of NCP retries before a timeout occurs, mark the status of other servers, and specify bindery service contexts.	NDS Trace to Screen; NDS Trace to File; NDS Trace Filename; NDS Client NCP Retries; NDS External-Reference Life-Span; NDS Inactivity-Synchronization Interval; NDS Synchronization Restrictions; NDS Server Status; NDS Janitor Interval; NDS Backlink Interval; NDS Trace File Length to Zero; Check Equivalent to Me; Bindery Context
System Fault Tolerance III (SFT III) Parameters	Test and customize the mirrored server environment.	Clear Extra ECB Space; Notify All Users of Mirrored-Server Synchronization; Server Failure-Notification Name; MSEngine Use Primary Server for DOS I/O; Check LAN Option; Check LAN Extra Wait Time; Use Diagnostic Responder to Validate LAN Functionality; Borrow-Short-Term-Memory-Ahead Amount; SFT3 Error-Wait Time; Secondary Take-Over Wait Time; Display Mirrored-Server-Too-Many-Hops-Away Message; Maximum Pseudo Hop Count; Enable Pseudo Hop Count; New End Address for Unclaimed Memory Block; New Start Address for Unclaimed Memory Block; MSL Error-Wait Time; Comprehensive MSEngine-Synchronization Check; IPX Internet-Down Wait Time; Display IPX Route to Other Server; MSL Deadlock Wait Time; Extra MSL Checking; *(continued)*

IOEngine Error-Log Use DOS; Always Down Server When Power Fails; Turbo Memory Sync; Secondary Server MSL Send Blocked-Recovery Option; Primary Server Send Blocked-Recovery Option; MSEngine Abend-And-Processor-Exception Recovery Option; Always Halt Secondary If Sync Error; IOEngine Abend-and-Processor-Exception Recovery Option; Machine-Check Recovery Option; Memory-Parity-Error Recovery Option; Secondary Server MSL Hardware-Recovery-Failure Recovery Option; Primary Server MSL Hardware-Failure Recovery Option; MSEngine Outputs Different Recovery Option; Secondary Server MSL Consistency-Error Recovery Option; Consistency-Error Recovery Option; Secondary-Server MSL Deadlock Recovery Option; Primary-Server MSL Deadlock Recovery Option; Stop on Server Test Unexpected Error; Restart Test Mode; Server Test-Minimum-Delay Minimum Delay Amount; Server Test-Minimum-Delay Amount; Restart Maximum-Random-Delay Amount; Server Test Maximum-Random-Delay Amount; Status Dump-File State; IOEngine Log-File State; Status Dump-File Overflow Size; IOEngine Error-Log File-Overflow Size

| Time-Synchronization Parameters | Control time synchronization, the TIMESYNC.CFG file, and time-zone settings. | TIMESYNC ADD Time Source; TIMESYNC Configuration File; TIMESYNC Configured Sources; TIMESYNC Directory Tree Mode; TIMESYNC Hardware Clock; TIMESYNC Polling Count; TIMESYNC Polling Interval; TIMESYNC REMOVE Time Source; TIMESYNC RESET; TIMESYNC Reset Flag; TIMESYNC Service Advertising; TIMESYNC Synchronization Radius; TIMESYNC Time Adjustment; TIMESYNC Time Source; TIMESYNC Type; TIMESYNC Write Parameters; TIMESYNC |

(continued)

Table S.4: SET Parameters (continued)

Category	Description	Parameters
		Write Value; Time Zone; Default Time-Server Type; Start of Daylight-Savings Time; End of Daylight-Savings Time; Daylight-Savings Time Offset; Daylight-Savings-Time Status; New Time With Daylight-Savings-Time Status
Transaction-Tracking System (TTS) Parameters	Guarantees that transactions (a set of write operations) is written to disk in its complete form, or is backed out if incomplete.	Auto TTS-Backout Flag; TTS-Abort Dump Flag; Maximum Transactions; TTS UnWritten-Cache Wait Time; TTS-Backout File-Truncation Wait Time
Miscellaneous Parameters	Various alert settings and other miscellaneous parameters.	Command-Line Prompt Default Choice; Command-Line Prompt Time-Out; Sound Bell for Alerts; Replace Console Prompt with Server Name; Alert Message Nodes; Worker Thread Execute In a Row Count; Halt System on Invalid Parameters; Upgrade Low-Priority Threads; Display Relinquish-Control Alerts; Display Incomplete IPX Packet Alerts; Display Old API Names; Developer Options; Display Spurious Interrupt Alerts; Display Lost Interrupt Alerts; Pseudo Preemption Count; Global Pseudo Preemption; Minimum Service Processes; Maximum Service Processes; New-Service-Process Wait Time; Automatically Repair Bad Volumes; Enable SECURE.NCF; Allow Audit Passwords; Allow Encrypted Passwords; SMP Stack Size; SMP Polling Count; SMP NetWare Kernel Mode; SMP Flush Processor Cache; SMP Intrusive-Abend Mode; SMP Developer Option; SMP Memory Protection

SFT

System Fault Tolerance, a data-protection scheme in NetWare that provides procedures allowing a user to automatically recover from hardware failures. In the three levels of SFT protection, each level includes the previous levels (for example, SFT III includes SFT I and SFT II).

See also **disk mirroring; disk duplexing; primary server; secondary server; System Fault Tolerance** (includes **Table S.9**).

SGMP

Simple Gateway-Monitoring Protocol, a network-management protocol that was the precursor to the Simple Network-Management Protocol (SNMP).

See also **Simple Network-Management Protocol.**

shadow RAM

Random-access memory (RAM) located in upper memory and that can be used as a place into which data and code can be copied from the computer system's read-only memory (ROM).

See also **memory; random-access memory; read-only memory.**

shareable

A term used to describe a file, device, or process that is available to multiple users and that they can use simultaneously if necessary.

Shareable (Sh) attribute

A file attribute, set by the NetWare operating system, that allows a file to be accessed by more than one user at a time.

See also **attribute.**

shared folder

A folder on a Macintosh networked computer that is available to other users either with or without restriction.

shared memory

Memory involved in an interprocess communication accessed by more than one program running in a multitasking operating system. Memory-management units such as semaphores are responsible for ensuring that applications do not collide or try to update from the same information at the same time.

See also **memory; semaphore.**

shared process

A process that can be serviced by a single server for multiple stations, all of which can communicate with the server.

shared services

Computer functions and resources that are used by multiple clients simultaneously from anywhere on the network.

shared-media network

A network configuration in which all nodes share the same line, thus making only one transmission possible at one time. Adding nodes to a shared-media network increases network traffic but does not increase capacity.

shareware

Computer programs that are made available to users for a trial period before the user is expected to pay a set amount to the shareware provider.

shell

Software that serves as the interface between the user and the operating system. The DOS operating system has a DOS command interpreter and the DOSSHELL program; Windows uses the Program Manager as a shell. The Macintosh environment uses the Finder; the UNIX environment uses the C shell and the Bourne shell.

shell account

An Internet account that allows a local computer to act as a terminal on a multiuser UNIX network connected to the Internet, which allows the use of all UNIX commands and the ability to store and process information on the host computer. The downside to a shell account is the inability to use a point-and-click interface, the inability to view graphics, and the fact that files are downloaded to the hard disk of the UNIX host machine (which means they must be downloaded from the host machine to the local computer).

shield

A sheath wrapped around a conductor wire and insulator in coaxial and twisted-pair cabling that helps to prevent external signals and noise from interfering with the signal transmission through the cable.

shielded cable

Cable manufactured with an insulated layer to protect against electromagnetic interference (EMI) and radio-frequency interference (RFI).

See also **cable; electromagnetic interference; radio-frequency interference.**

Shielded Distributed Data Interface (SDDI)

A network configuration that uses *shielded twisted-pair (STP)* cabling for the Fiber Distributed Data Interface (FDDI) architecture and protocols.

See also **Fiber Distributed Data Interface; shielded twisted-pair cable.**

shielded twisted-pair (STP) cable

A cable with a foil shield and copper braid surrounding pairs of wires that have a minimum number of twists per foot of cable length. Although it is considered bulky, STP is used for high-speed transmissions over long distances and is often associated with Token Ring networks.

See also **shielded cable; unshielded cable; unshielded twisted-pair cable.**

Shockwave

A multimedia package from Macromedia designed for efficient downloading and presentation of animation, sound, and related media types.

 **For more information about Shockwave, surf the Web to** `http://www.macromedia.com/shockwave.`

short

A cabling condition in which excess current flows between two wires because of an abnormally low resistance between the two wires.

short circuit

The accidental completion of a circuit at a point too close to its origin to allow normal or complete operation.

short machine type

A four-letter (or shorter) name that represents a DOS machine brand in NetWare (for example, IBM for an IBM computer). The same short-machine-type name is used with overlay files (for example, with IBM$RUN.OVL and CMPQ$RUN.OVL). The default short machine type, which is set in the NET.CFG file with the SHORT MACHINE TYPE parameter, is IBM.
See also **long machine type.**

shortcut

A keystroke (or keystroke combination) that is the equivalent of selecting a menu item, or a small Windows 95 file that acts as a pointer into a program, data file, or location on a network.

Shortest Path First (SPF)

A routing strategy in which packets are passed between routers according to the distance to the destination.
See also **Open Shortest Path First; routing; shortest-path routing.**

shortest-path routing

A routing algorithm that calculates paths to all network destinations wherein the shortest path is determined by the cost assigned to each link.

short-haul modem

A modem used to transmit information only over short distances (such as from one side of a building to another).

shout

The use of all-uppercase letters when composing an electronic-mail (e-mail) message or a posting on a Usenet newsgroup.
See also **electronic mail; Usenet.**

Show

An option of the NetWare NPRINT utility used to show the current status of printer ports.
See also **NPRINT utility.**

SHOW command

A control command that, when used in conjunction with an assigned number of a specific submenu, runs the specific submenu.

SHow option

An ITEM command option in an NMENU utility menu that displays in the screen's upper-left corner a DOS command being executed when an item in a menu class causes that command to be executed.

SHTTP

Service HyperText Transfer Protocol, a secure version of the Hypertext Transfer Protocol (HTTP) that provides encryption services, a digital signature, and authentication. SHTTP provides end-to-end secure communications.
See also **authentication; digital signature; encryption; HyperText Transfer Protocol.**

sideband

A modem frequency band either just above or just below the frequency used by the carrier signal in the modulation process that converts data along analog signals.

SIDF

System-Independent Data Format, a format used by the SBACKUP utility in NetWare that allows all data backed up with SBACKUP to be read by other backup applications with the capability of reading and writing in SIDF.
See also **SBACKUP.**

sig

signature, a set of identifying lines added to the end of an electronic-mail (e-mail) message or a Usenet newsgroup posting that usually include the name and telephone number of the message sender, a disclaimer, a quotation, and sometimes a graphical image created from ordinary American Standard Code for Information Interchange (ASCII) characters and symbols.
See also **American Standard Code for Information Interchange; electronic mail; Usenet.**

SIG

special-interest group, a group (often part of a user group or other organization) that shares information about a specific topic.

sign-trailing separate (STS)

A numeric data type in the COBOL programming language, represented as an American Standard Code for Information Interchange (ASCII) string. STS is right-justified and padded with leading zeros; it has the sign byte at the end.
See also **American Standard Code for Information Interchange.**

signal

A change in voltage or current over time described by the levels the current reaches and by the pattern with which the level changes over time. A peak is the highest level reached by a signal. A signal pattern is described as a waveform representing the level over time, with a sine waveform representing a clean signal and a square waveform representing an encoded digital bit. A signal can be either an electrical signal (one emanating from a power source) or a digital signal (one that represents a data transmission).

Signal-Quality Error (SQE)

A signal sent from the transceiver to the attached machine in an Ethernet 2.0 or 802.3 network to indicate that the transceiver's collision-detection circuitry is working properly. SQE is also known as a *heartbeat*.

See also **802.3; Ethernet; IEEE 802.*x*.**

signal-to-crosstalk ratio (SCR)

A ratio value representing the decibel level of a signal to the noise in a twisted-pair cable. The SCR is calculated specifically as the ratio between near-end crosstalk (NEXT) and the attenuation on a cable.

See also **near-end crosstalk.**

signal-to-noise ratio (SNR)

A measure of signal quality that uses a ratio between the desired signal and the unwanted signal (or noise) at a specific point in a cable.

signature (sig)

Identifying lines added to the end of an electronic-mail (e-mail) message or a Usenet newsgroup posting that usually include the name and telephone number of the message sender, a disclaimer, a quotation, and sometimes a graphical image created from ordinary American Standard Code for Information Interchange (ASCII) characters and symbols.

See also **American Standard Code for Information Interchange; electronic mail; Usenet.**

Simple Gateway-Monitoring Protocol (SGMP)

A network-management protocol that was the precursor to the Simple Network-Management Protocol (SNMP).

See also **Simple Network-Management Protocol.**

Simple Mail-Transfer Protocol (SMTP)

A standard electronic-mail (e-mail) protocol that provides specifications for mail system interaction and control message formats.

See also **electronic mail.**

Simple Network-Management Protocol (SNMP)

In the OSI Reference Model, a protocol in the Application Layer (Layer 7) that specifies a format for collecting network-management data and the exchange of that data between devices. Using Desktop SNMP services, a NetWare workstation can send status information to an SNMP-management program running on an Internetwork Packet Exchange (IPX) or Transmission-Control Protocol/Internet Protocol (TCP/IP) network. The two types of devices that make up the SNMP architecture are SNMP *agents* (a background process that monitors operation of the device and communicates with the outside world) and SNMP *managers* (network-management stations that collect messages from SNMP agents, generate reports, and handle data). Table S.5 shows the five operations on which SNMP functions are based.

Messages are delivered between groups of computers that are distinguished with 32-character, case-sensitive identifiers called community names. The *control community*

Table S.5: SNMP Operations

Operation	Description
GetRequest	Used by an SNMP manager to poll an agent for information.
GetNextRequest	Used by an SNMP manager to request the next item in a table or array.
SetRequest	Used by an SNMP manager to change a value within an agent's Management Information Base (MIB).
GetResponse	Used by an SNMP agent to satisfy a request from a manager.
Trap	Used by an SNMP agent to notify a manager of an event.

See also **Internetwork Packet Exchange; Management Information Base; OSI Reference Model; Transmission-Control Protocol/Internet Protocol.**

grants read and write access to MIBs. The *monitor community* grants read access to MIBs. The *trap community* identifies all messages originated by agents in response to traps.

Simple Network-Time Protocol (SNTP)

A variant of the Network-Time Protocol (NTP) in which the correct time is obtained from an official source and disseminated to servers across the network. The major appeal of this protocol is simplicity; it is not regarded as highly accurate (only to within several hundred milliseconds).

simplex

A communications mode that allows information to be transmitted in only one direction. Although the receiver may send control and error signals, it cannot send data to the sender.

Simplified Access Control (SAC)

Access-control guidelines presented in the Consultative Committee for International Telegraphy and Telephony (CCITT) X.500 Directory Services model.

See also **Consultative Committee for International Telegraphy and Telephony; SAC; X.500.**

Single Large Expensive Disk (SLED)

A storage method that uses only a single, high-capacity disk as a storage location.

See also **Redundant Array of Inexpensive Disks.**

Single Reference time server

The sole source of time on the NetWare network that provides time to Secondary time servers and to workstations.

single session

The only session connecting two logical units (LUs) in a Systems Network Architecture (SNA) network.

See also **logical unit; session; Systems Network Architecture.**

Single Sign-On (SSO)

A network login strategy in which a user needs only a single user ID and password to access any machine, application, or service on a network, provided the user has proper access and usage privileges.

Single-Attachment Concentrator (SAC)

A Fiber Distributed Data Interface (FDDI) network concentrator that serves as a termination point for a Single-Attachment Station (SAS) and that attaches to the FDDI network through a Dual-Attachment Concentrator (DAC).

See also **Dual-Attachment Concentrator; Fiber Distributed Data Interface; SAC; Single-Attachment Station.**

Single-Attachment Station (SAS)

A Fiber Distributed Data Interface (FDDI) network node that lacks the physical ports necessary to attach directly to both the primary and secondary rings on the network and that, instead, attaches to a concentrator.

See also **Fiber Distributed Data Interface.**

single-frequency transmission

A transmission method using radio waves in which the signal is encoded within a narrow frequency range and in which all energy is concentrated at a particular frequency range. Single-frequency transmissions are susceptible to jamming and eavesdropping.

single-mode fiber

A fiber with a narrow diameter, through which lasers are used to transmit signals. Only one route is used for the light wave to pass through the cable, making single-mode fiber popular in networks that transmit over long distances (such as telephone networks).

single-step multimode fiber

An optical fiber that has only a single layer of cladding, and a core wide enough to allow multiple light paths through at one time.

See also **cladding; fiber-optic cable.**

single-user system

A computer system designed to be used by only one user at a time. A single-user system is often a personal computer running DOS, System 7, OS/2, Windows 3.*x*, Windows 95, or Windows NT.

site

A group of computers (or even a single computer) that hosts a particular data collection, set of World Wide Web (WWW) pages that share a common entry-point address, or other network resource.

See also **World Wide Web (WWW).**

site license

A software-licensing agreement that applies to all installed copies of a software package at a specific location, rather than individual licenses for each copy of the software program. A site license may allow unlimited copies for internal use, or may limit the number of copies covered by the license agreement.

Sizzler

Products from Totally Hip Software that enable the conversion of digital movie and animation files to a proprietary format that can be supplied by standard server programs and displayed as *streaming files* (which can execute while they are still downloading). Windows and Macintosh software required for playback is available for Netscape Navigator and other compatible World Wide Web (WWW) browsers in the form of ActiveX controls.

See also **ActiveX; Netscape Navigator; Web browser.**

skin effect

A term used to describe the condition in the transmission of data at a fast rate over twisted-pair cable in which current flows most on the outside surface of the wire, thereby increasing resistance. Skin effect often results in a loss of signal.

Skip

A Novell Directory Services (NDS) Directory Schema term.

sky wave

A radio wave transmitted over a great distance before it is reflected back to Earth. A

sky wave is also known as an *ionospheric wave* because they take advantage of the ionosphere's reflection of high-frequency waves in a frequency-dependent manner.

SLED

Single Large Expensive Disk, a storage method that uses only a single, high-capacity disk as a storage location.

See also **Redundant Array of Inexpensive Disks.**

sliding-window flow control

A flow-control method in which a receiver grants permission to a transmitter to transmit data until a window is full, at which time the transmitter must stop the transmission until the receiver advertises a larger window. This type of flow control is common in transport protocols.

SLIP

Serial-Line Internet Protocol, an Internet protocol designed to run Internet Protocol (IP) over serial lines that connect two network systems. SLIP is being replaced by Point-to-Point Protocol (PPP).

See also **Point-to-Point Protocol.**

SLIST utility

In NetWare 3.*x*, a workstation utility that provides a list of file servers on the network and provides information about those servers.

slot time

The maximum elapsed time between the receipt of a packet by the first node on an Ethernet network and the receipt of a packet by the last node.

slots

A media-access method found in older ring topologies in which a ring is divided into fixed-sized slots that travel around the ring.

slotted ring

A ring topology utilizing slots as the media-access method. This topology was popular in the 1970s, but has been replaced by the Token Ring topology.

See also **Token Ring.**

SLS

secondary link station, a link station (other than the primary link station) that can exchange data with a primary link station, but not with other secondary link stations.

See also **primary link station.**

SLU

Secondary logical unit, a logical unit (LU) containing the secondary half-session for a particular logical-unit-to-logical-unit (LU-LU) session.

See also **half-session; logical unit; secondary half-session.**

SM

Standby Monitor, a network node (usually

found in Token Ring networks) that serves as a backup to the Active Monitor (AM) and is ready to take over in a timely and correct manner if the AM fails.

See also **Active Monitor; Token Ring.**

SMA connector

A fiber-optic connector utilizing a threaded-coupling mechanism to make the connection that can be used with either multimode or single-mode fiber. SMA connectors have been designed to meet military specifications.

SMAE

Systems-Management Application Entity, a component of the OSI Network-Management Model that implements the network-management services and activities at the Application Layer (Layer 7) in the network node.

See also **OSI Network-Management Model.**

Small Computer System Interface (SCSI)

An industry standard outlining the interconnection of peripheral devices (such as hard disk drives and tape backup systems) and their controllers to a microprocessor. The standard defines both hardware and software specifications for communication between a host computer and a peripheral device. A large degree of compatibility between SCSI (pronounced "scuzzy") devices is common.

See also **SCSI bus; SCSI disconnect; SCSI terminator.**

SMAP

Systems-Management Application Process, software in the OSI Network-Management Model that implements the network-management capabilities in a single node.

See also **OSI Network-Management Model.**

smart hub

An Ethernet or ARCnet network concentrator that has certain network-management facilities built into the firmware to allow a network administrator to control and plan network configurations. A smart hub is also known as an *intelligent hub.*

See also **concentrator; Ethernet.**

smart terminal

A terminal connected to a larger computer, having limited (or no) local disk-storage capacity and limited capability to perform operations independently of the larger computer.

SMASE

Systems-Management Application Service Element, SOFTWARE in the OSI Network-Management Model that implements the network-management capabilities in a single node.

See also **OSI Network-Management Model.**

SMB

Server Message Block, Microsoft's network protocol for distributed file systems, which lets one computer use the files and resources of another computer as if the two machines were locally connected.

SMDR

Storage-Management Data Requester, a NetWare feature that passes commands between the SBACKUP utility and Target Service Agents (TSAs).

See also **SBACKUP utility; Storage Management Services; Target Service Agent.**

SMDS

Switched Multimegabit Data Service, a packet-switched service that offers high-speed data throughputs for metropolitan-area networks (MANs). Described in a series of specifications produced by Bell Communications Research (Bellcore), this service utilizes the SMDS Interface Protocol (SIP) between a user device and SMDS network equipment. SMDS is being adopted by long-distance carriers and by providers of telecommunications equipment.

See also **Bellcore; metropolitan-area network (MAN).**

SMF

(1) Standard Message Format, a standard set of rules that defines the format of messages and how third-party application and gateway programs can interface with Message-Handling System (MHS) messaging products in NetWare.

(2) Systems-Management Function, services provided to manage particular network domains in the OSI

Network-Management Model. SMFs include Object Management, State Management, Relationship Management, Alarm Reporting, Event Report Management, Log Control, Security Alarm Reporting, Security Audit Trail, Access Control, Accounting Metering, Workload Monitoring, Summarization, and Test Management.

See also (1) **Message-Handling System;** (2) **OSI Network-Management Model.**

SMFA

Systems-Management Function Area, one of five domains defined in the OSI Network-Management Model, including Accounting Management, Configuration Management, Fault Management, Performance Management, and Security Management.

See also **OSI Network-Management Model.**

SMI

Structure-Management Information, a component in the Internet Protocol (IP) network-management model that specifies how information about managed objects is to be represented.

See also **Internet Protocol.**

SMODE utility

In NetWare 3.*x*, a workstation utility that specifies how a program uses search drives when looking for a data file. The eight search modes shown in Table S.6 are used to indicate how the program (executable file) searches for a data file.

Table S.6: SMODE Modes	
Mode	**Description**
0	No search instructions; default setting for all executable files.
I	Program searches according to a specified directory path. If no path is specified, the program searches the default directory and then all search drives.
2	Program searches according to a specified directory path. If no path is specified, the program searches only the default directory.
3	Program searches according to a specified directory path. If no path is specified, the program searches the default directory. Then, if the open request is read-only, the file searches the search drives.
4	This mode is reserved.
5	Program searches according to a specified directory path first, and then the search drives. If no path is specified, the program searches default directory and then the search drives.
6	This mode is reserved.
7	Program searches according to a specified directory path. If the open request is read-only, the program searches the search drives. If no path is specified, the program searches the default directory first. If the open request is read-only, the program searches the search drives.

SMS

Storage-Management Services, services that allow data to be backed up and restored independently of the hardware and file systems normally used for backup and storage. SMS-compliant software, including NetWare Loadable Module (NLM) programs, can run on NetWare servers.

See also **SBACKUP utility; SMS Device Interface; Storage-Management Data Requester; Storage-Management Services** (includes **Table S.7**); **Target Service Agent.**

SMS Data-Service Unit (SDSU)

A data-service unit that provides access to Switched Multimegabit Data Service (SMDS) through a High-Speed Serial Interface (HSSI) or through some other serial interface.

See also **High-Speed Serial Interface; Switched Multimegabit Data Service.**

SMS Storage Device Interface (SMSDI)

A set of NetWare routines that allows the SBACKUP NetWare Loadable Module (NLM) to access various storage devices and media. When more than one storage device is connected to the host, SMSDI provides SBACKUP with a list of available and unavailable storage devices and media, which SBACKUP then displays so the user can select an available backup device.

See also **NetWare Loadable Module; SBACKUP; Storage-Management Services.**

SMT

Station Management, a component in a Fiber Distributed Data Interface (FDDI) network, made up of services that ensure the correct operation of various network ele-

ments. SMT includes frame services, connection management, and ring management.

See also **Fiber Distributed Data Interface.**

SMTP

Simple Mail-Transfer Protocol, a standard electronic-mail (e-mail) protocol that provides specifications for mail system interaction and control message formats.

See also **electronic mail.**

SNA

Systems Network Architecture, a hierarchical, single-host network structure introduced by IBM in 1974 that includes descriptions of the logical structure, formats, protocols, and operational sequences for data transmission through, and configuration of, wide-area networks (WANs). The SNA model divides a hierarchical structure into seven layers, with each layer performing a specific function.

See also **control point; logical unit; physical unit; OSI Reference Model; Systems Network Architecture** (includes **Figure S.4** and **Table S.10**).

SNA Character Stream (SCS)

A printing mode in the Systems Network Architecture (SNA) model that provides various printing and formatting capabilities.

See also **Systems Network Architecture.**

SNA Distribution Services (SNADS)

A Systems Network Architecture (SNA) store-and-forward file and document handling service that uses Advanced Program-to-Program Communication (APPC) protocols to transport data.

See also **Advanced Program-to-Program Communication; store-and-forward; Systems Network Architecture.**

SNA gateway

A hardware or software device connecting a Systems Network Architecture (SNA) mainframe host to a local-area network (LAN).

See also **Systems Network Architecture.**

SNA Network Interconnection (SNI)

An IBM gateway that connects multiple Systems Network Architecture (SNA) networks.

See also **Systems Network Architecture.**

SNA/MS

Systems Network Architecture/Management Services, a network-management strategy based on the Systems Network Architecture (SNA) model to help plan, organize, and control an SNA network. This model includes five categories: Problem Management, Performance and Accounting Management, Configuration Management, Change Management, and Operations Management.

See also **Systems Network Architecture; Systems Network Architecture/Management Services** (includes **Table S.11**).

SNA/SDLC

Systems Network Architecture/Synchronous Data-Link Control, a communications protocol in the

Systems Network Architecture (SNA) model that transfers data between a host and a controller.

See also **Systems Network Architecture.**

SNADS

SNA Distribution Services, a Systems Network Architecture (SNA) store-and-forward file and document handling service that uses Advanced Program-to-Program Communication (APPC) protocols to transport data.

See also **Advanced Program-to-Program Communication; store-and-forward; Systems Network Architecture.**

snail mail

Traditional paper-based postal service.

SNAP

Sub-Network Access Protocol, a protocol in the OSI Reference Model, used on the middle three sublayers of the Physical Layer (Layer 1), the Data-Link Layer (Layer 2), and the Network Layer (Layer 3). The SNAP provides access to (and transfers data to) the *subnetwork*.

See also **OSI Reference Model.**

SNASVCMG

A mode defined in Advanced Program-to-Program Communications (APPC) used for CNOS negotiations.

SNDCP

Subnetwork-Dependent Convergence Protocol, a protocol in the OSI Reference

Model, used on the middle three sublayers of the Physical Layer (Layer 1), the Data-Link Layer (Layer 2), and the Network Layer (Layer 3) to handle details or problems relating to the subnetwork to which the data is being transferred.

See also **OSI Reference Model.**

sneakernet

File sharing by copying files onto floppy disks and physically transporting the floppy disks to another computer.

SNI

SNA Network Interconnection, an IBM gateway that connects multiple Systems Network Architecture (SNA) networks.

See also **Systems Network Architecture.**

SNICP

Subnetwork-Independent Convergence Protocol, a protocol in the OSI Reference Model, used on the middle three sublayers of the Physical Layer (Layer 1), the Data-Link Layer (Layer 2), and the Network Layer (Layer 3) to provide the routing and relaying capabilities needed to get data to its destination.

See also **OSI Reference Model.**

SNMP

Simple Network-Management Protocol, a protocol in the Application Layer (Layer 7) of the OSI Reference Model that specifies a format for collecting network-management data and the exchange of that data between devices. Using Desktop SNMP services, a NetWare workstation can send status infor-

mation to an SNMP-management program running on an Internetwork Packet Exchange (IPX) or Transmission-Control Protocol/Internet Protocol (TCP/IP) network. The two types of devices that make up the SNMP architecture are SNMP *agents* (a background process that monitors operation of the device and communicates with the outside world) and SNMP *managers* (network-management stations that collect messages from SNMP agents, generate reports, and handle data).

See also **Internetwork Packet Exchange; Management Information Base; OSI Reference Model; Simple Network-Management Protocol** (includes **Table S.5**); **Transmission-Control Protocol/Internet Protocol.**

SNMP trap handler

A trap handler used in the Simple Network-Management Protocol (SNMP).

See also **Simple Network-Management Protocol.**

SNP

Subnetwork Protocol, a subnetwork-layer protocol that provides the transfer of data through the local subnet. Some systems may require an adapter module to be inserted between the Internet Protocol (IP) and the SP to reconcile dissimilar interfaces.

SNPA

Subnetwork Point of Attachment, a data-link address used to configure a Connectionless-Mode Network Service (CLNS) route for an interface.

See also **Connectionless-Mode Network Service.**

SNR

signal-to-noise ratio, a measure of signal quality that uses a ratio between the desired signal and the unwanted signal (or noise) at a specific point in a cable.

SNTP

Simple Network-Time Protocol, a variant of the Network-Time Protocol (NTP) in which the correct time is obtained from an official source and disseminated to servers across the network. The major appeal of this protocol is simplicity; it is not regarded as highly accurate (only to within several hundred milliseconds).

soc newsgroup

An Internet newsgroup that discusses social topics.

socket

The portion of an internetwork address within a network node that represents the destination of an Internetwork Packet-Exchange (IPX) packet. Novell reserves socket number 451h for NetWare Core Protocol (NCP), 452h for Service-Advertising Protocol (SAP), 453h for Routing-Information Protocol (RIP), 455h for Network Basic Input/Output System (NetBIOS), and 456h for diagnostics, 8063h for Novell Virtual Terminal (NVT).

See also **Internetwork Packet Exchange; NetWare Core Protocol; Network Basic Input/Output System; Novell Virtual Terminal; Service-Advertising Protocol.**

socket client

A process or function that can make use of a socket to request and receive information and network services.

See also **socket.**

socket number

A unique value assigned to a socket, the maximum size of which depends on the number of bits allocated for the number.

soft error

An error in a Token Ring network that is not considered serious or a threat to the performance or continued operation of the network.

See also **hard error; Token Ring.**

software

Application programs that enable computers to perform functions and tasks.

software handshaking

A process in which control codes (XON and XOFF) in data are used to control the flow of data through the cable.

See also **XON/XOFF.**

software interrupt

A signal to the computer processor generated by an instruction in a software program that tells the processor to suspend and save its current activity, and then branch to an *interrupt service routine* (ISR).

See also **interrupt service routine.**

software license

An agreement to abide by certain prescribed conditions (such as defined rights of the user and limited liability of the software publisher) in the use of a software program.

software piracy

Illegally copying and distributing copyrighted software products.

Solaris

An operating system from SunSoft designed for UNIX environments and that supports a graphical user interface (GUI), electronic mail (e-mail), Network File System (NFS), and Network Information Services (NIS).

See also **electronic mail; graphical user interface; Network File System; Network Information Services.**

SONET

Synchronous Optical Network, a high-speed, fiber-optic network that provides an interface and mechanism for optical transmission of data. SONET features transmission rates from 51.84 megabits per second (Mbps) to 2.488 gigabits per second, an 810-byte packet frame, the capability of transmitting 80,000 frames per second, a four-layer (Photonic, Section, Line, and Path) hierarchy for implementation and management of frame transmissions, adjustable timing and framing during transmission, and support for drop-and-insert capabilities.

Source Address (SA)

A packet header field whose value represents the address of the node sending the packet.

See also **Destination Address.**

Source-Route Bridging (SRB)

An algorithm, often found in Token Ring networks, that provides a means of bridging local-area networks (LANs). This type of bridging assumes the complete source-to-destination route is placed in all frames being sent across the network, and that the frames can be stored and forwarded as indicated by the appropriate frame field.

See also **Token Ring.**

Source-Route Translational Bridging (SR/TLB)

A bridging method in which source and route nodes can communicate with a transparent bridge station with help provided by an intermediate bridge that translates between the two bridge protocols.

See also **transparent bridging.**

source-route transparent bridging

A proposed IBM bridging scheme that merges the transparent and Source-Route Bridging (SRB) strategies into one device to satisfy the needs of all nodes on the network. No translation would be performed between the bridging protocols.

See also **Source-Route Bridging; transparent bridging.**

source routing

IBM's method of routing frames through a network composed of multiple local-area networks (LANs) by specifying in each frame the route it is to follow. End-stations determine the route through a discovery process supported by source route bridges. NetWare source-routing programs allow bridges on IBM Token Ring networks to forward NetWare packets.

See also **Source-Route Bridging.**

source server

A server from which data files, bindery files, and other information is migrated to a NetWare 4 destination server during an upgrade.

Southeastern Universities Research Association Network (SURAnet)

An education-and-research network that connects hosts in 12 states of the Southeast and is part of the National Science Foundation Network (NSFnet).

See also **National Science Foundation Network.**

space parity

A type of parity in which the parity bit is set to 0 and used as the eighth bit in the byte.

See also **parity** (includes **Figure P.1** and **Table P.1**); **parity bit.**

Space Physics Analysis Network (SPAN)

A data-comparison network of the National Aeronautics and Space Administration (NASA) that has extensions to Canada, Japan, and many European countries.

spam

To post inappropriate commercial messages to a large number of unrelated, uninterested Usenet newsgroups.

See also **newsgroup; Usenet.**

SPAN

Space Physics Analysis Network, a data-comparison network of the National Aeronautics and Space Administration (NASA) that has extensions to Canada, Japan, and many European countries.

spanning

A technique involving the placement of frequently used segments of a file system or database on separate disks to improve input/output.

spanning tree

Either a network segment that has no logical loops, or a network structure that has a root node and one path that connects all the other nodes on the network. Used in bridged networks, this tree structure allows bridges to make routing decisions on the basis of the routing distance a path must span.

spanning-tree algorithm

On a multilooped, bridged network, a technique used to find the most desirable path between network segments. When multiple paths exist, this algorithm determines the most efficient path and limits the link between two networks to this single active path. If the path fails, the algorithm reconfigures the network to activate another path.

SPARC

Scalar Processor Architecture, a 32-bit Reduced-Instruction-Set-Computing (RISC) processor from Sun Microsystems, used in SPARCstation workstations.

See also **Reduced-Instruction-Set-Computing; SPARCstation.**

SPARCstation

A group of UNIX workstations from Sun Microsystems that range from small desktop systems to tower servers in multiprocessor configurations. The SPARCstation is based on the Scalar Processor Architecture (SPARC) processor.

See also **Scalar Processor Architecture.**

 **For more information about SPARCstations, surf the Web to** http://www.sun.com/desktop/products/workstations.html.

sparse file

A file that has at least one empty block, often created by a database program. Some operating systems save the entire file (including empty blocks) to disk. NetWare, however, conserves disk space by providing the capability to save only the portions of sparse files that contain data, rather than entire files with empty blocks.

special-interest group (SIG)

A group, often part of a user group or other organization, that shares information about a specific topic.

spectral width

A range of light frequencies emitted by laser. Spectral width is also known as *laser line width.*

speed matching

The capability of a destination device to use a buffer that allows a high-speed source to transmit data at its maximum rate, even if the destination device is a lower-speed device.

SPEED utility

In NetWare and IntranetWare, a server console utility that displays the speed at which the processor is running. The speed is determined by the clock speed of the central processing unit (CPU), the CPU type, and the number of memory wait states.

SPF

Shortest Path First, a routing strategy in which packets are passed between routers according to the distance to the destination.

See also **Open Shortest Path First; routing; shortest-path routing.**

spider

A program that attempts to visit every World Wide Web (WWW) site or other network node to collect the information necessary to create an index or map. A spider is also known as a *crawler* or *robot.*

See also **World Wide Web.**

spike

The occurrence of more than twice the nominal peak voltage in a line, usually caused by lightning and lasting a short while. A spike is also known as an *impulse*.
See also **power conditioning.**

splice

A transient signal, usually of very high amplitude, that lasts a short period of time.

split cable system

A broadband wiring scheme that incorporates a single cable bandwidth being divided between transmission and receiving capabilities. Common splits include a subsplit, midsplit, and highsplit.

split pair

The sending of a signal over wires from two different pairs in twisted-pair cabling, instead of over wires in the same pair.
See also **twisted-pair wiring.**

split-horizon routing

A routing technique in which routers that discover routes through an interface do not advertise the discovered routes through the same interface, because neighboring routers using that interface already know the information. Because split-horizon routing reduces routing traffic on the network, it is commonly used by distance-vector routing protocols.
See also **distance-vector protocol.**

splitter

An analog device that breaks a signal into multiple derived signals.

SPOOL utility

In NetWare 3.*x*, a server console utility that creates, changes, or displays spooler mappings (which are required to set up default print queues for the NPRINT and CAPTURE utilities, as well as supporting applications that make calls to printer numbers rather than to queues).
See also **CAPTURE utility; NPRINT utility.**

spooler

A device or software program that provides a queuing system for files that are waiting to be printed so that files can be printed while the computer performs other tasks.

SPP

Sequenced-Packet Protocol, a protocol in the Xerox Network System (XNS) for the Transport Layer (Layer 4) of the OSI Reference Model.
See also **OSI Reference Model; Xerox Network System.**

spread-spectrum transmission

The distribution of a radio transmission signal over a broad frequency range; the distribution pattern is based on either frequency hopping or on direct sequence coding.

Sprintlink

An Internet commercial network run by Sprint.

 **For more information about Sprint's networking products, surf the Web to** `http://www.sprintbiz.com/data1/index.html`.

Sprintmail

An electronic-mail (e-mail) service provided by Sprintnet and formerly known as Telemail.

SPS

standby power supply, an emergency power source designed to deliver a limited amount of power to a file server or other device in the event of a total loss of power that usually includes a battery charger, battery, and inverter. The SPS monitors power coming in from power lines (the primary source) and as long as that power is sufficient, bypasses the battery. When the primary source fails, the SPS switches to battery power (the secondary source) in a time period short enough usually to avoid data loss.

See also **uninterruptible power supply.**

SPX

Sequenced Packet Exchange, a NetWare protocol that enhances the Novell Internetwork Packet Exchange (IPX) protocol. To ensure successful packet delivery, SPX requests verification from a destination that data has been received, compares a verification value to a value calculated before

transmission, and, by matching those two numbers, acknowledges the packet arrived and that it arrived intact. SPX also has the capability of tracking data transmissions consisting of more than one packet (a transmission that has been split into several packets). If no acknowledgment is received within a specified amount of time, SPX retransmits the packets. If retransmissions fail to produce an acknowledgment, SPX notifies the operator that the connection has failed. SPX is derived from the Xerox Packet Protocol.

See also **Internetwork Packet Exchange.**

SPXCONFIG (NLM)

In NetWare and IntranetWare, a server console NetWare Loadable Module (NLM) that configures certain Sequenced Packet Exchange (SPX) parameters. The parameters include specifying the Watchdog Abort timeout, the Watchdog Verify timeout, the Ack Wait timeout, the Default Retry timeout, the maximum number of concurrent SPX sessions, the quiet mode, and Internet Packet Exchange (IPX) maximum socket table size.

See also **Internet Packet Exchange; NetWare Loadable Module; Sequenced Packet Exchange.**

SPXS utility

In NetWare and IntranetWare, a server console utility that provides STREAMS-based Sequenced Packet Exchange (SPX) services. This utility sets parameters in the IPXSPX.CFG configuration file.

See also **Sequenced Packet Exchange; STREAMS utility.**

Spyglass Enhanced Mosaic

The commercial version of a World Wide Web (WWW) browser from the National Center for Supercomputer Applications (NCSA), licensed by Spyglass, Inc. to other vendors. It serves as the foundation for other browsers, such as Quarterdeck Mosaic.

See also **NCSA Mosaic; Quarterdeck Mosaic; Web browser.**

SQE

Signal-Quality Error, a signal sent from the transceiver to the attached machine in an Ethernet 2.0 or 802.3 network to indicate that the transceiver's collision-detection circuitry is working properly. SQE is also known as a *heartbeat.*

See also **802.3; Ethernet; IEEE 802.x.**

SQL

Structured Query Language, a query language developed by IBM for the management of relational databases. Adopted by Oracle Corporation, SQL contains about 60 commands used to create, modify, query, and access data organized in tables. Used as either an interactive interface or as embedded commands in an application, SQL is a standard set by the American National Standards Institute (ANSI) and International Standards Organization (ISO).

See also **American National Standards Institute; International Standards Organization.**

SQL server

A server whose query procedures comply with the Structured Query Language standard.

See also **Structured Query Language.**

SR/TLB

Source-Route Translational Bridging, a bridging method in which source and route nodes can communicate with a transparent bridge station with help provided by an intermediate bridge that translates between the two bridge protocols.

See also **transparent bridging.**

SRAM

Static Random-Access Memory, a type of random-access memory (RAM) that can store only about one-fourth as much information as dynamic RAM (DRAM), but features access times of 15 to 30 nanoseconds, which is much faster than DRAM. Static RAM (or SRAM) retains its contents as long as power is applied and does not need constant refreshment, as does DRAM.

See also **dynamic RAM; memory; random-access memory.**

SRB

Source-Route Bridging, an algorithm, often found in Token Ring networks, that provides a means of bridging local-area networks (LANs). This type of bridging assumes the complete source-to-destination route is placed in all frames being sent across the network, and that the frames can be stored and forwarded as indicated by the appropriate frame field.

See also **Token Ring.**

SS

Sampled Servo, a recording technique for compact discs in which the contents are stored on a single, spiral track.

SS7

A standard from the Consultative Committee for International Telegraphy and Telephony (CCITT) that is applied to out-of-band signals. SS7 offers fast call setup and sophisticated information and transaction capabilities.

See also **Consultative Committee for International Telegraphy and Telephony.**

SSAP

Session Service-Access Point, in the OSI Reference Model, the service-access point for the Session Layer.

See also **Service-Access Point.**

SSCP

system-services control point, a control point in a host node that provides network services for dependent nodes.

SSCP-LU session

A session between a system-services control point (SSCP) and a logical unit (LU) in which the session enables the LU to request the SSCP to help initiate a logical-unit-to-logical-unit (LU-LU) session.

See also **logical unit; system-services control point.**

SSCP-PU session

A session between a system-services control point (SSCP) and a physical unit (PU) in which the session controls the network configuration by enabling SSCPs to send requests to (and receive messages from) individual nodes.

See also **logical unit; system-services control point.**

SSI

Server Side Includes, a set of commands enabling authors of World Wide Web (WWW) pages to insert variables in their Web pages (such as text from another file or the current date and time).

See also **World Wide Web; Web home page.**

SSL

Secure-Sockets Layer, a layer and type of network connectivity designed by Netscape Communications as part of the Secure-Sockets Layer (SSL) protocol. When a Uniform Resource Locator (URL) begins with *http*, it indicates an SSL connection.

See also **Secure-Sockets Layer (SSL) protocol; Uniform Resource Locator.**

SSL protocol

Secure-Sockets Layer protocol, a protocol designed by Netscape Communications that provides encrypted, authenticated communications across the Internet between World Wide Web (WWW) browsers and servers. A Uniform Resource Locator (URL) that begins with *http* indicates an SSL connection. With an SSL connection, each side is required to have a Security Certificate, the information from which is used to encrypt a message. This ensures that only the intended recipient can decode the message, that the message has not been tampered with, and that the message did indeed originate from the source that it claims to have come from.

See also **Security Certificate; Uniform Resource Locator; World Wide Web; Web browser.**

SSO

Single Sign-On, a network login strategy in which a user needs only a single user ID and password to access any machine, application, or service on a network, provided the user has proper access and usage privileges.

SSS

Server-Session Socket, a protocol in AppleTalk networks at the Session Layer (Layer 5) of the OSI Reference Model, containing the number of the socket to which Session Layer packets are sent.

See also **AppleTalk; OSI Reference Model; socket.**

ST (straight-tip) connector

A fiber-optic cable developed by AT&T, used in premises wiring and in networks.

ST-506

An interface drive type from Seagate Technologies that may be used in personal computer systems with less than 40MB disk

capacity and that features a relatively slow data-transfer rate of 5 megabits per second (Mbps).

stack manager

A software process that mediates between a driver for a Network Interface Card (NIC) and drivers for higher-speed protocols. Although typically loaded at the file server, this process may also be loaded at a gateway or workstation.

See also **Network Interface Card.**

standalone

A computer or peripheral not connected to a network.

standalone hub

An external hub with its own power supply that usually is a box with connectors for the attachment of nodes and possibly includes special connectors for linking to other hubs.

standard

Rules or procedures that have been agreed upon by industry participants.

Standard Message Format (SMF)

A standard set of rules that define the format of messages and how third-party application and gateway programs can interface with Message-Handling System (MHS) messaging products in NetWare.

See also **Message-Handling System; SMF.**

Standby Monitor (SM)

A network node, usually found in Token Ring networks, that serves as a backup to the Active Monitor (AM) and is ready to take over in a timely and correct manner if the AM fails.

See also **Active Monitor; Token Ring.**

standby power supply (SPS)

An emergency power source designed to deliver a limited amount of power to a file server or other device in the event of a total loss of power that usually includes a battery charger, battery, and inverter. The SPS monitors power coming in from power lines (the primary source) and as long as that power is sufficient, bypasses the battery. When the primary source fails, the SPS switches to battery power (the secondary source) in a time period short enough usually to avoid data loss.

See also **uninterruptible power supply.**

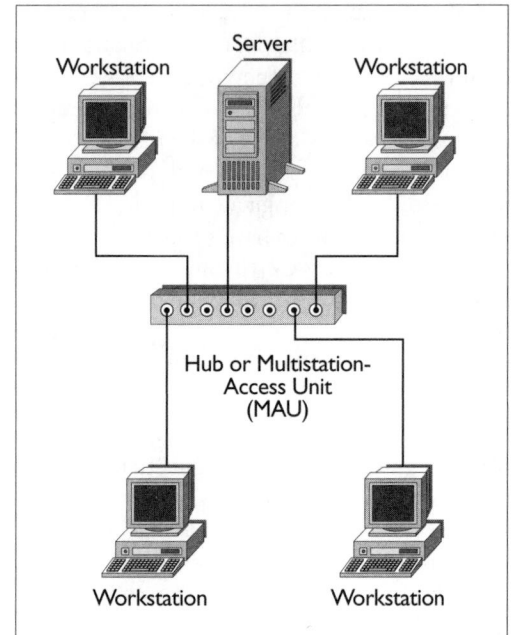

Figure S.2
Star topology

star topology

A network topology in the shape of a star that has a wiring hub (or concentrator) in the center of the configuration and the network nodes arranged around the hub, representing the points of the star. Each node in the network requires its own cable. The star topology does not adhere to any of the Institute of Electrical and Electronic Engineers (IEEE) standards for network configuration. Figure S.2 shows an example of the star topology.

See also **hub; Institute of Electrical and Electronic Engineers.**

star coupler

A coupler used to split a signal into more than two derived signals.

StarGroup

A network operating system from AT&T that usually runs on UNIX systems and provides support for common protocol suites, for Systems Network Architecture (SNA) and asynchronous gateways, for X.25 network routers, and other capabilities. StarGroup is based on the Microsoft LAN Manager.

See also **LAN Manager; Systems Network Architecture; X.25.**

StarKeeper

A network-management system from AT&T.

StarLAN

An AT&T network operating system that implements Carrier-Sense Multiple-Access/Collision Detection (CSMA/CD) protocols on twisted-pair cabling and that transmits at 1 megabit per second (Mbps). StarLAN 10 is a 10Mbps Ethernet version that uses twisted-pair or fiber-optic cabling.
  See also **Carrier-Sense Multiple-Access/Collision Detection; Ethernet.**

start bit

A bit used to start asynchronous communications timing, but not required in synchronous communications.
  See also **parity.**

Start Delimiter (SD)

A field that appears in a Token Ring data or token packet.
  See also **Token Ring.**

Starting Point search engine

A World Wide Web (WWW) metasearch engine that allows users to specify search terms and have results submitted from 1 of 16 different Web search engines. Uniform Resource Locators (URLs) are classified by subject matter, including Business, Entertainment, and Sports.
  See also **search engine; World Wide Web.**

STARTNET.BAT

A batch file that loads network drivers for NetWare on a personal computer workstation.

start-stop transmission

A method of transmission that synchronizes each character individually. No fixed interval exists between transmitted characters; start bits and stop bits coordinate the data flow.

startup disk

A disk containing all the necessary startup files to enable the computer to begin operation. A startup disk is also known as a *boot disk.*

STARTUP.NCF

A server boot file for NetWare and IntranetWare that loads the NetWare server disk driver, name spaces, some SET parameters, and other startup information.
  See also **SET utility.**

Starver

A NetWare Loadable Module (NLM) Behavior Testing utility that tracks how NLMs behave under scarce memory conditions by monitoring — and selectively refusing — their memory-allocation requests.
  See also **NetWare Loadable Module.**

star-wired ring topology

A hybrid physical topology that combines features of a star topology with those of a ring topology, connecting individual nodes to a central hub as an internal ring within the hub. The hub constitutes the ring, which must remain intact for the network to function. Advantages to a star-wired ring topology are that disconnecting a faulty node from the internal ring is relatively easy, fault isolation is relatively easy, the network layout is flexible and relatively easy to expand, individual hubs can be connected to form larger rings, and wiring to the hub is flexible. Figure S.3 shows an example of the star-wired topology.

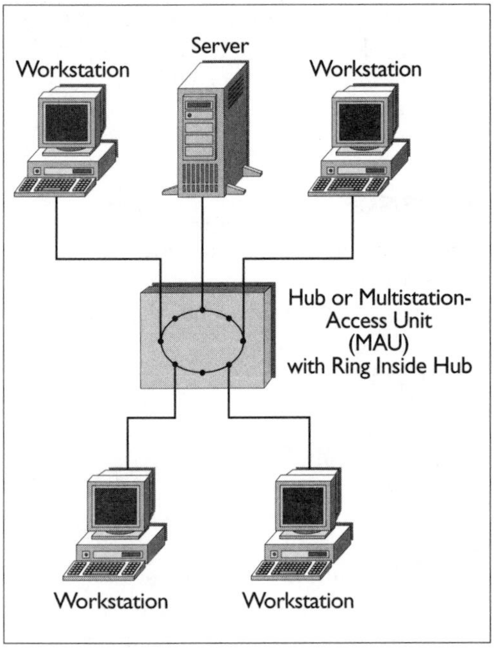

Figure S.3
Star-wired topology

state

A mode in Advanced Program-to-Program Communication (APPC) that determines which verbs a program is allowed to issue.

See also **Advanced Program-to-Program Communication.**

State or Province

A NetWare Directory Schema term and a selectable property for the Volume object in Novell Directory Services (NDS).

See also **leaf object; Novell Directory Services; object.**

stateless protocol

A protocol in which individual transactions may be repeated without affecting prior or future transactions, because each transaction is independent of its predecessor and its successor.

Static Random-Access Memory (SRAM)

A type of random-access memory (RAM) that can store only about one-fourth as much information as dynamic RAM (DRAM), but features access times of 15 to 30 nanoseconds, which is much faster than DRAM. Static RAM (or SRAM) retains its contents as long as power is applied and does not need constant refreshment, as does DRAM.

See also **dynamic RAM; memory; random-access memory.**

static routing

A method in which a Routing-Information Table is manually updated, rather than being updated automatically by the network system.

See also **Routing-Information Table.**

statically assigned socket

A socket with a number in the range of 1 through 127, reserved for use by clients such as the lower-level AppleTalk protocols.

See also **AppleTalk; socket.**

station

A server, router, printer, fax machine, or any computer device connected to a network by a Network Interface Card (NIC) and a communications medium.

See also **Network Interface Card; workstation.**

station address

A number that uniquely identifies a Network Interface Card (NIC). A station address is also known as a *node number*.

See also **Network Interface Card; node address; node number.**

Station Management (SMT)

In a Fiber Distributed Data Interface (FDDI) network, a component made up of services that ensure the correct operation of various network elements. SMT includes frame services, connection management, and ring management.

See also **Fiber Distributed Data Interface.**

station restrictions

Account restrictions imposed on a user that specify to which workstation(s) a user can log in.

statistical multiplexing

A method in which line time is dynamically allocated to each of the various attached terminals, according to whether the terminal is active or inactive at a particular moment. A statistical multiplexer is capable of analyzing traffic density and dynamically switching to a different channel pattern to speed up the transmission. Statistical multiplexing is also known as *stat mux*.

Statistical Time-Division Multiplexing (STDM)

A data-transmission method allowing the X.25 interface to maximize the use of bandwidth by dynamically allocating on demand portions of the available bandwidth to active devices. The X.25 interface provides a better throughput than Time-Division Multiplexing (TDM).

See also **Time-Division Multiplexing; X.25.**

Status

In Novell Directory Services (NDS), a selectable property for the AFP Server, Computer, Messaging Server, NCP Server, Print Server, Printer, and Volume objects.

See also **leaf object; Novell Directory Services; object.**

STDA

StreetTalk Directory Assistance, a popup window in StreetTalk that displays the name of every node or device attached to the network, as well as other information about the node or device.

See also **StreetTalk.**

STDM

Statistical Time-Division Multiplexing, a data-transmission method allowing the X.25 interface to maximize the use of bandwidth by dynamically allocating on demand portions of the available bandwidth to active devices. The X.25 interface provides a better throughput than Time-Division Multiplexing (TDM).

See also **Time-Division Multiplexing; X.25.**

STM

Synchronous Transfer Mode, a transport method used in broadband Integrated-Services Digital Networks (ISDNs) that uses Time-Division Multiplexing (TDM) and switching methods with up to 50 megabits per second (Mbps) of bandwidth for synchronous transmissions.

See also **Integrated-Services Digital Network; Time-Division Multiplexing.**

STM-x

Synchronous Transfer Mode-*x*, any of several channel capacities (denoted by *x*) that are defined by the Synchronous Digital Hierarchy from the Consultative Committee for International Telegraphy and Telephony (CCITT).

See also **Synchronous Transfer Mode-*x*** (includes **Table S.8**).

stop bit

A signal indicating the end of a character, or, in the context of a serial data transfer,

the distinction where one character starts and another stops.

See also **parity; serial communication.**

storage device

A device (such as an external tape-backup unit) used to back up data from a server or a workstation.

storage-device driver

Software designed to control the operation of a storage device attached to a compatible host adapter.

storage-device-driver database

A database file located on the host server that contains a list of supported storage device drivers.

storage-device interface (SDI or SMSDI)

A set of routines that enables the NetWare SBACKUP utility to access various storage devices and media. In the event that more than one storage device is attached to the host, the SDI provides SBACKUP with a list of storage devices and media.

See also **SBACKUP.**

storage-device-support driver

Software used with a Device-Independent Backup Interface (DIBI) and a storage-device driver.

See also **Device-Independent Backup Interface.**

Storage-Management Data Requester (SMDR)

A NetWare feature that passes commands between the SBACKUP utility and Target Service Agents (TSAs).

See also **SBACKUP utility; Storage-Management Services; Target Service Agent.**

Storage-Management Services (SMS)

Services that allow data to be backed up and restored independently of the hardware and file systems normally used for backup and storage. Table S.7 shows the SMS-compliant NetWare Loadable Module (NLM) programs and other software that can run on NetWare servers.

store-and-forward

A technique used in message switching that entails messages being stored temporarily at intermediate points across the network before being transmitted to the next destination. This method is commonly used on networks

Table S.7: SMS Programs for NetWare

Program	Description
SBACKUP utility	Provides backup and restore capabilities.
Storage-Management Data Requester (SMDR)	Passes commands between the SBACKUP utility and Target Service Agents (TSAs).
SMS Device Interface (SMSDI)	Passes commands between the SBACKUP utility and the storage devices and media.
Device drivers	Act on commands passed from the SBACKUP utility through the SMSDI to control the mechanical operation of storage devices and media.
Target Service Agents (TSAs)	Take data requests that are generated by the SBACKUP utility and pass them to the NetWare server (where data resides) and then return requested data back through SMDR to the SBACKUP utility.
Database TSAs	Take data and command requests from the host server (where SBACKUP resides) and the database (where the data resides) then return requested data back through SMDR to the SBACKUP utility.
Workstation TSAs	Take data and command requests from the host server (where SBACKUP resides) and the workstation (where the data resides) then return requested data back through SMDR to the SBACKUP utility.
Workstation Manager	Receives "I am here" messages from workstations available to be backed up and maintains an internal list of the names of these workstations.

See also **SBACKUP utility; SMS Device Interface; Storage-Management Data Requester; Target Service Agent.**

that are not available at all times and allows users to take advantage of off-peak rates when traffic and costs might be lower.

store-and-forward switch

A switch designed to first check a packet's integrity by confirming the Media-Access Control (MAC) address in an internal address table before sending it on to its destination port.

STP

shielded twisted-pair, a type of cable with a foil shield and copper braid surrounding pairs of wires that have a minimum number of twists per foot of cable length. Although it is considered bulky, STP is used for high-speed transmissions over long distances and is often associated with Token Ring networks.

See also **shielded cable; unshielded cable; unshielded twisted-pair cable.**

straight-tip connector

A connector for fiber-optic cable that maintains the alignment of the ends of connected fibers and that facilitates an efficient transmission of light signals.

stream

A full-duplex connection between a task and a device that can include an encapsulated processing module, or a second-level file opened for data transmissions.

stream I/O services

Services for standard read-and-write file operations in which data can be transmitted as characters, strings, blocks of memory, or under format control.

streaming

A transmission mode that allows a receiving system to begin processing or displaying the content of a file before an entire file has been received. When used with Internet files, this mode allows the user to hear, see, or interact with time-based multimedia files that have long playing times without waiting for similarly long download times.

streaming tape

A high-speed tape backup system that optimizes throughput because the tape is not stopped during a backup, but requires the computer and backup software to be fast enough to keep up with the tape drive.

STREAMS: Active Stream Handles

In NetWare 3.12, a resource appearing in the Available Options/Resource Utilization screen of the MONITOR NetWare Loadable Module (NLM) that tracks the number of communication streams that are currently in use.

See also **MONITOR; NetWare Loadable Module.**

STREAMS utility

In NetWare and IntranetWare, a server console utility that provides a common interface between NetWare and transport protocols (for example Internet Packet Exchange/Sequenced Packet Exchange, Transmission-Control Protocol/Internet Protocol, and Systems Network Architecture) that must deliver data and requests to NetWare for processing. This utility usually is automatically loaded by other modules when needed.

See also **Internet Packet Exchange/Sequenced Packet Exchange; Transmission-Control Protocol/Internet Protocol; Systems Network Architecture.**

StreamWorks

A product line from Xing Technology based on the Motion Pictures Expert Group (MPEG) standard designed to distribute real-time video and audio files to multiple recipients over the Internet or over an internal network.

See also **Motion Pictures Expert Group.**

 **For more information about StreamWorks, surf the Web to** `http://www.xingtech.com/sw_now.html`.

Street

A NetWare Directory Schema term and a selectable property for the Volume object in Novell Directory Services (NDS).

See also **leaf object; Novell Directory Services; object.**

StreetTalk

A distributed global naming and directory service on the Banyan Systems Virtual Network System (VINES) operating system.

See also **Virtual Network System.**

StreetTalk Directory Assistance (STDA)

A popup window in StreetTalk that displays the name of every node or device attached to the network, as well as other information about the node or device.

See also **StreetTalk.**

string

A series of alphabetical characters, or a category of data types that are used to store strings.

string-manipulation functions

Functions that are designed to manipulate strings of characters.

striping

Interleaving file systems or databases across multiple disks on a network in an effort to improve input/output performance.

Structure-Management Information (SMI)

A component in the Internet Protocol (IP) network-management model that specifies how information about managed objects is to be represented.

See also **Internet Protocol.**

Structured Query Language (SQL)

A query language developed by IBM for the management of relational databases. Adopted by Oracle Corporation, SQL contains about 60 commands used to create, modify, query, and access data organized in tables. Used as either an interactive interface or as embedded commands in an application, SQL is a standard set by the American National Standards Institute (ANSI) and International Standards Organization (ISO).

See also **American National Standards Institute; International Standards Organization.**

structured wiring

A planned cabling system for enterprise networks, expected to include provisions for both voice and data communications.

STS

sign-trailing separate, a numeric data type in the COBOL programming language, represented as an American Standard Code for Information Interchange (ASCII) string. STS is right-justified and padded with leading zeros; it has the *sign* byte at the end.

See also **American Standard Code for Information Interchange.**

STS bit

A bit that is set in the AppleTalk Transaction Protocol (ATP) header of a Transaction Response (TResp) packet to force the requester to immediately retransmit a Transaction Request (TReq) packet.

See also **Transaction Request packet; Transaction Response packet.**

stub network

An Internet Protocol (IP) network serviced by a proxy server, using a subset of an existing IP network address.

suballocation

A process of storing data in small blocks to save disk space.

subarea

The portion of a Systems Network Architecture (SNA) consisting of a subarea node and any peripheral nodes or other links attached to it.

See also **Systems Network Architecture.**

subarea node

A communication controller or host on a Systems Network Architecture (SNA) network that handles complete network addresses.

See also **Systems Network Architecture.**

subchannel

A subdivision of a communication channel based on broadband frequency and creating a separate channel.

subdirectory

A directory appearing below another directory in a file system hierarchy. (The *root directory* is commonly the highest directory in a file hierarchy and is the directory from which all other directories must branch.)

Sub-Distribution Frame (SDF)

An intermediate wiring center connected by backbone cable to a Main Distribution Frame (MDF).

See also **Main Distribution Frame.**

Sub-Network Access Protocol (SNAP)

In the OSI Reference Model, a protocol used on the middle three sublayers of the Physical Layer (Layer 1), the Data-Link Layer (Layer 2), and the Network Layer (Layer 3). The SNAP provides access to (and transfers data to) the *subnetwork*.

See also **OSI Reference Model.**

subnet layers

Network layers used by devices that relay transmissions between other devices. In the OSI Reference Model, subnet layers are the Physical Layer (Layer 1), Data-Link Layer (Layer 2), and the Network Layer (Layer 3).

See also **OSI Reference Model.**

subnet mask

In the Internet Protocol (IP) addressing scheme, a group of selected bits that identifies a subnetwork. All members of the subnetwork share the same mask value. A subnet mask is also known as a *subnetwork address mask*.

subnetwork

A portion of a backbone network partitioned by repeaters, bridges, or routers. Nodes on a subnetwork use a single protocol to communicate with each other. The subnetwork, which may include both nodes and routers, is connected to a larger network through an intermediate system that may use a routing protocol to communicate with nodes outside the subnetwork.

subnetwork address mask

An indication of how an Internet Protocol (IP) address is divided into subnetwork addresses and local host addresses. The network mask contains a 32-bit number with all ones for network and subnetwork portions of the complete IP address, and all zeros for the host address portions.

subnetwork addressing

The use of a single Internet Protocol (IP) address to identify a number of subnetworks.

Subnetwork-Dependent Convergence Protocol (SNDCP)

In the OSI Reference Model, a protocol used on the middle three sublayers of the Physical Layer (Layer 1), the Data-Link Layer (Layer 2), and the Network Layer (Layer 3) to handle details or problems relating to the subnetwork to which the data is being transferred.

See also **OSI Reference Model.**

Subnetwork-Independent Convergence Protocol (SNICP)

In the OSI Reference Model, a protocol used on the middle three sublayers of the Physical Layer (Layer 1), the Data-Link Layer (Layer 2), and the Network Layer (Layer 3) to provide the routing and relaying capabilities needed to get data to its destination.

See also **OSI Reference Model.**

subnetwork, level *x*

A network level created by dividing an oversized internetwork into a number of smaller networks to help routers keep track of routing information. For example, a *level-1 subnetwork* is managed by a *level-1 router*. All networks in this division are treated as part of the same network. Transmissions to a machine on one of the networks would be sent to the address of the level-1 router, rather than to the address of an individual network.

See also **level-1 routing; level-2 routing; level-3 routing.**

Subnetwork Point of Attachment (SNPA)

A data-link address used to configure a Connectionless-Mode Network Service (CLNS) route for an interface.

See also **Connectionless-Mode Network Service.**

Subnetwork Protocol (SP)

A subnetwork-layer protocol that provides the transfer of data through the local subnet. Some systems may require an adapter module to be inserted between the Internet Protocol (IP) and the SP to reconcile dissimilar interfaces.

subordinate object

A Novell Directory Services (NDS) object located within another object.

subordinate replica

A NetWare Directory replica automatically placed on a NetWare server when a parent Directory partition has a master, read/write, or read-only replica and the child Directory partition does not.

See also **NetWare Directory replica.**

subscribe

To sign up as a customer of an Internet service provider (ISP), add a name to a mailing list, or add a newsgroup to the list of pending articles a newsreader program presents to a user.

See also **Internet service provider; mailing list; newsgroup; newsreader.**

subscriber connector (SC)

A device that connects two components by plugging one connector into the other and that establishes a connection that must be broken (for example, by pressing a button or releasing a hatch). An SC works with either single-mode or multimode fiber.

substring

A subdivision of a string.
See also **string.**

subvector

In Systems Network Architecture (SNA), a data segment that is part of a message vector, consisting of a length field, a key describing the vector type, and other subvector-specific data.

See also **Systems Network Architecture.**

SuperHighway Access

A World Wide Web (WWW) browser from Frontier Technologies that offers a solid user interface to news, electronic mail (e-mail), and ftp clients, but offers limited configuration options.

See also **Web browser.**

superpipelining

A preprocessing method in which two or more execution stages are divided into two or more pipelined stages to improve microprocessor performance.

See also **pipelining.**

superscalar

A type of architecture for microprocessors, containing more than one execution unit and allowing the microprocessor to execute more than one instruction per clock cycle. The microprocessor determines whether an instruction can be executed in parallel with the next instruction in line; if it detects no dependencies, it executes the two instructions.

superserver

A high-performance computer specifically designed to be used as a network server and characterized by scalable input/output (I/O) channels, complex multiprocessing features, several central processing units (CPUs), large amounts of error-correction memory, cache memory, fault-tolerant features, and a large hard disk storage capacity.

superuser

A special UNIX privilege level for system managers that provides unlimited access to all files, directories, and commands.

supervisor

A person who is responsible for the administration and maintenance of a network, database, or both. Normally, a supervisor has access rights to all volumes, directories, and files.

See also **administrator.**

Supervisor right

A NetWare directory, file, object, and property right that grants a user all rights to directories, files, objects, and properties.

See also **access rights.**

Supported Connections

A NetWare Directory Schema term and a selectable property for the AFP Server object in Novell Directory Services (NDS).

See also **leaf object; Novell Directory Services; object.**

Supported Gateway

In Novell Directory Services (NDS), a protocol supported by the Messaging Server object.

See also **Novell Directory Services.**

Supported Services

In Novell Directory Services (NDS), a NetWare Directory Schema term and a selectable property for the Messaging Server and NCP Server objects.

See also **leaf object; Novell Directory Services; object.**

Supported Typefaces

In Novell Directory Services (NDS), a NetWare Directory Schema term and a selectable property for the Printer object.

See also **leaf object; Novell Directory Services; object.**

suppression

A power-conditioning technique that protects hardware against transients. The most common suppression devices are surge protectors that include circuitry to prevent excess voltage.

See also **power conditioning; surge protector.**

SURAnet

Southeastern Universities Research Association Network, an education-and-research network that connects hosts in 12 states of the Southeast and is part of the National Science Foundation Network (NSFnet).

See also **National Science Foundation Network.**

surface test

In NetWare, a test run by the INSTALL program to search a hard disk's NetWare partition for bad blocks. A *destructive test* destroys data as it makes several passes over

the disk surface while reading and writing test patterns. A *nondestructive test* pre-reads and saves existing data, reads and writes test patterns, and then writes data back to the hard disk. Volumes on the hard disk must be dismounted before the surface test can be run.

surge

A sudden increase in line voltage that usually lasts a short period of time and may be destructive.

See also **power conditioning.**

surge (packet-switched network)

A temporary increase in required bandwidth, measured in relation to a guaranteed bandwidth called the Committed Information Rate (CIR).

See also **Committed Information Rate.**

surge suppressor

A power-conditioning device placed between a computer and the Alternating Current (AC) line connection to protect the computer from power surges.

See also **power conditioning; surge.**

Surname

A selectable property for the User object in Novell Directory Services (NDS).

See also **leaf object; Novell Directory Services; object.**

SVC

switched virtual circuit, a circuit established dynamically (using call-setup and call-clearing procedures), that remains connected until a user or application shuts it down.

swap file

A file on a hard disk used to temporarily store parts of running programs that have been swapped out of memory to make room for other running programs.

See also **swapping.**

swapping

A process that involves exchanging one item for another item, which may occur with memory, processes, data, disk space, and so on.

switch (software)

An option that modifies the way a computer carries out a command.

switch (data)

A device that reroutes data to its destination, commonly found in switching networks where data is grouped and routed on the basis of predetermined criteria.

switch block

A set of switches mounted to form a single hardware component that can be used to control system configuration data or to set system addresses.

switch (Ethernet)

A device designed to direct traffic among several Ethernet networks. Normally, this device has multiple ports with which to connect subnetworks and multiple processors to handle traffic through the switch.

switched 56

A circuit-switched telecommunications service operating at 56 kilobits per second (Kbps) that can be leased from long-distance service providers.

switched digital access

A method in which a local telecommunications carrier mediates a connection to a long-distance line, connecting the user directly to the local carrier and from there to a long-distance carrier.

switched line

A network node connection established by dialing into the network.

Switched Multimegabit Data Services (SMDS)

A packet-switched service that offers high-speed data throughputs for metropolitan-area networks (MANs). Described in a series of specifications produced by Bell Communications Research (Bellcore), this service utilizes the SMDS Interface Protocol (SIP) between a user device and SMDS network equipment. SMDS is being adopted by long-distance carriers and by providers of telecommunications equipment.

See also **Bellcore; metropolitan-area network (MAN).**

switched network

A network in which temporary connections are established between two nodes when necessary. The routing of transmissions through these temporary connections is known as *switching* and is used for networks on which many nodes may be accessing the network simultaneously. The three most common types are circuit-switched networks, message-switched networks, and packet-switched networks.

See also **circuit-switched network; message-switched network; packet-switched network.**

Switched T1

A circuit-switched telecommunications service over a T1 line with a bandwidth of 1.544 megabits per second. The transmission may go through a multiplexer that breaks it down and transmits it across several slower channels.

See also **T1.**

switched virtual circuit (SVC)

A circuit established dynamically (using call-setup and call-clearing procedures), that remains connected until a user or application shuts it down.

switching element

A device that controls the mapping, scheduling, and forwarding of data during the transmission of a packet into a node and along the appropriate path to the packet's destination. The switching element consists of (1) an *input controller* that synchronizes each input with an internal clock, (2) an *output controller* that queues and buffers inputs, and (3) an *interconnection network* that provides a means of getting from an input channel to an output channel.

switching hierarchy

A hierarchy of five switch *levels* (or exchanges) that establish connections for long-distance telephone calls. The five levels are *regional centers* (or regional points), *sectional centers* (or sectional points), *primary centers* (or primary points), *toll centers* (or toll points), and *end offices*.

See also **exchange.**

synchronization

The process of ensuring that replicas of a NetWare Directory partition contain the same information as other replicas of that partition (*replica synchronization*) or that all servers in a Directory tree report the same time (*time synchronization*).

Synchronization Interval

A Novell Directory Services (NDS) Directory Schema term.

See also **Novell Directory Services.**

synchronization level

A specification that indicates whether corresponding transaction programs exchange confirmation requests and replies.

synchronization rules

The rules that file servers use to control simultaneous access to a file by multiple nodes on a network.

synchronization services

Services that provide applications with the capability to coordinate access to network files and other network resources.

Synchronized Up To

A Novell Directory Services (NDS) Directory Schema term.

See also **Novell Directory Services.**

synchronous

A data-transfer mode in which information is transmitted in blocks (or frames) of bits that are separated by equal time intervals. Both sending and receiving computers must precisely control the timing. This requires that special characters be embedded in the data stream to begin synchronization and to maintain synchronization during the transmission.

See also **asynchronous.**

Synchronous Data-Link Control (SDLC)

A protocol developed by IBM in the mid-1970s that supports a variety of link types and topologies. SDLC can be used with point-to-point and multipoint links, bounded and unbounded media, half-duplex and full-duplex transmissions, and circuit-switched and packet-switched networks. SDLC identifies *primary* network nodes as those controlling the operation of other stations and *secondary* network nodes as those being controlled by a primary network node. These nodes can be placed in a *point-to-point configuration* (which involves only a primary and secondary node), a *multipoint*

configuration (which involves one primary and multiple secondary nodes), a *loop configuration* (which involves a primary node connected to the first and last secondary nodes in a loop topology), and a *hub go-ahead configuration* (which involves the primary node using an outbound channel and the secondary nodes using an inbound channel).

Synchronous Optical Network (SONET)

A high-speed, fiber-optic network that provides an interface and mechanism for optical transmission of data. SONET features transmission rates from 51.84 megabits per second (Mbps) to 2.488 gigabits per second, an 810-byte packet frame, the capability of transmitting 80,000 frames per second, a four-layer (Photonic, Section, Line, and Path) hierarchy for implementation and management of frame transmissions, adjustable timing and framing during transmission, and support for drop-and-insert capabilities.

Synchronous Transfer Mode (STM)

A transport method used in broadband Integrated-Services Digital Networks (ISDNs) that uses Time-Division Multiplexing (TDM) and switching methods with up to 50 megabits per second (Mbps) of bandwidth for synchronous transmissions.

See also **Integrated-Services Digital Network; Time-Division Multiplexing.**

Synchronous Transfer Mode-x (STM-x)

Any of several channel capacities (denoted by x) that are defined by the Synchronous

Digital Hierarchy from the Consultative Committee for International Telegraphy and Telephony (CCITT). Table S.8 shows the transmission rates for STM-*x* channels.

Table S.8: STM-x Transmission Rates

STM Level	Transmission Rate
STM-1	155.52 megabits per second (Mbps)
STM-3	466.56Mbps
STM-4	622.08Mbps
STM-6	933.12Mbps
STM-8	1.244 gigabits per second (Gbps)
STM-12	1.866Gbps
STM-16	2.488Gbps

synchronous transmission

Network system operations in which events occur with precise clocking.

syntax

Rules of spelling and grammar applied to a programming language or to an operating system, including the exact sequence of command elements required for the command to be interpreted correctly.

syntax error

An error that occurs in a programming language or operating system syntax of commands (for example, a misspelling).
See also **syntax.**

SYS volume (SYS: volume)

The first volume created during NetWare server installation, containing the SYSTEM, PUBLIC, LOGIN, MAIL, DELETED.SAV, QUEUES, NLS, and ETC directories.
See also **SYSTEM directory.**

SYS:SYSTEM

SYSTEM directory, a directory (SYS:SYSTEM) created during the installation of NetWare. SYS:SYSTEM contains operating-system files, NetWare Loadable Module (NLM) files, and utilities for managing the network. The ADMIN user (or a user with ADMIN-equivalent rights) has rights to the SYS:SYSTEM directory.
See also **ADMIN object; NetWare Loadable Module.**

SYS: volume

Another way of writing **SYS volume.**
See also **SYSTEM directory.**

SYSCON utility

In NetWare 3.*x*, a workstation utility that controls accounting, file server, group, and user information. A network supervisor may also use this utility to control the network activities of workgroup managers.

sysop

systems operator, a person responsible for the physical operation of a computer system or a network resource who decides backup procedures and when maintenance should be performed on the system.

System (Sy) attribute

A directory and file attribute with which the NetWare operating system marks directories or files for its own exclusive use.

See also **attribute.**

System 7

A major revision to the operating system for the Macintosh computer, released in May 1991, that featured 32-bit addressing, aliases, and an Apple menu that could contain applications, the Applications menu, Balloon Help, colorized three-dimensional windows, faster printer drivers, built-in file sharing, and QuickTime. Since its initial release, several minor revisions have been released, as follows:

- *System 7.1.* Released in August 1992. Introduced a Fonts folder, but most other changes were core-level.
- *System 7 Pro.* Released in October 1993. Included an early version of PowerTalk and AppleScript.
- *System 7.5.* Released in late 1994. Introduced Macintosh Drag & Drop, QuickDraw GX, and Apple Guide.
- *System 7.6.* Released in early 1997.

system administrator

A person who is responsible for the daily operation and maintenance of the network system, including planning future expansions, installing new hardware and software, adding and removing users, backing up the system, assigning and changing passwords, monitoring system performance, and training users.

See also **network administration.**

Systems Application Architecture (SAA)

A set of IBM standards introduced in 1987 that defines a set of interfaces (and protocols) for future IBM software. The three main components of SAA are *Common User Access* (CUA), which defines a graphical user interface (GUI) for products designed for object-oriented environments; *Common Programming Interface* (CPI), which includes application program interfaces (APIs) and Structured Query Language (SQL); and *Common Communications Support* (CCS), which provides a common set of communications protocols.

See also **Application Program Interface; graphical user interface; Structured Query Language.**

system connect

The act of physically connecting to a host computer or to a network.

system console screen

A monitor display screen from which NetWare server console commands can be entered at the command line.

system crash

The point at which a network system becomes inoperable or no longer functions properly.

SYSTEM directory

A directory (SYS:SYSTEM), created during the installation of NetWare, that contains operating-system files, NetWare Loadable Module (NLM) files, and utilities for managing the network. The ADMIN user (or a user with ADMIN-equivalent rights) has rights to the SYS:SYSTEM directory.

See also **ADMIN object; NetWare Loadable Module.**

System Disk Drives

In NetWare 4.02 , the name of a screen from the MONITOR NetWare Loadable Module (NLM).

See also **MONITOR; NetWare Loadable Module.**

System Fault Tolerance (SFT)

A data-protection scheme in NetWare that provides procedures allowing a user to automatically recover from hardware failures. Table S.9 shows the three levels of SFT protection. Note that each level of protection includes the previous levels (for example, SFT III includes SFT I and SFT II).

System ID

A six-byte hexadecimal number used to identify a NetWare Link-Services Protocol (NLSP) router.

See also **NetWare Link-Services Protocol.**

System-Independent Data Format (SIDF)

A format used by the SBACKUP utility in NetWare that allows all data backed up with SBACKUP to be read by other backup applications with the capability of reading and writing in SIDF.

See also **SBACKUP.**

System login script

A type of login script that sets general environments for all users in NetWare 2.x and NetWare 3.x. The Container login script replaces the System login script in NetWare 4.x.

See also **Container login script.**

Table S.9: SFT Levels

Level	Name	Description
SFT I	Hot Fix	Provides protection against data being saved to faulty blocks on the server's hard disk.
SFT II	Disk Mirroring or Duplexing	Provides protection against hard disk failures by pairing two hard disks on the same channel (*disk mirroring*) or on different channels (*disk duplexing*).
SFT III	Server Mirroring	Provides protection from server failure through the use of a *secondary* (identical) server that immediately assumes control of network operations when the primary server fails.

See also **disk mirroring; disk duplexing; primary server; secondary server.**

system memory

System random-access memory (RAM) located between 640K and 1,024K and not usually addressed by DOS or applications. System memory can be addressed by computers with 80386 or 80486 microprocessors that use special control programs to make upper memory blocks (UMBs) in system memory.

See also **memory.**

System Module Information

In NetWare 4.02, a field name from the Available Options screen of the MONITOR NetWare Loadable Module (NLM).

See also **MONITOR; NetWare Loadable Module.**

System Modules

In NetWare 4.02, a name of a screen from the MONITOR NetWare Loadable Module (NLM).

See also **MONITOR; NetWare Loadable Module.**

system prompt

A monitor screen display that indicates the operating system is ready to receive a command.

system redundancy

Duplication of crucial system components to protect against failure. System redundancy in NetWare is provided in System Fault Tolerance III (SFT III) through mirrored network servers. Redundant cabling, power supplies, disk storage, gateways, routers,

Network Interface Cards (NICs), mirrored server links, and printers provide protection against other failures.

See also **System Fault Tolerance.**

system slide

Cabling that runs from a computer or network to a distribution frame.

See also **distribution frame.**

Systems-Management Application Process (SMAP)

Software in the OSI Network-Management Model that implements the network-management capabilities in a single node.

See also **OSI Network-Management Model.**

Systems-Management Application Service Element (SMASE)

A component that performs the work for a Systems-Management Application Entity (SMAE) in the OSI Network-Management Model.

See also **OSI Network-Management Model; Systems-Management Application Entity.**

Systems-Management Function (SMF)

Services provided to manage particular network domains in the OSI Network-Management Model. SMFs include Object Management, State Management, Relationship Management, Alarm Reporting, Event Report Management, Log Control, Security Alarm Reporting, Security Audit Trail, Access Control, Accounting Metering,

Workload Monitoring, Summarization, and Test Management.

See also **OSI Network-Management Model; SMF.**

Systems-Management Function Area (SMFA)

One of five domains defined in the OSI Network-Management Model, including Accounting Management, Configuration Management, Fault Management, Performance Management, and Security Management.

See also **OSI Network-Management Model.**

Systems-Management Application Entity (SMAE)

A component of the OSI Network-Management Model that implements the network-management services and activities at the Application Layer (Layer 7) in the network node.

See also **OSI Network-Management Model.**

Systems Network Architecture (SNA)

A hierarchical, single-host network structure introduced by IBM in 1974 that includes descriptions of the logical structure, formats, protocols, and operational sequences for data transmission through, and configuration of, wide-area networks (WANs). The SNA model divides a hierarchical structure into seven layers, with each layer performing a specific function. Table S.10 shows the seven layers and provides a brief description of each. Figure S.4 shows a comparison of

the SNA model to the OSI Reference Model.

The three lower levels of the model (Physical Control, Data-Link Control, and Path Control) are collectively referred to as the *transport network.* The distributed components of these three layers are responsible for transporting data through the network on behalf of network-addressable units (NAUs), which are components that can establish temporary, logical connections with each other. The following are the three types of NAUs:

- *Physical units* (PUs), which represent devices and communications links for the network
- *Logical units* (LUs), which serve as points of access for users on the network
- *Control points*, which include such network control functions as managing domain resources and monitoring and reporting on those resources.

SNA defines a hierarchical network configuration (consisting of subarea nodes and peripheral nodes), a peer-oriented configuration (consisting of Advanced Peer-to-Peer Networking and low-entry network nodes), and a hybrid configuration (consisting of one or more hierarchical network subnets with one or more peer-oriented subnets).

See also **control point; logical unit; physical unit; OSI Reference Model.**

 **For more information about the Systems Network Architecture, surf the Web to** `http://www.networking.ibm.com/app/aiwdoc/aiwsrc.htm.`

Table S.10: SNA Model

Layer	Description
Transaction Service (Layer 7)	Provides network-management services, such as distributed database access and document interchange.
Presentation Service (Layer 6)	Formats and transforms data for compatibility between different presentation media and coordinates the sharing of network resources.
Data-Flow Control (Layer 5)	Synchronizes data flow, coordinates the exchange of data, and groups data into units.
Transmission Control (Layer 4)	Performs error-control functions, coordinates the pace of data exchanges to match processing capacities, and encodes data for security.
Path Control (Layer 3)	Creates a logical channel between two nodes and controls data traffic on the network. Nodes perform routing and congesting control.
Data-Link Control (Layer 2)	Controls the transmission of data between adjacent network nodes over a single line. Nodes activate and deactivate links on command from their control points, as well as managing link-level data flow.
Physical Control (Layer 1)	Provides adjacent network nodes with either a parallel or serial interface. Includes both data communications equipment within nodes and the physical links (connections) between them.

Systems Network Architecture/Management Services (SNA/MS)

A network-management strategy based on the Systems Network Architecture (SNA) model to help plan, organize, and control an SNA network. This model includes five categories of management services, shown in Table S.11.

See also **Systems Network Architecture.**

Systems Network Architecture/Synchronous Data-Link Control (SNA/SDLC)

A communications protocol in the Systems Network Architecture (SNA) model that transfers data between a host and a controller.

systems operator (sysop)

A person responsible for the physical operation of a computer system or a network resource who decides backup procedures and when maintenance should be performed on the system.

system-services control point (SSCP)

A control point in a host node that provides network services for dependent nodes.

See also **SSCP-LU session; SSCP-PU session.**

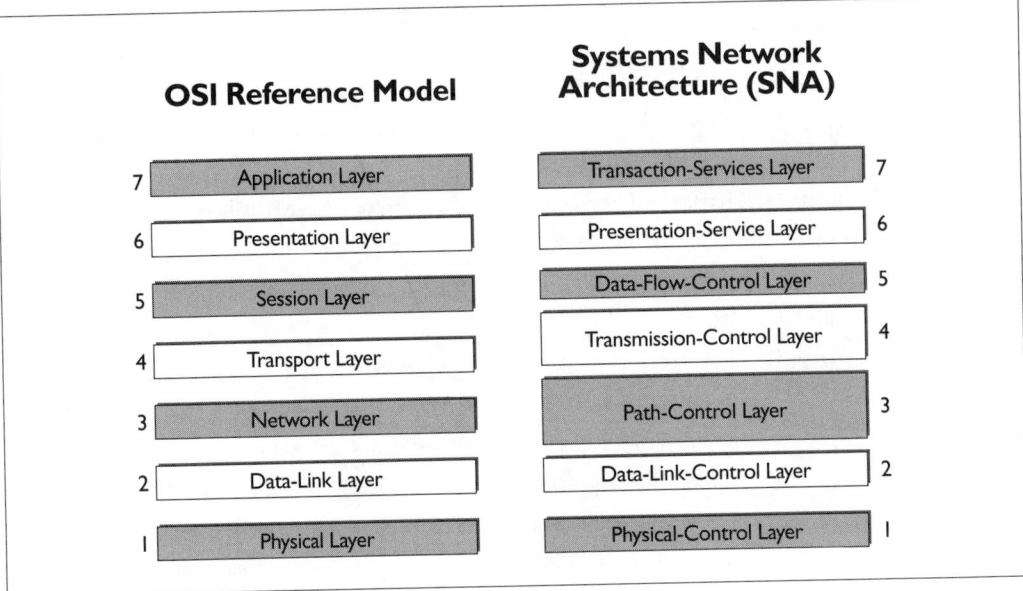

Figure S.4
Systems Network Architecture compared to OSI Reference Model

SystemView

A comprehensive network-management package, introduced by IBM in 1990, designed to replace NetView. SystemView supports more networking models than does NetView.

See also **NetView.**

SYSTIME utility

In NetWare and IntranetWare, a workstation utility that synchronizes the date and time on the workstation with those of the server.

Table S.11: SNA Management Services

Category	Description
Problem Management	Detects and corrects a condition resulting in a user's losing access to a system resource. This category includes problem determination, problem diagnosis, problem bypass and recovery, problem resolution, and problem tracking and control.
Performance and Accounting Management	Monitors the operation of the network, starts problem-management procedures, and fine-tunes network performance. This category includes response-time monitoring, availability monitoring, utilization monitoring, component delay monitoring, performance tuning, performance tracking and control, and accounting.
Configuration Management	Maintains information about network resources and provides information to other categories in SNA/MS. This category includes knowledge of the physical identification of resources and knowledge of the logical relationship between resources.
Change Management	Plans, controls, and applies changes to the network. This category includes hardware, microcode, and software changes.
Operations Management	Provides a means for querying and controlling distributed network resources from a centralized location. This category includes common operations and operations management.

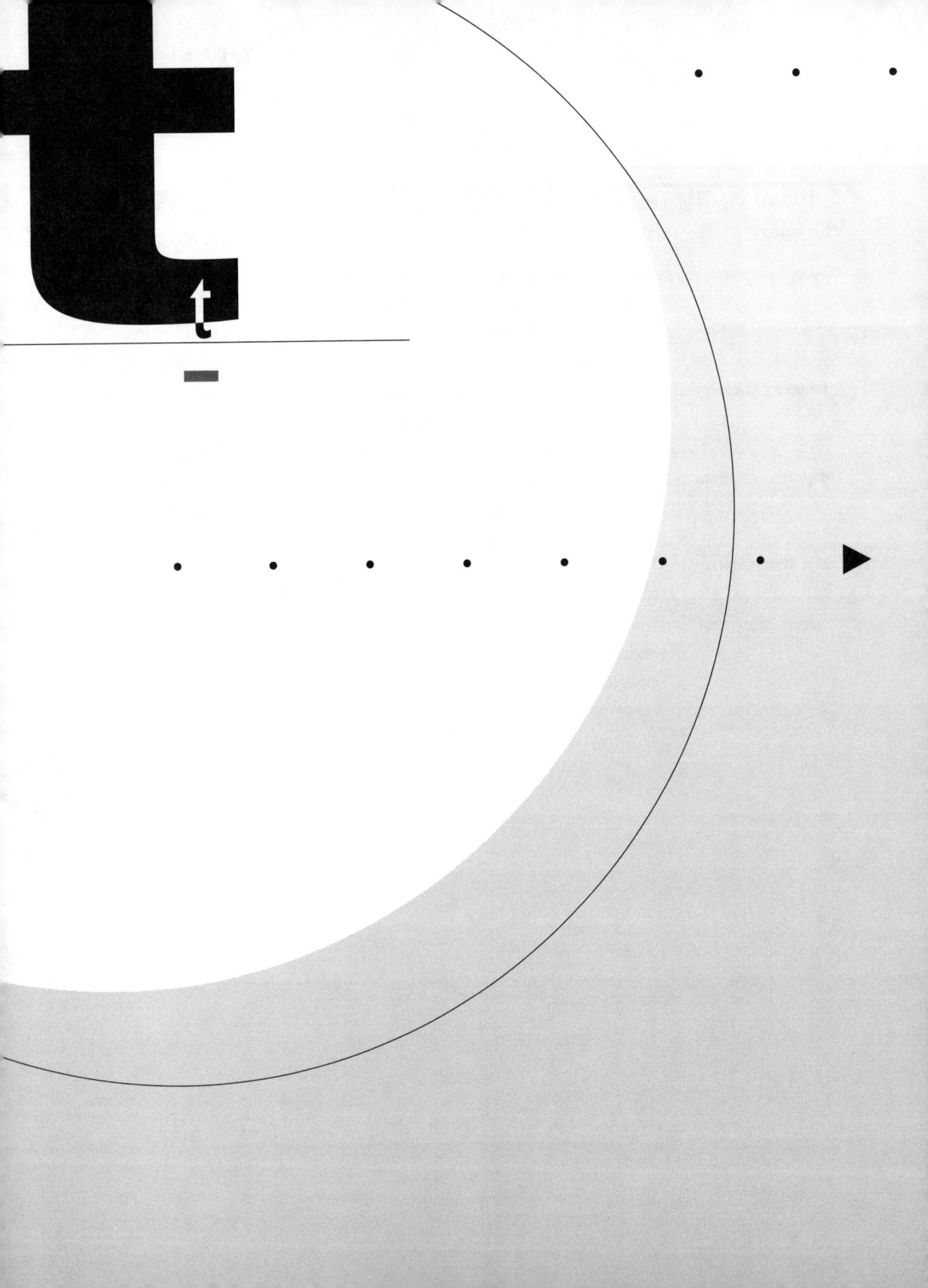

T

An abbreviation for *tera-*, which has a value of 2^{40} or 10^{12}, equivalent to about 1 trillion in the United States measuring system.

T1

A high-speed leased line developed by Bell, capable of transmitting telephone signals at up to 1.544 megabits per second (Mbps) in the United States. Theoretically, a T1 line should be able to transmit a megabyte of information in less than 10 seconds. Although not fast enough to transmit full-screen, full-motion video (which requires 10Mbps), T1 is the fastest speed commonly used to connect networks to the Internet.
See also **T1 Carrier, T-carrier.**

T1 Carrier

A digital-communications carrier used in North America, Australia, and Japan. Originally developed by AT&T to transmit voice conversations, it has been expanded to include data and image transmissions.

T1 multiplexer

A statistical multiplexer designed to split the 1.544-megabit-per-second (Mbps) T1 bandwidth into 24 separate 64-kilobit-per-second (Kbps) channels of digitized voice or data communications.
See also **T1.**

T1 small-aperture terminal (TSAT)

A satellite terminal used for T1 digital communications, with transmission rates as high as 1.544 megabits per second (Mbps).

T2

A communications service that provides the equivalent of four T1 channels, or 96 channels transmitting at 64 kilobits per second (Kbps) for a total bandwidth of 6.3 megabits per second (Mbps). Although not available commercially, this point-to-point service is used within telephone company networks.
See also **T-carrier.**

T3

A communications service that provides the equivalent of 28 T1 channels, or 672 channels transmitting at 64 kilobits per second (Kbps), for a total bandwidth of 44.736 megabits per second (Mbps). It is sometimes used to connect major nodes on the Internet and to form high-traffic internal networks.
See also **T-carrier.**

T4

A communications service that provides the equivalent of 168 T1 channels, or 4,032 channels transmitting at 64 kilobits per second (Kbps), for a total bandwidth of 274.176 megabits per second (Mbps). This point-to-point service is used for both voice and data transmissions.
See also **T-carrier.**

TA

Terminal Adapter, a device designed to mediate between an Integrated-Services Digital Network (ISDN) and devices that are not ISDN-compatible.
See also **Integrated-Services Digital Network.**

Ta-Ta For Now (TTFN)

A shorthand notation that sometimes appears at the end of an electronic-mail (e-mail) message or during an online forum.

TAC

Terminal-Access Controller, an Internet host computer designed to accept terminal connections from a dial-up line.

See also **dial-up line.**

TACACS

Terminal-Access-Controller Access System, a system designed by experts from the Defense Data Network (DDN) to restrict access to Terminal-Access Controllers (TACs) on the DDN.

See also **Defense Data Network.**

TAG

Technical Advisory Group, a committee of the Institute of Electrical and Electronic Engineers (IEEE), responsible for providing general recommendations and technical guidance to other IEEE committees.

See also **Institute of Electrical and Electronic Engineers.**

talk

An Internet newsgroup that conducts endless arguments about a wide range of topics.

See also **newsgroup.**

Talker

A World Wide Web (WWW) browser plug-in from MVP Solutions for Macintosh-based versions of Netscape Navigator (and compatible browsers). It creates synthesized speech from text files attached to a Web page.

See also **Netscape Navigator; Web browser.**

 **For more information about Talker, surf the Web to** `http://www.mvpsolutions.com/PlugInSite/Talker.html`.

tank circuit

A Token Ring network circuit that ensures accurate signal tracking and prevents the degradation of the signal.

tap

A connector used to attach cable without blocking the passage of information along that cable.

tape backup unit

An internal or external tape drive used to back up data from hard disks.

tape cartridge

A self-contained storage module for magnetic tape, which is frequently used as a backup storage medium.

tape drive

A peripheral device that reads from and writes to magnetic tape, often used as a backup medium for computer network systems. Since many backup software programs read the tape sequentially (always starting from the beginning of the tape to search for data), the tape drive is considered a slow backup device.

tape server

The combination of a tape drive and software that can back up files to — and restore files from — the tape drive. A tape server may include *archiving* capabilities to identify files that have not been accessed for a predetermined amount of time, and back up such files as well. No dedicated machine is required for a tape server.

See also **tape drive.**

TAPI

Telephony API, an Application Program Interface (API) that allows Windows applications to set up and control telephone calls. Developed jointly by Intel and Microsoft, TAPI functions independently of the telephone network and does not define a data-transmission method when a call is in progress.

See also **Application Program Interface.**

target

A server, workstation, or service on the NetWare network that has a Target Service Agent (TSA) loaded, which allows the target to have all its data backed up or restored.

See also **Target Service Agent.**

target coding

Coding used by an application receiving a transmission on a network. Such an application must be running on a network node

capable of using all seven layers of the OSI Reference Model.

See also **OSI Reference Model.**

target device

Devices aimed at performing specific functions. As an example, servers or workstations can contain files that are targeted for backup.

target server

A network server from which data is backed up or to which data is stored. Typically, the data is received from another network device.

Target Service Agent (TSA)

A program designed to process data that moves between a specific target and a backup engine that complies with NetWare's Storage-Management Services (SMS). When using the SBACKUP utility, the host server sends requests to the TSA. The TSA then receives the commands from SBACKUP, processes the commands so the target operating system can handle the request for data, pass the data request to the target, receive the requested data from the target and return it to SBACKUP in standard SMS format.

See also **SBACKUP; Storage-Management Services.**

Target Service Agent (TSA) resources

Categories of data created by each NetWare Target Service Agent (TSA and classified as either *major resources* or *minor resources*. These resources vary with each TSA, so the SBACKUP utility processes these resources in different ways.

Target Token-Rotation Time (TTRT)

A parameter value in a Fiber Distributed Data Interface (FDDI) network that specifies how much time passes before every node on the network gets access to the token.

See also **Fiber Distributed Data Interface; token passing.**

task

Collectively, an independent program and the network resources it uses (such as an operating-system process or part of an application).

Task Manager

A Novell DOS program designed to manage multitasking and task-switching operations.

task number

A unique number assigned to an individual program on a multitasking workstation.

task switching

A process that switches between applications, suspending one application in the background while running another.

TBMI2

A NetWare buffer that enables Internetwork Packet Exchange (IPX) and Sequenced Packet Exchange (SPX) programs to work in a task-switching environment.

See also **Internetwork Packet Exchange; Sequenced Packet Exchange.**

T-carrier

A digital-communications service that provides voice and data transmission at one of four Time-Division Multiplexing (TDM) levels. The TDM specification allows the bit stream of smaller carriers to be multiplexed into the larger ones, as shown in Table T.1.

TCNS

Thomas-Conrad Network System, an implementation of the Attached-Resource Computer Network (ARCnet) architecture developed by Thomas-Conrad that transmits at 100 megabits per second (Mbps). TCNS includes both ARCnet drivers and drivers for other operating environments; it requires the use of special Network Interface Cards (NICs). Although TCNS does use shielded twisted-pair (STP) or fiber-optic cables, it does not support unshielded twisted-pair cables (UTP).

See also **Attached-Resource Computer Network; Network Interface Card.**

T-connector

A T-shaped coaxial cable connector that connects two thin Ethernet cables and also provides a third connector for the Network Interface Card (NIC).

See also **Network Interface Card.**

TB

terabyte, a unit of measure equal to 2^{40} (approximately 1 trillion) bytes, most commonly used in the context of computer memory or disk-storage capacity.

Table T.1: T-Carrier Service Levels

Level	Channels	Transmission in Kilobits Per Second (Kbps)	Total Bandwidth in Megabits per Second (Mbps)
T1	24	64Kbps	1.544Mbps
T2	96 (equivalent of four T1 services)	64Kbps	6.3Mbps
T3	672 (equivalent of 28 T1 services)	64Kbps	44.736Mbps
T4	4,032 (equivalent of 168 T1 services)	64Kbps	274.176Mbps

TCM

trellis-coded modulation, a quadrature-amplitude-modulation technique that encodes data as a set of bits associated with both phase and amplitude changes. TCM is typically used in modems that operate at speeds of 9600 bits per second (bps) or higher.

See also **amplitude; phase; quadrature amplitude modulation.**

TCP

Transmission-Control Protocol, in the Internet Protocol (IP) suite, a transport protocol that provides connection-oriented, full-duplex streams of data and uses the IP for delivery.

TCP/IP

Transmission-Control Protocol/Internet Protocol, a suite of networking protocols that enables dissimilar nodes in a heterogeneous environment to communicate with one another. TCP/IP protocols handle media access, packet transport, session communications, file transfer, electronic mail, and terminal emulation. This suite and related applications were developed for the Department of Defense (DoD) during the 1970s and 1980s, specifically to permit different types of computers to exchange information with each other. TCP/IP is currently mandated as the official DoD protocol and widely used on UNIX platforms.

See also **OSI Reference Model; Transmission-Control Protocol/Internet Protocol** (includes **Figure T.3**).

TCP/IP Console (TCPCON)

In NetWare 4.*x* and IntranetWare, a server console NetWare Loadable Module (NLM) that monitors and gathers information from the local NetWare Transmission-Control Protocol/Internet Protocol (TCP/IP) node. This NLM enables a user to monitor activity in the TCP/IP network segments of the internetwork, view configuration information about selected TCP/IP protocols, view IP routes known to a TCP/IP node, view network resources supported by a TCP/IP node, and use the Simple Network-Management Protocol (SNMP) over TCP/IP, or the Internetwork Packet Exchange (IPX), to access TCP/IP information in any remote protocol stack that supports the TCP/IP Management Information Base (MIB).

See also **Internetwork Packet Exchange; NetWare Loadable Module; Simple Network-Management Protocol; Transmission-Control Protocol/Internet Protocol.**

TCP/IP Transport Software

NetWare operating-system software that includes a set of drivers having an interface with the Multiple-Link Interface Driver/ Open Data-Link Interface (MLID/ODI) drivers at the bottom layer, and an interface with the Berkeley-socket Application Program Interface (API) at the top layer.

See also **Application Program Interface; Multiple-Link Interface Driver; Open Data-Link Interface.**

TCPCON (NLM)

In NetWare 4.*x* and IntranetWare, a server console NetWare Loadable Module (NLM) that monitors and gathers information from the local NetWare Transmission-Control Protocol/Internet Protocol (TCP/IP) node. This NLM enables a user to monitor activity in the TCP/IP network segments of the internetwork, view configuration information about selected TCP/IP protocols, view IP routes known to a TCP/IP node, view network resources supported by a TCP/IP node, and use the Simple Network-Management Protocol (SNMP) over TCP/IP, or the Internetwork Packet Exchange (IPX), to access TCP/IP information in any remote protocol stack that supports the TCP/IP

Management Information Base (MIB).

See also **Internetwork Packet Exchange; NetWare Loadable Module; Simple Network-Management Protocol; Transmission-Control Protocol/Internet Protocol.**

TCPIP (NLM)

In NetWare 4.*x* and IntranetWare, a server console NetWare Loadable Module (NLM) that loads support for Transmission-Control Protocol/Internet Protocol (TCP/IP) on the network server.

See also **NetWare Loadable Module; Transmission-Control Protocol/Internet Protocol.**

TCU

Trunk-Coupling Unit, a physical device enabling a Token Ring network station to connect to a trunk cable.

See also **Token Ring; trunk.**

TDM

Time-Division Multiplexing, data transmission that dedicates a fixed bandwidth of the network medium to connected devices, regardless of whether the devices are active.

See also **Statistical Time-Division Multiplexing.**

TDMA

Time-Division Multiple Access, a method of communications in which a channel is made available to multiple parties simultaneously. Each party is allocated a time slot; its duration depends on two factors: (1) the number of parties who want to transmit and (2) the priority assigned the party to whom the time slot is allocated. Transmission packets must be reassembled at the receiving end.

See also **time slot.**

TDR

time-domain reflectometry, a technique used to diagnose cabling faults, calculating the length of the cable by measuring the time a reflected pulse takes to return to the TDR and multiplying that measurement by the Nominal Velocity of Propagation (NVP).

See also **Nominal Velocity of Propagation.**

Technical Advisory Group (TAG)

A committee of the Institute of Electrical and Electronic Engineers (IEEE), responsible for providing general recommendations and technical guidance to other IEEE committees.

See also **Institute of Electrical and Electronic Engineers.**

Technical and Office Protocol (TOP)

A version of Ethernet developed by Boeing Corporation, used in an engineering environment. TOP provides standardized protocols and services for use in real-world situations that may involve the exchange of formatted data or access to such data from remote locations. To accommodate a variety of file types, TOP provides Application Program Interfaces (APIs) built upon the OSI Reference Model, including Product-Definition Interchange Format (PDIF), Office Document Architecture (ODA), Office-Document Interchange Format (ODIF), Computer-Graphics Metafile Interchange Format (CGMIF), Graphics Kernel System (GKS), and File Transfer, access, and Management (FTAM) files.

See also **Application Program Interface; Ethernet; File Transfer, access, and Management; Office Document Architecture; OSI Reference Model.**

Technical Service Alliance (TSA)

A collaborative effort between Novell and numerous companies to solve technical problems for customers they share.

TECHWALK (NLM)

In IntranetWare, a server console NetWare Loadable Module (NLM) that records NetWare configuration information. This program may take from 5 to 60 minutes to complete (depending on the network configuration and network traffic) and dedicates the machine to the process during that period.

See also **NetWare Loadable Module.**

tee coupler

A coupler with three ports, used to split an incoming signal into two outgoing signals. It is commonly used in bus network topologies.

See also **bus network topology.**

telco

A shortened version of the term *telephone company.*

telecommunications

The electronic transmission of all types of information from one location to another over a communications link.

Telecommunications Industries Association (TIA)

An organization responsible for establishing cable standards for networking.

telecommuting

Working out of the home while using a computer, modem, and telephone to communicate with an employer's office.

teleconferencing

Linking audio, video, or computer systems by a communications channel to enable individuals who are geographically separated to participate in a discussion or meeting from a remote location.

TELENET

A public packet-switched network located in the United States.

Telephone

In Novell Directory Services (NDS), a NetWare Directory Schema term and a selectable property for the User object.
See also **leaf object; Novell Directory Services; object.**

Telephone Number

A selectable property for the following objects in Novell Directory Services (NDS):

Organization (O), Organizational Role, Organizational Unit (OU), and User.
See also **container object; leaf object; Novell Directory Services; object.**

telephony

A generic term used to describe the general field of voice telecommunications.

Telephony API (TAPI)

An Application Program Interface (API) that allows Windows applications to set up and control telephone calls. Developed jointly by Intel and Microsoft, TAPI functions independently of the telephone network and does not define a data-transmission method when a call is in progress.
See also **Application Program Interface.**

Telephony Services for NetWare

NetWare Telephony Services, a software/hardware package designed to integrate a NetWare network with a telephone private branch exchange (PBX). A hardware link is administered through the NetWare server and is used for all communication between the network and the PBX. Workstations must be configured with the proper software and must communicate with the PBX only through the server.
See also **private branch exchange.**

teleservices

Services defined for communications between two Integrated-Services Digital Network (ISDN) endpoints. Table T.2 shows common teleservices.

Table T.2: Teleservices

Service	Description
Telefax	Facsimile service that sends a fax on a B channel with control signals transmitted on a D channel.
Telephony	Speech communication over 3.1-kilohertz (kHz) bandwidths with the conversion sent over a B channel and control signals sent over a D channel.
Teletex	Text communication at 2400 baud with the user's transmission sent over a B channel and control signals sent over a D channel.
Telex	Interactive text communication.
Videotex	Graphics and text communication, usually one-directional.

See also **B channel; D channel; Integrated-Services Digital Network.**

Telnet

In the Transmission-Control Protocol/Internet Protocol (TCP/IP) suite, a protocol that governs character-oriented terminal traffic in the Application Level (Level 7) of the OSI Reference Model.

See also **OSI Reference Model; Transmission-Control Protocol/Internet Protocol.**

temperature sensor

A sensor located inside a computer that, when the temperature reaches a certain level, automatically turns on the computer's fan.

temporary swap file

A swap file created on a temporary basis that uses several noncontiguous pieces of hard-disk space. A temporary swap file does not occupy hard-disk space if the application that created it is not running.

See also **swap file.**

terabyte (TB)

A unit of measure equal to 2^{40} (approximately 1 trillion) bytes, most commonly used in the context of computer memory or disk-storage capacity.

termid

In Systems Network Architecture (SNA), an identification for a cluster controller on a switched line.

See also **Systems Network Architecture.**

terminal

A combination of a keyboard and display monitor capable of sending and receiving data over a communications link.

Terminal-Access Controller (TAC)

An Internet host computer designed to accept terminal connections from a dial-up line.

See also **dial-up line.**

Terminal-Access-Controller Access System (TACACS)

A system designed by experts from the Defense Data Network (DDN) to restrict access to Terminal-Access Controllers (TACs) on the DDN.

See also **Defense Data Network.**

Terminal Adapter (TA)

A device designed to mediate between an Integrated-Services Digital Network (ISDN) and devices that are not ISDN-compatible.
See also **Integrated-Services Digital Network.**

terminal-cluster controller

A device designed to connect one or more personal computers to a Front-End Processor (FEP) for a mainframe computer.
See also **Front-End Processor.**

terminal emulation

A software program or method of operation that enables a microcomputer to function as a *dumb terminal* attached to a mainframe computer, usually to facilitate telecommunications.
See also **dumb terminal.**

terminal server

Software that provides a transparent connection between a terminal and one or more host computers. This server may provide multiple terminals with access to a host, or it may provide terminals with the capability of switching between sessions on different host machines.

terminate-and-stay-resident (TSR)

A DOS program that remains in memory even when it is not actively running; a TSR can run while other applications are displayed on the monitor screen. Macintosh versions of TSRs are known as *Inits.*

termination

The placement of a terminating resistor at the end of a line, bus, chain, or cable to prevent signals from being reflected or echoed. If a signal echoes back along a line, bus, chain, or cable, it may become corrupted. In NetWare, the use of a Small Computer Systems Interface (SCSI) to connect a server's Host Bus Adapter (HBA) to a disk subsystem requires the termination of the bus, as do the hard disks connected to the respective controllers. Newer SCSI devices have automatic termination.

terminator

A device attached to the last node in a network or to the last peripheral device in a series.
See also **termination.**

test drive

The process of evaluating the functionality or performance of a software product by loading it and trying it in a real working environment.

Texas Higher Education Network (THEnet)

A network of more than 60 academic and research institutions in the state of Texas.

text-entry field

A field for entering text in a graphical utility.

text file

A file composed of text characters from the American Standard Code for Information Interchange (ASCII) character set, encoded in a format recognizable by most computers.

See also **American Standard Code for Information Interchange.**

text mode

A video-adapter mode used in personal computers. A personal computer in text mode (also known as *character mode*) displays characters on the screen from the built-in character set, but does not show graphics or a mouse pointer.

text utility

In NetWare 4.*x* software, one of two main types of utility (the other is *graphical*). Text utilities include *Command-Line Utilities (CLUs)* and *menu utilities*.

See also **Command-Line Utility; menu utility.**

TFTP

Trivial-File-Transfer Protocol, a version of the Transmission-Control Protocol/Internet Protocol (TCP/IP), but without password protection or user-directory capabilities.

See also **Transport-Control Protocol/Internet Protocol.**

TH

Transmission Header, in the Systems Network Architecture (SNA) model, an element added to the Basic Information Unit (BIU) at the Path-Control Layer (Layer 3).

See also **Basic Information Unit; Systems Network Architecture.**

THC Over X.25

A feature that provides Transmission-Control Protocol/Internet Protocol (TCP/IP) header compression (HC) over X.25 network links to assure link efficiency.

See also **Transmission-Control Protocol/Internet Protocol; X.25.**

The Internet Adapter (TIA)

A shareware program providing a Serial-Line Internet Protocol (SLIP) emulator for UNIX systems that enables the running of Windows Web browsers on UNIX systems.

See also **Serial-Line Internet Protocol; Web browser.**

THEnet

Texas Higher Education Network, a network of more than 60 academic and research institutions in the state of Texas.

ThickNet

Coaxial cable with a diameter of 1 centimeter (0.4 inch), used to connect Ethernet network nodes at distances up to about 1,000 meters (about 3,300 feet).

See also **Ethernet.**

thickwire

Coaxial cable that measures about half an inch in diameter.

804 · **ThinNet**

ThinNet

Coaxial cable with a diameter of 5 millimeters (0.2 inch), used to connect Ethernet network nodes at distances up to about 300 meters (about 1,000 feet).

See also **Ethernet.**

thinwire

A thin coaxial cable similar to that used for television and video connections.

third party

An outside vendor who supplies services or products to an organization or manufacturer.

Thomas

A World Wide Web (WWW) server that enables a user to browse, read, or search the full text of such legislative databases as bills before the U.S. Congress and the Congressional Record. In addition, a user may use links to other government Web sites. Named for Thomas Jefferson, this server is run by the Library of Congress.

See also **World Wide Web (WWW).**

For more information about Thomas, surf the Web to http://thomas.loc.gov.

Thomas-Conrad Network System (TCNS)

An implementation of the Attached-Resource Computer Network (ARCnet) architecture developed by Thomas-Conrad that transmits at 100 megabits per second (Mbps). TCNS includes both ARCnet dri-vers and drivers for other operating environments; it requires the use of special Network Interface Cards (NICs). Although TCNS does use shielded twisted-pair (STP) or fiber-optic cables, it does not support unshielded twisted-pair cables (UTP).

See also **Attached-Resource Computer Network; Network Interface Card.**

thrashing

Disk activity so excessive that the system spends all its time swapping pages in and out of memory, and spends no time executing an application. This may be caused by a poor system configuration that creates an undersized swap file, or by insufficient installed memory in the computer.

thread

A concurrent process that is actually part of a larger process or program. Multitasking operating systems allow single programs to contain several threads that all run at the same time.

thread global data items

A set of data items that have separate values for each thread. Data items for one thread cannot be referenced by another thread.

thread group

A group of one or more threads as defined by a program designer.

thread of execution

A separate execution within a program that either performs a request or polls for the occurrence of some event. Although polling threads are always running, they relinquish control after going through one polling loop.

threaded newsreader

A newsreader that enables the user to read groups of related articles (known as *threads*). This enables a user to choose to read or not to read a thread at a time, rather than one article at a time.
See also **newsreader.**

threaded-nut connector (TNC)

A connector that is threaded and screws into a jack to create a tight connection.

thread-group global data items

A method in which any change made to the value of a thread-group global data item affects all the threads in the thread group.
See also **thread.**

THREADS utility

In IntranetWare, a NetWare Loadable Module (NLM) that contains a library of functions constituting the thread package for IntranetWare. This NLM is automatically loaded by any module that needs it.
See also **NetWare Loadable Module.**

three-way handshake

A synchronization process for activities occurring when two protocols establish a connection. The three steps involved are the caller sending a packet requesting a connection, the called node returning a connect confirmation packet, and the caller sending an acknowledgment packet.

threshold

An attribute used in network management to indicate a cutoff point between significant (or critical) events and nonsignificant events.

throughput

A measurement of the total amount of useful information processed or communicated during a specific time period. Normally, this measurement is made according to the total number of bits transmitted in a second, including all bits transmitted or retransmitted.

throughput class

A class negotiation that specifies, on a per-call basis, the throughput of data that can be transferred on a virtual circuit (VC) at speeds of 75 bits per second (bps) to 64 kilobits per second (kbps).
See also **throughput; virtual circuit.**

throughput negotiation

A facility specifying whether to allow negotiation (on a per-call basis) of throughput for data that can be transferred on a virtual circuit (VC).
See also **throughput; virtual circuit.**

THT

Token-Holding Time, a parameter value used in Fiber Distributed Data Interface (FDDI) networks to adjust access to the network by specifying how long a node can hold the network token before it must be passed along to the next node in the sequence.
See also **Fiber Distributed Data Interface.**

TI

transaction identifier, under AppleTalk Transaction Protocol (ATP), a 2-byte integer that appears in the header of a Transaction Request (TReq) packet in a transaction. The transaction identifier uniquely identifies a request.

See also **AppleTalk Transaction Protocol; Transaction Request.**

TIA

(1) Telecommunications Industries Association, an organization responsible for establishing cable standards for networking. **(2) The Internet Adapter,** a shareware program providing a Serial-Line Internet Protocol (SLIP) emulator for UNIX systems that enables the running of Windows Web browsers on UNIX systems.

See also **(2) Serial-Line Internet Protocol; (2) Web browser.**

TIC

Token-Ring Interface Coupler, a device designed to provide direct connections between a Token Ring network and various types of mainframe equipment, including Front-End Processors (FEPs), aS/400s, and 3174 terminal cluster controllers.

See also **AS/400; Front-End Processor; terminal-cluster controller; Token Ring.**

tick

A time delay measuring about 1/18 of a second (or precisely 18.21 ticks per second). In NetWare, ticks are used to indicate how long it takes to reach the network. The number of ticks appears as part of each net-work entry in a Router-Information Protocol (RIP) packet.

See also **Router-Information Protocol.**

tie line

A private circuit that connects two or more points in a single organization and is usually leased from a communications carrier.

tight buffer

A layer stretched tightly over fiber-optic cable cladding to keep the fiber from moving around.

time

The period of measurement on a computer system used to "stamp" files with a time of creation or modification. A time period that occurs before noon on a 12-hour clock is noted as "a.m." A time period after noon on a 12-hour clock is noted as "p.m." If a.m. or p.m. is not specified, some computer operating systems (such as NetWare) assume that time values are entered as *military time* (on a 24-hour clock).

See also **time server; time stamp; time synchronization.**

Time-Division Multiple Access (TDMA)

A method of communications in which a channel is made available to multiple parties simultaneously. Each party is allocated a time slot; its duration depends on two factors: (1) the number of parties who want to transmit and (2) the priority assigned the party to whom the time slot is allocated. Transmission packets must be reassembled

Transmission packets must be reassembled at the receiving end.

See also **time slot.**

Time-Division Multiplexing (TDM)

Data transmission that dedicates a fixed bandwidth of the network medium to connected devices, regardless of whether the devices are active.

See also **Statistical Time-Division Multiplexing.**

time-domain reflectometery (TDR)

A technique used to diagnose cabling faults, calculating the length of the cable by measuring the time a reflected pulse takes to return to the TDR and multiplying that measurement by the Nominal Velocity of Propagation (NVP).

See also **Nominal Velocity of Propagation.**

time functions

Functions providing the capability to obtain and manipulate times and dates across the network.

time restrictions

In NetWare, login restrictions on a User account that designate blocks of time during which a user can and cannot access the network.

time-sequence diagram

A graphical representation of a sequence of events that shows time on a vertical axis

with the oldest event at the top and the most recent event at the bottom. The horizontal representation depends on the content of the diagram.

time server

A designated NetWare server that performs a particular time-synchronization function. Table T.3 shows the four types of time servers and describes the function of each.

time-slice multitasking

A multitasking process in which the operating system assigns the same small time period to each process in turn.

See also **cooperative multitasking; preemptive multitasking.**

time stamp

A unique code that includes the time and identifies an event that occurs in the NetWare Directory, such as when a password is changed or a Novell Directory Services (NDS) object is renamed. The NDS event must have a time stamp so that Directory replicas can be updated correctly. NDS uses time stamps to establish the order of events, record "real-world" time values, and set expiration dates.

time synchronization

A method that corrects inherent deviation of the time kept by clocks in all servers of a NetWare Directory tree so all servers report the same time and provide a time stamp to order Novell Directory Service (NDS) events.

Table T.3: NetWare Time Servers

Server	Description
Single-Reference time server	Determines the time for the entire network and provides time to Secondary time servers and to workstations. This time server is the only source of time on the network.
Primary time server	Synchronizes time with at least one other Primary or Reference time server and provides time to Secondary time servers and to workstations, as well as voting with other Primary or Reference time servers to determine a common network time. At least one other Primary or Reference time server that the Primary time server can contact is required.
Reference time server	Provides the time to which all other time servers and workstations synchronize, a time that may be synchronized with an external time source. Reference time servers vote with other Primary or Reference time servers to determine a common network time. A Reference time server, however, does not adjust its internal clock. Instead, the internal clock of the Primary server is synchronized with that of the Reference time server. Only one Reference time server is usually installed on a network.
Secondary time server	Obtains the time from a Single-Reference, Primary, or Reference time server, adjusting its internal clock to synchronize with network time. Secondary time servers also provide time to workstations.

Time-Synchronization Services

In NetWare 4.02, a field name in the System Modules screen of the MONITOR NetWare Loadable Module (NLM).

See also **MONITOR**; **NetWare Loadable Module**.

TIME utility

In NetWare and IntranetWare, a server console utility that displays the date and time kept by the network server's clock, shows the status of daylight-saving time, and provides time-synchronization information.

timeout condition

An error condition that occurs after a specified amount of time has elapsed without an expected event taking place. The error condition prevents the procedure from hanging up the computer system.

timeout

A technique used to specify an amount of time that may elapse before a particular event must take place.

TIMESYNC (NLM)

In NetWare 4.x and IntranetWare, a server console NetWare Loadable Module (NLM) that monitors the internal time on a server to ensure that the time reported by all servers is consistently synchronized across the network. Under most conditions, this NLM loads automatically when the server is started.

See also **NetWare Loadable Module.**

tip

One of the two wires in a twisted-pair wire; the other wire is called a *ring.*

Title

In Novell Directory Services (NDS), a NetWare Directory Schema term and a selectable property for the External Entity and User objects.

See also **leaf object; Novell Directory Services; object.**

title bar

A horizontal bar appearing across the top of a graphical utility screen that usually contains the name of the window.

TLAP

TokenTalk Link-Access Protocol, the protocol that allows TokenTalk to access a network.

See also **AppleTalk.**

TLI

Transport-Layer Interface, an Interprocess Communication (IC) mechanism providing protocol-independent support for server applications. In NetWare, the TLI is an Application Program Interface (API) that resides between the STREAMS utility and user applications.

See also **Application Program Interface; Interprocess Communication; STREAMS utility.**

TLI (NLM)

In NetWare and IntranetWare, a NetWare Loadable Module (NLM) that provides Transport-Level Interface (TLI) communications services.

See also **NetWare Loadable Module; Transport-Level Interface.**

TLIST utility

In NetWare 3.x, a workstation utility that provides a view of the trustee list of a directory or file. A user must be attached to a file server before viewing the trustee list of a directory or its files. A user must have the Access Control right in a directory to view the trustee list of that directory or its files.

See also **trustee; trustee rights.**

TN3270

Terminal-emulation software that allows a terminal to appear to the system as if it were an IBM 3270 Model 2 terminal.

TNC

threaded-nut connector, a connector that is threaded and screws into a jack to create a tight connection.

token

A special packet, used in some media-access methods, that is passed from node to node along a network according to a predefined sequence. The node possessing the token gets access to the network.

token-bus topology

A network architecture that uses token passing in a physical-bus configuration that connects its nodes in a logical ring. The token bus architecture supports both coaxial and fiber-optic cable in carrier-band or broadband networks. Transmission speeds in this type of network can reach 20 megabits per second (Mbps).

Token-Holding Time (THT)

A parameter value used in Fiber Distributed Data Interface (FDDI) networks to adjust access to the network by specifying how long a node can hold the network token before it must be passed along to the next node in the sequence.

See also **Fiber Distributed Data Interface.**

token passing

The circulation of an electronic token throughout a network to prevent multiple nodes from simultaneously transmitting on the network. A node must be in possession of the token before it can transmit across the network. Token passing is commonly used in Fiber Distributed Data Interface (FDDI), Token Ring, and Token Bus networks as a means of avoiding packet collisions.

See also **Fiber Distributed Data Interface; Token Ring.**

Token Ring

The IBM version of a local-area network (LAN): its ring structure uses a token-passing protocol of 4 to 16 megabits per second (Mbps) to regulate network traffic and avoid packet collisions. A Token Ring network with telephone wiring can support up to 72 devices; the same topology with shielded twisted-pair (STP) cabling can support up to 256 nodes, in star-shaped clusters of up to 8 nodes. Each cluster is attached to the same Multistation Access Unit (MAU); all MAUs are connected to the main ring circuit. One particular node on the ring, the *Active Monitor (AM)*, generates the token that starts the network communication process. Other nodes serve as *Standby Monitors (SMs)*, which track the activity of the AM and determine among themselves which is to replace the AM in case of failure. A Token Ring network also performs special activities, as shown in Table T.4.

Token-Ring Interface Coupler (TIC)

A device designed to provide direct connections between a Token Ring network and various types of mainframe equipment, including Front-End Processors (FEPs), aS/400s, and 3174 terminal-cluster controllers.

See also **AS/400; Front-End Processor; terminal-cluster controller; Token Ring.**

Token Ring topology

A local-area network (LAN) with a ring structure that uses a token passing to regulate network traffic and to avoid packet collisions. A controlling computer institutes token passing, which controls a node's right to transmit across the network. A node captures a token,

Table T.4: Token Ring Special Activities

Activity	Description
Beaconing	A signaling process by which network nodes announce the occurrence of hard (serious) errors on the network.
Neighbor notification	A process that tells each node about the upstream neighbor from which the node receives frames and the downstream neighbor to which the node transmits frames.
Ring insertion	A five-step process that enables a network node to join the network.
Ring purge	A process during which the AM dissolves the ring and rebuilds it, beginning with the token-claiming process.
Token claiming	A process during which an AM is chosen from among the available SMs.

sets its status to *busy*, and adds a message with a destination address. Every other node reads the token to determine whether it is the intended recipient; the actual recipient node collects the token, extracts the message, and returns the token to the sender. The sender then removes the message and resets the token to a *free* status, which indicates the token can be used by the next node in the sequence. Figure T.1 shows the Token Ring topology.

TokenTalk

An implementation of the AppleTalk protocol over Token Ring networks. TokenTalk is defined at the Physical Layer (Layer 1) and Data-Link Layer (Layer 2) of the OSI Reference Model, and uses the TokenTalk Link-Access Protocol (TLAP) to access the network. TokenTalk supports both 4 megabits per second (Mbps) and 16Mbps networks.

See also **AppleTalk.**

TokenTalk Link-Access Protocol (TLAP)

The protocol that allows TokenTalk to access a network.

See also **AppleTalk.**

Too Many Dirty Blocks

A field name that appears in the MONITOR NetWare Loadable Module (NLM).

See also **MONITOR; NetWare Loadable Module.**

tool

Hardware and software devices that simplify some tasks, make other tasks possible to complete, and are necessary for creating, running, and maintaining a network.

toolbar

A rectangle running either across or down a screen window within a particular program that contains a set of commands either in

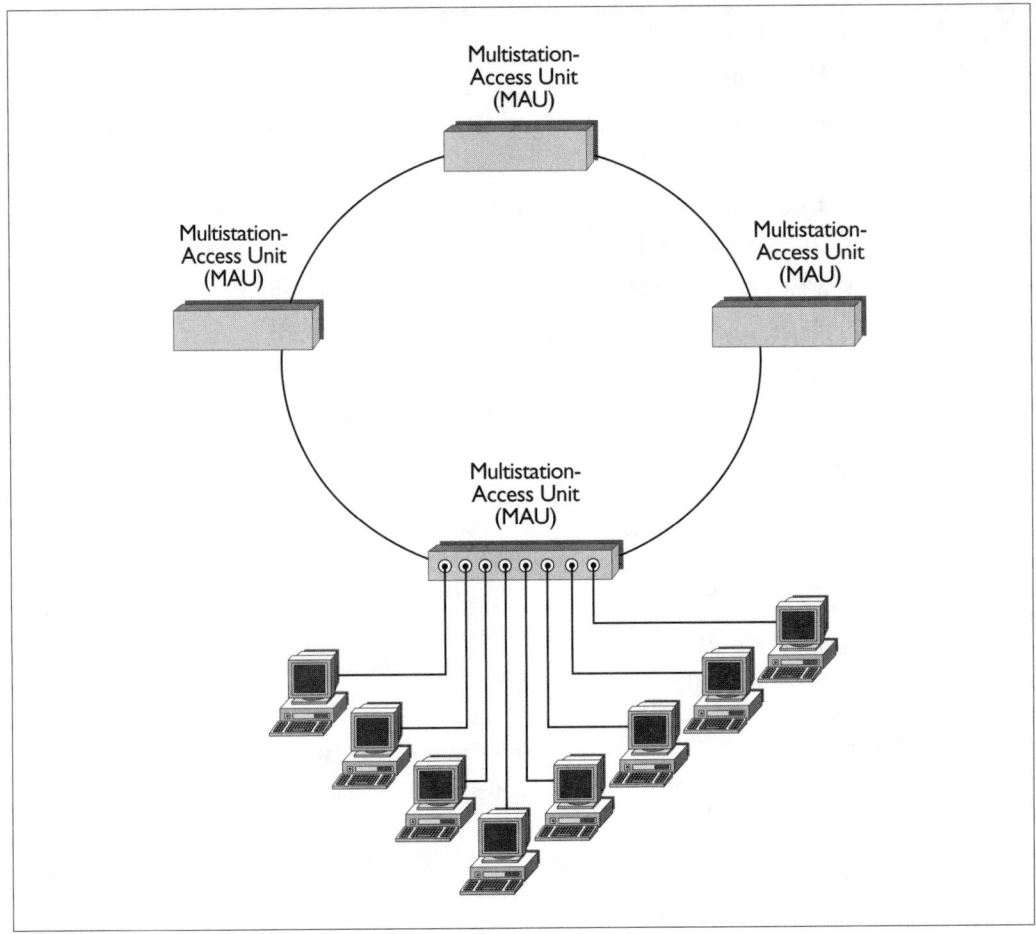

Figure T.1
Token Ring Topology

word form or icon form and that provides point-and-click access to frequently used commands.

ToolBook

A Windows application-development system from Asymetrix.

ToolVox

A World Wide Web (WWW) browser plug-in from VoxWare for Windows-based and Macintosh-based versions of Netscape Navigator (and compatible browsers) that plays back compressed sounds from files supplied by ordinary Web servers.

See also **Netscape Navigator; Web browser.**

For more information about **ToolVox, surf the Web to** `http://www.voxware.com/download.htm`.

TOP

Technical and Office Protocol, a version of Ethernet developed by Boeing Corporation, used in an engineering environment. TOP provides standardized protocols and services for use in real-world situations that may involve the exchange of formatted data or access to such data from remote locations. To accommodate a variety of file types, TOP provides Application Program Interfaces (APIs) built upon the OSI Reference Model, including Product-Definition Interchange Format (PDIF), Office Document Architecture (ODA), Office-Document Interchange Format (ODIF), Computer-Graphics Metafile Interchange Format (CGMIF), Graphics Kernel System (GKS), and File Transfer, access, and Management (FTAM) files.

See also **Application Program Interface; Ethernet; File Transfer, access, and Management; Office Document Architecture; OSI Reference Model.**

Top

A Directory Schema term for Novell Directory Services (NDS).
See also **Novell Directory Services.**

TopGun

A World Wide Web (WWW) browser plug-in from 7th Level, designed for Netscape Navigator (and compatible browsers), that displays animation in a proprietary format used for 7th Level's KidsWorld Web site.
See also **Netscape Navigator; Web browser.**

top-level domain

A level of the Internet Domain-Naming System (DNS) that appears as a child of the root domain (the highest level in the DNS). The Internet DNS uses domain syntax to help translate *hostnames* (which include the top-level domain as the rightmost component of the address) into *host addresses*. Top-level domains include generic worldwide domains, generic United States domains, and country domains. ISO-3166 defines two-letter and three-letter top-level domains from around the world. Table T.5 shows the generic domains, and Appendix D shows a listing of country domains in two-letter and three-letter formats. Figure T.2 shows the relationship between top-level domains.
See also **Internet address.**

Table T.5: Generic Top-Level Domains

Domain	Description
COM	Generic worldwide domain used for commercial organizations.
NET	Generic worldwide domain used for network service providers and Internet administration authorities.
EDU	Generic worldwide domain used for educational institutions, particularly four-year colleges and universities.
INT	Generic worldwide domain for organizations established through international treaties.

(continued)

Table T.5: Generic Top-Level Domains (cont.)	
Domain	**Description**
ORG	Generic worldwide domain for organizations not fitting into other generic worldwide-domain categories.
GOV	Generic United States domain for agencies of the federal government.
MIL	Generic United States domain for the U.S. Department of Defense.

The U.S. top-level domain is divided into several subdomains, which are shown in Table T.6.

topology

The physical layout of a network, including the cabling, workstation configuration, gateways, and hubs. The three basic types are the *star topology* (workstations connected to a server but not to each other), *ring topology* (server and workstations are cabled together in a ring), and *bus topology* (all workstations and the server are connected to a central cable). Each of these basic types has variations; some may be combined to create *hybrid topologies*.

See also **bus network topology; ring topology; star topology.**

Topology-Specific Module (TSM)

A **module** (a self-contained portion of a computer program written, tested, and compiled separately from the main program) designed to perform operations that are specific to a particular network topology.

Table T.6: U.S. Subdomains of Top-Level Domains	
Subdomain	**Description**
FED	Agencies of the federal government
DNI	Organizations with a presence in multiple states or regions
CC	Community colleges with a statewide presence
CI	City government agencies
CO	County government agencies
GEN	Organizations that do not fit into any other category
K12	Public school districts
LIB	Libraries
STATE	State government offices
TEC	Vocational and technical schools

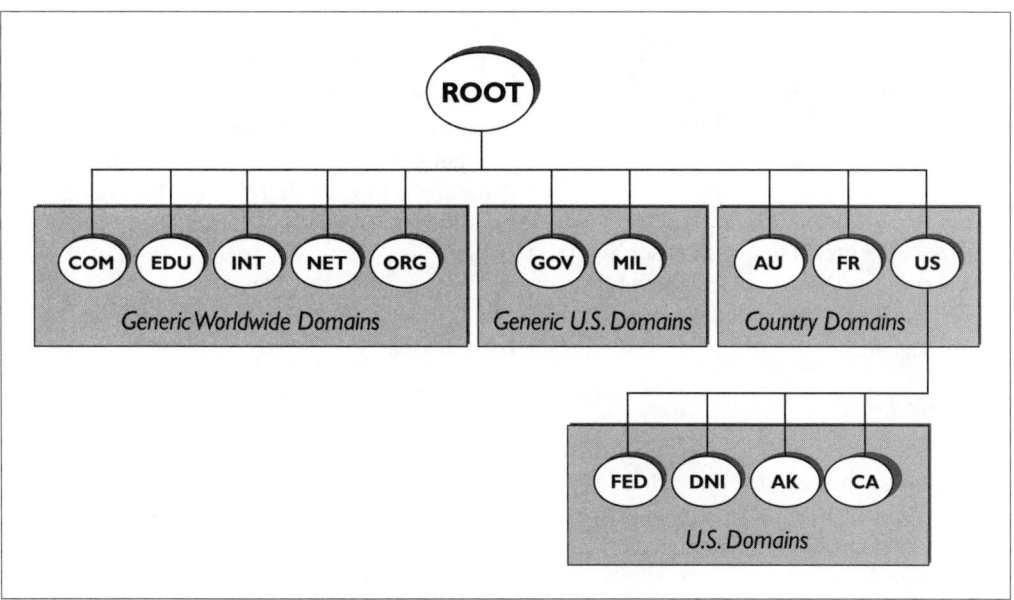

Topper

A World Wide Web (WWW) browser plug-in from the Kinetix division of Autodesk for Netscape Navigator and compatible browsers that displays interactive three-dimensional simulations based on such graphics formats as Virtual-Reality Modeling Language (VRML), Drawing Exchange Format (DXF), and 3D Studio (3DS).

See also **Netscape Navigator; Virtual-Reality Modeling Language; Web browser.**

ToS

Type of Service, a byte in the header of an Internet Protocol (IP) packet that specifies the kind of transmission being requested, including the delay, throughput, and reliability of the desired transmission.

Total Cache Buffers

A field name appearing in the Cache Utilization screen of the MONITOR NetWare Loadable Module (NLM).

See also **MONITOR; NetWare Loadable Module.**

TP

twisted-pair cable, cable with two or more pairs of insulated wires twisted together at a rate of six twists per inch; one wire carries the signal and the other is grounded. The two types of TP *are shielded twisted-pair (STP)* and *unshielded twisted-pair (UTP)*.

See also **shielded twisted-pair cable; unshielded twisted-pair cable.**

TP0

Under Open Systems Interconnection (OSI), a connectionless Transport Protocol (TP) in class 0 that is used for reliable transport over subnetworks.

TP4

Under Open Systems Interconnection (OSI), a connectionless Transport Protocol (TP) in class 4 that is used for reliable transport over subnetworks.

TPDDI

Twisted-Pair Distributed Data Interface, a network architecture that implements the capabilities of Fiber Distributed Data Interface (FDDI) on twisted-pair cabling.

See also **Fiber Distributed Data Interface.**

TPING (NLM)

In NetWare 4.*x* and IntranetWare, a server console NetWare Loadable Module (NLM) that sends an Internet Control-Message Protocol (ICMP) echo request packet to an Internet Protocol (IP) node on the network. This command line utility determines whether an IP target node is reachable.

See also **Internet Control-Message Protocol; Internet Protocol; NetWare Loadable Module.**

TP-PMD

Twisted-Pair, Physical-Media-Dependent, an implementation of the Fiber Distributed Data Interface (FDDI) standard that can attain 100 megabits per second (Mbps) on unshielded twisted-pair (UTP) cabling.

See also **Fiber Distributed Data Interface.**

Traceroute

A program that provides a map of the path a packet travels during transmission from source node to destination node.

track

A physical division of the platter on a hard disk that appears as a concentric circle where data can be stored.

See also **platter.**

TRACK OFF utility

In NetWare and IntranetWare, a server console utility that disables the display of the Router-Information Protocol (RIP) traffic screen (which provides information about all RIP packets being received or sent across the network).

See also **Router-Information Protocol.**

TRACK ON utility

In NetWare and IntranetWare, a server console utility that enables the server to display the Router-Information Protocol (RIP) traffic screen. This screen provides information about all RIP packets being received or sent across the network.

See also **Router-Information Protocol.**

Tracked Resource Types

In NetWare 3.12, a resource appearing in the Available Options/Resource Utilization screen of the MONITOR NetWare Loadable Module (NLM). The resource tracks those NLMs that add tracked resources to the operating system, ensuring as well that those resource types are unloaded when their NLMs are unloaded.

See also **MONITOR; NetWare Loadable Module.**

traffic

A flow of messages and data usually measured in bits transferred over a given time period by a communications channel or link.

traffic descriptor

In Asynchronous Transfer Mode (ATM), an element specifying the parameter values for Virtual Channel Connection (VCC) and Virtual Path Connection (VPC) that can be negotiated by entities involved in the connection. A traffic descriptor is also known as a *user-network contract.*

See also **Asynchronous Transfer Mode; Virtual Channel Connection; Virtual Path Connection.**

trailer

A part of a packet that includes the error-detection fields that follow the data contained in the packet. The header is the part of the packet that precedes the data contained in the packet.

transaction

A set of related operations constituting a logical unit of work. An application performing the transaction must specify whether all or none of these operations be performed.

Transaction Set

A Directory Schema term in Novell Directory Services (NDS).

See also **Novell Directory Services.**

transaction backout

The backing out of a transaction because of a system failure resulting from hardware problems and power outages, because of problems with applications running on a workstation, or because of user intervention at a workstation.

See also **Transaction-Tracking System.**

Transaction Bitmap

Under AppleTalk Transaction Protocol (ATP), a field that appears in a Transaction Request (TReq) packet to indicate how many buffers the requester has reserved for the packets that constitute the Transaction Response (TResp) message.

See also **AppleTalk Transaction Protocol; Transaction Request; Transaction Response.**

transaction identifier (TI)

Under AppleTalk Transaction Protocol (ATP), a 2-byte integer that appears in the header of a Transaction Request (TReq) packet in a transaction. The transaction identifier uniquely identifies a request.

See also **AppleTalk Transaction Protocol; Transaction Request.**

transaction program

An application program that performs transactions with one or more remote programs.

Transaction Release packet (TRel)

Under AppleTalk Transaction Protocol (ATP), a packet sent in response to a Transaction Response (TResp) packet to indicate that the requester received the entire response message.

See also **AppleTalk Transaction Protocol; Transaction Response.**

Transaction Request packet (TReq)

Under AppleTalk Transaction Protocol (ATP), a packet sent by a socket to request that a responding packet perform an action and return a response.

See also **AppleTalk Transaction Protocol.**

Transaction Response message

Under AppleTalk Transaction Protocol (ATP), a message that consists of up to eight Transaction Response (TResp) packets.

See also **AppleTalk Transaction Protocol; Transaction Response.**

Transaction Response packet (TResp)

Under AppleTalk Transaction Protocol (ATP), a packet sent in response to a Transaction Request (TReq) packet to speci-

fy the results of the requested operation.

See also **AppleTalk Transaction Protocol; Transaction Request.**

Transaction-Services Layer (SNA model)

The seventh layer (Layer 7) of the Systems Network Architecture (SNA) model. The Transaction Services Layer provides distributed network-management services such as database access and document interchange.

See also **Systems Network Architecture.**

Transaction-Tracking System (TTS)

A NetWare system designed to protect data from corruption by backing out incomplete transactions that result from the failure of a network component. A transaction may be saved improperly during a power interruption, failure of server or workstation hardware, of software, or of a transmission component (such as a hub, repeater, or cable). TTS makes a copy of the original data before it is overwritten by new data; when a transaction is backed out, data returns to the state it was in before the transaction began. TTS can protect against data corruption in any type of application that issues record-locking calls and stores information in records (including traditional databases, some electronic-mail applications, and some appointment schedulers in workgroup applications).

See also **record locking.**

Transactional (T) attribute

A file attribute set by the NetWare operating system that indicates the file is protected by the Transaction-Tracking System (TTS).

See also **attribute; Transaction-Tracking System.**

transactions list

A list that contains all recently received transactions, used to implement *exactly-once transactions*, and maintained by responders that comply with AppleTalk Transaction Protocol (ATP).

See also **AppleTalk Transaction Protocol.**

transceiver

A device that can transmit data, receive data, and convert from an Attachment-Unit Interface (AUI) Ethernet connection to another type of cabling. This term is a contraction of *transmitter/receiver*.

See also **Attachment-Unit Interface.**

transceiver cable

A cable, found primarily in Ethernet systems, that connects a Network Interface Card (NIC) to a transceiver.

See also **Ethernet; Network Interface Card; transceiver.**

transfer mode

A mode in which telecommunications data is transferred or switched (or both) in a network.

transfer time

The amount of time it takes a backup power supply to switch to auxiliary power in the event of a power outage affecting a network node.

Transistor-Transistor Logic (TTL)

A logic family for digital circuitry that can

operate at speeds in excess of 100 megahertz (MHz).

transit bridging

A bridging technique that encapsulates a frame being sent between two similar networks via a dissimilar network.

translation bridging

Bridging that resolves differences in header formats and protocol specifications. Translation bridging is required on networks that have dissimilar protocols for the Media-Access Control (MAC) Sublayer of the OSI Reference Model.

See also **Media-Access Control; OSI Reference Model.**

transmission code

A set of rules that govern how data is represented during a transmission. Examples include Extended Binary-Coded Decimal-Interchange Code (EBCDI), which represents data as 8-bit code, and American Standard Code for Information Interchange (ASCII), which represents data as 7-bit code.

See also **American Standard Code for Information Interchange; Extended Binary-Coded Decimal-Interchange Code.**

Transmission-Control Layer (SNA model)

The fourth layer (Layer 4) in the Systems Network Architecture (SNA) model. The Transmission-Control Layer performs error-control functions, coordinates the pace of data exchanges to match processing capacities, and encodes data for security. This layer establishes, maintains, and terminates

SNA sessions, sequences all data messages, and handles flow control for the session.
See also **Systems Network Architecture.**

Transmission-Control Protocol (TCP)

In the Internet Protocol (IP) suite, a transport protocol that provides connection-oriented, full-duplex streams of data and uses the IP for delivery.

Transmission-Control Protocol/Internet Protocol (TCP/IP)

A suite of networking protocols that enables dissimilar nodes in a heterogeneous environment to communicate with one another. TCP/IP protocols handle media access, packet transport, session communications, file transfer, electronic mail, and terminal emulation. This suite and related applications were developed for the Department of Defense (DoD) during the 1970s and 1980s, specifically to permit different types of computers to exchange information with each other. TCP/IP is currently mandated as the official DoD protocol and widely used on UNIX platforms. Figure T.3 shows the relationship between TCP/IP and the OSI Reference Model.

transmission group

In Systems Network Architecture (SNA), one or more parallel communications links that are treated as one communication facility for routing purposes.
See also **Systems Network Architecture.**

Transmission Header (TH)

In the Systems Network Architecture (SNA) model, an element added to the Basic Information Unit (BIU) at the Path-Control Layer (Layer 3).
See also **Basic Information Unit; Systems Network Architecture.**

transmission medium

The physical path (cabling, wires, microwaves, satellite transmissions) over which a transmission is carried.

transmission mode

One of four modes in which communication between a sender and receiver can take place. Table T.7 shows the four modes and provides a description of each.

Table T.7: Transmission Modes

Mode	Description
Simplex	One-way communication in which the sender can use the entire communication channel.
Half-duplex	One-direction communication, but going both ways, in which a sender can use the entire communication channel. To change directions, a special signal is issued and acknowledged.
Full-duplex	Two-way communication that goes both ways simultaneously. The sender and receiver each only get half the communication channel.

(continued)

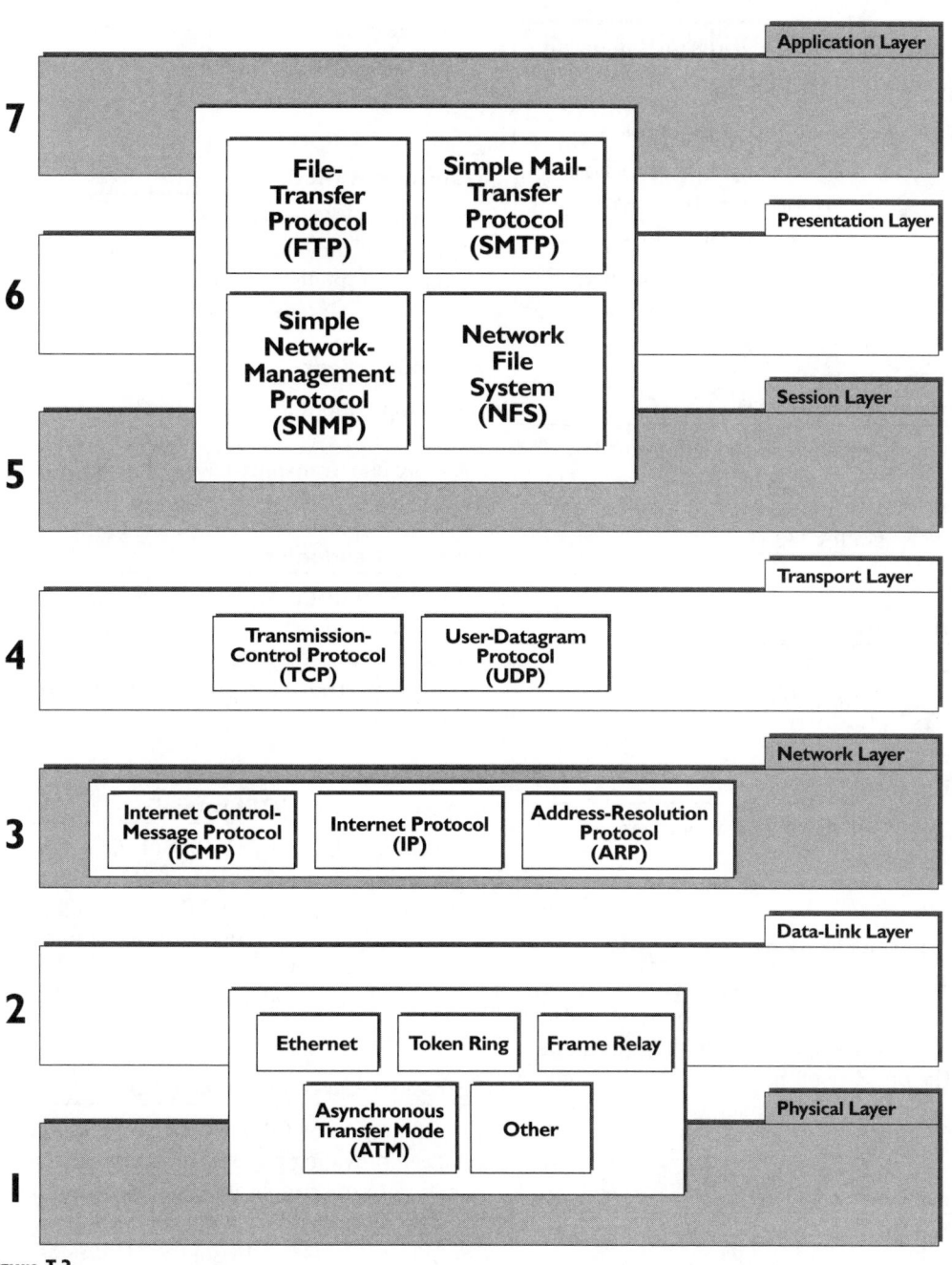

Figure T.3
TCP/IP and the OSI Reference Model
See also OSI Reference Model.

Table T.7: Transmission Modes (continued)

Mode	Description
Echoplex	Error-checking mode in which characters typed for transmission are returned to the sender's screen from the receiver for direct comparison with what was typed.

Transmit Data (TXD)

A hardware signal carrying information from one device to another, defined by the RS-232-C standard.
See also **RS-232-C.**

TRANSPAC

A European packet-switched network operated by France Telecom.

transparent

Capable of operating without being evident to the user.

transparent bridging

A scheme in which bridges pass frames one hop at a time, basing their hops on tables that associate end nodes with bridge ports. The presence of the bridges is transparent to the network's end nodes.

transparent LAN

A networking service in which two local-area networks (LANs) can communicate over telecommunications links without having to explicitly handle the long-distance connection.

transparent mode

A mode on a terminal display in which characters are displayed literally rather than being interpreted as commands.

transport client

An application or protocol that accesses Transport-Layer Interface (TLI) services.
See also **Transport-Layer Interface.**

transport endpoint

A channel that provides an endpoint for communication between a transport user and a transport provider.
See also **transport provider; transport user.**

Transport Layer (OSI model)

The fourth layer (Layer 4) in the OSI Reference Model. The Transport Layer provides reliable, end-to-end delivery of data and detects errors in the sequence of transmission.
See also **OSI Reference Model.**

Transport-Layer Interface (TLI)

An Interprocess Communication (IC) mechanism providing protocol-independent support for server applications. In NetWare, the TLI is an Application Program Interface (API) that resides between the STREAMS utility and user applications.

See also **Application Program Interface; Interprocess Communication; STREAMS utility.**

transport network

A private or public data network (usually packet-switched or circuit-switched) that transfers data between nodes.

See also **circuit-switched network; packet-switched network.**

transport provider

A protocol such as Datagram-Delivery Protocol (DDP) or AppleTalk Data-Stream Protocol (ADSP) that provides the services of the Transport-Layer Interface (TLI).

See also **AppleTalk Data-Stream Protocol; Datagram-Delivery Protocol; Transport-Layer Interface.**

Transport-Service Data Unit (TSDU)

A user data unit transmitted between two clients of a transport connection.

transport user

An application or protocol that accesses Transport-Layer Interface (TLI) services.

See also **Transport-Layer Interface.**

traps

Under Simple Network-Management Protocol (SNMP), operations used by an SNMP agent to notify an SNMP manager that major events have occurred.

See also **Simple Network-Management Protocol.**

Trash

A special folder on the Macintosh desktop that serves as a temporary repository for files that are marked for deletion but not yet officially erased.

tree structure

A flexible data structure representing the hierarchical organization of information. A tree consists of a *root* element with one or more elements branching out directly below it. Often the root is an abstract entity that has a purpose, but no real content. The elements below the root (also known as a *parent directory*) are called *children*; a child can, in turn, have children of its own beneath it. Various types of network directories are often represented in the tree structure.

See also **Directory tree.**

tree topology

A hybrid physical topology combining features of star and bus topologies. The starting end of the tree is the *head end* or *root end*. When several buses are daisy-chained together, branches are possible at the connections. A tree topology is also known as a *distributed bus topology* or a *branching tree topology*. Figure T.4 shows an example of a tree topology.

trellis-coded modulation (TCM)

A quadrature amplitude-modulation technique that encodes data as a set of bits associated with both phase and amplitude changes. TCM is typically used in modems that operate at speeds of 9600 bits per second (bps) or higher.

See also **amplitude; phase; quadrature amplitude modulation.**

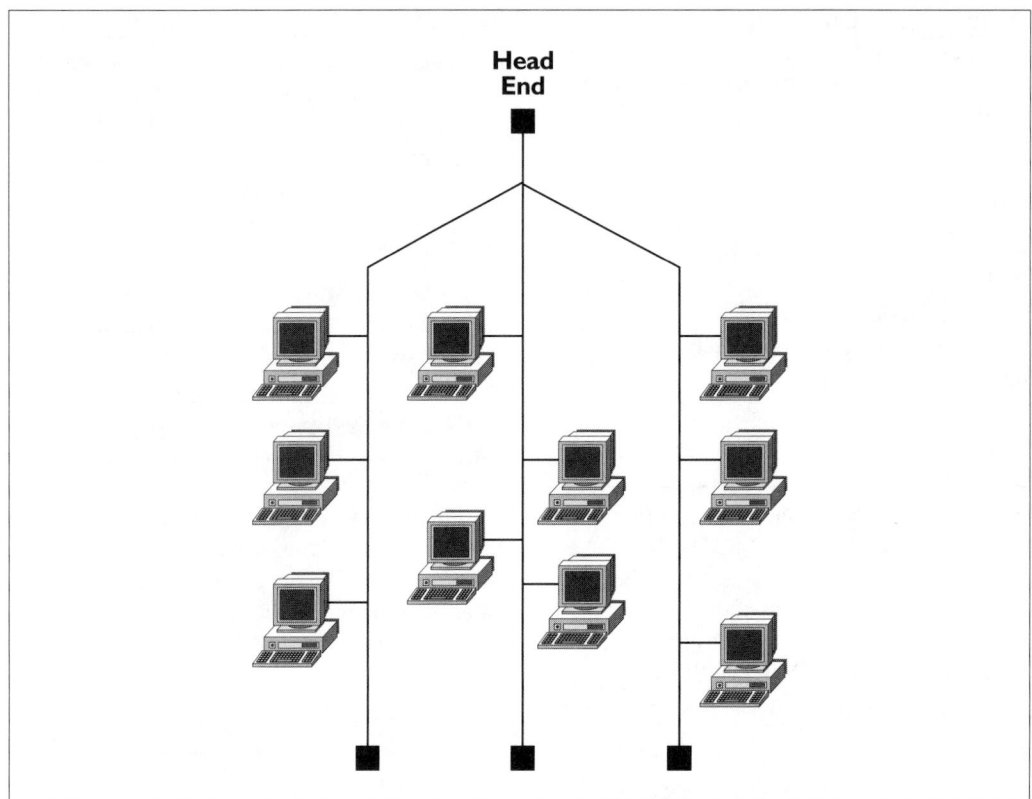

Figure T.4
Tree topology

TRel

Transaction Release packet, under AppleTalk Transaction Protocol (ATP), a packet sent in response to a Transaction Response (TResp) packet to indicate that the requester received the entire response message.

See also AppleTalk Transaction Protocol; Transaction Response.

TReq

Transaction Request packet, under AppleTalk Transaction Protocol (ATP), a packet sent by a socket to request that a responding packet perform an action and return a response.

See also AppleTalk Transaction Protocol.

TResp

Transaction Response packet, under
AppleTalk Transaction Protocol (ATP), a
message that consists of up to 8 Transaction
Response (TResp) packets.
See also **AppleTalk Transaction
Protocol; Transaction Response.**

triaxial cable

Coaxial cable consisting of an inner braid
surrounded by an inner jacket, surrounded
in turn by an outer copper braid, which is
surrounded by an outer jacket. The extra
shielding in triaxial cable provides grounding and improved protection.

Trivial File-Transfer Protocol (TFTP)

A version of the Transmission-Control
Protocol/Internet Protocol (TCP/IP), but
without password protection or user-
directory capabilities.
See also **Transport-Control
Protocol/Internet Protocol.**

Trojan Horse

A program that contains hidden instructions
to destroy files, programs, or File-Allocation
Table (FAT) information. The destruction
may be triggered by certain dates, times,
or user commands.
See also **File-Allocation Table.**

troll

The practice of posting a message on an
Internet newsgroup with apparent sincerity,
but with the real intention of eliciting a
reaction from readers.

trouble ticket

An error log used in network-fault management, particularly popular on distributed
systems.

TrueType

A font-rasterization and type-manager technology that creates scalable fonts by using
mathematical representations of their outline form. Jointly developed by Microsoft
Corporation and Apple Computer, TrueType
fonts can be converted to Adobe Type 1
fonts for output on PostScript printers.
See also **font; PostScript.**

Trumpet

A Windows-based newsreader program.
See also **newsreader.**

trunk

A transmission channel used to connect two
switching devices.

Trunk-Coupling Unit (TCU)

A physical device enabling a Token Ring
network station to connect to a trunk cable.
See also **Token Ring; trunk.**

trustee

In NetWare or IntranetWare, a user or
group granted the rights needed to work
with a directory, file, or object.
See also **trustee assignment.**

trustee assignment

Rights granted to NetWare or IntranetWare objects that are part of the directory, file, or object to which they grant access. In Novell Directory Services (NDS), a trustee assignment is stored in a *trustee list*, which in turn is stored in the object's Access-Control List property. The [Public] trustee assignment is special: Anyone who tries to access a file, directory, or object without any other rights is allowed only the rights granted to the [Public] trustee. Rights for files and directories are granted in the same manner, but rights to objects are different and have no effect on directories and files. Conversely, trustee assignments for files and directories have no effect on rights granted for objects. A trustee assignment for a file or directory enables a user to see the path to the root directory of the volume. A trustee assignment for an object does not automatically show the user the Directory tree to the root. Through *inheritance*, a trustee assignment to a directory, file, or object can provide access to the directory, its files, its subdirectories, or to the subordinate objects.

See also **access rights; access privileges; inheritance; rights.**

trustee node

An addressable, 128-byte entry in NetWare's Directory-Entry Table (DET), containing information about a trustee. Trustee nodes are maintained by the server.

See also **Directory Entry Table.**

trustee rights

Privileges granted to a user or group for a specific volume, folder, or file in NetWare

and that determine the kinds of tasks the trustee can carry out.

See also **trustee assignment.**

TSA

(1) **Target Service Agent,** a program designed to process data that moves between a specific target and a backup engine that complies with NetWare's Storage-Management Services (SMS). When using the SBACKUP utility, the host server sends requests to the TSA. The TSA then receives the commands from SBACKUP, processes the commands so the target operating system can handle the request for data, pass the data request to the target, receive the requested data from the target, and return it to SBACKUP in standard SMS format. (2) **Technical Service Alliance,** a collaborative effort between Novell and numerous companies to solve technical problems for customers they share.

See also (1) **SBACKUP;** (1) **Storage-Management Services.**

TSA resources

Target Service Agent resources, categories of data created by each NetWare Target Service Agent (TSA) and classified as either *major resources* or *minor resources*. These resources vary with each TSA, so the SBACKUP utility processes these resources in different ways.

TSAT

T1 small-aperture terminal, a satellite terminal used for T1 digital communications, with transmission rates as high as 1.544 megabits per second (Mbps).

TSDU

Transport-Service Data Unit, a user data unit transmitted between two clients of a transport connection.

TSM

Topology-Specific Module, a module (a self-contained portion of a computer program written, tested, and compiled separately from the main program) designed to perform operations that are specific to a particular network topology.

See also **topology.**

TSR

terminate-and-stay-resident program, a DOS program that remains in memory even when it is not actively running; a TSR can run while other applications are displayed on the monitor screen. Macintosh versions of TSRs are known as *Inits.*

TTFN

Ta-Ta For Now, a shorthand notation that sometimes appears at the end of an electronic-mail (e-mail) message or during an online forum.

TTL

Transistor-Transistor Logic, a logic family for digital circuitry that can operate at speeds in excess of 100 megahertz (MHz).

TTRT

Target Token-Rotation Time, a parameter value in a Fiber Distributed Data Interface (FDDI) network that specifies how much time passes before every node on the network gets access to the token.

See also **Fiber Distributed Data Interface; token passing.**

TTS

Transaction-Tracking System, a parameter value in a Fiber Distributed Data Interface (FDDI) network that specifies how much time passes before every node on the network gets access to the token.

See also **Fiber Distributed Data Interface; token passing.**

tunneling

Encapsulating and de-encapsulating one protocol in another. Specific definitions vary. In AppleTalk, tunneling is the process by which a router that supports the AppleTalk Update-Routing Protocol (AURP) encapsulates AppleTalk packets in Internet Protocol (IP) packets. The router then sends the resulting packets across the network under Transmission-Control Protocol/Internet Protocol (TCP/IP) to a router that supports AURP. In NetWare's Internetwork Packet Exchange (IPX) protocol, tunneling is the process by which a router running the IPTUNNEL or IPRELAY driver encapsulates IPX packets in User-Datagram Protocol/Internet Protocol (UDP/IP) packets, sending the resulting packets across the TCP/IP network to another router that runs IPTUNNEL or IPRELAY. The receiving router then removes the IP and AURP or UDP headers of the packets and forwards them to their destinations.

See also **AppleTalk; AppleTalk Update-Routing Protocol; Internet Protocol; Internetwork Packet Exchange; Transmission-Control Protocol/Internet Protocol; User-Datagram Protocol/Internet Protocol.**

Turbo FAT

Turbo File-Allocation Table, a special File-Allocation Table (FAT) index used when a file exceeds 64 blocks and must be quickly accessed.

See also **File-Allocation Table; FAT index.**

Turbo File-Allocation Table (Turbo FAT)

A special File-Allocation Table (FAT) index used when a file exceeds 64 blocks and must be quickly accessed.

See also **File-Allocation Table; FAT index.**

TUV

A German test agency responsible for certifying products to meet European safety standards.

TUXEDO

A Novell software program, originally developed by UNIX Systems Laboratory, that provides a high-level interface for transaction-management services in client-server systems. TUXEDO provides the capability of transferring data among platforms that differ in the way they represent data, while also monitoring and managing those transactions.

Development and support for TUXEDO has been transferred to BEA Systems, Inc.

 **For more information about TUXEDO Systems, surf the Web to** `http://www. beasys.com/products/ tuxedo/index.htm.`

twinaxial cable

A coaxial cable that has two cables inside a single insulating shield, commonly used with IBM AS/400 minicomputers.

See also **AS/400; coaxial cable.**

twisted-pair cable (TP)

Cable with two or more pairs of insulated wires twisted together at a rate of six twists per inch; one wire carries the signal and the other is grounded. The two types of TP are *shielded twisted-pair (STP)* and *unshielded twisted-pair (UTP)*.

See also **shielded twisted-pair cable; unshielded twisted-pair cable.**

Twisted-Pair Distributed Data Interface (TPDDI)

A network architecture that implements the capabilities of Fiber Distributed Data Interface (FDDI) on twisted-pair cabling.

See also **Fiber Distributed Data Interface.**

twisted-pair wiring

In balanced circuits, two wires that are spun around each other (usually loosely) to help alleviate any induced noise.

Twisted-Pair, Physical-Media-Dependent (TP-PMD)

An implementation of the Fiber Distributed Data Interface (FDDI) standard that can attain 100 megabits per second (Mbps) on unshielded twisted-pair (UTP) cabling.
See also **Fiber Distributed Data Interface.**

two-way channel

A channel allowing both incoming calls and outgoing calls.

TXD

Transmit Data, a hardware signal carrying information from one device to another, defined by the RS-232-C standard.
See also **RS-232-C.**

TYMNET

A public packet-switching network located in the United States.

Type

A Directory Schema term for Novell Directory Services (NDS).
See also **Novell Directory Services.**

Type 1 operation

A connectionless operation as defined by the Logical-Link Control (LLC) standard set by the Institute of Electronic and Electrical Engineers (IEEE).
See also **Institute of Electronic and Electrical Engineers; Logical-Link Control.**

Type 1-9 cable

Specifications set in the IBM Cabling System that define nine types of cable shown in Table T.8.

Table T.8: IBM Cabling System

Type	Description
Type 1	Shielded, twisted, dual-pair cable with 22-gauge solid connectors used to connect Token Ring networks.
Type 2	Shielded two-pair and unshielded four-pair cable (for a total of six pairs) with solid connectors and braided shield used to transmit voice and data.
Type 3	Four unshielded, solid, twisted pairs used to connect 16 megabits per second (Mbps) networks.
Type 4	Not defined.
Type 5	Dual fiber-optic cable used to connect Multistation Access Units (MAUs) in a Token Ring network.
Type 6	Shielded, two-pair, braided cable that serves as a short-distance patch.
Type 7	Not defined.
Type 8	Shielded dual-pair cable with no twists, serving as a flat cable placed beneath a carpet.
Type 9	Shielded, dual-pair, plenum cable (with solid conductors and a fire-resistant outer coating) that serves as a connector between floors.

See also **Multistation Access-Unit; plenum cable; shielded cable; Token Ring.**

Type 2 operation

A connection-oriented operation as defined by the Logical-Link Control (LLC) standard set by the Institute of Electronic and Electrical Engineers (IEEE).

See also **Institute of Electronic and Electrical Engineers; Logical Link Control.**

Type code

A four-character code that identifies the nature of a Macintosh file. Every Macintosh file has a Type code and a Creator code.

See also **Creator code.**

Type Creator Map

In Novell Directory Services (NDS), a NetWare Directory Schema term and a selectable property for the User object.

See also **leaf object; Novell Directory Services; object.**

Type of Service (ToS)

A byte in the header of an Internet Protocol (IP) packet that specifies the kind of transmission being requested, including the delay, throughput, and reliability of the desired transmission.

type-ahead buffer

Computer-system memory used to store the most recently typed keys on a keyboard. This feature is also known as a *keyboard buffer*.

t

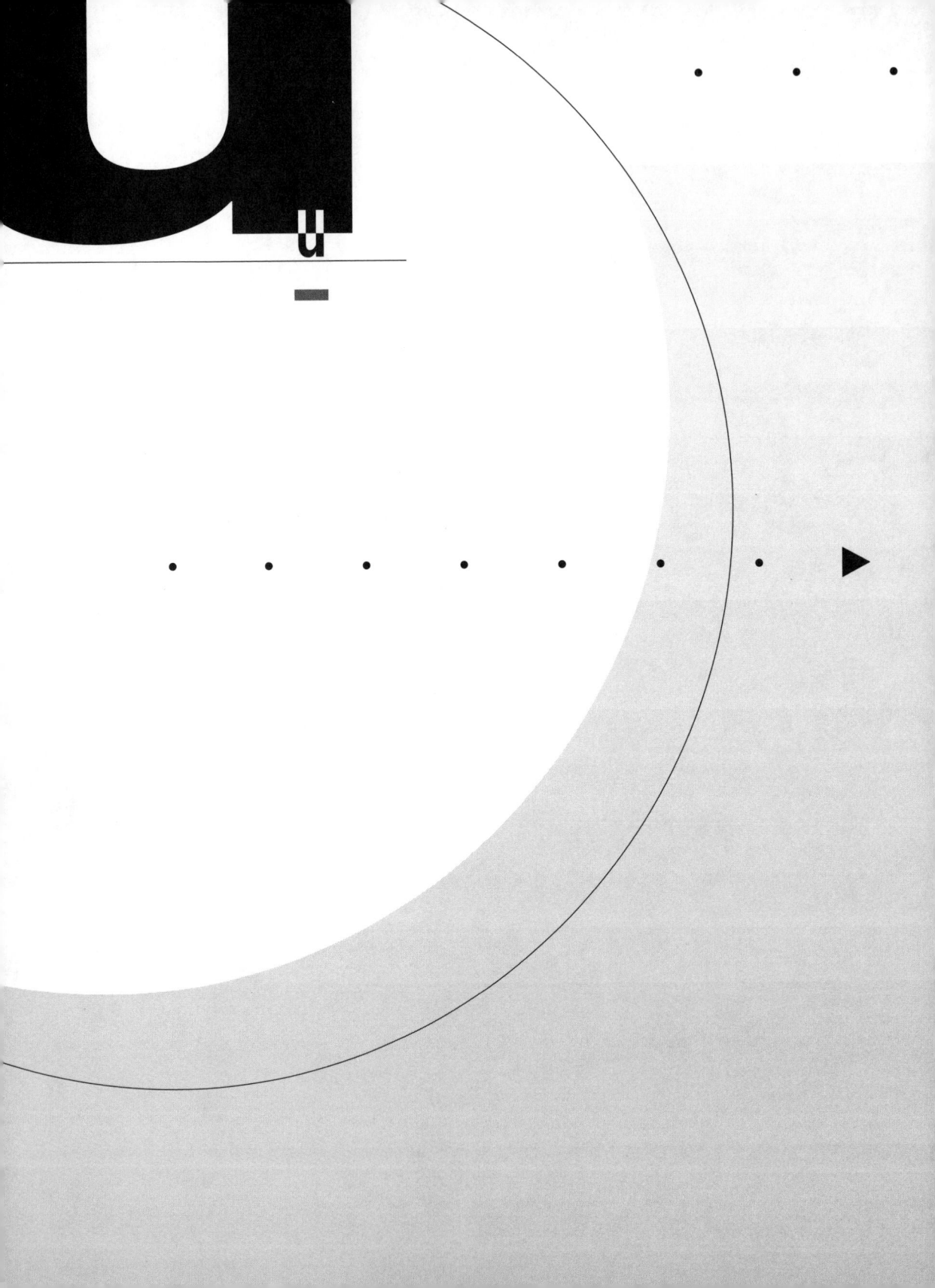

UA

(1) User Agent, an application process in the Consultative Committee for International Telegraphy and Telephony (CCITT) X.400 Message-Handling System (MHS) that gives users access to a Message-Transfer Service (MTS).
(2) Unsequenced Acknowledgment, a packet acknowledging the receipt of a Set Mode command in NetWare networks.

See also **(1) Consultative Committee for International Telegraphy and Telephony; (1) Message-Handling System; (1) Message-Transfer Service; (1) X.400.**

UAL

(1) User-Access Line, a line in an X.25 network that provides a connection between Data-Terminal Equipment (DTE) and a network. The user's Data-Communications Equipment (DCE) device, which may be a modem or multiplexer, provides the necessary interface to the network.
(2) User Agent Layer, an upper sublayer of the Application Layer (Layer 7) of the OSI Reference Model that provides an interface between user interaction and the Message-Transfer Layer (MTL) of the Consultative Committee for International Telegraphy and Telephony (CCITT) X.400 Message-Handling System (MHS).

See also **(1) Data-Communications Equipment; (1) Data-Terminal Equipment; (1) X.25; (2) Consultative Committee for International Telegraphy and Telephony; (2) Message-Handling System; (2) Message-Transfer Layer; (2) X.400.**

UAM

User-Authentication Method, a NetWare feature that compares the user name and password entered by a user at login with information stored in the NetWare Directory database, and then grants or denies the connection according to whether the comparison matches. NetWare supports an Apple Standard UAM and a NetWare UAM.

See also **clear-text UAM; NetWare User-Authentication Method.**

UART

universal asynchronous receiver/transmitter, an electronic module designed to combine the circuitry for transmitting and receiving, required for asynchronous communication over a serial line.

See also **asynchronous; asynchronous transmission.**

UBR

Unspecified Bit Rate, an Asynchronous Transfer Mode (ATM) service category that does not include the notion of a per-connection negotiated bandwidth. UBR does not make any traffic-related service guarantees.

See also **Asynchronous Transfer Mode.**

UDP

User-Datagram Protocol, a Transport Layer (Layer 4 of the OSI Reference Model) protocol in the Transmission-Control Protocol/Internet Protocol (TCP/IP) suite. UDP is not connection-oriented and does not acknowledge data receipt. This protocol is less reliable than TCP, but performs faster because it is does not establish and de-establish connections nor control data flow. This protocol is often bundled with the Simple Network-Management Protocol (SNMP).

See also **OSI Reference Model; Simple Network-Management Protocol; Transmission-Control Protocol/Internet Protocol.**

UIMPORT utility

In NetWare 4.*x* and IntranetWare, a workstation utility that imports user information from an existing database into the Novell Directory Services (NDS) database.

See also **Novell Directory Services.**

UL

Underwriters Laboratories, an independent agency that assesses conformity to standards and quality for manufacturers and other organizations.

See also **Underwriters Laboratories (includes Smart Link).**

ULP

Upper-Layer Protocol, a protocol in the OSI Reference Model that is higher than the current reference point, often the next-highest protocol in a particular protocol stack.

See also **OSI Reference Model.**

UltraNet

A 125-megabit-per-second (Mbps) network developed and maintained by Ultra Network Technologies.

UMB

upper memory block, a block of DOS memory between 640K and 1024K addressed by DOS and applications and defined by the Extended-Memory Specification (XMS). The unused portion of this memory area is known as the UMBs and is used to store terminate-and-stay-resident (TSR) programs and to load device drivers.

See also **memory; Extended-Memory Specification; terminate-and-stay-resident.**

UNA

Upstream Neighbor's Address, the address of a Token Ring network node from which a given node receives frames. Given the ring structure of the network, this address is unique at any given time in the operation of the network.

See also **Token Ring.**

unbalanced configuration

A configuration in the High-Speed Data-Link Control (HDLC) protocol that includes one primary station and multiple secondary stations.

See also **primary station.**

UNBIND utility

In NetWare and IntranetWare, a server console utility that removes a communication protocol from the local-area network (LAN) driver of a Network Interface Card (NIC) and disables communication on a specific NIC.

See also **Router-Information Protocol.**

unbinding

A NetWare process that removes a commu-nications protocol from Network Interface Cards (NICs) and from local-area network (LAN) drivers.

See also **Network Interface Card.**

unbundled software

An application or feature of an application sold separately from a computer system (in the case of an application) or from an application (in the case of a feature of an application).

UNC

Universal Naming Convention, a syntax used to specify a path to network resources. For example, in Windows 95, a UNC name of \\SERVER\APPS would specify the APPS subdirectory of the SERVER directory.

undervoltage

An electrical condition in which a voltage supply falls below its nominal value.

Underwriters Laboratories (UL)

An independent agency that assesses conformity to standards and quality for manufacturers and other organizations.

For more information about Underwriters Laboratories, surf the Web to http:// www.ul.com.

UNI

User-to-Network Interface, an interface used by a router to connect to and access Frame Relay network services. According to the ATM Forum that defines public and pri-vate access for Asynchronous Transfer Mode (ATM), the UNI occurs between an ATM end-system (such as a router) and an ATM switch. The UNI is also known as *subscriber network interface* in a Switched Multimegabit Data-Service (SMDS) environment.

See also **Asynchronous Transfer Mode; Frame Relay network.**

unicast address

An address that specifies a single network device.

Unicode

A 16-bit character representation defined by the Unicode Consortium that allows charac-ters for multiple languages to be represented and that supports up to 65,536 characters. NetWare stores all objects and their attributes in the Directory database in Unicode repre-sentation. DOS and OS/2 clients, however, use 256-character code pages, and not every character used on a given code page repre-sents correctly on a workstation using a dif-ferent code page. If a user changes code pages, a different set of Unicode translation tables are required to run NetWare utilities and to manage the Directory database. Therefore, when managing objects created in different code pages, object names and properties must be limited to characters common to all applicable code pages.

See also **code page; code-page switching.**

UNICON (NLM)

In IntranetWare, a server console utility that lets a user change to another server on the network and manage a different server; configure the server's global parameters; start, stop, and monitor certain services; configure and manage NetWare Domain Naming System (DNS) and the NetWare/IP Domain SAP/RIP Service (DSS); configure error reporting; and monitor performance and adjust parameters affecting performance.

See also **Domain-Naming System.**

unified messaging

A telephony service local-area networks (LANs) in which messages or information are accessed in a transparent manner (in other words, the messages or information can be displayed regardless of the format). Unified messaging is also known as *integrated messaging.*

Unified Network-Management Architecture (UNMA)

A network-management architecture developed by AT&T that relies on distributed processing. Based on Open Systems Interconnection (OSI) protocols, UNMA serves as an operating environment for the AT&T Accumaster Integrator network-management package. It provides a framework for dealing with nine management functions, including accounting management, configuration management, fault management, performance management, and security management, which correspond to the OSI Network-Management Model. The other management functions are integrated control, operations support, planning capability, and programmability.

See also **Open Systems Interconnection; OSI Network-Management Model.**

Uniform Resource Locator (URL)

An Internet address that consists of information about the document type and about the protocol used to transport it, the domain name of the machine on which the document is found, and the document's name represented as an absolute path to the file. Figure U.1 shows a sample URL.

Uniform Service-Ordering Code (USOC)

A commonly used sequence for wiring pairs.
See also **wiring sequence.**

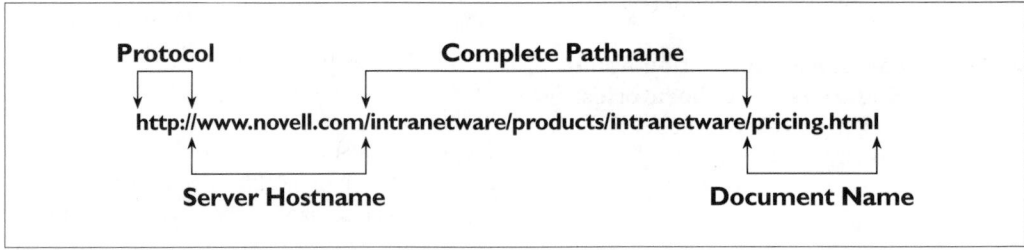

Figure U.1
Uniform Resource Locator

uninterruptible power supply (UPS)

A backup unit that provides uninterrupted power in the event of a power outage. An *online UPS* actively modifies power as it moves through the unit, so, if a power outage occurs, the unit is already active and continues to provide power. An *offline UPS* monitors the power line and, when power drops, the UPS is activated. If a UPS is attached to a server, the server can properly close files and rewrite the system directory to disk.

See also **power conditioning.**

unipolar

An electrical characteristic of internal signals in digital communications equipment that literally means one polarity.

See also **bipolar.**

unique password

A password unlike any other password used to log in to the NetWare network. If the network is configured to accept only unique passwords, it rejects any new password that is identical to one of the last eight passwords (or any password used for at least one day).

unity gain

The use of amplifiers to balance signal loss with signal gain in broadband networks.

universal asynchronous receiver/transmitter (UART)

An electronic module designed to combine the circuitry for transmitting and receiving,

required for asynchronous communication over a serial line.

See also **asynchronous; asynchronous transmission.**

universal in-box

A central delivery point for electronic mail (e-mail), faxes, and other types of electronic communication.

Universal Naming Convention (UNC)

A syntax used to specify a path to network resources. For example, in Windows 95, a UNC name of \\SERVER\APPS would specify the APPS subdirectory of the SERVER directory.

universal synchronous receiver/transmitter (USRT)

An electronic module combining circuitry for transmitting and receiving; required for synchronous communication over a serial line.

See also **synchronous; synchronous transmission.**

UNIX

An operating system originally developed by Dennis Ritchie and Ken Thompson at AT&T Bell Laboratories that allows a computer to handle multiple users and programs simultaneously. Since its development in the early 1970s, UNIX has been enhanced by many individuals and companies, particularly by computer scientists at the University of California at Berkeley (which is known as Berkeley Software Distribution UNIX, or

BSD UNIX). This operating system is available on a wide variety of computer systems ranging from personal computers to mainframes and is available in other related forms. AIX is an implementation that runs on IBM workstations, A/UX is a graphical version that runs on Macintosh computers, and Solaris runs on Intel microprocessors. UnixWare is the Novell implementation of UNIX. NetWare for UNIX is an Original Equipment Manufacturer (OEM) version of NetWare that can run on a UNIX host.

See also **Berkeley Software Distribution UNIX; NetWare for UNIX; UnixWare.**

 **For more information about UNIX user groups around the world, surf the Web to** `http://www.sluug.org/~newton/othr_uug.html`.

UNIX client

A UNIX computer, connected to a NetWare network, that stores and retrieves data from the server and runs executable network files. A UNIX client provides multitasking capabilities for multiple clients on a single station. To allow other NetWare clients to access UNIX applications, the UNIX client includes Internetwork Packet Exchange/Sequenced Packet-Exchange (IPX/SPS) and NetWare Core Protocol/Internetwork Packet-Exchange (NCP/IPX) protocols.

See also **Internetwork Packet Exchange; NetWare Core Protocol; Sequenced Packet Exchange.**

UNIX-to-UNIX Copy Program (UUCP)

An Application Layer (Layer 7 of the OSI Reference Model) protocol used by consenting UNIX systems to communicate with each other. In the early days of internetworking, this dial-up, store-and-forward protocol formed the basis for mail and news exchange.

See also **OSI Reference Model.**

UnixWare

Novell's implementation of the UNIX operating system. A Personal Edition of UnixWare is a single-user system for applications and an Application Server version is a multiuser, server system. UnixWare has been transferred to the Santa Cruz Operation (SCO) for future development and support.

Unknown Base Class

A NetWare Directory Schema term in Novell Directory Services (NDS).

See also **Novell Directory Services.**

Unknown object

A leaf object that represents a corrupted Novell Directory Services (NDS) object that cannot be identified as belonging to any other object class. The Unknown object has the Access-Control List, Back Link, Bindery, and Object Class selectable NDS properties

See also **leaf object; Novell Directory Services; object.**

Unknown Object Restriction

A NetWare Directory Schema term in Novell Directory Services (NDS).

See also **Novell Directory Services.**

UNLOAD utility

In NetWare and IntranetWare, a server console utility that unloads a module previously loaded with the LOAD command and unloads old NetWare Loadable Module (NLM) files so updated modules can be loaded. When a module is unloaded, all resources it used are returned to the system (if other modules depend on a particular module, it does not unload).

See also **LOAD utility; NetWare Loadable Module.**

unloading

A NetWare process that unlinks NetWare Loadable Modules (NLMs) from the operating system.

See also **NetWare Loadable Module.**

UNMA

Unified Network-Management Architecture, a network-management architecture developed by AT&T that relies on distributed processing. Based on Open Systems Interconnection (OSI) protocols, UNMA serves as an operating environment for the AT&T Accumaster Integrator network-management package. It provides a framework for dealing with nine management functions, including accounting management, configuration management, fault management, performance management, and security management, which correspond to the OSI Network-Management Model. The other management functions are integrated control, operations support, planning capability, and programmability.

See also **Open Systems Interconnection; OSI Network-Management Model.**

unnumbered frame

A frame used for system administration (such as link startup and shutdown, as well as mode specifications) in the High-Level Data-Link Control (HDLC) protocol.

See also **High-Level Data-Link Control.**

unreliable

A term often used to indicate that packet delivery on a network has not been verified.

Unsequenced Acknowledgment (UA)

A packet acknowledging the receipt of a Set Mode command in NetWare networks.

unshielded cable

Cable that has no outer foil shield to protect against electromagnetic interference (EMI) or radio-frequency interference (RFI).

See also **electromagnetic interference; radio-frequency interference; shielded cable.**

unshielded twisted-pair cable (UTP)

Cable containing two or more pairs of twisted copper wires; the greater number of twists, the lower the crosstalk. UTP is available in both voice-grade and data-grade versions. Ease of installation and low material cost make this cable appealing, but drawbacks include limited signaling speed and shorter maximum-cable-segment length.

See also **shielded twisted-pair cable.**

Unspecified Bit Rate (UBR)

An Asynchronous Transfer Mode (ATM) service category that does not include the notion of a per-connection negotiated bandwidth. UBR does not make any traffic-related service guarantees.

See also **Asynchronous Transfer Mode.**

up time

The time during which a computer or other device is functioning, but not necessarily available for use.

upgradable computer

A computer system designed to be upgraded when newer technology becomes available. Systems may differ in the degree that circuitry must be changed and how the upgrade is accomplished.

upgrade

A process involving the installation of a newer and more powerful version of hardware or software on a computer system.

uplink

Transmission of data from an Earth station to a satellite.

upload

A communications process involving the sending of files from one computer to another computer over a network or modem.

Upper-Layer Protocol (ULP)

A protocol in the OSI Reference Model that is higher than the current reference point, often the next-highest protocol in a particular protocol stack.

See also **OSI Reference Model.**

upper memory

DOS memory located above 640K and below 1024K, addressable by 16-bit micro-processors, keeping parts reserved for DOS and Basic Input/Output System (BIOS) functions. Upper memory is also known as *reserved memory.*

See also **memory.**

upper memory block (UMB)

A block of DOS memory between 640K and 1024K addressed by DOS and applications and defined by the Extended-Memory Specification (XMS). The unused portion of this memory area is known as the UMBs and is used to store terminate-and-stay-resident (TSR) programs and to load device drivers.

See also **memory; Extended-Memory Specification; terminate-and-stay-resident.**

UPS

(1) **uninterruptible power supply,** a back-up unit that provides uninterrupted power in the event of a power outage. An *online UPS* actively modifies power as it moves through the unit, so, if a power outage occurs, the unit is already active and continues to provide power. An *offline UPS* monitors the power line and, when power drops, the UPS is activated. If a UPS is attached to

a server, the server can properly close files and rewrite the system directory to disk. A backup unit that provides uninterrupted power in the event of a power outage. An *online UPS* actively modifies power as it moves through the unit, so, if a power outage occurs, the unit is already active and continues to provide power. An *offline UPS* monitors the power line and, when power drops, the UPS is activated. If a UPS is attached to a server, the server can properly close files and rewrite the system directory to disk.
(2) UPS (NLM). In NetWare and IntranetWare, a server console NetWare Loadable Module (NLM) that provides a software link between a server and an uninterruptible power supply (UPS), as well as activating UPS monitoring.

See also **(1) power conditioning.**

UPS monitoring

A NetWare process in which a server ensures that an uninterruptible power supply (UPS) unit is attached and functioning properly. In the event of a power failure, NetWare notifies users and, after a timeout period specified in the SERVER.CFG file, the server logs out remaining users, closes open files, and shuts itself down.

See also **uninterruptible power supply.**

UPS STATUS utility

In NetWare and IntranetWare, a server console utility used to view information about the uninterruptible power supply (UPS) attached to the server. The UPS utility must be loaded before this utility can work properly.

See also **uninterruptible power supply.**

UPS TIME utility

In NetWare and IntranetWare, a server console utility that changes the amount of time the server functions on battery power, changes the estimated time that the battery needs to fully charge, and changes the time interval between a power interruption and activation of the uninterruptible power supply (UPS). The UPS utility must be loaded before this utility can work properly.

See also **uninterruptible power supply.**

UPS_AIO (NLM)

In IntranetWare, a server console NetWare Loadable Module (NLM) used when an uninterruptible power supply (UPS) is connected to the server through a serial port. This NLM provides the software link between the server and the UPS.

See also **uninterruptible power supply.**

Upstream Neighbor's Address (UNA)

The address of a Token Ring network node from which a given node receives frames. Given the ring structure of the network, this address is unique at any given time in the operation of the network.

See also **Token Ring.**

upward compatibility

The capability of software to function with other, more powerful products likely to become available in the future. Upward compatibility is made possible by adherence to design standards.

See also **backward compatibility.**

URL

Uniform Resource Locator, an Internet address that consists of information about the document type and about the protocol used to transport it, the domain name of the machine on which the document is found, and the document's name represented as an absolute path to the file.

See also **Uniform Resource Locator** (includes **Figure U.1**).

U.S. classification levels

A set of classification levels established by the federal government for messages and information transmitted across the Internet that includes Top Secret, Secret, Confidential, and Unclassified. Each classification level is specified by an assigned 8-bit value.

Usenet

A cooperative network, initiated in 1979, that includes more than 10,000 hosts, a quarter million users, and a distributed conferencing service for users. The thousands of distributed bulletin boards on this network display messages according to hierarchical categories known as *newsgroups* and are accessed by users with *newsreader* programs. Individual Internet service providers (ISPs) determine which newsgroups to offer and with which systems to exchange messages. Newsreader programs use the Network News-Transfer Protocol (NNTP) to translate messages.

See also **Internet service provider; Network News-Transfer Protocol; newsgroup; newsreader.**

user

Someone who is authorized to log on to a network or database (or both) when security is installed and who has access rights to files and directories.

User

A NetWare Directory Schema term and a selectable property for the following objects in Novell Directory Services (NDS): AFP Server, Bindery Queue, NCP Server, Print Server, and Queue.

See also **leaf object; Novell Directory Services; object.**

User-Access Line (UAL)

A line in an X.25 network that provides a connection between Data-Terminal Equipment (DTE) and a network. The user's Data-Communications Equipment (DCE) device, which may be a modem or multiplexer, provides the necessary interface to the network.

See also **Data-Communications Equipment; Data-Terminal Equipment; X.25.**

user account

A NetWare security feature that determines under what name the user logs in to the network, the groups to which the user belongs, and the trustee assignments made to the user. This account is maintained by the network supervisor for every user on the network.

See also **trustee assignment; User object.**

User Agent (UA)

An application process in the X.400 Message-Handling System (MHS) specified by the Consultative Committee for International Telegraphy and Telephony (CCITT). The User Agent gives users access to a Message-Transfer Service (MTS).

See also **Consultative Committee for International Telegraphy and Telephony; Message-Handling System; Message-Transfer Service; X.400.**

User-Agent Layer (UAL)

An upper sublayer of the Application Layer (Layer 7) of the OSI Reference Model that provides an interface between user interaction and the Message-Transfer Layer (MTL) of the Consultative Committee for International Telegraphy and Telephony (CCITT) X.400 Message-Handling System (MHS).

See also **Consultative Committee for International Telegraphy and Telephony; Message-Handling System; Message-Transfer Layer; X.400.**

User-Authentication Method (UAM)

A NetWare feature that compares the user name and password entered by a user at login with information stored in the NetWare Directory database, and then grants or denies the connection according to whether the comparison matches. NetWare supports an Apple Standard UAM and a NetWare UAM.

See also **clear-text UAM; NetWare User-Authentication Method.**

User-Datagram Protocol (UDP)

A Transport Layer (Layer 4 of the OSI Reference Model) protocol in the Transmission-Control Protocol/Internet Protocol (TCP/IP) suite. UDP is not connection-oriented and does not acknowledge data receipt. This protocol is less reliable than TCP, but performs faster because it does not establish and de-establish connections nor control data flow. This protocol is often bundled with the Simple Network-Management Protocol (SNMP).

See also **OSI Reference Model; Simple Network-Management Protocol; Transmission-Control Protocol/Internet Protocol.**

user group

A group of users who meet to share tips and listen to industry experts discuss a computer or software product of common interest to the group. User group activities often include regular meetings, maintenance of a Bulletin Board System (BBS), or publication of a newsletter.

See also **Bulletin Board System.**

user hold

A hold placed on a NetWare print job by the queue user who owns the job or by the queue operator.

User ID (UID)

A selectable property for the User object in Novell Directory Services (NDS).

See also **leaf object; Novell Directory Services; object.**

User login script

A NetWare login script that sets environments specific to a user and that contains items not allowed in System or Profile login scripts. User login scripts, which are optional, execute after System login scripts and Profile login scripts.

See also **login script; Profile login script; System login script.**

user name

A name recognized by the network and with which a user gains access to a network server.

User object

A Novell Directory Services (NDS) leaf object that represents a person with access to the network and that stores information about the person it represents. The User object has the following selectable NDS properties: Access-Control List, Account Balance, Account Locked, Account Reset Time, Allow Unlimited Credit, Allow User to Change Password, Back Link, Bindery, City, Common Name (CN), Days Between Forced Changes, Default Profile, Default Server, Description, E-Mail Address, Facsimile Telephone Number, Fax Number, Full Name, Generational Qualifier, Given Name, Group Membership, Higher Privileges, Home Directory, Incorrect Login Attempts, Initials, Intruder Address, Language, Last Login Time, Last Name, Limit Grace Logins, Locality (L), Location, Locked By Intruder, Login Allowed Time Map, Login Disabled, Login-Expiration Date and Time, Login-Expiration Time, Login Grace Limit, Login Grace Remaining, Login Intruder Address, Login Intruder Attempts, Login Intruder Reset Time, Login Maximum

Simultaneous, Login Script, Login Time, Login Time Restrictions, Mailbox ID, Mailbox Location, Mailing Label Information, Maximum Connections, Message Server, Minimum Account Balance, Network Address, Network Address Restrictions, Object Class, Object Trustees (ACL), Organizational Unit (OU), Password Allow Change, Password Expiration Date and Time, Password Expiration Interval, Password Expiration Time, Password Minimum Length, Password Required, Password Unique Required, Passwords Used, Physical Delivery Office Name, Postal Address, Postal Code, Postal Office Box, Print Job Configuration, Printer Control, Private Key, Profile, Profile Membership, Public Key, Remaining Grace Logins, Require a Password, Require a Unique Password, S, SA, Security Equals To, Security Equivalences, Security Flags, See Also, Server Holds, Surname, Telephone, Telephone Number, Title, Type Creator Map, and User ID (UID). Table U.1 shows important management topics related to User objects.

User object ADMIN

Another name for the **ADMIN object,** a Novell Directory Services (NDS) User object (created in the process of installing NetWare 4.*x*) that has special privileges. These privileges include supervisory rights to manage an NDS Directory tree and to create or delete Directory objects. When the Directory tree is first created, ADMIN has a trustee assignment to the [Root] object. Because the trustee assignment includes the Supervisor object right, ADMIN can create and manage any object in the tree. Additional objects can later be given the

Table U.1: Management of the User Object

Management Area	Description
Account management	Users with Supervisor object rights to another User object can manage that User object and modify information about that user.
Group membership	Users can be assigned to Group objects and, when assigned to a group, the user inherits rights assigned to the group.
Home directory	The user's personal workspace is the home directory.
Login names	Login names are mandatory for User objects and can be up to 64 characters long (no special characters or control characters allowed).
Print-job configurations	A user may utilize default printing configurations or create a configuration for an individual print job.
Trustee rights	Adequate trustee rights must be granted to a user before the user can access specific directories or files.
User login scripts	This login script customizes the network environment for users. If no login script is used, a default login script executes.

See also **leaf object; login script; Novell Directory Services; object; trustee assignment.**

Supervisor object right if you need to decentralize control of the network. *Caution: Do not delete this object. If the ADMIN object must be deleted, another user must be granted full Directory rights beforehand.*

user profile

A record that specifies a user's access and usage privileges on a network system.

user template

A NetWare file that contains default information that can be applied to new User objects to give them default property values.

User templates are created in Organization and Organizational Unit objects.

User Template object

In IntranetWare, a leaf object used to create User objects in Novell Directory Systems (NDS). Through this object, a user can designate default values for User object creation (including NDS rights and file system rights). This object can only be used for setting up new users. This object replaced the older User object called User_Template found in earlier versions of NetWare 4.

See also **leaf object; Novell Directory Services; object.**

User Version

A selectable property for the Messaging Server object in Novell Directory Services (NDS).

See also **leaf object; Novell Directory Services; object.**

USERDEF utility

In NetWare 3.*x*, a workstation utility used by a supervisor to create multiple users, provide simple login scripts, set up home directories, set up minimal login/password security, assign account restrictions, assign disk space restrictions, and set up print job configurations.

USERLIST utility

In NetWare 3.*x*, a workstation utility used to view a list of current users for a given file server, view each user's connection number, view login time, view network addresses, view node addresses, and view the type of object attached to the server.

See also **Router-Information Protocol.**

username

A name assigned to a NetWare user account that the user types in to log in to the network and to gain access to network resources.

user-network contract

An Asynchronous Transfer Mode (ATM) element specifying parameter values for Virtual Channel Connection (VCC) and Virtual Path Connection (VPC) that can be negotiated by entities involved in the connection. A traffic descriptor is also known as a *traffic descriptor*.

See also **Asynchronous Transfer Mode; Virtual Channel Connection; Virtual Path Connection.**

User-to-Network Interface (UNI)

An interface used by a router to connect to and access Frame Relay network services. According to the ATM Forum that defines public and private access for Asynchronous Transfer Mode (ATM), the UNI occurs between an ATM end-system (such as a router) and an ATM switch. The UNI is also known as *subscriber network interface* in a Switched Multimegabit Data-Service (SMDS) environment.

See also **Asynchronous Transfer Mode; Frame Relay network.**

USOC

Uniform Service-Ordering Code, a commonly used sequence for wiring pairs.

See also **wiring sequence.**

USRT

universal synchronous receiver/ transmitter, an electronic module combining circuitry for transmitting and receiving; required for synchronous communication over a serial line.

See also **synchronous; synchronous transmission.**

utility

A program that adds functionality to a network operating system. For NetWare and IntranetWare, utilities support Windows,

OS/2, DOS, and UNIX environments. These utilities are designed to work at the server console (for example, to change memory allocations, monitor server operation, and control the utilization of server resources), on files, and at the workstation. Appendix E provides a breakdown of common NetWare and IntranetWare utilities, along with classifications as server console, file, and workstation utilities.

Utilization

A field name in the Cache Utilization screen of the MONITOR NetWare Loadable Module (NLM).

See also **MONITOR; NetWare Loadable Module.**

UTP

unshielded twisted-pair cable, cable containing two or more pairs of twisted copper wires; the greater number of twists, the lower the crosstalk. UTP is available in both voice-grade and data-grade versions. Ease of installation and low material cost make this cable appealing, but drawbacks include limited signaling speed and shorter maximum-cable-segment length.

See also **shielded twisted-pair cable.**

UUCP

UNIX-to-UNIX Copy Program, an Application Layer (Layer 7 of the OSI Reference Model) protocol used by consenting UNIX systems to communicate with each other. In the early days of internetworking, this dial-up, store-and-forward protocol formed the basis for mail and news exchange.

See also **OSI Reference Model.**

uudecode

The conversion of a file back to its original format from the uuencoded format. This encoding method is used to transfer both text and graphics files in many electronic-mail (e-mail) programs because it makes even binary files appear as strings of text characters. The encoding scheme was originally designed to work with the UNIX-to-UNIX Copy Program (UUCP). This term translates literally to "UNIX-to-UNIX decode."

See also **UNIX-to-UNIX Copy Program.**

uuencode

The encoding of a file to the uuencoded format. This encoding method is used to transfer both text and graphics files in many electronic mail (e-mail) because it makes even binary files appear as strings of text characters. The encoding scheme was originally designed to work with the Unix-to-Unix Copy Program (UUCP). This term translates literally to "UNIX-to-UNIX encode."

See also **UNIX-to-UNIX Copy Program.**

UUNET

A nonprofit organization that runs an Internet site that links the UNIX-to-UNIX Copy Program (UUCP) mail network to the Internet, maintains a File-Transfer Protocol (FTP) site, and runs a commercial Internet service provider (ISP).

See also **UNIX-to-UNIX Copy Program.**

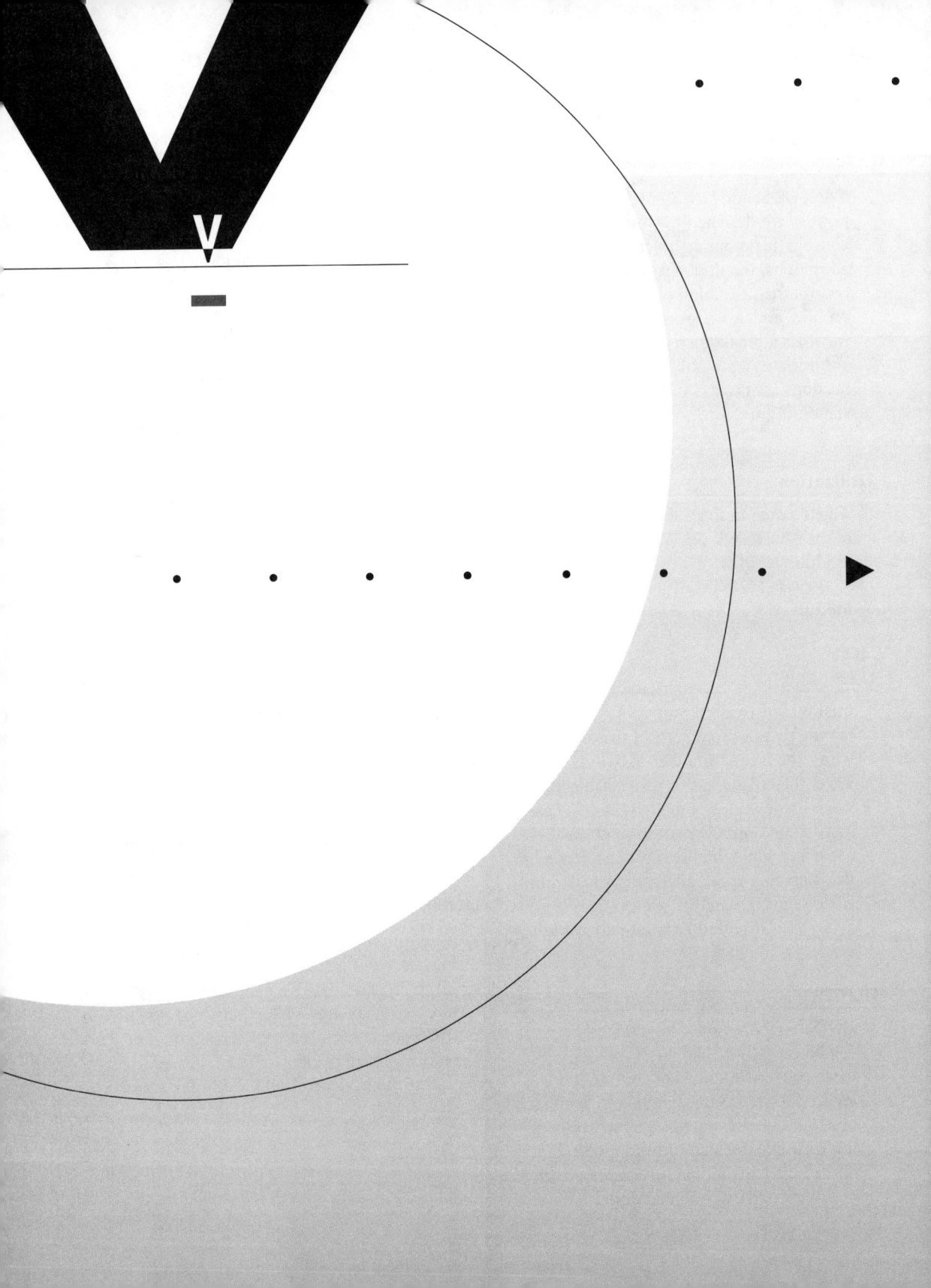

V.24

A Physical Layer (Layer 6 in the OSI Reference Model) interface used in many countries. V.24 is similar to the RS-232-C interface.

See also **RS-232-C.**

V.25*bis* dialing

A standard from the Consultative Committee for International Telegraphy and Telephony (CCITT) that describes in-band dialing on High-Level Data-Link Control (HDLC) bit-synchronous serial lines.

See also **Consultative Committee for International Telegraphy and Telephony; High-Level Data-Link Control.**

V.32

A modem that transmits at a speed of 9,600 bits per second.

See also **modem.**

V.35

A standard from the Consultative Committee for International Telegraphy and Telephony (CCITT) that describes data transmission at 48 kilobits per second (Kbps) using 60-kilohertz (KHz) to 108KHz circuits.

V_LONG (NLM)

A module used in the VREPAIR NetWare Loadable Module (NLM) to repair volumes using the LONG.NAM name space module (which enables a server to support Windows NT, Windows 95, and OS/2 long filenames and formats).

See also **LONG.NAM; NetWare Loadable Module; VREPAIR.**

V_MAC (NLM)

A module used in the VREPAIR NetWare Loadable Module (NLM) to repair volumes using the MAC.NAM name space module (which enables a server to support long filenames and formats on the Macintosh).

See also **MAC.NAM; NetWare Loadable Module; VREPAIR.**

V_NFS (NLM)

A module used in the VREPAIR NetWare Loadable Module (NLM) to repair volumes using the NFS.NAM name space module (which enables a server to support UNIX long filenames and formats).

See also **NetWare Loadable Module; NFS.NAM; VREPAIR.**

value

Contents of an object property in Novell Directory Services (NDS). Some properties may have multiple values (such as several telephone numbers for the Telephone Number property). While access rights control access to a property, they do not control access to individual values of a property.

See also **access rights; Novell Directory Services; object.**

value-added network (VAN)

A commercial network that adds services or features to an existing network.

value-added process (VAP)

A process designed to enhance the NetWare operating system features without interfering with normal network operation. A VAP runs on top of the operating system in a manner similar to a word-processing application or spreadsheet running on top of DOS.

value-added reseller (VAR)

A company that enhances the quality of a product (for example, by improving documentation, user support, service support, or system integration), repackages the product, and resells it to the public.

value-added server

A dedicated computer, separate from the network, that fulfills a specific function for network users (such as a print server or database server).

See also **print server.**

vampire tap

A hardware clamp used to connect one cable segment to another by penetrating the insulation of the network cable segment without cutting it. A needle on the tap pierces the cable insulation to make a connection with the cable.

VAN

value-added network, a commercial network that adds services or features to an existing network.

VAP

value-added process, a process designed

to enhance the NetWare operating-system features without interfering with normal network operation. A VAP runs on top of the operating system in a manner similar to a word-processing application or spreadsheet running on top of DOS.

vaporware

A term used to describe a software product announced for release on a specific date, but is still not released after that date has been passed by a significant amount of time.

VAR

value-added reseller, a company that enhances the quality of a product (for example, by improving documentation, user support, service support, or system integration), repackages the product, and resells it to the public.

Variable Bit Rate (VBR)

A connection method used in Asynchronous Transfer Mode (ATM) networks that transmits at varying rates and used for data transmissions whose contents are not time-sensitive. VBR is a *reserved-bandwidth* service, but instead of generating a constant bit rate, establishes a peak rate, sustainable rate, and maximum burst size.

See also **Asynchronous Transfer Mode.**

variable-length record

A record consisting of a variable-length portion (which may vary in size) and a fixed-length portion (which remains the same size in all records in a given file).

See also **Variable-Tail Allocation Table.**

Variable-Length Subnet Mask (VLSM)

A capability that optimizes available address space by specifying a different subnet mask for the same network number on different subnetworks.

See also **subnet mask.**

Variable-Tail Allocation Table (VAT)

An array that contains pointers to locations within the variable-length portion of a record.

See also **variable-length record.**

VAT

Variable-Tail Allocation Table, an array that contains pointers to locations within the variable-length portion of a record.

See also **variable-length record.**

VAX

A minicomputer manufactured by Digital Equipment Corporation.

See also **Virtual Memory System.**

VAX OSI Transport Service (VOTS)

A Transport Level (Level 4 of the OSI Reference Model) protocol used on Digital Equipment Corporation machines in a local-area network (LAN) or wide-area network (WAN).

See also **OSI Reference Model.**

VBI

Vertical Blank Interval, a transparent component of a television signal currently only used for closed captioning, but being devel-

oped by En Technology in its Malachi product to be used to download software.

See also **Malachi.**

VBR

Variable Bit Rate, a connection method used in Asynchronous Transfer Mode (ATM) networks that transmits at varying rates and used for data transmissions whose contents are not time-sensitive. VBR is a *reserved-bandwidth* service, but instead of generating a constant bit rate, establishes a peak rate, sustainable rate, and maximum burst size.

See also **Asynchronous Transfer Mode.**

VC

(1) **Virtual Channel,** a communications channel providing sequential, unidirectional transport of Asynchronous Transfer Mode (ATM) cells.

(2) **virtual circuit,** a circuit providing a connection-oriented service, or in packet-switching networks, a circuit that appears to be a physical point-to-point circuit connecting two end points and reliably conveying sequenced packets. In reality, a packet-switching VC shares the underlying links and relay systems with other network users.

See also (1) **Asynchronous Transfer Mode;** (2) **packet-switched network.**

VCC

Virtual Channel Connection, a logical, unidirectional connection between two entities on an Asynchronous Transfer Mode (ATM) that represents the basic switching level for ATM. A VCC may be switched or dedicated, preserves the order in which cells are transmitted, provides a quality of service

(QoS), and utilizes performance parameters to be negotiated by the entities involved in a connection.

See also **Asynchronous Transfer Mode.**

VCCI

Voluntary Control Council for Interference, a Japanese agency that examines interference generated by data-processing equipment.

VCI

Virtual Channel Identifier, a unique number identified by a 16-bit field in the header of the Asynchronous Transfer Mode (ATM) cell packet that identifies a virtual channel (VC) over which a cell packet is to travel. The VCI is used to route the cell to and from the user.

See also **Asynchronous Transfer Mode.**

VCPI

Virtual Control-Program Interface, specifications that allow DOS programs to run in protected mode on 80386 and higher machines, as well as executing cooperatively with other operating environments (such as memory-management programs). The VCPI was the first DOS extender.

See also **DOS extenders.**

VDOLive

A product line from VDOnet that provides access to real-time digital video pictures and audio to multiple users on Windows-based or Power Macintosh computers over the Internet or over internal networks.

 **For more information about VDOLive, surf the Web to** `http://www.vdo.net`.

VDT

Volume-Definition Table, a table stored in the NetWare partition that tracks such volume information as volume name, volume size, and the location of volume segments on various network hard disks.

See also **NetWare partition; volume segment.**

vector

A data segment consisting of a length field, a key describing the vector type, and vector-specific data in the Systems Network Architecture (SNA) model.

See also **Systems Network Architecture.**

vector graphics (images)

Graphical display rendered by using vector notation technology. Vector notation includes a starting point, length, and direction that a line is drawn from the starting point. Vector graphics are defined mathematically rather than as a set of dots. Users may manipulate a part of the image without redrawing, and may resize or rotate the image without distorting it.

See also **bitmap.**

Velocity of Propagation (VOP)

A value indicating the network signal speed as a proportion of the theoretical maximum possible speed. For example, VOP for electrically based local-area networks (LANs) range from 60 percent to 85 percent of maximum.

vendor

A person, organization, or company that manufactures and sells computer hardware or software (or both), as well as related services.

Vendor-Independent Messaging (VIM)

An Application Program Interface (API) between an application (such as an electronic mail program or scheduling program) and a message-related service (such as a message store-and-forward service or a directory service). VIM was developed jointly by Apple Computer, Borland International, Lotus Corporation, and Novell, and is comparable to Microsoft's Messaging Application Program Interface (MAPI).

See also **Application Program Interface; Messaging Application Program Interface.**

Veronica

Very Easy Rodent-Oriented Netwide Index to Computerized Archives, a service for the Internet that searches Gopher servers for any menus containing items that match specified search criteria.

Version

In Novell Directory Services (NDS), a selectable property for the AFP Server, NCP Server, and Print Server objects.

See also **leaf object; Novell Directory Services; object.**

version creep

Adding features to programs without taking care to provide compatibility with previous releases of a software product.

version number

A decimal number assigned by a developer to identify a particular hardware or software release with larger numbers indicating most recent releases. The number before the decimal point indicates a major revision to the product. The number following the decimal point indicates a minor revision. However, a minor product revision can produce a significant difference in performance.

VERSION utility

In NetWare 3.*x*, a server console utility that provides the server's version information, license information, and a copyright notice.

Versit

A joint effort by Apple Computer, AT&T, IBM, and Siemens Rolm Communications to create a specification for Computer-Telephony Integration (CTI) so that computers, networks, and personal digital assistants (PDAs) can communicate with telephones, Private Branch Exchanges (PBXs), and other devices.

See also **Computer-Telephony Integration; personal digital assistant; Private Branch Exchange.**

vertical application

An application whose functionality is limited to a narrow and specific market area of use (such as an accounting application or legal application).

Vertical Blank Interval (VBI)

A transparent component of a television signal currently only used for closed captioning, but being developed by En Technology in its Malachi product to be used to download software.

See also **Malachi.**

Very Easy Rodent-Oriented Netwide Index to Computerized Archives (Veronica)

A service for the Internet that searches Gopher servers for any menus containing items that match specified search criteria.

very-low-frequency (VLF) emission

Radiation emissions in the range of 2 kilohertz (KHz) to 400 KHz from a computer monitor and from common household electrical appliances. The emissions decline as a square of the distance from the source.

See also **electromagnetic interference; extremely-low-frequency emission; radio-frequency interference.**

very-small-aperture terminal (VSAT)

A satellite terminal used in digital communications capable of managing transmissions of up to 56 kilobits per second (Kbps) and that measures about 3 to 10 feet in diameter.

VESA

Video Electronics Standards Association, an association whose members include

manufacturers of video-graphics adapters and monitors, that sets standards for video on personal computers (particularly the standardization of Super VGA hardware).

VFS

Virtual File Storage, an intermediate transit format for File Transfer, Access, and Management (FTAM) that provides a set of common file operations that all FTAM systems understand.

See also **File Transfer, Access, and Management.**

VGA

Video Graphics Array, a video adapter from IBM that supports several graphics standards and provides several graphics resolutions, including 256 colors in a 640-by-480 display.

vi

A standard UNIX screen-based text editor used in many dial-up, text-terminal-style Internet accounts.

video adapter

An expansion board that provides text and graphics output to the monitor of a DOS computer system. This board plugs into the expansion bus in the computer.

Video Electronics Standards Association (VESA)

An association, whose members include video graphics adapter and monitor manufacturers, that sets standards for video on personal computers (particularly the standardization of Super VGA hardware).

Video Graphics Array (VGA)

A video adapter from IBM that supports several graphics standards and provides several graphics resolutions, including 256 colors in a 640-by-480 display.

video memory

An area of system memory used by hardware operating the computer's display or monitor.

See also **memory.**

videoconferencing

A multiparty teleconferencing technique that involves both audio and video transmissions, and that requires the use of a *video codec* (coder/decoder) to translate between video images and digital representations.

See also **code/decode.**

VIEW (NLM)

In IntranetWare, a server console NetWare Loadable Module (NLM) that provides a view of a file from the server, but does not permit any editing of the file.

See also **NetWare Loadable Module.**

View menu

A menu that provides access to options in a browser program.

viewer

A program used by Gopher, Wide-Area Information Servers (WAIS), and World Wide Web (WWW) clients to display nontext files (such as graphics, sound, or video files).

See also **Wide-Area Information Servers; World Wide Web.**

ViewMovie

A World Wide Web (WWW) browser plug-in from Ivan Cavero Belaunde for Macintosh-based versions of Netscape Navigator (and compatible browsers) that enables the display of movies in the Apple QuickTime format.

See also **Netscape Navigator; QuickTime; Web browser.**

For more information about ViewMovie, surf the Web to `http://www.well.com/ user/ivanski/viewmovie/ docs.html`

VIM

Vendor-Independent Messaging, an Application Program Interface (API) between an application (such as an electronic mail program or scheduling program) and a message-related service (such as a message store-and-forward service or a directory service). VIM was developed jointly by Apple Computer, Borland International, Lotus Corporation, and Novell, and is comparable to Microsoft's Messaging Application Program Interface (MAPI).

See also **Application Program Interface; Messaging Application Program Interface.**

VINES

Virtual Networking System, an operating system from Banyan Systems, based on a special version of the UNIX System V implementation, that provides all server functions. VINES can support up to four Network Interface Cards (NICs) per server for any topology while automatically managing protocol binding and translations required between the NICs for routing to different local-area network (LAN) segments. The console includes a complete set of built-in network-management tools.

See also **Virtual Networking System** (includes **Figure V.1**).

virtual

A term used to describe something conceptual, instead of something that actually exists.

virtual 8086 mode

A mode in computers equipped with the Intel 80386, 80486, or Pentium microprocessor that enables the microprocessor to emulate separate personal computer environments simultaneously; the operating system controls such external elements as interrupts and input/output (I/O). This mode is often used in OS/2 and Windows NT to multitask multiple DOS sessions.

Virtual Channel (VC)

A communications channel providing sequential, unidirectional transport of Asynchronous Transfer Mode (ATM) cells.

See also **Asynchronous Transfer Mode.**

Virtual Channel Connection (VCC)

A logical, unidirectional connection between two entities on an Asynchronous Transfer Mode (ATM) that represents the basic switching level for ATM. A VCC may be switched or dedicated, preserves the order in which cells are transmitted, provides a quality of service (QoS), and utilizes performance parameters to be negotiated by the entities involved in a connection.

See also **Asynchronous Transfer Mode.**

Virtual Channel Identifier (VCI)

A unique number identified by a 16-bit field in the header of the Asynchronous Transfer Mode (ATM) cell packet that identifies a virtual channel (VC) over which a cell packet is to travel. The VCI is used to route the cell to and from the user.

See also **Asynchronous Transfer Mode.**

virtual circuit (VC)

A circuit providing a connection-oriented service, or in packet-switching networks, a circuit that appears to be a physical point-to-point circuit connecting two end points and reliably conveying sequenced packets. In reality, a packet-switching VC shares the underlying links and relay systems with other network users.

See also **packet-switched network.**

virtual circuit number

A 4-bit logical group number and an 8-bit logical channel number used to identify which packets belong to which virtual circuits.

Virtual Control Program Interface (VCPI)

Specifications that allow DOS programs to run in protected mode on 80386 and higher machines, as well as executing cooperatively with other operating environments (such as memory-management programs). The VCPI was the first DOS extender.

See also **DOS extenders.**

virtual disk

A designated portion of random-access memory (RAM) made to act like a very fast disk drive. A memory disk is also known as a *RAM disk* or a *memory disk*.

Virtual File Storage (VFS)

An intermediate transit format for File Transfer, Access, and Management (FTAM) that provides a set of common file operations that all FTAM systems understand.

See also **File Transfer, Access, and Management.**

Virtual LAN (VLAN)

A network configuration that can span physical local-area networks (LANs) and topologies, and is created by software on an as-needed basis (for example, when multiple users require interaction during a large project).

virtual link

Software used to extend the backbone area of a network by linking two partitioned areas.

See also **backbone.**

Virtual Loadable Module (VLM)

A modular executable program in the NetWare DOS Requester that runs at each DOS workstation and enables communication with the NetWare server. VLMs provide backward compatibility and replace NetWare shells (NETX) used in early versions of NetWare. A *child VLM* program handles a particular implementation of a logical grouping of functionality (such as the NDS.VLM for NetWare 4 servers, BIND.VLM for bindery-based servers before NetWare 4, and PNW.VLM for NetWare desktop-based servers). Various transport protocols also have individual child VLM programs (such as IPXNCP.VLM, which handles Internetwork Packet-Exchange services, and TCPNCP.VLM, which handles Transmission Control Protocol functions). A *multiplexor VLM* program routes calls to the proper child VLM to ensure that requests to child VLM programs reach the appropriate VLM module.

See also **NetWare DOS Requester; NetWare Loadable Module.**

virtual machine

An operating system environment in which each executing application is under the illusion that it has gained complete control of an independent computer and that it can access all the necessary system resources.

See also **virtual 8086 mode.**

virtual memory

A memory-management technique in which information in physical memory is swapped out to a hard disk when necessary to provide applications with more memory space than is actually available in the computer. Programs and associated data are divided into *pages*. When more memory is needed, the operating system uses an algorithm based on frequency of use, most recent use, and program priority to determine which pages to write out to disk. Memory space occupied by pages written out to the hard disk then becomes available to the remainder of the system.

Virtual Memory System (VMS)

The operating system used on the VAX minicomputer from Digital Equipment Corporation.

Virtual Networking System (VINES)

An operating system from Banyan Systems, based on a special version of the UNIX System V implementation, that provides all server functions. VINES can support up to four Network Interface Cards (NICs) per server for any topology while automatically managing protocol binding and translations required between the NICs for routing to different local-area network (LAN) segments. The console includes a complete set of built-in network management tools. Figure V.1 shows how VINES compares to the OSI Reference Model.

Virtual Path Connection (VPC)

A cluster of logical Virtual Channel Connections (VCCs) between two entities in an Asynchronous Transfer Mode (ATM) network. All channels in a particular VPC connect the same two entities.

See also **Asynchronous Transfer Mode.**

Virtual Path Identifier (VPI)

An 8-bit field in the header of an Asynchronous Transfer Mode (ATM) cell header. This field indicates the virtual path over which the cell should be routed.

See also **Asynchronous Transfer Mode.**

Virtual Private Network (VPN)

A private network implemented over the Internet.

Virtual-Reality Modeling Language (VRML)

A graphics format used to construct and describe three-dimensional interactive images that requires a special VRML browser to receive the images and a special VRML server to transmit the images.

virtual route

A virtual circuit (VC) in the Systems Network Architecture (SNA) model. This logical connection between subarea nodes is a physical realization of an explicit route.

Virtual Telecommunications Access Method (VTAM)

Mainframe computer software for IBM machines running the Multiple Virtual Storage (MVS) or VM operating system that controls communications in the Systems Network Architecture (SNA) environment.

See also **Multiple Virtual Storage; Systems Network Architecture.**

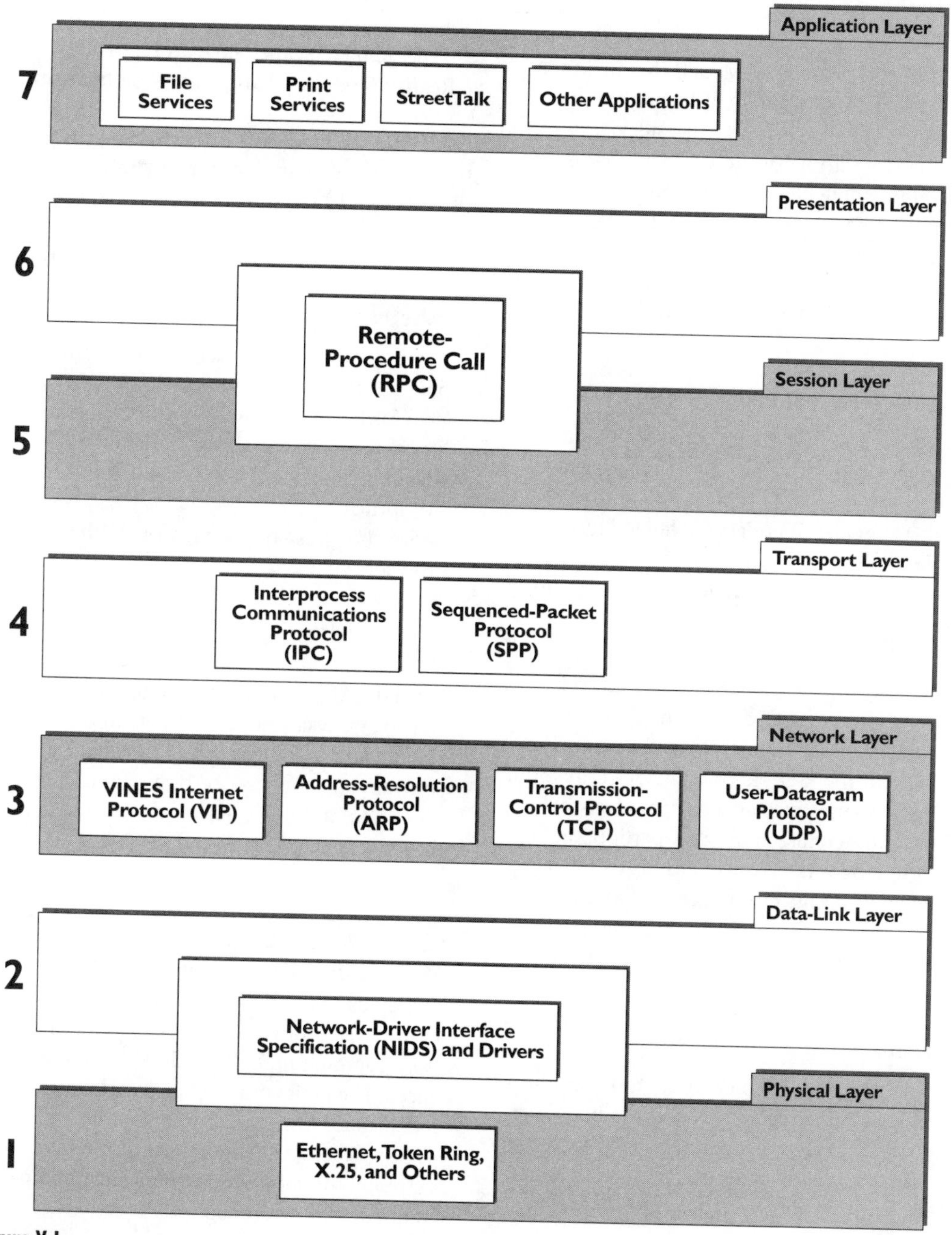

Application Layer

7

| File Services | Print Services | StreetTalk | Other Applications |

Presentation Layer

6

Remote-Procedure Call (RPC)

Session Layer

5

Transport Layer

4

| Interprocess Communications Protocol (IPC) | Sequenced-Packet Protocol (SPP) |

Network Layer

3

| VINES Internet Protocol (VIP) | Address-Resolution Protocol (ARP) | Transmission-Control Protocol (TCP) | User-Datagram Protocol (UDP) |

Data-Link Layer

2

Network-Driver Interface Specification (NIDS) and Drivers

Physical Layer

1

Ethernet, Token Ring, X.25, and Others

Figure V.1
VINES architecture

Virtual Terminal (VT)

A service on the Application Layer (Layer 7 of the OSI Reference Model) that makes it possible to emulate the behavior of a particular terminal. This capability alleviates concern with hardware-compatibility issues when remote clients are attempting to communicate with mainframe hosts. The VT acts as a translating intermediary between the remote client and the mainframe host.

See also **OSI Reference Model.**

Virtual-Terminal Protocol (VTP)

A Novell implementation of a Presentation Layer (Layer 6 of the OSI Reference Model) and Application Layer (Layer 7) protocol that provides a model of a general terminal for applications to use.

See also **OSI Reference Model.**

virus

A program designed to intentionally cause damage to a computer system, obviously without the user's knowledge or permission. Some viruses may attach themselves to other programs, to the disk partition table, or to a boot track on a hard disk so that when a specific event occurs, a specific time is reached, or a specific program is executed, the virus begins to damage the system.

Viscape

A World Wide Web (WWW) browser plug-in from Superscape for Windows-based versions of Netscape Navigator and compatible browsers that enables users to access interactive three-dimensional worlds based on

Virtual Reality Modeling Language (VRML) files.

See also **Netscape Navigator; Virtual Reality Modeling Language; Web browser.**

 **For more information about Viscape, surf the Web to** `http://www.superscape.com`.

VivoActive

A line of World Wide Web (WWW) browser plug-ins and compressor products from Vivo for Netscape Navigator (and compatible browsers) that enables users to play streaming digital video files created in Vivo's VIV format.

See also **Netscape Navigator; Web browser.**

VLAN

Virtual LAN, a network configuration that can span physical local-area networks (LANs) and topologies, and is created by software on an as-needed basis (for example, when multiple users require interaction during a large project).

VLF

Very-low-frequency emission, radiation emissions in the range of 2 kilohertz (KHz) to 400 KHz from a computer monitor and from common household electrical appliances. The emissions decline as a square of the distance from the source.

See also **electromagnetic interference; extremely-low-frequency emission; radio-frequency interference.**

VLM

Virtual Loadable Module, a modular executable program in the NetWare DOS Requester that runs at each DOS workstation and enables communication with the NetWare server. VLMs provide backward compatibility and replace NetWare shells (NETX) used in early versions of NetWare. A *child VLM* program handles a particular implementation of a logical grouping of functionality (such as the NDS.VLM for NetWare 4 servers, BIND.VLM for bindery-based servers before NetWare 4, and PNW.VLM for NetWare desktop-based servers). Various transport protocols also have individual child VLM programs (such as IPXNCP.VLM, which handles Internetwork Packet-Exchange services, and TCPNCP.VLM, which handles Transmission Control Protocol functions). A *multiplexor VLM* program routes calls to the proper child VLM to ensure that requests to child VLM programs reach the appropriate VLM module.

See also **NetWare DOS Requester; NetWare Loadable Module.**

VLSM

Variable-Length Subnet Mask, a capability that optimizes available address space by specifying a different subnet mask for the same network number on different subnetworks.

See also **subnet mask.**

VMS

Virtual Memory System, the operating system used on the VAX minicomputer from Digital Equipment Corporation.

voice mail

A computerized, store-and-forward, voice-messaging system. Prerecorded messages route a call to the intended recipient (perhaps a person, department, or mailbox), digitize the incoming message, and store the message on disk for review by the recipient.

See also **store-and-forward.**

voice-grade cable

Unshielded twisted-pair (UTP) telephone cable used for the transmission of voice signals, but not officially recognized as suitable for data transmissions.

VOLINFO utility

In NetWare 3.*x,* a workstation utility that provides information about each volume on the NetWare server, including the volume name, storage capacity of the volume, and the number of directories allocated for the volume.

See also **NetWare volume.**

volume

The highest level in the NetWare file system that represents the amount of hard-disk storage space, fixed in size. Volumes may be created on any hard disk that has a NetWare partition, with each server supporting up to 64 volumes. *Logical volumes* are divided into directories by supervisors and users with appropriate rights. *Physical volumes* are divided into volume segments, with each segment stored on one or more hard disks. Each hard disk can contain up to 8 volume segments belonging to one or more volumes, and each volume can consist of up to

32 volume segments. The NetWare INSTALL program creates the first volume named SYS:, and other volumes can be defined with assigned volume names of between 2 and 15 characters. When used as part of a directory-path designation, the volume name is followed by a colon (for example, SYS:PUBLIC). When a NetWare server starts, the volume becomes visible to the operating system, the volume's File-Allocation Table (FAT) is loaded into memory, and the volume's Directory-Entry Table (DET) is loaded into memory; the whole process is known as *mounting a volume*.

See also **Directory-Entry Table; File-Allocation Table; NetWare partition; volume segment.**

Volume

In Novell Directory Services (NDS), a Directory Schema term and a selectable property for the Bindery Queue and Queue objects.

See also **leaf object; Novell Directory Services; object.**

Volume-Definition Table (VDT)

A table stored in the NetWare partition that tracks such volume information as volume name, volume size, and the location of volume segments on various network hard disks.

See also **NetWare partition; volume segment.**

volume icon

An icon that looks like a filing cabinet on the NetWare desktop or a hard disk in the NetWare browser, and represents a volume on the NetWare server.

volume label

An assigned name used to identify a disk. Volume labels are set by the NetWare LABEL command.

Volume object

In Novell Directory Services (NDS), a leaf object that represents a physical volume on a network. The Volume object has the following selectable properties in NDS: Access-Control List, Back Link, Bindery, Common Name (CN), Description, Host Resource Name, Host Server, Locality (L), Object Class, Organization (O), Organizational Unit (OU), See Also, State or Province, Status, and Street.

See also **leaf object; Novell Directory Services; object.**

Volume Restrictions

A Directory Schema term in Novell Directory Services (NDS).

See also **Novell Directory Services.**

volume segment

A physical division of a NetWare or IntranetWare volume that can be stored on a hard disk. Each hard disk can contain up to 8 volume segments belonging to one or more volumes, and each volume can consist of up to 32 volume segments. Disk input/output (I/O) can be sped up by placing segments of the same volume on multiple hard disks because different parts of the same volume can be read from or written to simultaneously.

See also **volume; Volume-Definition Table.**

volume serial number

A unique number assigned by some operating systems during the formatting process for a disk. This number often is shown at the beginning of a directory listing.

volume table

A table containing the number of volumes mounted on a NetWare server, the name, size, and other information about each volume.

VOLUME utility

In NetWare and IntranetWare, a server console utility that lists mounted volumes for the current NetWare server, including block usage, number of blocks used, data streams, suballocation blocks, namespaces, number of directory entries, and number of extended attributes.

See also **NetWare volume.**

Voluntary Control Council for Interference (VCCI)

A Japanese agency the examines interference generated by data-processing equipment.

VOP

Velocity of Propagation, a value indicating the network signal speed as a proportion of the theoretical maximum possible speed. For example, VOP for electrically based local-area networks (LANs) range from 60 percent to 85 percent of maximum.

VOTS

VAX OSI Transport Service, a Transport Level (Level 4 of the OSI Reference Model)

protocol used on Digital Equipment Corporation machines in a local-area network (LAN) or wide-area network (WAN).

See also **OSI Reference Model.**

VPC

Virtual Path Connection, a cluster of logical Virtual Channel Connections (VCCs) between two entities in an Asynchronous Transfer Mode (ATM) network. All channels in a particular VPC connect the same two entities.

See also **Asynchronous Transfer Mode.**

VPI

Virtual Path Identifier, an 8-bit field in the header of an Asynchronous Transfer Mode (ATM) cell header. This field indicates the virtual path over which the cell should be routed.

See also **Asynchronous Transfer Mode.**

VPN

Virtual Private Network, a private network implemented over the Internet.

VR Scout

A line of World Wide Web (WWW) browser plug-in products from Chaco Communications for Netscape Navigator (and compatible browsers) that enables users to access interactive three-dimensional worlds based on Virtual-Reality Modeling Language (VRML) files with social-interaction features.

See also **Netscape Navigator; Virtual-Reality Modeling Language; Web browser.**

VRealm

A World Wide Web (WWW) browser plug-in from Integrated Data Systems, designed for Windows-based versions of Netscape Navigator (and compatible browsers). VRealm enables users to access interactive three-dimensional worlds based on Virtual-Reality Modeling Language (VRML) files with enhancements for object qualities and behaviors.

See also **Netscape Navigator; Virtual-Reality Modeling Language; Web browser.**

 **For more information about VRealm, surf the Web to** `http://www.ids-net.com/ids.`

VREPAIR (NLM)

In NetWare and IntranetWare, a server console NetWare Loadable Module (NLM) that corrects volume problems and removes name-space entries from Directory-Entry Tables (DETs). The version of this NLM must match the version of the operating system (for example, the NetWare 4 version of VREPAIR does not work on a NetWare 3 volume).

See also **Directory-Entry Table; NetWare Loadable Module; NetWare volume.**

VRML

Virtual-Reality Modeling Language, a graphics format used to construct and describe three-dimensional interactive images that requires a special VRML browser to receive the images and a special VRML server to transmit the images.

VSAT

Very-small-aperture terminal, a satellite terminal used in digital communications capable of managing transmissions of up to 56 kilobits per second (Kbps) and that measures about 3 to 10 feet in diameter.

VT

See **Virtual Terminal.**

VT100

A terminal manufactured by Digital Equipment Corporation in the late 1980s that has become an emulation standard for many computers communicating over the Internet.

VTAM

Virtual Telecommunications Access Method, MAINFRAME computer software for IBM machines running the Multiple Virtual Storage (MVS) or VM operating system that controls communications in the Systems Network Architecture (SNA) environment.

See also **Multiple Virtual Storage; Systems Network Architecture.**

VTP

Virtual-Terminal Protocol, a Novell implementation of a Presentation Layer (Layer 6 of the OSI Reference Model) and Application Layer (Layer 7) protocol that provides a model of a general terminal for applications to use.

See also **OSI Reference Model.**

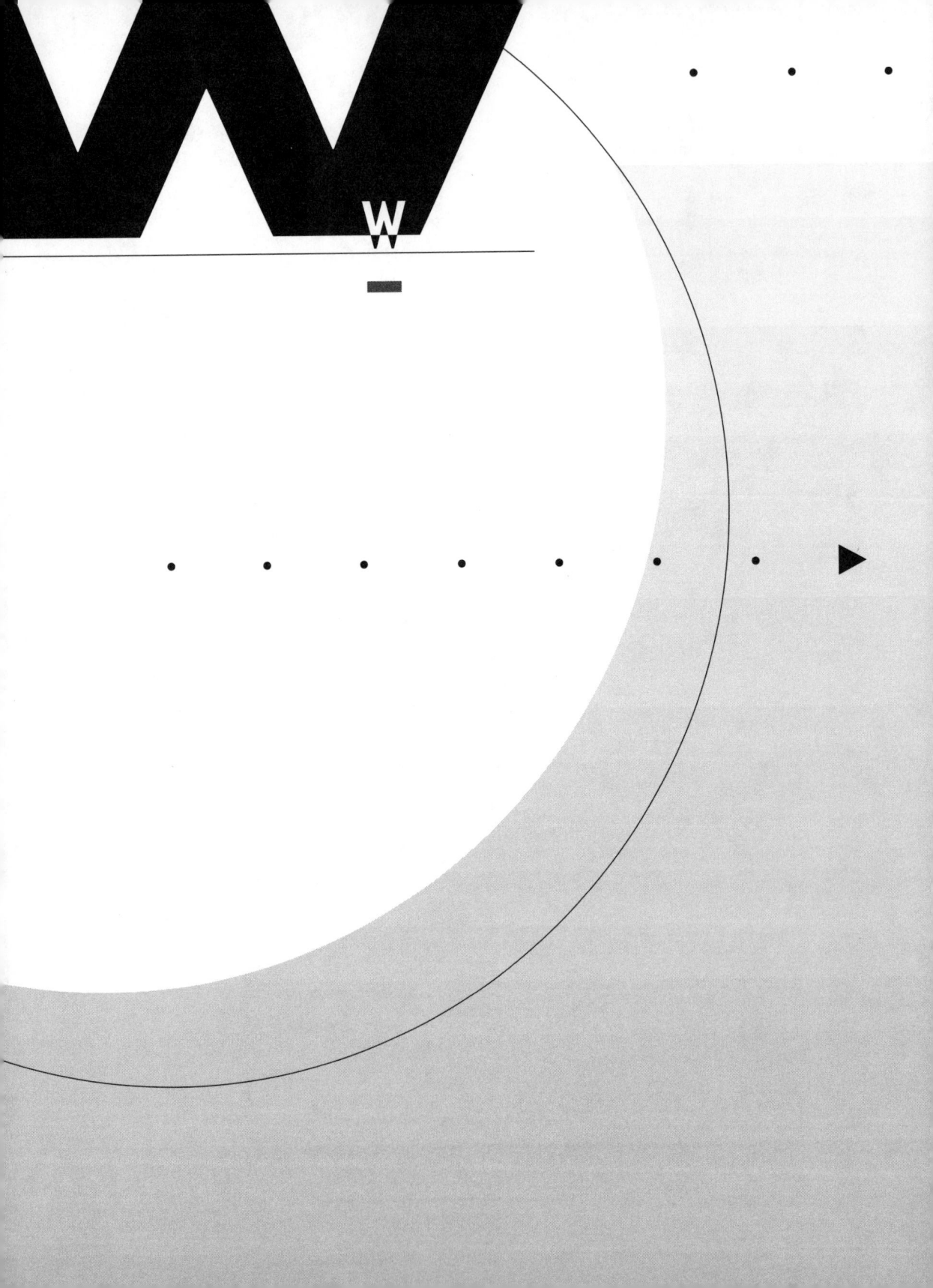

W3C

World Wide Web Consortium, an international industry association hosted by the Laboratory for Computer Science at Massachusetts Institute of Technology (MIT) and by INRIA and Keio University, with support from the Defense Advanced Research Projects Agency (DARPA) and the European Commission. W3C promotes standards for the Internet's World Wide Web (WWW).

See also **Defense Advanced Research Projects Agency; World Wide Web.**

WAIS

Wide-Area Information Service, an Internet service that searches specified source locations for files that contain user-specified keyword criteria. WAIS returns a list of files that match the user-defined data.

wait state

A period of time during which a processor is inactive and circuits or other devices operating at different speeds are synchronized.

wait time

A period of time (in seconds) designated as the amount of time to wait before signaling to the NetWare server that the normal power supply has been interrupted or has been shut off.

See also **uninterruptible power supply.**

WAN

wide-area network, a network encompassing a large geographical area (such as across a city or around the world). Local-area networks (LANs) connect to WANs by linking with a mainframe computer, a public data network, or another LAN.

See also **local-area network.**

WAN call destination

A NetWare remote call configuration for a wide-area network (WAN). Each call configuration equals one virtual circuit (VC) on one WAN link and contains parameters necessary for the WAN link driver to establish and maintain links to a given destination.

See also **virtual circuit.**

warm boot

Restarting a computer (without turning it off and on) after the operating system has been running for some time.

watchdog

A term used to describe packets designed to ensure all workstations are connected to the NetWare server. For example, if the server does not receive a packet from a workstation over a predetermined amount of time, a watchdog packet is sent to the workstation. If the workstation does not respond, another watchdog packet is sent. After a predetermined number of watchdog packets have been sent without acknowledgment, the server assumes the workstation is no longer connected and clears the workstation connection. The SET utility sets the period of time before the first watchdog packet, the period of time between watchdog packets, and the number of watchdog packets.

See also **SET utility.**

WATS

Wide-Area Telecommunication Service, a service that features unlimited use of a telephone circuit for specified periods and a fixed charge.

WAV (WAVE)

A Windows-based, digital, sampled sound format that uses a raw, uncompressed string of sampled recordings prefaced by a header.

waveform coding

An electrical technique that conveys binary signals.

wavelength

A measurement of the distance an electrical or light signal travels in a single cycle, used to encode particular transmissions.

Wavelength-Division Multiplexing (WDM)

A multiplexing process that involves the transmission of signals at different wavelengths along the same wire or fiber.

Wavelength-Selective Coupler

A splitter coupler that breaks an incoming signal into outgoing signals on the basis of signal wavelength.

WBC

Wideband Channel, a service that features unlimited use of a telephone circuit for specified periods and a fixed charge.

WDM

Wavelength-Division Multiplexing, a multiplexing process that involves the transmission of signals at different wavelengths along the same wire or fiber.

Web-Active

A World Wide Web (WWW) browser plug-in from Plastic Thought for Macintosh-based versions of Netscape Navigator and compatible browsers that displays pages with three-dimensional objects and television-like effects.

See also **Netscape Navigator; Web browser.**

Web browser

A client application for the World Wide Web (WWW) that enables the viewing of HyperText Markup Language (HTML) documents on the Web. When a hypertext link of interested is located, clicking on the link enables the browser to access the Internet host that holds the requested document. The browser has the capability to download information from the document, or to print the document through the computer operating system. Some browsers also maintain bookmarks, which allow users to easily access favorite Uniform Resource Locators (URLs).

See also **bookmark; hyperlink; hypertext; HyperText Markup Language; Uniform Resource Locator; World Wide Web.**

Web home page

A starting point for hypertext documents on the World Wide Web (WWW) that may be sponsored and maintained by individuals, organizations, or commercial interests, and has an assigned Internet address. A Web home page can provide access to information about an organization (or individual or commercial interest), access to other Web sites of interest, and a means for contacting the Web home page host.

See also **Internet address; Uniform Resource Locator; World Wide Web.**

Web robot

An electronic program that automatically retrieves information on the World Wide Web (WWW). Web robots are also known as *digital assistants*, *knowbots*, and *Web crawlers*.

See also **Knowbot; World Wide Web.**

Web Search Simple Search metasearch engine

A World Wide Web (WWW) metasearch engine that allows users to specify search terms and submit them to several different Web search engines, but each search engine must be accessed separately.

See also **search engine; World Wide Web.**

WebCrawler search engine

A World Wide Web (WWW) search engine that allows users to specify search terms and have 10, 25, or 100 results submitted along with a hotlinked title and a confidence rating from 0 to 100. However, this search engine does not provide a summary, nor does it provide a Uniform Resource Locator (URL).

See also **search engine; Uniform Resource Locator; World Wide Web.**

WebExplorer

An OS/2-based World Wide Web (WWW) browser from IBM that features several HyperText Markup Language (HTML) attributes (such as tables) and several customization options. WebExplorer also includes players for such multimedia file formats as Motion Pictures Expert Group (MPEG) and Audio Interchange File Format (AIFF). IBM offers automatic updates to this browser.

See also **Audio Interchange File Format; HyperText Markup Language; Motion Pictures Expert Group; Web browser.**

WebExplorer Mosaic

A World Wide Web (WWW) browser package from IBM that includes a licensed version of Spyglass Mosaic and electronic-mail (e-mail) client software. Installing this browser requires that virtual memory be enabled.

See also **Spyglass Enhanced Mosaic; Web browser.**

Webmaster

A person who is responsible for maintaining a World Wide Web (WWW) site.

See also **Web home page.**

WEBMGR

A Windows-based executable program, installed with the NetWare Web Server program that provides configuration management for the NetWare Web Server.

See also **NetWare Web Server.**

WebSter

A Windows-based World Wide Web (WWW) page-authoring tool from Alchemedia.

 **For more information about WebSter, surf the Web to** `http://www.` `alchemediainc.com/` `menu.html`.

WebTracks

A World Wide Web (WWW) browser plug-in from Wildcat Canyon Software for Windows-based and Macintosh-based versions of Netscape Navigator and compatible browsers that plays music supplied in Wildcat's WebTracks format or as standard Musical Instrument Digital Interface (MIDI) format.

See also **Musical Instrument Digital Interface; Netscape Navigator; Web browser.**

 **For more information about WebTracks, surf the Web to** `http://www.wildcat.com/` `Pages/WebTracks.htm`.

WebXpresso

A World Wide Web (WWW) browser plug-in from DataViews for Windows- and Solaris-based versions of Netscape Navigator (and compatible browsers) that displays three-dimensional graphics.

See also **Netscape Navigator; Web browser.**

where.com LinkSearch metasearch engine

A World Wide Web (WWW) metasearch engine that offers users access to 34 different Internet Uniform Resource Locator (URL) databases that are organized into categories of Web, Miscellaneous, Documents, Software, and Dictionaries.

See also **search engine; Uniform Resource Locator; World Wide Web.**

White Pages Directory

An Internet database that contains name and address information for users on a particular server or network. The White Pages Directory is a user-oriented database; the Yellow Pages Directory is a service-oriented database.

See also **Yellow Pages Directory.**

whiteboard

A term describing products that provide only software to enable users of a conferencing technology to work cooperatively on a document.

WHOAMI utility

In NetWare and IntranetWare, a workstation utility that provides a view of connection information. When logged in to Novell Directory Services (NDS), this utility displays the current tree name, a user's other names, a user's title, a user's description, a User ID, the name of the server, the version of the server, the server's connection number, the type of connection, and the date and time of login. When a user is attached to a server in bindery mode, this utility displays the user's workgroup manager, the user's security equivalences, groups to which the user belongs, the supervisor of the Bindery object, and the user's rights to files and directories on the server.

See also **Novell Directory Services.**

whois

A command used on some computer systems to generate a profile or description of a user. This command is used on the Internet to query the database at the Network Information Center (NIC) for an electronic mail (e-mail) address.

See also **InterNIC; Network Information Center.**

Whurlplug

A World Wide Web (WWW) browser plug-in from Apple Computer for Power Macintosh-based versions of Netscape Navigator and compatible browsers that enables users to access interactive three-dimensional worlds, complete with navigational controls and selectable objects.

See also **Netscape Navigator; Web browser.**

For more information about Whurlplug, surf the Web to `http://www.artifice.com/3d_gallery/whurlhelp.html`.

Wide-Area Information Service (WAIS)

An Internet service that searches specified source locations for files that contain user-specified keyword criteria. WAIS returns a list of files that match the user-defined criteria.

wide-area network (WAN)

A network encompassing a large geographical area (such as across a city or around the world). Local-area networks (LANs) connect to WANs by linking with a mainframe computer, a public data network, or another LAN.

See also **local-area network.**

Wide-Area Telecommunication Service (WATS)

A service that features unlimited use of a telephone circuit for specified periods and a fixed charge.

wideband

A communications channel capable of handling frequencies higher than the standard 3KHz voice channel.

Wideband Channel (WBC)

A channel with a 6.144 megabits per second (Mbps) bandwidth in a Fiber Distributed Data Interface (FDDI) network. An FDDI network can support 16 WBCs. When used in a packet-switched FDDI, WBCs can be grouped together to form a packet data channel, which transmits data at a minimum bandwidth of 78 kilobits per second (Kbps) and a maximum bandwidth of about 99 Mbps. When used on a circuit-switched FDDI, the WBC may be allocated to a single connection, or broken into slower channels, each of which can be used to connect a pair of network nodes.

See also **Fiber Distributed Data Interface.**

wildcard character

A character representing one or more unknown characters. The question mark (?) is used in many operating systems to represent a single unknown character in a filename or filename extension. The asterisk (*) is used in many operating systems to represent any number of unknown characters in a filename or filename extension.

WIN

Wireless In-Building Network, a wireless network confined to a single building.
See also **wireless network.**

window

A viewing area for graphical user interface (GUI) applications that can contain its own document or message. Window-based applications can display multiple windows simultaneously, each with its own boundaries and possibly containing a different document, message, menu, or other controls.

Windowing Korn Shell (WKSH)

A UNIX tool incorporating the MoOLIT toolkit used to develop windowing applications by providing a comprehensive prototyping facility for exercising the application early in the development cycle.

Windows 3.x

An operating system from Microsoft Corporation that features a multitasking graphical user interface (GUI) environment running on DOS-based computers and a standard interface based on drop-down menus, windowed regions on the screen, and a pointing device (such as a mouse). The three main components of Windows 3.x are the Program Manager (the primary shell program that manages the execution of applications and task switching), the Print Manager (which coordinates printing), and the File Manager (which manages files, directories, and disks). The standard Windows package includes a Write program (word processing), Paint program (graphics), Terminal program (communications), and other utilities.
See also **graphical user interface; Windows for Workgroups.**

Windows 95

An operating system from Microsoft that supports preemptive multitasking (multitasking under the control of the operating system) and multithreading (the capability to run multiple parts of a program). Included with the Windows 95 package is the Microsoft Network (MSN), which is an online service package providing electronic mail support, chat forums, Internet access, and information services. In addition to MSN, Windows 95 provides built-in support for peer-to-peer networking, as well as support for Transmission-Control Protocol/Internet Protocol (TCP/IP), Internetwork Packet Exchange/Sequenced Packet Exchange (IPX/SPX), Network Basic Input/Output Service Extended User Interface (NetBEUI), Network-Driver Interface Specification (NDIS), Open Data-Link Interface (ODI),

File-Transfer Protocol (FTP), Telnet, Serial-Line Internet Protocol (SLIP), and Point-to-Point Protocol (PPP). Windows 95 is the successor to Windows 3.x.

See also **File-Transfer Protocol; Internetwork Packet Exchange/Sequenced Packet Exchange; Microsoft Network; Network Basic Input/Output Service Extended User Interface; Open Data-Link Interface; Point-to-Point Protocol; Serial-Line Internet Protocol; Telnet; Transmission-Control Protocol/Internet Protocol.**

Windows accelerator

An expansion board or processor chip designed to speed up the performance of a personal computer's video hardware to give the impression that Microsoft Windows runs faster.

Windows client

A NetWare or IntranetWare workstation that boots DOS and gains access to the network either through the NetWare DOS Requester or the NetWare shell, and then runs Microsoft Windows.

See also **NetWare DOS Requester; NetWare shell.**

Windows for Pen Computing

A Microsoft application based on the Windows graphical user interface (GUI) and installed on portable computers designed to work with an electronic pen or stylus to produce screen output.

Windows for Workgroups

A Microsoft application based on the Windows 3.x graphical user interface (GUI) that includes added functions for limited networking of computers to allow users to share files, exchange electronic mail (e-mail), maintain a collective calendar of events, and so on.

Windows NT

A 32-bit, multitasking, portable operating system introduced by Microsoft in 1993 and based on the Windows graphical user interface (GUI), runs Windows and DOS applications, runs OS/2 16-bit applications, and includes 32-bit programs specifically designed to run under Windows NT. This operating system supports the DOS File-Allocation Table (FAT) system, the OS/2 High-Performance File System (HPFS), and its own NT File System (NTFS), as well as multiprocessing, Object Linking and Embedding (OLE), and peer-to-peer networking. Windows NT uses preemptive multitasking with applications capable of executing multiple threads. Figure W.1 shows a comparison of Windows NT to the OSI Reference Model.

Windows NT Advanced Server

A version of the Windows NT operating system that features centralized network management, security functions, disk mirroring, and support for Redundant Array of Inexpensive Disks (RAID) and uninterruptible power supply (UPS).

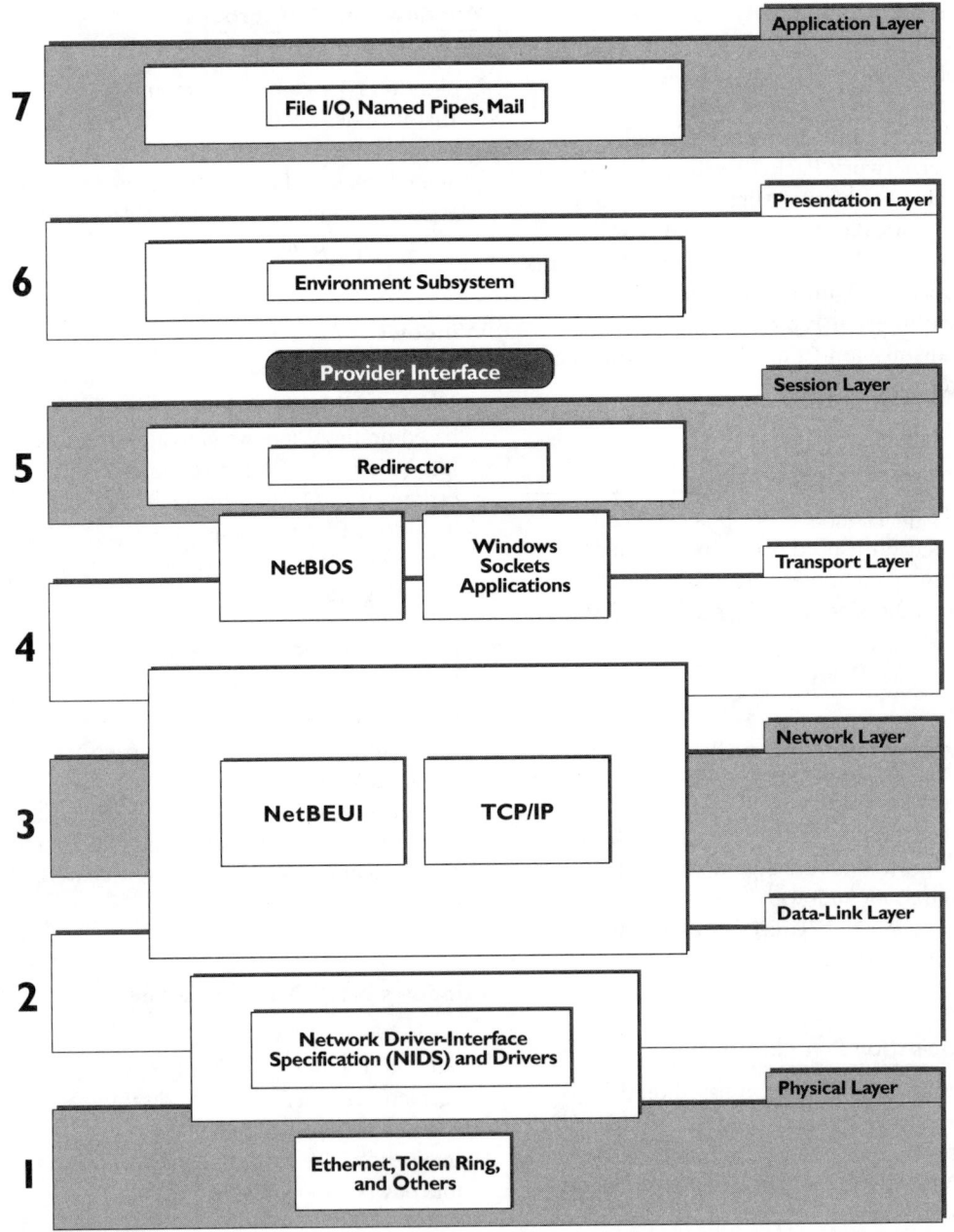

Figure W.1
Windows NT

See also File-Allocation Table; Graphical User Interface; High-Performance File System; NT File System; Object Linking and Embedding.

Windows Open-Services Architecture (WOSA)

An interface working at the system level that connects applications to services regardless of whether the services are provided on the network.

WinGopher

A graphical interface from Notis Systems used to navigate the Internet through a Windows client interacting with Gopher services, as well as Archie, Veronica, and TELNET protocols.

Winsock

A term describing the Application Program Interface (API) that implements the Transmission-Control Protocol/ Internet Protocol (TCP/IP) protocol stack in a Windows environment. In order for a Windows program to access the Internet, it must have access to the TCP/IP stack. Winsock is a contraction for "Windows socket."

See also **Application Program Interface; socket; Transmission-Control Protocol/Internet Protocol.**

WinWAIS

A Windows program that provides access to the Wide-Area Information Service (WAIS) system.

See also **Wide-Area Information Service.**

winWeb

A Windows-based World Wide Web

(WWW) browser from the TradeWave Galaxy, TradeWave's combination of business-oriented Web pages and Internet tools. The browser offers a built-in newsreader and electronic mail (e-mail) support. A Macintosh version of this product is called MacWeb.

See also **Web browser.**

WinZip

A Windows program that provides the capability to compress and decompress files in TAR, Gzip, UNIX compress, uuencode, BinHex, and MIME formats.

 **For more information about WinZip, surf the Web to** `http://www.www.winzip.com /info.htm.`

wire (solid)

An electrical wire with a central conducting element, normally a single wire of copper or other conductive material.

wire (stranded)

An electrical wire with a central conducting element, normally several strands of thin copper wire (or other conductive material) rolled tightly around each other.

wireless components

Components used in a wireless network that may include antennas or other transmitters and receivers not connected with wire or cable.

See also **wireless network.**

Wireless In-Building Network (WIN)

A wireless network confined to a single building.

See also **wireless network.**

wireless LAN

A local-area network (LAN) that uses a technology other than conventional cabling to connect to a main network. Available technologies include infrared (in which high-frequency light waves transmit data at distances up to 80 feet over an unobstructed path), high-frequency radio (in which high-frequency radio signals transmit data at distances up to 130 feet), and spread-spectrum radio.

See also **spread-spectrum transmission.**

wireless modem

A modem used on a wireless network that does not transmit over telephone lines.

See also **wireless network.**

wireless network

A network that does not use cable or wiring as a communications medium and that uses signals covering a broad frequency range. The frequency range (which may be a few megahertz to a few terahertz) determines the type of wireless network (for example, radio wave, microwave, or infrared network). Wireless networks are used to connect machines within a building, connect portable machines to a network, and connect mobile machines to a database.

See also **infrared network; microwave network; radio network.**

wiring (legacy)

Wiring that already exists within a building (business or residential) and may or may not be suitable for networking purposes.

wiring (premises)

Wiring that generally runs between outlets and any wiring centers or distribution frames in a house or office building. Connection to premises wiring is done with cords or cables that a user supplies.

See also **punch-down block; wiring center.**

wiring center

Components serving as a central termination point for one or more network nodes or for other wiring centers. A wiring center is designed to collect lines in a common location to continue a connection from that point on. Specific types of wiring centers include network hubs, concentrators, and Multistation Access Units (MAUs).

See also **concentrator; hub; Multistation Access Unit.**

wiring closet

A location in which premises wiring cables are gathered (usually in one or more punch-down blocks or distribution frames) and connect to various areas of central wiring in an office or building.

See also **distribution frame; punch-down block; wiring (premises).**

wiring sequence

The order in which the wiring pairs of twisted-pair cabling are attached to pins in a connector. Table W.1 shows common wiring sequences.

WIRL

A World Wide Web (WWW) browser plug-in from Integrated Vream for Netscape Navigator and compatible browsers that enables users to access interactive three-dimensional worlds based on Virtual-Reality Modeling Language (VRML) files with embedded multimedia and other enhancements.

See also **Netscape Navigator; Virtual-Reality Modeling Language; Web browser.**

WISCNET

A network that connects 27 campuses of the University of Wisconsin and a number of private colleges.

WKSH

Windowing Korn Shell, a UNIX tool incorporating the MoOLIT toolkit used to develop windowing applications by providing a comprehensive prototyping facility for exercising the application early in the development cycle.

word length

Either the standard data unit used in a computer (usually 8, 16, 32, or 64 bits), or the number of data bits in a communications data word.

Table W.1: Wiring Sequences

Sequence	Description
Uniform Service Ordering Code (USOC)	Originally developed by telephone companies; allows a six-wire plug to be plugged into an eight-wire jack.
10BaseT	Ethernet sequence for networks running over unshielded, twisted-pair (UTP) cable, compatible with three-pair or four-pair telephone cable.
Token Ring	Token Ring network sequence that makes it possible to use telephone cable for both voice and Token Ring networks simultaneously.
EIA-568A	Electronics Industries Association/Telecommunications Industry Association (EIA/TIA) specification for UTP wiring; backward-compatible with USOC.
EIA-568B	EIA/TIA specification for UTP wiring; used as the sequence for AT&T's Premises Data System (PDS).

See also **Electronics Industries Association; Ethernet; Premises Data System; Telecommunications Industry Association; Token Ring; Uniform Service-Ordering Code.**

workflow software

Any application program designed to describe or manage the steps required to complete a transaction or other type of task (such as flowcharting or computer-aided design programs).

workgroup

A group of two or more individuals on a local-area network (LAN) who share files, databases, and other network resources.

workgroup manager

A user classification in the NetWare 3 and NetWare 4 network operating systems that grants supervisory control over any user or user group created on the network.

working directory

The host server directory that contains log and error files for each backup session. In Windows, the default directory specified for an application.

Workspace

A Macintosh window that automatically opens when the NetWare for Macintosh application is launched and that provides access to NetWare entities.

workstation

A personal computer connected to a network and used to perform tasks through application programs or utilities. A workstation is also known as a *client* or a *station*.
See also **client.**

workstation manager

A software module in the NetWare Storage-Management Services (SMS) that receives ready messages from workstations available to be backed up and keeps the names of the workstations in an internal list.
See also **Storage-Management Services.**

Workstation Operating System (WOS)

The native operating system on a network workstation that may be different from the network server's network operating system, but is used to carry out tasks at the workstation.

workstation TSA

A NetWare Target Service Agent (TSA) in Storage-Management Services (SMS) that passes commands and data between the host server and the database where data to be backed up resides.
See also **Storage-Management Services; Target Service Agent.**

World-Wide Web (WWW)

An Internet protocol that enables users to search, access, and download information from a worldwide series of networked servers where information is dynamically interlinked. A Web client passes a user's request for information to a server, usually by way of a Web browser. The server and client communicate through a transfer protocol, usually the HyperText Transfer Protocol (HTTP). The server then accesses a Web page by using a Uniform Resource Locator (URL). Search engines are available to simplify access by allowing users to enter search criteria on a topic and have several

URLs returned for Web pages that pertain to the desired information. The number of available Web pages has grown from a few thousand in 1989 to several million today.

See also **HyperText Transfer Protocol; search engine; Uniform Resource Locator; Web browser.**

World Wide Web Consortium (W3C)

An international industry association hosted by the Laboratory for Computer Science at Massachusetts Institute of Technology (MIT) and by INRIA and Keio University, with support from the Defense Advanced Research Projects Agency (DARPA) and the European Commission. W3C promotes standards for the Internet's World Wide Web (WWW).

See also **Defense Advanced Research Projects Agency; World Wide Web.**

For more information about the World Wide Web Consortium, surf the Web to `http://www.w3.org/pub/WWW.`

World Wide Web Worm search engine

A World Wide Web (WWW) search engine that features adequate configuration options but often returns outdated hits.

See also **search engine; World Wide Web.**

WORM

Write Once, Read Many, an optical disc on which information can be recorded only once but can be read and reread many times. This medium has a high storage capacity suitable for archiving large amounts of information unlikely to change.

WOS

Workstation Operating System, the native operating system on a network workstation that may be different from the network server's network operating system, but is used to carry out tasks at the workstation.

WOSA

Windows Open-Services Architecture, an interface working at the system level that connects applications to services regardless of whether the services are provided on the network.

Write Once, Read Many (WORM)

An optical disc on which information can be recorded only once but can be read and reread many times. This medium has a high storage capacity suitable for archiving large amounts of information unlikely to change.

write-protect

To protect the information on a disk, file, or other medium against being overwritten. Methods include physically covering part of a floppy disk (or closing a notch) or issuing file commands.

Write right

A directory, file, and property access right in NetWare or IntranetWare that grants the right to open and write to files, and grants the right to add, change, or remove any values of a Novell Directory Services (NDS) property.

See also **access rights; Novell Directory Services.**

write-back cache

A disk-caching technique that either waits a specified length of time for a drop-in system load or waits for that drop to occur before writing information out to disk. A write-back cache improves hard-disk throughput by waiting until several disk writes can be made at the same time.

WSUPDATE utility

In NetWare 3.*x* and IntranetWare, a workstation utility that updates a file on multiple drives and subdirectories. This utility compares the date and time of the source and destination files. When the source file is more current, the utility updates the destination file

WSUPGRD utility

In Intranetware, a workstation utility that upgrades the Internetwork Packet Exchange (IPX) local-area network (LAN) driver on the workstation to the corresponding Open Data-Link Interface (ODI) driver.

See also **Internetwork Packet Exchange; Open Data-Link Interface; ODI/NDIS Support.**

WWW

World Wide Web, an Internet protocol that enables users to search, access, and download information from a worldwide series of networked servers where information is dynamically interlinked. A Web client passes a user's request for information to a server, usually by way of a Web browser. The server and client communicate through a transfer protocol, usually the HyperText Transfer Protocol (HTTP). The server then accesses a Web page by using a Uniform Resource Locator (URL). Search engines are available to simplify access by allowing users to enter search criteria on a topic and have several URLs returned for Web pages that pertain to the desired information. The number of available Web pages has grown from a few thousand in 1989 to several million today.

See also **HyperText Transfer Protocol; search engine; Uniform Resource Locator; Web browser.**

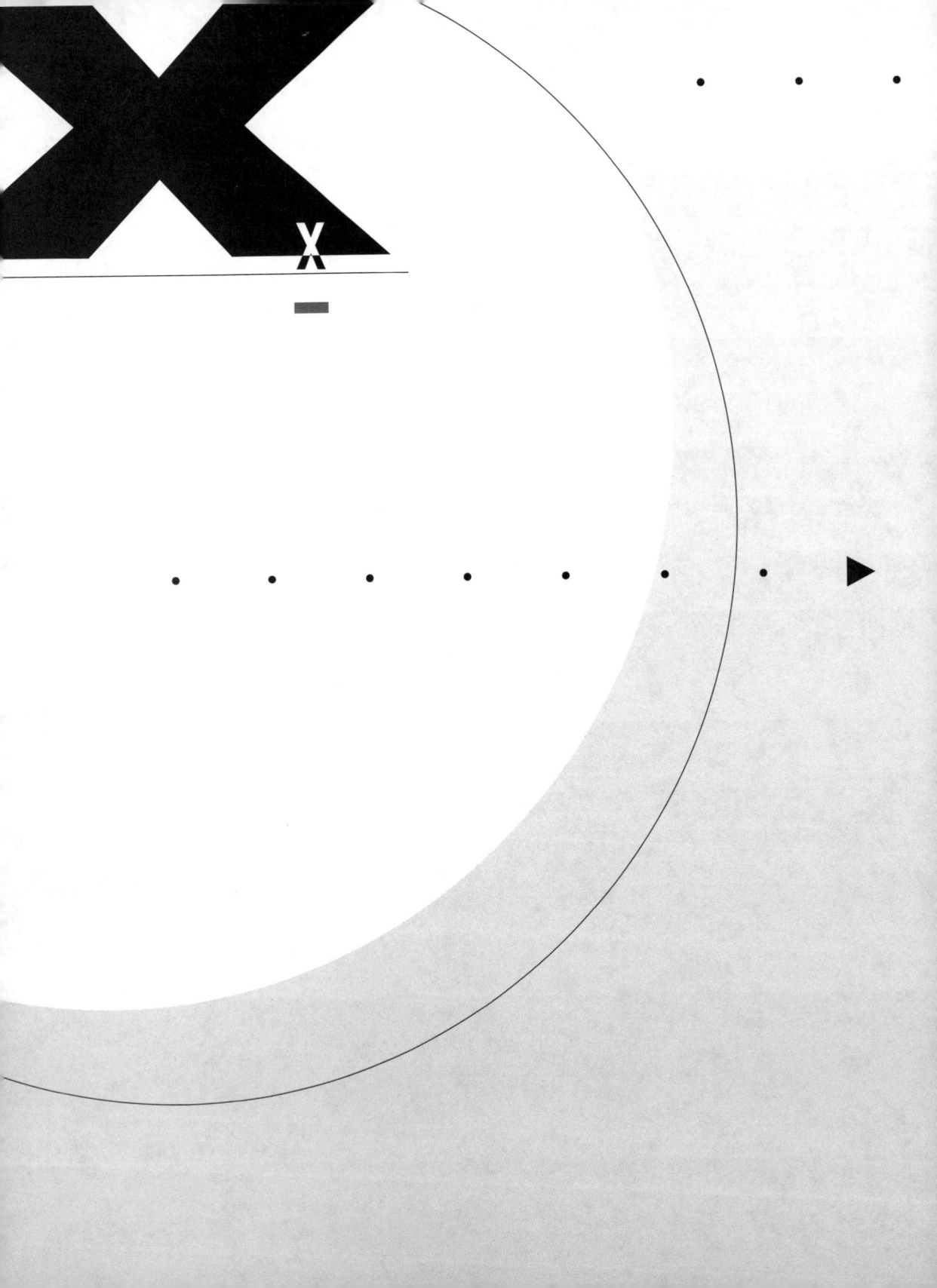

X Display Manager Control Protocol (XDMCP)

A protocol used by all X terminals to communicate with workstations on a UNIX network.

X Terminal

A graphical user interface (GUI) that enables a user to open numerous windows and perform multitasking operations on a UNIX system.

X Window System

A standard set of display-handling routines for UNIX workstations that allow the creation of hardware-independent graphical user interface (GUI) applications. The X Window System is a network-transparent, distributed system. An implementation from the Open Software Foundation (OSF) is known as *Motif*. An implementation from Sun Microsystems and Hewlett-Packard is known as *OpenLook*.

See also **graphical user interface**.

X.3

A standard from the Consultative Committee for International Telegraphy and Telephony (CCITT) that defines various parameters for a packet assembler/disassembler (PAD).

See also **Consultative Committee for International Telegraphy and Telephony; packet assembler/disassembler**.

X.21

A standard from the Consultative Committee for International Telegraphy and Telephony (CCITT) that defines a protocol for communications between a circuit-switched network and user devices. This standard describes the electrical connections, the transmission protocol, error detection and correction, and other aspects of the link. The X.25 standard parallels the Physical Layer (Layer 1), the Data-Link Layer (Layer 2), and the Network Layer (Layer 3) of the OSI Reference Model.

See also **Consultative Committee for International Telegraphy and Telephony; OSI Reference Model**.

X.25

A standard from the Consultative Committee for International Telegraphy and Telephony (CCITT) that defines how messages are encoded for transmission of electronic mail (e-mail) and graphics between dissimilar computers and terminals, as well as the contents for an electronic address and how the electronic envelope should appear. Users of an X.25 network contract with common carriers to use a packet-switched network and are charged for time on the network.

See also **Consultative Committee for International Telegraphy and Telephony; electronic mail**.

For more information about Series X Recommendations from X.1 to X.199, surf the Web to http://www.itu.int/itudoc/itut/rec/x/x1-99.html.

X.28

A standard from the Consultative Committee for International Telegraphy and Telephony (CCITT) that defines the interface between Data-Terminal Equipment (DTE) or Data-Communications Equipment (DCE) and a packet assembler/disassembler (PAD) in a public data network.

See also **Consultative Committee for International Telegraphy and Telephony; Data-Communications Equipment; Data-Terminal Equipment; packet assembler/disassembler**.

X.29

A standard from the Consultative Committee for International Telegraphy and Telephony (CCITT) that defines the interface between a computer and a packet assembler/disassembler (PAD).

See also **Consultative Committee for International Telegraphy and Telephony; packet assembler/disassembler**.

X.75

A standard from the Consultative Committee for International Telegraphy and Telephony (CCITT) that defines the interface between two packet-switched networks.

See also **Consultative Committee for International Telegraphy and Telephony; packet-switched network**.

X.400

A standard from the Consultative Committee for International Telegraphy and Telephony (CCITT) and Open Systems Interconnection (OSI) that defines a public or private international electronic-mail (e-mail) Message-Handling System (MHS). This standard specifies how messages are transferred across the network or between two or more heterogeneous networks, as well as the rules to follow when converting messages between transmission types (such as text and fax).

See also **electronic mail; Consultative Committee for International Telegraphy and Telephony; Open Systems Interconnection**.

X.400 Components

Components that make up the Message-Handling System (MHS) specified in X.400. Table X.1 shows the major components.

X.500

A standard from the Consultative Committee for International Telegraphy and Telephony (CCITT) and Open Systems Interconnection (OSI) that defines a means for locating electronic-mail (e-mail) users. This standard is similar to a telephone book.

See also **electronic mail; Consultative Committee for International Telegraphy and Telephony; Open Systems Interconnection**.

XII

Version 11 of the X Window System.

See also **X Window System**.

Table X.1: X.400 Components

Component	Description
Access Unit (AU)	A process providing a gateway between the MTS and other services.
Message Store (MS)	An archive for storing messages until they can be forwarded to their destinations.
Message-Transfer Agent (MTA)	A component of the MTS providing message forwarding to other MTAs or to the destination entity (such as an UA, MS, AU, or PDAU).
Message-Transfer System (MTS)	A process providing message transfer between users.
Physical-Delivery Access Unit (PDAU)	A special AU providing a gateway between the MTS and services that involve physical delivery.
User Agent (UA)	An application process providing access to the MTS.

X/Open

An independent international organization founded in 1984 to develop an open, multi-vendor Common Applications Environment (CAE) on the basis of the interfaces defined by the Institute of Electrical and Electronic Engineers (IEEE) and extended to cover additional open systems requirements. Novell turned over control of the UNIX operating system to X/Open in 1995.

See also **Common Applications Environment; Institute of Electrical and Electronic Engineers**.

For more information about X/Open, surf the Web to http://www.rdg. opengroup.org.

X3T9.5

A number assigned to the Task Group of Accredited Standards Committee for an internal working document on the Fiber Distributed Data Interface (FDDI).

See also **Fiber Distributed Data Interface**.

xarchie

A version of Archie (an Internet service for gathering, indexing, and displaying information) designed to run under the X Window System on a UNIX computer.

xB/tB Encoding

A term used to describe data-transmission schemes that serve as a preliminary to telecommunications or network signal encoding. Common translation schemes include 4B/5B, 5B/6B, and 8B/10B.

See also **4B/5B Encoding; 5B/6B Encoding; 8B/10B Encoding**.

XDMCP

X Display Manager Control Protocol, a protocol used by all X terminals to communicate with workstations on a UNIX network.

XDR

External Data Representation, a machine-independent syntax developed by Sun Microsystems as part of their Network File System (NFS), and used to describe data structures.

Xerox Network Systems (XNS)

A multilayer communications protocol originally developed by Xerox that supports a distributed file system in which users can access the files on other computers and can access printers as if they were local. Novell's Internetwork Packet Exchange (IPX) is a variation of XNS, although they do use different Ethernet encapsulation formats and IPX uses a proprietary Service Advertisement Protocol (SAP).

See also **Internetwork Packet Exchange; Service Advertisement Protocol**.

xgopher

A version of Gopher (a distributed Internet service used to access hierarchically organized information) designed to run under the X Window System on a UNIX computer.

Xmodem

A file-transfer protocol that divides data into blocks that consist of a start-of-header character, a block number, 128 bytes of data, and an error-checking mechanism. An Xmodem-CRC version offers cyclical redundancy check (CRC) capabilities to detect transmission errors.

See also **cyclical redundancy check**.

XMS

Extended-Memory Specification, the standard used to allow personal computers to access extended memory. DOS and Windows include an extended memory device driver called HIMEM.SYS, used to gain access to extended memory.

See also **memory**.

XNS

Xerox Network Systems, a multilayer communications protocol originally developed by Xerox that supports a distributed file system in which users can access the files on other computers and can access printers as if they were local. Novell's Internetwork Packet Exchange (IPX) is a variation of XNS, although they do use different Ethernet encapsulation formats and IPX uses a proprietary Service Advertisement Protocol (SAP).

See also **Internetwork Packet Exchange; Service Advertisement Protocol**.

XO bit

The third bit in a Control Information (CI) byte found in an AppleTalk Transfer Protocol (ATP) packet header that, when set, indicates a request for an exactly once (XO) transaction.

See also **AppleTalk Transfer Protocol**.

XON/XOFF

An asynchronous communications flow-control protocol that prevents a sending system from transmitting data faster than a receiving system can accept it. The receiving computer sends an XOFF control character to pause the transmission of data when the buffer becomes full, and then sends an XON character when it is ready to continue with the transmission.

Xpress Transfer Protocol (XTP)

A lightweight protocol designed as an alternative for traditional routing and transport protocols on high-speed networks. The protocol is streamlined through its packet structure and transmission, error-correction, and control strategies.

XRemote

A protocol that enables serial communications for an X Window System network.

XTP

Xpress Transfer Protocol, a lightweight protocol designed as an alternative for traditional routing and transport protocols on high-speed networks. The protocol is streamlined through its packet structure and transmission, error-correction, and control strategies.

xwais

A version of the Wide-Area Information Service (WAIS) designed to run under the X Window System on a UNIX computer.

See also **Wide-Area Information Service**.

Yahoo! search engine

A World Wide Web (WWW) metasearch engine from Yahoo! that provides a hierarchical series of categories from which users can search, and also provides a complete WWW search from outside the pre-established categories. When using the categories, Yahoo! presents a list of subcategories from which to choose. When using a keyword search, Yahoo! returns a list of Uniform Resource Locator (URL) addresses and summaries of each hit in the search result. Access to a variety of other search engines is manual (in other words, the search does not automatically default to another search engine).

See also **search engine; World Wide Web.**

 **For more information about Yahoo, surf the Web to** `http://www.yahoo.com.`

Yellow Pages

A term used to describe an online directory of businesses or services. Thousands of such directories exist on the Internet and range from directories categorized by geographical regions to those categorized by special-interest groups.

YMMV

Your Mileage May Vary, a cautionary note included in some Usenet newsgroup postings or other electronic-mail (e-mail) messages that indicates the reader may not get the same results as the author of the posting or message.

See also **electronic mail; Usenet.**

Ymodem

A file-transfer protocol that divides data into blocks that consist of a start-of-header character, a block number, 1K of data, and an error-checking mechanism. A variation of Xmodem, Ymodem also provides the capability to send multiple files in the same session and abort file transfer during a transmission.

Your Mileage May Vary (YMMV)

A cautionary note included in some Usenet newsgroup postings or other electronic-mail (e-mail) messages that indicates the reader may not get the same results as the author of the posting or message.

See also **electronic mail; Usenet.**

ZDL

Zero-Delay Lockout, a technology designed to prevent beaconing stations in a Token Ring network from inserting into the ring and causing network problems.
See also **Token Ring**.

zero-code suppression

A coding scheme in which a 1 is substituted in the seventh bit of a string of eight consecutive zeros.

Zero-Delay Lockout (ZDL)

A technology designed to prevent beaconing stations in a Token Ring network from inserting into the ring and causing network problems.
See also **Token Ring**.

zero-slot LAN

A local-area network (LAN) that uses existing serial and parallel communications ports on computers rather than requiring Network Interface Cards (NICs). Transmissions on existing ports are inherently slower than through NICs and the maximum cable length between workstations is severely limited. Zero-slot LANs are limited to two or three network nodes.
See also **Network Interface Card; parallel port; serial port**.

zero-wait-state computer

A computer that processes information without going through clock cycles, during which no instructions are executed, because the processor is waiting for data from a device or from memory (called *wait states*).
See also **wait state**.

zine

An expression of a personal view or of a group commitment to communicating an idea over the Internet. This term originally was a shortened version of *electronic magazine* or *electronic fanzine*.

ZIP

Zone Information Protocol, a protocol in the AppleTalk protocol suite that enables each router to maintain and access zone information for a network, and that enables nonrouter nodes on the network to obtain zone information.
See also **AppleTalk; zone**.

ZIP file

A file whose contents have been compressed using the PKZIP, WinZip, or compatible program. A ZIP file can contain one compressed file or several compressed files. Decompression requires either the PKZIP, WinZip, or compatible program, or that the file was compressed into a self-extracting archive that decompresses when its icon is double-clicked or when its name is entered at the command line.

ZIS

Zone Information Socket, a socket on an AppleTalk network associated with Zone Information Protocol (ZIP) services.
See also **Zone Information Protocol**.

ZIT

Zone-Information Table, a table in an AppleTalk network that contains the mappings of network numbers to zones, maintained by each router in the network.

See also **AppleTalk; zone.**

Zmodem

A file-transfer protocol that divides data into blocks, designed to handle larger data transfers than either Xmodem or Ymodem, that also includes checkpoint restart (a feature allowing an interrupted transmission to resume at the point of interruption).

See also **Xmodem; Ymodem.**

zone

An arbitrary group of nodes in an AppleTalk network that provides the capability to divide the network into smaller divisions. When a node connects to the network, it is automatically assigned to a zone. Zones are assigned names (which can be as many as 32 characters long) that are converted to addresses on the network by the Name Binding protocol (NBP) and are exchanged with the Zone-Information Protocol (ZIP). All zone names and addresses are kept in a zone information table within each router.

See also **AppleTalk; Name-Binding Protocol.**

Zone-Information Protocol (ZIP)

A protocol in the AppleTalk protocol suite that enables each router to maintain and access zone information for a network, and that enables nonrouter nodes on the network to obtain zone information.

See also **AppleTalk; zone.**

Zone-Information Socket (ZIS)

A socket on an AppleTalk network associated with Zone-Information Protocol (ZIP) services.

See also **Zone Information Protocol.**

Zone-Information Table (ZIT)

A table in an AppleTalk network that contains the mappings of network numbers to zones, maintained by each router in the network.

See also **AppleTalk; zone.**

zones list

A list that includes up to 255 unique zone names.

See also **zone.**

Z

Appendix A:
Acronyms and
Abbreviations

Table A.1 shows common networking acronyms and abbreviations.

Table A.1: Common Acronyms and Abbreviations

Acronym/ Abbreviation	Meaning
AA	Auto-Answer
AAL	ATM Adaptation Layer
AAR	Automatic Alternate Routing
AARP	AppleTalk Address-Resolution Protocol
AAUI	Apple Attachment-Unit Interface
ABI	application binary interface
ABM	Asynchronous Balanced Mode
ABP	Alternate Bipolar
ABR	area-boundary router
ABR	Available Bit Rate
ABUI	Association of Banyan Users International
AC	Access Control
AC	Alternating Current
AC	Application Context
ACDF	Access-Control Decision Function
ACE	Adverse Channel Enhancement
ACEF	Access-Control Enforcement Function
ACF	Advanced Communications Function
ACI	Access-Control Information
ACID	Atomicity, Consistency, Isolation, and Durability
ACL	access-control list
ACS	Asynchronous Communications Server
ACS	Asynchronous Communications Server
ACSE	Association-Control Service Element
ACU	Autocall Unit

(continued)

Table A.1: Common Acronyms and Abbreviations (continued)

Acronym/ Abbreviation	Meaning
ACU	Automatic Client Upgrade
AD	Administrative Domain
ADB	Apple Desktop Bus
ADC	Analog-to-Digital Converter
ADCCP	Advanced Data-Communications Control Procedures
ADDMD	Administrative Directory-Management Domain
ADMD	Administration Management Domain
ADN	Advanced Digital Network
ADPCM	Adaptive Differential Pulse Code Modulation
ADSL	Asymmetric Digital Subscriber Line
ADSP	AppleTalk Data-Stream Protocol
ADSU	ATM Data-Service Unit
AE	Application Entity
AEP	AppleTalk Echo Protocol
AFI	Authority and Format Identifier
AFP	Advanced Function Printing
AFS protocol	Andrew File System protocol
AFT	Application File Transfer
AI	Authentication Information
AIFF	Audio Interchange File Format
AIM	Analog Intensity Modulation
AIN	Advanced Intelligent Network
AIS	Alarm Indication Signal
AIX	Advanced Interactive Executive
AM	Account Management
AM	Active Monitor
AM	Amplitude Modulation
AME	Asynchronous Modem Eliminator
AMF	Account-Metering Function

Acronym/ Abbreviation	Meaning
AMH	Application Message Handling
AMI	Alternate Mark Inversion
AMP	Active Monitor Present
AMPS	Advanced Mobile Phone Service
ANF	AppleTalk Networking Forum
ANI	Automatic Number Identification
ANS	Advanced Network Services
ANSI	American National Standards Institute
AOL	America Online
AOM	Application OSI Management
AOW	Asia and Oceania Workshop
AP	Application Process
APD	Avalanche Photodiode
APDU	Application Protocol Data Unit
API	Application Program Interface
APIA	Application Program Interface Association
APPC	Advanced Program-to-Program Communications
APPI	Advanced Peer-to-Peer Internetworking
APPN	Advanced Peer-to-Peer Networking
AR	access rate
ARA	Attribute Registration Authority
ARAP	AppleTalk Remote-Access Protocol
ARCnet	Attached-Resource Computer Network
ARF	Alarm-Reporting Function
ARLL	advanced run-length-limited encoding
ARM	Asynchronous Response Mode
ARP	Address-Resolution Protocol
ARPA	Advanced Research Projects Agency
ARPAnet	Advanced Research Projects Agency Network

app.
a

(continued)

Table A.1: Common Acronyms and Abbreviations (continued)

Acronym/ Abbreviation	Meaning
ARQ	Automatic Repeat Request
ARS	Alternate Route Selection
ARS	Automatic Route Selection
AS	Autonomous System
ASCII	American Standard Code for Information Interchange
ASDSP	AppleTalk Safe Data-Stream Protocol
ASE	Application Service Element
ASI	Adapter Support Interface
ASIC	Application-Specific Integrated Circuit
ASN.1	Abstract Syntax Notation One
ASP	AppleTalk Session Protocol
ASVD	Analog Simultaneous Voice Data
ATA	ARCnet Trade Association
ATDP	Attention Dial Pulse
ATDT	Attention Dial Tone
ATFP	AppleTalk Filing Protocol
ATM	Asynchronous Transfer Mode
ATP	AppleTalk Transaction Protocol
ATPS	AppleTalk Print Services
ATXRP	AppleTalk Extended Remote Printer module
AUI	Attachment Unit Interface
AUP	Acceptable Use Policy
AURP	AppleTalk Update-Based Routing Protocol
AWG	American Wire Gauge
B8ZS	Bipolar with 8-Zero Substitution
BAC	Basic Access Control
BARRNet	Bay Area Regional Research Network
BBN	Bolt, Beranek, and Newman
BBS	bulletin board system

Acronym/ Abbreviation	Meaning
Bc	commited burst
BCC	Block Check Character
BCD	Binary-Coded Decimal
BCP	Byte-Control Protocol
BCUG	Bilateral Closed User Group
Be	excess burst
BEC	Backward Error Correction
BECN	Background Explicit Congestion Notification
BER	Basic Encoding Rules
BER	Bit Error Rate
BERT	Bit-Error-Rate Tester
BGP	Border Gateway Protocol
BIA	Burned-In Address
BIB	Bus Interface Board
BIND	Berkeley Internet-Name Domain
BIOS	Basic Input/Output System
BISDN	Broadcast Integrated-Service Digital Network
BITNET	Because It's Time Network
BIU	Basic Information Unit
BIU	Basic Interface Unit
BIU	Bus Information Unit
BLAST	Blocked Asynchronous/Synchronous Transmission
BLER	Block Error Rate
BLERT	Block-Error-Rate Tester
BLU	Basic Link Unit
BOC	Bell Operating Company
BPDU	Bridge-Protocol Data Unit
bps	bits per second
BRA	Basic-Rate Access

app.
a

(continued)

Table A.1: Common Acronyms and Abbreviations (continued)

Acronym/ Abbreviation	Meaning
BRI	Basic-Rate Interface
BSC	Bisynchronous Communication
BSD	Berkeley Software Distribution
BSD UNIX	Berkeley Software Distribution UNIX
BTAM	Basic Telecommunications Access Method
BTU	Basic Transmission Unit
BTW	By The Way
BUS	Broadcast and Unknown Server
CA	Certificate Authority
Cable, CATV	Community Antenna Television, or Cable Television
CAE	Common Applications Environment
CAN	campus-area network
CAS	Communicating Application Specification
CAT	Common Authentication Technology
CAU	Controlled-Access Unit
CAU/LAM	Controlled-Access Unit/Lobe-Attachment Module
CAV	constant angular velocity
CBC	Cipher-Block Chaining
CBDS	Connectionless Broadband Data Service
CBEMA	Computer Business Manufacturers Association
CBMS	Computer-Based Messaging System
CBR	Constant Bit Rate
CC	Clearing Center
CCIR	International Consultative Committee for Radiocommunications
CCIS	Common-Channel Interoffice Signaling
CCITT	Consultative Committee for International Telegraphy and Telephony
CCRSE	Commitment, Concurrency, and Recovery Service Element
CCS	Common Channel Signaling
CCS	Hundreds of Call Seconds

Acronym/ Abbreviation	Meaning
CCS 7	Common Channel Signaling 7
CD	Carrier Detect
CD	compact disc
CDA	Communications Decency Act
CDDI	Copper Distributed Data Interface
CDFS	CD-ROM File System
CD-I	Compact Disc-Interactive
CDM	Custom Device Module
CDMA	Code-Division Multiple Access
CDPD	Cellular Digital Packet Data
CD-ROM	Compact Disc Read-Only Memory
CD-ROM/XA	CD-ROM Extended Architecture
CELP	Code-Excited Linear Predictive Coding
Centrex	Central Exchange
CEPT	Conferénce Européene des Postes et Télécommunications
CERN	Conseil Européen pour la Récherche Nucléaire
CERT	Computer Emergency Response Team
CFB	Cipher Feedback
CGI	Common Gateway Interface
CHAP	Challenge Handshake-Authentication Protocol
CHRP	Common Hardware-Reference Platform
CICS	Customer-Information Control System
CICS/VS	Customer Information-Control System for Virtual Storage
CIDR	Classless Interdomain Routing
CIPX protocol	Compressed IPX protocol
CIR	Committed Information Rate
CIS	Compuserve Information Service
CISC	Complex-Instruction-Set Computing
CIX	Commercial Internet Exchange

app.
a

(continued)

Table A.1: Common Acronyms and Abbreviations (continued)

Acronym/ Abbreviation	Meaning
CLI	Command-Line Interface
CLID	Calling-Line Identification
CLNP	Connectionless Network Protocol
CLNS	Connectionless-Mode Network Service
CLP	Cell-Loss Priority
CLTP	Connectionless Transport Protocol
CLTS	Connectionless Transport Service
CLU	Command-Line Utility
CLV	constant linear velocity
CMC	Common Mail Calls
CMIP	Common Management-Information Protocol
CMIPDU	Common Management-Information-Protocol Data Unit
CMIPM	Common Management-Information Machine
CMIS	Common Management-Information Service
CMISE	Common Management-Information Service Element
CMNS	Connection-Mode Network Service
CMOS	Complementary Metal-Oxide Semiconductor
CMOT	Common Management-Information Services and Protocol Over TCP/IP
CMS	Conversational Monitor System
CMT	Connection Management
CN	Common Name
CNA	Certified NetWare Administrator
CNE	Certified NetWare Engineer
CNEPA	CNE Professional Association
CNI	Certified NetWare Instructor
CNT	Certified NetWare Technician
CO	Central Office
COCF	Connection-Oriented Convergence Function
CONP	Connection-Oriented Network Protocol

Acronym/ Abbreviation	Meaning
CONS	Connection-Mode Network Service
CORBA	Common Object-Request Broker Architecture
COS	Corporation for Open Systems
COSINE	Corporation for Open Systems Interconnection Networking in Europe
COW	Character-Oriented Windows Interface
CPE	Customer Premises Equipment
CPI	Computer-to-PBX Interface
CPIC	Common Programming Interface for Communications
cps	characters per second
CPU	Central Processing Unit
CRC	cyclical redundancy check
CREN	Corporation for Research and Educational Networking
CRF	Cable Retransmission Facility
CSA	Canadian Standards Association
CSFS	Cable-Signal Fault Signature
CSLIP	Compressed Serial-Line Interface Protocol
CSMA/CA	Carrier-Sense Multiple-Access/Collision Avoidance
CSMA/CD	Carrier-Sense Multiple-Access/Collision Detection
CS-MUX	Carrier-Switched Multiplexer
CSNET	Computer Science Network
CSNP	Complete Sequence Number PDU
CSU	channel service unit
CTI	Computer-Telephone Integration
CTS	Clear To Send
CTS	Computer Testing Service
CUA	Common User Access
CUG	Closed User Group
CUT	Control-Unit Terminal
CWIS	Campus-Wide Information System

app.
a

(continued)

Table A.1: Common Acronyms and Abbreviations (continued)

Acronym/ Abbreviation	Meaning
DA	Destination Address
DAA	Data-Access Arrangement
DAC	Digital-to-Analog Converter
DAC	Dual-Attachment Concentrator
DACS	Digital-Access and Cross-Connect System
DAL	Data-Access Languages
DAM	Data-Access Manager
DAMA	Demand-Assigned Multiple Access
DAN	Departmental-Area Network
DAP	Directory-Access Protocol
DARPA	Defense Advanced Research Projects Agency
DAS	Disk Array Subsystem
DAS	Dual-Attachment Station
DAS	Dynamically Assigned Socket
DASS	Distributed-Authentication Security Service
DAT	Digital Audio Tape
Data-PCS	Data Personal-Communications Services
dB	decibel
DBMS	database-management system
DBS	Direct Broadcast Satellite
DC	Direct Current
DCA	Document-Content Architecture
DCA	Defense Communications Agency
DCB	disk coprocessor board
DCD	Data-Carrier Detect
DCDB file	Domain-Control Database
DCE	Data-Circuit-Terminating Equipment
DCE	data-communications equipment
DCE	Distributed Computing Environment

Acronym/ Abbreviation	Meaning
DCS	Defined Context Set
DCS	Digital Cross-Connect System
DDB	Distributed Database
DDBMS	Distributed Database-Management System
DDCMP	Digital Data-Communications Message Protocol
DDD	direct distance dialing
DDE	Dynamic Data Exchange
DDL	Data-Definition Language
DDM	Distributed Data Management
DDN	Defense Data Network
DDN NIC	Defense Data Network Network Information Center
DDP	Datagram-Delivery Protocol
DDP	Distributed Data Processing
DDS	Dataphone Digital Service
DDS	Digital Data Service
DE	Discard Eligibility
DEA	Data-Encryption Algorithm
DECmcc	DEC Management-Control Center
DEK	Data-Encryption Key
DES	Data-Encryption Standard
DET	Directory-Entry Table
DFS	Distributed File System
DFT	Distributed-Function Terminal
DFWMAC	Distributed-Foundation Wireless Media-Access Control
DHCP	Dynamic Host-Configuration Protocol
DIA	Document-Interchange Architecture
DIB	Directory Information Base
DIBI	Device-Independent Backup Interface
DID	Destination ID

app. a

(continued)

Table A.1: Common Acronyms and Abbreviations (continued)

Acronym/ Abbreviation	Meaning
DID	direct inward dialing
DIP	dual in-line package
DIS	Draft International Standard
DISOSS	Distributed Office-Supported System
DIT	Directory Information Tree
DIX	Digital-Intel-Xerox
DL	Distribution List
DLC	Data-Link Control
DLCI	Data-Link Connection Identifier
DLL	Dynamic Link Library
DLS	Data-Link Services
DMA	Direct Memory Access
DMD	Directory-Management Domain
DMI	Desktop-Management Interface
DMI	Digital Multiplexed Interface
DNA	Digital Network Architecture
DNA	Distributed Network Architecture
DNIC	Data-Network Identification Code
DNIS	Dialed-Number Identification Service
DNS	Domain-Naming System
DOAM	Distributed Office-Applications Model
DOD	Direct Outward Dialing
DoD	Department of Defense
DOS	Disk Operating System
DOV	Data Over Voice
DP	data processing
DP	Draft Proposal
DPA	Demand-Protocol Architecture
DPC	Deferred Procedure Call

Acronym/ Abbreviation	Meaning
DPMI	DOS Protected-Mode Interface
DQDB	Distributed-Queue Dual-Bus
DRAM	Dynamic Random-Access Memory
DRDA	Distributed Relational-Data Architecture
DS	Digital Service
DS	Directory Services
DSA	Directory-Service Area
DSA	Directory System Agent
DSA	Distributed Systems Architecture
DSC	Data-Stream Compatibility
DSE	Data-Switching Equipment
DSI	Digital Speech Interpolation
DSOM	Distributed System-Object Model
DSP	Digital Signal Processor
DSP	Directory-System Protocol
DSP	Domain-Specific Part
DSPU	Downstream Physical Unit
DSR	Data Set Ready
DST	daylight-saving time
DSU	Digital Service Unit
DSU/CSU	Data Service Unit/Channel Service Unit
DSVD	Digital Simultaneous Voice and Data
DSX1/3	Digital Signal Cross-Connect Between levels 1 and 3
DTAM	Document Transfer and Manipulation
DTE	Data-Terminal Equipment
DTMF	Dual-Tone Multifrequency
DTR	Data Terminal Ready
DTR	Dedicated Token Ring
DTS	Digital Termination Service

(continued)

app.
a

Table A.1: Common Acronyms and Abbreviations (continued)

Acronym/ Abbreviation	Meaning
DUA	Directory User Agent
DUV	Data Under Voice
DXI	Data-Exchange Interface
EARN	European Academic and Research Network
EB	exabyte
EBCDIC	Extended Binary-Coded Decimal Interchange Code
ECB	Electronic Cookbook
ECB	Event-Control Block
ECB	Event-Control Block
ECC	Error-Correction Code
ECL	Emitter-Coupled Logic
ECMA	European Computer Manufacturers Association
ECN	Explicit Congestion Notification
ECNE	Enterprise Certified NetWare Engineer
ECTP	Ethernet Configuration-Test Protocol
EDI	Electronic Data Interchange
EDIFACT	Electronic Data Interchange for Administration
EDO	Extended Data Out
EDP	electronic data processing
EEMA	European Electronic-Mail Association
EEMS	Enhanced Expanded-Memory Specification
EEPROM	Enhanced Erasable/Programmable Read-Only Memory
EFF	Electronic Frontier Foundation
EFS	Error-Free Second
EFS	End Frame Sequence
EGA	Enhanced Graphics Adapter
EGP	External Gateway Protocol
EIA	Electronic Industries Association
EIB	Enterprise Information Base

Acronym/ Abbreviation	Meaning
EIRP	Effective Isotropic Radiated Power
EISA	Extended Industry-Standard Architecture
EKTS	Electronic Key Telephone System
ELAP	EtherTalk Link-Access Protocol
ELF	extremely low-frequency emission
ELS NetWare	Entry Level System NetWare
E-mail	electronic mail
e-mail	electronic mail
ED	End Delimiter
EMA	Electronic Mail Association
EMA	Enterprise Management Architecture
EMI	electromagnetic interference
EMM	Expanded Memory Manager
EMS	Expanded Memory Specification
ENS	Enterprise Network Services
EO	End Office
EOC	End of Content
EOF	end-of-file
EOT	end-of-transmission
EPP	Enhanced Parallel Port
EPS	Encapsulated PostScript
ERP	Exterior Routing Protocol
ES	end system
ESCON	Enterprise System-Connection Architecture
ES-IS	End-System-to-Intermediate-System
ESD	electrostatic discharge
ESDI	Enhanced Small-Device Interface
ES-IS	End-System-to-Intermediate-System
ESF	Extended Superframe-Format Framing

app.
a

(continued)

Table A.1: Common Acronyms and Abbreviations (continued)

Acronym/ Abbreviation	Meaning
ESN	Electronic Switched Network
ESnet	Energy Services Network
ETR	Early Token Release
ETSI	European Telecommunications Standards Institute
ETX	end-of-text
EWOS	European Workshop for Open Systems
FADU	File-Access Data Unit
FAL	File-Access Listener
FAQ	Frequently Asked Questions
FAT	File-Allocation Table
fax	facsimile
FBE	Free Buffer Enquiry
FC	Frame Control
FCC	Federal Communications Commission
FCS	Fiber-Channel Standard
FCS	Frame-Check Sequence
FDDI	Fiber Distributed Data Interface
FDL	Facility Data Link
FDM	Frequency-Division Multiplexing
FDMA	Frequency-Division Multiple Access
FDX	Full Duplex
FEBE	Far-End Block Error
FEC	Forward Error Correction
FECN	Forward Explicit Congestion Notification
FEP	Front-End Processor
FERF	Far-End Receive Failure
FEXT	Far-End Crosstalk
FID4	Format Identifier 4
FIFO	First In, First Out

Acronym/ Abbreviation	Meaning
FIX	Federal Information Exchange
FLAP	FDDITalk Link-Access Protocol
FLIH	First-Level Interrupt Handler
FLIP	Fast Local-Internet Protocol
FLP	Fast-Link Pulse
FNC	Federal Networking Council
FOIRL	Fiber-Optic Inter-Repeater Link
FPODA	Fixed Priority-Oriented Demand Assignment
FPS	Fast Packet-Switching
FPU	Floating-Point Unit
FQDN	Fully Qualified Domain Name
FRMR	Frame-Reject Response
FS	Frame Status
FSF	Free Software Foundation
FSP	File Service Process
FTI	Fractional TI
FTAM	File Transfer, Access, and Management
FTP	File-Transport Protocol
FTS	File-Transfer Service
FX	Foreign Exchange
FYI	For Your Information
GAN	global-area network
GB	gigabyte
Gb	gigabit
GDMO	Guidelines for the Definition of Managed Objects
GDS	Generalized Data Stream
GFC	Generic Flow Control
GFI	General Format Identifier
GGP	Gateway-to-Gateway Protocol

(continued)

app.
a

Table A.1: Common Acronyms and Abbreviations (continued)

Acronym/ Abbreviation	Meaning
GIF	Graphics-Interchange Format
GMT	Greenwich Mean Time
GoS	Grade of Service
GOSIP	Government OSI Profile
GPIB	General-Purpose Interface Bus
GSTN	General Switch Telephone Network
GUI	Graphical User Interface
HAL	Hardware Abstraction Layer
HAM	Host Adapter Module
HAT	Huge Variable-Length-Record Allocation Table
HBA	Host Bus Adapter
HCSS	High-Capacity Storage System
HDH	HDLC Distant Host
HDLC	High-Level Data-Link Control
HDX	Half Duplex
HEC	Header-Error Control
HEMS	High-Level Entity-Management System
HEPnet	High-Energy Physics network
HFS	Hierarchical File System
HIPPI	High-Performance Parallel Interface
HLLAPI	High-Level-Language Application Program Interface
HLM	Heterogenous LAN Management
HMA	High Memory Area
HMUX	Hybrid Multiplexer
HPFS	High-Peformance File System
HPPI	High-Performance Parallel Interface
HSCI	High-Speed Communications Interface
HSLAN	High-Speed Local-Area Network
HSM	Hierarchical Storage Management

Acronym/ Abbreviation	Meaning
HSSI	High-Speed Serial Interface
HTML	HyperText Markup Language
HTTP	HyperText-Transfer Protocol
HTTPD	HypertText-Transfer-Protocol Daemon
HVLR	Huge Variable-Length Record
Hz	Hertz
I/O	input/output
IA5	International Alphabet 5
IAB	Internet Architecture Board
IAC	Inter-Application Communication
IANA	Internet Assigned-Numbers Authority
IAP	Internet access provider
IBMNM	IBM Network Managment
IC	integrated circuit
ICMP	Internet Control-Message Protocol
IDA	Integrated Digital Access
IDAPI	Integrated-Database Application Program Interface
IDC	Insulation-Displacement Contact
IDE	Integrated-Drive Electronics
IDF	Intermediate Distribution Frame
IDG	Inter-Dialog Gap
IDI	Initial Domain Identifier
IDN	Integrated Digital Network
IDP	Internet Datagram Packet
IDPR	Interdomain Policy Routing
IDRP	IS-IS Interdomain-Routing Protocol
IDT	Interrupt-Dispatch Table
IDU	Interface Data Unit
IEC	International Electrotechnical Commission

(continued)

app.
a

Table A.1: Common Acronyms and Abbreviations (continued)

Acronym/ Abbreviation	Meaning
IEEE	Institute of Electrical and Electronic Engineers
IESG	Internet Engineering Steering Group
IETF	Internet Engineering Task Force
IFG	Interframe Gap
IFIP	International Federation for Information Processing
IFRB	International Frequency Registration Board
IFS	Installable File System
IGP	Interior Gateway Protocol
IGRP	Interior-Gateway Routing Protocol
IHL	Internet Header Length
IIH	IS-IS Hello
ILMI	Interim Local-Management Interface
IMAC	Isochronous Media-Access Control
IMAP	Internet Message-Access Protocol
IMP	Interim Message Processor
IMR	Internet Monthly Report
IMS	Information-Management Systems
IMTS	Improved Mobile Telephone Service
INETCFG	Internetworking Configuration utility
INOC	Internet Network-Operations Center
INTAP	Interoperability Technology Association for Information Processing
InterNIC	Internet Network-Information Center
INWATS	Inward Wide-Area Telephone Service
IO Engine	Input/Output Engine
IOC	Interoffice Channel
IONL	Internal Organization of the Network Layer
IP	Internet Protocol
IPC	Interprocess Communication
IPDS	Intelligent-Printer Data Stream

Acronym/ Abbreviation	Meaning
IPI	Intelligent-Peripheral Interfaces
IPM	Interpersonal Messaging
IPMS	Interpersonal Messaging Service, or System
IPng/IPv6	Internet Protocol Next Generation/version 6
IPP	Internet presence provider
IPSO	IP Security Option
IPX	Internetwork Packet Exchange
IPXODI	Internet Packet-Exchange Open-Data Interface
IR	Internet Registry
IR	Internet Router
IRC	Internet Relay Chat
IRDP	ICMP Router-Discovery Protocol
IRF	Inherited-Rights Filter
IRL	Inter-Repeater Link
IRM	Inherited-Rights Mask
IRN	Intermediate Routing Node
IRP	I/O Request Packet
IRP	Interdomain Routing Protocol
IRQ	Interrupt-Request Line
IRQL	Interrupt-Request Level
IRSG	Internet Research Steering Group
IRTF	Internet Research Task Force
IRV	International Reference Version
IS	Intermediate System
IS	Internet Standard
IS-IS	Intermediate-System-to-Intermediate-System
ISA	Industry-Standard Architecture
ISDN	Integrated-Services Digital Network
ISM	Industrial, Scientific, and Medical

app.
a

(continued)

Table A.1: Common Acronyms and Abbreviations (continued)

Acronym/ Abbreviation	Meaning
ISN	Information Systems Network
ISN	Internet Society News
ISO	International Standards Organization
ISODE	International Standards Organization Development Environment
ISP	International Standardization Profile
ISP	Internet service provider
ISR	interrupt service routine
ISU	Integrated Service Unit
ITC	Independent Telephone Company
ITR	Internet Talk Radio
ITT	Invitation to Transmit
ITU	International Telecommunications Union
IVD	Integrated Voice and Data
IVR	Interactive Voice Response
IWU	Internetworking Unit
IXC	Interexchange Carrier
JANET	Joint Academic Network
JCL	Job-Control Language
JDA	Joint Development Agreement
JDK	Java Development Kit
JEDI	Joint Electronic Data Interchange
JPEG	Joint Photographic Experts Group
JSA	Japan Standards Association
JTC	Joint Technical Committee
JTM	Job-Transfer and Manipulation
Jughead	Jonzy's Universal Gopher Hierarchy Excavation and Display
JUNET	Japanese UNIX Network
JVNCnet	John Von Neumann Center Network
Kb	kilobit

Acronym/ Abbreviation	Meaning
KB	kilobyte
kbit/s	kilobits per second
kbyte/s	kilobytes per second
KDC	Key Distribution Center
KDD	Kokusai Denshin Denwa
KIS	Knowbot Information Services
KMP	Key-Management Protocol
KSR	Keyboard Send and Receive
KTS	Key Telephone System
LAA	Locally Administered Address
LAM	Lobe-Attachment Module
LAMA	Local Automatic-Message Accounting
LAN	local-area network
LAN/RM	Local-Area Network Reference Model
LANAO	LAN Automation Option
LANE	LAN Emulation
LAP	Link-Access Procedure
LAP	Link-Access Protocol
LAPB Protocol	Link-Access Procedure Balanced
LAPD	Link-Access Protocol, D Channel
LAT	Local-Area Transport
LATA	Local Access and Transport Area
LBRV	Low-Bit-Rate Voice
LBS	LAN Bridge Server
LBT/LWT	Listen Before Talk/ Listen While Talk
LC	Local Channel
LCC/LCD	Lost Calls Cleared/ Lost Calls Delayed
LCD	liquid crystal display
LCGI	Local Common-Gateway Interface

app.
a

(continued)

Table A.1: Common Acronyms and Abbreviations (continued)

Acronym/ Abbreviation	Meaning
LCI	Logical-Channel Identifier
LCN	Logical-Channel Number
LCP	Link-Control Protocol
LCR	Least-Cost Routing
LCR	Line-Control Register
LDDS	Limited-Distance Data Service
LDM	Limited-Distance Modem
LEC	Local Exchange Carrier
LECS	LAN-Emulation Configuration Server
LED	light-emitting diode
LEN	Low-Entry Networking
LEOS	Low-Earth-Orbit Satellite
LES	LAN-Emulation Server
LFN	Long Fat Network
LID	Local Injection/Detection
LIFO	Last In, First Out
LIMS	Lotus-Intel-Microsoft Specifications
LIN	Language Identification Number
LIP	Large Internet Packet
LIPX	Large-Internet-Packet Exchange
LIT	Line-Insulation Test
LLAP	LocalTalk Link-Access Protocol
LLC	Logical-Link Control
LLC2	Logical-Link Control Type 2
LME	Layer-Management Entity
LMI	Local-Management Interface
LMMP	LAN/MAN Management Protocol
LMU	LAN Manager for UNIX
LMX	L Multiplex

Acronym/ Abbreviation	Meaning
LNI	Local-Network Interconnect
LNM	LAN Network Manager
LPC	Linear Predictive Coding
LPD	Line-Printer Daemon
LPP	Lightweight Presentation Protocol
LRU	Least Recently Used
LSAP	Link-Service Access Point
LSB	Least Significant Bit
LSL	Link-Services Layer
LSL	Link-Support Layer
LSP	License Service Provider
LSP	Link-State Packet
LSRR	Loose Source-and-Record Route
LTA	Line Turnaround
LTM	LAN Traffic Monitor
LU	logical unit
LUNI	LAN Emulation User-to-Network Interface
MAC	Media-Access Control
MAN	metropolitan-area network
MAP	Manufacturing Automation Protocol
MAPI	Messaging Application Program Interface
MAPI	Microsoft API
MAU	Medium-Attachment Unit
MAU	Multistation-Access Unit
Mb	megabit
MB	megabyte
Mbit/s, Mbps	megabits per second
MBONE	Multicast Backbone
MCA	MicroChannel Architecture

(continued)

app.
a

Table A.1: Common Acronyms and Abbreviations (continued)

Acronym/ Abbreviation	Meaning
MCF	MAC Convergence Function
MCI	Media-Control Interface
MD	Management Domain
MD5	Message Digest 5 Algorithm
MDF	Main Distribution Frame
MFM	Modified Frequency Modulation
MFS	Macintosh File System
MHS	Message-Handling System
MHSV	Multimedia Home Space Viewer
MHz	megahertz
MIB	Management Information Base
MIDI	Musical Instrument Digital Interface
MIME	Multipurpose Internet-Mail Extensions
MIPS	million instructions per second
MIS	Management Information System
MJ	Modular Jack
MLI	Multiple-Link Interface
MLID	Multiple-Link Interface Driver
MLP	Multilink Procedures
MLT	Multiple Logical Terminals
MM	Media Manager
MMF	Multimode Fiber
MMJ	Modified Modular Jack
MMS	Manufacturing Message Service
MMT	Multimedia Multiparty Teleconferencing
MMU	memory-management unit
MNP	Microcom Networking Protocol
MOO	Mud, Object-Oriented
MOP	Maintenance-Operation Protocol

Acronym/ Abbreviation	Meaning
MOTIS	Message-Oriented Text-Interchange System
MOV	Metal-Oxide Varistor
MP protocol	Multilink Point-to-Point protocol
MPEG	Motion Pictures Experts Group
MPI	Multiple-Protocol Interface
MPOA	Multiprotocol over ATM
MPR	Multiprotocol Router
MPR	NetWare Multiprotocol Router
MRM	Maximum-Rights Mask
MRU	Maximum-Receive Unit
MS	Message Store
ms	millisecond
MS DOS	Microsoft Disk Operating System
MSB	Most Significant Bit
msec	millisecond
MSL	Mirrored Server Link
MSM	Media-Support Module
MSN	Microsoft Network
MST	Minimum Spanning Tree
MTA	Mail-Transfer Agent
MTA	Message-Transfer Agent
MTBF	Mean Time Between Failures
MTL	Message-Transfer Layer
MTS	Message-Transfer Service
MTSO	Mobile-Telephone Switching Office
MTTR	Mean Time to Repair
MTU	Maximum-Transmission Unit
MUD	Multi-User Dimension
MUP	Multiple Uniform-Naming-Convention Provider

(continued)

app.
a

Table A.1: Common Acronyms and Abbreviations (continued)

Acronym/ Abbreviation	Meaning
MUSE	Multiuser Simulated Environment
MUSH	Multiuser Shared Hallucination
mv	millivolt
MVS	Multiple Virtual Storage
MX	Mail-Exchange Record
NA	Numerical Aperture
NAC	Network-Access Controller
NACSIS	National Center for Science Information Systems
NAEC	Novell Authorized Education Center
NAK	Negative Acknowledgment
NAL	NetWare Application Launcher
NAM	NetWare Application Manager
NAMPS	Narrow-Band Analog Mobile Phone Service
NAS	Network Application Support
NASI	NetWare Asynchronous Services Interface
NAU	network-addressable unit
NAUN	Nearest Active Upstream Neighbor
NBP	Name-Binding Protocol
NCB	Network-Control Block
NCC	Network-Control Center
NCCF	Network Communications-Control Facility
NCCP	Novell College Credit Program
NCP	NetWare Core Protocol
NCP	network-control program
NCP	Network-Control Protocol
NCS	Network-Control System
NCS	Network-Control System
NCS	Novell Consulting Services
NCSA	National Center for Supercomputer Applications

Acronym/ Abbreviation	Meaning
NCSC	National Computer Security Center
ND	names directory
NDD	NetWare Directory database
NDIS	Network Driver-Interface Specification
NDPS	Novell Distributed Print Services
NDS	Novell Directory Services
NEAP	Novell Educational Academic Partner
NEP	Noise-Equivalent Power
NET	Network-Entity Title
NetBEUI	Network Basic Input/Output Service Extended User Interface
NetBIOS	Network Basic Input/Output System
NEXT	near-end crosstalk
NFS	Network File System
NIAS	NetWare Internet-Access Server
NIC	Network Interface Card
NICE	Network Information and Control Exchange
NID	Next ID
NII	National Information Infrastructure
NIM	Network Interface Module
NIS	Network Information Services
NISDN	Narrowband ISDN
NIST	National Institute of Standards and Technology
NIU	Network Interface Unit
NLM	NetWare Loadable Module
NLS	NetWare Licensing Services
NLSP	NetWare Link-Services Protocol
NMA	Network-Management Architecture
NME	Network-Management Entity
NMP	Network-Management Protocol

app.
a

(continued)

Table A.1: Common Acronyms and Abbreviations (continued)

Acronym/ Abbreviation	Meaning
NMS	NetWare Management System
NMVT	Network-Management Vector Transport
NN	network node
NNI	Network-Network Interface
NNS	NetWare Name Service
NNTP	Network News-Transfer Protocol
NOC	Network Operating Center
NOS	Network Operating System
NPA	NetWare Peripheral Architecture
NPAP	Network Printing-Alliance Protocol
NPSI	Network Packet-Switch Interface
NREN	National Research and Education Network
NRM	Normal Response Mode
NRZ	Non-Return-to-Zero
NRZI	Non-Return-to-Zero Inverted
ns	nanosecond
NSA	Next-Station Addressing
NSAP	Network-Service Access Point
NSE	Novell Support Encyclopedia
NSE Pro	Novell Support Encyclopedia Professional Volume
NSF	National Science Foundation
NSFnet	National Science Foundation Network
NSP	Network Services Protocol
NTFS	NT File System
NTS	Novell Technical Support
NUC	NetWare UNIX Client
NUI	NetWare Users International
NVE	Network-Visible Entity
NVLAP	National Voluntary Laboratory-Accreditation Program

Acronym/ Abbreviation	Meaning
NVP	Nominal Velocity of Propagation
NVRAM	Nonvolatile RAM
NVT	Novell Virtual Terminals
NWADMIN	NetWare Administrator
OAI	Open Application Interface
OAM	Operations, Administration, and Maintenance Functions
OARnet	Ohio Academic Resources Network
OCR	optical character recognition
ODA	Open Document Architecture
ODBC	Open Database Connectivity
ODI	Open Data-Link Interface
ODINSUP	ODI/NDIS Support
OEM	original equipment manufacturer
OFB	Output Feedback
OFNP	Optical Fiber, Nonconductive Plenum
OFNR	Optical Fiber, Nonconductive Riser
OH	Off Hook
OIM	OSI Internet Management
OIW	OSI Implementers Workshop
OLE	Object Linking and Embedding
ONC	Open-Network Computing
ONN	Open-Network Node
OOP	object-oriented program
OPSF	Open Shortest Path First
ORB	Object-Request Broker
OS	operating system
OSI	Open-Systems Interconnection
OSI GOSIP	OSI Government Systems Interconnection Protocol
OSME	Open-Systems Message Exchange

app.
a

(continued)

Table A.I: Common Acronyms and Abbreviations (continued)

Acronym/ Abbreviation	Meaning
OSPF	Open Shortest Path First
OSTC	Open-System Testing Consortium
OTDR	Optical Time-Domain Reflectometry
PABX	Private Automatic-Branch Exchange
PAC	Privelege-Attribute Certificate
PACE	Priority Access-Control Enabled
PAD	packet assembler/disassembler
PAM	Pulse Amplitude Modulation
PAP	packet-level procedure
PAP	Password-Authentication Protocol
PAP	Printer-Access Protocol
PBP	Packet-Burst Protocol
PBX	Private Branch Exchange
PC	physical contact
PCI	Peripheral-Component Interconnect
PCI	Protocol-Control Information
PCL	Procedure Coverage Logger
PCM	Pulse Code Modulation
PCMCIA	Personal Computer Memory Card International Association
PCS	Personal Communications Services
PCS	plastic-clad silica
PD Stats	problem-determination statistics
PDA	personal digital assistant
PDAU	Physical-Delivery Access Unit
PDL	Page-Description Language
PDN	Public Data Network
PDP	Professional Developers Program
PDS	Premises Distribution System
PDS	Processor-Direct Slots

Acronym/ Abbreviation	Meaning
PDU	Protocol Data Unit
PEM	Privacy-Enhanced Mail
PEP	Packet-Exchange Protocol
PGP	Pretty Good Privacy
PHYSNET	Physics Network
PIC	Primary Interexchange Carrier
PID	Protocol ID
PIM	Personal Information Manager
PIN	Personal Identification Number
PING	Packet InterNet Groper
PIR	Protocol-Independent Routing
PIU	Path Information Unit
PLCP	Physical Layer Convergence Procedure
PLL	Phase-Lock Loop
PLP	Packet-Level Protocol
PLS	Physical-Layer Signaling
PLS	primary link station
PLU	primary logical unit
PMD	Physical-Media-Dependent
PMMU	paged memory-management unit
PNM	Physical Network Management
PNNI	Private Network-to-Network Interface
POP	point of presence
POP	Post Office Protocol 3
POSIX	Portable Operating-System Interface
POST	power-on self test
POTS	Plain Old Telephone Service
PPD	PostScript Printer-Definition file
PPP	Point-to-Point Protocol

(continued)

app.
a

Table A.1: Common Acronyms and Abbreviations (continued)

Acronym/ Abbreviation	Meaning
PPPRNS	Point-to-Point Protocol Remote Node Services
PRAM	Parameter RAM
PRI	Primary-Rate Interface
PRI	Primary-Rate ISDN
PRMD	Private Management Domain
PSN	Packet-Switch Node
PSNP	Partial-Sequence-Number PDU
PSTN	Public Switched Telephone Network
PTM	Pulse Time Modulation
PTT	Post, Telephone and Telegraph
PU	physical unit
PUP	PARC Universal Protocol
PVC	Permanent Virtual Circuit
Q-bit	Qualifier bit
QIC	quarter-inch cartridge
QLCC	Qualified Link-Level Control
QMS	Queue-Management Services
RACE	Research and Development Program in Advanced Communications in Europe
RAID	Redundant Array of Inexpensive Disks
RAM	random-access memory
RARE	Réseaux Associés pour la Réchérche Européenne
RARP	Reverse Address-Resolution Protocol
RAS	Remote-Access Services
RBHC	Regional Bell Holding Company
RBOC	Regional Bell Operating Company
RCGI	Remote Common-Gateway Interface
RDA	Remote Database Access
RDN	Relative Distinguished Name
RF	Radio Frequency

Acronym/ Abbreviation	Meaning
RFC	Request for Comments
RFI	radio-frequency interference
RFS	Remote File Service
RH	request/response header
RI	referencial integrity
RI	Ring Indicator
RI/RO	Ring In/ Ring Out
RIF	Routing-Information Field
RIP	Router-Information Protocol
RIPL files	Remote Internal Program Load
RISC	Reduced-Instruction-Set Computing
RJE	Remote Job Entry
RLL	run-length-limited
RMON	Remote Network Monitoring
RMS	Root Mean Square
RO	Receive Only
ROM	read-only memory
ROSE	Remote-Operations Service Element
RPC	Remote Procedure Call
RPG	Remote Password Generator
RPL	Remote Program Load
RSA	Rivesi, Shamir, Adleman Algorithm
RSRB	Remote Source-Route Bridging
RTMP	Routing-Table Maintenance Protocol
RTP	Routing-Table Protocol
RTS	Request To Send
RTSE	Reliable-Transfer Service Element
RTT	Round-Trip Time
RU	Request/Response Unit

app.
a

(continued)

Table A.1: Common Acronyms and Abbreviations (continued)

Acronym/ Abbreviation	Meaning
RXD	Receive Data
RZ	Return to Zero
RZI	Return-to-Zero Inverted
SA	Source Address
SAA	Systems Application Architecture
SAC	Simplified Access Control
SAC	Single-Attachment Concentrator
SAP	Service-Access Point
SAP	Service-Advertising Protocol
SAR	Segmentation and Reassembly
SAS	Single-Attachment Station
SATAN	Security-Analysis Tool for Auditing Networks
SCR	Signal-to-Crosstalk Ratio
SCS	SNA Character String
SCSI	Small Computer System Interface
SD	Start Delimiter
SDDI	Shielded Distributed Data Interface
SDF	Sub-Distribution Frame
SDI or SMSDI	storage-device interface
SDLC	Synchronous Data-Link Control
SDSU	SMS Data Service Unit
SDU	Service Data Unit
Session Identifier	Session ID
SET	Secure Electronic Transactions protocol
SFT	System Fault Tolerance
SGMP	Simple Gateway-Monitoring Protocol
SHTTP	Service HyperText-Transfer Protocol
SIDF	System-Independent Data Format
SIG	special-interest group

Acronym/ Abbreviation	Meaning
SLED	single large expensive disk
SLIP	Serial-Line Internet Protocol
SLS	secondary link station
SLU	secondary logical unit
SM	Standby Monitor
SMAE	Systems-Management Application Entity
SMAP	Systems-Management Application Process
SMASE	Systems-Management Application Service Element
SMB	Server Message Block
SMDR	Storage-Management Data Requester
SMDS	Switched Multimegabit Data Service
SMF	Standard Message Format
SMF	Systems-Management Function
SMFA	Systems-Management Functional Area
SMI	Structure-Management Information
SMS	Storage-Management Services
SMSDI	SMS Storage-Device Interface
SMT	Station Management
SMTP	Simple Mail-Transfer Protocol
SNA	Systems Network Architecture
SNA/SDLC	Systems Network Architecture/Synchronous Data-Link Control
SNADS	SNA Distribution Services
SNAP	Sub-Network Access Protocol
SNDCP	Subnetwork-Dependent Convergence Protocol
SNI	SNA Network Interconnection
SNICP	Subnetwork-Independent Convergence Protocol
SNMP	Simple Network-Management Protocol
SNPA	Subnetwork Point of Attachment
SNR	signal-to-noise ratio

app.
a

(continued)

Table A.1: Common Acronyms and Abbreviations (continued)

Acronym/ Abbreviation	Meaning
SNTP	Simple Network-Time Protocol
SONET	Synchronous Optical Network
SPAN	Space-Physics Analysis Network
SPARC	Scalar-Processor Architecture
SPF	Shortest Path First
SPP	Sequenced-Packet Protocol
SPS	Stand-by Power Supply
SPX	Sequenced-Packet Exchange
SQE	Signal-Quality Error
SQL	Structured Query Language
SR/TLB	Source-Route Translational Bridging
SRAM	Static Random-Access Memory
SRB	Source-Route Bridging
SRT bridging	Source-Route Transport
SS	Sampled Servo
SSAP	Source Service-Access Point
SSCP	system-service control point
SSI	Server Side Includes
SSL	Secure-Sockets Layer
SSL protocol	Secure-Sockets-Layer protocol
SSO	Single Sign-On
SSS	Server-Session Socket
STDA	StreetTalk Directory Assistance
STDM	Statistical Time-Division Multiplexing
STM	Synchronous Transfer Mode
STM-x	Synchronous Transfer Mode-x
STP	shielded twisted-pair
STS	sign-trailing separate
SURAnet	Southeastern Universities Research Association Network

Acronym/ Abbreviation	Meaning
SVC	switched virtual circuit
Sysop	System Operator
TA	Terminal Adapter
TAC	Terminal-Access Controller
TACACS	Terminal-Access-Controller Access System
TAG	Technical Advisory Group
TAPI	Telphony API
TB	terabyte
TCM	trellis-coded modulation
TCNS	Thomas-Conrad Network System
TCP	Transmission-Control Protocol
TCP/IP	Transmission-Control Protocol/Internet Protocol Suite
TCPCON	TCP/IP Console
TCU	Truck-Coupling Unit
TDM	Time-Division Multiplexing
TDMA	Time-Division Multiple Access
TDR	time-domain reflectometry
TFTP	Trivial File-Transfer Protocol
TFTP	Trivial File-Transfer Protocol
TH	Transmission Header
THEnet	Texas Higher Education Network
THT	Token-Holding Time
TI	transaction identifier
TIA	Telecommunications Industries Association
TIA	The Internet Adapter
TIC	Token-Ring Interface Coupler
TLAP	TokenTalk Link-Access Protocol
TLI	Transport-Layer Interface
TNC	threaded-nut connector

app.
a

(continued)

Table A.1: Common Acronyms and Abbreviations (continued)

Acronym/ Abbreviation	Meaning
TOP	Technical-Office Protocol
ToS	Type of Service
TP	twisted-pair cable
TPDDI	Twisted-Pair Distributed Data Interface
TP-PMD	Twisted-Pair, Physical-Media-Dependent
TRel	Transaction-Release packet
TReq	Transaction-Request packet
TResp	Transaction-Response packet
TSA	Target Service Agent
TSA	Technical Service Alliance
TSAT	TI small-aperture terminal
TSDU	Transport-Service Data Unit
TSM	Topology-Specific Module
TSR	terminate-and-stay-resident
TTFN	Ta-Ta For Now
TTL	Transistor-Translator Logic
TTRT	Target Token-Rotation Time
TTS	Transaction-Tracking System
Turbo FAT	Turbo File-Allocation Table
TXD	Transmit Data
UA	Unsequenced Acknowledgment
UA	User Agent
UAL	User-Access Line
UAL	User-Agent Layer
UAM	User-Authentication Method
UART	universal asynchronous receiver/transmitter
UBR	Unspecified Bit Rate
UDP	User-Datagram Protocol
UL	Underwriters Laboratories

Acronym/ Abbreviation	Meaning
ULP	Upper-Layer Protocol
UMB	upper-memory block
UNA	Upstream Neighbor's Address
UNC	Universal Naming Convention
UNI	User-to-Network Interface
UNMA	Unified Network-Management Architecture
UPS	uninterruptible power supply
URL	Uniform Resource Locator
USOC	Uniform Service-Ordering Code
USRT	universal synchronous receiver/transmitter
UTP	unshielded twisted-pair cable
UUCP	UNIX-to-UNIX Copy Program
VAN	value-added network
VAP	value-added process
VAR	value-added reseller
VAT	Variable-Tail Allocation Table
VBI	Vertical Blank Interval
VBR	Variable Bit Rate
VC	Virtual Channel
VC	virtual circuit
VCC	Virtual Channel Connection
VCCI	Voluntary Control Council for Interference
VCI	Virtual Channel Identifier
VCPI	Virtual Control-Program Interface
VDT	Volume-Definition Table
Veronica	Very Easy Rodent-Oriented Netwide Index to Computerized Archives
VESA	Video Electronics Standards Association
VFS	Virtual File Storage
VGA	Video Graphics Array

app.
a

(continued)

Table A.1: Common Acronyms and Abbreviations (continued)

Acronym/ Abbreviation	Meaning
VIM	Vendor-Independent Messaging
VINES	Virtual Networking System
VLAN	Virtual LAN
VLF	very-low-frequency emission
VLM	Virtual Loadable Module
VLSM	Variable-Length Subnet Mask
VMS	Virtual Memory System
VOP	Velocity of Propogation
VOTS	VAX OSI Transport Service
VPC	Virtual Path Connection
VPI	Virtual Path Identifier
VPN	Virtual Private Network
VRML	Virtual-Reality Modeling Language
VSAT	Very-Small-Aperture Terminal
VT	Virtual Terminal
VT	Virtual Terminal
VTAM	Virtual Telecommunications Access Method
VTP	Virtual-Terminal Protocol
W3C	World Wide Web Consortium
WAIS	Wide-Area Information Service
WAN	wide-area network
WATS	Wide-Area Telecommunication Service
WBC	Wideband Channel
WDM	Wavelength-Division Multiplexing
WIN	Wireless In-Building Network
WKSH	Windowing Korn Shell
WORM	Write Once, Read Many
WOS	Workstation Operating System
WOSA	Windows Open-Services Architecture

Acronym/ Abbreviation	Meaning
WWW	World Wide Web
XDMCP	X-Display Manager Control Protocol
XDR	External Data Representation
XMS	Extended-Memory Specification
XNS	Xerox Network Systems
XTP	Xpress Transfer Protocol
YMMV	Your Mileage May Vary
ZDL	Zero-Delay Lockout
ZIP	Zone-Information Protocol
ZIS	Zone-Information Socket
ZIT	Zone-Information Table

Appendix B: Standard ASCII Character Set

This appendix includes the American Standard
Code for Information Interchange (ASCII)
character set.

Decimal	Character	Decimal	Character	Decimal	Character	Decimal	Character
0	NUL (Null)	33	!	65	A	97	a
1	SOH (Start of Heading)	34	"	66	B	98	b
2	STX (Start of Text)	35	#	67	C	99	c
3	ETX (End of Text)	36	$	68	D	100	d
4	EOT (End of Transmit)	37	%	69	E	101	e
5	ENQ (Enquiry)	38	&	70	F	102	f
6	ACK (Acknowledge)	39	'	71	G	103	g
7	BEL (Audible bell)	40	(	72	H	104	h
8	BS (Backspace)	41	)	73	I	105	i
9	HT (Horizontal Tab)	42	*	74	J	106	j
10	LF (Line Feed)	43	+	75	K	107	k
11	VT (Vertical Tab)	44	,	76	L	108	l
12	FF (Form Feed)	45	-	77	M	109	m
13	CR (Carriage Return)	46	.	78	N	110	n
14	SO (Shift Out)	47	/	79	O	111	o
15	SI (Shift In)	48	0	80	P	112	p
16	DLE (Data-Link Escape)	49	1	81	Q	113	q
17	DC1 (Device Control 1)	50	2	82	R	114	r
18	DC2 (Device Control 2)	51	3	83	S	115	s
19	DC3 (Device Control 3)	52	4	84	T	116	t
20	DC4 (Device Control 4)	53	5	85	U	117	u
21	NAK (Negative Acknowledge)	54	6	86	V	118	v
22	SYN (Synchronous idle)	55	7	87	W	119	w

(continued)

Decimal	Character	Decimal	Character	Decimal	Character	Decimal	Character
23	ETB (End Transmission Block)	56	8	88	X	120	x
24	CAN (Cancel)	57	9	89	Y	121	y
25	EM (End of Medium)	58	:	90	Z	122	z
26	SUB (Substitution)	59	;	91	[	123	{
27	ESC (Escape)	60	<	92	\	124	|
28	FS (Figures Shift)	61	=	93	]	125	}
29	GS (Group Separator)	62	>	94	^	126	~
30	RS (Record Separator)	63	?	95	_	127	
31	US (Unit Separator)	64	@	96	`		
32	SP (Blank Space)						

Appendix C:
Novell Directory
Services (NDS) Object
and Selectable Properties

OBJECTS

PROPERTIES	AFP Server	Alias	Bindery Object	Bindery Queue	Computer	Country	Directory Map	External Entity	Group	List	Message-Routing Group	Messaging Server	NCP Server	Organization	Organizational Role	Organizational Unit	Print Server	Printer	Profile	Queue	Unknown	User	Volume
Access-Control List	x	x	x	x	x	x	x	x	x	x	x	x	x	x	x	x	x	x	x	x	x	x	x
Account Balance	x																				x	x	
Account Locked																	x	x			x	x	
Account Reset Time																					x	x	
Aliased Object Name		x																					
Allow Unlimited Credit	x											x			x						x	x	
Allow User to Change Password																					x	x	
Authority Revocation								x		x	x												
Back Link	x	x	x	x	x	x	x	x	x	x	x	x	x	x	x	x	x	x	x	x	x	x	x
Bindery Object Restrictions			x																				
Bindery Property	x	x	x	x	x	x	x	x	x	x	x	x	x	x	x	x	x	x	x	x	x	x	x

OBJECTS (continued)

PROPERTIES	AFP Server	Alias	Bindery Object	Bindery Queue	Computer	Country	Directory Map	External Entry	Group	List	Message-Routing Group	Messaging Server	NCP Server	Organization	Organizational Role	Print Server	Printer	Profile	Queue	Unknown	User	Volume
Bindery Type			X	X																		
CA Private Key											X			X								
CA Public Key											X			X								
Cartridge																	X					
Certificate Revocation								X	X		X			X								
Certificate Validity Interval											X		X	X								
City														X	X						X	
Common Name (CN)	X		X		X			X	X	X	X		X	X	X	X	X	X	X	X	X	X
Country (C)						X	X							X								
Cross-Certificate Pair								X	X	X	X			X								
Days Between Forced Changes																					X	
Default Profile																					X	X

OBJECTS (continued)

PROPERTIES	AFP Server	Alias	Bindery Object	Bindery Queue	Computer	Country	Directory Map	External Entity	Group	List	Message-Routing Group	Messaging Server	NCP Server	Organization	Organizational Role	Organizational Unit	Print Server	Printer	Profile	Queue	Unknown	User	Volume
Default Queue																		×					
Default Server																						×	
Description	×	×	×	×	×	×	×	×	×	×	×	×	×	×	×	×	×	×	×	×	×	×	×
Detect Intruder														×		×							
Device			×		×																		
DS Revision													×										
E-Mail Address							×	×	×	×	×			×		×						×	
External Name								×						×									
Facsimile Telephone Number									×	×	×			×		×						×	
Fax Number												×										×	
Full Name	×									×	×				×							×	
Generational Qualifier																						×	
GID									×	×												×	
Given Name																						×	

OBJECTS (continued)

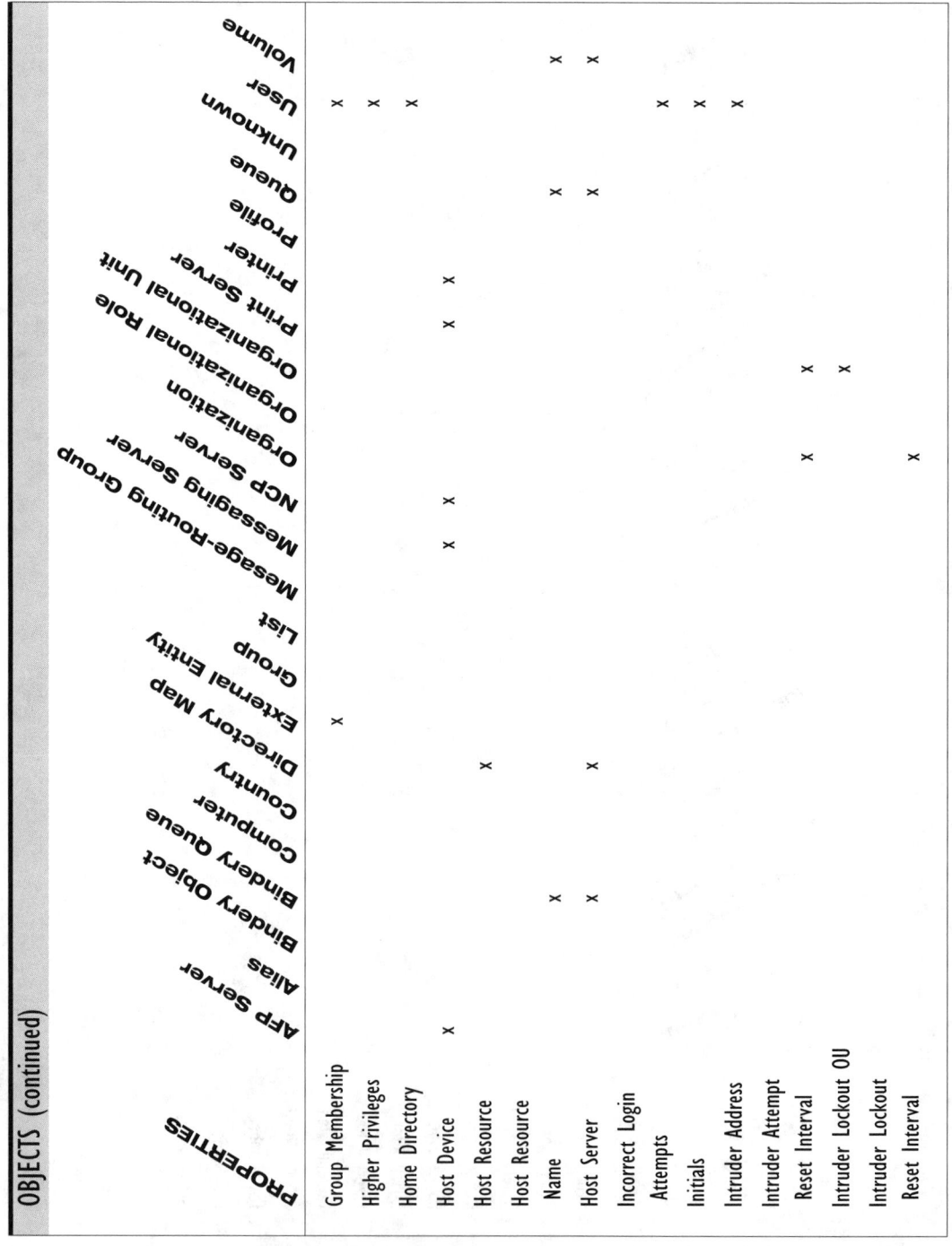

PROPERTIES	AFP Server	Alias	Bindery Object	Bindery Queue	Computer	Country	Directory Map	External Entry	Group	List	Message-Routing Group	Messaging Server	NCP Server	Organization	Organizational Role	Organizational Unit	Print Server	Printer	Profile	Queue	Unknown	User	Volume
Group Membership								x														x	
Higher Privileges																						x	
Home Directory																						x	
Host Device	x											x	x				x	x					
Host Resource							x																x
Host Resource			x				x																x
Name			x	x																			x
Host Server				x																x			x
Incorrect Login Attempts																						x	
Initials																						x	
Intruder Address																						x	
Intruder Attempt Reset Interval														x		x							
Intruder Lockout OU														x		x							
Intruder Lockout Reset Interval														x									

OBJECTS (continued)

PROPERTIES	AFP Server	Alias	Bindery Object	Bindery Queue	Computer	Country	Directory Map	External Entity	Group	List	Message-Routing Group	Messaging Server	NCP Server	Organization	Organizational Role	Organizational Unit	Print Server	Printer	Profile	Queue	Unknown	User	Volume
Language																						X	
Last Login Time																						X	
Last Name																						X	
Last Referenced Time									X	X	X			X									X
Limit Grace Logins																						X	
Locality (L)	X				X	X	X	X	X	X	X		X	X	X	X	X	X	X	X	X	X	X
Location																						X	
Locked By Intruder																						X	
Lockout After Detection													X		X								
Login-Allowed Time																						X	
Map							X															X	
Login Disabled																						X	
Login-Expiration Date and Time																						X	X

OBJECTS (continued)

PROPERTIES	AFP Server	Alias	Bindery Object	Bindery Queue	Computer	Country	Directory Map	External Entity	Group	List	Message-Routing Group	Messaging Server	NCP Server	Organization	Organizational Role	Organizational Unit	Print Server	Printer	Profile	Queue	Unknown	User	Volume
Login-Expiration Time																						X	
Login Grace Limit																						X	
Login Grace Remaining																						X	
Login Intruder Address																						X	
Login Intruder Attempts																						X	
Login Intruder Limit														X	X								
Login Intruder Reset Time																						X	
Login Maximum Simultaneous														X	X							X	
Login Script										X				X	X				X			X	
Login Time																						X	

OBJECTS (continued)

PROPERTIES	AFP Server	Alias	Bindery Object	Bindery Queue	Computer	Country	Directory Map	External Entity	Group	List	Message-Routing Group	Messaging Server	NCP Server	Organization	Organizational Role	Organizational Unit	Print Server	Printer	Profile	Queue	Unknown	User	Volume
Login Time Restrictions																						x	
Mailbox ID									x	x				x	x							x	
Mailbox Location									x	x				x	x							x	
Mailing-Label Information									x					x	x							x	
Maximum Connections																							
Member									x	x													
Memory																	x						
Message-Routing Group											x												
Message Server												x											
Messaging-Database Location											x											x	
Messaging Server													x										

app.
c

OBJECTS (continued)

PROPERTIES	Volume	User	Unknown	Queue	Profile	Printer	Print Server	Organizational Role	Organizational Unit	Organization	NCP Server	Messaging Server	Message-Routing Group	List	Group	External Entity	Directory Map	Country	Computer	Bindery Queue	Bindery Object	Alias	AFP Server
Messaging Server Type													×										
Minimum Account Balance		×							×	×													
Name																		×					
Network Address		×				×	×				×	×							×				×
Network Address Restrictions		×				×			×	×													
NNS Domain									×	×	×												
Notify				×		×	×																
Obituary		×		×	×	×	×	×	×	×	×	×	×	×	×	×	×	×	×	×	×	×	×
Object Class	×	×	×	×	×	×	×	×	×	×	×	×	×	×	×	×	×	×	×	×	×	×	×
Object Trustees (ACL)	×	×	×	×	×	×	×	×	×	×	×	×	×	×	×	×	×	×	×	×	×	×	×
Operator				×			×					×								×			×
Organization (O)	×	×		×	×	×	×	×	×	×	×	×	×	×	×	×	×		×	×	×	×	×
Organizational Unit (OU)	×	×		×	×	×	×	×	×	×	×	×	×	×	×	×	×		×	×	×	×	×

OBJECTS (continued)

PROPERTIES	Volume	User	Unknown	Queue	Profile	Printer	Print Server	Organizational Role	Organizational Unit	Organization	NCP Server	Messaging Server	Message-Routing Group	List	Group	External Entity	Directory Map	Country	Computer	Bindery Queue	Bindery Object	Alias	AFP Server
Owner						x							x	x	x				x				
Page-Description Language						x																	
Password Allow Change		x																					
Password-Expiration Date and Time		x																					
Password-Expiration Interval		x																					
Password-Expiration Time		x																					
Password Minimum Length		x																					
Password Required		x																					
Password Unique Required		x																					
Passwords Used		x																					

app.
c

OBJECTS (continued)

PROPERTIES	Volume	User	Unknown	Queue	Profile	Printer	Print Server	Organizational Unit	Organizational Role	Organization	NCP Server	Messaging Server	Message-Routing Group	List	Group	External Entity	Directory Map	Country	Computer	Bindery Queue	Bindery Object	Alias	AFP Server
Path																	X						
Physical-Delivery Office Name		X						X	X	X													
Postal Address		X						X	X	X													
Postal Code		X						X	X	X													
Postal Office Box		X						X	X	X													
Postmaster												X											
Print									X														
Print-Job Configuration		X						X	X	X	X												
Print Server						X																	
Printer Configuration							X																
Printer Control						X																	
Private Key		X									X	X	X										X
Profile		X												X	X								
Profile Membership		X												X	X								

OBJECTS (continued)

PROPERTIES	AFP Server	Alias	Bindery Object	Bindery Queue	Computer	Country	Directory Map	External Entity	Group	List	Message-Routing Group	Messaging Server	NCP Server	Organization	Organizational Role	Organizational Unit	Print Server	Printer	Profile	Queue	Unknown	User	Volume
Public Key	X												X			X	X					X	
Queue												X	X				X						
Queue Directory			X																	X			
Reference								X	X	X	X	X											
Remaining Grace Logins																						X	
Require a Password																						X	
Require a Unique Password																						X	
Reset Interval															X								
Resource	X										X	X				X							
Revision									X	X	X	X	X	X									
Role Occupant														X	X	X							
S	X							X						X	X	X						X	
SA	X							X					X	X	X	X						X	
SAP Name													X										

OBJECTS (continued)

PROPERTIES	AFP Server	Alias	Bindery Object	Bindery Queue	Computer	Country	Directory Map	External Entry	Group	List	Message-Routing Group	Messaging Server	NCP Server	Organization	Organizational Role	Organizational Unit	Print Server	Printer	Profile	Queue	Unknown	User	Volume
Security Equals To	X											X	X	X	X	X	X	X	X	X		X	X
Security Equivalences																						X	
Security Flags	X											X	X	X	X	X	X	X	X	X		X	X
See Also	X		X		X		X	X	X	X	X	X	X	X	X	X	X	X	X	X		X	X
Serial Number	X		X		X																		X
Server			X	X	X															X			X
Server Holds																		X		X			
State or Province						X								X		X						X	
Status	X				X						X	X	X				X	X	X	X		X	X
Street	X																						
Supported Connections	X												X										
Supported Services	X											X	X										
Supported Typefaces																		X					
Surname																						X	

OBJECTS (continued)

PROPERTIES	AFP Server	Alias	Bindery Object	Bindery Queue	Computer	Country	Directory Map	External Entity	Group	List	Message-Routing Group	Messaging Server	NCP Server	Organization	Organizational Role	Organizational Unit	Print Server	Printer	Profile	Queue	Unknown	User	Volume
Telephone																						x	
Telephone Number														x	x	x						x	
Title														x	x							x	
Type Creator Map								x															
User	x		x										x		x		x						
User ID (UID)																					x		
User Version												x											
Version	x												x						x	x			
Volume			x														x	x					

app.
c

Appendix D:
Country Codes for
Top-Level Domains

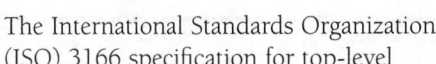

The International Standards Organization (ISO) 3166 specification for top-level domains defines the two-letter and three-letter country codes shown in this table.

Country	Two-Letter Code	Three-Letter Code	Number
Afghanistan	AF	AFG	004
Albania	AL	ALB	008
Algeria	DZ	DZA	012
American Samoa	AS	ASM	016
Andorra	AD	AND	020
Angola	AO	AGO	024
Anguilla	AI	AIA	660
Antarctica	AQ	ATA	010
Antigua and Barbuda	AG	ATG	028
Argentina	AR	ARG	032
Armenia	AM	ARM	051
Aruba	AW	ABW	533
Australia	AU	AUS	036
Austria	AT	AUT	040
Azerbaijan	AZ	AZE	031
Bahamas	BS	BHS	044
Bahrain	BH	BHR	048
Bangladesh	BD	BGD	050
Barbados	BB	BRB	052
Belarus	BY	BLR	112
Belgium	BE	BEL	056
Belize	BZ	BLZ	084
Benin	BJ	BEN	204
Bermuda	BM	BMU	060

Country	Two-Letter Code	Three-Letter Code	Number
Bhutan	BT	BTN	064
Bolivia	BO	BOL	068
Bosnia and Herzegovina	BA	BIH	070
Botswana	BW	BWA	072
Bouvet Island	BV	BVT	074
Brazil	BR	BRA	076
British Indian Ocean Territory	IO	IOT	086
Brunei Darussalam	BN	BRN	096
Bulgaria	BG	BGR	100
Burkina Faso	BF	BFA	854
Burundi	BI	BDI	108
Cambodia	KH	KHM	116
Cameroon	CM	CMR	120
Canada	CA	CAN	124
Cape Verde	CV	CPV	132
Cayman Islands	KY	CYM	136
Central African Republic	CF	CAF	140
Chad	TD	TCD	148
Chile	CL	CHL	152
China	CN	CHN	156
Christmas Island	CX	CXR	162
Cocos (Keeling) Islands	CC	CCK	166
Colombia	CO	COL	170
Comoros	KM	COM	174
Congo	CG	COG	178
Cook Islands	CK	COK	184
Costa Rica	CR	CRI	188
Côte d'Ivoire	CI	CIV	384
Croatia (local name: Hrvatska)	HR	HRV	191

Country	Two-Letter Code	Three-Letter Code	Number
Cuba	CU	CUB	192
Cyprus	CY	CYP	196
Czech Republic	CZ	CZE	203
Denmark	DK	DNK	208
Djibouti	DJ	DJI	262
Dominica	DM	DMA	212
Dominican Republic	DO	DOM	214
East Timor	TP	TMP	626
Ecuador	EC	ECU	218
Egypt	EG	EGY	818
El Salvador	SV	SLV	222
Equatorial Guinea	GQ	GNQ	226
Eritrea	ER	ERI	232
Estonia	EE	EST	233
Ethiopia	ET	ETH	231
Falkland Islands (Malvinas)	FK	FLK	238
Faroe Islands	FO	FRO	234
Fiji	FJ	FJI	242
Finland	FI	FIN	246
France	FR	FRA	250
France, Metropolitan	FX	FXX	249
French Guiana	GF	GUF	254
French Polynesia	PF	PYF	258
French Southern Territories	TF	ATF	260
Gabon	GA	GAB	266
Gambia	GM	GMB	270
Georgia	GE	GEO	268
Germany	DE	DEU	276
Ghana	GH	GHA	288

app.
d

Country	Two-Letter Code	Three-Letter Code	Number
Gibraltar	GI	GIB	292
Greece	GR	GRC	300
Greenland	GL	GRL	304
Grenada	GD	GRD	308
Guadeloupe	GP	GLP	312
Guam	GU	GUM	316
Guatemala	GT	GTM	320
Guinea	GN	GIN	324
Guinea-Bissau	GW	GNB	624
Guyana	GY	GUY	328
Haiti	HT	HTI	332
Heard and McDonald Islands	HM	HMD	334
Holy See (Vatican City State)	VA	VAT	336
Honduras	HN	HND	340
Hong Kong	HK	HKG	344
Hungary	HU	HUN	348
Iceland	IS	ISL	352
India	IN	IND	356
Indonesia	ID	IDN	360
Iran (Islamic Republic of)	IR	IRN	364
Iraq	IQ	IRQ	368
Ireland	IE	IRL	372
Israel	IL	ISR	376
Italy	IT	ITA	380
Jamaica	JM	JAM	388
Japan	JP	JPN	392
Jordan	JO	JOR	400
Kazakhstan	KZ	KAZ	398
Kenya	KE	KEN	404

Country	Two-Letter Code	Three-Letter Code	Number
Kiribati	KI	KIR	296
Korea, Democratic People's Republic of	KP	PRK	408
Korea, Republic of	KR	KOR	410
Kuwait	KW	KWT	414
Kyrgyzstan	KG	KGZ	417
Laos People's Democratic Republic	LA	LAO	418
Latvia	LV	LVA	428
Lebanon	LB	LBN	422
Lesotho	LS	LSO	426
Liberia	LR	LBR	430
Libyan Arab Jamahiriya	LY	LBY	434
Liechtenstein	LI	LIE	438
Lithuania	LT	LTU	440
Luxembourg	LU	LUX	442
Macao	MO	MAC	446
Macedonia, the Former Yugoslav Republic of	MK	MKD	807
Madagascar	MG	MDG	450
Malawi	MW	MWI	454
Malaysia	MY	MYS	458
Maldive Islands	MV	MDV	462
Mali	ML	MLI	466
Malta	MT	MLT	470
Marshall Islands	MH	MHL	584
Martinique	MQ	MTQ	474
Mauritania	MR	MRT	478
Mauritius	MU	MUS	480

app.
d

Country	Two-Letter Code	Three-Letter Code	Number
Mayotte	YT	MYT	175
Mexico	MX	MEX	484
Micronesia, Federated States of	FM	FSM	583
Moldova, Republic of	MD	MDA	498
Monaco	MC	MCO	492
Mongolia	MN	MNG	496
Montserrat	MS	MSR	500
Morocco	MA	MAR	504
Mozambique	MZ	MOZ	508
Myanmar	MM	MMR	104
Namibia	NA	NAM	516
Nauru	NR	NRU	520
Nepal	NP	NPL	524
Netherlands	NL	NLD	528
Netherlands Antilles	AN	ANT	530
New Caledonia	NC	NCL	540
New Zealand	NZ	NZL	554
Nicaragua	NI	NIC	558
Niger	NE	NER	562
Nigeria	NG	NGA	566
Niue	NU	NIU	570
Norfolk Island	NF	NFK	574
Northern Mariana Islands	MP	MNP	580
Norway	NO	NOR	578
Oman	OM	OMN	512
Pakistan	PK	PAK	586
Palau	PW	PLW	585
Panama	PA	PAN	591
Papua New Guinea	PG	PNG	598

Country	Two-Letter Code	Three-Letter Code	Number
Paraguay	PY	PRY	600
Peru	PE	PER	604
Philippines	PH	PHL	608
Pitcairn	PN	PCN	612
Poland	PL	POL	616
Portugal	PT	PRT	620
Puerto Rico	PR	PRI	630
Qatar	QA	QAT	634
Reunion	RE	REU	638
Romania	RO	ROM	642
Russian Federation	RU	RUS	643
Rwanda	RW	RWA	646
Saint Kitts and Nevis	KN	KNA	659
Saint Lucia	LC	LCA	662
Saint Vincent and The Grenadines	VC	VCT	670
Samoa	WS	WSM	882
San Marino	SM	SMR	674
Sao Tome and Principe	ST	STP	678
Saudi Arabia	SA	SAU	682
Senegal	SN	SEN	686
Seychelles	SC	SYC	690
Sierra Leone	SL	SLE	694
Singapore	SG	SGP	702
Slovakia (Slovak Republic)	SK	SVK	703
Slovenia	SI	SVN	705
Solomon Islands	SB	SLB	090
Somalia	SO	SOM	706
South Africa	ZA	ZAF	710

app.
d

Country	Two-Letter Code	Three-Letter Code	Number
South Georgia and the South Sandwich Islands	GS	SGS	239
Spain	ES	ESP	724
Sri Lanka	LK	LKA	144
St. Helena	SH	SHN	654
St. Pierre and Miquelon	PM	SPM	666
Sudan	SD	SDN	736
Suriname	SR	SUR	740
Svalbard and Jan Mayen Islands	SJ	SJM	744
Swaziland	SZ	SWZ	748
Sweden	SE	SWE	752
Switzerland	CH	CHE	756
Syrian Arab Republic	SY	SYR	760
Taiwan, Province of China	TW	TWN	158
Tajikistan	TJ	TJK	762
Tanzania, United Republic of	TZ	TZA	834
Thailand	TH	THA	764
Togo	TG	TGO	768
Tokelau	TK	TKL	772
Tonga	TO	TON	776
Trinidad and Tobago	TT	TTO	780
Tunisia	TN	TUN	788
Turkey	TR	TUR	792
Turkmenistan	TM	TKM	795
Turks and Caicos Islands	TC	TCA	796
Tuvalu	TV	TUV	798
Uganda	UG	UGA	800
Ukraine	UA	UKR	804
United Arab Emirates	AE	ARE	784

Country	Two-Letter Code	Three-Letter Code	Number
United Kingdom	GB	GBR	826
United States	US	USA	840
United States Minor Outlying Islands	UM	UMI	581
Uruguay	UY	URY	858
Uzbekistan	UZ	UZB	860
Vanuatu	VU	VUT	548
Venezuela	VE	VEN	862
Viet Nam	VN	VNM	704
Virgin Islands (British)	VG	VGB	092
Virgin Islands (U.S.)	VI	VIR	850
Wallis and Futuna Islands	WF	WLF	876
Western Sahara	EH	ESH	732
Yemen	YE	YEM	887
Yugoslavia	YU	YUG	891
Zaire	ZR	ZAR	180
Zambia	ZM	ZMB	894
Zimbabwe	ZW	ZWE	716

**app.
d**

Appendix E:
Common NetWare
and IntranetWare
Utilities

This table shows common utilities found in versions of NetWare and IntranetWare, along with classifications for the types of utilities.

Utility	Version			Utility Type		
	NetWare 3.12	NetWare 4.10	Intranet-Ware	Console	File	Work-station
ABORT REMIRROR		X	X	X		
ACONSOLE	X					X
ACTIVATE SERVER		X	X	X		
ADD NAME SPACE	X	X	X	X		
ADDICON			X			X
AFP			X			
AFPCON			X	X		
ALIAS			X	X		
ALLOW	X				X	
ATCON		X	X	X		
ATCONFIG			X	X		
ATOTAL	X	X	X			X
ATPS			X			
ATPSCON			X	X		
ATTACH	X			X		
ATXRP			X			
AUDITCON		X	X			X
BIND	X	X	X	X		
BINDFIX	X					
BINDREST	X					

Utility	Version			Utility Type		
	NetWare 3.12	NetWare 4.10	Intranet-Ware	Console	File	Work-station
BRGCON		X	X	X		
BROADCAST	X	X	X	X		
CAPTURE	X	X	X			X
CASTOFF	X					X
CASTON	X					X
CD		X	X	X		
CDROM		X	X	X		
CHKDIR	X				X	
CHKVOL	X			X		
CLEAR STATION	X	X	X	X		
CLIB	X	X	X	X		
CLS	X	X	X	X		
COLORPAL	X	X	X			X
CONFIG	X	X	X	X		
CONLOG		X	X			
CX		X	X			X
DHCPCFG			X	X		
DISABLE LOGIN	X	X	X	X		
DISABLE TTS	X	X		X		
DISKSET	X			X		
DISMOUNT	X	X	X	X		
DISPLAY NETWORKS	X	X	X	X		
DISPLAY SERVERS	X	X	X	X		
DOMAIN		X		X		

Utility	Version			Utility Type		
	NetWare 3.12	NetWare 4.10	Intranet-Ware	Console	File	Work-station
DOSGEN	X	X	X			X
DOWN	X	X	X	X		
DS Migrate			X			X
DSMERGE		X	X	X		
DSPACE	X			X		
DSREPAIR		X	X	X		
EDIT	X	X	X	X		
ENABLE LOGIN	X	X	X	X		
ENABLE TTS	X	X	X	X		
ENDCAP	X					X
EXIT	X	X	X	X		
FCONSOLE	X			X		
FILER	X	X	X			X
FILTCFG		X	X	X		
FLAG	X	X	X		X	X
FLAGDIR	X				X	
FPSM			X			
GRANT	X					X
HALT		X	X	X		
HCSS		X	X	X		
HELP		X	X	X		
HFSCD			X	X		
HFSCDCON			X	X		
INETCFG		X	X	X		
INITIALIZE SYSTEM		X	X	X		
INSTALL	X	X	X	X		

	Version			Utility Type		
Utility	NetWare 3.12	NetWare 4.10	Intranet-Ware	Console	File	Work-station
IPXCON		X	X	X		
IPXPING		X	X	X		
IPXS	X	X	X	X		
KEYB		X	X	X		
LANGUAGE		X	X	X		
LIST DEVICES		X	X	X		
LISTDIR	X				X	
LOAD	X	X	X	X		
LOGIN	X	X	X			X
LOGOUT	X	X	X			X
MACFILE			X		X	
MAGAZINE		X	X	X		
MAKEUSER	X			X		
MAP	X	X	X			X
MATHLIB	X	X	X	X		
MATHLIBC		X	X	X		
MEDIA		X	X	X		
MEMORY	X	X	X	X		
MEMORY MAP		X	X	X		
MENUCNVT			X			X
MENUNAME			X			X
MIGPRINT			X			X
MIGRATE			X			X
MIRROR STATUS		X	X	X		
MODULES	X	X	X	X		

	Version			Utility Type		
Utility	NetWare 3.12	NetWare 4.10	Intranet-Ware	Console	File	Work-station
MONITOR	X	X	X	X		
MOUNT	X	X	X	X		
MPDRIVER			X	X		
MSERVER		X	X	X	X	
NAME	X	X	X	X		
NCOPY	X	X	X		X	X
NCUPDATE		X	X			X
NDIR	X	X	X		X	X
NDS Manager			X			X
NETADMIN		X	X			X
NETSYNC3		X	X	X		
NETSYNC4		X	X	X		
NETUSER		X	X			X
NetWare Administrator		X	X			X
NetWare Application Manager			X			X
NetWare Directory Browser			X			X
NetWare File Migration			X			X
NetWare Login			X			X
NetWare Migration		X				X
NetWare Print Chooser			X			X

app. e

	Version			Utility Type		
Utility	NetWare 3.12	NetWare 4.10	Intranet-Ware	Console	File	Work-station
NetWare Tools (OS/2)			X			X
NetWare TSA (OS/2)			X			X
NetWare User Tools			X			X
NetWare Volume Mounter			X			X
NIT			X			
NLIST		X	X			X
NLMLIB			X			
NLS MANAGER			X			X
NMAGENT	X			X		
NMENU	X	X	X			X
Novell Application Launcher			X			X
NPAMS		X	X	X		
NPATH		X	X			X
NPRINT	X	X	X			X
NPRINTER (OS/2)			X			X
NPRINTER (Windows 95)			X			X
NPRINTER.EXE		X	X			X
NPRINTER.NLM		X	X	X		
NVER	X	X	X			X
NWIPCFG			X	X		

	Version			Utility Type		
Utility	**NetWare 3.12**	**NetWare 4.10**	**Intranet-Ware**	**Console**	**File**	**Work-station**
NWSTART			X			X
NWSTOP			X			X
NWXTRACT	X	X	X			X
OFF	X	X	X	X		
PARTMGR		X	X			X
PAUDIT	X					X
PCONSOLE	X	X	X			X
PING		X	X	X		
PMMON		X	X	X		
PRINTCON	X	X	X			X
PRINTDEF	X	X	X			X
PROTOCOL	X	X	X	X		
PSC	X	X	X			X
PSERVER		X	X	X		
PSERVER (Console Utility)	X			X		X
PUPGRADE		X	X	X		
PURGE	X	X	X			X
RCONSOLE	X	X	X			X
REGISTER MEMORY	X	X	X	X		
REINITIALIZE SYSTEM		X	X	X		
REMAPID		X	X			
REMIRROR PARTITION		X	X	X		
REMOTE	X	X	X	X		
REMOVE	X					X

	Version			Utility Type		
Utility	**NetWare 3.12**	**NetWare 4.10**	**Intranet-Ware**	**Console**	**File**	**Work-station**
REMOVE DOS	X	X	X	X		
RENDIR	X	X	X			X
REQUESTR			X			
RESET ROUTER	X	X	X	X		
RESTART		X	X	X		
RESTART SERVER		X	X	X		
REVOKE	X					X
RIGHTS	X	X	X			X
ROUTE	X	X	X	X		
RPL		X	X	X		
RPRINTER	X			X		
RS232	X	X	X	X		
RSPX	X	X	X	X		
SALVAGE	X				X	
SBACKUP	X	X	X	X		
SCAN FOR NEW DEVICES		X	X	X		
SCHDELAY		X	X	X		
SEARCH	X	X	X	X		
SECURE CONSOLE	X	X	X	X		
SECURITY	X					X
SEND		X	X	X		X
SERVER	X	X	X	X	X	
SERVMAN		X	X	X		
SESSION	X					X
SET	X	X	X	X		

	Version			Utility Type		
Utility	**NetWare 3.12**	**NetWare 4.10**	**Intranet-Ware**	**Console**	**File**	**Work-station**
SET TIME	X	X	X	X		
SET TIME ZONE		X	X	X		
SETPASS	X	X	X			X
SETTTS	X	X	X			X
SETUPDOC			X			X
SLIST	X					X
SMODE	X					X
SPEED	X	X	X	X		
SPOOL	X			X		
SPXCONFG	X	X	X	X		
SPXS	X	X	X	X		
STREAMS	X	X	X	X		
SYSCON	X					X
SYSTIME	X	X	X			X
TCPCON		X	X	X		
TCPIP		X	X	X		
TECHWALK			X	X		
THREADS			X			
TIME	X	X	X	X		
TIMESYNC		X	X	X		
TLI	X	X	X	X		
TLIST	X					X
TPING		X	X	X		
TRACK OFF	X	X	X	X		
TRACK ON	X	X	X	X		
UIMPORT		X	X			X
UNBIND	X	X	X	X		
UNICON			X	X		

**app.
e**

Utility	Version			Utility Type		
	NetWare 3.12	NetWare 4.10	Intranet-Ware	Console	File	Work-station
UNLOAD	X	X	X	X		
UPS	X	X	X	X		
UPS STATUS	X	X	X	X		
UPS TIME	X	X	X	X		
UPS_AIO			X			
USERDEF	X					X
USERLIST	X					X
VERSION	X			X		
VIEW			X	X		
VOLINFO	X					X
VOLUME	X	X	X	X		
VREPAIR	X	X	X	X		
WHOAMI	X	X	X			X
WSUPDATE	X		X			X
WSUPGRD			X			X

Appendix F:
Requests for
Comments (RFCs):
A Resource in Progress

Requests for Comments (RFCs)

Requests for Comments (RFCs) are documents available online in an ongoing series that discusses a wide range of computer-communication topics, including the Internet, protocols, procedures, programs, and concepts. When RFCs were first introduced in 1969, some included meeting notes, opinions on various subjects, and even humor.

Anyone can write an RFC. Documents submitted for RFC consideration are sometimes known as Internet Drafts. A primary source of Internet Drafts is the Internet Engineering Task Force (IETF). Working groups within the IETF cull the documents until they are ready for publication. When the IETF considers the document ready, it submits the Internet Draft to the Internet Engineering Steering Group (IESG). Upon approval by the IESG, the documents are then submitted by the IESG to the RFC Editor for publication consideration.

The publisher of the RFC document set, the RFC Editor, is responsible for the final editorial review of the documents. Chartered by the Internet Society (ISOC) and the Federal Network Council (FNC), the RFC Editor is located at and operated by the Information Sciences Institute (ISI) of the University of Southern California (USC). Only after the RFC Editor has approved a document is it then assigned an RFC number and published.

RFCs are distributed online by being stored in public-access files. Widespread distribution of RFCs is encouraged to stimulate discussion about computer-communication topics. Procedures, policies, and protocols cited in specific RFCs often are cited as source material when discussing these topics.

Table F.1 shows the current library of RFCs, listed in reverse numerical order, along with the document title, author(s), date of publication, and pertinent notes about the document. An RFC may add information about a topic discussed in a previous RFC (called an *update*) or it may completely replace an earlier update (called an *obsolete*). The *STD* abbreviation in the "Notes" column refers to the current edition of the "Internet Official Protocol Standards" (RFC 2200). The "FYI" refers to "For Your Information" documents and *BCD* refers to "Best Current Documents."

 **To find out more about the RFC Editor, point your Web browser to** http://www.isi.edu/rfc-editor/.

You can obtain RFCs via FTP from the following primary repositories: ds.internic.net, nis.nsf.net, nisc.jvnc.net, ftp.isi.edu, wuarchive.wustl.edu, src.doc.ic.ad.uk, ftp.ncren.net, ftp.sesqui.net, nis.garr.it, **or** ftp.imag.fr.

To learn more about submitting Internet Drafts for RFC consideration, download RFC 1543. To learn more about the IETF, surf the Web to www.ietf.org.

Note: Many RFCs date from earlier stages of modern computer history, before familiar standard usages emerged. As you browse the RFC titles in this table, you may notice that the spelling and punctuation of important terms and phrases can vary. They appear here with their original spelling and punctuation (or lack of it) left largely intact to preserve technical accuracy. When you search for or download an RFC, you may want to use its RFC number (in the leftmost column of Table F.1) as the primary means of identifying your choice. In addition, you may want to pay special attention to case sensitivity or try different spellings of keywords.

Table AF.1: RFC Index

RFC	Title	Author(s)	Date	Notes
2200	Internet Official Protocol Standards	J. Postel	June 1997	Obsoletes RFC 2000; STD
2182	Selection and Operation of Secondary DNS Servers	S. Bradner R. Bush R. Elz M. Patton	August 1997	
2181	Clarifications to the DNS Specification	R. Bush R. Elz	August 1997	Updates RFC 1034; updates RFC 1035; updates RFC 1123
2180	IMAP4 Multi-Accessed Mailbox Practice	M. Gahrns	July 1997	
2179	Network Security for Trade Shows	A. Gwinn	July 1997	
2178	OSPF Version 2	J. Moy	July 1997	Obsoletes RFC 1583
2177	IMAP4 IDLE command	B. Leiba	July 1997	
2176	IPv4 over MAPOS Version 1	K. Murakami M. Maruyama	June 1997	
2175	MAPOS 16 — Multiple Access Protocol over SONET/SDH with 16-Bit Addressing	K. Murakami M. Maruyama	June 1997	
2174	A MAPOS Version 1 Extension — Switch-Switch Protocol	K. Murakami M. Maruyama	June 1997	
2173	A MAPOS Version 1 Extension — 1 Node Switch Protocol	K. Murakami M. Maruyama	June 1997	
2172	MAPOS Version 1 Assigned Numbers	M. Maruyama K. Murakami	June 1997	
2171	MAPOS — Multiple-Access Protocol over SONET/SDH Version 1	K. Murakami M. Maruyama	June 1997	
2170	Application REQuested IP over ATM (AREQUIPA)	W. Almesberger J. Le Boudec P. Oechslin	July 1997	
2169	A Trivial Convention for Using HTTP in URN Resolution	R. Daniel	June 1997	
2168	Resolution of Uniform Resource Identifiers Using the Domain-Name System	R. Daniel M. Mealling	June 1997	

2167	Referral Whois (RWhois) Protocol V1.5	S. Williamson M. Kosters D. Blacka J. Singh K. Zeilstra	June 1997	Obsoletes RFC 1714
2166	APPN Implementer's Workshop Closed Pages Document DLSw v2.0 Enhancements	D. Bryant P. Brittain	June 1997	
2165	Service Location Protocol	J. Veizades E. Guttman C. Perkins S. Kaplan	June 1997	
2155	Definitions of Managed Objects for APPN Using SMIv2	B. Clouston R. Moore	June 1997	
2154	OSPF with Digital Signatures	S. Murphy M. Badger B. Wellington	June 1997	
2153	PPP Vendor Extensions	W. Simpson	June 1997	Obsoletes RFC 1661; obsoletes RFC 1962
2152	A Mail-Safe Transformation Format of Unicode	D. Goldsmith M. Davis	June 1997	Obsoletes RFC 1642
2151	A Primer on Internet and TCP/IP Tools and Utilities	G. Kessler S. Shepard	June 1997	FYI 30; obsoletes RFC
2149	Multicast Server Architectures for MARS-based ATM Multicasting	R. Talpade M. Ammar	May 1997	
2147	TCP and UDP over IPv6 Jumbograms	D. Borman	May 1997	Obsoletes RFC 1883
2146	U.S. Government Internet Domain Names	F. Networking Council (FNC)	May 1997	
2145	Use and Interpretation of HTTP Version Numbers	J. Mogul R. Fielding J. Gettys H. Nielsen	May 1997	

(continued)

app.
f

Table AF.1: RFC Index (continued)

RFC	Title	Author(s)	Date	Notes
2144	The CAST-128 Encryption Algorithm	C. Adams	May 1997	
2143	Encapsulating IP with the Small Computer System Interface	B. Elliston	May 1997	
2142	Mailbox Names for Common Services, Roles, and Functions	D. Crocker	May 1997	
2141	URN Syntax	R. Moats	May 1997	
2140	TCP Control Block Interdependence	J. Touch	April 1997	
2139	RADIUS Accounting	C. Rigney	April 1997	Obsoletes RFC 2059
2138	Remote Authentication Dial-In User Service (RADIUS)	C. Rigney A. Rubens W. Simpson S. Willens	April 1997	Obsoletes RFC 2058
2137	Secure Domain-Name System Dynamic Update	D. Eastlake	April 1997	Obsoletes RFC 1035
2136	Dynamic Updates in the Domain-Name System (DNS UPDATE)	J. Bound Y. Rekhter S. Thomson P. Vixie	April 1997	Obsoletes RFC 1035
2135	Internet Society By-Laws	Internet Society	April 1997	
2134	Articles of Incorporation of Internet Society	Internet Society	May 1997	
2133	Basic Socket Interface Extensionsfor IPv6	R. Gilligan S. Thomson J. Bound W. Stevens	April 1997	
2132	DHCP Options and BOOTP Vendor Extensions	S. Alexander R. Droms	April 1997	Obsoletes RFC 1533
2131	Dynamic Host-Configuration Protocol	R. Droms	April 1997	Obsoletes RFC 1541; obsoletes RFC 1533
2130	The Report of the IAB Character Set Workshop Held 29 February–1 March 1996	C. Weider K. Simonsen H. Alvestrand P. Svanberg	April 1997	

2129	Toshiba's Flow Attribute Notification Protocol (FANP) Specification	K. Nagami Y. Katsube Y. Shobatake	April 1997	
2128	Dial Control Management Information Base Using SMIv2	G. Roeck	March 1997	
2127	ISDN Management Information Base	G. Roeck	March 1997	
2126	ISO Transport Service on Top of TCP (ITOT)	Y. Pouffary A. Young	March 1997	
2125	The PPP Bandwidth Allocation Protocol (BAP); The PPP Bandwidth Allocation Control Protocol (BACP)	C. Richards K. Smith	March 1997	
2124	Light-Weight Flow Admission Protocol Specification Version 1.0	P. Amsden J. Amweg P. Calato S. Bensley G. Lyons	March 1997	
2123	Traffic Flow Measurement: Experiences with NeTraMet	N. Brownlee	March 1997	
2122	VEMMI URL Specification	D. Mavrakis H. Layec K. Kartmann	March 1997	
2121	Issues Affecting MARS Cluster Size	G. Armitage	March 1997	
2120	Managing the X.500 Root Naming Context	Chadwick	March 1997	
2119	Key Words for Use in RFCs to Indicate Requirement Levels	S. Bradner	March 1997	
2118	Microsoft Point-To-Point Compression (MPPC) Protocol	G. Pall	March 1997	
2117	Protocol-Independent Multicast-Sparse Mode (PIM-SM): Protocol Specification	S. Deering	June 1997	
2116	X.500 Implementations Catalog-96	C. Apple K. Rossen	April 1997	FYI 11; obsoletes RFC
2114	Data Link Switching Client Access Protocol	S. Chiang J. Lee H. Yasuda	March 1997	Obsoletes RFC 2106

(continued)

app.
f

Table AF.1: RFC Index (continued)

RFC	Title	Author(s)	Date	Notes
2113	IP Router Alert Option	D. Katz	February 1997	
2112	The MIME Multipart/Related Content-Type	E. Levinson	March 1997	Obsoletes RFC 1872
2111	Content-ID and Message-ID Uniform Resource Locators	E. Levinson	March 1997	
2110	MIME E-Mail Encapsulation of Aggregate Documents, Such as HTML (MHTML)	J. Palme A. Hopmann	March 1997	
2109	HTTP State Management Mechanism	D. Kristol L. Montulli	February 1997	
2108	Definitions of Managed Objects for IEEE 802.3 Repeater Devices Using SMIv2	K. De Graaf K. McCloghrie D. McMaster D. Romascanu	February 1997	Obsoletes RFC 1516
2107	Ascend Tunnel Management Protocol — ATMP	K. Hamzeh	February 1997	
2106	Data-Link Switching Remote-Access Protocol	S. Chiang J. Lee H. Yasuda	March 1997	Obsoleted by RFC 2114
2105	Cisco Systems' Tag Switching Architecture Overview	Y. Rekhter B. Davie D. Katz E. Rosen G. Swallow	February 1997	
2104	HMAC: Keyed Hashing for Message Authentication	H. Krawczyk M. Bellare R. Canetti	February 1997	
2103	Mobility Support for Nimrod: Challenges and Solution Approaches	R. Ramanathan	February 1997	
2102	Multicast Support for Nimrod: Requirements and Solution Approaches	R. Ramanathan	February 1997	

2101	IPv4 Address Behaviour Today	B. Carpenter J. Crowcroft Y. Rekhter	February 1997	
2100	The Naming of Hosts	J. Ashworth	Apr il 1997	
2099	Request for Comments Summary RFC Numbers 2000-2099	J. Elliott	March 1997	
2098	Toshiba's Router Architecture Extensions for ATM: Overview	Y. Katsube K. Nagami H. Esaki	February 1997	
2097	The PPP NetBIOS Frames Control Protocol (NBFCP)	G. Pall	January 1997	
2096	IP Forwarding Table MIB	F. Baker	January 1997	Obsoletes RFC 1354
2095	IMAP/POP AUTHorize Extension for Simple Challenge/Response	J. Klensin R. Catoe P. Krumviede	January 1997	
2094	Group Key Management Protocol (GKMP) Architecture	H. Harney C. Muckenhirn	July 1997	
2093	Group Key Management Protocol (GKMP) Specification	H. Harney C. Muckenhirn	July 1997	
2092	Protocol Analysis for Triggered RIP	S. Sherry G. Meyer	January 1997	
2091	Triggered Extensions to RIP to Support Demand Circuits	G. Meyer S. Sherry	January 1997	
2090	TFTP Multicast Option	A. Emberson	February 1997	
2089	V2ToV1 Mapping SNMPv2 onto SNMPv1 Within a Bi-Lingual SNMP agent	B. Wijnen D. Levi	January 1997	
2088	IMAP4 Non-Synchroniziong Literals	J. Myers	January 1997	
2087	IMAP4 QUOTA extension	J. Myers	January 1997	
2086	IMAP4 ACL extension	J. Myers	January 1997	
2085	HMAC-MD5 IP Authentication with Replay Prevention	M. Oehler R. Glenn	February 1997	
2084	Considerations for Web Transaction Security	G. Bossert S. Cooper W. Drummond	January 1997	

app.
f

(continued)

Table AF.1: RFC Index (continued)

RFC	Title	Author(s)	Date	Notes
2083	PNG (Portable Network Graphics) Specification Version 1.0	T. Boutell	January 1997	
2082	RIP-2 MD5 Authentication	F. Baker R. Atkinson	January 1997	
2081	RIPng Protocol Applicability Statement	G. Malkin	January 1997	
2080	RIPng for IPv6	G. Malkin R. Minnear	January 1997	
2079	Definition of X.500 Attribute Types and an Object Class to Hold Uniform Resource Identifiers (URIs)	M. Smith	January 1997	
2078	Generic Security Service Application Program Interface, Version 2	J. Linn	January 1997	Obsoletes RFC 1508
2077	The Model Primary Content Type for Multipurpose Internet Mail Extensions	S. Nelson C. Parks Mitra	January 1997	
2076	Common Internet Message Headers	J. Palme	February 1997	
2075	IP Echo Host Service	C. Partridge	January 1997	
2074	Remote Network Monitoring MIB Protocol Identifiers	A. Bierman R. Iddon	January 1997	
2073	An IPv6 Provider-Based Unicast Address Format	Y. Rekhter P. Lothberg B. Hinden S. Deering J. Postel	January 1997	
2072	Router Renumbering Guide	H. Berkowitz	January 1997	
2071	Network Renumbering Overview: Why Would I Want It and What Is It Anyway?	P. Ferguson H. Berkowitz	January 1997	
2070	Internationalization of the HyperText Markup Language	F. Yergeau G. Nicol G. Adams M. Duerst	January 1997	

2069	An Extension to HTTP: Digest Access Authentication	J. Franks P. Hallam-Baker J. Hostetler	January 1997	
2068	HyperText Transfer Protocol — HTTP/1.1	R. Fielding J. Gettys J. Mogul H. Nielsen T. Berners-Lee	January 1997	
2067	IP over HIPPI	J. Renwick	January 1997	Obsoletes RFC 1374
2066	TELNET CHARSET Option	R. Gellens	January 1997	
2065	Domain Name System Security Extensions	D. Eastlake C. Kaufman	January 1997	Updates RFC 1035; obsoletes RFC 1034
2064	Traffic Flow Measurement: Meter MIB	N. Brownlee	January 1997	
2063	Traffic Flow Measurement: Architecture	N. Brownlee C. Mills G. Ruth	January 1997	
2062	Internet Message Access Protocol — Obsolete Syntax	M. Crispin	December 1996	
2061	IMAP4 Compatibility with IMAP2BIS	M. Crispin	December 1996	
2060	Internet Message Access Protocol — Version 4rev1	M. Crispin	December 1996	Obsoletes RFC 1730
2059	RADIUS Accounting	C. Rigney	January 1997	Obsoleted by RFC 2139
2058	Remote Authentication Dial-In User Service (RADIUS)	S. Willens A. Rubens W. Simpson C. Rigney	January 1997	Obsoleted by RFC 2138
2057	Source-Directed Access Control on the Internet	S. Bradner	November 1996	
2056	Uniform Resource Locators for Z39.50	R. Denenberg J. Kunze D. Lynch	November 1996	
2055	WebNFS Server Specification	B. Callaghan	October 1996	
2054	WebNFS Client Specification	B. Callaghan	October 1996	

(continued)

app. f

Table AF.1: RFC Index (continued)

RFC	Title	Author(s)	Date	Notes
2053	The AM (Armenia) Domain	E. Der-Danieliantz	October 1996	
2052	A DNS RR for Specifying the Location of Services (DNS SRV)	A. Gulbrandsen P. Vixie	October 1996	
2051	Definitions of Managed Objects for APPC	M. Allen B. Clouston Z. Kielczewski W. Kwan R. Moore	October 1996	
2050	Internet Registry IP Allocation Guidelines	K. Hubbard M. Kosters D. Conrad D. Karrenberg J. Postel	November 1996	Obsoletes RFC 1466
2049	Multipurpose Internet Mail Extensions (MIME) Part Five: Conformance Criteria and Examples	N. Freed N. Borenstein	December 1996	Obsoletes RFC 1521
2048	Multipurpose Internet Mail Extensions (MIME) Part Four: Registration Procedures	N. Freed J. Klensin J. Postel	January 1997	Obsoletes RFC 1590
2047	MIME (Multipurpose Internet Mail Extensions) Part Three: Message Header Extensions for Non-ASCII Text	K. Moore	December 1996	Obsoletes RFC 1522
2046	Multipurpose Internet Mail Extensions (MIME) Part Two: Media Types	N. Freed N. Borenstein	December 1996	Obsoletes RFC 1521
2045	Multipurpose Internet Mail Extensions (MIME) Part One: Format of Internet Message Bodies	N. Freed N. Borenstein	December 1996	Obsoletes RFC 1521
2044	UTF-8, A Transformation Format of Unicode and ISO 10646	F. Yergeau	October 1996	

2043	The PPP SNA Control Protocol (SNACP)	A. Fuqua	October 1996	
2042	Registering New BGP Attribute Types	B. Manning	January 1997	
2041	Mobile Network Tracing	B. Noble G. Nguyen M. Satyanarayanan R. Katz	October 1996	
2040	The RC5, RC5-CBC, RC5-CBC-Pad and RC5-CTS Algorithms	R. Baldwin R. Rivest	October 1996	
2039	Applicability of Standards-Track MIBs to Management of World Wide Web Servers	C. Kalbfleisch	November 1996	
2038	RTP Payload Format for MPEG1/MPEG2 Video	D. Hoffman G. Fernando V. Goyal	October 1996	
2037	Entity MIB	K. McCloghrie A. Bierman	October 1996	
2036	Observations on the Use of Components of the Class A Address Space Within the Internet	G. Huston	October 1996	
2035	RTP Payload Format for JPEG-Compressed Video	L. Berc B. Fenner R. Frederick S. McCanne	October 1996	
2034	SMTP Service Extension for Returning Enhanced Error Codes	N. Freed	October 1996	
2033	Local Mail Transfer Protocol	J. Myers	October 1996	
2032	RTP Payload Format for H.261 Video Streams	T. Turletti C. Huitema	October 1996	
2031	IETF-ISOC Relationship	E. Huizer	October 1996	
2030	Simple Network Time Protocol (SNTP) Version 4 for IPv4, IPv6, and OSI	D. Mills	October 1996	Obsoletes RFC 1769
2029	RTP Payload Format of Sun's CellB Video Encoding	M. Speer D. Hoffman	October 1996	

**app.
f**

(continued)

Table AF.1: RFC Index (continued)

RFC	Title	Author(s)	Date	Notes
2028	The Organizations Involved in the IETF Standards Process	R. Hovey S. Bradner	October 1996	
2027	IAB and IESG Selection Confirmation, and Recall Process: Operation of the Nominating and Recall Committees	J. Galvin	October 1996	
2026	The Internet Standards Process — Revision 3	S. Bradner	October 1996	Obsoletes RFC 1602
2025	The Simple Public-Key GSS-API Mechanism (SPKM)	C. Adams	October 1996	
2024	Definitions of Managed Objects for Data-Link Switching Using SNMPv2	D. Chen P. Gayek S. Nix	October 1996	
2023	IP Version 6 over PPP	D. Haskin E. Allen	October 1996	
2022	Support for Multicast over UNI 3.0/3.1 Based ATM Networks	G. Armitage	November 1996	
2021	Remote Network Monitoring Management Information Base Version 2 Using SMIv2	S. Waldbusser	January 1997	
2020	Definitions of Managed Objects for IEEE 802.12 Interfaces	J. Flick	October 1996	
2019	Transmission of IPv6 Packets over FDDI	M. Crawford	October 1996	
2018	TCP Selective Acknowledgment Options	M. Mathis J. Mahdavi S. Floyd A. Romanow	October 1996	
2017	Definition of the URL MIME External-Body Access-Type	N. Freed K. Moore C. Cargille	October 1996	

2016	Uniform Resource Agents (URAs)	L. Daigle P. Deutsch B. Heelan C. Alpaugh M. Maclachlan	October 1996	
2015	MIME Security with Pretty Good Privacy (PGP)	M. Elkins	October 1996	
2014	IRTF Research Group Guidelines and Procedures	A. Weinrib J. Postel	October 1996	
2013	SNMPv2 Management Information Base for the User Datagram Protocol Using SMIv2	K. McCloghrie	November 1996	Obsoletes RFC 1213
2012	SNMPv2 Management Information Base for the Transmission Control Protocol	K. McCloghrie	November 1996	Updates RFC 1213
2011	SNMPv2 Management Information Base for the Internet Protocol Using SMIv2	K. McCloghrie	November 1996	Updates RFC 1213
2010	Operational Criteria for Root Name Servers	B. Manning P. Vixie	October 1996	
2009	GPS-Based Addressing and Routing	T. Imielinski J. Navas	November 1996	
2008	Implications of Various Address Allocation Policies for Internet Routing	Y. Rekhter T. Li	October 1996	
2007	Catalogue of Network Training Materials	J. Foster M. Isaacs M. Prior	October 1996	FYI 29
2006	The Definitions of Managed Objects for IP Mobility Support Using SMIv2	D. Cong M. Hamlen C. Perkins	October 1996	
2005	Applicability Statement for IP Mobility Support	J. Solomon	October 1996	
2004	Minimal Encapsulation within IP	C. Perkins	October 1996	

(continued)

app.
f

Table AF.1: RFC Index (continued)

RFC	Title	Author(s)	Date	Notes
2003	IP Encapsulation within IP	C. Perkins	October 1996	
2002	IP Mobility Support	C. Perkins	October 1996	
2001	TCP Slow Start, Congestion Avoidance, Fast Retransmit, and Fast Recovery Algorithms	W. Stevens	January 1997	
2000	Internet Official Protocol Standards	J. Postel	February 1997	Obsoletes RFC 1920; obsoleted by RFC 2200; STD 1
1999	Request for Comments Summary RFC Numbers 1900-1999	J. Elliott	January 1997	
1998	An Application of the BGP Community Attribute in Multi-Home Routing	E. Chen T. Bates	August 1996	
1997	BGP Communities Attribute	R. Chandra P. Traina T. Li	August 1996	
1996	A Mechanism for Prompt Notification of Zone Changes (DNS NOTIFY)	P. Vixie	August 1996	Updates RFC 1035
1995	Incremental Zone Transfer in DNS	M. Ohta	August 1996	Updates RFC 1035
1994	PPP Challenge Handshake Authentication Protocol (CHAP)	W. Simpson	August 1996	Obsoletes RFC 1334
1993	PPP Gandalf FZA Compression Protocol	D. Carr	August 1996	
1992	The Nimrod Routing Architecture	I. Castineyra J. Chiappa M. Steenstrup	August 1996	
1991	PGP Message Exchange Formats	D. Atkins W. Stallings P. Zimmermann	August 1996	
1990	The PPP Multilink Protocol (MP)	K. Sklower B. Lloyd G. McGregor D. Carr T. Coradetti	August 1996	Obsoletes RFC 1717

1989	PPP Link Quality Monitoring	W. Simpson	August 1996	Obsoletes RFC 1333
1988	Conditional Grant of Rights to Specific Hewlett-Packard Patents in Conjunction with the Internet Engineering Task Force's Internet-Standard Network Management Framework	G. McAnally D. Gilbert J. Flick	August 1996	
1987	Ipsilon's General Switch Management Protocol Specification Version 1.1	P. Newman W. Edwards B. Hinden G. Minshall	August 1996	
1986	Experiments with a Simple File Transfer Protocol for Radio Links Using Enhanced Trivial File Transfer Protocol (ETFTP)	W. Polites W. Wollman D. Woo R. Langan	August 1996	
1985	SMTP Service Extension for Remote Message Queue Starting	J. De Winter	August 1996	
1984	IAB and IESG Statement on Cryptographic Technology and the Internet	A. Weinrib	August 1996	
1983	Internet Users' Glossary	G. Malkin	August 1996	FYI 18; obsoletes RFC 1392
1982	Serial Number Arithmetic	R. Elz R. Bush	September 1996	Updates RFC 1034
1981	Path MTU Discovery for IP Version 6	J. McCann S. Deering J. Mogul	August 1996	
1980	A Proposed Extension to HTML: Client-Side Image Maps	J. Seidman	August 1996	
1979	PPP Deflate Protocol	J. Woods	August 1996	
1978	PPP Predictor Compression Protocol	D. Rand	August 1996	
1977	PPP BSD Compression Protocol	V. Schryver	August 1996	
1976	PPP for Data Compression in Data Circuit-Terminating Equipment (DCE)	K. Schneider S. Venters	August 1996	
1975	PPP Magnalink Variable Resource Compression	D. Schremp J. Black J. Weiss	August 1996	

app.
f

(continued)

Table AF.1: RFC Index (continued)

RFC	Title	Author(s)	Date	Notes
1974	PPP Stac LZS Compression Protocol	R. Friend W. Simpson	August 1996	
1973	PPP in Frame Relay	W. Simpson	June 1996	
1972	A Method for the Transmission of IPv6 Packets over Ethernet Networks	M. Crawford	August 1996	
1971	IPv6 Stateless Address Autoconfiguration	S. Thomson T. Narten	August 1996	
1970	Neighbor Discovery for IP Version 6 (IPv6)	T. Narten E. Nordmark W. Simpson	August 1996	
1969	The PPP DES Encryption Protocol (DESE)	K. Sklower G. Meyer	June 1996	
1968	The PPP Encryption Control Protocol (ECP)	G. Meyer	June 1996	
1967	PPP LZS-DCP Compression Protocol (LZS-DCP)	K. Schneider R. Friend	August 1996	
1966	BGP Route Reflection	T. Bates R. Chandra	June 1996	An alternative to full-mesh IBGP
1965	Autonomous System Confederations for BGP	P. Traina	June 1996	
1964	The Kerberos Version 5 GSS-API Mechanism	J. Linn	June 1996	
1963	PPP Serial Data Transport Protocol (SDTP)	K. Schneider S. Venters	August 1996	
1962	The PPP Compression Control Protocol (CCP)	D. Rand	June 1996	Obsoleted by RFC 2153
1961	GSS-API Authentication Method for SOCKS Version 5	P. McMahon	June 1996	
1960	A String Representation of LDAP Search Filters	T. Howes	June 1996	Obsoletes RFC 1558
1959	An LDAP URL Format	T. Howes M. Smith	June 1996	
1958	Architectural Principles of the Internet	B. Carpenter	June 1996	

1957	Some Observations on Implementations of the Post Office Protocol (POP3)	R. Nelson	June 1996
1956	Registration in the MIL Domain	D. Engebretson R. Plzak	June 1996
1955	New Scheme for Internet Routing and Addressing (ENCAPS) for IPN	B. Hinden	June 1996
1954	Transmission of Flow Labelled IPv4 on ATM Data Links Ipsilon Version 1.0	P. Newman W. Edwards B. Hinden G. Minshall	May 1996
1953	Ipsilon Flow Management Protocol Specification for IPv4 Version 10	W. Edwards F. Liaw T. Lyon G. Minshall	May 1996
1952	GZIP File Format Specification Version 4.3	P. Deutsch	May 1996
1951	DEFLATE Compressed Data Format Specification Version 1.3	P. Deutsch	May 1996
1950	ZLIB Compressed Data Format Specification Version 3.3	P. Deutsch J. Gailly	May 1996
1949	Scalable Multicast Key Distribution	T. Ballardie	May 1996
1948	Defending Against Sequence Number Attacks	S. Bellovin	May 1996
1947	Greek Character Encoding for Electronic Mail Messages	D. Spinellis	May 1996
1946	Native ATM Support for ST2+	S. Jackowski	May 1996
1945	HyperText Transfer Protocol — HTTP/1.0	T. Berners-Lee R. Fielding H. Nielsen	May 1996
1944	Benchmarking Methodology for Network Interconnect Devices	S. Bradner J. McQuaid	May 1996
1943	Building an X.500 Directory Service in the U.S.	B. Jennings	May 1996
1942	HTML Tables	D. Raggett	May 1996

(continued)

app.
f

Table AF.1: RFC Index (continued)

RFC	Title	Author(s)	Date	Notes
1941	Frequently Asked Questions for Schools	J. Sellers J. Robichaux	May 1996	FYI 22; obsoletes RFC 1578
1940	Source Demand Routing: Packet Format and Forwarding Specification (Version 1)	D. Estrin T. Li Y. Rekhter K. Varadhan D. Zappala	May 1996	
1939	Post Office Protocol — Version 3	J. Myers M. Rose	May 1996	Obsoletes RFC 1725; STD 53
1938	A One-Time Password System	N. Haller C. Metz	May 1996	
1937	Local/Remote Forwarding Decision in Switched Data Link Subnetworks	Y. Rekhter D. Kandlur	May 1996	
1936	Implementing the Internet Checksum in Hardware	J. Touch B. Parham	April 1996	
1935	What Is the Internet, Anyway?	J. Quarterman S. Carl-Mitchell	April 1996	
1934	Ascend's Multilink Protocol Plus (MP+)	K. Smith	April 1996	
1933	Transition Mechanisms for IPv6 Hosts and Routers	R. Gilligan E. Nordmark	April 1996	
1932	IP over ATM: A Framework Document	R. Cole D. Shur C. Villamizar	April 1996	
1931	Dynamic RARP Extensions and Administrative Support for Automatic Network Address Allocation	D. Brownell	April 1996	
1930	Guidelines for Creation, Selection and Registration of an Autonomous System (AS)	J. Hawkinson T. Bates	April 1996	
1929	Username/Password Authentication for SOCKS V5	M. Leech	April 1996	

1928	SOCKS Protocol Version 5	M. Leech W. Perry Y. Lee R. Kuris	April 1996	
1927	Suggested Additional MIME Types for Associating Documents	C. Rogers	April 1996	
1926	An Experimental Encapsulation of IP Datagrams on Top of ATM	J. Eriksson	April 1996	
1925	The Twelve Networking Truths	R. Callon	April 1996	
1924	A Compact Representation of IPv6 Addresses	R. Elz	April 1996	
1923	RIPv1 Applicability Statement for Historic Status	J. Halpern S. Bradner	March 1996	
1922	Chinese Character Encoding for Internet Messages	H. Zhu T. Kao W. Chang M. Crispin	March 1996	
1921	TNVIP protocol	J. Dujonc	March 1996	
1920	Internet Official Protocol Standards	J. Postel	March 1996	Obsoletes RFC 1880; obsoleted by RFC 2000; STD 1
1919	Classical Versus Transparent IP Proxies	M. Chatel	March 1996	
1918	Address Allocation for Private Internets	D. Karrenberg E. Lear R. Moskowitz Y. Rekhter G. de Groot	February 1996	Obsoletes RFC 1597; obsoletes RFC1627)
1917	An Appeal to the Internet Community to Return Unused IP Networks (Prefixes) to the IANA	P. Nesser	February 1996	
1916	Enterprise Renumbering: Experience and Information Solicitation	H. Berkowitz P. Ferguson W. Leland P. Nesser	February 1996	

(continued)

Table AF.1: RFC Index (continued)

RFC	Title	Author(s)	Date	Notes
1915	Variance for the PPP Connection Control Protocol and the PPP Encryption Control Protocol	F. Kastenholz	February 1996	
1914	How to Interact with a Whois++ Mesh	P. Faltstrom R. Schoultz C. Weider	February 1996	
1913	Architecture of the Whois++ Index Service	C. Weider J. Fullton S. Spero	February 1996	
1912	Common DNS Operational and Configuration Errors	D. Barr	February 1996	
1911	Voice Profile for Internet Mail	G. Vaudreuil	February 1996	
1910	User-Based Security Model for SNMPv2	G. Waters	February 1996	
1909	An Administrative Infrastructure for SNMPv2	K. McCloghrie	February 1996	
1908	Coexistence Between Version 1 and Version 2 of the Internet-Standard Network Management Framework	J. Case K. McCloghrie M. Rose S. Waldbusser	January 1996	Obsoletes RFC 1452
1907	Management Information Base for Version 2 of the Simple Network Management Protocol (SNMPv2)	J. Case K. McCloghrie M. Rose S. Waldbusser	January 1996	Obsoletes RFC 1450
1906	Transport Mappings for Version 2 of the Simple Network Management Protocol (SNMPv2)	J. Case K. McCloghrie M. Rose S. Waldbusser	January 1996	Obsoletes RFC 1449
1905	Protocol Operations for Version 2 of the Simple Network Management Protocol (SNMPv2)	J. Case K. McCloghrie M. Rose S. Waldbusser	January 1996	Obsoletes RFC 1448

1904	Conformance Statements for Version 2 of the Simple Network Management Protocol (SNMPv2)	J. Case K. McCloghrie M. Rose S. Waldbusser	January 1996	Obsoletes RFC 1444
1903	Textual Conventions for Version 2 of the Simple Network Management Protocol (SNMPv2)	J. Case K. McCloghrie M. Rose S. Waldbusser	January 1996	Obsoletes RFC 1443
1902	Structure of Management Information for Version 2 of the Simple Network Management Protocol (SNMPv2)	J. Case K. McCloghrie M. Rose S. Waldbusser	January 1996	Obsoletes RFC 1442
1901	Introduction to Community-Based SNMPv2	J. Case K. McCloghrie M. Rose S. Waldbusser	January 1996	
1900	Renumbering Needs Work	B. Carpenter Y. Rekhter	February 1996	
1899	Request for Comments Summary RFC Numbers 1800-1899	J. Elliott	January 1997	
1898	CyberCash Credit Card Protocol Version 0.8	D. Eastlake B. Boesch S. Crocker M. Yesil	February 1996	
1897	IPv6 Testing Address Allocation	B. Hinden J. Postel	January 1996	
1896	The Text/Enriched MIME Content-Type	P. Resnick A. Walker	February 1996	Obsoletes RFC 1563
1895	The Application/CALS-1840 Content-Type	E. Levinson	February 1996	
1894	An Extensible Message Format for Delivery Status Notifications	K. Moore G. Vaudreuil	January 1996	
1893	Enhanced Mail System Status Codes	G. Vaudreuil	January 1996	
1892	The Multipart/Report Content Type for the Reporting of Mail System Administrative Messages	G. Vaudreuil	January 1996	

(continued)

**app.
f**

Table AF.1: RFC Index (continued)

RFC	Title	Author(s)	Date	Notes
1891	SMTP Service Extension for Delivery Status Notifications	K. Moore	January 1996	
1890	RTP Profile for Audio and Video Conferences with Minimal Control	H. Schulzrinne	January 1996	
1889	RTP: A Transport Protocol for Real-Time Applications	H. Schulzrinne S. Casner R. Frederick V. Jacobson	January 1996	
1888	OSI NSAPs and IPv6	J. Bound B. Carpenter D. Harrington J. Houldsworth A. Lloyd	August 1996	
1887	An Architecture for IPv6 Unicast Address Allocation	Y. Rekhter T. Li	January 1996	
1886	DNS Extensions to Support IP Version 6	S. Thomson C. Huitema	January 1996	
1885	Internet Control Message Protocol (ICMPv6) for the Internet Protocol Version 6 (IPv6)	A. Conta S. Deering	January 1996	
1884	IP Version 6 Addressing Architecture	B. Hinden S. Deering	January 1996	
1883	Internet Protocol, Version 6 (IPv6) Specification	S. Deering B. Hinden	January 1996	Obsoleted by RFC 2147
1882	The 12 Days of Technology Before Christmas	B. Hancock	December 1995	
1881	IPv6 Address Allocation Management	S. Coya	December 1995	
1880	Internet Official Protocol Standards	J. Postel	November 1995	Obsoletes RFC 1800; obsoleted by RFC 1920; STD 1
1879	Class A Subnet Experiment Results and Recommendations	B. Manning	January 1996	
1878	Variable-Length Subnet Table for IPv4	T. Pummill B. Manning	December 1995	Obsoletes RFC 1860

1877	PPP Internet Protocol Control Protocol Extensions for Name Server Addresses	S. Cobb	December 1995	
1876	A Means for Expressing Location Information in the Domain Name System	C. Davis P. Vixie T. Goodwin I. Dickinson	January 1996	Updates RFC 1034
1875	UNINETT PCA Policy Statements	N. Berge	December 1995	
1874	SGML Media Types	E. Levinson	December 1995	
1873	Message/External-Body Content-ID Access Type	E. Levinson J. Clark	December 1995	
1872	The MIME Multipart/Related Content-Type	E. Levinson	December 1995	Obsoleted by RFC 2112
1871	Addendum to RFC 1602 — Variance Procedure	J. Postel	November 1995	Updates RFC 1602; obsoletes RFC 1603
1870	SMTP Service Extension for Message Size Declaration	J. Klensin N. Freed K. Moore	November 1995	Obsoletes RFC 1653; STD 10
1869	SMTP Service Extensions	J. Klensin N. Freed M. Rose E. Stefferud D. Crocker	November 1995	Obsoletes RFC 1651; STD 10
1868	ARP Extension — UNARP	G. Malkin	November 1995	
1867	Form-based File Upload in HTML	E. Nebel L. Masinter	November 1995	
1866	HyperText Markup Language — 2.0	T. Berners-Lee D. Connolly	November 1995	
1865	EDI Meets the Internet: Frequently Asked Questions About Electronic Data Interchange (EDI) on the Internet	W. Houser J. Griffin C. Hage	January 1996	
1864	The Content-MD5 Header Field	J. Myers M. Rose	October 1995	Obsoletes RFC 1544
1863	A BGP/IDRP Route Server Alternative to a Full Mesh Routing	D. Haskin	October 1995	

(continued)

app. f

Table AF.1: RFC Index (continued)

RFC	Title	Author(s)	Date	Notes
1862	Report of the IAB Workshop on Internet Information Infrastructure October 12-14, 1994	M. McCahill K. Sollins T. Verschuren C. Weider	November 1995	
1861	Simple Network Paging Protocol — Version 3 — Two-Way Enhanced	A. Gwinn	October 1995	Obsoletes RFC 1645
1860	Variable Length Subnet Table For IPv4	T. Pummill B. Manning	October 1995	Obsoleted by RFC 1878
1859	ISO Transport Class 2 Non-Use of Explicit Flow Control over TCP RFC1006 Extension	Y. Pouffary	October 1995	
1858	Security Considerations for IP Fragment Filtering	P. Ziemba D. Reed P. Traina	October 1995	
1857	A Model for Common Operational Statistics	M. Lambert	October 1995	Obsoletes RFC 1404
1856	The Opstat Client-Server Model for Statistics Retrieval	H. Clark	October 1995	
1855	Netiquette Guidelines	S. Hambridge	October 1995	FYI 28
1854	SMTP Service Extension for Command Pipelining	N. Freed C. Cargille	October 1995	
1853	IP in IP Tunneling	W. Simpson	October 1995	
1852	IP Authentication Using Keyed SHA	P. Metzger W. Simpson	October 1995	
1851	The ESP Triple DES-CBC Transform	P. Metzger P. Karn W. Simpson	October 1995	
1850	OSPF Version 2 Management Information Base	F. Baker R. Coltun	November 1995	Obsoletes RFC 1253
1849	Missing			

1848	MIME Object Security Services	S. Crocker N. Freed J. Galvin S. Murphy	October 1995	
1847	Security Multiparts for MIME: Multipart/Signed and Multipart/Encrypted	J. Galvin S. Murphy S. Crocker N. Freed	October 1995	
1846	SMTP 521 Reply Code	A. Durand F. Dupont J. Myers	October 1995	
1845	SMTP Service Extension for Checkpoint/Restart	D. Crocker N. Freed C. Cargille	October 1995	
1844	Multimedia E-Mail (MIME) User Agent Checklist	E. Huizer	August 1995	Obsoletes RFC 1820
1843	HZ — A Data Format for Exchanging Files of Arbitrarily Mixed Chinese and ASCII Characters	F. Lee	August 1995	
1842	ASCII Printable Characters-Based Chinese Character Encoding for Internet Messages	Y. Wei J. Li J. Ding Y. Jiang	August 1995	
1841	PPP Network Control Protocol for LAN Extension	J. Chapman D. Coli A. Harvey B. Jensen K. Rowett	September 1995	
1838	Use of the X.500 Directory to Support Mapping Between X.400 and RFC 822 Addresses	S. Kille	August 1995	
1837	Representing Tables and Subtrees in the X.500 Directory	S. Kille	August 1995	
1836	Representing the O/R Address Hierarchy in the X.500 Directory Information Tree	S. Kille	August 1995	

(continued)

app.
f

Table AF.1: RFC Index (continued)

RFC	Title	Author(s)	Date	Notes
1835	Architecture of the WHOIS++ Service	P. Deutsch R. Schoultz P. Faltstrom C. Weider	August 1995	
1834	Whois and Network Information Lookup Service Whois++	J. Gargano K. Weiss	August 1995	
1833	Binding Protocols for ONC RPC Version 2	R. Srinivasan	August 1995	
1832	XDR: External Data Representation Standard	R. Srinivasan	August 1995	
1831	RPC: Remote Procedure Call Protocol Specification Version 2	R. Srinivasan	August 1995	
1830	SMTP Service Extensions for Transmission of Large and Binary MIME Messages	G. Vaudreuil	August 1995	
1829	The ESP DES-CBC Transform	P. Metzger P. Karn W. Simpson	August 1995	
1828	IP Authentication Using Keyed MD5	P. Metzger W. Simpson	August 1995	
1827	IP Encapsulating Security Payload (ESP)	R. Atkinson	August 1995	
1826	IP Authentication Header	R. Atkinson	August 1995	
1825	Security Architecture for the Internet	R. Atkinson	August 1995	
1824	The Exponential Security System TESS: An Identity-Based Cryptographic Protocol for Authenticated Key-Exchange (E.I.S.S.-Report 1995/4)	H. Danisch	August 1995	
1823	The LDAP Application Program Interface	T. Howes M. Smith	August 1995	
1822	A Grant of Rights to Use a Specific IBM Patent with Photuris	J. Lowe	August 1995	

1821	Integration of Real-Time Services in an IP-ATM Network Architecture	M. Borden E. Crawley B. Davie S. Batsell	August 1995	
1820	Multimedia E-mail (MIME) User Agent Checklist	E. Huizer	August 1995	Obsoleted by RFC 1844
1819	Internet Stream Protocol Version 2 (ST2) Protocol Specification — Version ST2+	L. Delgrossi L. Berger	August 1995	Obsoletes RFC 1190
1818	Best Current Practices	J. Postel T. Li Y. Rekhter	August 1995	
1817	CIDR and Classful Routing	Y. Rekhter	August 1995	
1816	U.S. Government Internet Domain Names	F. Networking Council (FNC)	August 1995	Obsoletes RFC 1811
1815	Character Sets ISO-10646 and ISO-10646-J-1	M. Ohta	August 1995	
1814	Unique Addresses Are Good	E. Gerich	June 1995	
1813	NFS Version 3 Protocol Specification	B. Callaghan B. Pawlowski P. Staubach	June 1995	
1812	Requirements for IP Version 4 Routers	F. Baker	June 1995	Obsoletes RFC 1716
1811	U.S. Government Internet Domain Names	Federal Networking Council (FNC)	June 1995	Obsoleted by RFC 1816
1810	Report on MD5 Performance	J. Touch	June 1995	
1809	Using the Flow Label Field in IPv6	C. Partridge	June 1995	
1808	Relative Uniform Resource Locators	R. Fielding	June 1995	
1807	A Format for Bibliographic Records	R. Lasher D. Cohen	June 1995	
1806	Communicating Presentation Information in Internet Messages: The Content-Disposition Header	R. Troost S. Dorner	June 1995	
1805	Location-Independent Data/Software Integrity Protocol	A. Rubin	June 1995	

(continued)

app. f

Table AF.1: RFC Index (continued)

RFC	Title	Author(s)	Date	Notes
1804	Schema Publishing in X.500 Directory	G. Mansfield P. Rajeev S. Raghavan T. Howes	June 1995	
1803	Recommendations for an X.500 Production Directory Service	R. Wright A. Getchell T. Howes W. Yeong	June 1995	
1802	Introducing Project Long Bud: Internet Pilot Project for the Deployment of X.500 Directory Information in Support of X.400 Routing	H. Alvestrand K. Jordan S. Langlois J. Romaguera	June 1995	
1801	MHS Use of the X.500 Directory to Support MHS Routing	S. Kille	June 1995	
1800	Internet Official Protocol Standards	J. Postel	July 1995	Obsoletes RFC 1780; obsoleted by RFC 1880; STD 1
1799	Request for Comments Summary RFC Numbers 1700-1799	M. Kennedy	January 1997	
1798	Connectionless Lightweight Directory Access Protocol	A. Young	June 1995	
1797	Class A Subnet Experiment	Internet Assigned Numbers Authority	April 1995	
1796	Not All RFCs Are Standards	C. Huitema J. Postel S. Crocker	April 1995	
1795	Data Link Switching: Switch-to-Switch Protocol AIW DLSw RIG: DLSw Closed Pages, DLSw Standard Version 1.0	L. Wells A. Bartky	April 1995	
1794	DNS Support for Load Balancing	T. Brisco	April 1995	

1793	Extending OSPF to Support Demand Circuits	J. Moy	April 1995	
1792	TCP/IPX Connection Mib Specification	T. Sung	April 1995	
1791	TCP and UDP over IPX Networks with Fixed-Path MTU	T. Sung	April 1995	
1790	An Agreement Between the Internet Society and Sun Microsystems, Inc. in the Matter of ONC RPC and XDR Protocols	V. Cerf	April 1995	
1789	INETPhone: Telephone Services and Servers on Internet	C. Yang	April 1995	
1788	ICMP Domain Name Messages	W. Simpson	April 1995	
1787	Routing in a Multi-Provider Internet	Y. Rekhter	April 1995	
1786	Representation of IP Routing Policies in a Routing Registry (Ripe-81++)	T. Bates E. Gerich L. Joncheray J. Jouanigot	March 1995	
1785	TFTP Option Negotiation Analysis	G. Malkin A. Harkin	March 1995	Updates RFC 1350
1784	TFTP Timeout Interval and Transfer Size Options	G. Malkin A. Harkin	March 1995	Updates RFC 1350
1783	TFTP Blocksize Option	G. Malkin A. Harkin	March 1995	Updates RFC 1350
1782	TFTP Option Extension	G. Malkin 1350 A. Harkin	March 1995	Obsoletes RFC
1781	Using the OSI Directory to Achieve User-Friendly Naming	S. Kille	March 1995	Obsoletes RFC 1484
1780	Internet Official Protocol Standards	J. Postel	March 1995	Obsoletes RFC 1720; obsoleted by RFC 1800; STD 1
1779	A String Representation of Distinguished Names	S. Kille	March 1995	Obsoletes RFC 1485
1778	The String Representation of Standard Attribute Syntaxes	T. Howes S. Kille W. Yeong C. Robbins	March 1995	Obsoletes RFC 1488

(continued)

app. f

Table AF.1: RFC Index (continued)

RFC	Title	Author(s)	Date	Notes
1777	Lightweight Directory Access Protocol	W. Yeong T. Howes S. Kille	March 1995	Obsoletes RFC 1487
1776	The Address is the Message	S. Crocker	April 1995	
1775	To Be On the Internet	D. Crocker	March 1995	
1774	BGP-4 Protocol Analysis	P. Traina	March 1995	
1773	Experience with the BGP-4 Protocol	P. Traina	March 1995	Obsoletes RFC 1656
1772	Application of the Border Gateway Protocol in the Internet	Y. Rekhter P. Gross	March 1995	Obsoletes RFC 1655
1771	A Border Gateway Protocol 4 (BGP-4)	Y. Rekhter T. Li	March 1995	Obsoletes RFC 1654
1770	IPv4 Option for Sender-Directed Multi-Destination Delivery	C. Graff	March 1995	
1769	Simple Network Time Protocol (SNTP)	D. Mills	March 1995	Obsoleted by RFC 2030
1768	Host Group Extensions for CLNP Multicasting	D. Marlow	March 1995	
1767	MIME Encapsulation of EDI Objects	D. Crocker	March 1995	
1766	Tags for the Identification of Languages	H. Alvestrand	March 1995	
1765	OSPF Database Overflow	J. Moy	March 1995	
1764	The PPP XNS IDP Control Protocol (XNSCP)	S. Senum	March 1995	
1763	The PPP Banyan Vines Control Protocol (BVCP)	S. Senum	March 1995	
1762	The PPP DECnet Phase IV Control Protocol (DNCP)	S. Senum	March 1995	Obsoletes RFC 1376
1761	Snoop Version 2 Packet Capture File Format	B. Callaghan R. Gilligan	February 1995	
1760	The S/KEY One-Time Password System	N. Haller	February 1995	

1759	Printer MIB	R. Smith F. Wright T. Hasting S. Zilles J. Gyllenskog	March 1995	
1758	NADF Standing Documents: A Brief Overview	N. Directory Forum	February 1995	
1757	Remote Network Monitoring Management Information Base	S. Waldbusser	February 1995	Obsoletes RFC 1271
1756	Remote Write Protocol — Version 1.0	T. Rinne	January 1995	
1755	ATM Signaling Support for IP over ATM	M. Perez A. Malis	February 1995	
1754	IP over ATM Working Group's Recommendations for the ATM Forum's Multiprotocol BOF Version 1	M. Laubach	January 1995	
1753	IPng Technical Requirements of the Nimrod Routing and Addressing Architecture	J. Chiappa	January 1995	
1752	The Recommendation for the IP Next Generation Protocol	S. Bradner A. Mankin	January 1995	
1751	A Convention for Human-Readable 128-Bit Keys	D. McDonald	December 1994	
1750	Randomness Recommendations for Security	D. Eastlake S. Crocker J. Schiller	December 1994	
1749	IEEE 802.5 Station Source Routing MIB Using SMIv2	F. Baker E. Decker K. McCloghrie	December 1994	Obsoletes RFC 1748
1748	IEEE 802.5 MIB Using SMIv2	K. McCloghrie E. Decker	December 1994	Obsoletes RFC 1743; obsoleted by RFC 1749
1747	Definitions of Managed Objects for SNA Data Link Control: SDLC	J. Hilgeman S. Nix A. Bartky W. Clark	January 1995	
1746	Ways to Define User Expectations	B. Manning D. Perkins	December 1994	

(continued)

app.
f

Table AF.1: RFC Index (continued)

RFC	Title	Author(s)	Date	Notes
1745	BGP4/IDRP for IP — OSPF Interaction	K. Varadhan S. Hares Y. Rekhter	December 1994	
1744	Observations on the Management of the Internet Address Space	G. Huston	December 1994	
1743	IEEE 802.5 MIB Using SMIv2	K. McCloghrie E. Decker	December 1994	Obsoletes RFC 1231; obsoleted by RFC 1748
1742	AppleTalk Management Information Base II	S. Waldbusser K. Frisa	January 1995	Obsoletes RFC 1243
1741	MIME Content Type for BinHex Encoded Files	P. Faltstrom D. Crocker E. Fair	December 1994	
1740	MIME Encapsulation of Macintosh Files — MacMIME	P. Faltstrom D. Crocker E. Fair	December 1994	
1739	A Primer On Internet and TCP/IP Tools	G. Kessler S. Shepard	December 1994	Obsoleted by RFC 2151
1738	Uniform Resource Locators (URL)	T. Berners-Lee L. Masinter M. McCahill	December 1994	
1737	Functional Requirements for Uniform Resource Names	K. Sollins L. Masinter	December 1994	
1736	Functional Requirements for Internet Resource Locators	J. Kunze	February 1995	
1735	NBMA Address Resolution Protocol (NARP)	J. Heinanen R. Govindan	December 1994	
1734	POP3 AUTHentication Command	J. Myers	December 1994	
1733	Distributed Electronic Mail Models in IMAP4	M. Crispin	December 1994	
1732	IMAP4 Compatibility with IMAP2 and IMAP2BIS	M. Crispin	December 1994	
1731	IMAP4 Authentication Mechanisms	J. Myers	December 1994	

1730	Internet Message Access Protocol — Version 4	M. Crispin	December 1994	Obsoleted by RFC 2060
1729	Using the Z39.50 Information Retrieval Protocol in the Internet Environment	C. Lynch	December 1994	
1728	Resource Transponders	C. Weider	December 1994	
1727	A Vision of an Integrated Internet Information Service	C. Weider P. Deutsch	December 1994	
1726	Technical Criteria for Choosing IP: The Next Generation (IPng)	F. Kastenholz C. Partridge	December 1994	
1725	Post Office Protocol — Version 3	J. Myers M. Rose	November 1994	Obsoletes RFC 1460; obsoleted by RFC 1939
1724	RIP Version 2 MIB Extension	G. Malkin F. Baker	November 1994	Obsoletes RFC 1389
1723	RIP Version 2 Carrying Additional Information	G. Malkin	November 1994	Obsoletes RFC 1058; obsoletes RFC 1388
1722	RIP Version 2 Protocol Applicability Statement	G. Malkin	November 1994	
1721	RIP Version 2 Protocol Analysis	G. Malkin	November 1994	Obsoletes RFC 1387
1720	Internet Official Protocol Standards	J. Postel	November 1994	Obsoletes RFC 1610; obsoleted by RFC 1780; STD 1
1719	A Direction for IPng	P. Gross	December 1994	
1718	The Tao of IETF — A Guide for New Attendees of the Internet Engineering Task Force	G. Malkin	November 1994	FYI 17; obsoletes RFC 1539
1717	The PPP Multilink Protocol (MP)	K. Sklower B. Lloyd G. McGregor D. Carr	November 1994	Obsoleted by RFC 1990
1716	Towards Requirements for IP Routers	P. Almquist F. Kastenholz	November 1994	Obsoletes RFC 1009; obsoleted by RFC 1812
1715	The H Ratio for Address Assignment Efficiency	C. Huitema	November 1994	

(continued)

app.
f

Table AF.1: RFC Index (continued)

RFC	Title	Author(s)	Date	Notes
1714	Referral Whois Protocol (RWhois)	S. Williamson M. Kosters	December 1994	Obsoleted by RFC 2167
1713	Tools for DNS debugging	A. Romao	November 1994	FYI 27
1712	DNS Encoding of Geographical Location	C. Farrell M. Schulze S. Pleitner D. Baldoni	November 1994	
1711	Classifications in E-Mail Routing	J. Houttuin	October 1994	
1710	Simple Internet Protocol Plus White Paper	B. Hinden	October 1994	
1709	K-12 Internetworking Guidelines	J. Gargano D. Wasley	December 1994	FYI 26
1708	NTP PICS PROFORMA For the Network Time Protocol Version 3	D. Gowin	October 1994	
1707	CATNIP: Common Architecture	M. McGovern R. Ullmann	November 1994	
1706	DNS NSAP Resource Records	B. Manning R. Colella	October 1994	Obsoletes RFC 1637
1705	Six Virtual Inches to the Left: The Problem with IPng	R. Carlson D. Ficarella	October 1994	
1704	On Internet Authentication	N. Haller R. Atkinson	October 1994	
1703	Principles of Operation for the TPC.INT Subdomain: Radio Paging — Technical Procedures	M. Rose	October 1994	
1702	Generic Routing Encapsulation over IPv4 Networks	S. Hanks T. Li D. Farinacci P. Traina	October 1994	
1701	Generic Routing Encapsulation (GRE)	S. Hanks T. Li D. Farinacci P. Traina	October 1994	

1700	Assigned Numbers	Reynolds J. Postel	October 1994	Obsoletes RFC 1340; STD 2
1699	Request for Comments Summary RFC Numbers 1600-1699	J. Elliott	January 1997	
1698	Octet Sequences for Upper-Layer OSI to Support Basic Communications Applications	P. Furniss	October 1994	
1697	Relational Database Management System (RDBMS) Management Information Base (MIB) Using SMIv2	D. Brower R. Purvy A. Daniel M. Sinykin J. Smith	August 1994	
1696	Modem Management Information Base (MIB) Using SMIv2	J. Barnes L. Brown R. Royston S. Waldbusser	August 1994	
1695	Definitions of Managed Objects for ATM Management Version 8.0 Using SMIv2	M. Ahmed K. Tesink	August 1994	
1694	Definitions of Managed Objects for SMDS Interfaces Using SMIv2	T. Brown K. Tesink	August 1994	Obsoletes RFC 1304
1693	An Extension to TCP: Partial Order Service	T. Connolly P. Amer P. Conrad	November 1994	
1692	Transport Multiplexing Protocol (TMux)	P. Cameron D. Crocker D. Cohen J. Postel	August 1994	
1691	The Document Architecture for the Cornell Digital Library	W. Turner	August 1994	
1690	Introducing the Internet Engineering and Planning Group (IEPG)	G. Huston	August 1994	
1689	A Status Report on Networked Information Retrieval: Tools and Groups	J. Foster	August 1994	FYI 25

(continued)

app.
f

Table AF.1: RFC Index (continued)

RFC	Title	Author(s)	Date	Notes
1688	IPng Mobility Considerations	W. Simpson	August 1994	
1687	A Large Corporate User's View of IPng	E. Fleischman	August 1994	
1686	IPng Requirements: A Cable Television Industry Viewpoint	M. Vecchi	August 1994	
1685	Writing X.400 O/R Names	H. Alvestrand	August 1994	
1684	Introduction to White Pages Services Based on X.500	P. Jurg	August 1994	
1683	Multiprotocol Interoperability in IPng	R. Clark M. Ammar K. Calvert	August 1994	
1682	IPng BSD Host Implementation Analysis	J. Bound	August 1994	
1681	On Many Addresses Per Host	S. Bellovin	August 1994	
1680	IPng Support for ATM Services	C. Brazdziunas	August 1994	
1679	HPN Working Group Input to the IPng Requirements Solicitation	D. Green P. Irey D. Marlow K. O'Donoghue	August 1994	
1678	IPng Requirements of Large Corporate Networks	E. Britton J. Tavs	August 1994	
1677	Tactical Radio Frequency Communication Requirements for IPng	B. Adamson	August 1994	
1676	INFN Requirements for an IPng	A. Ghiselli D. Salomoni C. Vistoli	August 1994	
1675	Security Concerns for IPng	S. Bellovin	August 1994	
1674	A Cellular Industry View of IPng	M. Taylor	August 1994	
1673	Electric Power Research Institute Comments on IPng	R. Skelton	August 1994	
1672	Accounting Requirements for IPng	N. Brownlee	August 1994	
1671	IPng White Paper on Transition and Other Considerations	B. Carpenter	August 1994	
1670	Input to IPng Engineering Considerations	D. Heagerty	August 1994	

1669	Market Viability as an IPng Criterion	J. Curran	August 1994	
1668	Unified Routing Requirements for IPng	D. Estrin T. Li Y. Rekhter	August 1994	
1667	Modeling and Simulation Requirements for IPng	S. Symington D. Wood J. Pullen	August 1994	
1666	Definitions of Managed Objects for SNA NAUs Using SMIv2	Z. Kielczewski D. Kostick K. Shih	August 1994	
1665	Definitions of Managed Objects for SNA NAUs Using SMIv2	Z. Kielczewski D. Kostick K. Shih	July 1994	
1664	Using the Internet DNS to Distribute RFC1327 Mail Address Mapping Tables	C. Allocchio A. Bonito B. Cole S. Giordano R. Hagens	August 1994	
1663	PPP Reliable Transmission	D. Rand	July 1994	
1662	PPP in HDLC-Like Framing	W. Simpson	July 1994	Obsoletes RFC 1549; STD 51
1661	The Point-to-Point Protocol (PPP)	W. Simpson	July 1994	Obsoletes RFC 1548; obsoleted by RFC 2153; STD 51
1660	Definitions of Managed Objects for Parallel-Printer-Like Hardware Devices Using SMIv2	B. Stewart	July 1994	Obsoletes RFC 1318
1659	Definitions of Managed Objects for RS-232-Like Hardware Devices Using SMIv2	B. Stewart	July 1994	Obsoletes RFC 1317
1658	Definitions of Managed Objects for Character Stream Devices Using SMIv2	B. Stewart	July 1994	Obsoletes RFC 1316
1657	Definitions of Managed Objects for the Fourth Version of the Border Gateway Protocol (BGP-4) Using SMIv2	S. Willis J. Burruss J. Ito	July 1994	

(continued)

app.
f

Table AF.1: RFC Index (continued)

RFC	Title	Author(s)	Date	Notes
1656	BGP-4 Protocol Document Roadmap and Implementation Experience	P. Traina	July 1994	Obsoleted by RFC 1773
1655	Application of the Border Gateway Protocol in the Internet	Y. Rekhter P. Gross	July 1994	Obsoletes RFC 1268; obsoleted by RFC 1772
1654	A Border Gateway Protocol 4 (BGP-4)	Y. Rekhter T. Li	July 1994	Obsoleted by RFC 1771
1653	SMTP Service Extension for Message Size Declaration	J. Klensin N. Freed K. Moore	July 1994	Obsoletes RFC 1427; obsoleted by RFC 1870
1652	SMTP Service Extension for 8-Bit MIME Transport	J. Klensin N. Freed M. Rose E. Stefferud D. Crocker	July 1994	Obsoletes RFC 1426
1651	SMTP Service Extensions	J. Klensin N. Freed M. Rose E. Stefferud D. Crocker	July 1994	Obsoletes RFC 1425; obsoleted by RFC 1869
1650	Definitions of Managed Objects for the Ethernet-Like Interface Types Using SMIv2	F. Kastenholz	August 1994	
1649	Operational Requirements for X.400 Management Domains in the GO-MHS Community	R. Hagens A. Hansen	July 1994	
1648	Postmaster Convention for X.400 Operations	C. Cargille	July 1994	
1647	TN3270 Enhancements	B. Kelly	July 1994	
1646	TN3270 Extensions for LUname and Printer Selection	C. Graves T. Butts M. Angel	July 1994	
1645	Simple Network Paging Protocol — Version 2	A. Gwinn	July 1994	Obsoletes RFC 1568; obsoleted by RFC 1861

1644	T/TCP — TCP Extensions for Transactions Functional Specification	B. Braden	July 1994	
1643	Definitions of Managed Objects for the Ethernet-like Interface Types	F. Kastenholz	July 1994	Obsoletes RFC 1623; STD 50
1642	UTF-7 — A Mail-Safe Transformation Format of Unicode	D. Goldsmith M. Davis	July 1994	Obsoleted by RFC 2152
1641	Using Unicode with MIME	D. Goldsmith M. Davis	July 1994	
1640	The Process for Organization of Internet Standards Working Group (POISED)	S. Crocker	June 1994	
1639	FTP Operation Over Big Address Records (FOOBAR)	D. Piscitello	June 1994	Obsoletes RFC 1545
1638	PPP Bridging Control Protocol (P)	F. Baker R. Bowen	June 1994	Obsoletes RFC 1220
1637	DNS NSAP Resource Records	B. Manning R. Colella	June 1994	Obsoletes RFC 1348; obsoleted by RFC 1706
1636	Report of IAB Workshop on Security in the Internet Architecture — February 8-10, 1994	C. Huitema B. Braden D. Clark S. Crocker	June 1994	
1635	How to Use Anonymous FTP	P. Deutsch A. Emtage A. Marine	May 1994	FYI 24
1634	Novell IPX over Various WAN Media (IPXWAN)	M. Allen	May 1994	Obsoletes RFC 1551
1633	Integrated Services in the Internet Architecture: An Overview	B. Braden D. Clark S. Shenker	June 1994	
1632	A Revised Catalog of Available X.500 Implementations	A. Getchell S. Sataluri	May 1994	FYI 11; obsoletes RFC 1292; obsoleted by RFC 2116
1631	The IP Network Address Translator (Nat)	P. Tsuchiya K. Egevang	May 1994	

(continued)

app. f

Table AF.1: RFC Index (continued)

RFC	Title	Author(s)	Date	Notes
1630	Universal Resource Identifiers in WWW: A Unifying Syntax for the Expression of Names and Addresses of Objects on the Network as Used in the World-Wide Web	T. Berners-Lee	June 1994	
1629	Guidelines for OSI NSAP Allocation in the Internet	R. Colella R. Callon E. Gardner Y. Rekhter	May 1994	Obsoletes RFC 1237
1628	UPS Management Information Base	J. Case	May 1994	
1627	Network 10 Considered Harmful (Some Practices Shouldn't be Codified)	E. Lear E. Fair D. Crocker T. Kessler	July 1994	Obsoleted by RFC 1918
1626	Default IP MTU for Use over ATM AAL5	R. Atkinson	May 1994	
1625	WAIS over Z39.50-1988	H. Morris F. Schiettecatte	June 1994	
1624	Computation of the Internet Checksum via Incremental Update	A. Rijsinghani	May 1994	Updates RFC 1071
1623	Definitions of Managed Objects for the Ethernet-Like Interface Types	F. Kastenholz	May 1994	Obsoletes RFC 1398; obsoleted by RFC 1643; STD 50
1622	Pip Header Processing	P. Tsuchiya	May 1994	
1621	Pip Near-Term Architecture	P. Tsuchiya	May 1994	
1620	Internet Architecture Extensions for Shared Media	B. Braden J. Postel Y. Rekhter	May 1994	
1619	PPP over SONET/SDH	W. Simpson	May 1994	
1618	PPP over ISDN	W. Simpson	May 1994	
1617	Naming and Structuring Guidelines for X.500 Directory Pilots	P. Barker S. Kille T. Lenggenhager	May 1994	Obsoletes RFC 1384

1616	X.400(1988) for the Academic and Research Community in Europe	E. Huizer J. Romaguera	May 1994	
1615	Migrating from X.400(84) to X.400(88)	J. Houttuin J. Craigie	May 1994	
1614	Network Access to Multimedia Information	C. Adie	May 1994	
1613	Cisco Systems X.25 over TCP (XOT)	J. Forster G. Satz G. Glick R. Day	May 1994	
1612	DNS Resolver MIB Extensions	R. Austein J. Saperia	May 1994	
1611	DNS Server MIB Extensions	R. Austein J. Saperia	May 1994	
1610	Internet Official Protocol Standards	J. Postel	July 1994	Obsoletes RFC 1600; obsoleted by RFC 1720; STD 1
1609	Charting Networks in the X.500 Directory	G. Mansfield T. Johannsen M. Knopper	March 1994	
1608	Representing IP Information in the X.500 Directory	T. Johannsen G. Mansfield M. Kosters S. Sataluri	March 1994	
1607	A View from the 21st Century	V. Cerf	April 1994	
1606	A Historical Perspective on the Usage of IP Version 9	J. Onions	April 1994	
1605	SONET to Sonnet Translation	W. Shakespeare	April 1994	
1604	Definitions of Managed Objects for Frame Relay Service	T. Brown	March 1994	Obsoletes RFC 1596
1603	IETF Working Group Guidelines and Procedures	E. Huizer D. Crocker	March 1994	Obsoleted by RFC 1871
1602	The Internet Standards Process — Revision 2	A. Weinrib C. Huitema P. Gross	March 1994	Obsoletes RFC 1310; obsoleted by RFC 2026; updated by RFC 1871

(continued)

app.
f

Table AF.1: RFC Index (continued)

RFC	Title	Author(s)	Date	Notes
1601	Charter of the Internet Architecture Board (IAB)	C. Huitema	March 1994	Obsoletes RFC 1358
1600	Internet Official Protocol Standards	J. Postel	March 1994	Obsoletes RFC 1540; obsoleted by RFC 1610; STD 1
1599	Request for Comments Summary RFC Numbers 1500 — 1599	M. Kennedy	January 1997	
1598	PPP in X.25	W. Simpson	March 1994	
1597	Address Allocation for Private Internets	Y. Rekhter R. Moskowitz D. Karrenberg G. de Groot	March 1994	Obsoleted by RFC 1918
1596	Definitions of Managed Objects for Frame Relay Service	T. Brown	March 1994	Obsoleted by RFC 1604
1595	Definitions of Managed Objects for the SONET/SDH Interface Type	T. Brown K. Tesink	March 1994	
1594	FYI on Questions and Answers: Answers to Commonly Asked "New Internet User" Questions	A. Marine J. Reynolds G. Malkin	March 1994	FYI 4; obsoletes RFC 1325
1593	SNA APPN Node MIB	W. McKenzie J. Cheng	March 1994	
1592	Simple-Network-Management-Protocol Distributed Protocol Interface Version 2.0	B. Wijnen G. Carpenter K. Curran A. Sehgal G. Waters	March 1994	Obsoletes RFC 1228
1591	Domain Name System Structure and Delegation	J. Postel	March 1994	
1590	Media Type Registration Procedure	J. Postel	March 1994	Updates RFC 1521; obsoleted by RFC 2048
1589	A Kernel Model for Precision Timekeeping	D. Mills	March 1994	

1588	White Pages Meeting Report	J. Postel C. Anderson	February 1994	
1587	The OSPF NSSA Option	R. Coltun V. Fuller	March 1994	
1586	Guidelines for Running OSPF over Frame Relay Networks	O. deSouza M. Rodrigues	March 1994	
1585	MOSPF: Analysis and Experience	J. Moy	March 1994	
1584	Multicast Extensions to OSPF	J. Moy	March 1994	
1583	OSPF Version 2	J. Moy	March 1994	Obsoletes RFC 1247; obsoleted by RFC 2178
1582	Extensions to RIP to Support Demand Circuits	G. Meyer	February 1994	
1581	Protocol Analysis for Extensions to RIP to Support Demand Circuits	G. Meyer	February 1994	
1580	Guide to Network Resource Tools	E. EARN Staff	March 1994	FYI 23
1579	Firewall-Friendly FTP	S. Bellovin	February 1994	
1578	FYI on Questions and Answers: Answers to Commonly Asked 'Primary and Secondary School Internet User' Questions	J. Sellers	February 1994	FYI 22; obsoleted by RFC 1941
1577	Classical IP and ARP over ATM	M. Laubach	January 1994	
1576	TN3270 Current Practices	J. Penner	January 1994	
1575	An Echo Function for CLNP (ISO 8473)	S. Hares C. Wittbrodt	February 1994	Obsoletes RFC 1139
1574	Essential Tools for the OSI Internet	S. Hares C. Wittbrodt	February 1994	Obsoletes RFC 1139
1573	Evolution of the Interfaces Group of MIB-II	K. McCloghrie F. Kastenholz	January 1994	Obsoletes RFC 1229
1572	Telnet Environment Option	S. Alexander	January 1994	
1571	Telnet Environment Option Interoperability Issues	D. Borman	January 1994	Obsoletes RFC 1408
1570	PPP LCP Extensions	W. Simpson	January 1994	Updates RFC 1548

(continued)

Table AF.1: RFC Index (continued)

RFC	Title	Author(s)	Date	Notes
1569	Principles of Operation for the TPC.INT Subdomain: Radio Paging — Technical Procedures	M. Rose	January 1994	
1568	Simple Network Paging Protocol — Version 1(b)	A. Gwinn	January 1994	Obsoleted by RFC 1645
1567	X.500 Directory Monitoring MIB	G. Mansfield S. Kille	January 1994	
1566	Mail Monitoring MIB	N. Freed S. Kille	January 1994	
1565	Network Services Monitoring MIB	N. Freed S. Kille	January 1994	
1564	DSA Metrics (OSI-DS 34 (v3))	P. Barker R. Hedberg	January 1994	
1563	The Text/Enriched MIME Content-Type	N. Borenstein	January 1994	Obsoletes RFC 1523; obsoleted by RFC 1896
1562	Naming Guidelines for the AARNet X.500 Directory Service	G. Michaelson M. Prior	December 1993	
1561	Use of ISO CLNP in TUBA Environments	D. Piscitello	December 1993	
1560	The MultiProtocol Internet	B. Leiner Y. Rekhter	December 1993	
1559	DECnet Phase IV MIB Extensions	J. Saperia	December 1993	Obsoletes RFC 1289
1558	A String Representation of LDAP Search Filters	T. Howes	December 1993	Obsoleted by RFC 1960
1557	Korean Character Encoding for Internet Messages	K. Chon H. Je Park U. Choi	December 1993	
1556	Handling of Bi-Directional Texts in MIME	H. Nussbacher	December 1993	
1555	Hebrew Character Encoding for Internet Messages	H. Nussbacher Y. Bourvine	December 1993	

1554	ISO-2022-JP-2: Multilingual Extension of ISO-2022-JP	M. Ohta K. Handa	December 1993	
1553	Compressing IPX Headers over WAN Media (CIPX)	S. Mathur M. Lewis	December 1993	
1552	The PPP Internetwork Packet Exchange Control Protocol (IPXCP)	W. Simpson	December 1993	
1551	Novell IPX over Various WAN Media (IPXWAN)	M. Allen	December 1993	Obsoletes RFC 1362; obsoleted by RFC 1634
1550	IP: Next Generation (IPng) White Paper Solicitation	S. Bradner A. Mankin	December 1993	
1549	PPP in HDLC Framing	W. Simpson	December 1993	Obsoleted by RFC 1662
1548	The Point-to-Point Protocol (PPP)	W. Simpson	December 1993	Obsoletes RFC 1331; obsoleted by RFC 1661; updated by RFC 1570
1547	Requirements for an Internet Standard Point-to-Point Protocol	D. Perkins	December 1993	
1546	Host Anycasting Service	C. Partridge T. Mendez W. Milliken	November 1993	
1545	FTP Operation Over Big Address Records (FOOBAR)	D. Piscitello	November 1993	Obsoleted by RFC 1639
1544	The Content-MD5 Header Field	M. Rose	November 1993	Obsoleted by RFC 1864
1543	Instructions to RFC Authors	J. Postel	October 1993	Obsoletes RFC 1111
1542	Clarifications and Extensions for the Bootstrap Protocol	W. Wimer	October 1993	Obsoletes RFC 1532
1541	Dynamic Host Configuration Protocol	R. Droms	October 1993	Obsoletes RFC 1531; obsoleted by RFC 2131
1540	Internet Official Protocol Standards	J. Postel	October 1993	Obsoletes RFC 1500; obsoleted by RFC 1600; STD 1
1539	The Tao of IETF — A Guide for New Attendees of the Internet Engineering Task Force	G. Malkin	October 1993	FYI 17; obsoletes RFC 1391; obsoleted by RFC 1718
1538	Advanced SNA/IP: A Simple SNA Transport Protocol	W. Behl B. Sterling W. Teskey	October 1993	

(continued)

app.
f

Table AF.1: RFC Index (continued)

RFC	Title	Author(s)	Date	Notes
1537	Common DNS Data File Configuration Error	P. Beertema	October 1993	
1536	Common DNS Implementation Errors and Suggested Fixes	A. Kumar J. Postel C. Neuman P. Danzig S. Miller	October 1993	
1535	A Security Problem and Proposed Correction with Widely Deployed DNS Software	E. Gavron	October 1993	
1534	Interoperation Between DHCP and BOOTP	R. Droms	October 1993	
1533	DHCP Options and BOOTP Vendor Extensions	S. Alexander R. Droms	October 1993	Obsoletes RFC 1497; obsoleted by RFC 2131; obsoleted by RFC 2132
1532	Clarifications and Extensions for the Bootstrap Protocol	W. Wimer	October 1993	Obsoletes RFC 951; obsoleted by RFC 1542
1531	Dynamic Host Configuration Protocol	R. Droms	October 1993	Obsoleted by RFC 1541
1530	Principles of Operation for the TPC.INT Subdomain: General Principles and Policy	C. Malamud M. Rose	October 1993	
1529	Principles of Operation for the TPC.INT Subdomain: Remote Printing — Administrative Policies	C. Malamud M. Rose	October 1993	Obsoletes RFC 1486
1528	Principles of Operation for the TPC.INT Subdomain: Remote Printing — Technical Procedures	C. Malamud M. Rose	October 1993	Obsoletes RFC 1486
1527	What Should We Plan, Given the Dilemma of the Network?	G. Cook	September 1993	
1526	Assignment of System Identifiers for TUBA/CLNP Hosts	D. Piscitello	September 1993	

1525	Definitions of Managed Objects for Source Routing Bridges	E. Decker K. McCloghrie P. Langille A. Rijsinghani	September 1993	Obsoletes RFC 1286
1524	A User Agent Configuration Mechanism for Multimedia Mail Format Information	N. Borenstein	September 1993	
1523	The Text/Enriched MIME Content-Type	N. Borenstein	September 1993	Obsoleted by RFC 1563
1522	MIME (Multipurpose Internet Mail Extensions) Part Two: Message Header Extensions for Non-ASCII Text	K. Moore	September 1993	Obsoletes RFC 1342; obsoleted by RFC 2047
1521	MIME (Multipurpose Internet Mail Extensions) Part One: Mechanisms for Specifying and Describing the Format of Internet Message Bodies	N. Borenstein N. Freed	September 1993	Obsoletes RFC 1341; obsoleted by RFC 2045; obsoleted by RFC 2046; obsoleted by RFC 2049; updated by RFC 1590
1520	Exchanging Routing Information Across Provider Boundaries in the CIDR Environment	Y. Rekhter C. Topolcic	September 1993	
1519	Classless Inter-Domain Routing (CIDR): An Address Assignment and Aggregation Strategy	V. Fuller T. Li J. Yu K. Varadhan	September 1993	Obsoletes RFC 1338
1518	An Architecture for IP Address Allocation with CIDR	Y. Rekhter T. Li	September 1993	
1517	Applicability Statement for the Implementation of Classless Inter-Domain Routing (CIDR)	B. Hinden	September 1993	
1516	Definitions of Managed Objects for IEEE 802.3 Repeater Devices	D. McMaster K. McCloghrie	September 1993	Obsoletes RFC 1368; obsoleted by RFC 2108
1515	Definitions of Managed Objects for IEEE 802.3 Medium Attachment Units (MAUs)	D. McMaster K. McCloghrie S. Roberts	September 1993	
1514	Host Resources MIB	P. Grillo S. Waldbusser	September 1993	

(continued)

app.
f

Table AF.1: RFC Index (continued)

RFC	Title	Author(s)	Date	Notes
1513	Token Ring Extensions to the Remote Network Monitoring MIB	S. Waldbusser	September 1993	Updates RFC 1271
1512	FDDI Management Information Base	J. Case A. Rijsinghani	September 1993	Obsoletes RFC 1285
1511	Common Authentication Technology Overview	J. Linn	September 1993	
1510	The Kerberos Network Authentication Service (V5)	C. Neuman	September 1993	
1509	Generic Security Service API: C-Bindings	J. Wray	September 1993	
1508	Generic Security Service Application Program Interface	J. Linn	September 1993	Obsoleted by RFC 2078
1507	DASS — Distributed Authentication Security Service	C. Kaufman	September 1993	
1506	A Tutorial on Gatewaying Between X.400 and Internet Mail	J. Houttuin	September 1993	
1505	Encoding Header Field for Internet Messages	A. Costanzo D. Robinson R. Ullmann	August 1993	Obsoletes RFC 1154
1504	Appletalk Update-Based Routing Protocol: Enhanced Appletalk Routing	A. Oppenheimer	August 1993	
1503	Algorithms for Automating Administration in SNMPv2 Managers	K. McCloghrie M. Rose	August 1993	
1502	X.400 Use of Extended Character Sets	H. Alvestrand	August 1993	
1501	OS/2 User Group	E. Brunsen	August 1993	
1500	Internet Official Protocol Standards	J. Postel	August 1993	Obsoletes RFC 1410; obsoleted by RFC 1540; STD 1
1499	Request for Comments Summary RFC Numbers 1400-1499	J. Elliott	January 1997	
1498	On the Naming and Binding of Network Destinations	J. Saltzer	August 1993	

1497	BOOTP Vendor Information Extensions	J. Reynolds	August 1993	Updates RFC 951; obsoletes RFC 1395; obsoleted by RFC 1533
1496	Rules for Downgrading Messages from X.400/88 to X.400/84 when MIME Content-Types Are Present in the Messages	H. Alvestrand K. Jordan J. Romaguera	August 1993	Obsoletes RFC 1328
1495	Mapping Between X.400 and RFC-822 Message Bodies	H. Alvestrand S. Kille R. Miles M. Rose S. Thompson	August 1993	Obsoletes RFC 1327
1494	Equivalences Between 1988 X.400 and RFC-822 Message Bodies	H. Alvestrand S. Thompson	August 1993	
1493	Definitions of Managed Objects for Bridges	E. Decker P. Langille, A. Rijsinghani K. McCloghrie	July 1993	Obsoletes RFC 1286
1492	An Access Control Protocol Sometimes Called TACACS	C. Finseth	July 1993	
1491	A Survey of Advanced Usages of X.500	C. Weider R. Wright	July 1993	FYI 21
1490	Multiprotocol Interconnect over Frame Relay	T. Bradley C. Brown A. Malis	July 1993	Obsoletes RFC 1294
1489	Registration of a Cyrillic Character Set	A. Chernov	July 1993	
1488	The X.500 String Representation of Standard Attribute Syntaxes	T. Howes S. Kille W. Yeong C. Robbins	July 1993	Obsoleted by RFC 1778
1487	X.500 Lightweight Directory Access Protocol	W. Yeong T. Howes S. Kille	July 1993	Obsoleted by RFC 1777

(continued)

app.
f

Table AF.1: RFC Index (continued)

RFC	Title	Author(s)	Date	Notes
1486	An Experiment in Remote Printing	M. Rose C. Malamud	July 1993	Obsoleted by RFC 1528; obsoleted by RFC 1529
1485	A String Representation of Distinguished Names (OSI-DS 23 (v5))	S. Kille	July 1993	Obsoleted by RFC 1779
1484	Using the OSI Directory to Achieve User-Friendly Naming (OSI-DS 24 (v1.2))	S. Kille	July 1993	Obsoleted by RFC 1781
1483	Multiprotocol Encapsulation over ATM Adaptation Layer 5	J. Heinanen	July 1993	
1482	Aggregation Support in the NSFNET Policy Routing Database	M. Knopper S. Richardson	July 1993	
1481	IAB Recommendation for an Intermediate Strategy to Address the Issue of Scaling	C. Huitema	July 1993	
1480	The U.S. Domain	A. Cooper J. Postel	June 1993	Obsoletes RFC 1386
1479	Inter-Domain Policy Routing Protocol Specification: Version 1	M. Steenstrup	July 1993	
1478	An Architecture for Inter-Domain Policy Routing	M. Lepp M. Steenstrup	July 1993	
1477	IDPR as a Proposed Standard	M. Steenstrup	July 1993	
1476	RAP: Internet Route Access Protocol	R. Ullmann	June 1993	
1475	TP/IX: The Next Internet	R. Ullmann	June 1993	
1474	The Definitions of Managed Objects for the Bridge Network Control Protocol of the Point-to-Point Protocol	F. Kastenholz	June 1993	
1473	The Definitions of Managed Objects for the IP Network Control Protocol of the Point-to-Point Protocol	F. Kastenholz	June 1993	
1472	The Definitions of Managed Objects for the Security Protocols of the Point-to-Point Protocol	F. Kastenholz	June 1993	

1471	The Definitions of Managed Objects for the Link-Control Protocol of the Point-to-Point Protocol	F. Kastenholz	June 1993	
1470	FYI on a Network Management Tool Catalog: Tools for Monitoring and Debugging TCP/IP Internets and Interconnected Devices	R. Enger J. Reynolds	June 1993	FYI 2; obsoletes RFC 1147
1469	IP Multicast over Token-Ring Local-Area Networks	T. Pusateri	June 1993	
1468	Japanese Character Encoding for Internet Messages	J. Murai M. Crispin E. van der Poel	June 1993	
1467	Status of CIDR Deployment in the Internet	C. Topolcic	August 1993	Obsoletes RFC 1367
1466	Guidelines for Management of IP Address Space	E. Gerich	May 1993	Obsoletes RFC 1366; obsoleted by RFC 2050
1465	Routing Coordination for X.400 MHS Services Within a Multi-Protocol/Multinetwork Environment Table Format V3 for Static Routing	U. Eppenberger	May 1993	
1464	Using the Domain-Name System to Store Arbitrary String Attributes	R. Rosenbaum	May 1993	
1463	FYI on Introducing the Internet — A Short Bibliography of Introductory Internetworking Readings for the Network Novice	E. Hoffman L. Jackson	May 1993	FYI 19
1462	FYI on 'What Is the Internet?'	E. Krol E. Hoffman	May 1993	FYI 20
1461	SNMP MIB Extension for MultiProtocol Interconnect over X.25	D. Throop	May 1993	
1460	Post Office Protocol — Version 3	M. Rose	June 1993	Obsoletes RFC 1225; obsoleted by RFC 1725
1459	Internet Relay Chat Protocol	D. Reed	May 1993	
1458	Requirements for Multicast Protocols	R. Braudes	May 1993	

(continued)

app.
f

Table AF.1: RFC Index (continued)

RFC	Title	Author(s)	Date	Notes
1457	Security Label Framework for the Internet	R. Housley	May 1993	
1456	Conventions for Encoding the Vietnamese Language VISCII: Vietnamese Standard Code for Information Interchange VIQR: Vietnamese Quoted-Readable Specification	C. Nguyen	May 1993	
1455	Physical Link Security Type of Service	D. Eastlake	May 1993	
1454	Comparison of Proposals for Next Version of IP	T. Dixon	May 1993	
1453	A Comment on Packet Video Remote Conferencing and the Transport/Network Layers	W. Chimiak	April 1993	
1452	Coexistence Between Version 1 and Version 2 of the Internet-standard Network Management Framework	J. Case K. McCloghrie M. Rose S. Waldbusser	May 1993	Obsoleted by RFC 1908
1451	Manager-to-Manager Management Information Base	J. Case K. McCloghrie M. Rose S. Waldbusser	May 1993	
1450	Management Information Base for Version 2 of the Simple Network Management Protocol (SNMPv2)	J. Case K. McCloghrie M. Rose S. Waldbusser	May 1993	Obsoleted by RFC 1907
1449	Transport Mappings for Version 2 of the Simple Network Management Protocol (SNMPv2)	J. Case K. McCloghrie M. Rose S. Waldbusser	May 1993	Obsoleted by RFC 1906
1448	Protocol Operations for Version 2 of the Simple Network Management Protocol (SNMPv2)	J. Case K. McCloghrie M. Rose S. Waldbusser	May 1993	Obsoleted by RFC 1905
1447	Party MIB for Version 2 of the Simple Network Management Protocol (SNMPv2)	K. McCloghrie J. Galvin	May 1993	
1446	Security Protocols for Version 2 of the Simple Network Management Protocol (SNMPv2)	J. Galvin K. McCloghrie	May 1993	

1445	Administrative Model for Version 2 of the Simple Network Management Protocol (SNMPv2)	J. Davin K. McCloghrie	May 1993	
1444	Conformance Statements for Version 2 of the Simple Network Management Protocol (SNMPv2)	J. Case K. McCloghrie M. Rose S. Waldbusser	May 1993	Obsoleted by RFC 1904
1443	Textual Conventions for Version 2 of the Simple Network Management Protocol (SNMPv2)	J. Case K. McCloghrie M. Rose S. Waldbusser	May 1993	Obsoleted by RFC 1903
1442	Structure of Management Information for Version 2 of the Simple Network Management Protocol (SNMPv2)	J. Case K. McCloghrie M. Rose S. Waldbusser	May 1993	Obsoleted by RFC 1902
1441	Introduction to Version 2 of the Internet-Standard Network Management Framework	J. Case K. McCloghrie M. Rose S. Waldbusser	May 1993	
1440	SIFT/UFT: Sender-Initiated/Unsolicited File Transfer	R. Troth	July 1993	
1439	The Uniqueness of Unique Identifiers	C. Finseth	March 1993	
1438	Internet Engineering Task Force Statements Of Boredom (SOBs)	A. Chapin C. Huitema	March 1993	
1437	The Extension of MIME Content-Types to a New Medium	N. Borenstein M. Linimon	April 1993	
1436	The Internet Gopher Protocol (A Distributed Document Search and Retrieval Protocol)	F. Anklesaria M. McCahill	March 1993	
1435	IESG Advice from Experience with Path MTU Discovery	S. Knowles	March 1993	
1434	Data Link Switching: Switch-to-Switch Protocol	R. Dixon D. Kushi	March 1993	
1433	Directed ARP	J. Garrett J. Hagan J. Wong	March 1993	
1432	Recent Internet Books	J. Quarterman	March 1993	

(continued)

app. f

Table AF.1: RFC Index (continued)

RFC	Title	Author(s)	Date	Notes
1431	DUA Metrics	P. Barker	February 1993	
1430	A Strategic Plan for Deploying an Internet X.500 Directory Service	S. Kille E. Huizer V. Cerf R. Hobby S. Kent	February 1993	
1429	Listserv Distribute Protocol	E. Thomas	February 1993	
1428	Transition of Internet Mail from Just-Send-8 to 8-Bit-SMTP/MIME	G. Vaudreuil	February 1993	
1427	SMTP Service Extension for Message Size Declaration	K. Moore N. Freed J. Klensin	February 1993	Obsoleted by RFC 1653
1426	SMTP Service Extension for 8-Bit-MIME Transport	J. Klensin N. Freed M. Rose E. Stefferud D. Crocker	February 1993	Obsoleted by RFC 1652
1425	SMTP Service Extensions	J. Klensin N. Freed M. Rose E. Stefferud D. Crocker	February 1993	Obsoleted by RFC 1651
1424	Privacy Enhancement for Internet Electronic Mail: Part IV: Key Certification and Related Services	B. Kaliski	February 1993	
1423	Privacy Enhancement for Internet Electronic Mail: Part III: Algorithms Modes, and Identifiers	D. Balenson	February 1993	Obsoletes RFC 1115
1422	Privacy Enhancement for Internet Electronic Mail: Part II: Certificate-Based Key Management	S. Kent	February 1993	Obsoletes RFC 1114
1421	Privacy Enhancement for Internet Electronic Mail: Part I: Message Encryption and Authentication Procedures	J. Linn	February 1993	Obsoletes RFC 1113
1420	SNMP over IPX	S. Bostock	March 1993	Obsoletes RFC 1298

1419	SNMP over AppleTalk	G. Minshall M. Ritter	March 1993	
1418	SNMP over OSI	M. Rose	March 1993	Obsoletes RFC 1283
1417	NADF Standing Documents: A Brief Overview	T. Myer	February 1993	Obsoletes RFC 1295
1416	Telnet Authentication Option	D. Borman	February 1993	Obsoletes RFC 1409
1415	FTP-FTAM Gateway Specification	J. Mindel R. Slaski	January 1993	
1414	Ident MIB	M. St. Johns M. Rose	February 1993	
1413	Identification Protocol	M. St. Johns	February 1993	Obsoletes RFC 931
1412	Telnet Authentication: SPX	K. Alagappan	January 1993	
1411	Telnet Authentication: Kerberos Version 4	D. Borman	January 1993	
1410	IAB Official Protocol Standards	J. Postel A. Chapin	March 1993	Obsoletes RFC 1360; obsoleted by RFC 1500; STD 1
1409	Telnet Authentication Option	D. Borman	January 1993	Obsoleted by RFC 1416
1408	Telnet Environment Option	D. Borman	January 1993	Obsoleted by RFC 1571
1407	Definitions of Managed Objects for the DS3/E3 Interface Type	T. Brown K. Tesink	January 1993	Obsoletes RFC 1233
1406	Definitions of Managed Objects for the DS1 and E1 Interface Types	F. Baker J. Watt	January 1993	Obsoletes RFC 1232
1405	Mapping Between X.400(1984/ 1988) and Mail-11 (DECnet mail)	C. Allocchio	January 1993	
1404	A Model for Common Operational Statistics	B. Stockman	January 1993	Obsoleted by RFC 1857
1403	BGP OSPF Interaction	K. Varadhan	January 1993	Obsoletes RFC 1364
1402	There's Gold in Them Thar Networks! Searching for Treasure in All the Wrong Places	J. Martin	January 1993	FYI 10; obsoletes RFC 1290
1401	Correspondence Between the IAB and DISA on the Use of DNS Throughout the Internet	A. Weinrib A. Chapin	January 1993	

(continued)

app.
f

Table AF.1: RFC Index (continued)

RFC	Title	Author(s)	Date	Notes
1400	Transition and Modernization of the Internet Registration Service	S. Williamson	March 1993	
1399	Request for Comments Summary RFC Numbers 1300-1399	J. Elliott	January 1997	
1398	Definitions of Managed Objects for the Ethernet-Like Interface Types	F. Kastenholz	January 1993	Obsoletes RFC 1284; obsoleted by RFC 1623
1397	Default Route Advertisement in BGP2 and BGP3 Versions of the Border Gateway Protocol	D. Haskin	January 1993	
1396	The Process for Organization of Internet Standards Working Group (POISED)	S. Crocker	January 1993	
1395	BOOTP Vendor Information Extensions	J. Reynolds	January 1993	Updates RFC 951; obsoletes RFC 1084; obsoleted by RFC 1497
1394	Relationship of Telex Answerback Codes to Internet Domains	P. Robinson	January 1993	
1393	Traceroute Using an IP Option	G. Malkin	January 1993	
1392	Internet Users' Glossary	G. Malkin T. Parker	January 1993	FYI 18; obsoleted by RFC 1983
1391	The Tao of IETF: A Guide for New Attendees of the Internet Engineering Task Force	G. Malkin	January 1993	FYI 17; obsoleted by RFC 1539
1390	Transmission of IP and ARP over FDDI Networks	D. Katz	January 1993	Obsoletes RFC 1188; STD 36
1389	RIP Version 2 MIB Extension	G. Malkin F. Baker	January 1993	Obsoleted by RFC 1724
1388	RIP Version 2 Carrying Additional Information	G. Malkin	January 1993	Updates RFC 1058; obsoleted by RFC 1723
1387	RIP Version 2 Protocol Analysis	G. Malkin	January 1993	Obsoleted by RFC 1721

1386	The U.S. Domain	A. Cooper J. Postel	December 1992	Obsoleted by RFC 1480
1385	EIP: The Extended Internet Protocol A Framework for Maintaining Backward Compatibility	Z. Wang	November 1992	
1384	Naming Guidelines for Directory Pilots	P. Barker S. Kille	February 1993	Obsoleted by RFC 1617
1383	An Experiment in DNS-Based IP Routing	C. Huitema	December 1992	
1382	SNMP MIB Extension for the X.25 Packet Layer	D. Throop	November 1992	
1381	SNMP MIB Extension for X.25 LAPB	D. Throop F. Baker	November 1992	
1380	IESG Deliberations on Routing and Addressing	P. Gross P. Almquist	November 1992	
1379	Extending TCP for Transactions — Concepts	B. Braden	November 1992	
1378	The PPP AppleTalk Control Protocol (ATCP)	B. Parker	November 1992	
1377	The PPP OSI Network Layer Control Protocol (OSINLCP)	D. Katz	November 1992	
1376	The PPP DECnet Phase IV Control Protocol (DNCP)	S. Senum	November 1992	Obsoleted by RFC 1762
1375	Suggestion for New Classes of IP Addresses	P. Robinson	November 1992	
1374	IP and ARP on HIPPI	J. Renwick A. Nicholson	November 1992	Obsoleted by RFC 2067
1373	PORTABLE DUAs	T. Tignor	October 1992	
1372	Telnet Remote Flow Control Option	D. Borman C. Hedrick	October 1992	Obsoletes RFC 1080
1371	Choosing a Common IGP for the IP Internet (The IESG's Recommendation to the IAB)	P. Gross	October 1992	
1370	Applicability Statement for OSPF	A. Weinrib	October 1992	
1369	Implementation Notes and Experience for the Internet Ethernet MIB	F. Kastenholz	October 1992	
1368	Definitions of Managed Objects for IEEE 802.3 Repeater Devices	D. McMaster K. McCloghrie	October 1992	Obsoleted by RFC 1516
1367	Schedule for IP Address Space Management Guidelines	C. Topolcic	October 1992	Obsoleted by RFC 1467

(continued)

app.
f

Table AF.1: RFC Index (continued)

RFC	Title	Author(s)	Date	Notes
1366	Guidelines for Management of IP Address Space	E. Gerich	October 1992	Obsoleted by RFC 1466
1365	An IP Address Extension Proposal	K. Siyan	September 1992	
1364	BGP OSPF Interaction	K. Varadhan	September 1992	Obsoleted by RFC 1403
1363	A Proposed Flow Specification	C. Partridge	September 1992	
1362	Novell IPX Over Various WAN Media (IPXWAN)	M. Allen	September 1992	Obsoleted by RFC 1551
1361	Simple Network Time Protocol (SNTP)	D. Mills	August 1992	
1360	IAB Official Protocol Standards	J. Postel A. Chapin	September 1992	Obsoletes RFC 1280; obsoleted by RFC 1410; STD 1
1359	Connecting to the Internet: What Connecting Institutions Should Anticipate	ACM SIGUCCS	August 1992	FYI 16
1358	Charter of the Internet Architecture Board (IAB)	A. Chapin	August 1992	Obsoleted by RFC 1601
1357	A Format for E-mailing Bibliographic Records	D. Cohen	July 1992	
1356	Multiprotocol Interconnect on X.25 and ISDN in the Packet Mode	A. Malis R. Ullmann	August 1992	Obsoletes RFC 877
1355	Privacy and Accuracy Issues in Network Information Center Databases	J. Curran A. Marine	August 1992	FYI 15
1354	IP Forwarding Table MIB	F. Baker	July 1992	Obsoleted by RFC 2096
1353	Definitions of Managed Objects for Administration of SNMP Parties	K. McCloghrie J. Davin J. Galvin	July 1992	
1352	SNMP Security Protocols	J. Davin J. Galvin K. McCloghrie	July 1992	

1351	SNMP Administrative Model	J. Davin J. Galvin K. McCloghrie	July 1992	
1350	The TFTP Protocol (Revision 2)	K. Sollins	July 1992	Obsoletes RFC 783; obsoleted by RFC 1782; updated by RFC 1783; updated by RFC 1784; updated by RFC 1785; STD 33
1349	Type of Service in the Internet Protocol Suite	P. Almquist	July 1992	Obsoletes RFC 1248
1348	DNS NSAP RRs	B. Manning	July 1992	Updates RFC 1035; obsoleted by RFC 1637
1347	TCP and UDP with Bigger Addresses (TUBA), A Simple Proposal for Internet Addressing and Routing	R. Callon	June 1992	
1346	Resource Allocation, Control, and Accounting for the Use of Network Resources	P. Jones	June 1992	
1345	Character Mnemonics and Character Sets	K. Simonsen	June 1992	
1344	Implications of MIME for Internet Mail Gateways	N. Borenstein	June 1992	
1343	A User Agent Configuration Mechanism for Multimedia Mail Format Information	N. Borenstein	June 1992	
1342	Representation of Non-ASCII Text in Internet Message Headers	K. Moore	June 1992	Obsoleted by RFC 1522
1341	MIME (Multipurpose Internet Mail Extensions): Mechanisms for Specifying and Describing the Format of Internet Message Bodies	N. Borenstein N. Freed	June 1992	Obsoleted by RFC 1521
1340	Assigned Numbers	J. Reynolds J. Postel	July 1992	Obsoletes RFC 1060; obsoleted by RFC 1700; STD 2

(continued)

Table AF.1: RFC Index (continued)

RFC	Title	Author(s)	Date	Notes
1339	Remote Mail Checking Protocol	S. Dorner P. Resnick	June 1992	
1338	Supernetting: An Address Assignment and Aggregation Strategy	V. Fuller T. Li K. Varadhan J. Yu	June 1992	Obsoleted by RFC 1519
1337	TIME-WAIT Assassination Hazards in TCP	B. Braden	May 1992	
1336	Who's Who in the Internet Biographies of IAB, IESG, and IRSG Members	G. Malkin	May 1992	FYI 9; obsoletes RFC 1251
1335	A Two-Tier Address Structure for the Internet: A Solution to the Problem of Address Space Exhaustion	J. Crowcroft	May 1992	
1334	PPP Authentication Protocols	B. Lloyd W. Simpson	October 1992	Obsoleted by RFC 1994
1333	PPP Link Quality Monitoring	W. Simpson	May 1992	Obsoleted by RFC 1989
1332	The PPP Internet Protocol Control Protocol (IPCP)	G. McGregor	May 1992	Obsoletes RFC 1172
1331	The Point-to-Point Protocol (PPP) for the Transmission of Multi-Protocol Datagrams over Point-to-Point Links	W. Simpson	May 1992	Obsoletes RFC 1171; obsoleted by RFC 1548
1330	Recommendations for the Phase I Deployment of OSI Directory Services (X.500) and OSI Message-Handling Services (X.400) Within the ESnet Community	ESCC X.500/ X.400 Task Force	May 1992	
1329	Thoughts on Address Resolution for Dual MAC FDDI Networks	P. Kuene	May 1992	
1328	X.400 1988 to 1984 Downgrading	S. Kille	May 1992	Obsoleted by RFC 1496
1327	Mapping Between X.400(1988) / ISO 10021 and RFC 822	S. Kille	May 1992	Updates RFC 822; obsoletes RFC 1026; obsoletes RFC 1148; obsoleted by RFC 1495

1326	Mutual Encapsulation Considered Dangerous	P. Tsuchiya	May 1992	
1325	FYI on Questions and Answers: Answers to Commonly asked 'New Internet User' Questions	G. Malkin A. Marine	May 1992	FYI 4; obsoletes RFC 1206; obsoleted by RFC 1594
1324	A Discussion on Computer Network Conferencing	D. Reed	May 1992	
1323	TCP Extensions for High Performance	D. Borman B. Braden V. Jacobson	May 1992	Obsoletes RFC 1072; obsoletes RFC 1185
1322	A Unified Approach to Inter-Domain Routing	D. Estrin S. Hotz Y. Rekhter	May 1992	
1321	The MD5 Message-Digest Algorithm	R. Rivest	April 1992	
1320	The MD4 Message-Digest Algorithm	R. Rivest	April 1992	Obsoletes RFC 1186
1319	The MD2 Message-Digest Algorithm	B. Kaliski	April 1992	Obsoletes RFC 1115
1318	Definitions of Managed Objects for Parallel-Printer-Like Hardware Devices	B. Stewart	April 1992	Obsoleted by RFC 1660
1317	Definitions of Managed Objects for RS-232-Like Hardware Devices	B. Stewart	April 1992	Obsoleted by RFC 1659
1316	Definitions of Managed Objects for Character-Stream Devices	B. Stewart	April 1992	Obsoleted by RFC 1658
1315	Management Information Base for Frame Relay DTEs	C. Brown F. Baker C. Carvalho	April 1992	
1314	A File Format for the Exchange of Images in the Internet	D. Cohen A. Katz	April 1992	
1313	Today's Programming for KRFC AM 1313	C. Partridge	April 1992	Internet Talk Radio
1312	Message Send Protocol	R. Nelson	April 1992	Obsoletes RFC 1159
1311	Introduction to the STD Notes	J. Postel A. Chapin	March 1992	

(continued)

app. f

Table AF.1: RFC Index (continued)

RFC	Title	Author(s)	Date	Notes
1310	The Internet Standards Process	A. Chapin	March 1992	Obsoleted by RFC 1602
1309	Technical Overview of Directory Services Using the X.500 Protocol	S. Heker J. Reynolds C. Weider	March 1992	FYI 14
1308	Executive Introduction to Directory Services Using the X.500 Protocol	J. Reynolds C. Weider	March 1992	FYI 13
1307	Dynamically Switched Link Control Protocol	A. Nicholson	March 1992	
1306	Experiences Supporting By-Request Circuit-Switched T3 Networks	A. Nicholson	March 1992	
1305	Network Time Protocol (v3)	D. Mills	April 1992	Obsoletes RFC 1119
1304	Definitions of Managed Objects for the SIP Interface Type	T. Brown K. Tesink	February 1992	Obsoleted by RFC 1694
1303	A Convention for Describing SNMP-Based Agents	K. McCloghrie M. Rose	February 1992	
1302	Building a Network Information Services Infrastructure	D. Sitzler A. Marine	February 1992	FYI 12
1301	Multicast Transport Protocol	A. Freier	February 1992	
1300	Remembrances of Things Past	S. Greenfield	February 1992	
1299	Request for Comments Summary RFC Numbers 1200-1299	M. Kennedy	January 1997	
1298	SNMP over IPX	S. Bostock	February 1992	Obsoleted by RFC 1420
1297	NOC Internal Integrated Trouble Ticket System Functional Specification Wishlist ('NOC TT Requirements')	D. Johnson	January 1992	
1296	Internet Growth (1981-1991)	M. Lottor	January 1992	
1295	User Bill of Rights for Entries and Listings in the Public Directory	NADF	January 1992	Obsoletes RFC 1255; obsoleted by RFC 1417
1294	Multiprotocol Interconnect over Frame Relay	T. Bradley C. Brown A. Malis	January 1992	Obsoleted by RFC 1490

1293	Inverse Address-Resolution Protocol	T. Bradley C. Brown	January 1992	
1292	A Catalog of Available X.500 Implementations	R. Lang R. Wright	January 1992	FYI 11; obsoleted by RFC 1632
1291	Mid-Level Networks: Potential Technical Services	V. Aggarwal	December 1991	
1290	There's Gold in Them Thar Networks! or Searching for Treasure in All the Wrong Places	J. Martin	December 1991	FYI 10; obsoleted by RFC 1402
1289	DECnet Phase IV MIB Extensions	J. Saperia	December 1991	Obsoleted by RFC 1559
1288	The Finger User Information Protocol	D. Zimmerman	December 1991	Obsoletes RFC 1196
1287	Towards the Future Internet Architecture	B. Braden V. Cerf R. Hobby	December 1991	
1286	Definitions of Managed Objects for Bridges	K. McCloghrie E. Decker P. Langille A. Rijsinghani	December 1991	Obsoleted by RFC 1493; obsoleted by RFC 1525
1285	FDDI Management Information Base	J. Case	January 1992	Obsoleted by RFC 1512
1284	Definitions of Managed Objects for the Ethernet-Like Interface Types	J. Cook	December 1991	Obsoleted by RFC 1398
1283	SNMP over OSI	M. Rose	December 1991	Obsoletes RFC 1161; obsoleted by RFC 1418
1282	BSD Rlogin	B. Kantor	December 1991	Obsoletes RFC 1258
1281	Guidelines for the Secure Operation of the Internet	S. Crocker B. Fraser R. Pethia	November 1991	
1280	IAB Official Protocol Standards	J. Postel A. Chapin	March 1992	Obsoletes RFC 1250; obsoleted by RFC 1360; STD 1
1279	X.500 and Domains	S. Kille	November 1991	
1278	A String Encoding of Presentation Address	S. Kille	November 1991	

(continued)

app.
f

Table AF.1: RFC Index (continued)

RFC	Title	Author(s)	Date	Notes
1277	Encoding Network Addresses to Support Operation over Non-OSI Lower Layers	S. Kille	November 1991	
1276	Replication and Distributed Operations Extensions to Provide an Internet Directory Using X.500	S. Kille	November 1991	
1275	Replication Requirements to Provide an Internet Directory Using X.500	S. Kille	November 1991	
1274	The COSINE and Internet X.500 Schema	P. Barker S. Kille	November 1991	
1273	A Measurement Study of Changes in Service-Level Reachability in the Global TCP/IP Internet: Goals Experimental Design, Implementation and Policy Considerations	M. Schoffstall	November 1991	
1272	Internet Accounting: Background	D. Hirsh G. Ruth	November 1991	
1271	Remote Network Monitoring Management Information Base	S. Waldbusser	November 1991	Obsoleted by RFC 1757; updated by RFC 1513
1270	SNMP Communications Services	F. Kastenholz	October 1991	
1269	Definitions of Managed Objects for the Border Gateway Protocol (Version 3)	J. Burruss S. Willis	October 1991	
1268	Application of the Border Gateway Protocol in the Internet	P. Gross Y. Rekhter	October 1991	Obsoletes RFC 1164; obsoleted by RFC 1655
1267	A Border Gateway Protocol 3 (BGP-3)	K. Lougheed Y. Rekhter	October 1991	Obsoletes RFC 1105; obsoletes RFC 1163
1266	Experience with the BGP Protocol	Y. Rekhter	October 1991	
1265	BGP Protocol Analysis	Y. Rekhter	October 1991	
1264	Internet Routing Protocol Standardization Criteria	B. Hinden	October 1991	

1263	TCP Extensions Considered Harmful	L. Peterson S. O'Malley	October 1991	
1262	Guidelines for Internet Measurement Activities	A. Weinrib	October 1991	
1261	Transition of NIC Services	S. Williamson L. Nobile	September 1991	
1259	Building the Open Road: The NREN As Test-Bed for the National Public Network	M. Kapor	September 1991	
1258	BSD Rlogin	B. Kantor	September 1991	Obsoleted by RFC 1282
1257	Isochronous Applications Do Not Require Jitter-Controlled Networks	C. Partridge	September 1991	
1256	ICMP Router Discovery Messages	S. Deering	September 1991	
1255	A Naming Scheme for c=US	N. Directory Forum	September 1991	Obsoletes RFC 1218; obsoleted by RFC 1295
1254	Gateway Congestion Control Survey	A. Mankin K. Ramakrishnan	August 1991	
1253	OSPF Version 2 Management Information Base	F. Baker R. Coltun	August 1991	Obsoletes RFC 1252; obsoleted by RFC 1850
1252	OSPF Version 2 Management Information Base	F. Baker R. Coltun	August 1991	Obsoletes RFC 1248; obsoleted by RFC 1253
1251	Who's Who in the Internet: Biographies of IAB, IESG, and IRSG Members	G. Malkin	August 1991	FYI 9; obsoleted by RFC 1336
1250	IAB Official Protocol Standards	J. Postel	August 1991	Obsoletes RFC 1200; obsoleted by RFC 1280; STD 1
1249	DIXIE Protocol Specification	T. Howes B. Beecher	August 1991	
1248	OSPF Version 2 Management Information Base	F. Baker R. Coltun	August 1991	Obsoleted by RFC 1252; obsoleted by RFC 1349
1247	OSPF Version 2	J. Moy	August 1991	Obsoletes RFC 1131; obsoleted by RFC 1583
1246	Experience with the OSPF Protocol	J. Moy	August 1991	

(continued)

app.
f

Table AF.1: RFC Index (continued)

RFC	Title	Author(s)	Date	Notes
1245	OSPF Protocol Analysis	J. Moy	August 1991	
1244	Site Security Handbook	P. Holbrook J. Reynolds	July 1991	FYI 8
1243	AppleTalk Management Information Base	S. Waldbusser	July 1991	Obsoleted by RFC 1742
1242	Benchmarking Terminology for Network Interconnection Devices	S. Bradner	July 1991	
1241	A Scheme for an Internet Encapsulation Protocol: Version 1	D. Mills R. Woodburn	July 1991	
1240	OSI Connectionless Transport Services on Top of UDP — Version 1	K. Dobbins W. Haggerty C. Shue	June 1991	
1239	Reassignment of Experimental MIBs to Standard MIBs	J. Reynolds	June 1991	Updates RFC 1233
1238	CLNS MIB — for Use with Connectionless Network Protocol (ISO 8473) and End-System-to-Intermediate-System (ISO 9542)	G. Satz	June 1991	Obsoletes RFC 1162
1237	Guidelines for OSI NSAP Allocation in the Internet	R. Colella E. Gardner R. Callon	July 1991	Obsoleted by RFC 1629
1236	IP to X.121 Address Mapping for DDN	P. Asse	June 1991	
1235	The Coherent File Distribution Protocol	J. Ioannidis	June 1991	
1234	Tunneling IPX Traffic Through IP Networks	D. Provan	June 1991	
1233	Definitions of Managed Objects for the DS3 Interface Type	T. Brown K. Tesink	May 1991	Obsoleted by RFC 1407; updated by RFC 1239
1232	Definitions of Managed Objects for the DS1 Interface Type	F. Baker C. Kolb	May 1991	Obsoleted by RFC 1406

1231	IEEE 802.5 Token Ring MIB	E. Decker R. Fox K. McCloghrie	February 1993	Obsoleted by RFC 1743
1230	IEEE 802.4 Token Bus MIB	R. Fox K. McCloghrie	May 1991	
1229	Extensions to the Generic-Interface MIB	K. McCloghrie	August 1992	Obsoleted by RFC 1573
1228	SNMP-DPI — Simple Network Management Protocol Distributed Program Interface	G. Carpenter B. Wijnen	May 1991	Obsoleted by RFC 1592
1227	SNMP MUX Protocol and MIB	M. Rose	May 1991	
1226	Internet Protocol Encapsulation of AX.25 Frames	B. Kantor	May 1991	
1225	Post Office Protocol — Version 3	M. Rose	May 1991	Obsoletes RFC 1081; obsoleted by RFC 1460
1224	Techniques for Managing Asynchronously Generated Alerts	L. Steinberg	May 1991	
1223	OSI CLNS and LLC1 Protocols on Network Systems HYPERchannel	J. Halpern	May 1991	
1222	Advancing the NSFNET Routing Architecture	H. Braun Y. Rekhter	May 1991	
1221	Host Access Protocol (HAP) Specification — Version 2	W. Edmond	April 1991	Updates RFC 907
1220	Point-to-Point Protocol Extensions for Bridging	F. Baker	April 1991	Obsoleted by RFC 1638
1219	On the Assignment of Subnet Numbers	P. Tsuchiya	April 1991	
1218	A Naming Scheme for c=US	N. Directory Forum	April 1991	Obsoleted by RFC 1255
1217	Memo from the Consortium for Slow Commotion Research (CSCR)	V. Cerf	April 1991	
1216	Gigabit Network Economics and Paradigm Shifts	P. Kunikos	March 1991	

(continued)

app.
f

Table AF.1: RFC Index (continued)

RFC	Title	Author(s)	Date	Notes
1215	A Convention for Defining Traps for Use with the SNMP	M. Rose	March 1991	
1214	OSI Internet Management: Management Information Base	L. LaBarre	April 1991	
1213	Management Information Base for Network Management of TCP/IP-Based Internets: MIB-II	K. McCloghrie M. Rose	March 1991	Obsoletes RFC 1158; obsoletes RFC 1156; obsoleted by RFC 2013; updated by RFC 2011; updated by RFC 2012; STD 17
1212	Concise MIB Definitions	K. McCloghrie M. Rose	March 1991	STD 16
1211	Problems with the Maintenance of Large Mailing Lists	J. Postel	March 1991	
1210	Network and Infrastructure User Requirements for Transatlantic Research Collaboration — Brussels, July 16-18, and Washington, July 24-25, 1990	V. Cerf P. Kirstein B. Randell	March 1991	
1209	The Transmission of IP Datagrams over the SMDS Service	D. Piscitello	March 1991	
1208	A Glossary of Networking Terms	O. Jacobsen D. Lynch	March 1991	
1207	Answers to Commonly Asked 'Experienced Internet User' Questions	G. Malkin A. Marine	February 1991	FYI 7
1206	FYI on Questions and Answers — Answers to Commonly Asked 'New Internet User' Questions	G. Malkin A. Marine	February 1991	FYI 4; obsoletes RFC 1177; obsoleted by RFC 1325
1205	5250 Telnet Interface	P. Chmielewski	February 1991	
1204	Message Posting Protocol (MPP)	D. Lee	February 1991	
1203	Interactive Mail Access Protocol — Version 3	J. Rice	February 1991	Obsoletes RFC 1064

1202	Directory Assistance Service	M. Rose	February 1991	
1201	Transmitting IP Traffic over ARCNET Networks	D. Provan	February 1991	Obsoletes RFC 1051
1200	IAB Official Protocol Standards	J. Postel	April 1991	Obsoletes RFC 1140; obsoleted by RFC 1250; STD 1
1199	Request for Comments Summary RFC Numbers 1100-1199	J. Reynolds	December 1991	
1198	FYI on the X Window System	B. Scheifler	January 1991	
1197	Using ODA for Translating Multimedia Information	M. Sherman	December 1990	
1196	The Finger User Information Protocol	D. Zimmerman	December 1990	Obsoletes RFC 1194; obsoleted by RFC 1288
1195	Use of OSI IS-IS for Routing in TCP/IP and Dual Environments11	R. Callon	December 1990	
1194	The Finger User Information Protocol	D. Zimmerman	November 1990	Obsoletes RFC 742; obsoleted by RFC 1196
1193	Client Requirements for Real-Time Communication Services	D. Ferrari	November 1990	
1192	Commercialization of the Internet Summary Report	B. Kahin	November 1990	
1191	Path MTU Discovery	J. Mogul S. Deering	November 1990	
1190	Experimental Internet Stream Protocol, Version 2 (ST-II)	C. Topolcic	October 1990	Obsoleted by RFC 1819
1189	The Common Management Information Services and Protocols for the Internet	L. Besaw B. Handspicker L. LaBarre U. Warrier	October 1990	Obsoletes RFC 1095
1188	A Proposed Standard for the Transmission of IP Datagrams over FDDI Networks	D. Katz	October 1990	Obsoletes RFC 1103; obsoleted by RFC 1390
1187	Bulk Table Retrieval with the SNMP	J. Davin K. McCloghrie M. Rose	October 1990	

(continued)

app.
f

Table AF.1: RFC Index (continued)

RFC	Title	Author(s)	Date	Notes
1186	The MD4 Message Digest Algorithm	R. Rivest	October 1990	Obsoleted by RFC 1320
1185	TCP Extension for High-Speed Paths	B. Braden V. Jacobson L. Zhang	October 1990	Obsoleted by RFC 1323
1184	Telnet Linemode Option	D. Borman	October 1990	Obsoletes RFC 1116
1183	New DNS RR Definitions	R. Ullmann P. Mockapetris L. Mamakos C. Everhart	October 1990	
1182	Missing			
1181	RIPE Terms of Reference	R. Blokzijl	September 1990	
1180	A TCP/IP Tutorial	T. Socolofsky	January 1991	
1179	Line Printer Daemon Protocol	L. McLaughlin	September 1990	
1178	Choosing a Name for Your Computer	D. Libes	September 1990	FYI 5
1177	FYI on Questions and Answers — Answers to Commonly Asked 'New Internet User' Questions	G. Malkin A. Marine	September 1990	FYI 4; obsoleted by RFC 1206
1176	Interactive Mail Access Protocol — Version 2	M. Crispin	August 1990	Obsoletes RFC 1064
1175	FYI on Where to Start — A Bibliography of Internetworking Information	A. Yuan	August 1990	FYI 3
1174	IAB Recommended Policy on Distributing Internet Identifier Assignment and IAB Recommended Policy Change to Internet 'Connected' Status	V. Cerf	August 1990	
1173	Responsibilities of Host and Network Managers: A Summary of the 'Oral Tradition of the Internet'	J. VanBokkelen	August 1990	
1172	The Point-to-Point Protocol (PPP) Initial Configuration Options	R. Hobby	July 1990	Obsoleted by RFC 1332

1171	The Point-to-Point Protocol for the Transmission of Multi-Protocol Datagrams over Point-to-Point Links	D. Perkins	July 1990	Obsoletes RFC 1134; obsoleted by RFC 1331
1170	Public-Key Standards and Licenses	R. Fox	January 1991	
1169	Explaining the Role of GOSIP	K. Mills V. Cerf	August 1990	
1168	Intermail and Commercial Mail Relay Services	J. Postel	July 1990	
1167	Thoughts on the National Research and Education Network	V. Cerf	July 1990	
1166	Internet Numbers	S. Kirkpatrick	July 1990	
1165	Network Time Protocol (NTP) over the OSI Remote Operations Service	J. Crowcroft J. Onions	June 1990	
1164	Application of the Border Gateway Protocol in the Internet	J. Honig D. Katz M. Mathis Y. Rekhter J. Yu	June 1990	Obsoleted by RFC 1268
1163	A Border Gateway Protocol (BGP)	K. Lougheed Y. Rekhter	June 1990	Obsoletes RFC 1105; obsoleted by RFC 1267
1162	Connectionless Network Protocol (ISO 8473) and End System to Intermediate System (ISO 9542) Management Information Base	G. Satz	June 1990	Obsoleted by RFC 1238
1161	SNMP over OSI	M. Rose	June 1990	Obsoleted by RFC 1283
1160	The Internet Activities Board	V. Cerf	May 1990	Obsoletes RFC 1120
1159	Message Send Protocol	R. Nelson	June 1990	Obsoleted by RFC 1312
1158	Management Information Base for Network Management of TCP/IP-Based Internets: MIB-II	M. Rose	May 1990	Obsoletes RFC 1156; obsoleted by RFC 1213
1157	A Simple Network Management Protocol (SNMP)	J. Case J. Davin M. Fedor M. Schoffstall	May 1990	Obsoletes RFC 1098; STD 15

(continued)

app. f

Table AF.1: RFC Index (continued)

RFC	Title	Author(s)	Date	Notes
1156	Management Information Base for Network Management of TCP/IP-Based Internets	K. McCloghrie M. Rose	May 1990	Obsoletes RFC 1066; obsoleted by RFC 1158; obsoleted by RFC 1213
1155	Structure and Identification of Management Information for TCP/IP-Based Internets	K. McCloghrie M. Rose	May 1990	Obsoletes RFC 1065; STD 17
1154	Encoding Header Field for Internet Messages	R. Ullmann	April 1990	Updates RFC 1049; obsoleted by RFC 1505
1153	Digest Message Format	F. Wancho	April 1990	
1152	Workshop Report: Internet Research Steering Group Workshop on Very-High-Speed Networks	C. Partridge	April 1990	
1151	Version 2 of the Reliable Data Protocol (RDP)	B. Hinden C. Partridge	April 1990	Updates RFC 908
1150	F.Y.I. on F.Y.I.: Introduction to the F.Y.I. notes	G. Malkin J. Reynolds	March 1990	FYI 1
1149	A Standard for the Transmission of IP Datagrams on Avian Carriers	D. Waitzman	April 1990	
1148	Mapping Between X.400 (1988) / ISO 10021 and RFC 822	S. Kille	March 1990	Obsoletes RFC 987; obsoleted by RFC 1327
1147	FYI on a Network Management Tool Catalog: Tools for Monitoring and Debugging TCP/IP Internets and Interconnected Devices	R. Stine	April 1990	FYI 2; obsoleted by RFC 1470
1146	TCP Alternate Checksum Options	C. Partridge	March 1991	Obsoletes RFC 1145
1145	TCP Alternate Checksum Options	C. Partridge	February 1990	Obsoleted by RFC 1146
1144	Compressing TCP/IP Headers for Low-Speed Serial Links	V. Jacobson	February 1990	
1143	The Q Method of Implementing TELNET Option Negotiation	D. Bernstein	February 1990	
1142	OSI IS-IS Intra-Domain Routing Protocol	D. Oran	December 1991	

1141	Incremental Updating of the Internet Checksum	A. Kullberg T. Mallory	January 1990	Obsoletes RFC 1071
1140	IAB Official Protocol Standards	J. Postel	May 1990	Obsoletes RFC 1130; obsoleted by RFC 1200; STD 1
1139	Echo Function for ISO 8473	R. Hagens	January 1990	Obsoleted by RFC 1574; obsoleted by RFC 1575
1138	Mapping Between X.400(1988) / ISO 10021 and RFC 822	S. Kille	December 1989	Updates RFC 1026
1137	Mapping Between Full RFC 822 and RFC 822 with Restricted Encoding	S. Kille	December 1989	Updates RFC 976
1136	Administrative Domains and Routing Domains: A Model for Routing in the Internet	S. Ares D. Katz	December 1989	
1135	Helminthiasis of the Internet	J. Reynolds	December 1989	
1134	Point-to-Point Protocol: A Proposal for Multi-Protocol Transmission of Datagrams over Point-to-Point Links	D. Perkins	November 1989	Obsoleted by RFC 1171
1133	Routing Between the NSFNET and the DDN	J. Yu H. Braun	November 1989	
1132	Standard for the Transmission of 802.2 Packets over IPX Networks	L. McLaughlin	November 1989	
1131	OSPF Specification	J. Moy	October 1989	Obsoleted by RFC 1247
1130	IAB Official Protocol Standards	A. Weinrib A. Chapin	October 1989	Obsoletes RFC 1100; obsoleted by RFC 1140; STD 1
1129	Internet Time Synchronization: The Network Time Protocol	D. Mills	October 1989	
1128	Measured Performance of the Network Time Protocol in the Internet System	D. Mills	October 1989	
1127	Perspective on the Host Requirements RFCs	B. Braden	October 1989	

(continued)

app.
f

Table AF.1: RFC Index (continued)

RFC	Title	Author(s)	Date	Notes
1126	Goals and Functional Requirements for Inter-Autonomous-System Routing	M. Little	October 1989	
1125	Policy Requirements for Inter-Administrative Domain Routing	D. Estrin	November 1989	
1124	Policy Issues in Interconnecting Networks	B. Leiner	September 1989	
1123	Requirements for Internet Hosts — Application and Support	B. Braden	October 1989	Updated by RFC 2181; STD 3
1122	Requirements for Internet Hosts — Communication Layers	B. Braden	October 1989	STD 3
1121	Act One — The Poems	J. Postel L. Kleinrock V. Cerf B. Boehm	September 1989	
1120	Internet Activities Board	V. Cerf	September 1989	Obsoleted by RFC 1160
1119	Network Time Protocol Version 2 Specification and Implementation	D. Mills	September 1989	Obsoletes RFC 1059; obsoleted by RFC 1305; STD 12
1118	Hitchhiker's Guide to the Internet	E. Krol	September 1989	
1117	Internet Numbers	M. Stahl	August 1989	Obsoletes RFC 1062
1116	Telnet Linemode Option	D. Borman	August 1989	Obsoleted by RFC 1184
1115	Privacy Enhancement for Internet Electronic Mail: Part III — Algorithms, Modes, and Identifiers [Draft]	J. Linn	August 1989	Obsoleted by RFC 1319; obsoleted by RFC 1423
1114	Privacy Enhancement for Internet Electronic Mail: Part II — Certificate-Based Key Management [Draft]	S. Kent	August 1989	Obsoleted by RFC 1422

1113	Privacy Enhancement for Internet Electronic Mail: Part 1 — Message Encipherment and Authentication Procedures [Draft]	J. Linn	August 1989	Obsoletes RFC 1040; obsoletes RFC 989; obsoleted by RFC 1421
1112	Host Extensions for IP Multicasting	S. Deering	August 1989	Obsoletes RFC 1054; obsoletes RFC 988; STD 5
1111	Request for Comments on Request for Comments: Instructions to RFC Authors	J. Postel	August 1989	Obsoletes RFC 825; obsoleted by RFC 1543
1110	Problem with the TCP Big Window Option	A. McKenzie	August 1989	
1109	Report of the Second Ad-Hoc Network Management Review Group	V. Cerf	August 1989	
1108	U.S. Department of Defense Security Options for the Internet Protocol	S. Kent	November 1991	Obsoletes RFC 1038
1107	Plan for Internet Directory Services	K. Sollins	July 1989	
1106	TCP Big Window and NAK Options	R. Fox	June 1989	
1105	Border Gateway Protocol (BGP)	K. Lougheed Y. Rekhter	June 1989	Obsoleted by RFC 1163; obsoleted by RFC 1267
1104	Models of Policy-Based Routing	H. Braun	June 1989	
1103	Proposed Standard for the Transmission of IP Datagrams over FDDI Networks	D. Katz	June 1989	Obsoleted by RFC 1188
1102	Policy Routing in Internet Protocols	D. Clark	May 1989	
1101	DNS Encoding of Network Names and Other Types	P. Mockapetris	April 1989	Updates RFC 1034
1100	IAB Official Protocol Standards	A. Weinrib A. Chapin	April 1989	Obsoletes RFC 1083; obsoleted by RFC 1130; STD 1
1099	Request for Comments Summary RFC Numbers 1000-1099	J. Reynolds	December 1991	
1098	Simple Network Management Protocol (SNMP)	J. Case M. Fedor	April 1989	Obsoletes RFC 1067; obsoleted by RFC 1157
1097	Telnet Subliminal-Message Option	B. Miller	April 1989	

(continued)

Table AF.1: RFC Index (continued)

RFC	Title	Author(s)	Date	Notes
1096	Telnet X Display Location Option	G. Marcy	March 1989	
1095	Common Management Information Services and Protocol over TCP/IP CMOT	U. Warrier L. Besaw	April 1989	Obsoleted by RFC 1189
1094	NFS: Network File System Protocol Specification	Sun Microsystems, Inc.	March 1989	
1093	NSFNET Routing Architecture	H. Braun	February 1989	
1092	EGP and Policy Based Routing in the New NSFNET Backbone	J. Rekhter	February 1989	
1091	Telnet Terminal-Type Option	J. VanBokkelen	February 1989	Obsoletes RFC 930
1090	SMTP on X.25	R. Ullmann	February 1989	
1089	SNMP over Ethernet	M. Schoffstall M. Fedor J. Case	February 1989	
1088	Standard for the Transmission of IP Datagrams over NetBIOS Networks	L. McLaughlin	February 1989	
1087	Ethics and the Internet	A. Weinrib	January 1989	
1086	ISO-TP0 Bridge Between TCP and X.25	J. Onions M. Rose	December 1988	
1085	ISO Presentation Services on Top of TCP/IP-Based Internets	M. Rose	December 1988	
1084	BOOTP Vendor Information Extensions	J. Reynolds	December 1988	Obsoletes RFC 1048; obsoleted by RFC 1395
1083	IAB Official Protocol Standards	A. Weinrib A. Chapin	December 1988	Obsoleted by RFC 1100; STD 1
1082	Post Office Protocol — Version 3: Extended Service Offerings	M. Rose	November 1988	
1081	Post Office Protocol — Version 3	M. Rose	November 1988	Obsoleted by RFC 1225
1080	Telnet Remote Flow-Control Option	C. Hedrick	November 1988	Obsoleted by
1079	Telnet Terminal Speed Option	C. Hedrick	December 1988	RFC 1372
1078	TCP Port Service Multiplexer	M. Lottor	November 1988	TCPMUX

1077	Critical Issues in High-Bandwidth Networking	B. Leiner	November 1988	
1076	HEMS Monitoring and Control Language	G. Trewitt C. Partridge	November 1988	Obsoletes RFC 1023
1075	Distance Vector Multicast Routing Protocol	S. Deering C. Partridge D. Waitzman	November 1988	
1074	NSFNET Backbone SPF-Based Interior Gateway Protocol	J. Rekhter	October 1988	
1073	Telnet Window Size Option	D. Waitzman	October 1988	
1072	TCP Extensions for Long-Delay Paths	B. Braden V. Jacobson	October 1988	Obsoleted by RFC 1323
1071	Computing the Internet Checksum	B. Braden D. Borman C. Partridge	September 1988	Obsoleted by RFC 1141; updated by RFC 1624
1070	Use of the Internet as a Subnetwork for Experimentation with the OSI Network Layer	R. Hagens N. Hall M. Rose	February 1989	
1069	Guidelines for the Use of Internet-IP Addresses in the ISO Connectionless-Mode Network Protocol	R. Callon H. Braun	February 1989	Obsoletes RFC 986
1068	Background File Transfer Program	B. Braden	August 1988	BFTP
1067	Simple Network Management Protocol	J. Case M. Fedor M. Schoffstall J. Davin	August 1988	Obsoleted by RFC 1098
1066	Management Information Base for Network Management of TCP/IP-Based Internets	K. McCloghrie M. Rose	August 1988	Obsoleted by RFC 1156
1065	Structure and Identification of Management Information for TCP/IP-Based Internets	K. McCloghrie M. Rose	August 1988	Obsoleted by RFC 1155
1064	Interactive Mail Access Protocol: Version 2	M. Crispin	July 1988	Obsoleted by RFC 1176; obsoleted by RFC 1203

(continued)

app.
f

Table AF.1: RFC Index (continued)

RFC	Title	Author(s)	Date	Notes
1063	IP MTU Discovery Options	K. McCloghrie J. Mogul C. Partridge	July 1988	
1062	Internet Numbers	M. Stahl	August 1988	Obsoletes RFC 1020; obsoleted by RFC 1117
1061	Not Issued		January 1970	
1060	Assigned Numbers	J. Postel J. Reynolds	March 1990	Obsoletes RFC 791; obsoletes RFC 1010; obsoleted by RFC 1340; STD 2
1059	Network Time Protocol Version 1 Specification and Implementation	D. Mills	July 1988	Obsoletes RFC 958; obsoleted by RFC 1119
1058	Routing Information Protocol	C. Hedrick	June 1988	Obsoleted by RFC 1723; updated by RFC 1388; STD 34
1057	RPC: Remote Procedure Call Protocol Specification Version 2	Sun Microsystems, Inc.	June 1988	Obsoletes RFC 1050
1056	PCMAIL: A Distributed Mail System for Personal Computers	M. Lambert	June 1988	Obsoletes RFC 993
1055	Nonstandard for Transmission of IP Datagrams over Serial Lines: SLIP	J. Romkey	June 1988	
1054	Host Extensions for IP Multicasting	S. Deering	May 1988	Obsoletes RFC 988; obsoleted by RFC 1112
1053	Telnet X.3 PAD Option	S. Levy	April 1988	
1052	IAB Recommendations for the Development of Internet Network Management Standards	V. Cerf	April 1988	
1051	Standard for the Transmission of IP Datagrams and ARP Packets over ARCNET Networks	P. Prindeville	March 1988	Obsoleted by RFC 1201
1050	RPC: Remote Procedure Call Protocol Specification	Sun Microsystems, Inc.	April 1988	Obsoleted by RFC 1057

1049	Content-Type Header Field for Internet Messages	M. Sirbu	March 1988	Updated by RFC 1154; STD 11
1048	BOOTP Vendor Information Extensions	P. Prindeville	February 1988	Obsoleted by RFC 1084
1047	Duplicate Messages and SMTP	C. Partridge	February 1988	
1046	Queuing Algorithm to Provide Type-of-Service for IP Links	W. Prue J. Postel	February 1988	
1045	VMTP: Versatile Message Transaction Protocol: Protocol Specification	D. Cheriton	February 1988	
1044	Internet Protocol on Network System's HYPERchannel: Protocol Specification	K. Hardwick J. Lekashman	February 1988	
1043	Telnet Data Entry Terminal Option: DODIIS Implementation	A. Yasuda	February 1988	Updates RFC 732
1042	Standard for the Transmission of IP Datagrams over IEEE 802 Networks	J. Postel J. Reynolds	February 1988	Obsoletes RFC 948
1041	Telnet 3270 Regime Option	Y. Rekhter	January 1988	
1040	Privacy Enhancement for Internet Electronic Mail: Part I: Message Encipherment and Authentication Procedures	J. Linn	January 1988	Obsoletes RFC 989; obsoleted by RFC 1113
1039	DoD Statement on Open Systems Interconnection Protocols	D. Latham	January 1988	Obsoletes RFC 945
1038	Draft Revised IP Security Option	M. St. Johns	January 1988	Obsoleted by
1037	NFILE — A File Access Protocol	B. Greenberg	December 1987	RFC 1108
1036	Standard for Interchange of Messages	M. Horton	December 1987	Obsoletes RFC 850USENET
1035	Domain Names — Implementation and Specification	P. Mockapetris	November 1987	Obsoletes RFC 973; obsoleted by RFC 2136; obsoleted by RFC 2137; updated by RFC 1348; updated by RFC 1995; updated by RFC 1996; updated by RFC 2065; updated by RFC 2181; STD 13

(continued)

app.
f

Table AF.1: RFC Index (continued)

RFC	Title	Author(s)	Date	Notes
1034	Domain Names — Concepts and Facilities	P. Mockapetris	November 1987	Obsoletes RFC 882; obsoletes RFC 883; obsoletes RFC 973; obsoleted by RFC 2065; updated by RFC 1101; updated by RFC 1876; updated by RFC 1982; updated by RFC 2181; STD 13
1033	Domain Administrators Operations Guide	M. Lottor	November 1987	
1032	Domain Administrators Guide	M. Stahl	November 1987	
1031	MILNET Name Domain Transition	W. Lazear	November 1987	
1030	On Testing the NETBLT Protocol over Diverse Networks	M. Lambert	November 1987	
1029	More Fault-Tolerant Approach to Address Resolution for a Multi-LAN System of Ethernets	G. Parr	May 1988	
1028	Simple Gateway Monitoring Protocol	J. Case J. Davin M. Fedor M. Schoffstall	November 1987	
1027	Using ARP to Implement Transparent Subnet Gateways	S. Carl-Mitchell J. Quarterman	October 1987	
1026	Addendum to RFC 987: Mapping Between X.400 and RFC-822	S. Kille	September 1987	Updates RFC 987; obsoleted by RFC 1327; updated by RFC 1138
1025	TCP and IP Bake-Off	J. Postel	September 1987	
1024	HEMS Variable Definitions	C. Partridge G. Trewitt	October 1987	
1023	HEMS Monitoring and Control Language	G. Trewitt C. Partridge	October 1987	Obsoleted by RFC 1076

1022	High-Level Entity Management Protocol	C. Partridge G. Trewitt	October 1987	HEMP
1021	High-Level Entity Management System	C. Partridge G. Trewitt	October 1987	HEMS
1020	Internet Numbers	M. Stahl	November 1987	Obsoletes RFC 997; obsoleted by RFC 1062
1019	Report of the Workshop on Environments for Computational Mathematics	D. Arnon	September 1987	
1018	Some Comments on SQuID	A. McKenzie	August 1987	
1017	Network Requirements for Scientific Research: Internet Task Force on Scientific Computing	B. Leiner	August 1987	
1016	Something a Host Could Do with Source Quench: The Source Quench Introduced Delay (SQuID)	W. Prue J. Postel	July 1987	
1015	Implementation Plan for Interagency Research Internet	B. Leiner	July 1987	
1014	XDR: External Data Representation Standard	Sun Microsystems, Inc.	June 1987	
1013	X Window System Protocol Version 11: Alpha Update, April 1987	R. Scheifler	June 1987	
1012	Bibliography of Requests for Comments 1 Through 999	J. Reynolds J. Postel	June 1987	
1011	Official Internet Protocols	J. Postel J. Reynolds	May 1987	Obsoletes RFC 991; STD 1
1010	Assigned Numbers	J. Postel J. Reynolds	May 1987	Obsoletes RFC 990; obsoleted by RFC 1060; STD 2
1009	Requirements for Internet Gateways	B. Braden J. Postel	June 1987	Obsoletes RFC 985; obsoleted by RFC 1716; STD 4
1008	Implementation Guide for the ISO Transport Protocol	W. McCoy	June 1987	

(continued)

app.
f

Table AF.1: RFC Index (continued)

RFC	Title	Author(s)	Date	Notes
1007	Military Supplement to the ISO Transport Protocol	W. McCoy	June 1987	
1006	ISO Transport Services on Top of the TCP: Version 3	M. Rose	May 1987	Obsoletes RFC 983; STD 35
1005	ARPANET AHIP-E Host Access Protocol	A. Malis	May 1987	Enhanced AHIP
1004	Distributed-Protocol Authentication Scheme	D. Mills	April 1987	
1003	Issues in Defining an Equations Representation Standard	A. Katz	March 1987	
1002	Protocol Standard for a NetBIOS Service on a TCP/UDP Transport: Detailed Specifications	A. Weinrib	March 1987	STD 19
1001	Protocol Standard for a NetBIOS Service on a TCP/UDP Transport: Concepts and Methods	A. Weinrib	March 1987	STD 19
1000	Request for Comments Reference Guide	J. Postel J. Reynolds	August 1987	Obsoletes RFC 999
999	Requests for Comments Summary Notes: 900-999	J. Postel	April 1987	Obsoleted by RFC 1000
998	NETBLT: A Bulk Data Transfer Protocol	D. Clark M. Lambert L. Zhang	March 1987	Obsoletes RFC 969
997	Internet Numbers	J. Reynolds J. Postel	March 1987	Updates RFC 990; obsoleted by RFC 1020
996	Statistics Server	D. Mills	February 1987	
995	End System to Intermediate System Routing Exchange Protocol for Use in Conjunction with ISO 8473	International Organization for Standardization	April 1986	
994	Final Text of DIS 8473, Protocol for Providing the Connectionless-Mode Network Service	International Organization for Standardization	March 1986	Obsoletes RFC 926

993	PCMAIL: A Distributed Mail System for Personal Computers	D. Clark M. Lambert	December 1986	Obsoletes RFC 984; obsoleted by RFC 1056
992	On Communication Support for Fault-Tolerant Process Groups	K. Birman	November 1986	
991	Official ARPA-Internet Protocols	J. Reynolds J. Postel	November 1986	Obsoletes RFC 961; obsoleted by RFC 1011; STD 1
990	Assigned Numbers	J. Postel J. Reynolds	November 1986	Obsoletes RFC 960; obsoleted by RFC 1010; updated by RFC 997
989	Privacy Enhancement for Internet Electronic Mail: Part I: Message Encipherment and Authentication Procedures	J. Linn	February 1987	Obsoleted by RFC 1040; obsoleted by RFC 1113
988	Host Extensions for IP Multicasting	S. Deering	July 1986	Obsoletes RFC 966; obsoleted by RFC 1054; obsoleted by RFC 1112
987	Mapping Between X.400 and RFC 822	S. Kille	June 1986	Updates RFC 822; obsoleted by RFC 1148; updated by RFC 1026
986	Guidelines for the Use of Internet-IP Addresses in the ISO Connectionless-Mode Network Protocol [Working Draft]	R. Callon H. Braun	June 1986	Obsoleted by RFC 1069
985	Requirements for Internet Gateways — Draft	National Science Foundation	May 1986	Obsoleted by RFC 1009
984	PCMAIL: A Distributed Mail System for Personal Computers	D. Clark M. Lambert	May 1986	Obsoleted by RFC 993
983	ISO Transport Arrives on Top of the TCP	M. Rose	April 1986	Obsoleted by RFC 1006
982	Guidelines for the Specification of the Structure of the Domain Specific Part (DSP) of the ISO Standard NSAP Address	H. Braun	April 1986	

(continued)

app. f

Table AF.1: RFC Index (continued)

RFC	Title	Author(s)	Date	Notes
981	Experimental Multiple-Path Routing Algorithm	D. Mills	March 1986	
980	Protocol Document Order Information	O. Jacobsen J. Postel	March 1986	
979	PSN End-to-End Functional Specification	A. Malis	March 1986	
978	Voice-File Interchange Protocol VFIP	J. Reynolds W. Brackenridge J. Postel	February 1986	
977	Network News Transfer Protocol: A Proposed Standard for the Stream-Based Transmission of News	B. Kantor	February 1986	
976	UUCP Mail Interchange Format Standard	M. Horton	February 1986	Updated by RFC 1137
975	Autonomous Confederations	D. Mills	February 1986	
974	Mail Routing and the Domain System	C. Partridge	January 1986	STD 14
973	Domain System Changes and Observations	P. Mockapetris	January 1986	Updates RFC 882; obsoleted by RFC 1034; obsoleted by RFC 1035
972	Password Generator Protocol	F. Wancho	January 1986	
971	Survey of Data Representation Standards	A. DeSchon	January 1986	
970	On Packet Switches with Infinite Storage	J. Nagle	December 1985	
969	NETBLT: A Bulk Data Transfer Protocol	D. Clark M. Lambert L. Zhang	December 1985	Obsoleted by RFC 998
968	'Twas the Night Before Start-Up	V. Cerf	December 1985	
967	All Victims Together	M. Padlipsky	December 1985	
966	Host Groups: A Multicast Extension to the Internet Protocol	S. Deering D. Cheriton	December 1985	Obsoleted by RFC 988

965	Format for a Graphical Communication Protocol	L. Aguilar	December 1985	
964	Some Problems with the Specification of the Military Standard Transmission Control Protocol	D. Sidhu	November 1985	
963	Some Problems with the Specification of the Military Standard Internet Protocol	D. Sidhu	November 1985	
962	TCP-4 Prime	M. Padlipsky	November 1985	
961	Official ARPA-Internet Protocols	J. Reynolds J. Postel	December 1985	Obsoletes RFC 944; obsoleted by RFC 991; STD 1
960	Assigned Numbers	J. Reynolds J. Postel	December 1985	Obsoletes RFC 943; obsoleted by RFC 990
959	File Transfer Protocol	J. Postel J. Reynolds	October 1985	Obsoletes RFC 765; STD 9
958	Network Time Protocol (NTP)	D. Mills	September 1985	Obsoleted by RFC 1059
957	Experiments in Network Clock Synchronization	D. Mills	September 1985	
956	Algorithms for Synchronizing Network Clocks	D. Mills	September 1985	
955	Towards a Transport Service for Transaction-Processing Applications	B. Braden	September 1985	
954	NICNAME/WHOIS	E. Feinler K. Harrenstien M. Stahl	October 1985	Obsoletes RFC 812
953	Hostname Server	E. Feinler K. Harrenstien M. Stahl	October 1985	Obsoletes RFC 811
952	DoD Internet Host Table Specification	K. Arrenstien M. Stahl E. Feinler	October 1985	Obsoletes RFC 810

(continued)

app. f

Table AF.1: RFC Index (continued)

RFC	Title	Author(s)	Date	Notes
951	Bootstrap Protocol	J. Gilmore	September 1985	Obsoleted by RFC 1532; updated by RFC 1395; updated by RFC 1497
950	Internet Standard Subnetting Procedure	J. Mogul J. Postel	August 1985	STD 5
949	FTP Unique-Named Store Command	M. Padlipsky	July 1985	
948	Two Methods for the Transmission of IP Datagrams over IEEE 802.3 Networks	I. Winston	June 1985	Obsoleted by RFC 1042
947	Multi-Network Broadcasting Within the Internet	D. Mankins	June 1985	
946	Telnet Terminal Location Number Option	R. Nedved	May 1985	
945	DoD Statement on the NRC Report	J. Postel	May 1985	Obsoleted by RFC 1039
944	Official ARPA-Internet Protocols	J. Reynolds J. Postel	April 1985	Obsoletes RFC 924; obsoleted by RFC 961; STD 1
943	Assigned Numbers	J. Reynolds J. Postel	April 1985	Obsoletes RFC 923; obsoleted by RFC 960
942	Transport Protocols for Department of Defense Data Networks	National Research Council	February 1985	
941	Addendum to the Network Service Definition Covering Network Layer Addressing	International Organization for Standardization	April 1985	
940	Toward an Internet Standard Scheme for Subnetting	Gateway Algorithms and Data Structures T	April 1985	
939	Executive Summary of the NRC Report on Transport Protocols for Department of Defense Data Networks	National Research Council	February 1985	

938	Internet Reliable Transaction Protocol Functional and Interface Specification	T. Miller	February 1985	
937	Post Office Protocol — Version 2	M. Butler J. Goldberger J. Postel J. Reynolds	February 1985	Obsoletes RFC 918
936	Another Internet Subnet Addressing Scheme	M. Karels	February 1985	
935	Reliable Link-Layer Protocols	J. Robinson	January 1985	
934	Proposed Standard for Message Encapsulation	M. Rose E. Stefferud	January 1985	
933	Output-Marking Telnet Option	S. Silverman	January 1985	
932	Subnetwork Addressing Scheme	D. Clark	January 1985	
931	Authentication Server	M. St. Johns	January 1985	Obsoletes RFC 912; obsoleted by RFC 1413
930	Telnet Terminal Type Option	M. Solomon	January 1985	Obsoletes RFC 884; obsoleted by RFC 1091
929	Proposed Host-Front-End Protocol	M. Padlipsky	December 1984	
928	Introduction to Proposed DoD Standard H-FP	M. Padlipsky	December 1984	
927	TACACS User Identification Telnet Option	B. Anderson	December 1984	
926	Protocol for Providing the Connectionless Mode Network Services	International Organization for Standardization	December 1984	Obsoleted by RFC 994
925	Multi-LAN Address Resolution	J. Postel	October 1984	
924	Official ARPA-Internet Protocols for Connecting Personal Computers to the Internet	J. Reynolds J. Postel	October 1984	Obsoletes RFC 901; obsoleted by RFC 944
923	Assigned Numbers	J. Reynolds J. Postel	October 1984	Obsoletes RFC 900; obsoleted by RFC 943
922	Broadcasting Internet Datagrams in the Presence of Subnets	J. Mogul	October 1984	STD 5

app.
f

(continued)

Table AF.1: RFC Index (continued)

RFC	Title	Author(s)	Date	Notes
921	Domain-Name System Implementation Schedule — Revised	J. Postel	October 1984	Updates RFC 897
920	Domain Requirements	J. Postel J. Reynolds	October 1984	
919	Broadcasting Internet Datagrams	J. Mogul	October 1984	STD 5
918	Post Office Protocol	J. Reynolds	October 1984	Obsoleted by RFC 937
917	Internet Subnets	J. Mogul	October 1984	
916	Reliable Asynchronous Transfer Protocol	G. Finn	October 1984	RATP
915	Network Mail Path Service	M. Ivy	December 1984	
914	Thinwire Protocol for Connecting Personal Computers to the Internet	G. Delp D. Farber	September 1984	
913	Simple File Transfer Protocol	M. Lottor	September 1984	
912	Authentication Service	M. St. Johns	September 1984	Obsoleted by RFC 931
911	EGP Gateway Under Berkeley UNIX 4.2	P. Kirton	August 1984	
910	Multimedia Mail Meeting Notes	H. Forsdick	August 1984	
909	Loader Debugger Protocol	W. Milliken	July 1984	
908	Reliable Data Protocol	B. Hinden J. Sax	July 1984	Updated by RFC 1151
907	Host Access Protocol Specification	Bolt Beranek and Newman, Inc.	July 1984	Updated by RFC 1221
906	Bootstrap Loading Using TFTP	R. Finlayson	June 1984	
905	ISO Transport Protocol Specification ISO DP 8073	A. McKenzie	April 1984	Obsoletes RFC 892
904	Exterior Gateway Protocol Formal Specification	D. Mills	April 1984	Updates RFC 827; STD 18
903	Reverse Address-Resolution Protocol	R. Finlayson J. Mogul	June 1984	
902	ARPA Internet Protocol Policy	J. Reynolds J. Postel	July 1984	

901	Official ARPA-Internet Protocols	J. Reynolds J. Postel	June 1984	Obsoletes RFC 880; obsoleted by RFC 924; STD 1
900	Assigned Numbers	J. Reynolds J. Postel	June 1984	Obsoletes RFC 870; obsoleted by RFC 923
899	Request For Comments Summary Notes: 800-899	J. Postel	May 1984	
898	Gateway Special Interest Group Meeting Notes	B. Inden J. Postel M. Muuss J. Reynolds	April 1984	
897	Domain Name System Implementation Schedule	J. Postel	February 1984	Updates RFC 881; updated by RFC 921
896	Congestion Control in IP/TCP Internetworks	J. Nagle	January 1984	
895	Standard for the Transmission of IP Datagrams over Experimental Ethernet Networks	J. Postel	April 1984	
894	Standard for the Transmission of IP Datagrams over Ethernet Networks	C. Hornig	April 1984	
893	Trailer Encapsulations	M. Karels	April 1984	
892	ISO Transport Protocol Specification [Draft]	International Organization for Standardization	December 1983	Obsoleted by RFC 905
891	DCN Local-Network Protocols	D. Mills	December 1983	
890	Exterior Gateway Protocol Implementation Schedule	J. Postel	February 1984	
889	Internet Delay Experiments	D. Mills	December 1983	
888	STUB Exterior Gateway Protocol	L. Seamonson	January 1984	
887	Resource Location Protocol	M. Accetta	December 1983	
886	Proposed Standard for Message Header Munging	M. Rose	December 1983	
885	Telnet End of Record Option	J. Postel	December 1983	

(continued)

app. f

Table AF.1: RFC Index (continued)

RFC	Title	Author(s)	Date	Notes
884	Telnet Terminal Type Option	M. Solomon	December 1983	Obsoleted by RFC 930
883	Domain Names: Implementation Specification	P. Mockapetris	November 1983	Obsoleted by RFC 1034
882	Domain Names: Concepts and Facilities	P. Mockapetris	November 1983	Obsoleted by RFC 1034; updated by RFC 973
881	Domain Names: Plan and Schedule	J. Postel	November 1983	Updated by RFC 897
880	Official Protocols	J. Reynolds J. Postel	October 1983	Obsoletes RFC 840; obsoleted by RFC 901; STD 1
879	TCP Maximum Segment Size and Related Topics	J. Postel	November 1983	
878	ARPANET 1822L Host Access Protocol	A. Malis	December 1983	Obsoletes RFC 851
877	Standard for the Transmission of IP Datagrams over Public Data Networks	J. Korb	September 1983	Obsoleted by RFC 1356
876	Survey of SMTP Implementations	D. Smallberg	September 1983	
875	Gateways, Architectures, and Heffalumps	M. Padlipsky	September 1982	
874	Critique of X.25	M. Padlipsky	September 1982	
873	Illusion of Vendor Support	M. Padlipsky	September 1982	
872	TCP-on-a-LAN	M. Padlipsky	September 1982	
871	Perspective on the ARPANET Reference Model	M. Padlipsky	September 1982	
870	Assigned Numbers	J. Reynolds J. Postel	October 1983	Obsoletes RFC 820; obsoleted by RFC 900
869	Host Monitoring Protocol	B. Hinden	December 1983	
868	Time Protocol	K. Harrenstien J. Postel	May 1983	STD 26
867	Daytime Protocol	J. Postel	May 1983	STD 25
866	Active Users	J. Postel	May 1983	STD 23
865	Quote of the Day Protocol	J. Postel	May 1983	

864	Character Generator Protocol	J. Postel	May 1983	STD 22
863	Discard Protocol	J. Postel	May 1983	STD 21
862	Echo Protocol	J. Postel	May 1983	STD 20
861	Telnet Extended Options: List Option	J. Postel J. Reynolds	May 1983	
860	Telnet Timing Mark Option	J. Postel J. Reynolds	May 1983	STD 31
859	Telnet Status Option	J. Postel J. Reynolds	May 1983	Obsoletes RFC 651; STD 30
858	Telnet Suppress Go Ahead Option	J. Postel J. Reynolds	May 1983	STD 29
857	Telnet Echo Option	J. Postel J. Reynolds	May 1983	STD 28
856	Telnet Binary Transmission	J. Postel J. Reynolds	May 1983	STD 27
855	Telnet Option Specifications	J. Postel J. Reynolds	May 1983	STD 8
854	Telnet Protocol Specification	J. Postel J. Reynolds	May 1983	Obsoletes RFC 764; STD 8
853	Not Issued		January 1970	
852	ARPANET Short Blocking Feature	A. Malis	April 1983	
851	ARPANET 1822L Host Access Protocol	A. Malis	April 1983	Obsoletes RFC 802; obsoleted by RFC 878
850	Standard for Interchange of USENET Messages	M. Orton	June 1983	Obsoleted by RFC 1036
849	Suggestions for Improved Host Table Distribution	M. Crispin	May 1983	
848	Who Provides the 'Little' TCP Services?	D. Smallberg	March 1983	
847	Summary of Smallberg Surveys	J. Postel	February 1983	Obsoletes RFC 846
846	Who Talks TCP? — Survey of 22 February 1983	D. Smallberg	February 1983	Obsoletes RFC 845; obsoleted by RFC 847
845	Who Talks TCP? — Survey of 15 February 1983	D. Smallberg	February 1983	Obsoletes RFC 843; obsoleted by RFC 846

(continued)

Table AF.1: RFC Index (continued)

RFC	Title	Author(s)	Date	Notes
844	Who Talks ICMP, Too? — Survey of 18 February 1983	R. Clements	February 1983	
843	Who Talks TCP? — Survey of 8 February 1983	D. Smallberg	February 1983	Obsoletes RFC 842; obsoleted by RFC 845
842	Who Talks TCP? — Survey of 1 February 1983	D. Smallberg	February 1983	Obsoletes RFC 839; obsoleted by RFC 843
841	Specification for Message Format for Computer-Based Message Systems	National Bureau of Standards	January 1983	Obsoletes RFC 806
840	Official Protocols	J. Postel	April 1983	Obsoleted by RFC 880; STD 1
839	Who Talks TCP?	D. Smallberg	January 1983	Obsoletes RFC 838; obsoleted by RFC 842
838	Who Talks TCP?	D. Smallberg	January 1983	Obsoletes RFC 837; obsoleted by RFC 839
837	Who Talks TCP?	D. Smallberg	January 1983	Obsoletes RFC 836; obsoleted by RFC 838
836	Who Talks TCP?	D. Smallberg	January 1983	Obsoletes RFC 835; obsoleted by RFC 837
835	Who Talks TCP?	D. Smallberg	December 1982	Obsoletes RFC 834; obsoleted by RFC 836
834	Who Talks TCP?	D. Smallberg	December 1982	Obsoletes RFC 833; obsoleted by RFC 835
833	Who Talks TCP?	D. Smallberg	December 1982	Obsoletes RFC 832; obsoleted by RFC 834
832	Who Talks TCP?	D. Smallberg	December 1982	Obsoleted by RFC 833
831	Backup Access to the European Side of SATNET	B. Braden	December 1982	
830	Distributed System for Internet Name Service	Z. Su	October 1982	
829	Packet Satellite Technology Reference Sources	V. Cerf	November 1982	

828	Data Communications: IFIP's International 'Network' of Experts	K. Owen	August 1982	
827	Exterior Gateway Protocol (EGP)	E. Rosen	October 1982	Updated by RFC 904
826	Ethernet Address-Resolution Protocol, or, Converting Network Protocol Addresses to 48-Bit Ethernet Address for Transmission on Ethernet Hardware	D. Plummer	November 1982	
825	Request for Comments on Requests For Comments	J. Postel	November 1982	Obsoleted by RFC 1111
824	CRONUS Virtual Local Network	W. MacGregor	August 1982	
823	DARPA Internet Gateway	B. Hinden	September 1982	
822	Standard for the Format of ARPA Internet Text Messages	D. Crocker	August 1982	Obsoletes RFC 733; updated by RFC 987; updated by RFC 1327; STD 11
821	Simple Mail Transfer Protocol	J. Postel	August 1982	Obsoletes RFC 788; STD 10
820	Assigned Numbers	J. Postel	August 1982	Obsoletes RFC 790; obsoleted by RFC 870
819	Domain-Naming Convention for Internet User Applications	Z. Su J. Postel	August 1982	
818	Remote User Telnet Service	J. Postel	November 1982	
817	Modularity and Efficiency in Protocol Implementation	D. Clark	July 1982	
816	Fault Isolation and Recovery	D. Clark	July 1982	
815	IP Datagram Reassembly Algorithms	D. Clark	July 1982	
814	Name, Addresses, Ports, and Routes	D. Clark	July 1982	
813	Window and Acknowlegment Strategy in TCP	D. Clark	July 1982	
812	NICNAME/WHOIS	K. Harrenstien	March 1982	Obsoleted by RFC 954
811	Hostnames Server	K. Harrenstien E. Feinler	March 1982	Obsoleted by RFC 953

(continued)

app. f

Table AF.1: RFC Index (continued)

RFC	Title	Author(s)	Date	Notes
810	DoD Internet Host Table Specification	E. Feinler K. Harrenstien Z. Su	March 1982	Obsoletes RFC 608; obsoleted by RFC 952
809	UCL Facsimile System	T. Chang	February 1982	
808	Summary of Computer Mail Services Meeting Held at BBN on 10 January 1979	J. Postel	March 1982	
807	Multimedia Mail Meeting Notes	J. Postel	February 1982	
806	Proposed Federal Information Processing Standard: Specification for Message Format for Computer-Based Message Systems	National Bureau of Standards	September 1981	Obsoleted by RFC 841
805	Computer Mail Meeting Notes	J. Postel	February 1982	
804	CCITT Draft Recommendation T.4 [Standardization of Group 3 Facsimile Apparatus for Document Transmission]	International Telecommunication Union	January 1981	
803	Dacom 450/500 Facsimile Data Transcoding	A. Agarwal D. Mills	November 1981	
802	ARPANET 1822L Host Access Protocol	A. Malis	November 1981	Obsoleted by RFC 851
801	NCP/TCP Transition Plan	J. Postel	November 1981	
800	Request For Comments Summary Notes: 700-799	J. Postel	November 1982	
799	Internet Name Domains	D. Mills	September 1981	
798	Decoding Facsimile Data from the Rapicom 450	A. Katz	September 1981	
797	Format for Bitmap Files	A. Katz	September 1981	
796	Address Mappings	J. Postel	September 1981	
795	Service Mappings	J. Postel	September 1981	
794	Pre-Emption	V. Cerf	September 1981	
793	Transmission Control Protocol	J. Postel	September 1981	Obsoletes RFC 761; STD 7
792	Internet Control Message Protocol	J. Postel	September 1981	Obsoletes RFC 777; STD 5

791	Internet Protocol	J. Postel	September 1981	Obsoletes RFC 760; obsoleted by RFC 1060
790	Assigned Numbers	J. Postel	September 1981	Obsoletes RFC 776; obsoleted by RFC 820
789	Vulnerabilities of Network Control Protocols: An Example	E. Rosen	July 1981	
788	Simple Mail Transfer Protocol	J. Postel	November 1981	Obsoletes RFC 780; obsoleted by RFC 821
787	Connectionless Data Transmission Survey/Tutorial	A. Chapin	July 1981	
786	Mail Transfer Protocol: ISI TOPS20 MTP-NIMAIL Interface	J. Postel	July 1981	
785	Mail Transfer Protocol: ISI TOPS20 File Definitions	J. Postel	July 1981	
784	Mail Transfer Protocol: ISI TOPS20 Implementation	J. Postel	July 1981	
783	TFTP Protocol Revision 2	K. Sollins	June 1981	Obsoleted by RFC 1350
782	Virtual Terminal Management Model	J. Nabielsky	January 1981	
781	Specification of the Internet Protocol	Z. Su	May 1981	IP timestamp option
780	Mail Transfer Protocol	J. Postel	May 1981	Obsoletes RFC 772; obsoleted by RFC 788
779	Telnet Send-Location Option	E. Killian	April 1981	
778	DCNET Internet Clock Service	D. Mills	April 1981	
777	Internet Control Message Protocol	J. Postel	April 1981	Obsoletes RFC 760; obsoleted by RFC 792
776	Assigned Numbers	J. Postel	January 1981	Obsoletes RFC 770; obsoleted by RFC 790
775	Directory-Oriented FTP Commands	D. Mankins A. Owen	December 1980	
774	Internet Protocol Handbook: Table of Contents	J. Postel	October 1980	Obsoletes RFC 766
773	Comments on NCP/TCP Mail Service Transition Strategy	V. Cerf	October 1980	
772	Mail Transfer Protocol	J. Postel	September 1980	Obsoleted by RFC 780

(continued)

app.
f

Table AF.1: RFC Index (continued)

RFC	Title	Author(s)	Date	Notes
771	Mail Transition Plan	V. Cerf J. Postel	September 1980	
770	Assigned Numbers	J. Postel	September 1980	Obsoletes RFC 762; obsoleted by RFC 776
769	Rapicom 450 Facsimile File Format	J. Postel	September 1980	
768	User Datagram Protocol	J. Postel	August 1980	STD 6
767	Structured Format for Transmission of Multi-Media Documents	J. Postel	August 1980	
766	Internet Protocol Handbook: Table of Contents	J. Postel	July 1980	Obsoleted by RFC 774
765	File Transfer Protocol Specification	J. Postel	June 1980	Obsoletes RFC 542; obsoleted by RFC 959
764	Telnet Protocol Specification	J. Postel	June 1980	Obsoleted by RFC 854
763	Role Mailboxes	M. Abrams	May 1980	
762	Assigned Numbers	J. Postel	January 1980	Obsoletes RFC 758; obsoleted by RFC 770
761	DOD Standard Transmission Control Protocol	J. Postel	January 1980	Obsoleted by RFC 793; STD 7
760	DoD Standard Internet Protocol	J. Postel	January 1980	Obsoleted by RFC 777; obsoleted by RFC 791
759	Internet Message Protocol	J. Postel	August 1980	
758	Assigned Numbers	J. Postel	August 1979	Obsoletes RFC 755; obsoleted by RFC 762
757	Suggested Solution to the Naming Addressing, and Delivery Problem for ARPANET Message Systems	D. Deutsch	September 1979	
756	NIC Name Server — A Datagram-Based Information Utility	J. Pickens E. Feinler J. Mathis	July 1979	
755	Assigned Numbers	J. Postel	May 1979	Obsoletes RFC 750; obsoleted by RFC 758
754	Out-of-Net Host Addresses for Mail	J. Postel	April 1979	

753	Internet Message Protocol	J. Postel	March 1979	
752	Universal Host Table	M. Crispin	January 1979	
751	Survey of FTP mail and MLFL	P. Lebling	December 1978	
750	Assigned Numbers	J. Postel	September 1978	Obsoletes RFC 739; obsoleted by RFC 755
749	Telnet SUPDUP-Output Option	B. Greenberg	September 1978	
748	Telnet Randomly-Lose Option	M. Crispin	April 1978	
747	Recent Extensions to the SUPDUP Protocol	M. Crispin	March 1978	
746	SUPDUP Graphics Extension	R. Stallman	March 1978	
745	JANUS Interface Specifications	M. Beeler	March 1978	
744	MARS — A Message Archiving and Retrieval Service	J. Sattley	January 1978	
743	FTP extension: XRSQ/XRCP	K. Harrenstien	December 1977	
742	NAME/FINGER Protocol	K. Harrenstien	December 1977	Obsoleted by RFC 1194
741	Specifications for the Network Voice Protocol (NVP)	D. Cohen	November 1977	
740	NETRJS Protocol	B. Braden	November 1977	Obsoletes RFC 599
739	Assigned Numbers	J. Postel	November 1977	Obsoletes RFC 604; obsoleted by RFC 750
738	Time Server	K. Harrenstien	October 1977	
737	FTP Extension: XSEN	K. Harrenstien	October 1977	
736	Telnet SUPDUP Option	M. Crispin	October 1977	
735	Revised Telnet Byte Macro Option	D. Crocker	November 1977	Obsoletes RFC 729
734	SUPDUP Protocol	M. Crispin	October 1977	
733	Standard for the Format of ARPA Network Text Messages	D. Crocker J. Vittal	November 1977	Obsoletes RFC 724; obsoleted by RFC 822
732	Telnet Data Entry Terminal Option	J. Day	September 1977	Obsoletes RFC 731; updated by RFC 1043
731	Telnet Data Entry Terminal Option	J. Day	June 1977	Obsoleted by RFC 732
730	Extensible Field Addressing	J. Postel	May 1977	
729	Telnet Byte Macro Option	D. Crocker	May 1977	Obsoleted by RFC 735
728	Minor Pitfall in the Telnet Protocol	J. Day	April 1977	

(continued)

app.
f

Table AF.1: RFC Index (continued)

RFC	Title	Author(s)	Date	Notes
727	Telnet Logout Option	M. Crispin	April 1977	
726	Remote Controlled Transmission and Echoing Telnet Option	J. Postel D. Crocker	March 1977	
725	RJE Protocol for a Resource-Sharing Network	J. Day	March 1977	
724	Proposed Official Standard for the Format of ARPA Network Messages	D. Crocker J. Vittal	May 1977	Obsoleted by RFC 733
723	Not Issued		January 1970	
722	Thoughts on Interactions in Distributed Services	J. Haverty	September 1976	
721	Out-of-Band Control Signals in a Host-to-Host Protocol	L. Garlick	September 1976	
720	Address-Specification Syntax for Network Mail	D. Crocker	August 1976	
719	Discussion on RCTE	J. Postel	July 1976	
718	Comments on RCTE from the Tenex Implementation Experience	J. Postel	June 1976	
717	Assigned Network Numbers	J. Postel	July 1976	
716	Interim Revision to Appendix F of BBN 1822	D. Walden J. Levin	May 1976	
715	Not Issued		January 1970	
714	Host-Host Protocol for an ARPANET-Type Network	A. McKenzie	April 1976	
713	MSDTP-Message Services Data Transmission Protocol	J. Haverty	April 1976	
712	Distributed-Capability Computing System (DCCS)	J. Donnelley	February 1976	
711	Not Issued		January 1970	
710	Not Issued		January 1970	
709	Not Issued		January 1970	
708	Elements of a Distributed Programming System	J. White	January 1976	
707	High-Level Framework for Network-Based Resource Sharing	J. White	December 1975	
706	On the Junk Mail Problem	J. Postel	November 1975	

705	Front-End Protocol B6700 Version	R. Bryan	November 1975	
704	IMP/Host and Host/IMP Protocol Change	P. Santos	September 1975	Obsoletes RFC 687
703	July 1975 Survey of New-Protocol Telnet Servers	D. Dodds	July 1975	
702	September 1974 Survey of New-Protocol Telnet Servers	D. Dodds	September 1974	
701	August 1974 Survey of New-Protocol Telnet Servers	D. Dodds	August 1974	
700	Protocol Experiment	W. Plummer	August 1974	
699	Request for Comments Summary Notes: 600-699	J. Postel	November 1982	
698	Telnet Extended ASCII Option	T. Mock	July 1975	
697	CWD Command of FTP	J. Lieb	July 1975	
696	Comments on the IMP/Host and Host/IMP Protocol Changes	V. Cerf	July 1975	
695	Official Change in Host-Host Protocol	M. Krilanovich	July 1975	
694	Protocol Information	J. Postel	June 1975	
693	Not Issued		January 1970	
692	Comments on IMP/Host Protocol Changes, RFCs 687 and 690	S. Wolfe	June 1975	Updates RFC690
691	One More Try on the FTP	B. Harvey	May 1975	
690	Comments on the Proposed Host/IMP Protocol Changes	J. Postel	June 1975	Updates RFC 687; updated by RFC 692
689	Tenex NCP Finite State Machine for Connections	R. Clements	May 1975	
688	Tentative Schedule for the New Telnet Implementation for the TIP	D. Walden	June 1975	
687	IMP/Host and Host/IMP Protocol Changes	D. Walden	June 1975	Obsoleted by RFC 704; updated by RFC 690
686	Leaving Well Enough Alone	B. Harvey	May 1975	
685	Response Time in Cross-Network Debugging	M. Beeler	April 1975	

(continued)

app.
f

Table AF.1: RFC Index (continued)

RFC	Title	Author(s)	Date	Notes
684	Commentary on Procedure Calling as a Network Protocol	R. Schantz	April 1975	
683	FTPSRV — Tenex Extension for Paged Files	R. Clements	April 1975	
682	Not Issued		January 1970	
681	Network UNIX	S. Holmgren	March 1975	
680	Message Transmission Protocol	T. Myer	April 1975	Updates RFC 561
679	February 1975 Survey of New-Protocol Telnet Servers	D. Dodds	February 1975	
678	Standard File Formats	J. Postel	December 1974	
677	Maintenance of Duplicate Databases	P. Johnson	January 1975	
676	Not Issued		January 1970	
675	Specification of Internet Transmission Control Program	V. Cerf Y. Dalal C. Sunshine	December 1974	
674	Procedure Call Documents — Version 2	J. Postel	December 1974	
673	Not Issued		January 1970	
672	Multi-Site Data Collection Facility	R. Schantz	December 1974	
671	Note on Reconnection Protocol	R. Schantz	December 1974	
670	Not Issued		January 1970	
669	November 1974 Survey of New-Protocol Telnet Servers	D. Dodds	December 1974	
668	Not Issued		January 1970	
667	BBN Host Ports	S. Chipman	December 1974	
666	Specification of the Unified User-Level Protocol	M. Padlipsky	November 1974	
665	Not Issued		January 1970	
664	Not Issued		January 1970	
663	Lost Message Detection and Recovery Protocol	R. Kanodia	November 1974	

662	Performance Improvement in ARPANET File Transfers from Multics	R. Kanodia	November 1974	
661	Protocol Information	J. Postel	November 1974	
660	Some Changes to the IMP and the IMP/Host Interface	D. Walden	October 1974	
659	Announcing Additional Telnet Options	J. Postel	October 1974	
658	Telnet Output Line-Feed Disposition	D. Crocker	October 1974	
657	Telnet Output Vertical Tab Disposition Option	D. Crocker	October 1974	
656	Telnet Output Vertical Tabstops Option	D. Crocker	October 1974	
655	Telnet Output Formfeed Disposition Option	D. Crocker	October 1974	
654	Telnet Output Horizontal Tab Disposition Option	D. Crocker	October 1974	
653	Telnet Output Horizontal Tabstops Option	D. Crocker	October 1974	
652	Telnet Output Carriage-Return Disposition Option	D. Crocker	October 1974	
651	Revised Telnet Status Option	D. Crocker	October 1974	Obsoleted by RFC 859
650	Not Issued		January 1970	
649	Not Issued		January 1970	
648	Not Issued		January 1970	
647	Proposed Protocol for Connecting Host Computers to ARPA-Like Networks via Front-End Processors	M. Padlipsky	November 1974	
646	Not Issued		January 1970	
645	Network Standard Data Specification Syntax	D. Crocker	June 1974	
644	On the Problem of Signature Authentication for Network Mail	R. Thomas	July 1974	
643	Network Debugging Protocol	E. Mader	July 1974	
642	Ready Line Philosophy and Implementation	J. Burchfiel	July 1974	
641	Not Issued		January 1970	
640	Revised FTP Reply Codes	J. Postel	June 1974	
639	Not Issued		January 1970	
638	IMP/TIP Preventive Maintenance Schedule	A. McKenzie	April 1974	Obsoletes RFC 633

(continued)

app.
f

Table AF.1: RFC Index (continued)

RFC	Title	Author(s)	Date	Notes
637	Change of Network Address for SU-DSL	A. McKenzie	April 1974	
636	TIP/Tenex Reliability Improvements	J. Burchfiel	June 1974	
635	Assessment of ARPANET Protocols	V. Cerf	April 1974	
634	Change in Network Address for Haskins Lab	A. McKenzie	April 1974	
633	IMP/TIP Preventive Maintenance Schedule	A. McKenzie	March 1974	Obsoleted by RFC 638
632	Throughput Degradations for Single Packet Messages	H. Opderbeck	May 1974	
631	International Meeting on Minicomputers and Data Communication: Call for Papers	A. Danthine	April 1974	
630	FTP Error Code Usage for More Reliable Mail Service	J. Sussmann	April 1974	
629	Scenario for Using the Network Journal	J. North	March 1974	
628	Status of RFC Numbers and a Note on Pre-Assigned Journal Numbers	M. Keeney	March 1974	
627	ASCII Text File of Hostnames	E. Feinler	March 1974	
626	On a Possible Lockup Condition in IMP Subnet Due to Message Sequencing	L. Kleinrock H. Opderbeck	March 1974	
625	On-Line Hostnames Service	E. Feinler	March 1974	
624	Comments on the File Transfer Protocol	W. Hathaway J. White	February 1974	Obsoletes RFC 607
623	Comments on On-Line Host Name Service	M. Krilanovich	February 1974	
622	Scheduling IMP/TIP Down Time	A. McKenzie	March 1974	
621	NIC User Directories at SRI ARC	M. Kudlick	March 1974	

620	Request for Monitor Host Table Updates	B. Ferguson	March 1974	
619	Mean Round-Trip Times in the ARPANET	W. Naylor H. Opderbeck	March 1974	
618	Few Observations on NCP Statistics	E. Taft	February 1974	
617	Note on Socket Number Assignment	E. Taft	February 1974	
616	Latest Network Maps	D. Walden	February 1973	
615	Proposed Network Standard Data Pathname Syntax	D. Crocker	March 1974	
614	Response to RFC 607: Comments on the File Transfer Protocol	K. Pogran	January 1974	Updates RFC 607
613	Network Connectivity: A Response to RFC 603	A. McKenzie	January 1974	Updates RFC 603
612	Traffic Statistics December 1973	A. McKenzie	January 1974	
611	Two Changes to the IMP/Host Protocol to Improve User/Network Communications	D. Walden	February 1974	
610	Further Datalanguage Design Concepts	J. Hill	December 1973	
609	Statement of Upcoming Move of NIC/NLS Service	B. Ferguson	January 1974	
608	Host Names On-Line	M. Kudlick	January 1974	Obsoleted by RFC 810
607	Comments on the File Transfer Protocol	M. Krilanovich	January 1974	Obsoleted by RFC 624; updated by RFC 614
606	Host Names On-Line	P. Deutsch	December 1973	
605	Not Issued		January 1970	
604	Assigned Link Numbers	J. Postel	December 1973	Obsoletes RFC 317; obsoletes RFC 503; obsoleted by RFC 739
603	Response to RFC 597: Host Status	J. Burchfiel	December 1973	Updates RFC 597; updated by RFC 613
602	'The Stockings Were Hung by the Chimney with Care'	R. Metcalfe	December 1973	
601	Traffic Statistics November 1973	A. McKenzie	December 1973	

(continued)

Table AF.1: RFC Index (continued)

RFC	Title	Author(s)	Date	Notes
600	Interfacing an Illinois Plasma Terminal to the ARPANET	A. Berggreen	November 1973	
599	Update on NETRJS	B. Braden	December 1973	Obsoletes RFC 189; obsoleted by RFC 740
598	RFC Index — December 5, 1973	Stanford Research Institute	December 1973	
597	Host Status	E. Feinler	December 1973	Updated by RFC 603
596	Second Thoughts on Telnet Go-Ahead	E. Taft	December 1973	
595	Second Thoughts in Defense of the Telnet Go-Ahead	W. Hathaway	December 1973	
594	Speedup of Host-IMP Interface	J. Burchfiel	December 1973	
593	Telnet and FTP Implementation Schedule Change	A. McKenzie J. Postel	November 1973	
592	Some Thoughts on System Design to Facilitate Resource Sharing	R. Watson	November 1973	
591	Addition to the Very Distant Host Specifications	D. Walden	November 1973	
590	MULTICS Address Change	M. Padlipsky	November 1973	
589	CCN NETRJS Server Messages to Remote User	B. Braden	November 1973	
588	London Node is Now Up	A. Stokes	October 1973	
587	Announcing New Telnet Options	J. Postel	November 1973	
586	Traffic Statistics October 1973	A. McKenzie	November 1973	
585	ARPANET Users Interest Working Group Meeting	D. Crocker E. Feinler	November 1973	
584	Charter for ARPANET Users Interest Working Group	D. Crocker	November 1973	
583	Not Issued		January 1970	

582	Comments on RFC 580: Machine Readable Protocols	R. Clements	November 1973	Updates RFC 580
581	Corrections to RFC 560: Remote Controlled Transmission and Echoing Telnet Option	D. Crocker J. Postel	November 1973	
580	Note to Protocol Designers and Implementers	J. Postel	October 1973	Updated by RFC 582
579	Traffic Statistics September 1973	A. McKenzie	November 1973	
578	Using MIT-Mathlab MACSYMA from MIT-DMS Muddle	A. Bhushan	October 1973	
577	Mail Priority	D. Crocker	October 1973	
576	Proposal for Modifying Linking	K. Victor	September 1973	
575	Not Issued		January 1970	
574	Announcement of a Mail Facility at UCSB	M. Krilanovich	September 1973	
573	Data and File Transfer: Some Measurement Results	A. Bhushan	September 1973	
572	Not Issued		January 1970	
571	Tenex FTP Problem	B. Braden	November 1973	
570	Experimental Input Mapping Between NVT ASCII and UCSB On Line System	J. Pickens	October 1973	
569	NETED: A Common Editor for the ARPA Network	M. Padlipsky	October 1973	
568	Response to RFC 567 — Cross-Country Network Bandwidth	J. McQuillan	September 1973	Updates RFC 567
567	Cross-Country Network Bandwidth	P. Deutsch	September 1973	Updated by RFC 568
566	Traffic Statistics August 1973	A. McKenzie	September 1973	
565	Storing Network Survey Data at the Datacomputer	D. Cantor	August 1973	
564	Not Issued		January 1970	
563	Comments on the RCTE Telnet Option	J. Davidson	August 1973	
562	Modifications to the Telnet Specification	A. McKenzie	August 1973	
561	Standardizing Network Mail Headers	A. Bhushan J. White	September 1973	Updated by RFC 680

(continued)

app.
f

Table AF.1: RFC Index (continued)

RFC	Title	Author(s)	Date	Notes
560	Remote Controlled Transmission and Echoing Telnet Option	D. Crocker J. Postel	August 1973	
559	Comments on the New Telnet Protocol and Its Implementation	A. Bhushan	August 1973	
558	Not Issued		January 1970	
557	Revelations in Network Host Measurements	B. Wessler	August 1973	
556	Missing			
555	Responses to Critiques of the Proposed Mail Protocol	J. White	July 1973	
554	Not Issued		January 1970	
553	Draft Design for a Text/Graphics Protocol	C. Irby	July 1973	
552	Single Access to Standard Protocols	A. Owen	July 1973	
551	[Letter from Feinroth re: NYU, ANL and LBL Entering the Net, and FTP Protocol]	B. Fink	August 1973	
550	NIC NCP Experiment	P. Deutsch	August 1973	
549	Minutes of Network Graphics Group Meeting, 15-17 July 1973	J. Michener	July 1973	
548	Hosts Using the IMP Going Down Message	D. Walden	August 1973	
547	Change to the Very Distant Host Specification	D. Walden	August 1973	
546	Tenex Load Averages for July 1973	R. Thomas	August 1973	
545	Of What Quality Be the UCSB Resources Evaluators?	J. Pickens	July 1973	
544	Locating On-Line Documentation at SRI-ARC	N. Meyer K. Kelley	July 1973	
543	Network Journal Submission and Delivery	N. Meyer	July 1973	
542	File Transfer Protocol	N. Neigus	July 1973	Obsoletes RFC 354; obsoleted by RFC 765
541	Not Issued		January 1970	
540	Not Issued		January 1970	

539	Thoughts on the Mail Protocol Proposed in RFC524	D. Crocker J. Postel	July 1973
538	Traffic Statistics June 1973	A. McKenzie	July 1973
537	Announcement of NGG Meeting July 16-17	S. Bunch	June 1973
536	Not Issued		January 1970
535	Comments on File Access Protocol	R. Thomas	July 1973
534	Lost Message Detection	D. Walden	July 1973
533	Message-ID Numbers	D. Walden	July 1973
532	UCSD-CC Server-FTP Facility	R. Merryman	July 1973
531	Feast or Famine? A Response to Two Recent RFCs About Network Information	M. Padlipsky	June 1973
530	Report on the Survey Project	A. Bhushan	June 1973
529	Note on Protocol Synch Sequences	A. McKenzie	June 1973
528	Software Checksumming in the IMP and Network Reliability	J. McQuillan	June 1973
527	ARPAWOCKY	D. Covill	May 1973
526	Technical Meeting: Digital Image Processing Software Systems	W. Pratt	June 1973
525	MIT-MATHLAB Meets UCSB-OLS — An Example of Resource Sharing	J. Pickens	June 1973
524	Proposed Mail Protocol	J. White	June 1973
523	SURVEY Is in Operation Again	A. Bhushan	June 1973
522	Traffic Statistics May 1973	A. McKenzie	June 1973
521	Restricted Use of IMP DDT	A. McKenzie	May 1973
520	Memo to FTP Group: Proposal for File Access Protocol	J. Day	June 1973
519	Resource Evaluation	J. Pickens	June 1973
518	ARPANET Accounts	E. Feinler	June 1973
517	Not Issued		January 1970
516	Lost Message Detection	J. Postel	May 1973

(continued)

app.
f

Table AF.1: RFC Index (continued)

RFC	Title	Author(s)	Date	Notes
515	Specifications for Datalanguage: Version 0/9	R. Winter	June 1973	
514	Network Make-Work	W. Kantrowitz	June 1973	
513	Comments on the New Telnet Specifications	W. Hathaway	May 1973	
512	More on Lost Message Detection	W. Hathaway	May 1973	
511	Enterprise Phone Service to NIC from ARPANET Sites	J. North	May 1973	
510	Request for Network Mailbox Addresses	J. White	May 1973	
509	Traffic Statistics April 1973	A. McKenzie	April 1973	
508	Real-Time Data Transmission on the ARPANET	L. Pfeifer	May 1973	
507	Not Issued		January 1970	
506	FTP Command Naming Problem	M. Padlipsky	June 1973	
505	Two Solutions to a File Transfer Access Problem	M. Padlipsky	June 1973	
504	Distributed Resources Workshop Announcement	R. Thomas	April 1973	
503	Socket Number List	J. Postel	April 1973	Obsoletes RFC 433; obsoleted by RFC 604
502	Not Issued		January 1970	
501	Un-Muddling 'Free File Transfer'	K. Pogran	May 1973	
500	Integration of Data Management Systems on a Computer Network	A. Shoshani	April 1973	
499	Harvard's Network RJE	B. Reussow	April 1973	
498	On Mail Service to CCN	B. Braden	April 1973	
497	Missing			
496	TNLS Quick Reference Card Is Available	M. Auerbach	April 1973	
495	Telnet Protocol Specifications	A. McKenzie	May 1973	Obsoletes RFC 158

494	Availability of MIX and MIXAL in the Network	D. Walden	April 1973	
493	E.W., Jr Graphics Protocol	K. Kelley	April 1973	
492	Response to RFC 467	E. Meyer	April 1973	Updates RFC 467
491	What Is 'Free'?	M. Padlipsky	April 1973	
490	Surrogate RJS for UCLA-CCN	J. Pickens	March 1973	
489	Comment on Resynchronization of Connection Status Proposal	J. Postel	March 1973	
488	NLS Classes at Network Sites	M. Auerbach	March 1973	
487	Free File Transfer	R. Bressler	April 1973	
486	Data Transfer Revisited	R. Bressler	March 1973	
485	MIX and MIXAL at UCSB	J. Pickens	March 1973	
484	Not Issued		January 1970	
483	Cancellation of the Resource Notebook Framework Meeting	M. Kudlick	March 1973	
482	Traffic Statistics February 1973	A. McKenzie	March 1973	
481	Not Issued		January 1970	
480	Host-Dependent FTP Parameters	J. White	March 1973	
479	Use of FTP by the NIC Journal	J. White	March 1973	
478	FTP Server-Server Interaction — II	R. Bressler	March 1973	
477	Remote Job Service at UCSB	M. Krilanovich	May 1973	
476	IMP/TIP Memory Retrofit Schedule Rev 2	A. McKenzie	March 1973	Obsoletes RFC 447
475	FTP and Network Mail System	A. Bhushan	March 1973	
474	Announcement of NGWG Meeting: Call for Papers	S. Bunch	March 1973	
473	MIX and MIXAL?	D. Walden	February 1973	
472	Illinois' Reply to Maxwell's Request for Graphics Information NIC 14925	S. Bunch	March 1973	
471	Workshop on Multi-Site Executive Programs	R. Thomas	March 1973	
470	Change in Socket for TIP News Facility	R. Thomas	March 1973	
469	Network Mail Meeting Summary	M. Kudlick	March 1973	

(continued)

app.
f

Table AF.1: RFC Index (continued)

RFC	Title	Author(s)	Date	Notes
468	FTP Data Compression	B. Braden	March 1973	
467	Proposed Change to Host-Host Protocol: Resynchronization of Connection Status	J. Burchfiel	February 1973	Updated by RFC 492
466	Telnet Logger/Server for Host LL-67	J. Winett	February 1973	
465	Not Issued		January 1970	
464	Resource Notebook Framework	M. Kudlick	February 1973	
463	FTP Comments and Response to RFC 430	A. Bhushan	February 1973	
462	Responding to User Needs	D. Crocker	February 1973	
461	Telnet Protocol Meeting Announcement	A. McKenzie	February 1973	
460	NCP Survey	C. Kline	February 1973	
459	Network Questionnaires	W. Kantrowitz	February 1973	
458	Mail Retrieval via FTP	R. Bressler	February 1973	
457	TIPUG	D. Walden	February 1973	
456	Memorandum: Date Change of Mail Meeting	M. Kudlick	February 1973	
455	Traffic Statistics January 1973	A. McKenzie	February 1973	
454	File Transfer Protocol — Meeting Announcement and a New Proposed Document	A. McKenzie	February 1973	
453	Meeting Announcement to Discuss a Network Mail System	M. Kudlick	February 1973	
452	Not Issued		January 1970	
451	Tentative Proposal for a Unified User-Level Protocol	M. Padlipsky	February 1973	
450	MULTICS Sampling Timeout Change	M. Padlipsky	February 1973	
449	Current Flow-Control Scheme for IMPSYS	D. Walden	January 1973	Updates RFC 442
448	Print Files in FTP	B. Braden	February 1973	

447	IMP/TIP Memory Retrofit Schedule	A. McKenzie	January 1973	Obsoletes RFC 434; obsoleted by RFC 476
446	Proposal to Consider a Network Program Resource Notebook	P. Deutsch	January 1973	
445	IMP/TIP Preventive Maintenance Schedule	A. McKenzie	January 1973	
444	Not Issued		January 1970	
443	Traffic Statistics December 1972	A. McKenzie	January 1973	
442	Current Flow-Control Scheme for IMPSYS	V. Cerf	January 1973	Updated by RFC 449
441	Inter-Entity Communication — an Experiment	R. Bressler	January 1973	
440	Scheduled Network Software Maintenance	D. Walden	January 1973	
439	PARRY Encounters the DOCTOR	V. Cerf	January 1973	
438	FTP Server-Server Interaction	R. Clements	January 1973	
437	Data Reconfiguration Service at UCSB	E. Faeh	June 1973	
436	Announcement of RJS at UCSB	M. Krilanovich	January 1973	
435	Telnet Issues	D. Walden	January 1973	Updates RFC 318
434	IMP/TIP Memory Retrofit Schedule	A. McKenzie	January 1973	Obsoleted by RFC 447
433	Socket Number List	J. Postel	December 1972	Obsoletes RFC 349; obsoleted by RFC 503
432	Network Logical Map	N. Neigus	December 1972	
431	Update on SMFS Login and Logout	M. Krilanovich	December 1972	Obsoletes RFC 399
430	Comments on File Transfer Protocol	B. Braden	February 1973	
429	Character Generator Process	J. Postel	December 1972	
428	Not Issued		January 1970	
427	Not Issued		January 1970	
426	Reconnection Protocol	R. Thomas	January 1973	
425	But My NCP Costs $500 a Day	R. Bressler	December 1972	
424	Not Issued		January 1970	
423	UCLA Campus Computing Network Liaison Staff for ARPANET	B. Noble	December 1972	Obsoletes RFC 389

(continued)

app.
f

Table AF.1: RFC Index (continued)

RFC	Title	Author(s)	Date	Notes
422	Traffic Statistics November 1972	A. McKenzie	December 1972	
421	Software Consulting Service for Network Users	A. McKenzie	November 1972	
420	CCA ICCC Weather Demo	H. Murray	January 1973	
419	To: Network Liaisons and Station Agents	A. Vezza	December 1972	
418	Server File Transfer under TSS/360 at NASA Ames	W. Hathaway	November 1972	
417	Link Usage Violation	J. Postel C. Kline	December 1972	
416	ARC System Will Be Unavailable	J. Norton	November 1972	
415	Tenex Bandwidth	H. Murray	November 1972	
414	File Transfer Protocol (FTP) Status and Further Comments	A. Bhushan	December 1972	Updates RFC 385
413	Traffic Statistics October 1972	A. McKenzie	November 1972	
412	User FTP Documentation	G. Hicks	November 1972	
411	New MULTICS Network Software Features	M. Padlipsky	November 1972	
410	Removal of the 30-Second Delay when Hosts Come Up	J. McQuillan	November 1972	
409	Tenex Interface to UCSB's Simple-Minded File System	J. White	December 1972	
408	NETBANK	A. Owen J. Postel	October 1972	
407	Remote Job Entry Protocol	R. Bressler A. McKenzie	October 1972	Obsoletes RFC 360
406	Scheduled IMP Software Releases	J. McQuillan	October 1972	
405	Correction to RFC 404	A. McKenzie	October 1972	Obsoletes RFC 404
404	Host Address Changes Involving Rand and ISI	A. McKenzie	October 1972	Obsoleted by RFC 405
403	Desirability of a Network 1108 Service	G. Hicks	January 1973	

402	ARPA Network Mailing Lists	J. North	October 1972	Obsoletes RFC 363
401	Conversion of NGP-0 Coordinates to Device Specific Coordinates	J. Hansen	October 1972	
400	Traffic Statistics September 1972	A. McKenzie	October 1972	
399	SMFS Login and Logout	M. Krilanovich	September 1972	Updates RFC 122; obsoleted by RFC 431
398	ICP Sockets	J. Pickens	September 1972	
397	Not Issued		January 1970	
396	Network Graphics Working Group Meeting — Second Iteration	S. Bunch	November 1972	
395	Switch Settings on IMPs and TIPs	J. McQuillan	October 1972	
394	Two Proposed Changes to the IMP-Host Protocol	J. McQuillan	September 1972	
393	Comments on Telnet Protocol Changes	J. Winett	October 1972	
392	Measurement of Host Costs for Transmitting Network Data	B. Wessler	September 1972	
391	Traffic Statistics August 1972	A. McKenzie	September 1972	Obsoletes RFC 378
390	TSO Scenario	B. Braden	September 1972	
389	UCLA Campus Computing Network Liaison Staff for ARPA Network	B. Noble	August 1972	Obsoleted by RFC 423
388	NCP Statistics	V. Cerf	August 1972	Updates RFC 323
387	Some Experiences in Implementing Network Graphics Protocol Level 0	K. Kelley	August 1972	
386	Letter to TIP Users-2	D. Walden	August 1972	
385	Comments on the File Transfer Protocol	A. Bhushan	August 1972	Updates RFC 354; updated by RFC 414
384	Official Site Idents for Organizations in the ARPA Network	J. North	August 1972	Obsoletes RFC 289
383	Not Issued		January 1970	
382	Mathematical Software on the ARPA Network	L. McDaniel	August 1972	
381	Three Aids to Improved Network Operation	J. McQuillan	July 1972	
380	Not Issued		January 1970	

(continued)

app.
f

Table AF.1: RFC Index (continued)

RFC	Title	Author(s)	Date	Notes
379	Using TSO at CCN	B. Braden	August 1972	
378	Traffic Statistics July 1972	A. McKenzie	August 1972	Obsoleted by RFC 391
377	Using TSO via ARPA Network Virtual Terminal	B. Braden	August 1972	
376	Network Host Status	E. Westheimer	August 1972	Obsoletes RFC 370
375	Not Issued		January 1970	
374	IMP System Announcement	A. McKenzie	July 1972	
373	Arbitrary Character Sets	J. McCarthy	July 1972	
372	Notes on a Conversation with Bob Kahn on the ICCC	R. Watson	July 1972	
371	Demonstration at International Computer Communications Conference	R. Kahn	July 1972	
370	Network Host Status	E. Westheimer	July 1972	Obsoletes RFC 367; obsoleted by RFC 376
369	Evaluation of ARPANET Services January-March 1972	J. Pickens	July 1972	
368	Comments on Proposed Remote Job Entry Protocol	B. Braden	July 1972	
367	Network Host Status	E. Westheimer	July 1972	Obsoletes RFC 366; obsoleted by RFC 370
366	Network Host Status	E. Westheimer	July 1972	Obsoletes RFC 362; obsoleted by RFC 367
365	Letter to All TIP Users	D. Walden	July 1972	
364	Serving Remote Users on the ARPANET	M. Abrams	July 1972	
363	ARPA Network Mailing Lists	Stanford Research Inst.	August 1972	Obsoletes RFC 329; obsoleted by RFC 402
362	Network Host Status	E. Westheimer	June 1972	Obsoletes RFC 353; obsoleted by RFC 366
361	Deamon Processes on Host 106	R. Bressler	July 1972	
360	Proposed Remote Job Entry Protocol	C. Holland	June 1972	Obsoleted by RFC 407

359	Status of the Release of the New IMP System	D. Walden	June 1972	Obsoletes RFC 343
358	Not Issued		January 1970	
357	Echoing Strategy for Satellite Links	J. Davidson	June 1972	
356	ARPA Network Control Center	R. Alter	June 1972	
355	Response to NWG/RFC 346	J. Davidson	June 1972	
354	File Transfer Protocol	A. Bhushan	July 1972	Obsoletes RFC 264; obsoletes RFC 265; obsoleted by RFC 542; updated by RFC 385
353	Network Host Status	E. Westheimer	June 1972	Obsoletes RFC 344; obsoleted by RFC 362
352	TIP Site Information Form	D. Crocker	June 1972	
351	Graphics Information Form for the ARPANET Graphics Resources Notebook	D. Crocker	June 1972	
350	User Accounts for UCSB On-Line System	R. Stoughton	May 1972	
349	Proposed Standard Socket Numbers	J. Postel	May 1972	Obsoleted by RFC 433
348	Discard Process	J. Postel	May 1972	
347	Echo Process	J. Postel	May 1972	
346	Satellite Considerations	J. Postel	May 1972	
345	Interest in Mixed-Integer Programming MPSX on NIC 360/91 at CCN	K. Kelley	May 1972	
344	Network Host Status	E. Westheimer	May 1972	Obsoletes RFC 342; obsoleted by RFC 353
343	IMP System Change Notification	A. McKenzie	May 1972	Obsoletes RFC 331; obsoleted by RFC 359
342	Network Host Status	E. Westheimer	May 1972	Obsoletes RFC 332; obsoleted by RFC 344
341	Not Issued		January 1970	
340	Proposed Telnet Changes	T. O'Sullivan	May 1972	
339	MLTNET: A Multi-Telnet Subsystem or Tenex	R. Thomas	May 1972	

(continued)

Table AF.1: RFC Index (continued)

RFC	Title	Author(s)	Date	Notes
338	EBCDIC/ASCII Mapping for Network RJE	B. Braden	May 1972	
337	Not Issued		January 1970	
336	Level 0 Graphic Input Protocol	I. Cotton	May 1972	
335	New Interface — IMP/360	R. Bryan	May 1972	
334	Network Use on May 8	A. McKenzie	May 1972	
333	Proposed Experiment with a Message Switching Protocol	R. Bressler D. Murphy D. Walden	May 1972	
332	Network Host Status	E. Westheimer	April 1972	Obsoletes RFC 330; obsoleted by RFC 342
331	IMP System Change Notification	J. McQuillan	April 1972	Obsoleted by RFC 343
330	Network Host Status	E. Westheimer	April 1972	Obsoletes RFC 326; obsoleted by RFC 332
329	ARPA Network Mailing Lists	Stanford Research Institute	May 1972	Obsoletes RFC 303; obsoleted by RFC 363
328	Suggested Telnet Protocol Changes	J. Postel	April 1972	
327	Data and File Transfer Workshop Notes	A. Bhushan	April 1972	
326	Network Host Status	E. Westheimer	April 1972	Obsoletes RFC 319; obsoleted by RFC 330
325	Network Remote Job Entry Program — NETRJS	G. Hicks	April 1972	
324	RJE Protocol Meeting	J. Postel	April 1972	
323	Formation of Network Measurement Group (NMG)	V. Cerf	March 1972	Updated by RFC 388
322	Well-Known Socket Numbers	V. Cerf J. Postel	March 1972	
321	CBI Networking Activity at MITRE	P. Karp	March 1972	
320	Workshop on Hard Copy Line Printers	R. Reddy	March 1972	

319	Network Host Status	E. Westheimer	March 1972	Obsoletes RFC 315; obsoleted by RFC 326
318	[Ad-Hoc Telnet Protocol]	J. Postel	April 1972	Updated by RFC 435
317	Official Host-Host Protocol Modification: Assigned Link Numbers	J. Postel	March 1972	Obsoleted by RFC 604
316	ARPA Network Data Management Working Group	D. McKay	February 1972	
315	Network Host Status	E. Westheimer	March 1972	Obsoletes RFC 306; obsoleted by RFC 319
314	Network Graphics Working Group Meeting	I. Cotton	March 1972	
313	Computer Based Instruction	T. O'Sullivan	March 1972	
312	Proposed Change in IMP-to-Host Protocol	A. McKenzie	March 1972	
311	New Console Attachments to the USCB Host	R. Bryan	February 1972	
310	Another Look at Data and File Transfer Protocols	A. Bhushan	April 1972	
309	Data and File Transfer Workshop Announcement	A. Bhushan	March 1972	
308	ARPANET Host Availability Data	M. Seriff	March 1972	
307	Using Network Remote Job Entry	E. Harslem	February 1972	
306	Network Host Status	E. Westheimer	February 1972	Obsoletes RFC 298; obsoleted by RFC 315
305	Unknown Host Numbers	R. Alter	February 1972	
304	Data Management System Proposal for the ARPA Network	D. McKay	February 1972	
303	ARPA Network Mailing Lists	Stanford Research Inst.	February 1972	Obsoletes RFC 300; obsoleted by RFC 329
302	Exercising the ARPANET	R. Bryan	February 1972	
301	BBN IMP #5 and NCC Schedule March 4, 1971	R. Alter	February 1972	
300	ARPA Network Mailing Lists	J. North	January 1972	Obsoletes RFC 211; obsoleted by RFC 303
299	Information Management System	D. Hopkin	February 1972	

(continued)

app.
f

Table AF.1: RFC Index (continued)

RFC	Title	Author(s)	Date	Notes
298	Network Host Status	E. Westheimer	February 1972	Obsoletes RFC 293; obsoleted by RFC 306
297	TIP Message Buffers	D. Walden	January 1972	
296	DS-1 Display System	D. Liddle	January 1972	
295	Report of the Protocol Workshop 12 October 1971	J. Postel	January 1972	
294	On the Use of 'set data type' Transaction in File Transfer Protocol	A. Bhushan	January 1972	Updates RFC 265
293	Network Host Status	E. Westheimer	January 1972	Obsoletes RFC 288; obsoleted by RFC 298
292	E.W., Jr. Graphics Protocol: Level 0 Only	K. Kelley	January 1972	
291	Data Management Meeting Announcement	D. McKay	January 1972	
290	Computer Networks and Data Sharing: A Bibliography	A. Mullery	January 1972	Obsoletes RFC 243
289	What We Hope Is an Official List of Host Names	R. Watson	December 1971	Obsoleted by RFC 384
288	Network Host Status	E. Westheimer	January 1972	Obsoletes RFC 287; obsoleted by RFC 293
287	Status of Network Hosts	E. Westheimer	December 1971	Obsoletes RFC 267; obsoleted by RFC 288
286	Network Library Information System	E. Forman	December 1971	
285	Network Graphics	D. Huff	December 1971	
284	Not Issued		January 1970	
283	NETRJT: Remote Job Service Protocol for TIPS	B. Braden	December 1971	Updates RFC 189
282	Graphics Meeting Report	M. Padlipsky	December 1971	
281	Suggested Addition to File Transfer Protocol	A. McKenzie	December 1971	
280	Draft of Host Names	R. Watson	November 1971	
279	Not Issued		January 1970	

278	McKenzie, A.M, Melvin, J.T Sundberg, R.L, Watson, R.W, White, J.E Revision of the Mail Box Protocol	A. Bhushan B. Braden J. Heafner A. McKenzie	November 1971	Obsoletes RFC 221
277	Not Issued		January 1970	
276	NIC Course	R. Watson	November 1971	
275	Not Issued		January 1970	
274	Establishing a Local Guide for Network Usage	E. Forman	November 1971	
273	More on Standard Host Names	R. Watson	October 1971	Obsoletes RFC 237
272	Not Issued		January 1970	
271	IMP System Change Notifications	B. Cosell	January 1972	
270	Correction to BBN Report No. 1822	A. McKenzie	NIC NO 7958	January 1972
269	Some Experience with File Transfer	H. Brodie	December 1971	Updates RFC 122
268	Graphics Facilities Information	J. Postel	November 1971	
267	Network Host Status	E. Westheimer	November 1971	Obsoletes RFC 266; obsoleted by RFC 287
266	Network Host Status	E. Westheimer	November 1971	Obsoletes RFC 255; obsoleted by RFC 267
265	Heafner, J.F, McKenzie, A.M Melvin, J.T, Sundberg, R.L Watson, R.W, White, J.E. File Transfer Protocol	A. Bhushan B. Braden J. Heafner	November 1971	Obsoletes RFC 172; obsoleted by RFC 354; updated by RFC 294
264	Heafner, J.F, McKenzie, A.M Melvin, J.T, Sundberg, R.L Watson, R.W, White, J.E. Data Transfer Protocol	A. Bhushan B. Braden J. Heafner	December 1971	Obsoletes RFC 171; obsoleted by RFC 354
263	Very Distant Host Interface	A. McKenzie	December 1971	
262	Not Issued		January 1970	
261	Not Issued		January 1970	
260	Not Issued		January 1970	
259	Not Issued		January 1970	
258	Not Issued		January 1970	

(continued)

app. f

Table AF.1: RFC Index (continued)

RFC	Title	Author(s)	Date	Notes
257	Not Issued		January 1970	
256	IMPSYS Change Notification	B. Cosell	November 1971	
255	Status of Network Hosts	E. Westheimer	October 1971	Obsoletes RFC 252; obsoleted by RFC 266
254	Scenarios for Using ARPANET Computers	A. Bhushan	October 1971	
253	Second Network Graphics Meeting Details	J. Moorer	October 1971	
252	Network Host Status	E. Westheimer	October 1971	Obsoletes RFC 240; obsoleted by RFC 255
251	Weather Data	D. Stern	October 1971	
250	Some Thoughts on File Transfer	H. Brodie	October 1971	
249	Coordination of Equipment and Supplies Purchase	R. Borelli	October 1971	
248	Not Issued		January 1970	
247	Proffered Set of Standard Host Names	P. Karp	October 1971	Obsoletes RFC 226
246	Network Graphics Meeting	A. Vezza	October 1971	
245	Reservations for Network Group Meeting	C. Falls	October 1971	
244	Not Issued		January 1970	
243	Network and Data Sharing Bibliography	A. Mullery	October 1971	Obsoleted by RFC 290
242	Data Descriptive Language for Shared Data	L. Haibt	July 1971	
241	Connecting Computers to MLC Ports	A. McKenzie	September 1971	
240	Site Status	A. McKenzie	September 1971	Obsoletes RFC 235; obsoleted by RFC 252
239	Host Mnemonics Proposed in RFC 226 NIC 7625	B. Braden	September 1971	
238	Comments on DTP and FTP Proposals	B. Braden	September 1971	Updates RFC 171

237	NIC View of Standard Host Names	R. Watson	September 1971	Obsoleted by RFC 273
236	Standard Host Names	J. Postel	September 1971	Obsoletes RFC 229
235	Site Status	E. Westheimer	September 1971	Obsoleted by RFC 240
234	Network Working Group Meeting Schedule	A. Vezza	October 1971	Updates RFC 222
233	Standardization of Host Call Letters	A. Bhushan R. Metcalfe	September 1971	
232	Postponement of Network Graphics Meeting	A. Vezza	September 1971	
231	Service Center Standards for Remote Usage: A User's View	J. Heafner	September 1971	
230	Toward Reliable Operation of Minicomputer-Based Terminals on a TIP	T. Pyke	September 1971	
229	Standard Host Names	J. Postel	September 1971	Obsoleted by RFC 236
228	Clarification	D. Walden	September 1971	Updates RFC 70
227	Data Transfer Rates Rand/UCLA	J. Heafner	September 1971	Updates RFC 113
226	Standardization of Host Mnemonics	P. Karp	September 1971	Obsoleted by RFC 247
225	Rand/UCSB Network Graphics Experiment	E. Harslem	September 1971	Updates RFC 74
224	Comments on Mailbox Protocol	A. McKenzie	September 1971	
223	Network Information Center Schedule for Network Users	J. Melvin	September 1971	
222	Subject: System Programmer's Workshop	R. Metcalfe	September 1971	Updated by RFC 234
221	Mail Box Protocol: Version 2	R. Watson	August 1971	Obsoletes RFC 196; obsoleted by RFC 278
220	Not Issued		January 1970	
219	User's View of the Datacomputer	R. Winter	September 1971	
218	Changing the IMP Status Reporting Facility	B. Cosell	September 1971	
217	Specifications Changes for OLS RJE/RJOR, and SMFS	J. White	September 1971	Updates RFC 74
216	Telnet Access to UCSB's On-Line System	J. White	September 1971	

(continued)

app.
f

Table AF.1: RFC Index (continued)

RFC	Title	Author(s)	Date	Notes
215	NCP, ICP, and Telnet: The Terminal IMP Implementation	A. McKenzie	August 1971	
214	Network Checkpoint	E. Harslem	August 1971	Obsoletes RFC 198
213	IMP System Change Notification	B. Cosell	August 1971	
212	NWG Meeting on Network Usage	University of Southern California	August 1971	Obsoletes RFC 207
211	ARPA Network Mailing Lists	J. North	August 1971	Obsoletes RFC 168; obsoleted by RFC 300
210	Improvement of Flow Control	W. Conrad	August 1971	
209	Host/IMP Interface Documentation	B. Cosell	August 1971	
208	Address Tables	A. McKenzie	August 1971	
207	September Network Working Group Meeting	A. Vezza	August 1971	Obsoleted by RFC 212
206	User Telnet — Description of an Initial Implementation	J. White	August 1971	
205	NETCRT — A Character Display Protocol	B. Braden	August 1971	
204	Sockets in Use	J. Postel	August 1971	
203	Achieving Reliable Communication	R. Kalin	August 1971	
202	Possible Deadlock in ICP	J. Postel	July 1971	
201	Not Issued		January 1970	
200	RFC List by Number	J. North	August 1971	Obsoletes RFC 160; obsoletes RFC 170
199	Suggestions for a Network Data-Tablet Graphics Protocol	T. Williams	July 1971	
198	Site Certification — Lincoln Labs 360/67	J. Heafner	July 1971	Obsoletes RFC 193; obsoleted by RFC 214
197	Initial Connection Protocol — Reviewed	A. Shoshani	July 1971	
196	Mail Box Protocol	R. Watson	July 1971	Obsoleted by RFC 221

195	Data Computers-Data Descriptions and Access Language	G. Mealy	July 1971	
194	Data Reconfiguration Service — Compiler/Interpreter Implementation Notes	V. Cerf J. Heafner R. Metcalfe J. White	July 1971	
193	Network Checkout	J. Heafner	July 1971	Obsoleted by RFC 198
192	Some Factors which a Network Graphics Protocol Must Consider	R. Watson	July 1971	
191	Graphics Implementation and Conceptualization at Augmentation Research Center	C. Irby	July 1971	
190	DEC PDP-10-IMLAC Communications System	P. Deutsch	July 1971	
189	Interim NETRJS Specifications	B. Braden	July 1971	Obsoletes RFC 88; obsoleted by RFC 599; updated by RFC 283
188	Data Management Meeting Announcement	P. Karp	January 1971	
187	Network/440 Protocol Concept	D. McKay	July 1971	
186	Network Graphics Loader	J. Michener	July 1971	
185	NIC Distribution of Manuals and Handbooks	J. North	July 1971	
184	Proposed Graphic Display Modes	K. Kelley	July 1971	
183	EBCDIC Codes and their Mapping to ASCII	J. Winett	July 1971	
182	Compilation of List of Relevant Site Reports	J. North	June 1971	
181	Modifications to RFC 177	J. McConnell	July 1971	Updates RFC 177
180	File System Questionnaire	A. McKenzie	June 1971	
179	Link Number Assignments	A. McKenzie	June 1971	Updates RFC 107
178	Network Graphic Attention Handling	I. Cotton	June 1971	
177	Device-Independent Graphical Display Description	J. McConnell	June 1971	Updates RFC 125; updated by RFC 181

(continued)

app.
f

Table AF.1: RFC Index (continued)

RFC	Title	Author(s)	Date	Notes
176	Comments on 'Byte Size for Connections'	A. Bhushan R. Kanodia R. Metcalfe J. Postel	June 1971	
175	Comments on 'Socket Conventions Reconsidered'	J. Heafner	June 1971	
174	UCLA — Computer Science Graphics Overview	J. Postel V. Cerf	June 1971	
173	Network Data Management Committee Meeting Announcement	P. Karp	June 1971	
172	File Transfer Protocol	A. Bhushan B. Braden J. Heafner	June 1971	Updates RFC 114; obsoleted by RFC 265
171	Data Transfer Protocol	A. Bhushan B. Braden J. Heafner	June 1971	Updates RFC 114; obsoleted by RFC 264; updated by RFC 238
170	RFC List by Number	Stanford Research Institute	June 1971	Obsoleted by RFC 200
169	Computer Networks	S. Crocker	May 1971	
168	ARPA Network Mailing Lists	J. North	May 1971	Obsoletes RFC 155; obsoleted by RFC 211
167	Socket Conventions Reconsidered	A. Bhushan R. Metcalfe	May 1971	
166	Data Reconfiguration Service: An Implementation Specification	R. Anderson V. Cerf J. Heafner	May 1971	
165	Proffered Official Initial Connection Protocol	J. Postel	May 1971	Obsoletes RFC 123; obsoletes RFC 143; obsoletes RFC 145
164	Minutes of Network Working Group Meeting, 5/16 Through 5/19/71	J. Heafner	May 1971	

163	Data Transfer Protocols	V. Cerf	May 1971	
162	NETBUGGER3	M. Kampe	May 1971	
161	Solution to the Race Condition in the ICP	A. Shoshani	May 1971	
160	RFC Brief List	Stanford Research Institute	May 1971	Obsoleted by RFC 200
159	Not Issued		January 1970	
158	Telnet Protocol: A Proposed Document	T. O'Sullivan	May 1971	Updates RFC 139; obsoleted by RFC 495
157	Invitation to the Second Symposium on Problems in the Optimization of Data Communications Systems	V. Cerf	May 1971	
156	Status of the Illinois Site: Response to RFC 116	J. Bouknight	April 1971	Updates RFC 116
155	ARPA Network Mailing Lists	J. North	May 1971	Obsoletes RFC 95; obsoleted by RFC 168
154	Exposition Style	S. Crocker	May 1971	Obsoletes RFC 132
153	SRI ARC-NIC Status	J. Melvin	May 1971	
152	SRI Artificial Intelligence Status Report	M. Wilber	May 1971	
151	Comments on a Proffered Official ICP	A. Shoshani	May 1971	Updates RFC 127 RFCs 123, 127
150	Use of IPC Facilities: A Working Paper	R. Kalin	May 1971	
149	Best-Laid Plans	S. Crocker	May 1971	Updates RFC 140
148	Comments on RFC 123	A. Bhushan	May 1971	Updates RFC 123
147	Definition of a Socket	J. Winett	May 1971	Updates RFC 129
146	Views on Issues Relevant to Data Sharing on Computer Networks	P. Karp	May 1971	
145	Initial Connection Protocol Control Commands	J. Postel	May 1971	Obsoletes RFC 127; obsoleted by RFC 165
143	Regarding Proffered Official ICP	W. Naylor C. Kline J. Postel	May 1971	Obsoleted by RFC 165
142	Time-Out Mechanism in the Host-Host Protocol	C. Kline	May 1971	

(continued)

app.
f

Table AF.1: RFC Index (continued)

RFC	Title	Author(s)	Date	Notes
141	Comments on RFC 114: A File Transfer Protocol	J. Heafner	April 1971	Updates RFC 114
140	Agenda for the May NWG Meeting	S. Crocker	May 1971	Updated by RFC 149
139	Discussion of Telnet Protocol	T. O'Sullivan	May 1971	Updates RFC 137; updated by RFC 158
138	Status Report on Proposed Data Reconfiguration Service	R. Anderson V. Cerf J. Heafner	April 1971	
137	Telnet Protocol — A Proposed Document	T. O'Sullivan	April 1971	Updated by RFC 139
136	Host Accounting and Administrative Procedures	R. Kahn	April 1971	
135	Response to NWG/RFC 110	W. Hathaway	April 1971	
134	Network Graphics Meeting	A. Vezza	April 1971	
133	File Transfer and Recovery	R. Sundberg	April 1971	
132	Typographical Error in RFC 107	J. White	April 1971	Updates RFC 107; obsoleted by RFC 154
131	Response to RFC 116: May NWG Meeting	J. Heafner	April 1971	Updates RFC 116
130	Response to RFC 111: Pressure from the Chairman	J. Heafner	April 1971	Updates RFC 111
129	Request for Comments on Socket Name Structure	J. Heafner	April 1971	Updated by RFC 147
128	Bytes	J. Postel	April 1971	
127	Comments on RFC 123	J. Postel	April 1971	Updates RFC 123; obsoleted by RFC 145; updated by RFC 151
126	Graphics Facilities at Ames Research Center	J. McConnell	April 1971	
125	Response to RFC 86: Proposal for Network Standard Format for a Graphics Data Stream	J. McConnell	April 1971	Updates RFC 86; updated by RFC 177
124	Typographical Error in RFC 107	J. Melvin	April 1971	Updates RFC 107

123	Proffered Official ICP	S. Crocker	April 1971	Updates RFC 98; obsoletes RFC 66; obsoletes RFC 80; obsoleted by RFC 165; updated by RFC 127; updated by RFC 148
122	Network Specifications for UCSB's Simple-Minded File System	J. White	April 1971	Updated by RFC 269; updated by RFC 399
121	Network On-Line Operators	M. Krilanovich	April 1971	
120	Network PLI Subprograms	M. Krilanovich	April 1971	
119	Network Fortran Subprograms	M. Krilanovich	April 1971	
118	Recommendations for Facility Documentation	R. Watson	April 1971	
117	Some Comments on the Official Protocol	J. Wong	April 1971	
116	Structure of the May NWG Meeting	S. Crocker	April 1971	Updates RFC 99; updated by RFC 131; updated by RFC 156
115	Some Network Information Center Policies on Handling Documents	R. Watson	April 1971	
114	File Transfer Protocol	A. Bhushan	April 1971	Updated by RFC 141; updated by RFC 171; updated by RFC 172
113	Network Activity Report: UCSB Rand	J. Heafner J. White	April 1971	Updated by RFC 227
112	User/Server Site Protocol: Network Host Questionnaire Responses	T. O'Sullivan	April 1971	
111	Pressure from the Chairman	S. Crocker	March 1971	Updates RFC 107; updated by RFC 130
110	Conventions for Using an IBM 2741 Terminal as a User Console for Access to Network Server Hosts	J. Winett	March 1971	
109	Level III Server Protocol for the Lincoln Laboratory NIC 360/67 Host	J. Winett	March 1971	

(continued)

app.
f

Table AF.1: RFC Index (continued)

RFC	Title	Author(s)	Date	Notes
108	Attendance List at the Urbana NWG Meeting, February 17-19, 1971	R. Watson	March 1971	Updates RFC 101
107	Output of the Host-Host Protocol Glitch Cleaning Committee	R. Bressler S. Crocker	March 1971	Updates RFC 102; updated by RFC 111; updated by RFC 124; updated by RFC 132; updated by RFC 179
106	User/Server Site Protocol Network Host Questionnaire	T. O'Sullivan	March 1971	
105	Network Specifications for Remote Job Entry and Remote Job Output Retrieval at UCSB	J. White	March 1971	
104	Link 191	J. Postel S. Crocker	February 1971	
103	Implementation of Interrupt Keys	R. Kalin	February 1971	
102	Output of the Host-Host Protocol Glitch Cleaning Committee	S. Crocker	February 1971	Updated by RFC 107
101	Notes on the Network Working Group Meeting, Urbana, Illinois February 17, 1971	R. Watson	February 1971	Updated by RFC 108
100	Categorization and Guide to NWG/RFCs	P. Karp	February 1971	
99	Network Meeting	P. Karp	February 1971	Updated by RFC 116
98	Logger Protocol Proposal	E. Meyer	February 1971	Updated by RFC 123
97	First Cut at a Proposed Telnet Protocol	J. Melvin	February 1971	
96	Interactive Network Experiment to Study Modes of Access to the Network Information Center	R. Watson	February 1971	
95	Distribution of NWG/RFC's Through the NIC	S. Crocker	February 1971	Obsoleted by RFC 155
94	Some Thoughts on Network Graphics	J. Heafner	February 1971	
93	Initial Connection Protocol	A. McKenzie	January 1971	

92	Not Issued		January 1970	
91	Proposed User-User Protocol	G. Mealy	December 1970	
90	CCN as a Network Service Center	B. Braden	January 1971	
89	Some Historic Moments in Networking	R. Metcalfe	January 1971	
88	NETRJS: A Third-Level Protocol for Remote Job Entry	B. Braden	January 1971	Obsoleted by RFC 189
87	Topic for Discussion at the Next Network Working Group Meeting	A. Vezza	January 1971	
86	Proposal for a Network Standard Format for a Data Stream to Control Graphics Display	S. Crocker	January 1971	Updated by RFC 125
85	Network Working Group Meeting	S. Crocker	December 1970	
84	List of NWG/RFC's 1-80	J. North	December 1970	
83	Language-Machine for Data Reconfiguration	R. Anderson J. Heafner	December 1970	
82	Network Meeting Notes	E. Meyer	December 1970	
81	Request for Reference Information	J. Bouknight	December 1970	
80	Protocols and Data Formats	J. Heafner	December 1970	Obsoleted by RFC 123
79	Logger Protocol Error	E. Meyer	November 1970	
78	NCP Status Report: UCSB/Rand	J. Heafner J. White	October 1970	
77	Network Meeting Report	J. Postel	November 1970	
76	Connection by Name: User-Oriented Protocol	J. Bouknight	October 1970	
75	Network Meeting	S. Crocker	October 1970	
74	Specifications for Network Use of the UCSB On-Line System	J. White	October 1970	Updated by RFC 217; updated by RFC 225
73	Response to NWG/RFC 67	S. Crocker	September 1970	
72	Proposed Moratorium on Changes to Network Protocol	R. Bressler	September 1970	
71	Reallocation in Case of Input Error	T. Schipper	September 1970	
70	Note on Padding	S. Crocker	October 1970	Updated by RFC 228
69	Distribution List Change for MIT	A. Bhushan	September 1970	Updates RFC 52

(continued)

app. f

Table AF.1: RFC Index (continued)

RFC	Title	Author(s)	Date	Notes
68	Comments on Memory Allocation Control Commands: CEASE, ALL GVB, RET, and RFNM	M. Elie	August 1970	
67	Proposed Change to Host/IMP Spec to Eliminate Marking	W. Crowther	January 1970	
66	NIC — Third-Level Ideas and Other Noise	S. Crocker	August 1970	Obsoleted by RFC 123
65	Comments on Host/Host Protocol Document #1	D. Walden	August 1970	
64	Getting Rid of Marking	M. Elie	July 1970	
63	Belated Network Meeting Report	V. Cerf	July 1970	
62	Systems for Interprocess Communication in a Resource Sharing Computer Network	D. Walden	August 1970	Obsoletes RFC 61
61	Note on Interprocess Communication in a Resource Sharing Computer Network	D. Walden	July 1970	Obsoleted by RFC 62
60	Simplified NCP Protocol	R. Kalin	July 1970	
59	Flow Control — Fixed Versus Demand Allocation	E. Meyer	June 1970	
58	Logical Message Synchronization	T. Skinner	June 1970	
57	Thoughts and Reflections on NWG/RFC 54	M. Kraley	June 1970	Updates RFC 54
56	Third-Level Protocol: Logger Protocol	E. Belove D. Black R. Flegal	June 1970	
55	Prototypical Implementation of the NCP	M. Kraley J. Postel S. Crocker	June 1970	
54	Official Protocol Proffering	S. Crocker J. Postel M. Kraley	June 1970	Updated by RFC 57

53	Official Protocol Mechanism	S. Crocker	June 1970	
52	Updated Distribution List	J. Postel S. Crocker	July 1970	Updated by RFC 69
51	Proposal for a Network Interchange Language	M. Elie	May 1970	
50	Comments on the Meyer Proposal	J. Haverty	April 1970	
49	Conversations with S. Crocker	E. Meyer	April 1970	UCLA
48	Possible Protocol Plateau	J. Postel S. Crocker	April 1970	
47	BBN's Comments on NWG/RFC #33	W. Crowther	April 1970	Updates RFC 33
46	ARPA Network Protocol Notes	E. Meyer	April 1970	
45	New Protocol Is Coming	J. Postel S. Crocker	April 1970	
44	Comments on NWG/RFC 33 and 36	A. Shoshani	April 1970	Updates RFC 36
43	Proposed Meeting [LIL]	A. Nemeth	April 1970	
42	Message Data Types	E. Ancona	March 1970	
41	IMP-IMP Teletype Communication	J. Melvin	March 1970	
40	More Comments on the Forthcoming Protocol	J. Heafner	March 1970	
39	Comments on Protocol Re: NWG/RFC #36	J. Heafner	March 1970	Updates RFC 36
38	Comments on Network Protocol from NWG/RFC #36	S. Wolfe	March 1970	
37	Network Meeting Epilogue, Etc.	S. Crocker	March 1970	
36	Protocol Notes	S. Crocker	March 1970	Updates RFC 33; updated by RFC 39; updated by RFC 44
35	Network Meeting	S. Crocker	March 1970	
34	Some Brief Preliminary Notes on the Augmentation Research Center Clock	W. English	February 1970	
33	New Host-Host Protocol	S. Crocker	February 1970	Obsoletes RFC 11; updated by RFC 36; updated by RFC 47

(continued)

**app.
f**

Table AF.1: RFC Index (continued)

RFC	Title	Author(s)	Date	Notes
32	Connecting M.I.T. Computers to the ARPA Computer-to-Computer Communication Network	D. Vedder	January 1969	
31	Binary Message Forms in Computer	D. Bobrow W. Sutherland	February 1968	
30	Documentation Conventions	S. Crocker	February 1970	Obsoletes RFC 27
29	Response to RFC 28	R. Kahn	January 1970	
28	Time Standards	W. English	January 1970	
27	Documentation Conventions	S. Crocker	December 1969	Obsoletes RFC 24; obsoleted by RFC 30
26	Not Issued		January 1970	
25	No High Link Numbers	S. Crocker	October 1969	
24	Documentation Conventions	S. Crocker	November 1969	Obsoletes RFC 16; obsoleted by RFC 27
23	Transmission of Multiple Control Messages	G. Gregg	October 1969	
22	Host-Host Control Message Formats	V. Cerf	October 1969	
21	Network Meeting	V. Cerf	October 1969	
20	ASCII Format for Network Interchange	V. Cerf	October 1969	
19	Two Protocol Suggestions to Reduce Congestion at Swap Bound Nodes	J. Kreznar	October 1969	
18	[Link Assignments]	V. Cerf	September 1969	
17	Some Questions Re: Host-IMP Protocol	J. Kreznar	August 1969	
16	M.I.T	S. Crocker	September 1969	Obsoletes RFC 10; obsoleted by RFC 24
15	Network Subsystem for Time-Sharing Hosts	C. Carr	September 1969	
14	Not Issued		January 1970	
13	[Referring to NWG/RFC 11]	V. Cerf	August 1969	

12	IMP-Host Interface Flow Diagrams	M. Wingfield	August 1969	
11	Implementation of the Host-Host Software Procedures in GORDO	G. Deloche	August 1969	Obsoleted by RFC 33
10	Documentation Conventions	S. Crocker	July 1969	Obsoletes RFC 3; obsoleted by RFC 16
9	Host Software	G. Deloche	May 1969	
8	Functional Specifications for the ARPA Network	G. Deloche	May 1969	
7	Host-IMP Interface	G. Deloche	May 1969	
6	Conversation with Bob Kahn	S. Crocker	April 1969	
5	Decode Encode Language	J. Rulifson	June 1969	
4	Network Timetable	E. Shapiro	March 1969	
3	Documentation Conventions	S. Crocker	April 1969	Obsoleted by RFC 10
2	Host Software	B. Duvall	April 1969	
1	Host Software	S. Crocker	April 1969	

Appendix G
Graphical Review of
Network Topologies

This appendix provides a graphical review of some popular networking topologies. To clarify their differences and similarities, compare and contrast the figures. For more information, refer to Table AG.1, which arranges the topologies by type and cross-references the appropriate Encyclopedia entries.

Table AG.1: Representative Types of Network Topologies		
Type	**Appendix Figure**	**For More Information**
Bus	AG.1	See **Bus network topology**
Bridge, Backbone	AG.2A	See **Backbone bridge topology**
Bridge, Cascaded	AG.2B	See **Cascaded bridge topology**
Mesh	AG.4	See **Mesh network topology**
Ring	AG.5	See **Ring topology**
Ring, Star-Wired (Example of Hybrid Topology)	AG.8	See **Star-wired ring topology**
Star	AG.6	See **Star topology**
Star, Distributed	AG.3	See **Distributed star topology**
Tree	AG.7	See **Tree topology**

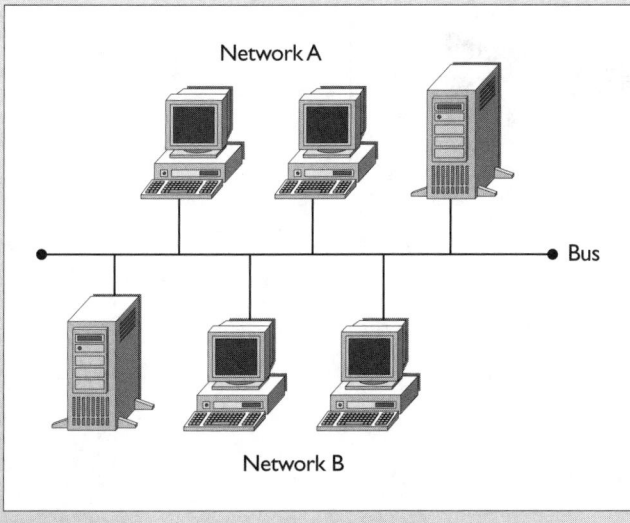

Figure AG.1
Bus topology

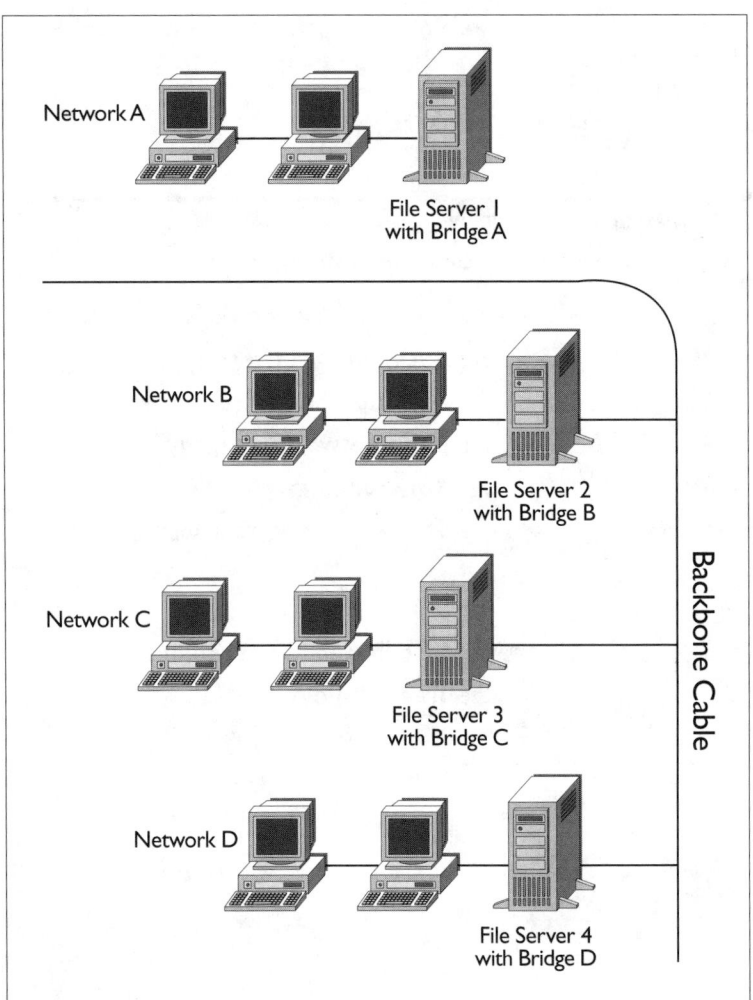

Figure AG.2A
Backbone bridge topology

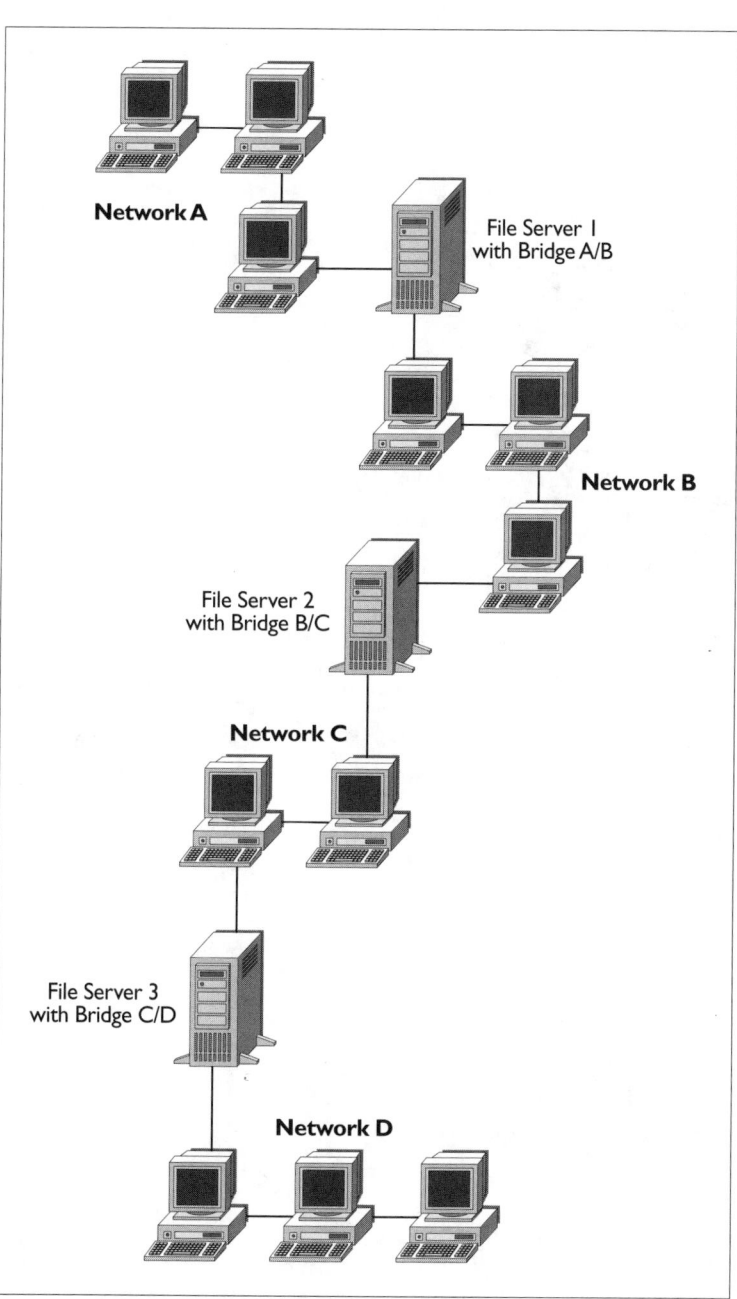

Figure AG.2B
Cascaded bridge topology

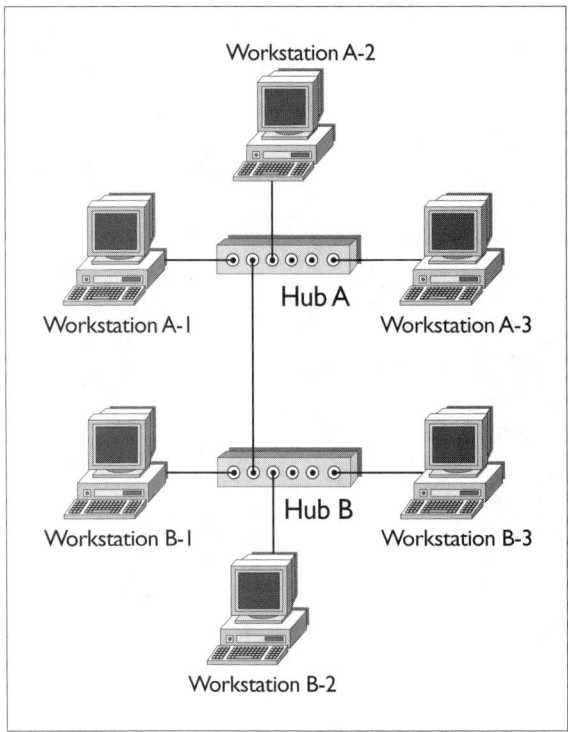

Figure AG.3
Distributed star topology

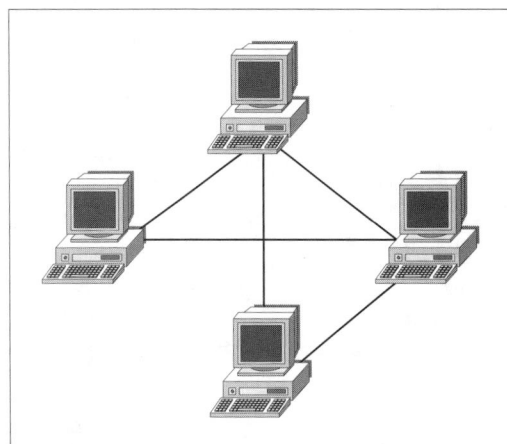

Figure AG.4
Mesh topology

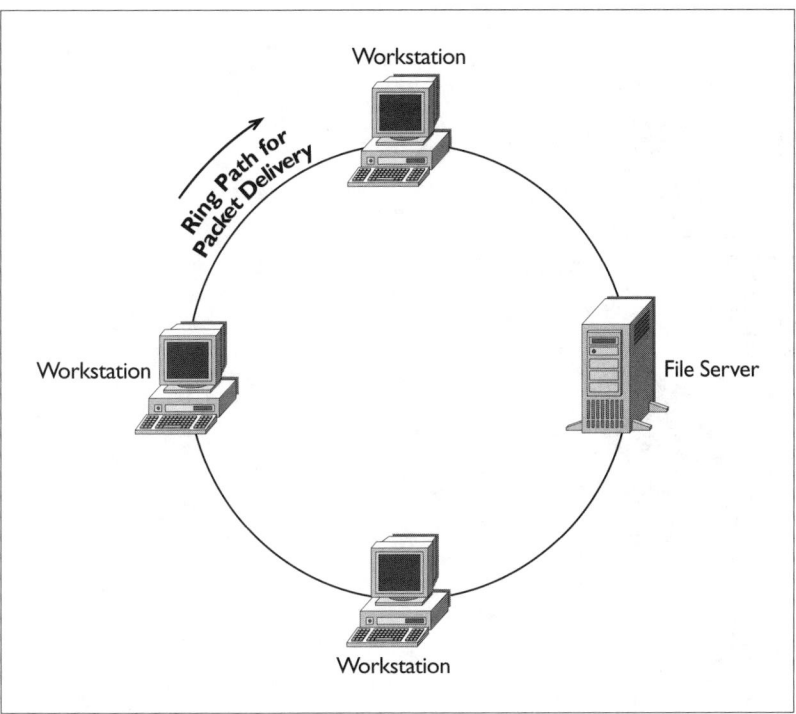

Figure AG.5
Ring topology

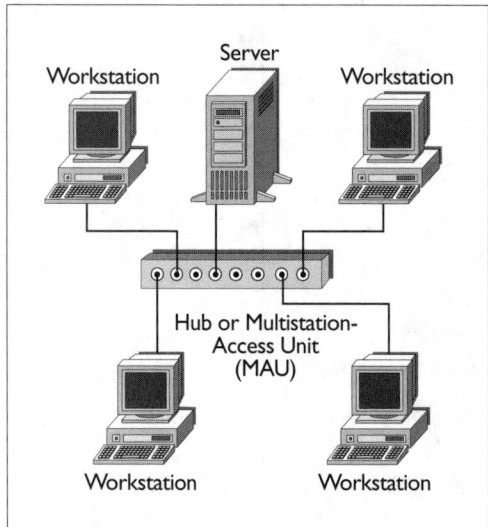

Figure AG.6
Star topology

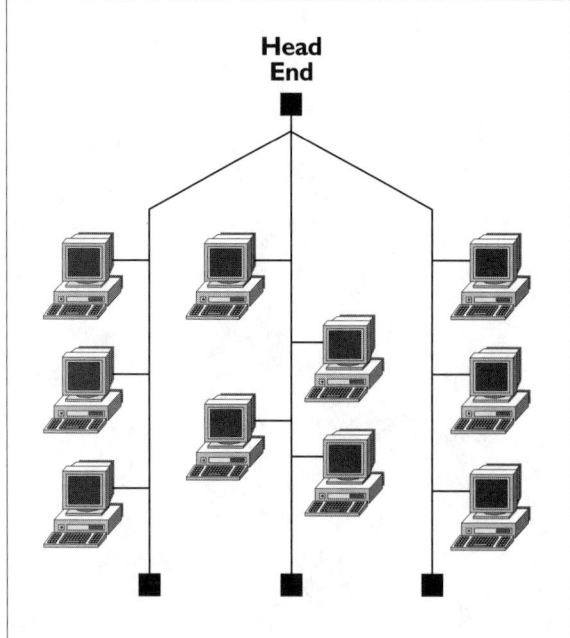

Figure AG.7
Tree topology

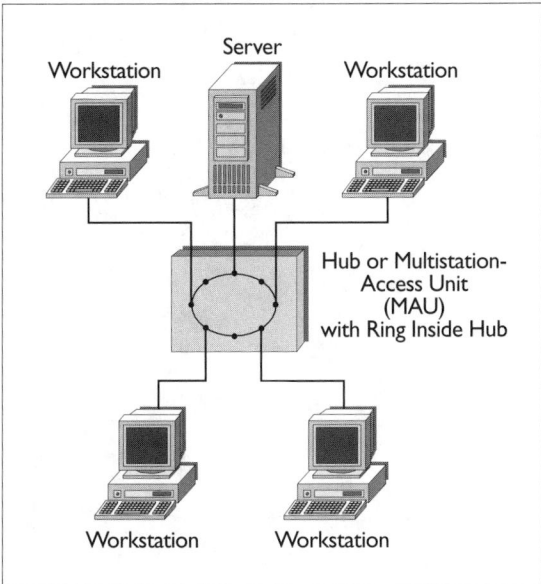

Figure AG.8
Star-wired ring (or hybrid) topology

Index

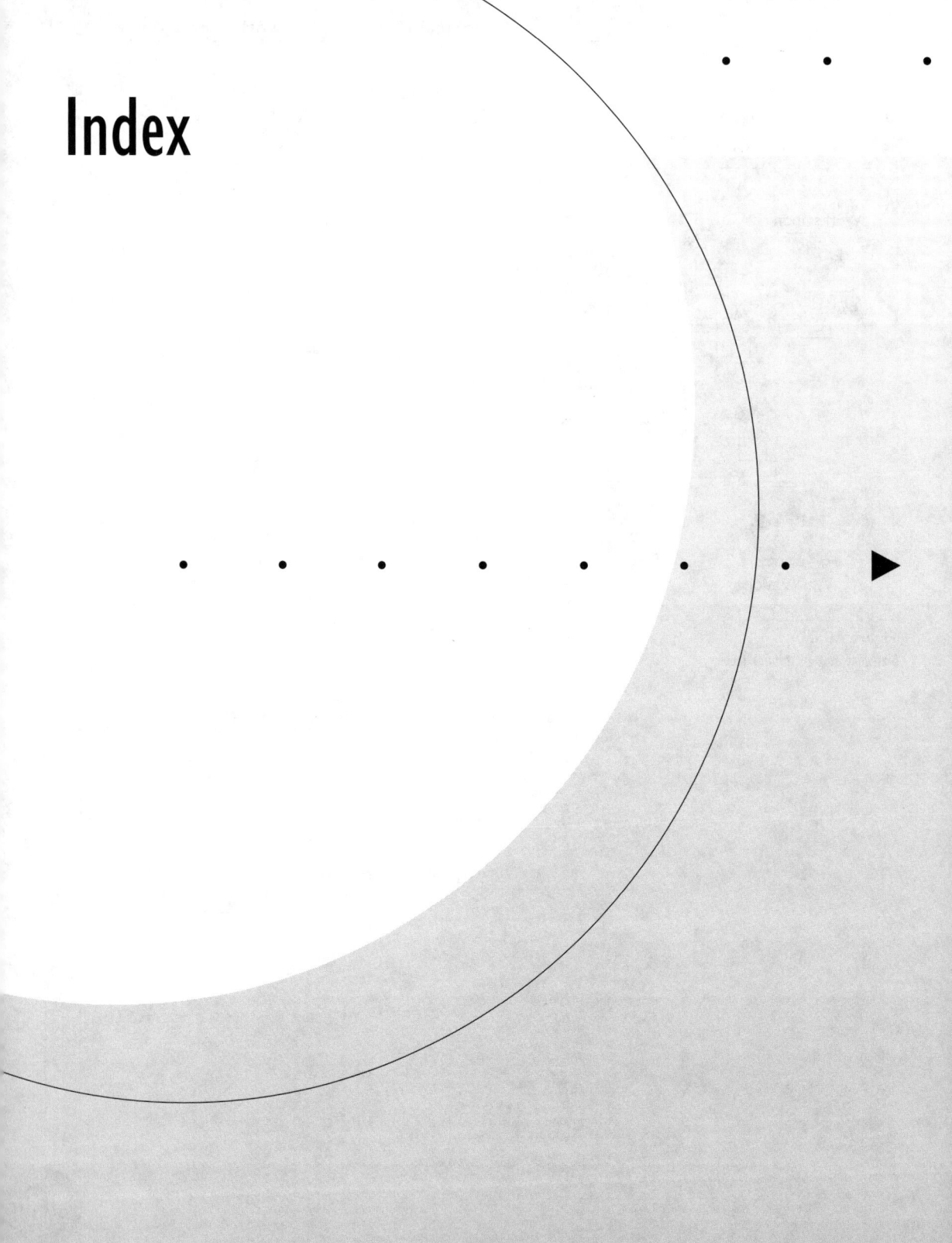

continued

continued

D

continued

continued

continued

Motion Pictures Experts Group (MPEG), 490
MOTIS (Message-Oriented Text-Interchange System), 471
MOUNT utility, 490
mounting, 490
mouse, 490
mouse pointers, 490-491
MovieStar plug-in, 491
MOVs (Metal-Oxide Varistors), 472
Mozilla team, 491
MP protocol (Multilink Point-to-Point protocol), 491
MPDRIVER NLM, 491
MPEG (Motion Pictures Experts Group), 490
MPI (Multiple-Protocol Interface), 491
MPOA (Multiprotocol Over ATM), 492
MPR (NetWare Multiprotocol Router), 492
MRMs (Maximum-Rights Masks), 459
MROM (mask read-only memory), 683
MRUs (Maximum-Receive Units), 459
MS (Message Stores), 469
ms (milliseconds), 478
MS-DOS (Microsoft Disk Operating System), 475
MS Windows client, 493
MSAUs (Multi-Station Access Units), 493
MSB (Most Significant Bit), 485
msec (milliseconds), 478
MSEngine (Mirrored Server Engine), 479
MSERVER utility, 493
.MSG filename extension, 298
MSLs (Mirrored Server Links), 479-480
MSN (Microsoft Network), 475
MST (Minimum Spanning Tree), 479
MTAs (Mail-Transfer Agents), 453
MTAs (Message-Transfer Agents), 470
MTBF (mean time between failures), 461
MTL (Message-Transfer Layer), 470
MTS (Message-Transfer Service), 470
MTSO (Mobile-Telephone Switching Office), 482
MTTR (mean time to repair), 461
MTUs (Maximum-Transmission Units), 459
mu-law standard, 495
mu symbol, 3
MUD, Object-Oriented (MOO) environment, 485
MUDs (Multi-User Dimensions), 495
multi-CPU architecture, 496
multi-homed hosts, 496
Multi-User Dimensions (MUDs), 495
multicast addresses, 495

Multicast Backbone (MBONE) network, 460
multicasting, 495
cooperative, 174
preemptive, 645-646
multidrop connections, 496
multidrop lines, 496
MultiFinder operating system, 496
multihoming, 496
multilayer boards, 496
Multilink Point-to-Point protocol (MP protocol), 491
Multilink Procedures (MLP) protocol, 481
multimedia, 497
multimedia extensions, 497
Multimedia Home-Space Viewer (MHSV) plug-in, 473
Multimedia Multiparty Teleconferencing (MMT), 481
multimedia packages, Shockwave, 747
Multimode Fiber (MMF), 481, 751
multipart e-mail format, 497
multipath signals, 497
multiple access, 497
multiple-byte characters, 498
multiple-domain networks, 497
Multiple-Link Interface (MLI), 480
Multiple-Link Interface Drivers (MLIDs), 480
Multiple Logical Terminals (MLTs), 481
multiple name-space support, 498
Multiple-Protocol Interface (MPI), 491
multiple protocols, 498
Multiple Uniform-Naming Convention Providers (MUPs), 498
Multiple Virtual Storage (MVS), 498
multiple-wait semaphores, 731
multiplexers, 498, 501
hybrid, 340
T1, 793
multiplexing, 498
M13 method, 449
statistical, 771
WDM, 868
multiplexor VLM, 499
multipliers, port, 641
multipoint connections, 499
multipoint lines, 499
multiport repeaters, 499
multiprocessing, 489, 499
multiprotocol encapsulation, 499
Multiprotocol Over ATM (MPOA), 492
Multiprotocol Router (MPR), 492
multiprotocol routers, NetWare, 535

Multipurpose Internet Mail Extensions (MIME), 478
multiserver networks, 500
Multistation Access Units (MAUs), 459
multitasking, 500, 807
multithreading, 500
Multiuser Shared Hallucination (MUSH) simulation, 500
Multiuser Simulated Environment (MUSE), 501
multiusers, 500
multivendor networks, 501
MUPs (Multiple Uniform-Naming Convention Providers), 498
MUSE (Multiuser Simulated Environment), 501
MUSH (Multiuser Shared Hallucination) simulation, 500
Musical Instrument Digital Interface (MIDI), 477
mutex mechanism, 501
mutual-exclusion semaphores, 731
mux (multiplexers), 498, 501
hybrid, 340
T1, 793
MUX Multipliers, 501
mv (millivolts), 478
MVS (Multiple Virtual Storage), 498
MX (Mail Exchange) records, 452

N

N-1 networks, 505
n abbreviation, 505
N (Normal) attributes, 562
N-Series connectors, 570
NA (Numerical aperture), 505
NACs (Network-Access Controllers), 505
NACSIS (National Center for Science Information Systems), 505
NAEC (Novell Authorized Education Centers), 505
Nagel's algorithm, 505
NAK (Negative acknowledgement) signals, 505
NAL (Novell Application Launcher) utility, 505
.NAM filename extension, 298
NAM (NetWare Application Manager) utility, 505-506
Name-Binding Protocol (NBP), 506
Name property, 506
name-space format, 507
name-space NLMs, 506-507
name-space support, multiple, 498
NAME utility, 507

continued

continued

continued

objects for, 676
operators for, 676
print, 649-650
sampling intervals for, 676
server mode for, 676
services for, 676
users of, 676
queuing
 Look-Ahead, 440
 Look-Back, 440
 priority, 653
queuing delays, 676
queuing theory, 677
QuickDraw printers, 677
QuickTime architecture, 677
QuickTime plug-in, 677
quintillions, prefix for, 255

R

RACE (Research and Development
 Program in Advanced
 Communications in Europe) project,
 679
rack-mount servers, 679
radio, cellular, 131
radio buttons, 679
radio frequency (RF), 679
radio-frequency interference (RFI), 679
radio networks, 613, 679
radio paging, 679
RAIDs (Redundant Arrays of Inexpensive
 Disks) architecture, 686-687
RAM (Random-access memory), 679,
 681. *See also* memory
 CMOS, 147
 NVRAM, 562
 page-mode, 614
 physical, 631
 PRAM, 616
 shadow, 745
 SRAM, 765
RAM chips, 679
RAM disks, 680
random access, 680
Random-access memory (RAM). *See*
 memory; RAM (Random-access
 memory)
ranges, network, 551
RARE (Reseaux Associes pour la
 Recherche Europeenne), 680
RARP (Reverse Address-Resolution
 Protocol), 680
RAS (Remote-Access Services), 680, 691
RBHCs (Regional Bell Holding
 Companies), 680

RBOCs (Regional Bell Operating
 Companies), 687-688
RC5 encryption algorithm, 681
RCGI (Remote Common-Gateway
 Interface), 681
RCONSOLE utility, 538, 681
rcp (Remote Copy) command, 681
RDA (Remote Database Access), 681
RDN (Relative Distinguished Name),
 681-682
read-after-write verification, 682
Read-Only (Ro) attributes, 682
read-only file mode, 682
read-only memory (ROM), 682-683
 boot, 101
 EEPROM, 259
 Flash EPROM, 302
Read-Only replicas, 682
Read rights, 682
Read Write (Rw) attributes, 682
Read/Write replicas, 682
ReadBind NLM, 682
README files, 682
real mode, 683
real-time systems, 683
RealAudio technology, 683
reassembly, 683
rebooting, 683
rec newsgroups, 684
rec (recreation) suffix, 683
Receive Data (RXD) signals, 684
Receive Only (RO) setting, 684
receive pacing, 684
Received Up To term, 684
Receiver Ready packets, 684
receivers, 684
reconfiguration bursts, 684
Record Manager, 684
recording, Sampled Servo technique for,
 720
records, 684
 adjacency, 27
 ascending order for, 56
 locking, 434, 684
 variable-length, 850
recovery, file, 294
rectifiers, 685
recursion, 685
recursive commands, 685
recursive copying, 685
Red Book, 685
red box package, 685
redefining keys, 404
redirect process, 685
redirection, 685
redirection areas, 685

redirectors, 685-686
redistribution process, 686
Reduced-Instruction-Set Computing
 (RISC), 686
redundancy, 686, 787
Redundant Arrays of Inexpensive Disks
 (RAIDs) architecture, 686-687
Redwood environment, 686
reentrant technique, 686
Reference property, 686
Reference time servers, 686
referential integrity (RI), 686
reflection loss, 699
reflectors, mail, 452
refraction index, 357, 687
Regional Bell Holding Companies
 (RBHCs), 680
Regional Bell Operating Companies
 (RBOCs), 687-688
register insertions, 687
REGISTER MEMORY utility, 687
Registered Disk Adapters resource, 688
Registered Hardware Options, 688-689
Registered MLID Boards resource, 689
registered resources, 689
regulation, power, 689
REINTIALIZE SYSTEM utility, 689
relational databases, 194, 689
Relative Distinguished Name (RDN),
 681-682
relay points, 690
relaying, 690
relays, 689
release timers, 690
releases, maintenance, 454
reliability
 data, 192
 line, 690
Reliable Transfer mode, 690
Reliable-Transfer Service Elements
 (RTSE), 690
remailers, anonymous, 43
Remaining Grace Login property, 690
REMAPID NLM, 690
REMIRROR PARTITION utility, 690
remirroring
 partitions, 690
 stopping, 15
remote access, 691
Remote-Access Services (RAS), 680, 691
remote booting, 691
remote bridges, 691
Remote Common-Gateway Interface
 (RCGI), 681
remote computing, 691
remote connections, 691

continued

CD-ROM Installation Instructions

CD-ROM Contents

The CD-ROM included with this book contains the following materials:

- Adobe Acrobat Reader
- An electronic version of this book, *Novell's Encyclopedia of Networking,* in Adobe Acrobat format

Installing the CD-ROM

The following sections describe the product and include detailed instructions for installation and use.

ADOBE ACROBAT READER The Adobe Acrobat Reader is a helpful program that will enable you to view the electronic version of this book in the same page format as the actual book.

NOVELL'S ENCYCLOPEDIA OF NETWORKING, ADOBE ACROBAT VERSION To install and run Adobe Acrobat Reader to view the electronic version of this book, follow these steps:

1. Start Windows Explorer (if you're using Windows 95) or Windows NT Explorer (if you're using Windows NT), and then open the Acrobat folder on the CD-ROM.

2. In the Acrobat folder, double-click ar32e30.exe and follow the instructions presented onscreen for installing Adobe Acrobat Reader.

3. To view the electronic version of this book after you have installed Adobe Acrobat Reader, start Windows Explorer (if you're using Windows 95) or Windows NT Explorer (if you're using Windows NT), and then open the Books\Novell's Encyclopedia of Networking folder on the CD-ROM.

4. In the Novell's Encyclopedia of Networking folder, double-click the chapter or appendix file you want to view. All documents in this folder end with a .PDF extension.